America's Most Influential Journalist

The Life, Times and Legacy of

THOMAS NAST

by JOHN ADLER

AMERICA'S MOST INFLUENTIAL JOURNALIST
The Life, Times and Legacy of Thomas Nast

ISBN 978-0-578-29454-4

First printing edition 2022.

www.ThomasNast.com

Harpweek LLC
P.O. Box 5304
Sarasota, FL 34277

Dedicated to three Nast scholars whose contributions to my knowledge greatly enhanced this book.

- The late Alice Caulkins
- The late Draper Hill
- Richard Samuel West

"WHERE THERE IS AN EVIL." "THERE IS A REMEDY"—(RIDICULE)

Table of Contents

Introduction

Most Americans have never heard of Thomas Nast, even though they are familiar with his legacy symbols: Uncle Sam, the Republican Elephant, the Democratic Donkey, and fat, jolly Santa Claus. However, the Supreme Court knew enough about him to cite him in a critical Freedom of the Press ruling that protects all journalists today.

In 1987, prominent Evangelical Christian pastor Jerry Falwell sued quasi-pornographic *Hustler Magazine* for libel, invasion of privacy, and intentional infliction of distress over the content of an advertisement "parody." Among other things, the caricature "portrayed respondent as having engaged in a drunken incestuous rendezvous with his mother in an outhouse." The core of *Hustler's* defense was that it was entitled to use "rhetorical hyperbole" to ridicule a public figure "who was seeking to impose his own view of morality upon society." Its viewpoint was supported by the Association of American Editorial Cartoonists and several other media-related organizations.

The Supreme Court, in an opinion written by Chief Justice William Rehnquist, ruled that "the First and Fourteenth Amendments prohibited public figures and public officials from recovering damages for the tort of intentional infliction of emotional distress without showing that the publication also contained a false statement of fact which was made with actual malice.

"Were we to hold otherwise, there can be little doubt that political cartoonists and satirists would be subjected to damage awards without any showing that their work falsely defamed its subject." The opinion goes on to include a paragraph about "Thomas Nast, probably the greatest American cartoonist to date," and cites "the passion and effectiveness of his graphic vendetta against Boss Tweed and his Tweed Ring as standing alone in the history of American graphic art."[1]

The Court's 1988 opinion echoed on an 1872 tribute to the 31-year old Nast in *The New York Times*.[2]

> *"Mr. Nast has achieved a reputation which many men of twice his age might well envy, and which will probably outlast the reputations of most men who profess to form and direct public opinion. His drawings are stuck upon the walls of the poorest dwellings, and stored away in the portfolios of the wealthiest connoisseurs. A man who can appeal powerfully to millions of people with a few strokes of the pencil, must be admitted to be a great power in the land. No writer can possibly possess a tenth part of the influence which Mr. Nast exercises. He addresses the learned and the unlearned alike. Many people cannot read 'leading articles,' others do not choose to read them, others do not understand them when they have read them. But you cannot help seeing Mr. Nast's pictures, and when you have seen them you cannot fail to understand them. When he caricatures a politician, the name of that politician ever afterwards recalls the countenance of which Mr. Nast has made him a present. An artist of this stamp — and such artists are very rare indeed — does more to affect public opinion than a score of writers."*

During the 150 years since the *Times* saluted him, Thomas Nast has been universally recognized as the father of American political cartooning and our nation's best-ever caricaturist. What hasn't been fully appreciated or validated to date, are his two concomitant achievements which, taken together, provide a new expanded perspective on his influence as a *journalist*, and his unique legacy as a *visual documenter* of our country's history during the crucial Civil War and Reconstruction era when the nation's fate and its system of government were at the heart of his depictions.

Journalist

After 27 years of immersing myself in Nast's life, work and legacy, my premise is that he was the **most influential journalist in American history**. An undated clipping in a Nast scrapbook helps explain why:

> *"Scathing editorials have no fear for political sinners. They well know that the public will forget them in a week if indeed they are read at all. But when a master of the pencil impales a man, he impresses his unhallowed inspiration on the general mind forever."*[3]

Nast was the first journalist who didn't own his paper to play a major role in shaping public opinion. However, he could not have done so without the quality, consistency, financial strength and resultant reach and dominance of *Harper's Weekly*, the country's leading illustrated newspaper. Its circulation exceeded 100,000 during the Civil War, reached as high as 200,000 in the course of major election campaigns, and came close to 300,000 at the height of his 1871 war against the Tweed Ring. Including passalong readership, Nast's cartoons always had half a million to a million or more viewers, a key factor in his influence.

During his quarter-century career at *Harper's Weekly* (1862-1886), Nast published almost 2,200 illustrations and cartoons. Its tabloid-size pages (16 x 11 inches) enabled him to cram as many as 40 recognizable characters into a double-page cartoon. Overall, he caricatured 450 different people; fewer than ten were women. Adding clout to his illustrations and cartoons, almost half of them were on large pages: 404 covers, 425 single pages and 130 double-pages (16 x 22 inches). To appreciate their contemporary impact, current viewers should keep in mind that they were created to be seen at those sizes.

In addition to Nast's artistic powers of persuasion and the editorial predominance of Republican *Harper's Weekly*, Nast's stature was unimpeded by any meaningful competition from other political cartoonists before military control of Reconstruction effectively ended in 1877. After 1864, Democratic-leaning *Frank Leslie's Illustrated Newspaper* had plenty of good illustrations, and circulation over 100,000, as the *Weekly's* only real competitor. However, it lacked *Harper's* editorial talent and prominence, and its several political cartoonists never came close to achieving Nast's fan base or his influence.

Both in his own time and today, Nast has been principally remembered for his primary role (with late but critical help from the *New York Times*) in bringing down Boss (William M.) Tweed and his ring of thieves. The corrupt and seemingly impregnable Tammany Hall (Democratic) chieftain who controlled New York City and State, had his eye on running his puppet (Governor John Hoffman) for the Presidency in 1872 against current President Ulysses S. Grant. Tweed reportedly complained: *"Let's stop them damned pictures. I don't care what the papers say about me — my constituents can't read; but damn it, they can see pictures."*

Nast generally led public opinion rather than followed it. Like most political cartoonists and editorial journalists, he was far from objective. Almost always, he preferred to be against a person or a cause, so he could serially pound the negatives — except when it came to his idol Grant, whom he treated much too leniently in the face of multiple scandals during his second term. (When Nast hadn't formed a strong opinion of somebody, he would draw him with his head peeping out from behind a wall or curtain, or else standing in profile or in shadow.) His beneficiaries, targets and, of course, he himself, recognized the extraordinary power and resultant influence that he wielded:

- For energizing Union morale and spurring enlistments during the Civil War, President Abraham Lincoln reportedly called Nast "*his best recruiting sergeant*."

- After winning his first term in 1868, Grant said that he "*was elected by the sword of Sheridan (*General Phil*) and the pencil of Thomas Nast*."

- Soon after Nast's celebrated victory over Tweed, Grant recruited him to work on his reelection campaign. Nast was lionized in Washington and filled his wife, Sallie, in on the details almost daily. Sensing a new peak of his influence, he wrote her on February 6, 1872, that he was seeing the President "nearly every day . . . it is funny how all the Senators are in a flutter about my being here and all are afraid that I will do them up . . . Darling the Power I have is terrible it frightens people, but darling you will keep a good look out for me, and will not let me use that Power in a bad cause."

- In 1872, Grant's opponent turned out to be Horace Greeley, the eccentric and easily caricatured editor of the *New York Tribune*. After being serially ridiculed in more than 80 Nast cartoons, Greeley grumbled that he "*didn't know whether he was running for President or the Penitentiary.*" (As it turned out, he was running for the cemetery because he died shortly after the election.)
- In 1876, Nast had policy differences with Republican candidate Rutherford B. Hayes, and did not actively support or even portray him during his campaign or his presidency. However, Nast despised Democratic nominee Samuel J. Tilden, and his merciless attacks before and after the disputed election undoubtedly influenced its outcome.

In summary, Nast's cartoons were influential in deciding four Presidential elections — 1864, 1868, 1872 and 1876 — during the critical Civil War and Reconstruction era. Almost all his cartoons excoriated the opposition, and every Republican candidate — Lincoln, Grant and Hayes — won. No journalist, then or later, could ever hope to achieve that level of editorial potency.

Nast essentially sat out the 1880 election because he believed Republican James Garfield lacked integrity and Democrat Winfield Scott Hancock was a personal friend. (Garfield won.) In 1884, he attacked Republican James Blaine, also for dishonesty, and backed Democrat Grover Cleveland. Cleveland won — giving Nast a perfect batting average — but he and *Harper's Weekly* (which also backed Cleveland) lost their power when much of their Republican base abandoned them. Three years later, Nast was a political "has-been" and faded from public view.

Visual Historian

A rural editor praised Nast from another viewpoint: "*In the future the volumes of his (Nast's) pictures will be read as the best history of the time.*"[4] Serendipitously, he was potentially correct, provided the context of his "pictures" is understood when looking at them today.

In fact, Nast wanted to be what he called a "history painter," but after giving it a try, he apparently recognized that he didn't have the artistic training (and perhaps the talent) to pursue painting as his primary occupation. Instead, he became an unsurpassed caricaturist and visual story-teller for the two decades before photography and printing technology could provide timely pictorial coverage of current events, people and issues.

Nast illustrated more than 100 books, including many children's tales. He used the same sequential approach in most of his serialized topical attacks, foreshadowing newspaper comic strips which first appeared in the 1890s. Innately, he seemed to understand that the essence of achieving political objectives during a campaign was to reinforce supporters, convince the undecided, and hopefully attract some of the opposition. They had the effect of repetitive television sound bites a century later. While repeating his basic message again and again, he varied his presentations in order to keep his content fresh and interesting.

To engage and persuade his audience, Nast effectively created a new visual language replete with symbols, caricatures, allegories, satire, puns and repetitive slogans. His readers understood his ocular shorthand, comprehended the minute details which more subtly reinforced his frontal attacks, and were familiar with his Shakespearean and other literary references. (He used Shakespeare in more than 100 cartoons, drawing from 23 of his 37 plays.)

All that was woven into the context of Nast's cartoons, which his fans and his haters instantly absorbed. Today it's difficult to appreciate his value as a visual historian without fully understanding the who, what and why of each one — and their serial effectiveness. Accordingly, my aim has been to provide today's readers with the same degree of insight and comprehension of his work that his original viewers had.

Content

This biography contains 1,000 Nast cartoons, illustrations, sketches and paintings — 800 of them from *Harper's Weekly* — plus 100 topic-relevant cartoons by other artists. Each has its characters identified and its often-subtle content and context explained.

Why so many? As mentioned previously, the power and influence of Nast's cartoons largely emanated from their repetition over weeks or months as his stories unfolded and he banged his points home. To cherry-pick his cartoons more than I already have done, could dilute the cumulative impact they convey.

There are numerous instances in this biography where I have referred to cartoons or context that appeared on previous pages. Rather than repeat, I have used asterisked referrals on the subsequent pages.

Index

The index is a uniquely valuable feature of this biography, so I want to call it to readers' attention up front. Its three parts are predicated on Nast's 1,000 depicted cartoons, illustrations, sketches and paintings, plus content and context related to them. I had to create it manually because digital indexing aids cannot read or interpret cartoons.

- **Nast's Life and Work**

  Personal Aspects
  Art
  Artistic and Literary Sources: e.g., Shakespeare (by play)
  Business Aspects
  Symbols: Impersonal Political, Personal Political, and International
  Cartoons by other Artists (by publication) e.g., Joseph Keppler (*Puck*)
  Newspapers/Publishers (most were Nast's targets)

- **Topics/Issues**

  Because of Nast's de facto role as a one-of-a-kind visual historian, the objective in mining his work was to create a unique resource for journalists, cartoonists, historians, educators, students, librarians, political scientists, politicians and the general public to be able to track Nast's caricatured individuals, topics and issues over three decades — including before and after *Harper's Weekly*. Ten major categories and dozens of sub-classifications comprise this section. Where applicable, Nast's characters are also referenced under their relevant categories.

  Civil War
  Reconstruction
  Presidents: Buchanan; Lincoln; Johnson; Grant; Hayes; Garfield; Arthur; Cleveland; Harrison
  Presidential Election Losers: Seymour; Greeley; Tilden; Hancock; Blaine
  Scandals
  Tweed Ring/Tammany Hall
  Ethnic/Religious/Radical (Political) Topics
  Recurring Political Issues: e.g., Civil Service/Spoils System; Immigration/Naturalization
  Recurring Financial/Business Issues: e.g., Inflation; Tariffs/Protectionism; Trusts/Monopolies
  Foreign Affairs and Countries (Even Afghanistan was in the news.)

- **People/Characters.** Nast drew more than 450 different characters. All but five were identified in the research for this biography; many were portrayed only once or twice, and they generally appeared in individual, non-serialized cartoons which were not selected for this biography. About half his characters are included here; all but two political figures (Anna Elizabeth Dickinson and Victoria Woodhull) were men. (Nast drew fewer than ten women, primarily actresses or opera singers.)

Nast's Bias

It should be noted, however, that several years ago Nast was effectively black-balled from election to the New Jersey Hall of Fame because he had denigrated the Irish with dozens of simian-featured stereotypes, as well as the Catholic Church in multiple cartoons. He had valid reasons for doing so — Irish riots, violence, drunkenness and electoral fraud, as well as the perpetual battles between Protestants and the Catholic Church over public funding and religious curricula for their respective schools. By today's standards, reasonable critics would be justified in calling Nast a bigot, but should recognize that much of the Protestant majority, including the management of *Harper's Weekly*, were in accord with those views.

HW April 13, 1867 233 (extract) **HW September 2, 1871 824**

THE USUAL IRISH WAY OF DOING THINGS

* * * *

To commemorate the hundredth anniversary of Thomas Nast's death in 2002, Pulitzer Prize-winning cartoonist Pat Oliphant wrote this tribute:[5]

> *In this tame era of one-newspaper towns, avaricious, bottom-line publishers and timorous editors beset by pressure groups and political correctness, it is useful for a cartoonist to reflect that once upon a time there was a place for controversy, outrage and anger in the daily press, and there once lived a man called Thomas Nast who became the high water mark for savage cartooning in America. He was a product of his time as we, trapped in our own time, are a product of ours.* ***And it is sad to think that were he drawing today, nobody would print his work for fear of giving offense.***
>
> *But I always take comfort in the fact that he was here, and that he left us such an example.*

Obviously, public opinion on some of the issues, people and events that Nast portrayed had changed over 150 years. While visionary in a myriad of ways, Nast reflected the views of his era, some of which are debatable or unacceptable when viewed through today's retroactive lens.

I have tried to refrain from obvious political comparisons to recent or current events or controversies. The content and context of the cartoons by Nast and his contemporaries has been explained as objectively as I can. For those with lingering concerns about Nast's lack of current political correctness, consider how organized baseball has dealt with similar issues.

The Baseball Hall of Fame received flak about whether some of its early entrants deserve to be there because of their racial attitudes. In response, a statement at the entrance reads: "Enshrinement in the National Baseball Hall of Fame reflects the perspective of voters *at the time of election*. The plaques on these walls recognize Members for their accomplishments in the game." (Italics supplied.)

Journalists, historians, other educators, politicians, students, librarians, cartoonists, print collectors and general readers should have a better understanding of Nast's accomplishments in the endless game of politics. They reflect the passions and prejudices of Americans as they dealt with topics and controversies that recur in the news today — and will in the future: Civil rights, political corruption, immigration, inflation, tariffs, education, ethnic and religious differences, elections, government expenditures, and foreign wars.

Today's readers may or may not agree with what Nast had to say — or how he said it — but my hope is that they will understand why he was the most influential journalist in American history.

Understanding Nast's Messaging Today

As with any political cartoonist, most of Nast's cartoons attacked people (Democratic Presidential candidates Boss Tweed, Jefferson Davis, Pope Pius IX) and causes (slavery, repression of Blacks, political corruption) without mercy. To do so, he employed ridicule, sarcasm, satire and exaggeration in his caricatures.

The irony which drove home Nast's points, occasionally included the N-word. He used it satirically by quoting the racist words of ex-Confederates and anti-Black Democrats, demeaning them by turning their own epithets against them. His audience knew that Nast strongly supported Blacks in their struggle for political equality, and understood that his ridicule was aimed only at white men he found obnoxious.

To better appreciate Nast's subtleties, in support of Black suffrage, consider the following two cartoons from the final months of the 1868 Presidential campaign. Nast's hero, Ulysses S. Grant, was running for his first term against Democrat Horatio Seymour.

The post-dated cartoon (opposite) appeared on August 26, seven weeks after the Fourteenth Amendment was adopted. Finally, Blacks were citizens (reversing the 1857 Dred Scott decision), but they still couldn't vote. Nast's central point was that Black veterans had earned the right to vote through their military service, rather than simply obtain it via their newly-granted citizenship.

Nast's sardonic title — "*This is a White Man's Government*" — was positioned at the top of the cartoon, an unusual placement for him; almost all his cartoons had their titles underneath. Here, he wanted to attract his viewers' attention to the caption before they looked at his image below. He quoted from the Democratic platform's reactionary declaration as his subtitle underneath.

The unwritten addendum to the title — "No Black Votes Allowed." — was conveyed by the three white supremacists stepping on a uniformed Black veteran to keep him from putting his vote into a ballot box. (He would have to wait 16 months until the Fifteenth Amendment allowing Black men to vote, was ratified in January 1870.)

The white supremacists included a stereo-typed, ape-faced Irish thug, whose shillelagh was marked "A Vote;" Nathan Bedford Forrest, a Confederate general and founder of the Ku Klux Klan, holding a Lost Cause dagger; and August Belmont, a wealthy banker and Chairman of the Democratic Party, waving a packet of $100 bills marked "Capital for Votes."*

The enraged expression on the Irishman's simian face marked him as a Civil War draft rioter. Seymour had been Governor of New York in July 1863, when Irish rioters protesting the Civil War draft, burned down the Colored Orphan Asylum and lynched several Black men. Seymour showed up a day late and addressed the rioters as "My Friends." Nast used the burning asylum and a lynched Black hanging from a lamp post to symbolize Seymour in this and several other cartoons. (Here, it comprised the background behind the Irishman but is difficult to distinguish. The asylum is clearly labeled and the lamp post with its victim hanging from it, is directly in front of and below it.) Of course, the original cartoon was about twice as large as this image, so Nast's symbolic details were readily apparent to his viewers.

The Irishman's "5 Points" hat band referred to the slum area where many impoverished Irish lived (today's Chinatown). In contrast, Belmont's "5 Avenue" (both had 5s), highlighted his wealthy home.

Forrest, the commanding central figure, wore a CSA (Confederate States of America) belt buckle and a "Fort Pillow" button; it was a reminder of his order to massacre almost 200 Black Union soldiers after they surrendered on April 12, 1864. "Remember Fort Pillow" subsequently became a battle cry for Black troops in the remaining year of the war.

---

*See p. 215 for further explanation

HW September 5, 1868 568

"WE REGARD THE RECONSTRUCTION ACTS (SO CALLED) OF CONGRESS AS USURPATIONS, AND UNCONSTITUTIONAL, REVOLUTIONARY, AND VOID.—DEMOCRATIC PLATFORM.

HW October 24, 1868 C

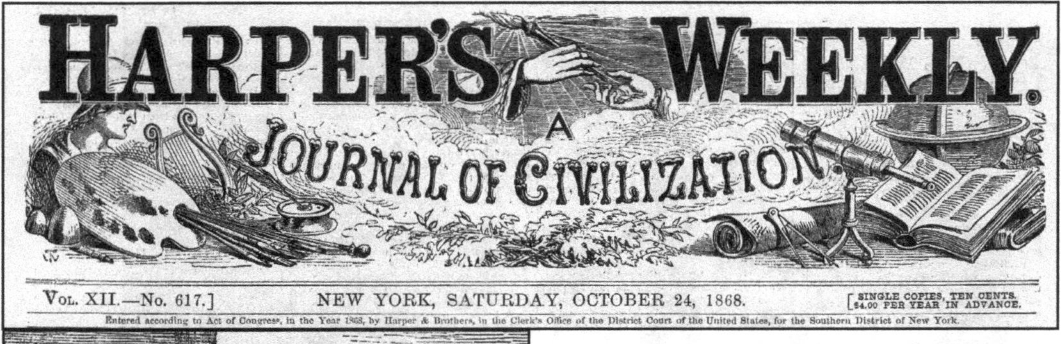

WHY "THE NIGGER IS NOT FIT TO VOTE."

With the election almost at hand, Nast taunted Seymour in a cover cartoon, using the N-word to highlight the Black man holding a ballot for the Grant-Colfax ticket, explicitly pointing out the actual reason why Democrats tried to suppress Black suffrage — the single most important issue during Reconstruction. Black voters helped Grant carry five former Confederate states; he won 26 to Seymour's 8.

While Nast's support of political equality for Blacks was primary to him, he also favored Chinese emigrants and Native Americans, especially in the later years of Reconstruction when their issues came to the fore.*

HW March 29, 1879 256

DIFFICULT PROBLEMS SOLVING THEMSELVES.

HW February 8, 1879 101 C

"EVERY DOG" (NO DISTINCTION OF COLOR) "HAS HIS DAY."
Red Gentleman to Yellow Gentleman. "Pale face 'fraid you crowd him out, as he did me."

---

* See p. 466 for context

Making History: Nast's Most Important Cartoon

In July 1864, President Abraham Lincoln's reelection chances looked dismal, primarily because the Civil War was dragging on in Georgia and Virginia. Northern morale was at a low. Within his cabinet, Postmaster General Montgomery Blair and, apparently, Secretary of War Edwin Stanton favored peace negotiations. Outside, New York publishers Horace Greeley (*Tribune*), James Gordon Bennett (*Herald*), Henry Raymond (*Times*), William Cullen Bryant (*Evening Post*), and former Mayor Fernando Wood, a leading Copperhead (Southern sympathizer) whose brother Ben published the *News*, supported the idea and beat their editorial drums.

Greeley wrote Lincoln, beseeching the President to authorize him to enter peace negotiations at Niagara Falls. Lincoln complied, provided that the Confederates committed up front to restoration of the Union and the elimination of slavery. Lincoln knew Jeff Davis would never agree, so that and a subsequent peace negotiation failed. Lincoln also was against any kind of armistice because it would have been perceived as a Confederate victory.

Thomas Nast, 23 at the time, took note. Although his reputation is largely based on his work for *Harper's Weekly*, he regularly contributed cruder unsigned cartoons, as early as 1859 and as late as 1873, to *Phunny Phellow*, a monthly humor publication. It provided him with ample space and uninhibited editorial freedom to develop his gifts as a caricaturist. The August 1864 issue reflected his imaginative sense of humor in a way that *Harper's Weekly* never would have permitted.

August 1864

American Antiquarian Society

Left to Right: Greeley, Bennett, Raymond, Bryant, Wood, Blair, Stanton, Lincoln

THE GRAND PEACE OVERTURE TO "OUR WAYWARD SISTERS."

Lincoln's prospects improved slightly on August 5, when Admiral David Farragut, lashed to the mast of his flagship, shouted "Damn the torpedoes! Full speed ahead!" on his way to capturing Mobile Bay. That was the first in a triad of critical Union victories.

The Democratic National Convention was scheduled to meet in Chicago during the last week of August to nominate George B. McClellan for President. Once the Union's top general, Lincoln had fired him almost two years earlier for his reluctance to fight. A key plank in the Democratic platform branded the war as "four years of failure."

The single most important and influential cartoon that Nast ever drew appeared in *Harper's Weekly* on August 24 (post-dated September 3), as the Convention was assembling. *Compromise with the South — Dedicated to the Chicago Convention* captured the very crux of the existential emotional and political stake at issue in the forthcoming election.

Nast's scathing caricature of an arrogant, exultant Jeff Davis shaking hands with a crippled Union soldier who — with his head bowed and his only leg shackled to a ball and chain — humbly accepted it. Columbia, representing the Union and modeled by Nast's wife, Sallie, wept at the gravestone marked "In Memory of Our Union-Heroes Who Fell in a Useless War."

HW September 3, 1864 572

DEDICATED TO THE CHICAGO CONVENTION.

As Davis's boot stomped on a Union grave and broke the sword of Northern Power, the cat-o'-nine-tails in his left hand was ready to flog his vanquished enemies. A black family in chains despaired behind Davis. The Union flag, upside down in distress, recited its successes, including emancipation, on its stripes; the Confederate flag detailed a list of atrocities.

Nast's original sketch included a bottom panel with three additional vignettes and a Copperhead snake coiled around the laurels of victory. One scene showed a slave auction — *To Have the "Union" as It Was* — and another showed blacks being forced *"Back into Slavery."* Fletcher Harper advised Nast to stay with his unsurpassable central theme — less was more — and the cartoon's powerful impact proved him correct.[6]

Separately, The *Weekly's* cover depicted General William T. Sherman holding a council of war with his staff, and quoted him underneath: "Gentlemen, I intend to place this Army southwest of Atlanta;" he captured the city on September 1, reviving Northern morale. It is conceivable that Nast's derisive image, plus the fall of Atlanta, stiffened McClellan's resolve to reject the "War is a failure" plank in his acceptance letter of September 8.[7] He decided that resigning as the nominee would be wrong, and that it was his duty to resolve the war on the one and only issue for which it had originally been fought — restoration of the Union.

John Hay Library, Brown University

PEACE

A TRAITOR'S PEACE

THAT THE

NORTHERN COPPERHEAD LEADERS WOULD FORCE UPON THE COUNTRY.

THE REBEL TERMS OF PEACE!!

"Save on our own terms, we can accept no peace whatever, and must fight till doomsday rather than yield one iota of them; and our terms are:

"Recognition by the enemy of the Independence of the Confederate States

"Withdrawal of Yankee forces from every foot of Confederate ground, including KENTUCKY and MISSOURI.

"Withdrawal of Yankee soldiers from MARYLAND, until that State shall decide, by a free vote, whether she shall remain in the old Union, or ask admission into the Confederacy.

"Consent on the part of the Federal Government to give up to the Confederacy its proportion of the Navy as it stood at the time of secession, or to pay for the same.

"Yielding up all pretensions on the part of the Federal Government to that portion of the old Territories which lies west of the Confederate States.

"An equitable settlement, on the basis of our absolute independence and equal rights, of all accounts of the Public Debt and Public Lands, and the advantages accruing from foreign treaties.

"These provisions, we apprehend, comprise the minimum of what we must require before we lay down our arms. That is to say, THE NORTH MUST YIELD ALL; WE NOTHING. The whole pretension of that country to prevent by force the separation of the States must be abandoned, which will be equivalent to an avowal that our enemies were wrong from the first; and, of course, as they waged a causeless and wicked war upon us, they, ought, in strict justice, to be required, according to usage in such cases, to reimburse to us the whole of our expenses and losses in the course of that war."

These are the terms of peace, and the "Enquirer" says further—

"As surely as we completely ruin their armies—and without that is no peace nor truce at all—SO SURELY SHALL WE MAKE THEM PAY OUR WAR DEBT, THOUGH WE WRING IT OUT OF THEIR HEARTS"

Citizens of the United States! These are the terms of peace to which you are invited by the Copperhead politicians of the country—the destruction of the Union—the giving up of Maryland, Kentucky, and Missouri, which have all voted by immense majorities for the Union—the surrender of a large part to our Navy—the loss of more than one half of our territory, *and the payment of the debt of the accursed rebellion of traitors*, by having it "WRUNG OUT OF OUR HEARTS!"

People of the United States! Will you give your assent to such a base surrender of our cause? If not, then repel the "Peace Organizations," and rally only with those who "keep step to the music of the Union," who stand by our brave soldiers in the field, and are for "Liberty and Union, now and forever, one and inseparable."

PRINTED FOR CONGRESSIONAL UNION COMMITTEE, WASHINGTON, D. C.

Please post this up.

Author's Collection

On October 16, the *Richmond Enquirer* published some new beyond-the-pale demands which were not in the platform at the Chicago convention. Among them were recognition of the Confederate States as an independent country; inclusion of three border states — Kentucky, Missouri and Maryland — in the Confederacy; and payment by the Union of the Confederate war debt.

Lincoln's reelection managers took Nast's cartoon, added "The Rebel Terms of Peace!!" to it, and made more than a million copies as campaign posters. In tandem with the trio of critical Union victories — by Farragut, Sherman, and on October 19, by General Phil Sheridan in the Shenandoah Valley (Sheridan's Ride) — the poster had a huge effect on the electorate.[8] Without those timely victories, however, the poster's impact would have been diluted. Nevertheless: **arguably, it was the single most effective visual campaign advertisement in any American presidential election — before or since.**

* * * *

Six weeks later, Nast's sequential punch broke new ground in pictorial satire when he took direct aim at *The Chicago Platform*. Although it didn't have the emotional impact of the much simpler *Compromise with the South*, its twenty vignettes, interwoven with extracts from the platform, revealed the true meaning of that document.

Nast's prize slap in the cartoon was at McClellan standing on board a ship covering his backside with his cap. The reference was to the "Gunboat Candidate," as McClellan was popularly mocked, going back to July 1, 1862, when he reportedly watched the Battle of Malvern Hill from the safety of the ironclad Galena in the middle of the James River, a mile away from the battle, in the finale to his failed Peninsular Campaign to capture Richmond. McClellan hesitated to use his numerically superior force because he erroneously believed that he was outnumbered by Lee's army. Underneath the cowardly general was a copperhead snake breaking the sword of Northern power, just as Jeff Davis did in *Compromise with the South.* The cumulative focal point of Nast's devastating attack on McClellan was to blend the general's fearful battlefield style with his acceptance of a contradictory nomination that he must have found humiliating on occasion.

(Nast reprised the theme thirteen years later when McClellan ran successfully for governor of New Jersey. From his command post on a Hudson River ferry — "This is not a gunboat" — Little Mac pleaded for more Democratic reinforcements, while keeping a "map of retreats" handy in case of defeat. Like the Republican elephant which Nast invented in 1874, he was not about to forgive or forget.)

HW October 27, 1877 837 C

"ALL QUIET ON THE" HUDSON.

"Mr." George B. M'Clellan In His Element Again—"Running For Something."

HW **October 15, 1864** **664-665**

Notable was the circular vignette at the lower left, featuring six Union stalwarts bowing to Jeff Davis. Sherman and Grant were in front, with Sheridan, Benjamin Butler, Farragut and General John Rawlins, Grant's chief of staff, behind them. Its counterpart on the right depicted Copperheads Clement Vallandigham, Indiana Congressman Daniel Voorhees, New York Governor Horatio Seymour, Fernando Wood and Vice Presidential nominee George Pendleton — all labeled as traitors.

Aid and Comfort to the Rebels Treasonable Speeches by Traitors at the North

Lincoln won a resounding victory with 70% of the military vote, 55% of the popular vote and an Electoral College landslide of 212 to 21. McClellan won only New Jersey and the Border States of Kentucky and Delaware. Republicans also consolidated control of Congress: 42/10 in the Senate and 149/42 in the House, a vital factor in the upcoming struggle over Reconstruction.

Fellow cartoonist Frank Bellew, (triangle signature) depicted Lincoln's success with an imaginative visual pun. Comparatively, it provides a solid example of what differentiated Nast — with his allegories and multiple vignettes — from his comic peers.

HW November 26, 1864 768

LONG ABRAHAM LINCOLN A LITTLE LONGER.

Santa Claus

Clement Moore personified the modern Santa Claus when he wrote his iconic *Twas the Night Before Christmas* in 1822. When the timeless verse was finally published in book form in 1848, St. Nick didn't look particularly warm or jolly. Ten years later, *Harper's Weekly* didn't capture Moore's description either.

HW December 25, 1858 817 C

SANTA CLAUS PAYING HIS USUAL CHRISTMAS VISIT TO HIS YOUNG FRIENDS IN THE UNITED STATES.

HW January 3, 1863 C

SANTA CLAUS IN CAMP.

Of all the symbols Nast created, popularized or inspired, Santa Claus is the most endearing, and probably will be the most enduring, as an irresistible holiday image — for both hearts and pocketbooks. However, his initial portrayal for *Harper's Weekly*, which appeared during Christmas week of 1862, depicted Santa in a brown furry suit.

However, the merry old Santa who appears in countless newspapers on Christmas Eve or Day every year, mirrors the artist's features. Santa was extremely personal to him and his family; they appeared in many of the 33 Santa Claus cartoons he drew for *Harper's Weekly* and the 21 he drew for *Harper's Bazar* over 24 years.

HW January 1, 1881 8-9

MERRY OLD SANTA CLAUS.

I hope this whets your appetite. Enjoy!

Sources and Acknowledgments

Albert Bigelow Paine

The only substantial biography of Thomas Nast was written by Albert Bigelow Paine, and published in April 1904, sixteen months after Nast's death. *Th. Nast: His Period and His Pictures* has been the basic sourcebook for all six subsequent efforts to chronicle the cartoonist's life and work.[1] I have used it extensively as well, but its lack of objectivity, errors, and omissions require critical commentary. (While it is unusual to introduce a book with a review of another book, it is essential here because "*the* Bible of Nastography" has been its cornerstone to date.)

Paine, 40, first met Nast, then 61, during the latter part of November 1901, at the Players Club in New York to which both belonged. Paine's ultimate objective was to write Mark Twain's biography, and he probably surmised that the path to Twain led through the humorist's good friend Nast. (His strategy worked so well that he became literary executor of Twain's estate.) Paine had authored other books but Nast's would be his first biography.

Nast should have been a biographer's dream. His ego led him to compulsively collect newspaper and magazine items about himself, probably using an early version of a clipping service. Whether favorable, unfavorable or downright venomous, they were pasted into scrapbooks, along with his own sketches, doodlings, invitations, letters, photographs and other ephemera. One horrific entry received at the height of the Tweed campaign was his printed portrait with his throat slit and a thread (representing a rope) around his neck — inscribed "A just doom for the pimp."

HW January 21, 1882 37

INNOCENCE ABROAD (IN SEARCH OF A COPYRIGHT).

Macculloch Hall Historical Museum

However, Paine was handicapped by two factors that he couldn't have anticipated when he undertook Nast's biography. First, his subject was deeply depressed because he had become irrelevant, was heavily in debt (having lost his savings via bad investments), and couldn't support his family. His oldest daughter Julia's death in 1899, may have also contributed.[2] Many of his former fans and foes thought he was dead — and he knew it. As his widow Sallie wrote Paine several years after his book was published to general acclaim: "I wish you could have known him before his nerves got the better of him, when he had that effervesing (sic) life and the merry spirits that were so natural to him. He was so original and lively."[3]

More damaging, Paine's interface with his primary source was cut short after seven months when Nast sailed for Guayaquil, Ecuador, on July 1, 1902. Desperate for the position's $4,000 annual salary, Nast accepted a diplomatic appointment from President Theodore Roosevelt in April. Anticipating his probable demise from yellow fever before he left, his silent prediction came true on December 7.

Paine p. 560

Sometime after he left *Harper's Weekly* (as 1887 dawned), Nast's depression must have deepened to the extent that he — previously a strong temperance promoter — began drinking. Paine noted that in a May 26 meeting with a potential publisher: "Nast and I got tight and had a quarrel because I said I didn't intend to read his great book of clippings until I had worked with him. All my silly."[4]

With Nast despondent and preparing to uproot his life, the quality and quantity of time that he gave to Paine in the five weeks after that meeting was less than ideal. Regardless, there was no way that Paine could be certain about everything that Nast told him, discern his embellishments and misrepresentations, or know about his deliberate or overlooked omissions. In Nast's defense, he was looking back over 55 years or so with a heavily stressed mind. His sketches and published work provided a voluminous base but, like a Swiss cheese, it had a lot of significant holes as the following examples demonstrate.

- During the Civil War, Nast was criticized by prominent frontline artists working for *Harper's Weekly* for two reasons: first, because he drew his illustrations and allegories safely at home in New York and also for taking too much credit (with his signature) for their "live" sketches which they sent to New York and he re-drew on woodblocks for publication. Nast had seen war and personal danger close up during the six months he had spent with Giuseppe Garibaldi's campaign to unify Italy in 1860; there, he also learned how to realistically re-create battle scenes. With that perilous experience behind him, he could draw credible military illustrations without leaving his wife and baby.

  Yet Nast told Paine that he first met General Benjamin Butler (a post-war favorite target) on a trip to Fort Moultrie, South Carolina (near Charleston) in the spring of 1863. False. Butler, who had been relieved of his command in New Orleans, was in New York and Washington during that period.[5]

  In the same paragraph, Paine wrote: "During these trips to the front he met and became the friend of General Sheridan, who invited the artist to establish headquarters in his camp." While Sheridan was in and around Murfreesboro, Tennessee that spring, Nast never went there and, if he had, Sheridan would not have issued such an invitation. (However, they became good friends several years later, probably leading Nast to gild the lily with Paine.) In between these two erroneous sentences, Paine implied that Nast drew from life the *Arrival of a Federal Column at a Planter's House* in Dixie. In fact, as *Harper's Weekly* explained in accompanying text on the preceding page — the illustration was based on content from a letter sent by "an officer in Dixie," which Nast then depicted.[6]

  Moreover, it is doubtful that Nast ever visited the front lines during the course of the war. He tried to get to Gettysburg before that key battle began on July 1, 1863, but was arrested because of his traveling companion's behavior, and spent the weekend in jail in nearby Carlisle, Pennsylvania. He tried again in December 1864 to see frontline action — this time at Fort Fisher near Wilmington, North Carolina — but literally missed the boat to his destination after making it as far as Fortress Monroe, Virginia.

- For a year beginning in June 1867, Nast's work didn't appear in *Harper's Weekly*. In addition to illustrating books, he spent much of that time creating a moving panorama show, comprising 33 nine-by-twelve foot panels dealing with slavery, the Civil War and President Andrew ("King Andy") Johnson. If the Grand Caricaturama had been successful, it might have altered Nast's career. However, it flopped financially, so Nast wasn't proud of it. Consequently, Paine gave it all of two sentences.[7]
- As mentioned previously, the humor magazine *Phunny Phellow* was an important comic outlet for Nast from 1859 until 1873. He supplied a cover, a center double-page, and a back page cartoon for dozens of issues. Nast may not have saved them or shown them to Paine, but their comic political content was certainly a more important aspect of his life than the three-plus casual sentences Paine gave them.[8] Eighteen are in this biography.
- Paine also made some careless errors. An important one was a misquote that distorted Nast's meaning in the previously quoted letter he wrote Sallie on February 6, 1872 about his power. Nast: "The power I have frightens *people*." Paine: "The power I have frightens *me*."[9]
- Finally, Nast himself didn't know the real background behind the most important decision he ever made — to marry Sallie Edwards — so Paine couldn't relate it. Tommy effectively "stole" his bride away from Jesse Haney, the publisher of the *Comic Monthly* who intended to marry her, to the amazement of their mutual friend, Thomas Butler Gunn. Gunn's diary, which neither Nast or Paine knew about, explained it all.*

After Nast sailed to Ecuador, Paine was totally dependent on his gleanings from the scrapbooks, letters, sketches, and the printed pages from *Harper's Weekly*, *New York Illustrated News* and other publications, to amplify his first-hand notes. Sallie helped where she could. Ultimately, he included 419 cartoons and illustrations, most from the *Weekly*, and without much context. As mentioned in the introduction, this biography has more than 1,000 — with context.

To Paine's credit, he produced an interesting, entertaining, well-written book which accentuated the positives and glided over or eliminated most of the negatives in Nast's life. He corrected Nast's spelling and grammar and occasionally deleted embarrassing portions from letters. (Conceivably, Paine may also have used that gentle treatment to indicate to Mark Twain what the humorist could expect if the two worked together.)

When comparing his subject to the leading European artists of the last two centuries, Paine exalted: "Most of them surpassed him in mere technique, and Nast himself was always the first to make this admission. But in fertility of thought, in originality of idea, in absolute convictions and splendid moral courage, in achievements that shall make men revere his name and memory, Thomas Nast was the peer of them all."[10]

Th. Nast: His Period and His Pictures appeared in April 1904 in *Pearson's Magazine*, in the first of six monthly installments. The Macmillen Company published the 583-page book in October. Pyne Press reprinted it in facsimile in the late 1960s.

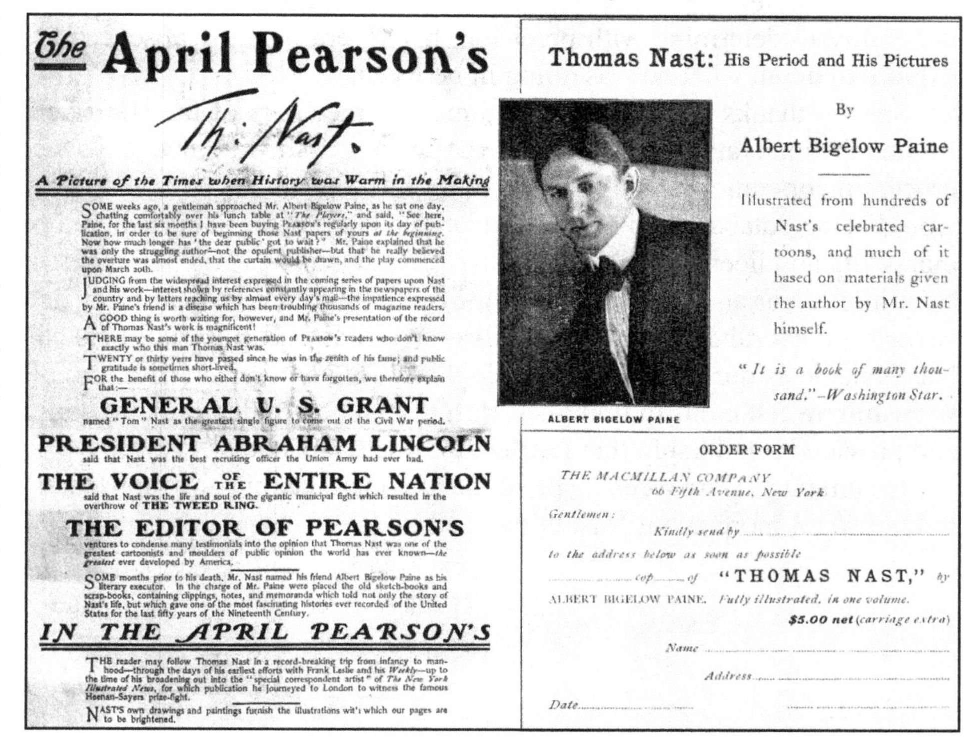

* See p. xxix

HarpWeek

After graduating from Dartmouth College in 1949 — with an MBA but without any history courses under my belt — my principal business experience was as a management consultant and entrepreneur. As an amateur historian, my consulting expertise paved the way for this book, and my actual road led through advertising.

More than fifty years ago, I started AdTel, Ltd., a market research business, which used novel dual-cable television to break new ground in measuring television advertising effectiveness and testing new products. By 1972, I had conducted several hundred meaningful tests, and became interested in the history of American advertising. One day, I answered a *New York Times* ad for the sale of some duplicate annual volumes of *Harper's Weekly* — America's de facto illustrated "newspaper of record" from 1857 to 1912 — and soon found myself the owner of a complete set of fifty-six volumes. Their sixteen lineal feet languished, mostly untouched on their custom-built shelves, for about twenty years.[11]

As a retirement hobby, I decided to have all 2,912 issues *manually* indexed. That included 173,000 ads, but it was the 10,000 cartoons and 65,000 illustrations by artists like Winslow Homer and Frederic Remington that really caught my attention.

My new company, HarpWeek LLC, manually indexed, scanned and retyped all 73,000 pages of *Harper's Weekly* over twelve years, with a staff of as many as fourteen historians working on it. *HarpWeek*, my proprietary digital database, has been licensed to more than 500 academic institutions and public libraries. (For this, and another database called *Lincoln and the Civil War*, I was awarded the 2003 e-Lincoln Prize in history, a big deal for a non-academic like me.)

When I delved deeper, the artistry and political impact of Thomas Nast's cartoons and illustrations totally captured my interest. Consequently, I had the indexers prepare a chronological listing of all Nast's work, including their size and location within each issue. Then we were able to identify 445 of the 450 people whom Nast drew. Finally, we indexed them by name, topic (e.g., Presidential Election Losers, Scandals, Civil Service Reform, Tariffs) and literary source, if any (e.g., Shakespeare by play and character).

These unique and exclusive compilations, along with relevant text, provided a complete visual record of Nast's quarter-century at *Harper's Weekly*. With them and the contextual **HarpWeek** database for a backbone, reporting and fleshing out Nast's life and work objectively became much more doable. A valuable by-product was the ability to determine with precision, his several lengthy absences from and returns to the periodical, and to explore in depth what he was doing in between.

Special thanks and credit go to three key members of the HarpWeek team. General Manager **Greg Weber** created the innovative database in the early days of the Internet, and successfully managed the indexing and data-processing operations — all with no footprints to walk in. Without Greg's exceptional skills and dedication, there would be no database and no biography. The late **Susan Severtson**, a librarian by profession, did a superb job of marketing and licensing our databases.

Chief historian **Robert C. Kennedy** also played a critical role. Before joining HarpWeek at its birth, Rob wrote his doctoral dissertation on George William Curtis, the political editor of *Harper's Weekly* for 30 years, and Nast's nemesis during his last decade there. He co-created (with me) 30 free Nast-related websites available at **www.harpweek.com**. In doing so, Rob researched in depth the historical context behind hundreds of cartoons, and provided scholarship that I utilized to write this book.

In summary, HarpWeek inspired me to undertake this biography, and was a useful starting point. But I needed to know a lot more about Nast to proceed.

Draper Hill

Without doubt, the late Draper Hill should have authored the definitive biography of Thomas Nast. A Harvard graduate and cartoon historian, he was obsessed with Nast for four decades, and probably spent more time on his avocation than he did on his day job as the political cartoonist for the *Detroit News*. In 1983, Draper took advantage of a Guggenheim Fellowship to study the Nast scrapbooks, letters and sketches in more than 20 libraries, museums and private collections. As a professional cartoonist, he had special insights into Nast's life and work, and understood him better — and certainly more objectively — than Paine did.

For example, Nast always believed he was born on September 27, 1840. Draper dug his birth certificate out of the municipal records in Landau, Germany, and found that his actual birthday was September 26.

However, after twenty-five years of collecting, researching and analyzing "everything Nast," Draper had at least three related problems: writer's block, deteriorating health, and an innate inability to organize his voluminous material into a coherent structure. Here is Draper as depicted by a fellow cartoonist, and as he accurately portrayed himself to me on a 2005 envelope, four years before he died at age 73.

Caricature by George Fisher

After meeting Draper in 1995, I commissioned him to help identify the 450 different individuals Nast drew in *Harper's Weekly*; his batting average was 99%. In retrospect, this turned out to be the key factor in documenting Nast's unique role as a visual historian.

However, it soon became clear that Draper's inertia when it came to writing Nast's biography trumped his encyclopedic knowledge. Moreover, his declining health increased the chances of that unduplicatable silo of Nastography disappearing forever when he died. Accordingly, I commissioned Draper to focus on four specific projects over six years (as "works for hire"):

- Write separate lengthy essays on Nast's 1871 and 1872 campaigns against Boss Tweed and Presidential candidate Horace Greeley, respectively, which led to my 2008 book on Nast vs. Tweed.[12*]
- Select, and sequentially explain in depth, Nast's 100 best/most important cartoons in *Harper's Weekly*; he reached 60 before he petered out. His research and artistic insights are reflected in explanations of almost all of those 60 cartoons included in this biography.
- Create a Nast biography as best he could. His 95-page biographical treatise was extremely disorganized — thoughts on people and topics scattered randomly throughout — but well written and chock full of details nobody else would have known.

In summary, this biography could not have been written without Draper's collective contributions. His spirit, as well as Nast's, lives within it.

---

* *Doomed by Cartoon: How Cartoonist Thomas Nast and The New York Times Brought Down Boss Tweed and His Ring of Thieves*

Richard Samuel West

Rich West also deserves a shout-out for his continuing invaluable assistance ever since we met in 1995. He is an extremely knowledgeable cartoon historian and has written extensively about several of Nast's contemporaries — especially Joseph Keppler who eclipsed Nast a few years after he founded *Puck* in 1877. That story is detailed, utilizing Rich's scholarship and *Puck's* cartoons to illustrate Keppler's emergence contrasted with Nast's decline. Rich's initial contribution to my project was an informative commissioned essay entitled *Nast in Decline*.[13]

More important, however, Rich enabled me to understand the first six years of Nast's career with as much insight as his next 25 at *Harper's Weekly*. Rich owns Periodyssey, a leading dealer in nineteenth century periodicals. Early on, he sold me the rare 1856-1862 volumes of *Frank Leslie's Illustrated Newspaper, New York Illustrated News*, and *Illustrated London News* in which Nast's illustrations and work appeared, as well as anti-Nast cartoons from various humor publications. Later, he sold me issues of several magazines from 1889-1895, in which Nast's work was published after he left *Harper's Weekly*.

Because of Frank Leslie's policy of keeping his illustrators anonymous, Nast's work during his 30 months there was unsigned; however, with help from Draper and Rich, we were able to identify it. Most significant for this biography, is the inclusion of Leslie's 1858 campaign against "Swill Milk" (contaminated by distillery slops), Nast's first municipal scandal. It was an important and amusing trailblazer, to which Paine devoted only one paragraph and none of the sardonic cartoons which led to a libel trial in court.[14]

In addition to covering the first international boxing championship in England (American John Heenan vs. Englishman Tom Sayers) and Giuseppe Garibaldi's 1860 campaign to unify Italy, Nast drew about 135 Civil War illustrations and 40 cartoons for *New York Illustrated News*. Paine covered the European adventure in depth, but totally ignored Nast's Civil War pictures for the *News*, even though they more than doubled the 62 he drew for *Harper's Weekly*. Neither has any subsequent author covered them; this biography does.

A number of those illustrations merely copied the sketches of frontline artists on to woodblocks. Other illustrations re-created battle scenes from written accounts when there were no artists' drawings available — as Nast had learned to do in Italy.

However, some of his cartoons were notable forerunners of his later pictorial victories, especially his first *serialized* attack on an individual. His despised target was pompous "Bull Run" (William H.) Russell, the influential *London Times* reporter who infamously predicted that the North would lose the Civil War after losing its first battle (from which he fled without seeing it). Russell's biased articles — intimating that England should support the South — were a potential game-changer that infuriated the North.

Over the years, Rich answered lots of questions for me. When I completed my final draft in book format, Rich carefully reviewed and edited about 750 pages of text and illustrations — challenging facts, assertions and conclusions while suggesting additions and deletions. Effectively, he edited my biography with a depth of overall knowledge that nobody else alive could have provided because they don't "speak Nast." Thank you, Rich!!

Having verified the book's accuracy, Rich also pressured me to get advice on improving the layout and presentation of its thousand-plus cartoons and illustrations from **Frank Pauer**, a graphic designer and cartoonist recently retired from the University of Dayton. Many of Frank's suggestions — including the cover — have been adopted, and I am grateful to him for making the biography's illustrated content easier to look at and comprehend.

Rich before I knew him

Alice Caulkins

The late Alice Caulkins was Curator of the Nast Collection at the Macculloch Hall Historical Museum across the street from his Morristown home, as well as President of The Thomas Nast Society. She, along with Jeffrey Eger and other volunteers, was responsible for inspiring and publishing more than 100 articles on diverse aspects of Nast's life. Over 16 years, beginning in 1987, *The Journal of The Thomas Nast Society* provided detailed information about Nast not available elsewhere: e.g., lists of the books he illustrated; reprints of informative articles by his contemporaries; and copies of the catalogues listing the memorabilia that Sallie auctioned off to raise money in the years following his death.

Alice gave me my earliest education about Nast. She wrote a commissioned essay for me on Nast's *Caricaturama*, which Paine basically ignored (as discussed previously). Only eight of the 33 historical panels survive; five of them, licensed from Macculloch Hall with Alice's assistance, are pictured in this biography.

Morton Keller

In 1968, the late Morton Keller, Professor of Political, Legal and Economic History at Brandeis University, focused on the context of Nast's cartoons (the only author to do so before me). In *The Art and Politics of Thomas Nast*, he carefully selected 241 cartoons from *Harper's Weekly*, and discussed "the political milieu from which they came" in a dozen thoughtful chapters.

30 years after his book was published, "Mickey" Keller wrote a commissioned essay for me, entitled *Thomas Nast and National Politics*. He covered the elections of 1864, 1866 (mid-term), 1868 and 1872 by putting Nast's extraordinary political cartoons into the broader context of their time.

Commissioned Essays

In addition to the essays discussed above, seven distinguished professors wrote commissioned papers for me in the late 1990s. They related Nast's specific cartoons to their academic specialties, and collectively provided me with many enlightening insights that have been incorporated into this biography.[15]

- The late **Albert Boime** of UCLA wrote *The Interactivity of Thomas Nast and High Art*. Al's unique analysis of how carefully-selected Nast cartoons were reflected in subsequent paintings by Edgar Degas and Vincent Van Gogh, was especially noteworthy.
- The late **Roger Fischer** of the University of Minnesota, Duluth, wrote *Thomas Nast and National Politics: 1876-1884*, picking up where Morton Keller left off (1864-72). Roger also was helpful in identifying some of Nast's later caricatures which Draper Hill wasn't sure about.
- **Thomas C. Leonard** of the University of California, Berkeley, wrote *Thomas Nast and the New Language of American Politics*. Tom's focus was on Nast's key role in developing a visual language for politics; its evolution on the Internet is dominant today.
- **Stephen Nissenbaum** of the University of Massachusetts wrote *Nast and Christmas*. Steve had just published a social and cultural history of Christmas so his essay on Nast couldn't have been more timely.[16]
- **Harry Rusche** of Emory University wrote *Oh For a Muse of Fire: Thomas Nast and William Shakespeare*. Harry taught Shakespeare, and his insights were extraordinary as he elaborated on "the aptness with which Nast chose his quotations." Nast's readers learned Shakespeare in school, so Harry's ability to explain context from both the playwright, and the situation Nast portrayed, has been extremely helpful.
- **Brooks Simpson** of Arizona State University, a Grant biographer, wrote *Nast and Grant* with special insight.

- **Mark W. Summers** of the University of Kentucky wrote *Thomas Nast and the Paper Tigers*. Mark's expertise was on the nineteenth century press and — often related — scandals from that era. A cartoonist himself, Mark's detailed acerbic commentary on individual cartoons added light and context on why Nast drew them. Equally important, Mark pointed out when Nast deliberately didn't comment at all, or did so impersonally, to protect President Grant in the face of widespread criminal behavior by his underlings.
- **Joshua Brown**, of the Graduate Center of the City University of New York — an expert on *Frank Leslie's Illustrated Newspaper* (the subject of his book)* — provided helpful guidance on Nast's work for that publication, gang battles in New York and other municipal topics relevant to Nast's early career. Josh also contributed some insightful editorial comments as my biography progressed. Thank you, Josh!

Other Input

With several hundred pages of commissioned essays added to my HarpWeek base, and Paine's biography as background, I traveled in Draper's footsteps by visiting a dozen libraries which had Nast collections, and studying his scrapbooks, letters, sketches, and relevant contemporary newspapers. Reviewing them enabled me to connect lots of small dots into a more complete narrative. For example, Nast's 1860 diary at the **Rutherford B. Hayes Library** in Fremont, Ohio, detailed his accounts receivable by client publication, as well as his daily European adventures in England, Italy and Germany; Librarian **Nan Card** was especially helpful to me in going through Nast's memorabilia.

Other important Nast-related material is at Brown University (The John Hay Library); Dartmouth College (Hood Museum); Princeton University; the University of Minnesota; The Huntington Library (San Marino, CA); New York Public Library; The Pierpont Morgan Library; and the New York Historical Society. Although I don't have specific names, I am grateful to all their librarians who walked the extra mile to help me.

Three institutions in particular hosted me on multiple occasions, and were extra-special resources.

• American Antiquarian Society

AAS in Worcester, MA was the first institution I visited back in 1995. Print curator **Georgia (Gigi) Barnhill** was especially helpful over the years, as were **Jackie Penny** and **Lauren Hewes** more recently. Most of the *Phunny Phellow* cartoons in the book came from AAS.

• Macculloch Hall Historical Museum

After Alice Caulkins retired, **Ryan Hyman** took over as Curator of the Thomas Nast Collection, located in a 210-year old house across the street from the Morristown home where Nast spent the last 31 years of his life. Ryan and photographer **Stan Freeney** provided me with the quality copies of unique Nast photos and drawings which are in this biography. The nucleus of the collection came from Nast's youngest child Cyril (born in 1878), a boyhood friend of the Museum's founder, W. Parsons Todd.

• Morristown and Morris Township Library

In its New Jersey History Center, the library contains many singular drawings, paintings and non-*Harper's Weekly* illustrations of its hometown celebrity. Curator **Chris Jochem** was especially helpful before she retired, and **James Lewis** and **Carolyn Dorsey** subsequently filled her shoes superbly over several intense and detailed days of study.

---

* *Beyond the Lines: Pictorial Reporting, Everyday Life and the Crisis of Gilded Age America (2002)*

• Missouri Historical Society: The Gunn Diaries

Thomas Butler Gunn, an Englishman, lived in New York from 1849 to 1863, and was a close friend of the various Edwards family members — particularly Sallie, whom Nast married. Gunn disliked Nast, but his daily jottings of young, unsophisticated Tommy's successful wooing of Sallie, as well as both their interactions with other key individuals in Nast's early business and social life, provided "I was there" accurate insights not available elsewhere, and unknown to Paine. Curator **Jaime Bourassa**, who oversaw the transcribing and typing of 800 Gunn Diary pages, printed out the 200 that related to Nast's personal life, saving me weeks of work, for which I am most grateful.

Cheryl Tomas

It has taken twelve years and dozens of yellow pads to write this biography. My truly indispensable heroine is Cheryl Tomas, who typed multiple drafts. With guidance from Frank Pauer, Cheryl also did the page layouts — not easy when sizing, labeling and integrating cartoons and illustrations with relevant context — and has also been involved with publishing, distribution and my **ThomasNast.com** website. Thank you, Cheryl!!

Greg Weber

As mentioned under HarpWeek, Greg Weber created the database on which this biography was conceived and predicated. Fifteen years after its completion, he volunteered to develop my **ThomasNast.com** website. Thank you, Greg!!

Editorial Considerations

• For quick identification and reference, periodical identification, date and page number for every cartoon and illustration has been included, even when the original didn't have this information adjacent to it. Covers have a "C" appended to the page number. Primary publications are denoted as follows:

HW	*Harper's Weekly*. (Sometimes referred to as *Harper's* or the *Weekly*.)
FLIN	*Frank Leslie's Illustrated Newspaper*. (Sometimes referred to as *Leslie's*.)
ICN	*Illustrated Chicago News*.
ILN	*Illustrated London News*.
NYIN	*New York Illustrated News*.
PP	*Phunny Phellow*.

• Within the biography itself, people of color are referred to as "black" (lower case). This terminology is in accord with the personal advice given to me by Dr. John Hope Franklin, a leading Black history scholar.[17] Today, "black" is capitalized, but it would have been inauthentic to have changed it from the way it was spelled in *Harper's Weekly* and nineteenth century cartoons.

HW August 26, 1871 804

THOMAS NAST, ARTIST OF "HARPER'S WEEKLY."

Chapter 1
Growing Up

Landau

After Napoleon Bonaparte's disastrous 1813 Russian campaign and his subsequent defeats in France, he abdicated in April 1814 and was exiled to the island of Elba in the Mediterranean. The victorious allied European powers — Britain, Austria, Russia and Prussia — were lenient with France and Napoleon. They exacted no war indemnities, let France keep her pre-Napoleonic boundaries, and permitted Napoleon to retain his title of Emperor and a pension, in a failed effort to promote stability in France.

Early the following year, Napoleon escaped from Elba and landed in France in March 1815. After his "Reign of a Hundred Days" ended with his defeat at the Battle of Waterloo in June, Napoleon abdicated for the second time and was exiled to the South Atlantic island of St. Helena off the African coast. This time the Quadruple Alliance imposed harsh terms on France, including the loss of significant territories, as the Congress of Vienna redrew the map of Europe. The small walled city of Landau which had been part of France since 1680, was ceded to the German Confederation on November 20, 1815.

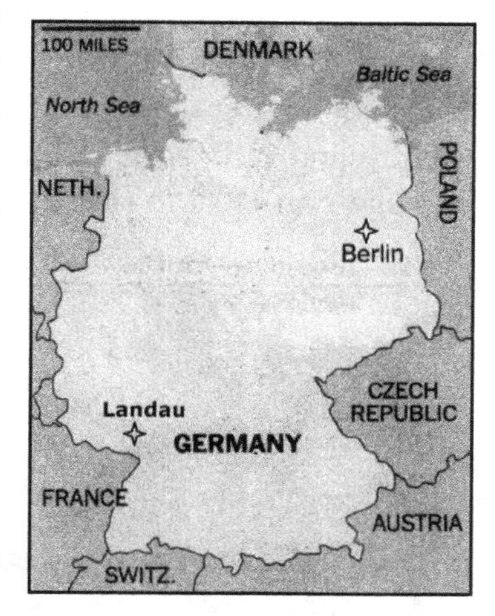

Landau, located several miles west of the Rhine River in the Palatinate, was originally settled early in the twelfth century. King Louis XIV of France fortified Landau at the end of the seventeenth century with a gigantic citadel to anchor the French border at the Rhine, and to defend against an attack from the northwest which never came. The 1815 Treaty of Paris transferred the city to the Kingdom of Bavaria, even though it was geographically separated from Bavaria.

Thomas Nast was born inside the Landau fortification in an old barracks building dating to 1759. He always celebrated his birthday on September 27, but his birth certificate — issued under the auspices of the King of Bavaria — confirms the day-earlier date of his birth as September 26, 1840. (See extract below).

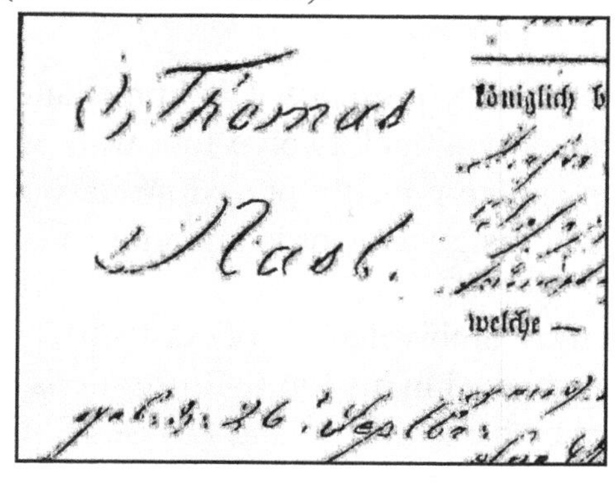

The Author at Thomas Nast's Birthplace in 1995.

Nast's father, Joseph Thomas Nast, played the trombone and/or trumpet in the Ninth Royal Bavarian Infantry Regiment Marching Band. Joseph, about 31 when Thomas was born, was the son of the music director of St. John's church in Nabburg, a small hilltop city not far from the Czech border. Joseph was raised in his father's tiny apartment at the top of the church's high drafty steeple. After his father died in 1827, Joseph joined the army and ultimately settled in Landau.

In 1834, Joseph married Apollonia Abriss, who was about eight years older. Apollonia, born in 1801, had left her French farm family around 1818 to work for a dyer in Landau. Thomas had three siblings who died in infancy or early childhood, and an older sister Carolina. Landau's population was about five to six thousand when the Nast family lived there.

Macculloch Hall Historical Museum

When he was 17, Tommy drew these penciled sketches of his father and mother.

Although his mother's native language was French, Tommy was raised in a German-speaking household. Pictures of the King and Queen of Bavaria hung over his parents' bed on either side of a crucifix. Both parents were observant Catholics at that time.

However, Tommy's aunt who, like his mother, had been born in Napoleonic France, gave her late Emperor a place of honor in her parlor with two popular prints. Napoleon's remains had been returned from St. Helena to Paris in the year of Nast's birth, and one of the prints was an engraving of his tomb in Les Invalides. The other showed the unmistakable silhouette of Napoleon surprising a dozing sentry, who then challenged him with a superfluous "Who goes there?" Tommy remembered the picture and utilized it in 1862 to portray General George B. McClellan (often derided as a "Little Napoleon"), and again in 1870 to ridicule Napoleon III at the time of his imminent defeat in the Franco-Prussian War of 1870.

HW November 15, 1862 725

THE ARMY OF THE POTOMAC — "LITTLE MAC" MAKING HIS ROUNDS

HW August 27, 1870 552

WHO GOES THERE? — "A FRIEND."

Tommy's early years were dominated by the city's military presence. His immediate backyard contained a bleak, almost windowless, seventy-foot tower, surrounded by a thick twelve-foot wall, which had served as the local prison for centuries. Tommy was the soldiers' pet and continually played military games in which he was always the "captain." The colorful uniforms, medals and insignia, swords and guns, martial music and barked orders all left a lasting impression on him.

Not surprisingly, Napoleon became the first — and most ambivalent — of Nast's lifelong handful of personal paragons. His three most prominent lifetime "heroes" portrayed in his future illustrations and cartoons were also successful military commanders: Giuseppe Garibaldi, Abraham Lincoln and Ulysses S. Grant. They were polar contrasts to his natural inclination to portray and ridicule "villains," of whom there were dozens that he found or created over the years.

During the 1830s and 1840s, political turmoil in the German states, as well as much of the rest of Continental Europe, caused unrest and uprisings, culminating in the several Revolutions of 1848 involving France, Italy, Hungary and Austria, as well as Germany. Napoleon I had imposed a workable system of local government on the Palatinate, but King Louis I of Bavaria and his ministers aborted many of the rights of its elected representatives, including a free press and a voice on tax issues and trade restrictions. Demands for trial by jury and a liberal constitution were ignored or refused. Adding to the stress of political turmoil by 1846, were lean grain harvests and the potato blight — best known for famishing Ireland but also devastating in Continental Europe — which resulted in inflated food prices and consequent bread and potato riots in the German states.

The combination of political agitation and economic distress motivated Joseph Nast, who had strong and outspoken liberal convictions, to emigrate to America as his empathetic military commander advised. In June 1846, he sent his wife, daughter and five-year old son to New York City. They had a memorable trip through Strasbourg and Paris, including some sight-seeing, before sailing in steerage from Havre on an American ship.

However, Joseph did not join his family until 1849 or 1850. First, he enlisted on a French warship and later on the Ohio, an American ship. Tommy had to live without his father during his first three to four formative years in his new country.

The Nast family's emigration was part of an increasing German flow. Incomplete U.S. immigration statistics show that about 8,000 German immigrants came to the U.S. in the 1820-30 decade, 152,000 in the 1830s and 435,000 in the 1840s. Many of them settled in the New York area, so the three-member Nast family had plenty of compatriots to relate to when they arrived in the summer of 1846, shortly before Tommy's sixth birthday. By 1855, almost one in six of the 600,000 New Yorkers was German-American.

New York

In the mid-nineteenth century, more than half of the city's residents lived in boarding houses. Many of them were run by women, especially widows, who provided crammed rooms and unappetizing meals, but put up with many eccentric, disorderly and dishonest tenants. Some catered to German-speaking immigrants, and it is likely that Apollonia Nast and her two children found refuge in one of them on Greenwich Street.

In 1857, eleven years after the Nast family arrived, Thomas Butler Gunn published a classic book called *The Physiology of New York Boarding-Houses*.[1] It was comically illustrated by Gunn, Alfred Waud and Frank Bellew, all of whom would become well acquainted with Tommy Nast in his teens and later life. Its thirty-three sardonic chapters included one on the German "Gasthaus," where the "needy contrived to lodge singly, or in twos and threes, with some fellow countrymen."

OUR BOARDING MISTRESS.

A TIPPERARIAN SOIREE MUSICALE, OVER THE HEAD OF A QUIET BOARDER.

Gunn's prototypical gasthaus also was located on Greenwich Street. He described it as an old fashioned Revolutionary War era mansion with a leaky roof and three or four rickety wooden steps off a stoop. It could accommodate up to twenty boarders, most of them recent immigrants. The men generally smoked pipes or cigars, played musical instruments and talked about the "vedder." Three meals a day were provided: "Huge dishes of baked pork swimming in grease, rank cow-beef, half warm sour-kraut, dishes of prunes and dried apples, soup apparently derived from cabbages, stale beer and moldy beans." The parlor had been converted into a lager-bier saloon, which was the focal place for relaxation.

After getting their initial bearings in the city, many of the German, as well as other immigrants, moved into homes where they rented spare rooms from the owners. When Apollonia and her two children made their first move to William Street, a few blocks away, it is likely that this was their arrangement.

Here, Dame Fortune smiled on Tommy. One of his new neighbors manufactured crayon sticks for artists. He gave some of his faulty crayons to Tommy, who drew indiscriminately and covered his walls with pictures. The seminal seed for an unsurpassed artistic career sprouted right there.

Dyslexia

The Nast family spoke only a Rhineland dialect of German at home, a circumstance that would have made education difficult for any young immigrant. Tommy, however, was also handicapped by dyslexia, a continuing impediment which would plague him for the rest of his life. Throughout his youth and his subsequent career, he would hear one thing and write another: “was” became “saw”; “science” emerged as “since”; etc. Some of his less carefully edited cartoons reveal his failure to overcome this inherent learning disability.

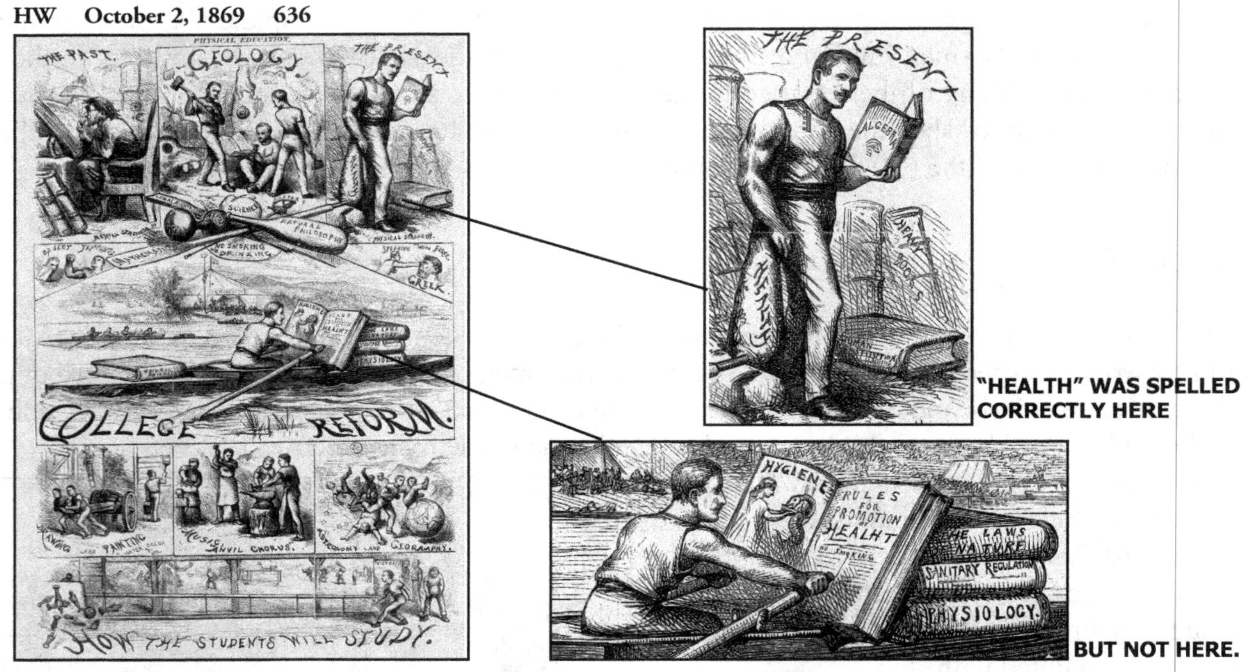

After Tommy married Sarah (Sallie) Edwards on his twenty first birthday, she edited the titles and other wording in his cartoons and illustrations and wrote almost all his correspondence. Asked on occasion, “if he ever wrote anything but his signature,” he answered: “Not if I can help it. My pen won’t spell right, anyway.” Sallie enabled him to focus his talent on his caricatures without worrying about his spelling or grammar, thereby eliminating his understandable innate and realistic concern of looking foolish to his public.

Nast always preferred to have his pictures speak for him, using small illustrations to convey his meaning. One story that he used to tell in later life, and which was repeated in a number of publications, concerned a young lady from Ohio who sent him a letter containing a formal proposal of marriage; she even included references. He responded with a cartoon of his wife and children labelled: “The only objections.”

Macculloch Hall Historical Museum

Like other apparent dyslexics — Leonardo da Vinci and Walt Disney were two whose artistic talents were exceptional — Nast's ability to draw, write and engrave on wood blocks for reproduction almost certainly was enhanced by his learning disability. Today, studies using M.R.I.'s and cognitive testing have demonstrated that dyslexics may have exceptional three-dimensional, "out-of-the-box," big picture thinking. Effectively, drawing minutely, *in reverse* and at high speed, was the silver lining in Nast's dyslexic cloud.

Handicapped by language and an inability to concentrate or to relate to his peers, as well as by dyslexia, Tommy Nast's seven years of public school education were disastrous. Before they ended at age thirteen in the spring of 1854, he had attended several different schools, some teaching in German and some in English. Regardless of the school, Tommy showed no aptitude for math or grammar or spelling — only for drawing. "Go finish your picture, Nast; you will never learn to read or figure" was what he remembered one teacher telling him.[2]

HW April 2, 1864 217

Nast's 1864 April Fool's Day cartoon contained a vignette of school as he probably remembered it. He may have pictured himself as the boy with the dunce cap marked "Fool" sitting against the teacher's desk. The teacher, with a switch in his hand, made fools suffer.

Life in the City

Life outside school must have been equally rough for young Tommy. The lower Manhattan Fifth and Sixth Wards were teeming with street urchins and gangs who probably found the short, fat boy with a German accent a tempting target for verbal and physical abuse. As mentioned earlier, until he was nine or ten, he had no father at home for guidance or protection; his mother spoke only German, so she couldn't make it easier for her son.

The Sixth Ward included the notorious Five Points (today's Chinatown); among other residents, its tenements were packed with Irish immigrant criminals, prostitutes and alcoholics. It's inhabitants, as well as those in other wards, included thousands of unwanted children who had no home and lived on the streets as best they could. Many of the young girls became prostitutes; the legal age of consent was 10. Some of those lowlifes belonged to the gangs, whose riotous 1857 brawl Nast covered for *Frank Leslie's Illustrated Newspaper*. While Tommy certainly had his share of encounters with Irish immigrants at school and in the streets during his youth, this assignment must have solidified his contempt for their sloth and almost continuous intoxication as he saw it. His impressions and prejudices stayed with him in his future cartoons, particularly many of those directed at the Tweed Ring more than a decade later.

In 1860, Nast drew a series of Five Points illustrations for the *New York Illustrated News*, which provided a candid picture of life in the slums (and were published without accreditation). The text and sketches depicted the sad plight of Irish immigrants, sleeping up to four to a bed at six cents each per night, and eating a plate of unappetizing food for another six cents. Drunkenness, prostitution, thievery, sickness and general misery were universal. Close to half of New York's Irish population spoke only Gaelic.

NYIN February 25, 1860 229

BACKGROUNDS OF CIVILIZATION. —A FIVE POINTS DINING AND LODGING ROOM, ON THE CORNER OF BAXTER AND WORTH STREETS.

BACKGROUNDS OF CIVILIZATION. —MRS. CROWN'S FIVE POINTS BAR-ROOM, ON CROWN'S CORNER, WORTH AND CROSS STREETS.

The Turners Society

An important part of Joseph Nast's life was membership in the New York Turners Society (the German Turnverein). First organized in Germany in 1811 in opposition to Napoleon, the 1848 revolutionary emigrants organized chapters in New York, Brooklyn and other cities in the East and Midwest, beginning about 1850. The Turners had singing societies, bands, parades, picnics, gymnastics, boat races, rifle tournaments, dances and last, but not least, lots of lager beer served to picnic-goers of all ages. Contacts with German emigrants who played a role in Tommy's future life probably were initiated via fellow Turner acquaintances of his father. The Seventh Annual Social Turnvest was described in a four-page article in *Frank Leslie's Illustrated News*, where Tommy worked at the time. They included a picture of his father seated drinking "A Mug of Lager Bier."

FLIN September 12, 1857 231

A FAMILY SCENE AT THE PICNIC

A HORN OF LAGER BIER AND MUG OF LAGER BIER.

Kossuth

A memorable event in Tommy's early years occurred after Joseph Nast took his eleven-year old son to a parade welcoming Hungarian nationalist Louis Kossuth to Manhattan in December 1851. Kossuth was a prime mover in the Revolution of 1848 when he tried unsuccessfully to gain Hungary's independence from Austria and, consequently, became a leader of European liberalism.

Kossuth was honored as much for the cause he represented as for himself, so he was a true hero to Joseph Nast and his compatriots. Although Kossuth met with President Millard Fillmore, was received by Congress, and delivered several hundred speeches around the country, the United States policy of non-interference in European affairs blocked his cause.

Kossuth's statue on the cover of the January 17, 1852 issue of Gleason's Pictorial (a pioneer illustrated weekly with little current news in it) was copied by the embryonic artist, praised by his teacher, and framed and hung by the desk of the school principal.

January 17, 1852

EQUESTRIAN STATUE OF LOUIS KOSSUTH, GOVERNOR OF HUNGARY

Fires

Fires were a common occurrence in everyday life. Back in 1835, 600 buildings were destroyed by a single large fire in New York. The sparks of stoves and gaslights, in close proximity to wooden structures, ensured that there would always be lots of action with clanging bells, running horses and heroic rough-and-tumble firemen. On occasion, even the steam fire engines themselves were known to explode. The excitement of running to and watching fires provided some of the memorable times in Tommy's childhood.

During his impressionable boyhood years, the Americus Engine Company No. 6, known as the "Big Six," was located half a mile or so from Tommy's home. Its foreman was none other than Bill Tweed, at that time a figure whom Nast looked up to, and later one of his favorite cartoon targets as Boss Tweed. The engine of the Big Six had a tiger painted on it, a front view with fierce distended jaws, which awed young Tommy. That emblem became the source for Nast's Tammany Tiger, which evolved into a key symbol in the destruction of the Tweed Ring more than twenty years later. The Big Six tiger itself had been copied from a French chromolithograph which Tommy probably saw hanging in the shop of a local coffee dealer.

Macculloch Hall Historical Museum

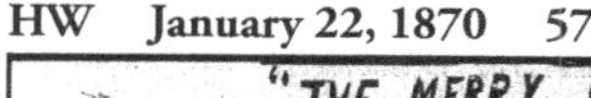

HW January 22, 1870 57

Nast's 1870 cartoon of Tweed leading the Big Six in a riotous brawl captured the action as he visualized it.

Collection of Independent Hose Company No. 1, Morristown. On Display at Macculloch Hall Historical Museum.

After he bought a home in Morristown, New Jersey in 1872, Nast prized his honorary membership in Independent Hose Company No. 1. He pictured himself celebrating its centennial twenty-five years later in this oil on canvas.

Theatre

After Joseph Nast, who had mastered English on board ship, reunited with his family in 1849 or 1850, he joined the Philharmonic Society and became a trombonist in the band at Burton's Theatre on Chambers Street. On May 31, 1862, Nast drew a page of nine cartoons — "A Few Military Terms Defined" — for the *New York Illustrated News*, all based on puns; in one of them he drew his father playing the trombone. Joseph had been dead for three years, but the resemblance between father and son was unmistakable.

Joseph's employer, William Evans Burton, was an actor, author, playwright, editor and entrepreneur who became the seminal contributor to Tommy's extracurricular education. Born in London, he came to America in 1834 when he was 30. He changed wives abruptly in July of that year — leaving the first one of eleven years in a hurry; marrying the second, an actress, on the same day; and then promptly crossing the ocean. He had theatrical ventures in Philadelphia, Baltimore and Washington, and also published *Burton's Gentlemen's Magazine* with Edgar Allen Poe as assistant editor. In 1848, he established himself permanently in New York when he bought Palmo's Opera House. He thoroughly renovated the run-down structure, erected a new proscenium, constructed private boxes, and had a new drop curtain painted. Many of his contemporaries considered his venture to be suicidal, but it flourished under Burton from mid-1848 until the spring of 1856.

Theatre was a primary entertainment in New York. Actors and actresses played specific roles in a number of plays, usually at the same theatre for a season. Some of them like Burton, Laura Keene, Lester Wallack and John Brougham went on to lease or buy their own theatres, and act in their own, as well as other old and new plays.

In mid-nineteenth century America, Shakespeare's plays were an inherent part of the school curriculum. The popular *McGuffey's Readers* incorporated many Shakespearean passages to help teach history, elocution, ethics, morality, and civics, in addition to reading and writing. After their schooling ended, even relatively uneducated people were attracted to Shakespearian theatre.

Possibly because he had no sons of his own, Burton became fond of young Tommy and provided him with his own special seat when he accompanied his trombone-playing father to the theatre. From there, Tommy could watch Burton play a number of Shakespearean roles: Falstaff in *The Merry Wives of Windsor*; Bottom in *A Midsummer Night's Dream*; Polonius in *Hamlet*; Caliban in *The Tempest;* and Dromio of Syracuse in *The Comedy of Errors*, among others. The lad also became familiar with Charles Dickens — Burton played Wilkins Micawber in *David Copperfield* — and many other Shakespearean, literary and mythological characters.

NYIN May 1860 408-409

VIEW OF THE OLYMPIC THEATER, LONDON, DURING THE PERFORMANCE OF THE FARCE "B B;" THE QUEEN, THE ROYAL CONSORT AND SUITE BEING PRESENT.—From A Sketch Taken On The Spot By Our Artist, Thomas Nast, Esq.

These characters would appear in future memorable Nast cartoons. He well understood that *Harper's* middle- and upper-class audience appreciated Shakespeare, Dickens, Aesop, the Bible and other literary allusions from their schooling, theatrical and everyday commercial experiences. His satirical cartoon implications and subtle references were not wasted on them.

Perhaps, the most important legacy that Burton left his young admirer was a vital love for the theatre. Whenever he could, Nast went to see a play, at home or abroad. In England in 1860 after the John Heenan - Tom Sayers championship fight, he drew Queen Victoria as part of the audience.

Not all the plays that Burton produced were of Shakespearean caliber. *Breach of Promise, or Second Thoughts are Best* and *A Kiss in the Dark* may have been more typical. One knowledgeable but upset reviewer opined that *Apollo in New York* was "remarkable only for its grossness and required a strong stomach to stand its vulgar and indecent allusions."

As a manager, Burton was considered to be a hard-working but strict taskmaster, warm-tempered but good-natured. As an actor, he was considered to be an exceptionally funny comedian, with extraordinary facial power but a tendency to be unnecessarily coarse and low-brow in some of his roles.

Burton was best known for his role as Timothy Toodles in a play of that name which he re-wrote from the original called *The Broken Heart, or The Farmer's Daughter*. A few months before Burton died in February 1860, Nast — then free-lancing — portrayed him as "Mr. Toodle" on the October 1859 cover of *Comic Monthly*. Forty years later, when Nast was desperately in need of income, he was commissioned to paint Burton as Toodles by William L. Keese, a drama historian and Burton's biographer. The picture was presented to the Player's Club at Gramercy Park in Manhattan to which both Nast and Keese belonged.

In later life Nast credited Burton with the primary responsibility for his own subsequent career as America's leading caricaturist. Beginning in 1873, and intermittently thereafter, Nast spent considerable time on the lecture circuit, visiting well over one hundred cities. He repeatedly told his audiences that he "had gathered his divine inflatus from watching Burton and afterwards sketching that gentleman's drunken scenes with charcoal upon his mother's prayer-book and his father's music lessons. The latter made a note of it."

More specifically, he related that after "seeing Burton at night, he would spend the next morning in practicing up on the well-remembered features." Then he would draw on a screen a vivid picture of Toodles "with his battered hat, cravat sticking straight into the air opposite an ear, and the drunken leer," as various newspapers reported. (Nast literally pasted dozens of reviews of his lectures in his scrapbooks).

Nast became a temperance zealot after the Civil War, especially attacking the Irish for their habitual drunkenness. It is ironic that he received some of his own career impetus from an inebriated theatrical character.

October 1859

Richard West, Periodyssey

BURTON, AS MR. TOODLE.

Nast's Lecture Sketch

WILLIAM E. BURTON AS "TOODLES"
Nast's 1899 Painting

Unfortunately for him, the entrepreneurial bug continued to bite Burton, and in 1856, he closed his Chambers Street Theatre to develop Burton's New Theatre on Bond Street uptown. That theatre failed three years later. Meanwhile, Joseph Nast had moved to the orchestra in Lester Wallack's newer theatre. Joseph was to die in March 1859 and Burton early the following year, but the combination of theatrical knowledge they gave to young Tommy provided him with a solid cultural and literary foundation for his chosen career. His volume of Shakespeare's plays would become the most dog-eared book in his library.

As he matured, Nast also used theatrical settings or stagings in many of his cartoons. He was partial to proscenium arches as an artistic device, and occasionally created a grand spectacle as in a coliseum.

HW May 20, 1865 312-313

HW March 30, 1867 200-201

AMPHITHEATRUM JOHNSONIANUM —(A Coliseum Scene)

HW October 7, 1871 948

In retrospect, Shakespeare's line of "All the world's a stage, And the men and women merely players" fit Nast like a glove. *(As You Like It*, Act II, Scene 7.) His caricatures were the "players" and his cartoon settings, the stage. In fact, by the way Nast groomed and dressed himself, and carefully cultivated his own public persona, he probably would have met Shakespeare's standard for an actor — with one fundamental exception: he was always uncomfortable facing an audience unless he had a crayon in his hand and a sketch pad next to him so he could effectively speak through his pictures.

In summary, the poor student who had trouble reading, writing and even speaking English in school, received the equivalent of a graduate course in theatre. He was to draw theatres, actors and actresses, and refer to and quote from Shakespeare's plays in more than 150 future cartoons and illustrations. The Players Club would become his New York City hangout for the last half of his life. (He moved to New Jersey when he was 31.) William Burton played a far more influential role in Tommy's education than he or anyone else realized at the time and possibly since.

Theodor Kaufmann

After Tommy dropped out of school at age 13, he clashed with his parents over his choice of career. In later life, Nast revealed that his father had threatened to strap him if he refused to enter the family occupation as a musician, or else accept an apprenticeship to a watchmaker. In a March 22, 1885 interview with the *Indianapolis Times*, Nast explained:

> *"I was never fit for anything but picture making . . . I had a turn for drawing when I was a small boy. I went to school like other boys, but I spent the study hours in drawing pictures on my slate . . . The teachers rather pitied me. They thought I was an idiot in other respects and finally concluded that it would be better to let me spend my time in drawing than in doing nothing. My parents had no sympathy with my desire to become an artist. I had to help myself unaided."*

That last sentence may not have been totally accurate. In mid-1854, Tommy was accepted for training in the studio of Theodor Kaufmann, a thirty-nine year old German-born revolutionary who had participated in an uprising in Dresden before emigrating to New York in 1850. It is likely that Joseph Nast knew Kaufmann through the Turners Society and arranged his son's apprenticeship. Thirteen-year old Tommy was Kaufmann's only pupil in the six months or so before his studio at 442 Broadway was destroyed by a disastrous fire on December 19, 1854, the day after he turned forty. Christmas was a sad day that year for Tommy and his now ex-teacher.

While Nast was learning about painting from Kaufmann, he assisted with his tutor's magnum opus, a cycle of eight large oils illustrating *The Development of Religious Liberty*. Kaufmann's descriptive commentary on this series stressed that his principal objective was to express his provocative ideas, as exemplified by a picture entitled *Martin Luther Nailing his Theses on the Door at Worms*.[3]

As Tommy worked on these paintings with his teacher, he was exposed to some pretty radical ideas for an unsophisticated boy of thirteen. For him, their discussions were the equivalent of having a tutor in philosophy, history and religion. Accordingly, the strong feelings that Nast later directed against Catholic political activism in general, and Pope Pius IX in particular, may have been partially incubated and certainly were reinforced by Kaufmann. Kaufmann left no doubt about where he stood with his picture of Luther whose views and actions initiated the Protestant Reformation.*

Just as Kaufmann learned from his German "history painters,"[4] his own pupil was influenced by Kaufmann in several ways. First was shaping Tommy's focus on becoming a "history painter," a phrase which was in vogue throughout the nineteenth century. Nast always wanted to be recognized as a topflight serious artist specializing in historical scenes. However, he came to realize that his talent for caricature was unique, and therefore more marketable and a better pathway to his burning desire for fame. Ultimately, he thought of political cartooning and history painting as sister arts and practiced them together. To ensure accuracy, he researched most of his subjects intensively in order to portray events and public personalities as clearly as possible, even when caricaturing them.

Second was Kaufmann's fierce intent, consistent with his German revolutionary days, to promote his own provocative ideas through his pictures. His young pupil certainly absorbed that lesson well.

Third, was Nast's visual and emotional introduction to the brewing conflict over slavery. In September 1850, the year that Kaufmann emigrated to America, Congress passed the Fugitive Slave Act, which forced federal and free-state officials, and even civilian bystanders, to collaborate in apprehending escaped slaves. The Act was an unprecedented expansion of federal power, enraged many whites who were previously neutral on the issue of slavery, and became a central theme of the 1852 presidential campaign between anti-slavery, Whig candidate General Winfield Scott, and Southern sympathizer Franklin Pierce. Democrat Pierce won 27 of the 31 states.

---

* Tommy's father Joseph probably inculcated some anti-Catholic ideas into his son's head prior to his association with Kaufmann because he believed the Pope was on the wrong side of the Revolution of 1848 and its precedent activities. Although born and raised Catholic in his early years, Tommy became an Episcopalian when he married Sallie Edwards.

In October 1850, as the Act's provisions became widely known and enforced, Kaufmann published and copyrighted a large lithographic print entitled *Effects of the Fugitive-Slave-Law*. It showed a group of four black men ambushed by a posse of six armed whites in a cornfield, with accompanying texts from the Bible (Deuteronomy) and the Declaration of Independence.[5] Tommy undoubtedly saw this print in Kaufmann's studio and had its significance explained to him; its quotation from the Declaration of Independence may well have been his introduction to that document and its importance to his adopted country.

Kaufmann's print must have brought the issue of slavery and the plight of southern blacks home to Tommy in a way that school never did or could have. His resultant positive attitudes toward emancipation for slaves, as well as civil rights and equal opportunity for blacks — and later his compassion for Chinese immigrants and American Indians — were influenced by his teacher's example of taking strong pictorial stands for his fundamental beliefs. In summary, the six months that Tommy spent under Kaufmann's tutelage probably contributed more to his academic education than any similar period before or after. Learning about painting may have been secondary to learning about national politics, religion, history, philosophy and self-expression.[6]

Alfred Fredericks

After the December 1854 fire ended his stint with Kaufmann, fourteen-year old Tommy progressed to the next stage with the help of Alfred Fredericks, a 30-year old English-born artist who had a studio on the same floor as Kaufmann. About fifteen years older than Tommy, Fredericks had emigrated to America in 1848. He became an important mentor in ways which Tommy's father and Theodor Kaufmann never could have. For openers, he let Tommy assist him in painting his panorama of the Crimean War.

The Crimean War began in mid-1853 when Russia moved aggressively against much smaller Turkey. Britain and France allied with Turkey, and ultimately forced Russia into submission after a year-long siege of Sebastapol on the Crimean Peninsula ended in surrender in September 1855. Another Treaty of Paris reversed Russia's territorial gains.

The Crimean War is memorable today primarily because of two British non-combatants. Pioneering nurse Florence Nightingale's introduction of novel sanitary practices into field hospitals significantly lowered British death rates from wounds and disease, while poet Alfred Lord Tennyson's *Charge of the Light Brigade* immortalized the disastrous British defeat at Balaklava.

However, the Crimean War also was responsible for some notable innovations in press coverage. It was the first to be covered live by "special artists," who were dispatched by the *Illustrated London News*. Even more important was the assignment by the *London Times* of William Howard Russell as the first foreign correspondent specifically dispatched to report on an active war from the front lines. Some of Russell's articles became the source of Crimean War news in American newspapers, primarily as excerpts or reprints from the *London Times*. Six years later, Russell would become the first of many "villains" whom Nast attacked serially (when the *Times* sent him to America to cover the incipient Civil War).

Fredericks probably kept up to date with his English homeland through the American press and/or the *Illustrated London News*, which was distributed from Boston about a month late. Perhaps of more importance as a model for some of Nast's future achievements, the Crimean War also was well caricatured by *Punch,* a twelve-year old British humor weekly, which featured cartoonists John Leech and John Tenniel. Regardless of what sources Fredericks used for his Crimean War Panorama — and showed to his young helper — Tommy received plenty of exposure to his future universe of pictorial journalism, as well as to current European geography and history.

As a blossoming landscape and figure painter, Fredericks was well connected at the prestigious National Academy of Design, considered to be the premier art school in America.[7] He saw to it that his young protégé was admitted, and Nast attended night classes for four years. He received standard academic training, and a good grounding in French and other European art and artists. His final student exhibit at the National Academy was a skillful drawing based on the famed armless Venus de Milo, which he audaciously entitled *The Finished Statue* in a foretaste of his future edgy cartoons.

The Academy also held an annual exhibition of original paintings by living artists — pictures never before exhibited — where artists could study and learn from the works of their contemporaries, and the public could buy. However, space on the Academy's crowded walls was extremely hard to come by. Illustrating that, Nast had three humorous cartoons published in the June 1860 issue of *Yankee Notions,* Thomas Strong's successful humor magazine. Called "Peeps in the Academy of Design," they featured Tommy himself trying to get his pictures hung, and suggest that he may even have sold one of them.[8]

PEEPS IN THE ACADEMY OF DESIGN.

Friend (To Artist Who Painted 121).— Why So Pensive, Tom?
Tom.—I Was Just Considering, Whether, If They Made A Hole In The Ceiling, My Picture Could Not Be Hung A Little Higher!

PEEPS IN THE ACADEMY OF DESIGN.

Friend (To Artist).—Why! Why! What's The Matter? Why So Pale? Bless Me! You're Fainting!
Artist—Oh! Oh! Look! Look! Just Look! See What's In The Corner Of My Picture!

During the day, along with his fellow students and, on occasion, Fredericks, Tommy visited art galleries to study, critique and sometimes copy the paintings he saw there. Among them was the Bryan Gallery of Christian Art, across the street from Wallack's Theatre where his father now worked. Founder Thomas Bryan was a wealthy, eccentric collector, who exhibited an odd assortment of several hundred old masters, many of which were erroneously attributed or fake copies. A passionate idealist who had studied art and begun assembling his collection in Paris, Bryan hoped to spark an American renaissance by exposing the public to eminent examples of the European tradition. (New York City had no public art museums until the Metropolitan Museum of Art opened in 1872). Bryan charged a 25 cent admission fee and admitted art students free.

Bryan, about 57, only five feet, three inches tall and stocky at 180 pounds, may have identified somewhat with the short, roly-poly Tommy Nast, whom he allowed to bring an easel to his gallery and copy the paintings. Paid visitors were attracted to Tommy and his work, and Bryan eventually made him door-keeper. This was Nast's first regular paying job because Bryan let him keep all the admission fees he took in over Bryan's own set minimum.

By mid-1856, when Tommy was almost sixteen, his father must have encouraged him to find a salaried position. Joseph Nast could not have found it easy to keep paying for his son's artistic education from his musician's wages of about ten dollars a week at Wallack's, supplemented by playing in a brass band at Dodsworth's Hall and Hotel, and with the Philharmonic Orchestra. Reciprocally, Tommy wanted to prove to his doubting parents that his ability to draw — as enhanced by Kaufmann, Fredericks and the National Academy — could provide him with enough income to contribute to both his own and his family's support.

Fredericks probably arranged an introduction to Frank Leslie in August 1856. Leslie had started his eponymous *Illustrated Newspaper* eight months earlier with lots of nerve and little capital. Fredericks began contributing illustrations to it on a free-lance basis in early 1856. His protégé went to see Leslie to ask for a job, and Thomas Nast's career as a pictorial journalist was launched.

Chapter 2
The Emergence of Frank Leslie

Henry Carter

Frank Leslie was almost twenty years older than Thomas Nast. He was born on March 21, 1821 and christened Henry Carter. His father, Joseph Leslie Carter, was a glove manufacturer in Ipswich, England, about 70 miles northeast of London. Like another glove manufacturer, John Shakespeare of Stratford, a century and a half earlier, Joseph wanted his son to carry on the family business. But like John's son William, Henry had a literary and artistic bent and followed his own path to inform and entertain the public while making a comfortable living.

When Henry was 17, his father sent him to London to work behind the counter in the glove department of Ellis & Everington, his uncle's dry goods store. Henry's flair and passion for engraving motivated him while the "dreary drudgery of the (retail glove) desk's dead wood" turned him off. He had to keep his artistic efforts hidden from his father and uncle who strongly discouraged and disapproved of them.

Accordingly, when submitting his engraved pictures to various publications, he adopted Frank Leslie as a pseudonym, utilizing his father's middle name. Thirty years later, Leslie said that he adopted his *nom de plume* for two reasons: his "uncertainty with regard to success" and a "feeling of pride" in establishing his own identity.[1] (His name change was formalized by the New York State Legislature in 1857).

After three years or so, Frank Leslie jumped the retail ship and emerged with his new identity and a new career when he joined the engraving staff of the fledgling *Illustrated London News.* Here he could work with "live wood." Turkish boxwood was what engravers used as their preferred surface for printing, and Leslie played an important role in refining a technique for speeding up the traditional engraving procedure. For the first time ever, readers could see for themselves what events looked like within a few days of their occurrence.

Fourteen years later, shortly before he hired Nast, Leslie published an informative article in his new eponymous illustrated newspaper, entitled *How Illustrated Newspapers Are Made*. He began by elaborating on **the distinction between a pictorial paper and an illustrated newspaper**: "The **pictorial paper** is merely the medium of presenting to the public pictures, whose merits consist in their abstract attractiveness, without regard to the passing events of the day. A pictorial paper, therefore gives literally nothing but pictures. An **illustrated newspaper**, on the contrary, not only furnishes its weekly gallery of art, but gives the current news, thus bringing the genius of the pencil and the pen promptly to illustrate the recorded event."

The *Illustrated London News*

The *Illustrated London News*, the first newspaper in the world to depict newsworthy events shortly after they happened, made its initial appearance on May 14, 1842. It was founded by Herbert Ingram of Boston, England just before his thirty-first birthday. Ingram had learned the printing, publishing and distribution business from the ground up, beginning as a printing apprentice.

After finishing his printing indenture, young Ingram moved to Nottingham where he worked hard as a news vendor, at all hours and in all kinds of weather, both delivering to homes and selling on the street. His first-hand familiarity with the life of a newsboy provided him with two significant insights that led him to start his paper.

First, Ingram noted that his customers, even the less literate ones, asked for news about London, regardless of what paper it was in. Second, he became aware that even a bad woodcut in an occasional issue of a paper would help him sell more than the usual number of copies. The name and concept of the *Illustrated London News* had their genesis in Ingram's gritty but educational experience as a newsboy.

Before starting his paper, however, Ingram also established his own printing, bookselling and news agency businesses. His original intent was to publish an illustrated crime journal, recognizing the appeal to readers.

During the pictorial's first month, on May 30, 1842, Queen Victoria and her husband, Prince Albert, were out riding in their open carriage, when a would-be assassin fired a pistol at them. His arm was knocked away at the last minute by a policeman and he missed. The *Illustrated London News* pictured the action five days later, a first for breaking news. A similarly unsuccessful attempt on the Queen's life was made seven years later.

ILN May 26, 1849 948

THE OUTRAGE.

ILN May 26, 1849 948

THE ARREST.

By January 1843 when he initiated his second volume of the *Illustrated London News*, Ingram had changed his target audience to "the RESPECTABLE FAMILIES OF ENGLAND" and his positioning to a "tone of high morality in every branch of public discussion" in literature, science, poetry and the cause of social advancement.

Readers responded. By 1851, the circulation of the *Illustrated London News* surpassed 130,000; it peaked at 250,000 for the 1852 funeral of the Duke of Wellington, Napoleon's conqueror at Waterloo. In less than two decades, the circulation of the *Illustrated London News* more than quadrupled that of the leading daily paper, the *London Times*.

Founder Herbert Ingram, the seventh generation of his family to bear that name, became a member of Parliament from Boston, while continuing as proprietor of his admired illustrated newspaper. Unfortunately, at age 50 in September 1860, Ingram and his sixteen-year old son drowned in Lake Michigan when their excursion ship was negligently rammed by another boat near Chicago. His English journal and its American imitators, *Frank Leslie's Illustrated Newspaper* and *Harper's Weekly*, would continue to thrive.

NYIN September 29, 1860 333

THE LADY ELGIN CATASTROPHE —THE LATE HERBERT INGRAM, ESQ., M.P., PROPRIETOR OF THE "ILLUSTRATED LONDON NEWS."

The Engraving Breakthrough

Before 1842, the boxwood blocks on which the illustrations were engraved were glued or cemented together when a larger illustration was required. Only one engraver could work on an illustration at a time, and the quick turnaround required to depict current news events was not achievable. Ingram's essential innovation enabled multiple engravers to work simultaneously on the same illustration. By dividing up the work, a large illustration could be completed in hours or a few days, rather than the weeks or months previously required, so a newsworthy event could be depicted on a relatively current basis

The inventor credited for the 1842 breakthrough that made illustrated newspapers feasible was Charles Wells of Lambeth, England.[2] Frank Leslie's timing was excellent because he saw what Wells devised, and refined it over time. The new process became the key to a successful career not only for Leslie as an engraver and publisher, but also for graphic artists like Nast and Winslow Homer.

Wells's novel technique was to fasten the required number of boxwood sections together with bolts inserted through channels in the back, so as to form a single smooth surface large enough for the illustration. The entire picture was then drawn on the enlarged surface of blocks combined within a single frame.

A master engraver sub-divided the blocks by loosening the screws or bolts in the back. The various pieces — as many as 36 in some of Nast's later double-pages — were then distributed to up to 20 or more artisans. Some of them had specialties like sky, foliage, children, animals, faces or landscapes, so their assignments went faster and their familiarity with their particular elements improved quality. The master engraver drew the segment-crossing lines and coordinated the finished blocks, so the entire picture blended and the segment lines weren't visible. On occasion, the master-joiner was sloppy or rushed and the white lines separating the blocks were all too apparent.

FLIN August 2, 1856 124-125

PREPARING BOXWOOD FOR ENGRAVINGS.

ENGRAVER AT WORK.

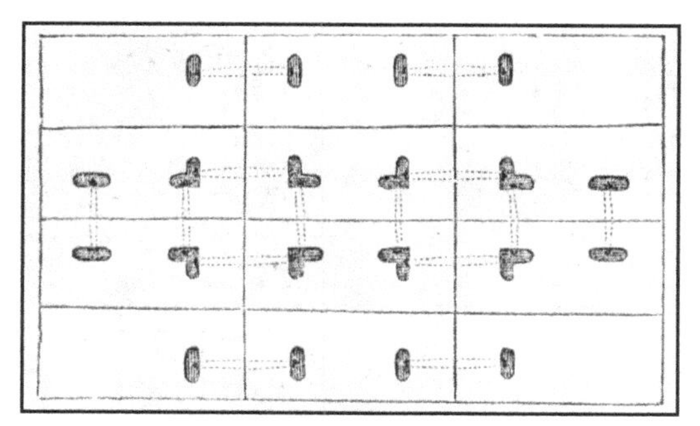

BACK OF BLOCK, SHOWING HOW IT IS FASTENED TOGETHER.

ENGRAVERS' ROOM.

In Turkey, boxwood trees had trunks which grew to seven inches in diameter. Boxwood was almost as hard as flint and could be cut with great precision; when carved to perfection, it provided bolder and richer effects than could be produced on copper or steel plates.[3] The artists' sketches and lettering had to be drawn or traced on the wood **in reverse**, so the printed images would appear correctly. As mentioned previously, that may have been the only circumstance where Nast's apparent dyslexia proved beneficial to him.

Woodblocks also were far more practical for the high-speed production process required for illustrated newspapers than the more laborious and time-consuming metal plates commonly used for printing much smaller runs of illustrated books. One block could print 100,000 impressions. However, the production process destroyed the woodblocks, and few cut but unused ones remain.

The actual art of engraving consisted of cutting a series of grooves into the wood, leaving the part of the wood which represented the lines in relief. When printed, the ink only took effect where the wood was left, so the lighter parts were where the wood was cut away with grooves. The unused Nast illustration below, *Cutting the British Lion's Tail,* comprised two joined woodblocks measuring about 3 ¼ by 5 ¼ inches each (shown actual size).

Macculloch Hall Historical Museum

Goodbye London

In contrast to his budding career at the *Illustrated London News* where he ultimately became a top engraver, Henry Carter/Frank Leslie's private life was a disaster. About the time of his twenty-second birthday in March 1843, he married Sarah Ann Welham, who was fifteen, not well educated, and pregnant with the future Henry (Harry) Leslie. Sarah Ann's mother had abandoned her husband and was living with a Mr. Thorp, thereby setting a poor example for her daughter (who would imitate it eight years later). Henry's marriage was the final straw for his father's family which became estranged from him. Two more sons followed: Alfred in 1845 and Scipio in 1847. To make domestic matters worse, Sarah Ann claimed to have caught a "loathsome disease" from her husband during her last pregnancy.

Frank struggled to support his family, frequently working sixteen-hour days. While he ultimately became lead engraver at the *Illustrated London News*, he also drew and submitted illustrations to other publications and took on outside engraving assignments. Meanwhile, he saw another start-up London pictorial newspaper fail. He knew that he couldn't save enough capital to succeed as an independent engraver in England, and his alienated family, which could readily have afforded to set him up in business, would not do so.

Accordingly, Frank decided to leave his family behind, probably permanently, and emigrate. He arrived in New York on July 7, 1848 with fifty pounds ($230) in his pocket. Sarah Ann was left almost destitute when Frank's uncle understandably declined to pay several notes his nephew had signed for his family's support.

Frank brought with him several letters of support. He had six solid years of engraving experience and some understanding of the newspaper business as his stock in trade. The 1849 *City Directory of New York* listed "Leslie, F. Engraver, 98 Broadway." What the 27-year old entrepreneur needed to do was to make useful contacts, accumulate capital, and find a formula for success as a novice publisher. It took him less than six years to accomplish those goals.

Hello New York

Leslie's door-opener in New York lay in his introduction to Phineas Taylor Barnum, unquestionably the master showman and promoter of his era. Barnum hired Leslie to produce an illustrated catalogue of his American Museum, which attracted almost 400,000 visitors annually at 25 cents each. Among many other exhibits, it featured giants, fat people, bearded ladies, exotic animals, the Siamese twins Chang and Eng, and "General" Tom Thumb, the 25-inch midget who had already spent three years touring Europe with Barnum.

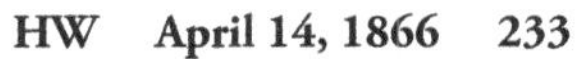

HW April 14, 1866 233

Nast's Sketch of Barnum

IN October 29, 1853 237

BARNUM'S AMERICAN MUSEUM, NEW YORK.

Barnum praised Leslie's illustrated catalog in his autobiography: "This he did in a splendid manner, and hundreds of thousands of copies were sold and distributed far and near, thus adding greatly to the renown of the establishment." While Barnum's circulation probably reflected his customary exaggeration, he respected Leslie's talent, and employed him in two future endeavors. Leslie capped off his 1848 initial year in New York by winning a medal from the American Institute for Wood Engraving.

Early on, Leslie learned a great deal about marketing and promotion from Barnum. One lesson which he absorbed well was always to use his own name and picture on any of his publishing ventures. Another negative lesson was to avoid Barnum's use of hype, exaggeration and even outright lies because it wouldn't help him in the newspaper business where other editors could shoot his stories down. For example, Barnum wrote in an October 1854 letter to an unidentified editor: "Will you have the kindness to announce that I am writing my life and that fifty-seven publishers have applied for the chance of publishing it . . . Such is the fact — and if it wasn't, why it still ain't a bad announcement."

Domestically, Leslie's life continued to be traumatic. Sarah Ann Leslie (as she was now known) and her three sons had arrived in New York in 1849, the year after Frank. Her husband supported them by engraving, printing and publishing on a free-lance basis. Ultimately, he housed them in a "well-furnished cottage" in Williamsburg (now part of Brooklyn) near the ferry to Manhattan, and then left them there for about six months while he accompanied Jenny Lind's tour. He sent Sarah Ann $25 from various cities, but had no other correspondence with his embittered wife.

When Frank returned to New York in early May 1851, he found his house occupied by strangers, with his two older children in the care of a poor woman who ran a day-school. They had been left five months earlier "for a few days" by Sarah Ann (following in her mother's footsteps), who had "eloped" with Thomas Croxon, a married man who had abandoned his wife. She had taken Scipio, then about three years old, with her, first to St. Thomas and then to Toronto. Frank tracked her down, ultimately reconciled, and then moved to Boston with his family.

There, he worked as an engraver for Frederick Gleason under a one-year contract beginning in the fall of 1851. *Gleason's Pictorial Drawing-Room Companion* had made its first weekly appearance on May 3, 1851, and Gleason needed additional skilled engravers for his featured illustrated articles. He was influenced by the success of the *Illustrated London News*. Unlike his English model, however, Gleason did not attempt to illustrate current news events.[4]

Leslie's conjugal situation remained muddled because Sarah Ann continued to see Croxon on the sly when her husband worked late. The Leslies were to continue their mutually adulterous marriage until they finally separated for good in December 1860. Their bitter divorce proceedings lasted for three years, from 1868 to 1871.[5]

Jenny Lind

One of Barnum's best known feats took place in 1850 when he promoted Jenny Lind's concert tour through America. Jenny, known as the Swedish Nightingale for her melodious soprano voice, had captivated European audiences for twelve years. Barnum bet his fortune — everything he owned or could borrow against — to sign her up to give 100 concerts for the unprecedented sum of $187,500, even though he had never heard her sing. At age thirty, she was smart enough to insist on having the entire amount deposited in her London bank account before she left for America.

Jenny arrived in New York on September 1, along with her baritone, Giovanni Belletti, and her conductor, Julius Benedict. No visitor had ever received a welcome like Barnum arranged. He met her ship at the entrance to New York Harbor. More than 30,000 cheering fans and a 200-person band were at the Canal Street pier to greet her. Before her first concert at Castle Garden, she made the rounds of the leading newspaper publishers. Serenades, speeches and plenty of flowers were augmented with merchandising offshoots for Jenny Lind gloves, bonnets, shawls, robes, sofas and pianos.

In total, Jenny gave 95 concerts under Barnum's auspices — 26 in New York (where 10-year old Tommy Nast attended at least one of them[6]) and 69 in sixteen other cities, including Havana, Cuba — during a 4,000 mile tour. Barnum unabashedly took the stage at a number of them to promote Jenny and himself. William Allen Butler, a lawyer and satirical poet, captured the promoter's essence in *Barnum's Parnassus*, published shortly after her arrival in New York.

So Jenny, come along! You're just the card for me,
And quit these kings and queens for the country of the free.
They'll welcome you with speeches, and serenades, and rockets,
And you will touch their hearts, and I will tap their pockets;
And, if between us both, the public isn't skinned,
Why, my name isn't Barnum, nor your name Jenny Lind!

Jenny, Butler and Barnum were right on the money. Jenny netted $177,000 after paying Barnum $32,000 to release her from her contract early, while Barnum came away with $535,000 before expenses. This was several times as much as Barnum netted from his museum during the nine-month tour.

Frank Leslie did not draw the initial New York cover of the program for Jenny Lind's tour. However, he engraved and publicized future programs, while serving as an advance man and assistant on the tour, along with Charles G. Rosenberg, a 33-year old author and music critic with an unsavory reputation, who had emigrated from England a year after Leslie. In 1851, the year the tour concluded, Rosenberg wrote and Leslie copyrighted a detailed chronicle of *Jenny Lind's Tour Through America and Cuba*, which was published by Street and Townsend.

Leslie's lengthy first-hand lesson in advertising and marketing from the unsurpassed, self-proclaimed "prince of humbugs" was well absorbed by the 30-year old entrepreneur-in-training. Leslie learned that promotion could be even more important than the product being sold, and he promoted himself to the usual anonymity of his staff in his subsequent publications, just as Barnum had done.

Thomas Strong: Illustration Pioneer

The *Illustrated London News* also became the first illustrated newspaper available in America when it established a Boston distribution office in 1843, its second year. While that office initially achieved a circulation of 300 copies a week, it didn't have to contend with the problems of producing the paper in this country. Ultimately, the paper established news agents in New York and other cities.

1845 saw the first full-page illustration of a current event in an American newspaper. In its edition of June 28, the *New York Herald* published six horizontal columns depicting President Andrew Jackson's memorial funeral procession. Jackson had died in Nashville less than three weeks earlier.

The picture was engraved by Thomas W. Strong, who was also a book and almanac publisher and print dealer. Strong, a 27-year old native New Yorker, was accused by rival publishers of using the same illustration for Jackson's funeral that had also been used to illustrate Queen Victoria's coronation in 1838 and President William Henry Harrison's funeral in 1841. The identifying captions above Strong's illustrations probably authenticated his drawing in this instance; however, on other occasions, he was not above using old images from other sources to illustrate totally different events. In fact, an ad for his own business stated that he had "Ten Thousand Wood Engravings on Hand."

Strong, a leading producer, wholesaler and retailer of valentines,had a large dose of entrepreneurship in his genes. Six years later, on June 7, 1851, he launched *The Illustrated New York News*, an eight-page paper, ten by fourteen inches, that sold for five cents a copy. The *Illustrated London News* was his model, but he warned his readers that it would take him a while to reach that journal's standard of excellence. Seven issues later, he changed his publication's name to *The Illustrated American News* and enlarged his pages to tabloid size. However, the content — illustrated fiction, short features, jokes, humorous sketches and news briefs taken from local dailies — didn't change at all.

After 24 issues and struggling to break even, Strong discontinued *The Illustrated American News* as of November 15, 1851. He claimed to have produced more than 300 engravings, but the stress on him as both editor and principal engraver was affecting his health. Meanwhile, his book publishing business was flourishing, the next valentine season was approaching, and he was preparing to launch the more successful *Yankee Notions* in January.

June 28, 1845

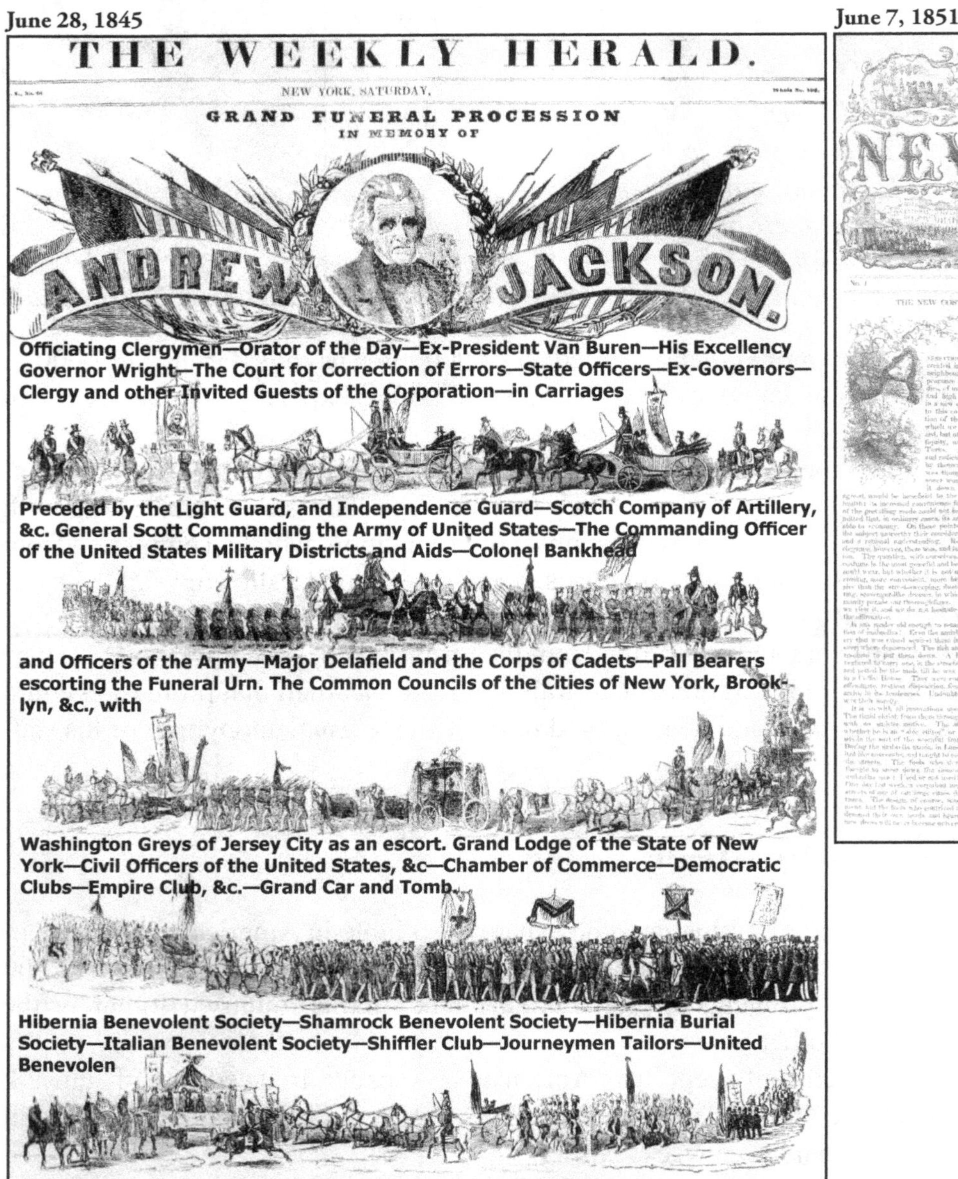
THE WEEKLY HERALD.

NEW YORK, SATURDAY,

GRAND FUNERAL PROCESSION IN MEMORY OF

ANDREW JACKSON.

Officiating Clergymen—Orator of the Day—Ex-President Van Buren—His Excellency Governor Wright—The Court for Correction of Errors—State Officers—Ex-Governors—Clergy and other Invited Guests of the Corporation—in Carriages

Preceded by the Light Guard, and Independence Guard—Scotch Company of Artillery, &c. General Scott Commanding the Army of United States—The Commanding Officer of the United States Military Districts and Aids—Colonel Bankhead

and Officers of the Army—Major Delafield and the Corps of Cadets—Pall Bearers escorting the Funeral Urn. The Common Councils of the Cities of New York, Brooklyn, &c., with

Washington Greys of Jersey City as an escort. Grand Lodge of the State of New York—Civil Officers of the United States, &c—Chamber of Commerce—Democratic Clubs—Empire Club, &c.—Grand Car and Tomb.

Hibernia Benevolent Society—Shamrock Benevolent Society—Hibernia Burial Society—Italian Benevolent Society—Shiffler Club—Journeymen Tailors—United Benevolen

June 7, 1851

THE ILLUSTRATED NEW YORK NEWS

SATURDAY, JUNE 7, 1851

THE NEW COSTUME

LADIES IN THE NEW COSTUME

Barnum and Beach's Illustrated News

On New Years Day 1853 a second *Illustrated News* was born in New York City. None other than Phineas T. Barnum was the self-styled "special partner," and the chief engraver was Frank Leslie who had recently completed his one-year contractual stint on *Gleason's Pictorial* in Boston. Leslie's previous relationship with Barnum on the American Museum and the Jenny Lind tour paid off for both of them in a city where engravers were in short supply. Their paper failed after 48 issues, but their overwhelming problems taught Leslie invaluable business lessons.

IN January 1, 1853 C

BIRTH OF THE NEW YEAR.

Barnum's two general partners were Alfred E. Beach and Henry D. Beach, two of the three sons of Moses Yale Beach who had acquired ownership of the flourishing *New York Sun.* The third Beach brother, Moses Sperry Beach, had succeeded his father as publisher of the *Sun* five years earlier, and had no time for the new venture. However, family connections enabled the *Illustrated News* to be headquartered and published in the *Sun* building.

Barnum and Beach's *Illustrated News* was the first American weekly that attempted to report and illustrate newsworthy events and people on a current basis. *Gleason's Pictorial* and Strong's similarly-named predecessor had pictorial features, but their reporting generally lagged several months behind the actual occurrences.

A number of new developments made the time ripe for the launch. Most important was the Post Office Act which took effect on September 30, 1852. Prior to that time, subscribers paid for postage at the post office of delivery, where a five-ounce periodical cost six and a half cents. Under the new system, the publisher absorbed the postal cost, which was reduced to one and a half cents. As intended, the Act facilitated the proliferation of newspaper and magazine subscriptions. Addressing was elementary; for example, "A. J. Robinson, Bangor" would be hand-written on the front or back page. However, nine months of experience convinced Barnum and the Beaches to note in their "Commercial Terms" column: "All subscription copies are carefully packed and sent from the Publication Office — the risks of mail transportation being then assumed by the subscribers."

A second major factor in the surge of new periodicals was the spread of the telegraph to obtain news faster. In March 1853, nine years after Samuel Morse's invention connected the thirty-four miles between Washington and Baltimore, the *Illustrated News* reported that 20,000 miles of telegraph wires were in operation and another 10,000 were under construction in the United States.

A third important element was the expansion of railroads. The Erie Railroad, whose owners would play a role in the Tweed Ring and some of Nast's future cartoons, commenced operations in 1836, while the New York and New Haven started up eight years later. 1853 saw the creation of the New York Central Railroad, which consolidated ten local lines running between Albany and Buffalo. Railroads speeded up delivery to newspaper offices of sketches made in the field, an essential development for illustrated newspapers. They also enabled the burgeoning New York City press readily to expand its distribution into the New England, Middle Atlantic, Mid-West and Southern states.

The concomitant negative of all railroads was frequent derailments, explosions and other tragedies. They provided circulation-boosting news stories and illustrations for the papers, but were devastating to passengers and their families. Barnum lived in Bridgeport, Connecticut, and commuted on the New York and New Haven Railroad. When an engineer drove his train through an open drawbridge in nearby Norwalk, killing and injuring some of Barnum's fellow residents, his paper covered the tragedy in depth with lists of the dead and injured, along with illustrations engraved by Leslie. 65 fatal railroad crashes were reported in the first seven months of 1853.

IN May 14, 1853 320

THE LATE RAILWAY CALAMITY AT NORWALK, CONN.

THE CATASTROPHE.

The Crystal Palace

In addition to these general factors, both Barnum and the Beaches had sound individual reasons for starting a new illustrated weekly. Barnum promoted his American Museum in almost every issue.

The Beach family's primary wealth came from their ownership of the *Sun*. While Moses Sperry Beach, its publisher since 1848, was not involved with the *Illustrated News* as an investor, he saw the possibility of adding engravings to the *Sun*, and also advertised the weekly *Sun* in the new publication.

His brother, 26 year-old Alfred Ely Beach, had left the *Sun* the previous year to become the editor and partial owner of *Scientific American*, then a seven year old weekly (and still around today as a monthly.) Alfred also was a talented inventor, and his interest in all branches of science was reflected in the *Illustrated News*.* For the youngest brother, Henry, it is likely that the new venture provided him with a publication to be involved with operationally, although under Barnum's dominance.

However, the decisive factor that brought the partners together almost certainly was the first American World's Fair, scheduled to open on May 1, 1853, on the four acres between 40th and 42nd Streets at Sixth Avenue (the present site of Bryant Park.) Barnum had attended an industrial exposition in Paris in 1844, and was impressed. In 1851, London had staged a huge and successful international exposition in a novel iron and glass hall called the Crystal Palace.

Now New York wanted its own World's Fair in its own Crystal Palace. Private investors, probably including Barnum and the Beach family, raised $300,000 for the venture. Barnum hoped to draw additional out-of-town customers to his museum while the Beaches could promote their *Sun* as well as the *Illustrated News*. Printing the *Official Catalogue of the New York Exhibition of the Industry of All Nations* would provide additional profits.

The architectural plan was approved in August 1852, and the construction contracts for the 173,000 square feet of exhibition space were signed in September. Barnum and the Beaches could reasonably expect the Exposition to meet its scheduled May 1853 opening and attract huge crowds of visitors. (This April Fools Day cartoon was published about six weeks prior to that date in their paper).

IN April 2, 1853 221

ANTICIPATED DOMESTIC INCONVENIENCES OF THE GREAT INFLUX OF VISITORS, AT NEW YORK, DURING THE GREAT EXHIBITION.

Frank Leslie followed his engraving of the initial cover with dozens of pictures like the construction of the Washington Monument, and the March 4 inauguration of Franklin Pierce as the fourteenth president. Additionally, the *Illustrated News*, like its predecessors and successors, invited "travelers, artists, naval officers and others" to submit sketches. "No good sketch will ever be denied publication." Payment was promised but not always received. These sketches, of course, had to be redrawn and then engraved on woodblocks before they could appear in the paper.

Leslie had plenty of problems trying to get the paper's engravings ready on a timely basis. He didn't have the requisite equipment for preparing and bolting the individual woodblocks necessary for preparing full-page illustrations. (A publisher's note in the July 30 issue referred to the "many disfigurements of engravings on account of the warping and cracking of woodblocks.") There were not enough competent engravers available, a situation which was aggravated by the increased demand for printing related to the upcoming Exposition.

* In 1870 Alfred built the city's first subway, using a giant fan to blow a car full of passengers through a pneumatic tube running under Broadway for several blocks.

The partners also faced severe operational difficulties which their publisher's notes explained and complained about frequently. Printing capacity was inadequate in light of the 70,000 circulation Barnum claimed to have reached within a month; the claim may have been Barnum hype, but the need for more steam presses was real. The existing presses operated around the clock, new ones would take several months to arrive, and orders for back issues could not be processed in spite of the demand for them.

Population growth provided an ever-growing market for newspapers as immigrants flooded into New York City and the rest of the country. The issues of slavery, western expansion, temperance, tariffs and politics continued to bubble. The literacy rate was high but people had few ways of visualizing who or what they were reading about in their daily or weekly papers.

Mathew Brady

Lastly, the explosion of photography, led by Mathew Brady, provided a ready base of portraits and pictures of static events for woodcut illustrations. Brady came to New York at age 21 in 1844, and improved the process of daguerreotyping — which had been invented by Louis Daguerre in Paris about six years earlier and came to America in late 1839 — to a commercially successful level. He opened his first gallery at Fulton Street and Broadway in 1849, and made his celebrity portraits and inexpensive cartes de visite available to publishers of books and periodicals.

By 1853, Brady was able to open a second studio at 359 Broadway over Thompson's Saloon. He had plenty of competition — the *Tribune* estimated there were 100 Daguerrean establishments in 1853 — but Brady's was predominant. The availability of ice cream, an exotic novelty in those days, in Thompson's Saloon probably helped draw customers to his retail gallery.

FLIN January 10, 1857

M.B. BRADY, ARTIST.
Ambrotyped By Brady.

Painting, 1866

From Grand Masquerade Ball *

IN November 12, 1853

BRADY'S GALLERY

Brady's portraits and cartes de visite provided a cornerstone for the fledgling illustrated newspaper industry, as well as for painters and illustrators who now could see what their subjects actually looked like even though they were not present. (Thomas Nast would maintain an extensive file of cartes de visite in his home studio from about 1865 on).

* See p. 158-161

Failure

Barnum paid close attention to the editing. He fired his first editor after he demanded complete control of the editorial columns; he got along better with his second editor but ultimately fired him too. The editorials in the paper were inconsistent at best. Barnum may have been handicapped by the Beach brothers' conception of an editor: "a good writer and compiler for about $1,000 or $1,500 a year," as Barnum put it. (However, that was a fair salary in those days).

The operational problems undoubtedly caused severe strains among the partners, and they must have been amplified by the delay of ten weeks in the opening of the Exhibition. President Franklin Pierce finally did the honors on July 14, 1853, with broad pictorial coverage in the *Illustrated News*. At least 4,000 exhibitors were represented. The gallery of paintings didn't open until another month passed.

IN July 30, 1853 43

INAUGURATION OF THE CRYSTAL PALACE — EXTERIOR OF SIXTH AVENUE CAR.

The *Illustrated News* signboard proclaimed: "Full Pictorial Coverage of the Exhibition"

Beginning July 2, the *Illustrated News* was cut back to eight pages with no advertising, and Alfred Beach was no longer listed as a partner. In the July 23 issue, Barnum printed a denial that he had sold his interest. Finally, on August 13, the paper returned to its sixteen-page size — Barnum's hokey touch was apparent in "double size with no change in price" — and Alfred Beach was again listed as a general partner.

The disagreement between the partners came to a head in October when more capital was needed. Barnum wanted to continue and offered to put up another $20,000, provided that each of the Beaches would match him and that Frank Leslie would be made managing editor. While Henry Beach may have been willing to continue — his brother Moses had the *Sun* and Alfred had *Scientific American* to occupy them — Alfred wanted out.

Consequently, the partners sold the engravings and good will to Frederick Gleason, Leslie's previous employer. Subscribers of the *Illustrated News* received *Gleason's Pictorial Drawing-Room Companion* until their subscriptions expired.

After the sale, Barnum still was not finished with the Crystal Palace. By late 1853, attendance fell off sharply, the Exposition was in financial trouble, and Barnum was urged to make it a paying proposition. He loaned it money, became a director, took the presidency in April, tried some special events, cut the fifty-cent admission price in half, and finally resigned later in July. When it closed officially in November 1854, it had debts of $300,000. Four years later, the vacant Crystal Palace burned down.

Without the upcoming Exposition, it is unlikely that Barnum and the Beaches would have taken a flyer on their paper, or that *Frank Leslie's Illustrated News* would have been started three years later and employed young Tom Nast.

Launch

For Frank Leslie, that stressful 1853 year with Barnum in the school of hard knocks turned into the springboard to a successful twenty-six year career as a publisher. He absorbed Barnum's philosophy: "Drive ahead, don't spare the steam, make all the noise possible, and by all means keep down the expenses."

Once Leslie saw that the Beaches were unlikely to continue supporting the *Illustrated News* with him as managing editor, he was ready to begin his entrepreneurial career as a publisher. He had experience with fashion reporting at all three illustrated pictorials he had engraved for, and he decided that a fashion magazine would provide him with the quickest road to profits. Accordingly, he hired an experienced fashion editor, and launched in January 1854, a month after the *Illustrated News* disappeared into *Gleason's Pictorial*. Learning from Barnum, he used the last November issues of the *Illustrated News* to announce the birth of *Frank Leslie's Ladies' Gazette of Fashion.* The magazine was successful, and enabled Leslie to add pages, increase the price and acquire his own steam printing presses by December 1854.

That same month Leslie acquired the *Illustrated New York Journal,* which had been started in August 1853 by a man named Orvis. Leslie renamed it *Frank Leslie's New York Journal of Romance, General Literature, Science and Art*, and engraved his picture on the front page as the handsome, determined 33-year old publisher; Barnum's self-promotion definitely had rubbed off on his protégé. He also "borrowed" George Thomas's cover angel's portrait drawn two years earlier for Barnum's fledgling paper.

PUBLISHED BY FRANK LESLIE, 12 & 14 SPRUCE STREET.

BIRTH OF THE NEW YEAR.—A Drawing By Thomas.

Leslie's New York Journal did not carry advertising in contrast to its predecessors and successors, and was dependent on subscribers who paid two dollars a year. Poaching liberally from English periodicals, it had lots of fiction, good coverage of scientific inventions, history features, travel pictorials, coverage of the Crimean War, and its share of jokes, cartoons and riddles.

The *New York Journal* served as his training vehicle for *Frank Leslie's Illustrated Newspaper,* which made its initial appearance on December 15, 1855. In March 1857, Leslie sold the *Journal* in order to concentrate on his *Illustrated Newspaper.*

The Newspaper Scene in 1856

In late 1855 when Leslie launched, his primary competition for readers and their pennies consisted of five well established dailies and one major weekly out of the dozens out there. The leaders and their circulations[7] included *The*:

Herald	58,000	***Tribune*** (Daily)	29,000	***Times***	42,000
Sun	50,000	***Tribune*** (Weekly)	163,000	***Evening Post***	12,000

The oldest current newspapers, dating back to the 1820s or earlier, had a mercantile clientele which needed the latest financial news — stock and commodity prices, money conversion rates and ship sailing schedules. About three-quarters of their content was advertising; clients usually contracted for a loosely defined block of space for $35 to $50 a year. Effectively, these papers were portable billboards, and their pages could be two by three feet, or larger.

Most of their circulation revenue came from annual subscriptions for eight to ten dollars, although collections were a continuing headache. Individual copies could be purchased at or near a publishing office for six cents. Their price, specialized content, and limited availability effectively restricted their circulation and utility to businessmen involved with shipping, manufacturing, wholesaling, retailing or related commerce.

The most respected financial newspaper was the *Evening Post*, owned and edited by famed poet William Cullen Bryant for half a century, beginning in 1829. Also noteworthy was the *Courier and Enquirer*, whose belligerent owner and editor, James Watson Webb, began his tenure in 1827 and ended it in 1861 when his failing paper was taken over by the newly-founded *World*. Other mercantile papers included the pro-slavery *Journal of Commerce* and the Republican-leaning *Commercial Advertiser*.

FLIN May 3, 1856 328

WILLIAM CULLEN BRYANT

HW September 4, 1858 561 C

GENERAL JAMES WATSON WEBB.

The market for newspapers changed drastically with the arrival of the daily penny press in 1833. Its disruption was equivalent to what happened to pictorial magazines like *Look* and *Life* when television caused their decline and eventual demise in the 1960s and 1970s. Four decades later, the media and advertising shake-up resulting from the advent of the Internet has been even more revolutionary. However, the same four major innovating factors — production technology, price, distribution and content — were responsible for the change in consumer behavior then as now.

Improvements in printing presses, like the introduction of steam, and later rotary presses, made faster and longer press runs feasible and permitted more recent news to be included. Paper-making improvements lowered costs and speeded up production. As a result, the new arrivals sold for a penny when they first came out, gradually going to two and even three cents after they were well established. That made them affordable to the mass market, a very high percentage of which was literate. Moreover, improved home lighting from oil or gas lamps made reading much easier than by candlelight.

However, the most important change was in the content of the new penny papers, which were aimed at ordinary people. It focused on local news with sensation, crime, sex, human interest and exposure of abuses in government, courts, churches, and financial institutions all in the mix. Then, as today, divorces and illicit sex attracted readers. The entertainment aspect ranked alongside the impact of news events.

In addition to revenue from circulation and commercial advertising, the penny papers often depended on job printing, including municipal notices and advertising, to maintain profitability. This usually required positive support for the politicians and office-holders who controlled those funds; negative articles or editorials could inhibit or foreclose financial lifelines.

Transplanting a system well established in London, the penny papers were distributed by newsboys who hawked them loudly and aggressively on the streets. The hordes of urchins, many of whom were homeless, augmented by unemployed men, bought their bundles of one hundred papers for sixty-seven cents and sold them for a dollar. Some boys had home routes and collected their weekly amount of six cents every Saturday. Many of them "graduated" to become gamblers, "roughs," or saloon-keepers.

FLIN September 3, 1859 210

PUBLICATION DAY OF THE "LEDGER" —SCENE AT ROSS & TOUSEY'S THE MOMENT OF ISSUING IT.

The *Sun*

On September 3, 1833, Benjamin Day, a 23-year old printer looking for additional income, revolutionized the New York newspaper world with the first appearance of his four-page, three-column, letter-size *Sun*. Features included daily coverage of the police-court report with humorous commentary on the human interest aspects of drunkenness, assault, theft, prostitution and wife-beating. Advertising, which constituted 75% of the content initially, and about 40% by 1856, included help-wanted ads.

Number 1 September 3, 1833

THE SUN.

PUBLISHED DAILY,

AN IRISH CAPTAIN.

THE FIRST ISSUE OF THE NEW YORK SUN.

While Day's initial purpose in starting the paper was to create additional profit for his printing business, within four months his circulation of 5,000 was the largest in the city. However, the financial panic of 1837 and an adverse libel suit prompted Day to sell the *Sun* for $40,000 to his brother-in-law, Moses Yale Beach, a decision he came to regret. By then the *Sun*'s circulation was 38,000.

Beach, who managed the mechanical and bookkeeping operations at the *Sun*, had previously invented a rag-cutting machine for manufacturing paper. He turned the *Sun* into a prosperous paper, mostly free from the controversies that enveloped all of the other leaders. A probable reason for that may have been that he avoided the editor changes and consequent resentments that took a toll on his competitors.

In 1848, Moses Yale Beach retired at age 48, having turned his thriving paper into both the circulation and advertising leader among all dailies. His sons — 26-year old Moses Sperry Beach and 22-year old Alfred Ely Beach — succeeded him. Alfred resigned in 1852 to take over *Scientific American* and then become P.T. Barnum's partner in the *Illustrated News*.

The *Herald*

The *Herald* was born on May 6, 1835 to forty-year old James Gordon Bennett, a true pioneer in American journalism, who had $500 to put into his venture. Bennett was a shrewd, energetic, hard-working Scotch emigrant, who had helped James Watson Webb edit the *Courier and Enquirer* before leaving that paper because of a strong disagreement over Jacksonian politics. Subsequently, the two men attacked each other in the press and, on two occasions, in violent physical fights started by Webb, which Bennett described in detail in his paper.

Bennett was an intense, unlikable egotist who relished comparing himself to Shakespeare, Napoleon and Moses. Benjamin Day wouldn't hire him for the *Sun* and Horace Greeley turned him down as a potential partner. However, he was a superb reporter, editor and innovator. His wife and two children usually resided in Paris, so he was free to spend all his time and attention on his paper.

Politically, Bennett was an ardent Democrat, who favored the South and supported Tammany Hall. He was a good economist, and his financial coverage was unsurpassed, even by the mercantile papers. He had resident correspondents in Albany, Washington, London, Paris, Vienna and Mexico City. While he supported the annexation of Cuba as a slave state, he also ran social protest exposes of slum housing, the debtors' prison, the almshouse and the lunatic asylum. Although his news coverage was broad, his editorial positions were biased in favor of slavery and the controversial Fernando Wood, New York's three-term Democratic mayor in the 1850s.

The *Tribune*

The first issue of the *Tribune* appeared on April 10, 1841, with Horace Greeley as publisher and Henry J. Raymond as editor. By the time of Frank Leslie's debut with his *Illustrated Newspaper,* Greeley's *Weekly Tribune* had the greatest local and national impact of any periodical in the country.

Greeley had learned the printing trade before he arrived in New York City at age twenty in 1831. He published an unsuccessful literary weekly called the *New Yorker* prior to starting the penny *Tribune* with the equivalent of $3,000, some of it borrowed. He was a quasi-socialist who promoted abolition, temperance, trade unions and other liberal causes. He was erratic as a personality, but talented as an editorial writer, and smart enough to pick superb managing editors to determine what content should go in each issue — and then to supervise its execution — as well as talented financial managers.

FLIN August 14, 1858 167

CHARLES A. DANA, EDITOR NEW YORK "TRIBUNE."

Raymond had a disagreement with Greeley after two years, and left to become managing editor at James Watson Webb's *Courier and Enquirer*. In his place, Greeley installed Charles A. Dana, who kept a steady hand on the tiller until he split with Greeley in 1862. Dana left to play an important role as Assistant Secretary of War, and then became owner and publisher of the *Sun* in 1868 when he and a syndicate bought it from Moses Sperry Beach. Raymond went on to start the *Times* in 1851.

Greeley could be vicious when he disagreed with anybody, including other publishers. When William Cullen Bryant suggested in his *Evening Post* that Greeley had once been soft in his opposition to slavery, Greeley's response in the *Tribune* was: "You lie, villain! Willfully, wickedly, basely lie!" He attacked pro-slavery publisher Bennett of the *Herald* as "the low-mouthed, blatant, witless, brutal proprietor of that sewer sheet."

During the sixteen years that Greeley and Bennett had disagreed on almost everything and pulled no punches in their respective papers, they had never actually met in person. Somehow they were coaxed into having breakfast together with an intermediary on September 30, 1856, but Leslie projected accurately that the "mutual struggle for supremacy" would begin again.

FLIN October 18, 1856 C

Greeley Bennett

A SKETCH OF CITY LIFE. —INTRODUCTION OF BENNETT AND GREELEY AT THE EVERETT HOUSE, UNION SQUARE, NEW YORK.

FLIN February 13, 1858 173

FOREIGN PARTY (TO HIS NEW YORK FRIEND)—"AW WHAT A STRIKING APPEARANCE! I SUPPOSE IT'S ONE OF YOUR BACKWOODSMEN?" NEW YORK PARTY—"MY GOOD SIR, YOU WILL HAVE TO GET POSTED; THIS IS ONE OF THE REPORTERS OF ONE OF OUR MOST EMINENT DAILY JOURNALS.

By 1856, Greeley had about 200 employees, including more than a dozen editors, under Dana's direct supervision. He also had foreign correspondents in several European capitals. One of them was Karl Marx, who was concurrently writing *Das Kapital* in London and had published the *Communist Manifesto* in 1848. Dana hired Marx to write monthly reports on the 1848 revolution and its aftermath in Europe. In actuality, Marx asked his colleague Friedrich Engels to do most of the writing because Engels had a better command of written English. Between them, they referred to Greeley as "that ass with an angelic face," but Marx needed the *Tribune's* weekly payments for his meal ticket. The relationship lasted for about ten years, beginning in 1851, and included several hundred dispatches, many of which were altered, discarded or published anonymously.

The *Times*

Henry Jarvis Raymond was a talented and ambitious man, both as an editor and as a politician. He received good training from both Horace Greeley and James Watson Webb, and was far more successful in the political arena than either of them. In 1850, he became the first editor of *Harper's New Monthly Magazine*, a post he retained for several years, even after founding the *New-York Daily Times* on September 18, 1851, when he was 31.

With George Jones as publisher and financial manager, the *Times* started with $100,000 in capital.[8] Raymond was given a 20% interest in exchange for his editorial services. The $100,000 contrasted with Bennett's $500 to start the *Herald* sixteen years earlier, and Greeley's $3,000 capital ten years previously.

FLIN August 23, 1856 176

HENRY J. RAYMOND

The rise of the *Times* — 20,000 circulation in its first year and 42,000 in 1856 — primarily came at the expense of the *Courier and Enquirer*. Raymond took away many of its readers, advertisers and staff from his former employer.

Raymond also started his public career with two terms in the state legislature, and one as Lieutenant Governor from 1854-1856. His political clout helped his paper and vice-versa. He supported the newly-formed Republican Party and John C. Fremont, its presidential candidate in 1856, and wrote the Party's first platform.

Leslie's Opportunity

In summary, all of these New York papers were doing well except for the *Courier and Enquirer*. Their reporters were far-flung and what they didn't cover directly, they picked up from competitors and from out-of-town papers. They had united to initiate and operate the Associated Press, and they had the telegraph to bring relative immediacy to their reporting. Many of them were politically ambitious, but they were much better at influencing politics and politicians through their editorial columns or their personal relationships than they were in gaining or succeeding in elected offices. As noted, their personal rivalries could be intense and vitriolic.

What all of them lacked was the visual capability to depict the personalities and events that they wrote about to their readers, except for occasional maps or other pre-existing material. Tightly packed with relatively small type, news columns did not have the impact of an illustration. Their readers generally did not know what the people they were reading about looked like.

This was the opportunity that Frank Leslie jumped at when he started his eponymous *Illustrated Newspaper* on December 15, 1855. He was long on experience but short on capital. However, his *Gazette of Fashion* and *New York Journal* were profitable, provided a revenue stream to support his new venture, and had enabled him to acquire his own steam presses about a year earlier.

Although Leslie could cover many local events with his own small staff, he sourced many items from the dailies, always with attribution. He made it a point to maintain the good will of their publishers by printing their flattering biographies and portraits in his paper. That was one thing that it would have been unseemly for them to do on their own.

As a pioneer without direct competition, Leslie had the luxury of charging ten cents an issue for the first year of his *Illustrated Newspaper*, even as he attempted to build circulation. He could also economize by copying illustrations from the *Illustrated London News* and other foreign papers.

Leslie's First Issue December 15, 1855

FRANK LESLIE'S ILLUSTRATED NEWSPAPER

No. 1.—VOL. I.] NEW YORK, SATURDAY, PRICE TEN CENTS.

JOHN BULL'S LAST GASCONADE.

(DR. KANE.)
THE ARCTIC EXPLORERS.

So Tommy Nast's timing was excellent when he applied to Frank Leslie for a job. Leslie had already hired Sol Eytinge, Jr., seven years older than Tommy, and he needed another talented recruit who would work cheap. The two damaging events that would darken Leslie's second year — the emergence of *Harper's Weekly* and the financial panic of 1857 — were not yet on the horizon. Tommy's stage was set and his real-life play was about to begin.

Chapter 3
Learning at Leslie's

Getting Hired

When 15-year old Thomas Nast walked into Frank Leslie's office in August 1856, he was met by a tall, imposing entrepreneur who had more in common with young Tommy than either of them knew. Both had rebelled against their fathers to pursue the artistic trade of their own choice, and both started with no resources except their incipient skills and drive.

Separately, both Nast and Leslie recalled the essence of that first interview many years after it took place. Nast described it to his biographer Albert Bigelow Paine about forty-five years later, and showed him the sketch he had drawn. Leslie described it in an interview with the *New York Sun* on June 24, 1877:

> "I remember as well as if it were only yesterday the first time Nast called on me. 'Twas late one afternoon, and I was just closing my office door, when a little fellow came up to me and said boldly and plainly, 'I want to draw for you, Mr. Leslie.'
>
> "I looked down at the speaker with some interest. He was a small undersized lad, below rather than over five feet, and from being accustomed to look up to people, I suppose, carried his head well back on his shoulders. Neck he didn't appear to have any of, his arms seemed shortened almost to disproportion, and his body was of the build one calls stuggy. His face was the most remarkable thing about him, next to his enchanting self-confidence . . . 'Indeed, my little man, want to draw for me, eh?' 'Yes, Mr. Leslie,' he said, 'and I have brought you these to show what I can do.' With that he opened a small portfolio and handed me some sketches, mostly crude and not particularly promising copies of the statues and curios at the odds-and-ends museum (where he worked). . .
>
> "'Ah, my little man,' I said, 'these are all very well, but you have a great deal to learn before you can draw for me.' Then as a means of getting rid of him — a means I had often employed before — I said: 'Now, look here, my little man, just to show me what you can do, go down to the Fulton ferry and make a sketch of the boats coming in. There are always a lot of people who will persist in jumping off before the boat touches the wharf, and I want to show as graphically as I can how stupid and dangerous the practice is'. . .
>
> "Well, I thought I had seen the last of him, but to my surprise, the next morning brought the little fellow back (with his sketch). 'Here is the sketch, Mr. Leslie,' said he. I took it, glanced over it, and saw that although his studies from still life were full of faults, his drawing of action had its good points. Besides, the youngster's activity and enterprise impressed me. So as to give him something to do, I put him in the artists' room to take the drawings to the engravers, sharpen the pencils, and so on. He was the busiest, most active little fellow I ever saw, always doing something, never idle."

Paine, p. 18

HOBOKEN FERRY, N.J.—THE ELYSIAN FIELDS.— GREAT RUSH OF VISITORS ON SUNDAYS.

Leslie remembered a few of the details incorrectly. He sent young Tommy to the ferry for the Elysian Fields, a recreational park in Hoboken, NJ, not to the Fulton ferry to Brooklyn. Never one to waste a free drawing, Leslie published it on October 11, 1856 without attribution.

The other detail, according to Nast's memory, was that Leslie took a half-page wood engraving block from his desk and told Nast to go upstairs "to Mr. Alfred Berghaus, our staff artist. He will show you how to whiten it. Then redraw your picture on this block."

FLIN March 24, 1860

ALBERT BERGHAUS

Alfred Berghaus was Leslie's leading artist from the first issue of his *Illustrated Newspaper* to Leslie's death in 1880. He probably was only about 20 years old when Nast encountered him, but he was over six feet tall and a towering blond presence to Tommy who was at least a foot shorter. Berghaus, like Nast, was born in Germany and had a strong German accent, a military bearing, and a remote, somewhat imperial presence.

In addition to Berghaus, Leslie had two other older, outstanding but well-compensated, artists working for him during the first year of his *Illustrated Newspaper* — Charles Parsons and Jacob Dallas. However, Leslie's limited capital forced him to seek out less costly artistic talent because he could no longer afford Parsons and Dallas by mid-summer of 1856.[1] He needed to hire young, unskilled novices with raw potential talent, and train them, with primary help from Berghaus. Nast's timely appearance, along with his other recruit, 23-year old Sol Eytinge, Jr., filled the bill.

The gruff Berghaus had to supervise these recruits, coordinating their assignments while assuring that the quality of their work met Leslie's standards. In addition, as Leslie's chief artist-reporter, he had plenty of his own work to keep him busy. He instructed Tommy to "make your drawing on dis block just der opposite as you have it on dot paper." With help, Nast's completed assignment satisfied Leslie sufficiently to sign up his happy, fifteen-year old neophyte artist for a four dollar weekly salary.[2]

Tommy was an industrious worker. He usually got up before dawn and labored far into the night. Leslie always had more than enough work for him, and appreciated his diligence. Ultimately, he received a raise from four to seven dollars a week.

During the two-plus years he spent working for Frank Leslie, Nast worked primarily as a "travelling artist," Leslie's term for his role. He was dispatched to cover accidents, meetings, parades and other events that Leslie thought would appeal to his readers. In addition, he undoubtedly picked up engraving skills from the master himself and from Alfred Berghaus. Several of his extended assignments served as important building blocks for Nast's later successes.

Sol Eytinge

Leslie's other recruit, Sol Eytinge, Jr., would play an important role in Nast's life for the next five years, while serving as his mentor and friend. The son of a Dutch-Jewish businessman, Eytinge was seven years older, tall, talented, and helpful to Tommy with technical tips. Nast reciprocated by filling in details and finishing sketches for Eytinge, who had a deserved reputation for being lazy, profane and drunk. His young protégé overlooked these faults, and was considered by some of his fellow artists to be Eytinge's flunky. Artist Alfred Waud, who disliked both, scorned them in an unpublished cartoon depicting Sol as an old clothes peddler with Tommy on his leash. This was a well-aimed barb at Sol — who was considered to be a good dresser, sensitive and kind-hearted — as well as at Nast.

Missouri Historical Society, St. Louis, MO

Thomas Butler Gunn Diaries, April 1862 (Probably drawn in 1858.)

Eytinge parted company with Frank Leslie two years later, after a row about money, idleness and drunkenness. Sol prospered on his own, working for the *New York Illustrated News* and *Harper's Weekly*, and becoming a respected book illustrator.

In addition to liquor and profanity, Eytinge was addicted to prostitutes. When Tommy first met Sol at Leslie's, Eytinge was living with Allie Vernon, one of six sisters who were "hawking their vendible commodities" to provide their daily bread.[2] (One of Sol's numerous siblings, younger by two years, was Rose Eytinge, who became a prominent actress. On June 17, 1869, Rose and Henry Raymond, founding editor of the *New York Times*, were enjoying some extra-marital, after-theatre intimacy when he had a stroke or heart attack in her home. His unconscious body was left on his doorstep around midnight, and he died the next morning.) Allie left her supposed second husband to join Sol, and evolved from mistress to wife. Prior to, and probably even after that, she reportedly slept with — and fixed up her sister Josey with — some of Nast's acquaintances, including publisher Jesse Haney and artist William Waud (Alfred's brother).[3]

In 1858, Allie Vernon changed her name to Margaret Winship, and was married to Sol by Reverend Henry Ward Beecher, with *Tribune* reporter Mortimer "Doesticks" Thomson serving as groomsman. Maggie's new name didn't cover up her old spots, and the Thomsons were perhaps the only married couple who would socialize with the Eytinges; they lived near each other in Brooklyn. When Mort's wife "Chips" died in childbirth at the end of 1858, Maggie attended the funeral and announced "I am now, after a fashion, married." Nast also was among the mourners, and must have heard her comment.

Tommy maintained his relationship with Sol for two more years, but didn't socialize. After he and Sallie Edwards were married in September 1861, the friendship ended badly when Tommy refused to permit his wife to meet Maggie Eytinge. She became a contributor to newspapers and magazines but, like Nast, many New Yorkers never let her forget her former occupation.

Mortimer "Doesticks" Thomson

On December 22, 1857, Leslie asked free-lancer Thomas Butler Gunn to accompany young Tommy to the Calico Ball, a charity event at the Academy of Music. Gunn, an Englishman, almost sixteen years older than Nast, was a fine writer and a fair illustrator. Five months earlier, he had published his classic, *The Physiology of New York Boarding-Houses*. (Gunn lived in a series of boarding-houses,changing almost every year on Moving Day, May 1, when his landlady generally rented a new abode.*

Tribune reporter Mortimer Thomson also covered the Calico Ball. Nast's vignettes spoofed both Thomson and himself — Little Waddley — as Thomson nick-named his short, plump accomplice.

FLIN February 13,1858

Nast
LITTLE WADDLEY AND HIS GREAT PARTNER.

Doesticks Nast
THE SKELETON SUPPER

Some of Thomson's culture rubbed off on his young friend. Personal conversations, public lectures, and satirical verse and columns all contributed to Tommy's extracurricular education, while Mort's house probably gave Nast his first taste of what genteel home life was like a year before he met Sallie. Two years after the Calico Ball, Nast caricatured Doesticks with a greatly changed appearance. He had heard Thomson lecture and was impressed.

THE COMIC MONTHLY **March 1860**

A POPULAR LECTURER AND AUTHOR—DOESTICKS.

Sometime during 1858, Tommy was smitten with Mort's cousin, Sarah Gay, whom he met at the Thomson home when she visited from Rochester. He made at least one trip to Rochester to see her before the relationship ended and Sarah subsequently became Mrs. Galusha. Sallie's discovery of this early short-lived romance caused a couple of bumps during Tommy's only other courtship, but they were resolved to his true love's satisfaction.

---

* See p. 3

Early Illustrations

FLIN September 13, 1856 213

DESTRUCTION OF THE LATTING OBSERVATORY.

Tommy's first two illustrations in *Leslie's* appeared in the September 13, 1856 issue. One had T.N. initials, and portrayed a Methodist Camp Meeting in Port Chester, NY. The other portrayed the fire which destroyed the Latting Observatory, a tall tower on 43rd Street near where the New York Public Library now stands. Nast had been fascinated with fires as a small boy, and now he had a chance to draw one large enough to warrant a city-wide general alarm. (In a city which today is primarily dependent on high-rise elevators, the Observatory's principal historical claim to fame was its location as the site of Elisha Graves Otis's first successful public demonstration of his improved steam-powered passenger elevator brake in 1853.)

Nast's third illustration appeared on September 27, the day he celebrated his sixteenth birthday, and was signed "T. Nast Del."** Leslie rarely let his artists sign their work, so this first-ever appearance of his last name was notable. Leslie was a strong Democrat who unequivocally supported James Buchanan's successful campaign against Republican John C. Fremont and American (Know-Nothing) Party candidate Millard Fillmore.

The *Monster Torch-Light Procession* for "Buck" (Buchanan) and "Brak" (Vice Presidential nominee John Breckinridge) included about 1,000 pitch torches illuminating the scene. **This was Nast's introduction to presidential election politics in which he was to play such an important future role.**

FLIN September 27, 1856 256

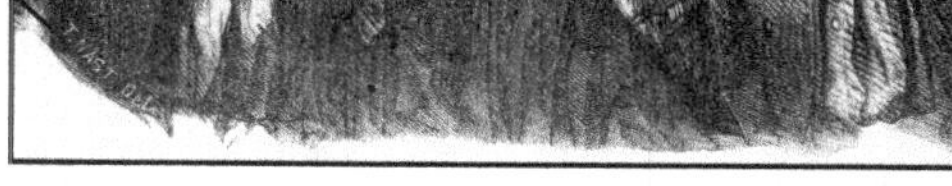

MONSTER DEMOCRATIC TORCH-LIGHT PROCESSION THROUGH UNION SQUARE, NEW YORK.

* Del." means "drawn by," an abbreviation of the word "delineator" from the Latin "delineauit."

During the summer of 1857, after sixteen-year old Tommy had been in his employ for a year, Leslie invited him to spend the weekend at the seaside resort of Long Branch, NJ. Subsequently the *Illustrated Newspaper* contained a long article by Leslie about the excursion, and included nine drawings by Nast; one of them showed the stocky young man with a sketch book in hand next to Leslie and his wife; another depicted a seasick, windswept passenger on the steamer to Long Branch holding on for dear life. **This almost certainly was Nast's first published comic portrait (probably of himself).**

FLIN April 22, 1857 181

VIEW OF LONG BRANCH, THIRTY MILES FROM NEW YORK CITY.

FLIN August 22, 1857 180

THE MAN WHO ENJOYED THE SAIL DOWN THE BAY TO LONG BRANCH.

Competition

Similarly to his mentor P.T. Barnum, Frank Leslie was under-capitalized in his first several years as a publishing entrepreneur. In August 1856, when he hired Nast and Eytinge at minimal wages to replace the high-priced Charles Parsons and Jacob Dallas, he also changed editors.

When the November 1856 issue of *Harper's New Monthly Magazine* announced the imminent birth of its sibling, Leslie immediately responded with a 40% price reduction from ten cents to six cents per copy. He still was a penny higher than *Harper's Weekly*, which was to be sold for a nickel.

Harper & Brothers was an ominous threat to Leslie in many ways. Started by James Harper in 1817, by 1825 it was the leading book publisher in the country. The *Monthly*, in its seventh year, had a ready supply of articles which could be adapted for the new *Weekly*. The Harper buildings had burned down in December 1853, but the modern new plant which replaced them in 1855 was iron-framed, considered fire-proof, and had the latest printing presses.

The Harper advantages — in contrast to Leslie — included superior management. Fletcher Harper was a bold and steady executive who was able to attract and keep top-flight editors and artists. His three older brothers – James, John and Wesley – supervised the book publishing, financial and operational aspects of the business, so Fletcher could focus on publishing the *Monthly* and the *Weekly*.

While hemmed in by *Harper's* on the revenue side, Leslie also was cramped by the dailies with regard to wages. Liberal crusader Horace Greeley had led a successful campaign to unionize the printing trade, and Leslie had to pay the going rates. Depending on the job, shift, experience and state of the economy, the pay for compositors, printers, reporters and editors was in the $9 to $15 a week range. The only place where Leslie had some wage flexibility was with artists, engravers, or the combination artist-reporter job he created and called "traveling artist." Nast was in that vulnerable category.

Leslie was innovative and persuasive, but often too impulsive. With his limited capital, the financial pressures on him were acute and his behavior could be erratic. Paine provided an undated amusing example of the interplay and results of these factors which probably happened in 1857 during Leslie's second year and *Harper's Weekly's* first.[4]

"Once, when the art department had not been paid for three weeks, a general demand was made on the treasurer, who told them to come back after luncheon . . . When they (returned), he informed them . . . that Mr. Leslie had just taken what money there was and gone. 'Gone! Took the money. Yes, he's bought a yacht and needed the money to pay for it.' They weren't paid for another ten days, after which there was a meeting of Leslie's creditors, and his affairs experienced one of those periodical readjustments which were a necessary part of his early career." He had learned well from Barnum.

Literally throwing caution to the winds in light of an approaching severe economic panic and recession, around this same time — August 15, 1857 — Leslie began publishing a German-language publication called *Illustrirte Zeitung* (Newspaper) that used the same material that appeared in his *Illustrated Newspaper*. Albert Berghaus and Nast, both of whom spoke German, probably were utilized for this new periodical. Here, Leslie was a follower of three German-speaking immigrants who had started a German language newspaper in 1852. They would ultimately retaliate by imitating Leslie, as well as *Harper's Weekly;* the *New York Illustrated News* made its debut in November 1859, and used the same content and illustrations in both their English and German language editions. Thomas Nast would become one of their featured artists in 1860, and initiate his first serial cartoon attack campaign the following year.

Nast's last year at *Leslie's* was 1858. His participation in two feature stories that year played an important role in his political and journalistic education as well as his future career.

Swill Milk

As 1858 dawned, *Frank Leslie's Illustrated Newspaper* claimed to have reached a circulation of about 100,000. *Harper's Weekly* had been competing with it for a year aiming at the upscale market, while Leslie primarily served the lower end. Initially, Leslie had used more illustrations than *Harper's*, but the *Weekly* was steadily increasing its pictorial content, following in its competitor's successful path.

Since there were no wars, crimes, calamities or scientific breakthroughs to capture the public's continuing attention, Leslie decided to create his own uproar, both to drive circulation and to one-up *Harper's Weekly*. On the cover of his May 8 issue, he began a public service campaign aimed at the poisonous swill milk trade.

The liquor distillers in Manhattan, Brooklyn and adjacent New Jersey fed the alcoholic, boiling hot residue of their distilling process — called slops or swill — to milk cows which were generally stabled in close quarters next to the distilleries; independent dairies obtained their swill in barrels. The cows soon became ill and died, but not before their impure milk sickened and often killed the babies who drank it. The milk was distributed to stores or directly to consumers from wagons whose signboards falsely claimed to carry fresh milk from upstate counties like Orange and Westchester. Additionally, the meat of the dead and diseased cows often was sold to the public through unscrupulous butchers, thereby compounding the public health problems.

FLIN May 8, 1858 C

EXPOSURE OF THE MILK TRADE — DRAGGING OUT A DEAD COW, JUST AFTER MILKING, FROM THE STABLES CONNECTED WITH THE DISTILLERY, CORNER OF FLUSHING AVENUE AND SKILLMAN STREET, BROOKLYN. From A Drawing Made On The Spot By Our Own Artist.

Leslie stated that he undertook this investigation with "no personal end to obtain, no injury to avenge, no malice to gratify." He later testified that he had first learned about swill milk from unillustrated — and therefore ineffective — articles in the *Sunday Dispatch* eight years earlier; had seen subsequent reports from the Academy of Medicine and public health committees; and had reviewed infant mortality tables. He later accused the swill milk operators of being responsible for the death of half a million infants and young children. Of course, while doing good for the public, he also did well for Frank Leslie as his circulation jumped 40% to 140,000.

However, the personal toll on Leslie went well beyond what he could have anticipated. He was sued for libel twice, physically threatened on several occasions, almost jailed, and unceremoniously thrown out of a public dinner. Never again in the remaining 32 years of his life, did Leslie undertake another public service campaign of any length, depth or risk.

For seventeen-year old Tommy Nast, his involvement and exposure provided an introduction to the political bombast and caricatures that matured during the Civil War and peaked during his famously successful campaigns against Tweed and Greeley. Just as Nast's cartoons caused Tweed to curse "those damned pictures," Leslie testified that the real-life illustrations of the stables brought home to his reading public the horrors of the swill milk trade in ways that the printed word by itself could not accomplish.

Leslie sent Albert Berghaus out to visit the stables and draw the sketches, and Nast participated as well. Nast was especially good at drawing figures and faces, and it is likely that the two collaborated on the vivid pictures as they appeared in more than a dozen issues of the *Illustrated Newspaper* between May and September 1858.

EXPOSURE OF THE MILK TRADE.—MILKING THE DYING COW. WHEN THE ANIMAL, FROM DISEASE AND ULCERATION, CAN NO LONGER STAND, MECHANICAL MEANS ARE USED TO SUPPORT IT WHILE UNDER MILKING, AND THE PROCESS IS CONTINUED UNTIL THE COW DIES. THE MILK IS USED WITH THE REST.

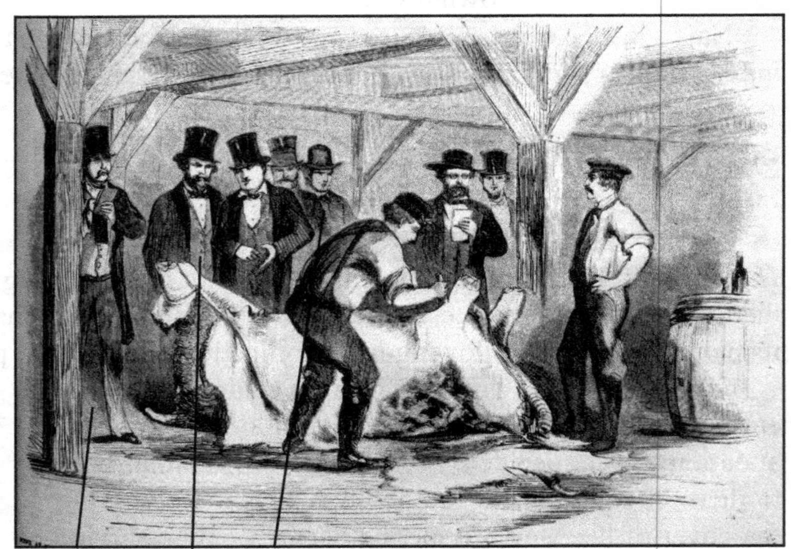

SCENE AT THE OFFAL DOCK, FOOT OF FORTY-FIFTH STREET, EAST RIVER. DISSECTING THE COW BROUGHT FROM THE SIXTEENTH STREET STABLES. THE HEALTH WARDENS, FRANK LESLIE AND HIS CORPS WITNESSING THE OPERATION AND TAKING NOTES.

Most of the men in the stables were rough Irish workers, who would have readily attacked their unwelcome visitors if police escorts had not been there to stop them. Commonly called "Hibernian milkmaids," they heaped verbal abuse on the "damned Dutchman," an appellation that certainly fit the German-accented Berghaus and probably Nast as well.

Leslie went further and hired detectives to follow the milk wagon drivers, and detail their routes by street and number, date and distillery. He published long lists as well as illustrations of the milk wagons with their false inscriptions of "Pure Country Milk."

FLIN May 15, 1858 384

ATTACK OF THE "MILKMAIDS," LED ON BY ONE STEPHEN SMALLEY, UPON ONE OF OUR ARTISTS, IN SKILLMAN STREET, BROOKLYN, BETWEEN THE STABLES.

Mayor Daniel Tiemann appointed a Swill Milk Investigating Committee, spearheaded by three crooked Aldermen: Mike Tuomey, owner of a saloon; Harrison Reed, a butcher; and Dan Tucker, a politician. At a minimum, what Leslie wanted was an ordinance stating "All dealers in swill milk shall have legibly painted on their wagons 'Swill-fed milk.'" If the poisonous beverage couldn't be expressly prohibited, at least its consumers would have some awareness of its danger.

The Aldermen predictably ignored Leslie's proposal, and Leslie responded with what probably was the most powerful local political cartoon of his entire publishing career. It showed Aldermen Tuomey, Tucker and Reed actively whitewashing the "Hibernian milkmaids" and their cows while passively accepting bribes. Importantly, no artist was credited with the cartoon; in fact, it may have been a joint effort of Berghaus, Nast and possibly Sol Eytinge. The anonymity totally frustrated the Aldermen when they sought to pin responsibility for the cartoon on a particular individual.

FLIN July 17, 1858 110

THE SIXTEENTH STREET DISTILLERY COW STABLES, COWS AND MILKMAIDS, UNDERGOING THE PROCESS OF WHITEWASHING BY ALDERMEN TUOMEY, TUCKER AND REED.

Tuomey promptly sued Leslie for libel, while Reed denounced the publisher in vile language at a Board of Health meeting. Leslie wanted to sue Reed, but his lawyer told him that slander was protected speech when made by a government official in a government hearing. However, Leslie retaliated in kind with a page of three cartoons — one for each Alderman — which appeared in the July 31 issue, available about a week before the first trial hearing in Tombs Police Court. One cartoon ridiculed Reed as a butcher; one taunted Tucker, who pronounced his v's as w's; and one admonished Tuomey who had threatened to throw a *Tribune* reporter overboard when he encountered him on a ship.

FLIN July 31, 1858 142

TAKEN AT HIS WORD

Mike O'Flan —*"Pat and I read ye tould the Aldermen t'other day, that swill fed beef was worth half a cent a pound more than any other kind of mate. Here's a beauty, yer honor' doesn't it look fatty and luscious? Arrah! Don't yer eyes water to look at it? Here's the baste, we've brought it on purpose for yer; hand us over the dimes and it's yours!"*

Ald. Reed —*"I don't deal in that kind of beef. I said that as an alderman, not as a butcher."* (Emphasis added)

ALDERMAN DAN TUCKER'S SOLILOQUY.

"I dare say I've often drinked swill milk—I dare say I drinks it now, but I don't want to know that it is swill milk, 'cos I shouldn't relish it, p'raps, so much. It's werry delicious, that I knows."(Vide Ald. Tuckers' speech at the Board of Health.)

ALDERMAN MIKE TUOMEY IN SEARCH OF A TRIBUNE REPORTER ON BOARD THE ERICSSON

"If I catch a Tribune reporter, I'll throw him overboard, G—d d —n him"

(Vide Tribune, July 6.)

Leslie printed the entire transcript of the July 27 hearing, and followed it up with three more cartoons. Reed's counsel, John Graham, proposed sending Leslie to jail. Leslie responded with a letter to the editor, entitled "Artists and Counselors," which he signed "AN ARTIST." He derogated Graham as a "milliner" and "the Narcissus of the New York bar," while saying *"the druggist who knowingly sells laudanum for tincture of rhubarb is hanged"* but, for hire, Mr. Graham defends *"the passing off of a slow poison as milk."* [5]

FLIN August 7, 1858 158

THE GREAT ORIGINAL NOSE EXHIBITION IN THE TOMBS.

Mr. Ashmead (Outside) —*Mr. Tuomey, has Mr. Reed got a nose like this?" (Shown Frank Leslie's Illustrated Newspaper.)*

Alderman Reed (Jumping Up) — *"Judge For Yourself—Here Is The Great Original Nose Itself!"* (Alderman Tuomey Silently Compares The Picture With The Original.)

MISS LACKADAISY RESOLVES TO SEND FRANK LESLIE'S ARTISTS TO THE PENITENTIARY.

Leslie's letter was an unknown but important serendipitous contribution to the First Amendment. He made the case for political cartoons as an expression of free speech in well expressed and unequivocal terms. It represents him at his emotional and rhetorical peak, and must have rubbed off on his budding young artist, Tommy Nast.

However, as a consequence of those subsequent cartoons, Leslie was again arrested for libel on complaints from Aldermen Reed and Tuomey. Attorney Graham again attempted to have Leslie jailed, both to protest the more recent cartoons and to prevent future caricatures from being published. Graham threatened physical violence and used scurrilous language, which the judge ignored. The trio's scheme to jail Leslie was thwarted when Leslie's friends provided $5,000 bail. In late September, a Grand Jury dismissed the libel complaints.

It took another year until Leslie could report progress. When the Annual Report of the City Inspector for 1859 was published, it called for the abolishment of swill milk as "a poison, utterly destructive of health and life, and responsible for many of the 13,000 children's deaths;" Leslie publicized it at length. Finally, almost three years after the start of Leslie's campaign, the sale of swill milk was abolished by New York State in March 1861. Leslie crowed in a cover story in the April 6 issue: "A Great Victory Won! Our Triumph Come at Last . . . Our work is accomplished — the Swill Milk trade is dead."

But not forever. The *Weekly* reported isolated instances in the late seventies and early eighties. 20 years after his first searing exposure to swill milk, Nast revisited the poisonous issue generically.

HW August 17, 1878 648

SWILL MILK.

Heenan vs. Morrissey

The second key event in Tommy Nast's last year at *Frank Leslie's Illustrated Newspaper* took place on October 20,1858 on Long Point Island, Canada, in Lake Erie, where Nast covered the heavyweight championship boxing match between John Morrissey and John C. Heenan. This was Leslie's first non-local assignment for Nast, who had turned eighteen about three weeks earlier.

Tommy was fortunate to get the job. According to Thomas Butler Gunn, "Sol Eytinge wanted to go sketch the fight, but Leslie wouldn't come down with $100 which he demanded for expenses. So little Nast went."[6]

Leslie did not let his young artist travel alone. He was accompanied by his friend "Doesticks" Thomson, who wrote about the match as a reporter for the *Tribune*.

The Heenan-Morrissey fight was important in its own right, but its significance to Nast's future career was far more meaningful. A little over a year later, Nast was to begin his next two-and-a-half year stint with the newborn *New York Illustrated News*, and his experience from the Heenan-Morrissey fight undoubtedly was the primary reason why the *News* wanted him.

Frank Leslie, as well as the editors at *Harper's Weekly*, condemned boxing as a brutal sport, "contrary to Christianity and even common humanity." Leslie's editorial, printed on the same page as his anonymous reporter's description of the fight, said that just as his paper printed pictures of "rotten cows and swill milk villainies," he was convinced that "the fidelity of our illustrations will do more to disgust the public with such bloodthirsty enormities than all the sermons that were ever preached."

Of course, both Leslie and his competitor recognized that the fight was the hot topic of the month and their readers demanded coverage. Although boxing was illegal in both the United States and England at that time, *Harper's Weekly* put it this way: "The popularity of prize-fighting as a newspaper topic is unquestionable. The best authority will sell a newspaper more quickly than the news of a presidential election, or of the loss of a steamer . . ." Hypocrisy prevailed. *Harper's* didn't send a reporter to cover the fight but relied on an article from the *Clipper* for updating its audience on the results.

Just getting to the fight was a strenuous experience, starting with a train trip to Buffalo. There Nast visited the bar of Izzy Lazarus, a 320-pound retired English prize-fighter, who hosted many of the New York ruffians. However, Leslie was alone in sending his artist to illustrate not only the fight, but some of the despicable class of people who attended it. Nast sketched 28 of these "distinguished and 'fancy' characters attending the fight."

FLIN October 30, 1858 346
Incidents In The Great Prizefight Championship Sketched On The Spot By Our Own Artist.

IZZY LAZARUS DRINKING WITH HIS FRIENDS IN HIS BAR-ROOM AT BUFFALO.

FLIN October 30, 1858 346
Incidents In The Great Prizefight Championship. Sketched On The Spot By Our Own Artist.

DAD CUNNINGHAM, THE RING KEEPER

Even then, Nast had the artistic skill to make his characters readily recognizable. For example, Theodore Allen (whom the *World* referred to in 1870 as "the notorious chief of the pickpockets and thieves"), Tom the Boatman, Big-Headed Riley, and Dad Cunningham were in the group. Cunningham, who had achieved his own notoriety five months before when he shot and killed a formidable gangster, was Morrissey's leading companion and one of 50 ring-keepers, 25 to a side, responsible for keeping the crowds away from the ring. Nast gave Cunningham his own sketch.

Because boxing was illegal, the fight was to be held on Long Point, a Canadian island in Lake Erie, about seven miles from the mainland and almost ninety miles from Buffalo. At midnight, three steamers set out for the eight-hour boat ride — one for each boxer and his adherents, and one for the reporters and the more respectable part of the crowd. Altogether, about 2,000 spectators watched the fight.

When the steamers arrived, they anchored about three-quarters of a mile from shore, where the passengers transferred to smaller boats. However, a sand bar kept the little boats away from shore, leaving the passengers to wade waist-deep through cold water or else pay a boatman a dollar for a piggy-back ride. Nast's steamer, the Kaloolah, was in bad shape; the small boats battled heavy seas, and he probably got soaked in the final stretch. Both Doesticks' reporting and Nast's illustrations gave Leslie's readers a good sense of their travails.

It took two hours to set up a 24-foot-square ring because there was no turf available, and it was against whatever rules existed to fight on sand. That problem and agreement on a referee — they ended up with two — took time, and it was almost four o'clock when the fight began.

FLIN October 30, 1858 342

GENERAL VIEW OF THE SCENE OF THE PRIZE FIGHT, AT LONG POINT, CANADA WEST. —From A Sketch By Our Own Artist.

John Morrissey

Born in Ireland and raised in Troy, NY, John Morrissey came to New York City in 1848 at age 17, unable to read or write, but a marvel with his fists in bar fights. He quit school after the third grade and after several back-breaking jobs, had his fill of manual labor. His new associates made their money through political rascality, prostitution, robbery and gambling. By 19, John had become literate and learned gambling from an honest man ("honesty pays better") named John Petrie. Dad Cunningham, who also worked for Petrie, became Morrissey's close friend.

The California gold rush was on, and Morrissey and Cunningham, backed by a loan from Petrie, travelled overland to San Francisco. They didn't find gold, but did well with a gambling establishment, set up for them by a wealthy Englishman whom they rescued from thieves. Morrissey decided to become a professional boxer, and won his initial battle. Two months later, Morrissey and Cunningham returned to New York. A year later, Morrissey slugged it out with a dissolute Englishman known as Yankee Sullivan for the American heavyweight championship, and won in the thirty-seventh round. The fight took place in Boston Four Corners, about 100 miles from New York, and Sullivan was arrested afterwards in Lenox, Massachusetts for his participation.

Morrissey fought with and against the hoodlum gangs which dominated the saloons, fraudulent politics, docks and general underworld of 1850s' New York. His notoriety, along with his reputation for honesty, led to John Petrie's making him a partner in his leading gambling establishment. (Later, Morrissey set up his own gambling house, one of the three most luxurious in the city).

When Fernando Wood ran successfully for Mayor in 1854, Morrissey helped him by threatening gang members who tried to take over ballot boxes. Morrissey learned a lot about buying votes, counting ballots, selling municipal offices and skimming office-holders' salaries.

Now 27, Morrissey was just under six feet tall, weighed about 187 pounds, and was in excellent shape. While training, he walked or ran more than 20 miles a day, watched his diet carefully and slept eight hours a night.

John C. Heenan

John Carmel Heenan was born in 1835, four years after Morrissey, and also was raised in Troy. They were acquainted but not friendly. Heenan was better educated than Morrissey, but not as intelligent, ambitious or self-disciplined. Like Morrissey, he also took the Overland Trail to California, where he became a blacksmith in the ironworks of the Pacific Steamship Company in Benicia, across the bay from San Francisco. He was dubbed the "Benicia Boy" and the name stuck to him for the rest of his life.

At six feet, two inches and 190 pounds, his fighting qualities soon emerged. A dour English trainer named Jim Cusick took Heenan in hand, and persuaded him to return East. Although he obtained a good job in the New York Customs House, he won a boxing exhibition in late 1857 and, in May 1858, challenged Morrissey by publishing a card in the *Clipper*, a sporting paper edited by Ed James. James became the promoter of the Heenan-Morrissey fight in conjunction with Frank Queen, the paper's owner.

In contrast to Morrissey, 25-year old Heenan was in terrible shape. An ulcerated lower leg sore had erupted six days before the fight, and it kept him in great discomfort and confined to his bed. Consequently, he was overweight and had little stamina, although his courage and pain threshold remained high in the ring.

The Marquess of Queensbury rules which govern modern boxing were not published in England until 1857, and did not come into general use in the United States until 1889. In Heenan's bare-knuckle fights with Morrissey, and later with Tom Sayers in England, a round was determined when a fighter hit the ground, whether he was wrestled, thrown or knocked down with a punch. Often, one fighter fell on top of the other, as happened in the first three rounds of the Heenan-Morrissey fight.

With his poor conditioning compounded by a wobbly leg, Heenan had to try to win quickly. He dominated the first round which lasted six minutes, but damaged two knuckles on his left hand when he hit a post after Morrissey ducked a punch. By the third round, his fatigue began to show, and he was unable to come out for the twelfth round. The fight lasted only 21 minutes and Morrissey retained his American championship.

Nast's drawings dominated Leslie's issue and became an important milestone in his life. He drew all the characters but one so that their features were readily recognizable. The exception was Morrissey.

In his drawing of the combatants shaking hands before the fight, Nast drew Morrissey accurately. But his depiction of Morrissey's face and head at the commencement and conclusion of the fight resembled simian Irish stereotypes, even allowing for Morrissey's bloodied and smashed up features. Perhaps, Nast was conditioned by the "Hibernian milkmaids" and dishonest Irish aldermen of the swill milk campaign. **This is the first apparent instance in which Nast, on his own initiative, used ape-like imagery to personify an uneducated, brutal Irish male figure.**

FLIN October 30, 1858 346

Incidents In The Great Prizefight Championship Sketched On The Spot By Our Own Artist.

THE COMBATANTS SHAKING HANDS BEFORE THE FIGHT.

FLIN October 30, 1858 343

THE GREAT PRIZE-FIGHT BETWEEN MORRISSEY AND THE BENICIA BOY AT LONG POINT, CANADA WEST —THE COMMENCEMENT OF THE FIGHT. —From A Sketch Taken On The Spot By Our Own Artist.

THE LAST ROUND IN THE GREAT PRIZE FIGHT —THE BENICIA BOY FAILING TO COME TO TIME. —From A Sketch By Our Own Artist.

After the Fight

Shortly after the fight, Heenan did everything he could to challenge Morrissey to a re-match. Morrissey refused, citing a promise to his young and beloved wife Susie, to give up boxing for good.

Morrissey later went into politics in a big way. He was elected to Congress in 1866 and 1868. He opposed the Tweed Ring from 1870 until its defeat the next year. He then struggled with "Honest John" Kelly for control of Tammany Hall but ultimately lost and founded a competitive faction called Irving Hall. He was only 47 when he died in May 1878 in Saratoga, New York, where he owned another successful gambling establishment.

In his obituary, *Harper's Weekly* said that John Morrissey "was regarded as a 'square man,' one who stuck to friends through thick and thin, and made open war upon his enemies." Even Nast, who caricatured him more than 26 times in the 1860s and 1870s, evidently grew to respect him. However, Nast always used boxing and gambling symbols when portraying Morrissey; boxing rings and political rings (like Tweed's and Tammany's) found common usage in his cartoons.

HW November 10, 1866 720

THE CONSERVATIVE CANDIDATE OF THE PEACE DEMOCRACY IN THE FIFTH CONGRESSIONAL DISTRICT. (MORRISSEY.)

HW November 29, 1873 1072

THE TAMMANY PHOENIX IS A FIGHTING-COCK.

Next for Nast

In addition to boxing, the Heenan-Morrissey fight provided Nast with at least one other reality experience. Growing up in a city dominated in certain neighborhoods by criminals who saw violence as everyday sport, had to affect Nast's view of his world in general and the fight environment in particular. He had drawn some of the illustrations for Leslie's article on the 1857 Independence Day riot between the Bowery Boys and the Dead Rabbits. Seeing these characters close up on this assignment — even though their fists, knives and guns remained mostly unused — made an indelible impact on the eighteen-year old illustrator.

Finally, the rugged steamship travel to the fight, as well as the sleepless night and long hours that preceded his actual drawings of the fight, showed that young Tommy had the mental and physical resources required for off-beat assignments like this one. The proof was in the accuracy and quality of his sketches.

A year later, George Wilkes, editor of the other leading sporting publication, the *Spirit of the Times*, negotiated with Heenan and the English champion, Tom Sayers, for a fight to take place in England in April 1860 for the championship of the world. Nast had become personally acquainted with Heenan when he pictured him breakfasting with his friends on the morning after his fight with Morrissey.

FLIN October 30, 1858 346
Incidents In The Great Prizefight Championship Sketched On The Spot By Our Own Artist.

THE BENICIA BOY AT BREAKFAST WITH HIS FRIENDS AT "BLOOMERS," OF BUFFALO, THE MORNING AFTER THE FIGHT

When the fight was close to being formalized, the *New York Illustrated News* was preparing for its debut. Nast's close friend and mentor, Sol Eytinge, probably was already working with the new publication's principals, and could have put the bug in their ear about sending Nast to cover the event, much as Leslie had done to gain a competitive edge the year before. They must have seen Nast as their circulation-boosting, prestige-building, Leslie-trumping weapon to make a big splash across the ocean with on-the-scene visuals of the training routines and the fight itself. Nast saw it as a way to establish his name — in contrast to Leslie's anonymous "Our Own Artist" — while building up his savings. Both were right — and wrong.

Chapter 4
Freelancing

Leaving Leslie

Several factors probably played a role in Nast's decision to leave Frank Leslie's employment after almost two and a half years. His father's health and ability to earn a living may have been key because Joseph Nast was to die less than three months later on March 15, 1859, resulting in Tommy becoming his family's breadwinner. He knew that his seven dollar weekly salary from Leslie wasn't totally secure in amount or date of payment, and that his pal Sol Eytinge was doing well financially as a freelance illustrator for periodicals and books. Eytinge probably encouraged him to leave and may have offered him space in his Brooklyn studio. His final illustrations in *Frank Leslie's Illustrated Newspaper* appeared in the post-dated issues of January 8 and 15, 1859.

In later life, Thomas Nast's management of his personal finances was disastrous. However, his initial entrepreneurial step, which he took in January 1859, turned out to be positive. In January 1860, he noted in his diary that his income for the year just ended was $1,083.17. That was triple what he would have made if he had stayed at Leslie's (and not had his salary cut, which well could have happened), and was ample to support himself and his widowed mother.[1]

Nast's work as a freelance artist appeared in ten different periodicals in 1859, including all three of the leading illustrated weeklies and five different comic periodicals. He made his freelance debut in *Harper's Weekly* in the March 19 issue; eight months later, he joined the newborn *New York Illustrated News*.

Leslie certainly didn't recognize Nast as a budding comic artist, even though Nast had drawn or assisted on several unsigned cartoons, especially during the Swill Milk campaign. When Leslie founded his *Budget of Fun* in January 1859, just after Nast left, he imported Henry Louis Stephens, a thirty-five year old well-regarded artist from Philadelphia, to draw for both his publications. Leslie was now competing with *Harper's Weekly* and needed to upgrade the capabilities of his art department.

As a new freelancer, Nast accepted an assignment from James Webb's *Sunday Courier* to accompany a detective on a tour of illegal gambling houses, and depict what he saw in the resultant articles. The personal publicity Nast received from the *Courier* probably got under Leslie's skin because he rarely gave credit to his artists by name. Leslie had feuded with the *Courier* in the past and now he exploded.

> *"It is the penalty of greatness to incur the envy of small minds, and so our Illustrated Newspaper disturbs the bile of those limited city weeklies which flourished upon flash stories and indecent advertisements. The waifs and estrays from our establishment, now a fledgling artist, now a learner in the engraving art, are snapped up with avidity, in the belief that whatever comes from our establishment must be good, and made much of, and puffed and crowed over in frantic delight. This is all very pleasant until they find out that had they been worth anything we should not have parted with them . . ."*[2]

As a "waif and estray," the "fledgling artist and learner in the engraving art" was about to launch a successful business career and to meet the girl he would marry.

Harper's Weekly

Nast's early mentor, Alfred Fredericks, was on the staff of *Harper's Weekly* in 1859, and it was he who encouraged Tommy to "make us a page of Police Scandal." The 1857 Metropolitan Police Act had been passed by New York Senate Republicans in Albany as part of a comprehensive effort to strip Democratic Mayor Fernando Wood of power and patronage after his reelection in 1856.[3] The two-year old state-controlled force was blasted in an investigative report in early March.

Nast's nine vignettes interpreted highlights of the criticism of the Metropolitan Police by depicting its alleged thievery, violence, bribery and extortion. He had to work quickly to get his sketches to the engravers; the report probably came into his hands on March 5th or 6th, and his pictures were in print on March 9, ten days prior to the March 19 post-dated issue. His father died less than a week later, so it was a bittersweet time for the 18-year old entrepreneurial artist.

HW March 19, 1859 190

THE NEW YORK METROPOLITAN POLICE

A PICTORIAL ANALYSIS OF THE REPORT TO THE LEGISLATURE.

1. These gentlemen, finding the garroting business on the decline, resolve to become guardians of law and order, and enter the Metropolitan Police.

2. Policemen are but men, and when young and fascinating women happen to get into the police-stations, who can blame them if they are civil and gallant?

3. As to poor devils, houseless wretches, with no good looks, and steeped in poverty and misery, can a high-bred policeman be expected to cringe to such as these? No, no; let them eat the bread of sorrow.

4. If a rowdy who votes with the Republicans happens to stick his knife into his neighbor's midriff, the judicious Metropolitan policeman instantly discovers a fight between two small boys at the next corner and hastens to interfere on behalf of law and order.

5. But if a poor wretch of a Democrat steals a loaf for his starving family, the zeal and fury of the Metropolitan police know no bounds, and the fellow is lucky if he be not brained on the spot.

6. A high-minded Commissioner scorns the idea of accepting a house bought by the members of the force; but somehow the house *is* bought, and the title-deeds are slipped into somebody's pocket without his knowledge and tremendously against his will.

7. The powers that be ask no favor; but when they want new clothes a friendly captain goes round with the hat, and as for the patrolman who declines to put in a quarter, he had better emigrate to California by the next steamer.

8. The consequence of which is, that the poor patrolman is unable to procure the food which his sick wife requires, and his children go without stockings and without new frocks.

9. The police service continues, however, to be admirably efficient, and quite a number of hack-carriages are actively employed on pressing police duty, as above depicted.

James W. Nye, a 45-year old lawyer, was President of the Metropolitan Police Board. Nast depicted him in Panel Six accepting a house as a bribe. He was ousted as a result of his notoriety.

Nye recovered by becoming Nevada's first territorial governor and, after statehood, its Senator. Nast got to know and like Nye, and drew him favorably as a happy court jester in 1872, contrasting him with Liberal Senator Carl Schurz whom he despised. Nast portrayed himself on Nye's jester stick.

6. A high-minded commissioner scorns the idea of accepting a house bought by the members of the force; but somehow the house is bought, and the title-deeds are slipped into somebody's pocket without his knowledge and tremendously against his will.

HW March 23, 1872 282

Nast

SEN. SCHURZ SITS IN FRONT OF SEN. NYE IN THE SENATE.

Two weeks later, Nast drew a second illustration for *Harper's Weekly:* "Street Scene in London – Winter Evening." Nast had never been to London, although he was to find his way there eleven months later to cover the Heenan-Sayers fight for the *New York Illustrated News*. It was a typical space-filling street scene, similar to those drawn by Alfred Fredericks, Winslow Homer and other periodical illustrators, and was Nast's last contribution to *Harper's Weekly* until he joined its staff three years later.

HW April 2, 1859 212

STREET SCENE IN LONDON. —WINTER EVENING

Phunny Phellow

The most important humor publication in Nast's professional career was *Phunny Phellow*, a monthly printed on inexpensive paper, which Street & Smith began publishing in 1859. As mentioned earlier, he commenced a fourteen-year relationship — which ended in 1873 when *Harper's* began paying him a $5,000 annual fee for exclusivity — by providing a front page, a back page and a center spread of cartoons which he didn't sign because they were "very roughly executed." ***Phunny Phellow* gave Nast his first opportunity to publish political caricatures on a regular basis. He now had the space and freedom for an ideal laboratory, where his skills as a caricaturist could be developed without public criticism.**

Nast opened in October 1859 with Horace Greeley. Greeley longed for more power in public life than he merited as editor of the *Tribune*. While he had served a term as a Congressman in 1848-1849, his one-time assistant and present competitor, Henry Raymond of the *Times*, outshone Greeley as Lieutenant-Governor of New York State, a more prestigious and influential position.

Greeley's most hated rival continued to be James Gordon Bennett, the *Herald's* equally powerful publisher. To needle Bennett, a facetious commentary in Greeley's *Tribune* of August 24, 1859, "The Right Man for the Right Job," proposed Bennett for Mayor; it noted that the two leading candidates for the next mayoral contest were deadlocked and drew attention to the supposition that both were considered "energetic and unscrupulous." The *Times* and the *Brooklyn Eagle* took the bait and endorsed Bennett, who reprinted their remarks but refrained from comment. On September 1, Bennett signed off by stating that his preferred candidate, former mayor Fernando Wood, would run again for mayor in the December 1859 election, (which he ultimately won).

Nast's first political cartoon for *Phunny Phellow* showed Greeley and the Scotch-born Bennett as *The Rival Jockeys Coming to an Understanding*. Greeley was holding a horse with the misspelled name of "Governer" and encouraging his rival, holding a (dark) horse marked "Mayor," to run for the governorship, which was not then at issue. Nast, still only 18, was making the apparent point that Republican Greeley, who despised Democrat Bennett and his politics, might want the governor's chair for himself at some future point.

Nast's second *Phunny Phellow* cartoon on the cover of the November issue again featured Greeley and Bennett. This time they were about to crush "small potatoes" Henry Raymond's *Times* between Bennett's "prize poompkin" *Herald* and Greeley's giant squash *Tribune*. The "Little Villain" Raymond had "No Where" to go.

PP October 1859

THE RIVAL JOCKEYS COMING TO AN UNDERSTANDING.
_H—E G—Y_—That's a fine looking nag you've got there, Jamie, and if you can't ride him to win, nobody can. You mount him, anyhow, and take the chances. I'll back you and holler on you as long as I've got a bit of wind left. _J.G. B—TT_—Hoot awa', mon! Ye'll no be pullin' the wull over my eyes. I did think o' ridin' him at first, but I've nae muckle faith in yer pretended friendship. Besides, I can do better, now. I feel extremely grateful to ye, for ye'r opinion o' my bonnie nag, an' I'm sorra I canna return the compliment. But honesty coonstrains me to say, mon, that your beastie has nae moor chance o' winnin' than a cat wud hae in tophet wi'out claws! Hoot awa', mon! Hoot awa'! We'll nae do for cronies, h—e! We'll nae do for cronies!

PP November 1859

THE "LITTLE VILLAIN" "NO WHERE."
**J.G. B——TT. —Have a care, ye little villain—have a care, mon! Dinna ye see i'm comin' wi' my prize poompkin? Ye canna charge me wi' ploom-guttin' this time!
H. G——Y. —Get out of the way, my friend—get out of the way! Don't you see me coming? You will surely be _squashed_ to death between the two of us!
H. RAY——D. —They've got me this time, sure enough! That is some pumpkin, and that is also some squash, while I can display nothing in the way of farm produce but a couple of small potatoes. I must attend to this in future!**

While these two cartoons were not memorable in themselves, they were Nast's first solo entries in the political ring. [4]

In the summer of 1859, Nast made another important connection with publisher Street & Smith's *New York Weekly,* which specialized in weekly installments of dime-novel-type fiction. He was commissioned to illustrate *Garibaldi, the Hero of Italy*, which commenced July 23, 1859, although he was not identified as the artist. The thirty-four chapter novel chronicled Giuseppe Garibaldi's flight as a hunted man in 1849 after his unsuccessful fight against the French in Rome. The series was timed to capitalize on Garibaldi's current 1859 victories over the Austrian armies. Tommy, of course, had no idea in July 1859 that he would be covering Garibaldi's campaigns in Sicily and Naples less than a year later as a neophyte war artist for two illustrated newspapers, and would be drawing the legendary architect of Italian unification from life.

Comics

When Nast set out as an entrepreneur, his best opportunity appeared to be the monthly comic magazines which needed the type of simplistic cartoons he could readily produce. Because his cartoons were rarely signed or initialed, he could freelance anonymously. By February 1859, he had three likely customers, with two more added before the year was over.

Probably his first comic client was a new children's magazine which lasted for just two issues in June and July 1859. *The Little Pig Monthly* hired Nast to illustrate the misadventures of a "fast" pig who ended up as sausage in the first issue, and the unfinished tale of a similar goose in the second. The magazine went broke, but the goose's story was completed in Nast's first book, *Laugh and Grow Wise*.

Nast's First Symbol: The Owl

The owl had been a symbol of wisdom dating back to the ancient Greeks and Athena, the Goddess of Wisdom. On his book's cover, it became the first symbol of dozens that Nast ultimately utilized. Art Young, a famous next-generation (after Nast) cartoonist, described his friend Nast as having "owl-like features."[5] Conceivably, young Tommy Nast may have had some glimmer of self-identification with the wise old bird. (When he finally published his own ill-fated eponymous paper 34 years later, the definitively self-imaged owl was again his symbol. However, Athena undoubtedly would have disavowed his wisdom at that point in his life.)

Nick-Nax and *The Comic Monthly*

The most important humor magazines for Nast's *personal* — as contrasted with his *professional* — career that he connected with during his freelancing year, were published by Jesse C. Haney, who had co-edited *Nick-Nax for All Creation* since its birth in 1856; he founded *The Comic Monthly* in March 1859 to compete with *Phunny Phellow* and Leslie's *Budget of Fun*. Both publications used the same office space, and sometimes the same illustrations, cartoons and jokes.[6]

Haney was well regarded for both his capability and his generosity. Cartoonists Frank Bellew, Thomas Butler Gunn, "Doesticks" Thomson, Sol Eytinge and artists Alfred and William Ward — along with Nast — all vied for his patronage.

Nast probably became acquainted with Haney at Pfaff's while he was working for *Leslie's*. Haney took a shine to the teenager and provided him with steady work on both his periodicals throughout the second half of 1859.

After Nast learned in late 1859 that he would be going to London in mid-February to cover the boxing match between John Heenan and the English champion Tom Sayers, he prepared a number of cartoons and caricatures which were published while he was in Europe. This humdrum one managed to get *Nick-Nax* (on the wall) into *The Comic Monthly* cartoon, although the dyslexic "j" in June" was backwards. The cartoon appeared in December 1860, but was drawn a year or so earlier.

THE COMIC MONTHLY December 1860

A SYMPATHIZING PAIR
Joe.—"*Getting on nicely, thank you. How's yours?*"
Dav. —"*Getting along first rate. I've been up two days and a night with it, and it's just beginning to color.*"
(Mutual admiration and examination of pipes follows.)

Nast's front and back pages in *The Comic Monthly* often targeted leading theatrical producers, impresarios, actors and actresses, including William Burton.* Each portrait probably was spawned by a free press pass to their performances, enhancing his cultural knowledge and theatrical passion.

* See p. 9

Nast's final cartoon for *Nick-Nax* was a double-page satire on lessons learned by youngsters in twelve different international cultures. His later stereotypes may have had their genesis here: A German drinking beer; an Irish lad brandishing his liquor bottle; an Indian holding his tomahawk; an American smoking his segars; and a Chinese with his hookah.

NICK NAX December 1859

1. Early Lessons of the German Boy. **2. Early Lessons of the English Boy.** **3. Early Lessons of the Irish Gossoon.**

4. Early Lessons of the Scotch Boy. **5. Early Lessons of the Spanish Youth.** **6. Early Lessons of Young America.**

10. Early Lessons of the Chinaman.

11. Early Lessons of the Indian.

12. Early Lessons of the Italian Boy.

Richard West, Periodyssey

Vanity Fair

Artist Henry Louis Stephens and his two brothers founded *Vanity Fair* on December 28, 1859. Its literary contributions often featured articles from the Bohemians at Pfaff's beer cellar. Nast contributed three cartoons at three dollars each before he left for England.

The first one *Vanity Fair* published was unsigned, but it dealt with Five Points and undoubtedly was a by-product of the series of illustrations on the miserable lives of its residents which appeared in the two issues of the *Illustrated News* following his departure for England. His first initialled cartoon was run-of-the-mill.

VF January 28, 1860 71

SCIENCE IN COW BAY.
Doating Mother. —Bless his 'ittle heart! He has ways about him, he has, so like his own father. He takes to that poker as nateral as if it was a jimmy!

VF February 25, 1860 35

AN AFFECTIONATE HUSBAND.
(Hp!) 'Taint late, o'ly (hp) eleven o'clock, (hp) mus' go home an' take my wife to the (hp) theatre.

* * * *

In summary, Tommy's freelancing year proved to be successful on many counts. He proved he could get work, tripled his income, and was hired by the *Illustrated News* (whom he thought would be a solid employer) to cover a stimulating overseas championship boxing match in the new year. Best of all, Jesse Haney — in addition to providing him with plenty of work — turned out to be a key spoke in Tommy's personal wheel of fortune. Their social friendship turned into the bridge that serendipitously led him to his bride and absolutely essential helpmate, Sallie Edwards.

Chapter 5
When Tommy Met Sallie

James Parton

James Parton was the original link between Jesse Haney, Thomas Nast and the Edwards family. Born in Canterbury, England on February 9, 1822, he arrived in Philadelphia at age five with his widowed mother. Despite their eighteen-year age difference, Parton would become one of Thomas Nast's closest friends.

Parton was one of the most eminent American biographers of his time. By 1859, when he met Nast, his lives of Horace Greeley and Aaron Burr were already published, and those of Andrew Jackson, Benjamin Franklin, Thomas Jefferson and Voltaire were still to come.

Jesse Haney, six years younger than Parton and twelve years older than Nast, was born and also raised in Philadelphia. In 1847, when he was 19, Haney came to a local school where Parton was tutoring. Parton trained him as a teacher and they became good friends.

George Edwards, Parton's uncle (his mother's brother), also emigrated to Philadelphia. The two families socialized in the Quaker City before 1848 when Parton moved to New York, and after 1854 when the Edwards family followed them. Parton introduced Haney to the Edwards family, and by 1856, both of them became regular visitors, along with Thomas Butler Gunn.

The Edwards Family

Born in 1798, George prospered in England, and had at least five children with his first wife. Hale and hearty, but not the smartest person in his family, his fortunes declined and his wife died. After he established himself in Philadelphia, George married Sarah Leach, who had been his daughter Anne's governess, and was fourteen years younger than he. It probably was more a marriage of convenience than of true love.

George's five children came to America with him. His older son married Sarah Leach's sister (so George and his son were brothers-in-law). That son, and his two married sisters, all lived in California. Anne and George's younger English-born son, also named George, lived on the east coast.

George and Sarah Leach Edwards had four American-born children as her first and his second family. John Darling Edwards, known as Jack, was 19, about seven months older than Tommy Nast when the future brothers-in-law first met. Sarah (Sallie) was 18, Martha (Mattie) was 16, and Elizabeth (Eliza) was 14. According to Gunn, Jack was always his mother's favorite, while Sallie frequently had a strained relationship with her.

Anne's decision to reject her cousin Jim Parton's three separate proposals while they lived in Philadelphia, turned out to be unfortunate for both of them. Gunn described Anne as "not ill-natured but sharpish and shallow, inclined to play school-mistress." In 1859, still unmarried and close to 40, she returned from working as a governess in Norfolk, and became part of her father's household. Her half-brother Jack considered her snobbish, and Sallie didn't like her.

Sarah, or Mrs. E., as Gunn referred to her, was a lively, energetic woman of 47, and probably the family's primary breadwinner and decision-maker. She was a skilled dress designer and seamstress, who operated a sewing room/retail shop on the ground floor of her home. She usually worked until eleven at night, helped by her daughters on occasion, as well as by hired sewers. The coming of the Civil War cut off her custom mail-orders from the South, and diminished the family's income.

George struggled to make a living as a jobber for Crockett, a company which manufactured quality oilcloth used as waterproofed cotton fabric. George procured paints and varnishes for the coating, dealing with suppliers located near Troy, NY. On occasion, he apparently also wholesaled paint, slate and other hardware items from suppliers in the area. That led to annual Edwards family vacations in Grafton Center, a small town fourteen miles southwest of Troy in the Catskill Mountains.

By 1859, George was complaining about feeling old and feeble at 61, although he would live another ten years. He maintained his jolly English visage and was best known for his exceptional recipe for punch, which he prepared almost every night. Gunn genially referred to him as paterfamilias or Mr. E.

The large rented house served not only as the Edwards home, Mrs. E.'s workshop and salesroom, but also as an entertainment center for up to fifty people on special occasions like Christmas. Several nights a week throughout most of the year, the finished basement had a merry salon-like atmosphere with George's punch as a centerpiece.

Parton, Gunn and Jesse Haney had been regulars since 1856 when the three girls were 11, 13, and 15. Of course, Parton had known them in Philadelphia when they were very young. The men were one to two decades older and had an avuncular, or even a somewhat pedagogic relationship, with their bubbly niece-like admirers. Other artistic or publishing notables who showed up on occasion included Mort Thomson, Leslie's reporter Augustus Rawlings, cartoonist Frank Bellew, and Haney's friend and publishing associate, Frank Cahill.

On May 16, 1859, Sallie turned 18, an age when marriage was a top-of-mind consideration. Mattie, 16, and Eliza, 14, were attractive flirts. Several additional admirers began to show up more frequently, including Edward Welles who had a talent for poetry. Another was soon to appear.

As previously mentioned, Tommy Nast first encountered Gunn, when Frank Leslie asked the free-lance writer and illustrator to accompany his eighteen-year old artist to the Calico Ball in December 1857.* Beginning eighteen months later, Gunn became a far more important factor in Nast's life because of his "Dutch uncle" relationship with Sallie Edwards. For most of that time, Gunn denigrated "Little Nast" — not inaccurately — as "podgey (fat), ignorant, selfish, uncultured and clownish, although hard working and generally in good humor." At five feet eleven, Gunn towered over Nast.

Gunn's best friend was Haney. Many of Gunn's other social friends — including Parton, Thomson, Frank Leslie, Sol Eytinge, Frank Bellew, artists Alfred and William Waud, and the entire Edwards family — played notable roles in Nast's life.

Nast himself never knew most of what Gunn recorded in his diaries. After Tommy married Sallie, Gunn came to fully respect and probably like him. Nast reciprocated by depicting Gunn as "Our Artist" in his 1864 cartoon *The Press on the Field*, probably as a tip of his hat to both Sallie and her former confidante.**

HW April 30, 1864 280

* See p. 36
** See p. 92

Sallie

On Sunday, June 19, Tommy Nast hit his lifetime personal jackpot when Jesse Haney brought him to the Edwards home at 745 Broadway as a substitute for Frank Cahill, a regular participant who was unavailable that day. As Gunn noted in his diary, Haney thought his eighteen-year old protégé would fill in adequately "in our little circle." If Haney had any vague thoughts of playing Cupid for Tommy, it would have been with Mattie or Eliza, who were four and two years younger than their new visitor — and definitely not for Sallie, for whom he had his own matrimonial intentions in mind.

It is highly unlikely that Tommy was aware of his mentor's romantic interest in Sallie because Haney apparently hadn't discussed the topic with anyone, including his intended. The single exception may have been Gunn, who was close enough to have shared a room with Haney three years earlier.

Nast certainly knew something about his patron's love life. As might be expected of a 31-year old bachelor with strong appetites for drink and sex, and enough money to readily afford them, Haney was uninhibited when out on the town. Gunn noted that his intimacies included Allie Vernon (whom Haney first introduced to Sol Eytinge), her sister Josey, his landlady, and innumerable brothel inhabitants.

Gunn was surprised to see Tommy there. In his diary, he noted that "Little Nast was an industrious little chap, German by birth (and exceedingly ungrammatically so). The girls noticed his assaults (on grammar) when he came out with 'There are some people what thinks ____!' He is good humored, I think, and unsophisticated, but shrewdly intent on money making. He does a good deal of drawing now, since his quitting Frank Leslie's, but works rather from knack and industry rather than perception. He was there for the first time and in high glee."

Almost four years later, in April 1863, just before he returned to his native England for good, Gunn was reminiscing with Tommy and Sallie in their home on West 44th Street. Sallie pointed out that her husband came of poor parents, had known privation, and in his early years "had to go to bed hungry on occasion because his mother had no food to give him." Gunn added, "At Leslie's he earned $5 a week and was mortally apprehensive of losing his place . . . Much of his apparent conceit is really the mask of his shyness and consciousness of his educational deficiencies."

At the time, however, with no real understanding of Nast's background, both Gunn and Haney were stunned by his behavior. "Tommy, growing up in this atmosphere, is brought to 745 (Broadway), when incontinently he falls head over ears in love with Sallie."

Sallie, of course, had no idea of Mr. Haney's (she probably called him that) romantic interest in her. She had known him since she was six years old, and regarded him as a somewhat pedantic and, on occasion, overly dogmatic friend. He was almost a polar opposite of Nast; small stature, large egos and an appreciation of cartoon humor were among the few characteristics they had in common.

As a social misfit, bubbly, unsophisticated Tommy inspired both ridicule and sympathy in the Edwards household. Mrs. Edwards liked him; perhaps her experience as a governess who climbed the social ladder, influenced her empathy for Sallie's unexpected suitor. He, in turn, recognized that she was the real brains in the family.

The girls dubbed their new friend "Roly-Poly." His inability to articulate and express himself often resulted in his clowning, pantomime and animated gesturing in social situations. Gunn referred to his "little buffooneries" and "his shoulder-shrugging and grimacing."

However, Gunn also noted that "the three Edwards daughters schooled him after their fashions." Sallie, who was considered the smartest, taught him how to dress and behave. Mattie, the prettiest, attacked Nast's language deficiencies; when he made a mistake in grammar or pronunciation, she would repeat it after him until he came to dislike her on occasion. Eliza, the most precocious, established solid rapport with Tommy and "laughed, reprehended or 'cut up' with him with her customary freedom."

There were three annual events on the Edwards family calendar. Every Fourth of July they enjoyed an elaborate picnic away from home. In August, they went on a three-week vacation to the same farmhouse in Grafton. At Christmas, they and their friends put on an elaborate theatrical entertainment for up to fifty guests in their home. The Edwards social circle was invited to participate in all of these happenings.

Tommy did so enthusiastically, to his great advantage in courting Sallie. They provided him with an opportunity to put his artistic talent to its best use, and to share both creative and romantic time with his newfound love.

Just over two weeks after meeting Sallie, Tommy joined her family and friends for their annual Fourth of July picnic, at Nyack, on the west side of the Hudson River. "Roly-Poly" subsequently illustrated the festivities in a "Picnic Book," which also included a poem by Edward Welles, another of Sallie's silent suitors. One short excerpt read:

> "I have bothered my head for a pun on the name of the young artist friend who along with us came, And is rushing along on the turnpikes of fame."[1]

Tommy and Sallie got to know each other better as they worked closely on the book, coordinating the Welles verse under Nast's sketches.

Caricature Of The Artist Of The Picnic Book, By Himself

"The Poet And The Artist" (From The Picnic Book)

Paine, p. 32 33

Less than a month after the picnic, Nast joined the Edwards family on their annual three-week vacation in Grafton. Getting there involved going up the Hudson River by steamboat or train, followed by a fourteen mile coach ride. As mentioned previously, George did occasional business in the area, and this was the family's third summer there. They stayed in the same large farmhouse, and went hiking, climbing, swimming and riding. Sallie displayed her talent as a superb horsewoman, but Tommy, who had never been in the saddle, refrained. His horrific first lesson would have to wait for their honeymoon, a little over two years later.

Macculloch Hall Historical Museum

Jesse Haney and Frank Bellew were in the Grafton entourage that year, but Gunn was not. Haney made his intentions known to Sallie, but her answer was ambivalent. Two months later, she gently but firmly discouraged his interest permanently. As a consolation prize, he would marry Mattie Edwards after the Civil War, and become Tommy and Sallie Nast's brother-in-law.

While in Grafton, Tommy continued to impress Sallie and her family with his artistic skills. In addition to sketching their travels in the hilly Catskills, Nast also drew portraits of the three sisters. In Gunn's opinion, only Sallie's was outstanding.

Paine p. 31

MISS SARAH EDWARDS
August 1859

Tommy told Sallie he was deeply in love with her and implored her to marry him. She put him off for the time being.

Haney and Gunn underestimated Nast, believing that he was not up to Sallie's standards. When Gunn perceived Nast's romantic interest, but knew nothing of his actual proposal, he wrote: "Poor little Nast! You are in for heart twinge, my boy!"

As Sallie and Tommy slowly became a couple, he took her to theatre and lectures, and accompanied her regularly on Sunday to hear Reverend Chapin's sermons. With his native German Catholicism long gone, he became an Episcopalian.

Tommy was persistent, and his good-hearted nature, energy and boyish enthusiasm — expressed in pictures as well or better than in words — eventually won Sallie over. He needed to accumulate a nest egg before they could marry, but he and Sallie came to an understanding around Christmas time. Haney acknowledged to Gunn in January that "Nast was the chosen one."

Their elaborate extravaganza made Christmas the most important day of the year for the Edwards family. When Gunn attended his first event in 1855, about twenty people assembled in the back workroom. Jim Parton and Haney wrote the program, and the latter performed magic tricks. Games, including charades and blind man's bluff, were played; songs sung; poems read; and toasts given.

In 1859, an elaborate handbill was prepared for *THEATRE DES EDWARDS*. The "Brilliant Galaxy" included Fanny Fern and her two daughters because she didn't want Jim to come alone. Total attendance was about fifty.

"Scenic Artist-in Chief, Signor Tommasso Nastonetti," prepared the scenery for the stage play in his "atelier." As Edward Welles, who had also written the verse for the Picnic Book, composed another poem referring to the portraits of Sallie, Mattie and Eliza that Tommy had painted at Grafton.[2]

> "'Twas ere that young artist of high and rare promise
> Whose surname is Nast and prenomen Thomas,
> Had come with his pencil to fill up the spaces
> On the walls of this room with three charming faces."

"Signor Haynau Heynhi" (Haney) had written a dramatic story about Bluebeard and played the part. Nast, attired as a French clown, played Bibbo, his valet and barber, all in pantomime. However, Signor Amodio Nassoletti did sing an aria from Ill Trovatorum which enthralled the audience while Sallie played the piano.

Four months later, when Nast was in England for the Heenan-Sayers fight, he wrote Sallie and included these two sketches in his letter.[3] After they were married the following year, Nast's first major gift to Sallie was a $350 piano, bought on credit.

The Edwards family gatherings not only provided Tommy with a real home-like social life for the first time, but also exposed him to informal discussions of art, music, literature, politics and history that broadened him educationally in ways that school never did or could have. His romance with Sallie was the icing on his cake, and her future role as his editor and muse was second only to her importance as his loving wife and mother of his five children.

PICKING THE NOTES TO THE "ASSEMBLED GUESTS."

Fanny Fern

In January 1856, Parton had married Fanny Fern, whose real name was Sara Payson Willis. Professionally, Fanny was a huge success as an author, earning $5,000 a year for a column in the *New York Ledger* which had a weekly circulation of 400,000. She sometimes wrote about taboo subjects like prostitution and venereal disease. *Ruth Hall*, her 1854 thinly-disguised autobiographical novel about her unhappy family life, was a best-seller. She often used her *Ledger* column in the same manner to publicize quarrels or disagreements with members of her extended family or social circle, or deride people she didn't like. Most of her readers were women who could readily relate to the candid, intimate, confessional style of her writing.

Gunn was a close friend of Parton's and strongly disliked Fanny. He knew that she seduced Parton before they married; he liked the sex but felt guilty about it; and he was "sick and tired of boarding-house discomfort." Fanny may even have told Jim she was pregnant, as Gunn intimated without confirming.[4] Gunn was particularly repelled by Fanny's aggressive feminism, sometimes expressed when she wore men's clothing.

Fanny could be stubborn, ill tempered and vituperative, as well as physically abusive to her husband. She knew that he previously had been involved romantically with his still unmarried cousin Anne Edwards (from George's first family) when both families lived in Philadelphia, and she was suspicious, despite his protestations, that all that was a thing of the past. The fact that James was Fanny's third husband and eleven years younger (48 in 1859), probably added fuel to her fire. According to Gunn, Fanny was promiscuous — traveling and sleeping with Oliver Dyer, her editor at the Ledger; attempting to seduce Jim's friends, including Jesse Haney; and "inviting Phallus-worship" by "habitual low-necked exposure of her bosom."

Unsurprisingly, Fanny was persona non grata to Jim's cousins in the Edwards home, where Mrs. E., in particular, detested her. Jim mostly socialized there without her, not infrequently to take refuge from her. On occasion, Fanny's jealousy of his time there spurred her to accompany him, so she could keep an eye on him in spite of the familial strains. On more than one occasion, he moved out or fled to his sister's home in Rochester, but she always was able to entice him back.

However, after Tommy and Sallie were married, the two couples had a warm relationship and even vacationed together. Here, they jointly celebrated New Years Day, joined by Jesse Haney, among others. [5]

HW January 2, 1864 8-9

Jim Tommy Gunn Haney Fanny Sallie

Marriage

A few weeks before Christmas, the newly-commenced *New York Illustrated News* enlisted Tommy for a series of assignments. Secretly, so as not to alert their established competition, the paper sent him to England in mid-February 1860 to cover the international boxing match between his old acquaintance, John Heenan, and the British champion, Tom Sayers.

The last time Sallie and Tommy were together was on Valentine's Day, as Tommy prepared to sail on the morrow. They began by going to the theatre. Sallie gave her fledgling fiance a lock of her hair, a ring, two handkerchiefs and her portrait (probably a carte de visite), and he gave her "jewels." They were informally engaged as he entered his self-named "time-trial" away from her. It had been all of eight months since Haney introduced them.

Sallie waited for her man. Although she expressed indifference about him to her social confidante Gunn on many occasions, she secretly wrote to Tommy at least four times, and her brother Jack did so on occasion as her designated substitute.

Tommy's growing fame and reputation undoubtedly was an important factor in keeping Sallie bound to him during his year's absence. After he had been away for four months, he wrote Sallie, "I came here to make a name to please you by that name so you will love me more."[6] His public recognition was also noted inside the Edwards social circle as the *Illustrated News* flaunted his European sketches and even his portrait.

Sarah and George Edwards both supported their daughter's marrying Tommy. Alfred Waud, who also worked for the *Illustrated News* at that time, disliked Nast and drew the cartoon showing him as Sol Eytinge's lapdog.* However, during a conversation in April 1861 after Tommy had announced his wedding plans, Alf recommended a jeweler to him, and told him about a specific diamond ring he had seen in his shop. Tommy bought the ring for $33, and he and Sallie Edwards became officially engaged.[7] The wedding was set for September 26, 1861, his twenty-first birthday. Sallie had turned twenty four months earlier.

Their marriage took place at 8 a.m., shortly after which they embarked on a long grueling train ride to Niagara Falls. "Thomas Nast & Lady" stayed at Cataract House for three nights which they put to good use; daughter Julia was born nine months later. Tommy splurged on Claret champagne and a carriage during their stay, but didn't do well on horseback. When Sallie felt ill, "Tommy borrowed some whisky and paregoric downstairs and dosed me until I felt relieved."

Macculloch Hall Historical Museum

Upon returning to New York after their three-day honeymoon, the newlyweds settled in at 282 West 44th Street. The household included Tommy's mother Apollonia and a servant girl to help Sallie, soon to discover she was pregnant, with her chores. It featured the piano which Tommy bought on credit as a present for his bride.

* See p. 35

Family

Julia was born on July 1, 1862. Ten months later, the Nasts moved to 64 East 89th Street, five houses from First Avenue, in Yorkville. That neighborhood, adjacent to the East River, was heavily populated with German immigrants. (Its centerpiece today is Gracie Mansion, home to the city's mayors.) Larger quarters provided Tommy with more space for a studio, totally necessary because he worked from home.

Their timing was extremely fortunate. On July 13, 1863, a little more than ten weeks after they moved, the Draft Riots broke out and the Colored Orphan Asylum, two blocks east of their former 44th Street home, was burned to the ground. Their new abode, which Tommy had just returned to after two weeks in Pennsylvania, was safe from the crazed mobs.

The following year, the family moved about two miles farther north to 24 West 125th Street, just off Fifth Avenue, in Harlem. Two more children would be born there: Thomas Edwards Nast (known as Tom, Jr.) on April 28, 1865 and Sarah Edith Nast (known as Edith) on July 3, 1868. The last two children were born in Morristown, New Jersey, after the Nasts moved there in the summer of 1871 as the Tweed campaign heated up: Mabel Nast on December 5, 1871 and Cyril Nast on August 28, 1879.

* * * *

Macculloch Hall Historical Museum

Sallie was integral to her husband's success. At home, she not only gave him the love and support he needed, but also read to him, corrected spelling and grammar in his cartoons, and sometimes suggested captions. They were a team in every way.

Moreover, she appeared as Columbia, the feminine symbol of the United States, in 158 cartoons. Only Uncle Sam, as the masculine symbol — whose image Nast modernized from its scraggly origin during the War of 1812 — outranked her with 185 depictions.

Tommy painted her classic beauty and stature in 1877 when she was about 37.

Apparently, the only time that Nast portrayed the entire Edwards family in *Harper's Weekly* was at Christmas 1864, when victory was close at hand. In one of seven supporting vignettes in a double-page allegory featuring Lincoln welcoming Jeff Davis and Robert E. Lee to the *Union Christmas Dinner*, George Edwards was giving a toast: "God Bless Our Soldiers and Sailors." Two-year old Julia stood on her high chair with her mother supporting her, while her father (back to the viewer) joined in. Jim Parton and Fanny Fern are recognizable, while Mrs. Edwards, Mattie and Haney (probably engaged by then), Eliza, Anne are almost certain. The young girl next to Nast may have been Fanny's daughter.

HW December 31, 1864 840-841

Back (L-R): Anne Edwards, Jim Parton, Sarah Edwards, Mattie Edwards, Jesse Haney, Fanny Fern
Front (L-R): George Edwards, Eliza Edwards, Thomas Gunn,, Tommy, Sallie & Julia
THE UNION CHRISTMAS DINNER. (extract)

Chapter 6
New York Illustrated News

The third version of a New York City periodical with "Illustrated News" in its title — after Thomas Strong's in 1851 and Barnum and Beach's in 1853 — appeared on November 19, 1859, as the *New-York Illustrated News*. Its original "proprietor," as he styled himself, was Rudolf Lexow who was born in Schleswig-Holstein (now Germany), in 1821. Lexow settled in New York City sometime after 1848, and in 1852 founded a German language newspaper which reached a circulation of about 20,000 by its fourth year, and included literature as well as news.

Why would Lexow, whose German-language publication was successful, launch a new illustrated newspaper into an arena already inhabited by *Frank Leslie's Illustrated Newspaper* and *Harper's Weekly*? Possibly, he wanted to hit back at Leslie who had invaded his turf by starting the German-language *Illustrated Zeitung* two years earlier, to serve "the influential and rapidly increasing population hailing from the Fatherland." Lexow saw how Leslie used the same content in both his English and German language publications, and decided to do the same. His reasoning may have been that the best defense was a good offense, and he pulled no punches in attacking Leslie.

Both Leslie and the Harpers were much better capitalized than Lexow. Leslie had his *Budget of Fun* and his fashion magazine to back up his *Illustrated Newspaper* venture. Harper Brothers was the country's leading book publisher, and also had *Harper's Monthly Magazine*, now a decade old, to go with *Harper's Weekly* and share the cost of facilities and staff. While a financial panic in the summer and fall of 1857 threatened both of Lexow's competitors, two years later they had far greater resources than he did to throw into the fray.

Nevertheless, Lexow launched with all guns blazing. The first year's issues were published under the auspices of J. Warner Campell & Co., probably to ensure fluent and idiomatic English. The price of six cents an issue, or three dollars a year, was identical to Leslie's and a penny more than *Harper's*. However, Lexow's name appeared only once in the text and never on the masthead of the sixty issues that were printed under his ownership.[1]

As previously mentioned, Nast's connection to the *Illustrated News* probably came through his friend Sol Eytinge who evidently went on Lexow's staff from the start. The championship fight between John Heenan and Englishman Tom Sayers already had been announced, and Lexow wanted Nast to give him a jump over Leslie, utilizing his experience with the Heenan-Morrissey battle a year earlier. Nast mailed his sketches from Europe directly to "Mr. Lexow."

Tommy's first year with the *Illustrated News* turned out to be a financial disaster, both for him and his employer. Nast told his biographer that he "was receiving the comfortable salary — considered really magnificent in those days — of forty dollars a week."[2] If that turned out to be the case, he would have earned about six times what Leslie had paid him in 1858, and about twice what he totaled as a free-lancer during 1859.

It is conceivable that Lexow used the forty dollar number as bait to get Nast on board. Tommy certainly had no written understanding, and his January 1860 diary provided convincing proof that he received $4 per illustration from the *Illustrated News* (vs. $7.50 from *New York Weekly*, $5 from *Phunny Phellow* and $3 from *Vanity Fair*).

All told, Nast collected $200 from the *News* for the fourteen weeks he spent in England, with no reimbursement for his expenses. $100 of that came before he left, and $100 from an advance that John Heenan gave his penniless friend in England, and then collected from the *News* with the threat of his fists. When his paper sent a reporter and an engraver to England several weeks later to complement Nast's efforts, they brought no money for their artist. Tommy did manage to scrape by financially with the help from Heenan and sketches he sold to the *Illustrated London News* (during his following six months with Garibaldi).

Lexow must have fallen far short of the circulation and advertising he needed to make the *Illustrated News* profitable. An employee, whom the *News* said was fired for "incompetence," took revenge by "concocting and issuing a malicious letter to the advertising public" about the paper's circulation. That letter probably was close to the truth in light of the other games Lexow played.

Why didn't Nast get paid? Did he think he was on a forty dollar a week salary plus expenses? Or four dollars a sketch plus expenses? Was Lexow unscrupulous enough to decide that he could give his naive nineteen-year old artist a hundred dollar advance and settle up when he returned? Or was money so short that Lexow paid the bills in front of him and let Nast fend for himself? Nast probably never knew the real reason, but the last alternative seems most likely.

NYIN January 5, 1861 132

JOHN KING, ESQ., PROPRIETOR OF THE "NEW YORK ILLUSTRATED NEWS."

Both Tommy and Sallie saw the purpose of his trip as two-fold. The first, which was to secure a financial nest egg for their marriage, failed completely when he returned with $1.50 in his pocket.

However, he did achieve his second objective of public recognition of his name and artistic abilities. Even in the short run, his growing fame and reputation probably were more important to him than the missing money. Undoubtedly, it was an important factor in keeping Sallie bound to him while he was away, as she commented confidentially to Gunn on occasion after the *Illustrated News* flaunted his sketches and even his portrait. Moreover, he developed additional artistic skills and knowledge before he returned home, and that too paid off in the future.

By the time Nast reappeared in New York in February 1861, the *Illustrated News* had been sold to its advertising agent, John King.

John Brown

Prior to leaving for England in mid-February 1860, Tommy completed several assignments for the *Illustrated News*. The biggest story of 1859 — John Brown's raid on the Federal armory in Harper's Ferry, Virginia (now West Virginia) on October 16 — was a polarizing event for the coming Civil War. Brown's intent was to seize weapons, arm 5,000 slaves in the surrounding counties, and eventually spur an insurrection. He failed, and all eighteen of his followers were killed outright or captured and executed; he himself was severely wounded. His trial began on October 27 and ended four days later when he was sentenced to hang on December 1.

November 19, 1859 C

THE ELECTION RIOTS AT BALTIMORE—DEATH OF MR. KYLE.

Meanwhile, his raid had a bombshell effect on the country. While even abolitionists agreed that the whole idea of sparking a slave insurrection through seizing the Federal armory was foolhardy, Brown's calm and even heroic demeanor throughout his imprisonment, trial and execution, made him a martyr in many northern eyes. (Less than two years later, *John Brown's Body* became a stirring marching song for Union soldiers).

On November 13, Tommy and Sallie attended a lecture on "Old Brown" given by Mortimer "Doesticks" Thomson. Gunn observed Nast and commented sardonically in his diary: "He would sit open-mouthed, swallowing all Mort's teachings as gospel." Jesse Haney and Gunn applauded while others hissed.

Lexow launched his *Illustrated News* in the middle of the uproar. The first issue featured election riots in Baltimore on its cover. The artist probably was on his way to cover Brown's imprisonment and execution and observed this scene on his way.

Mary Brown was allowed a last interview the day before her husband's execution, and then brought his body back to North Elba (in northern New York) for burial on December 8. Nast's initial assignment for the *Illustrated News* was to cover the story; however he was only identified as "Our Own Artist" when his illustration appeared on the cover of his paper's sixth issue, along with an inside sketch.

NYIN December 24, 1859 81 C
THE BURIAL OF JOHN BROWN

THE BURIAL OF JOHN BROWN, AT NORTH ELBA, DEC. 8, FROM A SKETCH BY OUR OWN ARTIST.

NYIN December 24, 1859 93

THE LAST VIEW OF JOHN BROWN'S BODY, FROM A SKETCH BY OUR OWN ARTIST.

Phrenology

One of Tommy's more stimulating assignments to him personally was a visit to the Fowler and Wells Phrenological Museum, which had been in business for 25 years and was an important advertiser in the illustrated weeklies. Conceivably, he could have tried to relate phrenology's guides to probable character with his own interest in caricature, and their common interpretation of what a person was really like based on both his physical characteristics and the bumps on his head. As Gunn noted six months later, "Nast had his head bumpologized and got a chart of his character from Fowler & Wells, and asserted that 'he could love but once' when, if unsuccessful, his prospects and happiness would be incurably blighted."[3]

Two days after Nast left for England, the *Illustrated News* featured an article about Fowler & Wells, along with two unsigned illustrations by him. Not coincidentally, Nast was provided with an eleven-page phrenological chart, including a write-up along the lines of what a fortune teller or amateur psychologist might prepare. On the last page, it made a point which Nast heeded: "You must try to steer the current of events, and beat against the wind when principle and duty point the way, not go on the bosom of the tide and float with the breezes as they happen to go."[4]

NYIN February 8, 1860 213

THE PHRENOLOGICAL MUSEUM OF FOWLER & WELLS, NO. 308 BROADWAY—EXAMINING ROOM.

Heenan vs. Sayers

Tommy kept a diary of his 13-day trip on the British steamship *City of Manchester.* He was the only one of the three passengers who shared the captain's table who didn't get seasick. He knew he was fortunate because, as he wrote Sallie a week later, heavy gales caused the steamship *Hungarian* to sink with the loss of all its passengers and crew. He drew dozens of humorous sketches, some of which, saved in a scrapbook, were published in Paine's biography.[5]

THE MOTION IS NOTHING WHEN YOU GET USED TO IT.

THE MEAL ON BOARD.

Nast's first call was on Frank Dowling, the editor of *Bell's Life*, a sporting publication which promoted the fight in England and represented Sayers — just as George Wilkes and his *Spirit of the Times* did for Heenan on the American side. Dowling also was responsible for selecting the site of the fight, as well as the referee. Dowling told him that Heenan was staying in the vicinity of Salisbury; Nast made the four-hour train trip the next day, and located Heenan at his rented quarters in Harnham.

Heenan greeted the young artist, whom he remembered from breakfast in Buffalo on the morning after his loss to John Morrissey.* He had long conversations with Tommy while training and at dinner. The *News* featured a hand-written note to the editor by Heenan, authenticating Nast's sketches, along with a picture of his warm welcome to his young friend; the inside included both a pictorial and a written account of Tommy's adventures. An interior page of the following issue contained two more Heenan illustrations; Nast pictured himself in both.

At 25, Heenan was only six years older than Nast. Heenan nicknamed his pal "The Little Dragsman," a play on the word "draughtsman." When he learned that Tommy was short of money because the *Illustrated News* had not sent him its promised remittances, he hosted Nast whenever he could.

Boxing was just as illegal in England as it was in America. However, the Pugilistic Benevolent Association did have established rules for the sport, which prohibited butting, hitting below the belt, gouging, biting, tearing flesh with fingers or nails, and falling on an antagonist knees first when he was down.

April 5, 1860

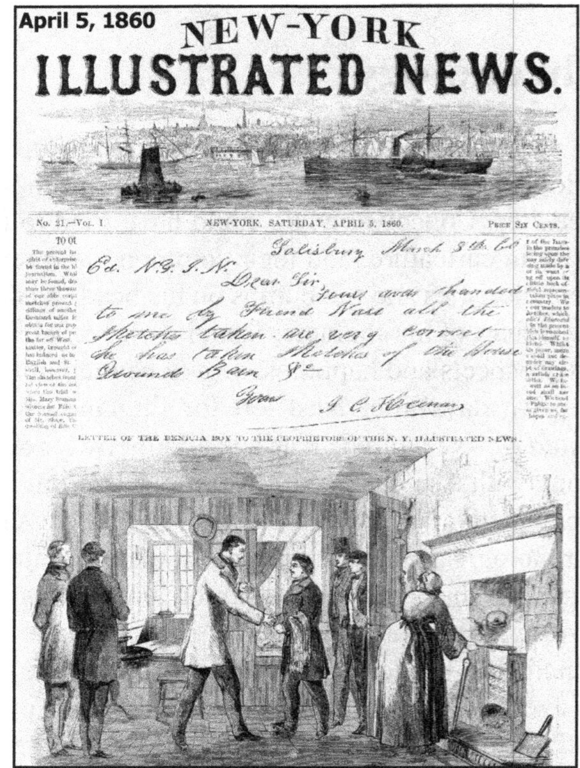

NEW-YORK ILLUSTRATED NEWS.

No. 21—Vol. I. NEW-YORK, SATURDAY, APRIL 5, 1860. Price Six Cents.

Salisbury March 8th
Ed. N.Y. I.N.
Dear Sir,
Yours was handed to me by Friend Nast all the sketches taken are very correct he has taken sketches of the House Ground Barn &c.
Yours J. C. Heenan

LETTER OF THE BENICIA BOY TO THE PROPRIETORS OF THE N. Y. ILLUSTRATED NEWS.

Heenan's trainer J.C. Heenan Thos. Nast The cook
A gentleman Heenan's trainer.
from New York Reporter of NY Clipper

THE RECEPTION OF OUR SPECIAL ARTIST, THOMAS NAST, ESQ., BY JOHN C. HEENAN, THE BENICIA BOY, AT THE HOUSE OF THE LATTER IN HARNHAM, WILTSHIRE.

* See p. 48

The newspapers, members of Parliament, churchmen and others tut-tutted hypocritically about the brutal sport while praying — if the fight indeed occurred — that their champion would win. It was the topic of the day for many weeks preceding the April 17 scheduled date. In fact, on the Tuesday that the fight took place, Parliament and many businesses shut down for the day.

The Commissioner of Police said that he would take steps to prevent the fight from being held within the Metropolitan Police District, but he could not be held responsible beyond that limit. However, the police in the countryside tracked Heenan as best they could, as he changed training locations three times. Once the cops raided just before daybreak, and Heenan ran out the back door in his nightshirt and hid in an outhouse. Running barefoot over hard, rocky ground he was caught, locked up, and finally released on bail put up by two bondsmen. That wasn't all bad because he was now virtually insured against further molestation. Nast, who stayed with Heenan, depicted the scenario.

Meanwhile, Tom Sayers trained tranquilly at Newmarket, undisturbed by the police. Nast also developed a cordial relationship with Sayers. While continuing to work as a bricklayer between fights, at 33, Sayers had only one defeat to mar his record.

The cover of the April 14 *Illustrated News* showed Nast being received by Sayers. George Wilkes, who promoted Heenan's end of the fight and described it in his *Spirit of the Times*, was also in the picture. The following week's issue depicted Nast at supper with Sayers and his trainer, as the young artist ingratiated himself with both sides.

NYIN April 4, 1860

Mr. Bryant Correspondent of the N.Y. Clipper. Mr. Th. Nast Mr. Thomas Sayers Col. Wilkes, Editor of Wilkes' Spirit of the Times

THE RECEPTION OF OUR SPECIAL ARTIST, MR. THOMAS NAST, BY THOMAS SAYERS, THE ENGLISH CHAMPION, AT HIS RESIDENCE, NEWMARKET.

In addition to polishing his interviewing style and rapport with his subjects, his three-month stay in London established Nast with his own artistic identity — able to imagine, create and draw the scenes he wanted and felt were important to his mission. However, what may be most impressive about the budding artist, whose public school education had ended six years earlier at age 13, was his apparent thirst for education, exploration and culture. In his first few days in London, Nast went to three theatres, Buckingham and Westminster Palaces, Westminster Abbey, St. Paul's Cathedral, the Bank of England and all the public parks. He immersed himself in what London was all about.

Not long after Nast sailed on February 16, the *Illustrated News* also sent reporter Francis Darragh to London to provide descriptions and context for Nast's illustrations. That took a load off the young artist who had to wear two hats for a while. The paper also sent engraver Andrew Anthony to engrave the fight pictures in London and on the ship back to New York, so as to beat its scorned competitor, Frank Leslie, to the journalistic punch.

Nast's portrait, probably the same picture he gave Sallie before he left, was featured in the May 5 issue along with Anthony's. He looked older than his nineteen years; the boy had become a man. With his name and picture in many of his published sketches, the fame and reputation he was seeking, was growing. Sallie received a descriptive love letter every time he sent a batch of sketches to the *Illustrated News*.

THOMAS NAST, ESQ., OF NEW YORK, A TALENTED ARTIST, WHO REPRESENTED THE NEW YORK ILLUSTRATED NEWS IN ENGLAND, ON THE OCCASION OF THE GREAT PRIZE FIGHT.

The Fight

After all the secrecy and distractions, the fight actually came off early on the morning of Tuesday, April 17, at a rural place called Aldershot, selected by Frank Dowling of *Bell's Life,* and outside the jurisdiction of the Metropolitan Police. The location was kept secret until nine o'clock Monday night, when the Railroad Company was notified to have a chartered train ready to leave from London Bridge station at four the next morning.

Sayers left his training camp at Newmarket in a horsebox used for transporting race horses in order to mislead the police and avoid arrest. He spent Monday evening in a hotel near the station. Nast re-created this scene as one of five vignettes on the cover of the May 12 *Illustrated News*.

SAYERS LEAVES NEWMARKET IN A HORSEBOX, TO MISLEAD THE POLICE AND AVOID ARREST.

Heenan traveled to London disguised in a curly wig, long whiskers, a slouched hat and a dark cape. He spent the evening hours at a friend's house near the station. Nast accompanied Heenan to a private entrance to the station shortly before 4 A.M. When they passed the car Sayers was in, the two disguised rivals were introduced for the first time while Nast and John Morrissey looked on. Morrissey had come over to help train Sayers by coaching him on Heenan's weak points.

Nast Morrissey

HEENAN AND SAYERS MEET FOR THE FIRST TIME ON THE MORNING OF THE FIGHT, AT THE RAILROAD TERMINUS BOTH BEING IN DISGUISE.

For miles along the way, every station had dozens of policemen to prevent landing "our cargo." When the train reached Hampshire County, the engineer was given instructions to stop only a few minutes before his train and the following one reached Aldershot.

The 1,200 or so knowledgeable ticket-holders followed the man in charge of the ropes and stakes to a meadow about 300 yards from the track where a ring was prepared. As a ruse, another party of "uninitiated" fans was led to a site about two miles away in case the police needed to be distracted. The two principals changed into their fighting costumes in their railroad cars and then, disguised in suits and caps, proceeded to the ring. The fight actually started shortly after seven.

The pre-fight agreement required that Heenan could not weigh more than 25 pounds more than Sayers. He came in at a trim 175 pounds, at least 20 pounds lighter than for the Morrissey fight when ill health and the resultant lack of exercise bloated him. He had significant physical advantages over Sayers in height, weight, reach, and age.

Heenan put these advantages to good use as Sayers was knocked down or slipped down in round after round. (A round ended when one of the boxers was on the ground). Moreover, at some point one of Heenan's punches evidently broke a bone in Sayers' right arm, effectively disabling it. Sayers did manage to partially close Heenan's left eye and was trying to blind him by smacking the other one.

In the 36th round, some of Sayers' backers who stood to lose their bets cried out "Police! Police!" They hoped that Heenan, as a stranger, would either jump out of the ring and forfeit, or else turn his head so that Sayers could hit him on his good right eye. Sayers had been warned of the ruse and ended that round and the next one with Sayers on the ground.

In round 38, Heenan bent Sayers' head under his arm and held him against the ropes while punching away, all of which was legal. This time some of Sayers' supporters went a step further, kicking and striking Heenan through the ropes, and dragging their beaten champion from his hold. In round 39, Sayers' cronies actually broke into the ring, causing the referee — none other than the promoter Frank Dowling — to disappear rather than stop the fight. Heenan stayed in the ring and continued to go after Sayers.

Sayers managed to make it into round 42, when the ruffians, who were about to lose their bets on him, cut the ropes and swarmed into the ring. At that point, the referee suddenly reappeared and suggested that "the men be taken away as it would be a pity to have two such game fellows injured." The police, who had actually been on the scene but remained inactive, were glad to oblige. Heenan took off running across the meadow to the train, and made it without being arrested.

"PEELERS" ARRIVE ON THE FIGHTING GROUND, BUT ARE KEPT OFF BY THE CROWD.

HEENAN LEAVING THE BATTLE-FIELD AFTER THE 42ND ROUND, RUNS WITH SURPRISING SPEED TO THE CARS.

Nast's five vignettes told the story effectively, on the May 12 cover, along with his text. Just before that, the *Illustrated News* put out a special "Championship Number" devoted to the fight. Nast's picture of the two fighters shaking hands in the ring was on the cover and a double page of the two in action, with their seconds and some of the ringsiders was the main feature. Nast portrayed himself, sketchbook in hand,

John Morrissey was depicted just outside the ropes in Sayers' corner. He had a $10,000 bet riding, and was accused of being the man who actually cut the ropes.

NYIN May 1860 408-409

Nast **Morrissey**

THE CHAMPION FIGHT BETWEEN HEENAN AND SAYERS ON THE 17TH APRIL. —From A Sketch By Our Own Artist, Thos. Nast, Esq., Engraved By A. V. S. Anthony, Esq., On Board The Vanderbilt, On Her Return Passage.

After the Fight

It was just after 9:30 AM when the fight was stopped. The two warriors had battled with each other and, in later rounds, the crowd, for over two hours. According to the rules of the Pugilistic Benevolent Association, the fight should have been continued in another location as soon as possible. If one fighter couldn't continue because of an injury, the other should have been awarded the prize money and the championship belt. Because of his injury, Sayers could not have continued the fight elsewhere within the prescribed week, so Heenan should have been declared Champion. However, two months later, both men were awarded a championship belt. Actually the boxers made far more money from exhibitions and appearances in the aftermath than they did from the fight itself — and with a lot less stress. Sadly, Heenan's life peaked in 1860 and he went downhill from there; both he and Sayers died before their fortieth birthdays.

Nast benefited from the close relationship he had developed with Heenan. As mentioned previously, when the "Little Dragsman" confided to his friend that he was broke, Heenan gave him twenty pounds which he had received as an advance from the promoter of his future sparring exhibitions and appearances with Sayers. In order to repay Heenan, Nast gave him an equivalent hundred dollar draft on the *Illustrated News*. Later in New York, Heenan told Nast that he collected by threatening to "punch their damned Dutch heads in if they didn't pay."

Immediately after the fight, Nast took the train back to London. With the help of two local artists he had previously hired and taken to see the fight, he finished the double-page sketch of the boxers in the ring within seven hours. He then turned it over to Anthony, who with the help of a second engraver, worked through the night on the large block Nast had given him. The next morning, Anthony travelled to Southampton to catch the steamship Vanderbilt, and finished engraving the central picture on the ship. Meanwhile, Nast went back to Heenan's room and sketched the boxer's late night interview with George Wilkes, as he lay in bed.

When the Vanderbilt docked in New York early on Saturday morning, April 28, Anthony took his engraved block directly to the printer. Nast's pictures of the fight, along with his and Anthony's portraits were in the post-dated May 5 issue, available on Monday April 30, less than two weeks after the fight.

That was the trump card for the *Illustrated News*, and it was played with great pride and self-praise. In the following May 12 edition, with five Nast vignettes on the cover and two more inside, the paper bragged that it had sold 153,000 of its regular edition and 26,000 extras for a total circulation of 179,000.

In summary, covering the Heenan-Sayers prizefight was the most momentous professional event in Thomas Nast's coming of age. Even though he was cheated of his wages, his stature as an enterprising, resourceful, tireless and skillful artist was established. After sketching an important horse race, which both Heenan and Sayers attended at Derby, and depicting Queen Victoria at theatre watching what appeared to be a boxing farce,* he was off to Italy to cover his soon-to-be hero, Giuseppe Garibaldi. America's first illustrator ever dispatched to cover an international sporting event (Morrissey in Canada, then Heenan) was also about to become the first to cover an overseas war.

---

* See p. 8

Chapter 7
Garibaldi

Background

Giuseppe Garibaldi, who effectively became the George Washington of Italy, was born in 1807 in Nice. The same 1815 Treaty of Paris which awarded Landau to Germany, also took Nice and Savoy away from France and gave them to the northern Italian country of Piedmont-Sardinia.

His family's business was fishing and coastal trading; he was a seasoned sailor at 15 and a ship captain at 25. Shortly thereafter, he became an Italian nationalist, and participated in an unsuccessful uprising in Piedmont in 1834. Sentenced to death in absentia, he went to South America where he fought for separatist movements in Brazil and Uruguay. He mastered guerilla warfare and helped Uruguay gain its independence from Argentina in 1846. That made him a hero in many European countries, especially Italy.

Italy, like Germany, France and Hungary, had its own revolution in 1848. Garibaldi returned from South America to participate, but this second uprising also failed. Still under a death sentence, and unwelcome as a potential revolutionary threat by the Piedmontese government, he again went into exile for about five years.

From August 1850 until April 1851, Garibaldi became a New Yorker; he even applied for American citizenship but never followed through. His friend and countryman, Antonio Meucci, had a candle-making business on Staten Island, and employed Garibaldi while putting him up in his cottage.[1]

In 1859, Garibaldi led still another revolt, this time in northern Italy against the Austrians. His success led to Lombardy's acquisition by neighboring Piedmont. In the aftermath, Garibaldi's reputation was even more enhanced, and northern Italy was united under King Victor Emmanuel II.[2] When Garibaldi launched his campaign to unify Italy in May 1860, the northern provinces were all under Piedmont's rule, except for Venice in the east which would remain under Austrian domination for another six years. The Papal States divided the country in the middle; it would take ten more years for them to exit the Pope's rule and complete Italy's unification.

The southern half of Italy, consisting of Sicily and Naples, was called the Kingdom of the Two Sicilies. It was under the rule of King Francis II who was despised by most of his own subjects, as well as by England, France and Austria, to whom he applied for help in vain when Garibaldi attacked.

Connecting with Garibaldi

Before Nast left London, he made arrangements with the *Illustrated London News* to publish his Italian sketches and pay him for the ones they used. The paper's primary illustrator in Italy was Frank Vizetelly, an experienced thirty-one year old "special artist," (who would come to America not long after, and cover the Confederacy for his paper during most of the Civil War). Vizetelly helped teach Tommy how to reconstruct an event by visiting the spot, interviewing eye witnesses, and even posing them on occasion to re-create a scene.

As mentioned previously, Tommy wrote Sallie that his primary reason for coming to Italy was to enhance his public image so that "you will love me more." However, he learned a number of valuable professional lessons during his six months there, some of them about what not to do: don't pursue hunches about vague rumors of impending battle action and thereby miss a major conflict by two days; conversely, don't lose the importance of an event by being too close to the reality of it.

Nast also asked William Luden Thomas, an engraver on the *Illustrated London News*, to whom he and Vizetelly mailed their sketches, to forward separate sketches to the *New York Illustrated News*. That paper proudly announced that "Our special artist, Mr. Nast, acting under our instructions, has repaired to Sicily to make drawings of the scenes and incidents connected with the present war between the troops of Garibaldi and those of the Royal party."[3]

Unfortunately, Nast missed Garibaldi's first conquering month in Sicily because his financial plight delayed his departure. With the help of the $100 advance from John Heenan, he finally made it to Genoa on May 27.

Nast put his extended time there to good use by getting well acquainted with John Peard, a large, bearded, Oxford-educated soldier of fortune, widely known as "Garibaldi's Englishman." Nast met Peard at the beginning of his adventure, and developed a quasi-paternal relationship with him. When Peard later learned that his artistic protégé had almost no money, he made him a paid aide-de-camp to himself. The *New York Illustrated News* played that up as "our special artist, now attached to Gen. Garibaldi's staff." It did not, however, relieve poor Tommy's financial distress.

ILN August 11, 1860 135

COLONEL PEARD, "GARIBALDI'S ENGLISHMAN." —From A Sketch By T. Nast.

NYIN October 27, 1860

COLONEL PEARD, COMMONLY KNOWN AS GARIBALDI'S ENGLISHMAN. From A Sketch By Our Artist, Thos. Nast, Esq., Now Attached To Garibaldi's Staff.

Garibaldi and "The Thousand" sailed south from Genoa to Marsala on the western tip of Sicily, about 60 miles from Palermo. On May 15, his force — outnumbered three to one — overcame strategic disadvantages at Calatafimi, and with a final bayonet charge routed the fleeing Neapolitans.

Garibaldi immediately declared himself Dictator of Sicily in the name of Victor Emmanuel. Effectively, he established an alternative government to the King of Naples, one that many on-the-fence Sicilians would now enthusiastically support. By June 6, after three days of heavy street fighting and difficult armistice discussions (held on the British warship *Hannibal* in Palermo's harbor), the Sicilian commander surrendered his 20,000 troops.

Meanwhile, 3,500 reinforcements had sailed from Genoa on June 9 to meet up with Garibaldi in Palermo. The three steamers had American captains and flew the American flag. The *Washington*, vastly overcrowded with 1,400 men, rifles and ammunition, also carried Nast, Peard, and Captain William de Rohan. The captain "strove to impress upon the young artist the fierce dangers of war, as well as the desirability of getting back to his mother at the first opportunity."[4]

One passenger wrote: "The volunteers were packed like herrings on this small steamer. The first day they got only a scrap of biscuit. There was plenty of food on board, but no getting at it. They cannot even lie down to sleep, and huddle together rolled up like balls. Many have to stand all night."[5]

Eight days of living like a canned sardine — in a ship manned mostly by Sardinians — gave nineteen-year old Tommy Nast his first taste of the hardships ahead.

NYIN July 21, 1860 165

SCENE ON BOARD THE SARDINIAN STEAMER "WASHINGTON," ON HER TRIP FROM GENOA TO SICILY, CARRYING VOLUNTEERS AND ARMS TO GARIBALDI. —From A Sketch By Our Own Artist, Th. Nast, Esq., Now At The Seat Of The Revolution.

ILN July 7, 1860 5

Captain Peard (Garibaldi's "Englishman") Nast

THE REVOLUTION IN SICILY. —VOLUNTEERS ON BOARD THE "WASHINGTON" PROCEEDING TO PALERMO. —From A Sketch By T. Nast.

Finally, on the night of June 17, the ship anchored in a cove well west of Palermo. The next morning Garibaldi, rowed by fishermen over a considerable distance, came on board to confer with Peard and Colonel Giácomo Medici, who was in charge of the 3,500 reinforcements.

This was Nast's initial look at the man he knew only by reputation. As he told Paine, Garibaldi was his hero from that hour.[6] Garibaldi's personal charisma and leadership, which attracted so many followers over his lifetime, made him the first in Nast's extremely selective lifetime pantheon. (Abraham Lincoln and Ulysses Grant were the other two).

Although Peard was several inches taller than Garibaldi (who was about five feet, nine), his long white-tinged beard often caused people who had never seen Garibaldi to mistake Peard for their hero. Peard had fought alongside Garibaldi in the 1859 campaign against Austria, and the friendship between "Garibaldi's Englishman" and his leader was common knowledge.

After coming ashore, it took Nast three days of hard travel — on foot, horseback and in a springless wagon with Captain Peard — to get to Palermo. The next day, Peard sent a letter to the *Boston Transcript*, published on July 16, and reprinted in both of Nast's respondent papers. His unscrupulous New York publisher printed Peard's comment: "We have with us a clever artist from the *New York Illustrated News*, who is making beautiful sketches. The *Illustrated London News* also have an artist here (Frank Vizetelly) and the *London Times* a correspondent." It followed with about 300 words of praise for Nast and itself, and positioned the article as the lead on its July 21 cover.

The next week the *Illustrated News* featured Nast's depiction of Garibaldi and his staff receiving Colonel Medici's 3,000 volunteer reinforcements in Palermo. By this time, Garibaldi had control of the city, the 20,000 Neapolitan soldiers had surrendered and been paroled, and some of them had joined Garibaldi's army. Later, he invited his officers to the royal palace, now his headquarters. There Captain De Rohan introduced Nast to Garibaldi, a sublime moment for the young artist.

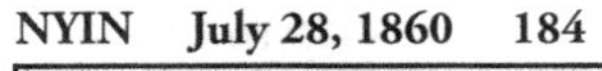
NYIN July 28, 1860 184

THE REVOLUTION IN SICILY.—RECEPTION OF COLONEL MEDICI'S VOLUNTEERS BY GARIBALDI AND HIS STAFF, AT PALERMO—From A Sketch Taken On The Spot, By Our Artist, Thomas Nast, Esq., Now At Palermo.

From Sicily to Naples

After Palermo, the next major battle took place July 20 at Milazzo, where Garibaldi defeated a much larger force of Neapolitans. Milazzo was about two-thirds of the way to Messina, where he could cross the straits to the road to Naples on the mainland. Effectively, the capture of Sicily provided the springboard to Naples.

Unfortunately, Nast missed the battle. With the assistance of Peard who gave him permission and loaned him money, Nast had gone to Naples on a British warship, hoping in vain to find some remittances. He toured the city with the English officers and even went to Pompeii. He returned to Palermo just in time to see Garibaldi's troopships leaving for Milazzo.

The embarrassed artist did manage to catch a ship later that night, arriving after the battle was over. His hard luck continued as he went without food and slept on paving stones. The *London Times* correspondent, among others, filled him in on perhaps Garibaldi's greatest feat of individual soldiery during the entire campaign. When he and his aide, Captain Missori, were attacked by a troop of cavalry. Missori shot the leaders' horses while Garibaldi killed the men with his saber. This battle was unplanned and it was only Garibaldi's tactics, courage and generalship that won the day. Nast imagined and recreated the scene of "Garibaldi Cutting Down the Neapolitan Soldiers" which, along with the *London Times* description, had to captivate his readers. Frank Vizetelly had taught him well, but his two other belated sketches of the battle went unpublished.

NYIN September 15, 1860 293

THE REVOLUTION IN SICILY. GENERAL GARIBALDI CUTTING DOWN THE LEADER OF A BAND OF HORSEMEN WHO HAD ATTACKED THE SICILIANS ON THE BRIDGE OF MELAZZO.

Garibaldi Cutting Down The Neapolitan Soldiers.
Our Special Artist, Thomas Nast, Esq., Who Is Now A Member Of Garibaldi's Staff, Has Sent Us From Sicily A Sketch Of The Personal Encounter Of Garibaldi With A Host Of Neapolitan Soldiers At The Battle Of Melazzo.

ILN August 11, 1860 138

After the well-fortified citadel outside Milazzo surrendered five days later, Garibaldi's men discovered a powder train running to the magazine, ready for explosion, a violation of the code of arms. Nast pictured it vividly.

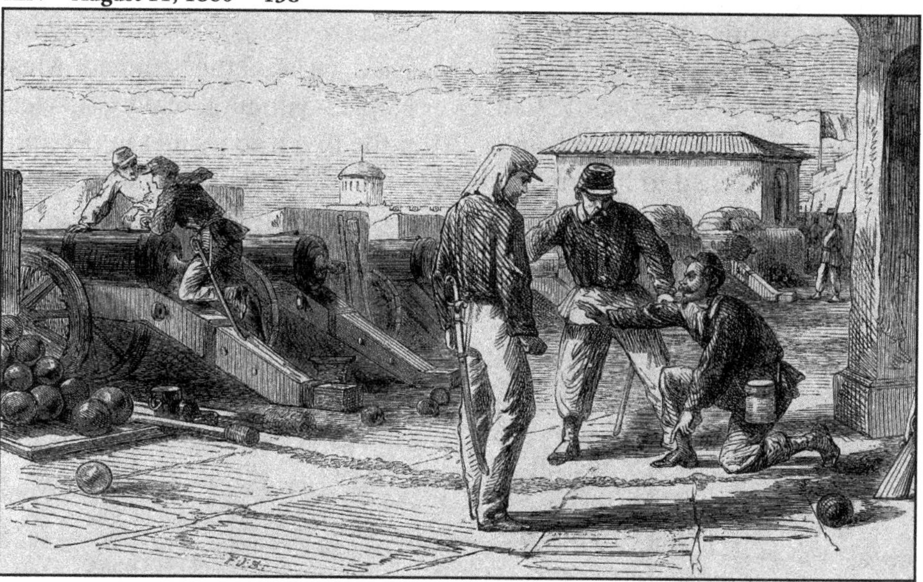

DISCOVERY OF A TRAIN LEADING TO THE POWDER MAGAZINE AT THE FORT OF MELAZZO—From A Sketch By T. Nast.

NYIN October 13, 1860 364

THE ITALIAN REVOLUTION. FIGHT OF THE NEAPOLITANS WITH THE GARIBALDIANS IN THE STREETS OF REGGIO.

When Garibaldi's men entered Messina on July 28, the Neapolitan general signed an agreement to surrender the city while keeping his 15,000 men in his "impregnable fortress" with no further hostilities to take place. That enabled Garibaldi to cross the straits without being fired on, a significant milestone in his plan to conquer Naples. He waited about three weeks to cross the Straits of Messina from a secret embarkation point to Melito (in the province of Calabria) and took nearby Reggio on August 22. Nast portrayed some of the fierce street-to-street fighting.

Some of the mainland Neapolitan soldiers revolted against their superiors. An unpublished Nast sketch showed General Brigasie on horseback being shot at close range by one of his soldiers in the Piazza in Melito.

Macculloch Hall Historical Museum

The map below depicts what Garibaldi actually did and what Nast covered. After landing in Marsala, Sicily in mid-May, his fabled "Thousand" men overcame 20,000 Neapolitan defenders to take possession of Palermo. He then won battles at Milazzo and Messina, crossed the Straits of Messina to conquer Reggio, and just over two weeks later, on September 7, took over Naples without a real fight. Meanwhile, King Victor Emmanuel's army of the north marched down to Naples. After the two leaders met in person, Garibaldi gave up his dictatorship voluntarily, and returned to his small island home of Caprera off the coast of Sardinia.

Nast and Garibaldi — May-November 1860

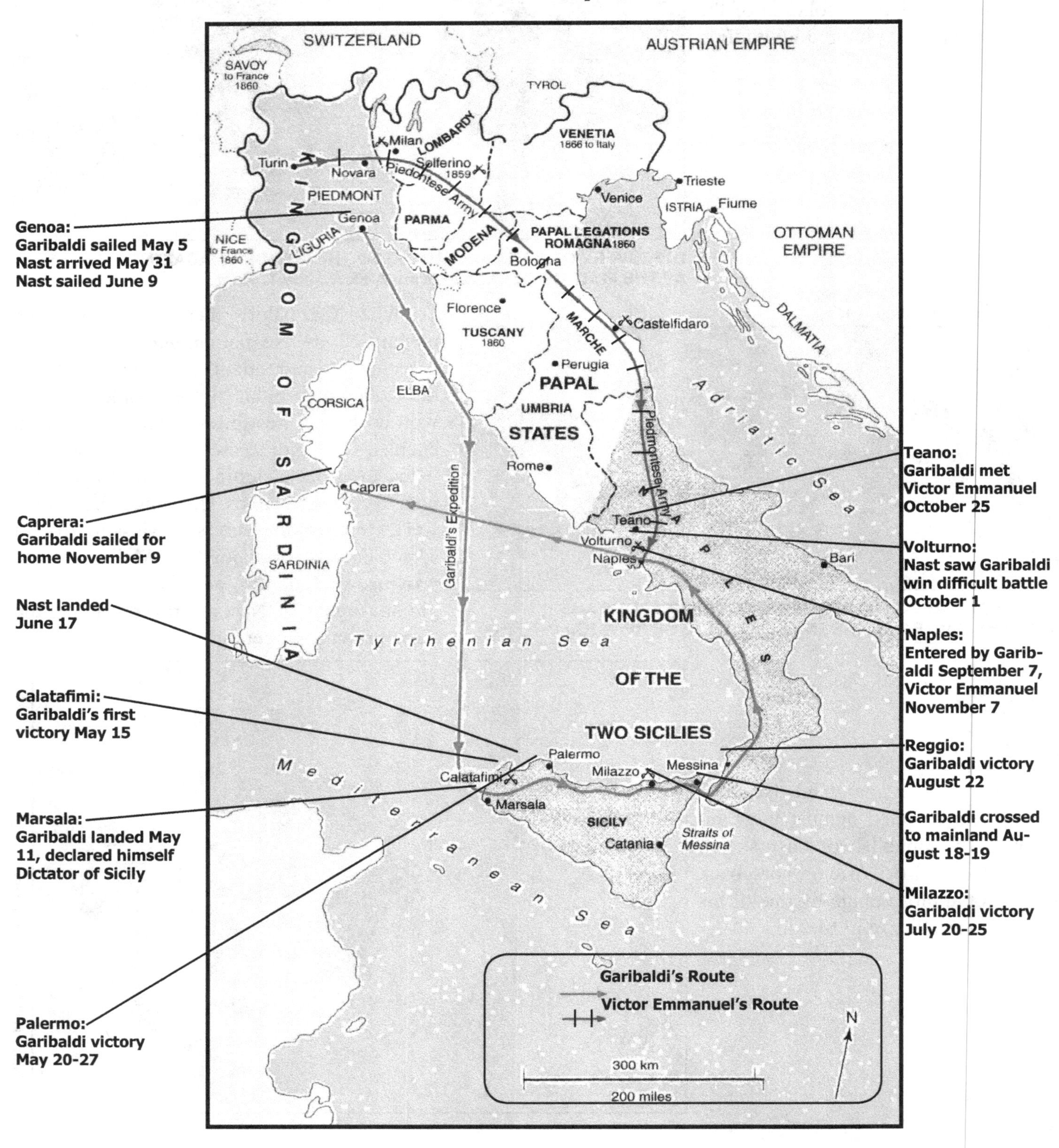

Tommy found time to write Sallie on July 30 from Messina with some personal news: "In my face I have quite a beard but will shave it off before I see you again." (This was his first experience with a beard, which became a significant feature of his future appearance.) He had not heard a word from America since he left England two months earlier, and he enclosed this letter in one sent to Sol Eytinge at the *Illustrated News* along with his sketches for proprietor Rudolph Lexow.

By this time, Nast was dressing like a Calabrian. He had his photo taken, picturing himself, sketchbook in hand, canteen on his belt, but still wearing his old hat, in the November 3 *New York Illustrated News*. A side paragraph was extremely complimentary: "He represents the true genius of true talent. . . He is true as an artist and as a man. He is industrious and zealous, too, beyond the ordinary standard. The conductors of the *Illustrated London News*, who constantly copy his sketches and avail themselves of his services, agree with us that the requirements of a true artist and a faithful cooperator are truly met. . ."

Paine, p. 52

THOS. NAST, ESQ, OUR SPECIAL ARTIST, NOW ATTACHED TO GARIBALDI'S STAFF, IN HIS CALABRIAN COSTUME.

The New York periodical paid him well in publicity if not in money. To take a dig at the London paper, which did pay him for his sketches, was outrageous for his resentful New York employer, who had not paid him anything since he left New York.

Tommy found time to write Sallie on July 30 from Messina with some personal news: "In my face I have quite a beard but will shave it off before I see you again." (This was his first experience with a beard, which became a significant feature of his future appearance). He had not heard a word from America since he left England two months earlier, and he enclosed this letter in one sent to Sol Eytinge at the *Illustrated News* along with his sketches for proprietor Rudolph Lexow.

After Reggio, Garibaldi travelled the few hundred miles to Naples virtually without opposition. The kingdom of Naples, with over six million people, was ripe for revolt. Military despotism, corruption of all kinds, highway robbers, mutinous mobs, and a starving peasantry were prevalent under the long rule of Ferdinand II. Ferdinand died the year before and his weak, inexperienced 24-year old son Francis II became King in May 1859. A year later, all that his subjects needed was a spark.

Garibaldi provided that. His legendary fame and exploits were reinforced by his accomplishments in Sicily along with his ability to communicate, relate to and inspire its citizenry. The Neapolitans were far more ready to support him than their despised King. Moreover, the majority of the Neapolitan troops were ready to quit or even to join the Garibaldians. They surrendered in droves.

Paine, p. 56

BOUND FOR NAPLES. ONE OF THE DAYS WHEN "JOE" HAD A HORSE

Colonel Peard had been ordered to go ahead of the army and scout out the enemy's country. Nast accompanied him, mounted on a donkey while Peard rode a bony horse. The large Englishman and "Joe, the fat boy"[7] as Peard called Nast, resembled Don Quixote and his faithful squire, Sancho Panza, The sketch was dated September 22, 1860.

Nast also related one particular incident to Paine that must have been a real highlight for him. He and Peard were napping in a vineyard. They awoke to find themselves surrounded by a Neapolitan army of 7,000 men. Peard asked to be taken to the commander, and told him: "You are our prisoners — Garibaldi is close behind." The commander was doubtful as to who was whose prisoner, so Nast was sent to fetch Garibaldi. The Dictator said he'd be along shortly and told Nast to have Peard prepare the surrender papers, so they would be ready when he arrived. What a role for the young artist, not yet 20!

Garibaldi, Peard and Nast entered Naples to cheering crowds on September 7. Riding in an open carriage, with Peard on the front seat next to the driver and Tommy himself facing the rear — identifiable by his unique headgear — Garibaldi was traveling down the main avenue from the palace to the cathedral. With flags flying and crowds pushing and shouting, Nast was in the middle of a scene he would never forget.[8]

ILN September 22, 1860 C

GARIBALDI'S ENTRY INTO NAPLES. —A Sketch In The Strada Di Toledo, By T. Nast.

Nast told Paine that as the carriage rode past a fort, the Neapolitan officers and gunners were ready to fire their guns. Garibaldi knew it and told his driver to stop directly in front of the guns which had their fuses already lighted. He stood up in the carriage and looked directly at the artillery men, whose officers then gave the command to fire. After a moment, the gunners threw away their fuses, flung their caps high in the air, and shouted with the crowd: "Viva Garibaldi! Viva Vittorio Emmanuele! Viva l'Italia!"

Danger

"The Thousand," Garibaldi's original fabled band of 1,080 volunteers — at least half of them Nast's age or younger — was to dwindle to 426 six months later; by then Garibaldi had conquered Sicily and Naples and turned the Kingdom of the Two Sicilies over to King Victor Emmanuel II. That 40% survival rate was indicative of the danger that Nast knew he was in and bravely tried to ignore as best he could.

Tommy wrote to Sallie from Palermo that there was danger that he might be killed but he was sure he wouldn't be, and that she should know how much he loved her if he was wrong. Frank Vizetelly reported to the *Illustrated London News* that one or two bullets went whizzing by his head while he was standing near his hotel room window.[9]

After Nast saw action a little too close up at the Battle of the Volturno on October 1, he wrote his friend and fellow illustrator, Sol Eytinge, and his wife Maggie in New York:

> *My dear Sol & Maggie This week I nearly got my head taken off by a shell. Now how would you like to see me come home without a head, without an arm, or only one leg? I myself think I would not look pleasant, what would my dearest Sallie say? . . .*

. . . I may thank God that I was not killed yesterday, by a shell that struck within a [yard?] from me in the road as I was going to St. Angelo. We [were] four. Col. Dowling, Captain Forbes, an officer and I went up the road without thinking a shell would fly this way because they stopped firing at midday (the Neapolitans I mean) well we were going along; very jolly, we heard a report near aus [us] a cloud of dust, which blinded aus all, Col. Dowling screamed a shell we all fell on the ground, that if it would bust we would escape, but it did not go off, to your [our?] great delight. I have heard bullets near my ear, but this time I thought it was up with me or aus. As we were on the mountain with [General Garibaldi's staff], they fired at aus but they did not quite come up the mountain, but struck two or three [yards] below aus. Sol you have no idea how very careless a person is when he is in war, why we did not think of this, any more than if a play ball would have come a yard from aus, at playing ball in Brooklyn [?] In war a man is not a man but a dreamer, he thinks of nothing but is always dreaming. So you see I will not awake till I come back again in New York, then my eyes will open, and I will see what a fool I was to come here and put myself in danger.

Nast's sketchbook showed "Col. Dowling's bayonet charge on the Neapolitan troops (in) the field on Monday Oct. 1." The casualties in the foreground brought Nast's description of the Volturno action vividly to life (and death). This sketch was never published.

Macculloch Hall Historical Museum

While informative, the other sketches of the Volturno battle that Nast's London and New York clients printed did not have the impact of the unpublished one — most certainly not on the sketcher himself.

NYIN November 17, 1860 20

INCIDENTS OF THE BATTLE OF VOLTURNO. BURNING OF THE DEAD AND WOUNDED. From A Sketch By Th. Nast, Our Special Artist, Now Attached To Garibaldi's Staff.

ILN October 20, 1860 379

THE BATTLE ON THE VOLTURNO. —THE NEAPOLITAN TROOPS PASSING ALONG A RAVINE. —From A Sketch By T. Nast.

NYIN December 1, 1860 52

THE ITALIAN REVOLUTION —THE ENGLISH DIVISION IN THE BATTLE OF THE 19TH OCTOBER, NEAR CAPUA. From A Sketch By Our Special Artist, Th. Nast, Now Attached To Garibaldi's Staff.

Almost three weeks after Volturno, in perhaps the last action Nast personally saw close up near Capua on October 19, he drew himself looking quizzically at Colonel Peard as men were fighting and dying all around him.

Nast's experience with the dangers of war was sufficient to last him a lifetime. During the Civil War, his illustrations — drawn in New York — were effective enough to draw Lincoln's praise and public support.

Conflict at the Top

Garibaldi sought to legitimize his victories by having plebiscites held on October 21 in both Naples and Sicily. Ninety-nine percent of the entire male population voted to become an integral part of Italy, with Victor Emmanuel as their constitutional King.

Nast drew a scene at a polling booth with himself prominently positioned on the far left sketching away. In the future, voting scenarios would be featured in a number of his cartoons, but most of the elections did not have the integrity of this one, his first ballot box drawing.

ILN November 10, 1860 450

THE VOTE FOR ANNEXATION AT NAPLES. —POLLING BOOTH AT MONTE CALVARIO. —From A Sketch By T. Nast.

While Garibaldi came up the Italian boot from the south to conquer Naples, King Victor Emmanuel left Piedmont and came down from the north. On October 25, the two met in Teano, north of Naples. Garibaldi had determined to cede power to the King, just as he had proclaimed himself Dictator (in the name of Victor Emmanuel) when he landed in Sicily six months earlier.

However, the two alpha men did not get along well, although Nast probably was not aware of that. Garibaldi asked to be made Viceroy of Southern Italy and was refused; he then turned down an offer to become a general in the Piedmontese army. Victor Emmanuel probably resented Garibaldi's unrivaled popularity with his new subjects, recognized that his courage and ability to lead posed a potential threat to his reign, and understood that Garibaldi was more of an improviser than a long-term strategist and planner.

Their stalemate had an uncanny replay ten months later. With the King's reluctant approval, President Lincoln, through his diplomatic emissary, offered Garibaldi the opportunity to become a major-general in the Union army; he was motivated by the disaster at Bull Run on July 21, 1861, when green Union troops panicked and fled. Garibaldi's fanciful response — to be commander-in-chief of the Army with contingent power to abolish slavery — ended discussions, but received publicity in the London and New York papers. An erroneous Nast cartoon showed the artist's incredulity.*

However, Garibaldi was sufficiently impressed by "the American President who has abolished slavery," to have his grandson — born in 1865 prior to the assassination — named Lincoln.[10]

* See p. 100

Nast's last war action picture featured a glum, impassive Victor Emmanuel. It was printed identically in both his London and New York papers. The action took place November 1 and victory was sealed the next day.

A week later, Garibaldi left for his island home of Caprera with almost no money or other tangible items to show for his achievements. Nast and Peard said their good-byes on board ship, as he depicted the scene for the *Illustrated London News*.

NYIN December 15, 1860 84

THE WAR IN NAPLES. VICTOR EMMANUEL GIVING COMMANDS TO COMMENCE THE BOMBARDMENT OF CAPUA.

Paine, p. 65

Nast Peard

FAREWELL VISIT OF GARIBALDI TO ADMIRAL MUNDY ON BOARD THE "HANNIBAL" AT NAPLES.

Garibaldi's 1860 campaign was the highlight of his career and established his stardom forever with his hero-worshipper, Nast. In fact, however, he had unsuccessful military and/or political adventures in 1862, 1866, and 1877, usually ending with his return to his home on Caprera. He was wounded, captured, imprisoned, pardoned, and exiled to Caprera on various occasions and, severely crippled by arthritis or rheumatism, frequently incapacitated for long periods.

In 1866, although Italy fought badly against Austria, it succeeded in acquiring Venice via France, just as had happened in 1859 with Lombardy being annexed by Piedmont after Austria turned it over to France. Nast portrayed Garibaldi hand-in-hand with Victor Emmanuel but in a subservient position.

HW July 14, 1866 436

**THE UPRISING OF ITALY.—
Drawn By Mr. Thomas Nast.**

HW September 9, 1871 833 C

LIKE PHOENIX, WILL RISE FROM ITS ASHES TO IMMORTALITY.

In July 1870, France declared war on Prussia and was soundly beaten. A significant side effect was that France had to pull her troops out of Rome where they had been keeping the Pope in temporal power for years. On September 19, the Italian army took over Rome from the Pope, completing the unification of Italy. Although Garibaldi played no role in the final chapter, Nast gave his hero equal billing with the King, when he portrayed the scene a year later.

In 1874, Garibaldi was elected to the Italian Parliament as a representative at large of Rome. Nast depicted his return early the next year midst the ruins of the Pope's temporal power.

HW February 20, 1875 161

GARIBALDI AT HOME — TIME WORKS WONDERS.

Nast's 1882 pictorial obituary of his primal hero featured the two key battles of the 1860 campaign in Sicily — Palermo and Milazzo were noted — but not the conquest of Naples, which must have left a distaste in the mouths of both the artist and his subject.

HW June 17, 1882 381

GIUSEPPE GARIBALDI:
DIED AT CAPRERA, JUNE 2.

The Long Way Home

In company with Lord Seymour, an English nobleman, Nast left Naples on November 30, with a warm embrace from his lifelong friend and father figure, Colonel Peard. His first sight-seeing objective was Rome, still under control of Pope Pius IX, supported by French troops. Nast visited the art galleries, but stayed away from the Vatican. The Coliseum left the strongest impression on him; two of his most important cartoons — one attacking President Andrew Johnson and the other Boss Tweed — utilized the Coliseum for dramatic effect.

HW March 30, 1867 200-201

Johnson
AMPHITHEATRUM JOHNSONIANUM.

THE TAMMANY TIGER LOOSE.

Tommy stopped in Florence and Milan on his way to Genoa, where he recovered the trunk he had left in storage six months earlier. Its contents included two sketchbooks — one of his ocean crossing and the other of his boxing-related scenes. Then he went on to Landau, through Switzerland and France, arriving four days before Christmas, in time for all sorts of celebrations. He stayed with his old aunt.

According to what he told Paine four decades later, the best thing that happened to him was a gift of forty dollars from a distant relative, who claimed to have borrowed it from his mother. That tale is contradicted by his diary. "During my stay here I found out I have an aunt from my father's side which has a little fortune which she would like to give over to aus." He called on her in Bamberg where she lived, but did not receive any money.[11] Consequently, he had to travel by third class rail to his great discomfort.

Overall, Tommy's visit to his birthplace was negative. He had an aversion to alcohol and tobacco, and noted in his diary that there was "too much beer and smoke." When his hosts denigrated Garibaldi, Nast listened grimly and bit his tongue.

From Landau, Nast went to London via Stuttgart, Munich and Paris, visiting cathedrals and art galleries, including the Louvre, along the way. When possible, he attended the local theatre.

On the way to Munich, he stopped in Nabburg, his father's birthplace, and saw another aunt whose husband was music director of the church, just as Tommy's grandfather had been. That gave him the chance to sleep in the same hard bed in the little steeple room where his father had spent his boyhood.

What his European experience did for the young artist, still only twenty, was establish his reputation, give him front-line experience under fire, teach him how to recreate scenes he didn't actually see, build his confidence, and enable him to observe firsthand the everyday life and culture of England, Italy, France and Germany. All that was priceless, and helped compensate for the mere $1.50 he had in his pocket when he arrived in New York on February 1.

As mentioned previously, the ownership of the *New York Illustrated News* had changed a month earlier with its first advertising agent, John King, now the proprietor. The paper's debt to Nast went unpaid, but he was offered enough of a "modest salary" — probably in the $25-35 a week range — for him to stay employed there.

Of course, Sallie was first and foremost on Tommy's mind. Her parents continued to see him as a loving, personable, hard-working and talented husband for their daughter, and were not overly concerned about his current financial condition. They formally consented to her marriage, now planned for Tommy's twenty-first birthday in late September. Before then, he would have some major events to cover.

Illustrated London News

Tommy's final European stop was London, where his journey began. Arriving on New Year's Day, he met with William Luden Thomas, the head engraver of the *Illustrated London News*, who had befriended Nast and managed his financial affairs while he was in Italy. They went to theatre together and Tommy stayed at his house. They would remain lifelong friends.

Thomas tried to talk Nast into working for his paper, but £1.1 ($5.50) per page was not persuasive, especially with Sallie eagerly waiting his return. Thomas did ask Nast to provide future sketches "about the Southern excitement," and the artist obliged with seven illustrations drawn from March through May 1861 — before Frank Vizetelly arrived on the scene for the London paper.

ILN May 11, 1861 434

MAJOR ANDERSON OF THE UNITED STATES ARMY, LATE COMMANDANT OF FORT SUMTER, CHARLESTON HARBOUR.

ILN May 11, 1861 435

THE MAIN BATTERY AT FORT SUMTER: GUNS BEARING ON FORT MOULTRIE AND THE CHANNEL DURING THE ACTION OF FRIDAY, APRIL 12.

ILN May 25, 1861 498

THE WAR EXCITEMENT IN NEW YORK: SCENE IN FRONT OF A FIRE-ENGINE HOUSE.

Chapter 8
The Civil War Begins

Abraham Lincoln campaigned, was nominated and elected while Nast was in Europe, so he probably knew little about the new president when he came back home. Lincoln's election was featured in the same issue of the *New York Illustrated News* as Nast's grisly picture of the burning of the dead and wounded at the Battle of Volturno.*

The day before his fifty-second birthday, Lincoln and his family left Springfield on a twelve-day trip to Washington. The train made numerous stops where Lincoln gave short non-controversial speeches, attended lunches or dinners, and sometimes spent the night in a hotel.

Between Cleveland and Buffalo, the train made a short stop in Westfield, NY, where Lincoln greeted and kissed Grace Bedell, who had written him a letter suggesting that he would look better with whiskers. Of course, he adopted her idea, thereby confusing papers like *Leslie's* and the *Illustrated London News*, which showed him clean-shaven.

ILN December 8, 1860 543

ABRAHAM LINCOLN, OF ILLINOIS, PRESIDENT ELECT OF THE UNITED STATES.—From A Lithograph Published By G. W. Nichols, NY.

NYIN March 2, 1861 C

LATEST PORTRAIT OF MR. LINCOLN—SKETCHED BY OUR OWN ARTIST.

Nast's new employer, John King, had some difficult decisions to make. Lincoln's trip to his inauguration was the top story, but two others required on-site coverage: Jefferson Davis' inauguration (February 18) in Montgomery and the brewing attack on Fort Sumter. Both of King's competitors were there and Leslie even had his own reporter and artist on Lincoln's train.

Nast drew the assignment. Lincoln's picture, including a growing beard, was his first depiction of the man who would become his second all-time hero. The text referred to Lincoln in "his new facial appointments."

Lincoln arrived in New York from Albany on February 19. Nast was in the huge crowd, and told Paine (perhaps fancifully) that he found himself directly in front of Lincoln at some point during the reception. Nast also drew the accompanying sketch under Lincoln's portrait.

MR. LINCOLN'S RECEPTION AT THE HUDSON RIVER RAILROAD DEPOT, THIRTIETH STREET, NEW YORK.

---

* See p. 80-81

NYIN March 9, 1861 281

MR. LINCOLN HOISTING A FLAG CONTAINING THIRTY-FOUR STARS TO THE STAFF ON THE TOP OF INDEPENDENCE HALL, PHILADELPHIA, AT SUNRISE, ON WASHINGTON'S BIRTHDAY. Sketched By Thos. Nast, Esq.

After two hectic days, including dinner with Vice President-elect Hannibal Hamlin, Lincoln left for Philadelphia. Nast was on the train and pictured Lincoln raising the 34-star American flag at Independence Hall on Washington's Birthday.

The Plot

After Philadelphia, the next scheduled stops were Harrisburg and Baltimore. While in Philadelphia, Lincoln received word from two different credible sources that there was a plot to kill him in Baltimore the next day.[1] The plan was to create a disturbance in the Baltimore station to distract the police, and then kill Lincoln with a knife or gun. Alternatively, there was talk of plans to blast the train off its track with explosives.

Lincoln decided to keep his date in Harrisburg, but to leave incognito after dinner. Detective Allan Pinkerton arranged for a special locomotive and coach to take Lincoln back to Philadelphia, accompanied by his friend and bodyguard, Ward Lamon. From there, he caught a train to Baltimore, arriving at 3:30 A.M. at the President Street station. Lincoln then travelled by carriage to Baltimore's other station a few miles away at Camden Yards, where he caught a 4:15 train to Washington. He arrived unrecognized at six Saturday morning, and went directly to the Presidential Suite at the Willard Hotel.

The reporters on Lincoln's train were caught flat-footed by the change from his written itinerary. One of them, Joseph Howard, Jr. of the *New York Times,* concocted a story that Lincoln had disguised himself in a Scotch plaid cap and a long military cloak. Effectively, Howard used his *Times* credentials to create a fable which was publicized by all the daily and illustrated weekly papers. Lincoln was derided for deviousness and even cowardice, and caricatured mercilessly.[2]

HW March 9, 1861 160

THE ALARM.
"On Thursday night, after he had retired, Mr. Lincoln was aroused, and informed that a stranger desired to see him on a matter of life and death. *** A conversation elicited the fact that an organized body of men had determined that Mr. Lincoln should never leave the city of Baltimore alive. *** Statesmen laid the plan, bankers indorsed it, and adventurers were to carry it into effect."

THE SPECIAL TRAIN
"He wore a scotch plaid cap and a very long military cloak, so that he was entirely unrecognizable."

NYIN March 9, 1861 280

Scotch Plaid Cap

ARRIVAL OF MR. LINCOLN AT THE CAMDEN STATION, BALTIMORE, AT 4 O'CLOCK ON THE MORNING OF FEBRUARY 23. Sketched By Thos. Nast, Esq.

Nast was the only artist or reporter who depicted Lincoln without the Scotch cap and cloak. Applying what he learned from Frank Vizetelly in Sicily, he went over all the details with the station master at Camden Yards depot. He depicted Lincoln in his standard top hat, but his editors changed that to a plaid cap. (In actuality, Lincoln was wearing an old overcoat and a soft wool hat; the plaid cap and long military coat never existed outside the rumor mill.)

The Inauguration

Nast stayed at the Willard Hotel, then Washington's residence of choice, along with the Lincolns and a host of other celebrities. He drew a couple of humorous sketches showing the tight sleeping arrangements, as well as the never-ending action in the lobby.

On February 25, two days after he arrived in Washington, Lincoln was introduced by his electoral runner-up, William Seward, a long time senator and soon to become Secretary of State — to the members of the Senate and the House. This was Nast's first look at his future figurative Congressional playground and a number of its inhabitants.

NYIN March 16, 1861 297

MR. LINCOLN AS HE APPEARED IN THE HOUSE OF REPRESENTATIVES, ON THE REPUBLICAN SIDE. FROM A SKETCH BY THOS. NAST.

Finally, March 4 arrived and Lincoln was inaugurated.

NYIN March 9, 1861 317

ARRIVAL OF MR. LINCOLN AT THE CAPITOL, ARM IN ARM WITH MR. BUCHANAN. ENTRANCE THROUGH THE EASTERN FRAME PORTICO. Sketched By Th. Nast, Esq.

The pivotal March 16 inauguration issue depicted Nast at his peerless best and careless worst. Inside was a superb sketch of the inauguration ceremony in front of the Capitol. (Its dome would be completed in 1866). Nast's two-double-page fold-out picture was twice the size of *Leslie's* photograph and *Harper's* drawing.

INAUGURATION OF PRESIDENT LINCOLN IN FRONT OF THE CAPITOL AT WASHINGTON. From A Sketch By Thomas Nast.

However, Nast's cover was a disaster, featuring a supposed image of Chief Justice Roger Taney administering the oath of office to Lincoln. Taney was two weeks shy of his 84th birthday, and the man in the picture looked to be in his forties.[3]

In its next issue, the *News* handled its unhideable cover page goof in a positive way — without apology — with a cover photo by Mathew Brady and a laudatory biography. There were no apparent jibes from *Leslie's* or *Harper's*.

NYIN March 16, 1861 C

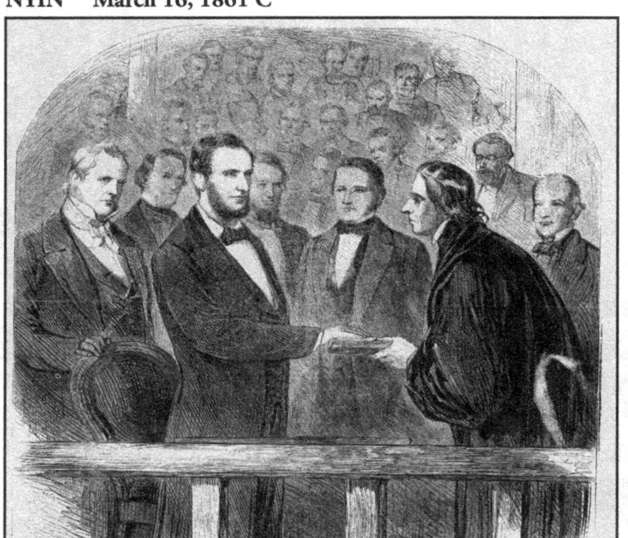

MR. LINCOLN TAKING THE OATH OF OFFICE IN THE FRONT OF THE CAPITOL. From A Sketch By Thos. Nast.

NYIN March 23, 1861 C

ROGER B. TANEY, CHIEF JUSTICE OF THE UNITED STATES SUPREME COURT.

The week before the goof, Tommy had sent a sketch of a "murderous attack" to a *News* artist who was to redraw his sketch on woodblocks, along with a note about the victim: "Do not draw his face in till I send Jim the photo."[4] Accordingly, it is possible that Nast depended on the same artist in New York to draw Taney's face. Nast was too far away to be able to observe Taney's age and features, and he probably did not have access to a Taney photograph. Regardless of who actually was responsible, Nast's name was on the picture.

Nast never told Paine about the error. However, he learned his lesson and kept an extensive file of cartes de visite in his home studio to use for future cartoons.

The Role of the Press

While devastating to the country as a whole, the Civil War provided a tremendous boost to the newspaper business in general and to the illustrated press in particular. Radio was a half century away and photography was limited to still pictures. (Photographers needed wagons, chemicals, special apparatus, long exposure times without movement, and far more mobility to shadow moving troops than their equipment allowed.) Accordingly, the demand for artists who could and would follow the armies continuously to sketch the skirmishes and battles, and to fill in the lulls in activity with scenes of everyday life, was almost insatiable.

Harper's Weekly, *Frank Leslie's Illustrated Newspaper* and the *New York Illustrated News* collectively employed more than fifty artists to cover live action during the course of the war. Many of the topflight ones worked for at least two of the weeklies at various times, although *Harper's* exerted the strongest pull from 1862 on. In addition, all three papers solicited, and promised to pay for, contributions from soldiers, sailors and civilians who drew acceptable sketches of incidents or battles.

The "specials" as they were called put up with horrifying living conditions and ever-present danger of injury, sickness, capture and, not infrequently, death. Most of them were young and adventurous, and willing to accept hardship and danger. With the two notable exceptions of Alfred Waud and Theodore Davis, none of them were at the front for all four years of the war, as burn-out and less hazardous or better-paying opportunities thinned their ranks.

Today's two best known Civil War artists probably are Winslow Homer and Thomas Nast, both of whom prepared most of their illustrations in the safety of their New York studios. Their reputations ride primarily on what they accomplished after the war — Homer with his paintings, and Nast with his political attack caricatures and Santa Claus cartoons.

Homer drew *News From the War* depicting Alfred Waud sketching at the lower left, and *Harper's Weekly* and other newspapers being read at the lower right. Homer began his illustration almost immediately after he returned from the Peninsular Campaign in late May 1862.

HW June 14, 1862 376-377

NEWS FROM THE WAR—Drawn By Our Special Artist, Mr. Winslow Homer.

Two years later, Nast covered similar territory with *The Press on the Field.* “Our artist,” shown at the upper left, was Thomas Butler Gunn. As in Homer’s picture, Nast’s small vignettes detailed an artist’s various activities: taking notes; sketching (a dead soldier close-up); getting the names of the wounded and dead (lower left center); drawing the complete picture from notes and quick sketches; and finally showing an original sketchbook. As *Harper’s* pointed out in its accompanying text, “that vast body of incident and adventure which finds no mention in official reports . . . is absolutely necessary to a proper appreciation of central facts and events.”

HW April 30, 1864 280-281

The leading daily newspapers from New York, Philadelphia, Boston, Washington, Chicago, Cincinnati, St. Louis and other Northern cities also had reporters in the field, often embedded with the Army of the Potomac or the various Western and Southern armies. Frequently, the illustrated weeklies would quote extensively from the dailies and then illustrate the credited articles, either with the work of a field “special” or a studio artist like Nast, who would recreate the reported scenario from scratch.

However, publishers had to be careful or their papers could be suspended and reporters jailed.[5] In February 1862, Secretary of War Edwin Stanton and others severely criticized James Gordon Bennett for publishing sensitive military information in his *New York Herald*. Nast chimed in with a half-page depiction of Confederate General "Prince John" Magruder, who was in charge of the defense of Yorktown at that time, reading the *Herald*, while Bennett, a defender of slavery, was preparing to feed him more secrets.

A second Nast cartoon featured editors Bennett, Horace Greeley of the *Tribune*, and Henry Raymond of the *New York Times* being strangled literally and figuratively by Stanton's orders.[6]

NYIN March 22, 1862 320

AID AND COMFORT TO THE ENEMY. —THE WAY MR. J. G. B***T DOES THE LOYAL BUSINESS.**

NYIN April 19, 1862 384

THE MODERN LAOCOON —RAYMOND, GREELEY AND BENNETT IN A FIX.

Contrabands

On May 22, 1861, Major-General Benjamin Butler took command of Fortress Monroe. Butler would become a future target of more than 65 Nast cartoons, but at this point he was on the side of Union angels as the initiator of an extraordinary turning point in Northern public opinion about slavery.

The next day, three slaves arrived at Fortress Monroe in a stolen rowboat, fleeing across the James River from constructing artillery across the harbor aimed directly at Butler's fort. They believed their owner was planning to send them to North Carolina to build more fortifications.[7]

Butler was a skilled lawyer and politician from Massachusetts. He was familiar with the Fugitive Slave Act of 1850, which Nast had learned about from his art teacher, Theodor Kaufmann. He understood that Lincoln had no intention of interfering with slavery at this early point in the war, but also knew that as a military commander, he had the right to seize any enemy property that was being used for military purposes.

When the owner's military emissary showed up to reclaim his slaves, Butler refused on the grounds that Virginia had seceded, and now as a "foreign country," it had no continuing rights under the Fugitive Slave Act. Since the South considered slaves as property, Butler would treat them as property too, and hold them as "contraband of war." The early trickle became a flood. Within three weeks, there were 500 contrabands within Fortress Monroe. Nationally, the hundreds eventually became tens of thousands during the course of the war.

Lincoln and his Cabinet passively agreed not to overrule Butler and the term "contrabands" quickly gained common usage on both sides. Two months later, Congress actively supported Butler by passing the First Confiscation Act. The more subtle aspect of the term "contraband" was that Unionists could readily support the principle of confiscation, while the idea of emancipation was premature at that time, except to a minority of dedicated abolitionists.[8]

Nast depicted Butler holding one of the artist's first Southern stereotyped villains at bay. Six months later, Flag Officer Samuel Dupont captured Port Royal, South Carolina. The Confederate military and white civilian population fled the coastal islands, leaving ten thousand contrabands behind. Now Nast stereotyped the contrabands, adding dialogue as well. However, the disparaging comical caricatures in theses early cartoons did not reflect his forthcoming empathy and strong support for blacks during the remainder of the War and Reconstruction.

NYIN June 15, 1861 96

CONTRABAND OF WAR.

NYIN December 2, 1861 80

THE WAY THE SOUTHERN NEGROES MET THE YANKEES.
Lor bress you, Massa Dupont, wese bin awaitin for you. Got all de best tings on dat da white man run away and left. Golly, feel almost good enuff to hug you. Take us right up Norf.

One of Nast's last efforts for the *Illustrated News* was to draw on woodblocks a sketch submitted by a soldier on one of the coastal islands. It showed his comrade removing a "hobble" from the ankle and foot of a contraband, who also had a yoke around her neck, attached by a chain to her foot.

NYIN May 17, 1862 32

UNION TROOPS REMOVING THE "HOBBLE" FROM ESCAPED SLAVES —A SCENE ON OTTER ISLAND, S. C. From A Sketch By Henry Stulen.

Alfred Waud

While in Washington covering President Lincoln's inaugural period, Nast drew a few first-hand sketches of military scenes as the volunteer Union army was first getting organized. However, he had had his fill of battlefield action with Garibaldi, and had learned enough from Frank Vizetelly in Italy to be able to transfer, fine-tune or recreate realistic scenes from sketches or reports prepared by others. He had spent a year away from Sallie, and was preparing to marry her at the end of September.

In the early spring of 1861, the *Illustrated News* hired Alfred Waud to embed himself with what would become the Army of the Potomac. Waud (pronounced "Wode" after its original Swiss "Vaud") was 32 when the war began, and considerably senior to fellow artists Nast and Theodore Davis (both 20) and Winslow Homer (25). Prior to his joining the *Illustrated News*, he designed the nautical scene with New York City in the background that was featured on the paper's masthead.

Physically, the tall, strapping, extroverted, full-bearded Alf Waud was courageous to an extreme, even firing a rifle at Confederate soldiers on occasion. One of the last of the more than 140 sketches he drew for the *Illustrated News* before he left for *Harper's Weekly* at the end of 1861, included a self-portrait as he crouched behind a pile of logs, sketchbook in hand, while a troop of Confederate cavalry passed by within shouting and shooting distance.

When Waud's sketches reached New York, they were turned over to Nast or another artist for drawing on woodblocks. On occasion, Nast modified or embellished Waud's sketches; often he added his own name or initials, so as to claim some credit, even though Waud's name was in the caption directly or as "Our Special Artist." Nast would not have been able to do that at *Harper's Weekly* or *Leslie's*, but his name had been touted by the *Illustrated News* as its "special artist," so he took full advantage of his opportunity for self-promotion. An early example was Waud's picture of a troop train in the build-up of the Union army prior to the Battle of Bull Run with Nast's name at the lower right.

NYIN December 28, 1861 C

REBEL HORSEMEN SCOUTING BETWEEN ANNANDALE AND FAIRFAX. Sketched By Our Special Artist, A.R. Waud

Waud quietly and understandably "detested" Nast as he wrote in a letter to a friend. Not covering the live action probably earned Nast demerits from Waud, but taking what he saw as Nast's unjustified self-promotion went beyond the pale. Of course, the roots of Waud's dislike went back several years to his time at *Leslie's* when Waud ridiculed him as Sol Eytinge's lapdog.*

NYIN May 18, 1861 20

Th. Nast

PASSAGE OF TROOPS EN ROUTE FROM ANNAPOLIS TO WASHINGTON. CHEERING THE PICKETS OF THE 69TH REGIMENT. A Sketch By A.R. Waud, Esq.

Nast's Role

On June 22, 1861, John King, who had purchased the *Illustrated News* six months earlier, was still its proprietor. A week later, Thomas B. Leggett & Co. had taken over. No announcement of the change in ownership was ever made, and King disappeared without a trace. Financial problems still plagued the paper, which did not — and probably could not — support as many quality artists on the front lines as its two competitors did.[9]

* See p. 35

During the initial fourteen months of the war, first Alfred Waud and then Arthur Lumley, did an excellent job of covering the Army of the Potomac in Virginia for the *Illustrated News*. Nast's role in tracing their sketches on woodblocks, and possibly even doing some engraving on occasion, was not of major importance. However, when it came to sketching battles where the *Illustrated News* did not have first-hand coverage — or when there were not enough sketches from the field to fill an issue — Nast played a key role in visualizing them for the paper's readers, although he didn't always identify himself as the artist. For example, after the Battle of Williamsburg on May 4-5, 1862, Henry Raymond, editor of the *New York Times*, provided vivid reporting on conditions he observed in a field hospital where both Union and Confederate wounded were operated on by the same surgeons. Nast's unsigned illustration captured the grisly scene all too well.[10]

Nast obtained two big advantages by covering the war from New York. First, it was relatively danger-free (except for the 1863 draft riots) and he could live a normal family life. Second, he received his weekly pay — probably in the $30-35 range — on a regular basis. He was too well known for his paper to lose him by playing games in the face of the strong demand for artists.

NYIN May 31, 1862 61

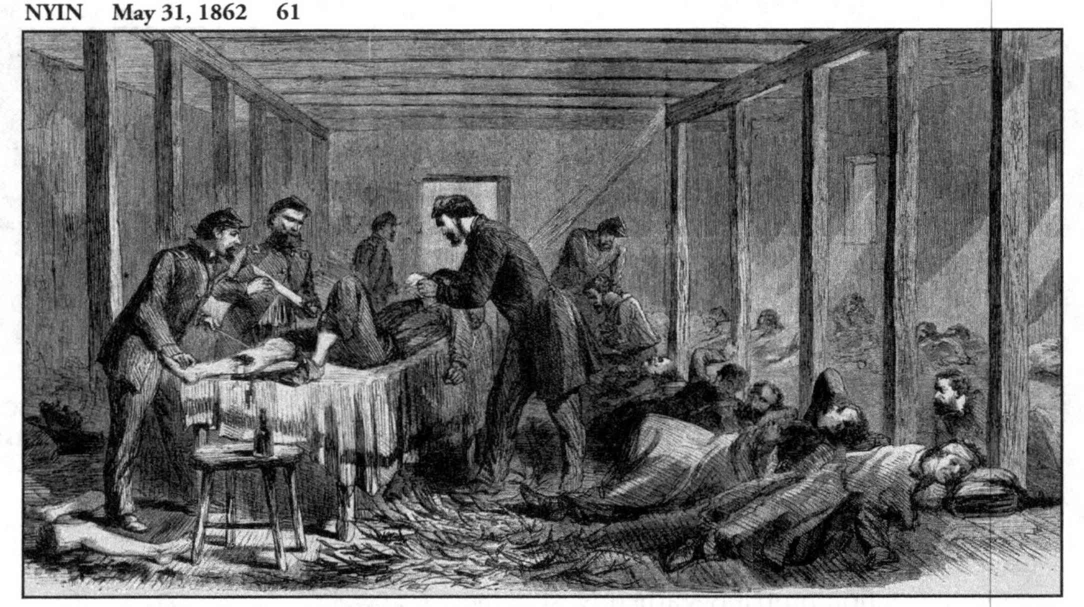

INTERIOR OF THE HOSPITAL ON THE BATTLE-FIELD OF WILLIAMSBURG — UNION AND REBEL DOCTORS ATTENDING.

The Battle of Bull Run

The first major battle of the Civil War took place on Sunday, July 21, 1861 at a narrow stream called Bull Run, about 25 miles from Washington. Strategically, Bull Run was important because it was close to Manassas Junction where two important railroads met.

Although the Confederates held commanding defensive positions, the 30,000 Union troops under the command of General Irvin McDowell anticipated victory. They began their attack before six in the morning and appeared to be winning by mid-afternoon. Then several thousand Confederate reinforcements arrived by rail, counter-attacked, and routed McDowell's green troops, many of whom fled in panic. Led by teamsters who cut loose their wagons from their horses, and followed by scattered groups of soldiers who threw away their supplies and equipment, the retreat became a stampede that lasted for several hours.[11]

In expectation of a pleasant Sunday afternoon rooting for their Yankees from a safe distance, many Congressmen and other Washingtonians came out in their carriages and enjoyed picnic lunches near Centerville, a small village about three miles closer to Washington. One of the spectators was William Howard Russell, the celebrated (especially in his own mind) foreign correspondent of the *London Times*, that city's most influential daily newspaper. He arrived around one o'clock with a friend in a carriage, followed by a tethered horse. He was joined at a feast of sandwiches and beer by Frank Vizetelly, his fellow English artist and reporter, who had been at the front in the morning, and now needed some refreshment.

ILN August 17, 1861 167

Vizetelly, Nast's artistic tipster in Italy, was dispatched by the *Illustrated London News* to cover the Civil War. He described the incredible panic, and drew the only accurate illustration of the rout to appear in any illustrated newspaper.

THE CIVIL WAR IN AMERICA: THE STAMPEDE FROM BULL RUN. — From A Sketch By Our Special Artist.

HW February 7, 1863 88

On the day after the battle, which had about 5,000 combined casualties, a Union field surgeon named Barnes began treating about 25 wounded soldiers as best he could under harrowing conditions. After leaving them for a break forced by enemy gunfire, he soon returned to find every last one bayonetted or cut to death, with some even being scalped. This "Southern Chivalry," reported in the Northern papers along with subsequent cold-blooded atrocities, was incorporated into a fervor-evoking series of allegorical illustrations that Nast drew for *Harper's Weekly* in 1862 and 1863.

Their repetitive influence on public opinion and resultant enlistments was so strong that it led to Lincoln reportedly calling Nast his "best recruiting sergeant."

In retrospect, the Bull Run debacle probably was a blessing in disguise for the North by serving as a wake-up call. It helped unify the public by arousing strong feelings of patriotism, and recognition that the Confederacy would not be a pushover. Lincoln replaced McDowell with General George McClellan as commander of the Army of the Potomac, with instructions to reorganize and train the troops into a fighting machine. (McClellan accomplished this effectively, although his subsequent reluctance to fight was to cause plenty of official and public discontent until Lincoln finally fired him fifteen months later).

"Bull Run" Russell

After Russell finished his leisurely picnic lunch, he rode his spare horse towards the battlefront three miles away. He soon encountered the first of the fleeing soldiers who shouted "We've been whipped" as they rode or ran past him. Once he grasped the dimensions of the rout, he fled back to Washington, arriving at his hotel about 11 PM.

Russell's paper, The *London Times,* had a strong influence on British public opinion and on Parliament, and Russell had the kind of prominence and respect for his reporting to make a difference. About 40, he had a law degree, was a fine writer, and knew the English politicians and aristocracy well. After arriving in Washington in April 1861, he met privately with President Abraham Lincoln and Secretary of State William Seward. He then left on an extensive tour of the South, visiting Charleston, Savannah, Montgomery and Memphis among other cities. He was accompanied by *Harper's Weekly's* 20-year old artist, Theodore Davis, who sketched his companion on several occasions.[12]

Three weeks before Bull Run, Nast drew his first Russell cartoon. Unsigned, it tweaked Russell for his drinking and pomposity, but was only a warm-up for the attacks that would begin after the full text of Russell's report on Bull Run in the *London Times* became known, and would extend over eight months.

NYIN June 28, 1861 128

POPULAR IDEA OF THE INSPIRATION OF W. H. RUSSELL, ESQ., BARRISTER-AT-LAW, &C., &C., &C., WHEN WRITING HIS LETTERS TO THE LONDON TIMES. From A Photograph.

In the interim, the Northern press expressed considerable concern about what effect Russell's words would have on English and French relations with the Confederacy. The *London Times* editorials strongly supported the South. England had recognized both sides as belligerents, and was supposed to respect the Union blockades of Southern harbors and remain neutral. The Confederacy was trying hard to be recognized by both England and France, and the Union was trying equally hard to prevent that. With the *London Times* and even the *Illustrated London News* favoring recognition, Russell's reporting was a major concern because of its potential to shape public opinion in England.

NYIN August 26, 1861 256

JOHN BULL AND THE AMERICAN LOAN.
No. Shylock —we did not come about the loan —we have money enough, and to spare at home. But we thought, since our English brethren had come to be ruled by such as you, and your hirelings yonder, that we had better keep an eye on you.

Nast drew four cartoons reflecting the Confederacy's attempts to obtain financial and logistical support from Europe, two of which featured Shakespearean references.

Shylock (from *The Merchant of Venice*), in front of the *London Times* office, was being sternly addressed by President Lincoln and General Winfield Scott (who had not yet been replaced by George McClellan) in their attempt to prevent a British loan to the Confederacy. The use of Shylock had an anti-Semitic tinge that probably referred to the Rothschilds, who were extremely important bankers in both London and Paris. Nast could not have known that August Belmont, the American representative of the Rothschild Bank, helped to negate English support for the Confederacy.[13]

In November, Nast's last cartoon on the subject of European funding for the South featured Jeff Davis trying to sell Confederate bonds collateralized by cotton. Nast used Shakespeare's Henry IV (Part I): "I can call spirits from the vasty deep" said Glendower to Hotspur; "Why so can I, or so can any man, but they will come when you do call for them?" replied Hotspur. That was a problem Davis never solved.

NYIN November 11, 1861 32

ALTERED CONDITION OF AFFAIRS.
***Jeff Davis.* —"I can call millions across the vasty deep."**
***European capitalist.* —"Ferry goot, but vill dey comes?"**

Russell's description of Bull Run, along with his diatribe, appeared in the *London Times* on August 6, and was available in America two weeks later. Like Vizetelly's report accompanying his sketch of the stampede, Russell's message about the panic was reasonably accurate; unlike Vizetelly, he fabricated accounts of the actual battle which he had not seen; nor had he interviewed any of its participants before he wrote his column in his Washington hotel room. Consequently, he was blasted in the Northern press.

The stage was set for Nast. A week after the Shylock cartoon, there was "London-Stout" Russell in all his complacent corpulence looking through his telescope at Bull Run fifteen (really three) miles away while eating a sandwich under a tree. His London notebook was at his side, along with seven bottles of his favorite beverage with its double meaning.

NYIN September 2, 1861 288

LONDON-STOUT RUSSELL AT THE BATTLE OF BULL RUN.

Two weeks later, Nast drew Russell having a nightmare. He was locked up in Fort Lafayette, a prison located on a small shoal at the entrance to New York Harbor (the Guantanamo of its day), used to hold "prominent rebels and traitors." Nast had published a sketch of Fort Lafayette two weeks earlier, so it was easy for him to put a face on the Fort and lay it on top of Russell's ample belly.

NYIN September. 16, 1861 320

THE SECESSIA NIGHTMARE.

The following week Nast drew the egotistical Russell using the first person singular pronoun twenty times in his dispatch, along with his nine bottles of London Stout. Next came Russell's ever-stouter figure with a slave under his foot and a pistol-wielding Confederate on his knee, reflecting his and his editor's beliefs (as Nast saw them).

NYIN September 23, 1861 336

LONDON STOUT RUSSELL'S LETTERS TO THE LONDON TIMES.

NYIN September 30, 1861 352

THAT FINE OLD ENGLISH GENTLEMAN, ALL OF THE LONDON TIMES.

Russell got a break from impalement while Nast was on his honeymoon. When Nast returned to he attack, his harpoon boomeranged, because he was wrong in ridiculing the *London Times* for reporting the discussion between Lincoln's emissary and Garibaldi. His caption quoted Garibaldi's unacceptable counter-offer as Lincoln's primary offer.*

The whole concept was incredible to Nast. Maybe he missed the rumors while on his honeymoon.

NYIN October 14, 1861 384

DEPLORABLE CONDITION OF THE EDITOR OF THE LONDON TIMES. Softening of the brain having supervened he produced the following rubbish —
"As if despairing of native genius and enterprise, the President at Washington has actually sent to ask Garibaldi to *accept the post of commander-in-chief, throwing into the bargain the emancipation of the slaves.* It costs us an effort to take in the extravagant oddity and humiliating character of this proposition." —*London Times.*

* See p. 82

That was all for Russell until the following year, when he was shown at the side of pompous "King" John Delane, the editor of the *London Times*, with all his subjects, even including Queen Victoria and the comic magazine *Punch*, bowing in obeisance. Russell had the plumed hat of a knight or noble, and his customary bottles of London Stout. Nast promoted himself with his initials on the inkwell in the right foreground.

NYIN February 22, 1862 256

ENGLAND'S MONARCH.

NYIN May 3, 1862 416

However, Nast had the last laugh in the spring of 1862 when Russell, along with Frank Vizetelly, was summarily prevented from accompanying General McClellan on his Peninsular Campaign by Secretary of War Edwin Stanton, who had them taken off their ship. Furious, Russell sailed for England several days later, while Vizetelly went South to travel with and sketch the Confederates for the rest of the war. Nast enjoyed himself drawing an angry Bull Run Russell with nary a bottle of London Stout in sight.

THE LAST OF BULL RUN RUSSELL. SKETCHED OFF THE "HIGHLAND LIGHTS."

Nast's serial attacks on Russell constituted a critical step in his development as an impactful visual journalist. For the first time, he found a comical target whom he could effectively torment or crucify again and again. Repetition became a hallmark of his success.

Dyslexic Christmas

Over the next quarter-century, Nast's family-oriented Christmas drawings would become a *Harper's Weekly* tradition. In 1861, however, his first Christmas tree had a double meaning: ten leading Confederate generals and politicians hanging as labeled ornaments.[14] The musician (right) probably was a memorial tribute to the artist's late father Joseph, who had played the trombone in Landau's military band.

Although Tommy had been married for three months, he evidently didn't have Sallie edit this cartoon. In the list of Southern cities, the two "N"s in Savannah were backwards; New Orleans was missing an "L" and ended with a backward "S"; and the "gard" in Beauregard was spelled "guard." These mistakes didn't detract from his usual pun, but they did illustrate Nast's lifelong problems with dyslexia and spelling.

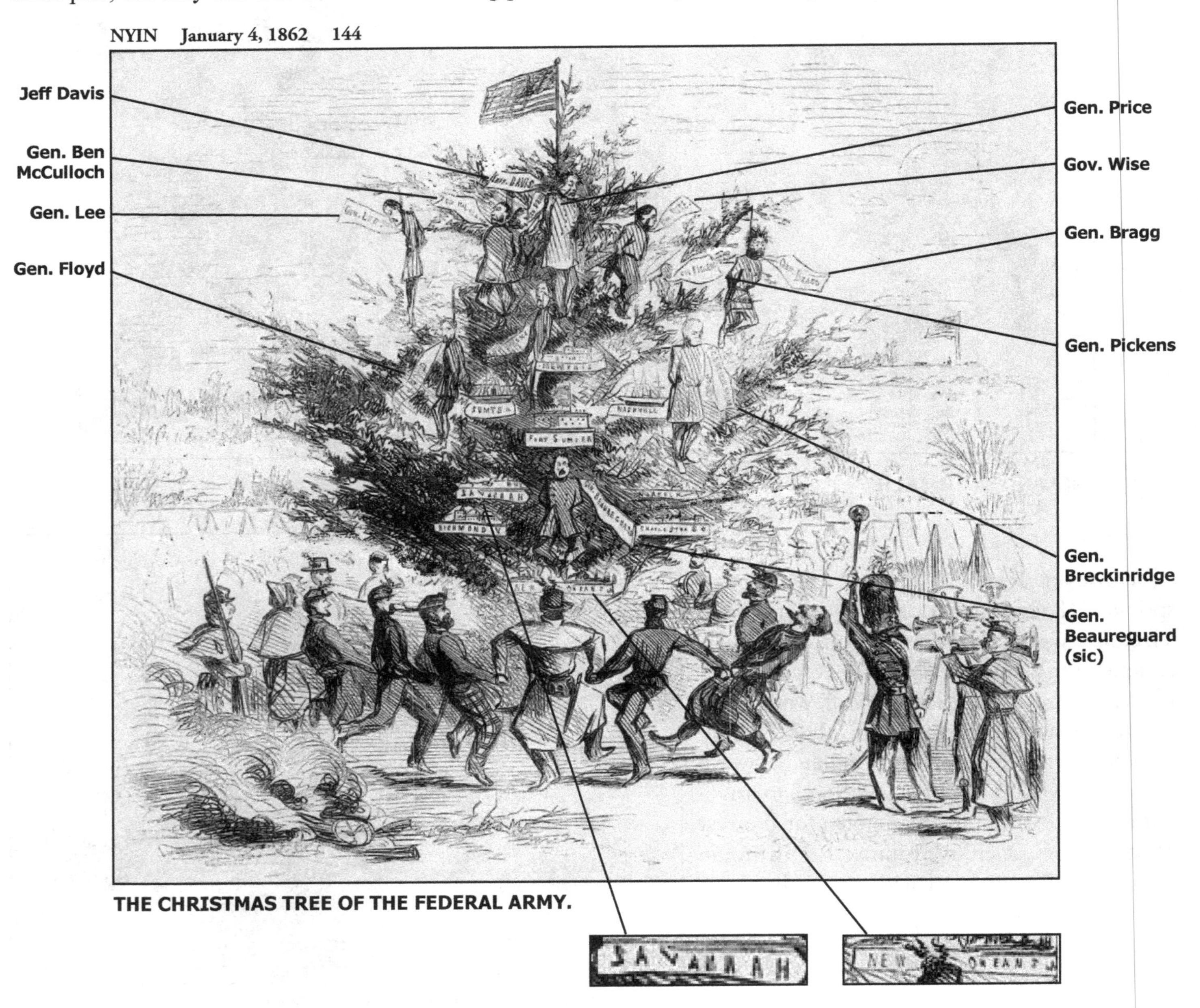

THE CHRISTMAS TREE OF THE FEDERAL ARMY.

The Emergence of Grant

The first Union attacks in the South occurred in early February 1862. Commodore Andrew Foote captured Fort Henry on the Tennessee River and turned it over to General Ulysses Grant and his 15,000 troops. The following week, Grant and Foote captured Fort Donelson on the Cumberland River. An artist named Adolph Schalter sketched a four-page illustration of the battle, and Nast drew it on woodblocks for the *Illustrated News*, prominently displaying his own name.

Grant's reputation was solidly established at Fort Donelson when he forced the last of three Confederate commanders — General Simon Bolivar Buckner — to accept terms of unconditional surrender. U. S. (Ulysses Simpson) Grant became U. S. (Unconditional Surrender) Grant to Nast and his subsequent audience of millions over the years. Grant later demanded the same terms from Confederate General John C. Pemberton at Vicksburg on July 4, 1863, thereby enhancing his reputation even more.[15]

Buckner had been put in the unfortunate position of having to accept an unconditional surrender by the cowardice of his two predecessors at Fort Donelson, Generals John Floyd and Gideon Pillow. Floyd had been Secretary of War from 1857 to 1860 under President James Buchanan, and knew that he would have been tried for treason if captured. When he realized the battle was lost, he turned his command over to Pillow, who immediately passed it down to Buckner before both men fled.

Nast paid tribute to Flag Officer Foote with a pun cartoon celebrating his victories, while Floyd and Pillow cravenly escaped.

NYIN March 8, 1862 288

THE WAY WE FOOTE THE REBELS.

Shiloh

After Grant's success at Fort Donelson, his army of 40,000 moved down the Mississippi Valley to Pittsburg Landing, a small steamboat dock on the Tennessee River. The ensuing battle, generally called Shiloh after a small church in the center of the action, was reminiscent of Bull Run in reverse but on a much larger scale. Its 24,000 casualties were almost five times greater than Bull Run; in fact, they exceeded the total from all previous American wars. Whereas Bull Run convinced the over-confident North that the South was no pushover, Shiloh made it clear to Grant and possibly Lincoln that only total conquest — or "subjugation" as Grant put it — would enable the Union to win the war.

If Grant and the Union had lost at Shiloh — which easily could have happened — the border states of Kentucky and Missouri might have joined the Confederacy, opening up the North to invasion through Ohio and/or Illinois. Lincoln would have had to switch from offense to defense in the West, with grave political and military repercussions.

To his well publicized discredit, Grant did not prepare his 40,000 men for a surprise attack. Accordingly, when Confederate General Albert Sidney Johnston's troops came out of the woods early Sunday morning April 6, the Union troops were routed and, after fifteen hours of fighting, fell back to the river in disorder. Only heavy shelling by two Union gunboats kept the Confederates from victory.

Albert Sidney Johnston, who was considered to be one of the South's best generals, bled to death when a bullet severed an artery in his leg. General Pierre Beauregard, a hero of Bull Run, took over, but put himself in Davis's doghouse for life by failing to mount the clinching attack at twilight of the first day when the Union troops were vulnerable. Even Grant, who had arrived from twelve miles away well after the battle started, was unable to do much more than hold a wavering line, significantly aided by the bombardment from Foote's gunboats.

That night, Union General Don Carlos Buell, arrived and ferried his 20,000 reinforcements across the Tennessee River. The next morning Grant counter-attacked, leading the charge, and surprising Beauregard. By mid-afternoon on Monday, after eight more hours of heavy fighting, the Confederates retreated back to Corinth, Mississippi.[16]

While the South lost perhaps its best general after Robert E. Lee and possibly Stonewall Jackson, the North had its two brightest future stars emerge as a team — Grant and William Sherman, who although wounded in the hand, distinguished himself throughout the battle. While Grant was a justifiable goat for his lack of planning and preparation before the battle, his leadership on the second day was instrumental in turning the tide. When tales of Grant's excessive drinking came to Lincoln's attention, the President backed his general, saying: "I can't spare this man; he fights." (In sharp contrast to McClellan, who was finally launching his unsuccessful Peninsular Campaign in Virginia after six months of idleness).

Frank Leslie's Illustrated Newspaper was the only paper in the country with an artist on the scene to sketch the Battle of Shiloh. Henri Lovie, a 34-year old German-born illustrator from Cincinnati, had covered several western states for Leslie and survived a threatened lynching by Confederate sympathizers in Kentucky. He drew more than twenty sketches of the action at Shiloh, pulling no punches about the North's near-disaster on the first day, and providing contextual detail for his illustrations.[17]

From the safety of New York, and utilizing dispatches from the front in the daily papers, Nast improvised an extra large picture of the battle on two foldout double-pages, featuring a fairly accurate picture of General Grant leading his final victorious charge. **This was Nast's first depiction of Grant, who would become his all-time hero and personal friend, and appear in more than 100 of his cartoons in *Harper's Weekly* — all but one of them (dealing with the scandals during his Presidency) positive.**

NYIN April 26, 1862

In the issue, the *Illustrated News* copied a long article by an unidentified reporter who noted: "Captain Carson was between General Grant and your correspondent when a cannon ball took off his head and killed and wounded several others." Nast could identify with that incident from his days with Garibaldi at Volturno when he had a similarly close call.

Leslie's Redux

Leslie promoted his live coverage of Shiloh and other battles. His on-the-scene staff of artists — perhaps as many as a dozen at its peak — provided action-packed drawings to his less educated audience; they probably overlooked his inconsistent editorial coverage compared to *Harper's Weekly*. In the early years of the Civil War, his circulation was about 150,000, about 30,000 more than the *Weekly*. However, *Harper's* thrived and was far more influential in shaping public opinion than *Leslie's*.

Meanwhile Nast's employer struggled.[18] Tommy left during May 1862, when Leslie lured him away for fifty dollars a week. Leslie's primary motivation in hiring Nast must have had more to do with harming his competitor —and possibly exacting some form of revenge on his former "fledgling artist" — than with buttressing his staff. Fifty dollars was a ridiculous salary; when the Harpers put Charles Parsons, an esteemed painter and illustrator, in charge of all their artists and engravers in April 1862, they paid him that rate. Leslie had the talented Frank Bellew on board to draw cartoons so Nast had no real role to play. Not long after, his salary was cut to thirty-five dollars a week, and by July 21 he was off the payroll.

One of the few cartoons that Nast drew for Leslie, *The American St. Patrick Driving Out the Reptiles*, **is noteworthy because it showed the Irish in a favorable light in marked contrast to dozens of his later cartoons.**

Colonel Michael Corcoran led the 69th New York Irish Regiment in a heroic charge and stand at Bull Run, when 600 of its 1,600 members were casualties. Alfred Waud sketched their bare-chested charge and Nast probably drew it on woodblocks. Corcoran was captured when he grabbed his regiment's colors and stood tall against the counter-attack of the Confederate cavalry in the late afternoon — in contrast to other Union troops fleeing around him. Corcoran was held prisoner for almost a year — until August 1863 when he was freed in an exchange. He was a true hero at a time when the Irish were frequently disparaged in the New York press. While pressing for Corcoran's release about a month before it took place, Nast gave St. Patrick the same Irish stereotyped face that he had used on John Morrissey at his championship fight with John Heenan four years earlier.*

FLIN July 5, 1862 224

THE AMERICAN ST. PATRICK DRIVING OUT THE REPTILES.
"And yer won't give up Corcoran, won't yer? But I'll make yor, ye spalpeens! Now take this! And this! And this!"

The stage was now set for Nast to join *Harper's Weekly* which did have a role for him that took full advantage of his talent. It is likely that Fletcher Harper, the *Weekly's* publisher, relished Nast's attacks on "Bull Run" Russell, whose lies in connection with Russell's Southern tour with Theodore Davis well before Bull Run, disgusted Fletcher. He hired "Tommy" (as he called him), and strongly backed the cartoonist right up until his death fifteen years later.

---

* See p. 46

Chapter 9
Harper's Weekly

Julia Nast was about a month old when her father joined *Harper's Weekly* in August 1862 as a free-lancer, probably getting paid at the same $30 per page rate as Winslow Homer. He needed the income, as well as the opportunity to supplement it by illustrating books and drawing for comic publications.[1]

During the war's first year, *Harper's Weekly* published more than 500 military-related illustrations with Fletcher Harper playing a key role in their selection and presentation. When Nast came aboard, *Harper's* had five artists at the front covering the major armies — Alfred Waud with the Army of the Potomac; Theodore Davis with Sherman's army; Henry Mosler with Buell's army; Alexander Simplot with Grant's army; and Angelo Wiser with Ambrose Burnside's army on the Carolina coast.[2] Contributing cartoonists included Sol Eytinge, William Newman and Frank Bellew (who swapped places with Newman after multiple disagreements with Frank Leslie).

Winslow Homer

Of course, the *Harper's Weekly* artist who achieved the most enduring fame was Winslow Homer. While Homer's reputation was built primarily on his later paintings, many of the hundred-plus drawings that Homer did for the *Weekly* between 1857 and 1875 schooled him in the finer aspects of composition and draftsmanship. However, even Homer found that the current art market wouldn't provide a living; he received only $60 for his magnificent 1862 painting of the *Sharp-Shooter*. That was a major reason that Homer continued to draw woodblock illustrations for *Harper's Weekly* and other publications for more than a decade after the war ended. Most of Homer's reputation as a Civil War artist was established later on, after his paintings had time to be appreciated.

During the course of the war itself, Homer drew 22 full or double-page illustrations for *Harper's Weekly* that directly related to military action and camp life; nearly all of them reflected scenes of the daily doings of soldiers.[3] Initially, *Harper's* may have intended to use Homer as a battlefield artist, but almost all of his Civil War drawings were produced in his New York studio. He did go to the front on three occasions — in October 1861 outside Washington; near Yorktown in April-May 1862; and probably for a brief time in May 1864 during Grant's Wilderness Campaign in Virginia. All his military illustrations were based on scenes he saw and sketched at the front.

Prior to Nast's arrival, Homer served for nine weeks as an embedded artist with George McClellan's Army of the Potomac during his ill-fated Peninsular Campaign. Homer's many sketches near Yorktown became the basis for both his *Harper's* military illustrations and his incomparable Civil War paintings. However, his experience with death, disease and the general cruelties of war left him emotionally scarred and disillusioned.

Moreover, Homer was frequently dissatisfied with the way that some of his sketches dispatched from the front were drawn or engraved on the woodblocks. Rubbing salt in his wounds, he received only $25 a page (instead of $30) to compensate for re-drawing his sketches.

HW November 15, 1862 724

THE ARMY OF THE POTOMAC —A SHARP-SHOOTER ON PICKET DUTY —From A Painting By W. Homer, Esq.

Homer's best Civil War illustration[4]

Author's Collection

OUR SPECIAL

Homer by Homer[5]

Like Homer, Nast preferred to draw in his home studio where his materials and cartes de visite were close at hand. Working at a safe distance, in relative peace and quiet all around, provided Nast and Homer a significant advantage over the battlefield artists in the quality of their work. They could draw directly on woodblocks without worrying about inaccurate transcribing by middlemen, and also had the opportunity to instruct their engravers first-hand (although execution wasn't foolproof).

Conversely, their illustrations generally had to fight for attention in the crowded sixteen-page issues of *Harper's Weekly*. Between eight and eleven pages of each issue were devoted to war-related sketches, maps, portraits and cartoons, so readers had plenty of visual content to engage their attention. Battle scenes by frontline artists had timely relevance and realism, and usually related to the press accounts of the action.

Nast was resented by some of the front-line artists. In addition to Waud who never liked him, Theodore Davis, who was Nast's age and drew more than 250 illustrations for the *Weekly*, told the *Evening Mail* in a March 1, 1868 interview: "It was Thomas Nast's province during the late war to make for himself the reputation of a war artist without the unpleasant necessity of exposing himself to either the hardships of campaign life or the dangers of the battlefield." Davis, who was arrested once and wounded twice, knew what he was talking about.

Nast's Impact

From the war's start at Fort Sumter to its effective conclusion at Appomattox, Nast produced about 260 illustrations. Only about forty had anything humorous in them. About 200 of the former and all but three of the latter were drawn for the *Illustrated News* before June 1862. As described earlier, Nast's primary assignment there was to take the battlefield sketches of Waud, Arthur Lumley and other embedded artists, as well as army amateurs, and redraw them on woodblocks.

Most of the three dozen or so cartoons that Nast drew for the *Illustrated News* were unremarkable and not always signed. They were equivalent to what Bellew, William Newman, John McLenan and others were churning out for the illustrated weeklies and the comics. The singular exception was Nast's **serialized** eight-month campaign against "Bull Run" Russell.*

* See p. 98-101

What then differentiated Nast from his fellow artists? Only two of his sixty-two wartime illustrations in the *Weekly* were sketched from what he actually saw — one in Philadelphia (on his hapless way to Gettysburg), and the other in New York during the draft riots. However, many of his 42 semi-allegorical illustrations or re-creations (e.g., four more draft riots scenes) had more emotional impact on *Harper's* readers than most of its sketched-from-life illustrations. Broadly, 24 of the 42 stressed Union positives and 18 vilified Confederates and their Northern sympathizers.

The *Weekly's* circulation was in the 120,000-plus range during the War. It claimed eight to ten "passalong" readers for each copy sold, so Nast's audience was about a million. Nast's semi-allegorical drawings helped establish the publication as a prominent leader in boosting Northern recruitment and morale; his five covers and thirty double-pages provided additional visual impact.

Essentially, Nast found a way to break fresh ground in the twilight zone between the factual reporting of battlefield artists — the bread and butter of any illustrated newspaper — and the energizing of public opinion. Fletcher Harper recognized Tommy's talent and encouraged him. Curtis often amplified his artist's efforts with related commentary and editorials, while Nast based some of his cartoons on what Curtis wrote; their pitch-and-catch game worked well.

In April 1865, the scholarly and conservative *North American Review* paid tribute to *Harper's Weekly* after first criticizing its on-the-fence pre-war position (to maintain its Southern subscriber base).

> *It was not until the 27th of April 1861, that Harper's Weekly found out that it had a country to be believed in, and learned that* ***compromise****, or surrender of right to wrong, was worse than war. Up to that time, it had tried to offend nobody, and it had succeeded in offending every earnest and right-thinking man. At length it was forced to have and to express opinions. . . .*
>
> *During the past two years it has been one of the most powerful of the organs of public opinion. Its vast circulation, deservedly secured and maintained by the excellence and variety of its illustrations of the scenes and events of the war, as well as by the spirit and tone of its editorials, has carried it far and wide. It has been read in city parlors, in the log hut of the pioneer, by every camp-fire of our armies, in the wards of our hospitals, in the trenches before Petersburg, and in the ruins of Charleston; and wherever it has gone, it has nerved the hearts and strengthened the arms of the people, and it has done its full part in the furtherance of the great cause of Union, of Freedom, and of Law.*
>
> *. . . Some of the symbolical pictures by Mr. Nast were among the most effective political tracts of the recent campaign, and merit preservation as embodiments of the popular imagination. . .*

As Nast with uncharacteristic modesty related nineteen years later: ***The war made me. . . My pictures appealed to the sentiment of the people and I became, so to speak, famous. My wit and satire, which today would hardly rise above mediocrity, was then considered wonderful.***[6]

Nast knew some of the artists at *Harpers* when he came aboard in August 1862, but John Bonner, the editor, was new to him. Earlier in the year, Nast had submitted a number of illustrations to the *Weekly* but Bonner rejected them all. Born in Canada, Bonner had been an editorial writer on the pro-slavery *Herald* before he became managing editor of *Harper's Weekly* in 1858. Although the *Weekly* did not oppose slavery then — some critics called it *Harper's Weakly* — its views changed during the early years of the war, while Bonner's did not. After Nast joined his staff, Bonner continued to reject or modify some of the newcomer's powerful anti-slavery sketches. He probably was more obstacle than mentor to his strong-willed artist. If not for Fletcher Harper's firm backing, Nast was unlikely to have stayed at his paper.

As mentioned previously, in April 1863, the Harpers hired English-born Charles Parsons as Superintendent of Art. Parsons, 43 at the time, would remain in that position for the next twenty-six years, leaving three years after Nast did. He was a good administrator, as well as a fine painter and illustrator, and he provided critical continuity for both Nast and the Harpers.

Nast had sixty-four drawings in *Harper's Weekly* before the war concluded at Appomattox on April 9, 1865; of these, only two were true cartoons, both small and on the back page. All related to military, civilian or political aspects of the war. Fourteen battle scenarios and half a dozen pictures of army life were competent but not noticeably different from those sketched by Waud and Davis at the front, or Homer in New York.

Phunny Phellow

In contrast to his serious, solemn and often grim Civil War illustrations in the *Weekly* — almost all of which were *signed* — Nast had a platform in *Phunny Phellow* where he could be unrestrained, even boisterous — and *anonymous*. Instead of depicting Lincoln and his generals as dignified and statesmanlike, he could portray Lincoln as an orchestra leader,* Gettysburg hero Winfield Scott Hancock as a pun-worthy vigilant rooster, or precocious George Armstrong Custer as the Pet of the Army.[7]

PP August 1864

PP October 1864 16

GENERAL HANCOCK ALWAYS READY FOR A FIGHT.

PP August 1865 16

GENERAL CUSTER, OR THE PET OF THE ARMY.

Confederate Atrocities

About a month before Nast joined *Harper's Weekly*, two Confederate colonels (soon to be generals) — Nathan Bedford Forrest in Tennessee and John Morgan in Kentucky, with commands of 800 to 1,000 men — each conducted devastating guerilla raids against troops under the control of Union General Don Carlos Buell. They not only caused significant casualties and captured valuable supplies, but they also demoralized Buell's army and Northern civilians who read about the defeats. Both Forrest and Morgan had fought against Grant and Buell at Shiloh, and decided that hit-and-run tactics would serve their cause better than traditional organized warfare.[8]

After General William Rosecrans replaced Buell in 1863, President Lincoln wrote Rosecrans: "In no other way does the enemy give us so much trouble, at so little expence (sic) to himself, as by the raids of rapidly moving small bodies of troops."

* See p. iv for full cartoon

Nast was familiar with abominable "Southern Chivalry" from his *Illustrated News* sketches of the scalpings and other atrocities at Bull Run and other battles and incidents reported in the Northern newspapers. At Pea Ridge, Arkansas, on March 7-8, 1862, 11,000 Union troops had routed 16,000 Confederates. 3,000 of the Confederate troops were Indians, primarily Creeks from the Indian Territory (now Oklahoma), under the command of Albert Pike. About twenty Union soldiers who lay on the field wounded or dead "were foully and fiendishly scalped, murdered and robbed" by this "Aboriginal Corps of Tomahawkers and Scalpers" as the *New York World* and *Tribune*, respectively, described their actions. Nast had included a grisly vignette of the scene in his depiction of the battle for the *Illustrated News*.[9]*

A prior Nast sketch for the *Illustrated News* was originally submitted by an Ohio soldier, along with a vivid detailed dialogue between captors and victims, and an account of how the culprits were caught and summarily executed. (Right)

NYIN February 22, 1862 C

MURDER OF TWO OF PLATT'S ZOUAVES, 34TH OHIO, BY EIGHT OF THE REBEL CHIVALRY, ON BEEF FORK, CABEL COUNTY, WESTERN VIRGINIA. Sketched By Ensign J. F. C. Hillen, Platt's Zouaves.

At *Harper's*, Nast's second illustration depicted *The Murder of General Robert McCook*, who was dumped from an ambulance and assassinated by guerillas on August 5. Nast drew his unsigned sketch from the report of a Philadelphia Press correspondent reprinted in the same issue.

HW August 23, 1862 541

THE MURDER OF GENERAL ROBERT L. MCCOOK, NEAR SALEM, ALABAMA

---

* See p. 97

Six months later, Nast drew his most vicious atrocity pictorial, reprising scenes of "Southern Chivalry" from Bull Run on. Comparisons with the brutal acts of modern terrorism, and its effects on video and internet audiences, are relevant.

HW February 7, 1863 88-89

Murder Of Two Of Piatt's Souaves, 34th Ohio — **Firing On U.S. Hospitals** — **Driving Negroes South** — **Southern Women Gloating Over Dead Union Soldiers** — **The Murder Of Gen. Robert L. McCook**

Throwing Sick And Wounded U.S. Soldiers In The Road To Die — **Pea Ridge** — **Hanging Union Men** — **Bull Run** — **Shooting U.S. Prisoners** — **Massacre Of Negroes At Murfreesboro Pike** — **No Quarter**

HISTORIC EXAMPLES OF SOUTHERN CHIVALRY, Illustrated By Thomas Nast —Dedicated To Jeff Davis.

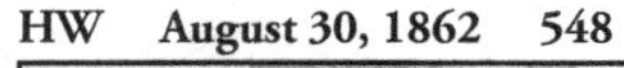

Guerilla Warfare

A week later with *John Morgan's Highwaymen Sacking a Peaceful Village in the West,* Nast unleashed the first of his full-scale, imaginative guerilla illustrations, depicting almost the entire gamut of criminal activities — murder, decapitation, arson and robbery — while intimating but not showing rape. The accompanying text was not as discreet when it talked about "making free with female purity" and "shrieks of agony . . . from outraged matrons and maidens," as well as "butchered children." Nast gave life to the inflammatory but realistic description.

HW August 30, 1862 548

JOHN MORGAN'S HIGHWAYMEN SACKING A PEACEFUL VILLAGE IN THE WEST.

Five issues later, Nast showed even more Confederate brutality and some of the same characters in *A Rebel Guerilla Raid in a Western Town.* The accompanying text described eyes being picked out by bayonets, and wounded soldiers having their throats cut ear-to-ear.

HW September 27, 1862 616

A REBEL GUERILLA RAID IN A WESTERN TOWN.

HW October 25, 1862 680

AFTER THE BATTLE —THE REBELS IN POSSESSION OF THE FIELD.

Nast's next negative illustration referred to the aftermath of the Union defeat at the Second Battle of Bull Run, which occurred two months earlier. A letter to the *New York Times,* reprinted in the *Weekly*, described the scene two miles from Centerville, the site of Bull Run Russell's infamy the previous summer. Confederates stripped and robbed the dead, and threw their bodies into trenches, which the *Times* reporter wrote about and Nast depicted in horrific detail. Even though these troops were not guerrillas, they knew that their actions violated all rules of warfare and decency, as they inadvertently admitted to the correspondent.

Finally, the Union struck back. In the same issue as Homer's *Sharp-shooter*, Nast drew *Surprise of the Guerrillas by a Squadron of United States Cavalry*. Nast's depiction of the Confederate horseman raised high out of his saddle by a sideways Union saber thrust from behind and protruding almost a foot out of his chest, would be difficult to duplicate in real life, but it made a vivid centerpiece for his picture.

HW November 15, 1862 728

THE WAR FOR THE UNION —SURPRISE OF REBEL GUERRILLAS BY A SQUADRON OF UNITED STATES CAVALRY.

Nast skipped his monthly guerilla exposé in December in favor of a Christmas Eve allegory. However, he used the model contrasting Union and Confederate behavior when he resumed his attack in January with *The War in the Border States*.

One oval showed Union soldiers marching through a village stripped clean by guerrillas, and trying to feed starving women and children with their own limited supplies; the other depicted a new widow and her children discovering the body of their murdered husband and father. The two main scenes in the circles were fringed with guerrillas, fleeing slaves, two freezing Union sympathizers behind bars and a burning bridge symbolizing the isolation of the survivors. The most grisly detail was in the bottom oval, where vultures had picked clean the bones and skull of a planter, leaving his vacant house in the background.

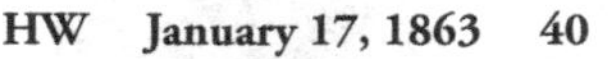

THE WAR IN THE WEST.

Prisoners

By mid-1863, guerillas gradually became less of a problem, and Nast turned his critical focus on the mistreatment of Union prisoners. During the first two years of the war, both sides exchanged most of their prisoners.[10] However, these exchanges were suspended in 1863, as the prisons filled after Chancellorsville, Gettysburg, Vicksburg, Chattanooga, Chickamauga and numerous other clashes.

Grant paroled 30,000 prisoners after Vicksburg because he didn't have the facilities to hold them. They were not supposed to rejoin the army until after they were formally exchanged for Union prisoners, but many of them did. Grant played hardball after he found out that the same men were recaptured in subsequent battles.

Prior to that, Nast drew *A Group of Union Prisoners Escorted Through a Rebel Town* with "the mingled curiosity and hatred with which they are regarded by some of the spectators, and the half-disguised sympathy shown them by others, especially the negroes." The extract was from the diary of a *New York World* correspondent who was imprisoned with the officers at Libby in Richmond. He was confined in one room with three others, who "were not permitted to stick a head out of the window on penalty of being shot."

HW June 13, 1863 373

A GROUP OF UNION PRISONERS ESCORTED THROUGH A REBEL TOWN.

HW December 5, 1863 781

THE PRISONERS AT RICHMOND—UNION TROOPS PRISONERS AT BELLE ISLE.

With the South suffering from shortages of all kinds by 1863, Union captives usually were almost starved, stripped of most of their clothing and valuables, given no blankets, and provided little or no shelter from the heat, cold and humidity. Most of the Union prisoners were sent to one of two military prisons situated on the James River in Richmond. Belle Isle was used only for enlisted men who numbered 15,000 or more at the end of 1863, according to a few who were exchanged. Nast illustrated the conditions at Belle Isle, as related by two returned prisoners.

After blacks began fighting for the Union and were captured, Jefferson Davis refused to exchange them, especially former slaves. Lincoln took a firm stand on principle and all exchanges stopped. In a satirical vignette in *The Chicago Platform*, a critically important 1864 pre-election cartoon, Nast showed a Union general imploring a "Man for Man" exchange while his Confederate counterpart thumbed his nose at him; ex-slaves were not men to be exchanged.*

HW October 15, 1864 664

* See p. x

Emphasizing Positives

An early contribution to the energizing of Northern opinion was *A Gallant Color-Bearer*, **the first of Nast's 404 covers in *Harper's Weekly***.

The accompanying text told the story of how a thrice-wounded New York soldier held on to his regiment's flag even when unconscious, marking him as a hero. Nast painted a watercolor of this scene in which the faces were far more lifelike than his engraver was able to translate onto woodblocks.[11]

HW September 20, 1862 C

A GALLANT COLOR-BEARER.

HW January 3, 1863 C

SANTA CLAUS IN CAMP.

The Christmas issue contained two allegories which drew widespread positive commentary. The cover featured *Santa Claus in Camp*. Although Santa's image had not yet evolved into the fat, jolly portrayal that Nast later made famous, it had a strong emotional impact on *Harper's* readers.

In a not-so-subtle inference to his year-earlier "hanging Christmas Tree" cartoon for the *Illustrated News*, Santa tightened a cord around a toy Jeff Davis's neck. A drummer boy with a jack-in-a-box, soldiers chasing a greased pig while another climbed a greased pole, and copies of *Harper's Weekly* all around showed a rare, somewhat playful Nast.

Christmas Eve, 1862 was a milestone in Nast's early career. **His sentimental allegory drew so much praise from the Harper brothers, as well as their public, that their young artist's power to draw what and how he wanted was virtually veto-proof.**[12] Nast's bold enlarged signature in the lower right re-emphasized his self-announced arrival as his own man.

The scene resembled a large valentine as it portrayed the love between a wife looking up at the moon and praying for her husband in the left oval while he, on picket duty in front of a camp-fire, gazed longingly at photographs of his family. Santa was preparing to go down the chimney with gifts for their sleeping children, while distributing packages (upper right) to the troops depicted in the related cover illustration. Below, the vignettes of soldiers marching, graves, and ships patrolling in a storm emphasized the realities of military life.

HW January 3, 1863 8-9

CHRISTMAS EVE, 1862.

Drummer Boys

As noted previously, Winslow Homer specialized in drawing scenes of army life for *Harper's Weekly*, as Edwin Forbes did for *Leslie's*.[13] During 1863, Nast drew his own impressions — some as pictures and some as topical vignettes.

Nast, who always enjoyed children, had a special appreciation for under-age drummer boys. In addition to serving as drummers and buglers, they assisted cooks, surgeons and supply officers, ran errands and delivered messages. Most were too small to carry or shoot heavy muskets. In his *Reveille in Camp* picture, they were the central feature.

HW July 11, 1863 444

REVEILLE IN CAMP —5 A.M.

Perhaps the most famous was Johnny Clem, who was allowed to join a Michigan Volunteer regiment in April 1861 as a nine-year old drummer boy. In September 1863, he escaped capture at Chicamauga by shooting a Confederate officer; a month later he was seized, but released shortly afterwards. The attendant publicity in Union newspapers may have inspired Nast's Christmastime tableaux.[14]

The artist depicted the non-military aspects of a Union drummer boy's life as he changed from a crying child on departure to a confident young man upon return. Nast stressed the positives: washing, eating, corresponding, and reassuring readers of camaraderie and protection by a group of caring soldiers. However, the bottom scene is questionable; in the unlikely event that a drummer boy was on the battlefield during action, he probably would have been helping with the wounded or running errands, not marching with the troops except possibly at the commencement of a battle before the fighting began.

HW December 19, 1863 805

THE DRUMMER BOY OF OUR REGIMENT —EIGHT WAR SCENES.

HW October 24, 1863 676

THE LIFE OF A SPY—IN NINE TABLEAUX.

Occasionally, Nast used his vignette format to focus on a particular segment of army life. *The Life of a Spy* illustrated the ups and downs of that occupation, utilizing the Napoleonic "Who Goes There" — the image in his aunt's bedroom in Landau — for one of the nine vignettes.

Chapter 10
Emancipation

Before the Proclamation

The question of how Lincoln would deal with the slavery issue was the elephant in the room from the day he was nominated for President. While Nast was in Italy with Garibaldi, *Harper's Weekly* published a cartoon comparing Lincoln to Charles Blondin, a famous French acrobat and tightrope walker, who had crossed the Niagara River the year before. It captured the unease of the black man on Lincoln's shoulders, as well as the indecision on the candidate's face as he resolutely balanced himself with the Constitution.

As discussed previously, in May 1861, General Benjamin Butler's order to treat escaped slaves engaged in military activity as "contrabands of war" became unofficial, and then official policy.* Sixteen months later, Lincoln essentially utilized Butler's rationale when he issued the Preliminary Emancipation Proclamation. The President emphasized that his freeing the slaves was a military strategy — to strengthen the Union while depleting the Confederacy of manpower — and de-emphasized any humanitarian considerations.

However, by declaring emancipation, Lincoln also inhibited England and France from recognizing or aiding the Confederacy. All previous political, economic or philosophical considerations were trumped by the proposed elimination of slavery.

HW August 25, 1860 544

THE COMING MAN'S PRESIDENTIAL CAREER, A LA BLONDIN.
MOTTO. —DON'T GIVE UP THE SHIP.

The four Border States — Missouri, Kentucky, Maryland and Delaware — contained more than 400,000 slaves, or about 10% of the four million total. If Missouri or Kentucky got upset about potentially losing its slaves and consequently joined the Confederacy, its action could have proved a tipping point. Moreover, Lincoln's war powers as Commander-in-Chief could only be used against states that had actually seceded, and did not apply to the Border States.[1]

In March 1862, Lincoln asked Congress to provide financial assistance to any of the four Border States that would agree to gradually emancipate their slaves in return for compensation of about $300 each to their owners. If they accepted, Lincoln favored a policy called Colonization which would have transported the freed slaves to Africa or the Caribbean area. Congress approved a month later, but the Border States never did.[2]

* See p. 93-94

NYIN April 12, 1862 308

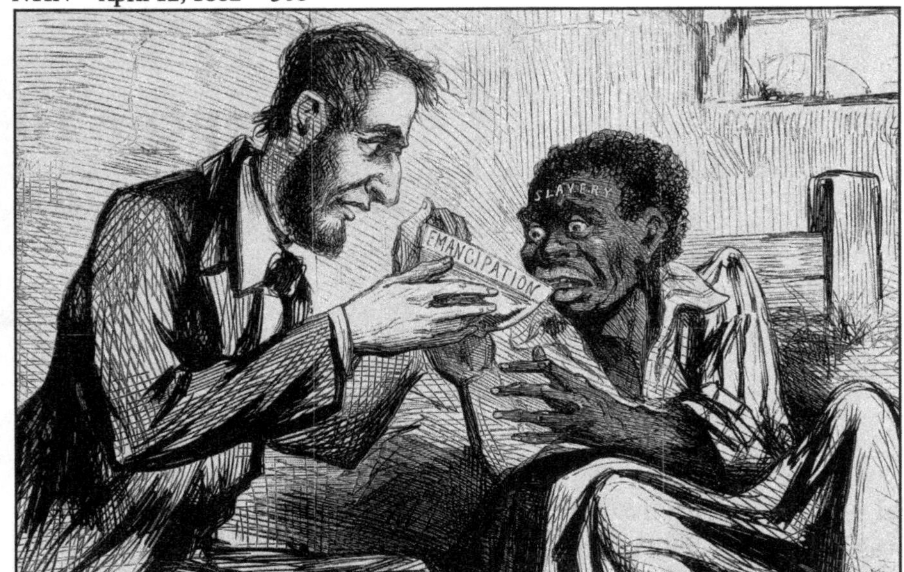

DOCTOR LINCOLN'S NEW ELIXIR OF LIFE —FOR THE SOUTHERN STATES.

Nast drew a crude but forceful cartoon for the *Illustrated News* while he was nearing the end of his time there. He used the word emancipation — a first for him — as it began to replace "abolition" in the Northern vocabulary.

In May 1862, another of Lincoln's mistake-prone generals, David Hunter, ordered slavery abolished entirely in South Carolina, Georgia and Florida. As he had done with General John Fremont in Missouri the year before, the President reversed Hunter's edict, and made it clear that he alone would be responsible for any decision on emancipation.

After General McClellan's fifteen-week Peninsular Campaign ended disastrously at Malvern Hill on July 1, 1862, his failure to capture Richmond made it apparent to Lincoln that there would be no quick end to the Rebellion. Recognizing that all-out war would be required to win, Lincoln made a strategic military decision — not a moral one — to use his war powers to free all 3.5 million slaves under Confederate control. Doing so would add more than 100,000 men to the Union ranks, while enabling whites currently in support activities like cooks, teamsters or hospital workers, to become front-line soldiers; ex-slaves also would prove to be good infantry men. Equally important, the Confederacy which used slaves to support its armies in just about every way except the actual firing of its guns, would now find some of those roles more difficult to fill.

Lincoln presented his emancipation proposal to his approving Cabinet in July. However, William Seward wisely advised waiting until after a military victory so it didn't look like a desperation measure, and the President concurred.

Antietam

On the night of September 4-5, General Robert E. Lee invaded Maryland en route to the Battle of Antietam. Alfred Waud painted an on-the-spot watercolor and sent his picture to *Harper's*.

Nast built on Waud's painting to evoke the drama of a gigantic rebel army stealthily crossing the Potomac by moonlight to gain a foothold on Union ground for the first time. Lee expected a royal welcome from Maryland's civilian population; he did not receive it (although Nast showed a cheering sympathizer). Lee moved on to "the bloodiest single day of the war" at Antietam, where more than 5,000 men died and another 21,000 were wounded or missing. The issue with Nast's illustration in it was on the newsstand a week earlier, three days after the Battle of Antietam took place, but before it was depicted in the weeklies.

HW September 27, 1862 613

THE REBEL ARMY CROSSING THE FORDS OF THE POTOMAC FOR THE INVASION OF MARYLAND.

HW October 4, 1862 C

GENERAL MCCLELLAN ENTERING THE TOWN OF FREDERICK, MARYLAND—THE POPULAR WELCOME.

McClellan should have won a clear-cut victory at Antietam because he had more troops (75,000 vs. 52,000) and an advance copy of Lee's plans which a Confederate soldier had lost. By procrastinating beforehand and not following up aggressively afterwards, he let Lee escape back to Virginia. Nevertheless, McClellan was considered the victor and Nast depicted him on the cover of the next issue receiving a hero's welcome in Frederick, Maryland.

Finally on November 7, Lincoln fired McClellan and replaced him with Ambrose Burnside. That action took place the day before Nast's untimely picture of "Little Mac" Making His Rounds appeared in the post-dated issue of the *Weekly*.

The Proclamation

Although the victory at Antietam was not decisive — as it could have been under a general like Ulysses Grant — it was still sufficient for Lincoln to proclaim that all slaves in states and/or territory within states controlled by the Confederacy would be emancipated on January 1, 1863.

Nast put a great deal of effort into his portrayal of Emancipation. The preliminary sketch in his Civil War scrapbook suggests that he began work shortly after Lincoln's September announcement.[3] His strong double-page allegory was twice rejected by John Bonner, the *Weekly's* pro-slavery editor. In the post-dated September 27 issue — available before the news of the Antietam victory or the Preliminary Proclamation was known — Bonner's editorial was captioned "Not an Abolition War." It resolutely emphasized: "The object of this war is restoration of the Union." However, three months later when the Emancipation Proclamation went into effect, Fletcher Harper saw to it that Bonner could no longer block Nast. By the end of 1863, Bonner was gone and George William Curtis, a strong abolitionist who had authored "The Lounger" column in the *Weekly* for five years, began his thirty-year career as editor.

Harper's Weekly printed the complete text of the Proclamation, as well as Winslow Homer's *A Shell in the Rebel Trenches* which clearly was timed to emphasize the utility of slaves at the front.

HW January 17, 1863 36

A SHELL IN THE REBEL TRENCHES.

The Emancipation of the Negroes finally emerged as a dramatic allegory in the next issue. The dominant center highlighted "a negro's free and happy home" where "the reward of faithful labor . . . belongs to the laborer only;" it included a framed image of Lincoln and a banjo on the wall, with "Union" inscribed on the stove. Below, Father Time had Baby New Year in his lap, who struck the shackles from the ex-slave on his knees. The horrors of slave life — whipping, branding, auctioning, being shot, chased by dogs — were depicted in excruciating detail on the left, contrasted with the benefits of public schools and paid work opposite.

Nast reached new artistic heights with his symbolized visualization of what the Proclamation would mean. No other illustrator or caricaturist of his era used such dramatic realism, detailed facial expressions and so few explanatory words — Public Sale of Negroes, Cashier, Public School — to capture its essence. His sketches spoke for themselves.

Eight years earlier, Theodor Kaufmann had inculcated the evils of slavery into his fourteen-year old public school-dropout pupil, while teaching him about history painting. How well Tommy learned!

HW January 24, 1863 56-57

THE EMANCIPATION OF THE NEGROES, JANUARY, 1863
THE PAST AND THE FUTURE. Drawn By Mr. Thomas Nast.

Nast's 247-page scrapbook in the John Hay Library at Brown University included 234 pencil sketches, 32 wash drawings and more than 600 cartes de visite, primarily from the Civil War, and mostly in chronological order. Significantly, the page after his sketch of the Emancipation Proclamation contained a wash painting of *Kingdom Comin'*, highlighting a black family's celebration. Nast emphasized the new era via the man at the forefront reading the *Tribune*. (In December 1864, *Kingdom Comin'* was on the cover of accompanying sheet music).

KINGDOM COMIN'.
We moved our things into Massa's parlor just to keep it while he's gone.

Consequences

Some of the first black soldiers in the Union army were South Carolina Sea Island Negroes who were freed as contrabands in November 1861. The official report of a colonel of the First Regiment of South Carolina Volunteers (colored) praised their valor in various victories in interior Georgia and Florida: "There is a fiery energy about them beyond anything of which I have ever read . . . It requires the strictest discipline to hold them in hand." Nast imagined and depicted *A Negro Regiment in Action* in a double-page illustration accompanying the *Harper's* article.

HW March 14, 1863 168

A NEGRO REGIMENT IN ACTION.

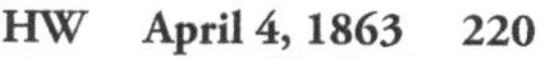

HW April 4, 1863 220

ARRIVAL OF A FEDERAL COLUMN AT A PLANTERS HOUSE IN DIXIE.

Three weeks later, *The Arrival of a Federal Column at a Planter's House in Dixie* showed unemancipated slaves in a non-threatening domestic environment because their white owners and overseers were away at war. The accompanying explanation, extracted from a Union "officer's letter in Dixie," noted that "These negroes . . . come and evince the most comical and unsophisticated manifestations of delight at our appearance." The facial expressions on Nast's characters tell the story well in a scene that was more like a book illustration than a wartime picture, and was later developed into a painting. (See p. 188)

Drawing Rations was notable for the black cook with a spoon in his hand, watching over his motley clientele with a look of concern on his face but confidence in his stance. This probably was the first time Nast drew a black person as just another unhighlighted character in a racially integrated scenario. However, his intent was clear because he drew a preliminary sketch of the cook by himself. (Now in his scrapbook.)

HW August 22, 1863 540

THE ARMY OF THE POTOMAC —DRAWING RATIONS.

As black soldiers proved their worth in battle, Nast depicted their integration into military life, a step beyond emancipation. His last illustration of life in the Army — *The Halt* — showed a white officer with his arm around a black helper at a pump. On the pump's other side, another black helper waited his turn, while a white surgeon filled his bucket. The three blacks in the picture, including a young boy, could be identified by their features as well as their skin color, but there was no hint of caricature or stereotyping in their appearance. Both Nast and the blacks had come a long way since his 1861 caricatures in the *New York Illustrated News*. Appearing in late September, the drawing was meant to reinforce the growing competence and success of the Union armies under Grant and Sherman.

HW October 1, 1864 628

THE HALT. —Drawn By Thomas Nast.

Gettysburg

During the first week of May 1863, Lee and Stonewall Jackson won a masterful victory over the Union army, now commanded by Joseph Hooker, at Chancellorsville, Virginia. (Lincoln had replaced Ambrose Burnside with Hooker after Burnside's disastrous defeat at Fredericksburg the previous December.) However, the victory proved pyrrhic for the Confederacy when Jackson was shot and mortally wounded by one of his own soldiers while reconnoitering at twilight.

Nevertheless, Lee, buoyed with over-confidence, crossed the Potomac with 75,000 men in June, to invade Pennsylvania and win a decisive battle. He counted on facing the same dazed Hooker he had beaten at Chancellorsville, but Lincoln replaced Hooker with George Meade three days before the battle. The two armies met at Gettysburg on July 1-3, and Lee lost. Gettysburg, along with Antietam, turned out to be the most critical Union victories of the entire war. Losses in either almost certainly would have changed its outcome.

Nast immediately gave Meade his due in *Phunny Phellow*.

PP August 1863 16

The Hero of Gettysburg.

American Antiquarian Society

On Gettysburg's second day, political General Dan Sickles almost cost the Union its critical victory. Smart — but egotistical, reckless and immoral to an extreme — Sickles deliberately disobeyed Meade's orders to hold his position on the heights of Little Round Top, and moved his 10,000-man Third Corps into the exposed Peach Orchard and adjoining Wheat Field, where his men were decimated by enemy fire.

HW May 25, 1867 324

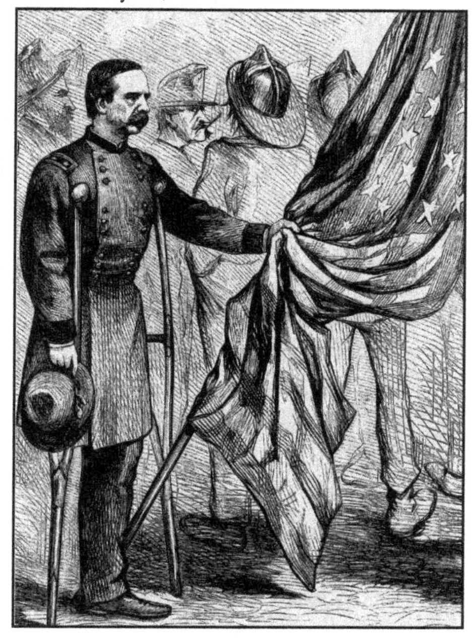

The Confederates almost capitalized on his blunder by charging the superior vacated space and taking control of the battle, but literally fell a few minutes short of doing so. Sickles' personal bravery on the field, plus his political connections — ultimately won him the Congressional Medal of Honor; he was probably more deserving of a court-martial. Of course, he blamed Meade for his own fiasco.

In addition to his reputation for military judgment, Sickles lost most of his right leg to a cannon ball, and came close to dying. (His conceit led him to donate his severed limb to the Army Medical Museum.) He was readily identifiable on his crutches in future Nast cartoons, as he often defied authority and was fired from other government positions. However, in 1876 he would play a key role in the post-election scramble for the Presidency.

Missing the Action

Gettysburg also turned out to be exasperating for Nast. *Harper's* sent its artist to find the coming battle and provide illustrations of it. He left by train for Philadelphia en route to Harrisburg on July 1, with the paper's letter of introduction (signed by editor John Bonner six months before George William Curtis replaced him), stating he had been "detailed for action." That night, he sent the *Weekly* six Philadelphia recruiting scenes with emphasis on enlisting colored soldiers.

Nast met up with a British cousin of his wife, arriving in Harrisburg, the state capital and a key railroad hub, on the afternoon of July 2. The artillery was blasting away forty miles to the south, during the second day of the battle at Gettysburg. Sallie's cousin was wearing a Confederate signal flag as a sash on his backside, and he and Nast were arrested as suspicious persons or even possible spies. With the Harpers apparently unreachable to verify Nast's authenticity over the coming weekend, he spent the next three days confined, frustrated and miserable. When he was finally released on Monday, July 6, the battle was over and there was nothing live to sketch. Fortunately for the *Weekly*, Alfred Waud did a splendid job of on-site coverage.

Draft Riots

By early 1863, it became obvious to President Lincoln and Congress that the Union Army needed more men than volunteers could supply. Military reverses, sickness, desertions, and low morale were significant problems. Congress responded by passing the Enrollment Act, which authorized the president to draft men for a period of up to three years, and created the bureaucracy to do so. It also allowed draftees who could pay either a $300 commutation fee or, alternatively, provide a substitute, to escape the draft, thereby inflaming those who had no way out.

New York City was a tinderbox with its resentful and volatile Irish population also worried about freed blacks coming North and taking their jobs as laborers. On Saturday July 11, the first draftees' names were drawn at the provost-marshal's headquarters. The names were published in the Sunday papers, and the pot began to boil. The next day, the worst riots that have ever occurred in this country exploded throughout the city and lasted four days. They were finally put down with the help of several regiments of soldiers who were ordered back from Gettysburg; it was their absence from the city that enabled the rioting to last as long as it did.

Monday's arson, assault and murder was primarily the work of potential Irish conscripts and their friends and relatives, including many blood-thirsty women. By Wednesday, criminal elements took the lead in looting, lynching and other pillage. The police were attacked and killed, and no home or business that the mobs associated with blacks or other anti-Irish social or political classes was safe. About 120 people died, including 21 blacks, several of whom were lynched. Property damage was extensive.

Although he had been unable to locate the war in Pennsylvania, Nast returned home on Sunday to find that the war effectively had come to him in New York. Sallie and one-year old Julia, along with his mother, were waiting for him in their Yorkville home on 89th Street near First Avenue.

Of all the horrendous atrocities committed by the mob during the riot, the most infamous was the burning of the Colored Orphan Asylum in the late afternoon of Monday, the first day. The building usually was home to six to eight hundred children, all of whom were safely evacuated due to the quick thinking of the orphanage's leadership.[4] Located on Fifth Avenue between 43rd and 44th Street, just north of today's New York Public Library, its property extended to Sixth Avenue. It was only two blocks from the 44th Street home that Tom and Sallie had left ten weeks earlier.

Nast probably saw about 2,000 rioters attacking the Asylum. They ransacked the four-story building and its two three-story wings, even carrying away the children's clothing, before setting it on fire. He sketched the horrific scene — no allegory . . . yet.

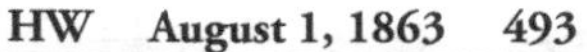

HW August 1, 1863 493

THE RIOTS AT NEW YORK —THE RIOTERS BURNING AND SACKING THE COLORED ORPHAN ASYLUM.

HW August 1, 1863 484

The *Weekly* had ten more ghastly illustrations in the same issue. Nast probably drew four of them and may have assisted on others. Understandably, none were signed.

One horrific sketch that became a symbol depicted *Hanging a Negro in Clarkson Street*. The innocent cartman was beaten insensible, hung and burned. Nast probably did not see this scene but recreated it from newspaper accounts, as he did with the two below.

HANGING A NEGRO IN CLARKSON STREET.

HW August 1, 1863 485

THE DEAD SERGEANT IN TWENTY-SECOND STREET.

DRAGGING COLONEL O'BRIEN'S BODY THROUGH THE MUD.

By Friday, the city was relatively calm, although the destruction was widespread. (Damaged property, which exceeded $30,000,000 in today's dollars, took years to be restored.) The provost-marshal's headquarters was in ashes, the rioters were exhausted, and the 4,000 soldiers returned from Gettysburg had restored basic order.

The black population of about 12,000 was devastated. Although volunteers provided some monetary relief, its sense of belonging was shattered and more than one-fifth left the city. Except for a few thieves caught red-handed, most of the culprits escaped prison. The draft, which had been suspended on Wednesday, was resumed a month later.

Horatio Seymour

Democratic Governor Seymour was the man to whom the stricken city looked to for leadership. He had been elected in 1862 on an anti-administration platform — as the Union army suffered continuing disappointments under McClellan — and was in tune with the Northern Copperheads who opposed the war, abolition and conscription.

In contrast to his fellow governors, Seymour deliberately avoided contact with the draft authorities. Unaware that conscription would commence the next day, he went on vacation to Long Branch on Friday, July 10, and didn't arrive in the embattled city until mid-day Tuesday. His first act proclaimed the city in a state of insurrection and ordered the rioters to desist.

HW October 31, 1868 700

MATCHED.(?) "A mob can revolutionize as well as a government."

GOVERNOR SEYMOUR'S SPEECH TO THE NEW YORK RIOTERS.

My friends,—I have come down from the quiet of the country to see what was the difficulty, to learn what all this trouble was concerning the draft. Let me assure you that I am your friend. [Uproarious cheering.] You have been my friends. [Cries of "Yes," "Yes" — "That's so"—"We are, and will be again."] And now I assure you, my fellow citizens, that I am here to show you a test of my friendship. [Cheers.] I wish to inform you that I have sent my adjutant-general to Washington to confer with the authorities there, and to have this draft suspended and stopped. [Vociferous cheers.] I now ask you as good citizens to wait for his return, and I assure you that I will do all that I can to see that there is no inequality, and no wrong done any one.—*New York Tribune, July 14, 1863.*

Next, Seymour addressed the mob in City Hall Park, calling them "My Friends." While his memorable salutation may have made sense under the circumstances, he would never live it down. When he ran for president against Grant in 1868. Nast repeatedly stigmatized him with it. He added the imagery of the burning Asylum and the hanging Negro to several cartoons, and an Irish ruffian looking at a dead black child in this one.

The riots had a critical legacy for Nast. Most important was increasing antipathy against the Irish, whose murderous behavior from men, women and even children — as depicted in the sketches — he would never forget. His anti-Irish feelings probably were originally kindled by childhood bullying, enhanced by gang warfare, and perhaps nurtured by the Nativist inclinations of the Harpers. But the impact of the infuriated mobs who could physically threaten him, his family and his employer were branded in his memory, and would be reflected repeatedly in his future cartoons. The following year, he moved uptown to 125th Street in Harlem.

Vicksburg

On July 4, the day after victory at Gettysburg, General Grant accepted General John Pemberton's unconditional surrender at Vicksburg after a long siege and constant shelling. His brilliant campaign opened the Mississippi River for Union commerce while cutting the Confederacy in two. In October, Grant moved east with a newly-expanded division and captured Chattanooga in late November after several well-executed battles, including Lookout Mountain. Utilizing Theodore Davis's frontline sketches, Nast drew one scene from each campaign.

As a result of his victories in the west during the past two years — Fort Henry, Fort Donelson, Shiloh, Vicksburg and Chattanooga — Congress unanimously passed a resolution of thanks to Major-General Grant and awarded him a gold medal. Nast's idolizing allegory — his first close-up of his hero — showed Columbia pinning it on him.[5]

HW December 26, 1863 829

THE CAPTURE OF LOOKOUT MOUNTAIN —GENERAL HOOKER FIGHTING AMONG THE CLOUDS.

HW February 6, 1864 C

THANKS TO GRANT.

Chapter 11
The Election of 1864

Military Success

In March 1864, Grant was promoted to Lieutenant-General and, subsequently appointed General-in-Chief. The war effort remained relatively stagnant until early May when Grant dispatched William Sherman's forces to split the Confederacy again by capturing Atlanta, a major communications, supply and manufacturing hub. Grant ordered Sherman to inflict all the damage he could on the enemy's war resources, an instruction which Sherman interpreted broadly over a wide front. Northern morale remained low until Atlanta finally fell on September 1, after four months of devastation.

HW April 2, 1864 212

GENERAL SHERMAN'S REAR-GUARD.

Before and during his campaign, hundreds of contrabands came into Sherman's camps seeking protection, and also slowing his advance. Nast's early depiction of Sherman's dilemma portrayed the helpfulness of his new "rear-guard." In another truly integrated, non-stereotyped, caricature-free Civil War illustration, at least half a dozen wounded soldiers were being carried or cared for by members of escaped black families. His comprehensive, empathetic scenario undoubtedly was calculated to reinforce positive feelings about the military contributions of former slaves.

Also in early May, Grant took command of George Meade's Army of the Potomac to begin a costly series of battles of attrition against Robert E. Lee at the Wilderness, Spotsylvania and Cold Harbor. Nast's only illustration of the campaign depicted a determined Grant watching as a battle raged around him.[1] In June, he initiated a siege of Petersburg, the gateway to Richmond, which lasted ten months, ending when the city fell a week before Lee surrendered at Appomattox on April 9, 1865.

HW June 18, 1864 392-393

THE CAMPAIGN IN VIRGINIA — "ON TO RICHMOND!"

1866 Painting From Grand Masquerade Ball *

With the election only three months away and Atlanta still holding out, the first of three 1864 bell-ringer victories — critical for both military and political reasons — came on August 5 when Admiral David Farragut captured Mobile Bay. The 63-year old naval hero made history when, lashed to the rigging and warned about sunken mines, he commanded "Damn the torpedoes! Full speed ahead!" After that, Nast always included Farragut, along with Generals Phil Sheridan and Sherman, just below Grant in his pictorial pantheon of Union heroes. In an 1866 caricature, Farragut sat on a torpedo with shells bursting all around, and a grenade or small bomb in his hand.

Fernando Wood

When the Civil War began, the Democratic Party in the North was split between War Democrats who supported Lincoln's military efforts to restore the Union, and Peace Democrats who supported a negotiated settlement to end the fighting. In the opinion of Republicans and many War Democrats, it was frequently difficult to distinguish between war opposition per se and overt support for the South.

Confederate sympathizers were commonly called Copperheads (after the poisonous snake), a name which they reveled in and flaunted on badges and banners. Their leaders — especially New York Mayor Fernando Wood, Ohio Congressman Clement Vallandigham and Governor Horatio Seymour — were prime targets for Nast's attacks. They supported slavery, endorsed its expansion into Western territories, and opposed civil rights for free blacks.

Fernando Wood served two terms as Mayor (1855-58) and regained the office for the 1860-61 term. However, his Mozart Hall Party, a Democratic faction opposed to Tammany Hall, lost in the November 1861 election. Wood had also advocated that New York City should secede from the state. Nast drew an unsigned cartoon for the *Illustrated News,* showing the former "Mare" being presented to Jeff Davis.

NYIN December 16, 1861 119

THE NEW YORK HACK MARE WOOD.
The city having thrown the above animal overboard, and Mozart Stables being now closed, his friends are about presenting him to Jeff Davis. He being eminently qualified for secesh business.

In early 1860, Fernando bought the *New York Daily News* for his older brother Ben, and sold it to Ben soon after. Ben turned it into the country's highest-circulation daily, with most of its readership among the lower-middle working class. It not only railed against "King Abraham Africanus I," but also discouraged enlistments and encouraged desertions. The government prohibited its distribution through the mails, seized its railroad shipments, and forced the paper to cease publication for eighteen months, until May 1863. (In early 1865, the War Department concluded that Confederate spies had been transmitting coded messages through the personal columns in the *Daily News*.)

* See p. 158-161

After the Emancipation Proclamation took effect in January 1863, the Copperhead movement became more explosive. Some Democrats who had supported the War when it was about restoration of the Union, violently opposed it when abolition became an equal objective. Vitriolic editor Chauncey Burr, began publishing *The Old Guard*, a Copperhead magazine. The first issue — six months *before* the draft riots — featured an engraved portrait of Horatio Seymour, while later issues similarly honored Vallandigham, Fernando and Ben Wood, and Indiana Congressman Daniel Voorhees.[2]

In June, an unsigned cartoon (not by Nast) depicted Wood as the devil who wanted to be an angel. Fernando, the Prince of Peace, was thumbing his nose at the Union, while his pugilistic clerk, probably Clement Vallandigham, was about to open Pandora's box.

HW June 20, 1863 400

THE PEACE-PREACHER AND HIS CLERK.
Rev. Fernando Wood. "Peace on earth, and good-will to rebels."

HW January 2, 1864 16

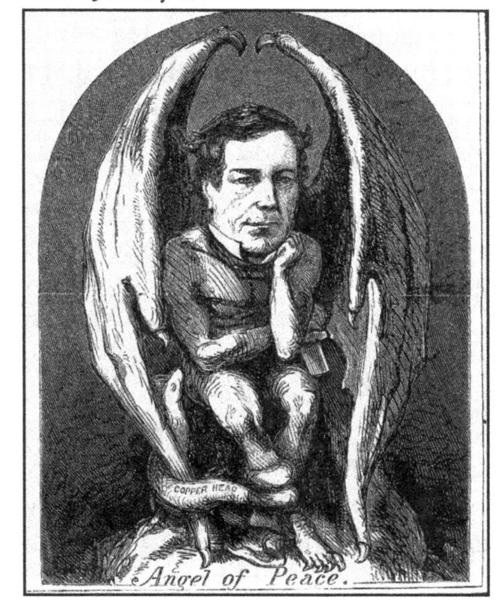

Six months later, Nast drew Wood as the *Angel of Peace* for the 1863 year-end issue of *Harper's Weekly*. Its double meaning played off the traditional New Year's symbol, as well as Wood's leadership role as a Peace Democrat, the polite name for his Copperhead faction. However, Wood's talon-edged wings, hair curled with demonic horns, and a namesake snake around his legs were less than subtle.

What is important about this small and otherwise insignificant cartoon is that Nast evidently considered it to be his first published caricature for *Harper's Weekly*. Nast always identified himself as a caricaturist — rather than a cartoonist — so this was a landmark for him.[3]

Clement Vallandigham

Vallandigham was the national leader of the Copperheads. An Ohio lawyer and legislator, he finished his second term in Congress in 1862 by strongly opposing Lincoln and the Republican majority. The next year, General Ambrose Burnside had him arrested for his traitorous speeches. He was convicted of treason, but Lincoln shrewdly exiled him to the Confederacy. Jeff Davis didn't want him either, so he made his way to Canada after running the blockade.

While in Canada, and after he returned to Ohio in June 1864, he participated in plotting riots, robberies and even abortive insurrections against the Union. He was instrumental in the Democratic Party's nomination of George McClellan to oppose Lincoln in 1864, and selected fellow Ohioan, George Pendleton, to be McClellan's running mate. McClellan, now 38, had been unemployed since Lincoln relieved him of command almost twenty-two months before. He was living in his home in New York, and thought himself better qualified than Lincoln to conclude the war and run the country.

The Democrats were energized by the stagnant war effort, as well as by significant public opposition to emancipation, the draft, the use of black troops, and the curtailment of habeas corpus and other civil liberties. If not for the flack he took for his role in the draft riots, Horatio Seymour probably would have been their candidate. Seymour did set the stage for his own nomination four years later by serving as chairman of the 1864 convention held in Chicago at the end of August.

Vallandigham prepared and enabled the Democratic "Peace Platform." His planks called for an immediate cessation of hostilities, a convention of all the states, and the restoration of peace upon the "basis of the Federal Union of the States." He understood that an armistice that withdrew the blockade could have allowed the confederacy to resupply from England and France, rebuild its Treasury, and discourage any military resumption. Implied was that states' rights would prevail and slavery would be reestablished.

The platform also included a plank that described the Civil War as "four years of failure." McClellan's continuing feelings of allegiance to the soldiers he had commanded, on top of the concurrent Confederate loss of Atlanta, made this declaration impossible for him to swallow. In his September 8 letter of acceptance, he repudiated Vallandigham's "failure" plank, stating: " could not look in the faces of gallant comrades of the army and navy . . . . and tell them that their labor and the sacrifice of our slain and wounded brethren had been in vain."

Meanwhile, Lincoln had been unanimously nominated in Baltimore in early June. By choosing Democrat Andrew Johnson of Tennessee as his running mate, the newly-formed National Union Party of Republicans and War Democrats sought to broaden electoral support. However, Lincoln's prospects looked dismal through August, primarily because the war was dragging on. When Sherman finally captured Atlanta on September 1, the tide turned. For the first time since Andrew Jackson won a second term in 1832, there was a reasonable chance that a sitting president could be reelected.

The Election

The impact of Nast's two cartoons on Lincoln's victory was discussed and illustrated in the Introduction.* ***Compromise with the South* was arguably the single most important and influential cartoon of his career, and *The Chicago Platform* reinforced it.**

Two more hard-hitting Nast cartoons appeared in the issue available a few days before the election. The cover story described forging of military votes, including accounts of Copperheads copying the names of dead Union soldiers from their graves and filling in the blank ballots with them, as well as changing and destroying military ballots.[4] The conspiracy was documented by Republican undercover investigators prior to the election, utilizing infiltration and intercepted mail. **This was Nast's maiden effort on fraudulent voting, which would become a recurring topic for him over the next two decades.**

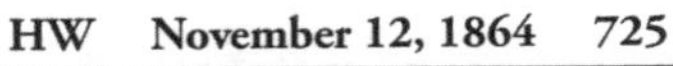

HW November 12, 1864 725

HOW THE COPPERHEADS OBTAIN THEIR VOTES.

* See p. v-xii

HW November 12, 1864 728

Election-Day, 8th November, symbolized the voting process. Columbia resolutely cast her ballot for "Union Lincoln" while her opposite, "Peace" (for Peace Democrats) with her hands tied behind her back by the "Traitors North" devil — copperhead snakes growing out of his head — looked disconsolately down. Nast referenced his kick-off cartoon of two months earlier with "No Compromise" featured below the title. Vignettes below showed soldiers and respectable citizens voting for Lincoln, contrasted with their Irish and ward-heeler counterparts casting ballots for McClellan (right).

Lincoln won a resounding victory with 70% of the military vote, 55% of the popular vote and an Electoral College landslide of 212 to 21. McClellan won only New Jersey and the Border States of Kentucky and Delaware. Republicans also consolidated control of Congress: 42/10 in the Senate and 149/42 in the House, an important factor in the upcoming struggle over Reconstruction.

Thanksgiving

Nast drew only two more cartoons before the Civil War ended and Lincoln was assassinated. Both were allegorical, full of symbolic detail, and featured Lincoln as a commanding central figure — the only times he played that role in a Nast cartoon during his Presidency.

Thanksgiving-Day honored Lincoln by bringing his family and his two secretaries together for the sole time in a Nast cartoon. The secretaries, John Nicolay and John Hay, who had been with the president since his Springfield days, appropriately stood immediately behind him. The cheering youngster was eleven-year old Tad. At the left was Mary Todd Lincoln, still mourning the loss of her son Willie two years earlier; Nast whitened her face to draw attention to her, but gave her an impassive expression.

On the far left, (with his hat next to Mary's face), Lincoln was saluted by a man who closely resembled Giuseppe Garibaldi. Nast apparently had his first hero hailing his second.

The officer shaking the President's right hand (probably Grant) had his left foot planted on a Confederate flag. This essentially mirrored Jeff Davis's foot in *Compromise with the South*.

HW December 3, 1864 776-777

The seven additional stories Nast told in his vignettes — with a minimum of words — are especially noteworthy. He began by thanking God for Union victories (upper right), and for Maryland freeing her slaves on November 1 — the first of the four Border States to do so.[5]

Napoleon III of France and John Bull were brooding in Europe, while Davis and Lee did the same in Rebeldom. Meanwhile "Blessed Peace-Makers" Sherman, Sheridan, Grant, Meade and Butler relaxed under a tent.

In Europe

In Rebeldom

Blessed are the Peace-Makers

A touch of Nast realism was apparent in the vignette at the lower left, While two of his comrades enjoyed their turkey dinner, a guard was on full alert with his rifle sighted, a reminder that the war was not yet over.

IN THE FIELD.

Chapter 12
Victory and Assassination

Christmas

The Union continued to enjoy major military success. After Thanksgiving, George Thomas destroyed Confederate General John Bell Hood's army in Franklin and Nashville, Tennessee. Thomas was immediately added to Nast's pantheon of Union generals.

Also in the weeks before Christmas, smashing Union victories in the Southeast, totally changed both Union and Confederate outlooks. Sherman — or "Billy the Conqueror" as Nast referred to him in his sketchbook — left Atlanta a week after the election, and completed his 285-mile "March to the Sea" when he arrived in Savannah on December 21. Along the way, the massive, two-wing operation destroyed railroads, crops, livestock, homes, farms and anything else considered of use to the Confederate war effort.

Except for the highlighted celebration of the happy Nast family in a separate vignette (at the bottom of the picture)* — of the 42 cartoons relating to Christmas that Thomas Nast drew for *Harper's Weekly, The Union Christmas Dinner* probably had the least to do with the holiday and the most to do with politics. Its allegorical political message was twofold: overtly, Sectional Reconciliation; more subtly but equally important, Reconstruction Policy.

The obvious focal theme was President Lincoln welcoming Davis, Lee and their associates to the Union Banquet Hall. The Northern governors — all recognizable — were seated at a long table opposite a row of empty chairs, each reserved for a specific Confederate state. An olive branch at the upper left and the return of the prodigal son at the upper right completed the allegorical imagery. If the Confederacy would lay down its arms, surrender unconditionally and be contrite, the Union — with Lincoln as its dominant forgiving father — would welcome Rebeldom back into the fold.[1]

HW December 31, 1864 840-841

* See p. 64

The prophetic vignette at the lower left anticipated Lee's surrender to Grant at Appomattox by exactly 100 days. Sherman was on Grant's right with George Meade, who won at Gettysburg and was Grant's second-in-command in Virginia, next to him. Thomas appeared for the first time in a Nast cartoon, receiving Hood's sword.

Confederate General Joseph Johnston was barely discernible behind Hood, who had replaced Johnston six weeks before the fall of Atlanta. In February 1865, Johnston was reassigned and led the Army of the Tennessee through the Carolina Campaign. His surrender to Sherman on April 26, seventeen days after Appomattox, marked the closing chapter of the war.

Equally important but less apparent, Nast was supporting Lincoln's Reconstruction policy in his struggle with Congress over the best way to reintegrate the seceded states back into the Union. Lincoln had pocket-vetoed the Wade-Davis Reconstruction bill, passed five months earlier, because its terms were too harsh. After his reelection, Congress refused to count the Electoral College votes or seat the representatives from Arkansas, Louisiana and Tennessee, as called for by Lincoln's plan. Nast emphasized Lincoln's policy by including a quote from his annual message to Congress on December 6, (on the floor in front of Lincoln): "The door has been for a full year open to all." While not as forcefully direct as *Compromise with the South*, or as complex as *The Chicago Platform*, *The Union Christmas Dinner* was a prime example of the way that Nast blended his artistic talent and political persuasiveness into a new approach to editorial journalism.

On December 13, armed with a letter of introduction from Curtis to Lincoln, Nast visited the White House and met briefly with the President.[2] It is conceivable that he showed Lincoln the preliminary sketch for the illustration. It is also likely that one of the reasons that Hay and Nicolay made their only appearance in a Nast cartoon — *Thanksgiving Day* — was to facilitate Nast's White House appearance.

Nast's objective was to see whether he could get an official commission to create history paintings for the Capitol which was then undergoing renovation. After being referred by another secretary to the Commissioner of Public Buildings, Nast was told that no work on the Capitol had been done during the past year — understandably — and only Congress could authorize future efforts. "So you see my darling," Nast wrote Sallie, "Here is no chance for your dear little hero."

Two days later, Nast went to Fortress Monroe. While there, he saw Alfred Waud and told him he planned to go to the front for a few days. Waud's comment was "God knows you need it," according to a letter Nast wrote to Sallie on December 15. However, General Benjamin Butler had sailed two days earlier in his unsuccessful expedition to capture Fort Fisher and close the port of Wilmington, North Carolina, the Confederacy's last remaining "gateway to the world." Nast missed the boat but he did get a good look at Fortress Monroe, where Jefferson Davis would be imprisoned about five months later, and pilloried by the cartoonist.

Surrender

The first half of April 1865 was dominated by two "A" news events — Appomattox and Assassination — separated by only five days. The second story so overwhelmed the first that neither *Harper's* or *Leslie's* gave Lee's surrender to Grant anywhere near the attention it merited. (The *New York Illustrated News* had faded away in August 1864.)

April 2 saw the successful end of the ten-month siege of Petersburg, the gateway to Richmond, as Grant completed his encirclement of the city. Lee evacuated Petersburg late that night.

While in church on that same disastrous Sunday morning, Davis received an urgent message from Lee, to get out of Richmond immediately. The city formally surrendered about four hours after Petersburg did so.

President Lincoln had been in the area for a few days prior, staying with Grant at City Point. Alfred Waud's back-page sketch of Lincoln's writing "All seems well with us" on a drum turned out the be the last depiction of the President — drawn live before his death — in any illustrated weekly. It was the same issue that contained the "Domestic Intelligence" report on Lee's surrender at Appomattox, and was post-dated to the day he died.

HW April 15, 1865 240

FROM OUR SPECIAL WAR CORRESPONDENT.
City Point, VA., April—, 8:30 A.M.
"All seems well with us."—A. Lincoln.

The next day, Lincoln joined Grant in Petersburg. Learning that Davis had fled, the Commander-in-Chief asked Admiral David Porter to take him up the James River to the Confederate Capital.

No photographer could move his wagon of supplies quickly enough to keep up with Grant's rolling victories or Lincoln's visit to Richmond. *Harper's* had artists Waud in Petersburg and A.W. Warren in Richmond, and a combined six illustrated pages from both cities in its post-dated April 22 issue — but no coverage of Lincoln's visit. (Neither did Leslie have an artist in Richmond, but he faked a picture credited to field artist Joseph Becker, but actually drawn by Albert Berghaus in New York.)

A year later, in honoring what would have been Lincoln's fifty-seventh birthday, Nast drew an illustration of *President Lincoln Entering Richmond, April 4, 1865*. An accompanying editorial made it clear that Nast's visual tribute was timed to coincide with historian George Bancroft's memorial address to a joint session of Congress delivered on February 12. For once, he had adequate time to prepare, so his research, creative imagination and careful execution made this the best example of "history painting" that he ever drew for *Harper's*.

According to Admiral Porter, the carriage expected to convey Lincoln and his party never showed up. Accordingly, they walked, accompanied by twelve of the ship's crew with bayonets fixed on their rifles. Nast's picture showed Lincoln holding his son's hand — it was Tad's twelfth birthday — with Admiral Porter just behind him and the naval guard out of sight. Eventually a four-horse carriage and a military escort caught up with them and brought them through the smoldering center of the Confederate capitol to Jeff Davis's residence. Lincoln sat at his rival's desk in a very personal victory celebration.

This was the first of only three occasions where Nast portrayed Lincoln as a flesh-and-blood person rather than as an emblematic figure (as he did in his 1864 Thanksgiving and Christmas allegorical cartoons). Nast captured the unique magic of the moment as eyewitness reporter Charles Coffin described it: "President Lincoln walked in silence acknowledging the salutes of officers and soldiers and of the citizens, black and white! It was the man of the people among the people. It was the great deliverer meeting the delivered . . . such wild indescribable ecstatic joy I never witnessed."[3]

HW February 24, 1866 120-121

PRESIDENT LINCOLN ENTERING RICHMOND, APRIL 4, 1865.

Lee continued to suffer losses. After an exchange of correspondence with Grant, Lee surrendered to him on Sunday, April 9 in the home of Wilmer McLean in Appomattox Court House (the name of the village).[4]

There were no reporters, artists or photographers in McLean's parlor to record the historic event. Lee, accompanied only by his aide, Colonel Charles Marshall, was in full dress uniform. Grant, whose better clothes were in a wagon far in the rear, wore a private's blouse, along with mud-splattered boots and trousers. The only special artist at the scene was Alfred Waud. For whatever reason — maybe he was late, or else blocked from going inside — Waud apparently never entered the house. He did sketch Lee as he left, and also some of Grant' exultant troops as they chopped up trees and even furniture for souvenirs.

For its April 22 issue which went to press before Lincoln died, the *Weekly's* Domestic Intelligence column had all of four-plus inches of small type devoted to the "Surrender of Lee's Army." That was its total coverage of the war's climactic event for the next half year — except for Nast who was the only artist to depict the surrender scene on a reasonably current timetable.

Almost seven months later, Colonel Batterby of the First New York Cavalry supplied *Harper's* with a vivid description of Appomattox and its immediate prelude, including at least five sketches. (Why the lag is unknown.) *Harper's* brief introduction to the text called "General Lee's Surrender at Appomattox Court House . . . *the most interesting event of the war.*" That "interesting event" couldn't compete with Lincoln's assassination, his elaborate and drawn-out funeral ceremonies, John Wilkes Booth's flight and death, and the capture and trial of his fellow conspirators. The *Illustrated London News*, quoting from the American daily papers, provided significantly more complete coverage. Finally, in the May 20 issue of *Harper's Weekly* — available in print about a month after the event — Nast's illustration appeared as part of an allegorical *Palm Sunday* cartoon. (Figuratively associating Lincoln's martyrdom with Christ's — both on Good Friday — was not unusual at the time.)

HW May 20, 1865 312-313

Nast probably had incomplete knowledge of who else was in the room with Grant, so he balanced his scenario with just Grant — wearing a dress coat and shined boots — and General John Rawlins.[5] Rawlins, who was about six-feet-five, towered over everybody even though he wasn't standing straight. However, Grant who was four inches shorter than Lee's six feet, was drawn an inch or so taller than the "Rebel General," as *Harper's* frequently referred to him. (Probably, this was Nast's intentional enhancement of his hero.)

On April 9, 1895 — exactly 30 years after Appomattox and almost ten years after Grant died — Nast completed *Peace In Union*, a nine-by-twelve foot picture of the participants and witnesses at the surrender. The picture had been commissioned the previous year by Herman Kohlsaat, a wealthy Chicago entrepreneur and friend of Nast, who knew Grant in 1860 when both of them and Rawlins lived in Galena. Kohlsaat donated Nast's masterpiece to the Galena public library on April 27, Grant's seventy-third birthday.

This time, he depicted Grant as shorter than Lee. In addition to Generals Phil Sheridan and Rawlins, the painting portrayed Lieutenant Colonel Ely Parker (between Grant and Rawlins on the right).[6]

Nast romanticized the picture by depicting Grant and his staff in dress uniforms.

Galena & U.S. Grant Museum, Galena, IL.

Left to Right: Gen. George A. Custer, Col. Theodore Bowers, Gen. Edward Ord, Col. Adam Badeau, Sheridan, Gen. Rufus Ingalls, Col. Horace Porter, Rawlins, Parker, Grant

Left to Right: Lee, Col. Charles Marshall, Col. Orville Babcock

PEACE IN UNION

Nast's Appomattox illustration in *Harper's Weekly* was informative and respectful, as befitted the sadness and gloom that pervaded the North. However, he reveled in using Lee for fodder in *Phunny Phellow* in a way that foretold the blooming caricaturist's post-war career. The cartoons below were drawn before Lincoln's assassination.

Nast anticipated Lee's surrender by almost a year.

After Appomattox, Nast celebrated with a double-page of Grant and his generals dancing around the cowering figures of Lee and Jeff Davis. Sheridan (left) and Sherman were high-kicking next to Grant, and Generals George Meade, Henry Halleck, George Thomas and Judson Kilpatrick were recognizable.

PP June 1864 C

General Grant.—-I've Rented This House From Abe Lincoln; And If You Don't Evacuate The Premises By 12 O'clock, I'll Take Possession By Main Force, For During The Last Three Years You've Been Most Troublesome.

PP May 1865 8-9

THE UNION QUADRILLE—LAST FIGURE—"ALL HANDS ROUND."

Uncle Sam's Rat Trap was in the same issue.

PP May 1865 6

Lee in Cage, Left to Right: Sherman, Thomas, Meade, Sheridan, Grant

UNCLE SAM'S RAT TRAP

Assassination

Lincoln was shot by John Wilkes Booth at 10:15 on Good Friday, April 14, while watching *Our American Cousin* at Ford's Theatre. He died at 7:22 A.M. the next morning in a house across the street from the theatre.

The normal closing dates for the next post-dated issue (April 22) would have been the Saturday of Lincoln's death. *Harper's Weekly* put an unattributed signed photograph of Booth on its cover, with an inside page depicting the assassination. Its readers could visualize Lincoln being shot, as well as Booth jumping to the stage for his escape out a rear door, where his horse stood waiting.

HW April 29, 1865 260

THE ASSASSINATION OF PRESIDENT LINCOLN AT FORD'S THEATRE ON THE NIGHT OF APRIL 14, 1865.

THE ASSASSINATION OF PRESIDENT LINCOLN AT FORD'S THEATRE —AFTER THE ACT.

Nast probably heard the news from Washington within a few hours and reacted with exceptional speed and feeling. He quickly made a pencil sketch of his proposed wood engraving at his home in Harlem, complete in every essential except for the grief-stricken figures of the soldier and sailor at the upper corners. Columbia was mourning at the martyred president's bier with her face covered. Normally, Sallie Nast would have posed but she was just thirteen days away from delivering Thomas Edwards Nast, (later known as Tom Jr.), their second child and first son, so Columbia's features were covered by her hand in this instance.

Nast raced downtown with his sketch to see the Harpers and reserve space in the next issue. The art deadline probably had passed, but he received an affirmative answer, provided he finished it in time. As he told an interviewer five years later, he worked all day Sunday and created a remarkably elegant double-page directly on a prepared woodblock.

In addition to the peak circulation of that issue of *Harper's Weekly* — in excess of 120,000 — Nast's illustration was engraved and sold separately as America mourned.

HW April 29, 1865 264-265

Nast had a second allegorical cartoon celebrating the end of the war in the same issue. He had taken a four-month "sabbatical" from *Harper's Weekly* to work on his paintings.[7] This re-introductory illustration was prepared in the five-day interim between Appomattox and Lincoln's murder and was already set to be printed. Called *The Eve of War — The Dawn of Peace*, it contrasted Fort Sumter in 1861 and 1865. Appearing opposite the depiction of Booth's attack and escape, it was anti-climactic.

For the next two months, Nast stressed religious aspects of life and death as Lincoln's funeral train travelled across the county. Memorial services were held in New York, Cleveland and Chicago, among other cities, before he was laid to rest in Springfield.

HW May 20, 1865 312

The President died the day before Easter, and Nast's *Palm Sunday* allegory pictured *The Saviour's Entry into Jerusalem.* (This was the first of the few times that Nast drew Jesus Christ in a *Harper's Weekly* illustration.) The text below offered an olive branch "to our erring and misguided brethren of the Southern states."

HW June 10, 1865 360-361

Thy Will Be Done **Our Savior**

Victory **Death**

EUROPE AND AMERICA.

Three weeks later, in a six-vignette memorial to "Our Martyred President" in *Victory and Death*, a black family prayed to Lincoln as "Our Savior." Another vignette showed his catafalque under a "Charity for All" Banner.

Nast waited two years to draw his last picture of Lincoln as a real person, timing it for the second anniversary of his death. On its cover page, the *Weekly* quoted an incident taken from *Six Months at the White House*, a book of reminiscences about the President which had been published in 1886 by Francis Bicknell Carpenter.[8]

Nast enjoyed drawing children as exemplified in his 1863 cartoon of the *Drummer Boy of Our Regiment*.* Now he illustrated *Abraham Lincoln and the Drummer Boy* as he would have done for a book. This is one of the few *Harper's Weekly* book-type illustrations that Nast drew, although he illustrated at least 110 books over the years for their authors or publishers.

HW April 27, 1867 264

ABRAHAM LINCOLN AND THE DRUMMER-BOY.

MR. LINCOLN AND THE DRUMMER BOY.
"Among the large number of persons waiting in the room to speak with Mr. Lincoln, on a certain day in November last, was a small, pale, delicate-looking boy, about thirteen years old. The President saw him standing, looking feeble and faint, and said—'Come here, my boy, and tell me what you want.' The boy advanced, placed his hand on the arm of the President's chair, and with bowed head and timid accents said: 'Mr. President, I have been a drummer in a regiment for two years, and my colonel got angry with me and turned me off; I was taken sick, and have been a long time in hospital. This is the first time I have been out, and I came to see if you could not do something for me.' The President looked at him kindly and tenderly, and asked him where he lived. 'I have no home,' answered the boy. 'Where is your father?' 'He died in the army,' was the reply. 'Where is your mother?' continued the President. 'My mother is dead also. I have no mother, no father, no brothers, no sisters, and,' bursting into tears, 'no friends—nobody cares for me.' Mr. Lincoln's eyes filled with tears, and he said to him, 'Can't you sell newspapers?' 'No,' said the boy, 'I am too weak, and the surgeon of the hospital told me I must leave, and I have no money, and no place to go to.' The scene was wonderfully affecting. The President drew forth a card, and addressing on it certain officials to whom his request was law, gave special directions 'to care for this poor boy.' The wan face of the little drummer lit up with a happy smile as he received the paper, and he went away convinced that he had one good and true friend, at least, in the person of the President."

Jefferson Davis

Of the many villains on Nast's lifetime list, Jeff Davis probably ranked first. He hated and despised Davis as a cowardly traitor who should have been tried, convicted and hanged for treason. Davis, a year younger than Lincoln, was a West Point graduate who after serving in the Mexican War, became a Mississippi planter, Congressman, Secretary of War (under Franklin Pierce), and Senator (the office he held when Mississippi seceded). He was inaugurated as provisional president of the Confederacy in Montgomery, Alabama in February 1861, and as president of the permanent government in Richmond a year later. Considered dictatorial and autocratic, he suffered from both ill health and ill temper.

After Petersburg fell to Grant, Davis fled south through Georgia and was captured on May 10 in Irwinsville, wearing his wife's overcoat and shawl. Cartoonists and illustrators, not including Nast, had great fun with that in *Harper's Weekly* and elsewhere. Secretary of War Edwin Stanton reportedly encouraged the cartoons, recognizing that humiliating Davis would dampen chances of the public's seeing him as a hero or a martyr.

---

* See p. 118

William Waud, Alf's brother, punned on the Confederacy's failure to gain recognition from England and France.

HW June 3, 1865 352

"AIN'T YOU GOING TO RECOGNIZE ME?"

However, the topic was too humorous for Nast to ignore entirely. His crude unsigned cartoon appeared on the cover of the July issue of *Phunny Phellow*.

PP July 1865

THE CAPTURE OF JEFF DAVIS OF THE C.S.A.

The *Weekly's* editorial page raged at Davis: "Booth, the murderer of one beloved man, at least died like a savage beast at bay. But Davis, with the blood of untold thousands of brave and noble victims upon his soul, will go down to posterity, cowering under a petticoat, the object of mingled horror and derision."[9]

HW June 17, 1865 373

THE CLOTHES IN WHICH DAVIS DISGUISED HIMSELF.
[From a photograph taken at the war department by Alexander Gardner.]

PP August 1865 C

JUSTICE DEMANDS IT, AND ANDY JOHNSON WILL DO IT!

A second editorial stated: "Treason is the highest crime known to the Constitution . . . Jefferson Davis must be tried for treason. If convicted he must be executed, unless for high reasons of state the President should commute his sentence." Nast graphically made the point in a following *Phunny Phellow* cartoon. Sallie was busy with newborn Tom Jr., so "axe" for "ask" slipped by the dyslexic artist.

Concurrently, Davis was reviled for the inhuman treatment of 45,000 Union enlisted men in Georgia's Andersonville Prison from February 1864 until almost the war's end. The men, who had been transferred from Belle Isle in Richmond, were deprived of most of their clothing and other possessions and given sparse rations of corn meal and beans. Malnutrition, poor sanitation, crowding, and exposure to Georgia's hot sun and humidity in the summer and cold in the winter, led to chronic diarrhea, dehydration and death. Discipline was strict, and men were shot on sight for approaching a "death line." 13,000 died.

Commandant Major Henry Wirz was tried and convicted in September 1865, when the shocking revelations of Anderson's horrors were front page stories. Wirz was hanged on November 10, the only Confederate executed for his military actions by the federal government after the war was over.

As a reviled impersonal symbol of the Confederacy, Andersonville was unsurpassed. A major issue at that time was whether Davis knew what was happening at Andersonville and, if he did, whether he too should be executed. The first question was never answered and he was never tried, although for other reasons.

On May 10, 1866, a year to the day after his capture, Davis was indicted for treason. Davis agreed that treason should be punished if committed by a citizen of the United States. His defense was that he had given up his citizenship when Mississippi seceded, and therefore he owed no allegiance to the U.S. As time passed, his trial was postponed several times. Public opinion, including *Harper's Weekly*, changed to oppose prosecution because there was nothing to gain; on the contrary, a ruling that the seceding states had the right to do so, could have upset the de facto applecart that victory had provided the Union with respect to secession.

Davis was confined at Fortress Monroe for two years under relatively easy conditions. His personal guards were removed after several months, and he was free to walk the grounds.

Nast never depicted Andersonville during the course of the war. However, a year after Davis's imprisonment, Nast contrasted the appalling conditions at Andersonville with the luxurious lifestyle Davis reportedly was enjoying in jail. Above Davis's head, Confederate sympathizer Horatio Seymour — Nast's villain from the 1863 draft riots and the future 1868 presidential campaign — was chatting with prison commander, General Nelson Miles. The corner vignettes (at the top) contrasted a prisoner entering and leaving the notorious prison, with (below) Davis entering defiantly and leaving a lot heavier amid fawning attendants.

HW June 30, 1866 409

President Andrew Johnson's frequent refrain, "Treason must be made odious," was an early example of Nast's hoisting his targets on their own verbal petards. (Horace Greeley became the best example in 1872.)

HW July 7, 1866 428

WHY HE CANNOT SLEEP

A week later Nast followed up with *Why He Cannot Sleep.* As the ghostly figure of Columbia pointed out Davis's responsibility for the atrocities and deaths at Andersonville, a gallows outside the window awaited him. War correspondent and author Charles Coffin wrote Nast that his cartoon "is better than all the speeches made in Congress during the session."

On May 13, 1867 after two years of imprisonment, Jeff Davis was bailed out of prison for $100,000 on the security of twenty men led by Horace Greeley. His trial was postponed to November, then to some indefinite time the next year. When all charges were finally dropped that spring, *Harper's Weekly* was in full accord.[10] In Nast's eyes, however, Greeley forever became a marked man for bailing Davis, and he used the act to repeatedly vilify Greeley in his 1872 presidential campaign against Grant.

Davis himself gradually faded away. His Mississippi mansion became a school for freed slaves. Three years later, in a final bit of irony, Nast depicted him as Iago lurking outside the Senate door as his former seat was occupied by Senator Hiram Revels (Othello). Born free in North Carolina, Revels became a minister and, elected by the Republican-controlled state legislature, the first black Senator. Welcoming him to the Senate were fellow Republicans (left to right) Henry Wilson (MA), Oliver Morton (IN), Carl Schurz (MO) and Charles Sumner(MA).

Nast never let up. When "Miss J. Davis" made a speech 12 years after his release, the cartoonist took another swing at "her."

HW July 5, 1879 536

JUDGING OTHERS BY OURSELVES.

"* * * But, whatever you and I may think about it, of one truth I am confident, I have never seen a reconstructed Southern Woman."—Miss J. Davis's Speech.

HW April 9, 1870 232

"TIME WORKS WONDERS."

Iago. (Jeff Davis.) "For that I do suspect the lusty moor hath leap'd into my seat: the though whereof doth like a poisonous mineral gnaw my inwards."—Othello

Chapter 13
President Johnson: First Year

Pre-Presidency

Born in Raleigh, North Carolina, six weeks before Lincoln, Johnson's parents were poor illiterates. He was relatively uneducated, and only learned to read comprehensively and to write after his wife taught him. Apprenticed to a tailor at fourteen, he ultimately settled in Greeneville in eastern Tennessee where slaves were relatively scarce. He was ambitious and a ferocious stump speaker, so he left tailoring for full time politics, working his way up the ladder as mayor, state legislator, five-term Congressman and two-term governor. In 1857, Senator Johnson made his debut on Capitol Hill.

As war approached, Johnson did his best to keep Tennessee in the Union. Failing, he was the only Senator who remained true to the Union after his state seceded. With demonstrated loyalty and intricate political knowledge of his state as primary qualifications. Lincoln appointed Johnson Military Governor of Tennessee in 1862. Two years later, he successfully organized a Unionist government in his home state.

Coming from a hardscrabble background, Johnson grew up with strong resentment towards men of wealth and power, especially the planter class which controlled Southern and national politics. He was outspoken, stubborn, inflexible, tactless, self-absorbed and relatively friendless. Compromise was foreign to him, as were the nuances of public opinion. These were the dominant attitudes and qualities, along with uncapped ambition, that Johnson brought to his unelected presidency.

Although Johnson had owned a few slaves at one time, he fully supported emancipation, but solely as a military necessity. While silently detesting Negroes, the future president told a black audience in Nashville in October 1864 that ***"I am your Moses,"*** implying that he would lead them to a promised land of Freedom, while also declaring that ***"Treason must be made odious and traitors must be punished and impoverished."*** With his strong anti-secession feelings, and his hatred of the wealthy politicians and planters who brought it about , Johnson undoubtedly meant what he said at the time. Nast would continually taunt Johnson with those words as events unfurled.

Settling In

After his access to the Presidency on April 15, Johnson had a political honeymoon for the rest of the year. All Lincoln's Cabinet members stayed on at his request; Secretaries William Seward (State), Hugh McCulloch (Treasury) and Gideon Welles (Navy) strongly backed Johnson through the rest of his term. He had the support of most Northern and Border State Democrats, as well as the splintered Republicans, although Congress was out of session until December 4 and let him alone.

As Lincoln stated and Johnson quoted, the paramount question to be decided after peace came was: How shall the States be restored to their practical relations in the Union? Along with that, the two intertwined issues were how to treat the former slaves, and what to do about suffrage for both Southern whites and blacks.

Johnson and Congress agreed that each of the eleven Confederate states must nullify their ordinances of secession, repudiate their debts, and ratify the Thirteenth Amendment abolishing slavery. (Passed on January 31, 1865, it was ratified in December). However, Johnson's *unrevealed* plan was to form a new political party — supported by conservatives and moderates from both North and South — with him as its leader and nominee for reelection in 1868.

In the post-War period, the so-called Liberal Republicans were in fact conservatives, content to let the role of blacks in society play out gradually over time rather than deal with it currently. Cabinet members Seward, McCulloch and Welles strongly supported this position, as did Henry Raymond, publisher of the *New York Times*, and concurrently a Congressman.

Radical Republicans were at the other end of the political spectrum. Under the leadership of Charles Sumner in the Senate and Thaddeus Stevens in the House, many of them wanted to treat the restored states as "conquered provinces." Confederate leaders should be tried for treason, kept from political roles, and be unquestionably repentant before receiving pardons (assuming they were not tried or convicted). Blacks were to receive equal civil and political rights — including suffrage — both as a matter of justice, and to ensure Republican control of the federal government as well as the individual Southern states. Specifically, the Radicals' overriding and justifiable fear was that if former Confederates — most of whom continued to believe in the "Lost Cause" — became eligible to vote and hold elective office, they would join with Copperheads, other Northern Democrats, and perhaps Conservative Republicans, to restore their majorities in Congress and on the Supreme Court, and keep hold of the Presidency (just as Johnson secretly schemed).

In the middle, were the Moderate Republicans. They agreed with the Radicals that it was essential to keep secessionist leaders out of power, and to maintain control of the federal government in Republican hands. They were concerned about immediate black suffrage because of potential adverse repercussions in the North, and the competency of black voters in the South. Ultimately, they were willing to compromise with the Radicals.

Currently, Congressional arithmetic provided the Republicans veto-proof majorities — 39-11 in the Senate and 140-43 in the House — if they all stuck together. If white-only additions from the restored stored states were seated in accordance with Johnson's proposed leniency, the Democrats could add as many as 22 votes in the Senate and more than 110 in the House. From veto-proof majorities to probable loss of control was not something that Republicans could allow to happen, and Johnson soon showed why.

Pardons

The first issue addressed was pardons. After several weeks of Cabinet discussion, Johnson issued an Amnesty Proclamation on May 29. It pardoned almost all rebels, restored all their property except for slaves and legal confiscations, and required only a nominal loyalty oath from them.

The Proclamation did not apply to many upper level Confederate military and political leaders, or to individuals with more than $20,000 in taxable property. They would have to apply directly to Johnson to have their electoral office-holding rights restored. That gave him personal contact and potential leverage with pliable Southern politicians and their backers whose support he would want in the future.

As early as its June issues, *Harper's Weekly* published the names of important Confederate Cabinet members, military men and politicians who had applied for Presidential pardons. Nast drew his only political cartoon over a four-month period (July - November 1865) featuring Columbia (symbol of America and posed by his wife) looking askance at a group of eighteen recognizable pardon seekers. The two in front were Robert E. Lee and Roger Pryor.

Pryor was not an obvious choice for a featured role. Before the war, he was a lawyer, newspaper editor, diplomatic emissary and Congressman from Virginia; during the war, he was a general close to Lee. Bearing a white flag of truce during the Petersburg campaign, he was captured and imprisoned at Fort Lafayette, where he served as a hostage to prevent a Union prisoner from being executed. Lincoln intervened to have him paroled and received him at the White House on his way back to Richmond.

Nast, somewhat subtly, featured Pryor as a symbol. When Fort Sumter was fired on to begin the Civil War, Pryor was invited to take the first shot. He declined and suggested Edmund Ruffin, who accepted the honor. Now Pryor represented the Confederacy asking for pardon on bended knee. (Six weeks earlier, Ruffin killed himself rather than apply for a pardon.) Pryor moved to New York where he had a successful career as a newspaper writer, lawyer and judge.[1]

The other prominent applicant was Alexander Stephens of Georgia, the second-ranking Confederate as Vice President. He was imprisoned for five months on an island in Boston Harbor and, still unpardoned, elected Senator when he returned to Georgia; however, Congress refused to let him take his seat. He was the only applicant to look Columbia straight in the eye, while holding out an actual petition for pardon.

Nast included many of the Southern politicians and generals: Governor John Letcher of Virginia, Generals Richard Ewell and John Bell Hood; former Secretary of State Robert Hunter; and Admiral Raphael Semmes. Also recognizable in the rear: Generals Braxton Bragg, Pierre Beauregard, John Gordon and James Longstreet; and Confederate Cabinet members Christopher Memminger (Treasury), John Reagan (Postmaster-General, who was captured with Jeff Davis), Stephen Mallory (Navy), John Breckinridge (War), and Judah Benjamin (State).[2]

Nast mistakenly included Robert Toombs, Davis's initial Secretary of State. Toombs fled to Cuba and then Paris before this cartoon was drawn. He never applied for a pardon, even after he returned in 1867.

On the facing double-page of this collection of suspiciously contrite Southerners, Nast again used Columbia to ask the straight-forward question about black suffrage: How could the rebels be allowed to vote if a black veteran who had lost a leg in the service of his country, could not? With a ballot box evident behind Columbia, Nast drove his point home.

HW August 5, 1865 488-489

PARDON.
Columbia—"Should I Trust These Men,

FRANCHISE.
And Not This Man?"

Reversal

In 1864 when Johnson was the Vice Presidential nominee, Copperheads like *New York World* publisher Manton Marble, Clement Vallandigham and John Van Buren blasted him as a renegade Democrat and an "insolent drunken brute." Van Buren, son of former president Martin Van Buren, had served as Attorney General of New York State and a leader of an anti-slavery movement. A political flip-flopper several times, he supported McClellan's Copperhead candidacy.

During his inauguration ceremony on March 4, 1865, Johnson was drunk and gave an incoherent speech in which he embarrassed Lincoln and himself, and gave fuel to his opponents' fire.[3] As 1865 progressed with Congress out of session until December, Johnson's "policy" took center stage. Seeing the lenient conditions he prescribed for the seceded states to rejoin the Union — and for the former Confederates to receive pardons, vote and hold office — his foes of a year earlier now praised him as a patriotic, wise and prudent statesman. In what would be Nast's last derisive political cartoon for more than seven months, he threw the Copperheads' words back at them, thereby taking a glancing shot at Johnson through guilt by association. He added former Mayor Fernando Wood in 1865. Vallandigham, the Copperhead leader, was about to serve the President a plate of candy and sugar plums.

HW November 11, 1865 13

Manton Marble John Van Buren Clement Vallandigham Fernando Wood

Top Left Corner:

"The drunken and beastly CALIGULA, the most profligate of all the Roman emperors, raised his horse to the dignity of consul—an office that, in former times, had been filled by the greatest warriors and statesmen of the republic, the SCIPIOS, the CATOS, by CICERO, and by the mighty JULIUS himself. The consulship was scarcely more disgraced by that scandalous transaction than is our vice-presidency by the late election. This office has been adorned in better days by the talents and accomplishments of ADAMS and JEFFERSON, CLINTON and GERRY, CALHOUN and VAN BUREN; and now to see it filled by this insolent, drunken brute, in comparison with whom even CALIGULA'S horse was respectable!—for the poor animal did not abuse his own nature."—*New York World*

Top Right Corner:

1865.

"Such did the Democratic masses find to be the record of ANDREW JOHNSON. They found as Civil Governor of Tennessee, member of Congress, or federal Senator, not one word or act of his which a national Democrat would not defend, and, as Military Governor of Tennessee, they appreciated the exigency in which he was placed. This cheered and delighted them."—*New York World.*

Bottom Left Corner:

1864.

"ANDREW JOHNSON is Military Governor of Tennessee, and this test oath is proposed by him, and substantially excludes every man opposed to the Administration from taking a vote. Talk to me of a Democrat sustaining all these usurpations, these violations of the Constitution and of the elementary principles of civil liberty! I submit that no man who has a democratic heart in his bosom and a democratic intellect in his head could fail to seize this occasion to drive from power the Administration that has been signalized by acts like these." JOHN VAN BUREN.

Bottom Right Corner:

1865.

"I look upon him [ANDREW JOHNSON] as a patriot and as a statesman who for twenty-five years has been distinguished in the service of his country in the various offices that he has filled, from the Legislature to Governor of the State, in both Houses of Congress, as Vice-President and President of the United States. I look upon him as patriotic, wise, and prudent." JOHN VAN BUREN.

Christmas Punch

On October 28, the President declared that the first Thursday in December would be Thanksgiving. Nast duly noted the day with an eight-vignette, double-page cartoon full of good feelings and with no politics in it.

His Christmas cartoon, however, was especially noteworthy on several counts. Most important, it featured Nast's depiction of Santa Claus as he has appeared ever since then. Utilizing Clement Moore's description in his 1822 poem, *A Visit from St. Nicholas*, Nast created the visage of the fat, jolly, white-bearded old elf — fur-clad, holding his long-stemmed clay pipe, and capped with mistletoe and holly — that predominates throughout the Western world. Only twenty-five at the time, he waited about fifteen years or so before incorporating his own features into Santa's face.[4]

HW December 30, 1865 824-825

ULYSSES THE GIANT KILLER

Below the holiday festivities (which occupied more than three-quarters of his double-page), Nast provided a Punch and Judy puppet show to deliver a strong political message to France and England about their North American transgressions. These shows had been popular in England since the seventeenth century and in America since the eighteenth. Nast's audience was familiar with Mr. Punch as a sly, untrustworthy, unpredictable character who violently assailed his opponents. He always dressed as a jester with brightly colored, mismatched clothes and a sugar loaf hat, and often had a hooked nose.

In 1863, Emperor Napoleon III had invaded Mexico — a violation of the Monroe Doctrine — and installed Maximilian, an Austrian Archduke, as emperor. The cartoonist's use of a puppet show to attack a puppet emperor would have been apparent to his audience. With the war over, Grant had good reason to be concerned about "Lost Cause" Confederates moving into Mexico from Texas, reorganizing a military force, and creating trouble. In June, he had urgently dispatched Phil Sheridan with 25,000 men to the Rio Grande. Sheridan wanted to attack, but Seward held him back, hoping to avoid European wars.[5]

Without using a single word other than his subtitle *Ulysses the Giant Killer*, Nast delivered his Christmas punch to Napoleon: "If you don't listen to Seward and get your 35,000 soldiers out of Mexico, our Army and Navy will do to you what Grant did to the Confederates." The artist was trying to provide a big stick to a man (Punch Seward) who wanted no part of swinging it.

ULYSSES THE GIANT KILLER (right side)

Seward was perfectly cast for Punch's role, including his prominent nose. He was pointing to Grant, who had the decapitated heads of Confederate Generals Hood, Lee and Ewell in front of him. John Bull (Britain) gasped in horror at the sight; Napoleon gazed fixedly at Grant, while holding his toddler son's hand. (Punch and Judy shows usually had a mistreated baby in them).

President Johnson, not interested in anything except Reconstruction, was conducting the orchestra in a disconcerted manner (under Lee's head). Recognizable generals behind Sheridan included Meade and Burnside.

As a final gesture, Nast drew a freed slave breaking his shackles (directly behind Lee's head). Earlier in December, Seward had announced that the Thirteenth Amendment had been ratified, thereby incorporating it into the Constitution.

On the left, Secretary of War Edwin Stanton, with apparent wings on his costume was studying Lee's head. Behind him was Sherman on his hobby-horse (in contrast to Sheridan, who was on a real horse with his sword raised); he wasn't going anywhere. Generals Thomas, Hooker and Kilpatrick were beside him. The American Navy represented a companion threat to Napoleon; Secretary Gideon Welles as Neptune, was backed up by Admirals Farragut and Porter.

ULYSSES THE GIANT KILLER (left side)

Except for the two Jeff Davis blasts available at the end of June 1866,* this was Nast's last political cartoon in *Harper's Weekly* for eight months. While he mostly devoted himself to painting, Johnson and Congress went at each other with their political cannons blazing away.

As 1866 ended, Nast celebrated in the January 1867 issue of *Phunny Phellow* with *A Few Unpleasant New Year's Calls*. Of his eight vignettes, the most prominent had Napoleon III facing off against Andy I. "When will you git out of Mexico?" "Whenever I pleases."

Napoleon finally withdrew his troops in 1867, leaving Maximilian (who willingly remained) to be captured and executed.

Hood Museum, Dartmouth College.

Mrs. Grundy

Nast was one of half a dozen or so cartoonists who contributed to *Mrs. Grundy*, a comic humor magazine that was launched on July 8, 1865 and expired after a dozen issues. The original Mrs. Grundy was a fictional self-righteous, priggish arbiter of social judgments in *Speed the Plough*, a 1798 English play by Thomas Morton. "What would Mrs. Grundy say?" became a humorous rhetorical question.

The magazine was patterned after London's *Punch*, but also had some American ancestry in *Vanity Fair* (which had expired in 1863). It was full of light verse, satire and cartoons, which played to local and domestic topics more than national or international events. The humor was strained and sophomoric.

MRS. GRUNDY July 8, 1865 3

Nast

* See p. 147-148

September 9, 1865 96

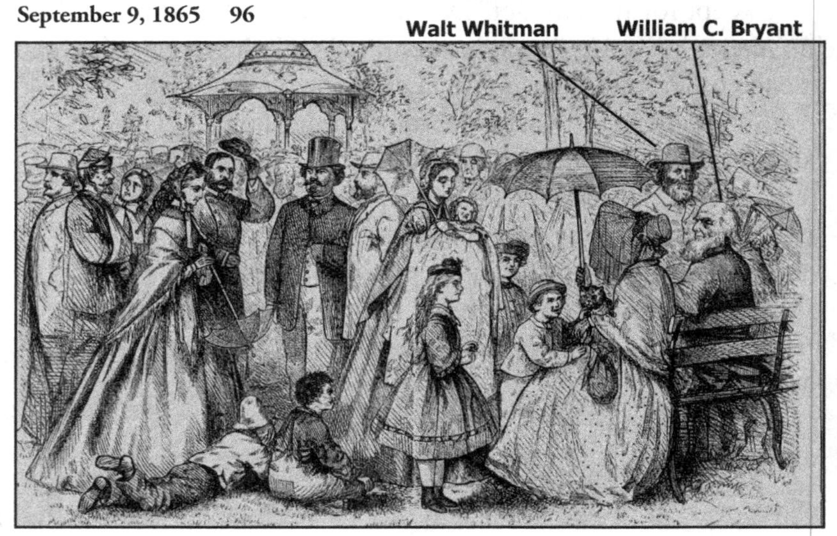

Of the eighteen cartoons that Nast drew — not all of them signed or initialed — an innocuous drawing of Central Park in which Walt Whitman appeared in company with poet and *New York Post* editor William Cullen Bryant is noteworthy. Nast almost certainly was acquainted with Whitman, but this probably was the only time that Whitman was clearly featured in one of his cartoons.

Macculloch Hall Historical Museum

Nast may have been the only beneficiary of *Mrs. Grundy* because he won a $100 prize for his unique cover. (As he noted on his contemporary photograph). He used his favored theatrical setting with a hundred hand-drawn recognizable faces in the audience. This remarkable feat made Nast justifiably proud, and foretold his ability to portray as many as forty caricatured identifiable individuals as tiny action figures in his future battles against Andrew Johnson, Horatio Seymour, Boss Tweed and Horace Greeley.

The audience included Generals George Meade, Phil Sheridan, Ulysses Grant, William Sherman, Ambrose Burnside and Benjamin Butler. The last two sat separately, probably because of their military failures. The international box featured King Victor Emmanuel II of Italy, Queen Victoria and the Prince of Wales, Emperor Napoleon III, and Pope Pius IX.

Ironically, Nast's subtle by-play on the cover — which was used on all twelve issues — was an anachronism by its second week. Phineas T. Barnum was in the front row, close by a scroll of "Weekly Lectures," which referred to the three-a-day moral discourses presented at his American Museum. Nast was inferring that Mrs. Grundy, the symbol of uptight morality, would be in total accord with the Barnum lectures.

Unfortunately, Barnum's Museum burned to the ground three days before *Mrs. Grundy* made her second appearance. With almost four thousand visitors a day, and receipts of about $300,000 a year, the Museum's going up in smoke was a major calamity. By the time *Mrs. Grundy* was buried, Barnum had arranged for the lectures to be given elsewhere while he rebuilt his museum.

To succeed, *Mrs. Grundy* needed a circulation of 6,000 to cover weekly expenses of about $600. Priced at a relatively high fifteen cents, it failed. As a *Harper's* cartoon by George Fox noted a week after her decease, "The poor old lady is since dead of a new disease called 'undeveloped humor.'" Nast was shown escaping (right rear) with a bagful of sketches.

HW September 30, 1865 624

POOR "MRS. GRUNDY!"

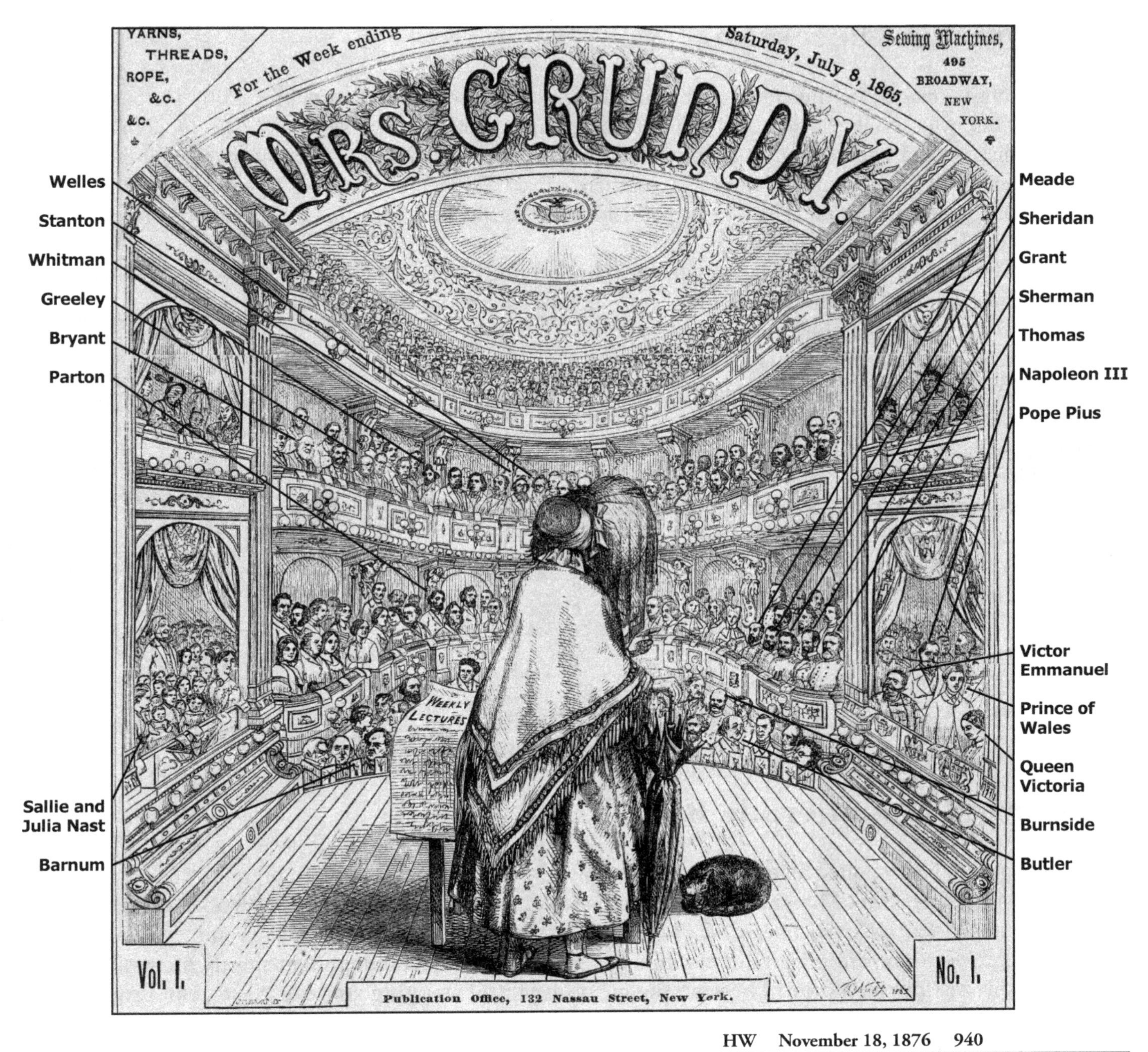

Nast continued to use Mrs. Grundy on occasion to lecture or assert a point, or as a symbol of gossip. Here, he attacked the anti-Grant press as his hero neared the end of his Presidency.

HW November 18, 1876 940

AFTER ELECTION.
"O, my prophetic soul!"

A Chronicle of Secession

During Nast's career, he illustrated more than 110 books — some of them published by Harper & Brothers — but only one was serialized in the *Weekly*. The singular exception was *Inside — A Chronicle of Secession*, a thinly-disguised novel which the firm acquired shortly after the Civil War ended and copyrighted the same year. It was written by William Mumford Barker, a Southern-raised, Princeton-educated, Protestant minister, under the pen name George F. Harrington. The *Weekly* published it in twenty-four installments during the first half of 1866, and followed it with a book.

Barker-Harrington was a Union sympathizer living in one of the "centers of secession," fictionally named Somerville. He based it on the events that happened around him, including controversies over escaping conscription, miscegenation, and false rumors about Lee's sweeping victory at Gettysburg. He had to bury his manuscript as he proceeded because discovery could have been fatal.

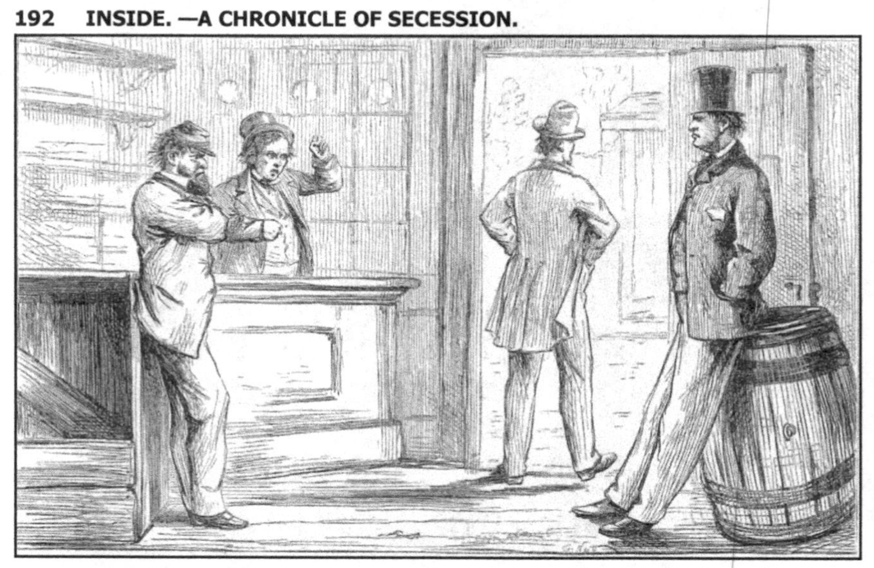

Miscegenation Argument.

For this Civil War reprise, Nast provided fifty-four illustrations, about two per issue. He probably completed these by the end of 1865, so he had plenty of time and some income for his other artistic pursuits the following year. Accordingly, he didn't resume regular cudgelling of President Johnson until September, when he made up for lost time with a vengeance.

The Grand Masquerade Ball

In early 1866, Nast spotted an advertisement by Max Maretzek, an Austrian immigrant, who had become the first successful impresario of Italian opera in New York. Maretzek had leased the New York Academy of Music, where he planned to give a masquerade ball on April 5. Nast contacted Maretzek to promote his idea of painting caricatures of prominent people for exhibition at the ball, and auctioning them shortly afterwards. The Bal d'Opera (as it was formally known) became **the most impactful stepping stone to Nast's career as an unsurpassed political caricaturist.**

They agreed on 60 pictures, all painted in tempura, and ranging from three-by-four to four-by-six feet. Nast had thirty days to complete them in order to meet the April 5 date for the social highlight of the season.

Nast co-ventured with Maretzek, agreeing to be reimbursed for his expenses, but not for his time. A week after the ball, the pictures were auctioned off for $1,100, which went into Nast's bank account. Maretzek also gave his artist a $250 gold watch. However, the acclaim and publicity that he received were probably as satisfying to him as his material rewards.[6]

In retrospect thirty years later, he thoughtfully added his own insight: "I had a good opportunity of noting the effects of the caricatures on the subjects . . . I noticed that every one of them who was present appeared to think the caricatures excellent until he came to his own, and then the change in his expression was great."[7] What more could a caricaturist want?

Other than his 54 prepared-in-advance, serialized *Chronicle of Secession* illustrations, the only Nast appearance in the *Weekly* over a sixteen-week period from February until mid-June 1866, was his double-page feature of the Bal d'Opera. Nast selected eighteen of his sixty caricatures to frame the masquerade. Excluding himself and Maretzek, half were from the political world and half from the entertainment world. Post-dated April 14, the issue probably was available the day before the ball.

His *Harper's Weekly* images suffered by comparison to his big-headed, small-bodied paintings as he rushed to complete them (as shown by Mayor John Hoffman). This was Nast's first of more than fifty depictions of Hoffman, a principal target during the artist's campaign against the Tweed Ring when he was Governor.

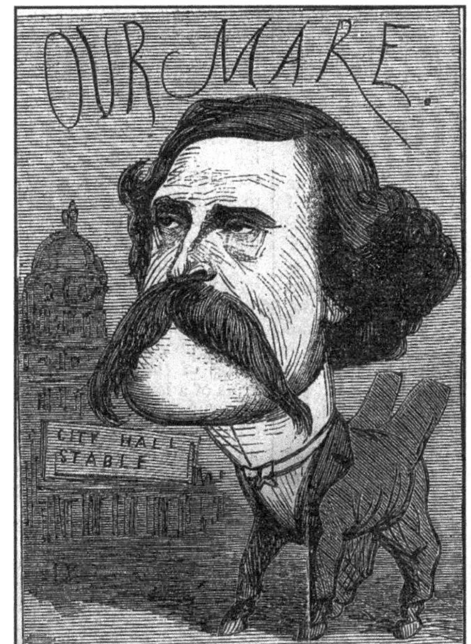

HARPER'S WEEKLY

PAINTED CARICATURE

HW April 14, 1866 232-233

GRAND MASQUERADE BALL GIVEN BY MR. MARETZEK AT THE ACADEMY OF MUSIC, APRIL 5, 1866. —By Thomas Nast

The imaginative centerpiece employed the artist's familiar theatrical setting, perfect for a masquerade ball. Two of his favorite international villains — the Pope and Emperor Napoleon III — received the full Nast treatment. Pius IX consorting with the Devil, left nothing to anyone's imagination. More subtly, Napoleon dangled his Mexican puppet emperor in front of an angry Queen Victoria, who appeared to be threatening to use her British navy to force the French emperor to get out of Mexico.

Pius IX Napoleon III Queen Victoria

Horace Greeley was shown innocuously walking his *NY Tribune* as a black-faced baby. Nast and Greeley were on the same side at this point in time, so the reference to his newspaper's promotion of abolition and civil rights for all blacks was positive — in deliberate contrast to Henry Raymond's *New York Times*.

Next to Greeley, Wendell Phillips, a rabid abolitionist orator for three decades, and current president of the Anti-Slavery Society, appeared as a woman holding her adopted black child. The *Times*, which supported Johnson's anti-black policy, commented in describing the auction: "Mr. Phillips and his nursling sold for $25, which was a good price considering the depreciated value of colored live stock."

Nast came down hard on popular Congregationalist preacher Henry Ward Beecher. Beecher had tremendous influence, emanating from his pulpit at Plymouth Church in Brooklyn, and reinforced by his theatrical lectures and widely read writings. A strong Lincoln supporter and Conservative Republican, he backed Johnson's Reconstruction policy of going easy on the South. Nast pulled no punches as Beecher played his flute to charm the CSA snake.

Ulysses Grant, “The Idol We Worship” — as Nast truly believed — was in a featured position (opposite Johnson), with his hugely swollen right hand. The rest of Nast’s usual lineup of generals — William Sherman, Phil Sheridan, Robert Anderson, Ben Butler and Ambrose Burnside (below, with his patronymic sideburns) — were included.

PAINTING

PAINTING

HARPER’S WEEKLY

Cyrus Field promoted the Atlantic Cable which ran from Ireland to Newfoundland. His cable had broken on several occasions since his first attempt in 1858, most recently in July 1865. Field had tears running down his face, a handkerchief in one hand and pieces of the broken cable in his other. However, he persevered and achieved success three months after the Ball, when a much stronger cable finally held.

PAINTING

HARPER’S WEEKLY

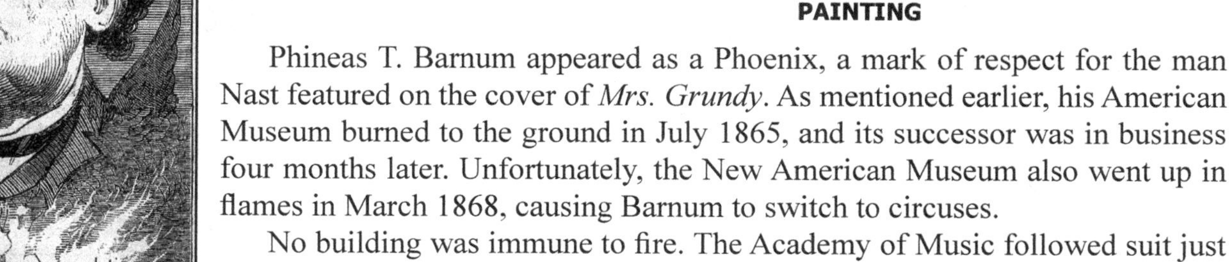

Phineas T. Barnum appeared as a Phoenix, a mark of respect for the man Nast featured on the cover of *Mrs. Grundy*. As mentioned earlier, his American Museum burned to the ground in July 1865, and its successor was in business four months later. Unfortunately, the New American Museum also went up in flames in March 1868, causing Barnum to switch to circuses.

No building was immune to fire. The Academy of Music followed suit just six weeks after the Ball. Nast’s timing was fortuitous.

HW April 13, 1867 232-233

GRAND MASQUERADE BALL OF THE ARION SOCIETY AT THE ACADEMY OF MUSIC, NEW YORK, MARCH 27, 1867.

A year later the Academy of Music had been rebuilt and the Grand Masquerade Ball had become an annual event sponsored by the German-American Arion Society. Nast was in his glory with a theatrical scene which featured all kinds of real and fanciful characters strolling and riding on four-wheel cycles.

In one of the best examples of pure wordless caricature ever drawn by Nast or anyone else, the artist portrayed four major national and international relationships and events — using only subtle facial expressions, postures and distance between characters to convey his messages — all within a three-inch high double-page strip.

On the far left, Queen Victoria was beating a drum while looking askance at a grim Mrs. Grundy; a distant Uncle Sam marched at her left. Britain was hated and scorned by Northern public opinion for her open support for the Confederacy.

In front of them rode a resolute President Johnson with an impassive Admiral Farragut on his left, and a taciturn Grant, noticeably distanced, on his right. Grant disagreed with Johnson's policies, but stayed on as the popular, heroic Army chief to help thwart the president's efforts to restore the South to its former political ascendancy. Johnson, whose primary goal was to win the 1868 presidential election as a Democrat, knew that Grant was likely to be the Republican candidate but couldn't risk firing him. Nast subtly captured the discordant relationship between the two.

On the far right, Nast depicted a stereotyped Irish hoodlum brandishing his sword. While celebrating St. Patrick's day with their annual parade several weeks earlier, the Ancient Order of Hibernians attacked the police. Nast had depicted the bloody battle in the previous issue, so his audience recognized his reprise.

In the middle, Nast composed a complicated six-character scenario summarizing the results of the seven-week war between Prussia and Austria in the summer of 1866. Prussia won, thereby gaining control of five North German states, with Emperor Napoleon III acting as mediator. As mentioned earlier, Napoleon also persuaded Austria to cede Venice to Italy (Prussia's ally in this war), even though the Italians, poorly led by King Victor Emmanuel II, lost two key battles on land and at sea.

Nast pictured a steadfast Napoleon pushing the unseen Italian King (under a woman's bonnet) reaching out to Garibaldi who was piloting a leery Pope Pius IX. Three years later, Napoleon started a war that he lost to Prussia; as a result, French troops pulled out of Rome, the Pope lost all temporal power, and Italy was unified at last. To complete the scenario, the contemplative, formally dressed Prussian Premier Otto von Bismarck, propelled his defeated adversary, Austrian Emperor Franz Joseph I, who was warily trying to hold off an avaricious Prussian eagle.

While the size, scale, topicality, visual impact and political implications of previous and subsequent Nast cartoons made them far more important, these overlooked miniature panels pinpointed the artist's ability as an unsurpassed caricaturist who didn't need any written identifications or words to make his subtle points.

Chapter 14
President Johnson: King Andy

Freedmen's Bureau

Johnson's honeymoon with Congress ended abruptly early in 1866 with the first of his many unsuccessful vetoes. Under Lincoln's administration, Congress had created the Freedmen's Bureau on March 3, 1865, as a temporary agency within the War Department. As the first federal agency dedicated to social welfare, its purpose was to assist the freed slaves by providing basic shelter, medical care, schools, and assistance in contractual labor negotiations. Suffrage was not in the bill.

After Congress passed a two-year extension of the Freedmen's Bureau on February 6 with unanimous Republican support, the President shocked the political universe by vetoing it two weeks later. His veto was sustained with the help of Conservative Republicans. He added fuel to the fire by openly declaring war on the Radicals, and blasting them for not seating newly-elected Southerners.

On Washington's Birthday, three days after his veto — and underestimating the damage that he had done to himself in Northern public opinion — Johnson spoke to a cheering crowd of supporters at the White House. Getting wound up by emotion, and probably hyped by liquor in a one-hour tirade, he told his audience that Thaddeus Stevens, Charles Sumner and Wendell Phillips — leaders of the Radical Republicans — were just as traitorous to the Union as Jeff Davis. When someone asked about including John Forney, the Radical Republican owner of the *Washington Chronicle* and the Secretary of the Senate, Johnson responded with: ***I do not waste my fire on dead ducks***. He and Forney had been good friends before the President reversed course.

In his Bal d'Opera, Nast depicted the Freedmen's Bureau literally, as Johnson — with a determined look — kicked it down the Congressional steps while small black figures escaped from its drawers. When the 60 pictures were auctioned off after the Ball, Johnson's portrait went for $50, the single highest price.

Nast also took the Dead Duck and flew with it. Later he used it as a recurring symbol of Johnson himself, as the President effectively became a lame duck for the last three years of his term.

HW April 14, 1866 232-233

Civil Rights and the Fourteenth Amendment

Johnson crossed the Rubicon when he vetoed the Civil Rights Bill on March 27; Congress overrode him two weeks later. Like the Freedmen's Bureau Bill, it had been introduced by Moderate Republicans. The President's words and actions made it clear to them that the only way they could preserve the victory of the war, ensure equality for blacks, and keep their party in power was to join the Radicals in opposing Johnson.

This was the first successful override of a presidential veto in the nation's history. It was followed in July by repassage of the Freedmen's Bureau Bill, overturning Johnson's February veto.

The Civil Rights Bill declared that blacks were citizens, nine years after the Dred Scott decision said they were not. It was supposed to protect them against Black Codes and other repressive restrictions; give them equal protection under the law with regard to contracts, land and property ownership; and affirm their right to sue and bear witness. Like the Freedmen's Bureau Bill, there was no mention of suffrage in it.

The Fourteenth Amendment process started in early 1866, and the Amendment was approved by Congress on June 11. It was intended to prevent the protections of the Civil Rights Act from being modified or repealed by a future Congress, just as the Thirteenth Amendment had done for the Emancipation Proclamation.

Johnson opposed it silently because he still hoped to keep the Moderate Republicans in his camp, and his formal approval wasn't required. His home state of Tennessee unexpectedly approved it on July 19, and was rewarded by Congress with readmission to the Union four days later; David Patterson, Johnson's son-in-law, was seated as a new senator.

The Amendment was a key element of Reconstruction and its ratification became a requirement for the ten remaining seceded states to be readmitted to the Union. Citizenship was defined to include all persons born or naturalized in the United States; federal debt was validated while Confederate debt was voided; apportionment was defined, and a state which interfered "in any way" with the right of adult male citizens to vote would have its representation reduced proportionately; and ex-Confederates were banned from holding state or federal office.[1]

The Fourteenth Amendment became part of the Constitution in July 1868. Seven of the Southern states elected delegates and held conventions, drafted new constitutions, enfranchised black male voters while disenfranchising many ex-Confederates, and seated Republican-dominated biracial legislatures. All but three were readmitted to the Union by the time Johnson left office.[2]

Race Riots

On May 1, 1866, three days of rioting broke out in Memphis, resulting in the deaths of 46 blacks and two whites, and the vandalizing and destruction of hundreds of black homes. The spark was the collision of two horse-drawn hacks with black and white drivers. The black population of Memphis had quadrupled during the Civil War, racial tensions were high, and white hostility towards blacks boiled over with the mostly Irish police force playing a major inflammatory role; the Irish population had ballooned when they moved to Memphis and took over offices and jobs formerly held by Confederates.

Johnson had clean hands with regard to the Memphis riot, but he bore primary responsibility for the New Orleans massacre which took place three months later on July 30. 25 delegates and 200 black supporters assembled in New Orleans to draw up a new state constitution. The Convention had been called by Louisiana Governor James Wells, who endorsed black suffrage and voting bans for former Confederates. Newly-pardoned Confederates, including Mayor John Monroe and State Attorney General Andrew Herron, mobilized the mostly ex-Confederate police to prevent the convention from taking place.

Phil Sheridan, the military commander, was in Texas that day. His understudy thought the Convention was to start six hours later than its actual plan; accordingly, there were no federal soldiers at the scene, nor had he received requested guidance from Secretary of War Stanton. Johnson had telegraphed Mayor Monroe, telling him that the military would be expected to sustain and not obstruct the local authorities.

The police attacked the black supporters outside the hall, and the delegates inside. 34 blacks and three white Radicals were killed, and more than a hundred others injured. *The Massacre of the Innocents* became notorious in the North, with Johnson receiving well-deserved blame; he expressed no remorse or sympathy for the victims.

HW September 8, 1866 569

Nast was in print late the following month with a dark ghoulish scene featuring symbolic Death rising over the slaughtered, while pointing at the murderous whites. Below, he issued a timely warning to Union men about New Orleans while raising the rhetorical question: Which is more illegal — the Civil Rights Convention or the massacre?

Eight months later, Nast's imaginative depiction of the New Orleans massacre used the Roman Colosseum as his setting.[3] He portrayed Johnson as Nero, figuratively fiddling with the Constitution as New Orleans rioted, an illusion to his indifference to the massacre. Looking over his shoulder was Secretary of State Seward as chief consul. Secretary of War Stanton turned his head away; Johnson wanted to remove him from office, while Stanton was determined to stay on and keep the President from interfering with the military in the South. (Eighteen months later, Johnson acted and impeachment followed.)

Monroe was leading his ex-Confederate police as they slaughtered the unarmed blacks on the Colosseum floor. Looking on were Cabinet members Gideon Welles (Navy), Hugh McCulloch (Treasury) and Alexander Randall (Postmaster General); Senator James Doolittle; Horatio Seymour who would run for Johnson's job in 1868; and Copperheads Manton Marble, John Hoffman,, Fernando Wood and Clement Vallandigham — Johnson supporters all. In the gallery on the other side, Johnson's enemies — Horace Greeley, Ben Butler, Wendell Phillips and popular lecturer Anna Elizabeth Dickinson could be readily identified. Speaker of the House Schuyler Colfax, a Radical, monitored the scene next to Doolittle.

To highlight his Nero analogy, Nast pulled out all the stops and depicted a Roman gladiator in the act of stabbing Jesus Christ. He pictured them in white to make sure they stood out.

Directly below Johnson, diminutive Union General Darius Crouch was sitting in the lap of the much larger South Carolina Governor James Orr alongside a labeled Copperhead snake. The two had the featured roles at the pro-Johnson National Union political convention in Philadelphia two weeks after the riot.

Most important, Grant had a firm hand on Sheridan's wrist, thereby inhibiting his unsheathed sword. Conversely, General George Armstrong Custer, a Johnson loyalist, watched the slaughter dispassionately.

HW March 30, 1867 200-201

AMPHITHEATRUM JOHNSONIANUM —MASSACRE OF THE INNOCENTS AT NEW ORLEANS, JULY 30, 1866.

Electoral Fall

The elections of 1866 became a referendum on Andrew Johnson versus Congress. Local issues were not the dominant factor that they ordinarily were in a non-presidential year.

Nast was busy painting and illustrating books during the first eight months of the year. When the election campaigns began in September, he used both the Memphis and New Orleans riots to whip up Northern emotion in a manner reminiscent of the "Southern Chivalry" and guerilla atrocities that were so effective during the Civil War. Johnson's continuing political misadventures gave Nast — now a committed caricaturist — plenty of fuel for his fired-up cartoons. He led off with *Andrew Johnson's Reconstruction and How It Works*. **This was the first of more than a hundred cartoons in which Nast used Shakespearean references — well understood by his readers — to make his points.**

Othello, the heroic and innocent Moor — one arm in a sling and the other holding an honorable discharge signed by Grant — was betrayed by the evil Iago, a symbol of hypocrisy and dishonesty. The wall behind them was plastered with Johnson's "I am your Moses" and other statements from his 1864 Nashville speech when he was Lincoln's running mate.

Above, the Memphis and New Orleans riots book-ended a slave auction and a lashing. Below, Johnson played his Constitution-flute to charm two snakes wrapped around a young black man — a Northern Copperhead and a CSA. Approving Cabinet members Seward and Welles looked on with interest, while an unhappy Stanton was disturbed. Pardons and vetoes were abundant.

Framing the snake-charmer, Nast contrasted New Orleans in 1862 with 1866. The left vignette showed General Benjamin Butler, Union Commander in charge of the recently-captured city, receiving a sword of surrender from a bowing Confederate, with underlying quotes from Iago and Othello — all under an American flag. The right had General Phil Sheridan bowing to Louisiana Attorney General Andrew Herron, a key conspirator in the New Orleans riot — under a Confederate flag and a picture of "General Lee and Staff." Underneath was Johnson's promise to Negroes — "You are now free" — and his rationale for leniency to the needy Southerners who "have suffered the loss of property."

HW September 1, 1866 552-553

The Tearful Convention

On August 14, 1866, the National Union Convention met in Philadelphia. It was Johnson's brainchild to defeat the Radical Republicans by uniting Conservative and Moderate Republicans, War Democrats, Copperheads and "Restored" (Johnson's terminology) Southerners into a political party that he would lead. He saw it as a means of integrating the Southern states on his terms — *My Policy* — and then winning the Presidency in 1868.

Henry Raymond made a personal, business and political decision to organize the Convention, write its platform, and promote Johnson and his new party in his *New York Times*. It cost him his seat in Congress (he didn't run against hopeless odds), and a third of his paper's circulation. Faced with Johnson's erratic behavior and the likely loss of his paper, Raymond broke with the President the following month; his political career was over, as were his relationships with many Republicans.

Only three of Johnson's cabinet members — Seward, McCulloch and Welles — supported his Convention; three others resigned. As mentioned previously, Stanton opposed Johnson, but stayed on to do what he could to obstruct the President's lenient policy in the South. Johnson ultimately replaced Postmaster General William Dennison with his assistant Alexander Randall, who was a floor leader and co-organizer of the Convention.

The highlight of the Convention was the arm-in-arm entrance of the massive South Carolina Governor James Orr and the diminutive Massachusetts former Union general, Darius Couch. The reconciliation reportedly brought "tears of joy" to many eyes, including Johnson's when he learned of it.

The Convention's Chairman and strict disciplinarian was Conservative Republican Senator James Doolittle of Wisconsin. He did not allow debate on Raymond's resolutions or anything else, believing the Convention's sole purpose was to support Johnson, not to debate his "Policy."

A critical internal problem that Raymond, Doolittle and Randall faced, was the appearance in Philadelphia of notorious Copperheads Clement Vallandigham and Fernando Wood as delegates. Nobody wanted them to contaminate the public persona of the National Union Convention, but they didn't give up easily.

Nast had fun, depicting a weeping Copperhead and a Confederate crocodile with plenty of tears. Raymond was kissing a Confederate, Randall was literally kicking out Wood and Vallandigham, and five potential debaters had locks on their mouths with Doolittle holding the key to "unbroken harmony."

Swingin' Round the Circle

Back in the winter of 1863, when he was the nationally known and respected Military Governor of Tennessee, Johnson went on a successful speaking tour of several major mid-western and eastern cities to drum up support for President Lincoln's policies and simultaneously blast his Copperhead opposition. Undoubtedly, his remembrance of the acclaim from that trip was a factor in his decision to undertake the first-ever presidential speaking tour to win the public over to his Reconstruction Policy. It became known as his *Swing Around the Circle*.

Leaving by train on August 28, 1866, two weeks after the Tearful Convention convened, Johnson spoke in more than two dozen cities in eighteen days. He gave the same speech in every city, so the crowds knew what to expect. He had been advised to avoid extemporaneous remarks that could interfere with his objective of selling his "policy" and denigrating the Radical Republicans. Seward master-minded the trip, assisted by Welles. Grant and Farragut were reluctant travelers, pressured to go along by their Commander-in-Chief.

The trip was an unmitigated disaster when too much whiskey and too many outrageous remarks disgusted and repelled his listeners. He advocated hanging Thad Stevens, Wendell Phillips and Charles Sumner; blamed the Radicals for the New Orleans massacre; challenged the legitimacy of Congress; supported the admission of unrepentant Confederates into government; slobbered "I do not care for dignity," and took bows when his audiences cheered "Grant! Grant! Grant!" Grant left the tour in Cincinnati when he could no longer suffer the behavior of the "drunken tailor," as some of his opponents labeled him. *Harper's Weekly* "defied any man to read the speeches uttered by the President without wincing with mortification," while others referred to the "Presidential orgy reeling across the astonished land."[4]

Nast had a field day with *Andy's Trip*. He used eight inches of text quoting Johnson's pre-presidential statements to answer his own question: "Where is the man or woman who can place his finger upon one single act of mine deviating from any pledge of mine?" The caricaturist's sub-headline, "Don't Get Mad, Andy", enlivened his seventeen searing vignettes, each of which told its own story.

One depicting the President bowing and issuing a pardon to the New Orleans riot instigator, Mayor John Monroe, while Thad Stevens and Wendell Phillips hung from a nearby gallows, was a forerunner of his next *Harper's Weekly* cartoon.

("HANG JEFF DAVIS.") "THEN I WOULD ASK YOU WHY NOT HANG THAD STEVENS AND WENDELL PHILLIPS?"

"THERE ARE VERY FEW MEN WHO HAVE BEEN ABANDONED BY THE PEOPLE UNLESS THEY HAVE DESERTED THEM FIRST" (THAT'S SO)

The staggered 1866 elections were underway, and the Republicans had already swept eight states, as Andy noted while standing outside "the Veto House." What effectively was a national referendum on Reconstruction added 18 Senate and 37 House seats to their veto-proof majorities. They also won every race for governor, and carried every state legislature where they ran candidates.

HW October 27, 1866 680-681

King Andy

While swinging round the circle, Seward made a speech from the balcony of a St. Louis hotel in which he compared his role as Secretary of State to President Johnson "who like kings and emperors, has ministers whose duty it is to be silent, and advise and record ..." A month later, a widely quoted (but false) rumor had Seward asking rhetorically: "Do you want Mr. Johnson as President, or do you want him as King?"

In his last cartoon before the remaining 1866 elections, Nast annointed King Andy I, asked the question, and answered "You pays your money and you takes your choice." Seward's speech perplexedly had referred to the "Constantinople of America," so Nast depicted Johnson as an oriental Emperor with Seward as his Grand Vizier.

Under an exotic canopy, King Andy wore his Dead Duck medallion on his royal robe, while looking menacingly beyond a despondent, shackled Lady Liberty. Johnson already was a lame duck who was destined to get much lamer in the coming months.

Nast had a subtle message for Seward as the Grand Vizier. With the *right* side of his face in profile, Seward pointed to the King's enemies ready for the chopping block. The inset below showed Seward dressed in his regular clothes, with his *left* profile revealing the scars from a near-fatal knife attack he suffered from would-be assassin Lewis Payne on the night Lincoln was shot. Nast was implying that talk about hanging or execution could result in unanticipated consequences.

Thad Stevens, the Radical leader in the House, was first on King Andy's enemies list with his head on the chopping block. Next in line were civil rights advocate Wendell Phillips; publisher John Forney; Senator Charles Sumner; Congressman Ben Butler who would lead the impeachment process; popular public speaker Anna Elizabeth Dickinson; Horace Greeley; soon-to-be Congressman and former general John Logan; and at the end of the line, none other than Nast himself, carrying a sketchbook.

Navy Secretary Gideon Welles looked on impassively — a plume in his crown, a lance in his hand, and a 290 medallion (symbol of the Confederate marauder *Alabama*) on his doublet. Perhaps he was the minister who disfavored the executions.

HW November 3, 1866 696

Suffrage

After Johnson's electoral disaster, Seward, Henry Raymond and others advised him to cooperate with Congress to get the Fourteenth Amendment ratified by the Southern states; alternatively, he could stay neutral and let Congress work directly with the states. Once the Amendment was ratified, the ten unreconstructed states could follow Tennessee's example by rejoining the Union, enfranchising their black voters, and gaining representation in Congress.

In December 1866, the reconvened Congress passed a bill granting suffrage to adult black males in the District of Columbia. It became law over Johnson's veto in January, an event Nast promptly recognized: Johnson, with a pocketful of vetoes frowned, as a black veteran voted for a Republican mayor. This particular veto took impeachment discussions up a notch.

HW March 16, 1867 172

THE GEORGETOWN ELECTION—THE NEGRO AT THE BALLOT BOX.

Southern Justice

Under Johnson's lenient eye, former Confederates in the southern states stepped up attacks on blacks, Union soldiers and reformers from the North. Confederate-dominated legislatures passed black codes that effectively reduced the freedmen to the same conditions they suffered under before emancipation.

In its January 12 issue, an editorial in *Harper's Weekly* described *Whipping and Selling American Citizens*, concluding with *"Is slavery dead?"* The *Domestic Intelligence* column provided the gory details.[5]

That became the question in Nast's accompanying cartoon. Effectively, he reprised *Southern Chivalry* from 1862 and 1863, using contemporary examples.

HW January 12, 1867 24

Negroes Sold as a Punishment for Crime. **Negroes Whipped as a Punishment for Crime.**

Prometheus Bound

The previous December, the Supreme Court had ruled that military tribunals could not try civilians, even in wartime, where civil courts were in operation. Grant, bound by that decision and immobilized by the open warfare between his Commander-in-Chief and the increasingly powerful Radical Republicans, was stuck.

Nast used a Greek myth to depict Grant as *Prometheus Bound*, along with an adaptive script and articles about insulting and killing Union soldiers in the South. During his vacation in the Catskills the previous summer, Nast had visited the studio of the late Thomas Cole and seen his monumental picture with the same title. Prometheus had stolen fire from the Gods and given it to mankind; Zeus punished him by having him chained to a rock and eternally tormented by a hungry eagle which feasted on his liver.

Johnson, of course, was the unseen, vengeful Zeus. Grant, bound by the Supreme Court ruling at his waist, presidential orders at his wrists, and "My Policy" at his ankles, was helpless to ward off the demonic furies of the Confederacy. However, on the left, the spectral goddess "Congress" urged her sister Columbia to go to the General's aid; at the lower right, the spirits of Northern states were rising to do just that "like flocks of clouds in spring's delightful weather." Congress concluded the dialogue with "And see! more come!"

This was the first time that Nast used classical mythology as the central theme of a cartoon. Over his career with *Harper's Weekly,* he would incorporate Greek and Roman gods and goddesses into his cartoons 69 times — exceptional for someone whose formal education ended at age thirteen.

HW March 2, 1867 137

SCENE.

A Ravine in the Southern States. Prometheus (Grant) is discovered bound to the precipice. Pantha (Columbia) and Ione (Congress) are sitting at his feet. Southern Furies, Minor Spirits, etc. TIME—Night. During the scene morn slowly breaks.

First Fury.

The hope of torturing him smells like a heap
Of corpses to a death bird after the battle

Second Fury.

We are the ministers of pain and fear,
And disappointment, and mistrust, and hate,
And clinging crime; and as lean dogs pursue
Through wood and lake some struck and sobbing faun,
We track all things that weep and bleed and live,
When the great King (Andy) betrays them to our will.

Ione.

Hark, Sister!—
Darest thou observe how the fiends torture him?

Third Fury.

Blood thou canst see, and fire, and canst hear groans;
Worse things, unheard, unseen, remain behind.

Pantheo.

Look, Sister, where a troop of spirits gather,
Like flocks of clouds in spring's delightful weather,
Thronging in the blue air!

Ione.

Ans see! more come!

INSULTS TO UNITED STATES SOLDIERS. WASHINGTON, Feb. 6.—A messenger has

REWARDS OFFERED FOR THE KILLING OF UNION OFFICERS IN TENNESSEE.

Author's Note: Gory details recited below.

Two months later, Nast again used *Southern Chivalry* as a model for *Southern Justice*. His demonic portrayal of *Justice*, with twisted features and copperhead snakes for hair, was perhaps as close to the apotheosis of evil as he ever drew. Her unbalanced lighter scale contained the valueless corpses of a Yankee, a black man (labeled "Nigger"), and a U.S. soldier, while a Confederate Southern Gentleman reclined peacefully on the weightier pan. The two large side panels also used the N-word, which Nast rarely employed, and then generally to hammer home anti-Confederate points as bluntly as he could.

The smaller vignettes at the top and bottom illustrated the atrocities described in the eleven news items (left text). The right text reiterated much of the language the President used in his veto of the Military Bill which was passed three weeks earlier.

HW March 23, 1867 184-185

Alaska

While Military Reconstruction dominated the news, the American public learned on March 31, 1867, that their country had just contracted to buy Alaska from Russia for $7,000,000 in gold. President Johnson called the recessed Senate into special session, and it approved the purchase (37-2) ten days later.

Russia sold because it needed the money and was worried about ultimately losing its territory, either through war with England (Canada's motherland) or annexation by the United States (as had happened with Texas). Consequently, the Russian minister to the U.S., Baron Edouard de Stoeckl, contacted Secretary of State Seward earlier in March. Johnson and Seward jumped at the deal, primarily in the nation's best interest, but also as a diversion from their losing battles with Congress over Reconstruction and the President's ugly public image.

Seward did a masterful job of persuasion, getting both Charles Sumner, Chairman of the Senate Foreign Relations Committee, and Thad Stevens to support the purchase and bring their colleagues on board. There was a much later battle in the House, which had to appropriate the funding, that wasn't resolved for another fifteen months even though the U.S. had taken title to the territory.

Harper's recognized the potential economic benefits of Alaska's fisheries, furs, timber and coal. Nevertheless, the *Weekly* opposed "Seward's Folly", as it editorialized about: taking on more debt; too much to do at home; the country shouldn't enter on a colonial system; Alaska's population of 50-60,000 Esquimaux and another 10,000 nondescripts living in a remote and barbarous National Ice-House would be expensive to maintain; and the whole idea was an "effort by Seward to regain some of that public consideration which he has so recklessly squandered." Its humor column called the walruses "cattle," and "supposed they gave ice cream". . . "the chief occupation of the natives is getting something to eat, and among strangers, to keep from being eaten."[6]

Nast strongly supported *Harper's* position. His back-page cartoon showed "Mother" Seward applying Russia Salve to pugnacious Andy's head.[7] On the Map of the Russian Fairy Land, Uncle Sam, trudging on snowshoes and carrying the flag, was being chased by a polar bear.

Looking in the mirror, Johnson saw himself as King Andy.

HW April 20, 1867 256

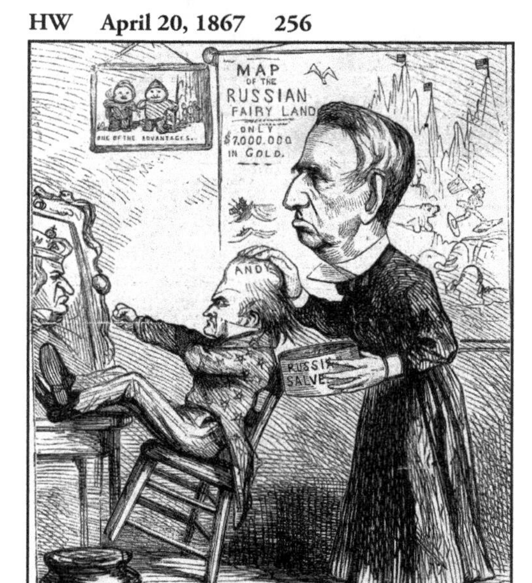

"THE BIG THING"
Old Mother Seward. "I'll rub some of this on his sore spot! It may soothe him a little."

Nast's cartoon for *Phunny Phellow* featured Columbus Seward discovering the North Pole with an American flag planted on it, while playful polar bears, seals, a walrus and three Eskimos watched apprehensively. Seward wore an "Andy" medallion while carrying a harpoon with an Andy - Copperhead pennant and a crown on top.

However, Nast's main political jab was at Henry Raymond and his *New York Times*. Raymond had been a consistent flip-flopper. He supported Johnson by organizing the National Union Convention and voting in Congress to sustain his vetoes of the Freedmen's Bureau and Civil Rights Act bills, but opposed him on the Fourteenth Amendment and the Military Reconstruction Bill.

In one of his most subtle but devastating caricatures, Nast played off the seals to depict an otherwise normal Raymond with flippers instead of hands — one black and one white. Nast probably couldn't have drawn this in the *Weekly*; Raymond had been the first editor of *Harper's Monthly* in the early fifties, and Fletcher Harper would have been upset at the pointed ridicule of his friend. In this instance, the *Times* backed Seward and Johnson on Alaska, while Horace Greeley who opposed the purchase, observed with dismay from the water; the *Tribune* and *Harper's Weekly* (figuratively) were in the same boat.

At this point in time, Nast was about to leave *Harper's* for a year as he explored painting, among other career paths. The satirical caption on his twelve-by-nineteen-inch image expressed his wistful hopes.

PP June 1867 8-9

THE DISCOVERY OF THE NORTH POLE BY COLUMBUS SEWARD. FROM AN ORIGINAL PAINTING BY THOMAS NAST, HISTORICAL PAINTER TO HIS MAJESTY KING ANDY.

N.B. This Painting is to be Placed in the Capitol at Washington, Price $50,000. Clarence Cork, the Art Critic (?) of the Tribune, says, “It’s the Worst Picture there.” And that’s Saying a Great Deal.

Military Reconstruction Acts

On March 2, 1867, Congress took decisive action against Johnson when it passed the first Military Reconstruction Act. The act stripped President of his power over the Reconstruction process and gave it to the Army, subject to Congressional oversight. The ten former Confederate states, divided into five military districts, were placed under the control of a Commander who had to be a brigadier or major general in the Regular Army. On March 11, 1867 — nine days after his veto was overridden — Johnson appointed the five military commanders whom Grant had recommended.

One of Commander Phil Sheridan's first actions in Louisiana was to remove from office New Orleans Mayor John Monroe, Attorney General Andrew Herron, and Judge Edmund Abell from office. Herron had failed to indict white law violators, while Abell didn't prosecute those who were arrested.

Three weeks after passing the first Military Reconstruction Act, Congress passed a second one, clarifying registration and election procedures. Nast celebrated with a smaller cartoon in which both a caricatured happy newly-enfranchised freedman and an unhappy "disfranchised" (sic) ex-Confederate accepted the situation.

HW April 13, 1867 240

HW May 25, 1867 324

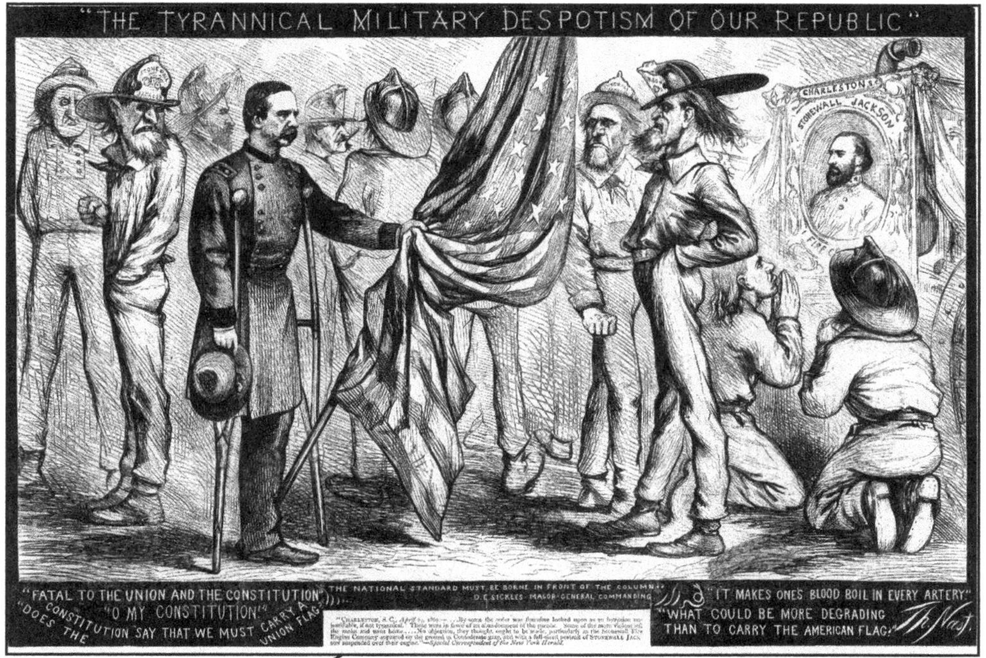

"CHARLESTON, S. C., *April* 29, 1867.—....By some the order was therefore looked upon as an intrusion unjustifiable, if not tyrannical. These were in favor of an abandonment of the parade. Some of the more violent left the ranks and went home.....No objection, they thought, ought to be made, particularly as the Stonewall Fire Engine Company appeared on the ground in Confederate gray, and with a full-sized portrait of STONEWALL JACKSON suspended over their engine."—*Special Correspondent of the New York Herald.*

Johnson appointed Dan Sickles as Military Commander of the Carolinas. General Sickles caught Nast's attention when he insisted that Charleston's Stonewall Jackson Fire Engine Company carry American flags on its parade equipment, over its fierce objections. As the accompanying editorial in *Harper's* pointed out, "the parade was to be a covert ovation in memory of the rebellion" in the place where it began, with a deliberate snub of the restored Union. For Nast, this was an opportunity to exalt the flag — his supreme symbol of patriotism — as well as take a slap at Johnson's much-too-lenient Reconstruction "policy."

Four months after the flag cartoon appeared, Johnson fired Sickles for insubordination. While absent from *Harper's*, Nast still contributed regularly to *Phunny Phellow*, and depicted the scene a few months later.

PP January 1868 C

OUR COMMANDER-IN-CHIEF DOING HONOR TO A HERO OF GETTYSBURG.

Conflict with Curtis: The Beginning

As Nast's caricatures of "King Andy" in *Harper's Weekly* gained continuing public acclaim, Nast received periodic letters from George William Curtis criticizing his Johnson caricatures; Curtis considered it unwise "to break finally and openly with our own Administration." Curtis's editorials would be forgotten, but Nast's pictures were "a blow beyond recall." Fortunately, Fletcher Harper allowed both his stars to fight their political opponents in their own ways.

The friction Curtis created was a significant factor in Nast's decision to leave the *Weekly* in May 1867 without a return date in mind. His plan was to create a traveling panorama, hopefully in partnership with humorist and publisher David Ross Locke of Toledo, Ohio. While he was negotiating with Locke before he actually left, he referred to his tense relationship with his editor, when he responded to a *Toledo Blade* article which Locke sent him: "The article in the *Blade* is first rate, particularly the little dig at the Harper's monopoly which tickles me, 'hit im again'" (sic).[8]

This was the first of several battles between Nast and Curtis, which flared up during the next three Presidential elections in particular, and would go against Nast after Fletcher died in 1877.

Prelude to Impeachment

The rumblings of impeachment grew louder and louder with Secretary of War Edwin Stanton at their epicenter. Johnson pressed him to resign, but Stanton refused. He wanted to be present to speak up in Cabinet meetings for stricter Reconstruction policies and enforcement, as well as to work behind the scenes with General-of-the-Army Grant and Congressional leaders.

In March 1867, Congress passed the Tenure of Office Act over Johnson's veto. It protected Stanton by forbidding a president from removing a Senate-confirmed appointee without the Senate's express approval. Johnson claimed that the law was unconstitutional so he didn't have to observe it *until* the Supreme Court upheld it.

Before Congress adjourned in July 1867, it passed the Third Reconstruction Act which Stanton helped draft. It explicitly made the state provisional governments subordinate to military rule, and enhanced the authority of military commanders.

Johnson responded by suspending Stanton on August 12, and appointing Grant as Acting Secretary of War. He evidently wanted to be seen as his pawn in order to damage him with Republicans. Grant accepted the position to prevent somebody more sympathetic to Johnson from assuming his authority. Congress was in recess so Johnson had not violated the Tenure of Office Act *yet*. After Congress reconvened, the Senate restored Stanton to office on January 25, 1868, and Grant stepped down.

HW April 14, 1867 232

To impeach a president required a vote by the House of Representatives; on February 13, after much debate led by ill and feeble Thaddeus Stevens, the House refused to impeach. That changed quickly. Eight days later, Johnson notified Congress that he had removed Stanton and replaced him with Adjutant-General Lorenzo Thomas. Three days after that, the House voted 147/47 to impeach the President for "High Crimes and Misdemeanors." In defiance of Congress, he deliberately violated a law which he had sworn to execute.

Events didn't go as planned for either side. Stanton refused to abandon his physical office and actually lived in it. Not only did he deny admission to his designated successor, but he had him arrested for trying to exercise his new responsibilities as Secretary of War.

Nast's portrait of Stanton was from the Bal d'Opera; "Mars" was Lincoln's nickname for his Secretary of War.

The Trial

The Senate formally received the specific charges against Johnson on March 4, 1868. The Eleventh Article, primarily written by Thaddeus Stevens, was essentially an omnibus of the other ten. After lots of discussion and delays, the Senate finally sat as a jury on March 30. Chief Justice Salmon Chase presided.

ICN April 24, 1867 C

Richard West, Periodyssey

Nast did go to Washington around the middle of March, hoping to see the action in the Senate. He had made an arrangement with the *Illustrated Chicago News*, a hopeful imitator of *Harper's Weekly*, which had recruited him to become its political cartoonist. In its first issue dated April 24, the newcomer boasted that it could "happily call him our own artist." In an ominous sign of its ill fate, the paper printed the date as 1867 — off by a year!

If the Chicago paper had been successful, Nast may well have ended his relationship with *Harper's*. Fortunately for him, his old employer and the public, it died with its eighth issue on June 13. Within two weeks — and after a year's absence — Nast was back where he belonged and Fletcher welcomed him warmly, but with a significant restriction; he now had to clear his submissions through Curtis.

While in Washington, he stayed at the home of his good friend, Brigadier General Norton Chipman. There, he drew an anticipatory never-published satire entitled *What a Fall Was There My Countrymen*; the line was taken from the beginning of Mark Antony's funeral oration in Shakespeare's *Julius Caesar* (Act III, Scene 2). An angry Columbia dumped King Andy out of his throne as his symbols of power, an orb and a scepter, went flying.[9]

The trial in the Senate dragged on for six weeks with its length working in Johnson's favor. When the vote on the Eleventh Article was taken on May 16, seven Republicans joined the Democrats in acquitting the President by 35/19. With the roll call taken in alphabetical order, Edmund Ross of Kansas provided the decisive vote.[10]

Continuing in the same vein, Nast drew *The Political Death of the Bogus Caesar*. It was a political parody of a painting by the renowned French artist Jean-Léon Gérôme entitled *The Death of Caesar*, and probably was intended for the first issue of the Chicago paper (April 24, 1868). However, it was never submitted as the trial dragged on and Johnson's acquittal became probable.[11]

Although Nast returned to *Harper's Weekly* in June 1868 and brought the block with him, Curtis and Fletcher decided to hold it for the issue of March 13, 1869 — an ideal time for its post-dated availability just prior to March 4, the date Johnson's term expired and Grant was inaugurated. The satire's proximity to the Ides of March when Caesar met his fate was a happy coincidence.

The impeached President lay dead on the floor, his vetoes beside him, his throne toppled over, and his orb of broken power at his feet. His own words — *Treason is a Crime and must be punished* — came back to haunt him from the wall.

Waving their swords triumphantly in their togas, the Roman senators who did the deadly deed were the Republican House managers of the President's trial in the Senate: George Boutwell (MA); John Logan (IL); John Bingham (OH); James Wilson (IA); Benjamin Butler (MA); and Thomas Williams (PA). Their instrument, the Tenure of Office Act, was legible on the floor.

HW March 13, 1869 164

Johnson

Left to Right: George Boutwell, John Logan, John Bingham, James Wilson, Benjamin Butler, Thomas Williams, Thaddeus Stevens

THE POLITICAL DEATH OF THE BOGUS CAESAR.

"Liberty! Freedom! Tyranny is dead!
Run hence, proclaim, cry it about the streets"

"Some to the common pulpits, and cry out
Liberty, Freedom, And Enfranchisement!"

The Aftermath

There were a number of reasons why impeachment failed. The political ones had to do with insufficient evidence; the threat to the traditional structure of government and the long-term effects on that; and the fact that Johnson only had nine months left in office. Ben Butler's weak but bombastic arguments were unconvincing, while the President's defense team — headed by former Attorney General Henry Stanbery and respected newcomer William Evarts — totally outlawyered him. Thad Stevens, who had led the impeachment effort in the House was failing rapidly and couldn't lobby for conviction; he died three months later.

Perhaps the most critical factor was the strong distaste that many Republicans had for fellow Senator Ben Wade of Ohio. As president *pro tem* of the Senate and acting Vice President of the country, Wade would have replaced Johnson in the White House; all knew that Wade should have recused himself from voting for impeachment because of his blatant conflict of interest. Important Moderates like William Fessender of Maine and James Grimes of Iowa preferred to keep Johnson in office for nine months more rather than have to deal with Wade. Ohioans must have agreed because Wade was not returned to the Senate that fall.

Nast's cartoon was published in the second issue of the *Illustrated Chicago News*. Prince Wade offered King Andy his crown back with appropriate Shakespearean dialogue. (*Henry IV, Part Two, IV).*

ICN May 1, 1868

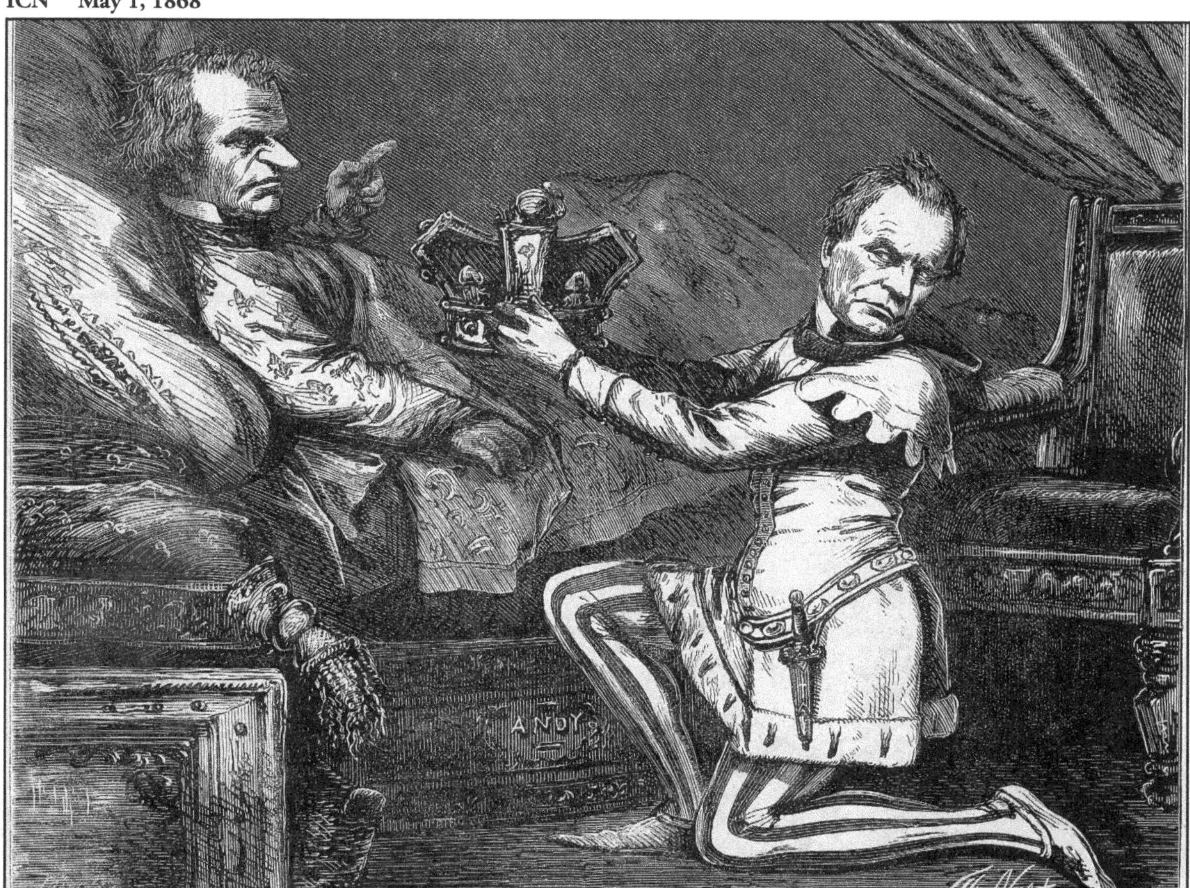

Hood Museum, Dartmouth College

SCENE AFTER THE VERDICT OF ACQUITAL.

Prince Wade – I never thought to hear you speak again.
King Andy—Thy wish was father, Ben, to that thought:
I stay too long by thee, I weary thee;
Dost thou so hunger for my empty chair.
That thou will needs invest thee with mine honors
Before thy hour is ripe? O, foolish youth!
Thou suk's't the greatness that will overwhelm thee.
Stay but a little' for my cloud of dignity
Is held from falling with so weak a wind,
That it will quickly drop; my day is slim . . . .
Thy life did manifest thou lov'ds't me not,
And thou will have me die assured of it;
Thou hid'st a thousand daggers in thy thoughts;
Which thou hast whetted on thy stony heart,
To stab at half an hour of my life.
What! Cans't thou not forbear me half an hour?
Then get thee gone. And dig my grave thyself;
And bid the merry bells ring to thine ear
That thou art crowned, not that I am dead.—
Shakespeare.

For the rest of his term, Johnson let military reconstruction proceed under Grant without making waves. Nast depicted him being rejected by the Democratic Party when — his hobby horse destroyed — King Andy uttered the famous last words of Shakespeare's *Richard III* in the battle which brought Henry VII to the throne. (Act V.)

HW July 25, 1868 480

"Give me another horse,—and bind up my wounds."

Alarm! Enter King * * * *.—"A horse! A horse! My kingdom for a horse!"
THE DEMOCRATIC CONVENTION, NEW YORK, JULY 9TH, 1868, DECLINE A.J. WITH THANKS.

HW October 31, 1868 695

"ALL QUIET ON THE POTOMAC."

Johnson went home to Greeneville, Tennessee after refusing to attend Grant's Inauguration.

On the last page of the same issue that depicted Caesar's demise, Nast turned to Shakespeare once again for King Andy's "*Farewell, a Long Farewell to All My Greatness*." Cardinal Wolsey spoke the line on learning of his dismissal by King Henry VIII. It is likely that this also was an unused relic of the *Illustrated Chicago News*.

Johnson appeared on the national stage once more when he was elected Senator from Tennessee in 1874. Nast was there to greet him figuratively just before he took office the following March. He only lasted five months before he died of a stroke.

HW March 13, 1869 176

"FAREWELL, A LONG FAREWELL, TO ALL MY GREATNESS!"

HW February 20, 1875 164

THE WHIRLIGIG OF TIME.
"Here we are again!"

Chapter 15
Historical Painter

Paintings

Given a choice, Thomas Nast would undoubtedly have chosen historical painting as his designated career. If he could have emulated Winslow Homer, his fellow artist at *Harper's Weekly,* he certainly would have preferred Homer's star status as a painter to that of the premier caricaturist that he was destined to become. Four years after his death, Leigh Leslie, an art critic who knew Nast and corresponded with him frequently in his later life, had this to say:

Thomas Nast's name is associated in the popular mind with cartoons, and it will go down in history as that of a pictorial satirist. The fame that Nast won with his pencil was great and merited, and it was gratifying to him. It was not satisfying to him, however. He wished to be known to future generations, not only as a pictorial satirist, but as a historical painter as well.

I do not know whether Nast was gifted with great talent for that higher form of art in which he aspired and labored to win distinction. But I do know this, that he valued highly his paintings of historical association, and I suspect that he never quite forgave his own generation for persistently denying him that claim to greatness as a painter which it so readily allowed him as a cartoonist.[1]

In fact, Nast was well prepared to become an historical painter, beginning with his six-month apprenticeship with Theodor Kaufmann after he dropped out of school at age thirteen. He had a solid knowledge of Dutch landscape, German and French romantic art, French academism and realism, as well as the work of French caricaturist and painter Honoré Daumier. However, Nast probably identified most closely with Gustave Doré, the French painter and illustrator, who was eight years older and came from Strasbourg, not far from Nast's birthplace in Landau. Nast got to know Doré and collected his work. They physically resembled each other, and developed similar over-sized egos as their accomplishments received increasing acclamation.

According to a letter Paine received after Nast's death from Nast's former colleague, who also knew Doré: "They had much in common . . . Tom patterned himself at one time on his resemblance to Doré, and favored the likeness by the trim of his beard. His hirsute adornments over time exceeded those of the Frenchman."[2] Nast had their two photographs from the early 1860s framed together in his home.

Macculloch Hall Historical Museum

Macculloch Hall Historical Museum

Self Portrait 1874

However, by 1869 Nast became disillusioned with Doré. In a response to his close friend Colonel Norton Chipman he wrote: "I endorse and highly appreciate your sentiments as to the comparison between me and Doré. In fact, I don't think he can hold a candle to me. I feel like some pumpkins and consider him small potatoes, speaking from a strictly regrettable point of view." Underneath, he sketched himself all swelled up, with Chipman looking at him admiringly.[3]

Additionally, Nast respected the English artists John Leech and John Tenniel. Leech joined *Punch* at its commencement in 1841, drew its first cartoon in 1843, and was its chief cartoonist until his death in 1864 when Tenniel succeeded him.

After Nast moved to Harlem in 1864, he filled all available wall space in his home with his pictures. Five years later, he portrayed the scene as Sallie dealt with Julia, Tom Jr., and baby Edith.[4]

Nast received a further psychic boost in April 1864 when a new book by art critic James Jackson Jarvis, described him as "an artist of uncommon originality of conception, lofty appreciation of national ideas and action, and a large artistic instinct."[5]

By then he was in full stride as a painter. The prime place to exhibit was the National Academy of Design, which had opened its palatial new white marble showplace at Fourth Avenue and 23rd Street on April 27, 1865. Nast had three paintings on display in the Academy's predecessor building in both 1862 and 1863, and two in 1864.

One of the 1864 paintings, *Faithful Unto Death*, depicted dead soldiers grouped around a gun under a rising moon. The *Weekly* called it "a true ballad of the war," but chastised the hanging committee of the Academy for placing it high in a corner out of sight.[6]

Currier & Ives

Currier & Ives created hand-colored lithographs that reproduced paintings by popular artists intended to appeal to the growing middle-class market. Priced from twenty cents to three dollars, they depicted a wide range of domestic scenes.

Nast painted five pictures that Currier & Ives used for their lithographs in 1863: once camp scene (*Preparing for Supper*) and four comics. In the year of Emancipation and the first enlisted black Union soldiers, *The Colored Volunteer* was especially timely.

THE COLORED VOLUNTEER.

DOMESTIC BLOCKADE

James Brust, San Pedro, CA.
THE COMMANDER-IN-CHIEF.

Another format that disseminated Nast's images to a wide audience was reproductive cartes de visite photographs (4 x 2 1/2 inch) designed to fill empty slots in family photo albums. Sometimes, Nast's own painting were photographed and his name and copyright designation appeared on the cartes de visite; more commonly, the lithograph was copied and distributed by other photographers, usually without credit to Nast or Currier & Ives.

Macculloch Hall Historical Museum
DOMESTIC BLOCKADE

Another painting of a different version of *Domestic Blockade* featured his beautiful, radiant Sallie holding one-year old Julia, facing a young boy dressed in a colorful Zouave uniform. Nast probably kept this picture for his family.

During the first four months of 1865, Nast took a sabbatical from *Harper's Weekly* to devote himself to painting. His principal effort was based on his *Weekly* illustration of April 4, 1863 — *Arrival of a Federal Column at a Planter's House in Dixie.** Nast hoped it would be the cornerstone for a career as a painter of contemporary historical scenes and subjects.

---

* See p. 123

Entitled *General Sherman's March Through Georgia — His Advance Arriving at a Plantation*, the approximate four-by-seven foot oil painting was on exhibit at the Academy's grand opening. Also referred to as *The Drink of Water*, Nast's picture was in good company with those of Albert Bierstadt, Thomas Hicks, Eastman Johnson and John Kensett.

But once again there was an insurmountable problem. As George William Curtis editorialized: "This is a picture that would richly reward your attention if you could see it. But you cannot" because the committee had hung the painting high over a door in a sunken panel.[7] This mistreatment of Nast's art — which had happened the year before and earlier* — was another portent of future disappointment in his subsequent efforts to gain recognition as a top flight painter.

Nast continued his attempts to become a top-tier painter for another several years. However, as pointed out earlier, even Winslow Homer continued to draw wood engravings for *Harper's Weekly* until 1875 because sales of his watercolor and oil paintings — sometimes of the same subjects as his prints — were insufficient to support him, even as a bachelor. By 1874, however, his watercolors were selling well and he soon devoted himself only to painting.

Another of Nast's better paintings during this five-year interim after the war, was *The Departure of the 7th Regiment to the War, April 19, 1861*. Nast had sketched the original march, which featured Colonel Robert Anderson, the hero of Fort Sumter, reviewing the troops from the balcony of jewelers Ball, Black & Co. Anderson, who surrendered the fort only five days earlier, had just landed in New York by steamer. Nast painted the five-and-a-half by eight-foot picture in 1869, and exhibited it at the National Academy of Design the following year. He was proud of having joined the Seventh Regiment after the war.[8]

Much to his regret, Nast understood by 1870 that his road to fame and financial stability would be paved by his skills as a political caricaturist. He put the same careful multi-faceted detail into his cartoons as he did with his paintings. He clearly understood that while his cartoons were ephemeral, they could bring him recognition, wealth and enough influence to accomplish his political goals.[9]

Nast's study for the final painting is in the Collection of The New-York Historical Society.

---

* See p. 13

The Grand Caricaturama

The social and financial success of the Grand Masquerade Ball inspired Nast to undertake the most entrepreneurial and potentially career-changing venture of his life. He believed that he could satisfy his passion for historical painting and his talent for caricature by combining them into a novel, attention-getting panorama.

Moving panoramas had been popular in the Unites States since the 1830s, anticipating the arrival of motion pictures on film by half a century. They consisted of thirty to fifty tall pictures, painted with impermanent water-based tempera, generally on cotton muslin similar to that used for theatrical scenes. The sequential pictures were unfurled between two tall spools, concealed from viewers by a knob or crank as part of an unseen control box; they were not intended to be viewed up close.

The rationale for the original panoramas was to bring the world to their curious viewers, similarly to current travel documentaries. They included spoken narratives, piano music, and occasional special visual or sound effects.

Nast undoubtedly saw a number of panoramas during his formative years, but the one that really impressed him was *Artemus Ward Among the Mormons*. Ward (pen name of Charles Farrar Browne) was a renowned humorist who went on a comic lecture tour through the West in 1863. Upon his return, he decided to spoof the popular Western panoramas.

He hired two artists to paint serious pictures, based partly on photographs of the people and places he had encountered, and wrote a humorous script which he delivered in a deadpan manner. The accompanying piano music was deliberately mismatched: soft romantic pieces for scalping scenes and military marches for sentimental panels. Before the curtain went up, Ward warmed up his audience with a long prologue that had little to do with his subject, but kept his audience laughing throughout.

The *Mormons* show opened on October 31, 1864, and ran for nine weeks in Dodsworth Hall. Prominent men were given free tickets admitting "the Bearer and **ONE** wife." However, the production was only moderately successful in New York, and then Boston. Ward changed course, replacing the serious, well-crafted panels with humorous scenes which parodied John Banvard's famous Mississippi River panorama and other popular Western themes.[10]

When *Mormons* reopened later in 1865, its transformation into the first completely comic moving panorama was successful. A road tour through several American and Canadian cities ended in London in January 1867, a time when Nast was planning his own Grand Caricaturama.

Nasby

Nast spent the best part of 1867 creating the Caricaturama, and poured all his artistic talent and a good share of his monetary resources into it. "I think I see a fortune in it" was how he put it when unsuccessfully wooing David Ross Locke as a partner who likely would have proved him correct.[11]

Nast probably was introduced to Locke by Boston publisher, Lee and Shepard, during 1866. (Nast illustrated books for the firm while it was preparing to publish Locke's first book under his pen name, Petroleum Vesuvius Nasby.) Seven years older than Nast, Locke (sequentially) partially owned and edited three small Ohio newspapers during the 1850s. In 1861, he moved to Finley, Ohio, purchased the *Hancock Jeffersonian*, and gained national recognition for his "Nasby Letters."

Nast recognized the need for a humorous script delivered by a topflight comic actor or lecturer to create the kind of total entertainment value that Artemus Ward brought to his *Mormons* show. His target was a Nast and Nasby extravaganza.

Paine p. 114

THE MEETING OF NAST AND NASBY

Using ungrammatical Kentucky dialect, phonic misspelling and biting humor, Nasby gave satiric voice to extreme Confederate thoughts and positions. His letters were widely reprinted and read, and — like Nast's allegorical cartoons — helped solidify Northern opinion. Kentucky-born President Lincoln was a strong Nasby fan. Nast and Locke became friends, and Nast illustrated Nasby's letters in two books:[12]

1867 — *Swingin Round the Cirkle by Petroleum V. Nasby . . . his Ideas of Men, Politics, and Things, as Set Forth in His Letters to the Public Press, During the Year 1866.*

1868 — *Ekkoes from Kentucky . . . . Being a Perfect Record uv the Dimocrisy, Dorrin the Eventful Year 1867; ez Seen by a Naturalized Kentuckian.*

DEDIKASHUN.

TO THE

MAN,

WHOEVER HE MAY BE, WHO SUCCEEDS IN BEIN ELECTED TO THE PRESIDENCY BY THE DIMOCRATIC PARTY, AND WHO SHALL, IMMEJITLY AFTER HIS INOGGERASHUN, APPINT ME TO THE POST OFFIS, FROM WICH THE TYRANT GRANT DISMIST ME, THUS ASURIN AN OLD DIMOCRAT, WHO NEVER SCRATCHED A TICKET, AND ALLUZ TOOK HIS LIKKER STRATE, A COMFORTABLE END TO AN UNCOMFORTABLE CAREER,

THIS VOLUME IS DEDIKATED,

BY THE AUTHOR,

WITH SENTIMENCE OF PROFOUND RESPECT,

PETROLEUM V. NASBY.

CONFEDRIT X ROADS
(wich is in the Stait uv Kentucky),
April 15, 1872.

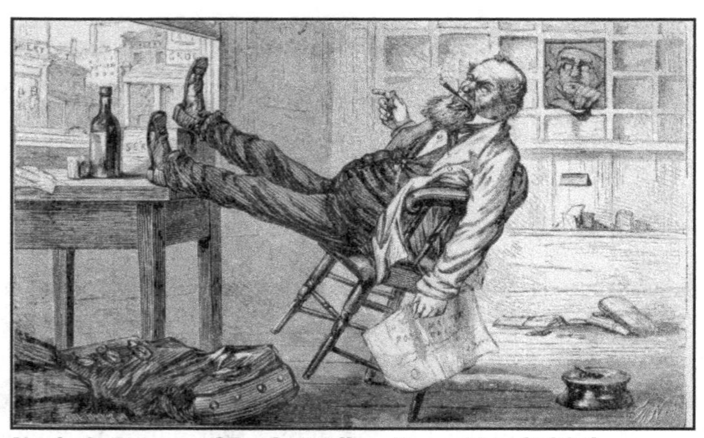

Nasby's Dream of Perfect Bliss. Page 194. (1867)

In early 1867, Locke wrote Nast about illustrating his books. Nast agreed but also told Locke that "ever since last spring when I was so successful with my caricatures for the Bal d'Opera, I have had panorama on the brain." He tried hard to convince Locke, suggesting that "even if you would not care to deliver the lecture written by you yourself, I would hire a competent actor to do so, who would get himself up to impersonate the ideal Nasby." He offered to let Locke do the accounting and banking, so that "we'll both make money and fame." He would add pictures "to keep it fresh. . . Strike while the iron is hot for the coming presidential campaign."[13]

"A great object would be to get a good manager to exhibit it. . . I hear that Artemus Ward had a good man and perhaps we might secure his services." Leaving no stone unturned, Nast went on to describe his plan for the Caricaturama — a dream sequence within an "American History Storyland" — and many of the preliminary sketches which he had already drawn.[14]

Unfortunately for Nast, Locke turned him down. He had managed several newspapers, knew the ins and outs of forecasting revenues and controlling costs, and evidently anticipated financial disagreements with Nast over anticipated ticket prices and expenses. He had recently acquired a controlling interest in the *Toledo Blade*, was working on his second Nasby book, and probably was leery about the lack of time and potential profitability. His judgment proved correct.[15]

If Nast and Locke had been effective partners — with Nast restricted to the paintings and Locke responsible for the narration, as well as most of the operational and all of the financial aspects — the Caricaturama almost certainly would have been successful. However, Nast's ego probably could not have accepted Locke as the final decision-maker, assuming Locke had proposed it. For example, if Locke had tried to eliminate Nast's hard-hitting attacks on Jeff Davis and Horace Greeley — which had nothing to do with their current common target, King Andy Johnson, and might have gratuitously alienated potential customers — Nast would have fiercely defended his right to have the final say on his artistic choices. "The painting must be done under my eye; everything depends on it," he told Locke.[16]

Their inability to connect in 1867 didn't end Nast's relationship with Locke. Five years later he illustrated *The Struggles (Social, Financial, and Political) of Petroleum V. Nasby*. It gave him an extra chance to tweak Horace Greeley, then running for President. In the book, Nasby cheered as Greeley signed the $100.000 bail bond for Jeff Davis on May 13, 1867, while its recipient looked warily on.

THREE CHEERS FOR JOHNSON GREELEY.

After Locke's rejection, Nast tried to enlist his friend Mark Twain, who was still relatively unknown but had lots of traveling, early publishing, and some lectures under his belt. Their collaboration could have been a winner, but Twain, though appreciative, turned him down. (In late 1877, Twain reversed the offer with a 50-50 split, but Nast said no, probably because he didn't want to travel so much. However, the two always remained close friends.[17])

The Program

Consequently, Nast proceeded on his own to create 33 approximately nine-by-twelve foot panels. The artist featured himself dozing in front of his easel in the first scene, and smiling contentedly in the last. Nineteen of the panels dealt with slavery, sectionalism and the Civil War, while twelve targeted King Andy.

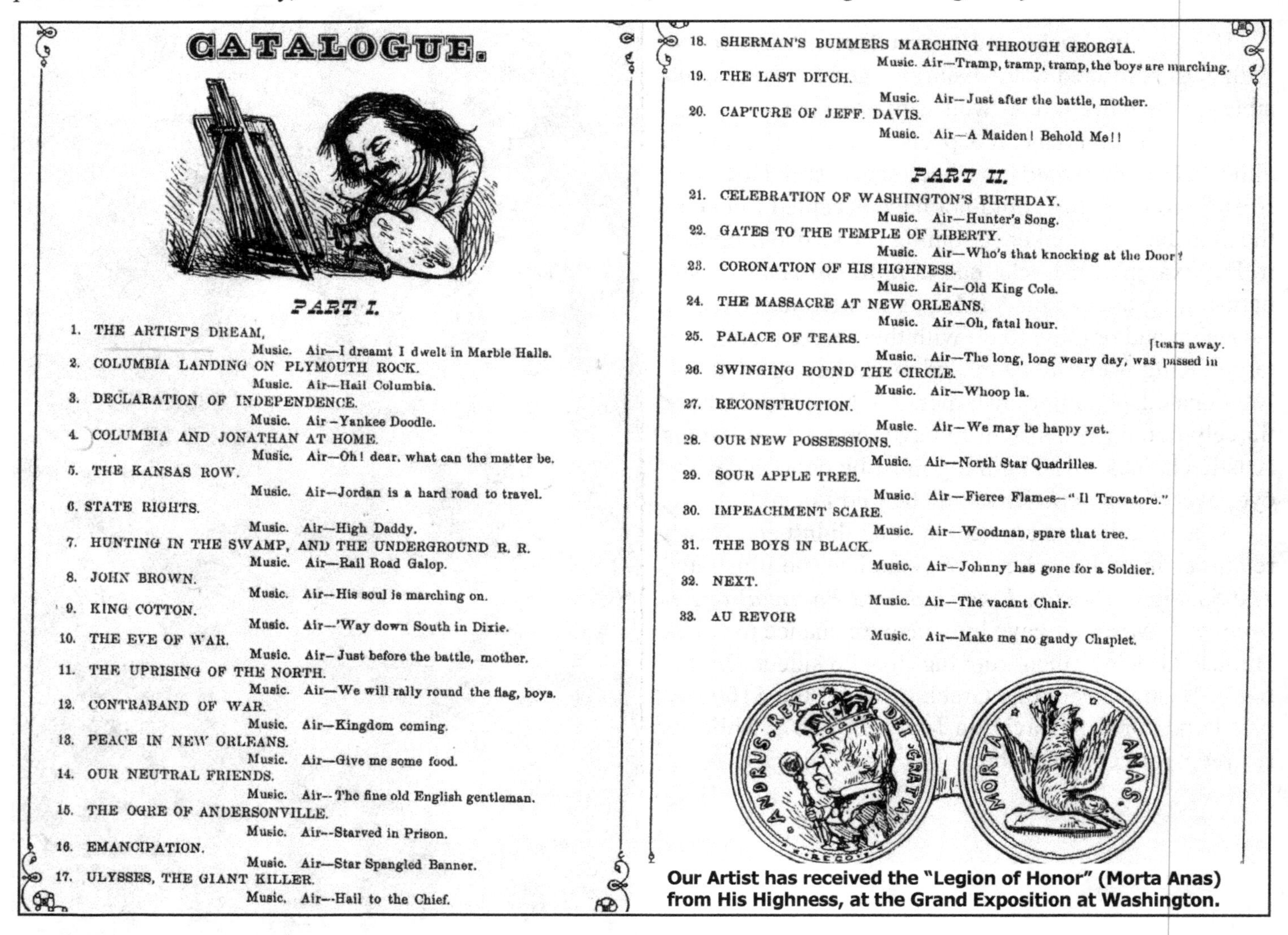

CATALOGUE.

PART I.

1. THE ARTIST'S DREAM.
Music. Air—I dreamt I dwelt in Marble Halls.
2. COLUMBIA LANDING ON PLYMOUTH ROCK.
Music. Air—Hail Columbia.
3. DECLARATION OF INDEPENDENCE.
Music. Air—Yankee Doodle.
4. COLUMBIA AND JONATHAN AT HOME.
Music. Air—Oh! dear, what can the matter be.
5. THE KANSAS ROW.
Music. Air—Jordan is a hard road to travel.
6. STATE RIGHTS.
Music. Air—High Daddy.
7. HUNTING IN THE SWAMP, AND THE UNDERGROUND R. R.
Music. Air—Rail Road Galop.
8. JOHN BROWN.
Music. Air—His soul is marching on.
9. KING COTTON.
Music. Air—'Way down South in Dixie.
10. THE EVE OF WAR.
Music. Air—Just before the battle, mother.
11. THE UPRISING OF THE NORTH.
Music. Air—We will rally round the flag, boys.
12. CONTRABAND OF WAR.
Music. Air—Kingdom coming.
13. PEACE IN NEW ORLEANS.
Music. Air—Give me some food.
14. OUR NEUTRAL FRIENDS.
Music. Air—The fine old English gentleman.
15. THE OGRE OF ANDERSONVILLE.
Music. Air—Starved in Prison.
16. EMANCIPATION.
Music. Air—Star Spangled Banner.
17. ULYSSES, THE GIANT KILLER.
Music. Air—Hail to the Chief.
18. SHERMAN'S BUMMERS MARCHING THROUGH GEORGIA.
Music. Air—Tramp, tramp, tramp, the boys are marching.
19. THE LAST DITCH.
Music. Air—Just after the battle, mother.
20. CAPTURE OF JEFF. DAVIS.
Music. Air—A Maiden! Behold Me!!

PART II.

21. CELEBRATION OF WASHINGTON'S BIRTHDAY.
Music. Air—Hunter's Song.
22. GATES TO THE TEMPLE OF LIBERTY.
Music. Air—Who's that knocking at the Door?
23. CORONATION OF HIS HIGHNESS.
Music. Air—Old King Cole.
24. THE MASSACRE AT NEW ORLEANS.
Music. Air—Oh, fatal hour.
25. PALACE OF TEARS.
Music. Air—The long, long weary day, was passed in tears away.
26. SWINGING ROUND THE CIRCLE.
Music. Air—Whoop la.
27. RECONSTRUCTION.
Music. Air—We may be happy yet.
28. OUR NEW POSSESSIONS.
Music. Air—North Star Quadrilles.
29. SOUR APPLE TREE.
Music. Air—Fierce Flames—"Il Trovatore."
30. IMPEACHMENT SCARE.
Music. Air—Woodman, spare that tree.
31. THE BOYS IN BLACK.
Music. Air—Johnny has gone for a Soldier.
32. NEXT.
Music. Air—The vacant Chair.
33. AU REVOIR
Music. Air—Make me no gaudy Chaplet.

Our Artist has received the "Legion of Honor" (Morta Anas) from His Highness, at the Grand Exposition at Washington.

Each scene received about two minutes of commentary while a female pianist played an appropriate song on the piano. The performance lasted for about an hour.

Nast hired comic actor William Norton to read a humorous explanatory text; however, the *New York Times* (whose publisher Henry Raymond was lampooned in some of the panels) commented that "the effect of the lecture was somewhat marred by the nervousness of the reader."[18] In retrospect, the difference between Norton and Locke or Twain, was a vital missing element. In Boston, a lyceum lecturer named Charles Brainard, also failed to provide the needed spark for what essentially was a multi-media entertainment.

In contrast to *Artemus Ward Among the Mormons*, which received more than ten positive reviews from a broad spectrum of New York papers two years earlier, the Caricaturama's reviews were mediocre to scathing. Even the latter complimented Nast's artistic talent and originality, but condemned him for "prostituting his ability" with his "coarse and scurrilous attacks."

The premier on Wednesday, December 4, 1867 at Dodworth Hall (806 Broadway) did not attract a full house, with tickets priced at 75 cents for reserved seats and 50 cents for general admission. The show ran for two weeks and box office results were disappointing.

When the Caricaturama moved to Boston's Horticultural Hall on March 30, 1868, ticket prices were reduced to 50 and 25 cents, respectively. Nevertheless, it failed to break even. Johnson's trial in the Senate began the same day, which may have been a distraction. The Boston run ended on April 16. Two days later, Nast was back in New York attending a ceremonial dinner for Charles Dickens, which highlighted the English author's final visit to America.

The financial failure of the Caricaturama must have hit Nast hard in his gut as well as his pocketbook. His pathway to earning a living through his first choice — historical painting — was no longer a possibility. His business acumen came up short. After a quick fling with the short-lived *Illustrated Chicago News* on the heels of the Caricaturama, his need to return to *Harper's Weekly* to provide a steady income and a national audience for his cartoons forced him to swallow some of his pride. By June 1868, he was back in harness.

As a watershed episode in Nast's career, the Caricaturama did have some pluses. Even the Democratic papers that detested its content praised the artist's conceptual and artistic talents. His role as a featured caricaturist for the nation's leading illustrated newspaper was set for the next sixteen years, along with the financial security, fame and political power to influence important events. Other than book illustrations and some later lecture tours and paintings, his course was channeled.[19]

These six paintings demonstrated Nast's unique ability to combine caricature with detailed "history painting." (The number referred to the picture's sequence within the Caricaturama.)

12. Contraband of War

General Benjamin Butler was no hero to Nast because of his military failures at Petersburg and Fort Fisher. Now as a Congressman, Nast recognized Butler would play a leading role at Johnson's trial if he were impeached. Nast honored him here for his 1861 feat in establishing the concept of contrabands,* perhaps implying that the spiked mace he used to deny the Confederate slave-retriever access to Fortress Monroe could also hypothetically be applied to the President.

The contrabands on top of the fortress wall jeered at the Confederate, while the crow (not an eagle) on top of the shield may have had a double meaning — Butler and the ex-slaves crowing, and the Confederate having to "eat crow" in spite of his cat-o'-nine-tails in one hand and a chain holding his slave-hunting dogs in the other.

Probably not coincidentally, the accompanying tune played was *Kingdom Coming*; Nast had illustrated the cover for the sheet music.**

* See p. 93-94

** See p. 122

15. The Ogre of Andersonville

Jeff Davis was never directly linked to the atrocities at Andersonville Prison, but Nast and many others believed he had to have known about them. Davis already had been released on bail provided by Horace Greeley and others when Nast painted him with devil's horns and a monstrous club pointing to a gallows with two Union prisoners hanging from it, while leaning over the stockade. The accompanying musical air was *Starved in Prison*.

29. Sour Apple Tree

Nast had come to despise Horace Greeley and never forgave him for his role in freeing Davis. He showed Greeley toting Davis in a long-handled bucket used for bailing water, while lighting flashed. The piece de resistance was the ghostly tree with a noose hanging from its branch-like hand; the reference was to "we'll hang Jeff Davis from a sour apple tree" to the tune of the popular song *John Brown's Body*. (Another earthier version was "We'll feed old Jeff Davis sour apples 'til he gets the diarhee" which was more relevant to Andersonville).

21. Celebration of Washington's Birthday

Nast led off his attack on Johnson with a reference to his surprise veto of the Freedmen's Bureau Bill, his drinking, and his comment about John Forney as a Dead Duck. Forney already was down flapping his wings, but abolitionist Wendell Phillips, Senator Charles Sumner and Congressman Thad Stevens were in range of the gun-toting President. In the background, Reverend Henry Ward Beecher, a Conservative Republican (also attacked in the Grand Masquerade Ball), was looking down his nose at the Radicals. The appropriate music was *Hunter's Song*.

Nast added a couple of special touches. Roger Whiskey was close behind the sometimes liquored-up President. In the right rear, Andrew Jackson (a fellow Tennessean) was on his emaciated horse; Jackson had backed Congress and Federal legislation over states rights and nullification when South Carolina wanted to secede in the 1830s. Contrarily, Johnson opposed almost every piece of federal legislation Congress sent him in favor of state laws, black codes and restrictive ordinances.

26. Swinging Round the Circle

Andy's trip featured an angry Johnson in a horse-drawn merry-go-round carriage, accompanied by Roger Whiskey, and holding his copy of the Constitution ("My policy"). Grant was behind him, stolid and smoking a cigar, followed by Naval Secretary Gideon Welles. Farragut was in front, an admiral sitting backward on his horse, while glaring at Johnson as if to say "What am I doing here?" Secretary of State William Seward led the procession, waving to the crowd.

The only restored original in existence is at the North Jersey History Center in the Morristown & Morris Township Public Library.

33. Au Revoir

Nast closed with his formally-dressed self-caricature, surrounded by painted exploding fireworks, probably made more realistic by dioramic lighting effects. His victor's laurel wreath was lowered onto his brow by two winged cherubs, one a smiling black devil, as the ringmaster exited in style.

Nast's Illustrated Almanacs

Two years after the Grand Caricaturama failed, Nast came up with a much simpler entrepreneurial project which embodied his earlier hope of becoming a historical painter. Around October 1870, *Nast's Illustrated Almanac* for 1871 appeared as a 72-page, (6 by 8 inches) paper-covered booklet priced at 25 cents ($5 today). It was published by McLoughlin Brothers — whose colorful children's books Nast had illustrated — and sold an astounding 36,000 copies in its first two weeks.[20]

Mostly ignoring domestic politics, Nast was at his whimsical, creative, humorous best. His masterpiece comprised 44 pages devoted to the 1871 calendar, including 12 fancifully illustrated American, British, Roman and French historical happenings. Some of his droller touches showed the birth of Napoleon with his hat on, Columbia as the first carpet-bagger landing on Plymouth Rock, and a sign on a glowering Henry VIII's wall warning "Post No Bills."

Following the calendar pages were six historical sketches, including *Henry VIII* and *The Landing of the Pilgrims*. All told, Nast had 105 illustrations in the Almanac, most of them small but witty.

LANDING OF THE FIRST CARPET-BAGGER ON PLYMOUTH ROCK, DECEMBER 22ND, 1620.

THE BIRTH OF NAPOLEON BONAPARTE, AUGUST 15TH 1769. THE BATTLE OF BOSWORTH, AUGUST 22ND, 1485. DOG DAYS.

LANDING OF COLUMBUS, OCTOBER 12TH, 1492.

BATTLE OF WATERLOO, JUNE 18TH, 1815.

ST. VALENTINE'S DAY. BIRTH OF WASHINGTON, FEB. 22, 1732.

FOURTH OF JULY—DECLARATION OF INDEPENDENCE, 1776—MARRIAGE OF COLUMBIA WITH BROTHER JONATHAN—CLEARING OUT OF FOREIGN RELATIVES

ASSASSINATION OF JULIUS CAESAR, MARCH 15TH, 44 B.C. DEATH OF QUEEN ELIZABETH, MARCH 24TH, 1603.

FALL AND DEATH OF CARDINAL WOLSEY, NOVEMBER 29TH, 1530.

Fletcher Harper noted the success of the initial *Almanac*, and arranged for the remaining four — its life, of course, not known at the time — to be published by his firm, beginning with 1872. Nast created it during the spring and summer of 1871 while his Tweed campaign was close to peaking, drawing 130 illustrations overall on 63 pages. He used the same seasonal carousel cover — featuring himself and Father Time — in all five years, so he didn't have to recreate it.

Under Fletcher's guidance, the calendar shrank to 13 pages of Nast's much smaller, less interesting Zodiac cartoons — no longer the featured presentation.

Fletcher evidently saw the *Almanac* as an advertising vehicle for Harper's books and periodicals, as well as other products. From two pages in 1871 (under McLoughlin Brothers) it went to 19 pages of ads in 1872; eight of them were for Harper's three periodicals and its book lists. Even the *Times* and the *Evening Post* took full pages, along with regular advertisers from the *Weekly's* food, drug, clothing and piano roster.

Nast added short stories and poems by well known American authors — Mark Twain, Petroleum Nasby, humorist Josh Billings — as well as Englishmen Alfred Tennyson, William Thackeray, and Charles Dickens (about characters from *Pickwick Papers*, which Nast had illustrated). Even John Hay, whom Nast had met in 1864 in the White House and who, as Secretary of State would send him to Guayaquil, Ecuador, in 1902, had a poem about the ills of *Ye Gambolier* (gambler).

[NEVER PUT OFF TILL TO-MORROW WHAT YOU CAN DO THE DAY AFTER TO-MORROW JUST AS WELL.—B.F.]

THE SUBLIME AND THE RIDICULOUS. "After You, Sir."

Although the *Almanac* was published through 1875, the last three years did not justify Fletcher's bet. Possibly because they were not solicited, no outside advertisers took space after 1872, and Twain dropped out as an author in 1875. Nast still had 80 to 90 illustrations in each issue — quite a few in silhouette — but there wasn't enough quality content to attract readers or advertisers.

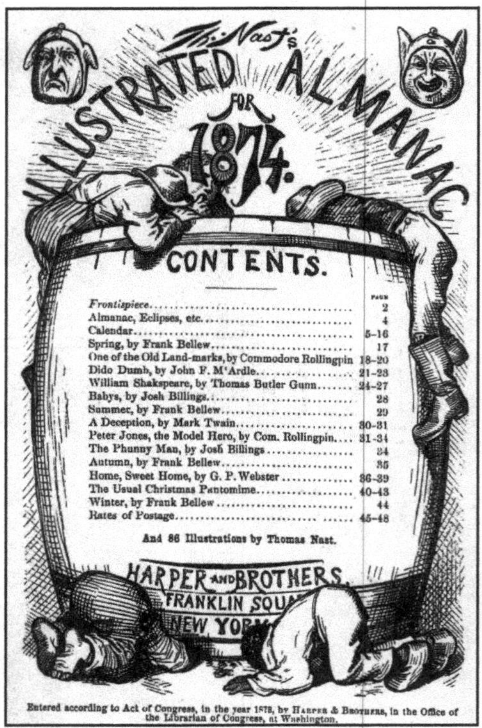

In retrospect, the *Almanac* — which was prepared during the summer and published in October — should have died a year or two earlier. Nast was still recuperating from the Greeley campaign and absent from *Harper's* when he prepared the 1974 edition in the summer of 1873. Fletcher wasn't about to alienate his hero cartoonist by rejecting it, even though the content was weaker than before.

CONTENTS.

A special feature was a four-page story about Shakespeare (sic) by Nast's old friend (from his courtship of Sallie days), Thomas Butler Gunn, whom he had visited in England during the spring. His old friend/rival, Frank Bellew, also contributed four illustrated pieces on the seasons. (As he said he would do after Nast gifted him $25 when Bellew was broke and ill after the Greeley campaign was over.)

By the summer of 1875, Nast was probably in total accord with Fletcher, to terminate the *Almanacs*. Fletcher's health was failing and that also may have factored into his decision.

Chapter 16
Harper's Bazar

On November 2, 1867, a month before the Caricaturama opened, *Harper's Bazar* made its debut as a family paper for women. It was Fletcher Harper's baby, born in spite of opposition from his reluctant — but finally agreeing — three older brothers. Its focus was on fashions in good taste, and included cut-out patterns in its supplement. Fletcher's model was the *Berlin Bazar*, which was already supplying colored fashion plates to Paris and London, and now gave Harper & Bros. the exclusive for America. Within six weeks its circulation exceeded 100,000.

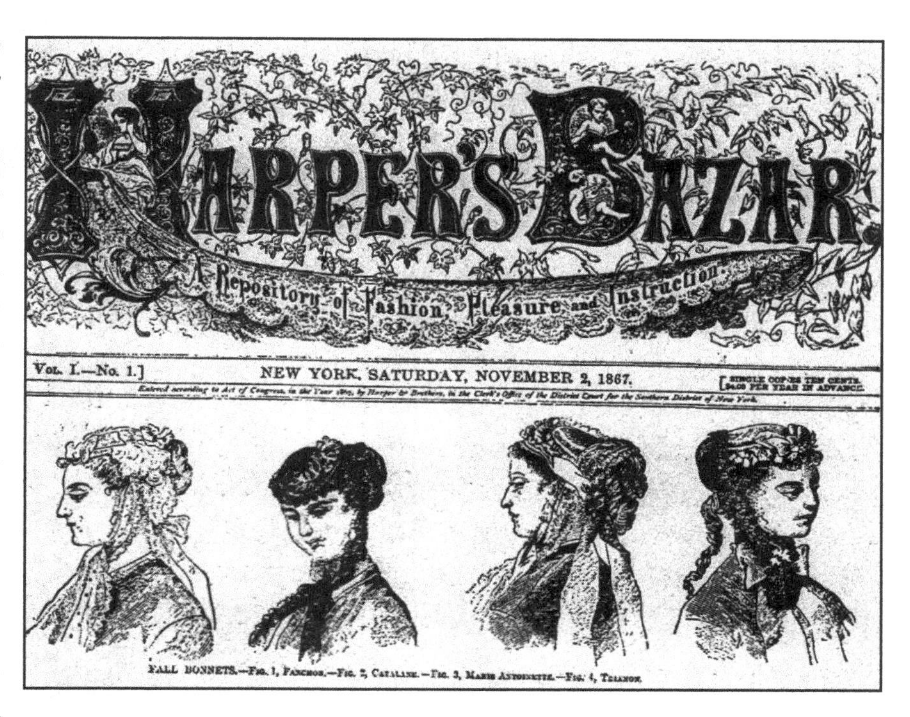
HARPER'S BAZAR
A Repository of Fashion, Pleasure and Instruction.
VOL. I.—No. 1.] NEW YORK, SATURDAY, NOVEMBER 2, 1867.
FALL BONNETS.—Fig. 1, Fanchon.—Fig. 2, Catalane.—Fig. 3, Marie Antoinette.—Fig. 4, Trianon.

The *Bazar's* masthead described it as *A Repository of Fashion, Pleasure and Instruction.* It included instructive cultural text; generally two serials quarterly; illustrations; and cartoons by Nast and others — mostly family-oriented rather than political.

An exception to political cartoons was a Nast farce, portraying Andy Johnson as a Presidential winner in 1868. *The Inaugural Ball — The Supper* depicted an intoxicated Johnson shoving oysters at Secretary of War Edwin Stanton, whose dismissal was the incident that resulted in the President's impeachment. Horace Greeley was in the background, and other characters were identifiable. Grant had been inaugurated a month before, so this was a fantasy.

HARPER'S BAZAR April 3, 1869 217

THE INAUGURATION BALL—THE SUPPER.

Nast drew only about half a dozen women in his political cartoons — a few singers and actresses, and two political figures: Lecturer Anna Elizabeth Dickinson and free lover Victoria Woodhull (who wanted to run for President in 1872). Only Woodhull was scorned.* His wife Sallie as Columbia — his female companion to Uncle Sam — served as a stand-in symbol for other American women.

* See p. 317-319

However, the *Bazar* gave him an opportunity to tweak women about their daily lives, and he seemed to enjoy it in the same illustrative style that he used in the *Weekly*, as well as in run-of-the-mill cartoons.

HARPER'S BAZAR September 4, 1868 568-569

Originally, *Marriage a la Mode* was a story and a play written by John Dryden in 1673. The great English artist and cartoonist, William Hogarth, popularized it with a series of six paintings in 1743. Its theme warned against the upper class practice of contractual marriage. Nast took it to a fantastic extreme by depicting the bride as an elephant. (Three years before he invented the Republican Elephant).

HARPER'S BAZAR April 1, 1871 200

MARRIAGE A LA MODE.

HARPER'S BAZAR July 3, 1869 425

"OH! BLESS US WITH ALL THESE THINGS!"

Equally sarcastic was his parody of worshipping the almighty dollar.

HARPER'S BAZAR June 24, 1871 393

LIKE MISTRESS LIKE MAID.

HARPER'S BAZAR October 23, 1869 688

COLD COMFORT TO A HUNGRY HUSBAND.
Pretty But Useless Wife. "The Cook left this morning, and I don't know how to Cook the Dinner, and—and—"

HARPER'S BAZAR December 11, 1869 800

THE WORST OF THESE WOMEN CLUBS.
Master Of The House (*the oppressed sex*). "Late again, my Dear!"
Emancipated Woman (*slightly under the influence of Strong Tea*). "Had no—*hic*—idea it was so Late—*hic*—my Darling!"

He often provided holiday scenes as well. President Grant, Secretary of State Hamilton Fish, and other Grant cabinet members were readily identifiable in the Thanksgiving series of ten vignettes, as were Sallie and their children in the center one. The turkey carver didn't look too much like Nast, but the proud papa was almost certainly him.

HARPER'S BAZAR November 27, 1869 760-761

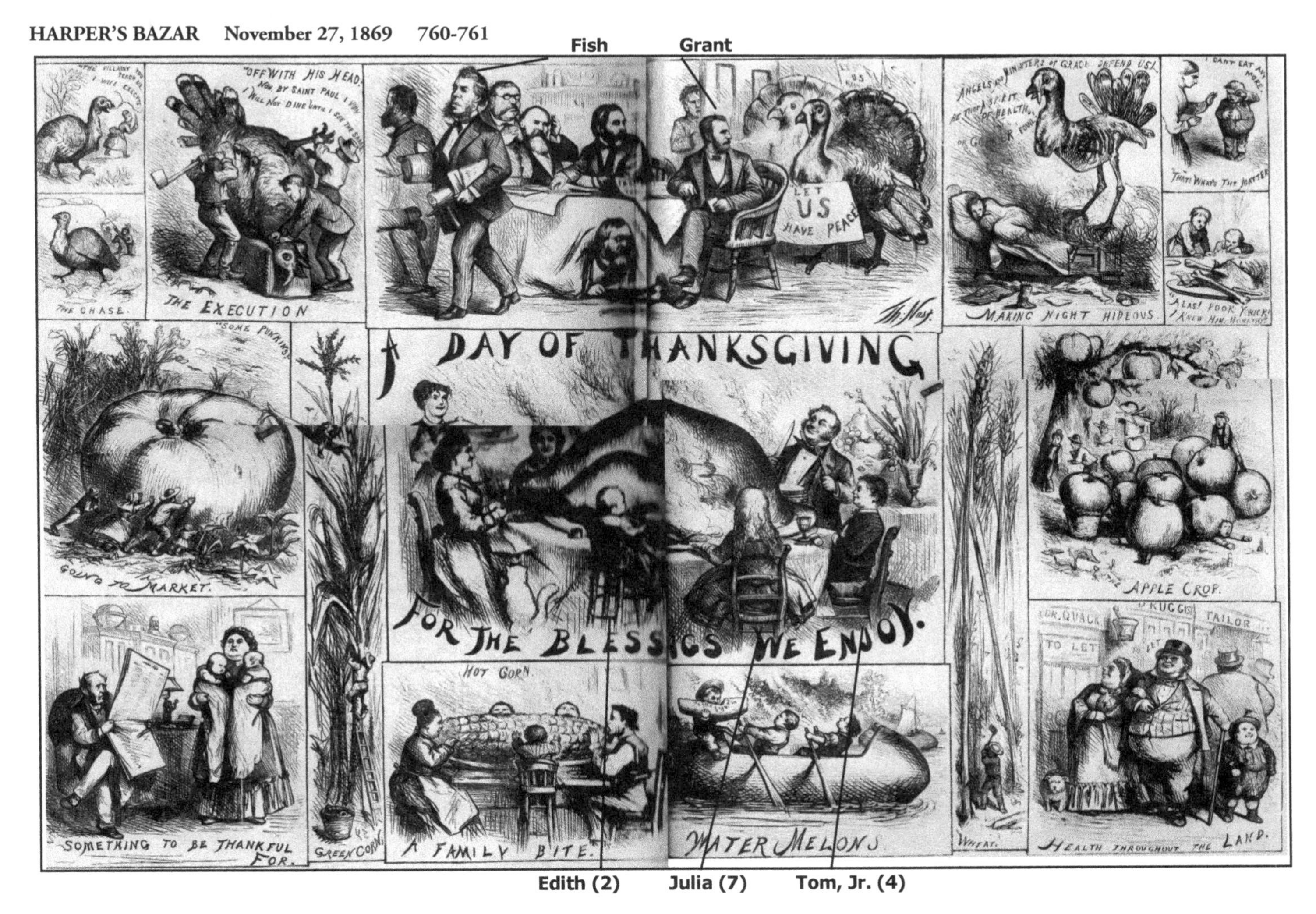

One of Nast's best festive illustrations was *Mother Goose Melodies*, which celebrated Christmas of 1870. Well over a dozen nursery rhymes were readily identifiable. Tommy (age 5) and Julia (9) were singing away at the piano, while Sallie rocked Edith to "Hushaby Baby" (lower right); not coincidentally, Father's bold signature was on the crib.

In total, Nast drew 74 cartoons for *Harper's Bazar* before he left the firm at the end of 1886 — or about four a year. 21 featured Christmas-related scenarios, many of them among his most memorable.

HARPER'S BAZAR January 7, 1871 8-9

MOTHER GOOSE MELODIES.

Chapter 17
The Election of 1868

Shortly after the Caricaturama closed in Boston, Nast previewed the coming presidential election with a *Cinderella* cartoon in the third issue of the *Illustrated Chicago News*. "Prince" Columbia was looking over eighteen possible candidates, but only Grant's dainty foot would fit his glass slipper. Other potential Republicans Ben Wade and Ben Butler had relatively small feet, but looked as dismal as their prospects. Schuyler Colfax, who would become Grant's Vice President, also was prominent.

ICN May 8, 1868 40

"Brick" Pomeroy, Pendleton, Sherman, Logan, Thomas, Howard, Fenton, Farragut, Colfax, Stanton, Sheridan

Hoffman, McClellan, Wade, Chase, Grant, Butler, Hancock, Seymour, Johnson

"CINDERELLA, OR THE GLASS SLIPPER." Drawn By Thomas Nast.

Among Democrats, George McClellan wore a dunce cap in front of Columbia, while King Andy Johnson's huge feet, labeled "My Constitution" and "My Policy" were the worst fit of all. The most likely Democratic nominee at that point in time was Chief Justice Salmon Chase, sitting on Grant's right with his feet almost covered by his judicial robe.

Nast's knowledge and subtlety with regard to the other candidates was prescient. He placed George Pendleton, a diehard Copperhead who had been McClellan's running mate in 1864, just above McClellan. Sure enough, Pendleton led on the first fifteen ballots. The leader on the sixteenth was Union General Winfield Scott Hancock (who would become the Democratic nominee in 1880). Eventually Horatio Seymour, who Nast stationed furthest from the Prince to emphasize the odds against him, won on the twenty-second ballot.

Chase

In 1864, Chase had flirted with the Republican nomination, but Lincoln maneuvered him out of the Cabinet (Treasury) into political exile as Chief Justice of the Supreme Court. Now Nast stressed the irony implicit in a strong and consistent champion of black suffrage — which Chase still was — pursuing the nomination of an unequivocally anti-black party.

Black suffrage was *the* crucial campaign issue in 1868. For Republicans, the only way to capture the Presidency and maintain control of Congress was to win black majorities in the Southern states. Conversely, Chase offered Democrats their best option to counter by attracting Conservative (liberal) and Moderate Republicans, as well as War Democrats, to his banner, along with white — and black — votes in the South.

However, Pendleton and his Negrophobic colleagues put ideology ahead of practicality and refused to accept a black suffrage plank, even though eight re-admitted states had agreed to it in their new constitutions. Consequently, Chase's name was withdrawn before the Convention began on July 4 in the new Tammany Hall.

The most damning of Nast's five cartoons taunting Chase was on the newsstands a few days earlier. Chase presided over the marriage of a forlorn colored man to a stereotyped Irish shrew representing the Democratic Party. In *Would You Marry Your Daughter to a Nigger?*, the artist left nothing to the imagination. The sardonic title was an old slogan used by Democrats and now thrown back in their faces.

Witnesses included vitriolic newspaper publishers Manton Marble (*World*), James Gordon Bennett, Sr. (*Herald*) and Congressman James Brooks (*Express*); Copperheads Seymour, Pendleton, Clement Vallandigham and Fernando Wood; politicians John Hoffman, John Morrissey, Montgomery Blair and James Doolittle; and Nast's Civil War/Lost Cause villains, Nathan Bedford Forrest and Raphael Semmes.

HW July 11, 1868 444

Seymour, James Brooks, Vallandigham, Pendleton, James Doolittle, Semmes, Forrest

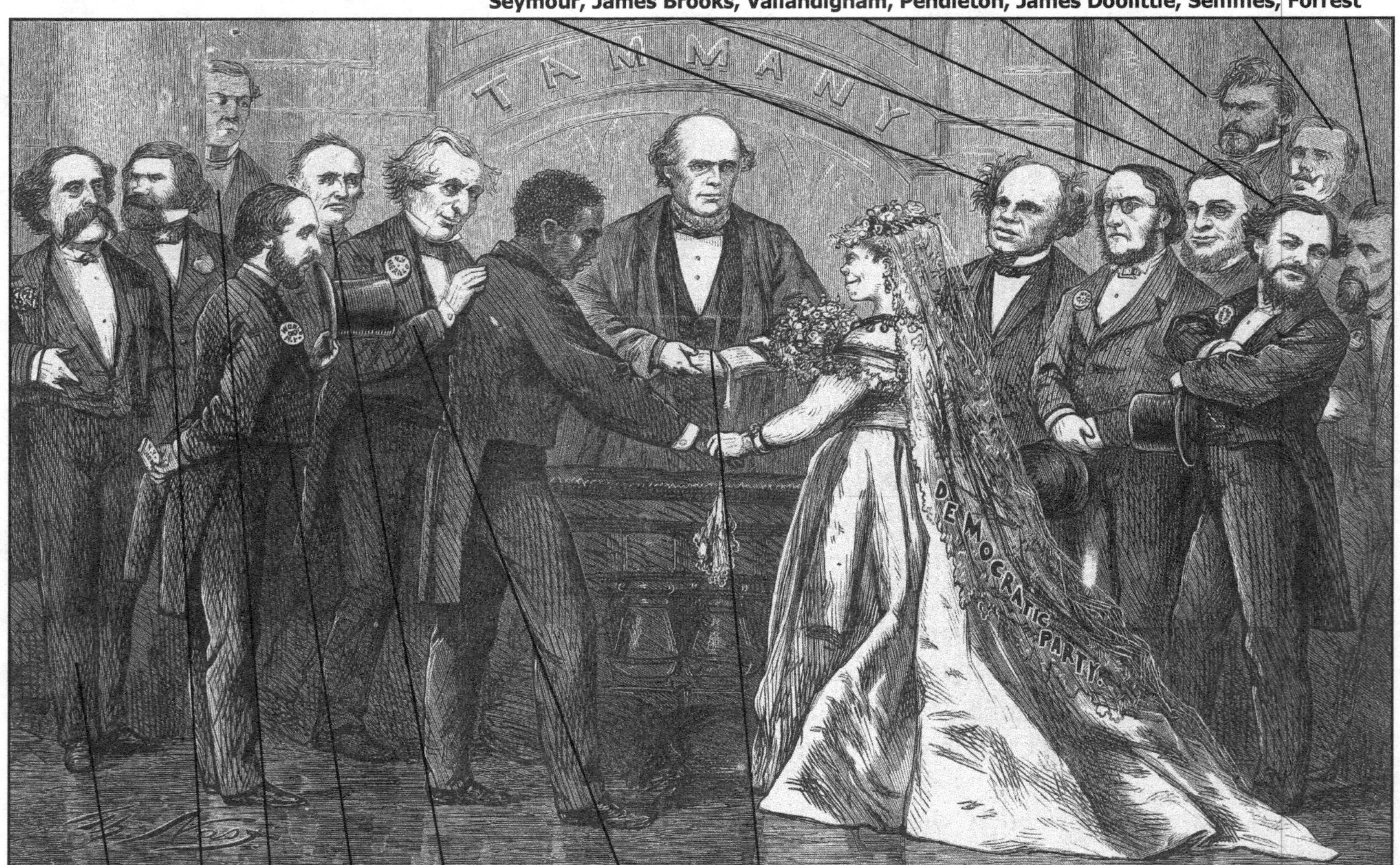

Hoffman, Morrissey, Wood, Marble, Montgomery Blair, Bennett, Sr., Chase

"WOULD YOU MARRY YOUR DAUGHTER TO A NIGGER?"

Grant

Beginning in 1867, Nast illustrated a number of children's books for leading publisher McLoughlin Bros. of New York, including *The Wonderful Adventures of Humpty Dumpty*. George Fox made the story into a musical extravaganza and Nast painted the scenery; opening on March 10, 1868, it ran for a record-setting 483 performances.

As mentioned previously, in mid-March, Nast spent time in Washington with his friend General Norton Chipman, hoping to witness Johnson's delayed impeachment trial.[1] Chipman had served with Grant at Fort Donelson, almost dying from wounds; later, he joined Grant's staff and was personally close to the general. Anticipating Grant's nomination, he commissioned Nast to draw a large picture to surprise the delegates meeting May 21 in Chicago. The *Illustrated Chicago News* handled the secret production.

The convention picture had an electric effect on its audience after a blank curtain rose to reveal a vacant chair (no Humpty Dumpty here) labeled "Democratic Nominee" opposite Grant; a bare-breasted Goddess of Liberty proclaimed "Match Him!!" Along with Grant's own slogan, "Let Us Have Peace," his campaign now had its two-word logo.

Nast probably sketched a promotional poster for Fox's *Humpty Dumpty*, which wasn't produced until after Grant's nomination.

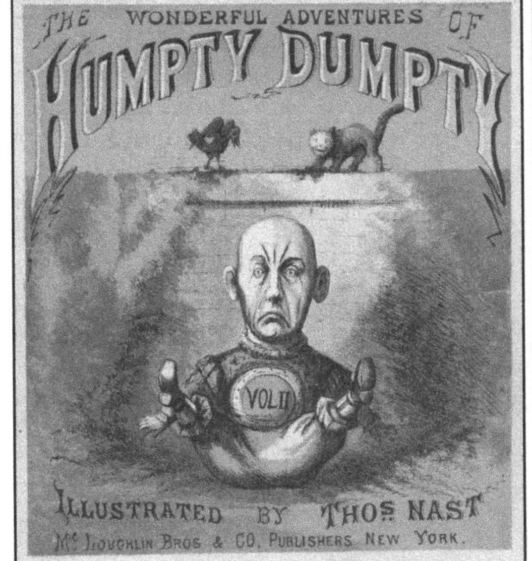

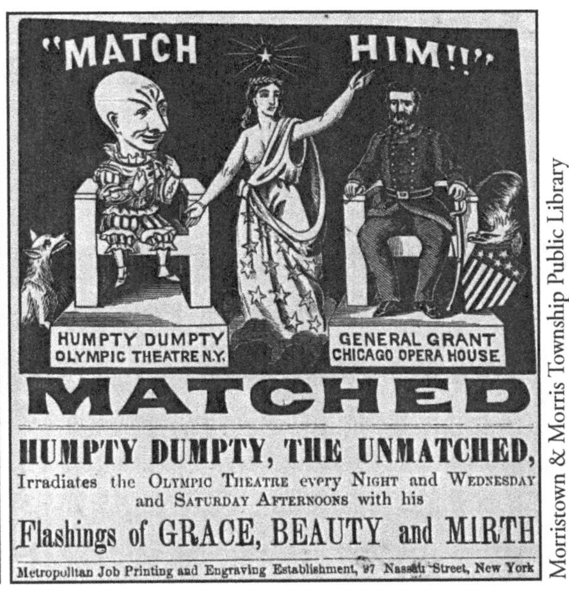

Morristown & Morris Township Public Library

HW October 31, 1868 700
"Let Us Have Peace." ***MATCHED.(?)*** **"A Mob Can Revolutionize As Well As A Government."**

The Republicans nominated House Speaker Schuyler Colfax to be Vice President. Colfax was an opportunistic, practical politician who lasted one term before scandal tarnished him.

As the bitter electoral contest neared its conclusion. Nast again used "Matched?," this time with a question mark. He contrasted Grant's demand for unconditional surrender at Vicksburg with Seymour's "My Friends" speech to the draft rioters just eleven days later.*

* See p. 127-128

Blair

The Democrats chose Frank Blair as Seymour's running mate, much to the future regret of their more moderate factions. Originally opposed to slavery, Republican Congressman Blair helped save Missouri for the Union. As a Union major-general, he served under Grant at Vicksburg and Sherman in Georgia. After the war, he clashed with Radical Republicans and became a "radical" Democrat. His letters and speeches were militant and racial; a loose cannon, his harsh words and abrasive personality frequently alienated many of his party's leaders.

In *Dignity and Impudence*, Nast contrasted Blair as a tiny dog of war glaring at Grant as the unperturbed watchdog of peace.

HW October 24, 1868 C

DIGNITY AND IMPUDENCE.
(for further particulars see Grant's and Blair's letters of acceptance.)

HW November 7, 1868 705

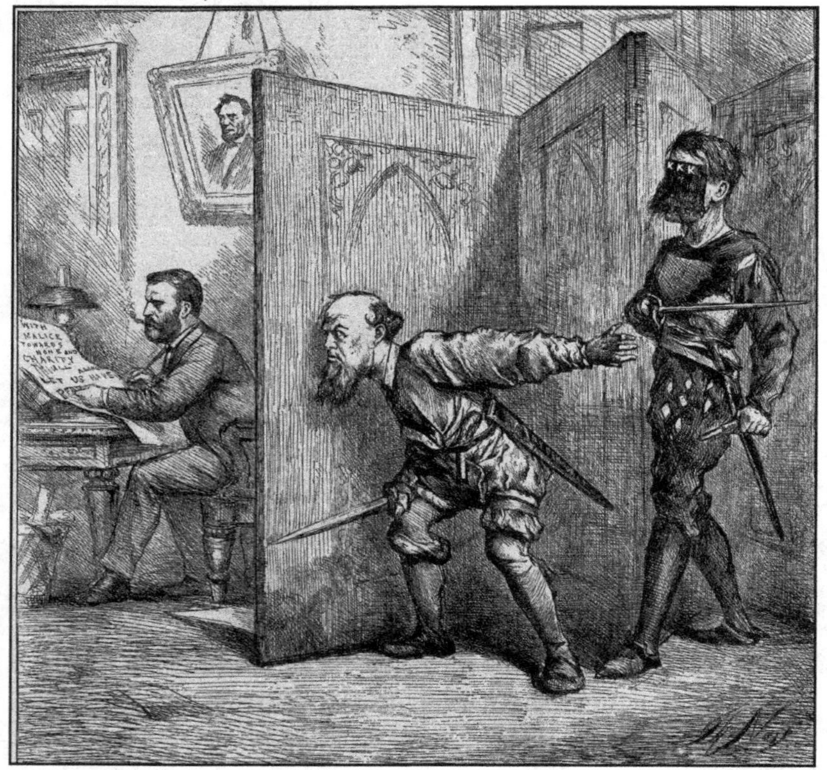

WILKES BOOTH THE SECOND.
"If he is elected by unfair means, or use of illegal power—if he does not receive a majority of the three hundred and seventeen votes of the Electoral College, fairly cast—if he seeks to override a majority in America, *he dies before his term of office shall one-fourth expire,* and the party that would thus unjustly elevate him to power shall be strangled in the blood it cries for."—*The Democrat, Oct. 13, 1868.*

Nast's strongest shot at Blair was on newsstands just before the election. The cover featured Blair as *Wilkes Booth The Second* under an editorial entitled "The Policy of Assassination." Marcus "Brick" Pomeroy, publisher of the "Red Hot" *New York Democrat* had made overt threats against Grant, and now stealthily led Blair, as a masked assassin branded with KKK on top of his mask.[2] Nast used theatrical costumes to allude to Booth's acting profession, and contrasted the intruders with Grant seated under Lincoln's picture while reading his second inaugural address: "With malice towards none and charity to all," and adding "Let us have peace."

Nast needed to establish new villains to represent the Confederacy. He chose three in particular: Nathan Bedford Forrest, Raphael Semmes and Wade Hampton.

Forrest

Poorly-educated Forrest had become a millionaire before the war by trading slaves, cotton, cattle and real estate around his native Memphis. He was a brilliant military tactician, distinguishing himself at Fort Donelson and Shiloh, and becoming a feared nemesis of the Union for his successful raids throughout the war. He hated blacks and became the first Grand Wizard of the Ku Klux Klan around April 1867. President Johnson pardoned him in July 1868.[3]

Forrest's conduct at Fort Pillow, TN on April 12, 1864 put him in the Union "Hall of Infamy" forever. His 1,500 troops overpowered the fewer than 600 defenders, and then massacred many of the survivors — including scores of blacks — *after they surrendered.* Black soldiers were shot or buried alive, and tents with wounded Union prisoners inside were set on fire. About three-quarters of the 262 black soldiers died.

Nast stigmatized Forrest with an ironic Fort Pillow "medal" when he skewered him in a dozen cartoons as a prominent white supremacy, Lost Cause symbol.

Raphael Semmes

Four days after Fort Sumter was attacked, Lincoln declared a blockade of all Southern ports. However, it was difficult to maintain a leak-proof blockade with 3,500 miles of Confederate coastline to cover. Moreover, England had no intention of observing the blockade, even though she recognized it as legitimate.

James Bulloch, a Confederate agent, was dispatched to Liverpool to try and get some warships built with the latest technology for attacking Northern merchant ships. In addition to damaging commerce and thereby forcing the Union navy to pay less attention to blockade duty while pursuing the raiders, the Confederacy also hoped that wealthy Northern traders would pressure Lincoln to abandon the war as their losses mounted.

As a private citizen, Bulloch contracted for two ships without revealing his true intention. He hired a local lawyer, who weaseled an opinion that a warship could be built under the Foreign Enlistment Act as long as it was not armed. If military equipment was added afterwards, he opined that England could not be held responsible.

The Confederacy's second ship, the *Alabama*, was the 290th constructed by the Laird shipyard. Nast used 290 as a symbol whenever he referred to the *Alabama* in subsequent cartoons. Effectively, Semmes became Nast's villainous poster boy for the American dispute with England (which wasn't resolved until 1872).

The three-masted schooner had the capability to store enough coal and supplies to spend six months at sea. Sneaking out of Liverpool, she sailed to the Portuguese Azores, where another English ship supplied her with heavy guns, other arms and coal, and Commander Semmes took charge. According to his diary, he captured 63 ships between September 1862 and June 1864 when the USS Kearsarge sank the *Alabama* off Cherbourg, France; he burned more than 50 of them.[4]

Semmes was 53 when he took command, old for the type of life he lived at sea for the next two years. He described his mostly English and Irish crew as "liars, thieves and drunkards" who expected to have "a jolly good time and plenty of license."

HW October 24, 1868 681

THE BOYS IN GRAY.

He undoubtedly needed his salty language and cold, reserved personality to deal with his undisciplined sailors. However, his impatience and lack of humility led to scorn and vilification beyond that visited on Lee and maybe even Forrest (who was hated but respected). The appellation of *pirate* that *Harper's Weekly* and others often used when referring to Semmes — as he did to himself — fanned the flames for Nast and others.

Semmes was called "Old Beeswax" by his crew because of his curlicued waxed mustache on which he prided himself. It was made to order for a caricaturist like Nast who repeatedly placed him in prominent positions in his post-war anti-Democratic Party cartoons as a "twin" of Forrest.

Wade Hampton

Nast used Hampton as a symbol of post-war Southern aristocracy opposed to blacks and Radical Republican reconstruction policies. The son and grandson of wealthy South Carolina planters, Hampton was among the richest men in the South before the war. As a cavalry general, he saw action in most of the leading battles and campaigns, and was wounded several times. Renowned for his intellect, courage and physical strength, he almost won the South Carolina governorship in 1865 as a write-in candidate against James Orr.

In one cartoon, Nast quoted Hampton: "Agree . . . and act firmly . . . that you will not employ anyone who votes the Radical ticket. Use all the means that are placed in your hands to control this element."[5] In another, Nast depicted Hampton worriedly shining an elegant black man's shoes, following his stated willingness to "send negroes to Congress (if) they will let us have the state."[6] Semmes and Forrest were spectators as former Governor Henry Wise of Virginia officiated at the wedding of a white suffragette to an overdressed, pompous black. A background poster read: "Seymour, the friend of colored orphans."

HW September 26, 1868 616

ALL THE DIFFERENCE IN THE WORLD.

Semmes

Forrest

"BUT—"

A week later, Nast displayed all his visual and verbal vitriolic symbols at a Democratic Barbecue celebrating the "Lost Cause Regained." Even "Moses" Johnson and a Copperhead snake were included, along with "New Orleans, Memphis, NY Riots, Fort Pillow, Mob Law, Slavery" and a skull and crossbones.

The Modern Samson was shorn of his suffrage hair by Southern Democracy, a Columbia-like figure representing the Lost Cause. The brandished swords, clubs and whips were to "make the Negro (late 'Nigger')" understand that we are the law and "Upon every occasion, organize a Ku Klux Klan," as promoted on Seymour's banner and chest.

Left to right: Hampton, Forrest, Lee, Seymour, Blair, Semmes and Hoffman.

HW October 3, 1868 632

THE MODERN SAMSON

August Belmont

An earlier cartoon, *This Is a White Man's Government*, introduced August Belmont as a symbolic character.* A wealthy German-Jewish financier who served as national chairman of the Democratic Party from 1860-1872, he lived in a Fifth Avenue mansion. As a War Democrat, he supported the Union and, as the American representative of the Rothschild Bank, he helped negate English support for the Confederacy. In 1862, he bought the *New York World*, installed Manton Marble as editor, and used it as a Democratic mouthpiece. Here he was waving a packet of $100 bills earmarked for buying votes.

Belmont joined forces with an ape-like Five Points Irish thug, and Forrest with a Lost Cause dagger in his hand and a lash in his pocket, to step on a black Union veteran, holding an American flag and reaching for a ballot box. Nast was emphasizing his belief that black men had *earned* the right to vote through their military service, rather than simply obtaining it via their newly-gained citizenship.

Seymour's draft riot symbols — the burning colored orphan asylum and the lynched black man — were in evidence along with an enflamed Southern school. The cartoon also became an enlarged campaign poster for Grant entitled *The New Rebellion*.

HW September 5, 1868 568

"THIS IS A WHITE MAN'S GOVERNMENT."

A Vote

5 Points

CSA

Capital For Votes

"WE REGARD THE RECONSTRUCTION ACTS (SO CALLED) OF CONGRESS AS USURPATIONS, AND UNCONSTITUTIONAL, REVOLUTIONARY, AND VOID.—DEMOCRATIC PLATFORM.

---

* Also discussed on p. vi

Twice Nast utilized Shakespeare's *Macbeth* for back-page cartoons attacking Seymour. The untitled first one depicted him as guilt-ridden Lady Macbeth, complicit in the murder of King Duncan, failing to wash out the stains of the draft riots. Coincidentally, Nast's initial allusion to Boss Tweed (as an obese, bearded, barely visible background figure) was here. However, Tweed and his associates kept a low public profile after the July Convention; Mayor John Hoffman served as Nast's symbolic link to Tammany Hall as part of the Democratic coalition.

Nast's later *Macbeth* cartoon, *The Democratic Hell-Broth*, included the text of William Croffut's poem mimicking the witches' incantation with a litany of Democratic sins and sinners. *Macbeth* was the only one of Shakespeare's 37 plays with witches in it; not coincidentally, the cartoon came out in the Halloween issue. Nast had Hampton stirring the pot, Blair holding his threatening acceptance letter, and Seymour wearing an *Alabama* 290 headband.

HW September 5, 1868 576

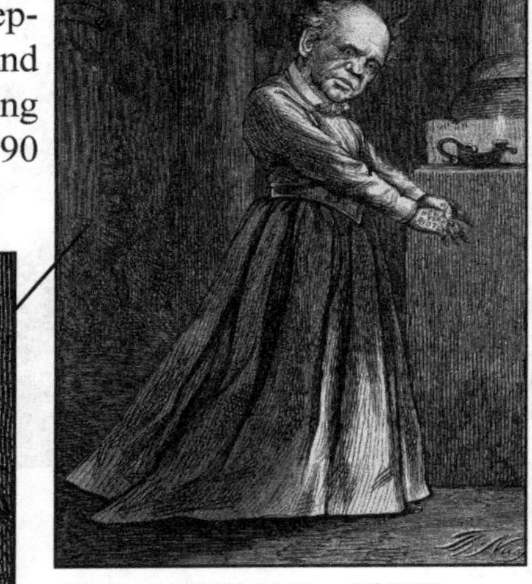

TIME, MIDNIGHT.—SCENE, NEW YORK CITY HALL.
Lady *****. "Out, damned Spot! out, I say!.....Here's the smell of the blood still: all the perfumes of Democracy will not sweeten this little hand. Oh! oh! oh!"**

HW October 31, 1868 704

THE DEMOCRATIC HELL-BROTH

**Double, double, toil and trouble,
Fire burn and caldron bubble.
Round about the hell-broth go,
In the motley fragments throw:**

**Hand of Treason, reeking red,
Poison-fang of Copperhead,
Bitter tear of refugee,
Curse of planter, prayer of slave,
Blossom from a martyr's grave,
Rod of "Moses," which he lost
When he pardoned Pharaoh's host,
Skull of prisoner at Fort Pillow,
Blood of freeman at Camilla,
Hampton's torch, Fred Douglass's fetter,
Booth's revolver, Blair's letter,
Toombs's whip and Forrest's sneer,
And a sigh from Dostie's bier,
Seasoned with guerilla's oath.**

**Seymour stirs the horrid broth—
Bound about his head a rag
From the Alabama's flag;
Cloak of canvas that the gale
Wrested from the pirate's sail;
Wand of witchery that bore
Treason's flag in '64.
With a weird and hissing sound
Rocks the caldron round and round,
And he cries, "Tis very good!
Lo! the cup of Brotherhood!"**

W.A. Croffut

The Boys in Blue

General Norton Chipman organized a huge three-day "Boys in Blue" convention of Union soldiers and sailors in support of the Republican campaign. Held in Philadelphia beginning September 30, it featured Nast's Caricaturama panels, augmented by fifteen additional commissioned pictures like *Seymour the Rioter* and *Grant the Quieter*.

Rutherford B. Hayes Library

The artist was compensated for his time and expenses, and received plenty of plaudits in person and in the press. Mixing with the celebrities and receiving accolades from them and attending journalists had to be one of the highlights of Nast's life.

Nast is like his work — quaint in person, full of ready drollery, incisive humor and subtle wit, ready with repartee, pun or bonmot; modest withal, turning the constant compliments that come to him with playful jest or amusing play on words. He sees everything and reads character just as his pencil traces the conception.[7]

Some of the new pictures were made into campaign posters.

Nast theatrically summarized the political battlefield with *Both Sides of the Question: The Boys in Blue* (and) *The Boys in Gray*. Grant stood resolute, seemingly breathing fire with his cigar, and staring steely-eyed at Seymour apprehensively stepping back. The artist sat in front of a dozen Union generals, nonchalantly sharpening his pencil; behind him was John Griswold, who was about to lose the race for governor to John Hoffman. Greeley was reading his *Tribune* behind Grant and Colfax while late arrival Henry Raymond, whose *Times* supported Johnson and was late to the Republican Party, came running in at the rear.

On the Democratic side, Blair was still brandishing a sword and Semmes a dagger, while Lee, Forrest and Hampton looked on. Jeff Davis sat dispassionately next to an apprehensive Seymour's feet, Johnson peered out of a trench, and McClellan — who disagreed with several planks in the platform — studied his former comrades through his field glasses (reminiscent of his cowardly performance on the *Galena* at the Battle of Malvern Hill).

HW October 24, 1868 680-681

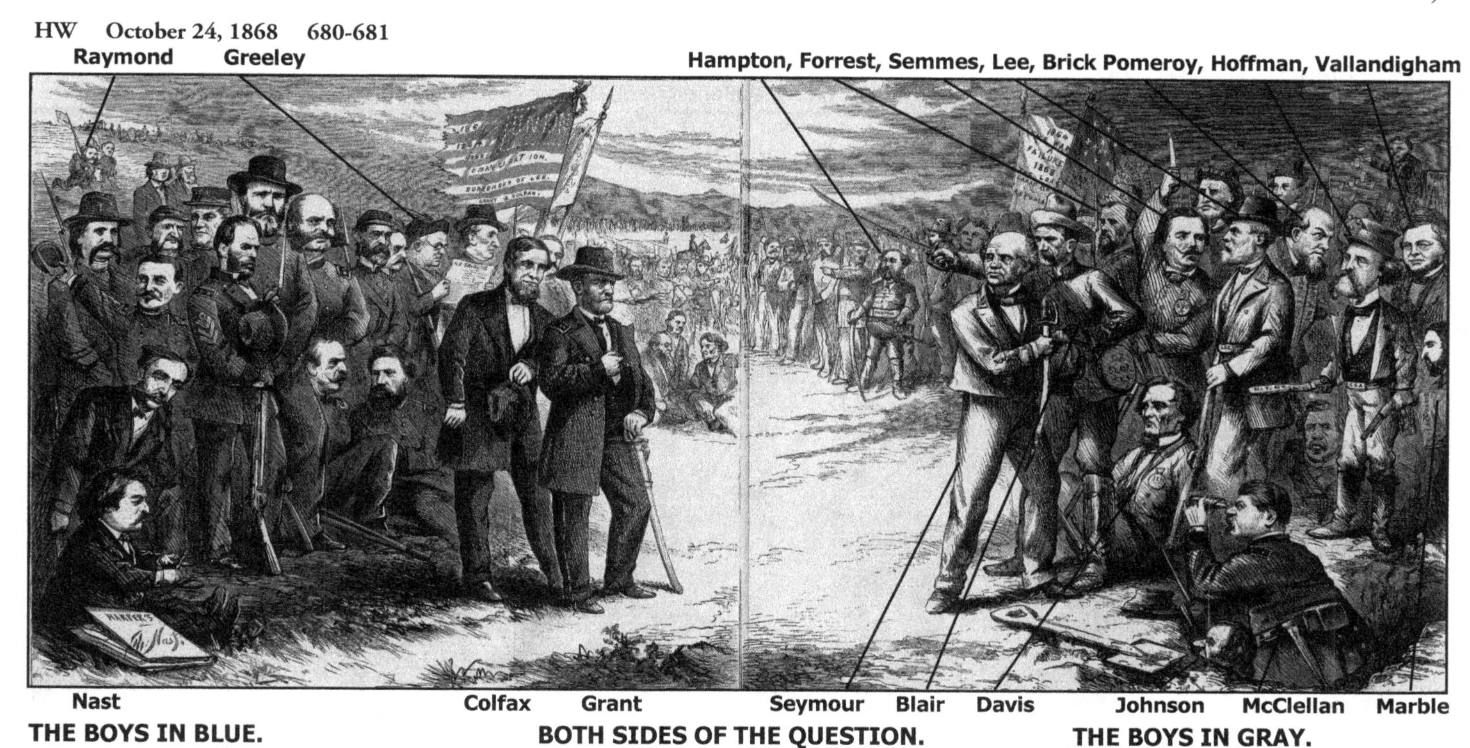

THE BOYS IN BLUE. BOTH SIDES OF THE QUESTION. THE BOYS IN GRAY.

Victory

Black votes in the five former Confederate states helped Grant carry 26 states and 214 electoral votes vs. Seymour's eight states and 80 electoral votes.[8]

The 53-47% popular vote was much closer. Only 300,000 out of 5,700,000 ballots separated the candidates, revealing just how divided the country was over the rights of the Freedmen.

HW October 24, 1868 C

WHY "THE NIGGER IS NOT FIT TO VOTE."

Nast's joyous sequel was available to readers eight days later. He was still sketching while behind him, Greeley was peddling his paper. In the rear, the "Peace (and) Union" stripes replaced the tattered Lost Cause banner.

Unconditional Surrender Grant held an olive branch over Seymour's head as the defeated candidate, his left arm in a sling, handed over his Lost Cause sword. In contrast, a still-defiant Blair was carried off in a litter by Forrest and Semmes, with Lee behind him watching Grant. Hampton was on his horse, about to scurry away.

A gleeful Nast obviously enjoyed tweaking the losing press. Below him, Raymond consoled a prostrate King Andy, his crown off and a veto sticking out of his pocket. Opposite, "Red Hot" Brick Pomeroy was cooling his feet in a bucket, while he, James Brooks (*Express*), Ben Wood (*Daily News*) and Manton Marble (*World*) considered what to do next. Belmont observed in a distressed, contemplative pose; afterwards, he was attacked with anti-Semitic slurs as a scapegoat for Democratic losses in the last three elections, but retained his post through the next one.

HW November 21, 1868 745

UNCONDITIONAL SURRENDER GRANT.

For Nast, the 1868 election was as much a winning referendum on the outcome of the Civil War as the 1864 contest had been. His tactics were similar: Eighteen cartoons attacked the Democrats from several directions, while seven were positive and four contrasted the two sides. **Grant reportedly attributed his victory to "the sword of Sheridan and the pencil of Thomas Nast."**

Chapter 18
President Grant: First Term

Understanding Grant

Ulysses Grant was the only president between Andrew Jackson (1828-36) and Woodrow Wilson (1912-20) to serve successive full terms. In contrast to Lincoln, he tended to see the presidency more as a reward than a responsibility; in contrast to Johnson, he worked through Congress, not against or around it.

Moreover, he was not well prepared for the political role of president. As a general and hard-driving military strategist and tactician, his orders were obeyed without much discussion. As his country's civilian leader, his knowledge of law, political intricacies, history, economics and salesmanship/persuasion was relatively weak. Accordingly, an innate sense of intellectual inferiority apparently made him reluctant to consult with or take advice from more knowledgeable potential or actual advisors.[1]

A singular exception when he first took office was John Rawlins, Grant's primary military advisor and first Secretary of War. Rawlins and Grant were close friends from their pre-war days in Galena. A lawyer by profession, Rawlins served as the principal sounding board for his relatively naive pal in a complex environment where political understanding, finesse, persuasion and patronage were the keys to success.

Unfortunately for Grant personally, as well as his presidency, Rawlins died from tuberculosis six months after he took office. With Rawlins gone, Grant lost the only person he trusted for objective political and moral guidance. If Rawlins had lived, Grant might have been protected from the poor advice and unethical behavior of a number of his relatives, cabinet officers and political associates.

Grant had a remote, introverted personality not easily penetrated. He now relied on Orville Babcock, whose wife was from Galena. Babcock had been one of his military secretaries, and became his personal secretary and gatekeeper. However, Babcock turned out to be a scoundrel, wheeling and dealing for his own benefit. Grant only found out in his last year as president.

Personal loyalty was an absolute requirement for Grant. Even when they were right, he was quick to get rid of dedicated and capable Cabinet members who disagreed with him openly, or opposed his policies or actions — because he considered them disloyal. Conversely, he defended Babcock and other knaves in the absence of "smoking guns." Essentially honest himself, he was blind to the misdeeds of others who passed his loyalty test. Scandals dogged both his terms, especially his second.

Black Friday

An early example involved his brother-in-law, Abel Corbin. Corbin, 61, had recently married Grant's 37-year old spinster sister, probably in part to gain access to the President. In conjunction with financier Jay Gould and his partner, playboy entrepreneur Jim Fisk — known for their manipulation of Erie Railroad stock and bribery of officials — Corbin tried to corner the gold market in the summer of 1869. He influenced Grant to appoint former general Daniel Butterfield, an old friend of Gould's, as Assistant-Treasurer, and Gould then bribed Butterfield.

Their game plan was to keep the supply of gold down and the price up by having Grant and Treasury Secretary George Boutwell refrain from selling any of the $14 million of gold in the Treasury. Fisk and Gould entertained Grant, gave him free travel on their steamboats and trains, and dropped hints about the government not selling.

Ultimately, Grant and Boutwell grew suspicious. Just before noon on Black Friday, September 24, Boutwell — with Grant's concurrence — intervened and sold $4 million in gold. The price dropped from $160 to $138 in a minute as panic and turmoil overwhelmed the market. More than 1,000 individual investors, 14 brokerage houses and several banks went under.

The uproar was made to order for a cartoonist, and the Democratic press clobbered Grant. However, Nast made no reference to Grant or Boutwell, while depicting Fisk and Gould as a couple of dead bulls pinned under the rubble, identifiable by their Erie Railroad tags, in a relatively bland back-page *Harper's* cartoon.

Four months earlier, Nast began drawing occasional cartoons for the *Evening Telegram*, a two-year old daily owned by the *Herald* and the first to have political cartoons; its staff included luminaries like Mark Twain and Walt Whitman. One of his first contributions featured Grant and Boutwell in Wall Street, with Grant pointing towards a golden bull on top of a paper stack of "Wars" (dealing with the South, England, France, Spain and Canada), and Boutwell holding a tablet for "Peace," "Economy" and "Reform."

EVENING TELEGRAM May 28, 1869 C

Richard West, Periodyssey

SECRETARY BOUTWELL IN WALL STREET.

HW October 16, 1869 672

"WHAT A FALL WAS THERE, MY COUNTRYMEN!"

This scandal was among the first of many unethical or outright dishonest actions involving Grant's relatives, friends, officials and their associates. To have paid more attention would have jolted Nast's almost paternal feelings for Grant. Even Nast's admiring and rarely critical biographer, Albert Paine, editorialized about his treatment of Black Friday: "It would seem now (Note: 35 years later) that this phase of plunder might have been entitled to further pictorial notice."[2]

Personally, Nast never had any use for Wall Street, and ultimately it would, through fraud, contribute to his financial ruin. An 1865 cartoon in the short-lived *Mrs. Grundy* featured its attendant evils spurred by the devil, as did his only relevant *Harper's* cartoon before Black Friday.

MRS. GRUNDY September 2, 1865

MEMPHISTOPHILES IN WALL STREET;
Or, the Devil to Pay among the Bankers and Brokers.

HW July 3, 1869 429

SIX DAYS WITH THE DEVIL AND ONE WITH GOD.
Business Man To Christianity. "I am too Busy to see you Now. Wait till Sunday."

The Fifteenth Amendment

The 1868 Republican platform strongly endorsed the Congressional mandate of suffrage for black men in the former Confederacy, while hypocritically asserting that it was up to the individual states in the rest of the country. Only eleven of the twenty-one Northern states and none of the five border states permitted black men to vote during the election.

Under strong Republican pressure, Congress passed a proposed Fifteenth Amendment in February 1869, which stated that the right to vote could not be denied because of "race, color, or previous condition of servitude." It took until March 30, 1870, for three-quarters of the states to ratify it and add it to the Constitution. Among the holdouts were New York, New Jersey and California (which feared a Chinese "invasion").

Towards the end of 1869, the Amendment's passage became clearer. In *Uncle Sam's Thanksgiving Dinner*, Nast went all out to endorse universal suffrage for all races and nationalities. Behind Uncle Sam was a picture of Castle Garden (the principal entry place for immigrants until 1890), invitingly labeled "Welcome." Along with Lincoln and Washington, Grant's portrait hung on the wall under "15th Amendment." This was Nast's first portrayal of Uncle Sam whose appearance would change in the near future.

Nast's all-encompassing guest list featured Columbia seated between a black man and a Chinese family, and Senator Carl Schurz next to a Native American. (His depiction of Schurz and his dinner companion was prophetic; as Interior Secretary in Rutherford Hayes' Cabinet, he was helpful to the Indian cause.) A cleaned-up Irishman was on Uncle Sam's left. Notably, Nast's close friend, General Norton Chipman made his only appearance in a Nast cartoon, next to the Chinese mother. As a reminder of Black Friday, Gould an Fisk were seated under Washington's portrait.

"Lo! The Poor Indian"

Grant appointed Ely Parker, his military secretary (and a Seneca who prepared the surrender documents at Appomattox) as Commissioner of Indian Affairs. Indian policy during the Grant administration was to move the tribes on to reservations to protect them, as well as Western travelers and settlers.

In 1869, Wendell Phillips, a leading abolitionist and former president of the Anti-Slavery Society, whom Nast had drawn as a woman holding her black child for his Grand Masquerade ball three years earlier,* had a new cause — American Indians. He gave a radical speech encouraging Indians to "tear up the rails (and) shoot passengers and conductors" on the Union Pacific Railroad, which had been completed two months earlier with the Golden Spike in Utah. "We see great good in this . . . The Pacific Railway is the Indians' *Alabama*. Haunt that road with such danger that none will dare use it . . . The Indian is no citizen and has the right to make war. An abolitionist may well glory in the Red men."[3]

Nast depicted Phillips as an Indian complete with tomahawk and knife, stretched across a track awaiting his fate if the train didn't stop.

HW July 10, 1869 436

"ALL HAIL AND FAREWELL TO THE PACIFIC RAILROAD."

In January 1870, Grant met with several tribal leaders, including Ogala Sioux Chief Red Cloud, in the White House. The following year, in a short article headlined *Lo! The Poor Indian*, *Harper's Weekly* commented: . . . "The history of our dealings with the Indians is one of uninterrupted injustice and wrong-doing. **Mr. Nast, who is a universal philanthropist, appears as the champion of this long-suffering race** . . . and makes a manly plea for justice toward them while we welcome to the polls the representatives of every clime and nationality . . . why, he asks, should we exclude the original owners of the soil? Is not Red Cloud also a man and a brother?"[4]

HW February 12, 1870 112

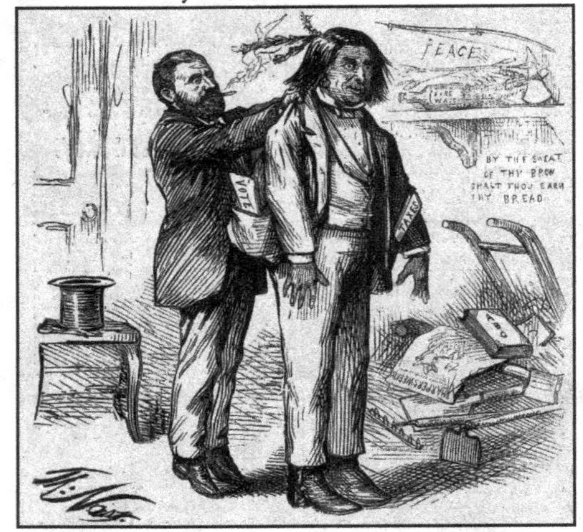

ROBINSON CRUSOE MAKING A MAN OF HIS FRIDAY.

Indian Chief. "Mr. President, we call here to-day to offer our fealty to you as our recognized Guardian and Ward, and to pray you, Sir, to continue our Good Friend and Father."

The President. "You are welcome; and in reference to continuing your 'Good Father,' as you say, I must answer that I have long thought that the two nations which you represent, and all those civilized nations in the Indian Country, *should be their own Wards and Good Fathers. I am of the opinion that they should become Citizens*, and be entitled to all the rights of Citizens—cease to be Nations and become States."

HW April 22, 1871 361

"MOVE ON"

Has The Native American No Rights That The Naturalized American Is Bound To Respect?

* See p. 160

Chinese Immigration

Anson Burlingame, a Republican Congressman from Massachusetts, served as Minister to China from 1861-67. The following year he switched hats, becoming "envoy extraordinary" of the Chinese emperor, and heading a diplomatic mission to foreign powers. Nast portrayed his "Celestial Excellency" sitting in the background while Columbia introduced a Chinese emissary to clearly identifiable European rulers. The bilateral Burlingame Treaty, signed in July 1868, recognized China's domestic sovereignty and established free immigration between the countries.

HW July 18, 1868 460

THE YOUNGEST INTRODUCING THE OLDEST.
America. "Brothers And Sisters, I Am Happy To Present To You The Oldest Member Of The Family, Who Desires Our Better Acquaintance."

While America needed unskilled laborers, especially for building railroads, contract "coolies" were banned by often-flouted law. Individuals faced abuse, especially from Irish immigrants who believed their jobs were threatened. Nast usually supported the Chinese and blasted the Irish thugs, reprising images of the 1863 draft riots in response to a failed bill introduced in Albany by Boss Tweed to penalize employers of "Heathen Chinese" in New York State.

HW February 18, 1871 149

THE CHINESE QUESTION.
Columbia — "Hands Off, Gentlemen! America Means Fair Play For All Men."

HW August 7, 1869 512

PACIFIC CHIVALRY.
Encouragement To Chinese Immigration

However, when the Chinese began to take over more skilled occupations like shoemaking, Nast evidently changed sides by criticizing Chinese "scabs" who replaced striking shoemakers in Massachusetts.[5]

HW July 16, 1870 464

THE MARTYRDOM OF ST. CRISPIN.

HW August 6, 1870 512

THE LATEST EDITION OF "SHOO FLY!"

The Democratic Donkey

Edwin Stanton, Grant's boss in the Lincoln and Johnson administrations, died the day before Christmas 1869. He had been ailing both physically and financially. Grant had announced his appointment to the Supreme Court, but he was unable to take his seat.

Manton Marble, editor of the *World*, was among the other Democrat (formerly Copperhead) publishers to smear Stanton, whose dismissal had resulted in Johnson's impeachment. With Aesop as his inspiration (in the first of seventeen Aesop-inspired cartoons), Nast depicted the Copperhead press as *A Live Jackass Kicking a Dead Lion*, with an American eagle looking askance in the background.

HW January 15, 1870 48

"A LIVE JACKASS KICKING A DEAD LION," AND SUCH A LION! AND SUCH A JACKASS!

LIBRARY OF CONGRESS 1833

"LET EVERYONE TAKE CARE OF HIMSELF."
(As the Jack ass said when he was dancing among the Chickens.)

A male donkey is known as a jack, and the "Jack-ass" had been used forty years earlier to denigrate Democratic President Andrew Jackson. Nast didn't originate the Party's symbol; to him, the donkey was a figure of derision, probably derived from Bottom the Fool, the perfect ass in Shakespeare's *A Midsummer Night's Dream*. On occasion, he also represented key Democrats and their party as foxes, wolves, jackals, vultures, geese and, of course, Copperhead snakes.

His creation of the Republican Elephant was still five years away. However, today's Democratic Donkey is traceable to Nast's initial use of it here, and his subsequent repetition and popularization of it.

Alabama Claims

Grant's best and most important advisor was Secretary of State Hamilton Fish, the only one of 25 cabinet members who served for a full eight years. Except for some abortive Caribbean ventures, Grant wisely delegated foreign affairs to Fish and — in contrast to many of his other good and bad cabinet officers — generally accepted his advice.

Fish was a dignified, austere, honest and independent gentleman, who had served in both the House and the Senate, and knew how to deal with Grant. Their wives, both named Julia, were friends. After sitting next to him at dinner in early 1872, Nast too respected Fish and never caricatured him negatively for *Harper's Weekly*, although his homely face easily would have lent itself to that if he had been an opponent. Nast did pun and draw him as an actual fish on occasion.

While the *Alabama* Claims settlement was in its final stages in mid-1872, Nast drew Fish as a "statesman" and Grant as a "sovereign" for London's *Vanity Fair*.

VANITY FAIR May 18, 1872

THE HONOURABLE HAMILTON FISH. "CONSEQUENTIAL DAMAGES."

VANITY FAIR June 1, 1872

Morristown and Morris Township Library

GENERAL ULYSSES S. GRANT. "CAPTAIN, TANNER, FARMER, GENERAL, IMPERATOR."

America's hostility towards England and France continued after the war ended. As Caleb Cushing, a prominent lawyer and diplomat wrote: "We charged and believed that Great Britain and her colonies had been the arsenal, the navy-yard and the treasury of the Confederates." He went on to accuse Britain of recognizing the belligerency of the Confederacy prematurely, of furnishing direct aid and supplies to the Confederacy in British ports, and of disregarding the obligations of neutrality to an extent to which would "have afforded to the United States just and ample cause of war."[6]

England probably could have achieved a modest settlement at the war's close in 1865, but her decision-maker, Lord Russell, refused. Nast made his case in *Phunny Phellow* in his first reference to Shakespeare's Lady Macbeth (France) trying to "wash this blood clean from my hands." John Bull Macbeth, with "Pirates" embellished on one bloody hand and "Alabama" on the other, quaked in the foreground, as a tiny British lion yapped at Uncle Sam (who was seeking a "Peaceful Settlement of All Damages to Our U.S. Commerce.") Nast entitled it *The Guilty Conscience; Or, Who's That Knocking at the Door?*.

PP July 1865

PROCLAMATION.
Whereas, The Southern Confederacy has been killed and swallowed up by that horrid demon of a Yankee;
Whereas, There will be no more blockade running for us;
Whereas, There can be no more fitting out of vessels for the Emperor of China;
Whereas, No more contraband-of-war articles, &c., can be sent to our dear lost Southern friends;
Resolved, That we consider the Southern Confederacy gobbled up, and that horrid demon of a Yankee anxious for more. We must fortify our frontiers in Canada, Mexico, England and France, and be constantly on our guard against that horrid demon.
In witness whereof we do set our bloody hands and seals.
BULL FROG.

(Upper left corner)

THE GUILTY CONSCIENCE; OR, WHO'S THAT KNOCKING AT THE DOOR?
Mr. John Bull Macbeth.—Whence Is That Knocking? How Is't With Me, When Every Noise Appalls Me? What Hands Are Here? Ha! They Pluck Out Mine Eyes! Will All Great Neptune's Ocean Wash This Blood Clean From My Hands?
Lady Nap. Macbeth.—My Hands Are Of Your Color; But I Shame To Wear A Heart So White, I Hear A Knocking . . . . . . & Little Water Clears Us Of This Deed; How Easy Is It Then.

In 1868, the Prince of Wales remarked that he wanted "every point in the dispute amicably settled." Nast noted that by having Columbia clip the wary British lion's claws.

HW August 1, 1868 488

THE BRITISH LION DISARMED.

When Fish took over in 1869, he and Grant agreed to wait for England to make the first move. Meanwhile Charles Sumner, Chairman of the Senate Foreign Relations Committee — and a powerful, arrogant, vitriolic Anglophobe — came out with beyond-the-pale demands: annexation of Canada, or payment of $2.5 billion for "indirect damages" (like extending the war); Fish's figure was $48 million.

At Sumner's request, and with Fish's approval, Grant appointed John Motley as Minister to England. Nast portrayed Motley following his instructions to cut off the British lion's tail in the *Evening Telegram*, and as the Angel of Peace in *Harper's Weekly*. However, Motley talked too much, exceeding his instructions, and was recalled in 1870.

EVENING TELEGRAM May 28, 1869 C

Richard West, Periodyssey

HW June 19, 1869 400

"LET US HAVE PEACE!"

MINISTER MOTLEY AS THE ANGEL OF PEACE

John Bull. "Glad To See You In That Rig, But What A Whopping Big Bill!"

In late 1869, Grant told Fish to put negotiations on hold for a year. Nast subtly alluded to that in a cartoon whose main thrust was a fierce attack on Pope Pius IX. As a casual spectator among European royalty, Grant had his back to the Pope, while Queen Victoria held the President's arm and looked imploringly at him — to no avail.*

HW November 27, 1869 760

HW December 17, 1870 824

Butler

"FE! FO! FI! FUM! I SMELL THE BLOOD OF AN ENGLISHMAN!"

A year later, Grant asked Fish to get the *Alabama* Claims settled before the next presidential election. About that time, Congressman Benjamin Butler was making verbal waves as Nast noted. Grant, who generally was passive about the subject, told Fish to forget about Canada and indirect claims, and make the deal.

Fish negotiated directly with the British minister, Sir Edward Thornton, and a Treaty of Washington was approved by the Senate and British Parliament in May 1871. Both Grant and Queen Victoria pushed their legislative bodies to support it, while Lord Russell withdrew his opposition.

---

* See p. 236 for complete cartoon

Under the Treaty, both sides agreed to settle all claims, as determined by an international tribunal of five arbiters in Geneva. In addition to British and American (Charles Francis Adams) representatives, it included members from Italy, Switzerland and Brazil — whom Nast portrayed without caricature.

On September 14, 1872, the Geneva Tribunal announced that Britain would pay the United States $15.5 million in gold to settle all the issues, including mutual fishing rights. Nast celebrated in the next available issue of *Harper's Weekly*, adopting William Tell, Switzerland's national hero, to make his point. He had stopped in Tell's hometown of Altdorf (formerly Uri) on his way home from Garibaldi's campaign, knew the legend, and relished precise pictorial arrows aimed at abusers of power — whether in England, France, the Vatican, New York or Washington.

John Bull aimed a "Peaceful Arbitration" arrow at the "*Alabama* Claims" apple on Uncle Sam's head while the Tribunal members — all identifiable — watched. In the background, the key European rulers — Franz Josef of Austria; Wilhelm I of Germany; Alexander II of Russia; and Victor Emmanuel II of Italy — observed with interest. In the "last scene" (inset), Uncle Sam held the arrow which pierced the "*Alabama* Claims" apple with "$15.5 million in gold" marked on its shaft, while John Bull embraced him in lasting friendship.

HW October 5, 1872 729

THE APPLE OF DISCORD AT THE GENEVA TRIBUNAL.

THE LAST SCENE OF THE WILLIAM TELL TRAGEDY.

Avoiding war with Britain through this settlement, was among the most enduring and significant accomplishments of Grant's entire presidency. However, Fish deserved almost all the credit.

Cuba

The standstill over the *Alabama* Claims during Grant's first two years cast a shadow over another critical issue: what to do about Cuba? When Grant took office, the eastern part of Cuba was in full revolt against Spain. The President and his Secretary of State had to determine whether or not to recognize the insurgents and their belligerency, or even independence. While both of them favored the rebels, Fish believed there was no precedent or justification in international law for recognition of an entity with no government, capital or administrative structure. Moreover, if the U.S. recognized Cuban belligerency, how could it question England's 1861 Declaration of Neutrality? Even though Spain had recognized the Confederacy as a belligerent, with strong Union resentment, a clash with Spain over Cuba made no sense with an already heavy war debt, outdated navy, and unresolved Reconstruction problems.

Nathaniel Banks, a Massachusetts politician and unsuccessful Union general, disagreed. As Chairman of the House Foreign Affairs Committee, he commissioned a report supporting some undefined actions to support the rebels. He presented it to the House, along with an impassioned speech on June 14, 1870.[7] Feeling Grant's pressure, the House turned him down two days later and Nast commented in the next issue with a pun. Also shown were wary Congressmen John Logan giving first aid to Banks, and Ben Butler, who favored the rebels but not enough to risk war with Spain.

Meanwhile, the President pushed as hard as he could for the annexation of Santo Domingo, now known as the Dominican Republic. Grant saw the independent country, whose corrupt dictator/president favored annexation, as a potential refuge for unhappy freedmen, increased commerce and a source of minerals. Unknown to Grant, his personal secretary, Orville Babcock, and other schemers stood to make fortunes in land development.

HW July 2, 1870 432

THE CUBAN SPARRING MATCH AT WASHINGTON.
General Banks Has The Floor

Grant believed he had Sumner on his side when he submitted a treaty of annexation to the Senate in January 1870. Six months later, the Senate rejected it by nine votes with Sumner leading the opposition. Grant came to despise Sumner, and the new Congress wisely replaced him as Foreign Relations Chairman in March 1871.

While Santo Domingo was a major issue for a year, with corruption charges about Babcock and others in the rumor mill, Nast never once commented on it.

However, Sumner's demotion led to his physical and mental breakdown the following year when his hatred of Grant caused him to abandon his lifetime cause of black civil rights, and to advise black voters to support Horace Greeley — despite Greeley's coalition including violent anti-black ex-Confederates and Ku Klux Klan members. Nast would have plenty to say about that.

Napoleon III

As the Civil War and early Reconstruction decade drew to a close, Nast devoted increasing attention to European affairs in general, and Napoleon III and Pope Pius IX in particular. Nast's hatred of both men had common ground in their enmity towards Garibaldi; French troops in Rome kept the Pope in temporal power and prevented the unification of Italy. Additionally, Napoleon's overt support of the Confederacy and his 1864 invasion of Mexico were unforgiveable.

The dictatorial Emperor made a fatal mistake when he was subtly provoked by Prussian Foreign Minister (soon-to-be Chancellor) Otto von Bismarck into declaring war on July 19, 1870. Seven weeks later, Napoleon was captured at Sedan (September 2) and imprisoned until Paris surrendered after a siege, and an armistice was signed in January 1871. He then went into exile in England where he died two years later. The *Treaty of Frankfort*, signed on May 10, awarded Prussia a billion dollars and the iron ore-rich provinces of Alsace and Lorraine.

Nast's focus on the Franco-Prussian War — undoubtedly sharpened by his early German and French roots and orientation — led to 19 relevant cartoons over about ten months. For openers, he attacked Napoleon III weekly. *Who Goes There? — A Friend*, featuring Death and Napoleon I, was the same image he remembered from his aunt's bedroom in Landau.*

HW August 20, 1870 544

THE FRENCH PHOENIX.

HW August 27, 1870 552

"WHO GOES THERE?"— "A FRIEND."

HW September 3, 1870 576

THE FRENCH EAGLE & THE ARROW.

* See p. 2

The next cartoon, *Dead Men's Clothes Soon Wear Out* — one of Nast's all-time best — was an adaptation of Paul Delaroche's 1846 painting of *Napoleon at Fontainbleau*. The French painter depicted Napoleon I sitting in gloomy contemplation of his imminent abdication and exile to Elba in April 1814. Nast incisively ridiculed Napoleon III's previous exploitation of his illustrious uncle's image by clothing him in the tattered remnants of his uniform, as failure and utter despair sunk in and his mustache drooped. The unrolled scroll at his right hand listed 60,000 dead and wounded, several defeats including Mexico, and a united Germany.

On occasion, Nast paid a compliment to artists like Delaroche and his pupil, Jean-Léon Gérôme, by utilizing their popularity to enhance his own work. As a frustrated history painter himself — having adopted caricature instead — he incorporated and even burlesqued the work of his notable rivals, thereby gaining some "academic respectability" for himself.[8]

HW September 10, 1870 588

NAPOLÉON
"DEAD MEN'S CLOTHES SOON WEAR OUT."

HW August 20, 1870 540

THE BEST OF FRIENDS MUST PART—"AU REVOIR"

After Napoleon and his country, the worst casualty of his disastrous war was Pope Pius IX. In preparation, the Emperor pulled out the last of his garrison guarding the Vatican. Nast commemorated the occasion by swatting both his villains with one blow, followed by two more cartoons featuring King Victor Emmanuel as he completed Italy's unification and moved its capital from Florence to Rome. The Pope became a self-declared "prisoner" in the Vatican.

HW January 7, 1871 16

"HOW IS THIS FOR HIGH?"

HW March 18, 1871 240

THROWN COMPLETELY INTO THE SHADE.

Shortly before the armistice was signed, King Wilhelm of Prussia became Kaiser Wilhelm I of Germany. Nast pictured him preening while "Mad King" Ludwig of Bavaria held up a mirror, and Bismarck with brushes and a palate painted the new map of Germany in the background.

In March, Nast again used the Delaroche image, this time with the unaltered original, to show Wilhelm's shadow eclipsing even Napoleon I, while the Kaiser held a map of a severed France.

Nast was so caught up in the war, that he illustrated and published a 25-cent pamphlet entitled: *The Fight at Dame Europa's School, Showing How the German Boy Thrashed the French Boy and How the English Boy Looked On.*[9]

"THE BAPTISM OF FIRE."

THE BULLY BOY THAT DID IT.

Chapter 19
The Pope

Catholicism

In his thoughts, words and pictures, Thomas Nast was a true patriot and idealist. Columbia (and her alter ego Justice) and Uncle Sam appeared more than 340 times in his *Harper's Weekly* cartoons as his personifications of America. Anything that threatened their safety, resoluteness or purity was his potential target.

Accordingly, Jefferson Davis ranked first among the cartoonist's all-time villains, as an unrepentant arch-traitor who tore his country apart. Collectively, Confederate politicians, militants, Copperheads and other sympathizers were tarred with the same brush (or pencil), but in a slightly less vituperative shade of black.

With personal loathing as the sole criterion, Pope Pius IX took second place on Nast's lifetime list — for the same reason he hated Davis.[1] As he saw it, the Pope — as the supreme authority over the American Roman Catholic Church — represented an ongoing threat to American unity and freedoms. However, with the sole exception of the Pope's *Declaration of Infallibility*, Nast attacked him and his hierarchy for their temporal rather than their religious beliefs — as a king, not a bishop, as *Harper's* put it.

Collectively, Irish-American thugs and drunks — almost all Catholic — sat in the adjacent pew to the Pope on Nast's hate list. His innate bias was shaped well before he first attacked the Pope (as mentioned previously) and had little to do with their religion per se. Nast grew up in streets and schools teeming with unruly Irish urchins and their elders. His English was limited and many of the Irish immigrants spoke only Gaelic. At *Leslie's*, he had exposure to Irish "milkmaids" and crooked aldermen during the Swill Milk campaign, large-scale gang battles, and the rough boxing crowd. At the *Illustrated News*, he depicted the miserable Irish home life and intoxication of Five Points. At *Harper's,* he witnessed the deadly Civil War draft riots led by the Irish. As an adult, it was their perpetual fighting and drunkenness, along with their allegiances to Tammany and aggression against the public school system, that kept his prejudice at a boil.

The Harper Brothers were ardent Methodists and nativists who understandably were distressed by the ever-increasing flood of Catholic immigrants threatening Protestant and Republican control of government, schools and public spending. Back in 1844, James Harper had been elected Mayor of New York City on a nativist platform.

Although the evidence is to the contrary, the Harpers denied being prejudiced against the Irish as a race or Catholicism as a religion. In April 1870, James Harper himself wrote a letter to a disturbed reader explaining his firm's policy.[2]

> *You misapprehend our position in supposing that we entertain any prejudice whatever against the Irish as a race. We do not. On the contrary, as the editorial columns of the Weekly show, we sympathize with them in their national trials and wrongs, and heartily acknowledge their great and patriotic services in the development and protection of our common country.*

But the Roman Catholic Church in this country, of which the Irish are the representative and most powerful element, has seen fit to enter the arena of politics, and arrays itself on one side of the most important political questions of the day, that of common school education; and while we hold that the private religious opinions of no man or body of men are a suitable subject for public criticism, and recognize the right of every one to worship God according to the dictates of his own conscience, whether he be Roman Catholic, Jew, or Protestant, we also maintain that when any Church, through its recognized leaders, takes sides on political questions, it becomes, as a political party, justly liable to political criticism.

Harper's Weekly, as a strictly political journal of pronounced opinions on all the great questions of the day, takes account of every element of political opposition, in whatever form it may appear; and it would just as readily criticize and condemn in the Methodist, Baptist, or any other Protestant denomination, as in the Roman Catholic, actions which it deemed harmful to the best interests of the people, and in no sense can it be called an opponent of the Roman Catholic religion or of the Irish race.

Very Truly Yours,

J.A. Harper

P.S.—Our periodicals are more directly under the supervision of Mr. Fletcher Harper.

During the 1870s and 1880s, the *Weekly* frequently included long vitriolic diatribes by columnists like Eugene Lawrence, who denounced priestly celibacy, convent life and other practices that had nothing to do with politics. Nast often played off Lawrence's abusive attacks with related cartoons but rarely dealt with American Catholic religious practices per se, focusing on public education, divided loyalties, and voting malfeasance.

Nast best expressed his philosophy through Columbia's lips in his 82-page 1871 book entitled *Miss Columbia's Public School*:

We acknowledge that among liberal Catholics, there are many worthy and estimable ones who never dream of intruding their religion into state affairs, but who are able to consider matters of government without reference to the Church. For such as those, we have only feelings of fraternal friendship, but for those turbulent bigots, who are continually dragging their Church into national affairs, there is no course left us but to compel them to conform to our rules, or to go back to where they came from. It is not ***their*** *country, as they seem to think; it belongs equally to all of us. All are welcome, irrespective of creed, color or nationality, and all have equal rights.*[3]

Among the fundamental liberties Miss Columbia taught was freedom of caricaturing, as noted in her First Lesson (right).[4]

Nast felt so strongly on the subject that he published the book at his own risk: "I thought I must do it even if I lost money," he wrote to his close friend, Colonel Norton Chipman.[5] After he laid out $500 for engraving the 75 illustrations, the publisher sold about 10,000 copies and Nast barely broke even. (Boss Tweed, who was at the peak of his battle with Nast, had his cronies delay publication until after the November election, gaining a small measure of revenge against his tormenter.)

When Nast went to work for Frank Leslie in 1856, New York's population was 48% native-born, 28% Irish immigrants, and 15% German immigrants like himself. About 90% of the Irish and half the Germans were Catholic.[6]

However, Nast grew to idealize his adopted country as a multiethnic republic and his cartoons reflected that. He strongly supported blacks, Indians and Chinese, as well as all sectarian religions except Papal-related Catholicism and polygamous Mormonism.

THE FIRST LESSON

Pius IX

The Revolution of 1848 affected Italy as well as France and Germany. For a while, Garibaldi occupied Rome, and the unpopular, disguised Pius IX escaped and remained in exile for more than a year. The Pope was restored in April 1850 by French troops, who protected his temporal power which had existed since the eighth century. He was outspoken in his opposition to the liberal reforms and representative governments brought about by the Revolution because they threatened both his temporal and ecclesiastical authority.

By 1864, Pius IX, 72, had held the Papacy for 18 years, supported by Napoleon III. That December, he issued his *Syllabus of Errors*, declaring: "It is an error to believe that the Roman Pontiff can and ought to reconcile himself to and agree with progress, liberalism and contemporary civilization." Accordingly, the *Syllabus* opposed public education and demanded church control of schools wherever possible.

Two years later, Garibaldi and King Victor Emmanuel II — the Pope's principal domestic enemies — almost completed the unification and liberalization of Italy with the recovery of Venice from Austria. France initiated that diplomacy, and removed many of its troops from the Papal States located in a band across central Italy. The now relatively defenseless Pope branded the King's government "illegitimate."

In November 1866, *Harper's Weekly* published an article about the Pope's private life and daily routine, praising him as a kind and unpretentious man.[7] That view changed drastically about two months later when the Pope, no longer having to answer to Napoleon, banned American and British Protestant worship within Rome. The *Weekly* responded by calling him a despot aiming specifically at America. *Harper's* article, which included the Pope's picture, inspired the first of Nast's Papal caricatures.

HW February 9, 1867 84

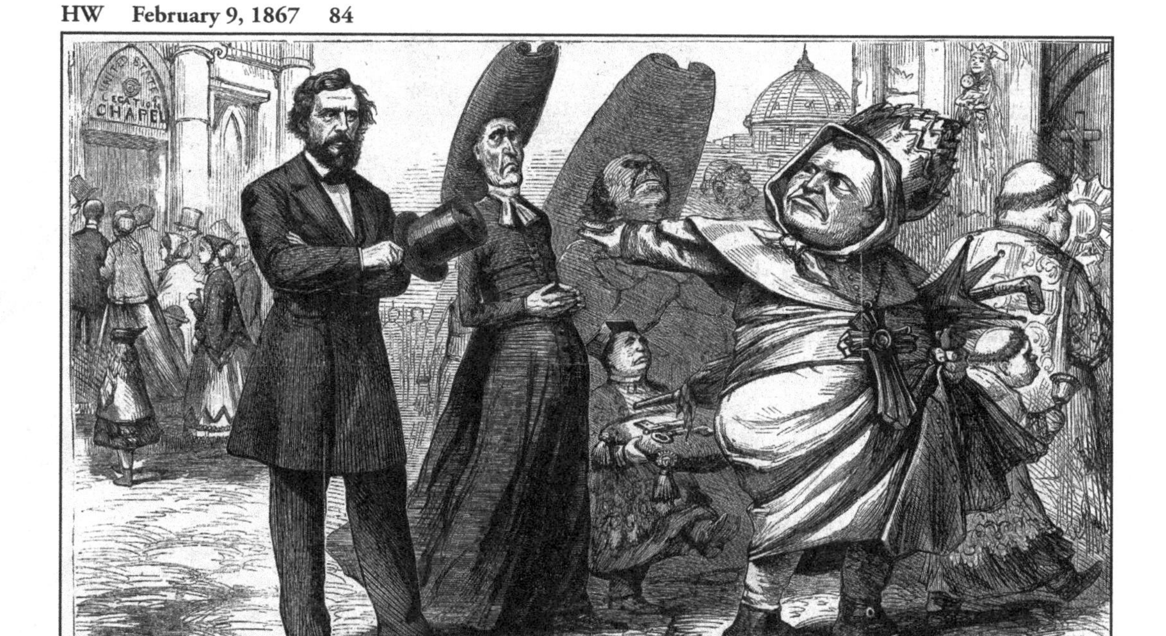

THE POPE ORDERING OUR MINISTER, MR. KING, TO REMOVE AMERICAN PROTESTANT WORSHIP FROM HOME.

Nast's serial campaign against Pius IX, and the Church began in 1867, lasted nine years, and included more than 75 cartoons in the *Weekly*. As discussed previously,* Nast's anti-Papacy beliefs were inculcated by his father, reinforced by his tutor Theodor Kaufmann, and cemented by his experiences in Italy with Garibaldi.

---

* See p. 11

"I Am Infallible"

Despite his foreseeable loss of temporal power, the Pope counter-attacked by convening an Ecumenical Council, the first in three centuries; more than 700 Roman Catholic clerics met for nine months, beginning in December 1869. Ultimately, it approved a *Doctrine of Papal Infallibility*: "The Roman Pontiff cannot err in defining matters of faith and morals." The European governments who formally protested included France, Britain, Austria, Spain and Germany.

The German Catholic revolt was led by Ignatius Dollinger, 71, an excommunicated priest and church historian dubbed "The Modern Luther." Nast quoted him: *"Do you in the United States comprehend what the (Infallibility dogma) involves? It imposes upon those who accept it the solemn obligation to violate civil law, to set themselves up in opposition to the ordinances of your Government whenever the Pope shall pronounce ordinances upon moral or religious grounds . . . It is the assumption of power on the part of the Pope to proclaim a higher law which . . . his children must obey,* ***though such obedience involves treason to the state and the overthrow of your government****."*

No wonder Nast's loathing of the Pope ranked alongside his hatred for Jeff Davis. In 17 cartoons, he attacked the Pope — not the Church per se — as an imperialist ruler for his Infallibility dogma. One of his first and best portrayed the demented-looking Pope biting his fingernails, sitting in front of the dark cave of the Ecumenical Council, marked "No Discussion Allowed." Other signs read: "Sovereign Authority and Subordination Unto the Pope;" "I am Chief, Father and Master Over All Christians;" and "I Am the Sole Judge of What Is Right and Wrong." Martyrs' skulls, skeletons and bones were scattered around him.

Nast's grim parody was rooted in *Pilgrim's Progress*, John Bunyan's 1678 allegorical tale, in which Christian, the leading Protestant knight, fought against the evils and temptations of the world. Separated by a wide chasm from the "crazy" (per Bunyan's text) Pope, the symbolic Christian faced his foe. Below were the opposed European Catholic rulers, including Victor Emmanuel (Garibaldi at his side) and Napoleon III, as well as Grant and Queen Victoria. Twenty lines of Bunyan's text were quoted underneath the caption.

HW November 27, 1869 760

Left to Right: Victor Emmanuel, Garibaldi Grant, Victoria Napoleon III (behind)

Two months later, Nast summarized the basic differences between the Old World and the New. In Europe, the rulers of France, Spain, Austria, Germany, Italy and England lined up behind Dame Europa as she tore Church and State apart. In America, the Pope blessed an Irish-Catholic pig-faced seamstress while she sewed Church and State together. A defiant Columbia, helplessly chained to a ballot box containing fraudulent votes that kept the Tammany Ring in power, glared defiantly at an Irish hoodlum threatening her with his shillelagh.

The accompanying text reported that the Roman Catholic Church received about 80% of state and city funding available for public schools, and more than $3 million in real estate. (The priest at the far right was holding a bag containing $1,000,000 in public school money.) Mention of the Pope's "letter of gratification" probably spurred Nast's cartoon. It was also an attack on Tweed — whose efforts secured the funding — and on the Irish whose support was critical for both the Church and the Ring.

The Public School Controversy

The fundamental rift in America preceded the 1846 assumption of the Papacy by Pius IX. As the massive influx of Irish immigrants and potential voters increased annually, New York Governor William Seward wanted to attract them to the Whig (pre-Republican) party. During 1840-42, he pressed the State Legislature to fund parochial schools. He partially succeeded; the Maclay Law permitted funding but prohibited religious instruction in any school, thereby giving him and Catholics half their loaf as a first step.

The primary objective of Protestant education was to provide the same fundamental liberal education to both native-born and immigrant children. Protestants did not want their First Amendment rights inhibited, nor did they want tax revenues used to support parochial schools of any denomination.

Conversely, many Catholics rejected Protestant "common" schools because they objected to lessons in history and religion which denigrated the authority and practices of their Church. Especially aggravating were readings from the St. James (Protestant) Bible. Rather than have their children "corrupted," they kept them out of school and then objected to their taxes being used to support those schools.

New York's first Archbishop, "Dagger John" Hughes, was consecrated in 1850. He became the most powerful Catholic in New York, and an outspoken supporter of Papal supremacy (ultramontanism) two decades before Pius IX declared himself infallible. Conversely, he believed that the fundamental weakness in Protestantism was its failure to recognize and impose religious authority. A child immigrant himself, he empathized with Irish rebels in their efforts to free their country from Protestant England.

Dagger John was effective. He succeeded in getting funding for Catholic schools and real estate for Catholic orphanages, hospitals and churches, as well as schools. He allied with Democrats in Tammany Hall as Irish voters helped keep them in power. When the Civil War came, he supported the Union and helped calm the draft riots. At his death six months later, *Harper's* praised him as wise and honorable, and noted the breadth of his social, moral and political influence. In retrospect, 21 years later when his "gentle and courteous" successor, John McCloskey (the first American Cardinal) died, the *Weekly* referred to Archbishop Hughes as "too active a politician and too polemical a prelate."[8]

Those positive feelings about Catholic leadership in New York evaporated soon after Pius IX erupted. Taking their lead from the Pope, outspoken Irish-American priests and media advocated the abolishment of public schools. Nast counter-attacked, quoting three Catholic media and a bishop to that effect, while a priest swept away the Bible and current textbooks. Another pointed to the infallible Pope, close by the keys to the Kingdom of Heaven.

HW April 16, 1870 256

FORESHADOWING OF COMING EVENTS IN OUR PUBLIC SCHOOLS

HW February 26, 1870 140

OUR COMMON SCHOOLS AS THEY ARE AND AS THEY MAY BE

After the Tweed Ring obtained more power in state as well as city government, Church schools received a large proportion of common school funding. Nast's three-vignette cartoon was, in effect, right on the money. Justice, with an Irish scale weighed down with "Fraudulent votes," gave bags full of state and local tax money to a gloating priest, while the public school representative got none. Below, ten different sectarian schools featured fighting everywhere, with a dominant Irish Catholic boy threatening in front.

As the Tweed Ring's power peaked, Nast showed the Boss and his cronies throwing out the old textbooks printed by Harper's, and substituting new books published by Tweed's New York Printing Company. This would have cost Harper Brothers at least $50,000 annually if Tweed had not been overthrown. There was some internal debate, but they stuck by Fletcher Harper who gave his siblings an ultimatum to continue the fight with him or go on without him.

HW May 13, 1871 440

THE NEW BOARD OF EDUCATION

At the height of the Tweed campaign, Nast launched one of his all-time best — some say also his most notorious — cartoons: *The American River Ganges*. Sub-titled *The Priests and the Children*, it accompanied Eugene Lawrence's scathing commentary of the same name on the preceding page. Lawrence pointed out that public schools in the "priest-ridden" city were crumbling while Catholic children were "taught a blind obedience to a foreign church."

A dozen crocodiles approached a beach full of cowering Protestant school children, ready to devour them. On closer inspection, the crocodiles were Catholic bishops, their miters turned into reptilian jaws.[9] As the glinting crocodiles closed in on their dinner, Mayor Oakey Hall, with Tweed at his side, dropped additional children from the public school to feed their appetites. Two Irish henchmen in the rear marched Columbia off to the gallows.

Across the water, Tammany Hall was annexed to "The Political Roman Catholic School." Nast's preliminary sketch labeled the river as "Holy See," but he dropped the pun. The Hall was a replica of St. Peter's Basilica in Rome, flying both Papal and Irish flags.

Four days after this cartoon appeared in print, the *Times*, which had been working in parallel with Nast to some extent, printed a sardonic editorial entitled *Pity the Poor Protestant*. "Next to the *Times*, which is credited with untold influence, our Catholic rulers fear the rebel Nast, who presents his incendiary ideas in such an attractive manner, that it overtaxes the ingenuity of the priesthood to contradict them."[10]

Nast's closest and grossest linkage between the Pope and Irish-Americans was based on a diatribe from the Catholic Bishop of Boston condemning Victor Emmanuel's takeover of Rome. A pig-faced Irish emissary kissed the dumped pontiff's toe with her snout in *America (?) Sympathizes with the Pope*. Behind her was a large Irish flag with a small upside-down (distressed) American flag in its corner. In front was a scroll declaring that "the Roman people have no rights," signed by a fictitious Patrick O'Blarny, Father Flatter and nine other Irish names on behalf of "The Irish United States of America." A smaller scroll was entitled "The Excommunication of the Italian Government."

On a positive note, Nast's hero Garibaldi cheered, directly over the Pope's head, in the artist's personalized symbol of triumph at its extreme.[11] Ballot boxes labeled "A Free Church in a Free State" and "The Will of the People" emphasized a plebiscite approving the King's takeover, which took place three months before this cartoon appeared.

AMERICA (?) SYMPATHIZES WITH THE POPE

HW September 30, 1871 916

THE PRIESTS AND THE CHILDREN

Another cartoon depicted Columbia as "State," rejecting applications from more than 20 different denominations including "Ritualistic" Catholic, "Heathen Chinee," Mormon, Quaker, Methodist, Baptist, Presbyterian, Lutheran and Jewish. Actual distributions for 1870 were $412,000 to Catholics, $29,000 to Episcopalians, and $14,000 to Hebrews, and lesser amounts to five other Protestant churches.[12]

HW February 25, 1871 172

CHURCH AND STATE — NO UNION UPON ANY TERMS

HW March 18, 1871 248

INMATES OF GLASS CHURCHES
"Welcome, Brother Baptist; I'm sure *you* will never throw stones at me again."

In fact, except for the Pope and his American vassals — as Nast saw and *Harper's* branded them — the artist tried to remain balanced about all religions. When the Baptists received city property for their Benevolent Society, a Catholic priest reprimanded them.

HW November 4, 1871 1041

THE GOOD-FOR-NOTHING, IN MISS COLUMBIA'S PUBLIC SCHOOL.
Dame Britannia. "Yes; the very same Boy that has given us so much trouble in my School. Well, Miss Columbia, 'Now you know how it is yourself!'"

Shortly before the election, Eugene Lawrence hit the heart of the issue in *The Pope and the Teacher*. He asserted that turning teachers into priests — combined with the decreed superiority of the Pope to all civil governments and his opposition to the rapid spread of knowledge and reform — would stop progress and endanger American unity.

In Nast's accompanying cartoon, Dame Britannia told Miss Columbia "Now you know how it is yourself." However, Nast's object lesson was more of an attack on the undisciplined, thuggish Irish child — whom Britannia supposedly knew well from her contentious relationship with the Catholics of Ireland — than a comment on Catholicism per se.

After Tweed and Tammany were beaten in the November elections, Nast illustrated *Romish Avarice*, another Lawrence diatribe in which he said that the Church "must prepare to be treated as a political faction rather than a Christian sect." For his cover-page blast, Nast showed the Democratic Party as Aesop's killed goose that laid the golden egg. The 17 labeled eggs all bore Catholic-related inscriptions, while the real estate map showed the site of the new St. Patrick's Cathedral.[13]

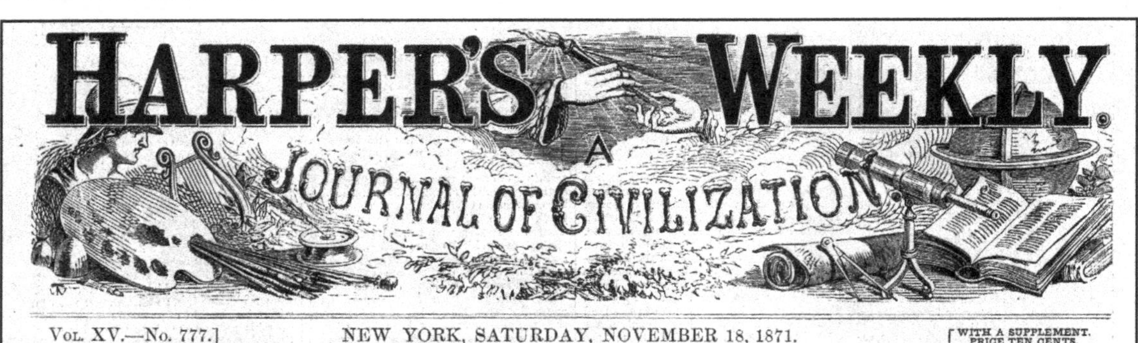

VOL. XV.—No. 777.] NEW YORK, SATURDAY, NOVEMBER 18, 1871. [WITH A SUPPLEMENT. PRICE TEN CENTS.

Entered according to Act of Congress, in the Year 1871, by Harper & Brothers, in the Office of the Librarian of Congress, at Washington.

ROMISH AVARICE.

BY EUGENE LAWRENCE.

M. COQUEREL—no incompetent authority—thinks the Romish Church the source of the grave troubles of his country, of the misfortunes of Italy and Spain. He repeats only the lesson of history; yet he could scarcely have been prepared to find in America the same fatal influence blighting the hopes of freemen. Of all the vices of the papal see not the least constant and dangerous has been avarice. Its passion for accumulating lands and endowments has disturbed and oppressed society in every European nation, impoverished England until, under HENRY VIII., it confiscated all the possessions of its priests, hastened the French revolution by enormous peculations, weighed down Italy and Spain until their suffering people have seized upon the wide domains of the papacy, exasperated Germany, and covered Mexico and South America with apparently endless misfortunes.

The same career of priestly rapacity has begun in our own city, and has advanced with more than European vigor. No savage king or servile despot of the Middle Ages was ever more bountiful to his Romish allies than our Democratic rulers. In Europe the wealth of the ruling sect was the slow growth of centuries. In New York two decades have sufficed to enrich the Romish Church from the public treasury. While taxation has risen to an intolerable severity, while the city debt has been steadily increasing until suddenly it is discovered that we are in a condition of almost hopeless insolvency, while enormous frauds have consumed the earnings of the poor and diminished the profits of the industrious, the lavish endowments of a foreign priesthood have never ceased, and millions have been squandered to maintain Catholic institutions, to preserve the integrity of the Romish faith.

How numerous these sectarian charities have become, how many Romish asylums, protectories, and private almshouses line the streets of our city, not many know; but every one is familiar with the large sums required for their support. An orphan house occupies a block of the most costly land of the city. The property on which it stands was granted on a perpetual lease, for a nominal rent, in 1846 or '47; it is maintained, in part, by a large yearly appropriation. Its annual cost to the city can not be less than one hundred thousand dollars, including the interest upon the value of the land; yet it is safe to say that all its inmates might be maintained in the public institutions, or lodged, at a moderate cost, in some country home. A cathedral of unusual size has sprung up next to the orphan asylum. It occupies a block of ground of enormous value. Grave suspicions rest upon the manner in which this land was obtained, and it would be well for its owners to satisfy the public mind by exhibiting their title. Fortunately for the city, one of the leases of the orphan asylum contains a clause of revocation, and was, no doubt, intended to enable the people to recall the grant whenever they should think proper to do so. Of the "Protectory," whose large endowment and excessive yearly cost every citizen is conscious of, it can only be said that all its beneficiaries might be cheaply provided for in the city institutions. The foundling asylum received half a million in land and money from the unstinted liberality of our present rulers. Its death rate is extraordinary: the public charities are prepared to supply its place, perhaps with more encouraging results.

We have noticed these institutions as the chief examples of their class; they are surrounded by a throng of similar charities, controlled by the Romish priesthood. For the honest laborers in the cause of humanity we have a lasting sympathy. We should rejoice to see the Romish Church pour forth its wealth in saving its poor from want, and softening the ills of its suffering people. But when it extracts such extravagant sums from an overburdened community, controls the city by a political party, and endows itself from the liberality of an unscrupulous faction, its charity is converted into selfish avarice, and it enters once more upon that course of ambitious greed which has forced every European nation to recall its gifts to the priesthood. Charity, we must remember, was the pretext under which Rome engrossed the fairest lands of Germany, and spoiled Italy and Spain.

If the Romish priesthood had possessed discretion, they would have carefully avoided any recurrence, in the New World, to that dishonest policy which has enraged against them the people of the Old. They would have come among us as one of many sects. They would have claimed no superiority except in humility and good deeds. They would have laid aside ambition; would have joined in no political movements; would have proved by an open reform that they had repented of their evil deeds in past history; were prepared to win a new reputation in all future ages. Unhappily they have entered boldly upon the opposite course. All that is bad in their past policy they would revive: the gentle teachings of FÉNÉLON, the ominous remonstrances of DÖLLINGER and HYACINTHE, they neglect. "The Catholic press of the United States," says, in effect, a foreign review, "is more bigoted and more hostile to freedom than the European: it teaches rebellion, persecution, and the final fall of the republic." The Romish Church has become once more an active political party. Its adherents vote on that side which promises them the largest share of power. It aims to rule in our wealthy cities. It has already become a source of discord and moral decay. It has suffered its officials to plunder the public without stint so long as it is allowed to share in the spoil. It has no word of reproof for its dishonest adherents. It must prepare in future to be treated as a political faction rather than a Christian sect; to be studied with keen accuracy by the patriot; reviewed by the swift insight of letters; pointed at by a HYACINTHE or a COQUEREL as a ceaseless cause of human woe; must deserve the rebukes of modern civilization, and sink beneath the scorn of the community it has rifled and betrayed.

As a political faction it can scarcely hope for any lasting success. It may hold New York in its grasp a few years longer. It may disturb the peace of quiet towns with riots and disorder. It may place in office men shameless and corrupt. But the same unpopularity that has followed the priestly rulers of Europe must attend them here, and any party that trusts for its victories to the support of a foreign Church will dwindle to a small minority. In Europe the firmest opponents of the Romish rule are Catholics who prefer the interests of their country to the advancement of the Church. The people of Italy, while still professing the faith of Rome, maintain their free schools, their liberal institutions, and have destroyed the temporal power in defiance of the anathemas of an infallible pope. It is a promising trait in our own politics that many intelligent and honest Catholics have denounced that dangerous policy upon which their Church has entered, would accept no bribes from dishonest rulers, and inculcate obedience to the laws.

Still, however, there must be a vigorous struggle, and it will demand all the watchful zeal of the patriotic to expel from our midst the corrupting influence of Romish politics. Only a year ago the nation was in signal danger. Possessed of New York, controlling its revenues, guiding the policy of the whole Democratic

KILLING THE GOOSE THAT LAID THE GOLDEN EGG.

"A certain man had the good fortune to possess a Goose that laid him a Golden Egg every day. But dissatisfied with so slow an income, and thinking to seize the whole treasure at once, he killed the Goose; and cutting her open, found her—just what any other goose would be."—ÆSOP.

Chapter 20
Tweed: Rise of the Ring

Tammany Hall

Tammany Hall — named after Tamarend, a Delaware Indian chief — began as a patriotic social organization prior to 1800, but soon became a Democratic political club whose support and tactics often decided New York City elections. As the number of poor, uneducated Irish immigrants — many speaking only Gaelic — surged in the middle of the century, they had no social network to turn to other than family, friends and Tammany Hall. Tammany mobilized them via patronage; employment as laborers and clerks; public works; real estate for parochial schools, churches, orphan asylums and hospitals; education subsidies; and, of course, sinecures, graft, violence and fraud. On occasion, Fernando Wood's Mozart Hall beat Tammany at its own game.

The "Big Four" Ring members — Bill Tweed, Peter Sweeny, Oakey Hall and Richard Connolly — all belonged to Tammany, with Tweed as Grand Sachem (chief) from 1863 until his downfall in late 1871. Dignified John Hoffman served as front man, first as Mayor and then as Governor.

Tweed confessed shortly before he died in prison in 1878. Asked to define "Ring," he responded: "A combination of men to do any improper thing." Nast often used "Tammany" and "the Ring" interchangeably.

Other crooked Tammany/Ring members included judges, law enforcement officers, city contractors, auditors, bookkeepers, and token Republicans. They milked the city for somewhere between $30 and $200 million. (Perhaps as much as $4 billion in today's dollars).

Naturalization Fraud

After Tweed consolidated power in 1863, he had the unqualified John McCunn elected judge by having his electoral counters increase McCunn's ballot box totals and decrease his opponents'. George Barnard, a Yale graduate and Tammany politician, who would play a critical role in both the Ring's maintenance and its fall, was elected judge in 1862. Albert Cardozo, father of future Supreme Court Justice Benjamin Cardozo, was Tweed's third corrupt judge. The new Boss became Deputy Street Cleaning Commissioner, which gave him patronage authority to employ thousands of Irish laborers.

From 1860-1867, average immigration to America from all countries was under 9,000 annually. In October 1868 alone — with the critical election coming up — McCunn, Barnard and Cardozo naturalized 57,000 new citizens (out of 60,000 for the entire year). As the *Tribune* noted and *Harper's* portrayed in a non-Nast cartoon: "McCunn manufactures citizens at the rate of 480 an hour." Almost all of the October immigrants were Irish.

HW January 22, 1870 56

The three requirements for citizenship included: age 21, arrival before age 18, and residency for five years. The crooked judges accepted blatantly false statements from lying applicants and witnesses who swore they met the legal requirements.

The scheme, however, went much deeper, encompassing thousands of *imaginary* Irish applicants, who were vouched for by the same Irish witnesses on the Ring's payroll, using phony names and addresses. Separately, the Ring provided blank Certificates of Naturalization, face-down in bulk, no questions asked, with names and addresses filled in later. Tweed's judges stamped them approved, sight unseen. District Attorney Hall ordered the election inspectors to accept these certificates as "conclusive evidence of the right of such person to vote."

Nast captured the scenario best in an illustration for his 1871 book. The four Ring leaders were rushing out to greet the arrogant immigrants from "Sweet Erin" and welcome them to New Cork.

Sweeny Hall Tweed Connolly

THE WELCOME TO NEW CORK.

Miss Columbia's Public School, p. 50

Repeating

As mentioned previously, the Irish support for the Ring peaked on Election Day when they were to vote illegally in as many election districts as possible, using false identifications and addresses — taverns, brothels and vacant lots included. In 1870, Mayor Hall created additional election districts to make repeat voting easier and less traceable.

Each district was supposed to have four inspectors, two from each party, to watch the actual voting. The Ring used bribes, drugged drinks, threats and even false arrests to neutralize Republican inspectors, facilitate repeat voting, and stuff ballot boxes. In 1868, Sheriff James O'Brien (who would later play a key role in the Ring's downfall) appointed 2,000 ruffians as deputy sheriffs with orders to arrest anyone who interfered with voting.

Nast subsequently depicted Tweed as Falstaff, capturing the essence of his memorable "Army," with Hoffman as a diminutive royal jester in front. (Falstaff was commissioned to raise an army for Shakespeare's King Henry IV, but he allowed the able-bodied to bribe their way out of service, and replaced them with the poorly-paid old, feeble and unfit, pocketing a handsome profit for himself.)

HW November 5, 1870 713

OUR MODERN FALSTAFF REVIEWING HIS ARMY.

Counting

After the polls closed and the ballot box shenanigans were complete, two canvassers in each district tallied the votes and forwarded the results to election headquarters. Now Tweed played his key card — counting.

While in jail shortly before his death, Tweed explained how he controlled elections: "Count the ballots in bulk, or without counting them announce the result in bulk, or change from one to the other, as the case may have been. The ballots made no result. The counters made the result."[1]

As the 1871 election approached, Nast banged away in conjunction with his repetitive campaign slogan: *What are you going to do about it?*

HW October 7, 1871 944

"THAT'S WHAT'S THE MATTER."
As long as I count the votes, what are you going to do about it? Say?

There were plenty of other tricks like dropping Republican votes into fake ballot boxes. Just before the election, Nast captured that, substituting a wastebasket, as the gang leered and the police looked on. The sub-caption: Boss. "You have the *Liberty of Voting* for any one you please; but we have the *Liberty of Counting* in any one we please."

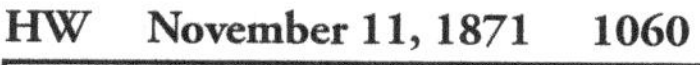
HW November 11, 1871 1060

GOING THROUGH THE FORM OF UNIVERSAL SUFFRAGE.
Boss. "You have the *Liberty of Voting* for any one you please; but we have the *Liberty of Counting* in any one we please."
"Do your duty as Citizens and leave the rest to take its course."—*New York Times*

Just as Nast picked up ideas from other artists, this cartoon may have influenced an important painting by Edgar Degas.[2]

Tweed's methods were effective. After the 1870 elections, Democrats controlled every branch of the New York State, City and County governments.

Boss Tweed

William Magear Tweed's Protestant ancestors emigrated from Kelso, Scotland (on the Tweed River) in the mid-1700s. Bill was a third-or-fourth-generation New Yorker, born on April 3, 1823.

For about 75 years after his death, Tweed's middle name was mistakenly thought to be Marcy; actually it was Magear, his mother's maiden name. He signed himself "W.M. Tweed" and didn't use his middle name. His eldest son was William Magear Tweed, Jr.

Bill was educated in public schools and learned bookkeeping at a private academy. His father Richard ran a chair-making business next to their home on Cherry Street. Bill and his brother (also Richard) worked with him and later took over the business which ultimately failed. Bill found employment with another chair manufacturer, Lorin Ingersoll, and also was involved with a brush-making business. Both enterprises provided income as Bill worked his way up the political ladder. He married the 19-year old daughter of his father's partner when he was 21, but became notorious for his "licentious excesses." In part, that may have been because his wife was frequently pregnant; they had ten children, two of whom died in infancy.[3]

The Ingersoll connection was important. Lorin provided financial help to Bill in 1868, when he successfully ran for the State Senate. Lorin's son James (nicknamed "Chairs") became Tweed's trusted confidante and the leading bagman for his Ring.

At 16, Bill began the first of eleven years service with the Americus Fire Engine Company No. 6, known as "Big Six." Volunteer fire companies frequently fought with each other or with onlookers, often to the detriment of the fires. Tweed, just under six feet and over 250 pounds as he matured, earned due respect as a brawler.* Ultimately, Tweed was elected leader of Big Six. His size, swagger, coarse sense of humor, and free-and-easy manner made him a natural.

During the 1840s, Tweed got to know many actual and would-be politicians, and by 1851 he had decided on a full-time political career. He had tried chair-making and brush-manufacturing and found they were not for him. That fall he was elected to the New York Board of Aldermen, part of the Common Council notoriously known as the "Forty Thieves." This was the group Frank Leslie took on (and Nast caricatured) in his 1858 Swill Milk campaign.**

Until the early 1850s, Tweed was anti-Catholic and even presided over a Nativist fraternal lodge in 1848-9. At the time, he was in accord with Tammany Hall. Democrats, as well as Nativists, were increasingly concerned about the rising tide of Irish and German immigration and its effect on the status quo. In 1852, Tweed was elected to his only term in Congress. He got a taste of Washington, found it dull, and was glad to return to New York.

During the latter 1850s and early 1860s, Fernando Wood dominated the city's politics as a perennial candidate for mayor; he won and lost three times. Tweed learned many of his political tricks and tactics from Wood while assembling his own alliances within Tammany Hall.

In 1857, he became an elected school official and a member of the Board of Supervisors. That Board was in charge of taxation, public improvements, revenue allotment and disbursements. Its twelve supervisors, six from each party, also had the power to appoint inspectors of elections. Tweed stayed on it until 1870, frequently as president.

During the Civil War, Tweed was a staunch Unionist, in contrast to Copperhead Wood who wanted the city to secede from the Union. In 1863, he became permanent chairman and Grand Sachem of the Tammany Society. Tammany reportedly made a deal with Wood, who agreed to go to Congress and stay out of New York politics, allowing Tweed to take uncontested total control.

He engineered his future Ring members on to his political chessboard: John Hoffman as Recorder (prosecutor/magistrate), soon to be Mayor and then Governor; Oakey Hall as District Attorney, eventually to replace Hoffman as Mayor; and George Barnard, Albert Cardozo, and John McCunn to do his bidding as crooked judges at various court levels. Innovative, boisterous, jovial, people-friendly, fearless, fond of high living — and totally unscrupulous — he was an ideal front man and commanding general.

---

* See p. 7
** See p. 39

Tweed loved ostentation, revelling in his image as "Boss," and maintaining a bold, commanding presence. He wore a huge ten-carat $15,500 diamond stick-pin which his nemesis continuously ridiculed as a symbol of greed. He owned a lavishly furnished house at Fifth Avenue and 43rd Street, close to where the newly-married Nasts once lived. He built a mansion in Greenwich and a $300,000 clubhouse on the water there for his Americus Club. He threw a wedding for his daughter which was the social event of 1871 and reportedly cost $700,000.

Tweed also had a reputation for generosity, although its sources were totally tainted. He did do some good with his ever-increasing tax levies by supporting parochial schools, orphan asylums, hospitals, homes for the friendless and dispensaries, and personally giving random gifts of food and coal.[4]

In 1870, he publicized a $50,000 Tammany Christmas contribution for the poor. Nast capitalized on that with Sweeny emptying the public treasury with one hand, while Tweed doled out cash with the other.

HW January 14, 1871 40

TWEEDLEDEE AND SWEEDLEDUM.
(A New Christmas Pantomime at the Tammany Hall.)
Clown (to Pantaloon). "Let's Blind them with *this*, and then take *some more*."

HW January 22, 1870 57

Tweed also was a made-to-order target for Nast, his only real-person image (Santa Claus and Uncle Sam excluded) who lives on today.* Tweed's corpulence, apparent aggressive posture, mostly bald head, and flashy diamond pin were a caricaturist's dream. Frank Bellew and other *Harper's* cartoonists depicting Ring members, had no choice but to adopt Nast's instantly recognizable imagery.

Ultimately, Nast depicted Tweed at least 120 times in *Harper's Weekly* during Tweed's lifetime, and another 25 after he died — more than any other real person. The "Boss" served as his bogeyman of evil, and his symbol of associated guilt for future villains.**

* See p. xiv

** Uncle Sam led with 186 followed by Columbia with 157. Ulysses Grant (105) and Horace Greeley (95) followed.

Peter Sweeny

Tweed had an alter ego in Peter Sweeny. A polar opposite of the gregarious Boss, Sweeny served as the Ring's stealthy strategist; however, he was uncomfortable playing any role requiring public appearances. Born two years after Tweed to an Irish-Catholic saloon-keeper with relatives who were priests, Sweeny graduated from Columbia College and became an extremely knowledgeable lawyer. He was deeply interested in history, art and literature in contrast to the non-intellectual Tweed.

In 1854, Sweeny became an Albany lobbyist for his uncle, a newly-elected State Senator. There he learned how to manipulate men and opportunities for political and financial gain.

Back in New York, Sweeny moved up the ranks in Tammany, but always preferred the background. His key post was City Chamberlain (Treasurer) and he later became Parks Commissioner. Initially, Nast and others believed he was the Ring's leader, and portrayed him as the "Chief of the Tammany Tribe."

HW December 4, 1869 777

Sweeny was of medium height and not too heavy. Not much there for a caricaturist, so Nast focused on his coarse, black, bristly hair. In his first solo portrait, Sweeny wore a "Steal (pun) Ring" headband and a tiger-head necklace adorned with shrunken skulls. He played his cards close to his vest, inspiring Nast to sometimes portray him in a buttoned-up overcoat.

Richard Connolly

"Slippery Dick" as he was generally known was the Ring's chief financial officer and numbers massager. Born near Cork, Ireland in 1810, he was thirteen to sixteen years older than the others. His schoolmaster father taught his son the fundamentals of accounting before young Dick left for Philadelphia and then New York. Connolly's resume included auctioneer's clerk, the Custom House, New York County Clerk, and manager and cashier of a bank, as well as a term as State Senator. He dabbled in politics in Tweed's Seventh Ward, and became active in Tammany Hall during and after the 1840s.

After Connolly was elected comptroller in November 1866, the "Big Three" became the "Big Four." An ace with figures, his manipulative skills and total control of the books made him the indispensable cog in the Ring's financial machinations.

However, Connolly was weak, cowardly, crafty and treacherous, and never gained the respect of his three peers. Obsequious to Tweed and Sweeny, he was arrogant, cold and oily to his clerks and others. Ultimately, he became the first of the Ring to crack under pressure. Nast never symbolized Connolly, although his face, portly figure and top hat were readily identifiable.

HW August 26, 1871 788

Oakey Hall

Abraham Oakey Hall, or A. Oakey Hall as he signed himself, was the Ring's advisor on most legislative and legal matters. Nast referred to him on occasion as "O.K. Haul."

Born three years after Tweed, he graduated from New York University, then dropped out of Harvard Law School to become a newspaper reporter in New Orleans. In 1854, he surfaced as a lobbyist in Albany, at the same time as Sweeny. Initially he was a Nativist, next a Republican, then a Democratic supporter of Fernando Wood who helped elect him District Attorney in 1862. With Wood in Congress and Tweed in power, Hall shifted allegiances once again and joined Tammany in early 1864.

HW August 26, 1871 788

If Tweed had been able to elect Hoffman as Governor in 1866, Hall would have succeeded him then as Mayor. With the help of fraudulent votes for Hoffman and himself in 1868, he had no trouble becoming "Mare" as Nast frequently portrayed him.

"Elegant Oakey" was a vain fun-loving charlatan who used suavity, flamboyance and wit to cover up his swindling. He was a poet, playwright, actor and punster whose jaunty manner, shameless insolence and fancy wardrobes helped him and the Ring disguise their schemes.

Hall was a small man with a heavy mustache and black beard. Nast focused on his owlish eyes and pince-nez glasses, worn on a black string, to accompany Tweed's corpulence and Sweeny's hair as personifications of their owners. Secondarily, he projected Hall's debonair manner, stage flair and foppish wardrobe to depict the flamboyant narcissist of the Ring.

HW September 23, 1871 896

Tweed Sweeny Connolly Hall

WHAT THE GERMAN DEMOCRATS HAVE DONE ABOUT IT.

After a while, Nast's symbols — Tweed's head, Sweeny's hair, and Hall's spectacles — became so well known to the public that they served as complete identifiers — as when the German Democrats threw the Ring overboard in August 1871. (Depicted in September as the Ring disintegrated).

John Hoffman

John Hoffman's elegant bearing, prominent chin and distinctive handlebar mustache made him a logical and appealing "respectable screen" for the Ring, and a favorite subject for Nast. Originally of Finnish stock (his Protestant ancestors had been in America since 1657), he was born five years after Tweed. A popular lawyer, he became affiliated with Tammany in 1854 and was elected Recorder (prosecutor and magistrate) six years later. In that capacity, his competence and severity in trying and sentencing 1863 draft rioters earned him bipartisan support for reelection.

Tweed tried unsuccessfully to have Hoffman elected Governor in 1866. Hoffman carried the city by 47,000 votes but lost the state by 5,000. The Democratic Party undoubtedly was hurt by President Andrew Johnson's antics and "policy" as Republican incumbent Reuben Fenton squeaked in. Two years later, the Ring's extensive vote frauds did make Hoffman Governor, while Fenton moved to the Senate.

Eleven years later with Tweed dead and Tammany disrupted, Nast portrayed Hoffman with Tweed's face and brains, and his own mustache and jutting chin.

HW October 4, 1879 788

HW October 10, 1868 656

A RESPECTABLE SCREEN COVERS A MULTITUDE OF THIEVES.

The Presidency

Tweed's next target reportedly was Washington. As early as January 1870, Nast drew a forboding 15-vignette cartoon entitled *Shadows of Forthcoming Events*. One scenario forecast Hoffman and Tweed as the Democratic ticket for 1872. However, as time passed, the rumored slate became Hoffman for President, Hall to replace him as Governor, and Tweed for Senator; another rumor had Tweed wanting to be ambassador to England. Comptroller Connolly would continue to hold the fort as the city's financial boss, while chief strategist Sweeny, rejecting any public office, would operate behind the scenes in either or both cities.

HW January 22, 1870 56

The Press

To ensure favorable publicity and continuing public support, the Ring bribed the press overtly and covertly. Mayor Hall distributed city advertising to 54 daily and 26 weekly newspapers in the city and state to keep them from attacking Tammany, even if not actively supporting it. Advertising included Oakey's speeches and comments along with legal announcements, and was paid for at two to five times normal rates.[5] Slippery Dick Connolly was known to withhold payment of selected advertising claims until newspapers complied with instructions to print specific stories or support bills in the State Legislature. Tweed paid a number of reporters directly, or with sinecure public payroll jobs, for writing favorable stories.

Manton Marble, a rabid and often dishonest Democrat, published the *New York World* and was a target of Nast's about two dozen times over the years. In 1869, however, he was on the same side as he editorialized: "Down with the shameless corruption of the Ring, O. Hall, W.M. Tweed." The following year, his advertising revenue from City Hall increased sixfold, as Nast quipped: "It's Love that makes the *World* turn round." While Marble balanced on his globe (*World*) as Cupid shooting arrows at Tammany dollars, his new message read: "Vote (often) for Hoffman, Hall and Tweed. Good and honest men."

Moreover, Tweed also awarded contracts for printing forms and regulations to selected newspapers. He controlled the extremely profitable New York Printing Company, which received almost all of the City and County government's printing business, as well as that from transportation, insurance and other private companies subject to municipal regulation.

HW November 12, 1870 727

"IT'S LOVE THAT MAKES THE *WORLD* TURN ROUND."

Going even further, Tweed, Sweeny, Jim Fisk and Jay Gould secretly put up $5,000 each to capitalize *Punchinello*, a satiric illustrated weekly. Top flight cartoonist Henry Stephens, who had worked for Frank Leslie and *Vanity Fair*, did his best to preempt the field by insuring gentle treatment of municipal government. First appearing on April 2, 1870, the paper expired with its Christmas issue.[6]

Earlier in 1870, Sheriff Jimmy O'Brien and former boxer-turned-politician John Morrissey challenged the Ring by forming a new political party called Young Democracy. Tweed killed it then, but both principals later had their revenge; O'Brien provided key evidence against the Ring, and Morrissey ultimately succeeded Tweed as Tammany Sachem.

When (now ex-Sheriff) O'Brien ran for Mayor against Oakey Hall later in 1870, Punchinello attacked publisher Charles Dana of the *Sun* for supporting him, as he threw mud at Governor Hoffman. Morrissey, with boxing gloves on, backed O'Brien,while Horace Greeley looked on approvingly with his *Tribune*.

PUNCHINELLO September 3, 1870 361

LAW VERSUS LAWLESSNESS.
The Virtuous Allies Of The New York "Sun" Engaged In Their Congenial Occupation Of Throwing Dirt.

The Charter

New York had both a city and an overlapping county government, providing duplicate opportunities for patronage and graft. The Common Council/Aldermen ("Forty Thieves") prepared the City budget, while the Board of Supervisors prepared the County budget. Each body could levy taxes and issue bonds. Some individuals worked for both simultaneously, drawing two salaries and essentially doing the same job. Others were sinecures whose only "work" was to collect their pay.

In order to gain total control, Tweed had to remove one final obstacle: the authority of the State Legislature to approve New York City and County tax bills. By reportedly giving over $1,000,000 in bribes to state legislators in April 1870, Tweed obtained a "reform" charter which provided home rule for the metropolis and was signed into law by Governor Hoffman. It not only deprived the public of all control over the amount and disposal of their tax dollars, but it ensured that Connolly could not be replaced as Comptroller (and financial fixer) for at least five years without his agreement. That turned out to be a critical provision 17 months later when the Ring came apart.

"Tweed's Charter" and related tax legislation (requiring additional bribes) established a "Board of Special Audit" — comprised of Mayor Hall, Comptroller Connolly and Tweed (as president of the newly-created Public Works Commission) — to pay pre-dated as well as current claims, 90% of which involved huge phony mark-ups on contractor invoices and reciprocal kickbacks.

Nast used Shakespeare's *Hamlet* (for the first of 14 times) to skewer Tweed in spite of his twin victories over the Legislature and O'Brien's faction of the Democratic party. Hamlet (Hoffman) lectured his bearded mother, Queen Gertrude, (Tweed) on corruption; "she" was dressed in an opulent gown and a Tammany crown. Meanwhile "O'Brien Democracy" lay dead with a sword sticking out of its belly, while a "Democratic Fight Over the Sacking of N.Y." raged in the background.

HW April 16, 1870 249

SENATOR TWEED IN A NEW ROLE.

Harper's, Nast and Democratic Party State Chairman Samuel Tilden strongly opposed the Charter. However, most of the co-opted press, including the *Times*, endorsed it, as well as the highly respected Citizens Association whose Republican secretary, Nathaniel Sands, was secretly on the Ring's payroll at an exceptional $75,000 a year (and would become a prominent Nast target).

Pay-offs

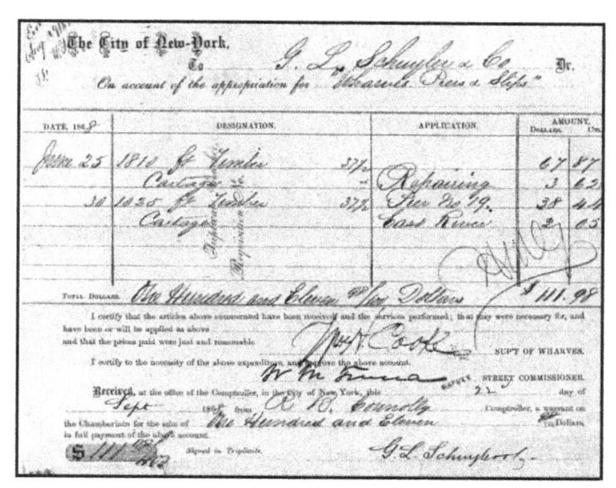

The City of New-York,
To G. L. Schuyler & Co. Dr.
On account of the appropriation for "Wharves, Piers & Slips"

DATE, 1868	DESIGNATION.		APPLICATION.	AMOUNT. Dollars	Cts.
June 25	1810 ft Timber	37½	Repairing	67	87
	Cartage			3	62
30	1025 ft Timber	37½	Pier No 49	38	44
	Cartage		East River	2	05

Total Dollars One Hundred and Eleven 98/100 Dollars $111.98

I certify that the articles above enumerated have been received and the services performed; that they were necessary &c, and have been or will be applied as above and that the prices paid were just and reasonable. Wm H Cook SUPT OF WHARVES.

I certify to the necessity of the above expenditure, and approve the above account. Wm M Tweed DEPUTY STREET COMMISSIONER.

Received, at the office of the Comptroller, in the City of New York, this 22 day of Sept 1868 from R. B. Connolly Comptroller, a warrant on the Chamberlain for the sum of One Hundred and Eleven 98/100 Dollars in full payment of the above account.

$111 98/100 Signed in Triplicate. G. L. Schuyler & Co.

The Ring had multiple income sources, almost all of them illegitimate. While taxes were the most prominent, bond issues were important and kickbacks from employees played a role. (Even a poor teacher had to pay $75 of her $300 annual salary to keep her job.)

Expenses for the city and county were paid from vouchers. This one from 1868 for wharf repairs was signed by the Superintendent of Wharves, approved by Tweed as Deputy Street Commissioner and countersigned by Connolly as Comptroller. After the Charter became effective in May 1870, the newly-established Tweed-Hall-Connolly Board of Audit took over.

The suggested kickbacks from the inflated invoices were 65% in 1870, up from 10% three years earlier. They were apportioned 25% to Tweed; 20% to Connolly; 10% to Sweeny; 5% to Hall; and 5% split between County Auditor James Watson and Board clerk Elbert Woodward who prepared the bills and presented them to Connolly for payment. Hall provided a second signature on the payment vouchers.

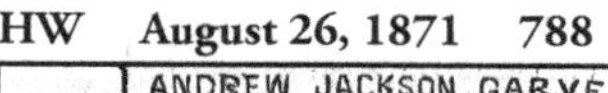

HW August 26, 1871 788

GARVEY

Many of the inflated invoices were for the new courthouse, finally completed for about $13,000,000, more than 50 times the original budget. Others covered fictitious repairs, supplies and rents. Edward Jones, who had the city's stationery contract, charged over $1,000,000 annually; his bills included jewelry and household furnishings selected by Ring members from a nearby luxury store.

The invoices were mostly funneled through three bagmen. John Keyser, a plumbing contractor was paid $2,000,000; Andrew Garvey, known as the "Prince of Plasterers," collected $3,000,000; and James "Chairs" Ingersoll, whose father Lorin once employed Tweed, had $5,000,000 pass through his hands. They also served as front men for other contractors' illegal bills.

James Ingersoll

Nast knew Jim Ingersoll as a fellow member of the Seventh Regiment. Both of them were at Saratoga together in July 1869, five months before his Ring campaign heated up. Sallie was by his side. Subsequently, at a testimonial for Ingersoll, Nast gave him multiple sketches of the event. Ingersoll also owned Nast's painting of the Regiment marching up Broadway in 1861.*

HW August 7, 1869 500

Nast Ingersoll

A SCENE AT SARATOGA DURING THE VISIT OF THE SEVENTH REGIMENT.

* See p. 188

Nast posed for this 1867 picture, taken by his good friend Napoleon Sarony, a renowned portrait photographer.[7]

The *New York Times*

While the *Times* played a critical role during the last 14 months prior to the Ring's November 1871 election defeat, it was silent before September 1870; as noted, it supported Tweed's new Charter in April, while also praising him as a "reformer," and hailing his appointment as Commissioner of Public Works. In return, the paper received about 7% of its total revenue from Ring ads and announcements.

Tweed effectively controlled the editorial commentary and endorsement of the *Times* through two of its board members: Leonard Jerome (whose daughter Jennie became Winston Churchill's mother), had joint real estate holdings with the Boss; and James Taylor, who owned 10% of the *Times* and minority shares in Tweed's New York Printing Company. Taylor had succeeded Henry Raymond as a director, when Raymond was fatally stricken in the company of his mistress in June 1869. (Oakey Hall was close enough to Raymond to have been one of his pall bearers.)

George Jones took over as editor (he already was the publisher) of the *Times*, but was inhibited by Taylor from assailing the Ring. When Taylor unexpectedly died from typhoid fever on August 22, 1870, Jones and his new managing editor, Louis Jennings, were free to attack a month later.

By then Nast, who first went after the Ring almost three years earlier, had already published ten cartoons, and the *Weekly* more than a dozen aggressive editorials.

HW November 6, 1869 720

Jones, Bryant, Greeley, Grant, Nast
"WE FIGHTS MIT SIGEL."

Nast disliked Henry Raymond because of his support for "King Andy" Johnson, but he respected George Jones. The previous year, he had depicted the heroic Jones and himself (along with President Grant, Horace Greeley and William Cullen Bryant of the *Evening Post*) campaigning for Civil War General and German community leader Franz Siegel, when he unsuccessfully ran for Secretary of State against Tammany.

In 1870, the *Times* had a circulation of about 35,000 for the daily paper and 20,000 for its weekly edition; *Harper's Weekly's* was more than five times as large. Both papers were read by a select audience of knowledgeable, influential and action-oriented readers, but *Harper's* had a pass-along audience exceeding a million.

It was a combination of the forceful editorials in both publications and incriminating disclosures in the *Times* — all amplified by Nast's 47 Ring-related cartoons — that finally brought the Ring down.

Chapter 21
Tweed: Attacking the Ring

Nast's First Shot: 1867

The October 1866 issue of *North American Review* carried a 52-page exposé by James Parton entitled *The Government of the City of New York.* The last line read: "The thieves must be driven out if it takes a bloody war, and it will cost a bloody war if it is not." *Harper's Weekly* praised and quoted from the article in detail.[1] Parton attended City Council and Aldermen's meetings in person and familiarized cousin Tommy (by marriage) with the gory details of what went on inside and outside those meetings.

Four months later, one councilman flung an inkstand at another, pistols were drawn and a riotous brawl ensued which the forewarned police broke up before too much blood was shed. Nast's consequent illustration included his first nondescript Tammany Tiger, boxer John Morrissey, lots of liquor, inkwells chained to their stands so they couldn't be thrown, and the word "steal" featured in three places. The man in front resembled Sweeny. The politicians aimed their pistols and Nast sharpened his rapier.

HW **February 9, 1867 88**

Nast's Second Shot: 1868

During the eight weeks Nast worked for the ill-fated *Illustrated Chicago News* during the spring of 1868, he sketched but didn't sign a drawing of New York City as a bed-ridden patient trying to cope with his Tammany afflictions; swollen leeches labeled "City Tax," "County Tax," and "State Tax" were sucking his blood. Regrettably, few people in New York saw it, although Horace Greeley's *Tribune* commented positively. If the Chicago paper had been successful — and Nast stayed with it instead of returning to *Harper's Weekly* — his life, fame, and the Tweed Ring's fate might have turned out quite differently. Instead, he spent most of his effort trying to get Grant elected, and didn't pay attention to the Ring or much else.

Hello, Bill Tweed: 1869

In August 1869, Bill Tweed unsuccessfully tried to remove August Belmont as national Chairman of the Democratic Party. Nast subsequently depicted Belmont as a Jewish scapegoat while Tweed made his first shadowy appearance in a Nast cartoon standing in front of an empty chair reserved for him. Nast had not yet dubbed him "Boss" because he didn't know whether Sweeny or Tweed was top dog.

HW September 11, 1869 592

Tweed

THE DEMOCRATIC SCAPEGOAT

Pope Hoffman

HW December 25, 1869 824

EXCOMMUNICATION OF MODERN CIVILIZATION.

GALILEO OF THE 19th CENTURY. "BUT NEVERTHELESS IT DOES MOVE."

After hammering the Pope during the fall of 1869, Nast tied him and the Ring together in the Christmas issue of the *Weekly* in an irreligious pair of facing cartoons. Nast's run-of-the-mill "so-called" *Oecumenical Council* which declared Pius IX infallible, depicted him excommunicating "Modern Civilization" represented by a terrestrial globe of liberalism and a reference to Galileo. In fact, it was a set-up for his punning, imaginative *Economical Council* — which was immediately opposite.

Here, Nast included all four principal Ring members for the first time. His *Economical Council* was all about money, not religion. Pius Hoffman I, wearing a Tammany papal crown and holding two "Tax Levy" golden keys, declared: "No discussion necessary for $ . . . that is condemned." Next to him, Sweeny was labeled Cardinal Antonelli (papal Secretary of State). "Infallible" signs applied to Pope Hoffman, Cardinal Sweeny and the Ring.

The supporting cast of bishops were identified on their miters or vestments. Their religious commandments written on the wall behind Tweed were: "Thou shalt steal, bear false witness, and vote often. They all looked on as the two Irish guards — labeled "repeater" and "fraudulent" — opened the box of "taxpayers' and tenants' hard cash" for distribution to the Ring.

The artist's insights and even clairvoyance were impressive. The man behind Connolly's right shoulder was Andrew Garvey, the "Prince of Plasterers," who took huge kickbacks for inflated construction, repairs and rent, and also served as front man for other illegal payments. What did Nast know almost two years before the Ring's downfall when he included him here? He drew Garvey in shadow, probably implying he suspected but wasn't sure. The other man in shadow was George Barnard, Tweed's favorite conniving judge.

Jim Fisk and Jay Gould were the key players in the "Black Friday" gold crash of three months earlier. They bought Tweed's political support for their Erie Railroad (on their miters) stock manipulations, in which they bested Cornelius Vanderbilt and his son William (shown here) for control of the railroad.

HW December 25, 1869 825

Bishops (Left to Right): William Vanderbilt, Jay Gould, Jim Fisk, Hall, George McLean, Garvey, Connolly, Barnard?, Tweed

Slaves

In the same issue as his Charter cartoon,* Nast portrayed the Irish as slaves to the Ring. He still was unsure whether Tweed or his key associate, Peter Sweeny, was the gang's leader but leaned towards Sweeny. In a burlesque of American Hiram Powers' sensationally erotic 1843 sculpture of a chained nude woman, Sweeny was an intimidating overseer, cat-o'-nine-tails in hand, watching over a grizzled Irish immigrant hand-cuffed to a "Democract" (sic) stump by an encircling "Tammany Ring." A ballot-box on the stump was topped by rum and whisky bottles, while five detailed vignettes depicted the Ring's fanciful recruiting process (top) and the reality of their employment (bottom).[2]

HW April 16, 1870 248

Moreover, in spite of their ever-higher taxes and real estate assessments, the city's residents didn't get much return as Nast depicted in a few casual vignettes in a previous cartoon. *The New Court-House* had "cartloads of money" in front and "More" as the title on the building. Sanitary conditions were terrible.

HW January 22, 1870 56-57

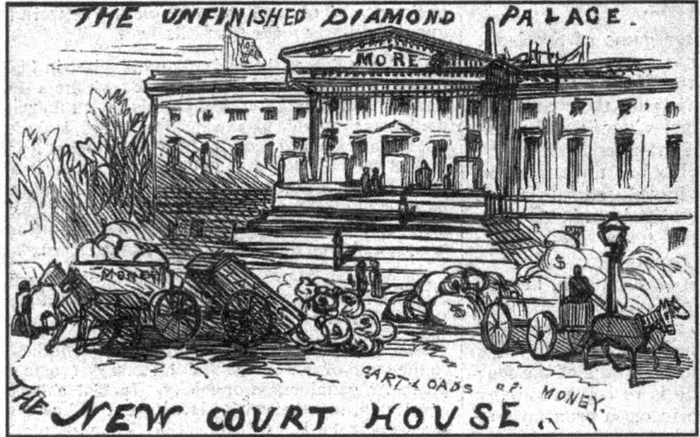

* See p. 252

Finding a Strategy

Nast knew that ridicule was probably the only effective way to attack the Ring, but there was no obvious approach. Tweed, Sweeny, Hall and Hoffman all had positive public images, while the press was largely controlled. Tammany excelled at keeping mouths and records closed, so meaningful information was hard to come by. In fact, until late 1870, Nast appeared unsure whether Tweed or Sweeny had the ultimate power within the Ring.

Shortly before that year's election, Tweed made his first cartoon appearance in five months; Nast had been focusing on the Pope, Napoleon's disastrous war with Prussia, Chinese immigrants and other miscellany. Now Tweed was the unmistakable *Power Behind the Throne*, although their respective headbands said "Sweed" and "Tweeny." Nast turned the *Tammany Kingdom* into *"Ringdom"* by doctoring the K.

As a wary King Hoffman sat on his throne, Nast reminded him that "he cannot call his soul his own." The Tammany Tiger evolved into a sharp-toothed snarler, and was the centerpiece in the royal seal of the "Kingdom of New York."

Although Tweed, Hall and Hoffman were all non-Irish Protestants, the Ring depended on Irish Catholics to maintain power. Without specific incriminating evidence with which to attack the Ring prior to July 1871, Nast tapped into nativist anti-Irish sentiment to establish his villains. Their general behavior and affiliation with the Pope, Catholic dogma, and the battle over sectarian education made it easy to do so.

HW October 29, 1870 697

Irish Heroes

An estimated 190,000 Irish-Americans participated in the Civil War, about 80% for the Union. Some of them saw military service as preparation for post-war action in Ireland. Many fought well, including New York's 69th Irish Regiment at Bull Run on July 21, 1861, when 600 of its 1,000 men were casualties. Two months later, at a benefit memorial for their widows and children attended by 70,000 New Yorkers, Captain Thomas Meagher spoke "for the vast majority of his countrymen . . . whose oath of loyalty to all the states (United States) ranks above that to Tammany or Mozart Hall."[3]

In one of Nast's rare (if not the only) cartoons praising an Irish-American per se — Colonel Michael Corcoran, the Regiment's heroic commanding officer who was in a Confederate prison when Captain Thomas spoke — he nevertheless gave *The American St. Patrick* simian features. Published just after the battle, the picture was one of his last contributions to *Frank Leslie's Illustrated Newspaper*.*

* See p. 106

After Nast joined *Harper's Weekly* about a month later, he didn't comment on actions involving German, Irish or other regiments or individuals based on their ethnicity. (However, he consistently portrayed black soldiers in a positive light.)

On occasion, Irish troops apparently were used as cannon fodder. In particular, Union cavalry general Hugh Judson Kilpatrick had a reputation for exhausting and needlessly sacrificing his men, earning him the sobriquet "Kill-Cavalry." Two months after Appomattox, Nast branded him "Kil-Patrick" when he drew the controversial officer riding a brutish Irishman in *Phunny Phellow*. (For some reason — maybe his jutting jaw, his being a Republican, or his anti-Irish reputation — Nast gratuitously inserted the relatively insignificant Kilpatrick into several post-war *Weekly* cartoons where he didn't really belong).

PP June 1865 10

KIL-PATRICK

Irish Villains

As part of Great Britain, Ireland was harshly governed by Protestants for centuries. In 1858, Irish nationists — often referred to as Fenians and primarily Catholics — established brotherhoods in Ireland and America whose primary objective was complete separation from England, using violence, if necessary, to achieve it. For example, when the Prince of Wales (the future King Edward VII), visited New York in 1860, Colonel Michael Corcoran refused orders to have his 69th Irish regiment honor him, and was being court-martialed when the Civil War broke out and he was needed at Bull Run.

In 1867, the Fenian Brotherhood attempted several revolts in Ireland. John Tenniel, the principal cartoonist at London's *Punch*, drew *The Fenian Guy Fawkes*. It referred to the failed "gunpowder plot" of 1605, in which Fawkes, a converted Catholic, almost blew up the English Parliament with the Protestant King James inside; his objective was to restore a Catholic monarch to the throne. The English commemorated the November 5 date annually until 1859.

The simian portrayal in Irish caricatures originated in England earlier in the nineteenth century. The stereotypical Irishman usually had distorted jaws, a large mouth, a snub nose with flaring nostrils, wild hair and an excessively-angled face — closer to an ape than a man. Occasionally, there were porcine features, relating to the frequency of pigs kept inside or outside Irish shanties. The intended effect, on both sides of the Atlantic, was to dehumanize the anti-authority rebels.

PUNCH December 28, 1867

THE FENIAN GUY FAWKES

HW September 2, 1871 824

THE USUAL IRISH WAY OF DOING THINGS

However, Nast improvised and added his own touches to the English stereotype. He believed that it was essential for the Irish to be portrayed as beastly types, not as individuals. (Even when he drew individuals like boxer John Morrissey early in his career, he gave him ape-like features.*) The simian Irishman consistently *symbolized* his anti-Tammany and pro-temperance themes and views. Moreover, the often violent and frequently drunken behavior of the Irish during the sixties and seventies made them ready targets.

* See p. 46

Every year, Irish Catholics celebrated St. Patrick's Day with a parade. In 1867, it turned into a major riot, with several policemen, some of them Irish, severely injured. Nast re-created the scene with two pig-faced and several apish, inebriated assailants using swords, pikes, bricks and shillelaghs.

HW April 6, 1867 212

Emperor Tweed

Nast also emulated his "King Andy" Johnson satire by attacking Tweed as royalty. A large lithograph of the Boss hung prominently in the offices of men who did business with the city The controlled press featured planted stories about Tweed, Hall and Hoffman. (Fewer about Sweeny who shunned most publicity.) Tweed's 280-pound stature and prominent diamond radiated power.

Accordingly, Nast dubbed him "Emperor," signaling to *Harper's* readership that even a Napoleon could be overthrown. As the Franco-Prussian war and its Paris Commune aftermath continued to make news through the spring of 1871, Nast used the defeated Napoleon III and his uncle's hat to ridicule Tweed.

In April, Tweed sheltered Hoffman (as Napoleon had done when he brought his 14-year old son to the front lines) from the exploding "Press that can't be bought" and the "Political reform meeting," while Sweeny cowered and Hall and the Tammany Republicans fled.

Later in a nine-vignette miscellany — six of them comparing New York with an enflamed Paris — Emperor Tweed sat on a volcano wondering when the eruption would come. The title, of course, came straight from Charles Dickens' novel.

HW April 22, 1871 368

"THE BAPTISM OF FIRE."
Emperor Tweed and the Prince Imperial.

HW July 1, 1871 604

A larger vignette featured Nast's version of the first rats leaving the Ring's ship: Governor Hoffman and *World* publisher Manton Marble. The issue was a State Legislature-approved proposed amendment to the Legal Code of Procedure, which would have blatantly violated the First Amendment to the Constitution by allowing courts, without trial by jury, to punish "free and public expression upon the conduct of judicial tribunals." Hoffman vetoed it at the urging of the American Bar Association and most of the press.[4] An angry Judge Barnard asked Emperor Tweed: "What is to protect me from slander?"

HW July 1, 1871 609

Barnard Tweed Sands Fields Hoffman Marble

The Leper

In early April, a Tammany alderman, also an Albany legislator, attacked a Republican assemblyman; his consequent expulsion left the Ring one vote short of the majority needed to pass its program. The 64 Republicans vowed to block his tax-levy and other key legislation, so Tweed adjourned the session to give himself time to find a bribe-taker.

After midnight, Orange Winans of Chautauqua County took $75,000 and Tweed achieved his goal. Winans, a 30-year employee of Fisk's and Gould's Erie Railroad, reportedly was promised a promotion; conversely, his job may have been at stake. Regardless, he made a terrible decision. Crucified in the press as a leper, abandoned by his wife and ostracized by his neighbors, Winans fled and disappeared forever.

Winans provided fodder for Nast who branded him both a traitor and a leper in *Harper's*. For the first time, Nast clearly identified Tammany Republicans Nathaniel Sands (Board of Education, Secretary of Citizen's Committee) and Tom Fields (Parks Commissioner, state senator) as members of the Ring, along with Winans' former employer Jim Fisk. In *Phunny Phellow*, his more humorous satire depicted Tweed winning Uncle Sam's auction, while Sands, Fields and Republican Police Commissioner Hank Smith watched.

HW May 6, 1871 416

MAKE ROOM FOR THE LEPER.

PP June 1871 5-6

Nathaniel Sands Hank Smith Orange Winans Tom Fields

EVERY MAN HAS HIS PRICE. THIS KIND OF SLAVERY NOT YET ABOLISHED.

American Antiquarian Society

The Beginning of the End

The Tweed Ring was partially unhorsed by a horse which belonged to James Watson. Previously jailed for unpaid debts, Watson had served as a collector in the sheriff's office before being appointed County Auditor in 1863. Under the Ring, he reported directly to Connolly, interfaced with contractors, and served as principal paymaster. He received 2.5% of the proceeds, which dwarfed his $1,500 salary.

Watson lived modestly, but splurged on fast trotting horses. A sleighing accident on January 24, 1871 left him critically injured, and his death three days later ultimately led to the Ring's downfall. The Boss and others kept a vigil at Watson's home to prevent the dying man from disclosing any compromising information. Tweed, Sweeny, Hall and Connolly all served as pallbearers.

In May 1869, the State legislature had approved a plan for widening and straightening Broadway from 34th to 59th Street. It was a fraudulent scheme in which Watson was closely involved. Nast depicted the architectural firm of Sweed Tweeny, with Hall sweeping away the dirt from the discarded public works project. Boss Sweed: "To make this *look straight* is the hardest job I ever had. What made Watson go sleigh-riding?"

HW March 4, 1871 200

GROSS IRREGULARITY NOT FRAUDULENT.

Game-changer

Jimmy O'Brien, an ambitious Irish-born politician, provided the key to unlocking the Ring. Only 26 when elected Sheriff in 1867 with Tweed's backing, he later rebelled against Tammany when the Boss refused to pay him $350,000 for fraudulent expenses.*

He began by founding Young Democracy, a political party which Tweed crushed in March 1870. The previous January, he had obtained a job in Connolly's finance department for William Copeland, an acquaintance who needed a favor. Copeland discovered the fraudulent accounting and, with O'Brien's encouragement, secretly made copies of incriminating vouchers. He brought them to O'Brien in late 1870.

In January 1871, (now ex-Sheriff) O'Brien tried to use Copeland's transcript for extortion. Tweed, Connolly and a reluctant Sweeny designated Auditor Watson to negotiate with O'Brien, but the sleighing accident foreclosed that possibility. Connolly fired Copeland in March, probably concluding that he was the leaker.

Connolly then promoted bookkeeper Stephen Lynes to take over Watson's fraudulent duties, and replaced Lynes with Matthew O'Rourke, a new hire. O'Rourke had been a newspaper reporter of military affairs and was familiar with military expense accounts. He quickly spotted extraordinary payments to Ingersoll & Co. in "Armories and Drill-Room" accounts for non-existent rents and repairs.

O'Rourke copied some of the fraudulent entries before he quit his job in disgust on May 19. In early July, he turned them over to *Times* publisher George Jones who promptly hired him to work with *Times* reporter John Foord and editor Louis Jennings.

The resultant news story, published on July 8,1871, was the first disclosure about the Ring's finances with actual proof of the frauds. It referred only to armory expenditures in excess of $500,000, not to the new courthouse. **Mayor Hall promptly dismissed the scandalous allegations, claiming that "all their troubles would soon blow over."**

---

* See p. 251

"Blow Over?"

Four days after the *Times* story broke, a terrible Irish-Catholic riot created further dissension within the Ring. Irish Protestants always observed their own holiday commemorating the July 12, 1690 Battle of the Boyne victory of William of Orange, the new Protestant King of England, over the deposed Catholic James II and his supporters. The previous year, spontaneous clashes resulted in four deaths, so in 1871, Mayor Oakey Hall ordered James Kelso, his police superintendent, to ban the Orange Day parade which he did on July 11.

"The resultant storm of indignation convinced Tammany leaders that they had made a great blunder," as the *Weekly* put it. Consequently, Governor John Hoffman, a Protestant, overruled Hall in a notice published in the papers on July 12, the day of the parade.

Hoffman, a Protestant, hoped to run for President in 1872 and had to be concerned about alienating non-Catholic voters outside New York.

Consequently, 5,000 National Guard members were ordered to safeguard the marchers and keep public order. The Guard's Seventh Regiment included Private Thomas Nast, whose vantage point on Eighth Avenue at 24th Street, five blocks from the parade's start, enabled him to sketch scenes of the ensuing melee after Irish Catholics began throwing rocks and other missiles; both sides used guns. The riot resulted in 62 dead, two of them fellow Guard members, and 120 injured.

The political consequences of the riot, amplified by the *Times* exposures, shook the Ring to its core. Mayor Hall, in particular, was vilified by both sides.

In print a week later, *Harper's* published the Hall and Kelso statements on its cover, surrounding an unsigned cartoon of Miss New York holding off an apish Irishman trying to attack her with a knife. Hoffman's statement was included on the following page.

HARPER'S WEEKLY

A JOURNAL OF CIVILIZATION

Vol. XV.—No. 761.] NEW YORK, SATURDAY, JULY 29, 1871. [WITH A SUPPLEMENT. PRICE TEN CENTS.

Entered according to Act of Congress, in the Year 1871, by Harper & Brothers, in the Office of the Librarian of Congress, at Washington.

TRUCKLING TO THE MOB.

THE MAYOR TO THE ORANGEMEN.

Just a week before the day appointed for the parade of the Orange societies Mayor Hall addressed the following letter to John J. Bond, Esq., the head of the Orangemen. It foreshadows the order signed by Superintendent Kelso, which evidently proceeded from the same pen:

Executive Department, City Hall, New York, July 6, 1871.

John J. Bond, Esq., G. M. L. O. I.:

Dear Sir,—From your letter to the Superintendent of Police, from your explanations to me, and from a letter which you addressed to the *Times* I learn that an order or association of individuals, over which you are the chief, propose to celebrate by a street procession and public picnic the victory achieved in 1690 by William III., one king of England, over James II., another king. Similar public celebrations in the country whence the events happened have always been attended by public disorders. Breaches of the peace have several times occurred in Canada and in the United States during celebrations of a like import. Last summer serious affrays in this city grew out of the public procession and picnic when participated in by your order. You seem to apprehend new disturbances this year on account of the proposed celebration, and I think I am justified by your written and published statements in inferring your own opinion to be that public disorder must necessarily result from your intended action, because of the religious as well as anciently political opposition to the event celebrated. Assemblages of any kind in places of public access, and public street processions of every character, have never become matters of popular right. In accordance, however, with the operations of free institutions they are generally permitted, and usually enjoy by popular assent much freedom of action, although often submitted to at considerable sacrifice of public comfort. They, therefore, become subjects for police regulation and supervision. If not an impossible, it is nevertheless a delicate task for the authorities to decide when this regulation and supervision shall begin, or how far it shall extend. The approximate rule seems to be that the greatest good and security of the greatest number should be consulted in the decision. Your proposed celebration appears to be unnecessary. And it certainly seems at first glance to be singular that a foreign event occurring nearly two hundred years ago, and with which American citizens can not actively sympathize, should become on our soil the subject for extensive commemoration. Moreover, ought not the feuds and animosities of old countries, from whence our adopted citizens come, be entirely merged in our citizenship? There is another danger, is there not, that collisions induced by their maintenance here would be taken advantage of by the dangerous classes, which always grow formidable by such opportunities? It has been said from the bench that no individuals ought ever to be permitted to publicly assemble with banners whose inscriptions would be calculated to inflame the passions of other men; and, in view of what took place last year, may it not be thought by even your well-wishers that a repeated participation by your organization would seem like a concerted effort to irritate the public peace? I could suggest many occasions for celebrating even American events which would result inevitably in producing public ill feeling and inviting public disorder. Suppose, for instance, that a considerable number of New York residents of Southern birth should propose to celebrate the battle of Bull Run, that occurred in this month, and should, by means of banners and music, succeed in arousing the bad temper of the hundreds of thousands who not only could never sympathize with the event, but, under much personal, sectional, or national feeling, deplore it; or suppose that, in view of recent events that have occurred in Europe, a body of French adopted citizens, furnished with banners and music distasteful in sight and sound to citizens of German birth, should march through sections of our city that are inhabited by the latter? I content myself at present with simply submitting to you these very general considerations, and with asking you whether it would not be more politic for you and your friends to forego any popular or public demonstration of the event to which you and they attach so much importance. Very truly yours,

A. Oakey Hall, *Mayor of the City of New York.*

GENERAL ORDER, NO. 57.

On discovering that the "glittering generalities" of his rhetoric had no effect upon the Orangemen, the Mayor directed Superintendent of Police Kelso to issue the following order prohibiting the parade:

Office of the Superintendent of Police of the City of New York, 300 Mulberry St., New York, *July 10, 1871.*

Captain ——, —— Precinct:

General Order, No. 57.—The Superintendent has been applied to by the Grand Master of the Orange Lodges in the United States to give police support to a celebration by a procession (through principal streets and avenues of the city of New York on the 12th inst.) in honor of the battle of the Boyne, and the surrender which was its consequence.

These several commemorative victories on the soil of Ireland by one English king over another one, nearly two centuries ago, engendered national differences which have descended from generation to generation with increasing acrimony, and large bodies of citizens participating in these feelings form parts of our community.

The Superintendent has been legally advised he should not aid any street celebrations that involve feuds and animosities belonging solely to the history of other countries than our own, and which experience has proved to endanger the public peace abroad and at home.

The proposed celebration, as is obvious to every one, belongs to the last-named class. Last year, upon the same calendar day, an unexpected public celebration of the foreign event just named was accompanied in the streets with inexcusable and deplorable affrays, by which four citizens lost their lives, despite the interference of the police. This violence was apparently unpremeditated, and resulted from what may be termed spontaneous excitement. This year, however, the procession has been announced much in advance, and unusual arrangements have been made to swell the numbers of participants by accessions from other parts of the State and from other States.

It is given out that some preparations for defense have been made by the members of the parading lodges. Indeed, the announced procession appears to have been especially organized beyond the magnitude of any previous ones, and is emphasized with announcements that apparently evince a determination to meet, if not to avenge, the events which attended last year's celebration, and some of its leaders have stated to the Superintendent that they considered a collision inevitable. It is needless [illegible] it would furnish the opportunity always sought for by the lawless and dangerous classes of the community to participate in, and to carry consequences so far as to endanger the safety of persons and property.

Recent disturbances have been announced from Great Britain by cable dispatches as incident to similar public demonstrations by the Orange Institution in that country. And upon a closer survey the Superintendent is convinced that if the proposed procession forms or moves with its banners and traditional music amidst many thinking, rash, and hot-headed spectators who are not in sympathy with the foreign feuds which the procession is intended to glorify, then the whole police (and perhaps much of the military) force of the city might be required to protect the procession, and large sections of the city most needing watching would be left unguarded.

If any procession (or occupation by marching order of the streets) were a matter of right, or could legally demand protection, then it should, at all hazards, receive escort and guard, because the authorities never should allow that which is matter of right to the populace to be ever lawlessly overawed. But legal decisions have settled that occupation of streets by processions is a mere matter of usage or toleration, and is always subject to police regulation and supervision. The surrender of thoroughfares to large organized bodies of men necessarily interferes with the individual rights of other citizens, and those thus engaged are, in the language of the law, permissible trespassers. The toleration of processions by citizens and authorities is perhaps due to the fact that street meetings and parades always represent some sentiment or occasion not at all calculated to provoke hot blood. In every subject-matter for police discretionary permission the inconvenience of the few ought to be surrendered to the widest security for the property and

BRAVO! BRAVO!—New York, July 12, 1871.

Bravo! Bravo!—New York, July 12, 1871.

As mentioned, Hall had responded to the *Times* exposé by commenting that "it would soon blow over." Nast threw the Mayor's words back in his face with *Something That Will Not "Blow Over."* His first-hand, double-page, six-vignette cartoon featured an enraged mob of Irish-Catholic thugs — now with pistols added to their swords and shillelaghs — charging a single unarmed marshal defended by Uncle Sam. Behind the retreating Protestants, a banner noted "Liberal Catholic Dollinger and Hyacinthe," focal excommunicated Catholic priests. In front, were European rulers opposed to the Pope, as well as a black, Chinese and Indian member of the Protestant melting pot. Two seven-stanza verses — *Columbia Speaks* and *Pat's Complaint* — not written by Nast, amplified the biting satire.

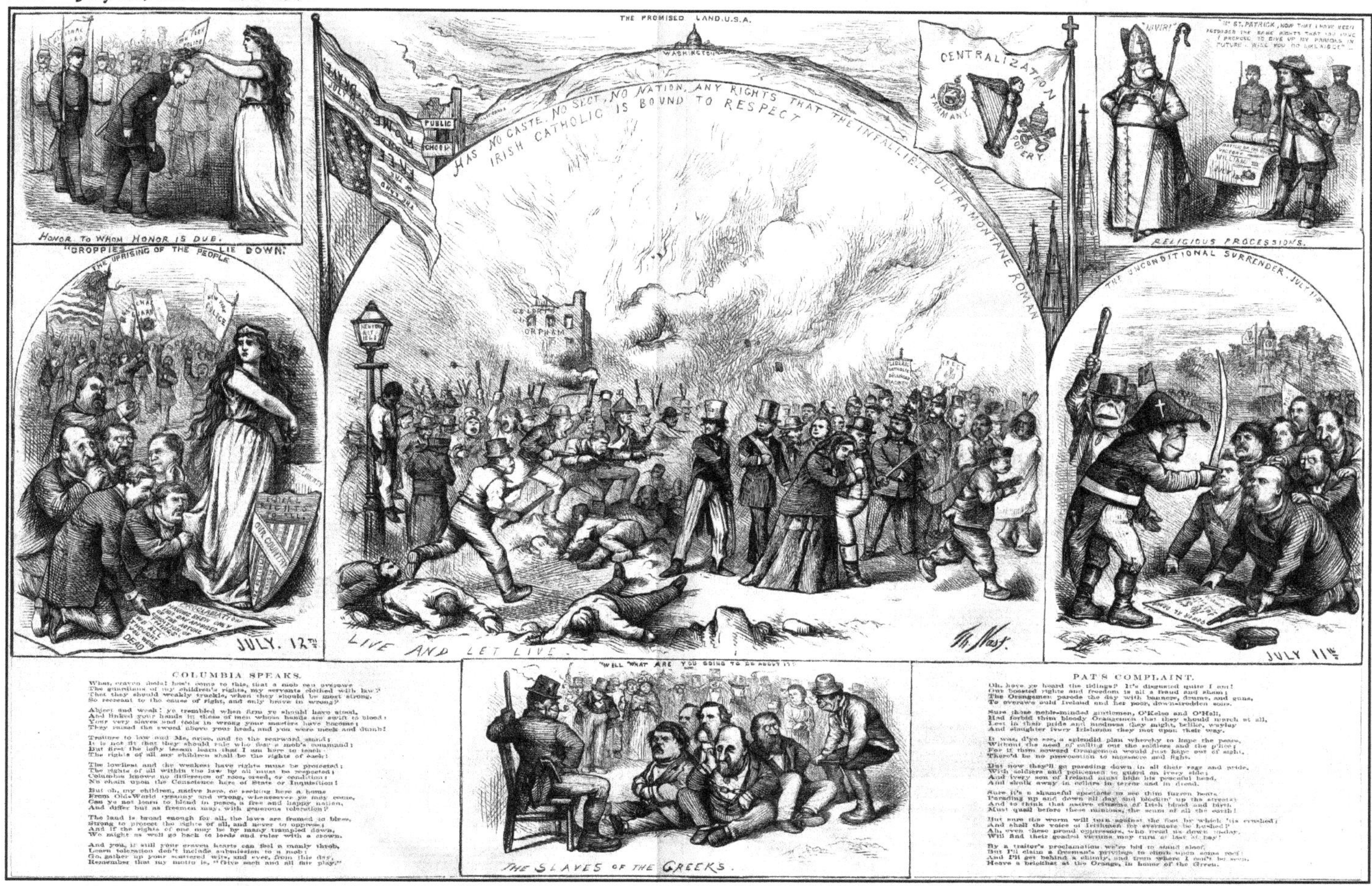

SOMETHING THAT WILL NOT "BLOW OVER"

Nast conspicuously reprised the lynched Negro and burning Colored Orphan Asylum from the Civil War draft riots. (Coincidentally, it was the eighth anniversary of their instigation). The Star Spangled Banner flying upside down next to a public school contrasted with an Irish "Centralization" flag emblazoned with the Popery and Tammany symbols.

His vitriolic text placed the blame squarely on the culprits, with no satire whatever: *Has no caste, no sect, no nation, any rights that the infallible ultramontane Roman Irish Catholic is bound to respect.*

In vignettes accompanying the Orange Day riot scene, Nast turned the tables and showed the principal ring members — including Sheriff Matthew Brennan and Police Superintendent James Kelso — as slaves of the Irish.

HW July 29, 1871 696-697

THE UNCONDITIONAL SURRENDER. JULY 11TH

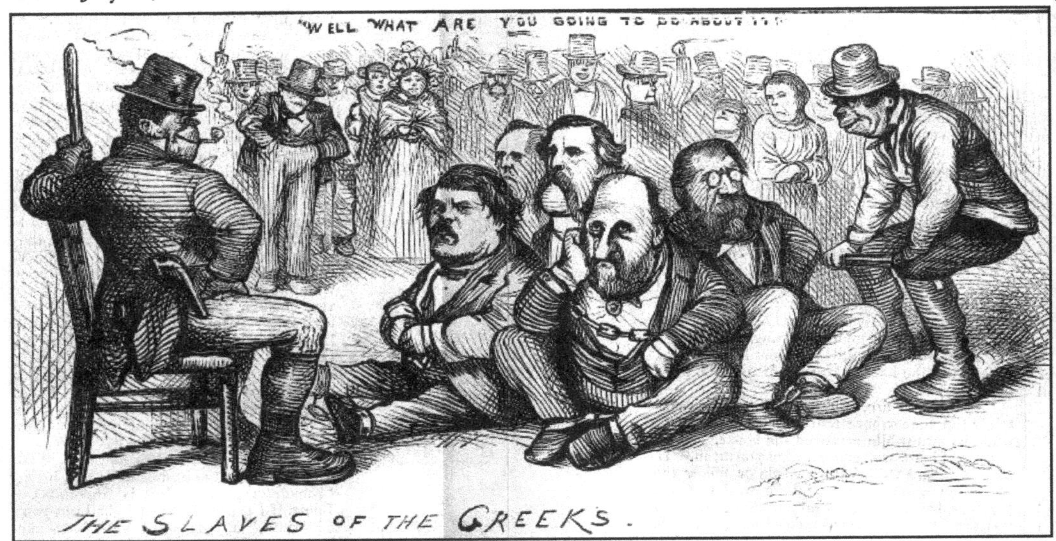

SOMETHING THAT WILL NOT "BLOW OVER"—July 11 and July 12, 1871

However, the riot was the unique exception to the Ring's daily control over its Irish "slaves." It provided them with employment as street-sweepers and laborers who could loaf as opportunities permitted. Their real work came at election time when they participated in naturalization fraud, voted repeatedly in as many as 20 or more districts each, stuffed ballot-boxes and threatened Republican voters.

HW January 22, 1870 56-57

* * * *

Nast disparaged the Irish well before and well after he drew this cartoon, but never more horrifically than here. In recent decades, he has been criticized for his anti-Irish and anti-clerical portrayals, and even kept out of the New Jersey Hall of Fame because of them. However, looked at through the eyes, events and consequent attitudes of his time, one can understand why he felt so strongly.

Chapter 22
Tweed: Breaking the Ring

What Are You Going to Do About It?

In addition to potent caricatures, Nast also needed a catchy slogan that, when repeated often enough, would incite his audience to vote Tweed and the Ring out of office in the November election, now less than six months away. As protests became more audible, an April 4 mass meeting at Cooper Union provided it when highly respected William Evarts — Republican lawyer, orator and future statesman — declared that the Ring leaders "boast of their corruption and despise honest men. They say **'What are you going to do about it?'** I think they will find out what we are going to do about it."

HW June 10, 1871 536

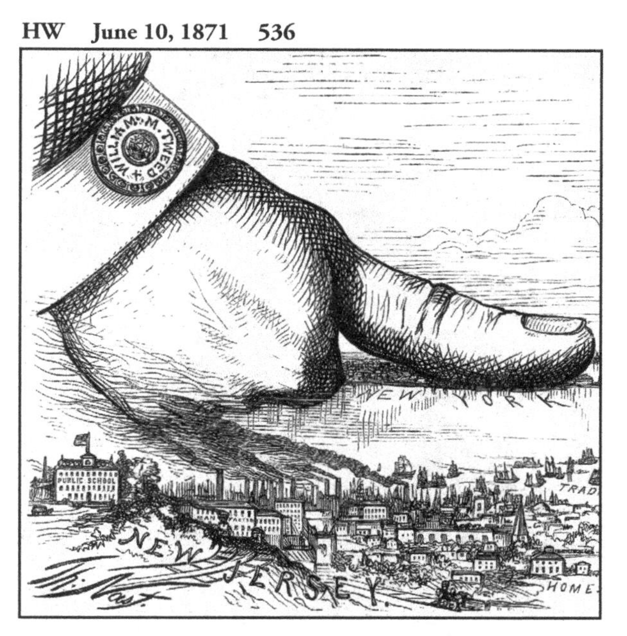

UNDER THE THUMB.
The Boss. "Well, what are you going to do about it?"

Nast adopted the question, added "Well" in front to make it more contemptuously combative. He put the words in Tweed's mouth, employed it as his serial punchline through to victory, and the *Times* echoed it. In conjunction with Nast's accompanying cartoon content, it inspired thousands of ordinary citizens to vote the Ring out of office.

The full slogan first emerged in *Under the Thumb* in which Nast emphasized the almost tangible power of Tweed's fist crushing Manhattan. In contrast, free and prosperous New Jersey beckoned across the Hudson, and Nast moved his family there about two months later.

Presidential Aspirations

As talk about Tweed's and Hoffman's national ambitions increased, Nast — who was determined to do all he could to help Grant get reelected in 1872 — had an extra burr under his artistic saddle. He responded to the threat with two major cartoons and several vignettes.

On to Washington featured Tweed and his not-so-merry men creeping furtively through the forest towards the White House where President Grant imperturbably was reading the paper and smoking a cigar. His campaign slogan "Let Us Have Peace for Another TERM" stated Nast's case. This apparently was Nast's only cartoon in which both Grant and Tweed appeared.

Hoffman was a cigar-store Indian and his Ring associates all wore feathers, based on the Tammany Society's designation of their leaders as "sachems" (Indian chiefs). Jim Fisk, Jay Gould and their lawyer Thomas Shearman of the Erie Ring were prominent, along with Archbishop John McCloskey, who had succeeded Dagger John Hughes, and his Irish followers (in the rear).

Nast wove some political subtleties into his cartoon that underscored his acumen. The title was a jab at Horace Greeley, whose 1861 "On to Richmond" editorial urging Lincoln to move forward prematurely, helped lead to the Union disaster at Bull Run. Now, Greeley had just returned from a southern trip in which he flew his own trial balloon for the 1872 Democratic nomination.

Even more astutely, Nast showed Sweeny perspiring and looking alarmed; he had dropped the handle of Hoffman's wheeled platform and grabbed Fisk's foot to halt his progress. Behind, Tweed also was sweating and appeared exhausted, and jester Hall looked concerned. Why?

As Nast explained to his biographer Albert Paine, Samuel Tilden had presidential ambitions of his own.[1] Tilden had been counsel for the Erie directors, when Tweed and Sweeny were on that board, and Tweed had unsuccessfully tried to dump him as Democratic National Chairman; Sweeny prevailed on Tweed to drop that effort. "Brains" Sweeny, who wanted no prominent public office for himself, probably saw the danger in blocking Tilden who knew where all the bodies were buried and would help reveal them shortly.

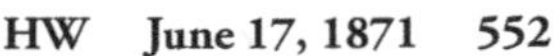

ON TO WASHINGTON.

Nast's final shot at the Ring's proposed takeover of Washington appeared two months later — after the *Times* published its financial revelations. Just prior to that, Tweed proclaimed in an Independence Day speech: "*We propose* . . . to wrest if possible the National Government from those who now, in our opinion, are betraying it." After the *Times* disclosures, followed by the Orange Day Riot, Hall boasted that "all their troubles would blow over," and that 1872 would see the Ring move on to Washington.

Playing off a *Times* editorial of which he must have had advance knowledge, Nast portrayed *The President of the United States and his Cabinet for 1872.(?)* This was Nast's class picture of the Ring, featuring de facto President Tweed smiling confidently in his office. A diminished Hoffman, in complete shadow, held an Erie bill, while George Washington wept on the wall behind him.

Nast's sardonic imagery fit like a glove in his supporting vignettes: Secretary of State (and Church) Sweeny; Attorney General Hall with his broom and duster for all kinds of dirty work; Secretary of War Ingersoll, who inflated armory bills; Interior Secretary Garvey, the "Prince of Plasterers" specialized in "white-washing;" Tom Fields, Tweed's Republican buddy and fellow state senator (who would figure prominently in Nast's post-disclosure cartoons) as Postmaster General; pompous Jim Fisk, who owned steamboats, as Navy Secretary; and, of course, Connolly about to open the U.S. Treasury safe: "There's money in it."

HW August 26, 1871 788

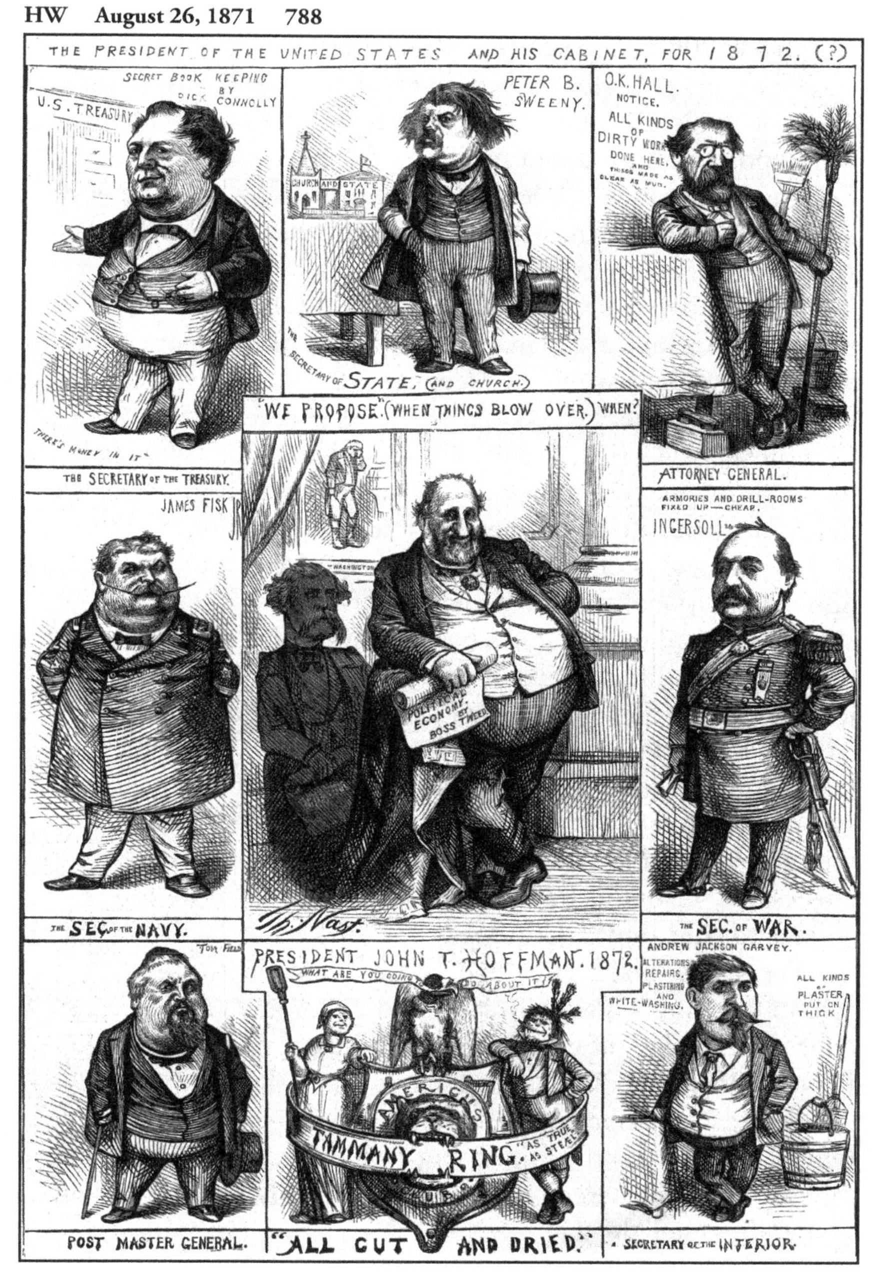

Below, the National Seal featured a vulture replacing an eagle, and a stereotyped Irish couple — she with a liquor bottle atop her pike — inside the Tammany "Steal" Ring. *E Pluribus Unum* was preempted by *What Are You Going to Do About It?*, Nast's catch-phrase slogan that became his campaign challenge to the voting public. "All Cut and Dried" harmonized with Hoffman's depiction as a cigar-store Indian, as well as Tweed's customary way of doing business.

HW August 26, 1871 804

THOMAS NAST, ARTIST OF "HARPER'S WEEKLY"

In the same issue of the *Weekly*, editor George William Curtis extolled Nast in a full column, along with an engraved photo of him by Mathew Brady: "The most cordially hated man in New York at the present day — hated by men whose friendship would be a dishonor — is Thomas Nast, the most successful, most widely known, and most gifted humorous artist whom the genius of America has produced."

Attempted Bribery

Nast took his annual vacation in July. After he returned, he was approached by a representative of the Ring and offered a six-figure bribe to go to Europe until the election was over. He told Paine he bargained the amount up to $500,000 before scornfully rejecting it.[2]

However, Nast was concerned about his health, safety and family. Malaria was around and his throat bothered him. (He evidently had catarrh.) A local priest urged his parishioners to harass him. He received hate mail featuring a noose with a "Doom for the Pimp" message. Accordingly, he moved his family to rented quarters in Morristown, New Jersey, while continuing to draw at his home in Harlem under police guard. The next year he bought a home in Morristown, where he lived for his last thirty years, while commuting 33 miles by rail to Manhattan whenever necessary.

Meanwhile, on the other disclosure front, Jimmy O'Brien took Copeland's transcript to the *Sun*. He had a solid relationship with Editor Charles Dana, who had supported him for Mayor against Oakey Hall the previous year,* and he knew Dana would be receptive. Unfortunately, Dana was away and he had to deal with Thomas Hitchcock who was in charge.

Hitchcock — rich, fiscally conservative, and a large shareholder in the *Sun* — didn't want to risk a criminal libel suit in courts dominated by Tammany judges like George Barnard. Accordingly, he turned O'Brien down, much to Dana's distress when he returned. Learning about O'Rourke's disclosures to the *Times* probably forced O'Brien's hand, so he appeared in George Jones's office around July 8, and turned Copeland's transcript over to him unconditionally and without compensation.[3]

Tweed tried to stop Jones by offering $5 million ($100 million today) for his stake in the *Times* or as a bribe. Rejected, Tweed attempted to buy Henry Raymond's widow's 34% ownership (Raymond had died in June 1869). Jones beat Tweed to the punch by arranging for E.B. Morgan, one of his original partners, to buy her stock for $375,000, they now owned 82% between them. **If Tweed had been successful, he could have asked for one of his crooked judges to shut down the paper.**

The *Times* disclosures and editorials played a major role in the Ring's downfall. Nast, the *Times* and *Harper's* continued to play off each other amid mutual praise. Back in November 1870, three elite businessmen — John Jacob Astor, Moses Taylor and Marshall Roberts — had investigated Connolly and certified that "the city's financial affairs were administered correctly and faithfully." After the first *Times* revelations in July 1871, Nast praised its "sharp editorials" for cutting off the tails of the prestigious "three blind mice."

HW July 22, 1871 680

THREE BLIND MICE.

Two Great Questions

The new revelations were splashed across the front page of the *Times* on July 22, and more came out over the next several weeks. Scorching editorials in the *Times* and *Harper's* continued while Horace Greeley's *Tribune* had little to say, finally asking *Who is Ingersoll's CO?* Nast had Ingersoll respond: "Allow me to introduce you to my CO?," pointing to a gargantuan Tweed covering a cowering Hall with his hat as Sweeny grabbed his coattails.

---

* See p. 251

Nast's second of *Two Great Questions — "Who Stole the People's Money?"* — was drawn on the same block of wood. This time, Tweed pointed to Ingersoll, in accord with the "'Twas Him" response. Nast's circle of accusers, cast as the Tammany Ring, were labeled with their specialties; Chairs, Plaster, Carpets; Carpenter, Gas Pipes, Awnings, Furniture, Old Board, and New Board. One character labeled "Tom, Dick and Harry" suggested that anyone who was willing to pay for a piece of the public pie could have a slice.

For Tweed, *Two Great Questions* was the final straw. It supposedly spurred his classic comment: **"Let's stop them damned pictures. I don't care so much what the papers write about me — my constituents can't read; but damn it, they can see pictures."**[4]

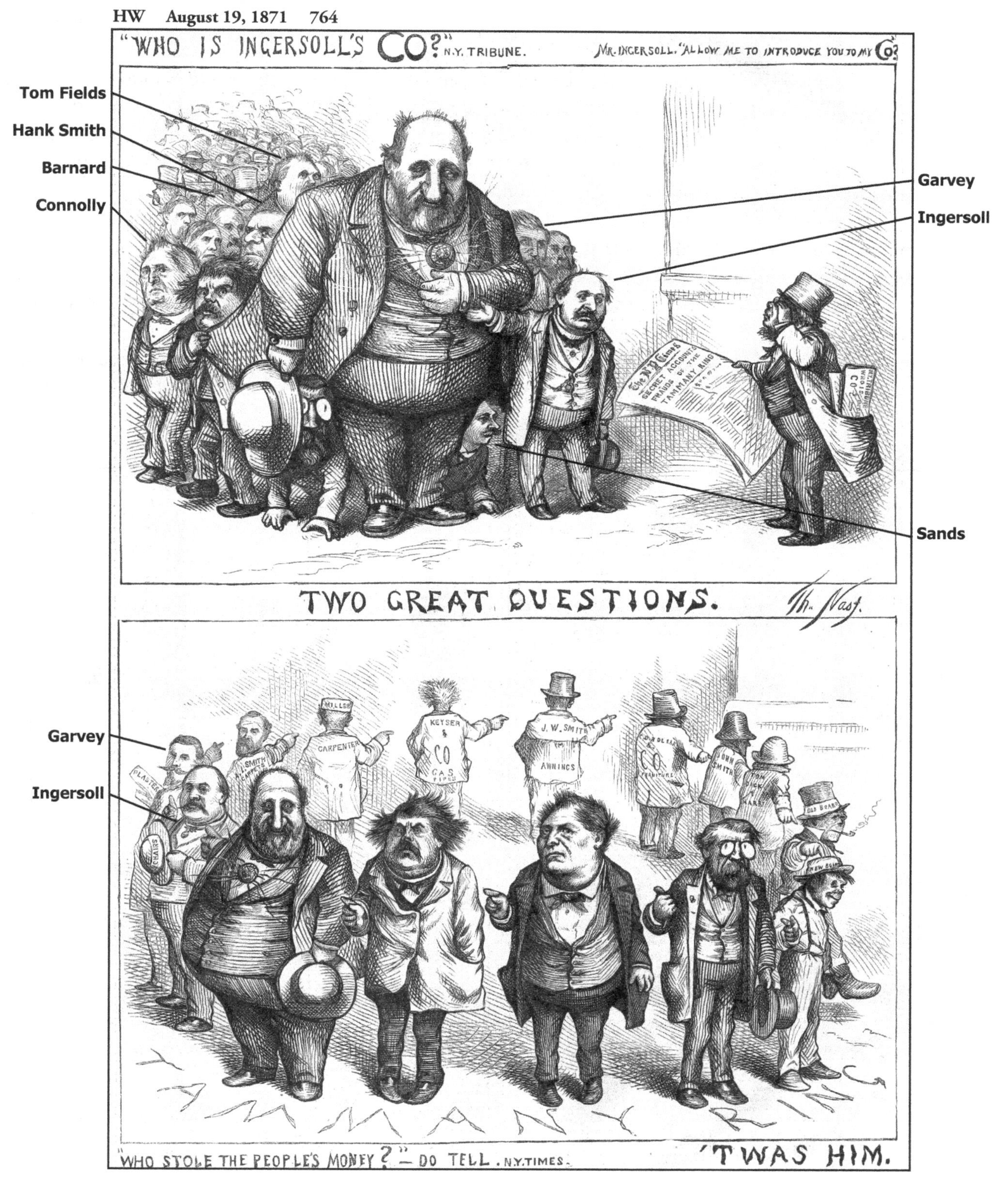

Convincing Tweed's Followers

The majority of *Harper's* normal circulation of about 135,000 went to middle and upper-middle income readers. To overthrow Tammany, Nast knew he had to attract and convince lower-class voters whose time, finances and literacy were limited. He appealed to them with three lifestyle-contrasting cartoons, which were ultimately made into campaign broadsheets and distributed in the relevant neighborhoods the week before election.

The Rich Growing Richer, the Poor Growing Poorer was in circulation the last week of August. It accompanied a double-page illustration of Tweed's mansion in Greenwich, Connecticut, and his bagmen's "summer palaces" in two-towns-away South Norwalk, along with the amounts their owners received during the previous two years.[5]

Separately, Nast depicted the Ring at Tweed's luxurious Americus Club on Long Island Sound in Greenwich, toasting their constituents: "May they live long, so that we may prosper." Connolly reclined on a bed of roses.

Below, a stern landlord handed a bill for "exorbitant" rent to an imploring housewife (modeled by Sallie Nast), whose daughter lay on a contrasting bed of thorns. Her despairing husband sat at a table with a pile of unpaid bills and a baby's coffin, while an empty market basket lay underneath.

An even stronger contrast followed two weeks later, as the Big Four made their last appearance as comparative equals. In *Wholesale and Retail*, they left the City Treasury with bulging pockets and police salutes as a smirking Tweed and conspiratorial Sweeny led the way. A worried Hall, behind his symbolic, attention-drawing spectacles, clung to Connolly's arm; the two were on the verge of a terminal confrontation a few days after this cartoon appeared on September 6.

This raw illustration, similar to some of his earlier boxing, Garibaldi and Civil War drawings, had no humor in it. Working families could empathize with its realism as applied to their everyday lives. Nast broke through their apathy, ignorance and fears in a way that words alone could not.

HW September 2, 1871 812

The Tammany Lords And Their Constituents.

HW September 16, 1871 865

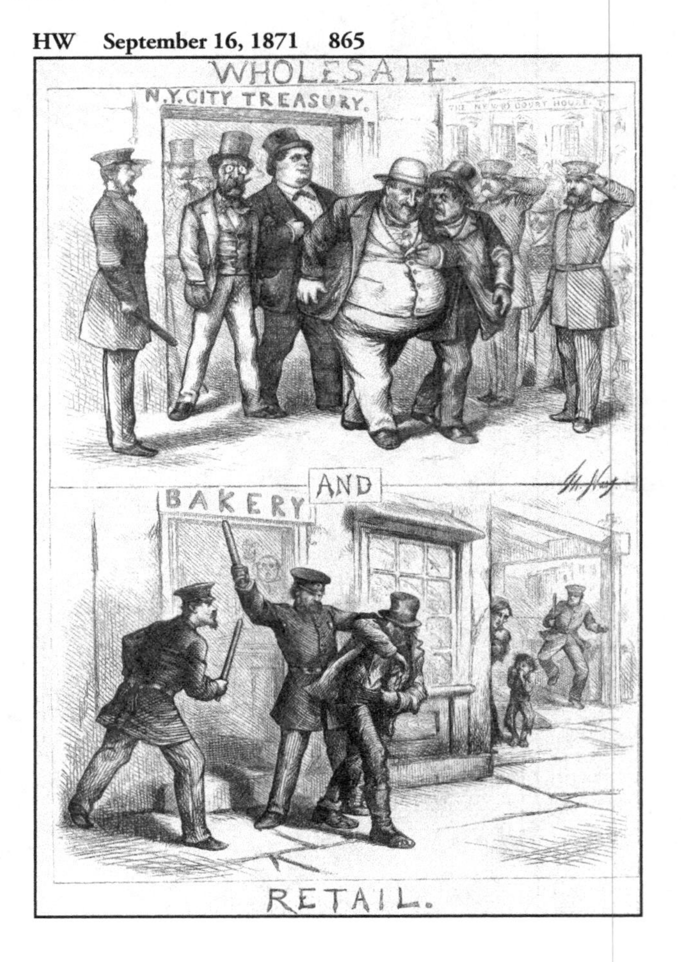

However, to ensure that the cartoon would be seen by Tweed's core voters who never would have looked at *Harper's Weekly*, a Republican reformer (who wrote to Nast) paid to have his motivational text incorporated into a widely-distributed campaign poster.

MEN OF NEW-YORK!

On the 5th day of May, 1870, your Mayor, your Comptroller, your "Boss," and your "Brains" passed a resolution to pay all claims against the city which had been declared valid by the old Board of Supervisors.

Within three months after the passage of this resolution, by means of fraudulent vouchers and of forged endorsements, SIX MILLIONS of Dollars were ROBBED from your City Treasury and divided up among these men and their followers. No wonder their classic features beam with content, their bellies are full, and their pockets are stuffed. Genial benevolence shines through their goggles.

See one of your poorer classes, whose wife, with scanty garment, vainly seeks to shelter herself from the piercing cold; whose child, with piteous cry, weeps for a crust of bread to stay the pangs of hunger. In a moment of despair, the father's hand seizes from the baker's well-stocked window, a bit of bread for his hungry baby. Oh, men with wives and children, how fearful is his sin! See how the vigilant guardians of your city's honor strike the thief down with their clubs. Away with the felon to jail.

Look at the other picture. Your big-bellied thief robs from your city treasury a Million of Dollars. He lives in his palace; he drives his carriage; he sports his diamonds; the bones he throws to his dogs are better food than your children get in many a weary week. Is this just? And yet the police take off their hats to him.

Men of New-York! you have the affidavit of one of the purest men of this city — SAMUEL J. TILDEN; you have the written statement of the first lawyer of the country — CHARLES O'CONOR — that your "Boss" took, in three months, as his share of the "stealings," One Million of Dollars. Think of it! It is more money than most of you would earn in one thousand years, and this man robbed it from you in three months!

In the classic language of the day, the "Boss" ought to let up. But he won't! Let us induce him to retire.
VOTE THE REFORM TICKET

A month later, Nast's final appeal to the "Workmen" depicted them looking at an empty safe with only debts inside, while "the four masters that emptied it" shared an apprehensive toast. This was a reminder rather than an action-provoking cartoon like its two precedents. Its primary purpose was to pound home **"What Are You Going to Do About It?"** which he had been battering the Ring with for four months.

HW October 14, 1871 960

THE CITY TREASURY

Tipping Point

Many of *Harper's* regular readers who had been on vacation as the *Times* disclosures rolled out, returned by September. The Citizens Association held a meeting of influential citizens from both parties on September 4, and formed a Committee of Seventy to lead the charge against the Ring. Committee President William Havemeyer, who would succeed Hall as Mayor in 1873, challenged the audience with Nast's slogan **"What Are You Going To Do About It?"**

HW October 21, 1871 978

THE ONLY THING THEY RESPECT OR FEAR.

In response, one audience member shouted out "Hang them." This echoed a *Nation* editorial from the previous week: ". . . the one consequence of thieving which Hall, Tweed and Connolly would now dread is a violent death. Public scorn, or even the penitentiary, has little terror for them"[6]

Nast followed up several weeks later, quoting the *Nation* in his cover-page cartoon full of subtle touches. Only the glitter of Tweed's large diamond could be seen. Hall and Sweeny trembled in fear, as their bent legs showed. Sweeny, his coat hastily buttoned up — probably to conceal secret papers — clutched at Tweed's jacket in desperation.

HW September 23, 1871 889

A GROUP OF VULTURES WAITING FOR THE STORM TO "BLOW OVER."—"LET US *PREY*."

As action against the Ring accelerated after the Committee of Seventy was formed, Nast engraved *A Group of Vultures Waiting for the Storm to Blow Over — Let Us Prey*.[7] His titular pun was the exclamation point for the rapacious quartet of Tammany predators hunkering down to attempt to ride out the storm of rising public indignation. It was in print by September 13 as the Ring was blowing apart.

The beaked Tweed, Connolly and Hall squatted on the supine figure of New York City, its fist clenched in defiance, as they stared in fear. The dog's muzzle at Hall's claws was reserved "for the Press," which the besieged Mayor was trying to silence or placate. Only Sweeny looked up at the giant boulder, dislodged by lightning, which was about to hit them. On their ledge, lay bones and skulls of "rent payer, tax payer, liberty, justice, law, suffrage and New York City Treasury."

Injunction

Lightning did strike unexpectedly about the time Nast prepared this cartoon. On September 7, in response to a petition from John Foley, a wealthy Irish-American pen manufacturer with no legal standing to sue, Judge Barnard issued a temporary injunction to prohibit Connolly from any further issuance of bonds or contracts. Eight days later after more hearings, he made the injunction permanent.

HW April 13, 1872 296

THE CLOWN IN THE JUDICIAL RING
To What Base Usage the Bench Is Put.

Barnard, a Yale graduate, had been a State Supreme Court Justice for nine years. He was known for his coarse behavior on the bench — feet up, whittling pine sticks, cracking bawdy jokes and drinking — while inevitably ruling for the Tweed and Erie Rings.

Why did Tweed's close friend double-cross him? Possibly Barnard heard lynching rumors. More likely, he had to decide between taking a huge bribe, or trying to keep his job by abandoning the obviously sinking ship. Regardless, he lost; when he was impeached six months later, Nast portrayed him as the clown he was reputed to be.

Robbery

On Saturday, September 9, a sub-committee of the Seventy, requested Connolly to produce his 1870 accounts and paid vouchers for inspection and audit the following Tuesday. On Sunday night, vandals — later revealed to be the janitor, his wife and his assistant — used a diamond to cut glass and unfasten a window in the office in the new courthouse where the papers were stored, and stole a dozen bundles of vouchers; much later they reportedly were found half-burned in a City Hall attic. Conveniently, the watchman was at dinner and ignored the broken window when he returned; the theft wasn't reported to the next-door police station until Connolly showed up the next afternoon.

The *Times* responded with "Heartless Robbery", a tongue-in-cheek editorial: ". . . people burst into a loud laugh when the story got wind, and went about asking each other with a broad grin, 'Have you heard of this robbery in the Comptroller's office?' Even the City Hall officials, instead of showing any proper feeling, went about saying, in the slang of the hour, that it was 'too thin.' Are their hearts made of stone?"

"*Too Thin*" was custom-made for Nast as he elongated Sweeny's hair, Tweed's diamond and Hall's glasses for *Harper's* cover. It also was made into a campaign poster.

HW September 30, 1871 905 C

Back on August 27, the *Times* had editorialized "Why Connolly was kept in office and how it was done?" The article explained how Tweed's (April 1870) Charter secretly cancelled the public's right to elect their comptroller, and made Connolly unremovable by anybody before 1875.

After the burglary, Hall tried to fire Connolly, his co-signer on the vouchers, and found he couldn't do so; their spat was the first public crack in the Ring. On September 15, the day Barnard issued his permanent injunction, Connolly went to see Samuel Tilden for advice. Tilden, Chairman of the State Democratic Party, now became a pivotal player behind the scenes. Although he refused to join the non-partisan Committee of Seventy for a year, he furtively furthered their efforts.

Nast always disliked Tilden whom he believed to be both deceitful and late to the reform movement. Nast battered him when he almost won the Presidency in 1876. For now, both were on the same side, although Tilden never gave Nast credit or referred to his cartoons.

Tilden advised Connolly that he had the legal right to designate his successor. The next day, at Tilden's suggestion, Connolly appointed Andrew Green, Tilden's close friend and former law partner, as his deputy — effective immediately.

Nast, who had attended a farewell dinner for Charles Dickens three years earlier and knew his stories well, used *Oliver Twist* to dramatically illustrate Connolly's downfall and abandonment as a dozen identifiable Ring members ran for their lives.[8] Hall, who was charged with malfeasance about a week after this cartoon appeared in print, was running away from Sweeny and Tweed.

In Hall's Tammany paper, the *Leader*, he declared that "The Democratic Party is behind him." Nast agreed, contributing *Which Nobody Can Deny*," as the "Honest Democrats" boot kicked his butt out of office. He followed with *Portraits of the Mayor's Grand Jury* — twelve identical portraits of Hall — in a prescient cartoon about three weeks before Hall was acquitted.

HW October 7, 1871 940

"STOP THIEF!"

Arrest

When Connolly sought Tilden's counsel in September 1871, he confided that exact copies of the stolen vouchers were in the possession of the Broadway Bank which Tweed controlled. An audit showed that $933,000 had been deposited to Tweed's account in just five months from May through September 1870, the initial period after the new charter passed and the Ring commandeered the city's and county's finances.

On October 24, Tilden filed an affidavit including a list of 190 vouchers totalling about $6,300,000 fraudulently extracted from the public treasury. Tweed was arrested three days later on a judicial warrant and immediately released on $1,000,000 bail.

Nast's cartoon appeared the day after the election. He depicted Sheriff Matthew Brennan making a jovial arrest of the amused Tweed while a smirking Sweeny, concerned Hall, and apprehensive Connolly looked on; Slippery Dick would be arrested a month later and Oakey had just survived his first trial. A stern Justice was pulling her sword from her scabbard to combat the *Tribune's* description: "Sheriff Brennan merely nodded to Mr. Tweed, bade him 'Good-day,' and laying his hand tenderly on his shoulder, said, laughingly, 'You're my man! It seemed like a deliciously cool joke, and, judging from the faces, it was."

HW November 18, 1871 1084

THE ARREST OF "BOSS TWEED" —ANOTHER GOOD JOKE.
The Shadow Of Justice. "I'll Make Some Of You Cry Yet."

Tammany Tiger

Nast first used the Tammany Tiger in September 1869 in a cartoon for the *Evening Telegram*, after Tweed unsuccessfully tried to remove August Belmont as Chairman of the Democratic National Committee. He adapted it from Big Six, Tweed's fire company.*

EVENING TELEGRAM September 10, 1869

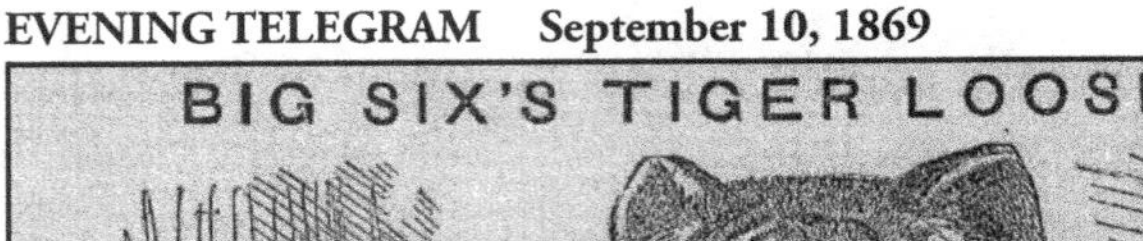

Richard West, Periodyssey

Now he used it for his campaign climax, along with five other cartoons — occupying four-plus pages in total — in the November 11 *Weekly*, available six days before the election. However, his keynote tiger had to compete for attention with Mrs. O'Leary's cow and the resultant Chicago fire, whose illustrations and descriptions were featured on the cover and several other pages.

Nast prepared this double-page cartoon well in advance of its publication. Now he flung ***What are you going to do about it?*** directly at *Harper's* 275,000 circulation and million-plus readers. Reprising the Colosseum from his 1867 *Amphitheatrum Johnsonianum*,** he pictured the action from the floor with the Ring members looking on apprehensively as the massive tiger — 11 inches from tail to paw — mauled Lady Liberty. Her "Republic" crown and sword of power lay in pieces; the "law" torn; the "ballot" bowl shattered; and Justice dead, scales and sword broken by her side.

Of the principal Ring members, only State Senator Tweed was on the ballot. He actually won but never took his seat. Sweeny's brother-in-law, Mike Norton, and Tweed's Republican buddy, Tom Fields, also running for the Senate, lost. The major victor was the State Attorney-General, whose office could now prosecute the Ring without interference.

Looking at Nast's career in its entirety, *The Tammany Tiger Loose* was probably the second-most impactful cartoon he ever drew, and among the tops in American political history.[9]

---

* See p. 7
** See p. 168

HW November 11, 1871 1056-1057

Hank Smith, Nathaniel Sands, Hoffman, Sweeny, Tweed, Connolly, Tom Fields, Hall, Garvey, Ingersoll, Fisk, Gould

"THE TAMMANY TIGER LOOSE — What are you going to do about it?"

Victory

"November 7, 1871 — The Tammany Ring Smashed — That's what the people did about it — Sweeny gone to grass — Haul done brown — Gov. Hoffman's veto power neutralized" were among the phrases Nast used in his cover cartoon which appeared eight days after the election.

Reiterating his depiction of Tweed as a Roman emperor (from *The Tammany Tiger Loose*), Nast's sequel featured the Boss as the exiled Roman general Marius sitting on the ruins of Carthage in 146 BC. His model was an 1807 painting by American John Vanderlyn. The last part of the title — *To the Victor Belong the Spoils* — was a take-off on the catchphrase of Jacksonian Democracy coined by New York Senator William Marcy in 1832.[10]

Wearing a headband of dollar signs (perhaps indicative of thorns), Tweed stared vacantly at his viewers. A gloomy tiger medallion hung from his huge emerald, his right hand held the remnant of a broken sword, and his left rested limply on an empty treasury safe. A sign noted that he won his State Senate seat by 10,000 votes, a third of what he wanted. As mentioned previously, he never took office.

The sign posted next to Tweed read "The Tammany Boys Whipped Out of Their Boats," which were scattered below identified by their owners' names. Sweeny's abandoned money bag labeled "Tammany Brains" lay unattended at the lower right, he had secretly resigned as Commissioner of Public Parks six days before the election, but withheld that news and its effective date until after the returns were official.

HW November 25, 1871 1097 C

"WHAT ARE YOU LAUGHING AT? TO THE VICTOR BELONG THE SPOILS"

If there was one single issue of *Harper's Weekly* when Nast reached his apogee of both skill and uncontroversial recognition, this was it. Including the cover, he dominated three of the first five pages. *Probably no American political loser has ever been caricatured as effectively after defeat.*

HW November 25, 1871 1100

SOMETHING THAT DID BLOW OVER — NOVEMBER 7, 1871.

Nast must have really enjoyed finalizing Oakey Hall's memorable forecast after the first *Times* revelation in July: "This will all blow over." *Something That Did Blow Over* featured the storm that destroyed Tammany Hall. Oakey hung from a teetering column with cash packets dropping from his pocket; Connolly was pinned under an empty safe; and Tweed, trapped under debris, was fanned by a "shiny-hat" lackey while a simian Irishman lifted a bottle to the Boss's lips. Sweeny, the only man in motion, was fleeing with his "Tammany Brains" moneybag.

On the facing page, Nast gave Sweeny his full due with a nine-vignette panel entitled *The Political Suicide of Peter "Brains" Sweeny*. One smaller scene (lower left center) depicted him sprawling dead over Connolly's lifeless body. However, Nast's key objective was to see Tweed go to prison, along with his three principal confederates. The bottom panel was a start.

HW November 25, 1871 1101

Chapter 23
Tweed: Aftermath

Sweeny

"Brains" Sweeny hated public appearances of any kind, especially in courtrooms, and fled to Montreal in December. From there, he eventually joined his brother James Sweeny in Paris. James, who fronted for Peter and collected Peter's share of the Ring's proceeds, died in France. Five years after he left, Peter Sweeny returned to New York, and settled the claims against him for $400,000 — all paid from James's estate — in June 1877, leaving him with millions of Ring money to spend over the last 34 years of his life.

Sweeny's payment was the only direct reparation New York City received from any of the four principal Ring participants.

Connolly

"Slippery Dick" went on leave after he appointed Andrew Green as his deputy in September. He formally resigned on November 18 and, to his surprise, was arrested on November 25 by Sheriff Matthew Brennan. Bail was set at $1 million, which he was prepared to meet. However, when prosecutor Charles O'Conor came to Connolly's house to collect, he unexpectedly raised the amount to $1.5 million. Connolly's wife Mary controlled the purse strings and refused the increase, thereby sending her husband to jail. On December 31, his bail was reduced to a reported $500,000, which she paid. He promptly fled to France via Canada, never to return. He died in Marseille nine years later.

Hall

"Elegant Oakey" was *The Last of the Four* as Nast put it. In October 1871, *before* the fall of the Ring, he faced a grand jury — charged with malfeasance for failing to audit vouchers but not with corruption or theft — and was not indicted although found "careless and negligent." Nast depicted the jury as a dozen identical portraits of Hall.

As "the last 'thorn of Tammany' left blooming alone, all his lovely companions are faded and gone," Hall topped a dead Tammany rose bush. Connolly peered from jail, Sweeny headed North to Canada, and Tweed danced on the shears of reform, trying to avoid being clipped.[1]

HW January 13, 1872 40

THE LAST OF THE FOUR.

Nast kept after Hall, featuring him in fourteen cartoons over the fifteen-month period until his term expired at year-end 1872. In January, Hall was Touchstone the Jester (from Shakespeare's *As You Like It)* reading: " 'Where Ignorance is Bliss, 'tis Folly to be Wise.' *I am in Blissful Ignorance of Every Thing that has happened since I have been Mayor of New York.*" Beyond Hall's left knee, the face of a second fool/jester peeked out with an expression of incredulity at Hall's statement.[2]

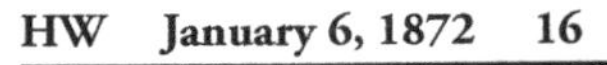
HW January 6, 1872 16

TOUCHSTONE.
Tammany (O.K.) Hall Jester (*Reads*). " 'Where Ignorance is Bliss, 'tis Folly to be Wise.' *I am in Blissful Ignorance of Every Thing that has happened since I have been Mayor of New York.*

HW March 23, 1872 240

THE SUDDEN APPEARANCE OF THE DEMON GARVEY.

In February 1872, Hall was indicted by a second grand jury on five misdemeanor charges, focused on a $41,563 warrant payable to Andrew Garvey for work on the new courthouse, and signed by Hall and Connolly. Garvey, who had escaped to Europe in September, returned as a surprise witness in exchange for immunity. His wife, intent on saving part of his ill-gained money, forced him to come back and testify candidly for the prosecution.[3] In Nast's cartoon, prosecutor Lyman Tremain was dressed as a sorcerer whose magic wand produced the "Demon" Garvey. Hall was shaken, his knees buckling, as Sweeny and Tweed fled in terror behind him. On March 12, the day before the cartoon was published, the jury foreman died and a mistrial was declared three days later. Hall escaped justice a second time.

In late October 1872, Hall was tried again. The jury deadlocked: seven Republicans for conviction and five Democrats against; Hall survived for a third time. While Nast attended Hall's trial at least once, he never caricatured it — probably because he was too busy attacking Horace Greeley as the Presidential election drew nigh.

Almost a year after he left office, Hall was tried a fourth time. A key issue for the jury was whether Hall could be convicted on simple neglect of duty or whether it had to be *willful*. The trial began on December 22, 1873 and ended on Christmas Eve. The judge ruled that *willful* applied, and told the jury that if a verdict wasn't reached by 10:30 p.m., they would be locked up for the night. Understandably, Hall was acquitted.

Nast probably anticipated that Hall would never be convicted. However, he knew that Hall was persona non grata with many of his former friends and in his upper-crust clubs. His socialite wife who had never mixed with her husband's political cronies or their wives, was extremely upset over his loss of respectability; ultimately, their marriage broke up. While Nast ignored the Mayor's legal exoneration, he understood that contempt and ridicule were almost as crushing to Oakey's flamboyant ego as the inside of a jail cell would have been.

In one of two cartoons available the day after Christmas 1872, Nast celebrated Hall's official exit from office by devastating him with a double-dose of ridicule. One embodied him as a victim of the "horse plague" which continued to afflict New York's equine population, as the dead mare/mayor was dumped off a refuse cart into the East River.

HW January 4, 1873 16

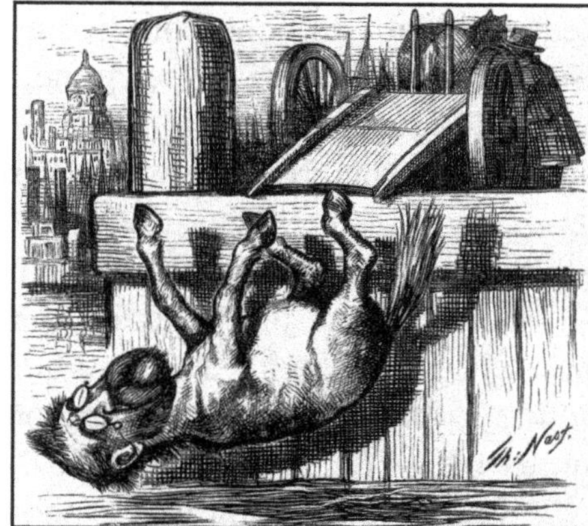

JANUARY 1, 1873.
The last of the Mare Disease with which this City has been so much afflicted.

HW January 4, 1873 4

THE FINGER OF SCORN
Shall Follow Them, If Law (Sometimes Called Justice) Can Not.

The Finger of Scorn, depicted Hall as a blind man being led away from City Hall by his seeing-eye bulldog (substituting for a tiger). His signboard read "Pity the Poor Blind Gentle Man Who Saw Nothing of the Ring's Stealings" while from behind City Hall, a dominant elongated finger pointed directly at him. Hercules was cleaning "this Mare's STABLE," while Tweed, Sweeny, Tom Fields and Judge Barnard scattered. Behind Hall, still-Governor Hoffman stood in front of an office sign: "Steamers to all parts of the world."

After leaving office, Hall resumed his law practice and had an unsuccessful venture as a playwright and actor while reportedly having affairs with actresses and other women. In March 1877, he abruptly disappeared; eventually, he turned up living in London — under an assumed name — with a woman who had preceded him from New York. Nast captured the situation with a pun and Hall's still-recognizable pince-nez symbol. His flight probably was prompted by Tweed's published statement that — facing life in prison — he was prepared to implicate his former associates in a full confession.[4]

Hall returned to New York for good in 1892. He died six years later with more debts than assets to show for his colorful life.

HW April 21, 1877 316

H'ALL THAT'S LEFT.

Hoffman

In the January 20, 1872 issue, Nast had four small Ring cartoons on a single page; two featured Tweed, one featured Hall, and one parodied an old English verse by Amelia Opie to satirize the Governor. With "Mother" Sweeny and "Father" Tweed gone, Nast depicted "Little Johnny T. Hoffman" as a helpless, weeping "orphan boy" mourning the death of his 1872 presidential hopes.

A week later, Nast showed Hoffman killing his proverbial father in a replay of French artist Jean-Léon Gérôme's *Death of Caesar*. (Also used to depict Andrew Johnson's political death three years earlier.*) He probably was stimulated by a current production of Shakespeare's *Julius Caesar* with Edwin Booth in the role of Brutus.

Hoffman had just repudiated Tweed in his annual message to the State Legislature, blaming the Ring for abuses of the Charter and for vote fraud. Aiming specifically at Tweed, he declared that anybody obtaining his office by bribery, false counting or illegal voting should be barred from it. Nast quoted at length from Hoffman under his *Et Tu, Brute? Then Fall, Caesar* caption.

Nast's central point was to show Brutus/Hoffman delivering a final thrust to his former mentor as he shielded his eyes from Tweed's face. In the background, a conspiratorial group of born-again reformers — including Tammany's ultimate successor, John Kelly, and publishers Manton Marble (*World*) and James Gordon Bennett, Jr. (*Herald*) fled into an archway. (Both Democratic papers had ignored the Ring's doings and backed its principals until the public revelations forced them to admit they were wrong.)

A year later, his term expired and, tarnished by his association with the Ring, Hoffman retired from politics and resumed his law practice. He died in 1888.

HW January 20, 1872 61

LITTLE JOHNNY T. HOFFMAN (THE ORPHAN BOY).

"STAY" (*some party*), "stay, for mercy's sake,
And hear a helpless orphan's tale:
Ah, sure my looks must pity wake!
'Tis want" (*to go to the White House*) "that makes my cheek so pale.
Yet I was once a mother's" (SWEENY) "pride,
And my brave father's" (TWEED) "hope and joy;
But in the" (*Tammany*) "proud" (?) "fight" they "died—
And I am now an orphan boy."

Not quite "AMELIA OPIE."

HW January 27, 1872 76

"ET TU, BRUTE?—THEN FALL, CÆSAR."

"Though the Charter was not all it should have been, it was the best that could then be obtained, and it promised relief from great and long continued wrong, under which the people of the City had been suffering, and from a system of government the abuses under which are now coming to light. The misconduct recently exposed was not a consequence from any of its provisions.

"The responsibility for the wrong-doing which has very justly aroused public indignation does not rest so much upon the Charter as upon individuals who held office in the City before the Charter was passed, and took office also under it.

"The complaints with regard to the late election in New York and Brooklyn, made through the Press, are chiefly of false counting of ballots and false returns by inspectors of election. The general suspicion of the existence of such an evil is almost as injurious as the practice itself: our people, if led to believe that it is carried on extensively, will neglect to vote, and will lose their habit of submitting quietly to the result of an election. The crime is, under our form of government, one of the worst, in its nature and in its effects, and should be punished accordingly. It is a practice which, if persisted in, is more likely to overturn our Government than any open war that can be levied against it. Effectual laws against bribery of the electors, and to take away an office obtained by bribery, thorough protection of the right of challenge on election day, severe penalties against miscounting of votes and against illegal voting, ought to suffice for the protection of the ballot, and will suffice if citizens, juries, and public officers will do their duty."—GOVERNOR HOFFMAN'S MESSAGE, 1872.

* See p. 182

Fisk and Gould

Before Grant's first election, Jay Gould and Jim Fisk controlled the Erie Railroad by fair means and foul; they issued stock and bonds like Monopoly money, and used bribery in the ordinary course of business. In 1868, they made Boss Tweed and Peter Sweeny board members, ensuring multiple corrupt rulings and injunctions from the Tweed Ring's favorite judge, George Barnard.

Nast depicted them more than a dozen times, most pungently when Fisk was buried three months after he had sued his ex-mistress, Josie Mansfield, and her new boyfriend, Edward Stokes, for blackmail after they threatened to reveal her cache of Jim's love letters. Seeing their scheme implode, Stokes shot Fisk in cold blood. (He was convicted of manslaughter and served only four years).

As the text below pointed out, "*Dead Men Tell No Tales*" was an attempt by Gould and his cohorts to scapegoat Fisk for all their sins. The State Legislature was about to vote on a Confiscation Act, which would have enabled Gould to "steal" 60,000 shares owned by English stockholders, and thereby maintain control of the Erie. The bill failed and Gould resigned a month after this cartoon appeared.

Especially notable was how the facial expressions and body language of each of Nast's characters told a story. Gould, going through the motions of respect by crossing his heart, but obviously planning his next move, had "stolen stocks" and "new schemes" sticking out of his pocket. In contrast, Tweed, who loved the ebullient "Jubilee Jim" like a brother, was weeping copiously. David Dudley Field, the lawyer for Tweed, Fisk and Gould — who would appear in 25 Nast cartoons — stood warily next to his client. A distressed Justice looked on, her scales totally unbalanced.

Standing by himself, an apprehensive Judge Barnard knew that his paymasters, Tweed and Gould, were out of power; he himself would be impeached and convicted six months later.

HW September 7, 1872 704

ANOTHER FALL, MY COUNTRYMEN! NEXT!

HW February 24, 1872 165

"DEAD MEN TELL NO TALES."
***Jay Gould.* "All The Sins Of Erie Lie Buried Here."**
***Justice.* "I Am Not Quite So Blind."**

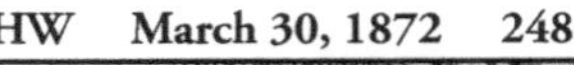
HW March 30, 1872 248

JUSTICE ON THE RAIL—ERIE RAILROAD (RING) SMASH UP.

Five weeks later, Nast drew a full page of the Erie Ring smash-up, including Gould's almost "stolen" English stock, Barnard, Field, and Gould's other counsel, Thomas Shearman. The lineman in the rear waved "clear track" for the new board of directors, whose names were on the individual cars. This was an incredible level of detail for any cartoonist then or now, and a good example of Nast's legacy as a visual historian.[8]

HW December 14, 1872 984

A "NORTHWESTERN" BLOW.
"When Rogues fall out, will Honest Men have their dues?"

HW January 18, 1873 64

HONOR AMONG —
Jay Gould. "For the Sake of Peace!"

Gould continued to appear in Nast cartoons, almost always with villainy involved. Later that year, he bested another dishonest speculator, Dan Drew, a blow from which Drew never recovered.

Gould also double-crossed his former partner, Henry Smith, in a different railroad stock maneuver, and Smith turned the Erie books over to the new directors. With his misdeeds revealed, Gould settled the claims against him for $9 million in securities and real estate. Perhaps, he also was influenced by the uproar over Credit Mobilier, the next railroad scandal, which was then in the middle of Congressional hearings. Nast, who didn't want to touch Credit Mobilier at that point in time, must have enjoyed finally depicting Gould as a loser.

Tweed

After Tweed resigned as Commissioner of Public Works on December 28, two key questions were: could he be convicted and, if so, would he escape? Nast depicted both queries as the New Year dawned.

HW January 6, 1872 8

CAN THE LAW REACH HIM—THE DWARF AND THE GIANT THIEF.

HW January 6, 1872 13

"STONE WALLS DO NOT A PRISON MAKE."
"No Prison Is Big Enough To Hold The Boss." In On One Side, And Out At The Other.

Two weeks later, Nast reveled in returning to his Emperor fantasies to commemorate Tweed's resignation, relating it specifically to Napoleon III's defeat at Sedan in September 1870, which ended the Franco-Prussian War.* In addition to the brooding Boss contemplating his future home in Sing Sing prison, Nast added two ironic German touches:

- Williamshöhe was the royal resort near Kassel in central Germany to which Napoleon III was temporarily exiled after his abdication.
- Sing Sing, located on the Hudson River — sometimes referred to as the "American Rhine" — was labeled "Die Wacht on Hudson." *The Watch on the Rhine* was a favorite drinking song of Prussian soldiers during the war.

Harper's large German-American audience must have appreciated Nast's nuances. In particular, he may have been tipping his hat to Oswald Ottendorfer, owner and editor of *Staats Zeitung*, the influential German-language daily, who deserved substantial credit for bringing along the German vote against Tweed.

HW January 20, 1872 61

AFTER SEDAN-WILHELMSHÖHE.

* See p. 230

The answers to Nast's predictive security concerns were accurate over time. Tweed's first trial was postponed for a year. Eighteen days after it started on January 13, 1873, a hung jury was dismissed; it was probable but never proved, that bribery played a role.

A second trial ended in Tweed's conviction on November 19, 1873. He was given a 12-year sentence by Judge Noah Davis, and jailed in the state prison on Blackwell's Island. Nast's cover cartoon had no humor in it.

HW December 13, 1873 1105 C

JUSTICE!

Tweed served 19 months on Blackwell's Island when the state's highest court freed him for his **criminal** conviction, ruling that Judge Davis's 12-year sentence had exceeded the statutory limit of one year. However, after gaining his freedom on June 22, 1875, he was rearrested the next day on **civil** charges that he had misappropriated more than $6 million in public funds. Unable to raise $3 million bail, he was sent to Ludlow Street jail and filed an appeal.

HW September 11, 1875 733 C

THE TABLES TURNED.
The Next Decision We May Expect.

His trial was scheduled for February 1876. Meanwhile, Nast drew four cartoons, blasting the Court of Appeals for overturning Tweed's criminal sentence. One cover featured Tweed turning the tables and thumbing his nose as he imprisoned Justice with her hair shorn and hands chained to a heavy ball behind her back.

Escape

By late November, Tweed determined to escape. Although **criminal** guilt no longer was an issue, a **civil** judgment for debt might keep him in jail forever. He could hide out locally until his last appeal was concluded and then decide what to do.

At Ludlow Street jail, Tweed was granted privileges and liberties allowed to people imprisoned for debt — but not to most other inmates — such as carriage rides and visits to his home and his adult children's homes. Reportedly, he paid a gang to plan and execute his escape while on a home visit.

Upon arriving at his house at 647 Madison Avenue on December 4, 1875, accompanied by the warden and another jailer, he saw the sign indicating that "tonight was the night." The prison officials knew nothing of the plot, and ate and drank liberally. After dinner, one guard rose to wash his hands in the dining room basin. Tweed excused himself to wash in another room, closing the door behind him and walking out the front door to a waiting carriage.

The hack drove him to the Hudson River where he was rowed across to Weehawken, New Jersey and taken to a deserted farmhouse. He was shaved, his hair clipped short, fitted with a reddish-yellow wig, and given gold spectacles. He became John Secor, an ailing businessman seeking rest and relaxation.

Tweed's escape was "humiliating" to Nast. Four days after it happened, the *Weekly* was in print with *Stone Walls Do Not a Prison Make*, a reprise of his predictive cartoon from almost four years earlier.

Tweed/Secor stayed in New Jersey for three months, paying close attention to the newspapers, many of which put successful pressure on the Court of Appeals to turn down Tweed's civil appeal. With two protectors, he moved to Staten Island for a while; in May, he sailed with them on a schooner to Florida.

There, he hooked up with a guide in his late twenties, whom he introduced as his nephew William Hunt. Hunt apparently did not know his companion's real identity. They camped out in the Everglades, and ultimately sailed from St. Augustine to Key West and then to Santiago, Cuba. They had false passports but no visas.

Arriving in Santiago on June 12, 1876, they were arrested by the Spanish military — Cuba was a Spanish possession — and held in custody. Word of the two Americans got back to the State Department in Washington, with Tweed's identity guessed. Republican officials from President Ulysses S. Grant and Secretary of State Hamilton Fish down wanted Tweed captured in order to provide political ammunition against current Democratic presidential candidate Samuel Tilden. Tweed's 1868 contribution of $5,000 to Tilden — when Tilden was Chairman of the New York State Democratic Party — was the link which Nast and others used as a cudgel.

By sweet-talking — possibly with money for American Consul Alfred Young in Santiago — Tweed was released from custody and sailed to Spain on July 27, almost literally "one step ahead of the sheriff." Consul Young was forced to resign soon afterwards as a result of Tweed's narrow escape.

Tweed's ship, the Carmen, took 42 days to arrive in Vigo, Spain on September 6, 1876. While it was in transit, the State Department, under the supervision of Minister to Spain Caleb Cushing, sent out wanted notices on Tweed to its consuls in Spanish port cities. No photographs were available in Spain, but some of Nast's cartoons were distributed to serve the purpose.

In particular, Nast's July 1 cover cartoon, *Tweed-Le-Dee and Tilden-Dum*, hit the mark. In print June 22, it was precisely timed to reach readers a week before the Democratic National Convention in St. Louis. Nast, correctly anticipating that Tilden would gain the nomination, challenged his claim to being a reformer and attacked his denial of Tammany Hall connections. Tilden was the unseen "twin" of "Reform Tweed," an escaped convict wearing a large "Tammany Police/Tammany Ring" belt while collaring a pair of juvenile sneak thieves. The caption insinuated that in a Tilden presidency, as in his current governorship, petty crooks would be arrested while major culprits like Tweed would be rewarded with public office.

The Vigo authorities identified Tweed from Nast's cartoon. Unable to read English and unfamiliar with the case, they assumed that the fugitive was guilty of kidnapping the two small urchins in the cartoon, and arrested him and his companion William Hunt.

HW July 1, 1876 525 C

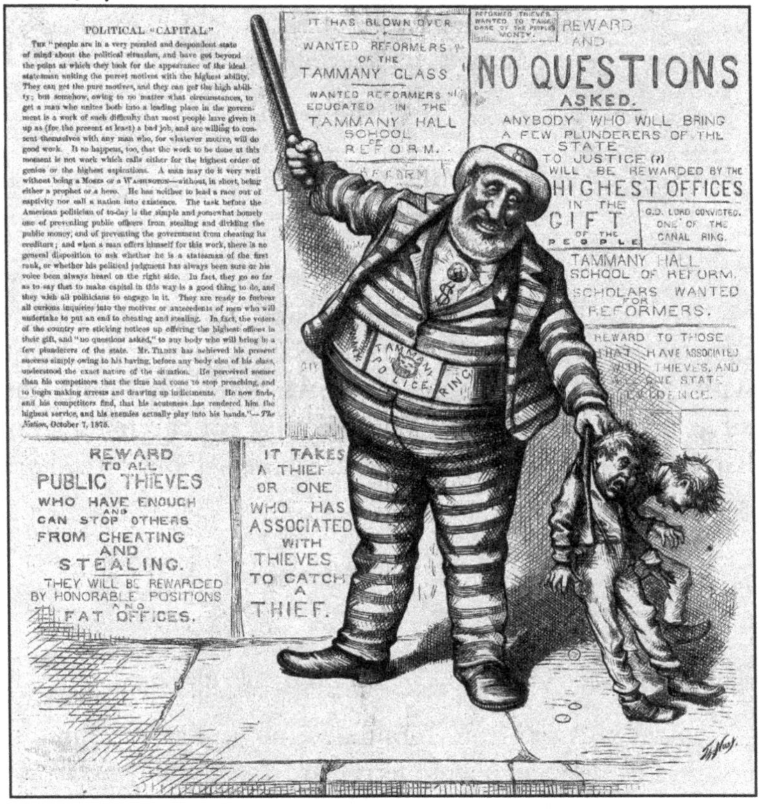

TWEED-LE-DEE AND TILDEN-DUM.
Reform Tweed. "If all the people want is to have somebody arrested, I'll have you plunderers convicted. You will be allowed to escape; nobody will be hurt; and then Tilden will go to the White House, and I to Albany as Governor."

Hunt was soon released and disappeared forever. Tweed spent three weeks in Spanish custody, after which he was returned to the United States aboard the Navy frigate *U.S.S. Franklin*, which departed Spain on September 27 and arrived in New York on November 23. While he was in transit, Nast celebrated with a pictorial pun featuring Secretary Fish as his ocean transport. The compressed Tweed actually lost more than 100 pounds on his two trans-Atlantic voyages, mostly from sea-sickness.

HW October 7, 1876 820

ANOTHER WHALE - JONAH CASE.

In the same issue, *Nast* and *Harper's* gloated by re-printing the *Tweed-Le-Dee and Tilden-Dum* cartoon from three months earlier with a new caption: *The Capture of Tweed — The Picture That Made the Spanish Officials Take Him for a Child-Stealer.*

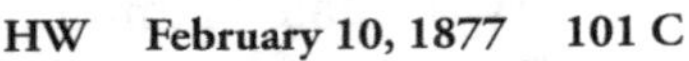

"THE BEST OF FRIENDS MUST PART."

The game was over for Tweed and he spent the remaining seventeen months of his life in the Ludlow Street jail. Soon after he returned, he reached a provisional deal with State Attorney General Charles Fairfield to surrender all his property and effects and make a full confession. Tweed followed through but was double-crossed by Fairchild. Tilden, now engaged in a close and bitter Electoral College dispute with Hayes (which he lost by one vote), supported the reneging as helpful to his own power-struggle.

For the first time ever, Nast drew a cartoon sympathetic to Tweed, as the former Boss stared at the duplicitous Tilden walking away with a broken piece of the "rotten Tammany Ring." *The Best of Friends Must Part* (from an old drinking song) was the same caption he used seven years earlier when Napoleon III abandoned Pope Pius IX.*

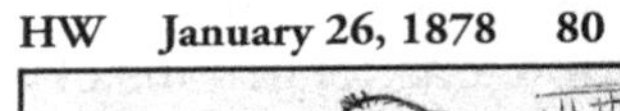

A year later, the New York Board of Aldermen approved a resolution calling for Tweed's release. Nast reflected that public sentiment with his last Tweed depiction drawn while his former target was still alive. The "poor Tweed-bird" looked skeptical in his jailor's grip, perhaps reflecting Nast's own mixed feelings about Tweed's release

A (JAIL)-BIRD IN HAND.

Under pressure from Tammany's current boss, John Kelly, the new attorney-general finally honored his predecessor's pledge and agreed to release Tweed on May 15, 1878, when the current legislative session ended. It was too late. William Magear Tweed died on April 12 from heart disease and other complications at age 55.

After drawing about 130 cartoons with Tweed in them, Nast chose not to comment pictorially upon the death of his most memorable foe.

---

* See p. 231

Credit

Looked at through the sole criterion of political persuasion, Nast's Tweed campaign was the zenith of his career. The Ring's power was almost impenetrable. The *Times* disclosures were critical towards moving that paper's and the *Weekly's* elite readers to act, but Nast was primarily responsible for bringing along the lower income, less educated and even illiterate masses whom the *Times* couldn't reach but whose votes were essential for victory. It helped that both were on the side of the angels and their joint persuasiveness overwhelmed their opposition when it literally counted.

During Nast's lifetime, the *Times* recognized his contribution.* When it wrote his four-column obituary on December 8, 1902, it commented: "Mr. Nast is generally credited with having had a great deal to do with the downfall of the Tweed dynasty."

However, during recent years, the paper has minimized or even ignored Nast. For example, on August 18, 2011, the *Times* ran a self-congratulatory editorial to commemorate the 200th birthday of George Jones, its founding publisher, whom it rightly lauded for his "journalistic enterprise and courage" in bringing down Boss Tweed. Self-strutting to a fault, it failed to even mention *Harper's Weekly* or Thomas Nast.

The Man Who Helped Stop Boss Tweed

In the 1860s and 70s, William M. Tweed — the apotheosis of big-city corruption — appeared to be unstoppable. Gorging on duck, oysters and tenderloin, he reigned supreme over New York City's patronage and politics. By one estimate, he and his Tammany Hall cronies purloined at least $1 billion and perhaps as much as $4 billion in today's dollars, much of it from the public purse.

He was finally brought low by his own greed, street battles between rival Irish groups, and, we proudly note, by the journalistic enterprise and courage of George Jones, this newspaper's founding publisher, who was born 200 years ago this week.

The beginning of the modern New York Times is generally dated to the paper's purchase in 1896 by Adolph S. Ochs. But, as David Dunlap of The Times noted in a City Room report on Tuesday, its roots go back to 1851 and a paper called the New-York Daily Times, edited by Henry Jarvis Raymond with Mr. Jones as publisher and business manager. When Mr. Raymond died in 1869, editorial direction fell to Mr. Jones, and with it the responsibility of tackling Tammany Hall.

The paper's biggest scoop was to obtain ledger items that showed, penny for penny, how Boss Tweed planned to pocket public money intended for the furnishing of a new courthouse. The Tweed forces offered Mr. Jones $5 million — equivalent to $100 million today — to back off. He refused, and the articles were published in July 1871. Two years later, Tweed was convicted of theft and sent to the Ludlow Street jail.

In those days, there were perhaps 10 major newspapers in the city, competing for headlines and readers. Today's media landscape is obviously very different. But some things are unchanged. Scoops are still exciting; even more rewarding is helping to ensure civic honesty.

As described earlier, the *Times* received its scoop on a silver platter, when Jimmy O'Brien and Matthew O'Rourke turned over copies of fraudulent accounting records. Its subsequent incriminating articles and forceful editorials obviously played a critical role in the Ring's demise. As the *Times* ping-ponged back and forth with Nast cartoons and George William Curtis editorials in *Harper's*, their joint efforts were magnified.

As discussed previously, Nast began his attacks on the Ring three years before the *Times* did, and had published ten notable cartoons before the *Times* first editorialized on September 20, 1870. Earlier that year, the *Times* had praised Tweed as a "reformer," hailed his appointment as Commissioner of Public Works, and supported his new Charter. It also received about 7% of its total revenue from Ring ads and announcements.

Why was the *Times* so late? Because it was controlled by the Ring through two of its board members, Leonard Jerome and James Taylor. As mentioned earlier, after Taylor died unexpectedly of typhoid fever on August 22, Jones and editor Louis Jennings were free to attack a month later.

---

* See p. iv

As the above editorial pointed out, Tweed tried to stop Jones by offering $5 million ($100 million today) for his stake in the *Times* or as a bribe. Rejected, Tweed attempted to buy Henry Raymond's widow's 34% ownership (Raymond died in June 1869). Jones beat Tweed to the punch by arranging for one of his original partners to buy her stock. If Tweed had been successful, he could have asked for one of his crooked judges to shut down the paper, and there would have been no *Times* for Adolph Ochs, patriarch of today's controlling Sulzberger family, to purchase in 1896.

Shortly after the election, Curtis praised the "courage, fidelity and ability of one great journal, the *New York Times*," which quickly responded: "Our victory . . . would hardly have been complete without its pictorial record by Nast, who has followed the thieves so sharply all through the fight."[6]

Nast drew 47 Ring-related cartoons in just over a year prior to the election, and added another 36 during the following six months. They brought tributes from all over the country. Two weeks after the election, editor Edwin Godkin of *The Nation* rhapsodized:

"To Mr. Nast it is hardly possible to award too much praise. He has carried political illustrations during the last six months to a pitch of excellence never before attained in this country, and has secured for them an influence on opinion such as they never came near having in any country. ***It is right to say that they brought the rascalities of the Ring home to hundreds of thousands who would never have looked at the figures and printed denunciations.***"[7]

When *Harper's Weekly* celebrated its 50th anniversary in 1907 (under non-Harper management), its cover featured Nast as a knight with his foot on Tweed's throat, as its dominant event. (Over the Civil War, the building of the West, and the Spanish War.) Nast had been dead for four years.

Chapter 24
The Election of 1872: The Liberal Republicans

Friendship With Grant

Impressed by Nast's pictorial triumph and acclaim, and concerned about reelection, Grant and his team recruited Nast with ardent wooing during a three-week visit to Washington, beginning January 26, 1872. He stayed with Colonel Norton Chipman, his good friend who had sought and received his help at the 1868 Republican Convention. Chipman was now the Congressional Delegate for the District of Columbia and an intimate of Grant. While there, Nast visited the President at the White House frequently and dined with him and his family at least four times.

Chipman also gave a dinner for Nast, where the guests included the Vice President, Cabinet members, Supreme Court justices, numerous senators, and the press; he sat next to Secretary of State Hamilton Fish. He also went to a dinner, and separately a reception, for House Speaker James Blaine whom he would skewer in future Presidential campaigns. Not coincidentally, Nast's first cartoons published after his return to New York featured Grant and Fish as victors and the British as losers in the Alabama Claims settlement.*

HW February 24, 1872 153 C

"WELL ROARED, LION," AND "WELL SHONE, MOON!"

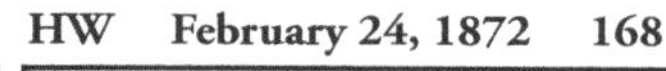

HW February 24, 1872 168

INDIRECT DAMAGES.

MR. DISRAELI "The Government still lacked a proper appreciation of the gravity of the question at issue between England and the United States. The American claims were greater than those which would follow total conquest."

* See p. 225-226

The President had been Nast's idol for almost a decade. Now they became personally close, a rarity for Grant. The Grants gave their new friend gifts for his children, which the recipient acknowledged pictorially in a letter whose salutation read "Dear Mr. and Mrs. General." (Julia was 9, Tom 6, Edith 3, and Mabel 2 months old). Their friendly relationship continued until Grant's death in 1885, and almost totally blunted Nast's objectivity towards the serious scandals in Grant's second term.

"The knife is a perfect success. Tom has been going around . . . stabbing people ever since he had it given to him, his young sister Edith in particular."

"Edith regards her medal as a most exact time keeper, carries it all around with her . . . gravely informing us at noon time that 'It is twenty-five of six.'"

"Julia's work basket gives her such pleasure, she meditates perpetrating a note of thanks on the subject . . ."

"The baby . . . manifests great intelligence for one of her tender age, expressing herself much pleased at my return."

While in Washington, Tommy filled Sallie in on the details almost daily, peaking on February 6 when he wrote that he was seeing the President "nearly every day . . . it is funny how all the Senators are in a flutter about my being here and all are afraid that I will do them up . . . **Darling the *Power* I have is *terrible* it frightens people, but darling you will keep a good look out for me, and will not let me use that *Power* in a bad cause.**"[1]

"What I Know About"

Horace Greeley was Grant's unexpected opponent. His nomination was a surprise to Republicans and Democrats of all stripes, and probably to himself, but he desperately wanted to be President.

As the editor of the *Tribune*, the nation's largest newspaper with a combined daily and weekly circulation of about 250,000 in 1870, a frequent traveler and political busybody, Greeley always had lots of influence. Once a close friend of William Seward, his homestate Governor and then Senator, he was instrumental in blocking Seward, the favorite, to make Lincoln's 1860 nomination possible.

At heart, Greeley was a quasi-socialist who promoted all sorts of fads and utopian causes over the years, many of them fringes like vegetarianism and spiritualism. More consistently, he was an early and steadfast abolitionist, pro-temperance and anti-tobacco. He founded a union for his printers (later Typographical Union No. 6), raised their wages 40%, but denounced their right to strike. He was an unwavering high-tariff protectionist who saw himself assisting American workers by opposing free trade.

Since 1853, Greeley had owned a 75-acre farm near Chappaqua, 35 miles north of New York City. In 1870, he published a book entitled *What I Know of Farming*. The title was Nast's springboard. He drew "**What I Know About** . . ." papers sticking out of Greeley's pockets in 59 cartoons.

Although he was a talented and prolific writer, Greeley took himself much too seriously and had no sense of humor. When a farmer wrote the *Tribune* to ask whether the agricultural know-it-all would "Advise putting manure on his strawberries," the temperance-minded editor responded: "That might do for people with tastes depraved by liquor but he preferred milk and sugar on his."

Greeley always had political ambitions. In 1866, Nast depicted him positively as a gesture to further reconciliation when he ran unsuccessfully for Congress, but scorned him the following year when he put up bail for Jeff Davis; for Nast, that was a treasonous act, never to be forgiven. Shortly before he went to Washington, he drew a two-panel cartoon, in which he baldly called Davis a traitor, as he aristocratically accepted his bail bond from a humble, bowing Greeley; the paper in Greeley's pocket read: "**What I know about bailing Jeff Davis**." In the adjacent panel, Greeley was about to sling "Tammany Mud" at "Patriot" Grant as he sat on the White House porch reading about Civil Service Reform.

HW January 20, 1872 52

WHAT I KNOW ABOUT HORACE GREELEY.

Politically, however, Greeley's only consistency was flip-flopping. As secession appeared likely after Lincoln's election, Greeley favored it — comparing it with 1776. After Fort Sumter, he vigorously backed the Union and the war, urging Lincoln "On to Richmond;" then he almost had a nervous breakdown when the Union's green troops were routed at Bull Run.[2] He was a constant thorn in Lincoln's side during the war and initiated somewhat deceitful peace negotiations in 1864.[3]* After the war, he was a Radical Republican who favored Andrew Johnson's impeachment.

The *Tribune* supported the Grant-Colfax 1868 ticket and opposed Seymour-Blair. The President's first term's achievements should have been satisfying to Greeley overall: The 15th Amendment finally passed in 1870, nominally securing suffrage for black men, Greeley's primary passion; Grant had used his military powers to combat anti-black violence in the Reconstructed South, especially by the Ku Klux Klan; the Amnesty Act pardoned almost all Confederates; the national debt had been substantially reduced; the economy was good; the Alabama Claims were essentially settled; and no major scandals had yet exploded.[4]

* See p. iii-iv

However, like other politicians and voters, Greeley had reservations about a second term for any president. None had completed two full terms since Andrew Jackson 31 years earlier, although three had died in office. Besides principle, there was significant Republican opposition to Grant's actions — primarily over patronage, his aggressive but unsuccessful push to annex Santo Domingo, and his blatant nepotism in appointments.

After taking office, Grant had conferred the exclusive right to recommend postmasters and other Federal officials on New York Senator Reuben Fenton and, to some vicarious extent, Greeley. Many of their postmasters, in particular, were incompetent and/or dishonest. Consequently, the President transferred patronage power to Roscoe Conkling, his friend and strong supporter, and New York's other Senator. In fact, this slap — more than any principle or other high-minded rationale — probably was responsible for the rupture between Fenton/Greeley and Grant.

The split climaxed in July 1870 when Grant replaced Fenton's man, Moses Grinnell, as Collector of the Port of New York with Tom Murphy, a corrupt low-life hack. Nast ignored the event, focusing on Napoleon III and his disastrous war against Germany, while the Tweed Ring-owned *Punchinello* captured its essence. Greeley, of course, targeted Murphy, who was forced to resign in November 1871. (Murphy's successor and close friend, Chester Arthur, would become the 21st President ten years later.)

PUNCHINELLO September 17, 1870 393

AT THE SARATOGA CONVENTION.
Horace Greeley, (to Roscoe Conkling.) "Don't Be Rash, Now; Remember That A Soft Answer Turneth Away Wrath."
Roscoe Conkling. "Let Us Have Peace, By All Means: But If That Fellow Reube Fenton Interferes With Me, He Had Better Look Out That I Don't Smash His Slate."

In a May 6, 1871 editorial, Greeley announced that he would not support Grant for reelection. He then went on a Southern tour which generated speculation that he wanted to be the Republican candidate. His remarks included: sectional reconciliation — "let by-gones be by-gones;" Grant should forgo reelection; and his own political future was "in the hands of my friends."

Harper's responded with two "bad idea" June 1871 editorials written by Curtis, and two Nast cartoons — all before the first Tweed Ring expose in the July 8 *Times*. Using one of Greeley's ironic nick-names — "Old Honesty" — Nast depicted him as the ancient Greek philosopher Diogenes looking for an honest man, and finding him in his own reflected image in a mirror shop.

With the election almost 17 months away, Nast's accompanying satire depicted farmer Greeley "plowing toward the White House" under the watchful eye of Liberal Republican Senator Fenton.

HW June 24, 1871 579

DIOGENES FINDS AN HONEST MAN AT LAST.

HW June 24, 1871 584

"WHAT I KNOW ABOUT FARMING."

Nast's first employer, Frank Leslie — a Democrat and a good friend of Greeley — published a "Horace Greeley for President" editorial on July 15, 1871, in his *Illustrated Newspaper*. Undoubtedly, the two conferred after Greeley returned from his southern tour. In the light of the *Times* disclosures of the Tweed Ring's finances a week earlier, they probably determined that Governor John Hoffman was no longer a viable presidential candidate.

Depicting Greeley

Greeley's physical appearance was truly unique. Owl-faced with a bemused expression, bald, plump and whiskered, he provided a natural image that was a caricaturist's dream. To that he added a long, loose white frock coat; he bought the first one many years before off the back of a recent Irish immigrant. Later, he added a broad-brimmed white hat. With papers always sticking out of his pocket, he intentionally, and probably somewhat naively, provided Nast and others with a symbolic appearance that was easy to ridicule.

After Greeley's nomination, Nast depicted his trademark outfit with a reprise of Oakey Hall's remark the previous year: *Something That Will Blow Over*. About the same time, he also provided a less fanciful portrait to London's *Vanity Fair*.

HW June 15, 1872 480

"SOMETHING THAT WILL BLOW OVER."

VF July 20, 1872

Morristown and Morristownship Library

HORACE GREELEY
"Anything to beat Grant."

Liberal Republicans

The Liberal Republican movement emerged in Missouri after the 1870 election of Benjamin Gratz Brown as Governor. Its platform advocated amnesty for all Confederates, Civil Service reform, universal suffrage (including women), and lower tariffs. Brown was a cousin of Frank and Montgomery Blair, worked in their law firm as a young man, and jointly owned a newspaper with Frank in the 1850s. Both Brown and Blair were delegates to the 1860 Republican Convention.

As discussed previously, Blair — a Union General who switched parties and became a militant anti-black Democrat — ran for Vice President with Horatio Seymour when they lost to Grant in 1868. Three years later, Blair emerged as a Democratic Senator with the support of Missouri's Liberal Republicans led by Cousin Gratz.

The other Missouri Senator was Carl Schurz, elected in 1869. Schurz, like Nast, was born in Germany. He fought in the 1848 Revolution, emigrated at age 24 in 1852, worked as a journalist, engaged in Republican state politics in Wisconsin, served as a controversial general during the Civil War, and was a Washington correspondent for Greeley's *Tribune* after it. He moved to St. Louis, edited a German-language newspaper, became a leading spokesman for German-Americans, and — ironically, in opposition to Blair — delivered the keynote address at the 1868 Republican convention.

Schurz was furious at Grant for the President's headstrong stance on Santo Domingo (among other matters), and his consequent loss of customary Missouri patronage as a result. Conversely, he and Senator Charles Sumner headed Grant's Republican Senatorial enemies list. After Brown's 1870 gubernatorial victory, Schurz joined him and others in birthing the anti-Grant Liberal Republican Party. However, he split with Brown the following year when the Governor understandably supported Blair's Senate bid. Ultimately, that paved the way for Greeley's nomination.

By late 1871, the prominent Liberal Republicans included Senators Schurz, Sumner, Fenton, Lyman Trumbull of Illinois and Thomas Tipton of Nebraska. On January 24, 1872, Schurz called for a national convention of Liberal Republicans to be held in Cincinnati, beginning May 1, to nominate a candidate for President. He expected Charles Francis Adams of Massachusetts — a steely-cold diplomat who served as Minister to England for Lincoln and Johnson, and was the son and grandson of former presidents — to be that candidate.

Adams too had broken with the Radical Republicans but Grant reluctantly appointed him as the American representative to the Geneva Tribunal. He was on his way to Europe to settle the *Alabama* Claims at the time of the Cincinnati Convention, and would not allow anyone to act on his behalf prior to it. Ultimately, he supported Grant.

In his cartoon demeaning *The "Liberal" Conspirators (Who, You All Know, Are Honorable Men)*, Nast quoted from Shakespeare's *Julius Caesar*, comparing Grant to Caesar; not coincidentally, it was published just before the Ides of March. Greeley was not yet a candidate but, clad in a toga, was reading his *Tribune* with a "What I Know About Bolting" paper in his pocket, while strolling past the White House. He was cast as Cicero, the Roman senator and enemy of Caesar, whom the other conspirators left out of the plot in Shakespeare's play. Ringleader Schurz, playing Brutus, disdained Greeley's potential candidacy.

THE "LIBERAL" CONSPIRATORS (WHO, YOU ALL KNOW, ARE HONORABLE MEN).

Lyman Trumbull

The 14-week interval between Schurz's call for the Cincinnati Convention and its commencement gave Nast time to draw 30 related cartoons, 25 of them attacking the Liberals. German-born Schurz was ineligible to run, but Illinois Senator Lyman Trumbull, Chairman of the Judiciary Committee, would gladly have accepted the nomination. Trumbull had been in the Senate since vanquishing Lincoln in 1855, and also resented his loss of patronage.

Trumbull recognized Nast's editorial power when they met during the caricaturist's Washington trip. Tommy sized him up in a letter to Sallie: "(He) is very polite to me, and very kind to me, but he is a very weak man, wants to be President, and thinks he better be on the right side of me."[5] Indeed, Nast treated him more gently than his fellow Senate bolters Schurz and Tipton, in an inspired reference to the bashful coach driver, Barkis, in Charles Dickens's *David Copperfield.*

HW March 23, 1872 232

Schurz and Trumbull created a tempest in a teapot in 1871 by charging that the government violated its neutrality toward Prussia by selling small arms to France during the previous year's Franco-Prussian War. Senator Conkling, Grant's close friend and ally, put that issue to rest after a Senate investigation. Nast ridiculed Trumbull via Shakespeare's *Macbeth.*

HW March 23, 1872 232

MACBETH TRUMBULL. "LAY ON, MACDUFF, AND DAMN'D BE HIM THAT FIRST CRIES HOLD, ENOUGH."

INVESTIGATION

N.B. MACBETH GOT ENOUGH, (IN THE PLAY)

INVESTIGATION

MACDUFF CONKLING.

Carl Schurz

Nast detested Schurz even more than Greeley, and attacked him about 60 times during Grant's presidency. At their first meeting in Washington in early 1869 when Schurz was a brand new Senator, they conversed in German. Schurz compared the American government unfavorably with Germany's, ending with "All the Americans are fools!" Nast's response: "Yes, they've sent you to the Senate!" set the stage for their stormy future relationship.

As not only the leader of the anti-Grant Liberal Republican faction, but also as a personally irritating, detestable liar (as he viewed him), Nast serially attacked Schurz over eleven consecutive weeks, well before and then after the Cincinnati Convention that ultimately nominated Greeley. In particular, he believed that the embittered, unlikable Senator blew up the problematic French Arms issue as a veiled attempt to turn the German vote against Grant. Accordingly, he cast Schurz as Iago, the evil villain from Shakespeare's *Othello*; as Don Quixote tilting at a windmill, with Tipton as Sancho Panza; and as a midget trying to corral the German vote.

HW March 30, 1872 241 C

Left to Right: Sumner, Schurz, Tipton, Trumbull, Greeley

UNITED STATES SENATE THEATRE.

Carl Schurz As Iago.

Iago (studying his part). **"I know not if't be true;**
But I, for mere suspicion in that king,
Will do, as if for surety"....

......"Divinity of hell!
When devils will their blackest sins put on.
They do suggest at first with heavenly shows,
As I do now,"—Shakespeare.

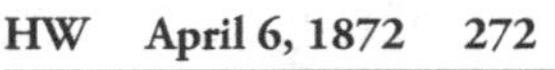
HW April 6, 1872 272

THE ONLY "EMERGENCIES" WE NEED FEAR (?).

Don Carlos Quixote And Sancho Tiptoe Panza On "The Path Of Duty." The French Arms Investigation.

HW April 20, 1872 320

WHICH IS THE BETTER ABLE TO POCKET THE OTHER?

HW May 11, 1872 384

CARL'S BOOMERANG.

Little Children Should Not Investigate (French) Fire-arms.

HW March 23, 1872 232

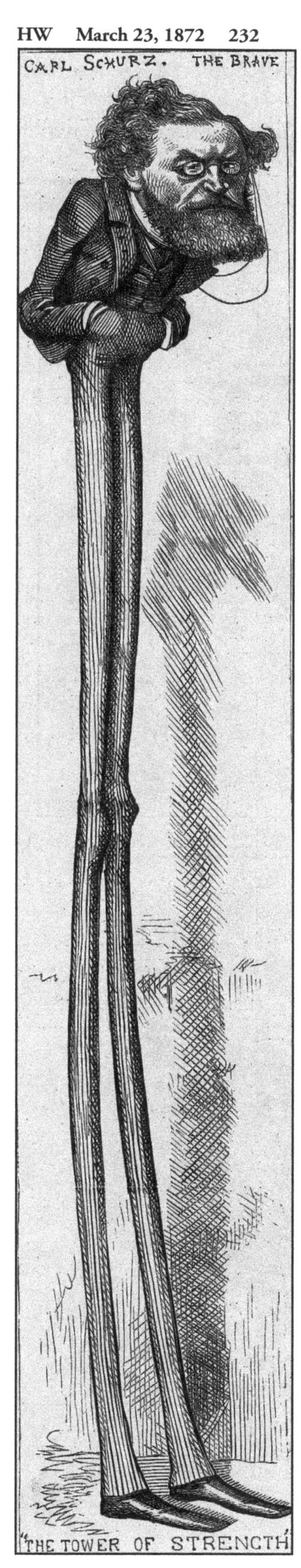

Schurz's long legs were his primary exaggerated feature for the caricaturist. Another attribute that Nast frequently "played to" was his musical talent, usually on the piano. Both before and after the Cincinnati Convention, he directly accused Schurz of lying about the French Arms controversy, among other subjects, via Shakespeare's *Hamlet*.

HW April 27, 1872 321 C

NOT SO EASILY PLAYED UPON.

U.S.G. "Will you play upon this pipe?"
C.S "My lord, I can not."
U.S.G. "*Tis as easy as lying*: govern these ventages with your fingers and thumb, give it breath with your mouth, and it will discourse most eloquent music. Look you, these are the stops."
C.S "But these can not I command to any utterance of harmony; I have not the skill."
U.S.G. "Why, look you now, *how unworthy a thing you make of me! You would play upon me; you would seem to know my stops; you would pluck out the hear of my mystery; you would sound me from my lowest note to the top of my compass*; and there is much music, excellent voice, in this little organ; yet can not you make it speak. *Why, do you think, I am easier to be played on than a pipe? Call me what instrument you will, though you can fret me, you can not play upon me.*"—Hamlet, Act III, Scene II.

After Greeley's nomination, several of the Liberal Republicans and journalists — anguished by what happened — met for a dismal dinner, during which Schurz played Chopin's *Funeral March*.

HW June 15, 1872 468

"PLAYED OUT!"

Several months later with Grant surging, Nast suggested through Uncle Sam that his disgusted piano-playing countryman go back where he came from. The message caught the attention of Joseph Keppler, a Vienna-born cartoonist living in St. Louis and working for a new German weekly called *Unser Blatt* (*Our Newspaper*) in the summer of 1872. Keppler's ambition was to replace Nast as the dominant American political cartoonist — which he eventually would do.

In perhaps his last cartoon drawn before he moved to New York in November to work for Frank Leslie, Keppler defended Schurz, his fellow St. Louis journalist, by attacking "Nasty." In the background, Grant was paying off a glamorous whore named *Harper's Weekly*.

The spout on Nast's pump repeated Uncle Sam's comment word-for-word.

UNSER BLATT October 26, 1872

Isn't that Nasty?

Missouri Historical Society

HW August 24, 1872 649 C

CARL IS "DISGUSTED WITH AMERICAN POLITICS."—*Frankfort Gazette*
***Uncle Sam.* "Look Here, Stranger, There Is No Law In This Country To Compel You To Stay."**

HW January 11, 1873 40

CARL'S POSITION
C. Schurz. "I finally declared that I had not passed from the Republican into the Democratic Party."— *(His Letter to the Democrats.)*

Nast was determined to have the last word. Two months after the election, he dumped Schurz into a wastebasket.

Charles Sumner

When Schurz first announced the Cincinnati Convention, he envisioned his close friend Sumner chairing it; in fact, Greeley's *Tribune* stated he would do so. Several weeks later, Nast sketched the two plotting to use the French Arms issue to attack Grant and attract the German vote. Preoccupied by poor health and an overwhelming desire for additional civil rights legislation, the Massachusetts Senator believed that Liberal Republicans aligned with Democrats could doom his precious cause. While he hated Grant, he found both Charles Francis Adams — his fellow homestate Republican whom he disliked — and Judge Davis unacceptable; he strongly distrusted Greeley, primarily for his Southern reconciliation policy among other reasons.

In print three weeks before the Convention, Nast depicted Sumner as Robinson Crusoe (from Daniel Defoe's 1719 novel) being unsuccessfully pressured and pushed by Schurz and Tipton into the Convention longboat, while stiffly avoiding eye contact with Greeley and his motley crew. Crusoe/Sumner's Man Friday — representing the country's black population — fearfully prayed on the bank as two shadowy KKK figures observed behind a tree. In the open sea beyond, the schooner *Democrat* — flying Tammany Ring, Truce and KKK banners — awaited the Liberals.

Nast's prediction was accurate. Sumner didn't attend the Convention or endorse Greeley until three months later.

HW April 20, 1872 313

James Doolittle, Blair, Seymour, Greeley, Jeff Davis, Schurz

Fenton, David Davis, Johnson, Trumbull, Sumner, Tipton

WILL ROBINSON CRUSOE (SUMNER) FORSAKE HIS MAN FRIDAY?

The Boat's Crew That Is Going Over.

Civil Service

FLIN 1872 (Date Unknown)

Paine, p. 247

WEIGHED IN THE BALANCE AND FOUND WANTING

U.S.G.; "Well, who'd have thought that the old white hat, boots and axe would have more weight than all these hangers-on of mine!"

Meanwhile, both Grant and Nast were regularly attacked by ardent Democrat Frank Leslie, in his *Illustrated Newspaper*. In 1871, Leslie hired former London cartoonist Matt Morgan for that specific purpose, paying him an exceptionally high $10,000 annual salary. (By contrast, he paid Keppler $30 weekly). Morgan was a capable portraitist but couldn't match Nast's caricature, wit or imagination. While crude, his low blows brought strong responses from Nast, and their respective outputs became increasingly vitriolic as the campaign progressed. He generally portrayed Grant as a dissolute drunk.

Here, intoxicated military dictator Grant, was supported by hangers-on Hamilton Fish, Senator Oliver Morton and even Boss Tweed (before Greeley affiliated with Tammany Hall). "Honest Tom" was written on a boot sticking out behind Fish, referring to Nast.

As noted, patronage was the rootstock of political power at federal, state and local levels. As that power shifted, men lost or gained jobs arbitrarily. Appointees often were required to kickback part of their salaries, hire unqualified and/or dishonest personnel, and promote specific measures. The spoils system was just that.

Grant did appoint a dozen or so relatives to official positions, including his father as a Kentucky postmaster and his brother-in-law, Casey Leet, as Collector of the Port of New Orleans. Leet turned out to be a crook, but *Harper's* defended the others. However, another *Leslie's* cartoonist, anonymous but skilled, drew the President's acceptance of "miscellaneous presents," nepotism, and fondness for alcohol in one strip entitled *My Policy* — a reference to Andrew Johnson's controversial term.

FLIN September 28, 1872 48

Addition **Division** **And Silence**

FLIN November 9, 1872 137

Morgan frequently drew Grant with bulldog puppies near him. The bulldogs reportedly were a gift to Grant from a man who was given an official position in return. The story was false but Morgan and Keppler chose to believe it, and used the puppies as a symbol for graft, and possibly also to treat Grant's cronies as lapdogs.

On January 11, 1872, the Republican National Committee met in Philadelphia and set June 5 as the date for their anointment of Grant for a second term. Greeley, the national committee-man for New York, refused to attend or be associated with the "Grant Convention," saying he wanted to stay independent. *Harper's* editor George William Curtis sharply criticized his good friend Horace in an editorial.

Curtis was the leading advocate for changing the system for hiring and firing federal employees. In June 1871, Grant had appointed him Chairman of a Civil Service Reform Commission, which spent six months coming up with proposed new regulations. Grant included them in his December annual report to Congress, and they became effective on New Year's Day. Of course, they became a prime topic for public debate.

Curtis spent considerable time in Washington and socialized with Sumner, Schurz and most of the other Liberal Republicans. About the time he criticized Greeley, he wrote Nast, addressing him as "My dear 'Nephew'" and signing "Your affectionate 'Uncle.'" He asked Nast not to demonize his Liberal Republican friends and specifically to refrain from "punching the Honorable Horace Greeley."

Morgan punched in early January 1872, with Grant as an uncomfortable schoolboy taking the new Civil Service exam from a stern Uncle Sam. Nast quickly responded with *Children Cry for It,* as the President fed Civil Service Reform gruel to unreceptive Liberal schoolchildren while a perplexed Greeley tasted it directly from a steaming bowl. Underneath the sub-caption, a lengthy quote from Grant's Congressional message explained his rationale.[6] Nast's image presented a strong, self-confident leader dominating his diminutive critics.

Out of about 70 cartoons portraying Schurz — many of them depicting his exaggerated long legs — this was the only time his stature was minimized. Conversely, Sumner was enlarged to stand out, probably as a message to Curtis not to interfere.

"CHILDREN CRY FOR IT."
U.S.G. "If You Can Stand It, I Can."
"If bad men have secured places, it has been the fault of the system established by law and custom for making appointments, or the fault of those who recommend for government positions persons not sufficiently well known to them personally, or who give letters indorsing the character of office-seekers without a proper sense of the grave responsibility which such a course devolves upon them. A civil service reform which can correct this abuse is much desired."—Grant's Message.

More Conflict with Curtis

Editor Curtis was on the horns of a personal dilemma that defied solution. There was no question about the candidate; Curtis believed that Grant deserved a second term, and Fletcher Harper made it clear to him that the *Weekly* would support the President if her ever wavered. Curtis knew Greeley well enough to editorialize before his nomination: "If there is one quality which is indispensable in a President, it is sound judgment. If there is a public man who is totally destitute of it, it is Horace Greeley."[7]

Unlike the 1868 election when Nast's return to *Harper's* after his Caricaturama year away (including the failure of the *Illustrated Chicago News*) was contingent on his receiving pre-approval from Curtis, the editor understandably lost that power during or after the Tweed campaign. Now he was reduced to begging Nast in person and in writing not to attack his close personal friends Schurz and Sumner too harshly.

When Nast ignored him with *Children Cry For It* — not only attacking his friend, but rubbing salt in this open wound: "I (Curtis) must bear the responsibility" Curtis exploded.

I am confounded and chagrined by your picture this week, in which my personal friends and those I asked you specifically to spare are exposed to what I think is not only ridicule but injustice . . . I support the President sincerely, but I respect the equal sincerity of my friends who differ . . . My dear Nast, I am very sorely touched by your want of regard for my friendship, for I asked you not to do this thing . . . I do not assume any right whatever to control your action or to dictate to you in any manner, but I respect the equal sincerity of my friends who differ. Today I am to dine with Mr. Sumner, but how can I eat his bread, knowing that the paper with which I am identified holds him up to public contempt? Yesterday, when I defended the President to Mr. Schurz, he shook my hand warmly, and said 'At least we agree on the point of Civil Service.' What will his feelings be when he sees **my paper**? . . . Very truly yours.[8]

Curtis appealed in vain to Fletcher, who solidly backed Nast. "Mr. Schurz has been very insulting to the President . . . and the policy of allowing him to escape without being made to appear ridiculous to the party he would ruin by persistent misrepresentation of its leaders" (is unacceptable).[9]

Nast believed, probably correctly, that Curtis was putting friendship ahead of principle. However, as the campaign developed and Greeley, Schurz and Sumner came out with inflammatory associates and contradictory statements, Curtis ultimately attacked them editorially without reservation.

The cartoon was published before Nast left for Washington. While there, Curtis confronted him and continued to give him a hard time. Tommy confidently wrote Sallie that if push came to shove, he thought Curtis would lose and leave.

Frank Bellew, who had observed their previous conflicts from the inside, captured the combatants current situation precisely in the short-lived *Fifth Avenue Journal* which currently employed him. As the sartorially elegant Curtis held up his dirty hands while helping to mix mud to throw at Greeley in 1872, he reprimanded Nast: "Don't spit in it, Thomas; it is not gentlemanly." Behind Nast, Fletcher Harper, Sr. and Jr. looked on in dismay.

FIFTH AVENUE JOURNAL (Date Unknown)

MIXING DAY AT HARPERS'.—MAKING MUD TO FLING AT GREELEY.

Chapter 25
The Election of 1872: The Nomination

Prelude to the Convention

When Carl Schurz issued his call for the Cincinnati Convention, the last person he wanted to see nominated was Horace Greeley, a vocal high-tariff Protectionist. Conversely, the outspoken editor mistrusted the Missouri Liberals both as free-traders and for their association with Frank Blair and other local Democrats.

Nast quickly followed up with an intuitive prediction about Greeley as a still-undeclared candidate. *Cincinnatus* was a reference to both the convention city and the legendary Roman patriot from whom its name was indirectly derived; he was summoned from his farm in 458 B.C. to become a dictator and defeat an enemy, after which he returned to farming and became an enduring symbol of civic virtue.[1]

With the White House and the Capitol in the distance, unpretentious Farmer Greeley was surprised to be tendered both the Liberal Republican and Democratic nominations from his other self, the distinguished journalist. Behind the farmer, a bucking Democratic donkey yoked to an uncooperative Liberal Republican ox wearing blinders, tried to bolt. Behind the editor, Schurz watched Greeley warily.

Gratz Brown lagged nonchalantly in the rear, nursing his own ambitions. Brown's appearance as a real character was noteworthy; after he was selected as Greeley's running mate, Nast couldn't immediately locate either of his two carte de visite photographs, and hastily drew him as a tag on Greeley's white coat. That symbol of insignificance was so successful that Nast used the tag, or occasionally an animal's tail, to demean Brown 41 times; subsequently, he appeared in the flesh only three other times, two of them thoroughly inebriated in accordance with his reputation and Greeley's abhorrence of liquor.

HW February 10, 1872 132

Schurz, Fenton, Gratz Brown

John Hay Library Brown University

CINCINNATUS
H. G. The Farmer Receiving the Nomination From H. G. the Editor.

The Convention

About a month before the Cincinnati Convention, Nast depicted it in a classic scene from *The Pickwick Papers* by Charles Dickens; he was about to illustrate that novel for Harper & Bros. and also had used short tales by Dickens in a series of five annual almanacs he published from 1871-1875.* Notably, he was one of 200 attendees at an exclusive farewell dinner for Dickens after his American lecture tour ended four years earlier; Greeley was the master of ceremonies and George William Curtis a featured speaker.

Five days after Schurz's January 24th call, Greeley had editorialized: "The Cincinnati Convention may prove a fiasco, or it may name the next President." Subsequently the *World*, published by Democrat Manton Marble, had suggested an alliance between Liberal Republicans and Liberal Democrats as the only way to beat Grant.

In a prescient parody, Nast picked up on both pronouncements. Greeley as Samuel Pickwick, Esq. "mounted the Windsor chair on which he previously had been seated, and addressed the club he himself had founded." Both political factions wanted reconciliation with the South; accordingly Jeff Davis, Andrew Johnson, and Copperheads Horatio Seymour and Fernando Wood were at the table passively listening.

Supreme Court Justice David Davis was among the leading candidates likely to attend, so Nast put him at the head of the table, his hands protesting what he was hearing. George Francis Train, an unconventional, self-promoted wild-card candidate, was seated between Justice Davis and Senator Reuben Fenton. Opposite, Gratz Brown, back to the viewer, had a "We Want the Nomination" sign in front of him.

HW April 13, 1872 284

Center (from behind): Gratz Brown
Left to Right: Jeff Davis, Seymour, Johnson, Wood, Tipton, David Davis, Train, Fenton, Trumbull, Greeley, Blair, Schurz

THE CINCINNATI CONVENTION, IN A PICKWICKIAN SENSE.
Horace Pickwick. **"Men and Brethren! A new leaf must be turned over, or there are breakers ahead. The Cincinnati Convention may prove a fiasco, or it may name the next President."**

Nast's little touches were notable. Greeley abhorred liquor and tobacco, so his cup contained water in contrast to wine glasses for others; Schurz and Blair smoked up a storm next to him. A sign on the door referred to the Pope's 1869 Declaration: "Investigate everything and everybody but us (The Liberal Infallibles)."

---

* See p. 202

The Deal

The principal issue dividing Greeley from his fellow Liberal Republicans was his Protectionism vs. their Free Trade. Schurz, Trumbull and David Davis insisted on that plank in their platform. No compromise position was possible so they punted: "Discussion of the subject was remitted to the people in their Congressional Districts and the decision of Congress, wholly free from Executive interference or dictation."

Unlike the other candidates Davis, Trumbull and Brown, Greeley did not attend the convention. He was well represented by Whitelaw Reid whom he had installed as his chief deputy to run the *Tribune* four years earlier. Reid now served as his campaign manager as well, and made a deal with Brown that facilitated Greeley's nomination. From Reid's standpoint, having his boss as the nominee would keep him out of the *Tribune* office and pave the way for Reid's takeover of the paper regardless of how the election turned out.

Heavy negotiating took place on May 1 in the absence of Schurz's political foes, Gratz Brown and Frank Blair, who arrived after midnight. When voting began, Adams led the first ballot with 205 votes; Greeley, aided by the tariff non-solution, polled a surprising 147. Subsequently, Brown withdrew and backed Greeley, thereby blocking Adams and gaining Greeley's endorsement for Vice President in return. Greeley squeaked in by eight votes on the sixth ballot after the Illinois delegates abandoned Davis and Trumbull, their home-state candidates.

Nast, anticipating victory by Adams, had nearly completed *Great Expectations*, again paying homage to Dickens. The "Liberal Mountain" was made of the mud which Liberal Republicans slung in their corruption charges against the Grant Administration. Nast may have been inspired by the eruption of Mt. Vesuvius a month earlier, and adapted the story from *Aesop's Fables*.

The Democratic National Committee favored Adams. Here, its Chairman, August Belmont, made his first campaign appearance next to firebrand Blair.

The face of the emerging mouse originally belonged to Adams. When Greeley won, Nast made a last-minute change, which explains why the unexpected nominee appeared twice.

In another late modification, Nast changed the look on Schurz's face to one of consternation. His hope to be Secretary of State — as shown by the paper in his hat — was gone. His Senatorial cabal wanted Greeley and his *Tribune* to support them; now they had the dismal prospect of supporting him.

HW October 21, 1876 860

Charles Francis Adams

HW May 18, 1872 392

Fenton **Tipton, Blair, Belmont**

Trumbull Schurz

"GREAT EXPECTATIONS."

"A (Mud) Mountain was once greatly agitated. Loud Groans and Noises were heard; and crowds of People came from all Parts to see what was the Matter. After long expectation and many wise conjectures from the by-standers, out popped a— Mouse!"

Curtis's Consternation

Curtis had known Greeley well for almost two decades, and considered him totally unqualified to be President. His editorial in the same post-convention issue focused on five of Greeley's bad ideas during the Civil War when he:

- *Would have allowed the Confederate States to secede*
- *Helped force Lincoln's army into the field before it was ready*
- *Begged Lincoln to try and buy peace by paying for the slaves*
- *Represented Mr. Lincoln's action in the Niagara Conference in a manner which Mr. Lincoln declared put him in a false position before the country*
- *Signed a letter to the loyal Governors after Mr. Lincoln was nominated in 1864, substantially asking whether he should not be set aside and a new candidate selected.*[2]

In the same issue, Nast depicted *Horace Greedey for President* with a lengthy pre-convention *Tribune* quote blasting Adams. His pocket paper read "What I know about blowing my own horn."

HW May 18, 1872 400

HURRA FOR HORACE GREEDEY FOR PRESIDENT.
"They will sustain Horace Greeley, whose presence on the ticket should be a guarantee to the country of the dignity and power of the reform movement; he would, they argue, carry an overwhelming Republican vote, and render the work of the Philadelphia gathering useless. They are equally frank in their repugnance to Charles Francis Adams, whose letter is regarded as frivolous and undignified. He is accused of courting Administration bounty by his careless, or, as they term it, slighting allusion to the Liberal Convention."—*N.Y. Tribune*, April 27.

Two weeks later, Nast portrayed Greeley strapped to the back of a wild horse on a ride from Cincinnati to (wherever), as Schurz and Tipton gesticulated anxiously from the edge of a cliff, along with a calmer Uncle Sam. The Modern Mazeppa involved the tale of a Polish nobleman; Nast had used it a decade earlier in *Phunny Phellow* with Jeff Davis in the lead role.[3]

HW June 1, 1872 428

THE MODERN MAZEPPA—"WHAT I KNOW ABOUT THE ROAD FROM CINCINNATI TO ——."

The Organ?

On May 15, Greeley announced that he would transfer editorial control of the *Tribune* to Whitelaw Reid and that his paper would cease to be a party organ for the duration of the campaign. An organ that was alleged not to be an organ was grist for Nast's mill. So a week after Mazeppa, he portrayed Reid as an organ-grinder with Greeley as his trained monkey begging for votes; Gratz Brown, of course, was the monkey's tail.

Greeley's tin-cup prospects comprised all of the Democratic factions — the Tweed Ring; Fernando and Ben Wood among other Copperheads; and even Jefferson Davis, Nathan Bedford Forrest and Rafael Semmes representing the Confederacy. The organ played *The Bonny Blue Flag*, a Confederate Civil War anthem.

Nast's real target was the upcoming national Democratic Convention scheduled for Baltimore. His shot was aimed at alienating Northern Democrats from the ex-Confederates, quoting Greeley from February 1871.

However, the Southerners appreciated Greeley's bailing Davis five years earlier, knew that he favored total amnesty, and went along with his "New Departure" — putting the "Lost Cause" behind them. He was their best hope of getting rid of military governance and regaining political power.

HW June 8, 1872 448

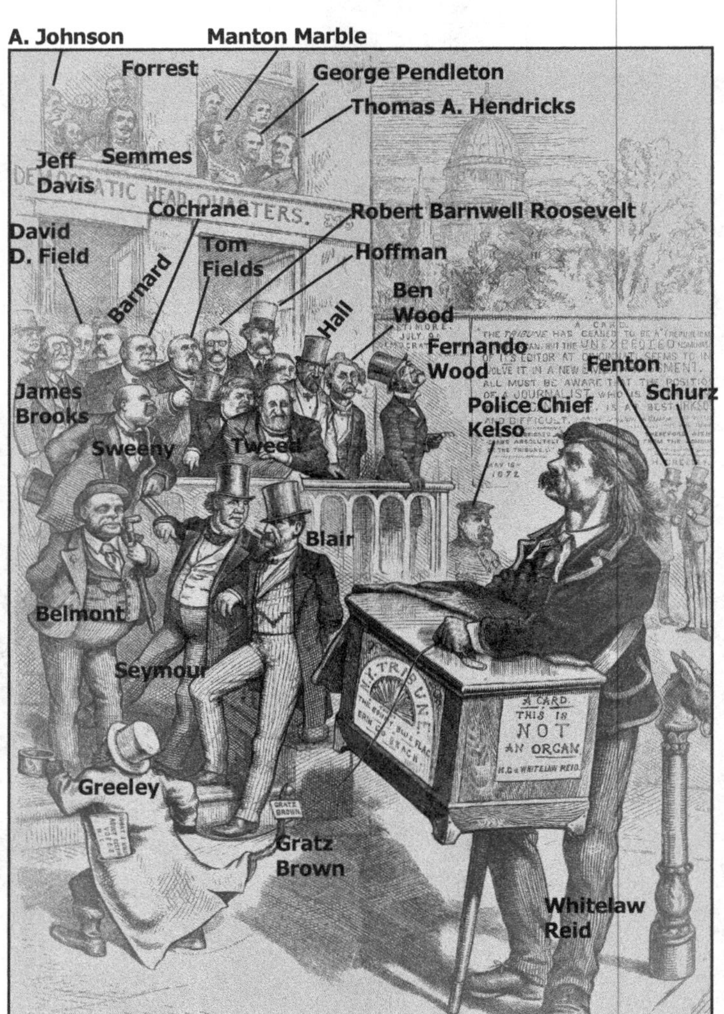

THE NEW ORGAN-(we beg the "Tribune's" pardon)-IZATION ON ITS "NEW DEPARTURE."—ANY THING TO GET VOTES.

"The brain, the heart, the soul, of the present Democratic Party is the rebel element at the South, with its Northern allies and sympathizers. It is rebel to the core to-day."—*New York Tribune* (old tune), February, 1871.

Schurz still found it difficult to endorse Greeley. As it became apparent that Greeley would also receive the Democratic nomination, the shell-shocked Liberal Republicans met at the Fifth Avenue Hotel on June 20 to seek some sort of *Anything to Beat Grant* rationale for rapprochement. Nast sequelled *The New Organ* with Schurz stiffly kissing the Greeley monkey — still attached to the organ — on the lips.

Nast found a second instrument — the lyre, usually played by Apollo, the Greek god of music — to attack the integrity of the *Tribune* and its publisher, "White Lie" Reid. Both were used to reinforce Greeley's obvious vulnerability on several future occasions.

HW July 6, 1872 536

"ANY THING TO BEAT GRANT!"

HW October 12, 1872 792

Shortly after *The New Organ* cartoon was in print, Manton Marble, editor of the *World*, who first suggested that the Liberal Republicans and Northern Democrats unite, had second thoughts about the Ring's lower-class "Scum and dregs of the community" being attracted to "Old Honesty's" bandwagon. Several weeks later, Nast brought "Tweed's Army" back to life.*

HW July 20, 1872 573

"OLD HONESTY."

"If he does still think that all the vilest classes ('*blacklegs, pugilists, keepers of dens, criminals, shoulder-hitters, rowdies, burglars,*' etc., etc.), all the scum and dregs of the community, are drawn to the Democratic party by '*a sympathetic chord,*' he disgraces himself in asking for Democratic suffrages."—*New York World,* June 6, 1872.

* See p. 244

The Deathbed Marriage

Nast caricatured the Democratic Convention in Baltimore well before it nominated Greeley. In print just a week later, he threw the kitchen sink at 32 unhappy Tweed-Ringers, other Democrats and Liberal Republicans attending the grotesque wedding party: *The Daughter of Democracy Has At Last Married a "Nigger!" (A Radical Black Republican)-July 10, 1872.*

The artist's ironic use of the "N-word" to criticize the negrophobia of distraught Democratic "friends of the bride" would not have bothered most contemporary readers. It reprised his 1868 cartoon on a similar theme.*

The dying lady had a bottle of Cincinnati Platform brandy by her bed (referring to the no-position tariff plank) as she extended her scrawny hand for Greeley's kiss. A "What I Know About Stooping to Conquer" paper stuck out of his pocket; however, there was no Gratz Brown tag on his coat (held by Reid) in a rare exception to Nast's incessant belittling of his running mate. The bride's labeled dowry of Tammany's fraudulent votes was emphasized by the belligerent masked Klansman with his hand on a stuffed ballot box.

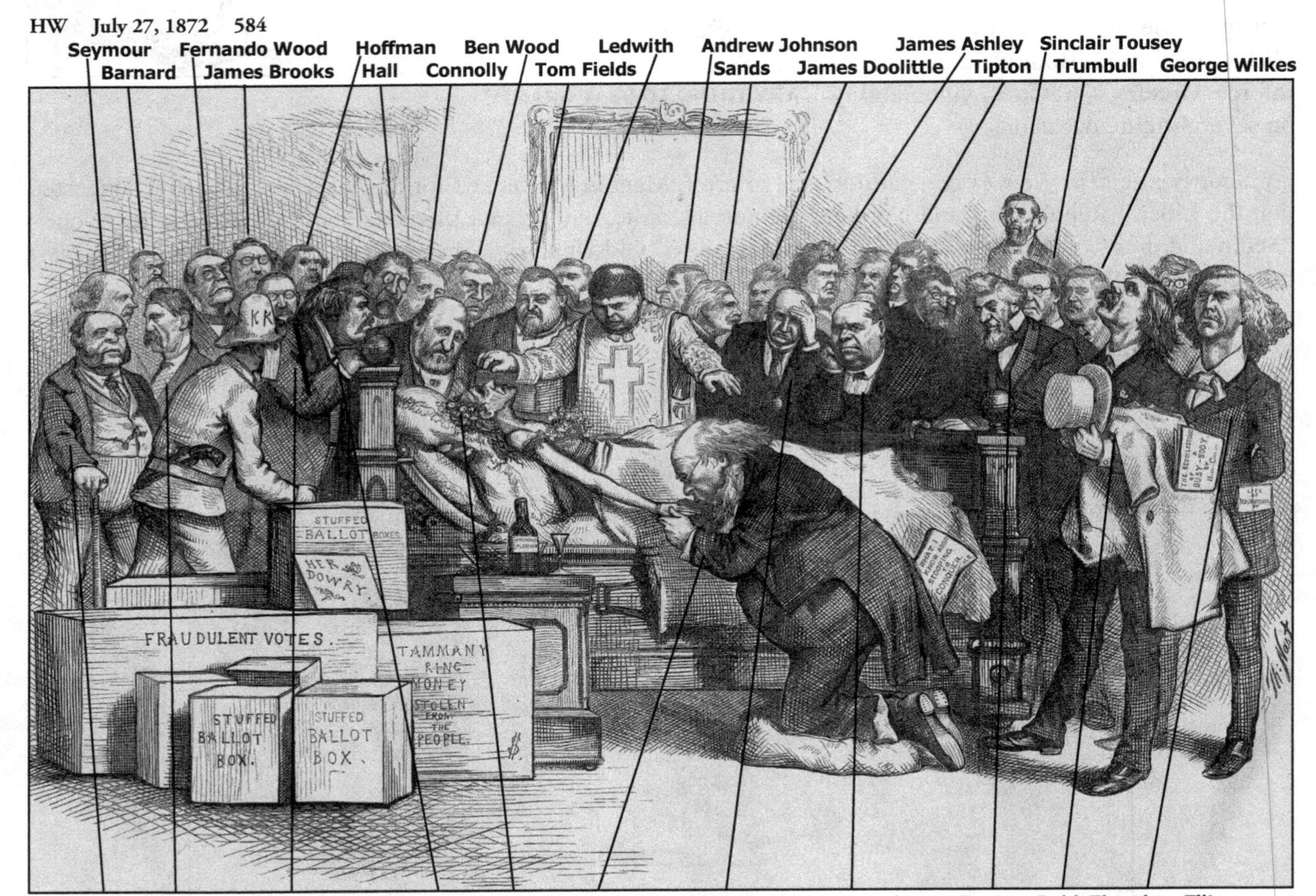

THE DEATH-BED MARRIAGE.
The Daughter Of Democracy Has At Last Married A "Nigger!" (A Radical Black Republican)—July 10, 1872.

* See p. 210

Free Love

In the 2,000-plus cartoons that Thomas Nast drew for *Harper's Weekly*, only two portrayed politically prominent public women. His first was a Radical Republican lecturer, Anna Elizabeth Dickinson, who stood in line to get her head chopped off as "King Andy" Johnson presided; Nast was behind her.*

His second featured a trailblazing feminist on a scathing full-page. Victoria Claflin Woodhull, whose notoriety as a proponent of Free Love — expressed in lectures and her unconventional weekly newspaper — must have "emanated from Satan" as *Harper's* described her in accompanying text. It contrasted her to an unhappy but wise wife "who is compelled to bear alone, the burden of a drunken (Irish-stereotyped) husband and her little children."

The text was also quoted from her women's rights lecture which produced strong mixed reactions three months earlier from 3,000 listeners at Steinway Hall. "*Yes, I am a free-lover. I have an inalienable, constitutional, and natural right to love whom I may; to love as long or short a period as I can; to change that love every day if I please.*"

HW February 17, 1872 140

"GET THEE BEHIND ME, (MRS.) SATAN!"

HW November 25, 1871 1109

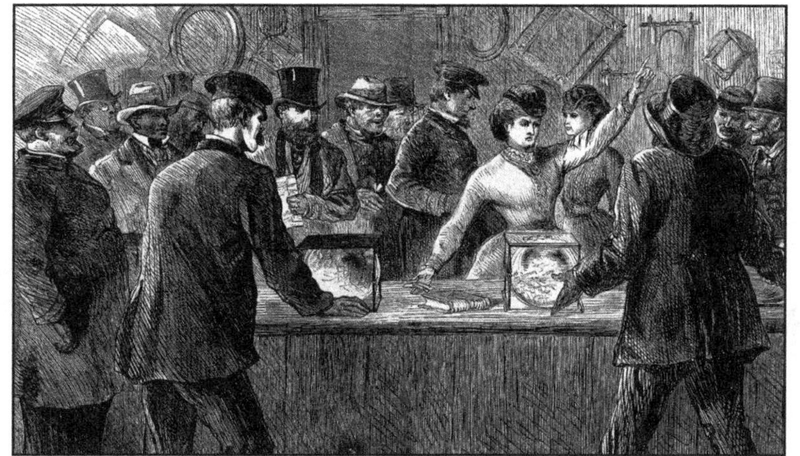

MRS. WOODHULL ASSERTING HER RIGHT TO VOTE.—
[From A Sketch By H. Balling.]

In addition to the morals issue, Nast had another reason for denigrating Woodhull. Almost two years earlier Victoria, then 32, announced in a long letter published in the *Herald* that she was the Equal Rights Party's candidate for President. That paper promptly ran an editorial supporting her, ignoring the Constitution's age requirement. Subsequently, she unsuccessfully attempted to vote in the November 1871 election (which vanquished the Tweed Ring), receiving publicity in *Harper's*.

Initially, Nast used Woodhull's Free Love platform to squelch any electoral diversion of votes from Grant. Three months later when Theodore Tilton became Greeley's campaign manager, Nast focused on her eulogistic biography, which Tilton had written and published as a 36-page pamphlet in September 1871. The author praised her purity, backed her as a leader of the Woman Suffrage movement, and became her sponsor and endorser in the public's estimation. *The Life of Mrs. Woodhull* became a scandalous symbol which Nast used to ridicule Tilton.

HW November 16, 1872 896-897

* See p. 173

The ten-cent “thrilling story” read “like a fairy tale” as its promotional advertisement proclaimed. Victoria Claflin, born in 1838, and her eight-year younger sister Tennessee — who changed her name to Tennie C. Claflin — were raised in Ohio, along with several siblings, by cruel huckster parents who changed residences and dishonorable occupations frequently. The girls were inseparable friends, beautiful and quick on their feet, but coarse and uneducated. They peddled their parents’ homemade phony cancer cures — and their bodies on occasion, along with attempted blackmail — but the family’s main income came from their skills as spiritual clairvoyants. Often, they were a step ahead or behind the sheriff and the courts.

At 14, Victoria attempted to escape by marrying Dr. Canning Woodhull, about twice her age. Several years later, she divorced him because of his temper, alcoholism and constant infidelity, but kept his last name. In St. Louis in 1866, she married Colonel James Blood, an intelligent Civil War hero. He educated both sisters in worldly affairs, his free love doctrine, and his activities as president of the local Society of Spiritualists. When the family moved to New York City two years later, Victoria divorced Blood but continued to live with him. Both practiced what they preached, as did Tennie.

Knowing that he would see anybody for ten minutes, their father introduced his daughters to America’s richest man, Commodore Cornelius Vanderbilt, who made his fortune in railroads and ships. Tall, steely, impassive, and coarse in manner like them, the recently-widowed, 74-year old introvert was consulting spiritualist physicians, faith healers, and a medium who brought him messages from his dead mother.

Bingo! He fell for the overtly seductive Tennie, 51 years his junior. He proposed, was rejected, but continued to see the girls and give them valuable stock tips. In early 1870, he backed the sisters when they opened the first female brokerage firm at 44 Broad Street, where he visited Tennie almost daily.

While Nast ignored the Vanderbilt story, *Harper’s* commented with two pointed (non-Nast) illustrations a week apart. *The Bewitching Brokers — Women on ‘Change* was a pun on the Stock Exchange. The other was a Winslow Homer cover of the two recognizable but unnamed sisters being chastised over the Tenth Commandment. Homer must have drawn this reluctantly because his signature was printed in miniscule type, although his initials were on a donkey’s collar (referring to “thy neighbor’s ox and his ass”).

HW March 5, 1870 160

THE BEWITCHING BROKERS — WOMEN ON ‘CHANGE.

HW March 12, 1870 161 C

“Thou shalt not covet thy neighbor’s house, thou shalt not covet thy neighbor’s wife, nor his servant, nor his maid, nor his ox, nor his ass, nor any thing that is his.”
“Lord, have mercy upon us, and write all these thy laws in our hearts, we beseech thee.”

The Tweed Ring's *Punchinello* also chimed in with a funny cartoon, diverting their public's attention from Tweed's new Charter.

PUNCHINELLO April 2, 1870 8

MESMERISM IN WALL STREET.
First Lady Broker, (entrancing subject.) "There, I've Got Him To The Point Now. Take Him At His Word, Quick."
Commodore V—-nd—rb—lt, (murmurs.) "Sell Me One Thousand Shares Central."
Second Lady Broker. "Booked!"

Some of Vanderbilt's 12 children were understandably worried about their father's relationship with the infamous Claflins. They brought up a distant relative and her daughter from Alabama, hoping that he would marry the widow, but in August 1869 he wed the daughter. However, that didn't stop his continuing intimacy with Tennie for eight months or so.

However, not long after these illustrations appeared, the relationship with Vanderbilt collapsed, soured by his new wife and Tennie's public testimony during a family-feud lawsuit ("Commodore Vanderbilt knows my power. I have humbugged people, I know. But . . .").

The sisters promptly rebounded by starting their own flamboyant newspaper, *Woodhull and Claflin's Weekly,* in May 1870. Its printing and paper stock were equivalent to *Harper's Weekly*, and it provided them with both wide local distribution and a national circulation for their unfiltered, politically incorrect viewpoints on women's rights, sexual freedom, spiritualism, labor activism, and even Communism. Two years later, they accused Vanderbilt of manipulating and watering stocks, among other nefarious practices: "Why Tammany was nothing compared to this great infamy."[4]

Theodore Tilton

Unseemly as the Vanderbilt saga may have seemed to some, the most notorious social scandal of the decade involved Woodhull, Tilton and Henry Ward Beecher, the country's most prominent clergyman. It turned out that all three were proponents of Free Love, two more openly than the third.

Beecher had preached at Plymouth Church in Brooklyn since 1847. He published and lectured widely and was a national figurehead for Christian morality. Over the years, however, consistent rumors spread about Beecher seducing some of his parishioners, cloaking his enticements in his religious eminence while telling them that God favored their intimacy with him and would bless them for it. Strong and avuncular, he would have been hard to resist.

Nast was wary of Beecher because of his backing of Andrew Johnson's Reconstruction Policy. He depicted Beecher as a Confederate snake-charmer for his 1866 Bal d'Opera.* Possibly, he too had heard the personal charm rumors.

---

* See p. 160

Back in 1855, Beecher had officiated at Theodore Tilton's marriage to Elizabeth Richards on Tilton's twentieth birthday. They had been friends for many years and Tilton worked for Beecher. Later, Tilton moved on to edit the *Independent* and the *Brooklyn Union*, both affiliated with Plymouth Church.

While Tilton was on a Western lecture tour in October 1868, Beecher, 55, seduced Elizabeth, convincing her that it was not criminally or morally wrong. He continued to make "pastoral" calls on her for about 18 months, especially when her husband was away. Once Tilton came home mid-day and found his wife and Beecher in her locked bedroom; Beecher, dressed but flushed, explained it away.

Finally, in July 1870, Elizabeth confessed to Theodore. Late that year, Tilton confronted Beecher, who persuaded her to recant. Then she confessed again, recanted, and confessed and recanted a third time. Beecher managed to keep the scandal quiet for a while, although both Tiltons confided in Elizabeth Stanton and Susan Anthony, the women's rights leaders, later that year. Tilton too had a long string of infidelities of which Elizabeth was aware in general; they may have included Susan Anthony.

On May 20, 1871, Victoria Woodhull published a card in the *World*, a mainstream Democratic daily:

> *"I know of one man, a public teacher of eminence, who lives in concubinage with the wife of another public teacher of almost equal eminence. All three concur in denouncing offenses against morality. I shall make it my business to analyze some of these lives."*

Woodhull continued to use her paper to promote her candidacy, as well as to see Tilton, whose *Golden Age* came out for Greeley in June 1871, as did *Leslie's Illustrated Newspaper.* After she reciprocated for his biography of her with fulsome praise in November, Leslie's comic monthly proclaimed "***Theodore Woodhull for President*** and ***Victoria Tilton for Vice.***"[5]

At her request, Tilton arranged a meeting for Victoria with Beecher. They found that they shared her Free Love philosophy, and practiced it on several occasions as she reported later.

Woodhull's relationship with Tilton ended in March 1872, prior to the Cincinnati Convention. He had worked for Greeley as a reporter early in his career, socialized with him, attended the Convention on his behalf, and collaborated with Whitelaw Reid on the successful negotiations with Gratz Brown. Reid ran the *Tribune* and Tilton managed Greeley's campaign as both became cannon fodder for Nast.

By September, Greeley's campaign was in trouble, so he went on a ten-day speaking tour. Nast drew a six-vignette cartoon which reprised his Andrew Johnson *Swingin' Round the Circle.** In one of the small rotating boats, he put Tilton and the Pope; "Free Love" and "Catholicism" were labeled on the side, and Tilton was displaying *The Life of Mrs. Woodhull* to the Pontiff. How Nast must have chuckled![6]

HW October 12, 1872 792

* See p. 171-173 & 195-196

Chapter 26
The Election of 1872: The Campaign

Having found the keys to ridiculing Greeley's running mate (Gratz Brown); campaign manager (Tilton); *Tribune* replacement (Reid); and Senatorial backers (Schurz, Sumner, Trumbull and Tipton), Nast focused on their unifying slogan — *Anything to Beat Grant*. He pounded repeatedly on three principal themes: Greeley's previous statements and actions; Confederate forgiveness and reconciliation; and acceptance of Tammany Hall/Tweed Ring support.

Hoist by his own petard

Greeley was haunted by his own record of hundreds of self-contradictions from the *Tribune,* as well as his many speeches and lectures. Grant's Congressional supporters raised $30,000 to hire more than 300 staffers for the search, which produced periodic pamphlets that provided Nast and other journalists with potent source material.

Harper's July 13 issue, in print a week before the Democratic Convention in Baltimore, contained three biting cartoons featuring Greeley's words and actions. The cover depicted the former abolitionist "thraeshing" (Nast's combination of thrashing (whipping) and threshing (farming) a black prisoner with a *Tribune* cat-o'-nine-tails lash. The backpage showed the editor eating his own "red hot" words.

HW July 13, 1872 545 C

WHAT H.G. KNOWS ABOUT THRAESHING.
And now "He comes among us to ask that we adopt *Him* as our Party Chief!" — *New York World,* June 6, 1872.

HW July 13, 1872 560

"RED HOT!"

Matt Morgan and others tried to respond in kind by referring to Grant's statements and actions early in the Civil War — declaring he was a Democrat, denouncing abolition as a primary war aim, and expelling Jews from his command. Their relative paucity and the General's subsequent hero status blunted Nast's rivals' efforts — in contrast to his repetitive piercing arrows.

During the campaign, Nast took occasional pot shots at Greeley for his consistent inconsistency. Using Greeley's close friendship with Phineas T. Barnum as his fulcrum, "What is It?" referred to an 1859 humbug at the American Museum when the showman billed a short black man as the missing link between apes and humans. (Darwin had recently published his theory of evolution). The candidate's white coat served as a billboard for his coalition's conflicting views on trade, temperance and the KKK.

Another Barnum sham was the Wooly Horse; he took a curly-haired horse, reversed it in its stall, and advertised it as "a horse with his head where its tail should be." Nast's "This is not the wooly horse" sign on Greeley's wooly hobby horse was an unsubtle reference to the "This is not an organ" *Tribune*.

HW July 13, 1872 548

BRINGING THE THING HOME. —(Dedicated To The Baltimore Convention.)

"When the Rebellious Traitors are overwhelmed in the Field, and scattered like Leaves before an angry Wind, it must not be to return to *Peaceful and Contented Homes. They must find Poverty at their Fire-sides, and see Privation in the Anxious Eyes of Mothers and the Rags of Children.*" —*New York Tribune*, November 26, 1860.

Two months later, Greeley appeared as a wolf in sheep's clothing, complete with his white coat and hat, a Gratz Brown tail, Tammany collar, KKK/CSA medallion, and a "What I know about lying — whoever says this is not a lamb is a liar and a villain" paper sticking out of his pocket. The damaging quote was from his Southern tour the previous year.

HW August 17, 1872 648

BARNUM'S NEW "WHAT IS IT."

P.T.B. "He is the most unselfish man I ever knew. His faith is so grounded in justice to all that no man, men, or clique can ever tempt him to wink at wrong-doing. He is sagacious, although almost celestial in his virtues," etc. ["Mr. Barnum's great Menagerie and Circus are now traveling through Ohio, Michigan, Indiana, Illinois, and Iowa."—*N.Y. Times.*]

Although it seemed blander than most of his other campaign cartoons, Nast considered *Bringing the Thing Home* — his third cartoon in that issue — to be one of the more effective satires he ever drew. Greeley, gloating over the devastation of the post-war South, in combination with his 1860 (actually May 1, 1861) inflammatory statement, was powerful enough for the Republican National Committee to distribute 1.5 million copies of a poster, with the cartoon on one side and 25 Greeley excerpts on the other, during the final weeks of the campaign.[1]

HW September 14, 1872 716

THE WOLF IN SHEEP'S CLOTHING.

"They propose to renew the fight, but not with gun and sabre. They expect to regain, as Democrats, through elections, the power they lost as rebels through war." —H. Greeley (The Prophet).

By late September, with *Anything to Beat Grant* as his inclusive theme, Nast climaxed Greeley's "own words" treatment with 19 separate quotes ranging from 1858 through 1871. They mercilessly deprecated an incongruous coalition of Liberal Republicans, assorted Democrats and Southern racists — now all his teammates or reluctant supporters. The 40 identifiable targets included Gratz Brown as other than a tag or animal's tail, one of the four times Nast humanized him in his 45 appearances.

Schurz played his own composition, *Swallowing the Greeley Pill (Boiled Crow)*, on the piano ("not an organ") as *The Keynote of the Campaign*. "A motley crew of office-seekers" (per the admiring *Times*) listened with individually customized looks of dread and despair on their faces. The quote from Greeley's speech of January 5, 1871 in the *Tribune* (bottom front) said it all: "General Grant will be far better qualified for that momentous trust in **1872** than he was in **1868**."

In addition to the Liberal Republican chorus around the piano, Boss Tweed and his cronies, and leading Northern Democrats, Nast included four notorious Confederates: Wade Hampton, Raphael Semmes, Jeff Davis and Nathan Bedford Forrest, founder of the Ku Klux Klan. A Klansman stood next to him for emphasis on Greeley's ill-fitting Southern reconciliation strategy, while Andrew Johnson peeked out from under a sofa.

THE KEY-NOTE OF THE CAMPAIGN.

Harper's next issue contained seven verses of *Swallowing The Greeley Pill: Mixed at Cincinnati, and Taken at Baltimore July 10, 1872*. It called him a "Chappaquack" who first mixed the pills and then became the pill that the Democrats and Southerners swallowed, but would throw up in November.

Tweed Again

In particular, Nast consistently used Greeley's own words to contaminate him with Tammany and Tweed. Three years earlier, the *Tribune* accused the Ring of "manipulating the Democratic Party for their individual aggrandizement and profit" and stealing the 1868 state vote from Grant by "the foulest, most audacious conspiracy and gigantic fraud."[2]

Nast also returned to the "Old Honesty" theme — reprising Diogenes — as Greeley shook Tweed's hand and a banner proclaimed **"It has blown over."** Next came Greeley as *The Cat's-Paw* (with Gratz Brown as its tail) to Tweed as the Tammany Tiger-cat reached for federal chestnuts (State, Treasury, Post Office, etc.) . Then Greeley whitewashed the Tammany Tiger, "chained Nov. 7, 1871," using a brush marked *NY Tribune/**Whitewash** Reid* and emphasizing "Reform" in four places. Nast reiterated his key Tweed slogan: **"What are you going to do about it?"**

HW August 3, 1872 605

DIOGENES HAS FOUND THE *HONEST MAN.*—(WHICH IS *DIOGENES* AND WHICH IS THE *HONEST MAN*?)

HW August 10, 1872 624

THE CAT'S-PAW.—ANY THING TO GET CHESTNUTS.

HW August 31, 1872 665 C

"WHAT ARE YOU GOING TO DO ABOUT IT, IF "OLD HONESTY " LETS HIM LOOSE AGAIN?

HW August 10, 1872 617 C

One of Nast's more imaginative Democratic Party-takeover cartoons featured Greeley as a Trojan horse — with Gratz Brown as his tail and Schurz as his coachman — outside the walled and moated fortress defending Washington. The KKK was climbing aboard, ready to open the gates after gaining access, while the Tweed gang, Liberal Republicans, Seymour and Blair, and even a stereotyped Irishman stood by in preparation for their government takeover. For the benefit of its readers, *Harper's* explained Virgil's tale of the Greeks' deceptive victory over Troy on the following page.

ANY THING TO GET IN.
You Can't Play The Old Trojan Horse Game On Uncle Sam.

Sumner's Bombshell

On July 29, Charles Sumner — in a total reversal of his single-minded lifetime cause — wrote a letter to "the colored citizens of the United States, telling them to vote for the Democratic ticket.

Harper's editor Curtis, Sumner's closest friend, was shocked: "His letter is a campaign document . . . which makes the Ku Klux Klan laugh with glee . . . He deliberately declares that the Democratic party has become Republican . . . Is the instinct of an oppressed race of no weight against Mr. Sumner's hostility to the President?"[2]

After previously admonishing Nast for belittling Sumner and his other Liberal friends, Curtis must have shuddered even more at Nast's cover on the same issue. In May 1856, Sumner had been caned in his Senate seat by South Carolina Congressman Preston Brooks because, two days before, Sumner had harshly berated his uncle, Andrew Butler, in a Senate speech condemning the evils of slavery. It took Sumner three years to recover and return to the Senate.

Now Nast had Sumner laying a flower on the grave of Bully Brooks as Schurz leered behind him. One of the messages in Sumner's hat read "Nothing in haste. Nothing in Vengeance. (Except to Beat U.S. Grant)."

HW August 17, 1872 633 C

WILL THE SENATOR FROM MASSACHUSETTS DO THIS, TO MAKE HIS WORDS GOOD?
"Pile up the ashes, extinguish the flames, *abolish the hate*—such is my desire."—Sumner's Letter, *July* 29, 1872.

FLIN August 24, 1872 376-377

THE MODERN MOSES TO HIS PEOPLE.

A week later, both Matt Morgan (in Leslie's) and Nast noted Sumner's endorsement. Morgan depicted Sumner as the Modern Moses, as he parted the Red Sea with Pharaoh Grant and his troops floundering in it, while Schurz and Greeley watched. "This good man Horace . . . has brought you to the Promised Land of equal rights to all . . . Honor and trust him, for he will never deceive you."

Morgan "honored" Nast by depicting him as one of the tiny drowning figures.

Nast's effort was much harder-hitting and imaginative. Greeley and Sumner attempted to entice a reluctant black man ("protected by Grant") to "clasp hands" with a KKK murderer, his fingers dripping blood and a mother and two children dead in front of him. For added emphasis on Greeley's link to Northern Democrats, the artist reprised the 1863 Draft Riots with the Colored Orphan Asylum and lynched blacks, a stereotyped Irish hoodlum, and a post-war burned schoolhouse in the background.

Understandably, Sumner soon left on a European vacation and avoided the electoral turmoil and disaster. Nast took note as Schurz glared and Greeley stared in dismay.

HW August 24, 1872 652

IT IS ONLY A TRUCE TO REGAIN POWER ("PLAYING POSSUM.").

HW September 21, 1872 744

"GOOD-BY! MY POOR BRAIN DEMANDS REST."

The public school issue flared less frequently, possibly because it was crowded out by Nast's other approaches. However, specific incidents like the banning of the Bible, gave rise to a Eugene Lawrence polemic and accompanying Nast cartoon on the same page — related to his "Any Thing to Beat Grant" unifying theme.

HW August 17, 1872 637

ROMISH POLITICS—ANY THING TO BEAT GRANT.
Irish Roman Catholic Invader. "The Y.M.C.A. want the Bible in the public school, assuming that this is a Christian country. *We want the Priest, the Brother, and the Sister in our public schools, not assuming, but endeavoring to effect, that this is a Catholic country."*—*St. Louis Western Watchman*, July 13, 1872.

Clasping Hands

Ever since Lee surrendered at Appomattox, Greeley's passion had been regional reconciliation. His lead in bailing Jeff Davis in 1867 was an early step. After the Cincinnati nomination, his May 20 acceptance letter stated his "confident trust that the masses of our countrymen, North and South, are eager to *clasp hands across the bloody chasm* which has too long divided them."

Many Northerners interpreted Greeley's embrace of the South as an attempt to undo their hard-earned military and political victories of the past twelve years, even as the Klan and other ex-Confederates continued their often-violent struggles to subjugate blacks and regain power, both locally and nationally. Conversely, recalcitrant Southerners saw Greeley as their best immediate hope for achieving those goals.

While Greeley's own replayed words and Tweed-Ringer images were Nast's bayonets, his grenades were the handshakes over the bloody chasm. On July 11, the day after Greeley won the endorsement of the ex-Confederates in Baltimore, the *Tribune's* front page featured a crude image of two clasped hands — one white and one black. For the artist, that was like giving candy to a baby.

Nast kicked off with a reprise of the post-Sumter attack (April 19, 1861) on the 6th Massachusetts Regiment as it marched through Baltimore to defend Washington. Greeley shook hands with a Confederate, whose feet were on a dead soldier, as Schurz and Fenton consoled the Regiment's home-state Senator Sumner in the rear.

Next came Greeley shaking hands with the spirit of John Wilkes Booth over Lincoln's grave, followed by Greeley and Sumner attempting to get a justifiably reluctant black man to shake hands with a Klansman (facing page). Then Andersonville Prison was the bloody chasm itself, with Greeley extending his arm over the stockade towards a tiny Confederate figure outside the far wall.

The following week, Nast drew what he probably thought would be the last of his serial "bloody chasm" attacks, with Grant reaching out to Greeley. However, Georgia had an early election, which used all kinds of violence, deceit and fraud against blacks to minimize Republican votes. *Harper's* described the gory details in a lengthy column, while Nast went to the chasm for the final time *before* the election.

HW August 3, 1872 596

BALTIMORE 1861 - 1872.
"Let us Clasp Hands over the Bloody Chasm."

HW September 21, 1872 732

"LET US CLASP HANDS OVER THE BLOODY CHASM."

HW September 28, 1872 745 C

CIRCUMSTANCES ALTER CASES.
U.S.G. "Let us Clasp Hands over the Bloody Chasm."

HW October 19, 1872 804

H.G. "LET US CLASP HANDS OVER THE BLOODY CHASM."
"A Great Victory has been won in Georgia . . . . The verdict in Georgia is certainly conclusive."—*New York Times, October 3, 1872.*

As mentioned previously, Greeley went on a ten-day speaking tour on September 18. During a Pittsburgh speech, he commented to the effect that in 1861 he had said that if the South wanted disunion, he would consent to it, and that would hold true in 1872 as well. After being blasted for "Secession Again" views, he retracted his "cat-out-of-the-bag" statement, as his supporter, ex-Governor Theodore Randolph, of New Jersey, fled in horror. Thanks to his befuddled target, Nast emphasized his most effective theme without referring specifically to the bloody chasm.

HW October 12, 1872 792

Gratz Brown

Embellishing Greeley's abhorrence of liquor, Gratz Brown's drinking problem rated a personal depiction rather than just a tag or a tail. *The Babes of the Wood* referred to an English children's story about two children who had been left to die in a forest so that their wicked uncle might steal their inheritance. Robins covered them with leaves to try to keep them warm.

Here, Greeley was in a deep sleep with his intoxicated running mate sprawled across his lap. The leaves were replaced by a blanket of ballots for Grant and Vice Presidential candidate Henry Wilson.

HW August 10, 1872 632

THE BABES OF THE WOOD.
Lost On The Way To The White House.

HW November 16, 1872 897

APOLLO AMUSING THE GODS.

At a Yale commencement dinner earlier that summer, Brown reportedly got so drunk that he buttered his watermelon. In a post-election cartoon with 25 recognizable characters in it, Nast prominently displayed Brown as Bacchus, the God of Wine, astride a watermelon with a large lump of butter at his side and a wreath of crabs around his head.*

HW July 31, 1875 628

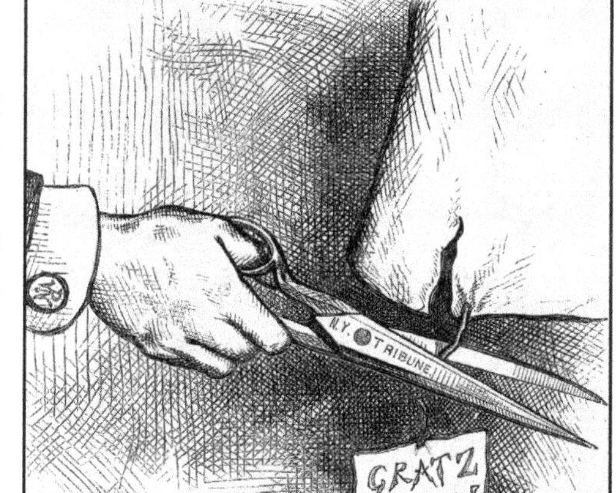

"THIS WAS THE MOST UNKINDEST CUT OF ALL."—SHAKESPEARE

Being debased 41 times as a small tag on a mockable candidate's coat was one of the more scornful campaign treatments any politician ever endured; even as a drunk, Gratz at least was a real person.

Three years later, Nast finally cut the Gratz Brown tag from the late publisher's coat. Reid wielded the proverbial scissors by accusing Brown of "profound and phenomenal ignorance" for his pro-inflation (soft money) stance.

* See p. 338

The Home Stretch

As the campaign headed into its final weeks, Nast used the home stretch as a theme for three successive issues. Its origin went back to an optimistic editorial which Reid published in the *Tribune* following Democratic losses in bellwether state elections on October 8: “Friends, we are on the homestretch, with every prospect of success.” A pro-Grant *Times* editorial wished “that Mr. Nast would draw a picture of it.”

Nast was ready with a *Tidal Wave* cartoon that probably was initially inspired by Matt Morgan’s biblical extravaganza featuring Charles Sumner as Moses.* Morgan followed that up two months later with a drowning Grant catching at straws to save himself. In the interim, the steamer *Metis* sank off Rhode Island after a collision with a schooner. Heavy loss of life, plus dramatic descriptions and illustrations in both pictorial weeklies, brought sea tragedies into public focus.

Nast’s wave engulfed 24 recognizable characters from the sinking “Liberal” and “Democrat” ships, while the “Grant” sailed serenely in front of the Capitol. Along with Reid and Greeley in the forefront, a desperate Schurz saw the German vote floating away from him while a small character on the packaged vote thumbed his nose.

HW October 26, 1872 832-833

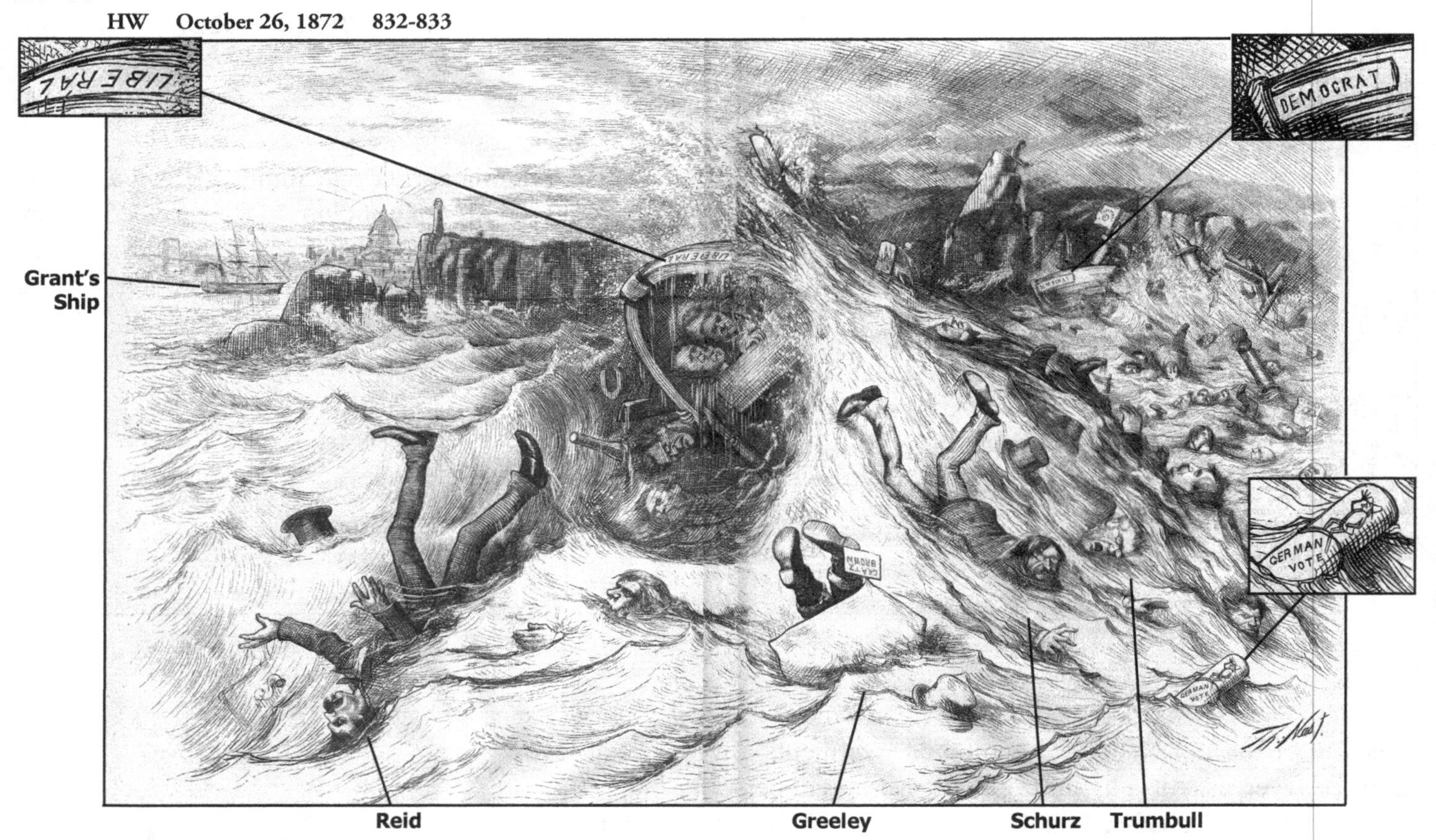

THAT “TIDAL WAVE.”—“WE ARE ON THE HOME STRETCH!”

---

* See p. 325

Nast's second *Home Stretch* cartoon was prophetic in ways the artist could not have foreseen, and its cleverness made it among the most controversial images of the campaign. Responding to Reid's bravado statement about the home stretch, the *Times* commented: "True. H.G. is going home to Chappaqua, and has every prospect of reaching there." Nast jumped on that.

His parody hit the newsstands on October 23, thirteen days before the election. Unfortunately, Mary Greeley died of consumption a week later in New York. Her husband of 37 years stayed with her around-the-clock during her final days, going sleepless at the cost of his own health. Her death and his doomed campaign broke him physically and mentally. He would die 30 days later in Chappaqua, having totally lost his mind.

The cartoon's overall design was a fake *Tribune* front page, dated the day after the election and "dear at any price." The masthead showed Greeley, facing backward, as disconsolate Father Time, while Reid, facing forward, banded to his "This is not an organ" organ, had his head viciously attacked by the American eagle perched on the stopped *Tribune* clock. Grant smoked contentedly on the roof of the Treasury building in the background.

Dominating the picture and the resultant controversy, was the image of the stricken candidate being carried on a stretcher from the Chappaqua railroad station to his farmhouse by his two closest associates, grim Senator Fenton and haughty *Tribune* publisher Reid. Nast's special touch was a shouting boy who was trying to return the Gratz Brown tag which had fallen off Greeley's coat. Tilton, weeping copiously, and Schurz, about to tip his hat, waited at the front gate.

HW November 2, 1872 848

"WE ARE ON THE HOME STRETCH."—*New York Tribune*, October 9, 1872.

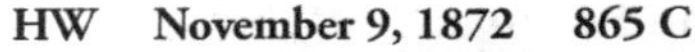
HW November 9, 1872 865 C

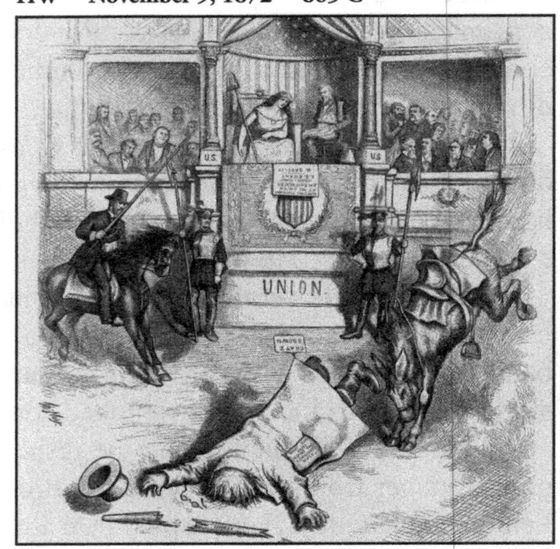

"HOME-STRETCHED."
November 5th His Borrowed Steed Will Home-Stretch Him.

Nast's last "Home-Stretched" cartoon also was drawn before Mary Greeley's death, and appeared on *Harper's* cover on the day after it. In a national joust between the candidates at the Union Amphitheatre, Grant looked on as Greeley lay face down, having been pitched from his saddle by a bucking "Democrat" donkey. His "Liberal" lance was broken, while a "What I know about riding the Democratic Mule" paper stuck out of his pocket. Vice President-elect Henry Wilson, Hamilton Fish and other identifiable Cabinet members watched from Grant's box, Columbia and Uncle Sam from another, and Schurz, Tilton, Reid, Fenton and Hoffman from Greeley's.

Wrap-ups

Nast's final pre-election shot at Greeley's unholy coalition of "pirates" appeared a week before the vote. In a parody of an 1851 French painting,[3] decoys Greeley and Schurz hailed Grant's "ship of state" as it crossed the bow of the buccaneer, well out of harm's way. First mate Reid fiddled away on his "This is not an organ" violin, standing on an about-to-explode "gun barrel of newspaper lies." Sumner, not part of the action, sat by himself reading *History of the Popes*, with Cardinal McCloskey nearby.

Crouching or lying out of sight were the pirates, "under false colors" listed on the sail over Reid's head — Journalism, Love, Peace, Reconciliation, Christianity and Reform. Jeff Davis was most prominent (in the forefront with "J.D." on his stocking cap to assure readers of his identity), along with Forrest, Semmes, Copperheads Fernando and Ben Wood, Seymour, Blair and the Tammany gang (headed here by Sheriff Matthew Brennan).

HW November 9, 1872 872-873

Reid, McCloskey , Tipton, Blair, Tilton, Schurz, Hoffman, Seymour

Sumner, Johnson, Fernando Wood, Hall, Brennan, Tweed, Ben Wood, Semmes, Forrest, Jeff Davis

"THE PIRATES," UNDER FALSE COLORS. —CAN THEY CAPTURE THE SHIP OF STATE?

On the same date, Matt Morgan's last pre-election cover in *Leslie's*, depicted a slouching, intoxicated King Grant directing Senators Roscoe Conkling and Simon Cameron to push Columbia into a yawning chasm of electoral fraud, as Senator Oliver Morton and Vice President Schuyler Colfax looked on.

FLIN November 9, 1872 C

Nast's brilliant response to Morgan's cartoon was in print eight days after the election. He effectively built on Morgan's concept by turning it upside-down. Now he could use the Bloodless (Sar)c(h)asm to: overtly pun; have Uncle Sam congratulated Grant on top of the now-sealed chasm; hang Greeley by his symbols; and envelop more than three dozen identifiable members of his losing coalition in Greeley's Inferno below. Caught by his Gratz Brown tag in the cleft at the top of the cave — with "What I Know about Chasms," "Oblivion" and "Running for President" papers sticking out of his pockets — Greeley dangled above his anguished Liberal Republican, Tammany, ex-Confederate and other Democratic party supporters.

Nast's subtle touches and expressions were among his best: Reid detached from his "Not an Organ"; Sweeny consoling Tweed; Seymour confronting an impassive Blair; Wade Hampton and Jeff Davis in shock; an emotionless Sumner reading a "Book on Foreign Treaties" (referring to the *Alabama* Claims settlement); Tilton in astonished disbelief, with his "Life of Mrs. Woodhull"; and Andrew Johnson trying to fend off a loose boulder.

HW November 23, 1872 912-913

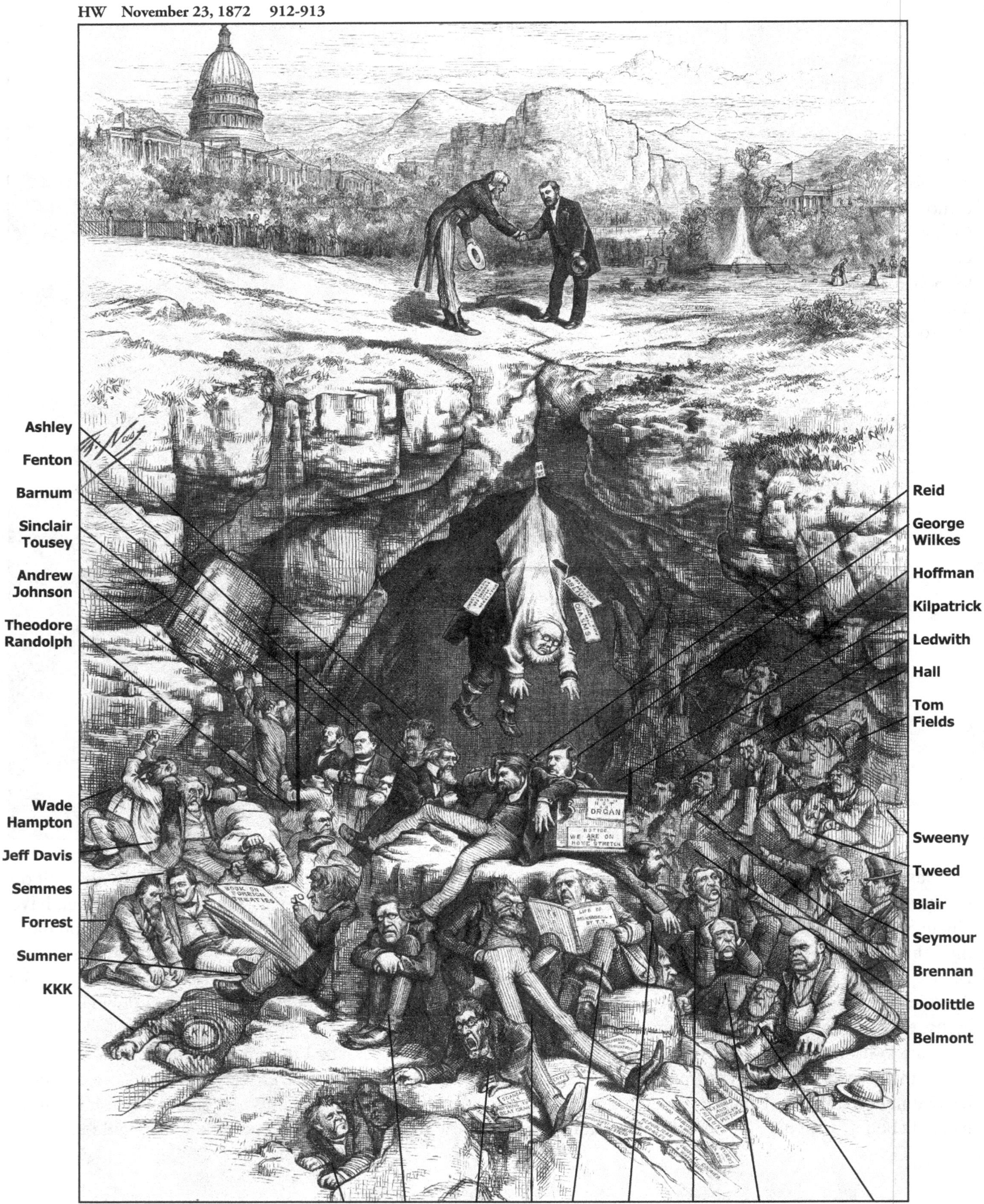

CLASPING HANDS OVER THE BLOODLESS (SAR)C(H)ASM.

"Go West"

HW October 12, 1872 792

Greeley had frequently advised people who asked him for career advice to "Go West, young man, go West."[4] A month before the election, Nast accurately forecast the post-election *Tribune* scenario when **White Lie** Reid would effectively fire his mentally-disturbed former boss.

Nast's contemporary *Phunny Phellow* cartoons were similarly predictive. The *Tribune* lost more than a quarter of its weekly circulation; its daily circulation of 45,000 was equal to the *Herald*, lower than the *Times* (50,000) and less than half that of the *Sun*. Greeley owned about 6% of its stock, but the other 21 shareholders could no longer depend on its dividends. Shortly after its founder's death, Reid put together a syndicate for $500,000 to gain 51% control, which his family maintained for the next 85 years; Jay Gould put up most of the money.

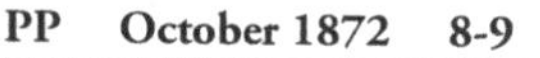
PP October 1872 8-9

WHERE THE TIDAL WAVE WILL LEAVE HIM, OR THE END OF THE CAMPAIGN.

PP November 1872 C

RIP VAN WINKLE (Greeley) waking, after his long dream of office, to find his once powerful blunderbuss useless.

Comic Relief

After his heavy workload over the past eight months, and the additional stress from his recent untimely *Home Stretch* cartoon, Nast was finally able to laugh as Election Day approached. *Apollo Amusing the Gods*, his Olympian Comic Opera, appeared the day after the election, but he probably drew it well in advance. He incorporated 28 identifiable characters: 10 Liberal Republicans, 11 Democrats and 7 members of the Tweed Ring.

"APOLLO AMUSING THE GODS."

He added a humorous explanation on the following page, including brief puns describing 11 of the mythological beings in a *Dramatis Personae.* He concluded with his rationale: *The reader will perceive that this was only an Olympian adaptation of the Liberal Farce first produced at Cincinnati last May and taken off the stage November 5.*

- **Greeley** was "Minerva, Goddess of Wisdom. Very much addicted to telling what She Knows About Every Thing in heaven and earth." The candidate stroked a donkey, pretending to be a lion.
- **Reid** played the lead role as "Apollo, God of Music, Poetry and Fable. He always preferred the lyre to the organ." (Double pun: Reid as a liar and *Tribune* not an organ.)
- **Fenton** was featured as Mercury, the God of Commerce but also Thievery. Nast added a fabled incident of the latter.

• **Sumner's** huge ego cast him as pompous Jupiter, the top god, and "the Thunderer . . . When he spoke, the whole senate of the gods was expected to tremble."
• **Schurz** glowered as "Mars, God of War. Exceedingly boastful and vain-glorious."
• Of course, **Tweed** was "Pluto, God of the Infernal Regions . . . His helmet had the power of making the wearer invisible when he wished to keep shady."
• Surprisingly, **Salmon Chase** was "Diana, Goddess of Chastity." This was one of Nast's better puns because Diana was principally known as Goddess of the Hunt. Chase had unsuccessfully "hunted" for the presidency on three occasions, so he was still "chaste," a pun on his name.
• As described and depicted previously, "**Gratz B**. Bacchus, God of Wine . . . riding on a buttered watermelon" received his most detailed actual portrait from Nast.
• T.T. Cupid (**Tilton**) . . . "Mischievous, wanton, and not above suspicion of gallantry among the fair," was adding to his "Life of Mrs. Woodhull."
• Another unexpected appearance was **James Gordon Bennett, Jr.** as "Neptune, God of the Sea, and Commander of the Olympian Yacht Fleet." Bennett had won the first Transatlantic Yacht Race and had been Commodore of the New York Yacht Club. As publisher of the *Herald*, he and Nast were on the same side in 1872, but would clash soon after Grant's second term began.
• **Manton Marble**, the crafty publisher of the *World* and a continuing adversary of Nast, was "Atlas, bearing the *World* on his shoulders: a very troublesome burden, apt to turn and shift about."

Grant won overwhelmingly on November 5, with almost 56% of the popular vote and a 286-18 electoral margin. Greeley only won six of the thirty-seven states. However, Tammany carried New York City for Greeley by 23,000 votes. Nast, however, was near collapse.

However, one fan note, in particular, must have cheered him.

Nast, you more than any other man have won a prodigious victory for Grant—I mean for Civilization and Progress. These pictures were simply marvelous, and if any man in the land has a right to hold his head up and be honestly proud of his share in this year's vast events, that man is unquestionably yourself. We all do sincerely honor you and are proud of you.

Yours ever,
Mark Twain

Nast as a Target

Nast first forged his reputation as an exceptional cartoonist during the Civil War, enhanced it during the Johnson Presidency, and reached the high point on his "turnpike of fame" with his nationally applauded victory over Boss Tweed. Because his opponents were generally despised by his, *Harper's*, and some of *Leslie's* readers, there wasn't much negative cartoon press.

That changed with Greeley, who was admired as an editor, publisher and well-meaning citizen, even though his public pronouncements were often controversial. He had many good friends in high places, including Frank Leslie. However, when he ran for President, many men who respected him as a person and a newspaper professional, disrespected and even ridiculed him as a politician; only their dislike or even hatred of Grant kept them on his side.

Fortunately for posterity, Nast collected cartoons which portrayed him negatively.[5] Matt Morgan's unsubtle efforts in *Leslie's* usually left Nast out of the picture, but a German-language publication in St. Louis, home to Schurz and Gratz Brown, retorted in kind.

However, the best anti-Nast cartoons during the Greeley campaign were drawn by Frank Bellew, his frequent colleague and occasional rival. As late as July 1871, Bellew, working for *Harper's* as a freelancer, had been pro-Grant and leery of Greeley and the KKK, but in 1872, he switched sides. *Leslie's* already had the high-priced Morgan, so Bellew was limited to small circulation periodicals like *Comic Monthly* and the short-lived *Fifth Avenue Journal* where his well-drawn attacks went relatively unseen.

KLADDERADATSCH

THE LION AND THE MONKEY
Dedicated to Mr. Thomas Nast

FIFTH AVENUE JOURNAL June 1872

MEN OF THE DAY
No. 1

Bellew's first effort depicted Nast sketching a fly impaled on a spike, surrounded by a portrait of "The Holy Grant," a dead cat, and sketches of "Greely (sic), a fool," Oakey Hall's spectacles, and Grant as an angry lion.

September 1872 C

AT LAST! THE MEETING OF THE CHIEFS.

Tweed and Grant embraced in front of the Harper & Bros. building, while Curtis and Nast looked on despondently.

An explanatory paragraph noted, "Mr. Nast can hardly hope to creep into history as a satirist. His work is much too blunt for that. Besides, his most careful productions seem prompted more by the spirit of prejudice than by a desire to vindicate principle or cripple vice."

In a sub-caption to his depiction of Greeley as a jolly good fellow, Bellew quoted from a recent speech by Grant's friend, Senator Roscoe Conkling, about "truth and decency having been driven away". . . by "a war of mud and missiles." Using verbal jujitsu — Conkling and Senator Oliver Morton, along with a grubby Nast and, surprisingly, Bellew's past and future editor, George William Curtis — were doing the actual mud-slinging.

FIFTH AVENUE JOURNAL (Date Unknown)

WHICH NOBODY CAN DENY.

On the same August 17th date that Nast resurrected Bully Brooks, Bellew depicted General Grant in 1862 with his foot on a dead black man, stating that he was indeed a Democrat. Both Nast and Curtis were observing, along with Grant's current Radical Republican supporters: Senators Roscoe Conkling and Oliver Morton and Congressman Benjamin Butler. An inset showed Grant — now labelled a Democrat — embracing a black.

Morton Conkling Butler
Curtis between Morton & Butler

Bellew's best shot purported to show *The Retreat from Washington* in March 1873 after a defeated Grant would leave office. Worthy of Nast, it depicted him sprawled in the foreground with his pencils scattered. Grant, an excellent horseman, was riding bareback, with disgraced ex-collector of the port Tom Murphy — a stark example of patronage gone wrong — clinging to Grant's waist. Hamilton Fish, Tweed, Conkling, Ben Butler and Oliver Morton were in the fleeing crowd in a scene reminiscent of Nast's *Oliver Twist* from the previous year. Surprisingly, Fletcher Harper, Jr., son of the *Weekly's* publisher, was carrying Curtis. (Evidently, there were no hard feelings because Bellew was back working for *Harper's* as a freelancer seven months later.)

In early 1873, Bellew was ill and financially stressed. Nast charitably sent him $25, for which his harsh depictor thanked him and offered to provide some free drawings for Nast's next Almanac. Bellew kept his promise.

FIFTH AVENUE JOURNAL October 12, 1872

Curtis & Fletcher Harper, Jr.

FRANK BELLEW'S CARTOON No. 2.

Fish

Tweed

Conkling

Butler

Morton

THE RETREAT FROM WASHINGTON MARCH 1873.

Probably in response to Nast's *Romish Politics — Anything to Beat Grant* cartoon, an unidentified Catholic publication responded. **Nast-y** was used in a number of diatribes and cartoons aimed at the artist, but its origin is unknown. (It wasn't here, and it wasn't Bellew, who always used a triangle to sign his work.)

THE SLANDERER AT HIS OLD WORK.

Chapter 27
Credit Mobilier

Ego

When the Greeley campaign was over, Thomas Nast was only 32 years old. He had fought and helped win six major historic contests: the Civil War, Lincoln's reelection, Johnson's repudiation, Tweed's downfall, and Grant's electoral victories in 1868 and 1872. He had rushed along the "turnpikes of fame" prophesied for him twelve years earlier when he was courting Sallie, and become the country's best known caricaturist.

He would live another 30 years; retain an exclusivity agreement with Harper & Brothers through 1886 (when he voluntarily withdrew); and draw three-quarters of his work for the *Weekly* during his final 14 years there. While some of his cartoons reached the relatively consistent artistic, satirical and journalistic heights of his first decade at *Harper's*, most did not.

The harsh reality was that Nast could no longer readily find glaring news-worthy targets to attack in *non-election years*, as he had with Tweed in 1870-71. Instead he steadfastly defended the Grant administration, even as his hero's public image diminished under the weight of anti-black militancy and corruption in the South; a five-year economic depression exploding in September 1873; an antagonistic Democratic Congress during his last two years; and multiple scandals which Nast largely ignored but competitive cartoonists did not.

Moreover, after Greeley lost and then died, Nast's self-confidence may have taken a hit alongside his physical relapse. He had to be bothered by the mud thrown at his shining post-Tweed reputation by anti-Grant editors, politicians and cartoonists, and maybe realized for the first time that his judgment was not infallible.

Nast's increasing use of self-caricature after the Greeley campaign probably related to his need for ego-boosting. No longer was he a passive bit-player as in King Andy Johnson's guillotine line,* or losing candidate Horatio Seymour's unconditional surrender to Grant.** From now on, he often portrayed himself as an active protagonist.

Less than two weeks after the election, Nast depicted himself in a quandary, alone in front of the *Times* building with signs proclaiming Grant's (and his own) successes, while the adjacent *Tribune* headquarters posted "The Greeley Triumph Postponed." In addition to uncertainty, there may have been feelings of depression in his self-expression.

HW November 23, 1872 920

OUR ARTIST'S OCCUPATION GONE.
Th. Nast. "It's all very funny to you; but what am I to do now?"

HW January 31, 1874 112

NOTICE—NO CARTOON THIS WEEK.
The News from Washington was too much for our Artist.

* See p. 173
** See p. 218

Health Issues

Despite the victory, Nast was near collapse. Two years of constant work — 252 cartoons produced over 100 weeks of Tweed and Greeley battles, compounded by flak over the latter's death — wore him out mentally and physically. He had long suffered from "chronic pharyngolaryngeal catarrh" (excess mucus leading to nasal and throat infections), an ailment whose effects were magnified by stress. The move from Harlem's malarial air to Morristown the previous year mitigated but didn't cure his condition. As he wrote his close friend Norton Chipman, if he didn't regain his health "this catarrh is pretty sure to go into consumption after a while."[1]

Adding to Nast's stress was concern about his mortgage. Chipman and his fellow Republicans wanted to raise a $10,000 testimonial fund to help their hero artist reduce his debt, but he refused because he wanted to maintain his political independence as he saw fit.[2]

Actually, 1872 had been a good year financially. As a free-lancer, Nast earned $18,000, $1,200 from his *Almanacs* and some from *Phunny Phellow*. (Not bad since Grant's salary was $25,000, probably for a lot fewer working hours). Beginning in 1873, *Harper's* paid him a $5,000 yearly retainer — plus $150 for a full-page cartoon — to ensure that his work didn't appear in any other periodical. (His annual *Almanac*, published for only two more years, provided him with additional compensation from the firm).[3]

His doctor, his friends Chipman and James Parton, and especially Sallie, convinced Nast to take time off by sailing to Europe in mid-March. He eased back on his workload, drawing only 22 cartoons for the *Weekly* over the next four months, none in February. His absence was noted, especially his silence as a Republican scandal exploded in Congress. He also completed the last of his 52 highly-finished illustrations for *The Pickwick Papers*, which Harper & Bros. published shortly afterward.

Credit Mobilier

Corruption was widespread in post-Civil War America, facilitated by the spoils and patronage system put in place by President Andrew Jackson. Politicians, appointees, judges, editors, reporters, businessmen, lawyers, lobbyists and bankers all participated. As today, both true and false allegations flew widely and wildly in the press.

During Nast's prime years, the expansion of the telegraph and the railroads were key drivers of the economy. Railroads, in particular, depended on government charters, land grants, subsidies and bonds. Consequently, they were subject to all kinds of corruption at local, state and federal levels — providing plenty of potential for caricaturists.

He had portrayed the Erie Railroad Ring of Jim Fisk and Jay Gould,* was familiar with Cornelius Vanderbilt and the New York Central, and had drawn a cartoon depicting fanatic Wendell Phillips lying across the track of the Union Pacific trying to stop its progress.**

The Union Pacific Railroad was probably the most important American construction project of the last half of the nineteenth century because it connected the Atlantic and Pacific coasts for the first time. The Congressional scandal surrounding it encompassed key Republicans — including both of Grant's Vice Presidents and two future Presidential candidates — and had a national impact comparable to that of Watergate, just over a century later.

---

* See p. 287
** See p. 222

George Francis Train

Credit Mobilier was initiated by Train, an eccentric shipping and railroad entrepreneur. An inveterate traveler with successful transportation businesses on four continents, Train claimed to be the inspiration for *Around the World in 80 Days*, Jules Verne's 1873 novel.

Train knew Lincoln personally and had discussed a transcontinental route with him in 1859. As President, Lincoln wanted the road built in hopes that it would cement California to the Union, but was too focused on winning the Civil War to have the government undertake huge railroad projects. In 1862, he backed the issuance of a Congressional charter to Train to build the Union Pacific from Omaha, Nebraska to California.

Train organized a construction company called Credit Mobilier of America, and assigned his contractual rights to it. (He named it after a French system of credit based on mobile personal property.) In the initial $1.4 million stock subscription, Train's $150,000 was "the pint of water that started the great wheel of the machinery."[4]

HW April 14, 1866 284

In addition to construction, Credit Mobilier's purported business objective was to purchase land along the railroad's prospective route and benefit by its rise in value. However, under the auspices of Train's selected president, Thomas Durant, and the company's ultimate financier, Oakes Ames, its nefarious operational goal was to create huge profits by inflating expenses billed to the government. Work which cost $16,000 to $48,000 a mile depending on specific topography, was charged at twice that or more. Without competitive bidding or realistic auditing, Credit Mobilier made a secret profit in excess of $16 million on an investment of less than $3 million.[5]

Train, always on the move to the next big thing, left the company around 1865, and later vigorously campaigned for the 1872 Presidency, making hundreds of speeches over three years. Nast depicted him in the 1866 Grand Masquerade Ball with an obvious pun, and also accurately included him at the Liberal Republican Cincinnati Convention six years later (although many of Train's extreme views favored revolutionaries like the Irish Fenians and the Paris Commune).

HW April 13, 1872 284

THE CINCINNATI CONVENTION, IN A PICKWICKIAN SENSE.

Train

Oakes Ames

The largest original shareholders, with a $200,000 investment, were the Ames brothers — Oakes and Oliver — wealthy pick and shovel manufacturers whose fortunes rose during the California gold rush and boomed during the Civil War. They also made swords and bayonets and were Massachusetts friends of Train (who began his career in Boston). Oakes became a Republican Congressman in 1863 and served on the Pacific Railroad Committee.

Construction started that year under Train and Durant, his president, promoter and engineer. They made little progress until 1865 when, reportedly at Lincoln's request, Oakes invested a large chunk of his family's capital. Grenville Dodge, a Union general and talented engineer who was familiar with the Western territory, took over construction in May 1866 and personally drove the final spike — steel, not gold — three years later in Promontory, Utah. Central Pacific president and California Governor Leland Stanford, who built the connecting piece from Sacramento through the Sierra Nevada range, did the reciprocal honors.

While Durant probably initiated the overcharging and Dodge continued it, Oakes installed his brother Oliver as president in 1866 and master-minded the scheme. To ensure Congressional good will when it came to subsidies, additional land grants (if needed), and possible contractual revisions — as well as to reward some of his friends — Oakes offered stock to more than a dozen key Republican legislators without revealing why their potential investment would be so profitable. Some refused or quickly returned their proffered shares, but not all. The takers paid far below its true value; some, without cash, had their bargain price deducted from larger future dividends.

The recipients included Grant's first Vice President, former Speaker Schuyler Colfax; his second, Henry Wilson (MA); Senators James Harlan (IA) and James Patterson (NH); and the chairs of the House Judiciary, Appropriations, and Ways and Means Committees. The sole Democrat, James Brooks, owner of the *New York Express* newspaper, was bought off with stock at his insistence, to ensure his silence as a member of the Pacific Railroad Committee.

Ames made a fatal mistake when he tried to squeeze out Henry McComb, one of Train's original shareholders. McComb sued him in Philadelphia, and produced three 1868 incriminating letters from Ames as evidence. News of the lawsuit broke the scandal wide open.

Charles Dana's anti-Grant *New York Sun* got hold of the story, which — erroneously, as it turned out — listed Speaker James Blaine as a recipient, along with a dozen others. The paper timed its September 4, 1872 release to damage Blaine who was up for reelection in Maine the following week.[6]

Blaine, in fact, did not receive stock in Credit Mobilier. However, he had blatantly used his influence as Speaker for financial gain in connection with other railroad legislation, then lied about it, and ultimately paid the political price over the next three Presidential elections.

"White Lie" Reid's *Tribune* ("not an organ") also piled on, hoping to revive an almost hopeless cause.

Three weeks after the *Sun's* first disclosure, Curtis commented in *Harper's* — blasting the "Greeley press" and doubting wrong-doing without definitive proof.[7] Over time, Curtis would vehemently defend Vice President Colfax and House Appropriations Committee Chairman (and 1880 Presidential candidate) James Garfield, neither of whom had totally provable clean hands, (although Curtis claimed they did).[8]

After Congress returned, House Investigating Committee Chairman Luke Poland (VT.) held explosive hearings during January. Ames and most of the recipients lied. The Committee Report issued on February 18 recommended that Ames and Brooks be expelled; to the disgust of *Harper's* and many others, they were "harshly censored" instead. Both died within three months.

September 4, 1872

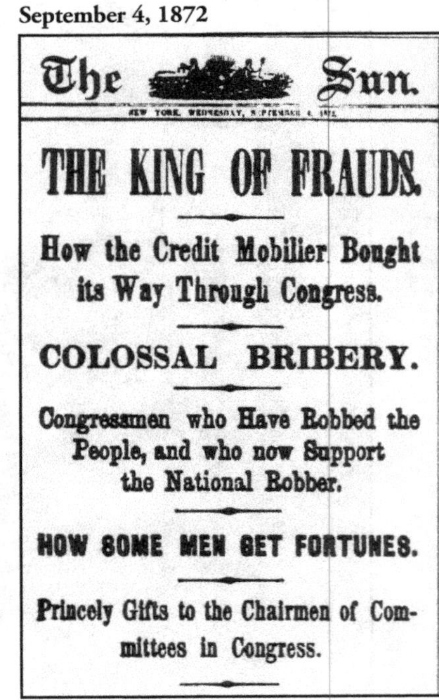

The Sun.

THE KING OF FRAUDS.

How the Credit Mobilier Bought its Way Through Congress.

COLOSSAL BRIBERY.

Congressmen who Have Robbed the People, and who now Support the National Robber.

HOW SOME MEN GET FORTUNES.

Princely Gifts to the Chairmen of Committees in Congress.

Chipman

All but one of the Congressmen tarred by the scandal were Republicans. (Brooks was the lone Democrat). Grant had no involvement, but both his Vice Presidents did. Norton Chipman, now a Congressional delegate from Washington and a close friend of both Grant and Nast, was in a quandary. He wanted to protect Grant whose month-away Inauguration was already shadowed by the fallout.

Accordingly, Chipman wrote Nast on January 26, 1873, asking him to hold off depicting the "dreadful disclosures": "The whole subject offers a rich theme for your pencil, but I doubt the wisdom of your availing yourself of it." Chipman accused the stock-takers of idiocy and cowardice for lying, cover-ups and misleading the public, "With absolutely an innocent transaction to start with, the actors in this matter have by their conduct magnified it into a stupendous fraud."[9]

Nast responded immediately and agreed to hold off for the time being: "The Credit Mobilier makes me sick, and I haven't the heart to touch it yet."[10] Nast's relationships with Chipman and Grant had grown to the point where loyalty superseded objectivity. Friendship triumphed, and Sallie and he spent a bitter cold Inauguration week as guests of the Chipmans. They visited Grant at the White House the evening before he was sworn in.

Nast and other cartoonists believed — with good reason — that Garfield was guilty and had lied. When the two crossed paths during an Inauguration event, Nast pointedly refused to shake the future President's hand.[11] Garfield would win without his help in 1880 as *Harper's* designated other cartoonists to support his candidacy.

Keppler

Accordingly, Nast was a blank slate during February. Into the vacuum, *Leslie's* fired away weekly through mid-March, with Nast-quality cartoons by Joseph Keppler, now a regular, and an occasional weak effort by Matt Morgan. For the first time, Nast had a strong competitor whose wit and skill were comparable, although Keppler's status and the editorial quality of his publication were not.

FLIN February 1, 1873 336

INJURED INNOCENTS.
First Boy— "I didn't touch it sir; I only smelt it." Second Boy— "I just took a little piece, sir, but I put it back again whole." Third Boy— "I just had a very small piece, sir; but I found it had a bad smell about it, and I didn't keep it." Fourth Boy— "I did have a piece, sir; but then I bought it for a penny, of that other boy, who said it was all right, and that you wouldn't mind it." Uncle Sam— "Very fine excuses; but still my cake is gone; and look, you rascals, there are crumbs on all your fingers!"

FLIN February 15, 1873 368

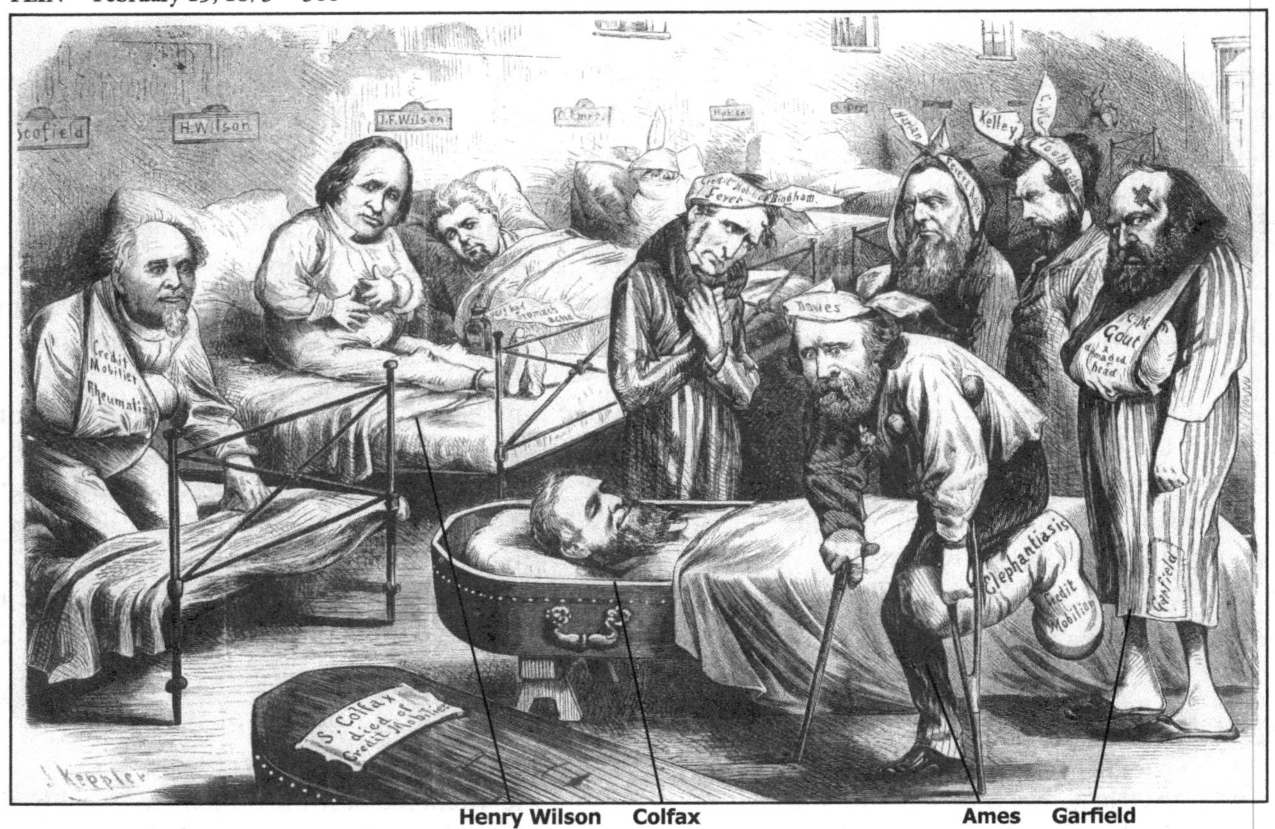

Henry Wilson Colfax Ames Garfield

THE DEAD, THE DYING AND THE CRIPPLED IN THE CREDIT MOBILIER WARD OF THE UNION PACIFIC HOSPITAL.

FLIN March 1, 1873 400

"Blaine escaped" Garfield

Henry Wilson Colfax Ames

WHAT IS FUN TO THE ELEPHANT IS DEATH TO THE CHICKENS.

Finally . . . Nast Returns

Of course, Nast's absence was noted with needling and derision by practically every consequential anti-Grant newspaper. Most of them had strongly supported Greeley, and this was a chance to get even with his chief tormentor. Finally, *Harper's* struck back with a full-column satire as the lead on the editorial page in the March 15 post-dated issue, available the day after the Inauguration, and probably written by Nast.

TOM NAST NOT DEAD! . . . Complete Success of the Kentucky Expedition . . . The Great Caricaturist Discovered in the Wilds of New Jersey. The text also explained that its celebrity artist had been busy illustrating a new *Harper's* edition of *The Pickwick Papers*.

Nast finally returned to pictorial action in the same issue, retaliating against a dozen of his press attackers by utilizing "the best defense is a good offense," as his somewhat lame theme. While Justice pointed an accusing finger at the disgraced Congressmen, she looked away from them to glare at "the Saints of the Press" while admonishing "Let him that has not betrayed the trust of the people, and is without stain, cast the first stone."

Quite obviously, the left half of the cartoon lacked the spirit and wit of Nast's reelection efforts, as if he reluctantly went through the motions of portraying the devastated culprits. Only Ames looked strong and steadfast, holding his stock certificates as "bait." Garfield was in shadow as though Nast wasn't absolutely certain about him. The *Tribune* quote underneath mirrored what Chipman had written in his letter, with a bow to his Inauguration host.

On the facing page, Nast's vitriolic juices were flowing again as he lit into both the local and national anti-Grant press. Dana of the *Spotted Sun*, Whitelaw Reid of the *Tribune*, James Gordon Bennett, Jr. of the *Herald*, Manton Marble of the *World*, Brick Pomeroy of the flame-throwing *Democrat*, Theodore Tilton (back at his *Golden Age*) and Joseph Howard of the *Star Forger,*[12] were all well depicted, as Nast had plenty of time to do so.

Notable among his targets were Horace White of the *Chicago Tribune*, Samuel Bowles of the *Springfield Republican* (stooping, rear view) and Henry Watterson of the *Louisville Courier-Journal* in the act of throwing mud. All were major players in instigating and supporting the Liberal Republican movement a year earlier.

Harper's political editor George William Curtis was ill during the first half of 1873, recuperating at his vacation home in Massachusetts. He didn't see the cartoon before publication, and never got over the inclusion of Colfax and Garfield (whom he believed to be innocent, as noted previously). The cartoon would cause both Curtis and Nast plenty of consternation when Garfield ran for President seven years later.

Nast closed out the specific subject a week later, depicting Brooks and Ames as *The Cherubs of the Credit Mobilier — From a Painting by Ben Butler*. Butler had defended Ames, his longtime Massachusetts friend, against expulsion, not surprising for the man whom Nast and others considered almost totally corrupt. He was smart enough to avoid the poisonous stock, and chose to make his Credit Mobilier money through legitimate legal fees.

As previously mentioned, both cherubs went to Heaven (or wherever) within three months.

Reverting to his innocuous, protective style, Nast warned the impersonal Senators, three of whom were guilty of taking bribes from Ames.

HW March 22, 1873 220

THE CHERUBS OF THE CREDIT MOBILIER — From A Painting By Ben Butler.

HW March 29, 1873 256

A WARNING TO THE UNITED STATES SENATE.
Don't let it come to this.

HW March 15, 1873 208-209

EVERY PUBLIC QUESTION WITH AN EYE ONLY TO THE PUBLIC GOOD.

"Well, the wickedness of all of it is, not that these men were bribed or corruptly influenced, but that they betrayed the trust of the people, deceived their constituents, and by their evasions and falsehoods confessed the transaction to be disgraceful."—*New York Tribune*, February 19, 1873.

Justice (To the Saints of the Press). "Let him that has not betrayed the trust of the People, and is without stain, cast the first stone."

"Finding" Nast

As with the Senate warning, Nast's parting shot at the press appeared while he was on the high seas to England. Following up on the *Harper's* satire that he was still alive, the missing man was discovered by Watterson, Bennett, Dana and Reid on their hunting expedition. In November 1871, Bennett's reporter, Henry Stanley, had found renowned explorer David Livingstone in Tanzania after a multi-year search. *Harper's* humorist paraphrased Stanley's famous greeting as "Commissioner" Watterson greeted his target with "Mr. Nast, I presume." "You bet, was the thrilling response."

The artist, who had been home-bound for several weeks earlier, took the occasion to draw his children at his Morristown home. His portraits of Julia (10), Tom Jr. (almost 8), Edith (4) and Mabel (15 months) provided one of the best family pictures he drew for publication. (Cyril's arrival was still more than five years away).

Nast greeted his strongly anti-Grant visitors with apparent cordiality but with large needles, as evidenced by the lances his children supported. Ardent Democrat Watterson, known for violent outbursts on occasion, had a knife and a pistol in his belt but tears in his eyes as he greeted his long-lost friend. Bennett, the yachter, wore a sailor suit and the "America Cup" on his lapel, and a carrion-eating vulture (rather than an eagle) on his *Herald's* flagpole. Snobby "White Lie" Reid, totally disinterested, brought up the rear.

Charles Dana, whose *Sun* had kicked off, and aggressively followed up, the Credit Mobilier scandal six months earlier during the campaign, was a special target with his hair curled into horns. Nast emphasized his short stature by depicting him as a native bearer, gripping his blunderbuss paper with both hands. In fact, the *Sun* had the largest circulation of any daily — about 100,000 — a tribute to the quality of Dana's news stories.

The script underneath suggested that it was Nast himself who wrote the satire about his "discovery" two weeks earlier. It was a prime example of his new need for ego-boosting by inserting himself as a principal into his cartoons.

HW March 29, 1873 248-249

THE MEETING OF NAST AND WATTERSON IN CENTRAL JERSEY.—[Drawn on the spot.]

"Mr. Watterson was so much overcome with joy at the sight of Nast that he felt strongly impelled to rush forward and throw his arms about the neck of the man whom he had traveled so far to find. 'The effort of restraint,' says Mr. Watterson, 'at the supreme moment of my journey, was positively painful; but in presence of those who certainly would have been unsympathetic, and possibly might have been hostile, the restraint was essential.' Then the Kentuckian advanced and saluted the adventurous Jerseyman. 'Nast, I presume?' The artistic stranger replied, simply, 'Yes;' but the more effusive Kentuckian exclaimed, 'Thank goodness that I have been permitted to see you!' The long-lost artist calmly rejoined, 'It is quite a wonderful event.'"—Correspondence Louisville Courier Journal.

Nast almost never drew his family or his home environment except in holiday cartoons. A rare exception came three years later when his dogs and his neighbor's children apparently made enough noise to disturb him. Over the years, the dogs made several appearances at Christmas time.

HW May 18, 1878 392-393

OUR NEIGHBOR'S CHILDREN.

Chapter 28
President Grant: Caesarism

Nast's Predicament

Nast arrived home from England in early June. He enjoyed his visit there, catching up with old friends William Thomas of the *Illustrated London News* and Colonel John Peard from the Garibaldi campaign, among others. However, he still didn't feel like his old self, and didn't make any more appearances in the *Weekly* until October — after a six-month absence.

Upon his return, Nast found his hero's administration facing several major crises which, along with the Salary Grab, would lead to heavy Republican losses in the 1874 mid-term elections. In supporting Grant, he could deal with three of those issues straight on: an economic depression which began in September 1873 with the collapse of Jay Cooke's investment bank; the specter of "Caesarism," a potential third term for Grant initially conjured up by the opposing press; and Reconstruction militancy in the South and increasing Northern apathy towards it.

However, when multiple scandals erupted involving men close to the President — his personal secretary, other close advisors, relatives, Cabinet members, Congressmen, wartime subordinates, and friends — Nast usually blunted his sword or sheathed it entirely. With one major exception, shielding his idol from direct or secondary blame preempted use of the weapon he had used so effectively to attack the Confederacy, King Andy Johnson, Boss Tweed and Candidate Greeley.

Salary Grab

Two weeks before Nast sailed, Congress was further disgraced by the passage of an act doubling Grant's salary from $25,000 to $50,000 for the coming term, and raising their own salaries by half from $5,000 to $7,500. What incited national anger was a provision championed by the always ethically-challenged Ben Butler, which provided Congressmen with two years of retroactive pay, secured by $5,000 bonus checks. The public uproar was loud enough to force repeal of the Salary Grab and a legal demand for repayment early in the next Congressional session, as Nast *impersonally* noted.

Not all Congressmen accepted back pay. Of the 102 incumbents who did, only 12 survived the 1874 nomination and election process.[1]

Nast clearly understood the effect of eliminating human faces from scandals. They became more abstract and difficult to attach personal blame, and less likely to reflect badly on the President.

HW December 27, 1873 1168

PECULIAR POSITION OF SOME MEMBERS WHEN ASKED TO REFUND THE BACK-PAY GRAB.

Lectures

When Nast sailed for England in mid-March, James Redpath, the owner of the Boston Lyceum Bureau, was one of his fellow passengers. A 40-year Englishman who emigrated to Michigan at age 16, he had worked as a reporter, Civil War battlefield correspondent, biographer of John Brown and, since 1868, the promoter of leading lecturers like Nast's friends Mark Twain and David Locke (Nasby).

HW November 15, 1873 1013

**THE LYCEUM COMMITTEEMAN'S DREAM—
SOME POPULAR LECTURERS IN CHARACTER.**

Redpath's sole purpose in booking passage was to sign up Nast for a 120-city tour, beginning in October 1873 and intermittently lasting almost two years. At the height of his fame for the Tweed and Greeley campaigns, Nast was hard to convince because of his overwhelming fear of public speaking. Undoubtedly, money to replace the income from other publications — now foreclosed by his new ($5,000 annually) exclusivity agreement with *Harper's* — was a decisive factor. He continued to draw his cartoons for the *Weekly* while on the road.

James Parton, his confidante and Sallie's cousin, wrote a script for him, which he bumbled or ad-libbed his way through, while also taking occasional requests from his audience. He gloried in self-portraiture as he told the story of his life.

The tour produced almost $40,000 for Nast, although he had to employ a helper for $15 a week plus expenses. Tickets sold for 50 and 75 cents. In Philadelphia, he earned $500 for a two-and-a-half hour lecture that attracted 3,000 people. He was able to pay off the mortgage on his home.[2]

However, Nast always considered his lecture income as "blood money." After his first self-terrifying performance on October 6 in Peabody, Massachusetts, he wrote Sallie that "The people seem pleased but I ain't . . . I offered Redpath money, buyout, but it was no go . . . This is like some horrible dream . . . I remain your Travelling Circus Boy."

As a pictorial entertainer, Nast generally captivated his audiences, although positive newspaper reviews often depended on whether or not the paper agreed with his politics. He told Sallie: "The interest people show in me is beyond description. When I draw, all eyes are on me to see how I do it. The silence is dreadful while I draw, and when I get through, the pleasure they manifest is very loud."[3]

Nast credited William Burton's Toodles as his inspiration for becoming a caricaturist, and often featured Andrew Johnson and Ben Butler as punching bags.

His last picture was drawn upside down, and its subject was not detected by the audience until it was reversed and the artist retired for the night.

Although he never felt comfortable on the stage, Nast gradually accepted it as a necessary source of income. He would make additional tours in 1884-5 and, after he had severed his connection with *Harper's*, in 1887-8.

Fake News

With a dozen or so rival daily papers for New Yorkers to read — each of them filled with similar Associated Press wire-stories — independent publishers often tried to create news by gossip mongering rather than just reporting it. They often relied on rumor, misinformation from inside sources, unverified allegations and even hypothetical interviews — not too different from today's Internet/cable/scandal sheet/fake news environment.[4]

Charles Dana's *Sun*, Whitelaw Reid's *Tribune*, Manton Marble's *World* and James Gordon Bennett's *Herald* were leaders of the pack. Nast constantly attacked them for their pro-Democrat and anti-Grant stories, especially scandals.

HW September 5, 1874 744

THE PRESS SPIES DOGGING ONE'S FOOTSTEPS.
If bitten by one of these Mad Hounds you will have the worst kind of Hydrophobia.

James Gordon Bennett, Jr.

Nast's next feud was with James Gordon Bennett, Jr., the wealthy, conceited, autocratic editor of the *Herald.* Junior was only 25 in 1867 when he inherited control of the paper from his crusty, intransigent, almost friendless father. Both men lived in the family mansion, and Senior counseled Junior until his death in June 1872.

In spite of his vast fortune, Junior — known, feared and despised as Gordon — was forever ostracized by New York "Society" after he arrived late and drunk at a party at his fiancee's house, urinated into the grand piano in full view of her family, and subsequently was horse-whipped by her brother.[5] Having been educated primarily in Paris where his mother and sister lived, Bennett moved there permanently in 1877, and ran both the New York and Paris *Heralds* from France.

Bennett was a smart dare-devil, who excelled in creating news as well as reporting it, as evidenced by his pioneering use of extraordinary investigations (e.g. finding explorer David Livingstone in Africa) and long personal interviews.

Caesarism

While Nast was still recuperating after his return from England in June 1873, Bennett's *Herald* livened up the dog days of mid-summer by accusing Grant of "Caesarism" — thirsting for a third term. Shakespeare's *Julius Caesar* was taught in many schools and performed in multiple theatres, so the public's familiarity was sufficient for Nast to satirize its scenes in ten cartoons. The catchy theme reverberated in the anti-Grant press, including Reid's *Tribune*, Dana's *Sun* and Henry Watterson's Louisville *Courier-Journal*. Nast had welcomed all four editors to his home in his prescient March cartoon.*

When Nast returned to *Harper's* in October, he went after Bennett with a vengeance, using Shakespeare to fight Shakespeare. Bennett was portrayed 30 times before the end of Grant's Presidency, usually as an ass (Bottom, the weaver) from *A Midsummer Night's Dream*. In an early shot, Grant vacationing at Long Branch, confronted the New York press with Bennett of the *NY Scarecrow* and Reid as asses and the foppish Dana of the *NY Biter* as an elegant hound. Nast's Grant declared that he could no more proclaim himself Caesar than eleventh century Danish/English King Canute could command the waves.

HW October 11, 1873 896-897

OUR MODERN CANUTE AT LONG BRANCH.
U.S.G. "I can no more proclaim myself Caesar than I can compel the Atlantic Ocean to recede, and you know it."

---

* See p. 349

Nast then tormented Bennett with his own "Sweet Music" played on harp (*Harper's Weekly*), with his sheet music containing an ass-headed Caesarism scarecrow. His heading pulled no punches, fighting fantasy with ridicule.

HW November 8, 1873 992

"WHERE THERE IS AN EVIL" (CAESARISM SCARE)
"THERE IS A REMEDY"—(RIDICULE)
J.G.B. (the would be Brutus). "I cry you mercy! stop! stop! I'll give in. I'll say no more about Caesarism."

The cartoon appeared in print on October 30. The next day, Bennett launched a hoax counter-attack in the *Herald* by soliciting charitable contributions for the "impecunious" cartoonist in a "Nast Fund." He appealed for aid for the "Distressed Artist/Black Board Martyr/Deserted Cartooner" who was so poor (false) he had to take to the lecture platform (true) to support his family (false). The compassionate deluge listed in succeeding issues included small coins, stamps and worthless bric-a-brac. One *Herald* column compared Nast's performance to the famous minstrel act of Dan Bryant, whose best known ditty began "Shoo Fly! Don't bother me!" Nast promptly responded in kind, dominating the scene.

HW November 22, 1873 1048

"SHOO, FLY!"

Other cartoonists jumped into the fray. Frank Bellew, now working for the newly-arrived *Daily Graphic*, portrayed Bennett auctioning off the statue of the dopey-looking American Caesar to Fletcher Harper, Jr. as his father shrugged and looked away.

DAILY GRAPHIC October 13, 1873

Fletcher Sr.

Auctioneer (J. G. Bennett)—"Going! Going!! Going!!! Gone!!!! Mr. Harper Has It. *(Aside)*—Thank Goodness, I've Got Rid Of The Old Thing At Last."

SELLING OUT THE IDEAS OF THE "HERALD'S" INTELLECTUAL DEPARTMENT.

Bennett and the opposition press didn't give up and neither did Nast. A year later, the Republicans were about to lose control of the House for the first time since the Civil War began. Nast drew an ironic "Third Term" cover cartoon, featuring a score of problems Grant faced, including "Office Seekers" as vultures.

The press — depicted as a pack of yapping dogs — specifically identified New York's *Herald*, *Sun*, *Tribune*, *News* and *Express*; the *Brooklyn Eagle*, *Chicago Tribune*, *St. Louis Republican* and *Washington Capitol* (with a muzzle). A teapot attached to the NY *Tribune's* tail, declared "this is not an organ."

In the same issue, Nast had a more jocular cartoon with Bennett on his third term hobby horse telling Whitelaw Reid that the *Herald*, not the *Tribune*, initiated the story. Paine pointed out that Nast's targets probably enjoyed the cartoon as much as the public.[6]

HW October 24, 1874 869 C

Tribune Herald Sun

A BURDEN HE HAS TO SHOULDER.

And they say, "He wants a Third Term."

HW October 24, 1874 876

THE HOBBY IN THE KINDER-GARTEN.

Junior Bennett. "You must take a back seat. I was on first."

Elephant

Seth Kaller, White Plains, NY

Bennett played a primary role in Nast's last pre-election cartoon, in which his supreme political symbolic legacy — the Republican Elephant — was born in *The Third-Term Panic*. At the time, and for seven cartoons afterward, it represented the Republican *Vote*, not the Republican *Party*. The Elephant's actual emergence on October 29 — six days before the election — paralleled the timing of the Tammany Tiger's birth three years earlier.

His choice of the ponderous pachyderm probably came from an ornament he had noticed on Grant's desk during his numerous visits to the White House. The black elephant had a gilt-metal blanket which lifted to reveal a brass and glass inkpot.[7]

Moreover, the elephant's characteristics fit Nast's needs for a Republican symbolic image. It was large, dominant, smart and usually well behaved, but stampeded out of control when frightened. Until that happened, it had exceptionally thick skin like Grant.[8]

THE FIRST REPUBLICAN ELEPHANT HW November 7, 1874 912

Tilden

THE THIRD-TERM PANIC.

"An Ass, having put on the Lion's skin, roamed about in the Forest, and amused himself by frightening all the foolish Animals he met with in his wanderings."—Shakespeare or Bacon

The ass in the lion's skin who scared the other animals was, of course, Bennett, braying about Caesarism. In *Aesop's Fable*, Reynard, the fox, said "I should have been frightened too if I had not heard you bray."

The panicked Elephant was about to trample the Democratic planks — favoring inflation, repudiating the national debt, de-fanging Reconstruction, and pushing phony Tammany reform — and plunge into the concealed trap of Southern claims, chaos and rum. The latter related to the ostrich burying its head in the Temperance sand because New York's Temperance Republicans had nominated a ticket that threatened to siphon off mainstream pro-liquor votes.

As usual, Reid was the uppity *Tribune* giraffe, while the *Times* — not generally portrayed by Nast — was a simon-pure unicorn with a monocle representing English-born editor Louis Jennings, whose valiant work had helped bring down the Tweed Ring in conjunction with Nast. The owl, a bird of prey with its beak probably a caricature of publisher Manton Marble's nose, represented the *World*, the mouthpiece of the upper-class "swallow-tail" Democrats, not the Tammany Hall Irish laborers; it carried an "Arithmetic" book forecasting a Democratic win, based on early victories in the flapping geese states of Ohio and Indiana.

Unfortunately, for Grant and the Republican Party, the predictions were all too accurate. While retaining the Senate, they lost control of the House, as well as many state governments.

In New York, Democrat Samuel Tilden won his race for Governor. Nast strongly disliked him, stemming from Tilden's belated arrival as a Tweed Ring enemy. On the *cover* of that same November 7 "Elephant" issue, Nast portrayed him as a "Tammany Rat" in several vignettes, plus one in which he depicted him as a fox. He then cast Tilden in the same "Reform (Tammany.K.K.)" sly fox role in the *The Third-Term Panic* cartoon, non-responsive to Bennett's bray while looking warily at the trampling "Republican Vote" elephant.

Wild Animal Hoax

Six days after the election and twelve days after Nast's first Elephant cartoon was in print, the *Herald* once again stirred up its readers with a front-page hoax. However, it didn't note that it was a hoax until the last of eight headings detailing the story, and many readers never got that far before panicking.

The article reported that on the previous day, all the wild animals in the Central Park Zoo had broken loose — killing 49 people, injuring 200, and leaving the city at the mercy of charging elephants and roving man-eaters. Possibly the editor and reporter who concocted the story and created a real frenzy of their own, were inspired by Nast's *Third Term Panic*. They claimed their "pure fabrication" was designed to "test the city's preparedness to meet a catastrophe."

Nast counter-punched immediately with a small back-page cartoon ridiculing Bennett — in print only two days after the *Herald's* Monday story terrorized New Yorkers. He probably finished it that same day and had *Harper's* hold the presses until the last possible minute.

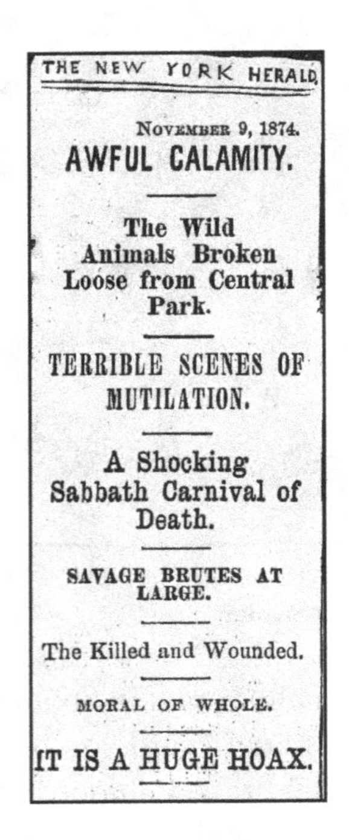
THE NEW YORK HERALD

NOVEMBER 9, 1874.

AWFUL CALAMITY.

The Wild Animals Broken Loose from Central Park.

TERRIBLE SCENES OF MUTILATION.

A Shocking Sabbath Carnival of Death.

SAVAGE BRUTES AT LARGE.

The Killed and Wounded.

MORAL OF WHOLE.

IT IS A HUGE HOAX.

HW November 21, 1874 964

"THE MAN WHO LAUGHS."
"Caesarism is dead. Now, boys, let the Animals loose in Central Park. That will raise hell!"

However, Nast had already prepared two Caesarism cartoons for the November 21 issue, well before the Wild Animal story ran. The cover depicted a Shakespearean scene featuring Bennett and Reid, with their broken pens and spilled ink featuring "The end of Grantism" and ""Caesarism is Dead."

HW November 21, 1874 949 C

"HOW MANY TIMES SHALL CAESAR BLEED IN SPORT."

BRUTUS BENNETT. "Only be patient, till we have appeas'd
The multitude, beside themselves with fear,
And then we will deliver you the cause,
Why I, that did love Caesar
when I struck him,
Have thus proceeded."

Shakespeare.

Inside, Nast had a follow-up Elephant cartoon which he must have prepared shortly after the first one — anticipating the disastrous election results. The agitated beast had fallen into the trap, pursued by hyenas and vultures representing the "Outs" who would now become the "Ins." Bennett the ass, brayed in the background while Tilden, still the Democratic Party fox, his eyes gleaming, was ready to pounce. The caption's inclusion of the word "Hoax," also must have been added just before the cartoon went to press.

Piling on the next week, Nast ridiculed Bennett on *Harper's* cover, as a sobbing little boy in a toga, being lectured by Minerva, the Roman Goddess of Wisdom. Of the 40 times he portrayed Bennett, this was probably the most brutal and humiliating.

HW November 21, 1874 960

CAUGHT IN A TRAP—THE RESULT OF THE THIRD-TERM HOAX.

HW November 28, 1874 969 C

THE "FUNNY" LITTLE BOY IN TROUBLE.

J.G.B., JUN. "I was ridiculed, mocked, and held up to scorn when I trotted out Caesarism, and the President of the United States said it was beneath his dignity to answer 'the mysterious influence' of the New York *Herald*. Now they say it was cruel to let Central Park wild animals loose, and that fellow that played so nicely with me on my hobby said I ought to be sent into the Tombs. But, oh, didn't I frighten the people!"

MINERVA. "If you had a little dignity it might prevent your indulging in so many practical jokes."

Correcting History: The Elephant Symbol's Origin

Historians, journalists and students have been unanimous and ***correct*** in giving Nast credit for inventing the Republican Elephant. They have been equally unanimous and ***wrong*** in attributing his source.

In 1972, respected columnist and author William Safire incorrectly gave partial source credit to Nast's seeing the *Wild Animal Hoax* in the *Herald*.[9] As noted above, the Hoax was published on November 9, twelve days ***after*** Nast's symbol appeared in print and two days ***after*** its publication date.

Safire and others following his lead also referred to the appearance of an elephant in *The Rail Splitter*, an 1860 Lincoln campaign newspaper published separately in Chicago and Cincinnati. In the Chicago version only, the image of a stampeding elephant was published on the back page as part of an advertisement for a Chicago shoe store. The elephant wore boots and carried a banner in its trunk labeled "For Good Boots and Shoes, go to Willet and Co's."

FATHER ABRAHAM October 18, 1864

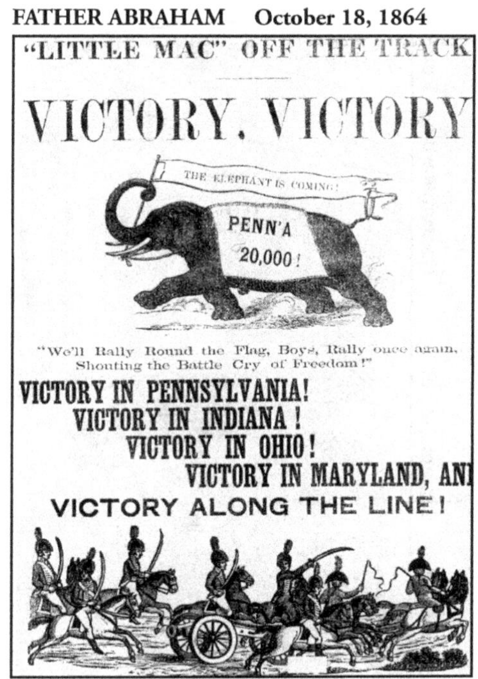

The elephant stood out because it was the only illustration on a crowded page of ads. Peculiarly, the ad was vertical and the elephant pointed north, probably so it could fit into a two-inch column. There was nothing political about the elephant; it was strictly an advertising gimmick — a primitive ancestor of Starkist's Charlie Tuna, Kellogg's Tony Tiger, the Pillsbury Doughboy and Keebler's Elves.

Finally, Safire and his followers pointed to the same elephant in an issue (October 18) of *Father Abraham*, an 1864 Lincoln Campaign vehicle published in small-town Reading, Pennsylvania. The identical elephant as in Willet's shoe ad appeared, this time without boots. The sign on its side proclaimed the Union's 20,000 victory margin in early state elections in Pennsylvania (as well as Indiana, Ohio and Maryland).

The elephant's trunk also supported a banner proclaiming "The Elephant is Coming." The phrase "to see the elephant" was Civil War slang for engaging in combat, making the dominating creature a natural visual symbol for celebrating political as well as military victories.[10] Four years apart, both campaign publications used the same stock image of an elephant. *Father Abraham* added six more stock images to its vertical half-page celebratory column.

Feast

Perhaps Nast's best Caesarism cartoon was timed to appear at Thanksgiving, as he feasted on puns. Once again, he went to Shakespeare's *Julius Caesar (Act I)*, quoting the negative question from Cassius.

Emperor Grant presided at a White House "Editorial Banquet," carving Bennett's "Intelligence Department" brain (Tete de Veau) as the piece de resistance. Behind him, Secretary of State Hamilton Fish held a staff topped by an American eagle, the current Republican Party symbol, while the *Brooklyn Eagle* newspaper was fair "game" — i.e., a cooked goose on a platter carried by Secretary of War William Belknap. Bespectacled Navy Secretary George Robeson bore a delectable dish containing Dana as a bony *Sun*fish.[11] Reid was a haughty roasted peacock. Manton Marble was a crab with its shell marked *N.Y. World*, another Nast pun on Marble carrying the world, but on his claws rather than his shoulders. Of course, the local Hibernian press was a pot of Irish stew, topped by Nast's stereotyped ruffian. For good measure, the generic offering included a dish of "Interviewers' Tongue," and casseroles of "Editors' Hash" and "Southern Press Gumbo."

The out-of-town anti-Grant press also included Henry Watterson of the *Louisville Courier-Journal* and Murat Halstead of the *Cincinnati Commercial* as "(very cool) cucumbers," and Samuel Bowles' *Springfield Republican* as "Bowles of Soup."

HW December 5, 1874 992

William Belknap Charles Dana George Robeson Samuel Bowles Manton Marble Henry Watterson Murat Halstead

Fish Grant James Gordon Bennett, Jr. Whitelaw Reid

"UPON WHAT MEAT DOTH THIS OUR CAESAR FEED THAT HE HATH GROWN SO GREAT?"—*Daily Press Question.*

The specter of Caesarism disappeared on May 29, 1875, when Grant wrote a long letter denying that he had any intention of seeking a third term. The *Weekly* published Grant's complete text underneath the cartoon.

The President was tired and discouraged by the continuing economic depression, scandals and Southern agitation, and uncertain of victory if he did receive the nomination.

Two months earlier, Nast had showed Bennett and Reid vainly trying to stab the apparition of Bottom the Ass in *A Moonshine Scene* from Shakespeare's *A Midsummer Night's Dream*. Now he finally had the last laugh.

HW March 27, 1875 256

A MOONSHINE SCENE.

We do it wrong, being so majestical,
To offer it the show of violence;
For it is, as the air, invulnerable,
And our vain blows malicious mockery."
—Shakespeare

HW June 19, 1875 496

WE ARE NOT PROUD.

Our Artist. "Didn't I told you so!"

In Grant's final year in office, Nast portrayed the press bowing to a skeptical Diogenes: The *Hoax* (*Herald*), *Tribulation (Tribune)* and *Moon-shine* (*Sun*), along with the daily *Canard*, *Hatchet, Busybody*, *Slanderer*, *Rumor* and *Innuendo,* were all included.

HW April 15, 1876 308

DIOGENES STILL LOOKING—"WE ARE THE GENTLEMEN YOU ARE IN SEARCH OF."

Chapter 29
President Grant: Scandals

Pulling Punches

In his first decade with *Harper's Weekly*, Nast became the most influential journalist in American History by playing hard offense. Confederates, Copperheads, Jeff Davis, Horatio Seymour, Pope Pius IX, Andrew Johnson, Boss Tweed and Horace Greeley were easy targets to attack, and difficult for their public supporters to effectively defend. During Grant's first term, he could focus on the Tweed Ring and then the President's reelection.

While Grant had some meaningful successes during his second term, the many scandals precipitated by his relatives, friends and associates put Nast in a quandary. As he wrote Sallie in early 1872, he had "terrible power" to influence events with his cartoons. He had no hesitation in using that power to reelect Grant, but as his friendship with the President ripened, his loyalty grew to a point where it superseded his objectivity.

After ability — and sometimes ahead of it — Grant valued loyalty in his friends and subordinates. With loyalty, came his trust and reciprocation. The President stood by his closest associates and was reluctant to believe that any of them would deliberately be involved in criminal behavior beyond questionable patronage practices like forced salary contributions to Republican Party coffers or campaigns. Although Grant would accept valuable personal gifts on occasion, he apparently never knowingly condoned, participated in or directly benefited from any of the corrupt activities that plagued his administration.

Both of his Vice Presidents, his two personal secretaries, at least five Cabinet officers, Washington city officials, his Minister to England, and several of his close relatives all betrayed his trust. They provided red meat for the press, including *Harper's,* on multiple occasions.

However, for the first and probably the only time in his long career, Nast violated his own self-imposed principles and flunked his personal ethics test by deliberately pulling about every punch he could. He was compromised not only by his extreme devotion to the President, but also by his friendship with some of the crooks. His mitigating strategy had several modes:

• Ignoring a scandal entirely, or treating it minimally — e.g., by naming it on one piece of paper or sign among many within a cartoon. When he found that he just couldn't ignore a widely-discussed Grant-related scandal, he often used a generic approach. Other times, he mitigated their impact by lumping them into congregates with the Tweed, Erie or non-Grant-related Rings like New York State's Canal Ring. Occasionally he attacked the "Press" for initiating or promoting coverage of specific corruption. Frequently, he used Columbia and Uncle Sam to play deflecting central roles rather than caricaturing the real culprits.
• Delaying any reference until a prosecution or trial was over; then, having taken note, drawing as few references (in future cartoons) as necessary to maintain some sort of personal credibility, while *Harper's* — which generally supported Grant — took a stronger tell-it-like-it-was approach.
• Avoiding casting personal blame on identified culprits whom he knew and liked and/or were close friends of Grant — Orville Babcock, Alexander Shepherd, Henry Cooke, and Horace Porter (his other personal secretary). Instead, he forfeited his greatest weapon — caricatured faces and figures — that had ridiculed Johnson, Tweed, Greeley and scores of others. By using anonymous stereotypes, a scolding Uncle Sam or Columbia, and symbols like walking whiskey barrels, he traded his harpoon for a feather-duster.

• Employing techniques like multiple "rings" around a barrel, or a diffusing mass of signs or papers, to dilute the importance of any one scandal, especially the one at hand.

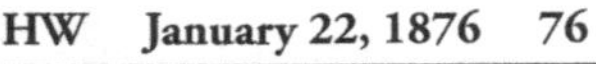
HW January 22, 1876 76

"From the Whiskey Ring"

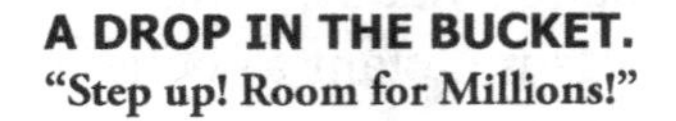
A DROP IN THE BUCKET.
"Step up! Room for Millions!"

HW March 25, 1876 256

IN FOR IT.
U.S. "I hope I shall get to the bottom soon."

The Freedmen's Savings Bank

About the time Nast returned to action at the *Weekly*, the Northern Pacific was at the root of still another railroad scandal. After its original promoter died, Congress revised its charter in 1869 to allow it to raise $100 million in construction bonds. Jay Cooke's Philadelphia investment bank obtained stock control and the right to sell the bonds, supported by his reputation for successfully selling government bonds during the Civil War. After a $50 million French loan fell through in 1871 because of the Franco-Prussian War, Cooke continued construction. Some of the funds came from government subsidies, helped by a loan (an indirect bribe) to Speaker James Blaine, and probably direct payments to other Congressional backers.

As Reconstruction commenced in 1865, the government chartered The Freedmen's Saving and Trust Company to provide a safe place for ex-slaves to keep their hard-earned money. Its investments were limited to government securities. In 1870, under heavy lobbying and related "benefits" from Cooke and others, Congress revised its charter to permit real estate investments — with fatal results.

The following year, Congress reorganized the District of Columbia as a territory. Grant then appointed Jay Cooke's dishonest, flamboyant brother Henry as its initial governor, and Washington political boss Alexander Shepherd as his deputy. Both men were close to Orville Babcock, Grant's powerful, unscrupulous private secretary, and part of the President's inner circle of sycophants. At Babcock's urging, Grant also appointed Henry Cooke and Boss Shepherd as lead directors of the Freedmen's Bank.

Concurrently, Babcock, a trained engineer whose building exploits had distinguished him as a young officer during the Civil War, served as Commissioner of Public Works, with Shepherd as his deputy. Shepherd, with Babcock's knowledge, was a silent partner in the DeGolyer Ring of paving contractors, which he administered while approving faulty construction, payments for work not done, and bloated invoices, while profiting from strategically-located real estate investments alongside planned roads and sewers.

Shepherd and Henry Cooke directed the Freedmen's Bank to invest in Jay Cooke's unsecured Northern Pacific Railroad bonds, as well as to finance the corrupt public works projects. In early February 1872 when Nast was being wined and dined by Grant and important politicians in Washington,* a newspaper item mentioned that he was about to caricature the bond-selling "syndicate." Jay, understandably worried, wrote Henry: was the story accurate? His brother reassured him that Nast, having been his guest the other day, had no such intentions.[1]

The railroad couldn't meet Jay Cooke's unrealistic sales projections and failed, bringing his banking house down with it on September 18, 1873. At least 14 other financial institutions collapsed, leading to a national panic and a crippling five-year depression. Grant, unaware of Cooke's peril, was staying at the banker's Philadelphia estate when the news broke.

A month before Jay Cooke & Co. collapsed, Jay forced Henry to resign, both as a Bank director and as Governor of D.C. — correctly anticipating that Henry's involvement would damage his firm. Grant, once again influenced by his personal friendship with Shepherd and by Babcock, appointed Shepherd to succeed Henry.

The Freedmen's Bank loans for public improvements also disappeared into an undocumented $17 million swamp of Washington debt. Consequently, 61,000 poor black depositors lost their savings when their trusted institution failed a short time later.

Nast, trying to protect Grant, produced a generic Wall Street cartoon which deliberately omitted the Cooke brothers but did show the "bust-up" of the "Northern Pole R.R. Co." and "The Bank of Inflation," the Fire & Brimstone Co., Nitroglycerine Co. and a Gambling House. Over the clock on the tower was "Moral," under it, "I told you so."

HW October 11, 1873 904

THE "LONG" AND "SHORT" OF IT IS A GENERAL "BUST" UP IN THE "STREET."

* See p. 295

In a cover cartoon a month later, Nast bent over backward, apparently to console Grant and his administration by blaming the press for continually publicizing the scandal. That went hand-in-hand with his contemporaneous Caesarism battle with the *Herald*, *Tribune* and *Sun*.

A week later, another generic cartoon attacked "Wildcat Speculators" and Railroad "Monopolists" without specific names but featuring the word "Panic."

HW November 15, 1873 1009 C

THE CONSOLING TRUTH.
Miss Columbia. "How is it that there are so many Defalcations and Betrayals of Trust?"
Uncle Sam (*Chief of U.S. Police*)."Every thing comes to the Surface in our Country; but on the other side of the Atlantic they have the Power of keeping their Frauds in the Dark."

HW November 22, 1873 1040

THE TRANSPORTATION PROBLEM.
Farmer "Granger." "I say, Mr. Wildcat Speculator, what am I to do now?"
Railroad "Monopolist." "Solve your own Problem, Mr. Farmer Despot."

HW January 10, 1874 40

THE SECRETARY OF WAR HAS CAUGHT A THIEF.
Now let us open the Drawer and see who it is!

Nast must have had at least some suspicion that Henry Cooke and Shepherd were the probable culprits in the bank's demise, but he kept them out of his only commentary. Instead, he featured Secretary of War William Belknap looking for a nameless thief in a Freedmen's Bureau drawer, reverting to his visual pun from Johnson's presidency.* He was smart to be cautious because the concomitant Congressional inquiry — which had to have known the truth — didn't name them either.

* See p. 165

December 3, 1874

New York Public Library

Anti-Grant papers attacked Nast unsparingly. A Washington cultural weekly called *The Arcadian* quoted from *The Capitol* while adding its own commentary and cartoon: **"There is one figure omitted in all Nast's cartoons that leaves each incomplete, and that is the toady. This artist licks the hand of power, be it clean or dirty . . . That Nast has genius makes this only the more to be regretted."** Comparing him to the renowned French artist, Gustave Doré, it also included an epitaph for his tombstone.

> Here lies Tom Nast
> Who's gone at last;
> Below he now holds revel;
> 'Mid groans and moans
> And dead men's bones
> Caricatures the Devil

Five years later, the economy was reviving at last, boosted by the Species Resumption Act (effective January 1879), but the Freedmen's Savings Bank was still winding up. Nast commented more vigorously but still generically.

As Nast left *Harper's* for the final time at the end of 1886, some of the Freedmen's Bank depositors were still waiting for their money — 13 years after the Bank failed. In one of his last six cartoons, he urged President Grover Cleveland to "Do your duty like a man" by repaying the million dollars still owed to them in 1887."

HW March 29, 1879 248

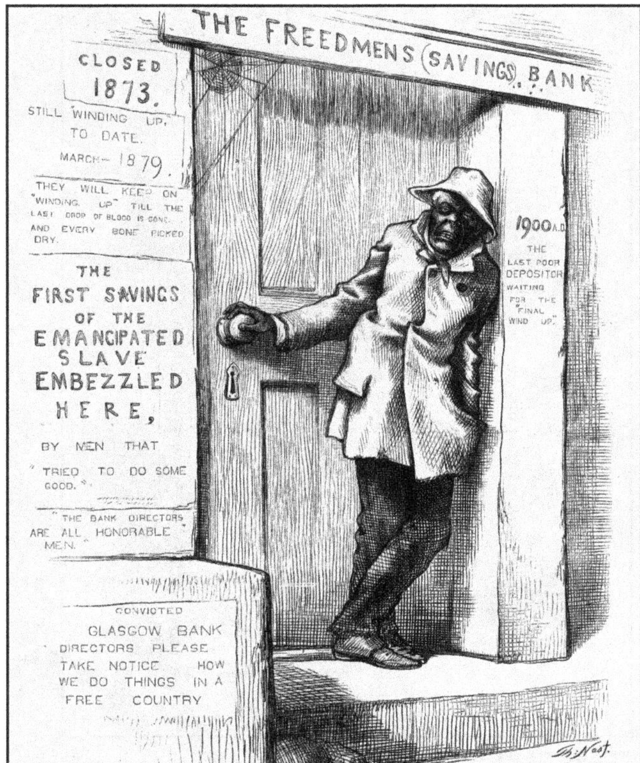

WAITING.
A Debt That The Republican Party Ought To Wipe Out.

HW January 1, 1887 13

THE PRESIDENT'S NEW-YEAR MESSENGER.
"This Year Do Your Duty, Like A Man."

The Shepherd Ring

As the Congressional investigation proceeded, Shepherd's corruption was exposed. He prohibited competitive bidding to ensure that the Ring in which he was a silent partner prevailed, and paid off the three leading newspapers with advertising to prevent its exposure. However, the Washingtonians whom he fleeced through assessments and ever-increasing taxes — including members of Congress — finally erupted. But Grant, prodded by Babcock, fired the city's *honest* Chief Engineer in the middle of his testimony against Shepherd's ring.

Congress reacted by voting overwhelmingly (211-22 in the House and 33-22 in the Senate) to reorganize the District's government by establishing a three-man Presidentially-appointed Commission to replace the Governor, and requiring Grant to select its chief. The President tried in vain to stall until the Senate adjourned; failing, he then submitted Shepherd's name which was overwhelmingly rejected the same day. However, Shepherd was never indicted and left public office with a net worth of about $500,000 ($10 million today).

Although Nast had met Boss Shepherd socially in 1872, Grant's unwavering support of him was too much for the cartoonist to tolerate after he learned that Boss Shepherd and Boss Tweed were like peas from identical pods. (Unfortunately, for Tweed, he didn't have a bunch of Congressmen and a President in his corner.) As Grant's crony, Shepherd's finished improvements in paved roads, closed sewers, and new gas and water mains positively changed the face of Washington from its primitive condition in which he found it — but at an unconscionable price.

Curtis, who supported Grant during his second term, blasted him in the July 4 issue, and again the following week. He noted that the Senate rejected Shepard by 42-6 although "a large number disgracefully evaded the vote."

At long last, Nast did not evade or avoid. **For the only time in 125 depictions, he attacked Grant head-on.** His *Harper's* cover portrayed his idol as seedy, shame-faced, stooped and scorned. While he probably felt almost patricidal, he knew that he had no choice, and perhaps he could help shock the President back towards political reality. In any event, his singular castigation did not affect their continuing friendship.

July 18, 1874

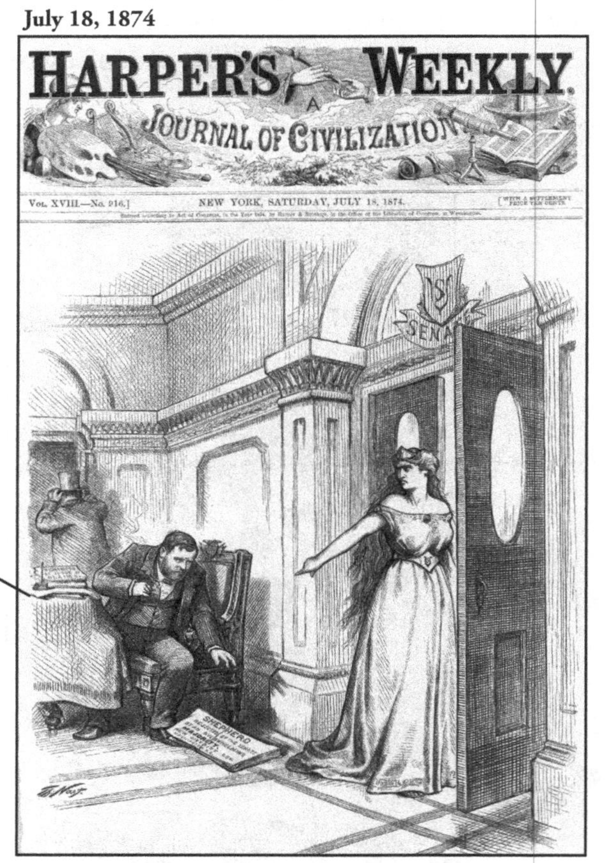

"DON'T LET US HAVE ANY MORE OF THIS NONSENSE. IT IS A GOOD TRAIT TO STAND BY ONE'S FRIENDS; BUT—"

Treasury Department (Sanborn Contracts)

The Shepherd cartoon also admonished Grant for another major scandal that Nast had commented on during the two preceding months. The witless culprit was Treasury Secretary William Richardson, an undistinguished Massachusetts lawyer, who served as George Boutwell's Treasury assistant. (Boutwell, a well-regarded Secretary, had filled Henry Wilson's Massachusetts Senate seat when Wilson became Vice President). Richardson had been a Civil War correspondent for the *Tribune* and knew Grant personally. Consequently, he authored *A Personal History of U.S. Grant*, which became a best seller during Grant's first electoral campaign. In appointing his unqualified, inept friend in the face of widespread opposition, the President opted for continuity over quality, and he paid the price.

While Richardson and Grant took the heat, John Sanborn set the fire and ethically-challenged Ben Butler helped supply the matches. Butler paved the way for his protege Sanborn to get a Treasury job under Boutwell in 1869. Three years later, Butler helped slip a provision into a Treasury Appropriations bill which authorized the Internal Revenue department to hire external contractors to collect taxes illegally withheld from the government. Sanborn left the Treasury payroll and became an official outside agent.

Because of Richardson's ignorance and stupidity in signing contracts without reading or knowing what was in them, Sanborn was legally able to bamboozle the government and its taxpayers in two ways: instead of the standard 10 percent commission, his contracts allowed him to keep half of what he collected; even worse, he was permitted to track down taxes that would have been paid in due course by businesses like railroads and distilleries, as well as individuals. Rather than specifying specific tax targets as required, he would list all the companies in railroad or distillery directories and take half of their legally remitted proceeds. Even when some firms paid their arrears before Sanborn started proceedings against them, Treasury officials paid him commissions as a sign of good faith. Moreover, some internal collectors had been advised to neglect their duty so that Sanborn could have more money to collect.

Butler probably shared in the proceeds. The House Investigating Committee found that Sanborn's expenses included unexplainable payments to lawyers whose offices were in the same Boston building as Butler's. It also concluded that while Secretary Richardson was grossly negligent, he was not aware of the specific corruption.

Heeding Butler's advice, Grant increased the uproar by failing to fire Richardson immediately. Finally, the Secretary resigned on grounds of ill health, and the President — in an attempt to save face — appointed him to the Court of Claims.

Nast's cover cartoon depicted Richardson as an ass, signing the resignation demanded by Uncle Sam, as his predecessor Boutwell (in portrait) looked on in dismay. A month later, Nast "upgraded" Richardson to a "square and honest blockhead," when the Investigating Committee accepted his plea of innocence. Subsequently; the Grant/Shepherd cartoon decried Richardson's appointment to the Court of Claims.

HW May 23, 1874 429 C

"THE NEXT THING IN ORDER."
(The Portrait Of The Secretary Of The Treasury Is Drawn As Mildly As Possible.)

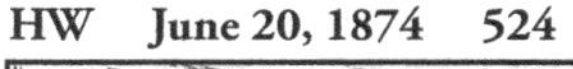
HW June 20, 1874 524

HEAD AND HANDS.
"Chiefs are not responsible for the defalcations of their subordinates."—*Decision of Investigating Committees.*

Orville Babcock

In addition to his hero worship, quasi-paternal relationship, and acclaimed campaign work for the President, Nast also was inhibited by his friendship with Babcock and never portrayed him in any cartoon (although he silently was as corrupt as any villain Nast ever skewered). The equivalent of today's presidential chief-of-staff, Grant's two private secretaries — Babcock and Horace Porter — served as his gatekeepers. Nast knew them from his frequent visits to the White House in early 1872, and maintained a humorous correspondence with Babcock.[2] Porter resigned at the end of 1873 to become president of the Pullman (sleeping car) Company.

A post-war sketch of Grant's staff included John Rawlins, his closest friend who died of tuberculosis at age 38 in September 1869. Knowing he was ill, Grant had made him Secretary of War. Rawlins was a strong personality, had unquestioned integrity, and could get Grant to accept his wise counsel in a role that nobody who came after him could replicate. If only he had lived, Grant would have had a lot less corruption to contend with during his Presidency.

Babcock, five years older than Nast, graduated from West Point in 1861, and first met Grant at Vicksburg. He served as Grant's aide-de-camp during the 1864 Overland Campaign, carried dispatches between Grant and William Sherman during the latter's Georgia campaigns, delivered Grant's surrender terms to Robert E. Lee, and then escorted Lee to Appomattox Courthouse. Based on that well-earned bond, the taciturn, remote President understandably depended on his smart, congenial secretary for counsel as well as execution of his requests and orders. Babcock took full advantage of his legitimate and unethical opportunities.

In addition to Babcock, two other future scoundrels on Grant's wartime staff were Rufus Ingalls, Grant's West Point classmate and Babcock's crony, and George Leet who wheedled his way into extortion schemes within the New York Custom House.

HW July 15, 1865 436

Seated Left to Right:
George Leet, Horace Porter, Rufus Ingalis

LIEUTENANT-GENERAL GRANT AND STAFF.

The Whiskey Ring

Of the several scandals that received notoriety during his second term, the Whiskey Ring had the most effect on the President because — probably unknown to him — Babcock was at the heart of it. Grant's personal interference kept Babcock out of prison, and Nast refused to implicate either of them.

The Whiskey Ring's origins dated to 1868 during Andrew Johnson's Presidency. Distilleries and rectifiers which were legally required to collect a 50 cents a gallon tax, colluded with Internal Revenue agents to not pay or record it. Profits were shared and some went into Democratic Party coffers.

After Grant took office, the conspiracy included Chicago, Milwaukee, Indianapolis, New Orleans (where Grant's brother-in-law, James Casey, was involved) and especially St. Louis. Unwilling distillers were forced to participate in order to stay in business. Only about a fourth of the shipped whiskey paid taxes — now 70 cents and by 1875, 90 cents a gallon. As with Johnson, some of the proceeds were used for political purposes, this time to benefit Republicans.

St. Louis was the Ring's headquarters, with General John McDonald, a wartime acquaintance of Grant, in charge. He ultimately went to prison and wrote *The Secrets of the Whiskey Ring* three years after his release, claiming that Grant knew about the conspiracy all along. That allegation was almost certainly false, but Babcock's role as Washington quarterback and bribe participant was accurate.

Treasury Secretary Benjamin Bristow, who had succeeded Richardson, noted the extreme revenue shortfalls and started an investigation in late 1874. He was in the process of sending honest agents to St. Louis, when the panicked McDonald asked Babcock to stop them. On December 13, 1874, Babcock telegraphed McDonald: "I succeeded. They will not go. I will write you. Sylph."

"Sylph" was Babcock's pet name for Louise Hawkins, a "luscious" courtesan whom he had met and become intimate with during a trip to St. Louis. The telegram would become a critical piece of evidence in Babcock's trial, 14 months away.

Some of the proceeds went to the Republican Party for use in election-related activities. The balance went to distillers, local revenue agents and facilitators, and Washington politicians like Babcock.

GEN. JOHN MCDONALD **GEN. O. E. BABCOCK** **SYLPH**

Source: *Secrets of the Great Whiskey Ring* by Gen. John McDonald 1880. Frontispiece, p. 107, 117

HW November 20, 1875 952

CALLING IN FRAUDS.
"Step up, Gentlemen. (?) Don't be Bashful!"

Bristow, a fearless Kentuckian, did everything he could to uncover the conspiracy, in spite of opposition from Babcock and Grant. Grant would have preferred to remove Bristow, but the inquiry was too far along to do so. In May 1875, Bristow's agents seized 16 distilleries without prior notice. Nast's delayed generic response came five months after a June indictment of McDonald and several others. More trials and convictions followed as 350 distillers and government officials were prosecuted.

When Grant learned what the St. Louis investigations were discovering, he had no idea of Babcock's involvement. Consequently, in July he instructed Bristow: "***Let no guilty man escape if it can be avoided***."

Babcock's "Sylph" letter was uncovered in August 1875. When Bristow confronted him with it, Babcock admitted authorship, gave him a false explanation, and repeated it to Grant. Bristow then showed the President indisputable proof that Babcock was guilty.

To repeat, during both his military and political careers, Grant's single most important qualification for his subordinates was personal loyalty. People who openly opposed him on an issue were branded as disloyal. Conversely, he carried his own loyalty to men like Babcock to extremes, influenced by the certainty that his personal secretary's conviction would incriminate him by association if not in fact.

Before Babcock's indictment in St. Louis on December 9, 1875, William Avery, a Treasury clerk and friend of the President, was convicted. Grant, through Attorney General Edwards Pierrepont, fired the special prosecutor for being too aggressive — in spite of his "let no guilty man escape" mandate. Later he pardoned Avery.

Two weeks before Babcock's trial began, Grant forced Pierrepont to issue an order to all involved District Attorneys to prohibit giving immunity to cooperating witnesses, thereby nixing plea deals and squelching critical testimony that could incriminate Babcock. Finally, in a last extraordinary effort four days after Babcock's trial began on February 8, 1876, Grant gave a five-hour deposition at the White House. Bristow and Pierrepont were present, and Chief Justice Morrison Waite acted as notary. The President could not be forced to answer any question or discuss any topic he wished to avoid. He disclaimed any knowledge of Babcock's involvement with the Ring, and affirmed his sterling character.

Babcock was acquitted on February 24 after jury deliberations lasting only three hours. Grant's deposition, probably augmented by payments to a majority of the jurors, did the trick. However, Babcock was forced to resign as private secretary by the end of March, and Grant appointed him Inspector of Lighthouses to get him out of Washington.

To his historical discredit and internal discomfort, Nast at first ignored and then depersonalized and distorted the Whiskey Ring findings. His two back-page cartoons blamed the distillers rather than their greedy political puppet-masters.

Let No Whiskey Escape appeared during Babcock's trial and made a poor joke out of Grant's "Let no man escape" proclamation. After Babcock did escape conviction, Nast paraphrased the slogan and attributed it to Bristow. During the remaining year of the Grant administration, he minimized the Whiskey Ring as one of many sordid rings going back to Tweed five years earlier.

HW March 4, 1876 196

LET NO WHISKEY ESCAPE.
U.S. "You will improve by keeping — the longer the better (as a Sample)."

HW March 18, 1876 236

PROBE AWAY!

Meanwhile, the talented Joseph Keppler, still at *Leslie's*, continued to lead the charge against Grant. His depiction of a wary Treasury Secretary Bristow carrying Babcock to the St. Louis court-house to face trial in the Whiskey Ring scandal — while a chained Grant wearing a Caesar collar barked in frustration — reinforced the relative **insignificance of Nast's impersonal cartoons.**

FLIN February 19, 1876

IMPOTENT RAGE.

War Department

William Belknap had served under General William Sherman in the March to the Sea and the Carolina campaign. After John Rawlins died in 1869, Belknap succeeded him as Secretary of War. The President knew both Belknap and his father from his army days, and Ulysses and Julia Grant maintained a close social friendship with him and his wife Amanda.

The War Department was responsible for the allocation and administration of Indian trading posts. It was estimated that a $15,000 investment in a trading post could produce a $40,000 annual profit, largely from cheating the Indians through a variety of corrupt schemes. Grant's brother Orvil, Julia's brother John Dent, Babcock's brother, and Belknap's New York friend Caleb Marsh, all owned trading posts.

Beginning in 1870, Marsh kicked back quarterly payments of $1,600 to Belmont's first wife Carrie. When Carrie died soon after, Marsh paid her sister Amanda who cared for Carrie's infant until it died, then paid Belmont directly until he married Amanda and shared the bribes. The six-year pay-off came to $20,000, more than a forty percent annual increment to Belknap's $8,000 salary.

Belknap's world crashed on February 29, 1876, after Marsh made a full confession to a Congressional Investigation Committee in his presence. A Republican member leaked word to Treasury Secretary Bristow early on March 2, who quickly told Grant.

Immediately afterwards, Grant's personal favorite Cabinet Secretary burst into the White House — totally distraught, weeping and confessing — and begged Grant to accept his one-sentence resignation. Grant obliged with his own single sentence: "Your tender of resignation as Secretary of War, with the request to have it accepted immediately, is received and the same is hereby accepted with great regret." Within an hour, both the resignation and its acceptance were in the hands of the Congressional Committee.

Grant's prompt acceptance was an error as he realized after he learned the length and depth of Belknap's corruption, and that his action had foreclosed irreversible impeachment. Ultimately, Belknap was impeached but not convicted on grounds that the Senate didn't have the authority to impeach a resigned official.

In this instance, Nast did draw a powerful double-page cartoon, turning the Belknaps into symbolic vultures reminiscent of his "Blowing Over" cartoon of the four Tweed Ring principals cowering on a cliff, but without any features.* Since Grant was really angry — both at Belknap and his own resignation mistake — Nast was on safe ground if he had used the bribe-takers' actual features. However, he probably wanted to pin-point haughty Amanda — known for her stylish clothes and parties, which she could not have afforded without the bribes — so he dressed her in peacock finery with an ermine collar, sitting on eggs of bribery, corruption, crime and dishonor. Belknap was labeled to ensure his identity, and had dirty dollars wrapped around his beak.

HW March 25, 1876 248-249

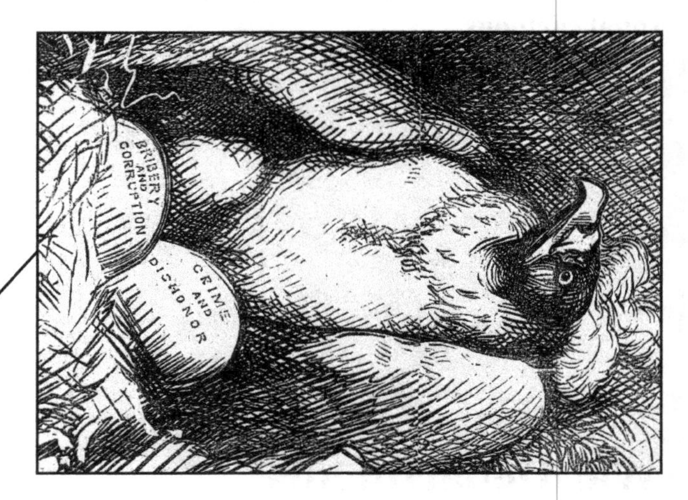

IT STRUCK (IN BLOWING OVER).—PICKING EVEN THE POOR SOLDIERS' BONES TO FEATHER THEIR NEST.

Interior Department

Columbus Delano was a former Ohio Congressman when Grant appointed him Commissioner of Internal Revenue, simultaneously with his inauguration in March 1869. During his 20 months there, Delano ignored rumblings about the Whiskey Ring.

In late 1870, Grant promoted Delano to Secretary of the Interior, the government's largest bureaucracy. His Western responsibilities included surveying, land grants and the Indian Bureau. Corruption was abundant and Delano's son John was deeply involved with fraudulent Indian, land, and surveying contracts, some of which his father knew about. Grant's brother Orvil — whom he was not close to but who could severely damage his reputation where the public was concerned — also was involved with bribes and pay-offs.

In March 1875, a whistle-blower sent convincing evidence to Bristow. Bristow showed it to Grant who declined to act "because it would be retreating under fire and be accepted as an admission of the charges." Delano offered to resign but Grant held off accepting until August, confirming in writing to Delano that he believed in his personal and official integrity.

If Grant hadn't accepted, he would have been faced with a probable resignation from Secretary of State Hamilton Fish and a certain one from Treasury Secretary Bristow, both of whom Delano tried to undermine. (He would have welcomed Bristow's but the public would not). However, he delayed the announcement until early October.

Nast must have been unhappy about his hero's procrastination, but he kept his powder dry. Finally, his condemnation shielded Grant directly but included the Freedmen's Bank and Treasury Secretary Richardson's Sanborn Contracts' fiasco in his sole commentary on Delano. Readers could interpret it as a second slap at Grant if they considered the cartoon carefully.

---

* See p. 274

HW November 13, 1875 925

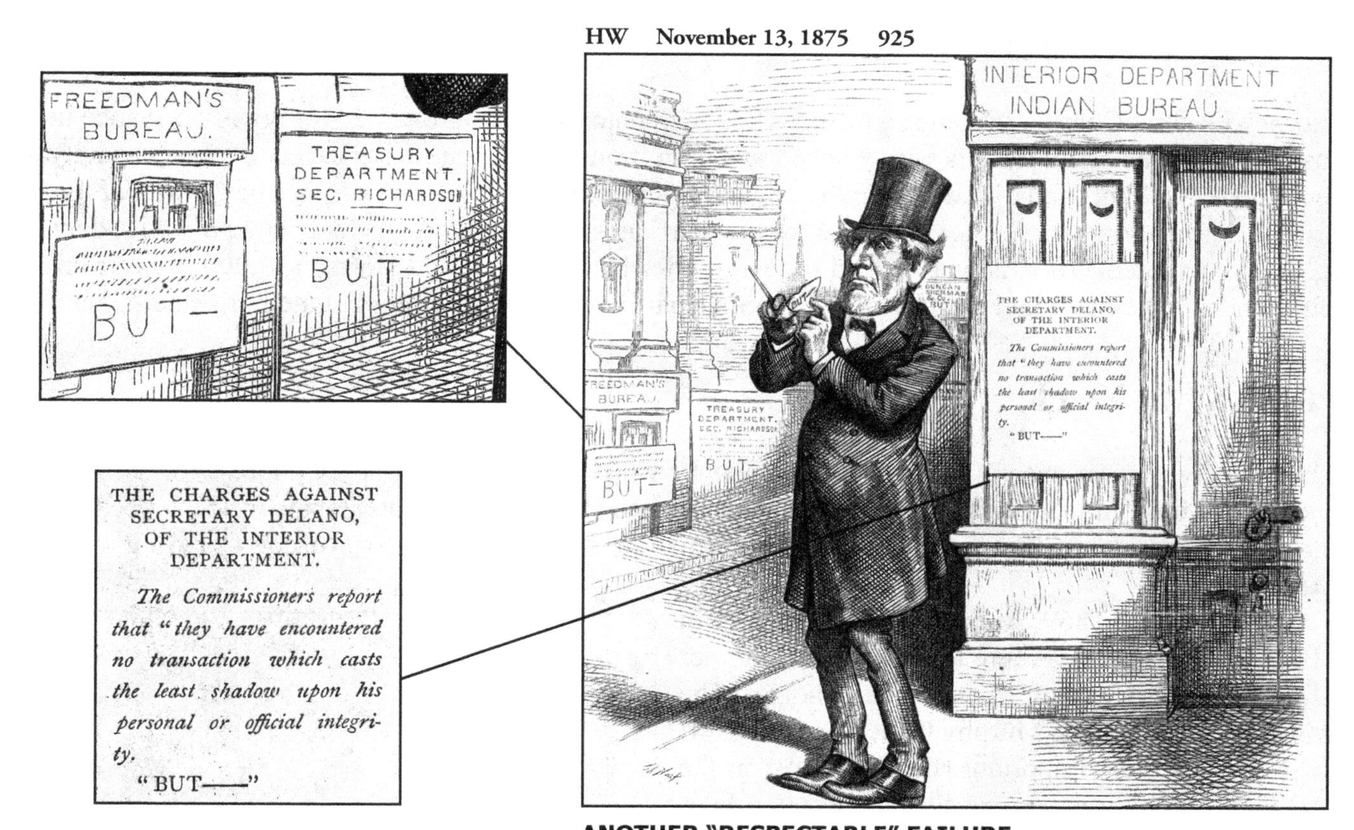

ANOTHER "RESPECTABLE" FAILURE.
Let Us Have No More "Buts" In Public And Private Business Transactions.

Navy Department

When small-time lawyer George Robeson became Secretary of the Navy in 1869 at an $8,000 salary, his net worth was about $20,000. After Congress investigated his department seven years later, his bank-book showed cumulative deposits of $320,000. The source of most of Robeson's new wealth was Cattell & Company, a Philadelphia grain merchant with no prior Navy contacts, which took generous commissions on contracts for food and other items and shared them with Robeson.

In July 1876, the Congressional Report accused Robeson of gross misconduct. Worse, it found a deplorably weak navy, as bloated expenditures went into repairing old, useless ships rather than building needed new ones. However, Cattell's records were sloppy, incomplete or missing, so payments to Robeson couldn't be traced. There was talk of impeachment, but that was already happening to the Secretary of War. By year-end, the disputed, still-undecided Presidential election obscured all other issues, so Robeson escaped justice. Two years later, his New Jersey constituents elected him to Congress.

Before the Congressional Report was issued, Nast depicted an over-zealous Democratic investigator reading buried ledgers on the ocean floor. At least his sub-heading accurately described the inquiry and mentioned Robeson — in his only commentary on the scandal.

HW May 27, 1876 432

BOTTOM FACTS.
"The House Naval Committee, in trying to get some evidence of corruption on the part of Secretary Robeson, went so far as to examine his private bank account for the six years prior to his entering the Cabinet, and to compare it with his account since he has been at the head of the Navy Department."—*Evening Post.*

Justice Department

Attorney General George Williams, a former Oregon Senator, was well regarded for his performance in office, but was burned by the actions of his wife whose social ambitions and expenditures exceeded their capacity to pay for them. In 1873, Grant tried to reward him by appointing him Chief Justice of the Supreme Court, but the Senate rejected the nomination because her expenses for fine carriages and similar items had been paid with department funds. Two years later, Williams was forced to resign after his wife tried to extort a $30,000 bribe from a New York firm under indictment by her husband's Justice Department. Nast never commented on either situation.

Port of New York

Tom Murphy was an unscrupulous New York hatter who was investigated by Congress for selling shoddy hats and caps to the Union army during the Civil War. He was elected to the State Senate in 1865, became a close friend of future president Chester Arthur, and a point man in the city for Senator Roscoe Conkling's expanding political machine.

In the summer of 1869, Murphy and Grant met in Long Branch, New Jersey, where they both had summer homes, and bonded over their mutual love of horses. The following year, Grant made Murphy Collector of the Port of New York, the most important patronage post in the country. This was a direct slap at Senator Reuben Fenton, and a major factor in Fenton's decision to back Horace Greeley against Grant two years later.

Murphy also was a real estate partner of Boss Tweed, and involved with him in the fraudulent scheme to upgrade Broadway which became an early step in his Ring's downfall.* After Murphy took over the Port, he devised multiple extortionary regulations for bilking importers and exporters, and was forced to resign about the time that the Ring blew up in 1871. His friend "Chet" Arthur replaced him as Collector.

Obviously, Murphy should have been a prime target for Nast. However, because Grant had appointed him, and Conkling and the Republican Party depended on him for patronage appointments and assessments, the cartoonist never once portrayed Murphy.

In 1880, Grant unsuccessfully tried for a third-term nomination. Keppler, now a co-owner of *Puck*, summarized many of the scandals from his second term by depicting all the villains, including Murphy, Williams and Babcock, in a cartoon that should have — but probably didn't — put Nast to shame for blatant omissions.

PUCK February 5, 1880

Top: Grant
(Left to Right) Middle: Shepherd, Robeson, Belknap
Bottom: Tom Murphy, Williams, Babcock

PUCK WANTS "A STRONG MAN AT THE HEAD OF GOVERNMENT"—BUT NOT THIS KIND.

* See p. 263

Chapter 30
President Grant: Second Term Issues

In addition to scandals and flack about a third term, Grant had three major domestic issues to deal with after his reelection: Reconstruction, Inflation and Civil Rights. Nast paid close attention to each of them.

The End of Reconstruction

As Grant's second term progressed, the economic depression sparked by the 1873 Panic choked the country's growth. Railroad construction came to a halt. The price of the South's agricultural mainstays — cotton, rice and sugar — barely exceeded their production costs. Many farmers, both white and black, were forced to become sharecroppers who scratched out a living. Economic pressure helped increase political turmoil past its boiling point all over the South.

By 1874, Republicans governed only four states of the Confederacy — Mississippi, Arkansas, South Carolina and Louisiana. Corruption, violence and intimidation were everywhere as the Democratic Party tried to retake control of cities, legislatures and governors. Grant strongly believed in enforcing the rights that blacks achieved through the Fourteenth and Fifteenth Amendments, but the majority of Southern whites scorned their carpetbagger governors, other officials from the North, scalawags (native white "renegades"), and elected black Republicans in their own states.

An increasingly key factor was a shift in Northern opinion, as exemplified by the Liberal Republicans in 1872. Upset by both the Panic and stories of widespread corruption, Northern Republicans lost interest in the plight of Southern blacks. Accordingly, in some instances, Grant was inhibited in how forcefully he could respond to local terrorism and political chicanery.

Mississippi

Mississippi was a good example. Although it sent the first black Senators to Congress — Hiram Revels, who took Jeff Davis's old seat,* and Blanche Bruce — violence and terror prevailed, and Grant refused to intervene. Northern Republicans told him that "there was no sense in trying to save Mississippi if the attempt to do so would lose Ohio." Nast took a shot at both sides: Adelbert Ames, the carpetbag governor (and Ben Butler's son-in-law), was left in an impossible position without Federal troops, and consequently resigned; the Legislature then withdrew the unwarranted impeachment changes against him. The poor black man sitting on a cotton bale had no escape.

HW April 29, 1874 353

KILLING POLITE.
The Mississippi Legislature Has Killed Itself By Withdrawing The Impeachment, And The Governor Has Killed Himself By Resigning His Office.

* See p. 148

Arkansas

Earlier in 1874, as two conflicting factions competed for state control in Arkansas, Grant did step in by backing the elected Republican — a former slaveholder and Union Army veteran — who re-enfranchised ex-Confederates among other actions. Many of his backers then switched to a carpetbagger supported by Democrats and anti-Grant Republicans. Making the best of a Hobson's choice, Grant recognized the Republican Governor and ordered his opposition to back down.

Nast dramatized his hero as a victorious knight stamping out corruption and fraud. Grant knew his Shakespeare well, so Nast used a quotation from the opening scene of *Romeo and Juliet* to praise him, substituting "President" for "Prince" at the end. While Grant appeared in several topical Reconstruction cartoons, this was the only one in which he was cast as the leading actor.

"Rebellious subjects, enemies to peace,
Profaners of this neighbor-stained steel,
Will they not hear?—what ho! you men, you beasts,
That quench the fire of your pernicious rage
With purple fountains issuing from your veins,
On pain of torture, from those bloody hands
Throw your mistemper'd weapons to the ground,
And hear the sentence of your moved" President
—Shakespeare

HW June 6, 1874 473

A STEP IN THE RIGHT DIRECTION.

South Carolina

South Carolina became a tipping point for Northern opinion. Its crooked, scalawag Republican Governor, Franklin Moses Jr., was elected in 1872 primarily by newly enfranchised black Republicans. He believed in social equality for blacks, entertained them in his mansion, and notoriously pardoned more than 400 of them and other criminals imprisoned for rape, assault, theft and other serious crimes.

Republican blacks also controlled the legislature, which was rife with disorder and corruption. On March 14, 1874, *Harper's* quoted direct dialogue from a *Charleston News* article and commented negatively on it. **In one of the few — and probably the strongest — anti-black cartoons that Nast ever drew, his stereotyped burlesque appeared on the *Weekly's* cover.**

Recent critics of Nast have cited this cartoon as proof that he ultimately turned his back on blacks. Not here. Just as he finally criticized Grant for ignoring Alexander Shepherd's corruption, Nast reflected the Northern mood after *Republican* black legislators abused their newly-gained power.

Overall, Nast strongly supported blacks in more than 140 *Weekly* cartoons. A dozen or so were friendly caricatures of the big grin, watermelon-eating type that projected blacks positively in that time, but would be unacceptably negative today. He endorsed black suffrage in several cartoons, but railed against political abuse in this singular case, as he did with whites hundreds of times, and with Grant after the Shepherd scandal dented his idol's image once too often. In summary, Nast conceivably was one of the most prominent national journalists and 1870s spokesmen for black civil and legislative rights, revisiting the topic repeatedly well after it was no longer popular.

However, Nast's outlier portrayal did draw immediate return fire from a young would-be competitor. Shortly before Nast sailed for Europe in March 1873 to recuperate from the Greeley campaign, the *Daily Graphic* — **the world's first pictorial daily** — appeared. Started by two Canadian engravers who had developed a method for reproducing photographs without using woodblocks, it was edited by David Croly, a seasoned journalist.[1]

The paper had welcomed Nast back when he returned to work in October, shamelessly self-promoting its proclaimed affinity to the nation's star cartoonist; two of his anti-Caesarism cartoons captured by the new process, were included in the cartoon. It also tried to woo him away from *Harper's*. Not succeeding, it attacked him.

October 1, 1873 C

MR. THOMAS NAST AT WORK AGAIN.

Harper's unusual cover appeared on March 4, ten days before the (post-dated) issue date of March 14. The quick turnaround *Daily Graphic* struck on March 11, directly attacking the artist with two "colored gentlemen" reciprocating in kind. ("Tu Quoque" translated to "You Too.") Editor Croly, an ardent anti-abolitionist and no friend of blacks, killed two birds with his single arrow.

March 14, 1874 C

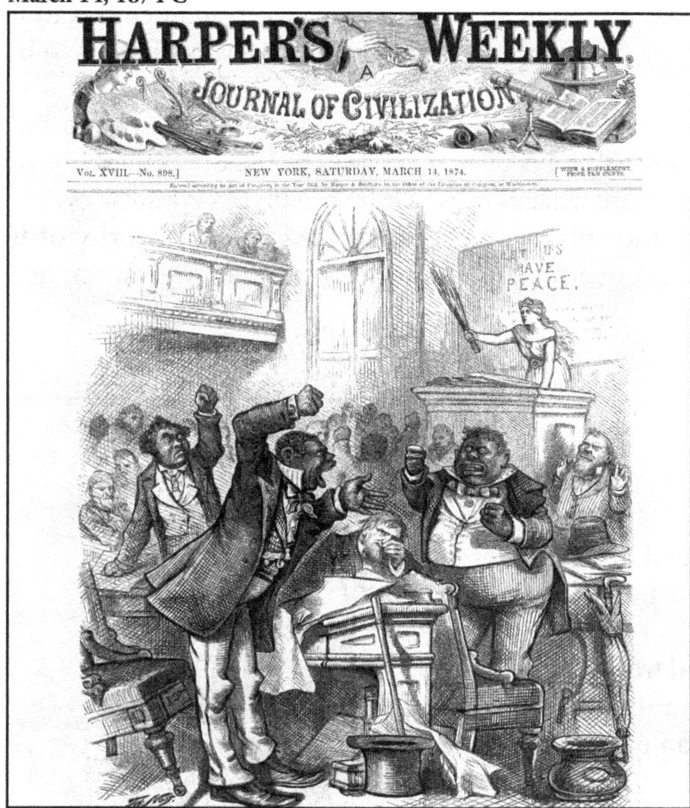

COLORED RULE IN A RECONSTRUCTED (?) STATE.
(The Members Call Each Other Thieves, Liars, Rascals, And Cowards.)
Columbia. "You are Aping the lowest Whites. If you disgrace your Race in this way you had better take Back Seats."

March 11, 1874 C

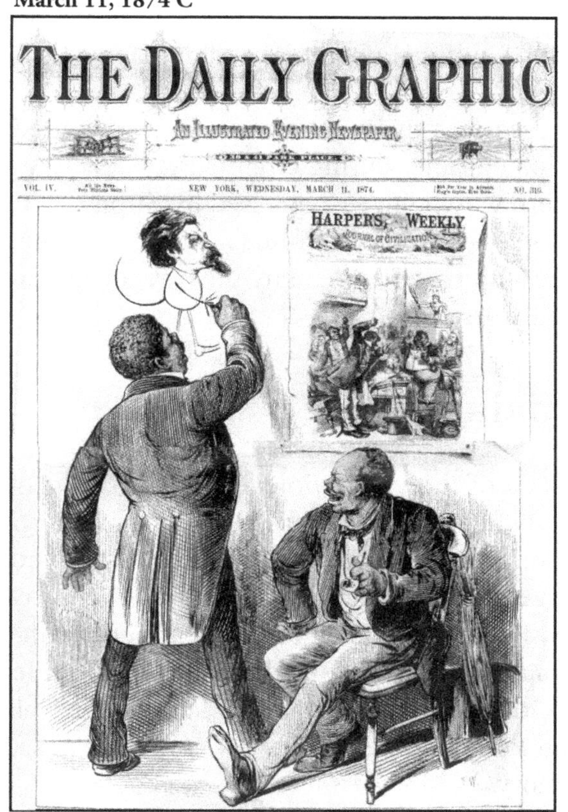

Artistic Colored Gentleman—"I Wonder How Harper's Artist Likes To Be Offensively Caricatured Himself?"
Second Colored Gentleman—"Golly, If Harper's Picture Is Nasty, Yours Is Nastier." **"TU QUOQUE!"**

Governor Moses became a whipping boy for Nast. With a salary of $3,500, he spent $40,000 on living expenses, raised through debt, taxes and fraud. Arrested for corruption and forgery, Moses couldn't be prosecuted until his term ended in late 1874. (His father was Chief Justice of the South Carolina Supreme Court.)

HW July 25, 1874 616

MOSES JUNIOR VIEWING THE PROMISED LAND FROM MOUNT RUIN.

HW August 29, 1874 709 C

FREEDOM, JUBILEE, AND PARDON.
He Is Doing Unto Others As He Would Have Done Unto Him.

HW September 26, 1874 792

THE COMMANDMENTS IN SOUTH CAROLINA.
"We've pretty well smashed that; but I suppose, Massa Moses, you can get another one."

Prominent New York lawyer (and former Mayor) George Templeton Strong reflected popular sentiment regarding South Carolina in September 1874. "Semi-brutal black voters are in a great majority and, under the leading of knaves and carpetbaggers, control the state and are sinking it into deeper ruin every day. Perhaps the unfortunate result of this experiment may open people's eyes and sooner or later bring about reaction at the North where it is sorely needed . . . The nigger majority is confiscating all their property by fraudulent taxation for the benefit of political operators and demagogues or rather 'zoogogues.' It may come to a war of races in bitter earnest."[2]

Moses was the most frequently caricatured Southern state official whom Nast personalized in his Reconstruction capacity during Grant's Presidency. Why? Probably because this was a prime opportunity to reflect the Northern viewpoint as expressed by Strong, without casting a shadow on Grant or stirring controversy about him.

Moreover, South Carolina's state legislature was the only one in which blacks held a majority of the seats. However, corruption in many other reconstructed state governments controlled by whites, apparently was as bad or even worse.

Louisiana

Some of the worst violence occurred in Louisiana, sparked by the White League and the Ku Klux Klan. Both openly advocated violent restoration of white supremacy; used assassination and mass murder to terrorize and kill black and other Republican officials and voters; and battled Federal and local forces in armed revolt.

Finally, Grant felt forced to intervene with federal troops after 3,500 New Orleans White Leaguers overwhelmed black militia and Metropolitan Police on September 14, and took possession of City Hall and an armory.

HW October 24, 1874 878

WORSE THAN SLAVERY

The November election literally was a war. Republican Governor William Kellogg was retained after the regulatory board discarded Democratic votes from parishes where fraud and violence altered the results. The President sent General Phil Sheridan to New Orleans after the *Democrats* requested federal troops, and surprised them by ordering him to ensure that the Republican government was duly installed.

The crucial event took place on January 4, 1875, when Kellogg asked Federal troops to clear out the seated Democratic majority — many of them fraudulently elected — and replace them with Republicans — many of them also illegally elected. Grant had asked Congress to act, but after sending a committee to New Orleans, it failed to do so.

Nast drew a dozen cartoons relating to the Louisiana crisis, many of them signboards referring to Grant's and Sheridan's messages. Others responded to attacks on them from newspapers and Democratic politicians across the country who assailed "bayonet rule," military dictatorship and Caesarism. The January 30, 1875 issue alone had five Nast cartoons. One — reminiscent of *Martin Luther Nailing His Theses on the Door at Worms*, which Nast had worked on with his tutor Theodor Kaufmann two decades earlier* — depicted Grant hammering on Congress. A smaller cartoon depicted a non-partisan bayonet, while quoting from Grant's message.

HW January 30, 1875 92

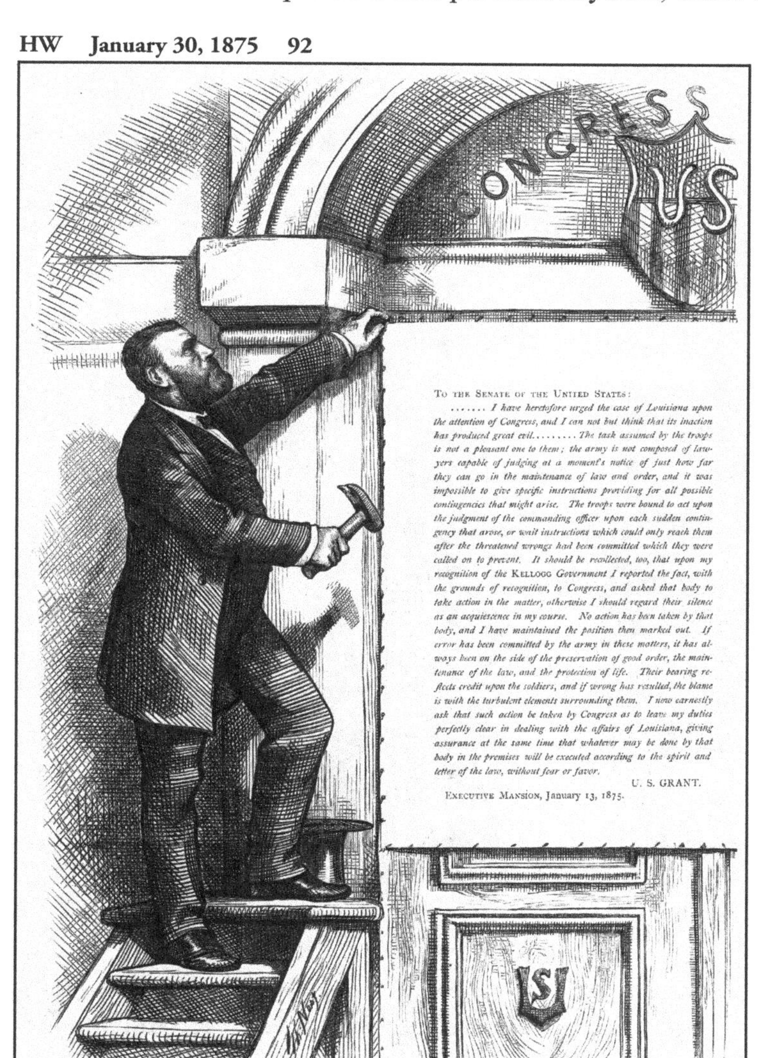

AT THE DOOR.
U.S.G. "If I hammer long enough, perhaps they'll wake up."

HW January 30, 1875 104

WHY IT IS NOT PARTISAN.
"With reference to Louisiana, it is to be borne in mind that any attempt by the Governor to use the police force of that State at this time would have undoubtedly precipitated a bloody conflict with the White League, as it did on the 14th of September. There is no doubt but that the presence of the United States troops upon the occasion prevented bloodshed and the loss of life. Both parties appear to have relied upon themselves as conservators of the public peace. The first call was made by the Democrats to remove persons obnoxious to them from the legislative hall, and the second was from the Republicans to remove persons who had usurped seats in the Legislature without legal certificates entitling them to seats, and in sufficient numbers to change the majority. Nobody was disturbed by the military who had a legal right at that time to occupy a seat in the Legislature."—From President Grant's Message.

* See p. 11

Open Conflict with Curtis

While Nast was praising Grant's reluctant decision to allow "bayonet action" when necessary, editor George William Curtis was strongly opposed: *A very great wrong here has been committed with the acquiescence of the Administration . . . a flagrant and fatal disregard of guarantees which are indispensable to free government . . . no need of rhetorical fury or brute force . . . Congress should do something.*[3]

In Nast's entire career at the *Weekly*, this probably was the most open conflict between the two strong-willed men. The week after Curtis raved (January 23), *Harper's* published Nast's five cartoons, but he was still only warming up.

He climaxed a week later with a dramatic encapsulation of "military despotism" as a public hoax perpetrated by the rabid press. Again, returning to Bennett's farce, he portrayed Grant's attackers as wild animals on the loose once more, this time blinded by the bayonets on their heads in reference to "bayonet rule." In the left insert, Grant — the King of Beasts — dropped his "sword of truth" into the den of Copperhead snakes while, opposite, he jammed his message down the throats of donkey Democrats.

HW February 6, 1875 116-117

THE BIGGEST SCARE AND HOAX YET!—THE WILD ANIMALS LET LOOSE AGAIN BY THE ZOOMORPHISM PRESS.

One day after the Hoax-picture issue, "an old party named Curtis" wrote Nast a long gentle "sermon" explaining why he disagreed. Even Fletcher Harper wrote him: "Don't get into a flurry, but learn to 'stoop to conquer.' Nobody out of Morristown can always have his own way. I'm sure you very well know that I don't."[4]

On previous occasions during the 1872 Greeley campaign and the "King Andy" Johnson Presidency, Fletcher had strongly backed his cartoonist when editorial disagreements arose. Why not now when Fletcher almost certainly agreed with Nast. Probably because John Harper, Fletcher's last surviving sibling, was close to death (after suffering a paralytic stroke several years earlier), and Fletcher didn't want to actively referee any longer. However, he still was able to effectively guarantee Nast editorial independence from Curtis until his own death two years later.

Sheridan, whom Nast knew and respected, had a solution: treat all the murderers and arsonists as "Banditti," and eliminate them accordingly. Nast liked the idea, but Congress didn't.

Nast echoed his Tweed campaign slogan (underline added).

HW February 6, 1875 124

LITTLE PHIL'S FIRE EXTINGUISHER.
"Would, if legal, soon put an end to the troubles and disorders."—U.S. Grant

HW March 6, 1875 192

Sheridan

"A REPUBLICAN FORM OF GOVERNMENT, AND NO DOMESTIC VIOLENCE."
Banditti. "The Northern and Southern Democratic Party *command you to suffer*, as it will place the United States Government in our hands. <u>So what are you going to do about it?</u>"

Congress did work out a compromise which kept Kellogg in office along with a Republican Senate, but gave the Louisiana House to the Democrats, while criticizing both factions for corruption and fraud. That got Grant off the hook, but the uproar in Congress and opposition from Fish and Bristow in his Cabinet convinced him that further military intervention was too politically risky. Moreover, the Senate rejected a House-passed Enforcement Act, with leading Republicans voting against it and further tying Grant's hands.

HW April 17, 1875 328

ANOTHER SCARE ENDED.
U.S.G. "What was all the Fuss about?"

Inflation

The money question was another major consideration which Congress, Grant and Nast dealt with during the President's second term. The Civil War had been financed with $400 million of paper money (called greenbacks because of their green ink) in addition to gold and silver (known as specie). Beginning in 1865, Treasury Secretary Hugh McCulloch redeemed $44 million of greenbacks until Congress stopped him in 1868.

Westerners, in particular, wanted the recalled greenbacks — which were backed by government bonds and not by gold — reissued to help farmers and pay off railroad bonds with cheaper currency. Hard-money opponents, including Eastern bankers, wanted to pay off the national debt, contract the money supply and resume specie payments.

The Panic of 1873 brought the subject to a boil in Congress and the press. Nast took note in December with the first of his 122 cartoons on monetary policy. Since paper money was made from rags, he created the Rag Baby to represent inflation, sometimes referring to it as the Money-Bag in its 32 appearances over the next ten years.

HW December 20, 1873 1141

BY INFLATION YOU WILL BURST.
Uncle Sam. "You stupid Money-Bag! there is just so much Money in you; and you can not make it any more by blowing yourself up!"

HW February 12, 1876 136

"HUSH-A-BYE (RAG) BABY, BE STILL!"

Grant was in the middle. Remembering his first-hand experience as a farmer and a tanner, he could empathize with failing Western growers and manufacturers. With the President's approval, Treasury Secretary William Richardson had increased the money supply by reissuing $26 million of the previously redeemed $44 million in greenbacks. However, several of his strongest Senate supporters — among them Oliver Morton (IN), John Logan (IL), Matthew Carpenter (WI) and Simon Cameron (PA) — pushed an Inflation Bill which Congress passed with, large majorities on April 14, 1874, and sent to the President for his widely expected signature.

Grant contemplated for a week and then vetoed the bill, astonishing Congress and the opposition press. His veto message emphasized two critical points: any short-term benefit would be far outweighed by long-term damage to the national economy; and the Republican platform and his campaign promises called for early resumption of specie payments. It was one of the most important and politically courageous decisions of his Presidency — praised by many of his liberal opponents and criticized by some of his conservative supporters.

Nast finally had an important issue that he could jump into without equivocation — skewering even Republicans who were on the wrong side. In particular, he went after Ben Butler, still a Massachusetts Congressman, and one of his favorite all-time targets (with 64 appearances in the *Weekly*). His cock-eye, unethical if never-quite-proved dealings, autocratic and sometimes chameleon-like behavior, and frequent failures, made him a caricaturist's dream come true. He was a leader of the Salary Grab, had defended his friend Oakes Ames in the Credit Mobilier scandal hearings, and led the charge in the House for the Inflation Bill.

As the Civil War wound down in 1865, General Butler had failed to execute General Grant's orders to attack Fort Fisher and close the Wilmington, North Carolina port, and subsequently was effectively fired from the Army. He became "Bottled-up" Butler in the popular press. Nast had a good time with that as Butler failed again.

HW April 11, 1874 309 C

HW May 9, 1874 396

Before the Bill Passed

HW May 16, 1874 409

After Grant's Veto

HW May 16, 1874 416-417

DEAD ASSES KICKING A LIVE LION.

In addition to Butler, Nast's prime targets in the same celebratory issue, were the mid-Western Republican Senators Logan, Morton, Carpenter and Thomas Ferry (MI), and Ohio Democrat Allen Thurman who played a major role when inflation heated up again during the Hayes administration. Cameron and fellow Pennsylvanian, Congressman William Kelley, also were included. The cartoonist gleefully reversed Aesop's Fable to depict them as *Dead Asses Kicking a Live Lion.*

The following week, in a politically unusual cartoon featuring Grant and Hamilton Fish taking a bow, Nast depicted several of his consistent Liberal targets cheering the decision — including Carl Schurz, Whitelaw Reid (*Tribune*), Manton Marble (*World*), Henry Watterson (*Louisville Courier-Journal*), Murat Halstead (*Cincinnati Commercial*), and Horace White (*Chicago Tribune*). All of them had been strong Greeley backers two years earlier.

HW May 23, 1874 432

Fish Grant Halstead Watterson

Labor Capital Marble Schurz Reid White

PUBLIC OPINION—APRIL 22, 1874.

When the opposition press described the cartoon as "Brutal," "Disgraceful" and "Degrading," Curtis responded with a *Harper's* editorial criticizing inflation, while explaining that it was a hard topic to caricaturize in the abstract, and strongly supporting his cartoonist.[5]

With that unusual endorsement, Nast doubled down by inserting himself in a tableau on the Senate floor, bowing deeply and sarcastically apologizing to the offended quartet. His Shakespearean titles were casually derived from *Julius Caesar* (Act V, Scene I) and *Winter's Tale* (Act III, Scene 2).

HW June 6, 1874 480

Left to Right: Logan, Morton, Cameron, Carpenter

"PEEVISH SCHOOL-BOYS, WORTHLESS OF SUCH HONOR."

"Apollos, pardon my great Profaneness; oh, pardon me, that I descend so low!"

As Nast told his biographer Paine, his Republican targets were angry. Senator John Logan complained to Nast's friend Norton Chipman: "Little Nast thinks he can teach statesmen how to run the government! Anybody might think he runs it himself!"

Of course, Chipman defended his friend. "Never mind, Logan; it is a distinction to be really caricatured by Nast. Just think what it would be to indicated by a tag." (Remembering Gratz Brown from two years before.)[6]

Benjamin Bristow became Treasury Secretary in June 1874. He worked closely with Ohio Senator John Sherman to craft the Specie Payment Resumption Act which would allow greenbacks to be redeemed for gold. Grant called for its approval in his December message to Congress, and it passed on January 14, 1875. By restoring the gold standard, effective four years later, and further contracting the nation's money supply, its objective was to slowly restore the nation's finances to the stability they had prior to the Panic of 1873. It worked and the economy finally rebounded in 1879.

Nast couldn't resist a final shot at the bill's leading opponents, using a slight variation of his Tidal Wave cartoon from the Greeley campaign three years earlier.* *Harper's* cover featured Grant as Captain of the Ark of State steering a straight course towards resumption. A dove of peace flew overhead as a message to the insurgents to return to the fold.

HW January 9, 1875 25 C

"TO THIS WE SHOULD RETURN WITH THE LEAST PRACTICABLE DELAY."—U.S. GRANT.

Three years later, Nast would repeat this cartoon as the Hayes administration fought off efforts to repeal redemption and freely monetize silver. In the revival, he inserted himself as a principal with one of the strangest and strongest political statements he ever made.

* See p. 330

Capital and Labor

The continuing depression, which the Panic of 1873 had initiated, saw an increase in labor strife. Nast generally avoided specific issues and preached unity between capital and labor. He tended to empathize with the working man — as he did to win their votes against Tweed — except where violence, anarchy or loosely-defined "communism" was involved.

Nast often used "Death" as a symbol of radical political philosophies. His home studio included a skeleton, connected at the joints by a series of wires, to enhance his ability to project Death's postures and movements in a lifelike manner.

In January 1874, New York communists organized a public rally of workingmen in Tompkins Square on the Lower East side. *Harper's* supported the forceful intervention of the police to suppress the resultant violence; its editorial concluded with: "Communism is a foreign product, which can hardly be made to flourish on American soil."[7] Nast's cover cartoon showed Death wearing a "communists" sash as it motioned a family towards the melee.

A month later, Nast addressed the Grangers (associations of Western farmers, which had originated in 1867), who wanted more inflation to pay off their debts. This time, communism was a foreign, poisonous mushroom. Its insinuation here really wasn't warranted because the Grangers favored a different economic policy having nothing to do with Communism.

HW February 7, 1874 121 C

THE EMANCIPATOR OF LABOR AND THE HONEST WORKING PEOPLE.

HW March 7, 1874 224

A FOREIGN AND POISONOUS WEED.
U.S. "That's right, Mr. Granger; I thought you would not have *that* in your *field*."

Separately, in the same issue with Death (as Communism) on the cover, Nast portrayed a skeptical Labor and Capital, looking askance — although joined by a loose umbilical cord — as *The American Twins*. This was his first use of a labor cap, which would become standard as his symbol of the working man.

Eleven weeks later, he definitively sided with Labor, as Capital lied about inflation. This was in the same issue as his *Public Opinion* cartoon, in which Labor and Capital joined the Liberals in applauding Grant and Fish for the President's veto of the Inflation Bill.

HW February 7, 1874 136

THE AMERICAN TWINS.
"United we stand, Divided we fall."

HW May 23, 1874 444

INFLATION IS "AS EASY AS LYING."
Capital. "By dividing this One Dollar it becomes Two, which makes more money. I pay you these 'Two Dollars' for Wages, you see."
Labor. "But when I go to buy Bread I find them only worth one; so I don't see it."

Civil Rights Act

With strong support from President Grant, Congress finally passed the Civil Rights Act in February 1875, prohibiting discrimination against blacks by railroads, hotels and theatres. However, it had no real teeth and few black litigants were able to take advantage of it. For Nast, it provided several humorous opportunities to tweak ex-Confederates and others who opposed the bill. However, eight years later, the Supreme Court ruled the Civil Rights Act unconstitutional in an 8-1 vote.

Another "wild animals" cover cartoon depicted Kentucky Congressman John Y. Brown as a fierce tiger attacking Civil Right Act advocate Ben Butler during the debate over that measure. Questioned by Speaker James Blaine over his language (inferring that Butler was a murderer who sold his victim's dead bodies for gold), Brown lied and was subsequently censured. It was the first of Blaine's 90 appearances in a Nast cartoon, and one of the few that didn't attack him.

Fernando Wood and Ohio Congressman Samuel "Sunset" Cox were trying to hold Brown back until the Democrats took control. Interestingly, both Cox and a Congressional friend of Brown sent Nast better likenesses (cartes de visite) for the caricaturist to use for his future skewering.

HW February 27, 1875 169 C

Blaine
Wood
Cox
Brown
Butler

GENTLEMEN YOU MUST NOT LET YOUR WILD ANIMALS LOOSE TILL THE NEXT SESSION.
JOHN THE YOUNG BROWNSTEER
VERY CIVIL RIGHTS IN THE HOUSE OF REPRESENTATIVES

THE TROUBLE HAS COMMENCED— A TALE OF ANXIETY.

HW February 27, 1875 184

THE HOUR OF MARTYRDOM HAS COME.
"Now I must marry my daughter to a Nigger."

HW April 17, 1875 316

REQUIRED TO LIVE UNDER A NEW ORDER OF THINGS.

Two church-related Civil Rights cartoons (dated April 3) were based on a story from the *Times* in the same issue::

> *"It was known here Sunday morning that the Civil Rights Bill had passed both Houses of Congress, and needed only the signature of the President to become a law. On that very morning, in Manchester, just across the river from Richmond, a negro woman marched into the Meade Memorial Episcopal Church, just before the services began, and took a front seat beside a lady. The lady at once rose, went into the vestry-room, and informed the rector, Rev. Mr. Samms. Mr. Samms considered the situation for a few moments, and then determined that, as the easiest way out of the difficulty was perhaps the best way, he would dismiss the congregation without having any services, which he did promptly. — New York Times."*

HW April 3, 1875 277

THE GOOD (PURE WHITE) SHEPHERD.

HW April 3, 1875 288

THE JUBILEE, 1875.
"Hi, Massa Peter, you can't objec' to open de gates fo' me now!"
N.B. Pure White Churches please take notice.

In a follow-up cartoon Nast, strongly pro-temperance, wound up by killing two of his birds with one harpoon.

HW April 24, 1875 336

A PRIVILEGE.
Wife. "I wish you were not allowed in here."

* * * *

In addition to a Democratic House of Representatives, the 1874 elections saw Democrat Samuel Tilden beat Republican John Dix for Governor of New York. Dix had replaced Tammany's John Hoffman two years before. Now Nast had a despised new target to attack, along with some old causes.

Chapter 31
The Election of 1876: Tilden

Background

Samuel Jones Tilden, 62, the Democratic candidate for President in 1876, was smart, knowledgeable about business, and a canny but devious politician. As perhaps the most eminent railroad lawyer in the country prior to the Civil War, he became wealthy and owned a comfortable home in New York City's elegant Gramercy Park neighborhood. Personally, he was a cautious, introverted, dyspeptic, hypochondriac who remained a confirmed bachelor and had few close personal friends.

As a rising politician, Tilden managed Horatio Seymour's successful campaign for Governor in 1862, and was his campaign chairman in 1868 when he was nominated on the twenty-second ballot to oppose Grant for the Presidency. In between, he played an important role in George McClellan's nomination to succeed Abraham Lincoln in 1864. Working closely with Copperheads, he was tainted to some extent, although he supported the Union and consulted with Lincoln and Secretary of War Edwin Stanton on occasion.

The Tweed Ring

Tilden became chairman of the New York State Democratic Party in August 1866. While the Tweed Ring was consolidating its power at both local land state levels, Tilden kept quiet. During the 1868 campaign for governor, a letter went out under Tilden's signature, to all county leaders asking for pre-election vote count estimates to be used in "adjusting" the returns. Mayor Oakey Hall may have forged the signature, but Tilden knew about it and did nothing to disclaim it at the time.[1]

To his credit, he opposed Tweed's new 1870 charter, which passed with the help of bribes. Tweed, who despised Tilden, unsuccessfully tried to depose him as state chairman.

As discussed previously, after the first *Times* exposé of the Ring's accounts, it took Tilden two months to surface. After that, he played a meaningful role in replacing Slippery Dick Connolly, and bringing the Ring down. However, Nast and *Harper's* never forgave Tilden for being late to Tweed's comeuppance.

Just before Tilden's 1874 election as governor, Nast pictured him as a Tammany Rat in a "historical" six-vignette cover cartoon. After "saving his reputation by the skin of his teeth" by walking away as Tammany crumbled (upper right), he presided as a hooded fox at a Reform meeting as "The shrewd lawyer and astute politician for the part he played in the campaign which overthrew Tammany."

HW November 7, 1874 909 C

The Chairman Of The Democratic State Central Committee.

A TAMMANY RAT.

Canal Ring

Tilden's first major action after he was elected Governor was to attack the Canal Ring. The Erie Canal's 363 miles between Albany and Buffalo opened up the Northeast to the rest of the country, and cut transportation costs by 95%. Completed in 1825, the system added another 160 miles by 1862.

As with the construction of the railroads, the maintenance of the canal provided numerous opportunities for corruption via kickbacks for surveys, maps and estimates; work not done; and unconscionable overcharging. Canal commissioners, engineers, inspectors and two tame judges were involved in an $11 million fraud that Tilden exposed through an Investigating Commission. Both Democratic and Republican legislative leaders masterminded the Ring.[2]

Nast reluctantly and sarcastically gave Tilden his due in another multi-vignette cover cartoon — *The Little Boy Getting Brave* as he attacked the Sing-Sing prison birds (vultures) . . . *Now Let Him "Achieve* Greatness."

(Extract from upper left)

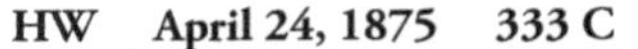
HW April 24, 1875 333 C

A FEW SKETCHES

Portraying Tilden

In February 1875, a month after his inauguration, Tilden suffered a stroke which distorted his countenance. Until he became a likely presidential candidate a year later, Nast harpooned him without showing the effects of his malady.

Nast's change in portrayal probably came from more than just caricature. Although Tilden was well known as a hypochondriac, his emergence as a post-stroke candidate gave some Democrats cause for concern about his health; in fact, he looked about ten years older than his age (62). Nast wasn't overly subtle in transmitting that to his audience.

HW November 6, 1875 893 C

IT SOUNDS WELL!—THE PROLOGUE BEFORE THE FARCE.

HW October 28, 1876 880

REFORM IS NECESSARY EVEN IN S.J.T.

The Pope (Again)

Before and after Tilden's election as governor — and the continuing scandals in the Grant administration that Nast dealt with lightly or not at all — the Pope, the Catholic Church, and the continuing battle over education funding provided substance for his cartoons over the years. Sometimes, he used European settings to portray the Pope's troubles with King Victor Emmanuel of Italy, Chancellor Otto van Bismarck of Germany, and Prime Minister William Gladstone of England. Gladstone had published a pamphlet which he was beating the Pope with while the King watched through his window.

HW January 25, 1873 80

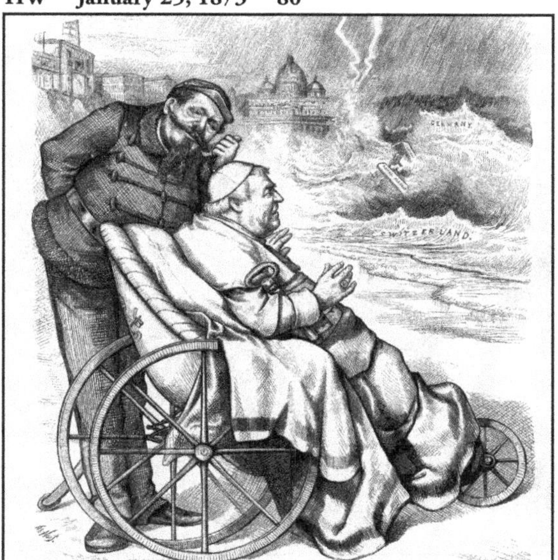

THE UNPROTECTED FEMALE AT THE HOLY SEA SIDE.
V.E. "What Are The Wild Waves Saying, Saying, Sister, To Thee."

HW January 16, 1875 57

AMPHITHEATER FLAVIUS, ROME, MDCCCLXXV.—CAESAR HAVING THINGS RENDERED UNTO HIM.

The Catholic press responded in kind, depicting Nast as Fletcher Harper's pet monkey.

THE FREE LANCE, NY May 1, 1875

Nast Collection, New York Public Library

THE ROCK THEY SPLIT ON.
Gladstone, Bismarck, Victor Emmanuel, Fletcher Harper and Tom Nast (in chorus)—*We must give this up! We hurt ourselves more than the Pope! This rock is so firm, it must be the "Rock of Ages."*

As the probability of Tilden's nomination for president increased during 1875, Nast attacked him and his party for promoting parochial educating at the expense of public schools. He repeated *American River Ganges*, his notorious crocodile cartoon from the Tweed campaign.*

October's cartoons featured Grant emphasizing the separation of Church and State. They provided a rare opportunity to praise the President while simultaneously bashing his would-be successor.[3]

HW October 16, 1875 836

POCKETING THE MISSING PLANK.
But They Are Sure To Put Their Foot In It Some Day.

HW October 23, 1875 860-861

Church and State.

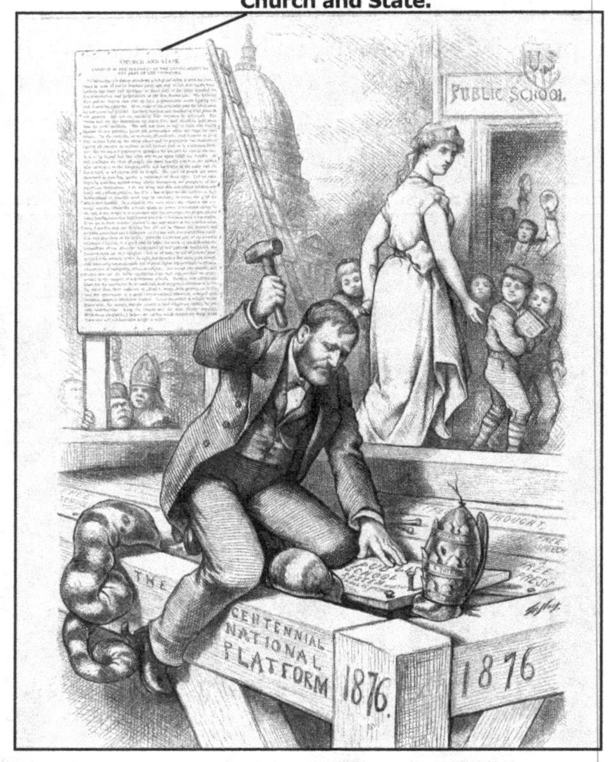

THE PLANK—HITTING THE NAIL ON THE HEAD.

* See p. 240

HW October 23, 1875 868

THAT MISSING PLANK.
U.S. Grant. "You have dropped something."
S.J. Tilden. "O!—It's—of no account."

HW October 30, 1875 873 C

THE POPE'S BIG TOE.
"If we are to have another contest in the near future of our national existence, I predict that the dividing line will not be Mason and Dixon's."—Grant's *Speech on our Public School System.*

Reform

Nominated overwhelmingly on the second ballot at the Democratic Convention in St. Louis in late June 1876, Tilden presented himself as the "Reform Candidate." As a general theme, "Reform" was the Democrats' antidotal slogan against the Grant administration's multiple instances of corruption and nepotism. In fact, it had more to do with replacing Republican officeholders — especially in Southern white governments — than with proposed structural or procedural changes to assure that honest men would be elected.

Tilden had an encyclopedic knowledge of law, legislatures and courts. Nast used his expertise as a boomerang embodied in "Red Tape," both figuratively and literally.

HW October 16, 1875 833 C

OUR MODERN MUMMY.
Tammany Tweedledee. "She is going to punish us!"
Canal Tweedledum. "That's the best joke yet."

HW February 19, 1876 141 C

MORE!
State of New York, Executive Chamber, Albany, *January* 18, 1876.
***To the Senate*:**
In answer to the resolution of the Senate—more appropriations, more power, more attorney-generals, more district attorneys, more marshals, more deputy-marshals, more counsels, more legislation,. more laws, more commissioners to investigate, more trials, more cases, more reports, more suits, more opinions, more resolutions, more annual messages, more penalties, more proofs, more civil action, more whereas, more red tape, more—that's all—for conducting these trials.
All-Of-A-Twist.

HW August 12, 1876 664

SLIPPERY SAM.

HW October 14, 1876 828

Nast also came up with an obscure legal term — "usufruct," which Tilden probably employed in his railroad law practice — to tarnish the candidate. (The ominous-sounding but politically innocent and neutral definition: the right to enjoy all the advantages of another's property, provided that such property is not destroyed or damaged.) Nast branded him with it as an epithet — creating nouns, verbs and adjectives as he saw fit — to imply fraud.

For example, Tilden's age — 47 when the Civil War began — and poor health kept him out of the Army. In contrast, his Republican opponent Rutherford Hayes — 38 when the War started — became a low-level general who was wounded four times and noted for his bravery in over 50 engagements.

BETWEEN TWO FIRES.
Soldiers. "Whose side were you on?"
Reformed Usufruct. "I—I was—busy in court with a *Railroad Case.*"

Tweed (Again)

Nast had successfully rejuvenated Tweed as a bogeyman during the Greeley campaign, when it was far more timely to do so. Four years later, Tweed had escaped from jail and was off the scene. Nevertheless, Nast frequently tied him to Tilden in several effective ways, ignoring the total enmity between them and the fact that Tweed on the lam was not Tilden's responsibility.

During the 1868 campaign when John Hoffman was elected as Tweed's puppet governor with thousands of fraudulent votes, Tilden — as Chairman of the State Democratic Committee — accepted a $5,000 ($100,000 today) contribution from Tweed. Additionally, Nast accused Tilden of a deliberately unaggressive "still hunt" for Tweed and his fellow Ring members.

Tilden, with no family to support and conservative spending habits, had accumulated a fortune estimated to be as much as $10,000,000. Nast used a barrel of his potential vote-buying dollars to implicate the candidate on several occasions. The symbol became more important in the election's aftermath when attempted vote-buying by the Democrats turned into a scandal.

HW September 30, 1876 789 C

AN "AGGRESSIVE "STILL HUNT."
"Governor Tilden has for years, like a hound on the scent, followed the members of the Ring patiently, secretly, and diligently."—Mr. Hewitt.

HW September 30, 1876 804

THE BARREL CAMPAIGN IS A FAILURE.

As the campaign progressed into the fall, Nast had lots of fun linking his old nemesis to his new one. Tweed, who had sailed from Cuba to Spain in July, was captured when he landed in Vigo, Spain on September 6. Recognized by the Spanish authorities from Nast's Tweed-Le-Dee and Tilden-Dum cartoon which the State Department had distributed,* the artist gloated by repeating it with a revised caption.

HW October 7, 1876 821

THE CAPTURE OF TWEED—THE PICTURE THAT MADE THE SPANISH OFFICIALS TAKE HIM FOR A "CHILD-STEALER."
[Republished From "Harper's Weekly" For July 1, 1876.]

Several cover cartoons included Tweed's 1868 campaign contribution. In the final one, available two weeks before the election, Tweed picked Tilden's pocket to retrieve it, while both thumbed their noses at the public.

HW September 9, 1876 729 C

A BOX STEW; OR, AN ENVIABLE POSITION.
Usufructuary Tilden. "William, we *would* miss you —until I am in the White House." (Hard on Tweed.)

HW September 16, 1876 749 C

"ANY THING FOR A CHANGE."
Exile Tweed To Usufructuary Tilden. "Let us usufruct or change. That's the best thing you can do about it."

HW October 28, 1876 865 C

'WILLIE, WE HAVE MISSED YOU!'

* See p. 291

Inflation (Again)

Indiana Governor Thomas Hendricks, the runner-up to Tilden, reluctantly accepted the Vice Presidential slot on the ticket. The two men had a major policy difference — hard vs. soft money. Tilden had always been a specie supporter, but Hendricks, with a large agricultural base, favored greenbacks so Western farmers could pay back their debts with cheaper currency.

"Honest John" Kelly, Tammany Hall's political boss, strongly opposed Tilden who had crimped his wings. He was instrumental in getting Hendricks to run with Tilden. Their contrary positions on such a critical issue relating to the continuing economic slump, gave Nast his primary graphic campaign motif.

He also disparaged gambler (and former boxer) John Morrissey, who had effectively lost his battle with Kelly for control of Tammany Hall. (Nast's portrayals of Morrissey went back longer than any of his other current characters — to 1858 when, as an illustrator for his first employer, Frank Leslie — he covered the Morrissey-Heenan fight in Canada). Now Morrissey would become a symbolic Democratic Party loser.

This was Nast's first use of the Tiger as a symbol for the Democratic Party. The Tammany Tiger had evolved.

HW July 22, 1876 589 C

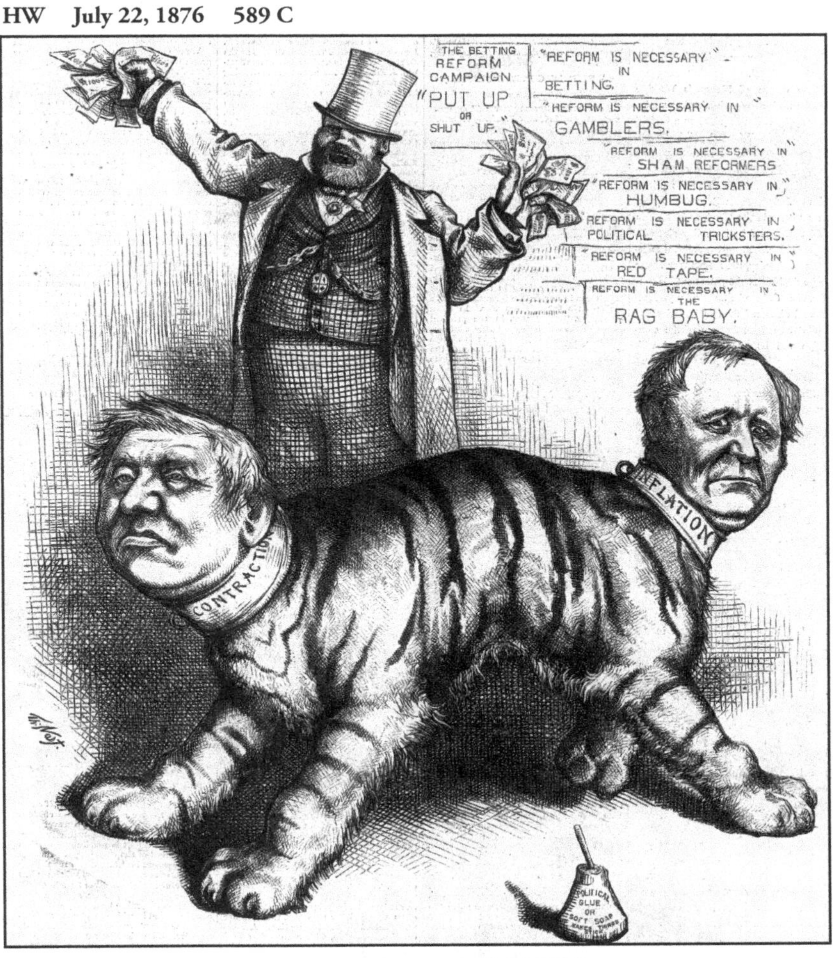

THE DEMOCRATIC (DEFORMED) TIGER "FIXED."
"Reformed 'Gambler Statesman.'" "I'll bet $10,000 that this is the greatest Deformed (*Reformed*, I mean) Animal going; $10,000 that it is going to lick every thing else in the Field; $10,000 that this double-headed Tiger can be turned any way to gull the American People; $10,000 that nobody could tell now that he had ever lost his Head or his Tail."

As discussed previously,* Grant had vetoed the "Inflation" Bill of 1874 and signed the Specie Payment Resumption Act which was to become effective on January 1, 1879. In August 1876, the Democratic House repealed that fixed date, but the Republican Senate refused to go along.

Nast resurrected his Rag Baby, which by now had also been adopted by several other cartoonists to symbolize inflation. Two August satires featured the mismatched pair as a married couple nursing their soft Rag Baby. Their depictor really enjoyed himself, knowing along with the public, that Tilden was a confirmed bachelor.

---

* See p. 386

In the first, *Hen(dricks)-Pecked*, Father Tilden fed the Rag Baby "Democratic Platform Soothing Syrup while Mother stoked the fire in their "House of Reform." Three weeks later, the inebriated Rag Baby thumbed his nose as Mother Hendricks happily watched. Father Tilden had fed it "High Bock Beer" when "Congress Water" didn't work.

Nast's little touches added to the comedy: Tweed, known to be on a ship to Spain, was in a sailor suit in a picture on the wall, flanked by Morrissey as "the champion reformer or deformer;" the clock was at the eleventh hour with time about to run out for the Democratic ticket.

August 5, 1876 629 C

HEN(dricks)-PECKED.
Mrs. Tilden. "Nurse the Baby, while I stir up the Fire."

August 26, 1876 689 C

A HARD SUMMER FOR THE SOFT RAG BABY.
Mr. Tilden. "Now don't wake it, dear; the second bottle did it."
Mrs. Tilden. "You are a wonderful Nurse, darling. See! the Angels are whispering to it."

Simultaneously and serially, Nast used the money question (as it was called) to portray the Democratic duo as a two-headed tiger.

HW August 5, 1876 644

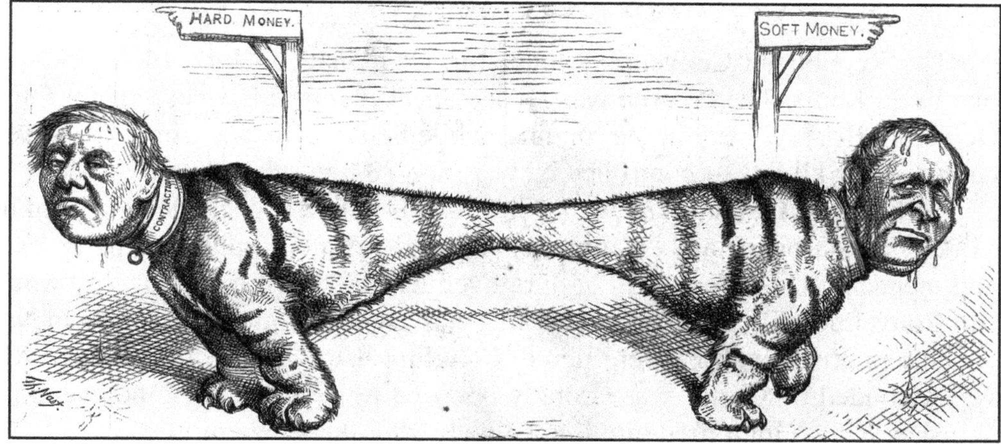

THE ELASTIC DEMOCRATIC (DEFORMED) TIGER.
They pull together so very nicely.

HW August 26, 1876 704

BY REPEALING THEY RESUME—BY RESUMING THEY REPEAL.
Extremes have met, and now you can't tell, which is which.

HW October 28, 1876 868

"THE ELEPHANT WALKS AROUND"—AND THE "STILL HUNT" IS NEARLY OVER.

In August, gambler Morrissey holding $10,000 apparently stolen from Tilden's usufruct barrel, was betting that the money question would be resolved.

Two months later, the Republican elephant, with Uncle Sam as its pilot, squashed both halves of the tiger as Morrissey stood by, a loser with empty pockets. The elephant still represented the vote, not the party. Triumphant public schoolers cheered in the howdah.

Hayes

The Republican Convention opened in Cincinnati on June 14, 1876 — two weeks before the Democratic one in St. Louis. The favorite was House Speaker James Blaine. Senator Oliver Morton and Treasury Secretary Benjamin Bristow were in the running, while Senator Roscoe Conkling — whose malaria would keep him from campaigning all fall — controlled New York's 70 favorite son votes.

Early on the first day, *Harper's* editor Curtis gave a speech blasting Conkling for his arbitrary control of New York State patronage and "usurpation and abuse of the Republican party, excluding other voices in its councils and menacing the very system of our government."[4] Their open hostility would erupt again at the State Republican Convention fifteen months later, in a clash which would reverberate in Nast's career at the *Weekly*.

The internal rivalries were fierce. Conkling hated Blaine and disliked Morton. Bristow, whose nomination was seconded by Curtis, was strongly opposed by Grant because he had exposed Orville Babcock's role in the Whiskey Ring. Grant fired him immediately after the convention.

Blaine had an excellent track record as Speaker of the House for six years, and Minority Leader for the last two. He was popular throughout the country, better qualified to be President than any other nominee, and desperately wanted the job. But details of his using his office for profiting from railroad securities, public exposure, and deceit and lies to cover up, combined with justified doubts about his integrity, to cost him critical support from Morton's and Bristow's backers when the deadlock broke.

HW June 24, 1876 505 C

"CONTINUE THAT I BROACHED IN JEST."—Shakespeare.

Depicting himself as a proud schoolboy, Nast predicted a slate of Hamilton Fish and Ohio Governor Rutherford Hayes in a cartoon available the day the Convention opened. Although Fish would have been Grant's choice, the cartoonist and the President knew that the 67-year old Secretary of State wanted only to complete his eight years as the cabinet's effective anchor, and then return to private life. Nast's cover title, *"Continue that I Broached in Jest"* from Shakespeare's *Taming of the Shrew* (Act I, Scene II), may have implied a comparison between the resolute Fish and the intractable nag of the play. (Modernized in the musical *Kiss Me Kate*).

HW July 8, 1876 545 C

"WHY WE LAUGH."

Nast's whimsical prophesy came partially true with the nomination on the seventh ballot of Hayes as a compromise candidate, narrowly beating Blaine when the other candidates — including Conkling, whose hatred of Blaine proved stronger than his dislike of Hayes — consolidated their votes behind him. The egotistical artist celebrated with a tip of his hat to himself in *"Why We Laugh,"* and included an accurate *"Declaration of Principles,"* the last of which expressed the gratitude of the American people to President Grant and his Administration.

The Republican Party had adopted the 17 "Principles" at its Convention. Curtis editorialized on them the previous week, but conspicuously omitted the one pertaining to Grant, along with several others. Nast took a subtle poke at Curtis, while continuing his refusal to portray Hayes, even as he cheered the result.

HW July 29, 1876 616

Hayes picked up support from Republican moderates, and Curtis strongly backed him on *Harper's* editorial pages. Whitelaw Reid's *Tribune* and Carl Schurz returned to the Republican fold after their misadventure with Horace Greeley four years earlier, so Nast reprised Schurz's piano playing from that campaign.

GETTING IN TUNE.

Discord with Curtis (Again)

There were several important issues on which Nast was in accord with Hayes. He was a strong anti-inflationist, the key platform on which he narrowly won his Ohio races. He had supported public schools against the Catholic Church, and had waved the bloody shirt effectively in his Ohio campaign oratory.

However, two larger issues for Grant — and therefore for Nast — turned them against Hayes personally, even though they obviously wanted their party to hold the presidency. Most important for Grant was that Hayes leaned towards ending the increasingly unpopular Reconstruction policy, permitting the three former Confederate states still under Republican control — Florida, Louisiana and South Carolina — to govern themselves. This would put black rights, which the President had tried to protect, in permanent danger, and conceivably put control of both Congress and even the Presidency in Democratic hands.

Perhaps equally damaging in Grant's mind — and to his yet unspoken and perhaps unformed potential quest for a third term in 1880— was Hayes's pledge to a one-term presidency if he won. The President criticized Hayes for that, and refused to accept his subsequent apology as he, Nast and others interpreted Hayes's unsolicited statement as an open attack on Grant's record. (Fix it and get out.)

For Nast, Hayes's endorsement of Civil Service reform was another implicit criticism of Grant and his political control of patronage. This put the cartoonist at sharp odds with Curtis, who spearheaded that issue for many years and had chaired Grant's ineffective Reform Commission during his first term.

Nast felt so strongly about Hayes reversing Grant's policies that he refused to depict the nineteenth president, either before or after his election. That stand brought him into serious conflict with Curtis. Fletcher Harper was mortally ill and absent, so Nast had no consistent champion inside the firm. His losing battles with Curtis continued throughout the Hayes Presidency and, off and on, through the rest of his last decade at *Harper's Weekly.*

Consequently, he portrayed Miss Columbia (posed by his wife Sallie) ambivalently preparing to spin the Wheel of Fortune in *The Political Lottery.* Her apprehension and uncertainty probably reflected his own feelings.

The dominant two-page vertical cartoon was based on Shakespeare's *Merchant of Venice* (Act III, Scene 2), where Portia's suitor, Bassanio, had to blindly try to select her hand. Columbia was a featured symbol of the National Centennial Exhibition in Philadelphia, which began on July 4, shortly after the Conventions.

HW November 11, 1876 912-913

THE POLITICAL LOTTERY.
"And Here Choose I. Joy Be The Consequence!"—Shakespeare.

Nast's non-prediction was right on the money. It took almost four months after the election to determine the winner in a no-holds-barred contest laden with attempted bribery and corruption.

Chapter 32
The Election of 1876: Electoral Scramble

Dan Sickles

Blundering Civil War general, wily career politician, scheming diplomat, and notorious womanizer Dan Sickles was infamous on many counts.* In 1853, as secretary to future President James Buchanan at the American Embassy in London, he left his young pregnant wife at home in New York, and brought a prostitute to live with him in London, where he had the audacity to introduce her to Queen Victoria. Six years later, Democratic Congressman Sickles murdered his wife's lover — Washington District Attorney Philip Key (son of *Star-Spangled Banner* composer Francis Scott Key) — in cold blood. He escaped conviction and probable execution on grounds of temporary insanity. (The first ever; his lead lawyer was Edwin Stanton, who became a life-long friend). In his diary, noted New York lawyer George Templeton Strong wrote "One might as well try to spoil a rotten egg as to damage Dan's character."[1]

After Grant was first elected, he appointed Sickles as Minister to Spain, over the strong objections of Secretary of State Hamilton Fish, who despised him. During his five years in Madrid, he had a lengthy affair with deposed Queen Isabella II, and contravened American policy by trying to provoke war with Cuba. Nast portrayed an angry Fish swallowing Sickles' forced resignation as England and Spain watched. A piquant side scene showed Grant watching onshore as Navy Secretary George Robeson rowed his replacement, Caleb Cushing, across the Atlantic.

HW January 24, 1874 73 C

A HARD FISH TO CATCH.
John Bull To Spain. "It's difficult Fishing here!"

To his credit, however, late on Election Night, November 7, 1876, Sickles made a serendipitous major contribution to the Republican Party when he visited its almost deserted headquarters at the Fifth Avenue Hotel to check out various state telegrams comprising the returns. The lone clerk told him Tilden had been elected and the Republican *Tribune* confirmed that in its first edition headline.[2]

---

* See p. 125 and 179-180

In particular, Sickles looked at the returns from Florida, Louisiana and South Carolina — the three Southern states still controlled by Republican governors. Tilden had 184 votes and needed one more. If Hayes could hold the 19 combined votes from the three questionable states — plus those from late-returning Oregon and California — he would edge out Tilden with 185. There were still 28 days left before the official returns had to be submitted to Congress.

Sickles convinced some newly-arrived and other sleeping politicians to send identical telegrams to the key Republican official in each of the three vital states: "With your state sure for Hayes, he is elected. Hold your state."

About 4 A.M., Democratic National Committee Finance Chairman and U.S. Senator from Connecticut, William Barnum (a third cousin of P.T.), wired the *Times* to ask about the counts in Florida, Louisiana and South Carolina. *Times* editor John Reid, an ardent Republican, had been queried separately by a New York Democratic leader, and deduced they must be worried. Accordingly, his first edition headline read "A Doubtful Election." Reid promptly hurried to Republican headquarters, convinced Party leaders that the election could be won, and sent off another set of telegrams to the three state leaders under National Committee Chairman Zach Chandler's signature.[3]

Both parties now pulled out everything they could think of in their attempts to control the decisive 20 votes. While Nast disliked Hayes, he preferred him and a Republican presidency to that of the despised Tilden. As events unfolded, his targets provided him with plenty of arrows over a two-year period.

Oregon, where the eligibility of one of its three delegates was in doubt, was a late addition to the list.

The South

The overall issue in the post-election scramble was Southern power in general, and "home rule" — local control of the last three unreconstructed states — in particular. Two weeks before the election, Nast featured $2.5 billion in fanciful claims for the $olid South, including refunds for destroyed supplies and a cotton tax, and rent for Andersonville Prison.[4]

HW November 4, 1876 885 C

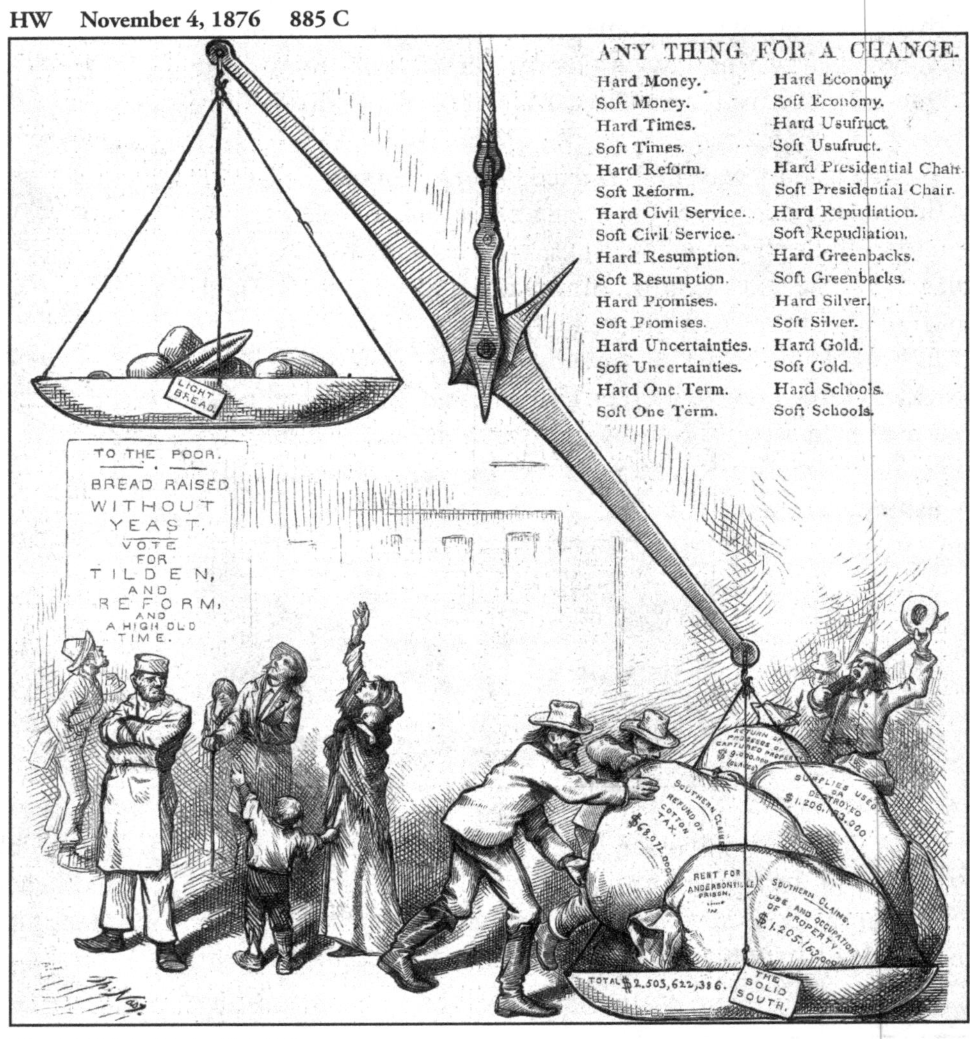

THIS WILL BE A CHANGE.

Violence in the South continued to flare during the campaign, but paled in comparison — at least in the Northern public eye — to the previous two years. A notable exception was a July 5th riot in Hamburg, South Carolina — a tiny black-controlled community across the Savannah River from Augusta, Georgia. When a racial confrontation took place on Independence Day, beginning with a dispute over free passage on a public road, white reinforcements crossed the river. Six blacks were massacred in cold blood while one white was killed. Nast had two cartoons in the same issue, linking Tilden to the same bloody shirt that the cartoonist had waved so effectively against Greeley four years earlier.[5]

HW August 12, 1876 652

THE "BLOODY SHIRT" REFORMED.
Governor Tilden. "It is not I, but the Idea of Reform which I represent."

HW August 12, 1876 656-657

DECLARATION OF EQUALITY.—
***Justice.* "Five More Wanted."**

Not all of Nast's Republican audience agreed with him. Strong had written in his diary on September 2, 1874: "Sporadic riots and lynchings among Southerners are exaggerated by the newspapers into a war of races and a reign of terror for the fall election. In poor sorely punished South Carolina, . . . semi-brutal black voters are in a great majority and, under the leading of knaves and carpet-baggers, control the state."[6]

A fortnight later, he added: "The governments of South Carolina and Louisiana are, I fear, mere nests of corrupt carpet-baggers upheld by a brutal nigger constituency. But have we here in New York any right to look down on them? Our civic rulers are, as a class, utterly base, and a Celtocracy is as bad as a niggerrocrasy, and in some respects worse." Departing from his usual positive depiction of blacks, Nast depicted that actual scenario in a cover cartoon after the election.

HW December 9, 1876 985 C

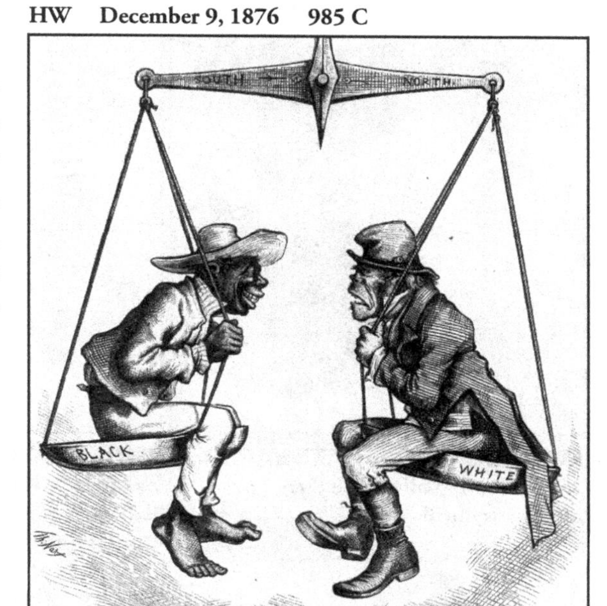

THE IGNORANT VOTE—HONORS ARE EASY.

Henry Watterson

To try to keep violence and fraud at a minimum, President Grant dispatched troops to all three of the Southern Republican states about two weeks before the election. The leading Southern Democrats didn't want another Civil War, so the troops on the whole served their peacekeeping purpose. Tilden was in full agreement.

However, Henry Watterson, the fiery editor of the *Louisville Courier-Journal* and a freshman Congressman, planned a Washington speech calling for 100,000 "peaceful citizens" to assemble in Washington to demand Tilden be declared President. Watterson, known for his violent outbursts and heavy drinking, was supported by Oswald Ottendorfer, the leading German-language publisher with strong influence over the German vote.

In spite of their huge political differences, Nast and Watterson maintained a needling friendship that was important to both of them. For openers, Nast satirized Grant's secret order to General William Sherman to divert four artillery companies en route to New York — represented by four toy soldiers — to Washington. In the same issue, he also targeted "wind bag Noodledorfer" along with Watterson.

HW December 9, 1876 1000

4—00,000 MORE.

HW December 9, 1876 996

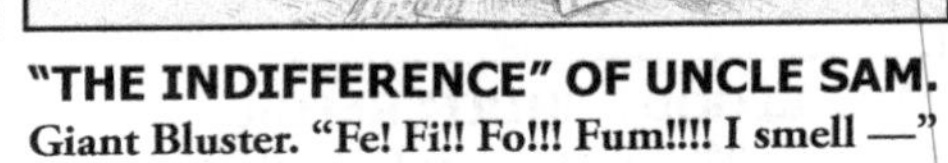

"THE INDIFFERENCE" OF UNCLE SAM.
Giant Bluster. "Fe! Fi!! Fo!!! Fum!!!! I smell —"
Uncle Sam. "Oh, give us a rest!"

HW February 3, 1877 93

FIRE AND WATER MAKE VAPOR.
What a cooling off will be there, my countrymen!

HW March 10, 1877 188

"ONE TOUCH OF NATURE MAKES"— EVEN HENRY WATTERSON GIVE IN.
"Let us have peace. I don't care who is the next President," cries our bold Patriarch at *the* First *arrival.*
"The Hon. Henry Watterson has just been presented with a son—weight, 11 pounds."— *Washington Correspondence.*

Watterson gave his actual speech on January 8, 1877 at Ford's Theatre after reviewing and toning it down with Tilden in New York. Nast responded with fellow publisher Murat Halstead of the *Cincinnati Commercial* pouring ice water on Watterson's "Red Hot" head. Nast showed a bunch of unplayed cards — labeled "reform tricks" — coming out of the publisher-Congressman's sleeves. According to biographer Paine, Watterson later complained that his fellow poker players assumed the cards were real "and I haven't been able to get into a game since."[7] Score one for Nast! He made up after the inauguration with a celebration of Watterson's newborn son, a picture the fiery father mounted in his home.

Watterson may have been unique — a continuing target whom the artist really liked and probably respected.

South Carolina

With violence as an election influence reasonably well neutralized, attention focused on the so-called returning boards for each of the four contested states. The members of those boards were to review the returns from each county (parish in Louisiana) and determine the actual counts. There was plenty of opportunity for fraud and bribery at both local returning board and state levels. Many of the crooked twists didn't emerge until two years after the election.

The Democratic schemers — not including Tilden himself — evaluated their chances for knavery. South Carolina's black voter population outnumbered its whites four to three, and its five-member returning board was all Republican and majority black. Hayes appeared to have a 600-1,000 vote majority, buttressed by the board's throwing out returns from two counties, citing Democratic fraud and intimidation, and ignoring similar charges against black Republicans. Daniel Chamberlain, its carpet-bagger governor, certified the state's seven electoral votes for Hayes on November 22 and sent its electors to Congress.

Unknown until Tilden testified to a Congressional investigating committee in February 1879 was that his nephew, William Tilden Pelton, was in the middle of a bribery attempt to buy South Carolina's votes for $60,000 to $80,000 two days before the board's certification. Pelton met in Baltimore with South Carolina Congressman Smith Weed, and communicated to his best friend Edward Cooper (son of wealthy, renowned industrialist and philanthropist Peter Cooper) that he would "draw upon him the next day for the money."

Edward Cooper told Tilden about "the offer," and Tilden telegraphed his nephew not to negotiate, accusing him of "officious meddling" when he returned. Public information about the offer never surfaced at the time, so Nast and the press didn't know about it.[8] However, Pelton would play a major in the Florida vote scenario, which Nast portrayed with relish when it surfaced.

Colonel Pelton, 40, had lived in his uncle's house for eight years and served as military secretary to the Governor. Unsuccessful in business, he had no direct control over potential bribery funds, but the outside world assumed he was representing his uncle. Tilden testified that he saw little of his nephew "who went out early and came home late."

Abram Hewitt

Hewitt, Chairman of the Democratic National Committee, was the ringmaster for early bribery attempts in Florida and Oregon. Wealthy from prewar coal and iron investments, he was Tilden's neighbor in Gramercy Park. Married to Edward Cooper's sister, he had a close friendship with Pelton as well as his uncle.

Recognizing the importance of Florida's four electoral votes, Hewitt dispatched Senator Barnum, his Finance Chairman, to Tallahassee. Before he went, Hewitt sent him a letter authorizing him to "buy more mules," understood as "votes." Unfortunately, the letter became public, and Nast referred to it in a cover cartoon published six days before the election, in the same issue as *The Political Lottery*.

Tilden was featured dumping his barrel of usufruct dollars into a ballot box with Hewitt's message to Barnum behind him and his $5,000 contribution to Tweed sticking out of his pocket. A sign on the far side of the barrel equated "The Shot-Gun Policy South" with "The Barrel Policy North."

However, the cartoon was aimed at New York, and the sub-title echoed Tweed's "What Are You Going to Do About It?" Below were lengthy quotes from the 1868 message that went out under Tilden's signature requesting pre-election vote estimates, and Greeley's letter to Tilden a year later, calling on him to stop illegal voter registration in the city.

Literally, it was as bald an on-the-money accusation as Nast could make. The only inaccuracy was that the projected bribe money would not come from Tilden but from his Democratic associates. The nominee was honest in that regard, although his awareness became suspect and Pelton continued to live in his home.

HW November 11, 1876 905 C

THE CIRCULAR.

ROOMS OF THE DEMOCRATIC STATE COMMITTEE, *October 27, 1868.*

MY DEAR SIR,—Please at once to communicate with some reliable person, in three or four principal towns and in each city of your county, and request him (expenses duly arranged for at this end) to telegraph to WILLIAM M. TWEED, Tammany Hall, at the minute of closing the polls, not waiting for the count, such person's estimate of the vote. Let the telegraph be as follows: "This town will show a Democratic gain [or loss] over last year of—[number];" or this one, if sufficiently certain: "This town will give a Republican [or Democratic] majority of ——." There is of course an important object to be attained by a simultaneous transmission at the hour of closing the polls, but not longer waiting. Opportunity can be taken of the usual half-hour lull in telegraphic communication over lines before actual results begin to be declared, and before the Associated Press absorb the telegraph with returns and interfere with individual messages, and give orders to watch carefully the count. Very truly yours,

(Signed) SAMUEL J. TILDEN, Chairman.

LETTER TO A POLITICIAN.

....Now, Mr. TILDEN, I call on *you* to put a stop to this business. You have but to walk into the Sheriff's, the Mayor's, and the Supervisors' offices in the City Hall Park, and say there must be no more of it—say it so that there shall be no doubt that you *mean* it—and we shall have a tolerably fair election once more. Probably a good part of the Fifty Thousand supplied last Fall with bogus Naturalization Certificates will offer to register and to vote—some of them pretending not to know that they are no more citizens of the United States than the King of Dahomey is—but very few will vote repeatedly unless paid for it; and we shall not be cheated more than Ten Thousand if you simply tell the boss-workmen that there must be no more Illegal Voting instigated and paid for.

Will you do it? Your reputation is at stake. The cowardly craft which

"would not play false,
And yet would wrongly win,"

will not avail. If we Republicans are swindled again as we were swindled last Fall, you, and such as you, will be responsible to God and man for the outrage. Prosecutors, magistrates, municipal authorities, are all in the pool; we have nothing to hope from the ministers of justice, and the villains have no fear of the terrors of the law. I appeal to you, and anxiously await the result. Yours,

NEW YORK, *October 20, 1869.* HORACE GREELEY.

THE PROSPECT IN NEW YORK.
"What Are You Going To Do About It?"

HW December 2, 1876 980

GO SOUTH, YOUNG MAN.

Barnum had a reputation for political trickery. Two weeks after the election, Nast showed him en route to Florida with instructions from Hewitt to buy one more "electoral" mule for Tilden. Tammany politician and gambler John Morrissey accompanied him with the (betting) "pools, not the country, at stake."

Hewitt accused the well-regarded New York Postmaster of being responsible for the leak of his letters, a charge which he probably knew was false, and was denied. In the same *Harper's* issue, the Democratic-leaning *Nation* was quoted about "Mexican Poison" in an article which discussed using Republican scalawag fraud to offset Democratic White League terror and assassination in Louisiana. Nast captured both topics by featuring the Mexican Don Quixote tilting at a post office windmill, while Sancho Usufruct (Tilden) trailed "behind" in search of a county to rule."

HW January 27, 1877 61 C

THE MEXICAN DON QUIXOTE.
Don Hewitt (*on his journey in search of a country for Sancho Usufruct to rule*). "I wonder if there is any thing left of the Post-Office after my charge upon it? and what shall I destroy next?"

Oregon

Both sides essentially agreed that Hayes won the state by at least 1,000 votes. A legitimate question was raised immediately over the eligibility of one elector who earned $268 annually as a postmaster; the Constitution prohibited federal employees from serving as electors. On the advice of an Oregon Senator, John Watts resigned his postmastership, voted as an elector, and hoped to be reappointed by Hayes. The Republican Secretary of State certified Watts and the other two Republican electors, tentatively providing the single vote that ultimately decided the election.[9]

Meanwhile, Hewitt saw the Oregon vote as crucial for another reason: it would set a precedent for the three Southern states by forcing Congress to go behind the certificates of the returning boards and get into the merits of the individual county votes. Accordingly, he successfully pressured Oregon Governor Lafayette Grover to appoint E.A. Cronin, the runner-up to Watts and a Democrat, as the replacement delegate. Grover then certified Cronin and the two Republican electors, and dispatched Cronin to Washington with a potential tie-breaking Democratic vote.

HW January 13, 1877 36

CRONIN "ORGANIZED HIMSELF."

Nast must have chuckled when he portrayed Cronin as a tramp, his first usage of that symbol. Tramps had become more numerous and visible during the economic slump and unemployment that persisted from 1873 until 1879. In fact, the word "tramp" had a new meaning before the 1870s; it meant a walk of some length.

However, Oregon election law required that in case of a vacancy, the other two electors should select a replacement. They did so, reappointing the former postmaster. Meanwhile, Hewitt and Pelton sent encrypted telegrams to a shady Democratic middleman from Nebraska, offering $8,000 for "legitimate legal expenses" as a bribe to Cronin and possibly Governor Grover as well. Their actions became public,[10] revealing that the $8,000 was sometimes referred to as a "pig" (rather than a "mule").

Nast threw boulders at Hewitt and his Gramercy Park (Tilden's residence) glass house, naming Cronin, Grover, Pelton, Tilden, middleman J.N.H. Patrick, and Tammany boss John Kelly. His stones included $8,000, "Cipher Dispatch" and "Bribery." The cover cartoon was published two days before Congress voted to declare Hayes as the nineteenth president.

HW March 10, 1877 181 C

HEW(ITT) DOWN.
Throwing Stones Is Not A Very Safe Business.

Louisiana

Louisiana's eight electoral votes appeared to be Tilden's best opportunity in the three Southern states. The first count gave him a 7,700 vote plurality. Accordingly, both parties sent top "visiting statesmen" to oversee the Returning Board. Henry Watterson was the self-appointed leader of the Democrats.

The Returning Board was all Republican, two whites and two blacks. It was chaired by James Madison Wells who had been removed as a Reconstruction governor by General Philip Sheridan as a consequence of the 1866 New Orleans race riot massacre,* and now served as surveyor of the Port of New Orleans.

"Mad" Wells was looking for a bribe. Watterson received a $250,000 proposal — $100,000 each for Wells and his white deputy, and $25,000 for each of the two blacks — but he either failed to pursue it or was unsuccessful in doing so.

Toward the end of November, Wells dispatched John Pickett, a disreputable former soldier and adventurer, to seek a million dollar bribe from Hewitt in New York. Along the way, Pickett conspired with Joseph Maddox, a Treasury Department agent in Washington, and then met with Hewitt and later Pelton in New York. Hewitt turned him down, but Pelton was interested. While there, Pickett also talked to John Morrissey who told him that he thought the Oregon vote was sewed up (for only $8,000), which made his proposed Louisiana bribe unnecessary. He compared buying politicians to buying pigs.

Somehow the proposed bribe was exposed, and Pickett was questioned on the record by David Field, a well known attorney who had represented Tweed and the Erie Ring. Nast jumped on that, featuring Morrissey and a large pig. The jewel in the title referred to the large diamond that Tweed (and now Morrissey) wore on his chest, as the former Boss peeked out behind him.

HW February 24, 1877 141 C

A JEWEL AMONG SWINE.

"You must remember that this was on Sunday, and it was not in a bar-room. *He said that he would buy these fellows as readily as he would buy pigs, or words to that effect*, in which I coincided with him in the interest of forty millions of people; but he said that we all knew that Tilden was elected, and that he had just received, or the public had just received, information from Oregon which made it unnecessary to resort to any such measure. That was about the purport of my conversation with Mr. Morrissey."—Colonel Pickett.

With Federal troops on stand-by, Hayes's fellow Ohioans — visiting Senators John Sherman and Stanley Matthews — and other national figures keeping the pressure on in New Orleans, Democratic bribe attempts remained unsuccessful. The Returning Board threw out all the votes from two parishes and some from others — 15,000 altogether, of which 13,200 were Tilden's. There was plenty of misconduct on both sides, especially Democratic threats and violence, but the apparently unbribed electors stayed with their Republican roots.[11]

* See p. 167-8

Florida

The Returning Board in Florida consisted of three state officials, two of them Republicans. The original canvas showed Tilden ahead by 91 votes out of 48,791 cast. Attorney General William Cocke, the lone Democrat, promptly sent a telegram to a Baltimore newspaper stating: “I do not think the Radicals (Republicans) can cheat the Democrats out of the state.”[12]

Manton Marble tried to ensure that result by bribing Samuel McLin, a Confederate Army deserter, who served as Secretary of State and Chairman of the Returning Board. Separately from William Barnum’s and Abram Hewitt’s attempts, he sent at least fifteen encrypted telegrams to Tilden’s nephew, William Pelton, at Tilden’s home where Pelton lived. However, the unsuccessful attempts didn’t come to light until a year and a half after Hayes was inaugurated. Six months after that, Tilden swore to a Congressional committee that he had no knowledge of the telegrams which employed the same cypher code he used in his business transactions.

The Returning Board contested fourteen counties of which five were critical; a handful of counties had novel tactics which included “galvanized” ballots, where the Republican emblem was listed over Democratic names, fooling illiterate voters who recognized the symbol but couldn’t read.[13]

The Board reviewed thousands of false affidavits from voters and officials. Unbribed but promised new appointed positions, the two Republicans discarded 1,030 more Democratic ballots than those of their own party, and Hayes consequently won by 930 votes. Subsequently, Board Chairman McLin was appointed Justice of the New Mexico territory but not confirmed by the Senate.

Exposure

The Marble-Pelton bribery scheme unexpectedly came to light more than a year into the Hayes Administration. In May 1878, the Democratic House, still smarting over Tilden’s loss, formed an investigating committee chaired by Clarkson Potter (NY) to try to prove that “Rutherfraud” Hayes was an illegitimate President. Nast pictured a piece of “Pottery” with the White House turned upside down.

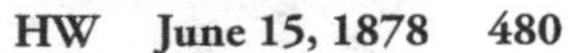
HW June 15, 1878 480

A NEAT DESIGN.
A Bit of Work just from the Potter.

HW October 18, 1879 833

Clarkson Potter

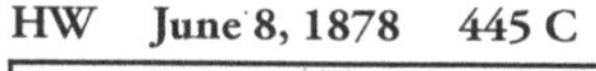
HW June 8, 1878 445 C

Although the committee was stacked with Hayes's political enemies, its investigation foundered after several weeks because of weak evidence and the President's openness. Nast's early depiction of the committee as a camel — appearing two weeks after its formation — was more predictive than he could have guessed.

THE DEMOCRATIC CAMEL.

Suddenly, the political witch hunt backfired, providing Nast a tremendous opportunity to continue flaying Tilden without praising Hayes. The *Tribune* learned that a Republican Senate committee had a batch of incriminating telegrams, probably obtained illicitly from Western Union. Playing cat-and-mouse beginning in August, it printed bits and pieces of the translated telegrams over several weeks. In an expanded edition on October 7, it published its first major exposé detailing correspondence between Marble, C.W. Woolley (a Democrat "fixer") and Pelton. It explained how it acquired and deciphered the telegrams, including the coded originals and their translations.

HW October 26, 1878 856

AN APPEAL TO MARBLE.
"Tis Time; Descend; Be Stone No More."—Shakespeare

The reluctant Potter Committee was forced to investigate. Marble wiggled and lied, but Pelton confessed. Some of the telegrams were addressed to "Russia," Tilden's code name, but the Committee accepted his denial and found him innocent. However, the revelations ruined his chances for the 1880 election, as well as preventing his party from using vote fraud as an issue in that campaign. Curtis referred to him as the "Sage of Ciphers."

Nast's first shot was a blast at Marble, whom he had occasionally targeted as the inconsistent publisher of the Democratic *World*, but now had solid evidence of his public shaming. Accordingly, he toyed with his old adversary, once again using *The Winter's Tale* from Shakespeare as the source of his pun.

Cipher Mumm(er)y

After clashing with his now all-powerful editor, Curtis, in July of 1877, Nast took a self-enforced three-month leave from the *Weekly*. One of his last cartoons featured Tilden and Hendricks as embalmed Egyptian mummies, waiting for the 1880 campaign. It was the first of fourteen images over seven years that would use the mummy theme.

In addition to the embalming (enduring life) feature, Nast emphasized the shriveled stroke victim's apparent health problems. Now, the mum part of "mummy" took on a third meaning, referring to Tilden's stoic silence during the entire post-election controversy.

HW July 7, 1877 524

EMBALMED—THAT THEY MAY KEEP UNTIL 1880—OR LONGER.
Mummy Hendricks To Mummy Tilden: "I am glad I am not so feeble as you."

HW November 2, 1878 869

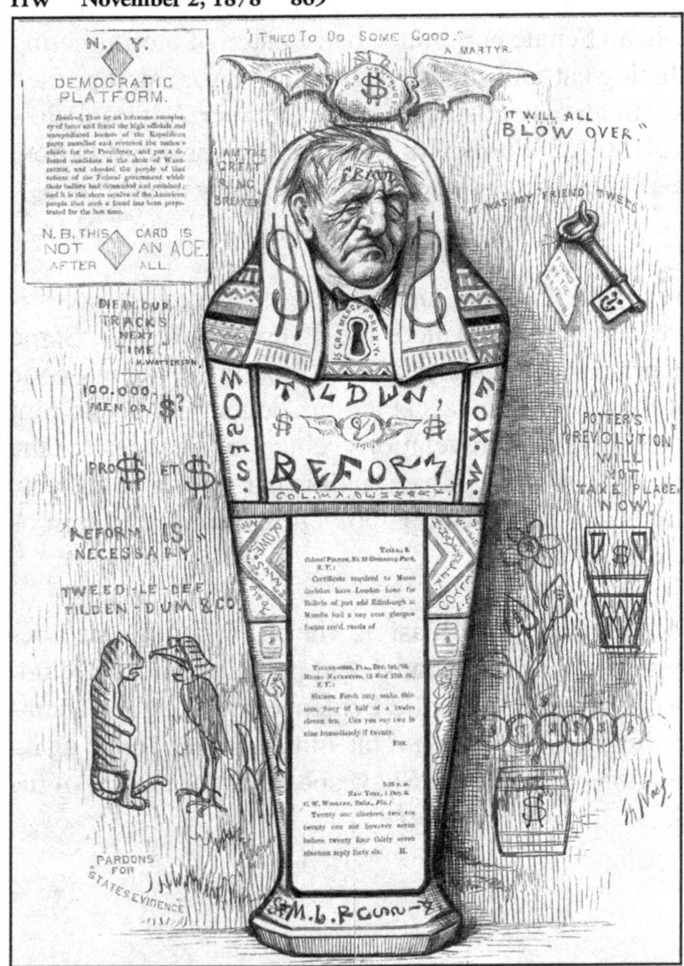

CIPHER MUMM(ER)Y.
Exhumed By The New York Tribune.—**[See Page 875.]**

The *Tribune's* revelations sparked new creativity in Nast's cartoons. They enabled him to add another layer of symbolism, inventively uniting the encryption of the encoded telegrams, the pictorial language of Egyptian hieroglyphics, and his own visual emblems and verbal puns into a complex riddle that his readers could appreciate and solve without undue difficulty. His first response incorporated several inspired pieces into the puzzle.

- *Code names*: Moses (Marble), Woolley (Fox), Tilden (Russia), and Pelton (Denmark).
- *Tilden's residence* at 15 Gramercy Park: The key ("found by the Tribune") was to the right of Tilden's face while the keyhole was under his chin.
- *The $ symbol*: On a prehistoric Egyptian bird over Tilden's head and on his chest; on a sprouting barrel of flowers (lower right); and on an Egyptianized container (above the barrel).
- *Henry Watterson*: Two direct quotes on the left: "Die in our tracks next time," and "100,000 men or $?" A needle about the "N.Y. Democratic Platform" accusing the Republican party of fraud, and here attributed to Watterson, noted that "this card is not an ace after all," (referring to his earlier cartoon demeaning Watterson. (See p. 388).
- *Tweed*, who died in prison earlier that year, still was referenced three times, including Oakey Hall's memorable phrase "It will all blow over."

The Bribe Correspondence

Nast printed three encoded messages on the sarcophagus, and the *Weekly* printed the *Tribune's* translations on a separate page, along with explanations.

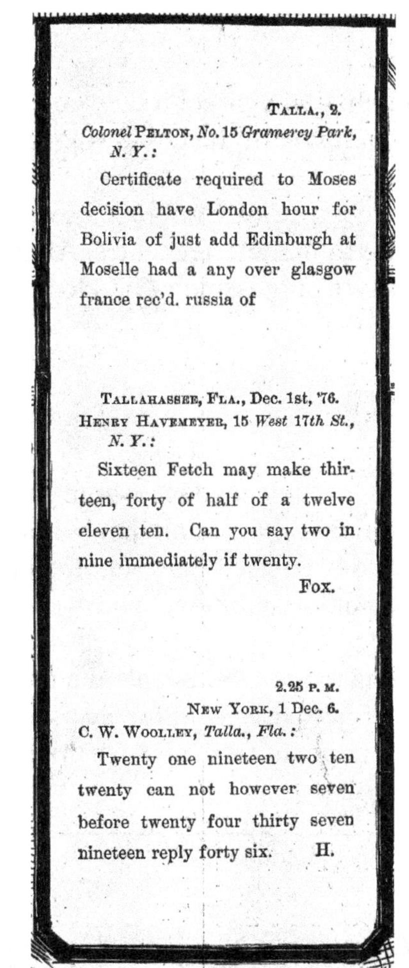

TALLA., 2.
Colonel PELTON, *No.* 15 *Gramercy Park, N. Y.*:
Certificate required to Moses decision have London hour for Bolivia of just add Edinburgh at Moselle had a any over glasgow france rec'd. russia of

TALLAHASSEE, FLA., Dec. 1st, '76.
HENRY HAVEMEYER, 15 *West 17th St., N. Y.*:
Sixteen Fetch may make thirteen, forty of half of a twelve eleven ten. Can you say two in nine immediately if twenty.
FOX.

2.25 P. M.
NEW YORK, 1 Dec. 6.
C. W. WOOLLEY, *Talla., Fla.*:
Twenty one nineteen two ten twenty can not however seven before twenty four thirty seven nineteen reply forty six. H.

[Translation.]

"Tallahassee, *December* 2.

"*Colonel Pelton, 15 Gramercy Park*:

"Have just received a proposition to hand over at any hour required Tilden decision of Board and certificate of Governor for $200,000. Marble"

[Translation.]

"Tallahassee, *December* 1.

"*H. Havemeyer, 15 West Seventeenth Street, New York:*

"Board may make necessary expense of half of a hundred thousand dollars. Can you say will deposit in bank immediately if agreed?"

There can be no doubt of the meaning of this proposal. The reply was as follows:

[Translation.]

"New York, *December* 1.

"*C.W. Woolley, Tallahassee, Florida*:

"Telegram received. Will deposit dollars agreed; (you) can not, however, draw before vote member received."

The top dispatch was dated December 2, three days before the Returning Board had to make its decisions and certification to Congress. Sent by Marble to Pelton, it requested $200,000.

The remaining messages involved C.W. Woolley, an obscure Pennsylvania politician who had been sent to Florida with pre-arranged cipher codes, and Henry Havemeyer, a wealthy member of the Sugar Trust family. Both men were deeply involved with racing trotter horses, which probably initiated their otherwise unlikely connection. Woolley requested $50,000 on December 1, the day before Marble's message. Pelton wanted the cheaper deal and told his Florida envoys to consult. However, his dispatch was scrambled and the resultant delay killed any possibility of a deal.

The Electoral Commission

The certifications from all 37 states were due in Congress on December 6, 1876. Ultimately, Florida and Louisiana submitted three sets, and South Carolina and Oregon two; Democratic factions authored the extras.

The Constitution required the President pro-tem of the Senate, Republican Thomas Ferry of Michigan, to open the certificates and "count the votes;" however, it wasn't clear who should count in disputed circumstances. The Democratic House wanted to count by itself, or in conjunction with the Senate; the Republicans wanted Ferry to count.

Other critical unprecedented questions included:

• Which set of returns should be counted?
• Could the counting body go behind the face of a certificate and investigate the evidence on which it was based?
• Could that body disqualify an elector, as Governor Grover, in violation of the state constitution, tried to do in Oregon?

If Congress could not agree, then a Democratic filibuster that went past the March 4 inauguration date could throw the election into the Democratic House (as happened in 1824), and Tilden would win. In fact, that was his preferred strategy.

With so much uncertainty in both parties, and with Inauguration Day only six weeks away, Congress agreed to appoint an Electoral Commission to debate and decide the outcome for each of the four contested states. After a week's discussion, both houses approved a 15-man Commission on January 26: five Congressmen (3:2 Democrats), five Senators (3:2 Republicans) and five Supreme Court Justices.

David Davis

The designated Justices included two Democrats, two Republicans and Davis, an independent whom the Congressional Democrats believed would vote their way. Their support of the Commission hinged on that belief.

Davis, who had been Lincoln's campaign manager in 1860 (and subsequently administered his estate), had been appointed to the Court two years later. He was known to have his own presidential ambitions, and was a candidate for the Liberal Republican nomination at its 1872 Cincinnati Convention.*

To the total surprise of both national parties, the Illinois Legislature elected Davis to the U.S. Senate the day before Congress finally approved the Commission. Davis, not wanting to alienate either party with his decisive electoral vote, accepted and resigned from the Court, thereby keeping his presidential hopes alive in his own mind.

HW February 17, 1877 121 C

EX -JUDGE DAVID DAVIS (NOW SENATOR), AT HOME,
After Wandering Abroad For Many A Year.

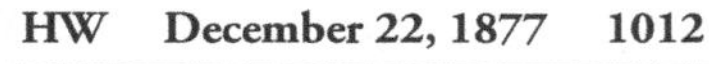

HW December 22, 1877 1012

THE MANDARIN IN THE SENATE.

* See p. 310

Nast appeared to understand Davis's ambition, and tweaked the 300-pounder on his political neutrality over the years. Before Tilden dropped out of the 1880 chase for the Democratic nomination, Nast portrayed Davis as his potential running mate, carrying Tilden's sarcophagus on his back.

HW June 21, 1879 493

THE DAVID DAVIS BOOM.
The "Independent" Senator, By Sitting On The Party-Line Fence So Long, Has Completely Obliterated It.

HW June 5, 1880 361

NOT A BAD IDEA.
It Will Take "*A Strong Man*" To Carry Him To The White House.

Joseph Bradley, a Republican appointed to the Court by Grant in 1870, became the decisive fifteenth vote in place of Davis. All four disputed states were decided for Hayes by 8-7 margins. The final count was announced to Congress about 4 A.M. on March 2. The Inauguration was two days away.

Nast commemorated Hayes' victory as passively as he could with a 185-vote flag flying over Fort Sumter in a small back-page cartoon. He dedicated the small back-page cartoon to New York Congressman David Field who had unsuccessfully argued Florida's case before the Commission. (Field was a frequent target when he represented Boss Tweed, Jim Fisk and other Tammany figures.*)

HW March 10, 1877 196

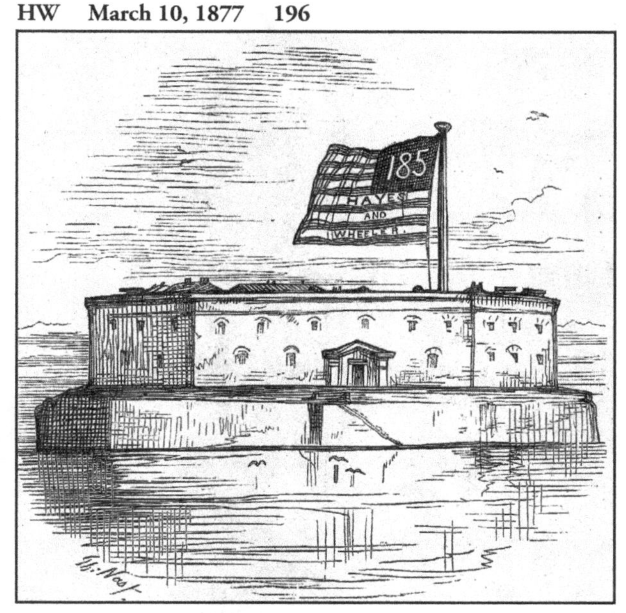

YOU CAN'T "GOBBLE" IT UP.
Mr. D.D. Field, you might as well go to sleep, the Flag is all right.

* See p. 287

Military Reconstruction's End

For Southern Democrats, replacing "Bayonet Rule" with "Home Rule" was a more important issue than the Presidency. Florida had elected a Democratic governor, but carpetbaggers Daniel Chamberlain in South Carolina and Stephen Packard in Louisiana still were in charge.

To foreclose the possibility of a filibuster in the Democratic House, secret negotiations during February and a final oral agreement reached at a hotel conference six days before the Inauguration, provided for the withdrawal to their barracks of Federal troops in South Carolina and Louisiana. That enabled ex-Confederates Wade Hampton and Francis Nicholls to take over as Governors in early April, and effectively ended Reconstruction.

One of the Southerners who played a key role in the entire post-election drama — and who was well respected by his peers in both parties — was Mississippi Congressman Lucius Q.C. Lamar. Referring to the Louisiana Returning Board, he commented: "The fraudulency of returns certified by the carpetbagger returning board was so patent . . . that the (Electoral) Commission dodged the question of fraud by denying its own power under the Constitution to go behind the returns."

After Lamar's death in 1893, an unsent note was found in his papers: "The Commission has not ventured to say that Tilden was not elected; they have simply declared that they are technically disabled from examining if he was."[14]

In the immediate aftermath, Nast gave both parties a kick in the same issue. For Tilden, it was simple with his barrel falling apart. For the winner, he used the Elephant in a new role in what he clearly saw as a mixed blessing.

HW March 24, 1877 227

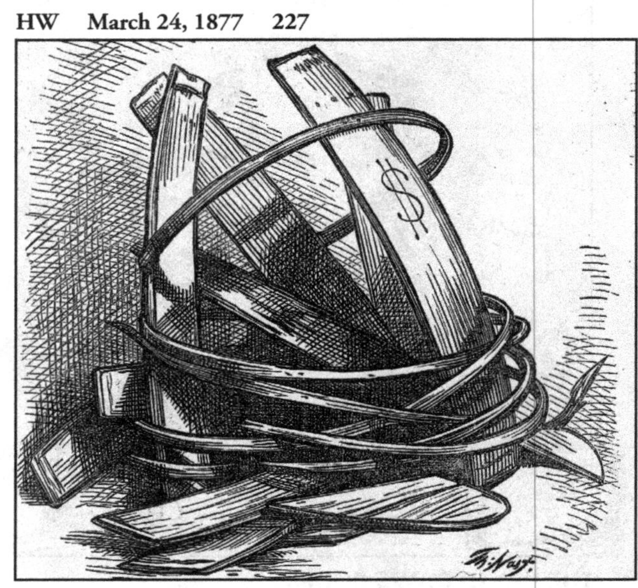

GONE TO SMASH.

HW March 24, 1877 232

"ANOTHER SUCH VICTORY, AND I AM UNDONE."—PYRRHUS

In its first nine appearances, the Elephant represented the Republican vote but not the Party itself. Unlabeled here, the battered creature symbolized the Pyrrhic victory of the Party.[15] Other than the tombstone of the Democratic Tiger, "Greatly mourned by the bereaved filibusters," and a laurel victory wreath on its bandaged head, all Nast's touches were negative.

Sagging and exhausted, its right eye covered by the bandage, one foreleg in a sling and a crutch by the other, a tourniquet on its limp trunk, sticking plasters (band-aids) all over its body, and its tail severed, Nast's symbol seemed to be warily assessing its prospects out of its good eye, It was oblivious to the tiny vultures circling over its head.

In a personal sense, the election results also had a pyrrhic dimension for Nast. At age 36, he was on the political and even artistic downside of his career as several new impediments loomed, especially the increasing conflict with his editor.

Chapter 33
Power Struggle with Curtis: Early Rounds

Inherent Conflict

Obvious to its audience and its competitors, there was no love lost between the two leading political and pictorial journalists at *Harper's Weekly*. George William Curtis believed that "his paper," as he referred to it, should speak with one voice and unquestionably it should be his.

As he wrote Nast in late January 1872: "The one thing I have striven for in the conduct of this paper is unity of sentiment. I don't think the pictures and the text should be at variance."[1]

However, Curtis's expressed philosophy contained far more than met the eye. When the two differed, he abhorred the thought and fact that Nast was able to sell his pictorial passions more effectively than his own carefully crafted editorials could persuade *Harper's* audience. The reality was that Nast was more influential.

Probably, equally, or even more important to Curtis, he objected to Nast lambasting his close friends like Senators Carl Schurz and Charles Sumner, even when they obviously deserved it. Continuing in the same January 1872 letter, he wrote: "It is possible to criticize a man severely in words without the least ridicule, but it can't be done in pictures . . . I protest to you as a friend against the injustice done to other friends, and *in a way of which I must bear the responsibility*."

Nast showed the letter to Fletcher Harper, who made the final decisions when his two indispensable journalists disagreed. Fletcher liked and admired both men, and believed that "his paper" — which, of course, it was — benefited from both their diverse viewpoints.

A few days later, Nast wrote Sallie that Fletcher and the other Harpers who saw the letter, would back him over Curtis, "who knew which side his bread was buttered on;" additionally, Fletcher had told him that "he was right oftener than Curtis." [2]

That last point was accurate because Fletcher and Nast were harder-hitting conservatives than Curtis, who often lost his objectivity when it came to Nast's current Liberal Republican targets. Moreover, Nast had just come off his victorious Tweed campaign, where his cartoons did far more for *Harper's* circulation (reaching almost 300,000 on occasion), profit and reputation than Curtis's editorials and commentary. A superb businessman, Fletcher couldn't afford to lose Nast, and was certain he wouldn't lose Curtis.

On occasion, Curtis publicly recognized and even acclaimed Nast's independence, as in this July 18, 1874 editorial.

> *A newspaper commenting upon a recent drawing by Mr. Nast, says that if he lives long enough, he will caricature "every prominent man in the country, no matter what his style of politics or style of religion." If this means that Mr. Nast will use his skill wantonly and for the mere sake of levity, we are very sure that the paper is mistaken. But if it means that he will not hesitate to use his pencil in the cause of what he believes to be truth and justice and liberty and sound principles of government and pure administration, against those of every party and every church who assail or injure them, then it merely does him justice. But in such a course, Mr. Nast does only what every independent editor or writer for the press now does.*

The post-dated editorial was in print on July 8. The next day Nast wrote to thank Curtis and define his goal of objectivity. [3]

Dear Mr. Curtis,

I cannot allow this occasion to pass, without writing to you to thank you for the kindness with which you have defined my position in this week's paper.

To be entirely independent and impartial is my chief aim, and I consider that my duty towards any fellow citizens is performed exactly in proportion as I am unpredjudiced (sic) in the use of my pencil.

Yours truly,
Th: Nast.

Unfortunately for both of them, Curtis was really just giving lip service to what he didn't believe. On occasion, he resented the bluntness, lack of good taste and immediate emotional impact of Nast's cartoons, even when they may have been in accord with his political views. When they differed, he suffered, complained, and censored when he could.

Accordingly, the continuing struggle between editorialist and cartoonist became a dominant factor affecting Nast's career — more so than his biographer Albert Paine, or any subsequent commentator, realized. To appreciate how and why it so affected him, it is critical to understand the interplay and events that began less than four years after Nast joined the *Weekly* in August 1862.

George William Curtis

The gulf between their backgrounds couldn't have been wider. Nast arrived as a five-year old German immigrant. Handicapped by language, dyslexia, inability to concentrate and frequent school changes, he dropped out at age 13. His ability to draw was exceptional, so he began working for *Frank Leslie's Illustrated Newspaper* at 15. Much of his cultural education came from the theatre, where his father played in the orchestra. Short, fat, poor and barely literate, he had few friends.

Born in 1824, patrician Curtis was 16 years older than Nast. The first ancestral Curtis arrived from England in 1636, and his mother's family in the 1700s. His father was a bank president, and his mother's forbears included a Chief Justice and a U.S. Senator. His blue blood education included private tutoring; 18 months at Brook Farm, a Utopian community; some of the next two years on a Concord, MA farm in close proximity to future literary greats like Ralph Waldo Emerson, Nathaniel Hawthorne and James Russell Lowell; and four years back-packing around Europe and the Middle East with his older brother. When he returned at age 26, he had a deep knowledge of world history, art, music, literature, French, German and Italian. [4]

Curtis began his relationship with Harper & Brothers shortly after his arrival when the firm published his travel books. His "Easy Chair" column first appeared in *Harper's Monthly* in 1853, and continued until his death four decades later. "The Lounger" column — short essays on life and culture — commenced in the *Weekly* in 1857, its first year. In summary, Curtis had developed a strong relationship with Fletcher and his brothers for a decade before Nast came on board.

Curtis posed for this carte de visite in 1862, the year before he became editor.

In late 1863, Fletcher finally fired his pro-slavery editor, John Bonner — who had rejected or delayed some of Nast's cartoons — and replaced him with Curtis, who reveled in his new role. Curtis appreciated the added value of the *Weekly's* illustrations as he wrote to an old friend the week after Lincoln died.

"I am perfectly free to say what I think upon all public questions in Harper's Weekly without the least trouble or responsibility for the details of the paper, and with no necessity of even being in the office. The audience is immense . . . (sometimes) more than 200,000. Its circulation is among that class which needs enlightenment . . . and access is secured to it by the character of the paper as an illustrated sheet."[5]

Like Nast, Curtis generally didn't go into the Harpers office on Franklin Square more than once a week; Thursday was his regular day to write and deliver editorials. He lived in a comfortable home on Staten Island and raised his family there. He frequently lectured on the Lyceum circuit, so traveling from home gave him the freedom to do what he wanted when he wanted. He also had a vacation home in Ashland, Massachusetts, where he spent considerable time.

Both Curtis's stature and his income were enhanced in 1869. After Henry Raymond suffered a fatal heart attack or stroke in the home of his mistress (actress Rose Eytinge) in June, *New York Times* publisher George Jones tried to hire Curtis as his replacement, at twice his current pay. (Raymond had been making $10,000, but the size of the offer to Curtis is unknown. Raymond also received a $5,000 salary as a concurrent Congressman.)[6]

At Fletcher's suggestion, Curtis took time to reflect, and then decided to stay at *Harper's*. When he told Fletcher, his salary was doubled on the spot to match the offer from Jones. Over and above his personal relationship with Fletcher, there were several apparent reasons why Curtis made this pivotal career decision.

First, he valued his life style, family time, and the ability to work from home or readily go on the lecture circuit. Next, from a prestige viewpoint, he could wield more influence from his current pulpit where circulation was three to six times the 35,000 of the *Daily Times*, and passalong readership much higher.

Lastly, Raymond's *Times* had supported Johnson's "policy;" opposed the Civil Rights and Military Acts, as well as impeachment; consequently alienated Republican Party Radicals whom Fletcher and the *Weekly* supported; and would avoid criticism of Tweed and his connivers for another 15 months while the Boss's two business partners controlled its board.* Belatedly, Raymond reluctantly shifted his allegiance and supported Grant for President in 1868.**

Curtis enjoyed his initial taste of politics when he worked closely with the Republican Party's first Presidential nominee, John C. Fremont, who lost the 1856 election to James Buchanan. Shortly afterward, Fremont attended Curtis's Thanksgiving Day wedding to Anna Shaw, daughter of a wealthy outspoken abolitionist who lived on Staten Island. (Why Curtis resided there.) [7]

Subsequently, Curtis was a delegate to every national and most New York State Republican Party conventions for the rest of his life. In 1860, he backed his good friend William Seward over Lincoln, but later admitted "(Lincoln) is wonderfully acute, simple, sagacious, and of antique honesty! I can forgive the jokes and the big hands, and the inability to make bows. Some of us who doubted were wrong."[8]

Curtis and Nast marched to the same drummer during the Civil War. Along with Lincoln and Fletcher, he recognized that the impact on recruiting and morale created by Nast's illustrations couldn't be matched by any editorial writer, no matter his skill with words.

Fletcher Harper

Although he was the youngest of the four Harper brothers, Fletcher was the most talented and entrepreneurial. A natural leader, motivator and manager, he was the marketing genius responsible for initiating and operating the firm's periodicals: the *Monthly Magazine* (1850), the *Weekly* (1857) and the *Bazar* (1867). He started the school book business (1841), and played the major role in literature acquisitions. His brothers managed functional aspects of the business: production (James); finance and purchasing (John); and correspondence and proof-reading (Joseph Wesley, known as Wesley).

---

* See p. 254

** See Nast's clever portrayal on p. 217

Mathew Brady took this photograph in February 1863 of Fletcher, James, John and Wesley.

Fletcher took particular interest in the *Weekly*, especially in the selection, placement and layout of its illustrations. He had a quasi-paternal relationship with Tommy (as he called him) Nast, who was 34 years younger. He recognized the journalistic power of Tommy's illustrations and cartoons to attract and keep subscribers, and found Nast's hard-nosed attitudes toward ex-Confederates, Pope Pius IX, the Irish, and Greeley aligned with his own. Most important, he was willing to take heat from critics who couldn't understand why the editorial and pictorial viewpoints expressed in his paper were not always in agreement.

Round One to Nast

After Andrew Johnson became President in April 1865, both Nast and Curtis gave him the benefit of any political doubt for the rest of the year. When Johnson sided with the South and clashed with the Radical Republicans in the Senate in 1866, Nast attacked with his "King Andy" cartoons. Curtis responded with several critical letters to Nast, creating what would become on-going tension between them. As discussed previously, that friction was a significant factor in Nast's decision to leave the *Weekly* in May 1867 — to create his Caricaturama — without a return date in mind.

Curtis claimed that he was defending Johnson out of respect for the office, not the man, and that Nast's ridicule went too far. Equally likely, Curtis was influenced by his old friend William Seward, who remained loyal to the President, and whom Nast depicted alongside King Andy in several hard-hitting cartoons.* (Seward remained as Secretary of State until Johnson left office). Fletcher's views coincided with Nast's, so the defamatory cartoons kept coming in spite of Curtis's complaints.

Johnson's impeachment and trial took place during Nast's absence. Curtis's attitude toward the President had hardened over time. He wrote a friend that he "should have voted to convict the impeached President, although he respected the Senators who voted for acquittal." In retrospect, Curtis was somewhat relieved that impeachment failed.[9] Nast and probably Fletcher disagreed.

---

* See p. 168 and 173

Round Two to Curtis

After both the Caricaturama and the *Illustrated Chicago News* failed, Nast returned to *Harper's Weekly* in June 1868 after a year away. It is conceivable that Curtis played a role in that, assuming they saw each other on May 21 at the Republican Convention in Chicago.* Back in March, Norton Chipman had commissioned Nast to draw a large picture to surprise the delegates; the *Illustrated Chicago News* handled the secret production before it folded in June. When "Match Him!!" unexpectedly appeared on a large painted curtain, not only did the delegates cheer wildly — which Curtis took in — but Grant had his campaign slogan along with "Let Us Have Peace."

Both Curtis and Fletcher were strong Grant supporters, so they welcomed Nast back — with one new binding restriction: Nast had to clear all his cartoons through Curtis before they were accepted. Fletcher raised Nast's pay to $150 a page — he was still a freelancer with no exclusivity clause — but Nast, with no bargaining power, had to submit to Curtis's control. The condition was so distasteful to him that he apparently never mentioned it to his biographer Paine.

However, a letter that he wrote to Curtis two months later, at his Massachusetts vacation home, clearly laid out the changed relationship among the three as his campaign against Horatio Seymour and Frank Blair was moving into high gear.[10]

> *My dear Mr. Curtis August 3, 1868*
> *I received your last expressing approval of my newest subjects.*
> *Today, I send down a half-page block for which I would like you to write a few lines if you could, as I feel that it wants an explanation. I enclose a sketch of it. It will be for the paper that goes to press next Monday. I call it "Predjudice." (sic, Curtis did not write an explanation).*
> *"The White Man's Government" is finished, all but Belmont's head. I am not satisfied with the photos that I have and am waiting for the last from Mr. Brady. This will be for the week after the above mentioned. (Getting Mathew Brady's carte de visite delayed the issue date by a week, while demonstrating Nast's quest for perfection).*
> *I have also drawn a two column comic of "Ulysses the Giant-Killer," but before I take it in, I would like the subject to have your sanction, for if I show Mr. Fletcher Harper anything new, something upon which you have not refused your approval, he is at a total loss as to what to say about it, and must likely refuse.*
> *Of late, he has become tender of other peoples feelings, and wishes to beware of giving offense to anyone. He does not wish too much nigger, wants to avoid the horrible and come out strong on the beautiful. But whenever I see him look doubtful, I exclaim, "Mr. Curtis has approved of this," and then he condescendingly observes, "oh! well then, you can go on with it."*

HW August 22, 1868 540

PREJUDICE.
"What! won't these stupid White Geese even let me go to School without hissing and biting at me?"

Fletcher probably had *Would You Marry Your Daughter to a Nigger?* in mind; it had been published a month earlier.** However, the term was in common usage then and was not considered offensive by most people.

* See p. 211
** See p. 210

Ulysses the Giant-Killer finally appeared as a back-page cartoon after the election. Grant, smoking a cigar, threw the heads of Seymour and Blair on to the same heap where he had deposited the heads of eight prominent identifiable rebel generals at the close of the War. Surprisingly Forrest and Semmes didn't make the scene, possibly because of space limitations.

HW November 21, 1868 752

ULYSSES THE GIANT-KILLER.
Columbia. "Throw them on the same Heap!"

After November 1868, Nast made only four appearances in the *Weekly* until June 1869. Two were published as Johnson left office, including *The Political Death of the Bogus Caesar*, originally intended for the *Illustrated Chicago News* and drawn a year earlier.*

However, Nast drew two cartoons which were never published but showed his intense feelings about censorship. One was probably drawn in 1869 or 1870 and hung in the Harper business office for many years. Called *Small Potatoes Before the Supreme Court*; it depicted the artist, standing among his laurels while showing a picture to the various department heads, including Curtis. Paine identified the "judges," and quoted Fletcher saying to Henry Alden, the *Monthly's* editor: "We are the only respectable ones. He left us out."[11]

SMALL POTATOES BEFORE THE SUPREME COURT.

During the spring of 1870, Nast sketched for his own wry amusement — or emotional catharsis — a picture of Curtis lecturing him with an extended forefinger from his *Editor's Easy Chair,* as he whittled the lead in his pencil: "Don't make it too sharp, Tommy, or you'll spoil the POINT." Of course, stiff and formal Curtis probably never would have addressed him other than by his last name. The artist's retort — "I must be cruel, only to be kind," was derived from Hamlet's response to his mother (Act III, Scene 4).

* See p. 182

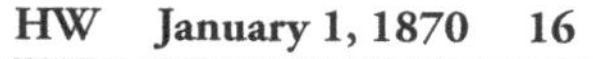
HW January 1, 1870 16

Author's Collection, Originally from Draper Hill

OH!!!

From Nast's viewpoint, he had not only a censorship but also a pocketbook issue with Curtis. The editor's private wastebasket had at least one signed but discarded woodblock in it. A proofsheet hanging on the wall implied that it was an intended cover cartoon of Pope Pius IX, slipping on a 19th Century hillside and dropping a basket of doctrinal eggs. After likely conferring with Fletcher — who despised the Pope as much as Nast did, but had given his editor control over his artist the previous year — Curtis finally published it in the 1869 Christmas issue (post-dated January 1, 1870), but on the back page and reduced to a small two-column picture entitled *Oh!!!*

Curtis's shrinkage, which was repeated for six subsequent anti-papal cartoons, also shrunk Nast's income from the $150 he received for a full page.

Curtis, a Unitarian but not a nativist, did not feel as antagonistic toward the Pope as the ardent Methodist and nativist Harpers did. Consequently, Fletcher subsequently hired Eugene Lawrence, strident anti-papist and anti-Catholic, to write most of the *Weekly's* vitriolic editorials about the Pope, the Church and the public school controversy.

Round Three to Nast

As 1870 progressed and 1871 exploded, the cartoonist's role and resultant public acclaim in bringing down the Tweed Ring, made him too valuable for Curtis or even Fletcher to interfere with or censor his efforts. His effect on circulation, profits, and saving the Harper's schoolbook business, put Curtis into the shade. All prior clearances or censorship disappeared as the Grant Administration reached out to Nast to help win a second term in 1872.

That became a factor during the Greeley campaign when Curtis literally begged Nast in writing and in person not to attack his friends Carl Schurz and Charles Sumner too harshly. As noted previously, Nast had a sound basis for believing that Curtis was putting friendship ahead of principle.*

* See p. 308

On August 1, 1872 — three days after Sumner abandoned his lifetime cause to urge blacks to vote for the Ku Klux Klan-supported Democratic ticket, Curtis wrote Nast requesting him "not to introduce Mr. Sumner in any way into any picture."[12]

My Dear Nast:

Since Webster's "Seventh of March" speech nothing in our political history has seemed to me so sad as Mr. Sumner's letter. He is my dear friend, a man whose service to the country and to civilization have been immense, who deserves all honor and regard from all honorable men. The position of such a man may be criticized in writing, because in writing perfect respect may be preserved. But it is not so with the caricaturing pencil. You see what I am coming to. You are your own master, and your name is signed to your work. But it is nevertheless supposed that I, as editor, am responsible for what pains me the more because of my friendship and my difference. Besides, the caricature puts a false sense upon what is written and covers the expressions of the most sincere regard with an appearance of insincerity. There are thousands of good men who feel as I do about it, and I hope that your friendship for me will grant my request that you will not introduce Mr. Sumner in any way into any picture.

Very sincerely yours,
George William Curtis

Nast responded: "The effect that the fact of Sumner's heroic past, and the prestige derived therefrom, made the Senator's present attitude all the more a menace to the cause of right."

In his reply on August 22 — eight days after he had seen Nast's merciless cartoon linking Sumner to the KKK in print* — Curtis clearly explained how he differed from Nast and Fletcher Harper in what a cartoon should provide: "A good-humored laugh or a moral denunciation."[13]

My Dear Nast,

I am very much obliged by your note. I did ask you not to caricature Sumner, Greeley, Schurz and Trumbull, because at that time I thought it was bad policy — and I think so still!

The exact difficulty which I feel is this, that it is wrong to represent as morally contemptible men of the highest character with whom you politically differ. To serve up Schurz and Sumner as you would Tweed, shows, in my judgment, lack of moral perception. And to one who feels as I do about those men, and who knows that he is about right! every picture in which you defame them is a separate pain. **There is a wide distinction between a good-humored laugh and a moral denunciation.**

Your are very good to have answered me at all. I know how I differ from you and from our friends in Franklin Square upon this point, and I have wished only to free my conscience by protesting. I shall not trouble you any more, and I am,

Very truly yours,
George William Curtis

* * * *

Fletcher undoubtedly recognized that the personal gulf between his two star journalists was too wide ever to be bridged over. However, Nast was too important to the *Weekly's* circulation and bottom line to have him leave — or help a competitor — so paying Nast $5,000 annually for exclusivity achieved his purpose.

Incompatibility and conflict were assured for the next 14 years before Nast left *Harper's* for good. Nast confided to his Morristown lawyer and close friend that Curtis "would sometimes treat him as an inferior hired draftsman, not as the pictorial editor he ascribed to himself."[15]

Conversely, two years after Curtis died in 1892, Edward Cary, a former reporter for the *Times*, published his biography, including scores of letters. There was not a single mention of Thomas Nast in the book.

* See p. 326

Chapter 34
Power Struggle with Curtis: Tipping Point

Grant's Second Term

Nast and Curtis continued to express their differing viewpoints during the balance of Grant's Presidency, and the press took note. Approaching its second anniversary in 1875, the *Graphic* captured the Nast vs. Curtis disagreement over Grant's use of Federal troops to pacify Louisiana and determine control of its state government. A.B. Frost (who would join *Harper's* art staff the following year) pictured the two standing back-to-back, along with two accompanying limericks. Nast — greatly slimmed down and much younger — was obviously favored over "This jealous old party named Curtis." Their internal battle was out in the open, more than two years before the decisive game-changing blow-up.

Other ephemeral papers joined in. Frederick Opper, a 19-year old novice on the staff of *Wild Oats*, a leading comic paper of the 1870s, tweaked Nast on several counts, including his anti-Catholicism. (After spending four years at Leslie's, Opper joined *Puck* in 1880 and stayed for 18 years.)

June 14, 1876

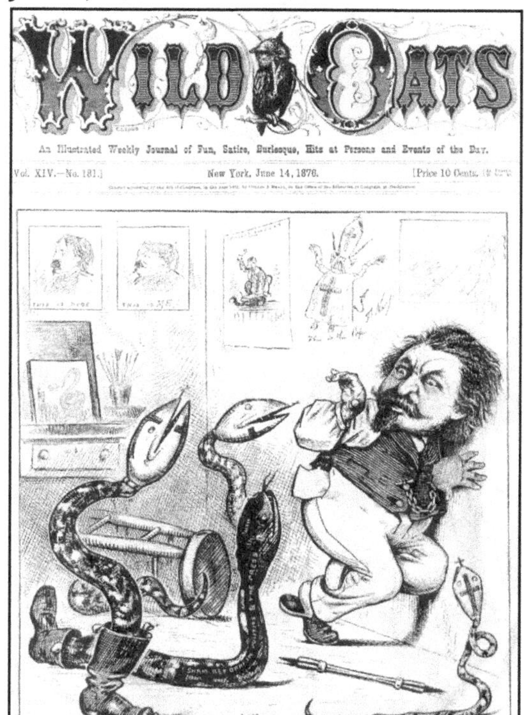

TOMMY SEES SNAKES AGAIN.—A T.-NAST-Y CARTOON.

February 3, 1875

LOOK ON THAT PICTURE AND ON THIS.

"Great wits are sure to madness near allied,
And thin partitions do their bounds divide."

There was an old party named Curtis,
Who said, "Nast, you surely will hurt us
If truer than I
Your pencil you ply,"
This jealous old party named Curtis.

There was a young party called Nast:
His eye on his picture he cast,
And said, "Yes, 'tis better,
More true to the letter!"
This egregious young person called Nast.

As previously mentioned, Curtis worked out of his home on Staten Island. On Thursdays, he would come into *Harper's* composing room, write his editorials and hand them to his compositor as he finished a page.[1] He rarely encountered Nast who also worked out of his home, delivering or sending in his completed drawings on woodblocks of the stipulated size. Curtis generally didn't see the cartoons until after the *Weekly* was published on Wednesdays, ten days prior to the cover date.

As the nominating conventions approached in mid-June 1876, Curtis left Grant relatively alone, but blasted his scandal-tainted associates — William Belknap, Orville Babcock, Columbus Delano and Alexander Shepherd, in particular. Separately, he attacked New York Senator Roscoe Conkling, who would have liked the nomination for himself and controlled New York's delegates.

Curtis favored Kentuckian Benjamin Bristow, whom Grant had fired as Treasury Secretary for being too diligent in prosecuting the Whiskey Ring scandals by indicting his personal secretary and close friend, Orville Babcock.* Curtis seconded Bristow's nomination at the Republican convention.

Nast was convinced that Curtis's editorials were helping Democratic prospects. Accordingly, for his own quiet satisfaction, he apparently pictured Curtis as a jackass — although that wasn't recognizable to anyone not in the know. The Democratic Party, depicted as a fox, was standing on the Curtis-implied jackass, to crown Grant as a scapegoat — his sins, spelled out on the goat's horns, included the blunders of Congress and carrying out the Republican platform. Other previously used Democratic symbols including a goose, hare and bear observed, while the press, as a pack of dogs and other personified beasts, howled away.

The grubby jackass had a highlighted caterpillar and worm crawling on his snout, as well as several rats nearby. Other than the shaggy hair, there was no physical resemblance or textual inference to Curtis. Silently to his public, and like a diary entry to himself, Nast vented his contempt for his editor via the vermin on and around him.

HW May 13, 1876 388-389

Curtis

THE CROWNING INSULT TO HIM WHO OCCUPIES THE PRESIDENTIAL CHAIR.

* See p. 373-374

Nast opposed Hayes because the new President's policies on Southern pacification in particular, and Civil Service reform — championed by Curtis — to a lesser degree, controverted Grant's. Nast did support Hayes on other key topics like hard money and funding the army.

However, Curtis refused to let Nast attack Hayes directly. If the two agreed on a certain issue, or Curtis didn't have an opinion, Nast had a green light; otherwise, his only option was to ignore the subject. When Nast's estate went on the auction block in 1906, it contained more than 75 photographs of Grant and exactly one of Hayes.

Fast forward almost a year to April Fools' Day, *The Day We Celebrate*, when Hayes had been President for a month. Late the preceding December, Curtis had been the keynote speaker at a formal banquet, where he referred to himself as a Puritan and a Pilgrim as he talked about peaceful resolution of the Hayes-Tilden electoral deadlock.[2]

The foppish jackass presiding in Nast's matching cartoon had the same full-face features as its predecessor. This time it wore luxuriant "mutton chop" side-whiskers and parted its shaggy hair in the middle — as Curtis did — and had a fool's cap on the tapestry over its head. The toast — "We are not all dead yet" — was relevant to the restrictions Curtis placed on Nast with regard to President Hayes after his Inauguration.

Perhaps the biggest shock was that the cartoon was printed. Assuming that Curtis saw it in advance, he probably couldn't admit to anybody that he was the target. Moreover, it was on the cover, so if he did see it before publication, it may have been too late to reject it. **Without question, this was the strongest personal attack on his editor that Nast ever made in *Harper's Weekly.***

HW April 7, 1877 261 C

"THE DAY WE CELEBRATE"—(APRIL 1).
Toast: "We are not all dead yet."

HW January 5, 1907 19

GEORGE W. CURTIS
(Portrait from 1892 in his HW obituary)

Post-election Reaction

After the election on November 7, a delegate from the Republican National Committee was dispatched to Morristown with a check for $10,000 in recognition of Nast's contributions. Possibly they wanted his active support for Hayes. He rejected the money and any implication that went with it, saying Harper Brothers had already paid him.[3]

As previously noted, Nast featured himself as a political participant even when his wings were somewhat clipped. Three weeks after the election, he was on *Harper's* cover sharpening his hardest pencil for "more hard labor", and on the back page, keeping cool in a polar refrigerator.

HW December 2, 1876 965 C

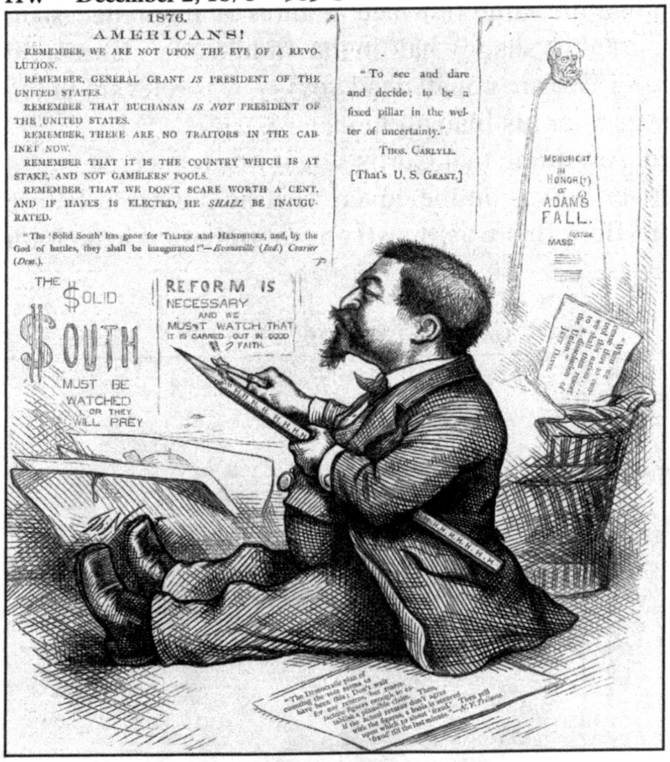

NO REST FOR THE WICKED—SENTENCED TO MORE HARD LABOR.

HW December 2, 1876 980

"KEEP COOL!" TEN DAYS AFTER THE ELECTION.

Supporting Curtis

Four weeks later, Nast actually supported Curtis in probably the most scatological cartoon he ever drew for *Harper's*. Edwin L. Godkin, editor of the *Nation*, and Curtis got into a spitting contest about their respective degrees of support for Hayes before the election.

In an editorial entitled "Independence of Party," appearing in print the day after the election, Curtis blasted Godkin for feigning independence while tacitly supporting Tilden. He used his restraint of Nast to make his point.

Harper's Weekly sincerely desired the success of Hayes and Wheeler as promoting the best interests of the country. But what proof should we have given of our faith and hope if Mr. Nast had filled the paper of trenchant cartoons of conspicuous Republicans, and we had occupied these columns with "digs" and stabs at the party? If an independent paper decides to sustain a party candidate, it will undoubtedly do so in an independent manner.[4]

Godkin responded the following week, and concluded with a statement promising to say more about "campaign party journalism (with illustrations), which we think one of the most immoral and debauching agencies of our time." He didn't follow up on his promise so, a month later, Nast dressed as a courtier, delivered in person a large box of Blue Pills, a leading constipation remedy, "*to be taken before writing editorials to the plebians*."

Well over a century before four-letter words regularly appeared in the popular media, Nast baldly told Godkin that his commentary was full of shit. He complemented his central theme with all sorts of anal-personality "warnings" from the editor, and reprinted the *Nation's* earlier messages in full.

HW December 30, 1876 1061

"WITH THE UTMOST RESPECT"—OUR ARTIST AS THE GOOD (?) SAMARITAN.

Probably in appreciation of that supportive cartoon, Curtis printed extracts from a glowing English magazine article about Nast which occupied two full columns on an editorial page. The author was Thomas Butler Gunn, Nast's one-time critic and current friend.[5]

However, the good will evaporated quickly. Over the four months following the Inauguration, Nast contributed 40 cartoons to the *Weekly*, featuring the Russian-Turkish War, other European topics and anything but the Presidency, while Curtis poured praise on Hayes.

Note: Turkey lost. Nast depicted England (John Bull), Germany (Bismarck), Austria (Franz Joseph) and Russia (Czar Alexander II) cutting up the Turkish empire.

HW June 30, 1877 497 C

PEACE RUMORS.

Let Us Have (A) Peace (Piece).

The Turk wishes he was a Christian

The daily papers continually commented about missing Nast's pictorial commentary on the Hayes Administration, as did increasing numbers of letters to the Harper Brothers establishment. Finally, "Brooklyn Joe" Harper — Fletcher's successor as chief executive — handed Nast one such letter, and was told that Nast was ready when he was. Joe reiterated that the "no attack" policy would remain.

"The general disposition seems to be to stand back and give the President's policy a chance." Nast asked if he could put that into a cartoon. Joe agreed "if you keep Hayes out of it."

Nast responded with Uncle Sam forcing the protesting artist into a chair in the Blue Room of the White House, with his sketches falling on the floor. He was pointing his pencil (in the form of a dagger) towards a public notice from Gen. Disposition: "Watch and pray. Stand back and give the President's policy a chance." With a Shakespearean quote from *Twelfth Night* as a title, Nast reappeared on the *Weekly's* cover. [6]

HW May 5, 1877 341 C

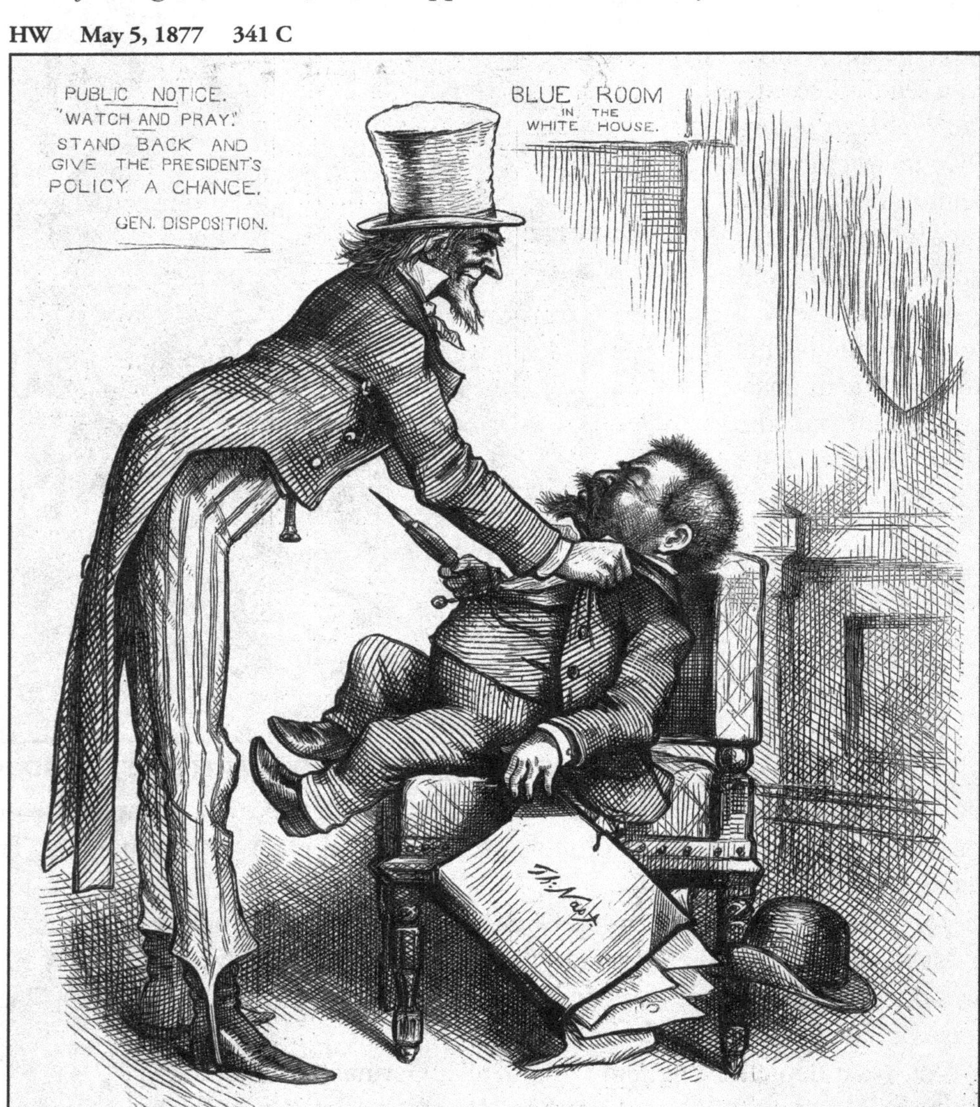

"NAY, PATIENCE, OR WE BREAK THE SINEWS."—Shakespeare

U.S. "Our Artist must keep cool, and sit down, and see how it works."

According to what Nast told his biographer Paine, Joe Harper asked whether "that fellow choking you was intended for me or Mr. Curtis?" Nast responded: "Neither. It represents a policy, not an individual. Policy always strangles individuals."[7]

Eight days after the cartoon appeared in print, Nast gave a small dinner party for Ulysses and Julia Grant at his home in Morristown. Joe Harper and one of his relatives were among the invited guests. Shortly afterwards, the Grants left on a two-year trip around the world.

Scissors

There was an old tale about a stubborn wife who, in a dispute with her husband, persisted in shouting "Scissors!" until he tossed her into a river. She repeated "Scissors!" every time her head rose above the water. When she was pushed under the surface one last time, she raised her hand and used her fingers to imitate the action of the opening and shutting blades. The parable served as a symbol of journalistic resistance.

During the Hayes Presidency, Nast used it to illustrate his enforced silence. It first appeared three days after Inauguration Day, with the anti-Grant, carping press as the nagging spouse. Coincidentally, the unsigned, run-of-the-mill, pro-Hayes cartoon alongside it displayed the relative flaccidity of Nast's substitutes.

HW March 17, 1877 216

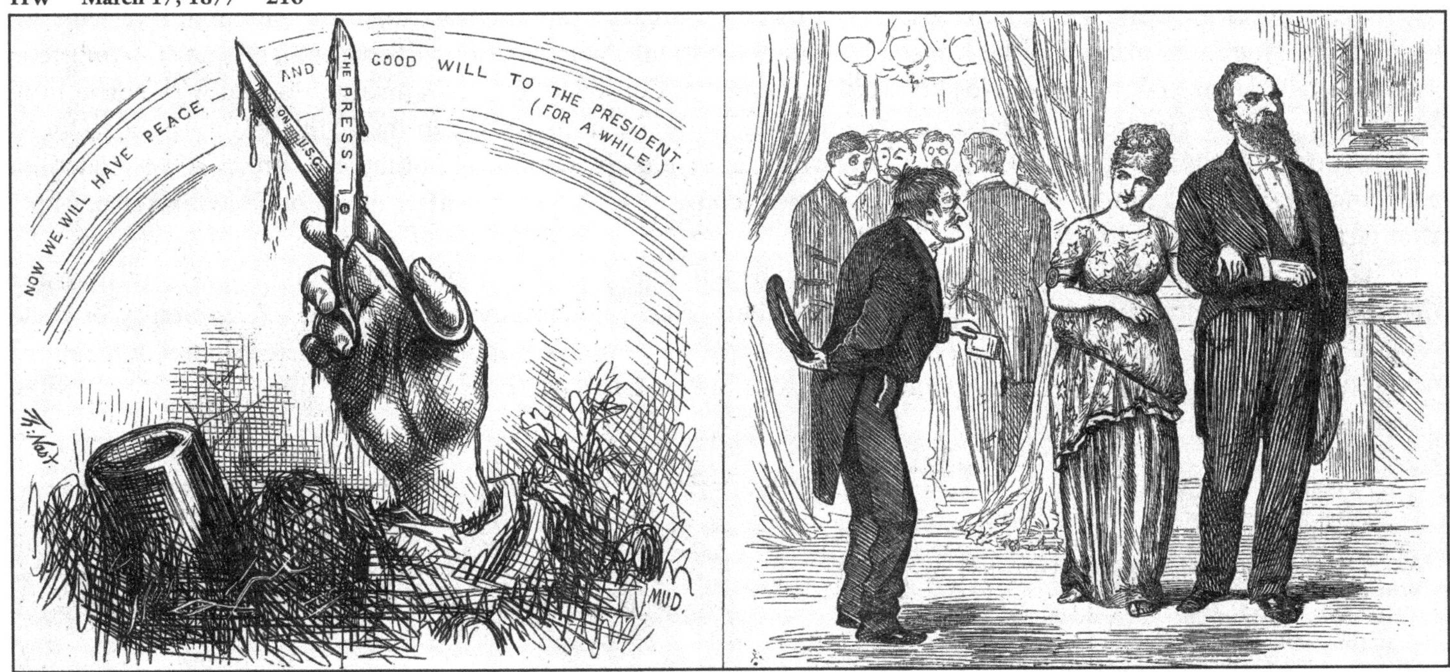

March 4, 1877.

Mrs. U.S. "Thanks, Mr. Tilden. I have promised to dance this set with Mr. Hayes."

The Final Straw

As previously mentioned, when Fletcher, the last of the four Harper brothers, died on May 29, 1877 after a long illness, Nast lost his counselor and protector. Fletcher had taken a much less active role in the business during the preceding two years, but his vitality kept his conflicted players within a civil understanding until the election was decided. The firm's second generation leader, Joe Harper ("Brooklyn Joe"), didn't have the combination of seniority, internal stature, experience and ability that his uncle had, to be able to manage two yoked but dissonant horses. He tipped the scales in favor of Curtis.

HW June 16, 1877 457 C

FLETCHER HARPER.

For Nast, the 1877 straw that broke the camel's back had nothing to do with Hayes or politics. It was an already-engraved cartoon featuring James Russell Lowell, the accomplished poet, Harvard professor, linguist, noted satirist, and Curtis's friend of 30 years. Lowell had spoken for Hayes at the Republican Convention, and was appointed Minister to Spain as a reward. Curtis editorialized that Lowell was well qualified to represent his country despite his lack of diplomatic experience.

Hayes also asked Curtis to be Minister to England, but was turned down. With Fletcher near death, and his solid relationship with Joe Harper promising him complete editorial control, Curtis undoubtedly believed — correctly — that as a close advisor to the President, he would have far more influence over domestic policy in general, and Civil Service Reform (his top priority) in particular, than he would in London. He explained that to Jamie Lowell in a warm letter dated July 9, shortly before his best friend sailed for Spain.[8]

A year earlier, Lowell had written a short poem, full of sarcasm, commemorating the Centennial International Exhibition, which was printed in the *Nation*. Nast decided to take some of Lowell's barbed critiques of American society and have the poet read them to skeptical, uninterested European rulers, themselves loaded with corruption, debt and nepotism. He drew Lowell as Dante, reciting to Beatrice (as Spain) in the 13th Century poet's *Divine Comedy*, using a photograph of the original picture as his model. It was not an unkind caricature of the preaching poet, and was scheduled to be published on Independence Day 1877, one year after the Centennial and two weeks after Curtis's flattering editorial.

Unamused; and perhaps overly sensitive because he had rejected his own diplomatic plum, Curtis went to Joe Harper to kill the cartoon and the poem, which Nast had printed underneath. Harper ran it by Secretary of State William Evarts, who saw no harm. Nevertheless, Curtis persisted on the principle that Nast should not demean his cultured friends, an apparently spiteful carryover from his unsuccessful censorship attempts during the Greeley campaign five years earlier.[9]

THE WORLD'S FAIR, 1876.
Columbia, puzzled what she should display
Of true home make on her Centennial Day.
Asked Brother Jonathan; he scratched his head
Whittled awhile reflectively and said,
"Your own invention and own making, too?
Why any child could tell ye what to do —
Show 'em your Civil Service and explain
How all men's loss is everybody's gain;
Show your new patent to increase your rents
By paying quarters for collecting cents;
Show your short cut to cure financial ills
By making paper dollars current bills;
Show your new bleaching process, cheap and brief,
To wit, a jury chosen by the thief;
Show your State Legislature; show your Rings,
And challenge Europe to produce such things
As high officials sitting half in sight
To share the plunder and to fix things right.
If that don't fetch her, why you only need
To show your latest style in martyrs —TWEED
She'll find it hard to hide her spiteful tears
At such advance in one poor hundred years.
From the "Nation." **—J.R.L.**

THE UNPUBLISHED CARTOON OF MINISTER LOWELL.

Nast was so enraged by this unforeseen exclusion of his engraved and scheduled Fourth of July-appropriate woodblock, that he declared his own independence and went on strike for three months. Only one proof impression of the cartoon survived; it was sold at auction in April 1906. Lowell's poem was posted on the back, together with a note: *Accepted by Harper's, rejected by Curtis; a long silence followed.*

During his "vacation," Nast thoroughly enjoyed spending time at home and on excursions with his family. He was wealthy — a millionaire in today's dollars — and had no debts, his mortgage having been paid off after his 1873-74 lecture tour. Remembering his stage fright and loneliness from that "blood money" (as he termed it) venture, he now rejected repeated tour offers of $1,000 a week or $20,000 for the season from experienced promoter J.B. Pond.[10]

After more than two months away, Nast received some sound guidance from James Parton, his close friend and Sallie's cousin, after they sent him a proof of the Lowell cartoon. "If that picture is rejected for any reason, it is plain that Thomas Nast and the rejector thereof cannot work in concert. You could never be sure of having anything accepted . . . On the other hand, there cannot be two editors to one paper . . . Mr. Curtis must possess all the power of an editor, and in that case you could never work under him . . . I hold him in very high esteem, but between him and you, there could never be any harmony, no more than between a nightingale and a falcon." In concluding, however, Parton advised Nast to stay calm, enjoy life and do nothing for the moment.[11]

David Croly at the *Daily Graphic* and Frank Leslie also reached out to Nast. Leslie had lost his star cartoonist in September 1876, when Joseph Keppler left to found German-language *Puck*, to be followed six months later by the English-language version.

Conkling vs. Curtis

As Hayes was choosing his cabinet, New York's political boss, Senator Roscoe Conkling, pressured him to make his protégé, Tom Platt, Postmaster General. There were about 40,000 postmasters in the county, fewer than 2,000 of whom required Senate confirmation.[12] That would have provided Platt, and effectively Conkling, with significant national political leverage.

As mentioned previously, Conkling didn't like Hayes but, reluctantly, had helped him win the 1876 nomination as the lesser of two evils. (His arch-enemy, House Speaker James Blaine, was worse.) After Hayes turned him down and selected Democrat David Key, Conkling blasted him as "Rutherfraud" and opposed most of Hayes's nominations in the Senate for the remainder of the President's term. Key, of course, replaced thousands of Republican postmasters with Democrats.

In response to Conkling, Hayes threatened his political hegemony by attacking his de facto control of the New York Custom House which provided 1,000 patronage jobs. Hayes singled it out as a national bellwether for Civil Service Reform, while collectors in other important ports were left relatively undisturbed.

Previously, in late June, Hayes had issued an order prohibiting political assessments, and the management of political organizations, campaigns and elections by Federal civil servants; however, he was leery of emasculating most Republican Party organizations, so he moved much slower than Curtis, who pushed Hayes hard for Civil Service Reform, wanted. Violation of that order by Alonzo Cornell, who refused to give up his Chairmanship of the Republican State Committee — while serving under Custom House Collector Chester Arthur as his deputy (called Naval Officer) — gave Hayes grounds to remove them.

He issued an order to that effect on September 6, 1877, three weeks before the Republican Party Convention convened in Rochester. However, Conkling successfully opposed their replacement nominees in the Senate, so Hayes had to wait until July 1878 when Congress was in recess, to suspend them and temporarily install their successors.

Defying Hayes, Cornell opened the Convention on September 26, and then turned the gavel over to Conkling's flunky, Tom Platt. Shortly, a gloves-off battle erupted between Curtis and Conkling, which subsequently opened the door for Nast's return to the *Weekly*.

Curtis commenced by lashing out at Conkling. He asserted that the Senator always won his Federal cases because his legal opponents and judges owed their appointments to him. Looking directly at Conkling, he blistered those "blinded by the flattery of parasites or their own ambitions."

The personal ferocity of Conkling's return volley shocked even his supportive assemblage: "Who are these men who, in newspapers or elsewhere, are cracking their whips over me and playing schoolmaster to the party? . . . Some of them are the man-milliners, the dilettanti and carpet knights of politics . . . For extreme license in criticism of administrations and of everybody connected with them, broad arguments can be found. **Many might be found in the files of the journal made famous by the pencil of Thomas Nast."**[13]

The epithet "man-milliner" painted Curtis as effeminate if not homosexual. When Conkling's son published the full text of his father's speech he used three asterisks in place of the actual term.[14] Perhaps the Senator remembered Frank Bellew's 1872 cartoon of Curtis in a dress with a sampler of Civil Service reform.

FIFTH AVENUE JOURNAL 1872

MEN OF THE DAY (AFTER TO-MORROW).

HW October 20, 1877 817 C

HALT!
Sentinel Hayes. "You can't come in here, Gentlemen, with that Flag!"

The situation was ripe for a cartoon. Nast was still on strike, but would not have touched the subject if he wasn't. Curtis must have conscripted Charles Reinhart, better known as an illustrator and painter, to draw a cover cartoon worthy of Nast. In print two weeks after the convention and a week before his own return, Nast may have foreseen a potential internal threat to himself in Reinhart's concept, puns and execution.

Chester Arthur, ironically the next Vice President and then President, was "a bigger man than old Grant," as his satchel stated. (Six inches taller and at least 100 pounds heavier, while showing his "influence" to Hayes). Cornell (behind Arthur wearing "Reward for Service" on his lapel) and Conkling pushed Arthur forward. Lapdog Platt was loose on his leash, barking at Hayes. The Spoils System flag behind Conkling and the full text of Hayes's reform order reinforced the picture.

Nast's Return

Conkling's vitriol and Nast's favorable mention in it set off a conflagration in the press, and provided the spark for his return to *Harper's* about three weeks later. What became apparent to Joe Harper, and probably to Curtis as well, was that the *Weekly* needed its popular cartoonist more than he needed it.

Prior to Nast's departure in early July, he had provided 18 of the 28 covers for 1877. When he returned in late October, he was featured on the first six and 29 of the next 32 covers, running through the first half of 1878.

Of course, circulation had fallen off as *Harper's* readers deplored their magnet's absence. Immediately after Nast's return, the next issue contained a novel subscription offer: 61 issues for the four dollar price of 52. The text proclaimed "No pains will be spared to render the . . . periodical as interesting and attractive in the future as (it) has been in the past."[15]

Joe Harper didn't make the same mistake twice. When the Nast family travelled through Europe in the summer of 1878, he made sure his readers knew about it. Moreover, Nast must have prepared a number of cartoons in advance that appeared while he was away. His work was on 34 covers in 1878 and on 40 the following year.

In his first cover cartoon after his return, Nast took a less than subtle shot at Hayes's Southern policy, which had further empowered the Reconstructed states without pacifying them. His ex-Confederate tiger licked its Democratic chops after devouring the Republican lamb and peas ("peace," and conceivably "ap*pease*ment"), while feeling "Pretty 'solid', thank you." This was Nast's Tammany-style tiger at its best — without wordy platitudes or handcuffs.

HW November 3, 1877 857 C

THE MILLENNIUM.
The Tiger And The Lamb Lie Together.

Mark Twain

Nast had been back at the *Weekly* for about a month when he received an offer from Mark Twain that could have — and, in retrospect, probably should have altered his career.[16] Twain proposed an equal partnership on the lecture circuit, and outlined a complete business plan, with Nast's share projected in the $30,000-$37,000 range for an 18-week tour.

Nast was five years younger than Twain. They had known each other for more than a decade, probably since Twain first published in *Harper's Monthly* in December 1866. A year later, Nast unsuccessfully tried to get Twain to join him on the Caricaturama tour after David Locke had turned him down.* Beginning in the early seventies, when Twain came to New York, he would socialize with publishing notables. Twain also contributed humorous articles to three of Nast's five annual *Almanacs* (1872-74), which the cartoonist illustrated.**

---

* See p. 191
** See p. 202

Twain was riding high, having published *Tom Sawyer* the previous year. So the link-up of America's leading humorist and caricaturist would have been a powerful draw, as he wrote Nast:

Hartford, Nov. 12, 1877

My Dear Nast: —

I did not think I should ever stand on a platform again until the time was come for me to say, "I die innocent." But the same old offers keep arriving that have arriven every year and every year declined. (Note: $500 a night for Louisville, St. Louis, Toronto, etc.) I have declined them all, just as usual, though sorely tempted, as usual.

Now, I do not decline because I mind talking to an audience, but because (1) travelling alone is so heart-breakingly dreary, and (2) shouldering the whole show is such a cheer-killing responsibility.

Therefore, I now propose to you what you proposed to me in November 1867, ten years ago (when I was unknown), viz., that you stand on the platform and make pictures, and I stand by you and blackguard the audience. I should enormously enjoy meandering around (to big towns — don't want to go to the little ones) with you for company.

My idea is not to fatten the lecture agents and lyceums on the spoils, but put all the ducats religiously into two equal piles, and say to the artist and the lecturer: "Absorb these."

For instance — this being the plan: — pay the lecture bureau two percent of gross receipts to engage halls and arrange dates and routes for us. Take an agent with us to tend door and shoulder all details for $70 to $75 a week, he to pay his own expenses. Perform at a dollar a ticket only in towns capable of furnishing from $800 to $1,200 audiences. Have fifty cent or seventy-five cent admissions also in halls and theatres where there are galleries, if considered expedient.

Take a hall in New York for two weeks (with privilege of extending the time if necessary); go from there elsewhere, and come back with two or three weeks more at the end of the tour. Begin February 1 and perform one hundred times — call the gross results $100,000 for four months and a half and the profit from $60,000 to $75,000. (I try to make the figures large enough, and leave it to the public to reduce them.) . . .

You and I can cram any house in America as full as it can hold.

Well, you think it over Nast, and drop me a line. I am not proposing a novel business. In California and Nevada, I always ran my own show, took all the money myself and pocketed the whole profit. The agent got nothing but a salary. I know this business from A to Z. We should have some fun.

Yours truly,
Samuel Clemens

Twain believed he had the business skills and experience to make the tour successful, and Nast had no reason to doubt him. (Years later, Twain went bankrupt when several business ventures failed, but the lecture circuit was well within his capability.) Moreover, Nast could have continued free-lancing cartoons on an opportunistic basis without artistic handcuffs from Curtis. Hitching his wagon to Twain's would have been stimulating as well as lucrative.

Perhaps if Nast had received Twain's proposal before he returned to *Harper's*, he would have accepted. Undoubtedly, his continuous interaction with Sallie and his children dominated his life, and the familial bonds grew even stronger during his "strike-vacation" when his children had no school and were free to play with him all day long. Conversely, he didn't like being away from home, remembering his stage fright and loneliness on his lecture tour four years earlier.

So Nast stayed where he was comfortable and declined Twain's offer. In retrospect, it was the worst career decision he ever made. He was 37 years old and his life was on a downward slope.

Puck

In addition to a restless readership, Joe Harper and his cousins had cause to worry about incipient frontal competition. *Puck*, an aspiring humor magazine co-owned by Joseph Keppler, was now seven months old and attracting notoriety. Although its circulation was just a few thousand, the Harpers were familiar with Keppler's abilities ever since Frank Leslie hired him late in the Greeley campaign five years earlier.

Two years older than Nast, Keppler had quite a bit in common with him. Both their fathers came to America to escape the revolutions of 1848. However Vienna-born Joseph didn't arrive until 1867 when he was 29, after receiving his artistic training and experience in Europe.[17]

Keppler had worked as Frank Leslie's principal cartoonist until October 1876, when he left to start a German-language *Puck*. Leslie, an autocrat and ardent Democrat, had alienated his artist with too many instructions and prohibitions. He began publishing his English-language humor magazine *Puck* on March 14, 1877, just after Hayes was inaugurated. Democrat Keppler, who disliked being forced to favor Tilden while at *Leslie's*, probably preferred him over Hayes, but was not so doctrinaire that he wouldn't give Hayes a chance.

Two months after English-language *Puck's* birth, it saluted the new President as St. George slaying a fierce dragon by removing the last Federal troops from Louisiana and South Carolina. Near the end of his term — a month before the 1880 election — Keppler expressed his opinion of Cinderella Hayes vs. Grant and Conkling. Two of the jars in Hayes's cabinet represented Presidential vetoes.

PUCK May 20, 1877

THE MODERN ST. GEORGE.

PUCK October 13, 1880

THE CINDERELLA OF THE REPUBLICAN PARTY AND HER NAUGHTY SISTERS

Understandably, Nast envied Keppler's new editorial freedom because his own hands remained somewhat tied for his final decade at *Harper's*, while his skilled rival could draw on any subject and in any manner he wanted. (Nast's craving to have equity in his own publication would not be realized for another 15 years, and then it never came close to success). Balancing the scales somewhat, although the Harpers may not have known about the *Daily Graphic's* courting Nast while he was on strike, they probably did have to contemplate losing him to a rival publication like the *Graphic* or *Puck* if the rift became permanent. (Nast's and Keppler's egos and political differences almost certainly would have prevented them from collaborating at *Puck*, but the Harpers couldn't take that possibility for granted.)

In turn, Keppler envied Nast's place in the sun; his primary goal was to achieve equal or greater stature. He made that clear with his first cartoon as he literally created *A Stir in the Roost*. His chief target, dressed in finery, stood apart as cock-of-the-walk, holding a copy of *Harper's Weekly*. Frank Leslie, his ex-boss, was the plumpest hen, tethered to his family of small publications. Readily identifiable editors included Whitelaw Reid (*Tribune*), Ben Wood (the Civil War Copperhead with his *Daily News*), George Jones (*Times*), James Gordon Bennett, Jr. (*Herald*), Charles Dana (*Sun*), William Cullen Bryant (*Evening Post*), E.L. Godkin (*Nation*), and David Croly (*Daily Graphic*).[18]

Although both artists were born Catholic, they despised Pius IX, his associated American Catholicism, and the intemperate, pugilistic Irish. Keppler's depiction of the infallible Pope and his groveling followers was as harsh as any that Nast ever drew. It was notable for the effect of color, as well as his punning: "Charity Begins at Rome" and Puck's bag of "Puckerings" — not so different from Nast.

June 13, 1877

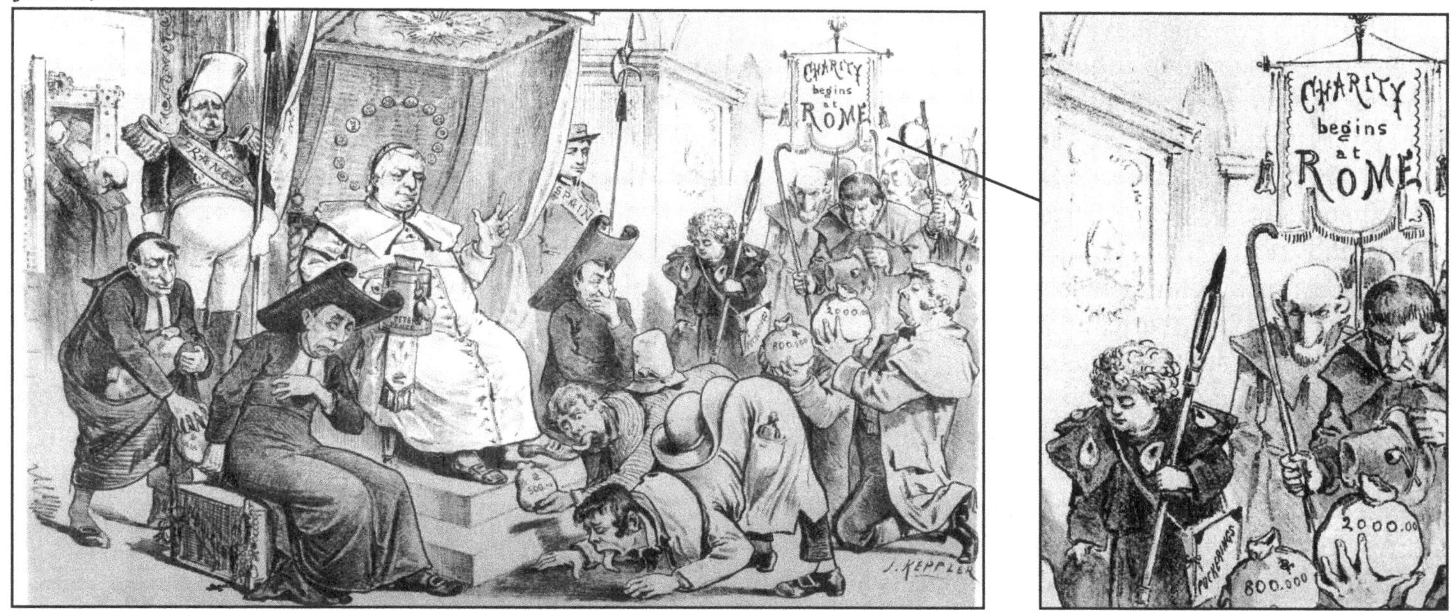

THE NEW PILGRIMS' PROGRESS — ENLIGHTENED AMERICANS PAYING HOMAGE TO "INFALLIBILITY"

Like Nast, Keppler inserted himself into his cartoons on occasion. After four years of picking on them, ten of his "victims" — including Grant, Ben Butler, Tilden and Conkling — corrected their caricatures as he dreamed in his hammock.

August 10, 1881

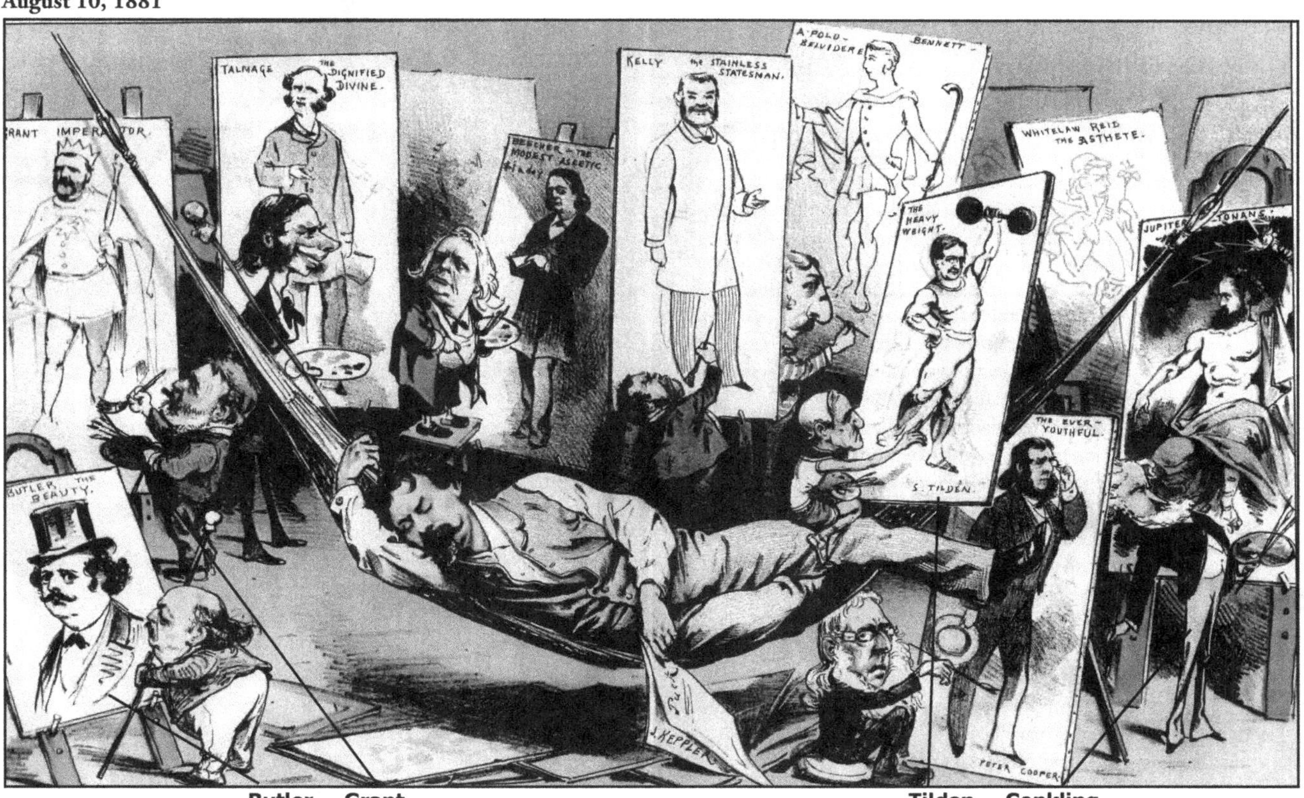

A MID-SUMMER DAY'S DREAM

Over his career, however, Nast's cartoons were blunter than Keppler's. He was promoting his point of view — good vs. evil with not much in between. Keppler had a broader political vision, doubtful that either side was totally correct or even truthful. His objective was to enlighten and entertain through colorful, more gentle satire, even when he had a pointed message.[19] However, he fully equalled and frequently surpassed Nast in imagination, creativity and execution during their overlapping decade (1877-1886).

Keppler's principal advantage was his use of color. His lithographs were drawn on stone — not woodblocks — and his pioneering printing technology created an impact. To use color effectively, Keppler needed a quality printing partner. He had that and much more in Adolph Schwarzmann, a German immigrant of the same age, who worked for Frank Leslie for ten years where the two became friends. Their partnership agreement gave Keppler totally free artistic rein, while Schwarzmann turned out to be a solid administrator and financial manager.

When both *Puck* and Hayes reached their first anniversaries in March 1878, the magazine's circulation was several thousand. However, most of its distribution was in metropolitan areas, so politicians and businessmen in New York, Washington, Chicago, St. Louis and other influential cities quickly came to appreciate (or not) Keppler's and his fellow caricaturists' artistry. Moreover, long-time editor Henry Bunner added humor, fiction and articles to round out the content.

English-language *Puck* survived its first year only because its German-language sister helped support it. Keppler drew nearly all the 150 or so lithographs and many of the ads because he couldn't afford to hire other talent.[20] James Wales, 26, had succeeded Keppler as *Leslie's* chief cartoonist in 1876, and joined him on *Puck* in January 1879. However, he left two years later to help found *Judge*, a Republican rival.

As Nast's fall-on-his-sword (or pencil) causes became fewer, he tended to replace some of his active detailed creativity with passive devices like platitudes from Columbia and Uncle Sam, or overuse of signboards. Would-be rivals, who envied Nast's national recognition and status, noticed and attacked. Early in *Puck's* third year, Wales took a direct shot at Nast's puns, signboards and predictable style, even including Nast's wife Sallie, his model for Columbia. Looked at through a different lens, it was a backhand compliment to his somewhat receding reputation — as the caption suggested.

June 14, 1879

Our independent artist, finding ideas very scarce this week, has quietly left the last page to be filled by the unfortunate editor, who has been forced to avail himself of one of his esteemed friend Mr. Thomas Nast's patent double-back-action reversible cartoons, suitable to all occasions, and to all weathers.

What is sauce for the *Harper's* is sauce for *Puck*. The reader can select for himself an idea appropriate to the young woman in the picture. Behold the works of the editorial genius. You pays your money and you takes your choice of ideas. This is a genuine Nast caption.

PUCK SENDS HIS COMPLIMENTS TO MR. NAST ONCE MORE.

Chapter 35
President Hayes: Civic Issues

Civil Service Reform

During Nast's absence in the summer of 1877, Curtis preached Civil Service Reform and continually praised the Hayes Administration. After Nast's return in October, the cartoonist and his editor generally agreed on almost all key issues during the remainder of Hayes's term: hard money, low inflation and faithful debt repayment; Southern obstruction, violence and electoral fraud; fair treatment of blacks, Indians and Chinese; support of the financially-starved Army; and non-sectarian public education.

Civil Service Reform was an apparent exception. Actually, Nast probably believed in the cause as strongly as Hayes did, but because Curtis was its principal proponent along with disliked Interior Secretary Carl Schurz, Nast was reluctant to give the President credit or support. He treated the subject impartially when he dealt with it at all.

The existing patronage system went back to President Andrew Jackson and New York Senator William Marcy, who coined the phrase "To the victors belong the spoils." Nast used the statue of Jackson on his horse as his spoils symbol. As discussed previously, Grant appointed Curtis as Chairman of a new Civil Service Reform Commission in June 1871, and implemented its recommendations as the year ended.*

Supporting his hero after his 1872 reelection, Nast depicted "Unconditional Surrender" Grant closing the door on sleazy Senator and Pennsylvania political boss Simon Cameron and his puppet, newly-elected Governor John Hartranft; both wore banditti hats and carried weapons. Perhaps Nast selected Cameron for his legendary definition of an honest politician as "one who when bought, stays bought."

HW December 7, 1872 945 C

NO SURRENDER.
U.S.G. "I Am Determined To Enforce Those Regulations."

HW March 31, 1877 256

CIVIL SERVICE REFORM.
Office-Seeker. "St. Jackson, can't you save us? Can't *you* give us something?"

* See p. 307

Less than four months after the Cameron cartoon appeared, Grant filled the third-ranking spot in the New York Custom House, ignoring Curtis's Civil Service rules and appointing Tom Murphy, whom Curtis abhorred for good reason. Curtis resigned with a petulant letter that did him and his cause no good. Grant appointed a successor, but after Congress refused to fund the Commission, he gave up the reform effort. Nast later depicted his hero as a nurse holding the abandoned Civil Service baby.

After reform became moribund, Nast let it alone for the rest of Grant's Presidency, and commented dispassionately at the beginning, middle and end of Hayes's term.

HW April 3, 1875 288

CAN A MAN BE A NURSE?
U.S.G. "Both parties say they love it. But —"

HW April 28, 1877 325

IN MEMORIAM—OUR CIVIL SERVICE AS IT WAS.

However, by early December 1877 — only two months after his strike ended — Nast must have smiled when Curtis admitted: "those who are most disposed to support the Administration have been disappointed that its course seems at times to be both timid and inconsistent," referring both to Civil Service and the South.[1]

Early on, Nast gave Hayes (and Curtis) a compliment by depicting Jackson riding a hog instead of a horse. Two years later, a Democratic wolf backed off from a Republican vulture as they fought over offices in the Senate; Nast blasted both sides for their greed. A month before Hayes's term ended in 1881, the best Nast could do was a wordy, uninteresting illustrated monologue.

HW April 19, 1879 316

THE GRAB-BAG.

HW February 5, 1881 81 C

OH, THE DEGRADATION OF IT!
Office-Holder. "One might as well be an Army or Navy Officer, or a mere *Machine*, if Civil Service Reform is to be enforced! . . . We will have to submit to examination as to competence for office, just as if a Statesman wasn't able to fill any position! . . . And then promotion according to routine and merit! One would have to wait a lifetime for a Cabinet position! . . . No, no! Let us stick to the old, time-honored Jacksonian system."

HW March 12, 1881 165

1877 — 1881

Curtis, however, was determined to give Hayes his end-of-term tribute. He commissioned Alfred Fredericks — Nast's old mentor who tutored him when he was 14 and facilitated his first two cartoons for *Harper's Weekly* in 1859 when he was 18 — to anoint Hayes with the same royal treatment that his protégé had used for Grant. It was not coincidental.

New York Custom House

Initially, Hayes implemented Civil Service Reform in two primary areas: the Interior Department and the New York Custom House. The first was easy because Secretary Schurz, always a leading advocate, could finally put his Department's money where his mouth was. He totally reorganized Interior's personnel based strictly on merit entrance exams, pay and promotions, and elimination of mandatory assessments and illegal political activities.

The second created a political hurricane. Grant had appointed Tom Murphy, a disreputable machine politician, as Collector in 1870.* He was kicked out the following year and replaced by Chester Arthur. Arthur and his deputy, Alonzo Cornell, operated more honestly than Murphy while collecting 70% of the nation's revenue, controlling a thousand jobs, and minimizing their predecessors' illegal profiteering and graft.

As discussed in the previous chapter, Hayes began the process to remove Arthur and Cornell in September 1877, with the aim of breaking Conkling's control of the state's patronage. Conkling successfully opposed their replacement nominees in the Senate, so Hayes had to wait until July 1878 when Congress was in recess, to suspend them and temporarily install their successors.

After the Senate reconvened in December 1878, Hayes resubmitted his nominations. Much to Conkling's bitter surprise, he lost the battle to block them when too much ego antagonized some of his prior supporters. Rubbing salt in his wounds, Hayes appointed spoilsmen to customs posts in New Orleans, St. Louis and Boston. However, to the chagrin of both Hayes and Curtis, Cornell was elected New York's Governor in 1879.

---

* See p. 378

Nast knew Conkling through their mutual relationships with Grant, and appreciated his ironic praise when he attacked Curtis at the Republican state convention, thereby paving the way for the cartoonist's return to the *Weekly* after his three-month strike. But Conkling had worn out his welcome with Nast, as well as with the stalwart (pro-Grant) wing of the Republican Party; Nast attacked him for going after his own side rather than the Democratic Tiger (upper left). Cornell was a tag on the Stalwart Bull's tail, in a replay from Gratz Brown on Horace Greeley's white coat.

HW November 22, 1879 924

NOW THEN, BUTT AWAY!
"A Bull, escaping from a Tiger, entered a cave which some shepherds had largely occupied. A he-Goat was left in it, who sharply attacked him with his horns. The Bull quietly addressed him: 'Butt away as much as you will. I have no fear of you, but of the Tiger. Let that monster go, and I will soon let you know what is the respective strength of a Goat and a Bull.'" A Fable

A month later, Nast hit Conkling again, capturing his essence as the 1880 Presidential contest approached and he jockeyed for position.

Conkling was six foot, three with erect posture and a Van Dyke beard. He deliberately set himself up for caricature by twirling a curl into the center of his forehead, and puffing up the hair on both sides of his head to make it more noticeable.[2] Here, Nast sprouted the curl to emphasize its owner's vanity.

HW December 20, 1879 981 C

BORROWED PLUMES—MR. JACKDAW CONKLING.
Eagle. "Perhaps you would like to pluck me."

Starving the Army

During the middle of Grant's second term, funding a standing Army and Navy became an issue as the economy's slump worsened. Moreover, after the Democrats won the House in 1874, they had overt political reasons for minimizing or even eliminating the Army, which they correctly viewed as a barrier against election violence and fraud.

Its Constitutional responsibility to assure honest voting was a bone in the throats of the many ex-Confederates now serving in Congress, and as governors, mayors and other elected officials. By getting rid of any military presence at the polls, they schemed to eliminate Republican votes — and, if necessary, voters — in the South, and thereby take control of Congress and ultimately win back the Presidency.

However, the Army's primary role was to provide security for forts and to protect Western emigrants, settlers and miners against hostile Indians. Its 25,000 soldiers also had to police 13,000 miles of borders with Mexico and Canada against violence and smuggling. Many of them living in poor and perilous conditions didn't get paid for months at a time. Disabled Union veterans serving in non-military jobs in Washington were displaced by ex-Confederates.

From 1874 through 1879, Nast published two dozen cartoons attacking Congressional cuts in military funding, often using a skeleton to symbolize the Skeleton Army.

HW May 30, 1874 449 C

"THERE IS NOTHING MEAN ABOUT US."
Uncle Sam. "What Congress proposes to reduce our Army and Navy to!"

HW August 8, 1874 649 C

THE MERE SHADOW HAS STILL SOME BACKBONE.
"Our Standing Army" Stands In Spite Of Political False Economy.

HW February 12, 1876 128-129

FOOD FOR THE TRICKY "STATESMAN" AND DEATH TO OUR HONORABLE ARMY.
"The *Line* Is Being So Reduced That We Can No Longer *Fight It Out.*"

HW February 15, 1879 137

In appreciation of his efforts, the *Army and Navy Journal* raised funds (limited to 25 cents per contributor) for an 1879 testimonial to Nast *in recognition of the patriotic use of his rare abilities as the artist of the people*. The Tiffany, sterling silver, gold-tinted army canteen rested on the back of two eagles; its face displayed Nast receiving a decoration from Lady Liberty (probably taken from his wife Sallie's portrayal in one of his cartoons.) 3,500 soldiers and sailors paid for it.

Nast's friend, General Winfield Scott Hancock was scheduled to make the presentation — the year before he became the Democratic Presidential nominee. Unfortunately, he was ill, so his substitute told the artist: *"At a time when the Army and the Navy were in their utmost straits, you were a friend . . . Your little finger was stronger on the trigger than the pens and voices of the ablest and loudest orators who were against us.*"[3]

THE NAST TESTIMONIAL FROM THE ARMY AND NAVY OF THE UNITED STATES.

Vetoes

Shortly after Hayes took office in March 1877, Congress adjourned without passing an appropriation to support the Army. The President called it back for an extra session, and barely secured sufficient funding to cover fiscal 1878-9. Uncle Sam and the drooping American Eagle were unhappy.

When the next round of appropriations came up in 1879, Hayes again called Congress back for an extra session as the issue came to a full boil. The House had been Democratic for two terms; now the Senate had 30 of its 43 Democratic majority from the South. While Congress was debating a bill in April that included a rider prohibiting a military presence at national or state electoral sites, Nast and many others feared for the outcome. His cover cartoons brought back Andersonville and Jeff Davis as specters from the Civil War; he envisioned — correctly — the current political battle as the potential next chapter of that epic struggle.

HW May 5, 1877 356

EXTRA SESSION OF CONGRESS SOON.
Our Uncle—when he thinks of it.

HW April 12, 1879 281 C

"HISTORY REPEATS ITSELF"— A LITTLE TOO SOON.
U.S. Skeleton Army. "Uncle, this reminds me of Andersonville."

HW April 19, 1879 301 C

"WE HAVE COME TO STAY."

Hayes, who was considered weak, wobbly or wrong-headed by many Republicans — often including Nast and, on occasion, even Hayes's good friend, editor Curtis — was at his strongest on both vital interlocked issues: "National protection at National elections, and not allowing Congress to usurp his power to share in legislation." He knew that if he compromised, he would ruin himself, his party and his country.[4]

During the two months before Congress adjourned on June 30, Hayes vetoed five separate appropriation bills that contained language or riders he found objectionable. When push came to the final shove, Democrats couldn't adjourn without passing an acceptable bill because enough of them joined with Republicans and Greenbackers to keep Congress in session. Two days before the fiscal year ended, Hayes won the fight and received the funding he needed.[5]

DAILY GRAPHIC June 3, 1879

HAYES AT BAT FOR THE UNION.

HW August 23, 1879 676

WHO BACKED DOWN?
(As soon as they feel a little refreshed.)

If there was any critical action during Hayes's term that deserved a public pat on the back from Nast, this was it. Grant was his hero when he vetoed the Inflation Bill five years earlier, but Hayes was ignored after he was equally resolute. The *Daily Graphic* gave the President personal credit in a simple cartoon, but Nast couldn't bring himself to do so.

Indians

Most Americans living outside the South viewed the Army primarily as a bulwark against Indian outrages. During the last year of the Hayes Administration, Curtis editorialized: "There are but three ways in which the Indians can be regarded — as a foreign people, as wards of the nation, or as ordinary citizens. Our practice has been to treat with tribes as nations, but under this pretext we have imposed our own will upon them as wards. To carry out this policy by supplies of food and clothing, there is a system of civilian agencies, and the army is summoned only when there are actual outbreaks of the Indians, escapes from reservations, or raids upon settlements. The net result . . . is enormous expense, wrong and crime, and general impatience or indifference with the whole subject."[6]

Arguably, the most memorable Indian attack in American history was Sitting Bull's massacre of George Armstrong Custer and more than 300 soldiers at Little Big Horn, Montana Territory, on June 26, 1876, during Grant's final year in office. Nast's own pictorial hatchet was at its most devastating as Democratic Congressional appropriator Fernando Wood shook hands with a masked Klansman and Sitting Bull, holding his bloody tomahawk; they had found another way to *reduce* the size of the Army. In contrast to his blatant overuse of signboards in many of his post-Grant cartoons, Nast's subtle use of them here complemented his stomach-turning scenario to drive his point home on the *Weekly's* cover.

HW July 29, 1876 609 C

THE NEW ALLIANCE.
"We stand here for Retrenchment, and Reducing the Army of the United States."

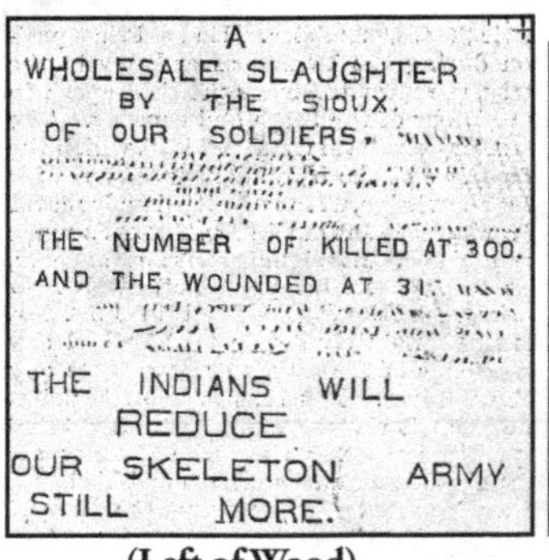

(Left of Wood)

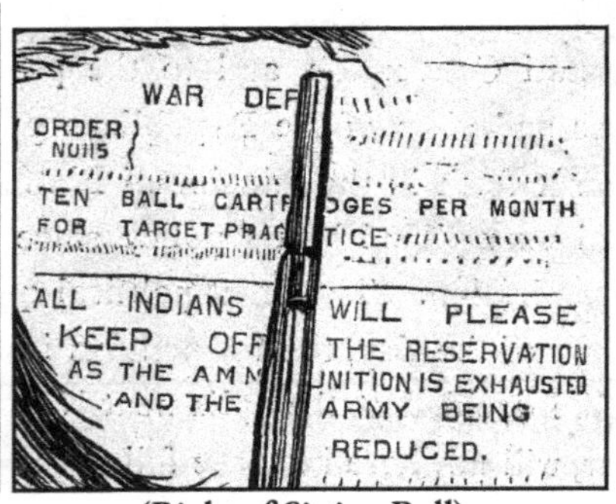

(Right of Sitting Bull)

HW August 5, 1876 632

A follow-up cartoon two weeks later was even more gruesome and not as subtle.

NOTICE.

Indians had better finish their work with Promptness and Dispatch, while the Economical Democratic Mania *lasts, for as soon as they have a* Great Democratic Father *in the White House the Confederate Army will take the place of the Ex-United States Army, and then the Indians will be compelled to sign Treaties of Peace.*

Indians out of ammunition, and in favor of reducing the United States Army still further, will find supplies awaiting their orders at the nearest Agencies.

United States soldiers are requested not to fire off cartridges without a special permit from the House of (Mis)-representatives.

"BILL PASSED PROVIDING FOR TWO NEW MILITARY POSTS" BY THE GENEROUS DEMOCRATIC HOUSE.

Initially, Secretary of the Interior Carl Schurz did a good job of weeding out corruption in the Indian Bureau, cleaning up after the disgraced Secretary of War, William Belknap.* As Schurz pulled eight little Belknaps (modeled on Tweed and labeled Fraud, Corruption, Dishonesty, Rascality and Irregularities) out of the Bureau's drawers and sent the jailbirds flying off to prison, Nast gave "him and them their dues" in a cover cartoon. This probably was Nast's only favorable portrayal of Schurz in 70 cartoons.

HW January 26, 1878 65 C

THE SECRETARY OF THE INTERIOR INVESTIGATING THE INDIAN BUREAU.
Give Him His Due And Give Them Their Dues.

HW January 25, 1879 51 C

NO MORE OUTBREAKS.
C. Schurz. "I do not repel, but invite, inspection and observation on the part of military officers." (See by Mr. Schurz's letters how he likes it.)

Although Nast had been a champion for Native Americans throughout Grant's Presidency,** and probably still favored their eventual citizenship and assimilation, he had two reasons for portraying them negatively during Hayes's term. The first was relatively petty — his antipathy towards Schurz, who was in a struggle with Commander of the Army William Sherman, among others, for control of the Indian Bureau. Exactly a year later, Nast reversed his favorable portrayal of Schurz (also in a cover cartoon), believing that the Indian Bureau should be put back under the War Department where it was before Belknap's hasty resignation and impeachment.

* See p. 375-376
** See p. 222

Nast's second reason for portraying Indians negatively was to gain leverage against reducing the size of the Army by depicting their atrocities — similar to the way he influenced Northern opinion during the Civil War by portraying Confederate outrages.

Before 1878 was over, Nast pictured Schurz as a bureaucrat, facing off against Generals Sherman and Phil Sheridan for control of the Indian Bureau. The following week he demeaned Schurz as a failed theorist, lecturing a surviving settler whose family and homestead had been destroyed by jubilant Indians. Finally, he showed Schurz coming to his senses.

HW December 21, 1878 1005 C

THE NEW INDIAN WAR.

Now, No Sarcastic Innuendoes, But Let Us Have A Square Fight.

HW December 6, 1879 964

MAKING WHITE MEN "GOOD."

Little Hatchet. "Me know nothing about White River massacre. White man bad; steal, kill, get drunk, and lie. Me good—make pale face '*good*' too."

HW December 28, 1878 1040

PATIENCE UNTIL THE INDIAN IS CIVILIZED—SO TO SPEAK.

Secretary of the Interior. "There are two methods of Indian management possible: either to herd and coral the Indians under the walls or guns of a military force, so to speak, so as to watch them and prevent outbreaks; or to start them at work upon their lands, to educate them, and to civilize them.....There are in the Army a great many gentlemen who have good ideas about the Indian Service, but it is one thing to have ideas, and another to carry them out, and I think that the patient labor and care of detail necessary to raise the Indian tribes to a state of civilization would not be found among the officers of the Army."

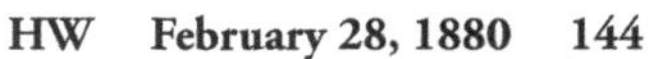

HW February 28, 1880 144

ORDERS FROM SCHURZ.
The appropriations of Congress for the White River Utes were shipped last Fall. They destroyed their supplies during the attack on Thornburgh, and during the massacre at the White River Agency. The Indians can't destroy their cake and have it too.

THE (INDIANS) INTERIOR DEPARTMENT COMING TO ITS SENSES.

Secretary Schurz. "Wilful waste makes woful want."

Guarding the Polls

The Democratic Congress's declared primary motivation for minimizing the Army centered on political control, not safety from Indians or external invaders. Once all the Reconstructed States had re-established "Home Rule" at the start of Hayes's Presidency, their next goal was to keep it by controlling state and local elections through threats, violence and ballot box fraud. To accomplish that, they tried to eliminate what they called "Federal Interference" at the polls, an Army responsibility enshrined in the Constitution "on application of the Executive." Their initial approach in Congress had been to minimize the Army by not appropriating funds; in 1879, they switched to attaching riders to appropriation bills — funding the Army but prohibiting its presence at or near polling places.

A few weeks after returning from his 1877 self-imposed break from *Harper's*, Nast hammered home his point, using several stereotypes, including a simian Irishman, a Communist, a New York gangster reborn as a Southern planter/politician, and a masked Klansman watching a lynching; however, a dozen signboards and an explanatory quote from the Constitution were integral to his concept. Two years later, the battle was lost.

HW December 1, 1877 948

LIFE, LIBERTY, AND PROPERTY MUST BE PROTECTED.
"The United States shall guarantee to every State in this Union a Republican form of Government, and shall protect each of them against Invasion; and, on application of the Executive (when the Legislature can not be convened), against Domestic Violence."— United States Constitution.

HW October 18, 1879 821 C

DEATH AT THE POLLS, AND FREE FROM "FEDERAL INTERFERENCE."

Lucius Lamar

Mississippi Senator Lucius Quintas Cincinnatus Lamar (also his father's name) was a close friend of Jefferson Davis, a favored acquaintance of editor Curtis, and a respected post-Reconstruction Congressional leader of the South. That qualified him as a symbolic statesman in seven Nast cartoons.

During the Grant-Greeley 1872 campaign, Nast and Curtis had clashed over the artist's disdainful treatment of the arrogant Massachusetts Senator Charles Sumner, Curtis's beloved and admired friend. Sumner's last wish before he died on March 11, 1874, at his home in Washington, was for passage of the Civil Rights Bill, a passionate cause for both men. Curtis gave the principal eulogy at his funeral.

Congress paid tribute on April 27. Amazing the spellbound House and the entire national political establishment, Lamar, a polar political opposite of Sumner — and who had never met him while a Congressman — eloquently praised his breadth of knowledge, powerful oratory and "instinctive love of freedom" for former slaves. In particular, he noted Sumner's desire for reconciliation with the South, which jibed with his own strong belief.[7]

Curtis gave Lamar's 1874 eulogy scant attention in the *Weekly*, but did become friendly with him. After Hayes became President and Reconstruction ended with the removal of Federal troops from Louisiana and South Carolina, Lamar remarked that Hayes "is full of the idea of being a great Pacificator."[8]

In late January 1878 "Free Silver" currency and the integrity of the national debt became a major issue. Lamar broke with his home state legislature and strongly supported Hayes. Again, his political courage was praised, even by his Senate opponents; Curtis responded with a long editorial lauding and quoting his speech. "No Senator has shown himself more worthy of universal respect" or "has shown the manly courage which becomes an American Statesman." Curtis also quoted extensively from Lamar's oration.[9]

Recognizing his as a politician respected by both Democrats and Republicans — as well as by Curtis — Nast never directly attacked Lamar or portrayed him as a "rough." He depicted him as powerful and potentially explosive, but was wary of Lamar's repression of black suffrage. Although Lamar fully accepted the Fourteenth and Fifteenth Amendments — and didn't support (at least openly) violence against blacks to suppress their votes - cratic ticket.

HW January 12, 1878 36

THE ESTABLISHMENT NEEDS CONSTANT ADVERTISING.

HW December 21, 1878 1016

"POOR IGNORANT BLACK MAN" WANTS TO KNOW, AND YOU NOBLE WHITE GENTLEMAN DO TELL.

Black Question. "Whom do you mean by the People?"
White Answer. "How dare you wave the Bloody Shirt again?"
Echo From A Naturalized Foreigner. "If Misther Lamar lived up our way, I would be afther showing him that *I am one* of the People!"

Early on, Nast illustrated the pressure on blacks and Southern White Republicans.

HW December 8, 1877 972

THE COLOR LINE IS BROKEN.

HW March 2, 1878 180

"PACIFICATION."

Pacific Male To Uncle Sam. Yes, kind Uncle, it works like a charm; all the white Republicans in the South who were not killed during the election campaign we are putting in jail as fast as possible, and after we have the Republicans in the North locked up too, we sha'n't have any more trouble."

With truly humorous situations hard to come by, Nast never tired of portraying Southern blacks as superior to ignorant whites. Below right, Postmaster General David Key, the only Democrat in Hayes's Cabinet, reacted to the shooting of an on-duty black South Carolina Postmaster, by shuttering the office.

HW January 18, 1879 52

THE COLOR LINE STILL EXISTS—IN THIS CASE.

HW November 1, 1879 876

IF, LOCKED BY KEY.

First Citizen (S.C.). "The Federal Government thinks to punish us by stopping the mail!"

Second Citizen. "It's only those cussed ignorant niggers that care so much for reading and writing."

Exodus

Conditions worsened for many Southern blacks during the Hayes Administration. Their lives were threatened if they voted Republican. Northern teachers left, their replacements weren't as good, and school years often were shortened. Black children hired out as laborers were whipped. Wages were paid in plantation scrip not redeemable outside, and inside only at exorbitant prices for supplies.

By 1879, the black exodus to Kansas, Indiana and other Northern and Western states became a stampede, assisted by so-called colonization organizations (reminiscent of the underground railroad.) In Lamar's Mississippi, they embarked at Vicksburg, sailed to various Kansas ports on the Missouri River, and often found their way to Topeka. As Curtis pointed out in the *Weekly*, "The chief check on (Southern) outrage is emigration."[10] Many Mississippi planters were devastated.

Nast took great pleasure in portraying adventurous blacks besting Southern whites, and even their new job competitors, as they voted with their feet.

HW April 26, 1879 321 C

***HE* (THE SOLID SOUTH) WILL SOON BE "LET ALONE."**

"Massa, I leave you because you '*kill us with* Kindness.' There is too much Freedom *at the Polls*, and I am going where the '*bad Yankees*' live, and where there is 'Wicked Bayonet Rule.' Niggers can't stand so much '*Kindness*;' it makes them 'Impudent' and 'Ungrateful.'"

HW May 31, 1879 421 C

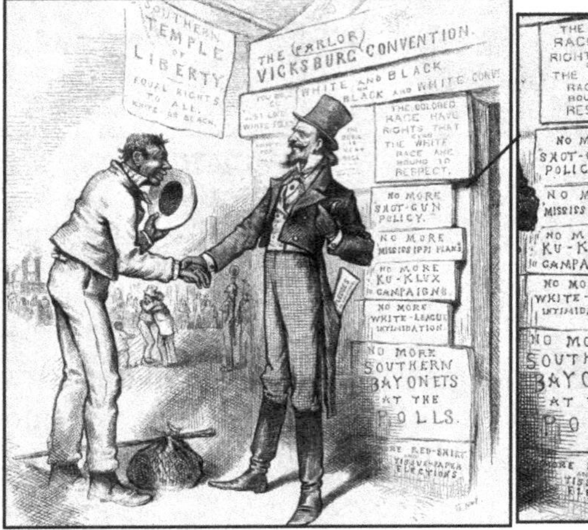

ANOTHER STEP TOWARD CIVILIZATION.

Mr. Solid Brutus. "Why, Mr. Exode Caesar, you are a Man and a Brother after all. So step into my parlor."

HW January 31, 1880 65 C

ANOTHER INVESTIGATION COMMITTEE.

Self-Appointed Gent. "An' what right have you, sure, to be afther laving your native place an' coming here? Spake!"

Northern Election Concerns

As the next Presidential election appeared on the horizon, Senator Thomas Bayard of Delaware was a leading Democratic candidate. Nast envisioned Lamar thinking about running, but disqualified him because of notorious violence in Mississippi's Yazoo county four years earlier. (White men broke up a Republican rally, killed several prominent blacks, and drove out the carpetbagger sheriff who had assisted black families with education and real estate.)[10]

HW November 15, 1879 916

LAMAR IS LOOKING AT A *STAR*—BUT DOES NOT SEE THE *PIT*.

Somewhat ironically, Nast was concerned about the Democrats winning the Presidency in 1880, which would lead to Southerners taking charge of the country. (The irony relates to his close friendship with Hancock, the ultimate Democratic candidate.)

First, he outlined the Southern "Bulldozer" three-step strategy: having won control of the Southern states, the Democratic Tiger would focus on Northern state elections, and then the Federal elections.

HW May 10, 1879 361 C

THE BULLDOZER.
"Three Bulls for a long time pastured together. A Tiger lay in ambush in the hope of making them his prey, but was afraid to attack them whilst they kept together. Having at last, by *guileful speeches, succeeded in separating them,* he attacked them without fear, as they fed alone, and feasted on them one (by one?) at his own leisure."

Six months later, referring to violence in Maryland elections, Nast had a Northern "rough,' ready to shoot voters. He quoted William Chandler, the Republican politician, who had been instrumental in preserving the electoral vote for Hayes, and now spelled out the arithmetic for Democratic success.

HW November 22, 1879 925

THE ROUGH IS READY.
The Southern Epidemic Will Spread North If Not Checked.

VOTING POWER OF THE SOUTH.

MR. CHANDLER dwelt at some length upon the Election Laws, and claimed that the Southern end of the republic didn't want any safeguards put upon the purity of elections, because they would interfere with the operations of the Ku-Klux at the polls. Said Mr. CHANDLER, "Give them permission to perpetrate the same kind of fraud and violence in New York city and Cincinnati as has been perpetrated in the South, and those two cities, with the solid South, will give them the Presidency of the United States, and by fraud and violence they would hold it for a generation."

Finally, he reincarnated Tweed's spirit as a smirking Southern "rough" with an overt replay of his 1871 cartoon.

HW October 7, 1871 944

"THAT'S WHAT'S THE MATTER."

HW December 13, 1879 969

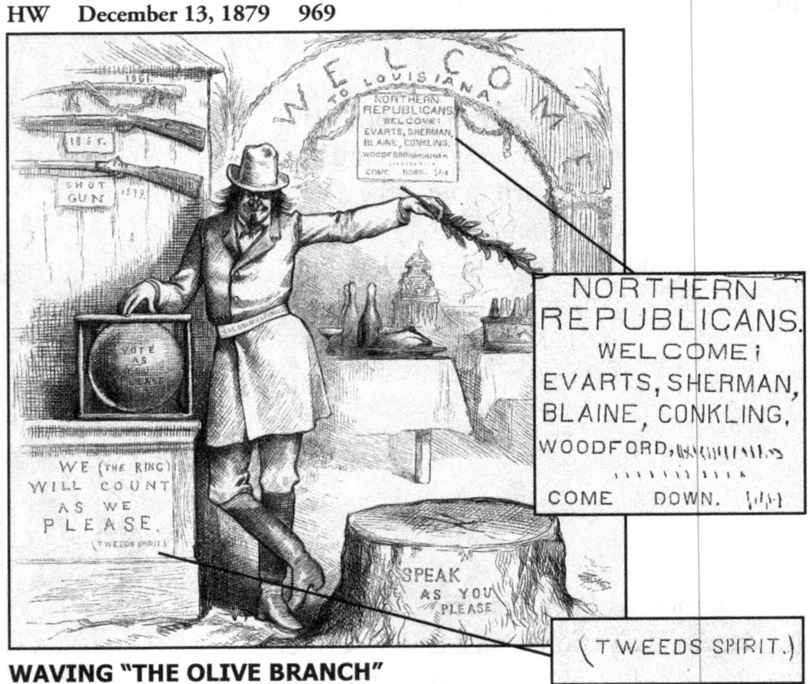

WAVING "THE OLIVE BRANCH" OR WEARING OF THE TWEED.

Chinese Exclusion

The question of Chinese exclusion became an important issue during the Hayes Administration. The 1868 Burlingame Treaty permitted voluntary but not contractual immigration. Many of the 130,000 Chinese in California, Nevada and Oregon in 1877, came to construct the Central Pacific Railroad, and stayed to dominate the current textile, shoemaking and laundry industries. They did not assimilate well, had different living habits, and were considered a significant threat to white labor because of their willingness to work for lower wages. They constituted about a quarter of California's labor force, and even more in San Francisco.[12]

Denis Kearney — an Irish immigrant, agitator and anarchist — led a violent movement to shut down Chinese immigration. His headquarters was on an open sand lot adjacent to San Francisco's new city hall. Nast, who strongly supported the Chinese, targeted Kearney nine times over the five years of the exclusionary movement.

HW March 20, 1880 177 C

THE IDES OF MARCH.
Don't—Put Him Out Of His Misery.

BRUTUS WANTED!

KILL ME!
I AM PREPARED TO DIE!
And not only would the streets of San Francisco run in blood, but also New York, Boston, Chicago, and other Eastern cities.
I will leave a list of names of persons who must be guillotined when I am gone.—MY WILL.
MY LIFE AS A SACRIFICE!
Kill me! KILL ME!! KILL ME!!!
I will be glad to be taken out of my MISERY!
DENIS KEARNEY,
AGITATOR AND MARTYR.

(Center)

THE SAND-LOT THEATRE.
DENIS KEARNEY AS JULIUS CÆSAR
BRUTUS?

(Upper Right Corner)

HW April 10, 1880 225 C

SOCIAL SCIENCE SOLVED.
The Modern Archimedes. *"Eureka! Eureka!"* "Constant Vigilance" (committee) "is the price of Liberty" in San Francisco.

While Kearney became a symbol for Chinese exclusion, both the Democratic and Republican platforms adopted anti-Chinese planks in 1876. Senator James Blaine, who hoped to win the Republican nomination in 1880, expected to secure the electoral votes from California, Nevada and Oregon by pushing for a Chinese Exclusion Bill. Nast, who disliked Blaine for his railroad chicanery, ridiculed him for his anti-Chinese stance in several cartoons.

Both the Senate and the House passed a bill which limited Chinese immigration, thereby violating the Burlingame Treaty. Hayes vetoed it on March 1, 1879, three days after two Nast cartoons appeared in print. *The Civilization of Blaine* cover showed him coddling a black for his vote, while stepping on the Burlingame Treaty and ignoring the Chinese.

HW March 8, 1879 181 C

THE CIVILIZATION OF BLAINE.
John Confucius. "Am I not a Man and a Brother?"

HW March 8, 1879 196

"AH SIN WAS HIS NAME."
The Heathen Chinee. "That is just what I have been longing for."

HW February 5, 1881 96

CELESTIAL.
The Yellow Dragon. "Of course, I did not hope to suit *you*, but this is for my friend, Uncle Sam, and it will even enable *you* to get better accustomed to this land of freedom, which you have adopted and which protects you."

Hayes sent a three-man commission to China to renegotiate the Treaty. Just after the 1880 election, the revised treaty enabled the US to regulate, limit and suspend — but not prohibit — the immigration of Chinese laborers.[13]

In supporting the Chinese, as he did blacks and (for the most part) Indians, Nast frequently compared or contrasted their mistreatment.

HW April 6, 1878 280

HARD TO PLEASE THE "WHITE TRASH."
U.S. "I hate the 'Nigger' because he is a citizen, and I hate the 'Yellow Dog' because he will not become one."

HW February 8, 1879 101 C

"EVERY DOG" (NO DISTINCTION OF COLOR) "HAS HIS DAY."
Red Gentleman to Yellow Gentleman. "Pale face 'fraid you crowd him out, as he did me."

HW March 29, 1879 256

DIFFICULT PROBLEMS SOLVING THEMSELVES.

A major difference between the three minority groups was that, as noted, most Chinese planned to return to China after they accumulated sufficient wealth — a significant factor in their acceptance of low wages and miserable living conditions. Nast enjoyed an unusual exception in this cartoon.

HW May 22, 1880 336

A PARADOX.
"A Chinaman has declared his intention to become an American citizen"—the consequences.

Chapter 36
President Hayes: The Money Question

Silver

Grant tried to put the money question to bed when he vetoed the Inflation Bill (relating to greenbacks) in 1874, and signed the Resumption Act (relating to gold) in January 1875; it was scheduled to become operative four years later, in the middle of Hayes's Presidency.* Nast created the Money Bag and the Rag Baby to symbolize inflation, and used them effectively to back his idol and sting the Western Republicans who opposed him.

During 1875, Nast illustrated a small paperback book by David Wells entitled *Robinson Crusoe's Money* and published by Harper & Brothers in January 1876. Wells was a financial expert, who had served as a Revenue Commissioner for both Abraham Lincoln and Andrew Johnson, and strongly opposed inflationist policies, including the new threat, "free silver." That experience gave Nast better insight into the technicalities of the money question than he could otherwise have obtained.

Author's Collection

Before 1873, the country was on a bimetallic standard where both gold and silver were coined at a fixed ratio. That year, in what silver proponents later called the "Crime of '73," silver was quietly removed as legal tender except for small change; nobody seemed to notice or object.

HW March 16, 1878 220

DANCE TO YOUR DADDY.
The Dear has Swallowed the Silver Dollar (412 ½ Grains) and is Reviving.

Soon afterwards, new discoveries in Nevada in the Comstock lode and other large silver deposits — boosted by novel mining equipment and techniques, and transported on new railroads — provided a surplus. The interests of Western miners in reactivating silver currency, and Western farmers in paying off mortgages and other debts in cheaper currency, converged. Nast depicted the Rag Baby after it swallowed the new overvalued silver dollar, which was worth about 92 cents initially.

Nast's title related to silver backers referring to the "dollar of the daddies" — their metal co-existing with gold from Alexander Hamilton's time as the first Secretary of the Treasury. (Ignoring the fact that he paid the young country's debts in gold.)[1]

---

* See p. 389

The money question was of prime importance to Hayes. He was determined to pay down the $2 billion national debt with gold, to ensure specie resumption in January 1879, and to limit further inroads from greenbacks and "free" (unlimited) silver. On this particular issue, the President had some unusual Congressional supporters like Conkling and Blaine. Nast believed in, and probably admired, Hayes's determination and hard-earned success, but never gave him any more personal public support than he did during his campaign against Tilden. Nevertheless, by attacking the inflationists with several serialized approaches (as he had Tilden), Nast undoubtedly helped him.

Soft-Soap

Henry Watterson, Nast's longtime personal friend and political target, gave him an exceptional opening when he editorialized in his *Louisville Courier-Journal* that voters could decree that even soft-soap money could be used as currency to "repudiate the whole debt." Nast responded with the Devil ladling soft-soap money from the U.S. Treasury: "In God We Trust — but the Devil is to Pay." After the fall elections ten months later, Watterson still couldn't let the Devil loose because Hayes had effectively neutralized his Congressional opponents, and Species Resumption was a month away.

HW January 19, 1878 48

"IDEAL MONEY."
"Universal Suffrage can, if it likes, repudiate the whole debt; it can, if it likes, decree soft-soap to be currency."—*The Louisville Courier-Journal.*

HW November 30, 1878 948

CHAINED.
Henry Watterson (the keeper). "I am very sorry, but I can't let you go just yet."

Greenbacks

Without fanfare, Nast also introduced another symbol to represent the Greenback Party, which had organized two years earlier. James Weaver, a former Republican, was a prominent promoter; he was elected to Congress from Iowa in 1878 and received three percent of the popular vote for President in 1880. Nast depicted him as Weaver the Ass from Shakespeare's *A Midsummer Night's Dream*.

Here, Weaver was in the same Congressional boat as the Democratic fox, trying to pull the national credit over Inflation Falls. Nine months later, both were flailing in the water, vultures overhead, as "Our Credit" was safe and Resumption ahead.

HW February 23, 1878 145 C

CAN HE?
"Now pull him over the Falls, and see if he can reach the Point again."

HW November 9, 1878 892-893

HELP!

Stand from Under!

While Nast never fully depicted Hayes himself — positively or negatively — in any cartoon, he did portray the President and his Cabinet **without their heads** (in the same issue as his only favorable reference to Interior Secretary Carl Schurz.) In perhaps his best caricature of the Hayes era, his double-page capture of the national credit crisis made a difficult visual concept easy to understand.

A week after the first Soft-soap cartoon, the banged-up Republican Elephant lost its trunk-hold on "Our National Credit" as it came crashing down on the posturing, headless Administration. Schurz was readily recognizable with his pince-nez and long legs; Hayes and Treasury Secretary John Sherman less so except for their stances. Bankruptcy boulders from banks, insurance companies and factories were about to hit them, along with "Repudiation" of the debt and "Southern Claims" left over from the Civil War.

Subsequently, Hayes came out reasonably well, ensuring that resumption would take place as scheduled a year later, and the national debt would be supported by gold. Congress passed the compromise Bland-Allison Act which mandated that Treasury buy $2-4 million dollars of silver monthly, to be coined into standard dollars, worth about 92 cents and convertible into legal tender silver certificates. Hayes vetoed the bill, Congress passed it over his veto at the end of February 1878, and Treasury Secretary Sherman minimized its effect by staying with the lower $2,000,000 purchase level.

HW January 26, 1878 72-73

STAND FROM UNDER!

Allen Thurman

Democrat Thurman, Ohio's senior Senator and a national leader of his party, initially favored hard money. After the Species Redemption Act passed in January 1875, Thurman realized he had to soften his position and promote greenbacks if he wanted to win favorite-son endorsement from Ohio Democrats for the next year's Presidential nomination. Nast needled him with two Rag Baby cartoons; the second featured hard-money candidate Samuel Tilden choking the inflation symbol, while Thurman pretended not to be home.

HW September 4, 1875 716

THAT IRREDEEMABLE RAG BABY.
This Is A Nice Position For A "Hard-Money" Bachelor To Be Place In!

HW October 9, 1875 813 C

"HOLY MURDER!!!"
Governor Tilden And The Ohio Rag Baby.

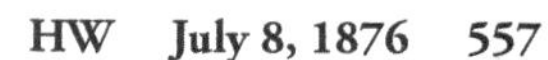
HW July 8, 1876 557

The 1876 Democratic platform included Repeal of the Resumption Act, due to take effect on January 1, 1879. A week before its candidates — hard-money Tilden, and soft-money Thomas Hendricks for Vice President — were known, Nast depicted the Democratic Tiger decapitated in a prison cell, with Uncle Sam as the jailor. A placard noted that the favorite son of Ohio, the Rag Baby, was running for the Presidency.

While the cartoon wasn't noteworthy for its message, it was the first instance where Nast created a steel trap to symbolize inflation. 22 trap-centric cartoons followed in 1878 alone, which the cartoonist used to visually drumbeat the political and economic trap that greenbacks and free silver represented, both in themselves and from the Democratic Party.

THE DEAD LOCK—AND NOW THE DEMOCRATIC TIGER HAS LOST THE HEAD.

Stanley Matthews

After Hayes took office, his principal monetary opponent — and Nast's primary target — was Stanley Matthews, Ohio's junior Senator and fellow Republican. After Hayes appointed Senator John Sherman, another Ohio friend, as Treasury Secretary, the Ohio legislature — with the President's blessing — chose Matthews as his replacement to serve out the last two years of Sherman's term. They attended Kenyon College together and served as officers in the 23rd Ohio Regiment during the Civil War. Later, they became in-laws. (Hayes's wife Lucy's brother married Matthews's sister.) During the Electoral Controversy, Matthews had gone to New Orleans as a "visiting statesman" on Hayes's behalf, represented him before the Electoral Commission, and played a key role in the pre-Inaugural compromise that assured "Home rule" would replace "Bayonet rule" in Louisiana and South Carolina. Matthews now turned on his close friend and political ally, as well as on his predecessor Sherman, by leading the charge in the Senate for "free" unlimited silver currency and more inflation.

HW November 17, 1877 897 C

THE OFF YEAR.
Moral.—**Don't try unsound experiments with a substantial animal.**
N.B.—Stanley (Mathews) was not successful in *his* Exploring Expedition.

Nast first depicted Matthews as an explorer riding the Republican Elephant, who was shattering the "Communism" and "Tricky Currency" planks of the recently lost Ohio state election. Nast's feeble pun equated "explorer" Stanley Matthews with Henry Stanley, the *Herald* reporter who found explorer David Livingston in Tanzania six years before.

Shortly after Congress convened in December 1877, Matthews introduced a resolution that all U.S. bonds could be legally redeemed in 92 cent (412.5 grains) silver dollars. Before the January 25 vote, Nast referred to the resolution as *The Tweed-ization of Silver*. Matthews was a pawnbroker, returning a silver watch in place of the gold one "Me. Bloated Bondholder" had hocked. Below the counter, a beat-up cloth umbrella "will be returned for a silk one."

Nast focused on Matthews's full mustache that came down on his round beard. Within a month, that feature evolved into a jagged animal trap which the artist had first used generically with the Tiger seven months earlier. Now he personalized it, as Matthews led the legislative battle for free silver. After Congress passed the Matthews Resolution, Uncle Sam's foot was stuck in it — initially as *The First Step Toward National Bankruptcy*.

HW January 19, 1878 45 C

THE TWEED-IZATION OF SILVER.
S. Matthews (Rep., Ohio). "Yes, Mr. Bloated Holder, you gave me a Gold watch and chain, but now I can legally return a Silver one."

HW February 16, 1878 125 C

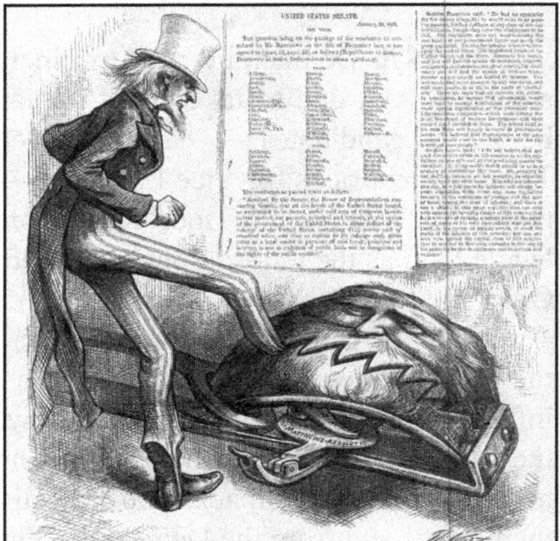

THE FIRST STEP TOWARD NATIONAL BANKRUPTCY.

The Matthews Resolution, which Nast printed in full, also contained a tricky but successful political trap. Because it was "concurrent" rather than "joint," it did not require the President's signature and could not be vetoed. Conkling tried in vain to adjust the wording. Nast and all the politicians understood its author's craftiness in setting his trap.[2] To focus blame as he saw it, the cover cartoon listed the Senatorial yeas and nays.

Nast tweaked the Republican renegade further by playing with his name and abbreviating "Stanley" to its first two letters. Now the soft-money strategist became St. Matthew, the Biblical Apostle, who previously had been a despised tax collector. An alarmed Uncle Sam had his foot trapped in St. Matthews' Resolution as its author smiled.

As mentioned earlier, the impact of the Matthews Resolution was lessened by the Bland-Allison Act which Congress passed over Hayes's veto on February 28. It limited the amount of silver which the Treasury was required to buy to two to four million dollars a month. Treasury decision-maker Sherman generally stayed with the minimum.

The blame soon shifted to Uncle Sam. In probably the roughest, most despicable image of his 185 depictions, America's trapped national symbol appeared as a dishevelled, cigar-puffing bum — leaning perilously off-balance — as Hayes's veto and "honest debts" lay under the trap in the Congressional spittoon. Above, the ghostly spirit of tax-happy King George III made his only appearance in a Nast cartoon, as he admonished the principle-setting, first president in a large double-page combining illustration and caricature. Nast must have been especially proud of his picture because Uncle Sam's good foot rested on his signature block to draw attention to it.

HW March 23, 1878 232-233

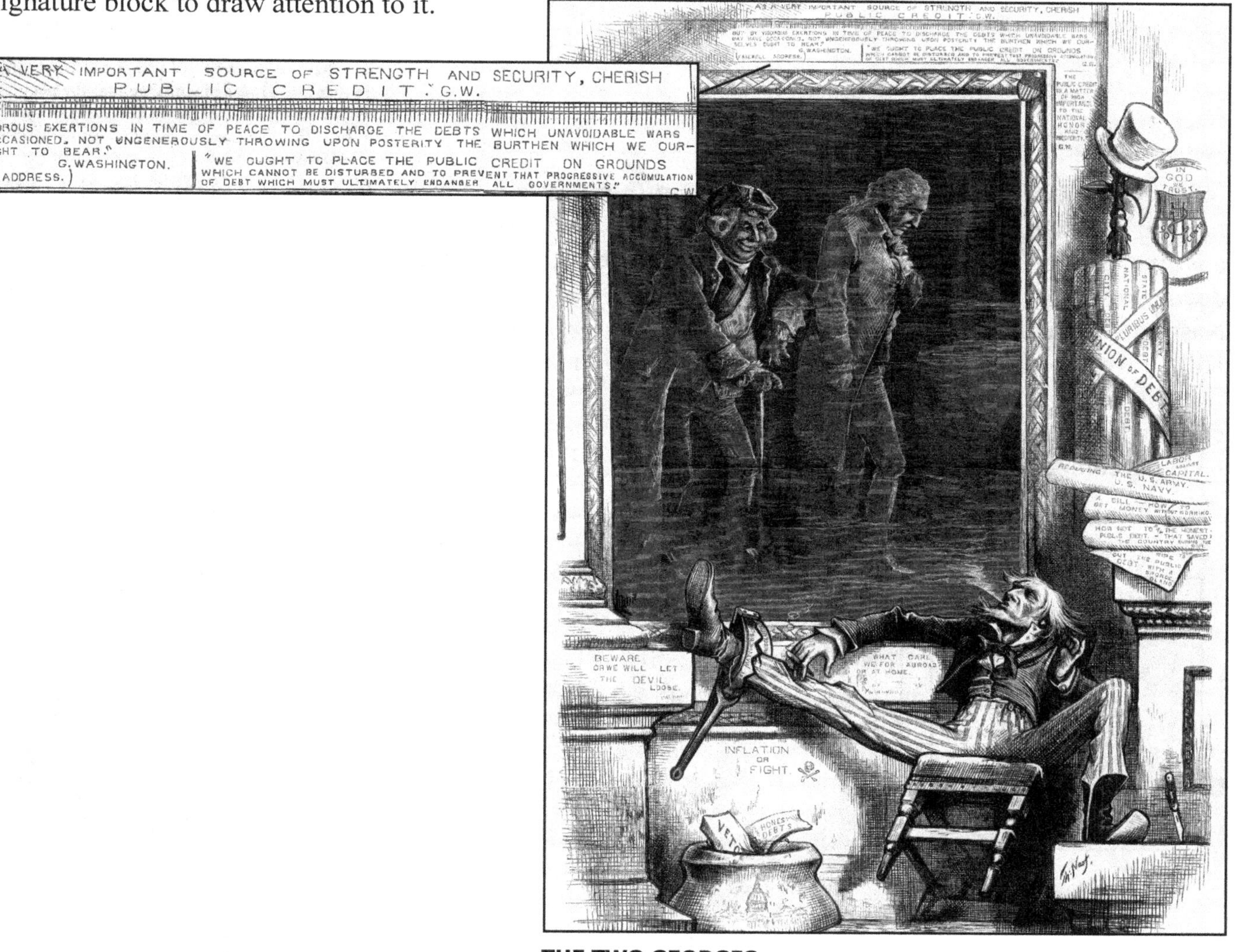

THE TWO GEORGES.
George III to George Washington. "I say, George—Daddy—is that the free and enlightened Cherub for whom you fought? Don't you think you had better write another Farewell Address to him?"

Six weeks later, Nast followed up with wordy Columbia giving a sulky Uncle Sam "Hail Columbia" in a long, preachy sub-title. This time George Washington's aphorism and portrait reiterated the importance of maintaining public credit. Slyly referring back to his "This is not an organ" (with regard to the *Tribune's* role in the Greeley campaign), the trap claimed "This is not a trap." Another dig labeled Congress as "Gab House."

HW May 4, 1878 345 C

GIVING U.S. HAIL COLUMBIA.

Columbia. "You have disgraced your good name by coining dollars which are not dollars, and benefited nobody (not even the Silver Ring) but the European silver-sellers......Then your Secretary is compelled to ask favors of the 'Wall Street sharks' and 'bloated bondholders,' that you may fulfill your promise of Resumption; and it will not be the first time, either, that they have helped you out of a tight place......Do close that Gab House of yours, so that the people may know how they stand, and be able to resume business......There, now, be sulky when you are found fault with, and say that I am not patriotic, and don't love my people!"

In May 1878, the Democratic-stacked Potter Committee was trying to gather evidence that the electoral returns in Louisiana and Florida were fraudulent.* The supervisor of registration in one Louisiana parish produced a written commendation from Matthews in his unsuccessful attempt to get a consulship (because other fabricated documents and testimony discredited him). However, Matthews took heat for his recommendation of a rascal, and Nast must have laughed as he depicted *The Trapper-Trapped* in a "Civil-Service trap for machine politicians." Killing two birds, he also nailed the Potter Commission in his timely series about its backfires.

Nast never let up on Matthews. After his two-year Senate term expired, he returned to Ohio. His reason according to his artistic nemesis: "Because he does not want his salary in silver," which by that time was worth only 83 cents compared to a gold dollar.

HW June 29, 1878 505 C

THE TRAPPER-TRAPPED.

HW January 24, 1880 64

REFUSING THEIR OWN.

* See p. 418-421

As a lame duck in January 1881, Hayes sent Matthews's nomination to the Supreme Court to the Senate, which rejected it. Incoming President James Garfield, a fellow Ohioan, renominated Matthews; this time he was confirmed by a 24-23 vote, as Nast noted in the last of his 15 cartoons depicting his hapless victim, now almost slipping off the court's bench. Curtis editorialized that Matthews did not belong on the Court because of his views.[3]

HW February 19, 1881 128

LET US HAVE JUDGES ABOVE SUSPICION AND ABOVE PAR.

HW March 19, 1881 191

KEEPING THE BENCH ABOVE SUSPICION OF DISHONEST MONEY.

HW June 11, 1881 387

ON—BY THE SKIN OF HIS TEETH.

Circulation

On occasion, Nast expanded his use of the silver trap by portraying it as the cause of inflation via Uncle Sam's increasingly swollen leg: as over-valued silver piled up in the Treasury, it didn't circulate like gold. He updated Uncle Sam's condition towards the end of each year.

Just before resumption began, the first bulge appeared as Sam contemplated petitioning Congress for relief.

HW December 14, 1878 985 C

THE SOONER THE BETTER.

A year later, the swelling was much larger as Uncle Sam pleaded with Treasury Secretary Sherman to do something about the silver situation.

HW November 29, 1879 948

RESUMPTION (?)
U.S. "There is no circulation in that leg, and it's swelling every day more and more. Mortification will set in, and I am sure my other leg will be affected. Now, Dr. Sherman, something must be done, and quick, too."

HW December 13, 1879 980

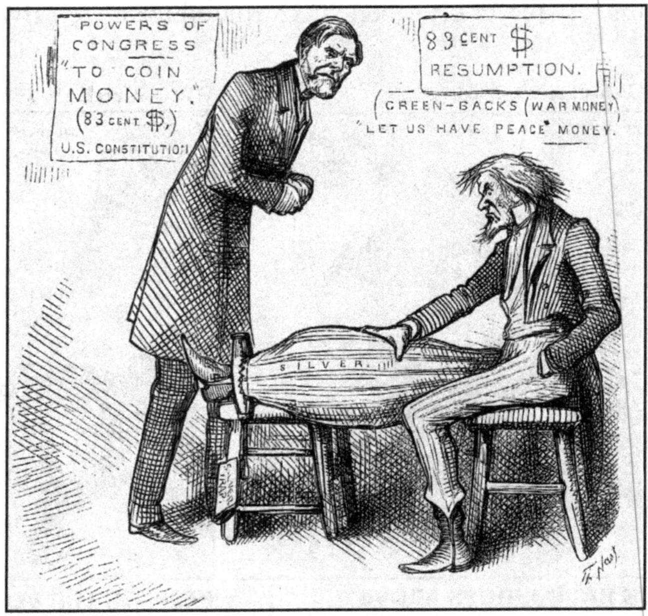

BE SOUND IN MIND AND BODY.
Uncle Sam. "As long as I keep these outstanding notes on my mind, which I am well able to pay, I am violating the laws of my constitution; and how can I expect my body to recover when my mind is not at ease?"

After Hayes became a lame duck in 1880, an almost unrecognizable Uncle Sam had his leg inflated to the point where he couldn't even get out of bed. Nast noted that "silver (political money) goes into the U.S. Treasury and stays there" — with no circulation — while "gold (real money) goes around the world."

HW December 25, 1880 836

DOCTORS DIFFER.
U.S. The Congress of doctors has met. Now Tinkering and Experimenting will begin; but that will give *No Relief to the Circulation*.

Shylock

The money question sparked perhaps the most astonishing cartoon of himself that Nast ever drew. He felt so strongly about upholding the national credit by limiting greenbacks and denying so-called "free silver," that he cast himself as Shylock the Jew from Shakespeare's *Merchant of Venice*.

Three years earlier when Grant signed the Resumption Act, Nast had depicted him leading "The Ark of State" while the Act's Republican promoters floundered in the waters of inflation.* Now he "indorsed" that cartoon, while adding his slate: "No objection to the METAL but to the MEDALLER. Yours truly. Shylock Jew. Bloated Bond-holder. Gold bug." On the outside of the slate, he added: "If this is being a Jew, I am one."

HW February 23, 1878 156

OUR ARTIST INDORSING THE ABOVE CARTOON, PUBLISHED JANUARY 9, 1875.

During Nast's career, there was widespread prejudice against Jews, and Nast occasionally used Shylock as his stereotype to denigrate Democratic Party Chairman and financier August Belmont for his heritage. He depicted him as a vote buyer** and a scapegoat.*** During the 1872 campaign, he showed Liberal Republicans Horace Greeley and Reuben Fenton asking Shylock Belmont for money and votes, quoting Shakespeare's vile text in full.

HW July 6, 1872 528

"SHYLOCK, WE WOULD HAVE MONEYS AND VOTES."
Shylock. "Well then, it now appears, you need my help:
Go to, then; you come to me, and say,
Shylock, we would have moneys; You say so;
You, that did void your rheum upon my beard
And foot me, as you spurn a stranger cur
Over your threshold; moneys is your suit,
What shall I say to you? Should I not say,
Hath a dog money? is it possible
A cur can lend three thousand ducats? or
Shall I bend low, and in a bondsman's key
With 'bated breath and whispering humbleness,
Say this,—
Fair Sir, you spit on me on Wednesday last;
You spurn'd me such a day; another time
You call'd me—dog;and for these courtesies
I'll lend you thus much monies?......
I would be friends with you, and have your love,
Forget the shames that you have stain'd me with,
And supply your present wants."
—Merchant Of Venice, Act I, Scene III.

* See p. 389
** See p. 215
*** See p. 256

HW January 22, 1881 64

"DAS DEUTSCHE VATERLAND" IS ABOVE CRITICISM.
"Froth. "I will cut you into small pieces if you say dem mean tings again!"

Nast may have been influenced by his hero Grant's earlier turnaround towards Jews. Fed up with renegade Jewish cotton traders who violated Treasury regulations, thereby aiding the Confederacy, Grant issued his infamous Order No. 11 to General William Sherman expelling *Jews as a class* from his army. As he later admitted, Grant made an extraordinary mistake by not limiting his order to miscreants. His timing was terrible too, coming in December 1862; Jews were ejected weeks before the Emancipation Proclamation freed the slaves. Lincoln revoked Grant's order while approving "expelling traders and Jew peddlers."[4]

Asked to clarify his intent by a leading Jewish lawyer in 1868, Presidential candidate Grant responded that his order was directed against miscreants "whose religion was in no way material to the issue." The recipient, Simon Wolf, wrote a letter exonerating Grant which was published widely, and was appointed Recorder of Deeds for the District of Columbia shortly after the inauguration. It gave him a lobbying role with Congress for Jewish issues.

In 1870, Grant appointed Wolf's friend, Edward Salomon, as Governor of the Washington Territory. Six years later, he attended the opening of a synagogue, and also invited delegates to an American Hebrew Congregations convention to the White House.[5] Grant's about-face probably rubbed off on Nast who never used Shylock again.

Nast rarely mentioned Jews in subsequent cartoons. He did forcefully attack anti-Semitism in Germany in 1881, and in Russia the following year in a cartoon with no humor in it.

HW February 11, 1882 96

LIVE AND LET LIVE IN RUSSIA.
"Your money, Jew, or your life!"—*The cry for ages.*

Chapter 37
The Election of 1880: The Candidates

Downswing

As Nast entered his last decade with the Harpers, four factors combined to reduce his journalistic influence and power. All of them were apparent in 1880.

- Printing technology changes
- Stronger outside cartoon competition
- The emergence of inside cartoon competition
- More oppressive censorship from editor George William Curtis

Printing Technology Changes

First, the Harpers forced Nast to change his artistic technique in 1880 by switching from drawing directly on woodblocks with a soft pencil to using a pen and ink on paper. Their new photo-chemical process eliminated the jobs and expense of wood engravers, while speeding up the production process. The change took place gradually over the year.

There were three potential advantages for Nast: he no longer had to wrestle with woodblocks, draw in reverse, or have to make his cartoons at the same size they were to be reproduced. However, for Nast personally, the change generally resulted in lower quality artistry because he had less control over line width; the bold lines and cross-hatching of his soft pencil gave way to thinner, sparser lines of a steel pen, which were less impactful.

The old and then the new techniques were used in successive Christmas cartoons at the beginning and end of 1880. Both had his own features incorporated into Santa Claus. His detailed cross-hatching and thicker, blacker lines gave the earlier one more intensity.

HW January 3, 1880 8-9

ANOTHER STOCKING TO FILL.

HW January 1, 1881 8-9

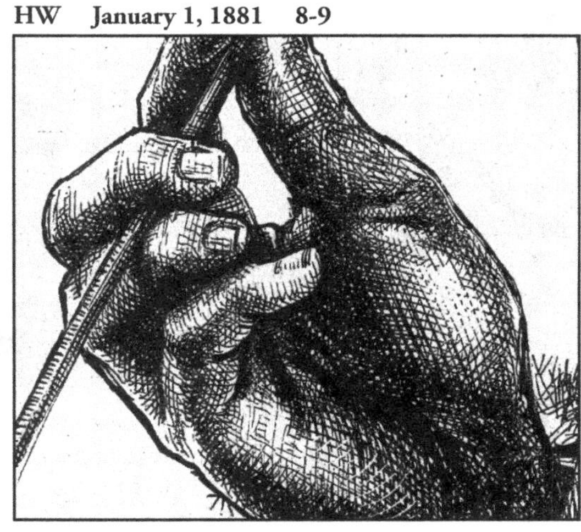

MERRY OLD SANTA CLAUS.

Nast told his biographer Paine that the smooth hard surface of the boxwood was easier for him to draw on than the yielding paper of the new procedure. He also noted that, on occasion, the imperfect chemical engraving process resulted in its acid biting into his lines and affecting or even destroying his more delicate touches.[1]

Opposition papers noted that his hand was losing its skill. That obviously didn't bother the Harpers because he drew 34 cover cartoons in 1880 and 31 in 1881.

Republicans

While on his European trip during the summer of 1878, Nast had seen W.S. Gilbert's and Arthur Sullivan's ground-breaking operetta, *HMS Pinafore*, which had opened in London in May. It made enough of an impression that he used it in five subsequent cartoons. In the third of these, Nast cast leading candidates James Blaine, Roscoe Conkling and Zachariah Chandler as sailors on the U.S.S. Pinafore, singing verses from their Gilbert and Sullivan campaign song 15 months before the election.

Chandler, a Michigan Senator, had chaired the Republican National Committee, and done a good job cleaning up the Indian Bureau, Patent Office and other corrupt operations as Secretary of the Interior during Grant's second term. (He had replaced the disgraced Columbus Delano.)* However, Chandler died unexpectedly three months after his depiction here.

Nast was on target with Blaine, but Conkling would represent Grant rather than himself at the Chicago Convention which still was ten months away. They would go head-to-head through 35 ballots.

HW August 2, 1879 612

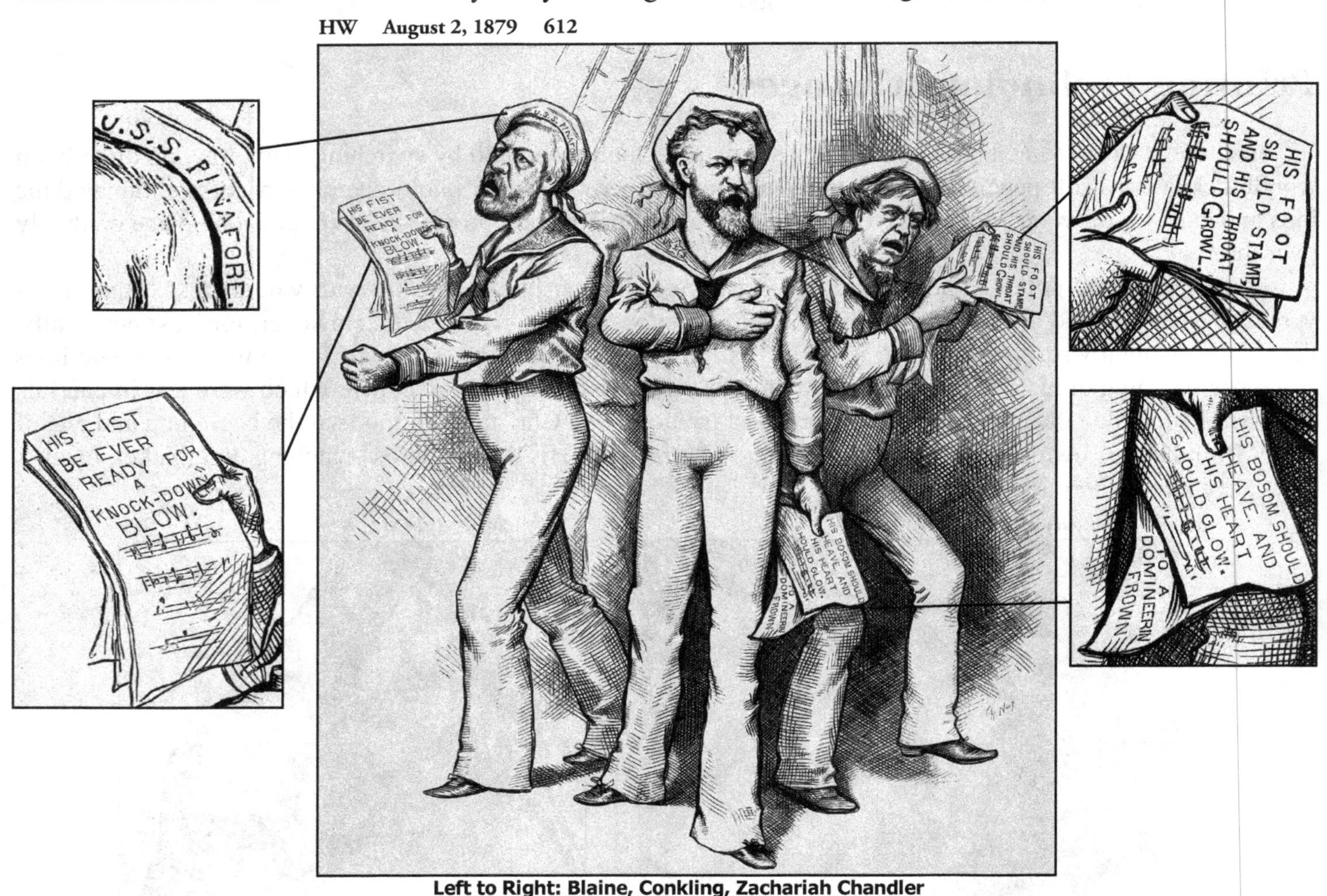

Left to Right: Blaine, Conkling, Zachariah Chandler

THE CAMPAIGN SONG.

Trio And Chorus.—Ralph Conkling, Boatswain Blaine, And Boatswain's Mate Chandler.

* See p. 376

Grant

Grant had left on a two-year world tour, shortly after dining with the Nasts at their Morristown home in May 1877. The Grants traveled with Nast's friend John Russell Young, a former managing editor of the *Tribune* in the sixties, and a European reporter for the *Herald* in the seventies. From time to time, Nast pictorially noted a few of the many honors Grant received in Europe and Asia; the acclaim helped restore his damaged reputation.

While "on the Red Sea" in February 1879, Russell wrote Nast to alert him that *Grant, (his friend) and I spend most of our time looking out at the water, and scheming for a third term!!!! You never knew such a schemer as the General. He sits up for hours and hours, late and schemes. Don't tell Mr. Harper about this (because) it will distress him . . . The General sent you his kindest wishes and Mrs. Grant sent you her love.*[1]

HW October 11, 1879 808-809

THE RETURN OF ULYSSES.

After Grant landed in San Francisco on the steamer *Tokio* to an unprecedentedly large public welcome in September 1879, *Harper's* described the events in two full laudatory columns. Nast alluded to Homer's *Odyssey* in his prosaic double-page *The Return of Ulysses*.

As time passed, a potential third term for Grant was widely discussed. Led by Senator Roscoe Conkling — who hated Blaine — conservative Republican Stalwarts like Illinois Senator John Logan and Pennsylvania Senator Don Cameron pressed for Grant's nomination. However, Grant himself was now uncertain that he wanted it, although he would have accepted if the convention vote went his way. Nast thought a third term run was a bad idea for his hero and for the country, and ignored Grant except for an inconsequential May 1880 cover mocking German anti-Grant sentiment in Ohio. (He must have had his Caesarism cartoons in mind).*

PUCK March 31, 1880

Belknap Cameron Robeson Logan Shepherd Murphy

THE POLITICAL "ARMY OF SALVATION."

Joseph Keppler, who loathed Grant, took out his cudgel. His first barb in February 1880 — *Puck Wants A Strong Man at the Head of Government — But Not This Kind* — featured six crooked Grant appointees held up by the trapeze artist President.**

Several more Keppler cartoons followed, many with artistry and wit comparable to Nast's best against Andrew Johnson, Boss Tweed and Horace Greeley. In March, Keppler utilized the Salvation Army which came to America the previous year. (14 years after its 1865 founding in London.) Substituting Grant as the Savior (of his country) for Jesus Christ on his irreligious banner, Conkling led a chorus of scandalized crooks — George Robeson, William Belknap. Tom Murphy, Alexander Shepherd — and patronage bosses Cameron and Logan. Opportunistically, Keppler also took a shot at the Temperance movement.

---

* See p. 354-364
** See p. 378

A week before the June 2 Republican Convention opened in Chicago, Curtis came out strongly against Grant: *We do not allege Grant's personal complicity in scandals, but all Republicans know that he was chiefly indignant not with those who compromised his good name and the success of the party, but with those who sought to punish the offenders.*[2] Curtis suggested that Vermont Senator George Edmunds might be a good candidate.

Simultaneously, Keppler depicted Grant's "Strong Government" train steam-rolling past the "Third Term Crossing," guided by Conkling, Logan and Cameron. Elihu Washburn, Grant's longtime Illinois supporter and himself a long-shot candidate, held a "Clear the Track" sign for Grant.

What probably caught Nast's attention were a despondent George William Curtis and Carl Schurz looking at the run-over body of the Republican Party, while Puck wept alongside.

PUCK May 26, 1880

TO THE CHICAGO CONVENTION.

Immediately after Grant lost, Keppler rejoiced in his defeat in a cartoon worthy of Nast at his best. Using Grant's greatest military accomplishment as a boomerang, *The Appomattox of the Third-Termers — Unconditional Surrender*, Keppler depicted Grant and Conkling in abject defeat, while Sherman and Blaine pulled down their third-term flag. Behind Garfield, Curtis cheered while Schurz and Puck smiled.

Keppler got in his last licks at Grant, with a full roster of his Administration's scandal figures identified by their military tents, banners, or labeled caps. Orville Babcock's "Headquarters of the Crooked Whiskey Department offered bourbon samples. Others included Cabinet officers Belknap (War), Columbus Delano (Interior) and George Williams (Justice), as well as crooked machine politicians Murphy (New York Port), Shepherd (Washington) and Don Cameron (Pennsylvania).*

PUCK June 16, 1880

THE APPOMATTOX OF THE THIRD TERMERS —UNCONDITIONAL SURRENDER.

---

* See p. 370-375

Blaine

James Blaine, who represented the moderate "Half-breed" wing of the Republican Party, would be Grant's principal opponent at the convention. Nast knew Blaine personally, but distrusted him because of his shady railroad dealings which had blown up during the Congressional investigation of 1876, and contributed to his failure to win that nomination which ultimately went to Hayes.

During his nominating speech for Blaine at the 1876 Convention, renowned Illinois orator Robert Ingersoll likened him to "an armed warrior, *a plumed knight*, marching down the halls of Congress and throwing his shining lance . . . against the brazen forehead of every traitor to his country and every maligner of his reputation." Blaine was worried that the phrase might be misapplied to suggest a white feather, but his principal artistic "maligner" went much further than that during the next two presidential elections when he targeted the Plumed Knight 62 times.

Nast also disdained Blaine's support for Chinese exclusion. During 1879 and into 1880, Nast drew several cartoons ridiculing Blaine for his anti-Chinese stance. Blaine, who had always supported black rights, was looking to secure the California, Nevada and Oregon electoral votes by backing Denis Kearney, the violent labor agitator who led the exclusionary movement.*

In the same pre-convention issue that Curtis blasted Grant, Nast's post-dated cover featured "The Plumed Knight" wearing his bloody shirt, and about to don his hat. Appearing more like leeches than feathers, Blaine's plumes included the Republican nomination, Communists (referring to Kearney), and the "machine of bluster and brag." Hedging his bet, Nast's vignette (on the left) showed Blaine's "boom balloon" exploding while "Defeat Sure" was on the shadowed apparition below.

HW June 5, 1880 353 C

"THE PLUMED KNIGHT."

Blaine's charisma was acclaimed as his "magnetic" personality which attracted followers and votes. Nast turned that upside down by portraying him as a magnet with scandals, corruption and controversial issues sticking to him. His head was propped on one of Nast's symbolic barrels of dollars used to buy votes or political favors. Kearney was attached as his potential vice president, beside a Chinese coolie. At his feet was the Credit Mobilier scandal (Nast knew he was innocent), and the fraudulent railroad bonds, and "smoking gun" Mulligan letters (explaining his deceit), which had cost him the 1876 nomination.

HW May 8, 1880 300

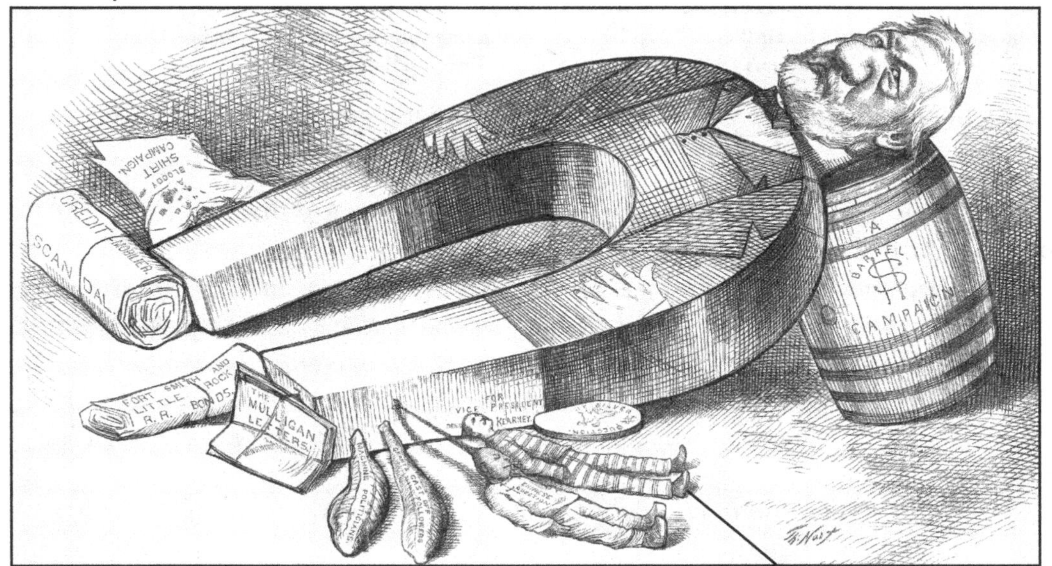

THE "*MAGNETIC*" BLAINE; OR, A VERY HEAVY "LOAD"-STONE FOR THE REPUBLICAN PARTY TO CARRY.

* See p. 464

Early in his confrontation with Blaine, Nast experienced a rare case of his targeted victim hitting back. Blaine had effectively controlled the Republican Party in Maine for two decades. In September 1877, Alonzo Garcelon, a Democrat and Surgeon-General during the Civil War, was elected Governor by the Maine Legislature with the help of a large Greenback Party vote. A year later, Garcelon and his confederates falsified the returns, throwing out 37 duly elected Republicans so as to keep the government in Democratic hands. Looking for meat for his cartoons, and finding electoral fraud, Nast drew Garcelon as he knocked on Tilden's door, and three other times.

When Blaine learned about the fraud, he rushed to Augusta with 100 armed men; his home faced the state capitol. Garcelon called out the state militia and civil war almost broke out. Garcelon sensed he was losing public opinion; agreed to peaceful intervention by Maine's Gettysburg hero, General Joshua Chamberlain; and accepted the decision of the state Supreme Court. The displaced Republicans were restored and elected a Republican governor.

Consequently, Nast depicted Blaine as an Indian chief about to swing his huge war club until Chamberlain dissuaded him. Both men had feathered headdresses — or plumes in Blaine's case. (Nast's title referred to expelled Governor Smith, linking him to Tilden and his cypher nephew Pelton.)

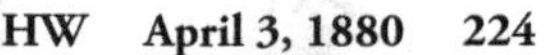

HW April 3, 1880 224

QUACKS OF A FEATHER.
He will be "at home," and the doctors will agree.

HW February 7, 1880 88

THE SMITHS GIVE A GREAT DEAL OF TROUBLE.
Powhatan Blaine. "Just let me give him one whack to show how *strong* I am."
Pocahontas Chamberlain. "No, don't, Jim; you'll make a mess of it."

Three days after the cartoon was published, Blaine wrote Nast from Washington, making a good case.

"My Dear Mr. Nast:

I am perhaps as willing a victim as ever was caricatured for the entertainment of the public. But, of course, I do not like to be totally and inexcusably misrepresented on an important issue.

Having spent seventy anxious days and nights in Maine for the express purpose of settling all our troubles without violence or the slightest infraction of law, I do not see the justice of painting me as an Indian with a war club, anxious to strike and only prevented by the interposition of General Chamberlain.

I would be glad as a matter of mere personal curiosity to learn any fact or rumor or hearsay that justified you in thus presenting me. If I was ever widely known for any public act or policy, it was for precisely the reverse of that which you present.

I have always had a strong belief in your sense of right and justice, and I leave you to do what seems meet and proper in your eyes."[3]

Nast never responded in a cartoon or in print, or in any known letter.

Sherman

Another candidate was John Sherman, who was well regarded as Hayes's Secretary of the Treasury and for his prior service as an Ohio Senator. Blaine made a fatal mistake when he tried to woo Ohio's delegation away from their favorite son months before the Convention. He secured 9 of their 44 electors, but the others were so bitter that they decisively backed their fellow Ohioan, James Garfield, when the stand-off between Grant and Blaine ended on the 36th ballot.

Two months prior to that unanticipated but conclusive event, Nast depicted the two battling Senators as their historical Roman counterparts, Julius Caesar and Pompey. In 49 B.C., Pompey (Blaine) turned against Caesar (Sherman) in the Roman Senate, condemning Caesar as an enemy of the state (Ohio). Here, both were spoilsmen, linked to the statue of Romulus and Remus, the legendary founders of Rome, suckling (for spoils) at a she-wolf's teats. His title, *The Die Is Cast*, referred to Caesar's edict to his troops in Gaul (modern France) to cross the Rubicon River into Italy and march on Rome.

Nast called upon his store of Italian history, which he probably learned during his somewhat comparable campaign accompanying Garibaldi in 1860, and amplified watching Shakespeare's plays.

HW April 17, 1880 252

"THE DIE IS CAST"—CAESAR AND POMPEY IN OHIO.
Sherman. "If the Republicans of Ohio do not fairly and fully in their Convention express a preference for me, and support me with substantial unanimity in the National Convention, my name will not be presented to that Convention with my consent.
Blaine. "Well, what of it?"

Garfield

As planned, Garfield nominated his fellow Ohioan with a well-received speech, which some thought tooted his own horn as much as Sherman's. Later, he gave a second impressive address which resulted in Blaine's delegates switching to him, thereby denying Grant a third term. Acknowledging defeat, Conkling moved to make Garfield's nomination unanimous, stormed out of the hall, and retaliated by withholding support from Blaine when he was the candidate in 1884.

Arthur

New York's 35 electoral votes, largely controlled by Conkling, were accurately seen as key to the election. In both a practical and conciliatory gesture, the Republican National Committee wanted the embittered Conkling to approve a candidate for Vice President. Conkling refused, but Chester Arthur, his former lieutenant, accepted the nomination over his political mentor's strong objections.

The November election actually did hinge on New York. Garfield — with Arthur on the ballot — won the state by 20,000 votes, the popular vote by 10,000, and the electoral college by 214 to 155. If he had lost New York, the count would have been 190 to 179 against him.

Arthur was a questionable choice at best. He was a close friend of Tom Murphy, who was known for selling shoddy caps to the government during the Civil War, was in real estate deals with Boss Tweed, and was forced to resign as New York's Port Collector — where his friend, President Grant, had installed him — for fraud and corruption.*

Arthur, a lawyer by profession and a notorious high-living playboy, replaced Murphy at the Port. President Hayes fired him in July 1878, with the aim of breaking Conkling's control of the state's patronage. After Arthur joined Garfield on the ticket, Sherman wrote to a friend: "He never held an office except one that he was removed from."[4]

While Curtis was happy with Garfield and unhappy about Arthur, Nast was apparently stuck for another four years with a candidate whom he disliked. With the Democratic Convention coming up in two weeks, *Harper's* stayed relatively quiet.

Tilden

The math for Democratic victory in 1880 was pretty simple. The Party was certain to carry the Solid South and the Border States. To win, it was essential to capture New York's 35 electoral votes and, hopefully, Indiana's 15.

In early 1879, New York's Tilden appeared to have the best chance, but after the Potter Committee's investigation backfired with the *Tribune's* cipher revelations, his chances diminished significantly.** Nast kept using his cipher-mummy symbol to remind his public of Tilden's shadiness and health problems. In December 1879, he put him on ice with the frosty Charles Francis Adams. By May, rumors of his withdrawal were getting louder; Tammany leader John Kelly, Tilden's arch-enemy in the battle to control New York State, listened to the mummy with "Fraud" stamped on its forehead, in one of Nast's best Tilden cartoons.

HW December 13, 1879 976

ON ICE.
$.J.T. "I only place myself here to keep respectably fresh."
"There is a whisper to the effect that after himself he desires Mr. Charles F. Adams nominated."—*Daily Press.*

HW May 15, 1880 305 C

"IT IS WHISPERED AGAIN THAT TILDEN HAS GIVEN IN."
The Hon. John Kelly. "*Louder*! Louder!! LOUDER!!!"

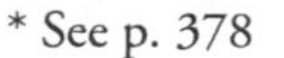

* See p. 378
** See p. 418-421

HW July 10, 1880 433 C

BOOM!!!—SO NEAR, AND YET SO FAR.
S.J.T. "By Jupiter! can't they understand a joke? Catch me believing in lightning-rods again!"

On June 20, two days before the Convention began, Tilden's brother Henry showed up with his letter of withdrawal. In Nast's final mummy stab — and his last *Weekly* cover for five weeks due to his editor's censorship — Nast depicted the result as lightning from the Cincinnati Convention striking General Hancock at his headquarters on Governors Island in New York harbor as Tilden despaired in his sarcophagus.

Bayard

Well before Tilden's prospects evaporated, longtime aristocratic Delaware Senator Thomas Bayard assumed that he was the 1876 loser's residual heir.[5] Bayard was a strong believer in states' rights, which enhanced his appeal to the South. He claimed that he could conciliate both sectors, a proposition which Nast attacked without mercy, mostly in words.

However, Nast respected Bayard's advocacy of hard money and financial soundness. In late 1879, he depicted Bayard preventing the Democratic Donkey from falling into financial chaos; meanwhile, Treasury Secretary Sherman, holding 83-cent silver certificates, watched the Republican Elephant slumber on the edge of the same precipice as it "let well enough alone." **This was the first joint appearance of the two permanent party symbols in a Nast cartoon**.

HW December 27, 1879 1001

STRANGER THINGS HAVE HAPPENED.
Hold On, And You May Walk Over The Sluggish Animal Up There Yet.

HW November 29, 1879 948

"THE SOUTH NEEDS SYMPATHY AND RESPECT."—SEN. BAYARD.
Solid North To Solid South. "I regret that you had to surrender after rebelling against our country, and still have such unpleasant duties to perform as killing niggers, white Republicans, and independents. That Yazoo County affair, too, must have been very annoying. And then disagreeable necessities, like bulldozing, tissue-paper ballots, and counting yourselves in, forced upon you! And last, but not least, the grievance of being compelled to repudiate your debts! But I sympathize with you deeply, and respect you in spite of all!"—(Will this style do, Mr. Bayard?)

Hancock

The other leading candidate was Major General Winfield Scott Hancock. Now 56, he graduated from West Point in the same class as Grant, George McClellan and Stonewall Jackson. He had a superb military record in both the Mexican and Civil Wars, highlighted by his critical battle-saving leadership at Gettysburg where he turned back Pickett's charge on the decisive final day. He served under Grant in the bloody 1864 Overland Campaign, where Brigadier General Hayes served under him. Two years later, Grant promoted Hancock to Major General in the regular Army, where he battled Indians. Currently, he commanded the Army's Atlantic Division headquartered at Fort Jay (then Fort Columbus) on Governor's Island in New York Harbor, a position he returned to after the election.

Why was Hancock — a man with no political experience — even a candidate? A lifelong Democrat, he had been mentioned as a possibility in 1868 when Horatio Seymour ran against Grant; it would have been two acclaimed generals facing off. Now, with Grant a strong potential nominee just three weeks earlier, a matching top-level general — with no associated scandals — would help offset the potential Republican candidate's unique advantage as a military savior. Editor Curtis queried: "Is it because he is a Union Soldier that General Hancock is an acceptable candidate to the Democratic Party, or because, being a Union soldier, he enables the party to assert its loyalty?"[6]

President Hayes had replaced hard-bitten Phil Sheridan as military governor of Louisiana with the softer Hancock, who made a favorable impression upon the South. Like Bayard, Hancock believed in states' rights. While he promised to enforce the Reconstruction Amendments, he opposed Federal supervision of elections. Accordingly, both candidates were acceptable to the South, as well as the other Democratic factions.

With Grant was no longer the opponent for a Democrat, Hancock's only dubious edge was that his politically clean slate limited criticism of him to that fact, compared to Garfield whose reputation was tainted. As it turned out the other side of that coin — political naivete — was a significant factor in his defeat.

The Convention

The Democrats met in Cincinnati on June 22, While *Harper's* ignored the event pictorially, Keppler continued on track with a neutral preview of the coming horse race. As a Democrat who distrusted Garfield, he probably didn't care which candidate won, as long as it wasn't Tilden.

During 1873, Keppler had six cartoons about Credit Mobilier in *Frank Leslie's Illustrated* Newspaper.* Having denigrated Garfield then, he wasn't about to let him off the hook now. Mounted on the Republican steed, Garfield was handicapped by Credit Mobilier, another scandal called DeGolyer, and his running mate Arthur, as Uncle Sam and Columbia surveyed his opposition.

Lead jockey Tilden had two heavy weights to bear: the Cipher scandal and "income taxes," an 1876 accusation that he had failed to pay them during the Civil War. Behind him were Bayard and Hancock, as well as four identified outside possibilities including House Speaker Samuel Randall.

Hancock was nominated on the second ballot.

PUCK June 23, 1880

THE POLITICAL HANDICAP — WHO WILL RIDE THE DEMOCRATIC ENTRY?

* See p. 345-346

Chapter 38
The Election of 1880: The Campaign

Nast's Handcuffs

The election of 1880 played a relatively minor role in American history, but it was a watershed event for Thomas Nast. After eight years of conflict, editor George William Curtis, no longer overruled by the late 8 Harper, Sr., "housebroke" his star cartoonist by putting him in a public straight jacket.

When Nast lacerated Curtis's Liberal Republican friends like Carl Schurz and Charles Sumner during the 1872 Greeley campaign, he ignored his editor's protests. When Curtis rejected Nast's cartoon slightly needling his friend James Russell Lowell early in the Hayes Administration, Nast left and the *Weekly's* circulation suffered.* The Harpers learned that they needed Nast as much as he needed them, and Joe Harper and his irreplaceable artist reached an uncomfortable truce before he returned. Nast never depicted Hayes, but did support him on key issues like hard money and funding the military. Curtis was thwarted because he had no competent cartoonists who could (or would) portray Hayes positively in other than a humdrum manner.

Nast had opposed Hayes because the new President overturned his idol's (Grant) policies with regard to active Southern pacification and passive Civil Service reform — not because of his integrity. With Garfield, Nast never would forgive the candidate's questionable involvement with the Credit Mobilier scandal, and possibly other issues that Keppler poked at in *Puck*, but Nast never mentioned previously and couldn't refer to now.

Curtis had total editorial control and he point-blank refused to let Nast disparage his good friend Garfield. That left Nast in a bind. Because of his personal friendship with Hancock, he didn't feel comfortable attacking him as forcefully as he had denigrated the candidate's four Democratic predecessors: Samuel Tilden, Horace Greeley, Horatio Seymour and George McClellan.

While Curtis had the whip hand, neither he nor the Harpers wanted Nast to leave as he had in 1877, disturbing the artist's fan base and significantly reducing the *Weekly's* circulation and income. This time, he developed an alternative that gave him total pictorial control, while keeping Nast on board. He used five current *Harper's* illustrators to draw pro-Garfield cartoons on occasion, but mostly to attack Hancock without reservation. Arthur B. Frost, William A. Rogers and Thure de Thulstrup were the best known, along with Thomas Worth and Michael Woolf. Curtis announced his policy in a pro-Garfield endorsement, published in mid-July and enforced immediately.

HARPER'S WEEKLY.

SATURDAY, JULY 24, 1880.

HARPER'S WEEKLY
FOR THE
PRESIDENTIAL CAMPAIGN.

The attention of our readers is respectfully directed to the advertisement in another column of HARPER'S WEEKLY for the present political campaign. The WEEKLY will cordially and heartily support Republican principles and the Republican candidates, and will do everything in its power to promote the success of the party which has preserved the Union, and which has for twenty years controlled the destinies of the nation. Besides the full discussion in its editorial columns of the vital issues of the campaign, *its pages will present political cartoons, sketches, and comics by THOMAS NAST and other well-known artists, employed especially for this purpose,* and every legitimate and proper means will be used to insure the triumph of the Republican national ticket at the polls in November.

* See p. 440

For emphasis, Curtis shelved Nast's completed cartoon intended for the cover of the same July 24 issue. A reporter for the *World* who had seen the cartoon about two weeks earlier while interviewing Nast at his Morristown home, described it as "different branches of the Democratic Party surrendering to General Hancock." In its place, Curtis used a mediocre unsigned cartoon, probably by Thulstrup, which essentially made the same point.

When the *World* reporter who had seen the shelved cartoon made a return visit, he asked Nast about that and his rumored break with Curtis. Nast responded: "The Harpers can answer that a great deal better than I can because they have perfect control of the paper, both editorially and pictorially."

The reporter followed up with Joe Harper, who "politely but firmly intimated that that was a question with which the public could have no legitimate concern." When his comment was reprinted widely, one paper added: "but the public did concern itself in the subject several years ago, rather to the financial loss of Messrs. Harper."[1]

HW October 23, 1880 685

THE FRIEND OF THE FREEDMEN.

Nast had drawn the first two post-convention political cover cartoons in July, but then he was absent from three issues in a row, and his place usurped by other cartoonists as far as the public could tell. Curtis had made his point to his artists and to his readers, so Nast reappeared on the last three August covers. In the interim, the *World's* first interview and Nast's subsequent absence were noted in newspapers around the country.

After Curtis had "housebroken" Nast, he continued to feature his work although sparingly compared to the previous Presidential campaigns. During the 22-week period from Hancock's nomination through November 1880. Nast drew 15 covers; his colleagues drew 7. Collectively, they also had 11 full or double-pages, while Nast had 16. Including small cartoons, Nast had 56 appearances in total during the campaign.

Curtis played his cards well and achieved his primary objectives. Most important, he kept Garfield from being attacked, as well as receiving praise on occasion as with de Thulstrup's uninspired illustration (right). Additionally, he kept Nast onboard as *Harper's* readership demanded and, by doing so, eliminated the possibility of his prime cartoonist working elsewhere to the detriment of Garfield's campaign and *Harper's* circulation.

Garfield's Baggage

As previously mentioned, once Garfield was nominated, his Credit Mobilier entanglement flared. Keppler agreed with Nast that its stain on him was indelible. Indeed, while the Congressional Investigating Committee exonerated Garfield from "any suspicion of corruption, it implies that he prevaricated in his testimony."[2]

Curtis strongly disagreed with the Committee's finding, published while Nast was absent during his six-month sabbatical recovering from the strain of the Tweed and Greeley campaigns. Curtis editorialized that Garfield's "political life has covered him with honor and (nothing) can deprive him of the esteem and gratitude of his countrymen."[3]

The Investigating Committee had censured Congressman Oakes Ames, who master-minded the scandal, and died soon afterwards. Ames testified that Garfield was on the list of Congressmen who were offered nominally-priced stock in return for their potential influence on Union Pacific Railroad legislation, and that he received a $329 dividend. Garfield testified that after a long delay, he never accepted or paid for the stock, but did borrow $300 from Ames which he subsequently repaid; Ames swore he had no recollection of that.

As the 1880 campaign proceeded, *Harper's* readers remembered Nast's 1873 cartoon. When a subscriber asked: "Mr. Editor — How can you reconcile (your) present support of General Garfield with the views of him . . . expressed in 1873?," Curtis answered: "The views of this journal . . . are to be found in its editorial columns," and reprinted his 1873 commentary in the same article.[4]

Nast had pictured Garfield, standing directly behind Ames, as one of the guilty Congressmen in his devastating and well-remembered cartoon of March 15, 1873.* A month after Garfield was nominated, his campaign biography was published; 57 of its 356 pages were devoted to his defense of the Credit Mobilier charges.[5]

The Democratic National Committee also reprinted this part of the cartoon with each character's name under his picture, the *Harper's Weekly* masthead on top, and columns of old newspaper commentary on the Congressional investigation strategically included. The widely-circulated poster effectively hoisted Garfield on Nast's petard, much to Curtis's discomfort.

EVERY PUBLIC QUESTION WITH AN EYE ONLY TO THE PUBLIC GOOD.

Puck

As mentioned earlier, when Joseph Keppler came to New York from St. Louis in 1872 to work for *Frank Leslie's Illustrated Newspaper*, his ultimate personal goal was to surpass Nast as America's leading political cartoonist. He achieved that by the close of the 1880 campaign through a combination of Nast's handcuffs and his own creative, colorful *Puck* cartoons that caught the public's attention. *Puck's* circulation zoomed to 85,000 — close to *Harper's* — while its advertising boomed even as it raised its rates twice in 13 months.[6]

James Wales, Keppler's lieutenant, used the back-firing 1873 cartoon for a triple master-punch. First, he ridiculed his rival as a dart-throwing, bareback rider on a hobby-horse (blanketed with *Harper's Weekly)*, Nast's own symbol for a person with questionable authority. Second, Nast's target held by Marshall Jewel, Nast's good friend and Chairman of the Republican Party, was a rough parody of his own Credit Mobilier cartoon. Last but not least, was his pun on Nast's name as he loudly proclaimed his superiority, which his victim was helpless to answer.[7]

SHIRKING THE FEAT.
Nast—"I went through that Ring in 1873; but I can't go through it again. I am not that kind of a Jim Nast."

* See p. 348 for complete cartoon

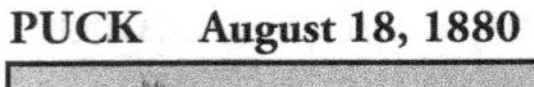

PUCK August 18, 1880

IT MAKES HIM SICK.

Continuing to attack where Nast couldn't tread, Keppler depicted Garfield reeling from the effects of smoking a pipe full of Credit Mobilier tobacco, left over from his nomination. Small clouds of "Loss of Votes," "Public Censure," and a "Smoky Record" wafted in the air nearby.

A week later, Keppler drew *Forbidding the Banns*, a risqué cartoon that was far and away the best by any artist during the campaign — **and comparable to Nast at his zenith**.

Of course, Curtis, Joe Harper, or even the late Fletcher Harper, would almost certainly have rejected any Nast cartoon as ribald as this one, no matter whom he was skewering. Keppler answered only to himself, as he widened the distance between him and Nast in the public mind.

As the ballot box minister was about to pronounce Uncle Sam and Garfield — his disreputable intended bride, falsely clad in virgin white — man and wife, Democratic National Chairman William Barnum, holding Garfield's illegitimate baby, ran in to stop the ceremony. The baby, bewhiskered like his parent, wore a "$329" blanket, the sum Garfield was accused of accepting as a Credit Mobilier dividend. The "bride's" response was classic: "But it was such a little one."

Looking on were bearded bridesmaids Carl Schurz and *Tribune* editor Whitelaw Reid, in front of Republican National Committee Chairman Marshall Jewel. Groomsmen Chester Arthur, John Logan and Roscoe Conkling watched with concern.

PUCK August 25, 1880

Barnum Jewel Schurz Reid Arthur Logan Conkling

FORBIDDING THE BANNS.
The Bride (Garfield): "But It Was Such A Little One!"

A second black mark for Garfield — frequently made in the press but usually not in the relevant cartoons — was the 1873 Salary Grab, approved by him as Chairman of the Appropriations Committee. It provided Congressmen with two years of back pay, a provision that was revoked the following year following public outrage.* Garfield devoted 12 pages of his campaign biography to his rationale: first, that it was a provision he didn't like in a much larger appropriation bill that needed his approval; second, he had returned his own check to the Treasury.[8]

* See p. 351

DeGolyer

In 1873 — the same year as Credit Mobilier exploded — Washington's notorious political boss, Alexander Shepherd, contracted with DeGolyer-McClellan Company of Chicago to cover the city's dirt streets with its patented wooden paving blocks. DeGolyer retained Garfield, Chairman of the House Appropriations Committee, to make a one-time appearance before the Washington Board of Public Works, ostensibly to defend the patent and attest to the product's durability. Substituting for DeGolyer's regular attorney *only* on that occasion, Garfield was paid $5,000 — equivalent to his prior year's Congressional salary.

In his official capacity, Garfield endorsed the project and enabled its funding, despite DeGolyer's reputation for poor work. When the fraud was exposed, Garfield said he was only involved with the patent and knew nothing about the deceit. He rationalized his decision in his campaign biography without mentioning his $5,000 fee.[9]

Nast had indirectly referenced the scandal back in 1874 when he drew his only negative cartoon of Grant.* Curtis totally ignored DeGolyer, while Keppler taunted Garfield with it on several occasions.

In summary, there was plenty of smoke with which to blacken Garfield, and Keppler took full advantage of it while Nast was silenced.

Hancock's Vulnerabilities

Both Nast and Keppler agreed that the Democratic candidate was a good man of strong character, but were dismayed by the unreconstructed Confederates, Tammany patronage seekers, and inflationists who comprised his principal backers. Hancock's political blank slate was unblemished, but he had nothing but his Army career — which most Southerners scorned — to establish his qualifications for President.

While Nast was minimized at *Harper's* when the first campaign cartoons appeared, Keppler cleverly defined the pluses and minuses for both parties. Heavyweight Hancock shouldered the Democratic donkey, which was blinded by "Stupidity" and literally earmarked with "Inflation" and "Greenbackism." Tammany Boss John Kelly, dressed as an Irish leprechaun and carrying a "To the Victor Belong the Spoils" banner, was astride the sheathed blade of Hancock's sword, pulling the donkey down by its tail. Its rear end was marked "Secessionist Sympathy," its foot had a "Lost Cause" ribbon, and its saddle straps included "Pro Slavery," "Copperheadism" and "States Rights."

Opposite, lightweight Garfield, uncomfortably clinging to the Republican Party steed, with his baggage — Credit Mobilier, the DeGolyer contract, and a wary Arthur — in a sling on his back, tried to steer his reluctant mount towards Washington. As Keppler aptly put it, Hancock carried his Party while the other Party carried his opponent. The differences between the candidates, were readily apparent, as were the differences in artistry between Nast and Keppler.

PUCK July 28, 1880

HE CARRIES THE PARTY. **THE PARTY CARRIES HIM.**

* See p. 370

Pulling Punches

Prior to his nomination, Nast had Hancock in his small pantheon of heroes. He had caricatured him as a fighting cock for *Phunny Phellow* in 1864 and painted him for a publisher a year later.[10]

PHUNNY PHELLOW October 1864

GENERAL HANCOCK ALWAYS READY FOR A FIGHT.

Rutherford B. Hayes Library

As with Grant, Phil Sheridan and other Union generals, Nast developed a personal friendship with Hancock. The general lived in New York, and was even scheduled to present the Army-Navy testimonial cup to Nast the previous year when illness prevented him from doing so.* **Unlike any other candidate whose election he opposed over six presidential campaigns (1864-1884) and numerous state elections, Nast treated Hancock mildly in 20 of 23 cartoons during his run.**

Hancock had gained considerable weight after the war. Initially, Nast tweaked him on his size. The first cartoon related to the Democrats failure to fund the Army during the Hayes Administration; the other chided Democrats for nominating Hancock after years of attacking Grant, an excellent rider, as the "Man on Horseback" for his military control over the South and other forceful actions.

HW July 17, 1880 464

"REVENGE IS SWEET."
Democratic Citizen. "What did you nominate Hancock for?"
Democratic Statesman. "To reduce the army."

HW July 24, 1880 480

BEHIND AGAIN.

* See p. 454

Nast almost always portrayed Hancock as a stately figure dressed in full regalia. Generally, the cartoons lacked bite, dealing with the hungry Democratic tiger looking for spoils, or the lack of ammunition to effect change.

HW August 14, 1880 521

GENERAL INSPECTION.
General Hancock And General Vacancy.

HW September 4, 1880 568

GENERAL LOOKOUT.
A Hard Fort To Attack With The Material You Have.

Puppet

Going in, the Democrats were confident that they would hold the eleven Confederate and four Border states, and enough Northern states, including pivotal New York, to win the election. Then the naive Hancock would be a puppet in their hands. The obvious attack point for *Harper's* was to portray that early and often. With Nast reluctant to go all out, Frost, Rogers and Gillam all met the challenge with 14 cartoons among them.

Initially, Curtis called on A.B. Frost who was 25 when the Harpers first engaged him as a freelancer in 1876. He published eight cartoons attacking Tilden during that campaign, then spent the next two years in England, studying and mastering cartooning to a level where his execution was on a par with Nast's in his prime.

Overtly continuing his efforts to both supplement and discipline Nast, Curtis gave the July 31 cover to Frost, who drew *The Democratic Trojan Horse*, a well-executed cartoon reminiscent of Nast's 1872 attack on Greeley.* Frost made the point that Hancock was only a figurehead, Tammany's John Kelly was his brain, and spoilsmen and the South were ascending. Tilden (with his barrel) was being hoisted up, alongside his crooked fixer-nephew, William Tilden Pelton,. Even the 1868 Democratic candidates, Seymour and Frank Blair, were ensconced on top, while Henry Watterson led his post-1876 election proposed charge of 100,000 men at the bottom. Ohio's Senator Thurman was carrying his rag baby up the ladder, followed by Southern politician Wade Hampton brandishing his sword.

HW July 31, 1880 481 C

THE DEMOCRATIC TROJAN HORSE.
Forewarned, Forearmed. The Defenders Of The City Will Not Be Misled By A "Superb" Figure-Head.

HW July 31, 1880 484

Kelly Watterson Voorhees Fernando Wood

Belmont Hampton Jeff Davis

GENERAL HANCOCK GULLIVER, HOW DO YOU LIKE IT AS FAR AS YOU'VE GOT?

Nast's *Gulliver* appeared three pages later. Drawn horizontally (landscape-style), Nast may have known that he was unlikely to make the cover (vertical only). Nast's Lilliputians (from Jonathan Swift's 1726 novel) climbing on Hancock's face included Watterson and a symbolic Irish drunk. In a subtle reference to the Biblical Samson, Boss Kelly was cutting off Hancock's hair with a knife, while former Democratic Party Chairman August Belmont whispered in the nominee's ear. Hampton and Jeff Davis lurked in the rear behind Copperheads Fernando Wood and Indiana Senator Daniel Voorhees; the latter had an 85 cent dollar around his neck.

While both cartoons were imaginative and essentially made the same point, Frost's probably had more impact.

---

* See p. 324

Shortly after these cartoons appeared, Wade Hampton, a leading spokesman for the ex-Confederacy, provided some live ammunition for the Republicans. A wealthy South Carolina planter and slave-owner before the war, Hampton became a notable general, then Governor in 1876, and a U.S. Senator three years later. Both Nast and Keppler often used Hampton — with his luxuriant, easily caricaturable mustache — to personify the South.

The overriding ironic factor in the campaign was nominal ex-Confederate support for Hancock, in spite of his stature as the hero of Gettysburg. He was grudgingly acceptable to the South because he had lightened up on New Orleans after he replaced hard-bitten Phil Sheridan as its military governor during the Hayes administration. Hancock also favored state rather than Federal supervision of elections — the key to regaining Southern political control after Reconstruction ended — because it enabled suppression of black and Republican votes.

In late July, Hampton made a speech that stripped the veil from any pretense of sectional unity under Hancock. In a straight-forward cartoon, reminiscent of his 1868 campaign *"This is a White Man's Government."** Nast clearly depicted the irony of Hampton's announcement.

HW September 11, 1880 580

"THE WAR IS OVER?"

"CONSIDER what LEE and JACKSON would do were they alive. *These are the same principles for which they fought for four years.* Remember the men who poured forth their life-blood on Virginia's soil, and do not abandon them now. Remember that upon your vote depends the success of the Democratic ticket."—WADE HAMPTON'S *speech as originally reported in The Staunton Valley Virginian, July* 29, 1880.

"Pause before you cast your vote. Think how LEE would have voted. Think what JACKSON would have done before he would have cast a vote calculated to divide his beloved Virginia. I ask you to remember those who have died on your soil, *and to remember that the principles they died for are again on trial to-day.*"—WADE HAMPTON *in The Staunton Vindicator* (*Democratic*) *of July* 30, 1880.

WADE HAMPTON'S DILEMMA.
Southern Democrat. "If you did not say it, we shall lose votes."
Norther Democrat. "If you did say it, we shall lose votes."

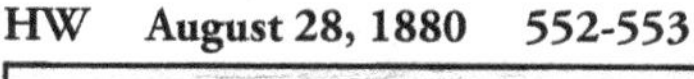
HW August 28, 1880 552-553

THE "SILENT (DEMOCRATIC) MAJORITY."
General Hancock Will Miss Them On Election Day.

Hampton's words inflamed Nast to a level that overrode his personal feelings for Hancock. His initial response shockingly and aggressively skewered Hancock more severely than any other time during the campaign. It must have torn at his conscience to depict his friend gazing pensively at the graves of the rebels his troops had killed during Pickett's charge on the conclusive day that ensured the critical Union victory at Gettysburg.

Moreover, for the only time during the campaign, Curtis promoted "Mr. Nast's impressive cartoon," as he excoriated Hancock on the preceding editorial page: "He now joins hands with men who openly avow that they are still rebels at heart, and that if they obtain control of the government, will undo everything that was accomplished by the war."

* See p. 215

Even after Hampton's incendiary remarks, Nast continued to depict Hancock in a stately manner — but now demeaned him as a puppet or slave. Robert Toombs, an ex-Confederate General and Secretary of State, and Georgia politician — who was so anti-Union that he refused to request a post-war pardon — augmented Hampton as an outspoken would-be manipulator, as Nast returned to *Gulliver's Travels*. A sign in the background had Toombs demanding "All Union Soldiers Must Go" and "The Southern (Civil War) Debt Must Be Paid Somehow."

Two weeks before the election, Nast actually had Hancock in chains, his hands manacled behind his back by a Democratic House and Senate. Worse, a Solid South "Master" threatened him with a cat-o'-nine-tails. The ballot box read "Solid for Hancock. No count necessary."

HW September 18, 1880 596

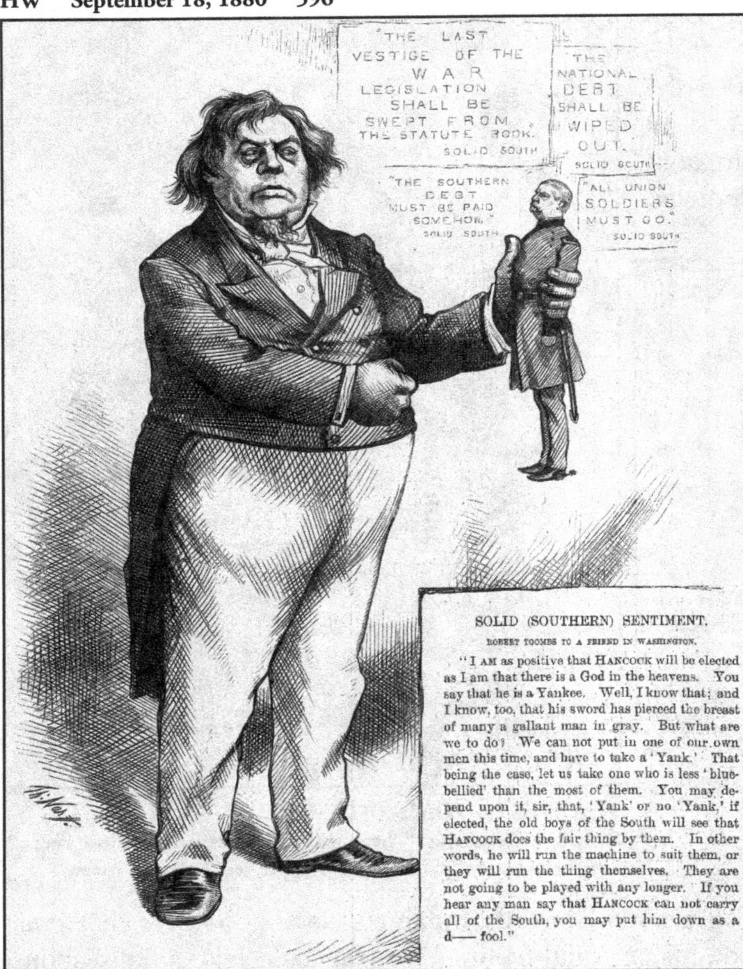

SOLID (SOUTHERN) SENTIMENT.

ROBERT TOOMBS TO A FRIEND IN WASHINGTON.

"I AM as positive that HANCOCK will be elected as I am that there is a God in the heavens. You say that he is a Yankee. Well, I know that; and I know, too, that his sword has pierced the breast of many a gallant man in gray. But what are we to do? We can not put in one of our own men this time, and have to take a 'Yank.' That being the case, let us take one who is less 'blue-bellied' than the most of them. You may depend upon it, sir, that, 'Yank' or no 'Yank,' if elected, the old boys of the South will see that HANCOCK does the fair thing by them. In other words, he will run the machine to suit them, or they will run the thing themselves. They are not going to be played with any longer. If you hear any man say that HANCOCK can not carry all of the South, you may put him down as a d— fool."

HE WILL BE GULLIVER IN THE HANDS OF BROBDINGNAGIANS.

Brobdingnag Toombs. "You may depend upon it, sir, that, 'Yank' or no 'Yank,' we will 'yank' you!"

HW October 30, 1880 701

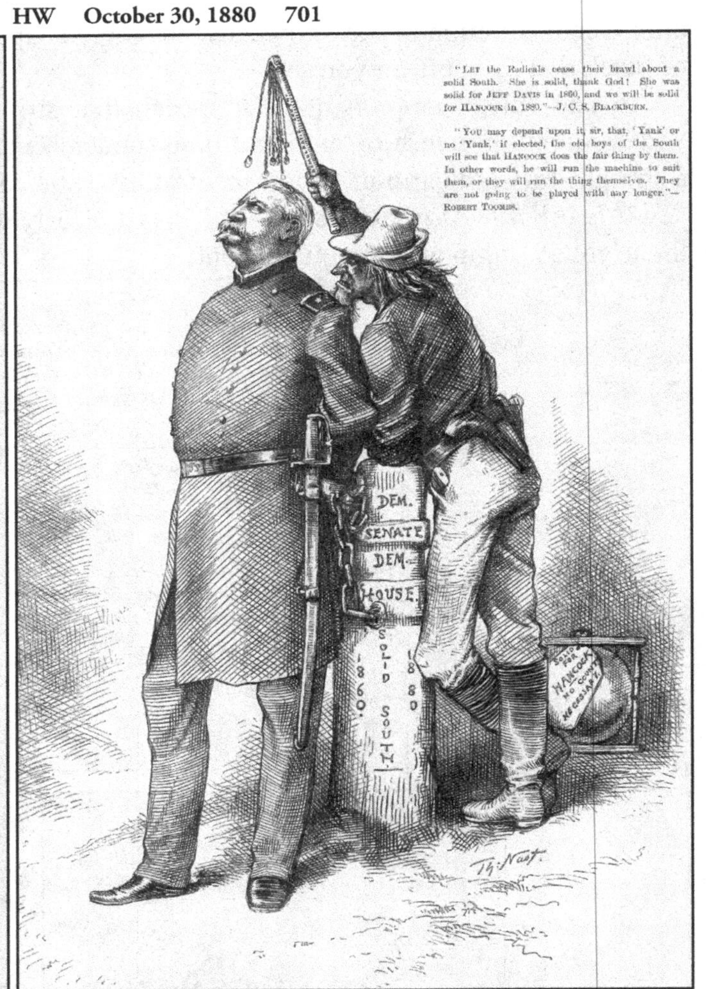

MASTER AND SLAVE.

Solid South. "I *count you* In—and you will be as a Rag Baby in my hands."

English

There was one candidate whom Nast felt free to attack without pulling his punches. In fact, William English took the brunt of the assault that Nast would have preferred to wage against Garfield or a Democrat who wasn't a personal friend.

English of Indiana received the Democratic nomination for Vice President for two reasons — geography and personal wealth — both of which backfired. Indiana's 15 electoral votes were considered critical and, as an early-voting state, it could serve as a bell-cow. (Unfortunately, it went Republican.)

Perhaps more importantly, English's $2,000,000 fortune derived from his hard-nosed mortgage business, was expected to help finance the campaign, particularly in Indiana. As Curtis wrote: "It was not the man, indeed, it was the bar'l that was nominated at Cincinnati." However, English made clear in his acceptance letter that his barrel was shut; moreover, his harsh treatment of his debtors came under attack. Late in the campaign, Nast drew a cover cartoon of English contemplating foreclosing a mortgage on the White House.

HW October 30, 1880 689 C

THE HEIGHT OF ENGLISH'S AMBITION.

In an earlier cover cartoon, Nast punned: "Praise but no money . . . in plain *English.*" In the same issue, he followed up with a somewhat prophetic cartoon distinguishing between "hard" money and "soft soap" (purchased votes). A month after Garfield's Inauguration, at a celebratory dinner for Stephen Dorsey, the Secretary of the Republican Party who presumptuously took full credit for its victory, Vice President Arthur bragged that Dorsey's "soft soap" had bought enough votes to swing the Indiana election.[11] Garfield, who chose not to attend, may not have known about the corruption before then; neither, of course, did Nast.

HW August 21, 1880 529 C

A TAIL PRAISING ITS HEAD.
Governor's Island Swarming With Democrats.

HW August 21, 1880 541

HARD (*UP*) MONEY CAMPAIGN.
"Hang it, General, it's only Soft Soap!"

A.B. Frost continued his sophisticated, punchy cartoons attacking Hancock and English directly. On his October 9 cover, Democratic editor Henry Watterson was turning the grindstone to sharpen Hancock's axe for repellent causes that made the candidate sweat: Confederate principles, Civil War claims and patronage. A skeptical Tilden, who was sitting on his barrel in the August cartoon, now warily poured a few coins from it into Hancock's collection basin.

HW August 28, 1880 557

CHORUS OF HUNGRY DEMOCRATS.

"Come, Bill, fork over the needful. Do you think we'll work for you for nothing?"

"It is now becoming apparent that Mr. English, of Indiana, who has been so confidently looked to to open his two-million barrel for General Hancock's benefit, is a miser. An Indianian who has known him from boyhood declares that the contribution of even one hundred thousand dollars to the canvass would kill him. He can spare blood easier than money. His name is connected with no charity. Treasury clerks who served with him in the department at Washington say his chief occupation was making small loans to his associate clerks at most usurious rates of interest, and that he always insisted on his pound of flesh."—*Buffalo Express.*

HW October 9, 1880 641 C

THE DEMOCRATIC AXE-GRINDER.

"A Change Is Necessary"—In Order To Get Democratic Axes Ground.

HW October 9, 1880 648-649

ANOTHER KIND OF "SILENT (DEMOCRATIC) MAJORITY."

Six weeks after putting Hancock at the site, Nast came back with the same setting to scorch Vice Presidential nominee English as he stared at the tombstones of his foreclosed mortgage victims while vultures circled overhead.

W.A. Rogers joined Harper & Brothers in 1877 at age 23, and stayed for 25 years, illustrating books as well as the firm's periodicals. . Self-taught, his prior experience consisted of two years at the newly-founded *Daily Graphic*. He drew five cartoons attacking Hancock, which were less sophisticated than Frost's , but gave Curtis additional offensive strength to offset Nast's inhibitions.

Here, Hancock was about to set off a torpedo aimed at the White House. English sat on his bar'l, while Boss Kelly and Ben Butler, among others, waited for the explosion.

HW October 16, 1880 661

NOW OR NEVER—THE WHITE HOUSE OR "BUST"!

Rogers's best cartoon borrowed directly from two of Nast's in the Tweed and Greeley campaigns, respectively. First, the double-page predicted Hancock's cabinet, just as Nast did for Tweed's puppet, Governor John Hoffman in 1871;* then Rogers borrowed from Nast's *Apollo Amusing the Gods* as Greeley lost to Grant the following year.**

A Change in the Cabinet depicted Hancock in despair with John Kelly (State); Daniel Voorhees (Treasury, with his 85-cent silver dollars); Henry Watterson (War); Wade Hampton (Navy); Benjamin Faceabout Butler (Interior, after changing parties for the umpteenth time; Fernando Wood (Postmaster General); Robert Toombs (Attorney-General) and Jefferson Davis as a "welcome visitor").

A subtle but faint background map divided the (South), Kelly's (Northeast) and Butler's (Mid-West). Hancock was allotted the tiny District of Columbia. While Rogers's drawing skills were not up to Nast's or Frost's, his sense of humor was equivalent.

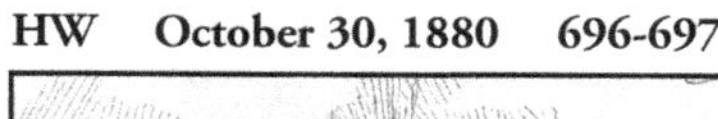

HW October 30, 1880 696-697

A CHANGE IN THE CABINET—DOES THE COUNTRY WANT IT?

---

* See p. 269

** See p. 336-337

The accompanying text took particular aim at Wood and Toombs for their Civil War conduct.

HW October 30, 1880 695

"A CHANGE IN THE CABINET."

OUR artist, in his striking double-page drawing, presents a timely warning of the tendency of the Democratic demands in favor of a "change" in the government under the leadership of the man of whom General GRANT said that he was "crazy to be President, ambitious, vain, and weak, and would easily be controlled by the South." The group, as shown in the picture, is made up as follows:

Secretary of State.—JOHN KELLY, of New York, successor to WILLIAM M. TWEED as Boss of the Tammany Hall Party.

Secretary of the Treasury.—DANIEL W. VOORHEES, of Indiana, the renowned advocate of the 85-cent dollar.

Secretary of War.—HENRY WATTERSON, of Kentucky, leader of the valiant host of a hundred thousand men, *all on paper.*

Secretary of the Navy.—WADE HAMPTON, of South Carolina, champion defender of "the principles for which LEE and JACKSON fought for four years."

Secretary of the Interior.—BENJAMIN FACEABOUT BUTLER, the Massachusetts statesman who, "in a very impressive manner," predicted a political revolution in Ohio and Indiana. But the revolution went the wrong way for him.

Postmaster-General.—FERNANDO WOOD, of New York, who, while Mayor of this city, in January, 1861, sent the following memorable dispatch to ROBERT TOOMBS, of Georgia:

"*Hon. Robert Toombs, Milledgeville, Georgia:*

"In reply to your dispatch, I regret to say that arms intended for and consigned to the State of Georgia have been seized by the police of this State, but that the city of New York should in no way be made responsible for the outrage.

"As Mayor, I have no authority over the police. If I had the power, I should summarily punish the authors of this illegal and unjustifiable seizure of private property. FERNANDO WOOD."

Attorney-General.—ROBERT TOOMBS, of Georgia, one of the "old boys of the South who will see that HANCOCK, Yank or no Yank, does the fair thing by them." This is the unreconstructed ex-senator who said that "HANCOCK will run the machine to suit them, or they will run the thing themselves. They are not going to be played with any longer."

To such a cabinet JEFFERSON DAVIS would be hailed as "a welcome visitor." He could then point with complacency to the boastful prophecy he made twenty years ago, when the prison doors closed behind him, in these words, "The principle for which we contend is bound to re-assert itself, though it may be *at another time and in another form.*"

Adding to his pummeling power to secure Garfield's victory, Curtis brought in 24-year old Bernhard Gillam a month before the election. In his five cartoons, he either flattered or teased Nast (possibly both), by blatantly referring to Nast's Tweed and anti-Papal cartoons in three of his first four forgettable cartoons.

HW October 9, 1880 652

Watterson, Tilden, Kelly, Solid South, Barnum

FALSTAFF HANCOCK AND HIS RAGGED REGIMENT.

HW November 6, 1880 708

English (crying), Watterson, Barnum

Tilden

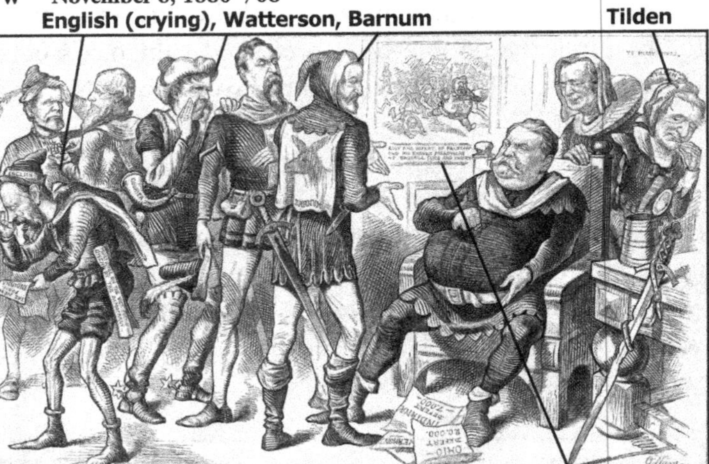

"CALL YOU *THAT* BACKING OF YOUR FRIENDS? A PLAGUE UPON SUCH A BACKING!"

HW October 30, 1880 700

THE NEW PILGRIM'S PROGRESS.

"They came to where two roads met, and here stood a man called Flattery, who tried to induce Christian [Uncle Sam] to leave the straight road and trust to *his* guidance. 'No,' said Christian; 'my strong friend, Great Heart, has guided me, so far, safely on my way, and I should be but tempting Providence to *change* now!"

Help from *Puck*

Although Joseph Keppler leaned Democratic, his crowded cartoon of an astonished Hancock looking at the headless Donkey and its horrendous Confederate elements, savaged the party as forcefully as Nast ever did. The South end of the animal was branded with “secession” and “states rights;” Party Chairman William Barnum and Southerners Hampton and Lucius Lamar were pushing the reluctant general towards it. But it was the wide array of Confederate keepsakes in the *Democratic Curiosity Shop* that was reminiscent of Nast’s gruesome Civil War cartoons.* They included a slave-tracking bloodhound with a dead black child at its feet, a whipping post next to a “lamp post for lynching ‘niggers’”; an Andersonville skeleton, Jeff Davis’s female disguise when he was captured, John Wilkes Booth’s pistol, and even the cane that Congressman Preston Brooks used to beat Senator Charles Sumner senseless while sitting at his desk in the Senate in 1856.

Of more recent vintage, Keppler also depicted the key to the cipher dispatches that Barnum and his co-conspirators used to try and buy the contested 1876 election for Tilden.**

The Northern end of the horse was labeled “Inflation,” and highlighted by the Rag Baby symbol that Nast had created four years earlier.***

PUCK September 1, 1880

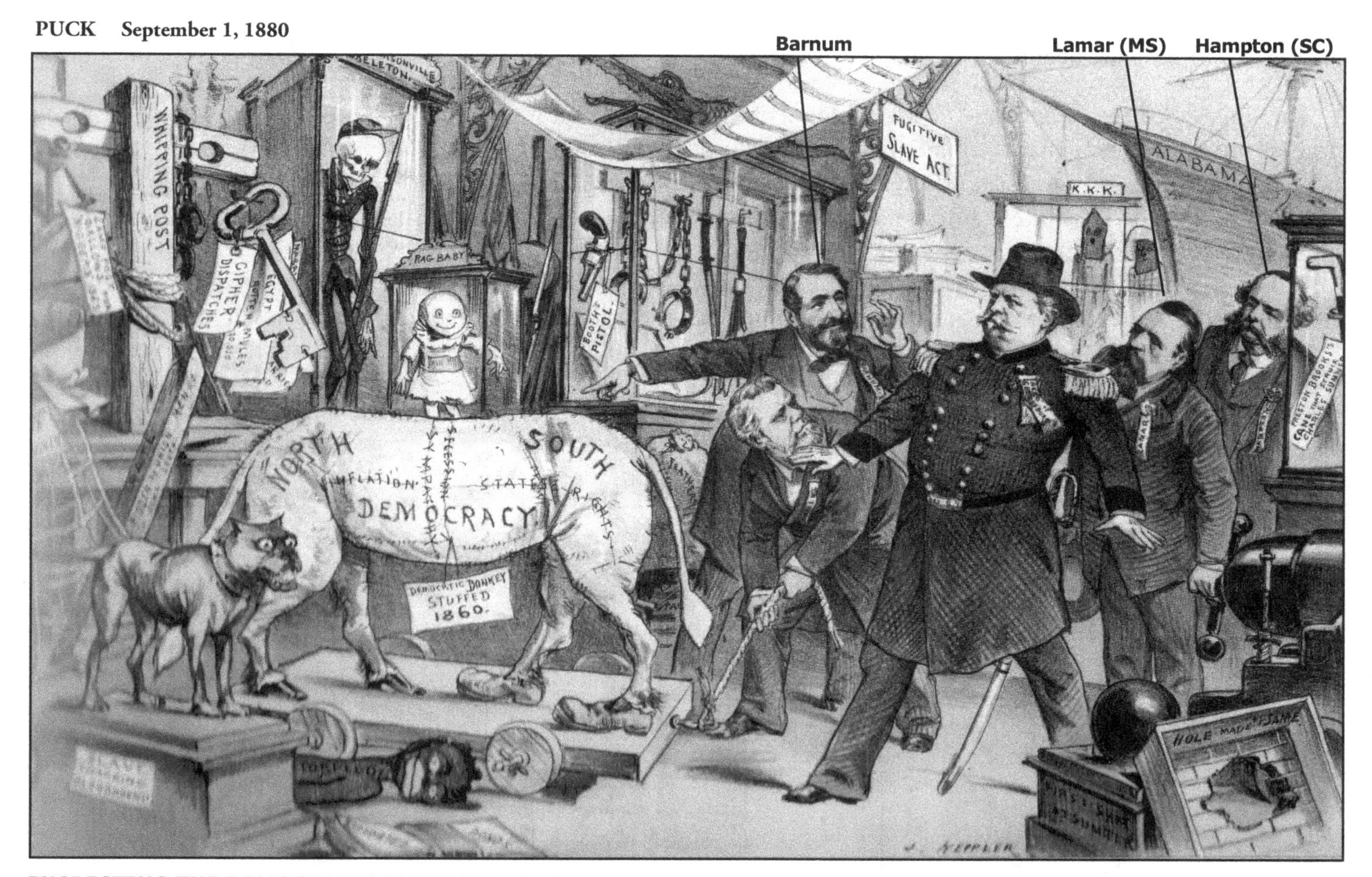

INSPECTING THE DEMOCRATIC CURIOSITY SHOP

* See p. 112
** See p. 420-421
*** See p. 386

Greenback Party

The Democratic platform called for hard money, a position that Nast had always endorsed. In protest, the inflationist Greenback Party nominated Iowa Congressman James Weaver as its third-party candidate. He ended up winning almost three percent of the popular vote after being the first Presidential candidate to *extensively* tour the country during his campaign. (Greeley went on a ten-day tour in 1872.)*

Nast once again turned to Shakespeare, as he ridiculed Weaver with Bottom, the weaver in *A Midsummer Night's Dream*, in a series of five cartoons beginning three months before both conventions, while Weaver was imploring his fellow Congressmen to print more paper money and equate it with gold.

Bottom was always dressed as an Athenian and adorned with the head of a vacuous ass. In Nast's first cartoon after Weaver's nomination, Columbia (as Titania, the Fairy Queen) awoke from a love-potion to hear her suitor singing "More greenbacks! More! More!" while his campaign banner was inscribed on the face of the moon. The keynote stab, of course, was Shakespeare's "Thou art *as wise* as thou art beautiful."

HW July 3, 1880 420

"A MIDSUMMER NIGHT'S DREAM" NOMINATION.
The Queen Of Fairies (Columbia). "What angel wakes me from my flowery bed?.... Thou art *as wise* as thou art beautiful."—Shakespeare

In September, the Greenback Party elected its Maine candidate for Governor. Hancock promptly made a huge mistake by telegraphing his congratulations to the victor, and was criticized by both Northern Democrats like Senator Bayard and Southerners like Hampton. His political naivete was obvious, and he admitted his mistake.

His friend Nast called him "General Went-off Halfcock" and tagged him with Weaver's Rag Baby. First, he waved his handkerchief — a white flag of surrender; two weeks later, he hid the upside-down baby behind his back while taking heat from Bayard. "Con-fusion" in Nast's title referred to Hancock's mistaken thought about combining the Greenback and Democratic Party votes.

HW October 9, 1880 645

A FINANCIAL MISTAKE.
General Went-Off Halfcock—Kissing "*Soft*" Babies Is Sure To Offend "*Hard*" Fathers.

HW October 23, 1880 684

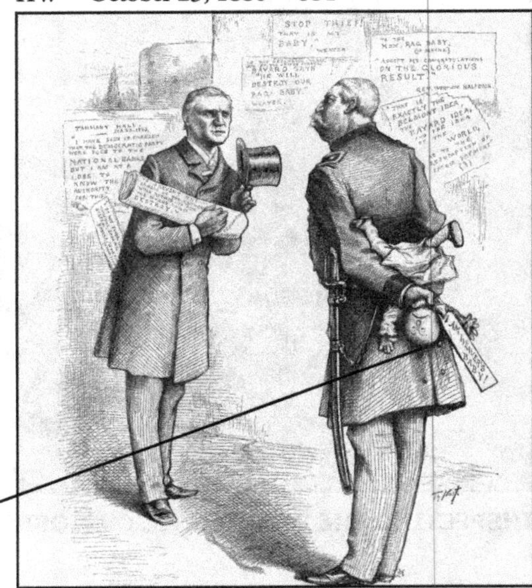

RESUMPTION—OF WHAT?—*CON-FUSION.*
General Went-Off Halfcock. "Resumption is a glorious result."
Senator Bayard. "I was for resumption, and I am now for resumption, and the Democratic candidates for President and Vice-President want the same kind of resumption that I do—a real and not a sham resumption."

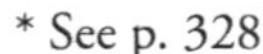

* See p. 328

Tariffs

Hancock's political naivete peaked late in the campaign over the tariff issue. After the Civil War, the first federal income tax and most other taxes were repealed, and tariffs provided ample revenue for peacetime government. The Democratic platform supported free trade and tariffs for revenue only.

Congressmen from states with heavy manufacturing constantly pushed for higher protective tariffs. Pennsylvania's William "Pig Iron" Kelley, prodded by his constituent oil, coal and iron industrialists, was their active leader. Nast, who believed in free trade, targeted Kelley during the seventies.

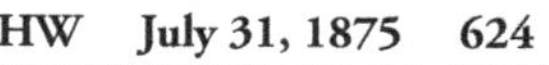

HW July 31, 1875 624

IRON AND BLOOD—THIS "DON'T SCARE WORTH A CENT."

HW September 6, 1879 701 C

A HIGH OLD TARIFF TIME.
Bismarck (*to* Mr. W.D. Kelley, *of Pennsylvania*). "The (protection) you teach me I will execute, and it shall go hard (with American imports) but I will better the instruction (a very high tariff)."

On October 7 — less than a month before the November 2 election — Hancock made his second major mistake during an interview with a reporter from the Democratic-leaning *Paterson Daily Guardian* in protectionist New Jersey.

Candid to a fault, he said that "the tariff, while important, was mostly talk, a matter of schedules which Congress developed for local interests . . . He was not a free trader . . . a little incidental protection was alright . . . ***The tariff is a local question.***"

In fact, although Hancock's response was political heresy, it was basically accurate. However, the interview created an uproar, especially within the Democratic Party; Henry Watterson, who had created the "Tariff for Revenue Only" slogan and steered it into the platform, raged at his candidate. Senator Theodore Fitz Randolph, a Morristown neighbor of Nast's, wrote Hancock for a further explanation. The general floundered deeper, responding that "protection has built up our industries and he stands upon the platform for revenue only, and that all talk about free trade is folly." Curtis included the text in his editorial of November 6, appearing four days before the election: *General Hancock Explains Again.*

Nast's cover cartoon for that issue referred to the unhappy candidate as "General Went Off Full-cock," a doubling of his "Half-cock" appellation from his Greenback Party candidate mistake. In a following cartoon, Hancock sported a placard: "Taffy is a Local question and should be left to the Candy Stores. Free Trade is folly."

HW November 6, 1880 712

"A CHANGE IS NECESSARY"—"WHO SHOULD WITHDRAW?"

HW November 6, 1880 713

A CAMPAIGN OF "CHANGES."
General Hancock. "Come, gentlemen, the time is short. If any more changes are wanted, speak up quickly!"

On the facing page, W.A. Rogers had a much more interesting cartoon, also on the subject of change.

Garfield Wins

The election was extremely close with each candidate winning 19 states, and Garfield edging Hancock by 10,000 votes (48.3% to 48.2%) in the popular vote and 214 to 155 in the electoral college. New Jersey was the only Northern state that Hancock won. As mentioned previously, if he had captured New York's 35 votes, he would have been President.

HW November 13, 1880 721 C

"A LOCAL QUESTION."
"Who Is *Tariff*, And Why Is *He* For Revenue Only?"

Nast's best known cartoon of the 1880 campaign tackled Hancock's tariff remark directly, but was deliberately timed to appear (in the post-dated issue) the day after the election when it couldn't impact the result, a point Nast made in a wall sign. As New Jersey Senator Fitz Randolph discussed "A Local Question" with his befuddled candidate, Hancock — assuming that "Tariff" was a person — asked "Who is *Tariff*, and why is *he* for revenue only?"

Four pages later, Nast lightly criticized Hancock again, while putting the primary blame for staining his war record on his Southern, ex-Copperhead, and Tammany promoters.

HW November 13, 1880 725

Hampton, Lamar, Toombs, Wood, Kelley, Voorhees, Butler

WHAT A PITY!

Miss Columbia (housekeeper). "Ever since you've put him up, and handled him, how you have besmeared him, and you've even turned his head!"

Keppler's campaign wrap-up also appeared the day after the election. It depicted the Biblical Republican Delilah using a "Tariff Issue" scissors to cut off the "Democratic Samson's" locks, as he lay in a stupor after drinking the "wine of self-confidence." Garfield and others watched from behind a curtain.

PUCK November 10, 1880

THE REPUBLICAN DELILAH STEALTHILY DEPRIVES THE DEMOCRATIC SAMSON OF HIS STRENGTH.

Aftermath

Immediately after the election, Nast sought to repair his relationship with Hancock, as his friend returned to his Army post in New York Harbor. When Hancock died just over five years later, Nast drew a solemn cover and Curtis praised him as a patriotic hero and stainless gentleman, but a victim whose nomination was a trick by his party to recover power by a pretence.

HW November 20, 1880 744-745

"NO CHANGE IS NECESSARY, GENERAL HANCOCK; WE ARE TOO WELL SATISFIED WITH YOUR BRAVE RECORD AS A UNION SOLDIER."

February 20, 1886 C

HARPER'S WEEKLY
A JOURNAL OF CIVILIZATION
NEW YORK, SATURDAY, FEBRUARY 20, 1886

MAJOR-GENERAL WINFIELD SCOTT HANCOCK, U.S.A. DIED FEBRUARY 9, 1886.

Nast's campaign finale showed *The Republican Pachyderm Alive and Kicking*, with its two front feet on a mat entitled "The Cause for which Lee and Jackson Fought," on the edge of a precipice. Democratic Committee Chairman Barnum and Tammany chief Kelly were sprawled behind him. Falling into the chasm were English, carrying his mortgage on the White House and a foreclosure sign; Weaver's Rag Baby; the Democratic tiger (having lost its head); and Hampton's change of address to "Columbus (sic), S.C."

For the first time in about six months, Nast could relax and have fun with a cartoon. He separated Democratic New Jersey from the stub of the elephant's tail and noted below his signature "Not From New Jersey."

HW November 20, 1880 737 C

THE REPUBLICAN PACHYDERM ALIVE AND KICKING.

Nast was on the cover. Gillam gave Curtis what he wanted four pages later in the same issue; Nast probably would have quit before he would have done so.

The battle of 1880 was over and Curtis, along with Garfield, claimed victory.

A year later, Gillam was working for *Puck*.

HW November 20, 1880 741

VICTORY!

PUCK November 10, 1880

THE WAKE OF THE REMAINS OF THE DEMOCRATIC PARTY.

Keppler, who had also denigrated Garfield during the campaign, celebrated the Democratic defeat rather than the Republican victory. At their wake, the regular Democrats were asleep or roaring drunk, while party renegades — Tammany's John Kelly and Massachusetts politician Ben Butler (out of office in 1880) — danced a jig.

The Morey Letter

Less than three weeks before the election, a New York paper ill-named *Truth*, published a fraudulent letter, supposedly in Garfield's handwriting, to a fictional H.L. Morey. It falsely stated that Garfield favored cheap Chinese labor and (implied) unlimited immigration, and was written on Congressional stationery. Abram Hewitt and Senator William Barnum — Nast's Democratic targets during the Tilden post-election scramble — authenticated the text and Garfield's handwriting for *Truth's* editor before he published. The letter was quickly shown to be a forgery, but the consequent uproar in the West cost Republicans the electoral votes of California and Nevada, as well as a Senator from each state. That created a 37-37 deadlock.[12]

The Morey letter gave Nast one last shot at Hewitt and Barnum for their attempted bribery of elections on Tilden's behalf after the 1876 election.* Keppler also depicted a probably drunk Barnum and a sleeping Hewitt in his *Wake* cartoon.

HW December 4, 1880 769 C

THE HEAT OF THE LAST POLITICAL CAMPAIGN.
The Innocent Hewitt Always Gets Hold Of The Wrong End.

* * * *

In summary, the 1880 campaign was predictive of Nast's forthcoming decline in at least three important regards:

- Curtis was clearly more powerful.
- Frost and Rogers, in particular, were capable of giving Curtis what he wanted at the time, weakening Nast's in-house leverage. However, his presence was still important for *Harper's* circulation and profits.
- Keppler had achieved his goal of replacing Nast at the pinnacle of political cartooning as Garfield's Presidency began.

---

* See p. 413-416

Chapter 39
President Garfield

Thomas Nast actually celebrated Garfield's Inauguration with the only positive depiction of the President that he ever drew. Hailed by normally combative factions — North and South, Capital and Labor — Nast proclaimed that prosperity was at hand.

HW March 26, 1881 193 C

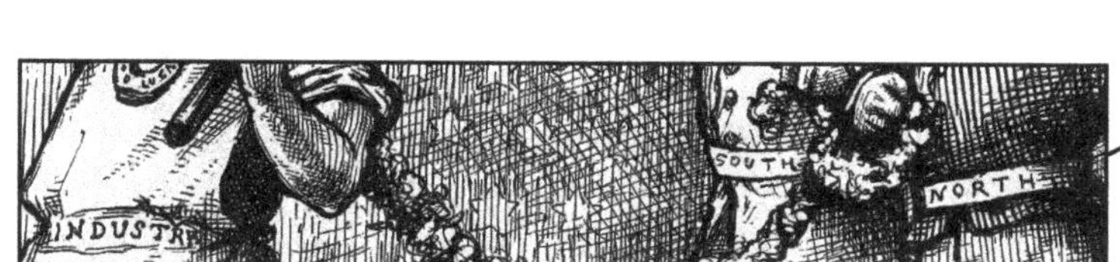

THE REAL CONNECTING LINK— THIS LOOKS LIKE BUSINESS

Conkling

Garfield's first order of business was cabinet selection. Well before his inauguration, he announced that James Blaine would be his Secretary of State. That set off a battle royal with Roscoe Conkling, who had hated Blaine for 15 years before the Convention and even more afterwards.

Reluctantly, at Grant's urging, Conkling had campaigned with the former President in the early-voting states of Ohio and Indiana, and aided significantly in winning them. In return, Conkling believed — probably correctly — that Garfield had committed to letting him select the occupant of one of the six remaining cabinet posts, especially Treasury or Postmaster General. Treasury controlled the ports, but both offered plenty of patronage, spoils and political assessment potential.

Conkling's choice for Treasury Secretary was New York Congressman and successful businessman, Levi Morton, a logical choice since Garfield had offered him the Vice Presidency at the Republican Convention. (Conkling successfully pressured Morton to reject it before second choice Chester Arthur accepted. He became Benjamin Harrison's Vice President eight years later). Garfield then offered Morton the Navy Department, which Conkling again pressured him to reject; he ended up as consul general in Paris.

Garfield also took Conkling's alternative requested cabinet post away from him by appointing New York Postmaster Thomas James to be Postmaster General. James who was honest, competent and a Conkling supporter, accepted over his leader's strong objection; in doing so, he switched his allegiance, just as Arthur had done when he accepted the Vice Presidential nomination.

Platt

In mid-January 1881, the New York Legislature met to elect a junior Senator. After some backroom dealing, Thomas Platt was chosen — upon his firm verbal commitment to support all of President Garfield's nominations, even if Conkling opposed them. Platt was considered to be Conkling's flunkey, sometimes referred to as "Me Too." He was sworn in on March 3, the day before Garfield.

Three weeks later, the Garfield vs. Conkling rivalry boiled over. First, the President tried to conciliate the Senator by sending nine of his suggested New York nominees to the Senate for approval, thereby angering the Blaine faction. The next day, possibly at Blaine's instigation, he nominated State Senator William Robertson as Collector of the New York Port. Robertson had led the 19 delegates who defied Conkling by voting for Blaine, and ultimately Garfield, at the Republican Convention. No redder flag could have been waved at the soon-to-be castrated Conkling bull than to elevate this traitor to New York's top patronage position.

To accomplish this, Garfield first removed Edwin Merritt, the well-regarded current Collector, whom President Hayes had appointed in 1878 to replace Conkling's henchman, Chester Arthur. Merritt became consul general in London and three other appointees were shuffled to make room. The slap at Conkling was obvious because Merritt's term as Collector still had two years left.

HW May 14, 1881 309 C

IS THERE TO BE A POWER BEHIND THE THRONE?

Nast sided with Garfield, but refused to portray him. In the first of several cartoons depicting Garfield as a Roman emperor — but only from behind — toga-clad Senators Conkling and Blaine struggled for power. Blaine was physically closer, more determined, and had a better grip.

"Me Too" Platt was in a bind. He had pledged to support any Garfield nomination — even Robertson's — so he couldn't vote against him. Instead, he talked Conkling into both of them resigning, getting vindicated by prompt reelection and then, unfettered, blocking Robertson in the Senate. Two days later, the Senate approved Robertson by acclamation.

Their resignations on May 16 shocked the country, and provided Nast with his best target since Tilden. He quickly responded with several successive covers.

The first showed Platt as the bell-sheep's tail (reminiscent of Gratz Brown, Horace Greeley's 1872 running-mate). The second played on Conkling as the spoiled spoilsmaster, even as the localized Columbia (here, New York State) prepared to whip them both.

HW June 4, 1881 357 C

HW June 11, 1881 373 C

THE SPOILE-ED.

New York (meaning business). "I know what you DO want!"

W.A. Rogers and Bernhard Gillam also chipped in, portraying Garfield positively, as Nast never would do.

HW June 4, 1881 368

HW June 18, 1881 393

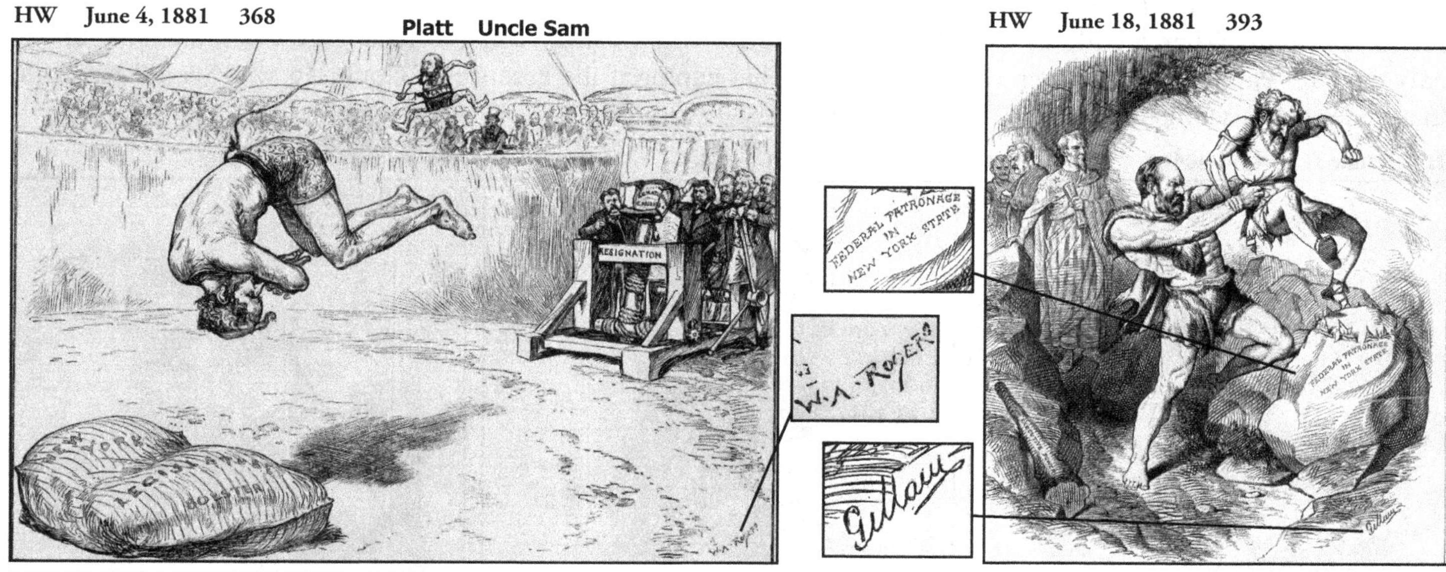

THE GREAT CATAPULT FEAT—NOT AT ALL GRACEFUL, AND VERY RISKY.

HERCULES TEARS THESEUS FROM THE ROCK TO WHICH HE HAD GROWN.

HW June 25, 1881 405 C

A FALLING OFF—OF BOSSES.

On occasion, Blaine struck out too. Garfield nominated former Republican National Committee Chairman and Senator, William Chandler, as Solicitor General, without first clearing it with Attorney General Wayne MacVeagh, who protested and threatened to resign. Blaine advised the President to play hardball and not withdraw the nomination, but the Senate rejected it, as Nast's cover cartoon depicted. Blaine still retained power, even though he was one step below the top.

Conkling, completely powerless, was sprawled upside down below the bottom step. Platt lay underneath him. Conkling clutched his sign noting Robertson's confirmation and his own resignation from the Senate.

Nast reluctantly depicted Garfield, but only with a rear view. The President apparently was wearing a crown of thorns.

With a target he relished, and Curtis and the Harpers in full accord, Nast went back to his old style and let his pictures deliver the message without wordy signboards, sub-titles, or even titles on occasion. His "lost head" series said it all. When a child observed the much shorter Grant vainly trying to recapitate Conkling, she reportedly asked: "Papa, why doesn't he stoop a little?" That captured the essence of Conkling who would never do that under any circumstances.[1]

HW June 18, 1881 404

HW July 2, 1881 421 C

Note: Nast didn't even use titles in these two cartoons.

HW July 23, 1881 508

HOW TO GET A REST THIS SUMMER.

Conkling and Platt spent six weeks through the end of June unsuccessfully trying to convince the alienated New York Legislature to reelect them. After 31 ballots, Platt resigned on July 1, prompted by scandal. Tipped off, several anti-Conkling legislators used a step-ladder to peer into Platt's hotel room and observe him cavorting with a woman who had been observed sneaking into the Delevan Hotel.

Prior to Conkling's resignation, Vice President Arthur was his confidant; they roomed in the same Washington boarding house. When Conkling was in Albany in late May to woo the Legislature, Arthur joined him, and received severe public criticism. Six weeks later, Nast's cover shamed him as a detestable flunky for doing so.

Almost three years later, Arthur had turned out to be a good President. Nast and a Harper executive called on him in a vain attempt to get him to run for another term, and thereby keep James Blaine from getting the Republican nomination. Arthur brought up the cartoon and told Nast that he had not gone to Albany to conciliate Conkling. It was worse. His old boss had ordered him — the Vice President — to explain in person why he and Garfield had reneged on their patronage pledge.[2]

HW July 16, 1881 453 C

OUT-"SHINING" EVERYBODY IN HUMILIATION AT ALBANY.

New York: "I did not engage you, Vice-President Arthur, to do this kind of work."

HW August 6, 1881 529 C

PLUCKED OF HIS PLUMAGE (OR PATRONAGE).
The Jackdaw Is Again Nothing But A *Jackdaw*.

Replacements for Conkling and Platt were elected in July. Nast gave Jackdaw Conkling his last rites by plucking the plumage from his cartoon of 18 months earlier in which he depicted him as a Jackdaw (a small crow) with his turkey-gobbler strut. His plumes represented his Senate seat and his control over the New York State Legislature and Governor; the national eagle was asking if he wanted to pluck its feathers for the 1884 nomination.*

Now he had lost all his patronage (plumage), as well as control of the Stalwart faction. He retired to private life and a successful law practice, and would use whatever influence he had left against Blaine in the 1884 election.

Control of the Senate

As discussed previously,** the Senate was deadlocked at 37-37. Democratic Senator William Mahone of Virginia broke the Senatorial tie by voting with the Republicans. He founded the Readjusters Party with two primary objectives: first, readjust the state debt by assigning one-third to West Virginia (which had seceded from its parent in 1863); second, remove the poll tax from Negroes to encourage their voting. This brought Mahone, an ex-Confederate general, into direct conflict with Senator Ben Hill of Georgia, leader of the Solid South "Bourbon" Democrats. To accomplish the coup, David Davis, the Illinois Democrat whose surprise switch from the Supreme Court to the Senate in January 1877, cost Democrats control of the Electoral Commission and Tilden the Presidency, was elected President pro tem of the Senate as an Independent. When he didn't vote on a specific bill, Republicans had the majority.***

---

* See p. 452
**See p. 510
*** See p. 422-423

Nast, who enjoyed tweaking Davis for his girth and indecisiveness, pictured him as a circus clown reading his own poem: "Wiggle waggle from the Supreme Bench to the Fence." After Republicans Conkling and Platt resigned, control shifted for two months, and Ben Hill became the ringmaster until their replacements were seated.

HW April 2, 1881 209 C

U.S. CIRCUS.
Wm. Mahone(to Bourbon Hill). "Now stop your slashing around, and let the Elephant appear."

HW April 16, 1881 245 C

THE "READJUSTING" PERFORMANCE.
N.B.—Republicans, *a straw has broken a camel's back before.*

HW June 4, 1881 371

BEN HILL MASTER AGAIN.

HW July 9, 1881 452 **Mahone vs. Hill**

THE NEXT POLITICAL CONDITION—SOUTH.

Star Route Frauds

New Postmaster-General Thomas James uncovered a major fraud which began under Democrat David Key, his predecessor in the Hayes Administration. After four long years, Nast finally had a scandal that he could attack without inhibition, as he did a dozen times before it finally fizzled out.

In western states with small populations and large areas for the Post Office to cover, four-year mail contracts were awarded to low bidders who agreed to deliver with "certainty, celerity and security." Their routes were marked on postal registers with three small stars (asterisks). Star Route compensation could be increased unilaterally by the Second Assistant Postmaster-General, Thomas Brady, who was appointed by President Grant in 1876 and continued through the Hayes and into the Garfield administrations.

Brady, colluding with crooked Arkansas Senator Stephen Dorsey and Dorsey's brother, increased the payments astronomically. For example, Dorsey's Ring obtained a 24-route contract for $55,000 and collected $501,000 in total.[3] By the time James took over, Dorsey had left the Senate and become Secretary of the Republican National Committee.

Nast created a symbol by double-punning on Key's name and party, as Brady led his don*key* and its $ mailbag along a Star Route. In the same issue, he used the signs of the Zodiac for a plethora of puns although his readers had to have good eyesight to appreciate them. A prosaic James was about to use his "Investigation" telescope to peer at the astrological signs in the Star Route Ring, while the fraudsters fell off it into the Penitentiary for Fallen Stars.

The 40-foot refracting telescope at the Naval Observatory in Washington — the world's largest at the time — was Nast's model. He probably had seen it because he was interested in astronomy, kept a telescope at home, and often went out to observe the sky at night.

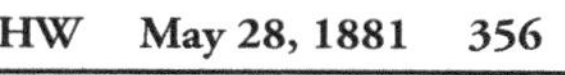

General Brady

STAR ROUTE.

THE GREAT REFRACTING TELESCOPE AT WASHINGTON, D.C.

Postmaster-General James, Let Us Have The Whole Truth, Even If The Political Heavens Fall.

Nast's heavenly puns began behind James's head.

- Capricorn, the Goat, was eating $.
- Sagittarius, the Archer, was riding a U.S. mail horse, with a bagful of $.
- Scorpio, the Scorpion, was Ring-leader Dorsey.
- Libra's scales were unbalanced as "Millions of Fraud $" outweighed honesty.
- Virgo was a "fraudulent mail" route.
- Leo the Lion's tail had a "Gen. Brady" sign, "Leo's Share," at the top of the Star Route Ring.
- "Honest" Cancer the Crab reflected Garfield's statement to "Go ahead regardless of whom you hit. I direct you not only to probe this cancer to the bottom, but to cut it out."
- The Gemini Twins were the Tweed and Star Rings, a set-up for Nast.
- Taurus was a Bull "Dozer," a term for violent unreconstructed Ex-Confederates.
- Aries the Ram was butting open the Treasury.
- Pisces the Fish were the "Fish-y" House and Senate.

Nast followed up with James emptying a mailbag and about to stamp on Scorpion Dorsey who had dropped out, along with Brady and "USPS — $1000 a mile," as falling stars. The donkey and the "New Star Route to Prison" were featured at the top.

Ultimately, the case went to trial in March 1882 and dragged along into September. Eloquent Chicago lawyer Robert Ingersoll, an influential Republican politician and counsel for the "Fallen Stars" (as Nast put it), got his clients acquitted to his later regret and repentance. Nast and most Republicans were really unhappy about the "suits" against the "conspirators" being squashed, but pleased that the obnoxious Dorsey was disgraced and out of the political picture for good. Nast closed his case in December with Columbia appealing to Hercules to cleanse the Star Route stable.

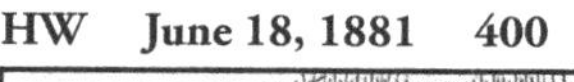

HW June 18, 1881 400

THE NEW (U.S.P) *STAMP* ACT—APPROVED.

HW September 23, 1882 593 C

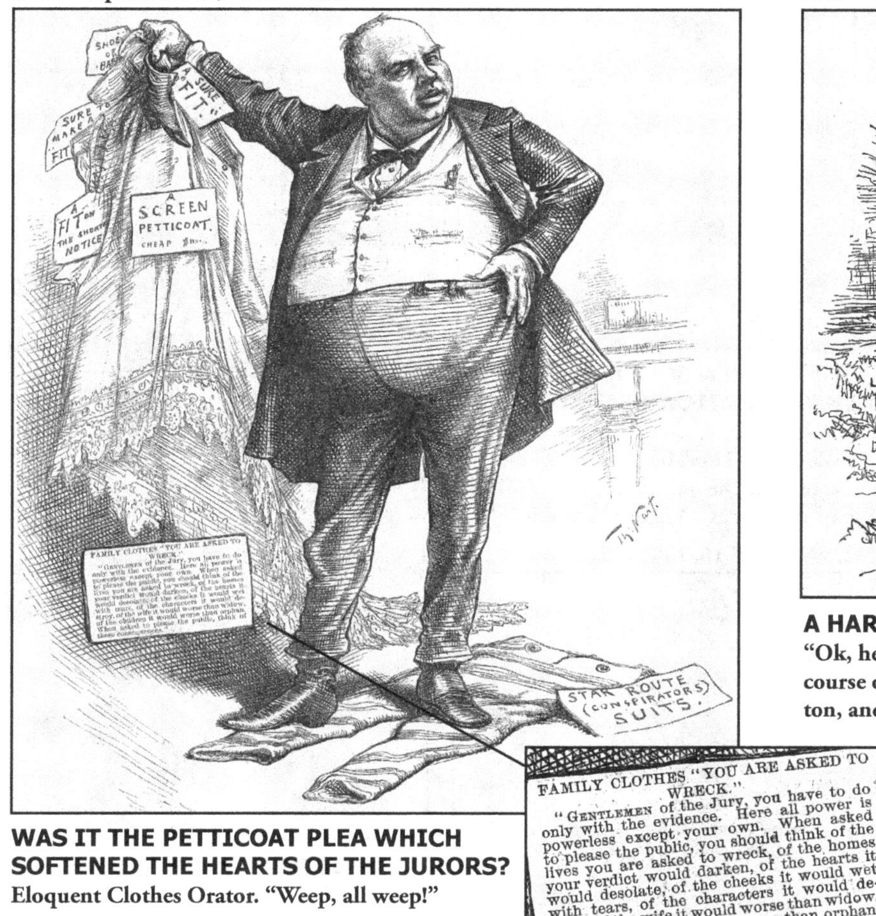

FAMILY CLOTHES "YOU ARE ASKED TO WRECK."

"GENTLEMEN of the Jury, you have to do only with the evidence. Here all power is powerless except your own. When asked to please the public, you should think of the lives you are asked to wreck, of the homes your verdict would darken, of the hearts it would desolate, of the cheeks it would wet with tears, of the characters it would destroy, of the wife it would worse than widow, of the children it would worse than orphan. When asked to please the public, think of these consequences."

WAS IT THE PETTICOAT PLEA WHICH SOFTENED THE HEARTS OF THE JURORS?
Eloquent Clothes Orator. "Weep, all weep!"

HW December 9, 1882 792

A HARD JOB FOR JUSTICE.
"Ok, help me, Hercules! even if you have to change the course of the Potomac through the whole of Washington, and cleanse out all the departments."

Civil Service

With the strong backing of his editor, Civil Service Reform leader George William Curtis, Nast published a series of attacks on the spoils system, beginning even before Garfield's inauguration. They were prophetic in view of the motive behind his assassination four months later.

King Log and King Stork referred to *Aesop's Fable* in which the frogs appealed to Jupiter for a leader to rule over them, and ultimately received a stork who devoured them. Nast's stork was the Senate, answering the frogs' petitions for more government control with bills for more spoils. A beleaguered Uncle Sam had his right leg swollen with 85 cent silver and his left arm in a sling with the increasing tariff.

HW March 5, 1881 157

KING LOG AND KING STORK.
U. Sam (Jupiter). "Look before you leap. I find myself trammelled by the powers behind the throne."

HW March 19, 1881 189

PAN-IC IN SESSION.
Death To Us (The People) And Fun For Them ("Statesmen").

Davis and Mahone were included as the price of their support, which was predicated on patronage.

HW March 12, 1881 172

THE CITIZEN SOLDIER AT THE INAUGURATION OF GENERAL GARFIELD.
Columbia. "Don't be alarmed, noble 'Statesman,' he only comes for a Holiday, and not as a Victor For Spoils."

HW April 30, 1881 277 C

OUR STUMBLING BLOCK.

HW April 16, 1881 260

BETWEEN THE TWO, THEY WILL LICK THE PLATTER CLEAN.

HW June 4, 1881 372

EVEN VICTORS QUARREL OVER BOOTY.
Democratic Brigand (*to Columbia, bound*). "If you had allowed me to capture you, all this would not have happened."

Assassination

Garfield's active Presidency ended at 9:20 A.M. on Saturday, July 2, just short of four months after it began. Accompanied by Secretary of State Blaine, he entered Union Station to begin a trip to New England, where Williams College, his alma mater, would be his first destination. Suddenly, he was hit by two bullets at close range.

The shooter was Charles Guiteau, 39, a mentally unbalanced, undistinguished lawyer and itinerant preacher. He had approached Garfield in the White House seeking a job, and determined to kill him when he didn't get one. Arrested at the scene and asked for a motive, he shouted, "I am a Stalwart (pro-Grant, anti-Garfield) and want Arthur for President."

The entire country went into shock. Even the *Charleston News and Courier* editorialized: "Such events as the tragedy yesterday lift people above personal and sectional considerations, and make the whole country kin."[5] That also applied to Thomas Nast, who dealt gently with Garfield while maintaining his practice of not drawing him as a recognizable individual.

Curtis grieved as much as anybody, both because of his warm friendship with Garfield and his wariness of Arthur. Six days after the event, he published a Friday special edition, a first and probably the last for the Harpers. It included a cover photograph of Guiteau, and a W.A. Rogers illustration of his second shot into the President's back, which ultimately proved mortal.

July 8, 1881 473 C

SPECIAL EDITION.
HARPER'S WEEKLY
JOURNAL OF CIVILIZATION

THE TRAGEDY AT WASHINGTON—THE ASSASSIN CHARLES JULES GUITEAU.

HW July 8, 1881 476

THE TRAGEDY AT WASHINGTON—THE ASSASSIN FIRING THE SECOND SHOT AT PRESIDENT GARFIELD.

Garfield remained in critical condition in the White House until early September when he was taken by train to the seashore at Elberon, New Jersey (part of Long Branch). He died there on September 19.

Nast drew a double-page illustration of Columbia shedding tears as she anticipated Garfield's death. His blood was on the floor near Lincoln's with her Fourth of July laurel wreath nearby. This was the kindest portrayal of a longtime political adversary that Nast ever created; only idols like Lincoln, Garibaldi and Grant received laudatory pictorial prayers and eulogies.

Continuing in the same vein, Nast drew Columbia praying beside a four-stanza poem entitled *God Save the President!* It appeared shortly after Garfield arrived in Elberon. Two issues later, Columbia prayed over his tomb in a black-bordered cover and with a three-verse mourning poem rhyming "a hero's fall" with "Death comes after all!" It is likely that Curtis, not Nast, supplied the text to *After All*.

HW July 23, 1881 488-489

AT LIBERTY'S DOOR.

Guiteau's Trial

Garfield's assassination was widely and correctly blamed on the Spoils System, and led to Civil Service reform eighteen months later, with Arthur's unexpectedly strong backing. Nast attacked right away, as Guiteau's office-seeking arrow felled the spoils vulture, with its wings representing both political parties. He followed with a generic spoilsman involuntarily caught up in the wave of reform.

HW July 23, 1881 512

A FABLE LESSON.
The American Vulture. "It is a double grief to me that I should perish by an arrow feathered from my own wings."

HW July 30, 1881 528

A GUILTY CONSCIENCE.
Statesman. "I have no offices to give, I AM A CIVIL SERVICE REFORMER!"

With in-depth artistic coverage by *Harper's*, Guiteau's trial began in mid-November and dragged on as the insanity issue was debated. In a cover cartoon, Nast portrayed him as a total lunatic, sitting on Garfield's grave and playing with a skeleton; the jurors were roaring with laughter at what they were seeing.

Despite his obvious insanity, Guiteau was convicted in January 1882 and sentenced to death. After appeals ran their course, he was hanged on June 30.

Nast concluded his Guiteau depictions with a direct reference to the Spoils System as the Devil. It was the start of a successful year-long Civil Service Reform campaign, which included several aspects of the inherent evils of patronage.

HW December 10, 1881 817 C

FROM GRAVE TO GAY.

HW January 7, 1882 4

A NEW YEAR'S CALL.
Mr. Fallen Angel, *alias* Insane Spirit, *alias* Etc. Etc. I want you to understand one thing, Mr. Guiteau, I won't have my reputation ruined by you. It was I that inspired you, you whelp, and you know it. *Au revoir.*"

Chapter 40
President Arthur

Welcoming Arthur

Both Joseph Keppler and Thomas Nast must have prepared their cartoons before Garfield died. Possibly *not* coincidentally, both used Shakespeare's *King Henry IV* for a central theme. Prince Hal had led a dissolute life with disreputable companions; when he assumed the throne, he renounced them and became well respected.

The contrast between the two cartoons emphasized the growing gap between the old and new "kings of caricature." Blending color, facial expressions and clever dialogue into a masterpiece of dramatic irony, Keppler depicted the new President as King Chester I, turning away Conkling and his cronies: "Master Shallow" Platt, and Star Route scandal masterminds Stephen Dorsey and Thomas Brady. Next to Arthur was Senator John Jones of Nevada, a mining magnate and close friend, whose home the Vice President lived in after Conkling resigned and left Washington. Jay Gould and William Vanderbilt held Arthur's cloak, as Grant and Senator John Logan looked on.

PUCK October 5, 1881

A GRAND SHAKESPEAREAN REVIVAL.

Sir John Conkling—Stand here by me, Master Shallow Platt; I will make the King do you grace. Do but mark the countenance he will give me.

My King! My Jove! I speak to thee, my heart!
King Chester I—I know thee not, old man! Fall to thy prayers!

Presume not that I am the thing I was;
For heaven doth know, so shall the world perceive.
That I have turned away my former self;
So will I those that kept me company!
(2nd Part of King Henry IV, Act V, Sc. 5.)

HW October 15, 1881 689 C

At the other end of the scale, Nast prepared another emblematic cover cartoon. Justice was about to hand the incoming President her sword; Columbia, the Constitution; and Mercury, representing trade, the great seal. The title was an actual quote from Garfield: "God reigns, and the Government at Washington still lives."

Keppler's *Puck* cartoon appeared on September 28, a week before the October 5 publication date on its masthead. It is probable that Nast saw the cartoon, hastily turned to his well-worn copy of Shakespeare and added appropriate text from *King Henry IV*. The last line: "So said Prince Henry when he became King" is what arouses suspicion of a last-minute addition to his post-dated October 15 cover cartoon, published on October 5.[1]

"GOD REIGNS, AND THE GOVERNMENT AT WASHINGTON STILL LIVES."—GARFIELD

"I do commit into your hand
The unstained sword that you have used to bear;
With this remembrance,—That you use the same
With the like hold, just, and impartial spirit
As you have done 'gainst me. There is my hand:
My voice shall sound as you do prompt mine ear;
And I will stoop and humble my intents
To your well-practiced, wise directions—
*****
And with his spirit sadly I survive,
To mock the expectation of the world;
To frustrate prophecies; and to raze out
Rotten opinion, who hath writ me down
After my seeming. The tide of blood in me
Hath proudly flow'd in vanity, till now:
Now doth it turn, and ebb back to the sea;
Where it shall mingle with the state of floods,
And flow henceforth in formal majesty.
Now call we our high court of parliament;
And let us choose such limits of noble counsel,
That the great body of our state may go
In equal rank with the best-govern'd nation."
—So said Prince Henry when he became King.

Effectively, and possibly unrealized even by himself, the old "king of caricature" was recognizing the new king. It probably was a momentous transition point for Nast, and must have increased both his frustration with his *Harper's* handcuffs, and his determination to acquire his own paper where he could compete on equal terms.

As President, Arthur did turn over a new leaf. As he left office in March 1885, *Harper's* paid "a warm tribute to his public character and career . . . The expectation and the apprehension that Mr. Arthur would surround himself with advisors drawn from a faction of his party, and that he would be the instrument of influences which had been openly hostile to President Garfield, were soon dispelled . . . There is no reason to suppose that the Garfield administration would have been more satisfactory than that which filled the larger part of his term."[2]

Coming from Editor Curtis, this was higher praise than his close friend, President Hayes received when his term ended. It was reflected in another prosaic Nast cartoon on the cover of the same issue.

HW March 7, 1885 145 C

THE COMPLIMENTS OF THE SEASON—MARCH 4.
Cleveland To Arthur. "I hope that I may leave the house in as good order as you have."

Civil Service Reform

Arthur's major surprise was his diligence in pursuing Civil Service Reform. The spoils system was predicated on two fundamental interconnected parts. Most important was patronage, the awarding of jobs and political offices in return for votes and money. Keppler caught that in full flower, depicting Arthur as a political magician trying to satisfy his diverse Republican factions. It appeared a week after his welcome to the new "King."

PUCK October 12, 1881

A PRESIDENTIAL CONJUROR.

The complementary necessity was political assessments on the patronage recipients, essential for funding the electoral machinery that kept their layers of bosses in power. Although laws were passed to make contributions optional, there was nothing "voluntary" about them as Nast and *Harper's* frequently noted. Michigan Congressman Jay Hubbell, who headed the Republican Committee that proclaimed assessments, was Nast's whipping boy; he was defeated for reelection that fall.

HW July 1, 1882 416

POLITICAL ASSESSMENTS.

"The Committee is authorized to state that such voluntary contribution from persons employed in the service of the United States will not be objected to in any official quarter."—*Circular of the Republican Congressional Committee.*

HW July 8, 1882 429

"VOLUNTARY CONTRIBUTIONS."

The (Political) Wolf and the Fold (of Laborers, Clerks, Errand-Boys, Women, and Girls in the Public Services).

HW November 25, 1882 752

HUBBELL AT HOME EVEN ABROAD.

The Pendleton Act

Senator George Pendleton, an Ohio Democrat, was the man who proposed, pushed and ultimately succeeded in getting Civil Service Reform enacted into law. A Copperhead during the Civil War, he was George McClellan's running mate in 1864; Nast attacked him on both counts. A year later, he voted against the Thirteenth Amendment which ended slavery. In 1868, he led on the first 15 ballots before New York Governor and fellow Copperhead, Horatio Seymour, received the Democratic Presidential nomination. Becoming less extreme over the next decade, Pendleton replaced Stanley Matthews in the Senate in 1879, and later became Chairman of the Democratic Caucus.

Garfield and Pendleton knew each other from Ohio and national politics. After Garfield was shot, the Senator introduced the Pendleton Act to establish a merit system for Federal appointments through competitive examinations, tenure for fixed terms, prohibition of political assessments, and a permanent, three-member Civil Service Commission appointed by the President with Senatorial consent.

President Arthur put his substantial weight behind the Act. After a long, contentious battle, final Congressional passage came in early January 1883, resulting in 13,000 Federal offices being placed under Civil Service rules by executive order. Nast referred to the bill on several occasions, primarily when Pendleton's own Democratic Party, especially Tammany and John Kelly, gave him grief.

HW September 16, 1882 591

THE OUT-DEMOCRATS.
Tammany Hall. "Shake hands, that's the kind of Civil Service Reform I believe in."
Senator Pendleton, in his speech delivered at Mount Gilead, Ohio, remarked: "It has been said that the abandonment of the spoils system will exclude Democrats from office when the day of our victory shall come. Not at all. On the contrary, I believe that the adoption of this policy as our party creed will hasten the day of the victory of our party, and its adoption as a law will, under any administration, fill many offices with Democrats. I believe Democrats will stand any test of examination, and in a fair field will not come out second best. Who shall do them the discredit to say that in any of the essential elements of character, or capacity, or fitness, they are inferior?"

HW December 16, 1882 805

DR. ARTHUR'S PRESCRIPTIONS.
Now That The Cause Is Ascertained He May Hope For Relief.

When the bill looked doubtful a month before passage, Nast's battered Uncle Sam was crippled by 85-cent silver in his inflated leg, his eye patch said "Spoils System," and the wall signs related to the Pendleton Act.

HW January 13, 1883 28

THE CIVIL SERVICE BILL PASSED THE HOUSE JANUARY 4, 1883.

ALL HONOR TO SENATOR PENDLETON.
Pendleton To Hawley (in strict confidence). "I thank you for your help and congratulations, but find myself in a peculiar position. Your party supports me, while my party gives me the cold shoulder."

A month later, Nast honored Congressman Pendleton (something unimaginable a decade earlier) and Republican Senator Joseph Hawley of Connecticut, who headed the Senate Civil Service Committee. The Senate passed the Act on December 27; the House on January 4, 1883. Nast probably drew the humdrum illustration-cartoon in advance, and then added the House passage date just before publication.

Mormons and Polygamy

In late 1881, the issue of polygamy came to a head in Congress. There were roughly 140,000 Mormons in the Utah Territory, including about 12,000 in plural marriages. The founding Harper brothers, strict Methodists, detested polygamy; the second issue of the *Weekly*, dated January 10, 1857, listed the members of the Utah Legislature, along with their number of wives and amusing parenthetical comments. (Future Congressional Delegate George Cannon was not on the list.).

Polygamy was a constant thorn in the side of Congress, which included a non-voting Delegate from Utah. It had been prohibited by the 1862 Morrill Act, which Lincoln deliberately chose not to enforce. Ten years later, "Brigham Young vowed he would 'cram polygamy down the throats of Congressmen,' and withdrew Utah's Delegate from Congress because 'he was the husband of only one wife,' and selected Apostle George Cannon, who (then) had four wives to replace him. Spasmodic efforts had been made to oust the apostle from his seat in Congress, but he maintained his position by the humiliating quibble that he was the husband of 'only one wife,' knowing as he does that the other 'women' are not recognizable in a court of law as 'wives.'"[3]

(*Harper's* editor Curtis, who wrote the above words after Young died on August 29, 1877, probably didn't know that Cannon was the nephew of John Taylor, the man who succeeded Young as Chief Apostle.)

AVERAGE ALLOWANCE OF WIVES TO LEGISLATORS IN UTAH.

A correspondent of the San Francisco *Herald* gives the following list of the members of the Legislature of Utah with the number of their wives:

Members of Council.	*No. of Wives.*
Heber C. Kimball, President of the Council	57
Daniel H. Wells, Councilman (cross-eyed)	19
Albert Carrington (cripple and near-sighted)	12
Orson Pratt (cripple and near-sighted)	7
Wilford Woodruff (cripple and near-sighted)	12
John Stoker (cripple and near-sighted)	8
Lorin Farr (cripple and near-sighted)	3
Lorenzo Snow (cripple and near-sighted)	25
Leonard E. Harrington (cripple and near-sighted)	3
Isaac Morley (seventy-two years old)	5
John A. Ray (from Texas)	2
George A. Smith (cripple and near-sighted)	5
Grand total—men 13; women	171
Members of House of Representatives.	
J. M. Grant, Speaker, has	6
W. W. Phelps (printer of Morgan's book)	8
A. P. Rockwood (an old man)	3
Edwin D. Wolley (a small man)	5
J. W. Cummings (cripple)	10
Hosea Stout (lawyer from Kentucky—three dead)	1
S. W. Richards (young and handsome lawyer)	15
Jesse C. Little (lawyer of Boston, Mass.)	3
William Snow (Vermont laborer)	8
P. H. Young (older brother of Brigham—tailor)	5
C. V. Spencer (of Massachusetts—quite small) has but	2
Ezra S. Benson (old and homely)	15
James C. Snow (quite poor)	3
Aaron Johnson (has three sisters, and altogether)	6
Lorenzo H. Hatch (wagon maker)	2
Jacob G. Bigler (farmer)	10
George Peacock (farmer)	10
John Eldridge (phrenologist—two dead)	1
Isaac C. Haight (coal digger)	12
Jesse N. Smith (lawyer)	2
John D. Parker (old and deaf)	3
Jesse Hobson (ox teamster)	10
J. C. Wright (hotel keeper)	5
James Brown (dairyman)	7
Enoch Reese (farmer, &c.)	2
W. A. Hickman (one of the Danites)	3
Total—members 26, and wives	157
Officers of the House.	
Thomas Bullock (Clerk and an Englishman)	4
J. Grimshaw (Assistant Clerk and an Englishman)	5
Chandler Holbrook (Foreman and deaf)	4
Jacob F. Hutchinson (Messenger)	2
Joel H. Johnson (Chaplain)	7
Total	22

Brigham Young having 68 wives, these 40 men have 420 women among them.

Other than depicting the Mormon Tabernacle to represent one of 20 different denominations included in a Church vs. State cartoon eleven years earlier, Nast refrained from commenting on the Mormons before late 1881.* *Harper's* scornful editorial blast probably inhibited any humorous portrayal by Nast. However, Keppler — six months after *Puck's* birth — came up with a classic "memorial," basing it on an illustration in Mark Twain's 1872 *Roughing It*.[4]

PUCK September 5, 1877

IN MEMORIAM BRIGHAM YOUNG.
"And the place which knew him once shall know him no more."

Nast did get involved when momentum built in Congress to ban plural marriage by forbidding polygamists to hold office, vote or judge elections, and to appoint a commission to conduct Utah's elections. He used a stout old man with an umbrella as a symbol in four cartoons.

HW December 31, 1881 889 C

CONSTANCY IS A JEWEL.
Mormon. "I'll live in defiance of both."

HW January 28, 1882 61

"VIOLATORS OF THE LAWS OF THE LAND."
Columbia. "Even (G.Q.) Cannon shall not open these Doors to you."

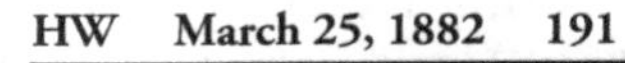

HW March 25, 1882 191

PURE WHITE "MORMON IMMIGRATION" ON THE ATLANTIC COAST.
More *cheap* "help-mates" for Mr. Polygamist.

---

* See p. 241

HW May 6, 1882 288

BURST THE OTHER DAY AT WASHINGTON, D.C.

Republican Senator George Edmunds of Vermont sponsored an eponymous law which passed in March 1882 and made polygamy a felony. Delegate George Cannon was expelled; Nast punned by picturing him as cannon fodder.

HW December 22, 1883 824

ST. NICK'S COMPLIMENTS TO THE MORMONS.

For Christmas 1882, Nast prepared his final cartoon on the Mormons, but *Harper's* chose not to print it. A year later, when Nast had left the magazine and was too ill to return, the *Weekly* — desperate for a Christmas cartoon from him — finally printed it.

However, the Edmunds Act failed to accomplish its purpose. The Mormon Church claimed that ecclesiastical marriages could not be dissolved by Territorial laws, especially ones that pre-dated the law. President Arthur was not going to use military force, so he recommended repeal in his December 1883 annual message to Congress.

A second Act (Edmunds-Tucker), passed in 1887, disincorporated the Church and was upheld by the Supreme Court in 1890. Delegate Cannon, who ended up with six wives and 32 children, hid out until 1886, when he served a six-month prison term.

After the Supreme Court ruling, Cannon helped write the Church's *Manifesto*, prohibiting plural marriages, which was published in September 1890 and became a major factor in revitalizing the Church.

Chinese Exclusion

Another major political issue came to the fore early in 1882 when the new Congress enacted a 20-year ban on Chinese laborers entering the country. Although 228,000 Chinese had arrived over the past two decades — primarily to build the Union Pacific and other railroads — most of those who survived took their accumulated savings and returned to China. The 1880 Census recorded 105,000 Chinese.

As discussed previously, the campaign to ban them was led by Denis Kearney.* Nast now broadened his attack from just Kearney to include his updated Irish stereotype.

HW March 25, 1882 192

WHICH COLOR IS TO BE TABOOED NEXT?
Fritz (*to Pat*). "If the Yankee Congress can keep the *yellow* man out, what is to hinder them from calling us *green* and keeping us out too?"

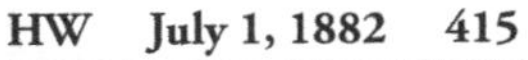
HW July 1, 1882 415

NOW "THE AMERICAN MUST GO."
"We have a new gospel of Americanism in this evening of the nineteenth century—a gospel that declares Kearney shall be supreme in California, and shall close the 'golden gate' against the Chinaman; and which prescribes that in the East the commissions of our ministers shall be countersigned by an Irish 'suspect.' 'The American must go.'"—From *The Hour*.

HW April 15, 1882 236

THE VETO.
Arthur (a connoisseur). "It would be unreasonable to destroy it, and would reflect upon the honor of the country."

On April 4, President Arthur vetoed the 20-year ban, to high praise from *Harper's Weekly* among others. In addition to its length, he objected to passport and other restrictions. It also counteracted an 1880 treaty with China that allowed the United States to regulate, limit or suspend the immigration of Chinese laborers if the influx seemed to threaten public order; no such threat was apparent. Nast praised President Arthur in his cartoon published the day after the veto.

* See p. 464

The 20-year ban was primarily a Democratic-backed bill. After the veto, more Republicans came on board to support a 10-year ban containing all the provisions that Arthur objected to in his rejection message. This time, he signed it to biting criticism from Nast and editor Curtis.

HW April 22, 1882 256

AT LAST THE DEMOCRATIC TIGER HAS SOMETHING TO HANG ON.

HW May 20, 1882 317

(DIS-) "HONORS ARE EASY."
Now both parties have something to hang on.

The *Weekly's* editorial, entitled *The Chinese Panic*, blasted the Republican Party, and sarcastically suggested that the same "principle of discrimination against foreign immigration" be applied to the Irish for "their records of crime, disorder and danger to the free-school system."[5]

This act was the first legal restriction on immigration in the country's history.

Before President Arthur vetoed the 20-year ban, Nast commented with the Castle Garden immigrant reception building as his scenario. After a separate treaty was signed with Korea (then spelled Corea), he revisited the building's law library. The various legal volumes included "On Color and Pigtails," as well as "Bribes," "Duties," and "Antiques."

HW April 1, 1882 207

E PLURIBUS UNUM (EXCEPT THE CHINESE).

HW August 19, 1882 527

A DISTINCTION WITHOUT A DIFFERENCE.
"You no stoppee me? me no China manee, me Corea manee; allee sammee Melican manee."

Rivers and Harbors

Muddying up a separate Congressional swamp were the annual pork-barrel Rivers and Harbors bills, aimed at pet projects — often participated in directly or indirectly by their sponsors — and attracting reelection votes. The cost to taxpayers rose from $4 million in 1870 to $11.5 million in 1881 to a proposed $18.7 million in July 1882 when an omnibus bill came to Arthur's desk. Courageously, he vetoed it, earning plenty of praise from Nast and *Harper's*, but Congress was able to override the bill.

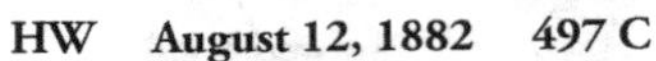
HW August 12, 1882 497 C

PRESIDENT ARTHUR, HIT HIM AGAIN! DON'T LET THE VULTURE BECOME OUR NATIONAL BIRD.

HW September 2, 1882 560

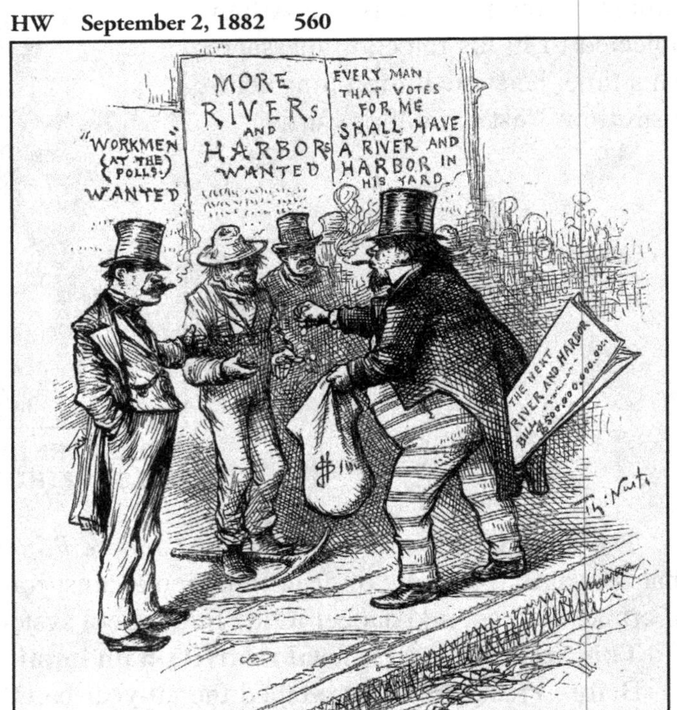

NO HONEST WORKMAN WILL GET ONE CENT OF IT.
Statesman. "When I go back to Congress, I'll make the United States like Venice—canals everywhere."

Boss Kelly

John Kelly eventually succeeded Boss Tweed as Tammany Hall's chief Sachem, and controlled or attempted to control both city and state politics for about ten years. A tough, scheming, corrupt politician, he often fought his fellow Democrats for power, sometimes enabling Republican victories in the process.

Relatively short and stocky, he was an easy target for Nast who usually commented on him rather than attacking him head-on as he did Tweed. Kelly, born poor in 1822, was a grate-setter and mason by trade, Catholic and pro-Irish, and a fearsome boxer. Unlike his political rival, John Morrissey, he never turned pro.

In the 1850s, Kelly was an Alderman, then served two terms in Congress, and spent six of the eight years through 1867 as Sheriff. In 1868, he ran for Mayor against Tweed's choice, Oakey Hall. At the last minute, he dropped out and went to Europe for three years, presumably well compensated by Tweed for doing so. Although his morals were on a par with the Tweed Ring, he was absent during its heyday, and dubbed "Honest John" because of his non-participation. He made up for that after his return in the fall of 1871, shortly before the Tweed Ring was beaten at the polls. By 1875, Kelly gained effective control of Tammany after vying with Morrissey.*

* See p. 47

Battles with Fellow Democrats

Consequently, Morrissey formed Irving Hall and competed and battled with Tammany until his untimely death from pneumonia in 1878 at age 47. Kelly ruled Tammany until his nervous breakdown in 1884 (two years before he died), resulted in Richard Croker's reign. Over the years, Nast featured Morrissey duking it out with Kelly, usually to Honest John's disadvantage.

HW November 27, 1875 972

"TRUTH CRUSHED TO DEATH WILL RISE AGAIN."—Boss Kelly

"Truly, an honorable fight and a glorious victory! In after years, when an upright and God-fearing Republican shall review on his death-bed the events of a well-spent life, doubtless his thoughts will linger long, and with sweet satisfaction, upon the proud day when he joyfully enrolled himself as a follower and supporter of Wood, the lottery dealer; Hall, the unconvicted relic of Tweedism; and Morrissey, the prize-fighter. In the blissful consciousness of having taken so exalted and ennobling a part in the great work of reform, he may feel that he has not lived in vain, for, in the memorable year 1875, he helped John Morrissey to punish Tammany for trying to clean itself."—N.Y. Tribune, Nov. 5

HW July 29, 1876 624

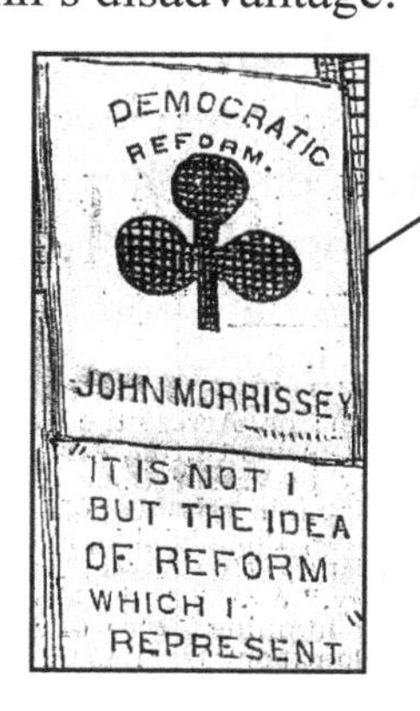

THE LATEST FASHION.

"Whoever says that *I am not* a Reformer, I'll lamm him."

HW November 24, 1877 932

HON. J. MORRISSEY'S GAME

Knocking Spots out of "Hon." J. Kelly.

Nast punned on "Honest" vs. "Honorable"

HW October 4, 1879 788

EVEN TAMMANY SACHEMS DRAW THE LINE SOMEWHERE.

Ex-Governor (*counted in by* Tilden) Hoffman. "I resign. I could go Boss Tweed and his gang. But a Boss that upsets a dainty morsel fresh from the Barrel like that, I cannot stand."

When Samuel Tilden was elected Governor in 1874, Kelly lost some of his power. He fought Tilden and opposed his nomination for President in 1876, when he was instrumental in getting Thomas Hendricks — whose inflationary views clashed with Tilden and provided Nast with plenty of fodder — as his running mate.*

Mayor Smith Ely appointed Kelly as City Controller in 1876, and he reduced the city's debt during his two terms. In 1879, he ran for Governor against Democratic incumbent Lucius Robinson, and pulled enough votes to let Republican Alonzo Cornell win with a 35,000 (4%) plurality. Now Kelly was on the outs with all three prominent former Democratic governors: Tilden, Robinson and John Hoffman. As a result, outgoing Mayor Edward Cooper refused to reappoint him Controller when Kelly's term ended in 1880.

Nast's cartoon referred to Tilden's financial barrel, and his failed backing of Governor Robinson — portrayed as a dead duck lying at Kelly's feet.

* See p. 403-405

Grover Cleveland for Governor

As the 1882 fall elections approached for New York's governor and the city's mayor, Nast — like an old fire-horse — burst forth with flames of creativity for the relatively short course of the campaign. His primary target was Kelly and the spoils system; however, in Grover Cleveland, he had his first positive role model since Grant a decade earlier.

Republican Governor Alonzo Cornell had a credible record after being elected in 1879 as Conkling's man, over Curtis's opposition and with Kelly's splinter-ticket help. He probably deserved reelection, but Conkling now hated and, therefore, blocked him. President Arthur persuaded Treasury Secretary Charles Folger to become the Republican Candidate, but he wasn't supported by Nast, Curtis or Blaine's Half-breed faction.

The Democrats met in late September and nominated dark horse Cleveland, a lawyer and current Mayor of Buffalo. He had two major advantages: first, a reputation for honesty, respectability, and efficiency; second, a clean record and no political quarrels. That made him acceptable to all the competing party factions. John Kelly reluctantly threw his Tammany votes behind Cleveland to clinch his nomination, seeing Cleveland as his potential front man, much as Tweed had done with John Hoffman.*

Nast and *Harper's* broke their Republican consistency by endorsing a Democrat. Nast even showed some passion, rarely visible since the Greeley campaign ten years earlier. This time, however, his path was trickier — praising Cleveland while damning Kelly.

His solution was to depict Cleveland as a head angel, complete with a crown, wings and a clean robe over his portly body. Kelly, also stout but much shorter, usually was a Tammany Indian Chief, with a dirty shirt — always trying to manipulate the angelic Cleveland.

Nast's initial Cleveland cartoon — one of ten portrayals in 1882 — excelled any of his subsequent depictions of Cleveland during his Presidential campaign two years later (when Nast supported him against James Blaine). It appeared on the first of three successive covers following his nomination for Governor, and was especially noteworthy for its subtle details.

Kelly and an Irving Hall spoilsman — the Democratic Party factions (wings) — were adjusting Cleveland's wings so that *they do not clash*; however, the wings were upside down, making it difficult, if not impossible, for the head angel to fly, even as he complacently admired himself in the mirror. The Irving spoilsman's dirty coat hung on the wall, awaiting whitewash and powder to cover it up, while a bottle stuck out of his back pocket.

HW October 14, 1882 641 C

THE NEW ANGELIC FLYING MACHINE.—(Patent Applied For.)
Grover Cleveland (*head angel*). "Be careful in adjusting the wings; see that *they do not clash.*"

* See p. 259

The following week, Nast lamented that Tammany's stains were too ingrained to rub out. His list covered the 1860-1882 period, and included Copperheads, Civil War draft riots, ballot box stuffing, fraud, spoils and corruption — all of which he had attacked in his free-swinging days. The buckets contained water from Lakes Erie and Ontario, probably a reference to the Canal Ring scandals which Tilden had tackled in 1874,* and Cleveland knew all about from his three years as Sheriff of Erie County.

HW October 21, 1882 657 C

"AY! THERE'S THE RUB!"—YOU CAN'T CHANGE THE NATURE OF THE ANIMAL.

HW October 28, 1882 673 C

DEEP DIPLOMACY.
John Kelly. "I'll let them have their way *before* election, but *I* am boss *afterward*, and don't you forget it."

The next week's cover added a major new prediction: Cleveland flying towards the White House in 1884. While his biographer Paine gave Nast credit for prognostication, Nast had to be aware of similar scuttlebutt echoing at the time of the future President's nomination in Albany a month earlier.[3] Nevertheless, his prediction must have made an impression on his readers.

The cartoon's main thrust, of course, showed Kelly and Irving Hall blowing smoke for reform and honest government promises, while the written proposals, with tiny wings attached, lay in a wastebasket.

* See p. 396

In addition to the cover, the November 4 pre-election *Weekly* contained six other Nast cartoons — the most for any issue since the *Home Stretch* of the Greeley campaign a decade earlier. One page had three cartoons, all of them aimed at Kelly.

Most unusual and noteworthy was a book-like illustration adapted from Charles Dickens's *Oliver Twist*. (Nast had illustrated part or all of several Dickens stories and had attended the author's farewell New York dinner in 1868). Here, master-burglar Kelly (Bill Sykes), standing on the shoulders of Irving Hall, was pushing diminutive Cleveland (Oliver) through a small window of the Public Treasury. It was a dark night scene, so Nast's heavy cross-hatching differentiated it from almost all his other cartoons.

However, the cover itself was uninspired, depicting Columbia leery of the lurking Tammany Tiger.

HW November 4, 1882 701

Bill Sykes. "As soon as I've got you in, open the front door for me."

Two weeks later, after Republican Folger was swamped by almost 200,000 votes, a disturbed Columbia admonished the Tiger to "Behave yourself," while a quote from Governor-elect Cleveland referred to the next election, keeping it and him in the current spotlight. (The Democratic turnout was almost the same as in the 1880 election, but about 200,000 Half-breed Blaine Republicans stayed home because they resented President Arthur's forced imposition of Folger as their candidate, or voted for the Prohibition Party candidate.)[6]

HW November 4, 1882 689 C

LOOK BEFORE YOU LEAP!

HW November 18, 1882 721 C

NOW, THEN, BEHAVE YOURSELF.

"THE result in 1884 will depend almost entirely upon the conduct of the two parties during the intervening period."
GOVERNOR-ELECT CLEVELAND.

Mayor

The month before the election, Kelly selected Franklin Edson, a prominent businessman, as his choice for Mayor. He correctly believed that Edson would be more malleable than the current Mayor, William R. Grace, a successful shipping entrepreneur, who constantly battled Tammany. Nast depicted Cleveland as a Tammany curse and Grace's expulsion as a blessing.

HW November 4, 1882 701

A BOSS WARNING.
Angel Kelly (*to head angel*). "If you don't do as I dictate, I'll smash you. I've done it to bigger men than you."

HW November 4, 1882 701

MAKING HIS TOY HORSE REAR.
Chief Kelly. "Whoa, there! What an independent-spirited animal this is! I fear I shall not be able to manage it."

HW November 4, 1882 704

THE CITIZENS' MOVEMENT MEANS BUSINESS.

Nast first introduced Edson as Pegasus, the winged horse from Greek mythology, as the "bargain mayor" hobby horse for "N.Y. City," in a vignette in his *Deep Diplomacy* cartoon.* The wings made the horse somewhat difficult to manage before the election, but were under control when *On to Washington!* after it.**

Edson's opponent was Allan Campbell, the city's comptroller, who had replaced the outraged Kelly in that job (by Grace's predecessor, Edward Cooper). Originally the County Democracy, a new reform party, nominated Campbell, and Nast, *Harper's* and most Republicans supported him. Nast's cartoon was published on October 25, but somehow Kelly enticed or browbeat the reformers to switch their allegiance to Edson after that date, and Campbell lost by 20,000 votes.

HW January 20, 1883 48

THE CLEAN SHIRT PERIOD AT AN END.
Mayor Edson's *dis*-appointments to the people and appointments of Tammany.

Once Edson took office, Nast was quick to get rid of his clean shirt.

However, two years later, Edson split with Tammany, and William Grace became Mayor again.

* See p. 535
** See next page

Victory and Defeat

After the election, Nast used the same "*On to Washington*!" title that related to Tweed eleven years earlier — but in a much simpler cartoon.* The earlier prospect of Tammany controlling the Presidency after the 1872 election was much slimmer with Governor John Hoffman than with Governor Cleveland in 1884.

Personally, Nast knew he had a tough fight in front of him with regard to Kelly. In the same issue as *On to Washington*!, he was totally candid about who lost.

HW November 18, 1882 736

"ON TO WASHINGTON!"

Before

HW October 21, 1882 671

THE FLAG OF TRUCE (OR DECOY).
"What, surrender without a fight, and give them a walk over? Not much."

After

HW November 18, 1882 727

GOT LEFT.

Nast was not used to losing political battles even though Curtis had neutralized him during the Hayes and Garfield administrations. From here on, it would only get worse. Two years later even winning would turn out to be losing as his prediction for Cleveland came true.

* See p. 268

Chapter 41
Irreparable Losses

Squeezed

Harper & Brothers was doing very well financially in the early 1880s. Its sales from books, the *Weekly*, the *Monthly*, and the *Bazar* were in the range of $4 million; it had more than 700 employees; and as the country's largest book publisher, it had about 4,000 titles in print.[1]

As discussed previously, Nast's authority and derived leverage at *Harper's* almost disappeared after Fletcher, the last of the four founding brothers, died in 1877. Initially Curtis alone was Nast's primary censor, but by 1882, the younger Harpers were participating. Five sons of the first generation had entered the firm in 1869, and eight from the third generation had joined by 1882. "While exclusively a family concern, it was customary to treat the young Harpers as far as possible alike, paying them liberal salaries, and then leaving them largely to their own devices to display their business capabilities, a policy not always conducive to hard work."[2]

As the 1880s progressed, the *Weekly* became more family-oriented, featuring valentines, holiday events, and literature on its covers, with less emphasis on politics. While Nast's cartoons were still important to his fan base, other artists like W.A. Rogers and A.B. Frost were more in tune with the broader social content that the firm wanted to co-feature.

Nast was in "no-man's land." Over a six-year period (1877-83), he reported to three different Harpers: second-generation Joseph W., Jr. ("Brooklyn Joe"); John W.; and J. Henry (Harry), Fletcher's capable grandson, who skipped Harvard at his grandfather's suggestion to join the firm, and became a partner at age 29 in 1877, the year his grandfather died.

What understandably bothered Nast most was having his acceptance-rejection decisions made by a committee that included several Harpers and Curtis (when available), with unclear criteria. As his rejections increased, his confidence, creativity and morale declined, along with his income. He was paid $150 for a full-page, plus his $5,000 annual retainer for exclusivity.

As shown below, Nast's income from full pages dropped by $9,000, or 74%, from 1879 to 1882. While the total number of cartoons was about the same in both years, his covers shrank from 39 to 13 — from an average of three every four weeks to just one — and his $150 full pages dropped from 81 to 21.

	Covers	Other Full Pages	Double Pages	Total Full Pages	Income from Full Pages	Total Cartoons
1879	39	34	4	81	**$12,150**	138
1880	34	29	4	91	**$10,650**	121
1881	31	10	4	49	**$ 7,350**	109
1882	13	6	1	21	**$ 3,150**	137
1883	-	-	-	-	-	13

However, in addition to the $3,150 from his full pages, Nast also earned an estimated $5,900 from 118 smaller cartoons (probably at $50 each). Adding in his $5,000 retainer, he earned about $14,000 in 1882.

With better business judgment, Nast should have been able to handle a drop of about $11,000 from his 1879 income of about $25,000 ($500,000 today) from *Harper's*. His 1880 assets were worth about $125,000, the equivalent of about $2.5 million today. Although he had moved to Morristown nine years before, he still owned his previous property in Harlem, worth about $30,000, and about $60,000 in government securities. Unfortunately, in his quest for additional capital to fund his own paper, he had lost most or all of the value of his government bonds by selling them to speculate in mines, patents, railroads and other ventures that ultimately proved worthless.[3]

Moreover, Nast's $14,000 from *Harper's* was far more than he could have earned at any other publication. For example, Bernhard Gillam, who had worked for *Harper's Weekly* in 1880,* was making $100 a week at *Puck*; when *Puck* refused to give him a raise to $125 after his anti-Blaine cartoons were instrumental in doubling its circulation in 1884, he accepted $150 and a 20% equity interest to switch to *Judge* the following year. Budding star Eugene (Zim) Zimmerman, 23, earned $80, up from $35, when he moved with Gillam.[4]

Hemmed in both editorially and financially, Nast believed that his only salvation was to redouble his efforts to establish his own paper. He had tried unsuccessfully to attract outside backers over the past several years, so it would require self-funding, using his own depleted capital as an investment base and increasing it as best he could.

Competition

Nast's distress must have been intensified by the emergence and varying success of four competitors — two of them new. Of course, he would have had to battle them for circulation if he had launched.

- ***Leslie's Weekly*** — Frank Leslie had died of cancer in January 1880, leaving his publishing company with debts of $300,000. His widow and successor, Miriam, changed her name to Frank Leslie and successfully resuscitated her company, making it a much stronger competitor. For example, when she learned about President Garfield's attempted assassination shortly after he was shot at 9:20 A.M. on Saturday, July 2, 1881, she sent artists to Washington on the next train.** One returned with sketches on the midnight train. By working around the clock, she had the story printed and on the streets by Tuesday, one day ahead of *Harper's Weekly*, which also expedited its issue. She reportedly netted $50,000 from that journalistic coup.[5]
- ***Puck*** — During 1880, Joseph Keppler had replaced Nast as the country's leading cartoonist. By 1884, *Puck* achieved a profitable circulation in the range of 80,000, with an expanding staff of 400. Nast envied Keppler's editorial freedom but probably didn't know that his net worth was about $600,000.
- ***The Judge*** — Perhaps even more irritating to Nast was the emergence of *The Judge* — an imitation of *Puck* — on October 29, 1881. When James Wales, 29, an American-born cartoonist, was denied the opportunity to obtain equity in *Puck* where he was Keppler's principal lieutenant, he left to co-found a competitor. (Under his art direction, *The Judge* was unprofitable, so he returned to *Puck* in 1885 — at a salary of only $60 a week — and died of an accidental drug overdose late the following year).

  In 1885, *The Judge* was sold to William Arkell, who dropped "The" from its title, and induced Bernhard Gillam to leave *Puck* and become his lead cartoonist. *Judge* evolved into a successful Republican-oriented humor weekly, whose views opposed Democratic-leaning *Puck*. It ultimately outlived all its competitors, including *Harper's Weekly*.
- ***Life*** — Founded by three recent Harvard graduates — who also were alumni of the *Lampoon*, the college's humor magazine — *Life* appeared as a picture weekly on January 4, 1883. After a slow start, it was profitable after nine months, and reached a circulation of 50,000 within a few years.

---

* See p. 502
** See p. 521

The neophytes who founded *Life* had a good vision of the evolving market, as well as financial smarts. Entrepreneur and chief cartoonist John Mitchell used his $10,000 legacy to pay his printer weekly in advance, while business manager Andrew Miller carefully watched the cash flow. The following year, recent Columbia graduate John Kendrick Bangs became editor. (In 1888, Bangs joined Harper & Bros, stayed until its financial reorganization in 1901, and edited *Harper's Weekly* during his last three years there.)

In looking back at *Life's* success in particular, it is striking to observe how these 21-22 year-old novices possessed the contemporary and complementary artistic, literary and management skills which 42-year old Nast lacked. Equally important, they weren't locked into the political likes, dislikes and rigidities that prevented Nast from providing the enlightened and more entertaining satire that appealed to Reconstruction-fatigued audiences of the 1880s. The Harpers and their competitors realized that, but Nast probably didn't fully comprehend — at that point in his life — that time already had passed him by.

Leaving

On the Ides of March 1883 — always a notable date for Nast who used Shakespeare's *Julius Caesar* in eleven cartoons — he composed a letter to John W. Harper, the finance-oriented manager to whom he then reported. He had already submitted the last of his 14 cartoons accepted for 1883. Harper replied immediately, and Nast kept the $5,000 exclusivity retainer in place as "H.B." (Harper Brothers), suggested.[6]

My dear Mr. Harper:

Since you have taken exclusive charge of my drawings, they have appeared less and less frequently in the *Weekly*, and I think I have observed faithfully the letter of the agreement. For some years past my work has been refused at times, but some reason has been assigned for it, generally that the subjects were adverse to the interests of the house.

Of late, however, no such motive could apply, for noticing how often they were suppressed I have been careful to avoid doubtful subjects. Still they have met the same fate persistently, and whenever you have selected any for publication you have invariably chosen the smallest.

Hence, I am forced to the conclusion that for some reason unknown to me, my drawings are no longer of use to you, and that under those circumstances you certainly cannot care to continue the arrangement with me. . . .

Of course, nothing having been said up to January 1, I naturally considered the agreement binding for another year, and have refused good offers. But as it is, I have decided that it would be best for both parties to bring it to a close at the end of the first quarter, April 1.

The agreement as to the retainer, made ten years ago, may also expire at the same date.

Yours truly,

Th. Nast.

My dear Nast:

Your dynamite communication of the 16th inst, in which you decide to exchange old friends and long friendships for new, came to hand, very singularly, on St. Patrick's Day. The conduct which you criticise has not been that of any one member of our firm exclusively, but we have advised with one another, as is our habit in other business questions. Whenever your work had been omitted, there have been good reasons, in our judgment, for such omissions, and explanations have been made frankly when you have given us an opportunity to do so by your presence. In many instances, I think, you have agreed with us. Recently you have avoided me altogether, but I did not suspect it was from any unfriendly feelings; I supposed it merely accidental. From your point of view, I am not surprised at your expressions; but you ought to remember that we have to consider these matters from a business standpoint, as well as from their artistic merits.

I shall submit your letter to the firm, for whom it is intended, and in any event I shall hope that our friendly intercourse of so many years may not be interrupted because we differ in questions relating wholly to business.

Yours very truly,

John W. Harper.

P.S. — Perhaps you had better not disturb the retainer feature just now, but take more time to consider before cutting loose from Your Franklin Square Friends,

H.B.

The Year Away

Nast's full year off began well. In May 1883, he went to London; spent time with old friends, artists, writers, and some of Grant's acquaintances to whom he had an introduction, as well as statesmen and politicians; he even attended a concert at Buckingham Palace.[7]

The previous year, Nast had attacked England in 25 cartoons, for its bombardment of Alexandria and conquest of Egypt in order to gain control of the Suez Canal. He must have had some interesting conversations when that subject came up, assuming his audience was familiar with his work.

HW July 22, 1882 461

THE END OF THE MASQUERADE—AND THE BRITISH LION IS GOING FOR HIS SHARE.
Lord Granville (*Foreign Secretary*). "It is painful—by jingo, it is, too—to be obliged—you know—to use force against the weak—you know—you know."

August 26, 1882 529 C

Prime Minister Gladstone
THE BURNING OF ALEXANDRIA.
It Sounds Like Charming, Bewildering Music, But Nevertheless Seems Like *An Overture From Nero*.

HW November 11, 1882 708

AS OF OLD (THE BRITISH) CAESAR WILL GROW FAT IN EGYPT.

One cartoon complimented James Russell Lowell, now Minister to England, as he knocked the crown off the British Lion's head. The French title translated to: "Shame on him who thinks ill of it" (the motto of the chivalric Order of the Garter). The cartoon must have had special significance for Nast because it was Curtis's arbitrary rejection of Nast's July 1877 mild tweak of Lowell, Curtis's close friend, that led to his previous self-separation from *Harper's*.* It is likely that Nast met Lowell in London at one or more of his numerous dinners with literary, artistic and political celebrities.

By early summer, he was back, enjoying Saratoga and then Morristown. The Nasts and the Grants exchanged visits, the first time he had seen the General since his world tour began six years before. The generous returns on their Grant and Ward investments had to be a prominent topic of conversation. (See next page).[8]

While in Montreal during October, Nast developed pneumonia which prostrated him. It took a vacation in Florida for him to finally regain his health before he returned to Morristown in February 1884.

HW April 15, 1882 240

"HONI SOIT QUI MAL Y PENSE."
The Democratic view of the American Minister's duty at the Court of St. James.

Return to *Harper's*

The Harpers had heard plenty from Nast's supportive readers, and needed to know whether his decision to leave was final. They wanted him back for the upcoming Presidential election, and had replaced stern, financially-oriented John W. with third-generation J. Henry (Harry) to manage the periodicals. Harry was only ten years younger than Nast, they were social friends and their families were close. They met for dinner in September 1883, six months after Nast left and before he became ill. J. Henry wrote him a warm fish-or-cut-bait letter the next day, but Nast deferred a decision.[9]

Dear Nast:

I have thought and worried over what you told me when we separated last night.

I then understood you to say, but I hope my inference is incorrect, that you have concluded to sever your connection with us. I have not since mentioned the matter to any member of the firm, but I think I ought to know what your determination is, for they have now apparently given me charge of the *Weekly*. Nothing has been done as yet to fill the void in that journal which your absence has created, and I consequently feel that if you have irrevocably made up your mind to leave us that we must make some attempt to fill that vacancy. I can't add anything to what I have already said to persuade you to take up your pencil for us, but the *Weekly* must endeavor to forge on again, and if we fail to secure the services of the old-experienced and well-beloved staff who have fought with us through so many successful campaigns, we will, alas, be compelled to hunt around among the untried and uncongenial lesser lights to prepare for the fight which is hard upon us.

I write without consulting anyone, and will look for your answer, I must own, with sad misgivings. I know, however, that whatever decision you may make will be from a conscientious sense of duty, and I remain as ever,

Faithfully yours,
J. Henry.

---

* See p. 440

"Brooklyn Joe" Harper, now serving as managing partner, wrote Nast again in late October, after learning of his illness. More personal visits and letters followed, during which Nast agreed to return when he felt better. The *Weekly* printed an announcement to that effect at year-end, in conjunction with his previously rejected Mormon Christmas cartoon.[10*]

Grant and Ward

In order to raise more capital, Nast sold his Harlem property in early 1883 and invested the $30,000 proceeds with the well-regarded brokerage firm of Grant and Ward. The Grant in the firm was the General's middle son, Ulysses Jr., known as Buck (after the Buckeye state of Ohio where he was born). Buck had graduated from Harvard and Columbia Law School, and was personable, smart and wealthy in his own right.[11]

The Ward was Ferdinand, a native of Geneseo, New York, and a scoundrel and liar who would steal from family, friends, partners and investors without exception or conscience. He did so by running up bills, borrowing, and promising fictitious investment returns, and then refusing to pay or reneging on his commitments. He had personal charm and an almost hypnotic selling ability, but underneath he was a sociopath, totally devoid of any moral sensitivity or responsibility.[12]

HW May 24, 1884 337

FERDINAND WARD

Ferdinand's brother Will roomed with Buck Grant in 1879. Will — talented, honest and generous — introduced Buck to Ferdinand, and on July 1, 1880, the brokerage firm of Grant and Ward was formally established. Ferdinand's objective was to use the name, reputation and aura of Buck's father to attract investors whom he could fleece; he achieved that goal in October 1880, two weeks before Garfield's election.[13] Early on, Ferdinand made clear to Buck that he alone would do all the investing and keep the books.

Ultimately, the Grant family — the General and his three sons — invested almost $2 million with Ward. Each of the Grants was to receive $2,000 monthly until 1884, when it would increase to $3,000.[14] With the Grant family and probably others whom he knew, reportedly getting wealthy, Nast's judgment appeared sound when he put his remaining savings into Grant and Ward and reinvested his unexpectedly large reported dividends in hopes of eventually earning enough to start or buy his own paper.

Ward's working partner was James Fish, President of Marine National Bank, who owned a quarter share and received his monthly dividends in full. Fish, 58, and a lonely widower, socialized with Ferdinand and his wife daily. His bank lent huge sums, not all of them with security, to Grant and Ward at his partner's request. Fish almost certainly was aware that Ward was running a huge Ponzi-scheme, with new money used to pay dividends to previous investors. Many, like Nast, reinvested their huge returns.

Ward sometimes played poker with the General and his wealthy friends including Roscoe Conkling and Nelson Tappan, the City Chamberlain who was New York's top money man; some of them also invested. Tappan made a Tweed-like deal to tap city funds.[15] Both former Mayor William Grace and current Mayor Franklin Edson made large personal investments; Edson had employed Ward for six years as a clerk on the Produce Exchange which he presided over.

In 1883, Ward invented phantom Federal government supply contracts to borrow against; none ever existed. Even Fish, his crooked bank partner, believed they were real and loaned money against them without ever seeing them.[16]

---

* See p. 529

When the inevitable crash came on May 6, 1884, Grant and Ward owed $14.5 million and had less than $60,000 in assets. Fish was out $2 million. Grant's sons lost their homes.[17]

Fish was arrested in May but was free on bail until his trial which took place a year later. He was convicted in June 1885 and sentenced to ten years in prison in Auburn, New York.

Ward's trial didn't begin until four months later, but he was jailed in Ludlow Street — where Boss Tweed had died six years earlier — and then at the much harsher Tombs. He was convicted in late October and sent to Sing Sing prison for an identical ten years.[18] Both men were paroled early for good behavior.

While Nast understandably ignored their trials, *Puck* did not. Bernhard Gillam drew a wonderful barber shop scene shortly after Fish's conviction. Dressed in prison garb, Fish had just left the barber's chair while Ward — still in civilian clothes — appeared to be wary about entering, although the confident barber was stirring his shaving cup. As Ward's October trial was set to begin, Frederick Opper referred to the Delaroche painting and cast Ward as *The "Little Napoleon of Wall Street" in Exile*.

PUCK July 8, 1885

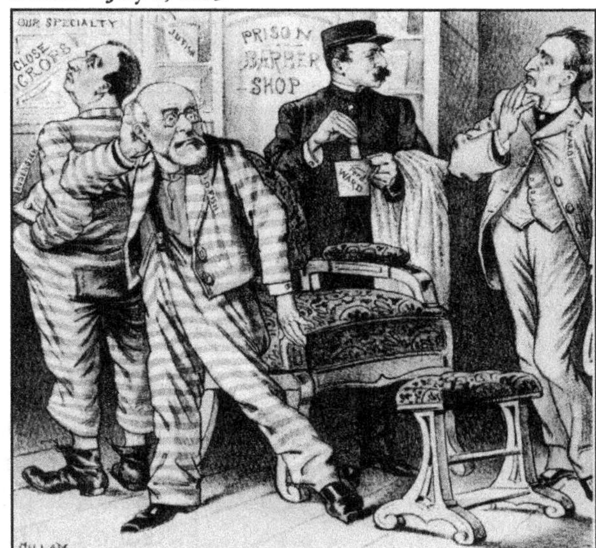

THE PRISON BARBER SHOP.

PUCK October 21, 1885

THE "LITTLE NAPOLEON OF WALL STREET" IN EXILE.
The Friends of His "Flush" Days Don't Care to Know Him Now.

Nast's Anguish

Harper's initially referred to the crash as "Monaco on Wall Street." The following week, Nast drew an emotional cartoon which, figuratively if not literally, portrayed an anguished Grant and himself. Against a background of Wall Street and Trinity Church, it depicted both large and small investors entangled in ticker tape and about to fall into a wastebasket.

HW May 31, 1884 356

THE TAPE THAT ENTANGLES BOTH LARGE AND SMALL.

Nast never published another cartoon related to his loss. However, he laid out his internal torment in an unpublished storyboard of *The Old-Old Story*.[19]

Morristown and Morris Township Library

He also depicted his emotional agony in two rough drawings in a very private sketchbook (not a scrapbook), almost certainly intended for visualizing his innermost thoughts, and not for anyone else's eyes. One depicted Sallie beating his own hapless self with a broom, while a stupefied figure (probably Grant) looked on; the other showed Sallie crying, still holding the broom.[20]

Author's Collection

Thomas Nast was a proud, proud man — a true egotist. Now his pride surrendered to a bad fall, and his inner self emerged in his own private reflections. They were a forerunner of both his internal and external decline over the last 18 years of his life.

Grant's Last Year

Ward's principal victim, of course, was General Grant whom he used and abused to the bitter end. Grant trusted his friends to a fault — Orville Babcock was a prime example — and he had even gone the extra mile to borrow a last-day $150,000 from William Vanderbilt at Ward's urging; he had pledged most of his assets as security for the loan. His despondency was worsened by the subsequent discovery that he had incurable cancer of his tongue and throat. Although his constant cigars were the primary culprit, the public blamed Ward for contributing to the declining health and ultimate death of its national hero.

In January 1885, Vanderbilt demonstrated his regard for Grant by proposing to the General that his many public awards and mementos — which the railroad tycoon now possessed — be presented to the Federal Government. Grant accepted, but turned down Vanderbilt's further offers to cancel his $150,000 debt, pay off his real estate mortgages, and set up a trust fund for his wife Julia.[21]

Also, as 1885 dawned, a widespread movement was underway in Congress to restore General Grant to his retired rank in the Army and enable him to receive a $5,000 annual pension. However, there was opposition in the House, and the Retirement Bill didn't pass until March 3, the last day Congress was in session. President Arthur signed the bill as his final official act and his successor, Grover Cleveland, signed Grant's commission as one of his first. Nast's pre-passage efforts in several cartoons undoubtedly helped.

HW March 7, 1885 160

1862 —FEB. 16— 1885

VICTORY FOR OUR HOUSE. SHAME AND HUMILIATION ON OUR HOUSE.

HW April 11, 1885 232-3

OUR ULYSSES.

April 9, 1865—A Never-To-Be-Forgotten Deed.

HW March 14, 1885 176

JUST BEFORE THE CURTAIN WENT DOWN.

A month later, Nast commemorated the twentieth anniversary of Appomattox with a double-page tribute, his last of 125 cartoons portraying Grant while he was alive; all but one were positive.* **Notably, none of Nast's post-1880 cartoons referenced Grant's Presidency.**

* See p. 370 for the exception

Grant determined to write and publish his memoirs in order to pay off the loan to Vanderbilt, replace the capital he had lost and provide sufficient income for his wife Julia to live comfortably. Working incessantly through pain and failing health, he barely finished his two-volume *Personal Memoirs* before he died on July 23, 1885. Thanks to the generosity and entrepreneurship of Mark Twain who published them, 300,000 sets were sold and his estate received $420,000 (about $10 million today). Nast was given one of 25 copies earmarked by the General for his special friends.[22]

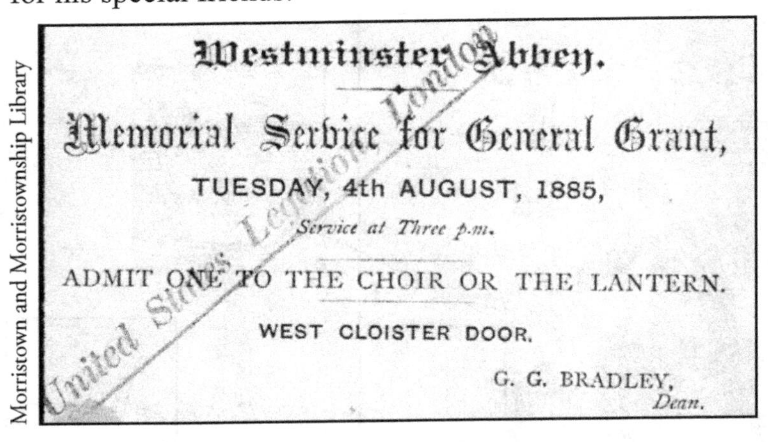
Westminster Abbey.

Memorial Service for General Grant,

TUESDAY, 4th AUGUST, 1885,

Service at Three p.m.

ADMIT ONE TO THE CHOIR OR THE LANTERN.

WEST CLOISTER DOOR.

G. G. BRADLEY, Dean.

United States Legation London

Morristown and Morristownship Library

During the last seven months of 1884, Nast focused on his bitter anti-Blaine nomination and election campaigns, while his hero suffered and wrote. Grant was living in his comfortable East 66th Street home, so it is likely that Nast visited him on occasion. Six weeks before he died, Grant was moved on a special train to Mount McGregor near Saratoga, where the cooler air made it easier to breathe. Nast never saw his friend and idol again. He was in London when Grant died and saved the ticket for his memorial service at Westminster Abbey in a scrapbook.

After Grant's death, Nast eulogized him with another reference to Appomattox, as Columbia mourned. This was Nast's final tribute to his idol. It was a huge double loss — both friend and fortune — and, along with his sliding career, understandably deepened his depression and outlook on life.

Nast couldn't resist one last shot at Jeff Davis who still had four years to live. His apparent image was on the front of Grant's shield in both cartoons, portrayed as the Devil with horns.

HW August 1, 1885 504-5

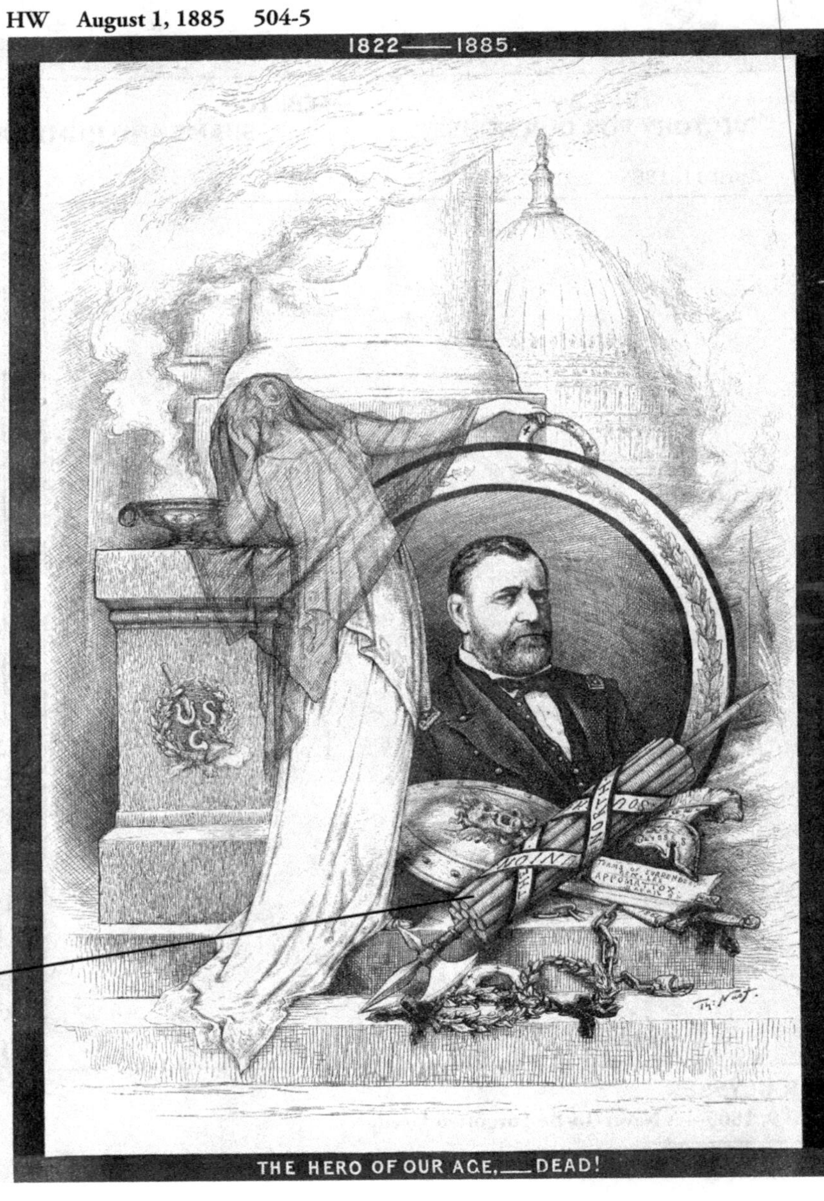

THE HERO OF OUR AGE,—DEAD!

Chapter 42
The Election of 1884: Blaine

Nast's Return

As election season dawned, the Harpers were finally able to celebrate the return of their "missing link."

HARPER'S WEEKLY.

NEW YORK, SATURDAY, MARCH 8, 1884.

THOMAS NAST.

The readers of HARPER'S WEEKLY *will extend a cordial welcome to* MR. THOMAS NAST *on his return to his old field of labor. They will be glad to learn that his sojourn in Europe, and his subsequent visit to the genial shores of Florida, have resulted in the complete restoration of his health, and that he re-enters the arena with renewed energy and zeal.*

HW March 8, 1884 149 C

THE SACRED ELEPHANT.
This Animal Is Sure To Win, If It Is Only Kept Pure And Clean, And Has *Not Too Heavy A Load To Carry.*

The cover said it all as the artist greeted the sacred Republican Party Elephant. The vacant chair on top was awaiting a nominee who was pure and clean, and didn't have too heavy a load to carry. That candidate definitely was *not* the betting favorite, James Gillespie Blaine.

However, Nast knew that Blaine was likely to win and — if that happened — he could no longer support the Republican Party. Consequently, he portrayed himself as the tiniest and least consequential figure in any of his full-page cartoons.

The Republican Convention

The Convention began on June 3 in Chicago. Shortly before, *New York Times* publisher George Jones announced that his paper would not support Blaine if he received the nomination. He asked George William Curtis and the Harpers to join him, but they held off until the candidate was known.

Curtis attended the Convention as Chairman of New York's delegation — a compromise choice between Blaine's Half-breeds and Roscoe Conkling's Stalwarts. Naively, he thought he might be able to stem the inevitable Blaine tide. When Blaine won on the fourth ballot over President Chester Arthur, Curtis acquiesced in making the nomination unanimous. He also served on the committee that selected Illinois Senator John Logan as his running mate. After Curtis returned and announced he would not support Blaine for whom he had voted, he and *Harper's Weekly* drew harsh criticism and thousands of cancellations from angry and disgusted Republicans.[2]

During the 1880 campaign when Blaine had battled ex-President Ulysses Grant for the nomination, and James Garfield won as the compromise candidate, Nast attacked Blaine as "The Plumed Knight," as well as the "Magnetic Man" whose railroad securities scandal and subsequent lying about it stuck to him.* The *Times* declaration probably spurred Nast to turn his March prediction into fact with a prepared-in-advance and post-dated cartoon that was available about the time the Convention was over.

In addition to his sticky scandal, Blaine's "magnet" also referred to his widely known personal magnetism or charisma. Here, it was almost breaking the Republican Elephant's back, thereby crushing its Civil Service Reform plank.

HW June 14, 1884 388

TOO HEAVY TO CARRY.

* See p. 483

Mugwumps

The breakaway Republicans — both positively and derisively called Mugwumps — formed a virtual Independent Party which backed Democrat Grover Cleveland's candidacy. Mugwump purportedly was an Algonquin Indian word for chief; Republicans scornfully redefined the term as a partisan fence-sitter with his "mug" on one side and his "wump" on the other.

The initial Mugwump meeting was held at J. Henry Harper's home on June 17. George William Curtis presided, Nast received one of about 150 invitations and probably attended; Carl Schurz took the lead. For the first time in four Presidential elections going back to 1868, Nast and Curtis were in total unanimity. Even Schurz, whom Nast disliked and had tormented as the Liberal Republican leader in 1872, were spokes in the same wheel.*

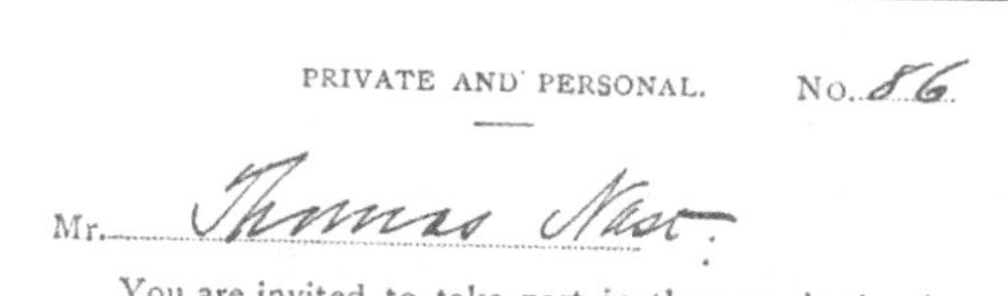

PRIVATE AND PERSONAL. No. 86

Mr. Thomas Nast.

You are invited to take part in the consultation in regard to the action necessitated by the results of the Republican Convention, to be held at the residence of J. Henry Harper, Esq., ~~262~~ 269 Madison Avenue, on Tuesday evening, June 17th, at eight o'clock.

As the consultation is private, you are asked to hand this card to the attendant at the door, signing it on the back. If it be not possible for you to be present, kindly return this card at once, with any expression of your opinion, to George Haven Putnam, 27 West 23d Street, New York.

While Nast was reconciled to Cleveland's candidacy, he actually preferred President Arthur. "He had given the country an honest and very respectable administration, and I thought it the proper thing to nominate him next. Blaine it was impossible to support."[1]

A week after the *Too Heavy to Carry* cartoon, he depicted himself walking away from the Republican ticket — with Blaine as a "Dainty Dish" of plumed crow.

In addition to Jones, other prominent Mugwumps included *Nation* editor Edwin L. Godkin, *Evening Post* editor Horace White, and Reverend Henry Ward Beecher. The *Daily Graphic* harpooned Nast, Curtis and Godkin a week after they formally organized.

HW June 21, 1884 395

PLUMED CROW.

THE NEW SALVATION ARMY

The Devil-Teasers After Diabolus Blaine And On The Happy Road To The New Political Jerusalem.

* See p. 302-303

Mugwump vilification was intensified because Republican Party leaders knew that a Cleveland victory probably would result in more Civil Service Reform than the Pendleton Act of 1883 provided.* Expanding the Act to include more than the 13,000 Federal employees currently covered, would further restrict patronage, the lifeblood of the party system.

Curtis had been the foremost proponent of Civil Service Reform for at least 14 years, so he, along with Schurz, led the Mugwump movement. The intellectual Curtis, in particular, was depicted as effeminate by Frank Beard in the Republican comic *The Judge*, which reveled in it. Below he was identifiable by his corset — also conveying uptightness — while Beecher, Schurz and Jones were labeled. (Curtis was pictured as a seduced woman on the issue's cover. See p. 578). All four were hooded and hanging from a limb, as ominous vultures awaited.

August 16, 1884

Left to Right: Beecher, Schurz, Jones, Curtis

---

* See p. 526

Civil Service

Curtis editorialized that "the personality of the candidates will be more vigorously scrutinized than ever before because there is no great supreme issue of national peril or national policy which will engross the attention of the people, and this scrutiny invites defeat."[3] While Blaine's corruption and false testimony in a railroad securities scandal was Nast's and the Mugwumps' overriding objection to Blaine's potential Presidency, they also decried his record as a spoilsman who rejected Civil Service reform.

HW August 9, 1884 525

HIS LETTER OF ACCEPTANCE.
J.B. (*devilish sly*). "Civil Service Reform! I just *love it!* In fact, I'm a regular *masher* on that subject."

Guano

Another reason the Mugwumps disliked Blaine was his imperialist foreign policy during his brief tenure as Garfield's Secretary of State in 1881. "Jingo Jim" as his critics referred to him, resigned after Arthur took office; the new President soon reversed Blaine's initiatives in Latin America and the Pacific.

One of Blaine's aggressive actions came back to haunt him in 1884. He had hoped to mediate a territorial dispute between weak Peru and stronger Chile. In the process, he improperly pressed the American Minister to Peru to support a questionable $50 million dollar claim of a dubious American citizen to valuable guano and nitrate deposits in Peru. His predecessor, William Evarts, had rejected the proposition.

The claimant's lawyer, Stephen Elkins, a former West Virginia Congressman, was not only a close friend of Blaine, but also had given him valuable advice on profitable investments. When Congress investigated the 1881 circumstances, Blaine was severely criticized. Guano became a secondary scandal during his campaign, although far behind the railroad securities in importance. Elkins became his campaign manager.

Tariffs

Blaine did his best to focus his campaign on the assertion that protective tariffs were *the* key issue of national importance. He reversed his 1880 support for "Tariffs for Revenue Only," and now promoted "High Tariffs Protect the Working Man." The other side of that issue — protecting monopolies — became increasingly relevant in the public mind, and Nast hammered it home as the campaign progressed.

Nast taunted Blaine's claim of helping working men and farmers with his protective tariffs. He told Blaine directly that he was full of guano when it came to helping farmers.

HW August 2, 1884 508

POOH POOHING MOTHER EARTH AND THE TOILER.
Western Farmer. "So it is your protection, and your twenty years in Congress, that make the soil so rich."

HW October 11, 1884 663 C

STOP TICKLING *US*, AND ANSWER WITHOUT DODGING.
American Labor. "Does public plunder for private gains protect American labor?"

HW August 9, 1884 523

THE "GREAT AMERICAN" GAME OF PUBLIC OFFICE FOR PRIVATE GAIN.
This is not "*Protection*"; this is *very* "*Free Trade*" with the people's money.

Twenty Years of Congress

Blaine was proud of his Congressional achievements. He was elected to the House in 1863, served three terms as speaker (1869-1875), and became a Senator late in 1876.

After he resigned from Arthur's cabinet, Blaine took time off to write his memoirs: *Twenty Years of Congress: 1861-1881* (Lincoln to Garfield). It was published in two volumes, the first in the spring of 1884 — timed to coincide with the start of his Presidential campaign — and the second in 1886. (Earning Blaine $200,000-300,000.[4])

Nast used the title to taunt Blaine by tagging his carpetbag with "Twenty Years of ______," just as he had labeled Horace Greeley with "What I Know About ______" twelve years before.* On occasion, he also put Tweed's defiant "What are you going to do about it?" into Blaine's mouth, and ultimately brought the ghost of Tweed himself into the picture for direct comparison.

HW June 28, 1884 420

VERY DEMOCRATIC.
J.B. "Well—what are you going to do about it?

HW September 27, 1884 627 C

GRAVE REGRETS.
The Spirit Of Tweed. "If I hadn't been *too previous*, and had only belonged to the Republican party, and had been a big enough boss to get myself nominated, what a brilliant, intense American statesman I might have been!"
J.G.B. "And besides, I had the Star Route Defender, Bob Ingersoll, christen me the *Plumed Knight*, and have the *New York Tribune* defend me *through thick and thin*."

Blaine's Railroad Deal

Born in 1830 and raised in Pennsylvania, Blaine went to Kentucky at 17 after graduating from Washington and Jefferson College. He married Harriet Stanwood in June 1850. In 1854, he moved to Augusta, Maine, where her family had roots, to become publisher and co-owner of the *Kennebec Journal*. Harriet's brothers Jacob and Eben helped finance the purchase.

Jacob Stanwood established himself as an entrepreneur in Boston, where one of his associates was Warren Fisher, a railroad contractor. James Mulligan served as Fisher's bookkeeper, and helped Stanwood as well. When Mulligan and Stanwood had a dispute at some point in the seventies, Blaine arbitrated in favor of his brother-in-law, and the embittered clerk quit or was fired.

---

* See p. 296-297

Fisher had a contract to build the Little Rock and Fort Smith Railroad, which was to run, with its planned Southern extension via the El Paso route, through "the richest land of the Southwest," as Blaine described it.[5] In early 1869, Speaker Blaine pushed a bill enabling a government land grant to the railroad. Apparently, he had no known specific incentive to do so other than the normal course of legislation.

However, after the bill passed, Blaine saw an opportunity for himself to make money by acting as an agent to sell the railroad's bonds. Consequently, he wrote Fisher with a proposition: He would sell $130,000 of bonds and, in return, would receive $130,000 of land grant bonds and $32,500 of first mortgage bonds as his commission.

In the letter, Blaine assured Fisher of his capability: ***I do not feel that I shall prove a dead-head in the enterprise if I once embark on it. I see various channels in which I can be useful***. Blaine got his deal, and Nast and other cartoonists subsequently got their campaign ammunition.

HW August 16, 1884 542

"THE FOREMOST MAN OF THE TIME."—*Blaineism.*
"I do not feel that I shall prove a dead-head."

HW August 30, 1884 569

THE KNIGHT OF THE MONEY-BAG.

Initially, Blaine probably was unable to sell the securities. As a final resort in October 1869, he approached the Cooke brothers with an urgent proposition for them to pay him $91,500 cash in exchange for $252,500 in various Little Rock and Fort Smith securities. He told Henry Cooke he could help get a Congressional subsidy for their Northern Pacific Railroad (which did happen seven months later),* and met with Jay Cooke in early November. Jay said his timing was off and turned Blaine down, but did make him a personal loan at some point thereafter.

In a November 10, 1869 last gasp letter to Jay (which came to light many decades later), Blaine virtually incriminated himself: "Are you not willing to aid me when you can do so with profit to yourself at the same time? *Just how your subscription to the enterprise will aid me, I need not explain. Sufficient that it is so. Your participation in the future would be of no benefit to me*."[6]

Ultimately, Blaine sold the Little Rock and Fort Smith bonds to friends and acquaintances in Maine. However, the deal backfired when the bonds lost most of their value within two years. Blaine was concerned about his friends, as well as his reputation, so he asked wealthy railroader Tom Scott to bail them out as a favor to him. Scott was president of the Union Pacific for a year beginning in April 1871, and then took over the Texas Pacific in July 1872. Complying with Blaine's request, Scott bought $75,000 of the Maine investors bonds for $64,000 — a price far in excess of their current value — and parked them in the Union Pacific's treasury; his bailout occurred within weeks of the House passing a bill subsidizing his railroad. Blaine was never asked to redeem the bonds, nor was his connection to them known for about five years.

---

* See p. 366-367

The Mulligan Letters — First Edition

In April 1876 — two months before the Republican nominating convention — the House Judiciary Committee undertook an investigation of the Union Pacific. In addition to Scott, outside witnesses included Fisher and Mulligan, who brought a number of letters from Blaine to Fisher that their writer believed had been destroyed. Scott and Fisher cleared Blaine to the Committee, but Mulligan testified truthfully about Blaine's commission of $162,500 in free bonds.

Immediately after the hearing was abruptly adjourned at Blaine's instigation, he confronted Mulligan in a hotel room, asked to look at the letters while promising to return them, and did so. In a follow-up meeting, Blaine pocketed the letters to Mulligan's consternation, and stormed out. The next day, he read parts of them to the Committee and a packed gallery. He ignored chronology (1864 to 1876) and omitted unfavorable parts, but he survived to stay on as a Senator while losing the nomination to Hayes.* On April 24, Curtis editorialized "that *in the absence of other evidence*, the speech of Mr. Blaine was a complete vindication."

As mentioned earlier, the Mulligan Letters were also an issue in 1880 when, after a battle with Grant's followers, Garfield won as a compromise candidate.** As Nast had emphasized in 1876, the Mulligan Letters were the essence of the dominant scandal sticking to the "magnetic" Blaine.

HW May 8, 1880 300

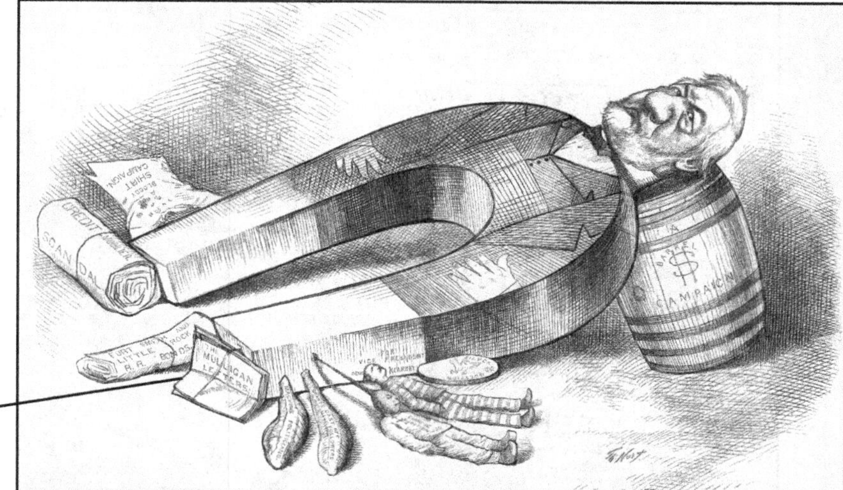

THE "MAGNETIC" BLAINE; OR, A VERY HEAVY "LOAD"-STONE FOR THE REPUBLICAN PARTY TO CARRY.

The Mulligan Letters — Second Edition

On August 5, 1884, Schurz gave a 49-page speech in Brooklyn, claiming that the Mulligan letters by themselves should disqualify Blaine. His scathing tirade was widely distributed in print.[7]

A month later, Schurz was contacted by a Boston law firm which had additional Blaine-Fisher correspondence belonging to its client James Mulligan. After delegated Mugwumps met with Mulligan and inspected the letters, they were published on the front page of the *Times* and in other papers on September 15, seven weeks before the election. Blaine acknowledged their authenticity, claimed they reflected his integrity, and encouraged Republican newspapers around the country to reprint them — consequently reviving the public's interest.

However, one letter marked confidential blew up in Blaine's face. It had been written eight days *before* he made his melodramatic defense on the floor of the House on April 16, 1876, reading parts of the original batch. It asked Warren Fisher to do him "a very great favor" by copying and immediately returning a draft of an enclosed letter from Fisher to Blaine distorting the facts and exonerating the candidate.

---

* See p. 406

** See p. 483

Blaine's transmittal letter closed: ***The letter is strictly true, is honorable to you and to me, and will stop the mouths of slanderers at once. Regard this letter as strictly confidential . . . Kind regards to Mrs. Fisher.***

Sincerely,
(Burn this letter) J.G. Blaine

Fisher neither replied nor burned the two letters. They provided fuel to Nast and other cartoonists, as well as to Cleveland marchers carrying torch-lit paper signs while chanting: "Burn this letter. Burn this letter. Kind regards to Mrs. Fisher."[8] The next issue of *Harper's Weekly* included six Nast cartoons and Blaine's game-changing letters.

HW September 27, 1884 637

SLIPPERY JIM DICTATING HIS LETTER OF EXONERATION TO HIMSELF.
[See Letter in Supplement.]

The *Tribune*

Whitelaw Reid's *Tribune* was Blaine's most prominent newspaper supporter. Nast portrayed Reid going down for the count when hit by the second edition of the Mulligan letters. In a more prosaic cartoon, Blaine's carpetbag was full of both bonds and the letters as Mulligan rebuffed him.

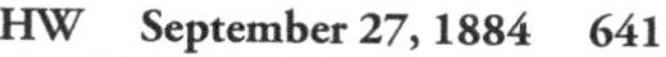
HW September 27, 1884 641

KNOCKED OUT OF NEWS FOR TWENTY-FOUR HOURS.

HW September 27, 1884 642

BRAZENING IT OUT.

J.G.B. "So you will give them to the public, will you? Well, *there is not a word in them that is nor entirely consistent with the most scrupulous integrity and honor.*"

Reid had joined the *Tribune* as managing editor in 1868, and bought a controlling interest after Greeley died in 1872 with capital loaned by Jay Gould. (In return, Gould received positive press and, conceivably, the ability to promote stocks up or down in its columns.) In 1881, Reid married the daughter of a wealthy financier, and subsequently bought out minority stockholders and paid off what, if anything, remained of his debt to Gould.

Reid and Blaine were close personal friends and the *Tribune* became Blaine's mouthpiece as early as the 1880 election. Blaine often inserted anonymous squibs and news items into its columns and used pseudonyms in letters attacking Republicans who disagreed with him.

However, the *Tribune's* labor relations contributed to Blaine's defeat in New York State. In 1883, when his printers as a unit joined the Typographical Union Number Six, Reid replaced them with strikebreakers. The printers' newspaper, the *Boycotter*, told its 3.500 members to "Boycott the *Tribune* and James G. Blaine." If half of them — who otherwise would have supported their ex-employer's candidate — did so, they would have been the difference in Blaine's 1,047 vote loss in New York.

HW November 15, 1884 761

CAMPAIGN MUD.
"The *Tribune* lies, but never surrenders."—
N.Y. Times, Nov. 7.

Nast depicted Reid fifteen times during the 1884 campaign, culminating with his "scissors" cartoon appearing the week after the election; Reid was drowning — going under for the last time — still supporting Blaine. (See p. 439 for an explanation of the "scissors" tale.)

The Tattooed Man

Almost two months before his nomination, *Puck's* Bernhard Gillam stole Nast's thunder by indelibly marking Blaine with tattoos of his various scandals. Using Blaine himself as a signboard became *the* outstanding symbol of the campaign as Gillam repeatedly displayed him in sophisticated color cartoons worthy of Nast at his best.

Gillam began in April with *The National Dime Museum*, where about two dozen political aspirants and influencers were depicted. In addition to the Mulligan Letters, Blaine's tattoos included Guano Statesmanship, Northern Pacific Bonds, Bribery, Bluster, and Anti-Chinese Demagoguery.* Nast's symbolic roots were present in the Tammany Tiger and in Tilden as a mummy. (Just as they had been when Gillam was at *Harper's Weekly* in 1880 to attack Winfield Hancock in the last month of that campaign).**

President Arthur was a snake charmer, Boss Kelly a trained pig, Senator John Logan the wild man of Borneo, and potential Vice Presidential candidates Robert Lincoln, a non-plumed helmeted knight in striped red shorts. Other potential candidates included Ben Butler, William Evarts, David Davis, Roscoe Conkling, and Curtis favorite George Edmunds.

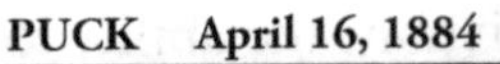
PUCK April 16, 1884

THE NATIONAL DIME-MUSEUM—WILL BE RUN DURING THE PRESIDENTIAL CAMPAIGN.

* See p. 465
** See p. 502

Phelps

Congressman William Walter Phelps of New Jersey was a wealthy dilettante and former minority stockholder in the *Tribune*, and another of Blaine's closest personal friends. Phelps had sold Blaine the land at Dupont Circle on which he built his Washington home.

On April 27, Phelps published a letter in the Sunday *Tribune* in which he defended Blaine from the impact of the Mulligan letters, partially by accusing honest Senator Edmunds of a similar railroad transaction. Edmunds immediately responded, Phelps backtracked, and *Harper's* published both letters.[9]

Gillam responded with *"Love's Labor's Lost."* Phelps with sandpaper, and Reid with Borax and a scrubbing brush, were unsuccessfully trying to remove Blaine's tattoos as he winced in pain.

PUCK May 7, 1884

"LOVE'S LABOR'S LOST."

Nast's references to Phelps generally were trite and unimaginative, illustrating the widening gap between him and the *Puck* artists. However, Phelps was a well known horticulturist (for the gardens at his New Jersey estate), so Nast's floral references were relevant jabs.

HW July 26, 1884 489

SOUND POLITICAL ARGUMENTS.
William Walter Phelps (*the Jersey Lily*). "I say, my dear boy, is there anything more to be done, after that letter of mine, in Blaine's defense?"
Whitelaw Reid (the *New York Daisy*). "Oh yes, my dear Bangtry; we must call those who do not protect Mr. Blaine's record, *Free-traders*, and *Britishers*, and Dudes, and all that sort of thing, you know."

HW August 2, 1884 505

POLITICAL ENCHANTMENT.
Sir Plumed Knight. "So sweet and peaceful!"
Sir William Walter Bangtry. "It's too, too utter! Just let me put in a 'skeeter,' so there may be a little sting in it."
The "Tribune" Daisy. "Washington or Lincoln never cooked anything so delicious as this."

HW September 6, 1884 590

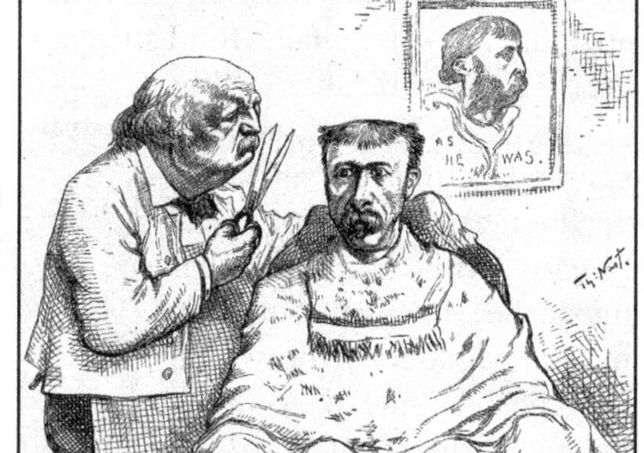

FUSION IN NEW JERSEY.
Ben, The Barber. "Those who ape the British Aristocracy in this country wear clothes which are imported, can only be waited upon by British servants, ***and cut their whiskers, even, British fashion,*** so as to appear un-American as possible."
Wm Walter P. Bangtry. "Yes, yes, but please don't cut my bang off; and must I wealiy wear homespun clothes?"

When the Mulligan letters were first exposed in 1876, Schurz commented that "Blaine had wallowed in spoils like a rhinoceros in an African pool."[10] Reid and Phelps tried to defend their candidate by claiming his letters were no concern of the public. This time, Nast was more creative.

HW October 11, 1884 674

GLORYING IN THEIR SHAME.
The Thick-Skinned Animal Going Around The Circle.

Just before Blaine was nominated in Chicago, 10,000 copies of Gillam's latest masterpiece appeared locally in *Puck.* To make sure that it had the desired impact on the delegates, it was re-printed on large broadsheets and distributed in the hotels. Retrospectively, it ranks with the best and most influential political cartoons in any American election campaign.

Gillam's inspiration was Jean-Léon Gérôme's 1861 scandalous painting *Phryne Before the Areopagus*. (An ancient Greek Tribunal). Reid stripped away Blaine's cloak to reveal his tattoos as well as a magnetic pad, while the 21 recognizable tribunal members gasped, smiled, smirked, grimaced or threw up their hands. "Black Jack" Logan (with his handlebar mustache) laughed out loud in the second row; he would become Blaine's running mate. Curtis couldn't look and turned away in disgust (far right).

PUCK June 4, 1884

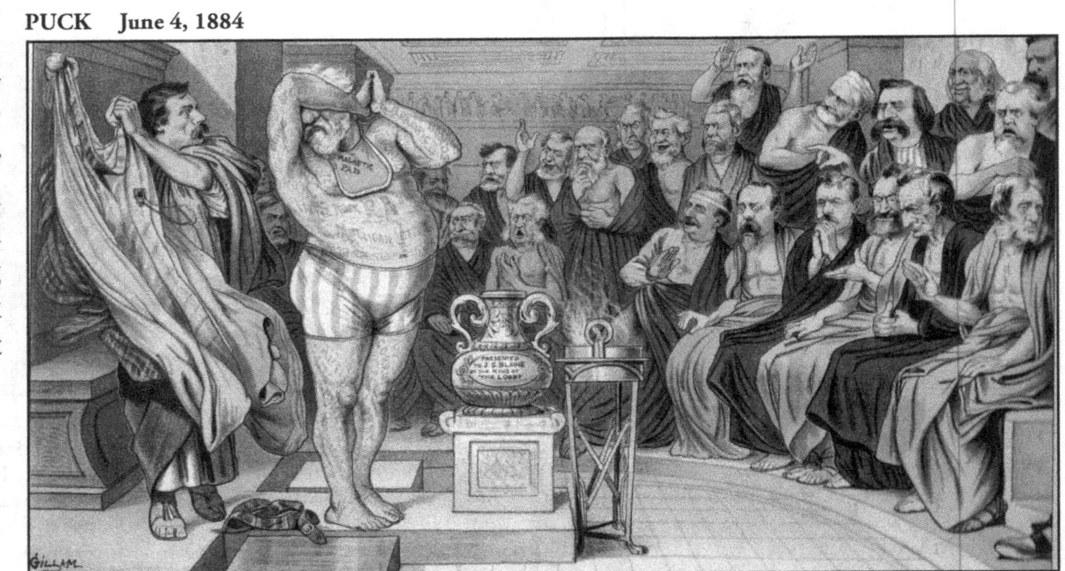

PHRYNE BEFORE THE CHICAGO TRIBUNAL.
Ardent Advocate—"Now, Gentlemen, don't make any mistake in your decision! Here's Purity and Magnetism for you—can't be beat!"

The Judge (pro-Blaine) quickly countered with two weak efforts. The first showed Blaine laughing at a *Tattooed Man* cartoon. The second compared him to Garfield, Lincoln and Washington — all with tattoos but without writing on them. However, Lincoln held the Emancipation Proclamation and Washington the Declaration of Independence. Blue boxer shorts were featured in both.

LET THOSE LAUGH WHO WIN.

THE JUDGE June 28, 1884

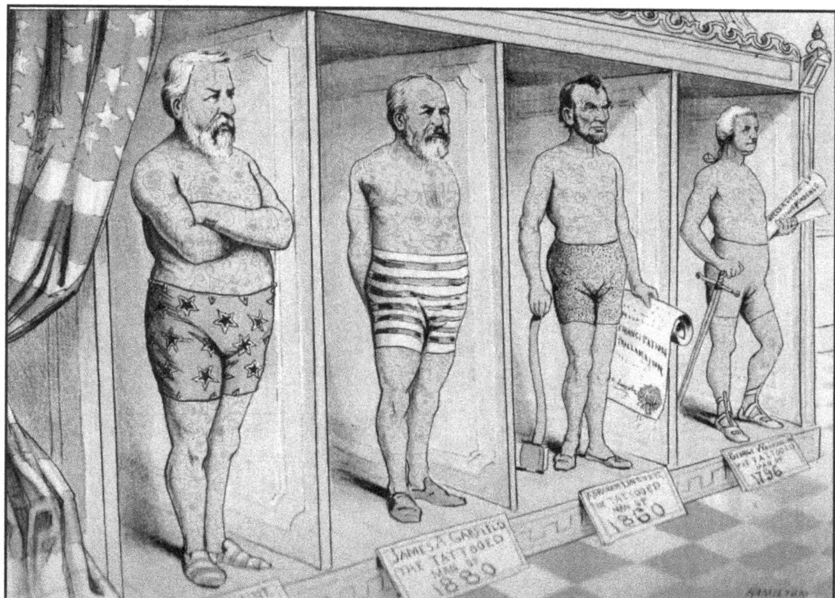

MEN WHOM THE AMERICAN PEOPLE HAVE LEARNED TO ADMIRE HAVE BEEN TATTOOED.

In between *The Judge* cartoons, Gillam's boss, Joseph Keppler, adopted and built on the tattooed man. His initial effort depicted "Republican Revolt" as *The Writing on the Wall*. Blaine, wearing a cabbage leaf (symbol of petty theft) for a hat, shielded himself with the *Tribune*, as his backers — with Reid gesticulating in the middle — were in an uproar. "Black Jack" Logan, dressed as an Indian, was at his side. William Vanderbilt, Jay Gould and Cyrus Field were in front of a bowl of "Monopoly Stew." Robert Ingersoll, the man who dubbed Blaine "The Plumed Knight" at the 1876 Convention, was at the far right.

The Biblical analogy referred to King Belshazzar's sumptuous feast for royalty at which a hand appeared out of nowhere to write strange words on the wall. The prophet Daniel interpreted them as a promise of divine judgment on the King who died that night. Belshazzar's feast would be the subject of another cartoon by a new artist in a renovated daily newspaper — appearing just before the election — which was instrumental in Blaine's defeat.

PUCK June 18, 1884

THE WRITING ON THE WALL

A month later, Keppler showed Blaine losing his presidential race against time and his tattooed shadow while his dismayed friends watched. Phelps was peeping out of Blaine's tent pleading with Reid — carrying a bucket of whitewash and his *Tribune* — to do something; Reid, looking helpless, had no answers. One of his supporters appeared to be waving a white handkerchief of surrender as Stephen Elkins, his wealthy campaign manager, tried to pull it out of his hand. *Puck* continued to beat the anti-monopoly drum, so wreaths from Gould, Field and Sage hung on Blaine's tent.

PUCK July 30, 1884

HE CAN'T BEAT HIS OWN RECORD.
Chorus of Friends—"Go in, Jim—brace up! Can't you do any better than that?"

Clean Shirt

Blaine had been know for raising the bloody shirt issue when he successfully fought against pardoning Jeff Davis. In a long speech to Congress in January 1876, Blaine didn't exclude him as the "head and front of the rebellion," but solely because "he was the author, knowingly, deliberately, guiltily of the great crime of Andersonville." [11]

In 1880, Nast told him it was "the only thing you have" in his unsuccessful bid for the nomination. The *Weekly* reprinted the cartoon as one of several anti-Blaine reprises in 1884.

HW June 5, 1880 353 C

"THE PLUMED KNIGHT."
Blaine, "please keep your shirt on"—
(it's the only thing you have).

Now that he was the candidate, Nast added a clean shirt to Blaine's 1884 wardrobe, replacing the old bloody shirt. However, his new shirt was on upside down as Reid tried to adjust it.

HW June 28, 1884 405

A ROARING FARCE—THE PLUMED KNIGHT IN THE CLEAN SHIRT.
Trying It On.
Whitelaw Reid (*to audience*). "Ladies and gentlemen, allow me to introduce to you our next—"
J.G.N. (*behind the curtain*). "Wait a minute! *There's something wrong!*"

HW July 2, 1884 489

MAKING THE BEST OF IT.
Whitelaw Reid. "I'll fix it so that no one will notice it, and make it all right in to-morrow's *Tribune*. Washington and Lincoln *always wore their shirts this way.*"

Blaine thought he had a chance to pick up some electoral votes from the Solid South, especially in West Virginia (which had some slaves but had split off from Virginia during the Civil War), where his manager Elkins and other coal and iron pro-tariff businessmen were based. During the two weeks he spent touring Ohio, he did spend some time in neighboring West Virginia, which also voted in October. He won in Ohio but lost West Virginia and his bid to crack the South. Immediately, he reversed course, donned the bloody shirt, and attacked the ex-Confederates who were intimidating potential black Republican voters.

HW October 18, 1884 685

THE CLEAN SHIRT—A BAD FIT.
Sir Blaine. "I haven't felt so uncomfortable for twenty years. Ever since I put this on I've had to defend myself. Oh, give me back my old shirt!"
Hired Editor. "Patience, my dear boss. Washington and Lincoln always put on the bloody shirt for the last week of the campaign—just too late for the brigadier-generals to hear of it.

HW November 1, 1884 721

THE LAST WEEK OF THE CELEBRATED BREAKDOWN.
Richard Is Himself Again, In His Bloody Shirt.

Chapter 43
The Election of 1884: The Other Candidates

Flashback

When Grover Cleveland ran for Governor of New York in 1882, both Nast and Curtis strongly supported him — the first time that they endorsed a Democrat for major office. Tammany Hall and Irving Hall — the two wings of the New York City Democrats — actively opposed him.* Those alignments didn't change two years later, but the internecine struggle among Democratic factions grew even more bitter, now that it was on a national level.

When Nast returned to *Harper's* in the spring of 1884, he picked up where he left off in 1882 by pummeling Boss Kelly, while praising Cleveland. He also had a new local hero, 25-year old Theodore Roosevelt, whom he portrayed for the first time — without caricature. State Assemblyman Roosevelt was minority leader of the Assembly and active in Civil Service reform. However, Roosevelt campaigned for Blaine in October, and Nast — disappointed — didn't refer to him again before leaving the *Weekly*.

HW April 19, 1884 249

REFORM WITHOUT BLOODSHED.
Governor Cleveland And Theodore Roosevelt At Their Good Work.

HW May 10, 1884 293 C

OUR NEW WATCHMAN, ROOSEVELT.
Our Political "Boss and Henchman" Must Go.

---

* See p. 534-536.

Tilden

There was early talk about re-running the 1876 Democratic ticket of Samuel Tilden and Thomas Hendricks. Hendricks liked that idea because of Tilden's frail health. At 70, Tilden tottered on a cane, had a useless arm, and spoke in whispers. He knew he was dying from the effects of a second stroke earlier in the year, and withdrew by letter on June 10, a month before the Democratic Convention. Nast quoted his statement in a cover cartoon, as Tammany (Kelly) and Irving Hall sank his symbolic sarcophagus beneath the waves, while the Democratic Party ship foundered.

HW June 21, 1884 389 C

"I OUGHT NOT TO ASSUME A TASK WHICH I HAVE NOT THE PHYSICAL STRENGTH TO CARRY THROUGH."—(Tilden's Declination.)

Nast followed with a pair of cartoons depicting the two factions achieving harmony by splitting their patronage grab bag.

HW June 21, 1884 404

NEW YORK DEMOCRATIC HARMONY.
One to the Other: "HALVES!—I Mean—Harmony."

HW June 28, 1884 419

PEACE AND HARMONY AMONG NEW YORK DEMOCRATS (?)

Cleveland

The Democratic Convention opened on July 8 in Chicago. Curtis had endorsed Cleveland the previous week in *Harper's*, but there was competition from nationally respected Senators Thomas Bayard and Allen Thurman. Tammany fought hard to defeat Cleveland, but its delegates were forced to vote for him when the Convention majority favored unit rule. (All delegates had to vote for a state's majority candidate.)

Wisconsin delegate General Edward Bragg, a Civil War hero and former Congressman, seconded Cleveland's nomination with an endorsement for the ages: "They (young men of Wisconsin) love Cleveland for his character, but also *for the enemies he has made*." Kelly's outspoken deputy, Tom Grady, responded: "On behalf of his enemies, I accept your statement." (Grady hated Cleveland because the Governor had blocked his re-nomination for State Senator after Grady repeatedly opposed him in the legislature.)[1]

HW July 19, 1884 465

AN INDEPENDENT VICTORY.
The Democratic Party Was Compelled To Nominate A Man With A Clean Record—one whose knees will not yield, even to Boss Kelly.

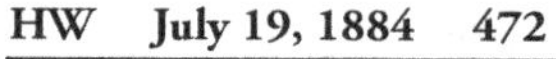
HW July 19, 1884 472

THE REPUBLICAN BOSS.
The Boss of Bosses.
J.G.B. "H'm, you're not such a big boss after all, are you? *But I'll see you later.*"

Nast not only visualized their declarations, but also threw them back at Blaine in the same issue — substituting "friends" for "enemies."

Hendricks was nominated as Vice President in a concession to old-line Democrats, especially Kelly who liked him.

Benjamin Butler

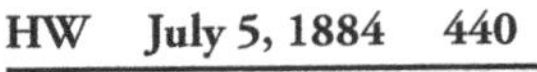
HW July 5, 1884 440

EXACTLY SO.
"Butler, Kelly, and Pryor meet"—of course,
to nominate men above suspicion.

The innuendo in the sub-title — "I'll see you later" — had a solid basis in fact. Two weeks earlier — well before the Convention — Nast's back-page cartoon depicted Kelly scheming with Butler and Butler's lawyer, Roger Pryor. (The last time Nast depicted Pryor was in 1865, when he and Robert E. Lee were begging Andrew Johnson for Presidential pardons. An ardent Confederate, Pryor moved to New York that year, and eventually became Butler's law partner).*

Their mutual objective, of course, was to keep Cleveland from being elected. Butler had turned Democrat in 1874, after being a Radical Republican and leading President Andrew Johnson's impeachment trial. He was elected Governor of Massachusetts in 1882 on a Greenback/Democratic ticket, but was defeated for a second term. Over his mostly unsuccessful military and successful legal career, he developed a reputation for shadiness and dishonesty.

HW July 12, 1884 441 C

THE BOSSES' CONVENTION.
Democratic Boss Kelly to Republican Boss Blaine. "I hope I can manage MY Convention as well AS YOU DID YOURS. If I don't, *I'll see you later.*"

Butler really, really wanted to be President. Before the Convention, he received nominations from the Greenback and Anti-Monopoly parties, but didn't accept them until he could try to swing the Democrats his way. He never had a chance because the South despised him for his actions in 1862 as military commander in New Orleans when he earned the nickname "Beast." Ultimately, Butler couldn't even find a Democrat to nominate him, so he accepted the minor party nominations in August and ran as the People's Party candidate. When the election results were in, he received less than two percent of the vote compared to Greenback candidate James Weaver's three percent in 1880.

The specifics of the proposed deal called for Tammany to support Butler, thereby damaging Cleveland by diverting otherwise-Democratic votes. In the following issue — still available before the Convention — Nast's cover cartoon showed a super-confident Kelly and sinister Butler entering the Democratic circus from the stage door, while cagey Blaine pondered the deal. Curtis discussed the potential bargain in an accompanying editorial.

* See p. 151

About the same time, Joseph Keppler had a compelling cartoon in *Puck*, which Nast could never have gotten away with in *Harper's*. Kelly was dressed in Indian garb, including his henchman Grady's tomahawk. Circus clown Butler, embracing Kelly (who evidently smelled something bad), appeared to be urinating and defecating; his multiple sausage-linked, apparent turds included nominations from the Tammany, Greenback, Women's Suffrage, Pauper and Convict Parties. Meanwhile, the young Independent Party was hoisting a Cleveland flag, as the Democratic Party hailed it.

PUCK July 16, 1884

A FLAG THE INDEPENDENTS WILL FIGHT UNDER.

PUCK October 22, 1884

HELPING THE RASCALS IN.—A BURGLAROUS SCHEME THAT MAY BE SUDDENLY SPOILED.

A pre-election Keppler cartoon was the best on this subject. Blaine, on Butler's shoulders via Dana's back, was trying to break into the White House. Only the Independent voter, club in hand, could stop him.

Kelly supported Butler for a couple of months. In early September, he reluctantly switched Tammany's backing to Cleveland as the safer choice — or the lesser evil — for Tammany's future. His lieutenant, Tom Grady, who had been so vehement at the Convention, didn't follow.

Doubling down, in late July Butler met secretly with Blaine's team led by Navy Secretary William Chandler. The Republicans agreed to pay Butler's campaign $5,000 a month to ensure he stayed in the race. They reasoned that he would attract more Democratic than Republican votes to his People's Party.

Butler barnstormed extensively in the Midwest, Northeast, and county-by-county in New York State. Although he represented the working class, he traveled in a luxury railroad car. That, and rumors of his deal, didn't help his vote totals. When all was done, he received only 17,000 votes in New York. He claimed he was swindled in Brooklyn and Long Island City — and was proved correct a decade later — but the Republican Party was in no position to protest.

The *Sun*

In June 1884, Charles Dana's *Sun*, which he had owned for sixteen years, was New York's leading newspaper; its 150,000 circulation doubled Whitelaw Reid's *Tribune's* 75,000. The *Sun* leaned Democratic, supporting Horace Greeley in 1872 and Tilden in 1876. However, Dana held a personal grudge against Cleveland for refusing to appoint a close friend to the Governor's staff in Albany, and he also opposed Cleveland's low-tariff policy. There was no way he would support the Democratic nominee this time around.[2]

Accordingly, the *Sun* became Butler's only meaningful press backer, while inadvertently providing cartoonists with plenty of ammunition. In addition to ridicule, his Butler endorsement cost Dana half his circulation, most of which was picked up by the newly revitalized *World*.[3]

In a cover cartoon, Nast portrayed "widow" Butler (Butler's self-referral as a person who knew his way around) being stroked by Dana and Republican Reid. Dana's *Sun*flowers were strewn in front, while Butler held his inflation Rag Baby and a silver spoon. (He had been derisively labeled "Spoons" after confiscating silverware from its Confederate owners in captured New Orleans.)

HW September 13, 1884 591 C

"OUR FRIENDS, THE ENEMY."
The Charming Widow. "Oh! you naughty, naughty men, will you ever abuse your good, true, and beautiful one *again*?"

HW November 15, 1884 762

A COLD DAY FOR THE POLITICAL TRAMP.
Benj. F. Butler. "The *Sun* don't shine worth a cent."

Created before the election results were known and published the day after, Nast featured Dana aptly glaring down at Butler, whom he labeled a political tramp. Obviously, Dana was referring to the "Burn this letter" chant of Cleveland's backers.

The *World*

The *World* had been Democratic since Party Chairman August Belmont acquired it in 1862 and installed minority owner Manton Marble as editor. Marble bought it outright in 1869, but sold it to Tom Scott after the election controversy of 1876-7 in which he played a sinister role.* Scott purchased it for the Pennsylvania Railroad (he was president) even though it was unprofitable because he believed it would be useful for pursuing railroad benefits. After two years, Scott sold the *World* to Jay Gould.

Under Gould, circulation fell below 20,000 and the paper lost $40,000 a year. In May 1883, he sold the *World* to Joseph Pulitzer, who had just arrived in New York from St. Louis, where he owned the successful *Post-Dispatch*. Pulitzer's younger brother Albert had preceded him to New York, founded the *Morning Journal* with capital of only $25,000, priced it at a penny, and achieved circulation of 100,000.[4]

Joseph Pulitzer paid $346,000 for the *World* with its 15,000 circulation and three-cent price. He cut its price to two cents and, within four months, forced the *Times* and *Herald* to match him. The *Tribune* went from four to three cents, and the *Sun* was already at two cents. Within a few years, the *World's* circulation reached 600,000 and profits exceeded $500,000.[5]

In addition to price and the latest printing equipment, Pulitzer utilized an adaptation of the relatively new half-tone photographic process — which the *Daily Graphic* had developed — to highlight pictures in many issues, including on the front page. He appealed to readers' emotions by featuring stories of crime, sex and catastrophe with copious illustrations, and soon expanded the paper to 24 pages.

For the 1884 election, Pulitzer hired cartoonist Walt MacDougall at $50 a week — a first for a daily newspaper. (James Gordon Bennett's *Evening Telegram* contained political cartoons every Friday in the late 1860s).** MacDougall began in August and ultimately drew the single most impactful cartoon of the campaign three days before the election. The preceding week, he attacked Butler, depicting Dana paying him while the candidate dropped votes into Blaine's hat; Logan, Elkins and Reid looked on approvingly.

WORLD October 20, 1884

"ONLY A 'BLIND' FOR BLAINE"
B.F. Butler's candidacy

Politically, the *World* was as strongly Democratic as the *Tribune* was Republican, and targeted a working class audience. It was pro-labor, favored higher taxes and lower tariffs, opposed big business, and led the charge against monopolies. Of course, Pulitzer admired Cleveland and detested Blaine and Butler.

* See p. 418-421
** See p. 220, 227, 278

John St. John

The fourth significant candidate was John P. St. John of the Prohibition Party. Only two states, Kansas and Maine, constitutionally banned alcoholic beverages, but other states were considering doing so. St. John had served two terms as Republican Governor of Kansas, but lost in 1882 and split with the Republicans in an acrimonious aftermath. He then went on the lecture circuit, promoting prohibition at fifty dollars a lecture.

Maine voted in September, ahead of potential stormy November weather. Blaine lived in Augusta, the capital, and was on the point of a political sword. If he voted for retaining prohibition in Maine, he would probably lose the beer-drinking Germans and, consequently, the state of Ohio, which also voted early — on October 15. That could lead to losses in other Mid-West states like Indiana. Before Maine voted, Nast pictured Blaine's dilemma in a cover cartoon. A week later, budding star cartoonist Eugene Zimmerman followed in *Puck*.

HW August 23, 1884 543 C

HE THINKS HE CAN.
"Can he (Blaine) satisfy, or, at least, pacify, then (the Germans) without angering irreconcilably the Prohibition Republicans? He is as smart as he is said to be if—he can."—*New York Sun.*

PUCK September 3, 1884

"A MAGNETIC STATESMAN"

With no politically acceptable choice, Blaine dodged by not voting and declaring prohibition *a local issue*, just as Winfield Hancock had incorrectly done with tariffs in the 1880 campaign. He won Maine easily, then went on an extensive tour of Ohio and other Mid-West and Northeast states, beginning September 17, just after Maine voted. Nast had a new drum to beat.

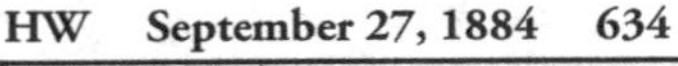

HW September 27, 1884 634

THE TEETOTAL DODGER.
St. John. "Mr. Canvasser, you are not going to dodge me and call me a local issue."

HW October 4, 1884 654

AT HIS OLD TRICKS AGAIN OUT WEST.
James .G. Blaine. "I will now, in confidence, *take in* 50,000,000 people."

When he was 19, St. John had married a woman, separated after two months, and divorced seven years later at her request; both remarried. They had a son, whose education St. John paid for, and whose career he fostered. There was nothing dishonorable or that unusual about the situation.

However, Republicans were worried about St. John pulling votes away from Blaine, especially in dry-leaning areas like upper New York State. When they couldn't induce him to drop out late in the campaign, their smear artists got hold of the story, collecting phony affidavits that turned St. John into an abusive husband who abandoned his starving, ill-clad wife.

Newspaper stories gulled the public, but boomeranged when they incited St. John into doubling down on his efforts in specific counties where Blaine was vulnerable. Both *Puck* and Nast had fun with that in the weeks preceding the election.

PUCK October 15, 1884

St. John.—"It's cold, and lonesome, and not exhilarating—but I like it—oh, I like it!"

HW October 25, 1884 707

COLD WATER COMFORT.

St. John. "I shall neither withdraw from the canvass nor assume a neutral position."

New York was key to the election, so the Democratic Party pitched in with $25,000 to fund St. John's efforts, provided that he confine the last weeks of his campaign to upstate New York. He made about 40 speeches and his efforts paid off. Blaine received almost 12,000 fewer votes north of New York City than Garfield did in 1880, and his loss was greatest in Western New York.[6]

Roscoe Conkling

While Conkling had retired from active politics after the 1880 election, he still had influence with the Stalwart (formerly pro-Grant) faction of the Republican Party. He had hated Blaine for most of Blaine's "Twenty Years in Congress," going back to when Blaine accurately likened him to a strutting turkey-cock. When a Republican committee called at his law office to negotiate for his support, he responded: "Gentlemen, you have been misinformed. I have given up criminal practice."

Other Stalwarts were justifiably concerned that Blaine would replace them with his Half-breed supporters. Consequently, they either voted for St. John or refrained altogether. Stormy weather upstate also kept many potential voters home.

As previously mentioned, Blaine lost New York State and the election by 1,047 votes.

Chapter 44
The Election of 1884: The Campaign

Maria Halpin

John St. John's marital story was the last of three that provided fodder to the electoral campaign. The first and most notorious almost sank Grover Cleveland's ship before it left its pier.

On July 21, ten days after his nomination, the *Buffalo Evening Telegraph* (in Cleveland's home city) broke a partially true story about his prior relationship with an attractive 33-year old widow named Maria Halpin, and telegraphed it nationwide. The disreputable paper's scandalous falsehoods were embellished by two local ministers, giving them substance. If the purported facts had come out two weeks earlier, Cleveland would not have been the Democratic candidate; if they had emerged two months later, he would have lost the election.

Maria moved from Pennsylvania to Buffalo in 1871, leaving two children behind, and found a good job in a clothing store. She probably slept with several men, including Cleveland and his close friend and law partner, Oscar Folsom. In September 1874, she gave birth to a son and claimed that bachelor Cleveland was his father; her hope was to have him marry her. Neither Marie nor Cleveland knew the boy's paternity, but he accepted the responsibility because the other possible fathers were married. Accordingly, he agreed to provide child support.

Maria named her son Oscar Folsom Cleveland, and admitted to her lawyer that Cleveland had never made any promise of marriage. Folsom had died in a tragic carriage accident in July 1875, and Cleveland had been appointed administrator of his estate. He watched over his widow Rose, and acted like a guardian of her 13-year old daughter Frances. (Nine years later when he was 49, Cleveland would marry Frances in the White House).

Even while nursing, Maria began drinking heavily and neglected her son. Alarmed, Cleveland went to a former county judge whom he knew, and asked him to take control of the family matter without involving him. The judge institutionalized Maria with her consent, and ultimately committed baby Oscar to the Protestant Orphan Asylum. He was adopted by a distinguished family, exited from Cleveland's life, and had a successful career.[1]

All these events from 1874-1876 had been kept out of the press, so now they created an uproar. Immediate first-hand digging by Mugwump investigators determined the actual facts, and forced the lying clergymen to apologize for their false tales, and the *Evening Telegraph* to admit that its story was based on untrue rumors. There had been no seduction or breach of promise, and Maria had been intimate with other men.

Cleveland's prompt response was "Tell the truth." After accepting uncertain paternity, he had conducted himself honorably thereafter. In personal interviews, he convinced key Democrats, Mugwumps and clergymen — including powerful preacher Henry Ward Beecher (whose adultery was far more sinful than anything Cleveland did) — of the actual circumstances. *Harper's Weekly* never printed Maria Halpin's name, and Nast ignored the story.

Once the facts were clear, Blaine believed them and wished the Republican press would drop the story so he could concentrate on the protective tariff issue.

Puck quickly came to Cleveland's defense by attacking Blaine in successive weeks. His campaign manager, Stephen Elkins, and Ben Butler's backer, Charles Dana's *Sun*, were fruitlessly pushing the dogs of clerical and common slander in the second one. Cleveland was composed in both.

PUCK August 13, 1884

HE INSTITUTED THE ORDEAL—CAN HE STAND IT HIMSELF?
Uncle Sam,—"We have heard from Mr. Cleveland. Now then, Mr. Blaine, *you* made this issue; it is your turn to step up and— *Tell the Truth*!"

PUCK August 20, 1884 C

THOSE DOGS WON'T FIGHT—THEY ARE DYING OF STARVATION.

However, *The Judge* wouldn't let the juicy story fade away. At the same time that *Puck* counter-attacked, Frank Beard portrayed Curtis as a seduced woman cradling her Independent Party love child, while holding a folded *Harper's Weekly* umbrella to shelter him further if necessary. A National Theatre poster featured Cleveland as the lead actor in *Led Astray*. The witty cartoon was entitled *The Mistake of a Lifetime*.

August 16, 1884 C

THE MISTAKE OF A LIFETIME.

September 27, 1884 C

ANOTHER VOICE FOR CLEVELAND.

Coincidentally or not, on the same date that *Harper's* printed the complete second edition of the Mulligan letters, Beard illustrated the current mocking verse:

Ma, Ma, Where's My Pa?
Gone to the White House.
Ha! Ha!! Ha!

The story simmered quietly, but flared up again five days before the election. On October 28 and 29, Maria apparently signed two affidavits, the second of which accused Cleveland of rape. When she told him she was pregnant, she said he verbally abused her and she never saw him again. The *Chicago Tribune*, owned and published by arch-Republican Joseph Medill, printed the affidavits on October 30-31.

Alarmed by Medill's account, the Democrats went all out to track Maria down. She pronounced the affidavits false, and told a *World* reporter: "I have no quarrel with Mr. Cleveland. He is a good, plain, honest-hearted man who was always friendly to me and used me kindly. Joseph Pulitzer's *World* printed the interview on November 2, and the *Detroit Free Press* and probably other Democratic papers followed the next day.[2]

As it played out, the Halpin scandal probably didn't cost Cleveland many votes. In retrospect, it may have harmed Blaine more by diverting time that could have been spent much more effectively to promote protective tariffs, the key plank in his campaign.[3]

Blaine's Marriage Scandal

Both to offset the Halpin story and warn Republican papers not to exploit it, the Democrats attacked Blaine's marriage. His recently published campaign biography said that he had married Harriet Stanwood in Pittsburgh on March 29, 1851, and their son was born on June 18. Harriet went home to her mother in Maine and Blaine returned to Kentucky to teach. On August 7, the *Indianapolis Sentinel* broke its story: "There is hardly an intelligent man in this country who has not heard that James G. Blaine betrayed the girl whom he married, and then only married her at the muzzle of a shotgun."[4] (Actually, her father died six years before).

Blaine answered by hiring Senator Benjamin Harrison of Indiana to sue the *Sentinel* for libel and $50,000 in damages. He knew the charges could not be proved and wanted a retraction, but he got the opposite. The paper pushed ahead with some hard questions it wanted Blaine to answer under oath.

In response, William Walter Phelps — Blaine's friend and current house guest — released a letter from Blaine himself claiming that he and Harriet had been secretly married in Millersburg, Kentucky, on June 30, 1850. There had been two now-deceased witnesses, no minister, no license, no public notice, and Blaine was a minor. (He was 20, Harriet 22.) Blaine later felt doubts about its validity, and arranged the second marriage with a license when he was 21.[5]

Looked at realistically, Blaine and Harriet probably considered themselves engaged and had an intimate relationship, and she became pregnant in the fall of 1850. His reported marriage date of June 30 was a Sunday, an unlikely day for any Protestant wedding. However, their marriage of 34 years was a happy one, the libel suit was postponed, (and then withdrawn after the election), and the issue probably didn't affect many votes

Someone did approach Cleveland to sell him "proof" of Blaine's situation. Cleveland bought the bundle and promptly burned it without inspection. Neither he nor Blaine publicly protested against defamation of the other's character.[6]

The Irish Vote

There were about two million Irish-born Americans in 1884, most of whom had strong feelings about England's harsh treatment of their mother country and its rebellious population. When Blaine was Secretary of State during Garfield's brief administration in 1881, he had taken a hard line with England on that and other issues. (After Chester Arthur succeeded the assassinated President, he replaced Blaine with Frederick Frelinghuysen, a prominent New Jersey politician, who reversed his predecessor's English policy).

Blaine expected to receive a minor but significant share of the estimated half-million Irish votes in New York State. He was supported by the *Irish World* and *Irish Nation* editors, while other Irish factions stayed with their Democratic roots. Protestant *Harper's Weekly* with its editorial blasts against sectarian schools, Nast's anti-Irish cartoons, and Eugene Lawrence's anti-Catholic diatribes, couldn't expect to sway many pro-Blaine Irish voters.

However, Nast found a way to inject the Irish vote issue into his campaign against Blaine. In his first cartoon on the subject, he viewed the Republican effort as an attempt to avoid discussion of Blaine's record.

HW July 19, 1884 463

FE! FI! FO! FUM!
To Distract Our Attention From Blaine's Record, The Managers Are Springing This Little Toy Upon Us.

On July 28, the self-described Irish-American Independents in New York held a rally for Blaine. The week before the pre-announced meeting at Chickering Hall, Nast attacked Blaine in two cartoons. The cover depicted him pleading with the Irish by promising to "twist the British Lion's tail for you," while the back page depicted him feeding the opposite line to John Bull (representing England).

HW July 26, 1884 473 C

IS THIS "THE TRUE AMERICAN POLICY"!
Sir Knight (*on his knees again*). "Yes, my letter of acceptance is gentle as a sucking dove; but when I get in, I'll screech like an American War-Eagle, and I'll twist the British lion's tail for you; I'll protect you from British dungeons after you've killed innocent women and children with dynamite. Who could do more for you?"

HW July 26, 1884 488

A SHAM-FIGHT CAMPAIGN.
Sir Knight. "My dear cousin John, you're not at all alarmed at this anti-British war-cry, I hope? It is only to get the Irish vote from the Democratic party, and make up—"
J.B. "Yes, for, the disgusted Republicans that have left you."

After the meeting, Nast followed up with Blaine thumbing his nose at his Irishman while embracing him. A picture of the previous cover cartoon hung on the wall, and the pro-Blaine *Tribune's* quote of a "remarkable meeting" was below. What Nast found remarkable was Blaine's anti-Irish nativist "Know Nothing Record" sticking out of his carpetbag. A week later, Blaine was on his knees to the British Lion, wanting to twist his tail off now and return it after the election — (a la Mulligan Letters).

HW August 9, 1884 526

"THE SPREAD OF AMERICAN IDEAS."
"The meeting of Irish-Americans at Chickering Hall last night was a remarkable one."—*N.Y. Tribune, July 29.*

HW August 16, 1884 541

"THOROUGHLY AMERICAN, YET SEEKING PEACE."—*Blaineism.*
The So-Called Intensely American Knight (to *British Lion*). ""Please let me twist your tail off; I will return it to you after election—(*a la Mulligan Letters*)."

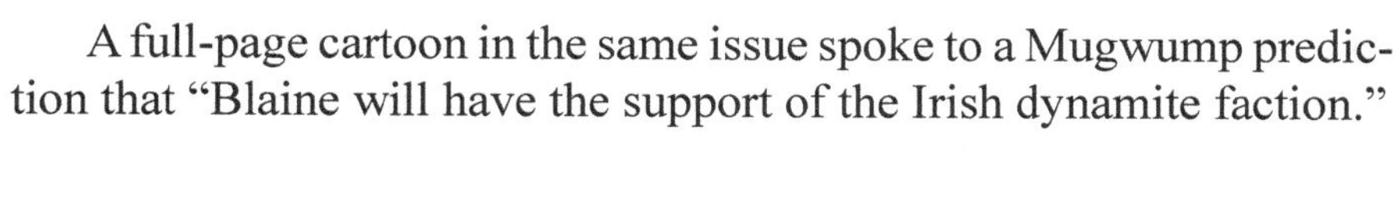

A full-page cartoon in the same issue spoke to a Mugwump prediction that "Blaine will have the support of the Irish dynamite faction."

HW August 16, 1884 530

THE SO-CALLED "INTENSELY AMERICAN CANDIDATE."
Dynamite Dictator. "I hope that the wire will flash the tidings of this magnificent demonstration to the English Aristocracy, telling them that the Irishmen of America intend to put James G. Blaine in the Chair of George Washington."
Uncle Sam. "Gammon! The English Aristocracy is nothing to me. No true Irish-*Americans* are dynamiters—and I think I have something to say about this."

Blaine's Tour

As discussed previously, after the Maine vote in mid-September, Blaine immediately left for a two-week tour of Ohio. Its success convinced him to spend another month barnstorming the Mid-West and Pennsylvania, returning to upper New York State the last week in October.

Early on, Nast depicted the Plumed Knight on his steed covered with the second edition of Mulligan letters; *Harper's* had printed all of them the week before. Blaine's banner was emblazoned with his old Tweed slogan: "What are you going to do about it?"

Blaine's six weeks on the road were both exhausting and unexpectedly expensive. His New York advisors, led by Whitelaw Reid, beseeched him to preside at a fund-raising banquet at Delmonico's Restaurant on Wednesday, October 29. Money was desperately needed to pay off local politicians by the final weekend before election. Over the objections of his campaign manager, Stephen Elkins, Blaine reluctantly agreed about ten days before the scheduled event.

HW October 4, 1884 661

THE BRAZEN KNIGHT OF THE WHITE FEATHER ON HIS ROUND TRIP FOR VOTES.

The Three R's

However, the single most influential incident — not only of Wednesday, October 29, but also of the entire campaign — had nothing to do with the dinner at Delmonico's. It took place mid-morning when Blaine was welcomed by a group of four to five hundred ministers at the Fifth Avenue Hotel. He had checked in the night before at the end of his long tour, where his wife and children awaited him.

The meeting had been organized in advance by Reverend R.W. McMurdy, who headed a small secretive Republican group intended to help secure the clerical vote for Blaine. McMurdy sent more than a thousand invitations to New York State ministers of multiple faiths, but those who attended were primarily Methodist and Presbyterian, and unfamiliar to the general public. The original designated speaker was stuck in Philadelphia, so the almost unknown Samuel Burchard was the compromise choice — solely because he was the oldest. (In his seventies.)

Frank Mack, the Associated Press lead reporter in New York, was the only journalist allowed. He, and his two shorthand stenographers, stationed themselves close to Blaine on the steps leading to the large ballroom where the audience was seated. He noticed that Blaine looked extremely pale and weary, with deep circles under his eyes and a faraway look in them. After a brief introduction by the Chairman, the large-framed Dr. Burchard took over.

Romanism

". . . We are your friends, Mr. Blaine. Not withstanding all the calumnies against you, we stand by your side. We expect to vote for you next Tuesday. . . We are Republicans, and ***we do not propose to leave our party and identify with the party whose antecedents have been Rum, Romanism, and Rebellion.*** *We are loyal to our flag, we are loyal to you."*

Mack looked at Blaine's face which was impassive. He probably had assumed that all the talks had been vetted, and was thinking about his own remarks which would follow. He certainly had not understood the potential impact of the explosive middle word — *Romanism* — in Burchard's improvised alliteration. Mack did, and dispatched his first stenographer back to the AP office.

Blaine could have fixed matters by denouncing the use of "Romanism." His mother was Catholic and his sister was a mother-superior in a convent, so it would have been natural for him, all political considerations aside. But he hadn't comprehended and he didn't rebut. Mack sent the second stenographer to the AP office with what Blaine did (and did not) say.

When Blaine's supporters quickly filled him in, he sent for Mack who was about to leave, only to learn that the two shorthand stenographers were too far along for him to do anything about it. Soon, a Democratic operative at the AP office took the transcript to Cleveland's campaign manager, Arthur Pue Gorman, who immediately publicized it with press releases, banners and placards. The Democratic *World* printed the complete text on Thursday morning, in the same issue in which it ridiculed the previous night's fund-raising dinner on its cover.

By Friday, Democratic papers throughout the country were editorializing about "The Three R's." On Saturday night, thousands of Democrats paraded through New York streets with signs about both of Wednesday's Republican debacles — "Romanism" and the banquet. On Sunday, Catholic parishioners heard all about it in their Sunday sermons, after seeing plenty of placards as they came in.

Finally understanding that the issue wasn't going away, Blaine tried to explain himself on Saturday night in a New Haven speech: "*Although Protestant by conviction and connected with a Protestant church, I should esteem myself of all men the most degraded if, under any pressure or any temptation, I should in any presence, make a disrespectful allusion to that ancient faith in which my revered mother lived and died.*"

In retrospect, Burchard's comment cost Blaine the electoral votes of New York, New Jersey and Indiana. It had its greatest effect on Irishmen who were undecided or looking for a reason to remain Democratic; those committed to Blaine probably stayed loyal.[7]

Burchard, ridiculed and reviled, became known as *the man who opened his mouth and swallowed a Presidency*. Well after he resigned his pulpit and left the ministry the following year, he was introduced to the AP reporter on a social occasion. Frank Mack discussed the incident at the close of a three-page article in *Harper's Weekly* twenty years later.[8]

> *"It is the renewal of an acquaintance," I remarked.*
> *"Have I met you before?" he asked, and peered down at me with his dimmed eyes.*
> *"I stood before you when you addressed Mr. Blaine in the 1884 campaign," I smiled.*
> *A queer look crept into his face — a compound of wan smile and far regret.*
> *"Ah, well," he mused, "it was a bitter, bitter thing; but it comes to me sometimes now that I may have been, after all, a humble instrument in the hands of a greater Power."*

Jay Gould

Meanwhile, in late August, Nast had introduced Jay Gould into his cartoons as Blaine's monopolist money-man. The second of eight Gould depictions not only featured his long-deceased partners Jim Fisk and Boss Tweed,* but also referred to the upcoming, well-publicized banquet, it even listed the expected attendees on the issue's cover.

HW August 23, 1884 557

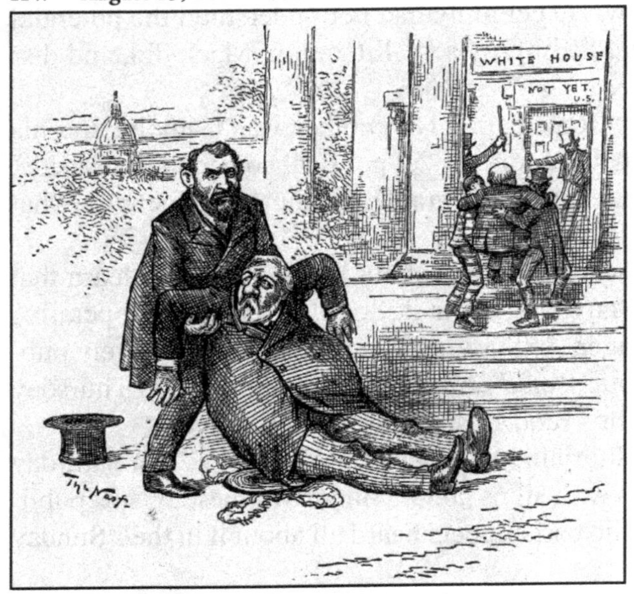

MY DEAR MONOPOLY GOULD.
If you help me to get in, I see various channels in which I know I can be useful to you. Very hastily and sincerely your friend, P.K. (Plumed Knight)

HW October 25, 1884 695 C

A JOB LOT.
Jay Gould. "I see numerous channels in which you could be useful, my dear knight—even more so than my late, but now silent, partners."
G. Blaine. "Very well; as long as I'm let in on the ground-floor it's all right."

A week later — with the election less than two weeks away — Gould was in three post-dated cartoons dealing with Fort Boodle (Nast's word for graft), along with Ben Butler.

HW November 1, 1884 715 C

THE BLAINE TARIFF FRAUD.
Chorus of Working-Men. "Duped, by gosh!"

HW November 1, 1884 726

HIGHWAY POLITICS.
A Vote For Butler Is A Vote *Lost*— *Or* Stolen.

HW November 1, 1884 730

THE GREAT BOODLE MONOPOLY.
"I do fear they will build up the worst railroad monopoly ever seen in this country."—Thurman.

---

* See p. 287

Belshazzar's Feast

Campaign manager Elkins knew that the dinner was a bad idea, and not only because his candidate would be exhausted. The economy was in recession, and the public image of monopolists and so-called money kings living it up while their employees and other were struggling, could cost Blaine votes. He declined to participate so Gould, William Evarts and Atlantic Cable entrepreneur Cyrus Field did the organizing. Their sole purpose was to raise enough money to grease various New York grass roots bosses during the five-day run-up to election.

As mentioned earlier, the guest list of the financial and political invitees was known in advance. On Thursday morning, Pulitzer's pioneering daily *World* trumped all its competitors (including the weeklies) with Walt MacDougall's cartoon at the top of its front page: *The Royal Feast of Belshazzar and the Money Kings*; the accompanying article was headlined *Mammon's Homage*. With plenty of time to prepare, MacDougall depicted 20 recognizable men eating Gould Pie, Lobby Pudding, Monopoly Stew and Patronage Cake. Some of the portrayed guests — notably Elkins and William Vanderbilt (seated next to Blaine, with a crown) did not attend.

In front of the banquet table, an impoverished family begged for leftovers. In response, Reid, in the next day's *Tribune* (Friday), identified the man as Cleveland, and asked its readers to guess who the woman and child were.

October 30, 1884

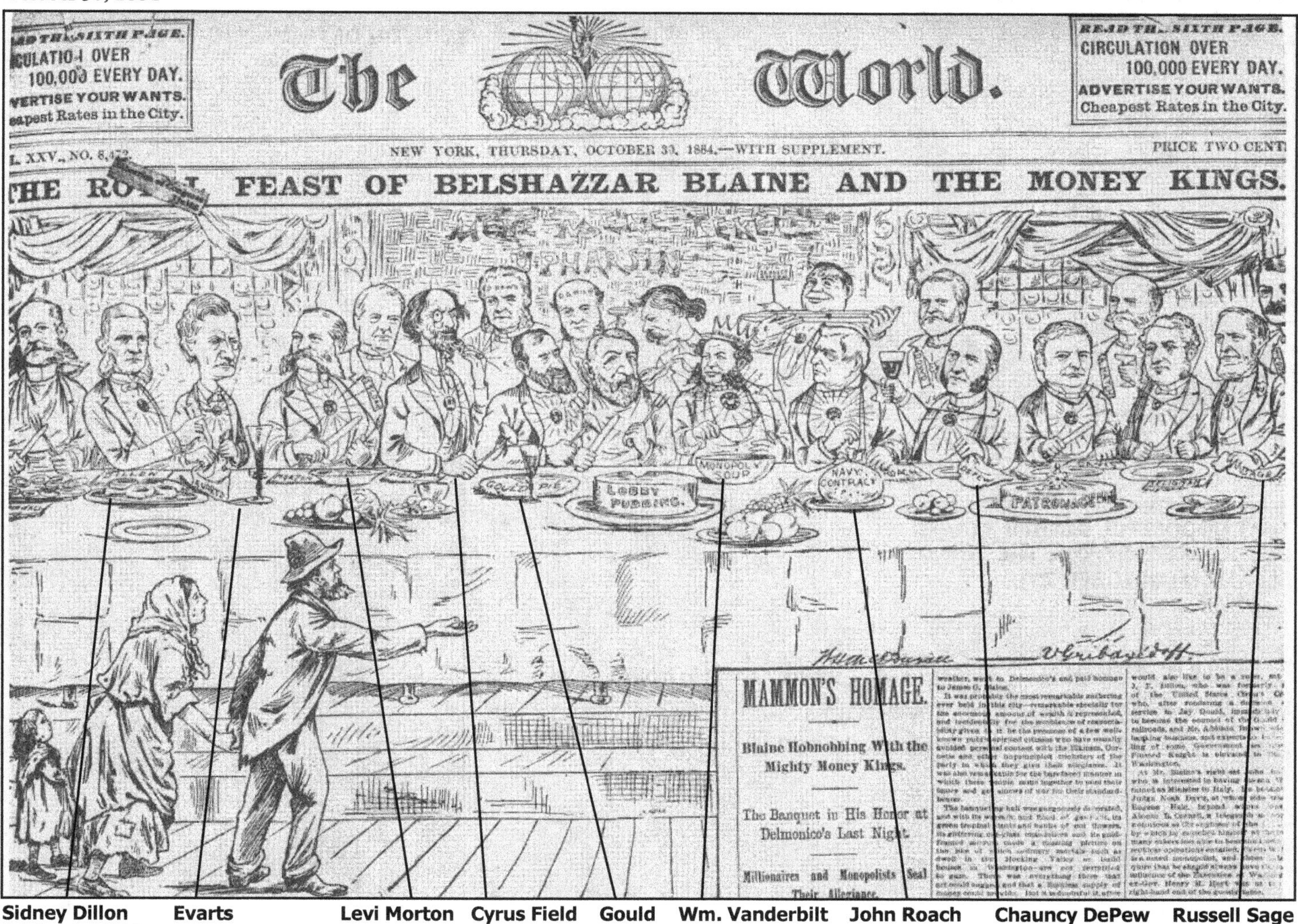

By Friday, Arthur Gorman saw to it that copies of the cartoon were on placards posted all over the city, as well as on posters carried by chanting marchers.

Nast's Wind-up

Nast continued to attack as word of the dinner spread. His post-dated November 8 cover cartoon appeared in print on the day of the dinner, with a list of probable attendees posted between Gould's late notorious partners, Jim Fisk and Boss Tweed. Gould was mesmerized by the election returns coming in on his stock ticker.

HW November 8, 1884 731 C

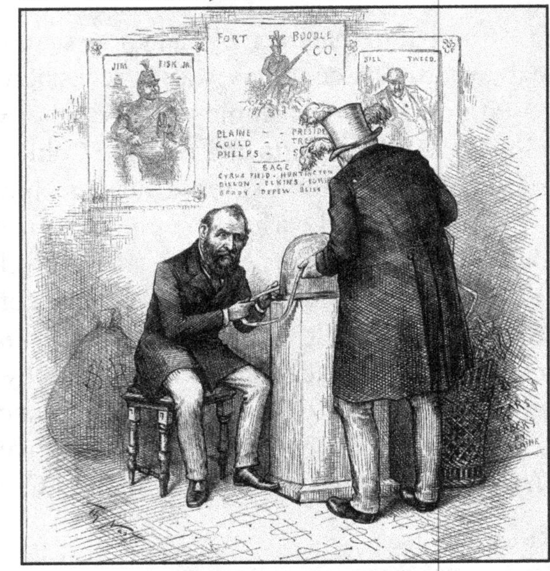

ELECTION DAY—WATCHING THE RETURNS.

HW November 15, 1884 758

THAT BOODLEFUL DINNER AT DELMONICO'S BEFORE THE ELECTION (OCTOBER 29).

A week later, Gould was offering soap (cash) to 4 in exchange for four judges on the Supreme Court, jobs, and help with his Union Pacific and Western Union enterprises. An alarmed William Evarts was blowing a White House soap bubble with them inside. The action took place at Delmonico's boodleful (a pun on "beautiful" and "full of boodle") dinner.

After the election was decided, Gould — who owned Western Union — was depicted on his knees with a *hand-written* telegram begging Cleveland to keep "the business interests of this country" safe.

HW November 22, 1884 778

NO *UNION PACIFIC* FOR THE PRESIDENT-ELECT.

Payoffs

The Republicans were short of cash for several reasons. Political assessments, which had always been a dependable source of funds, had been reduced by Civil Service reform, especially the Pendleton Act of the previous year.* Major Republican donors had not come through and, as mentioned, Blaine's tour had run up unanticipated heavy expenses.

Unfortunately for Blaine, most of the potential contributors ducked. Others committed but welshed when Blaine lost. However, Jay Gould did come up with $50,000, which was turned over to Republican boss James O'Brien (Boss Tweed's old political foe) for distribution to local politicians. O'Brien pocketed the money and never gave any to the ward leaders for whom it was intended. As Chief of the Bureau of Elections, nobody had any recourse against him.

Keppler's cartoon in *Puck* showed O'Brien's sleigh, with Blaine huddled and Reid about to throw the New York City child to the Tammany Wolf. Cleveland had made a personal call on Kelly earlier in the month and probably reached an understanding on votes now for patronage later. Reid knew about that and had given up hope for a Republican surge in the city.

PUCK October 29, 1884

A SACRIFICE TO THE POLITICAL WOLF.
Republican Desperation And The Peril Of New York City.

* See p. 526-527

Fraud

Tammany only controlled New York County. Brooklyn had its own powerful political boss, Hugh McLaughlin, who backed Cleveland at the Convention (in contrast to Kelly), and delivered a 15,000 vote majority for him in the election. However, still another local absolute ruler, John McKane, switched about 8,000 actual votes from Ben Butler to Cleveland — decisive when he won the state by fewer than 1,100.

McKane had total control of Gravensend, which included Coney Island, Brighton Beach and Manhattan Beach. (The area would not be annexed to Brooklyn for another ten years). He ruled with an iron fist over business licenses, gambling, beach concessions and, of course, voting. His opponents were brutally beaten with truncheons, sometimes by him personally, and lost their licenses and ability to do business.

Elections took place in the municipal building where McKane scrutinized every voter, as well as the counting of their ballots. Ten years later, he was convicted of his 1884 transfer of votes, and sent to Sing Sing Prison for six years.

Why Blaine Lost

Although Cleveland probably was the better man for the office, many factors which neither candidate could control, made him extremely lucky to win New York State — and consequently the election — by a mere 1,047 votes.

Upstate (north of New York City and Suffolk County), John St. John's Prohibition Party took about 25,000 votes from Blaine. Roscoe Conkling's enmity probably cost a few thousand more. But terrible weather on Election Day may have been the decisive factor, hurting Republican turnout. They lost almost 17%, 13,000 votes, from their total in the 1880 election.[9]

But Blaine still would have won except for Burchard's *Rum, Romanism and Rebellion*. If only he had ignored Reed and accepted Elkins' advice to return to his home in Maine and skip New York. . . .

Of course, Nast, the Harpers and the Mugwumps celebrated. A sign outside Nast's home in Morristown summed it all up.[10]

THE WORLD SAYS THE INDEPENDENTS DID IT
THE TRIBUNE SAYS THE STALWARTS DID IT
THE SUN SAYS BURCHARD DID IT
BLAINE SAYS ST. JOHN DID IT
THEODORE ROOSEVELT SAYS IT WAS THE SOFT SOAP DINNER
WE SAY BLAINE'S CHARACTER DID IT
BUT WE DON'T CARE WHAT DID IT
IT'S DONE

The Price Nast Paid

In 1881, Curtis unknowingly predicted what would happen to *Harper's Weekly* three years later. "If a journal be Republican or Democratic, it can educate and advance opinions which it approves, so long as it is done without alienating Republican or Democratic sympathy. But if the Republican journal should suddenly declare Democratic views, or vice versa, its prosperity would be instantly checked."[11]

The Harpers significantly underestimated the financial damage to the *Weekly* when it abandoned its Republican base. Circulation and advertising fell drastically, never to really recover. Originally estimated at about $100,000 when they made the decision to lead the Mugwump movement, the financial loss significantly exceeded that as book and other periodical customers left in droves. The slumping economy was an additional drag.[12]

At 44, Nast had the roughest year of his life to date. Most of his savings disappeared in May with the failure of Grant and Ward. Working for the same cause, Keppler and Gillam clearly outshone him in both creativity and colorful execution, as proved by *Puck's* sharply increased circulation, advertising and profits.

Moreover, he was continually demeaned in *The Judge* and other humor magazines like the San Francisco *Wasp*, as his prior cartoon successes effectively hoisted him on his own petard time and again. Short, with his distinctive goatee and a flowing mustache, he was easy to caricature. Cartoonist Frank Beard frequently portrayed him as the pet monkey of organ-grinder Curtis, just as Nast had done with Horace Greeley and Whitelaw Reid in 1872.* Eventually, he evolved into just a tail wrapped around a pen, similar to Nast's portrayal of Gratz Brown, Greeley's running mate.

Here, Beard parodied Nast with several blowbacks in a double-page satirical (but not artistic) masterpiece. The title — *Anything to Beat Blaine* — echoed 1872's *Anything to Beat Grant*. The subtitle "Let us shake hands over the bloody chasm" was embodied by monkey Nast reaching over it to shake hands with the ghost of Boss Tweed, while Curtis did the same with current Tammany Boss Kelly. Child Nast in a dress to go with Curtis's feminine outfit, was apparently standing on a large snake with his current face as its head. Nast's old Tweed cartoon, with his persistent query "What are you going to do about it?" was in the foreground, while the other key Ring members — Oakey Hall, Peter Sweeny and Richard Connolly were identifiable in the rear. *Times* publisher George Jones held the Independent Republican plank: "To bridge the bloody chasm."

THE JUDGE October 29, 1884

ANYTHING TO BEAT BLAINE.
"Let us shake hands over the bloody chasm."
Ghost Of Boss Tweed.—"Go right along, gentlemen; you are now arrayed against my old enemy, the Republican Party"

* See p. 314

In *The Judge's* most obvious take-off, cartoonist Louis Dalrymple simply replaced Greeley and Senator Charles Sumner attempting to entice a black man into shaking hands with a KKK murderer with figures of Nast and Curtis; the rest of the cartoon was unchanged.

HW August 24, 1872 652

IT IS ONLY A TRUCE TO REGAIN POWER ("PLAYING POSSUM.").

THE JUDGE August 30, 1884

A NAST CARTOON (Slightly changed.)
Geo. Wm. Curtis And Th. Nast To Colored Republican.— "*Let us embrace the Democracy, 'twill purify the Republican Party.*" (See *Harper's Weekly*, August 24, 1872.)

All told, *The Judge* ridiculed Nast in more than a dozen cartoons in 1884, and followed up sporadically the following year. It also came up with accompanying verses, one of which Nast showed to his biographer Albert Paine.

Poor, poor T. Nast,
Thy day is passed —
Thy bolt is shot,
Thy dye is cast —
Thy pencil point
Is out of joint —
Thy pictures lately disappoint.

Nast was used to being targeted in cartoons, going back to 1872 when Frank Bellew went after him in the *Fifth Avenue Journal*.* What hurt most now was the loss of dozens of friends and thousands of admiring fans. Even Nasby (David Ross Locke), whom he had hoped to partner with in his Caricaturama, and whose books he had illustrated, published a critical letter in *x-roads*. General Grant, fading rapidly in his final year, favored Blaine and must have been unhappy with his old friend.

* * * *

In retrospect, however, *The Judge* might have been wiser to focus more on Cleveland and low tariffs rather than on Nast, Curtis and the Mugwumps. Despite its clever cartoons, it probably didn't swing many votes. Its continuing financial problems led to the previously mentioned sale to William Arkell the following year.

A year later, Walt MacDougall depicted the decline of Mugwump influence over Cleveland. Cheap Mugwump mummies were for sale, including *Harper's Weekly* (with Curtis as its figurehead), *Puck*, the *Evening Post*, and the *Times*. Republican Headquarters also was closed and an emaciated Reid was on crutches. Cleveland definitely was his own man.

"AND JONES HE PAYS THE FREIGHT."

* See p. 338-339

Chapter 45
President Cleveland: Civil Service Reform

Introduction

Grover Cleveland's first two years in office, coincided with Thomas Nast's last two at *Harper's Weekly* (1885-86). He and editor George William Curtis continued their Mugwump support of the Democratic President — to a far greater extent than Cleveland's own party did. Civil Service reform was both a decisive and divisive factor.

During the two-year span, Nast drew 350 cartoons for the *Weekly*, far more than in any comparable period. (He spent early July to early September 1885 in Europe, and several weeks in September - October 1886 in Colorado, drawing a few date-neutral cartoons before he left — like the tribute to Grant upon his death on July 23.*

About 50 dealt with Civil Service. In about two dozen cartoons, he reincarnated the Tammany Tiger to represent the patronage-starved Democratic Party, beginning immediately after the election with a dominant double-page.

HW November 15, 1884 747 C

WHAT IT MEANS.

HW November 29, 1884 786-787

BEWARE! FOR HE IS VERY HUNGRY AND VERY THIRSTY.
"Ability and zeal in the service will be the measure of usefulness. The rules of the Civil Service Commission will govern all minor appointments."—Grover Cleveland.

---

* See p. 548

Prior to Cleveland's Inauguration on March 4, Nast continued to feature Civil Service reform. He even depicted the President as an elephant, the only time a Democrat played that role, previously and hereafter, reserved for Republicans.

HW January 10, 1885 32

A GENTLE HINT TO OFFICE-SEEKERS.
"I regard myself pledged to this."—(Letter of President-elect to Civil Service Reform League.)

HW February 28, 1885 144

HAVE THE DEMOCRATS AN ELEPHANT ON HAND?
"A Southern Congressman, having paid a visit to the President-elect, is much dissatisfied with the lack of interest Governor Cleveland showed in his suggestion that the offices should be 'filled with Democrats' as soon as possible. To this Mr. Cleveland replies: 'I fear there will be some disappointment about that. You know that we are greatly indebted to many Republicans, and that *our party is pledged to civil-service reform.*' When the Congressman returned to Washington he said to his friends: 'Gentlemen, we've got a big elephant on our hands.'"—*Daily Paper.*

HW February 21, 1885 127

"TAMMANY HALL IS GOING TO THE INAUGURATION."—*News.*
They Can't Help Themselves.

As the Inauguration drew near, Nast showed an ailing Boss Kelly — arm in a sling and using a cane — leading Tammany to its funeral. Actually, Kelly's health declined, and he turned over control of Tammany to Richard Croker about that time. He died the following year.

HW March 7, 1885 145 C

THE COMPLIMENTS OF THE SEASON—MARCH 4.
Cleveland to Arthur. "I hope that I may leave the house in as good order as you have."

Nast's Inauguration cover greeted the new President and praised the outgoing one (whom he had favored for renomination). President Arthur had done a relatively good job implementing the new Civil Service regulations. As the *Weekly* noted, he set a precedent by replacing about half of the Republican office holders whose terms had expired with new Republican appointees, all of whom had to pass examinations to qualify.

According to Curtis, "reform" to most Democrats "means turning out a Republican — however capable, honest and experienced — and turning in a Democrat, capable and honest if God wills and it should so happen. To Cleveland, however, reform means the retention of subordinate employees who do not deserve dismissals; the serving out their terms by other officers who do their work properly and do not meddle with politics; and even the reappointment of officers of that kind."[1]

Cleveland followed through shortly after his inauguration by reappointing Republican Postmaster Henry Pearson of New York to a four-year term. At the same time, he sent a nomination to the Senate to replace the reputed alcoholic crook who was running the Rome, New York, Post Office. When the Senate failed to act, Cleveland couldn't fire the man because of Civil Service regulations, but he did suspend him.[2] Nast emphasized the President's assertiveness.

HW April 18, 1885 255

IT MAY NOT BE CIVIL, BUT IT'S RIGHT!
"I shall do all that is in my power to rid the public service of officials who exhibit such loose ideas of their duty to the Government. The fact that I have before me documents signed by many residents of the city where this Postmaster is located, and who belong to both political parties, asserting their entire confidence in his honesty and fidelity demonstrates the unfortunate facility with which such papers may be obtained, and gives rise to an unpleasant suspicion touching a too prevalent standard of political honesty."—*The President of the U.S.*

Among the outspoken complainers was Senator James Eustis of Louisiana, who came into office at the same time as Cleveland, and demanded patronage. He was supported by publisher John McLean of the *Cincinnati Enquirer*, an occasional Nast target. Nast used the biblical story (St. Matthew) of Jesus multiplying five loaves and two fishes to feed several thousand people, to make his point. (During his second term, Cleveland would appoint Eustis as Ambassador to France after getting to know the Senator better.)

Nast couldn't resist giving Eustis an extra tweak. During the Civil War, he had served as a Judge Advocate in the Confederate Army. At the bottom of the Louisiana mat on which Eustis Pelican was standing, "Union Offices & Confederacy" was written, with the last word crossed out.

However, Cleveland soon encountered problems in making good on his Civil Service reform pledges under pressure from Democratic politicians, thereby disappointing both Nast and Curtis. Two months later, the *Weekly* published a generic cover cartoon that Nast had drawn before he left for Europe, showing Cleveland dropping the applications of "well trained practical politicians" into a wastebasket.

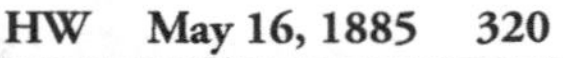
HW May 16, 1885 320

SENATOR EUSTIS PELICAN AT THE WHITE-HOUSE DOOR.
"If there is not a change soon, the volcano of discontent will belch forth in such a way as to leave the Louisiana Senator's opening fun only a faint echo."—Johnny McLean.

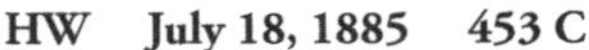
HW July 18, 1885 453 C

WHAT THE POSITION OF A PRESIDENT OF THE UNITED STATES REALLY IS.

Hendricks

Cleveland had accepted Thomas Hendricks as his running mate because it pacified Boss Kelly — both of them spoilsmen — and could help win his home state of Indiana. (It did). However, Cleveland made clear that there would be no spoils for the Vice President, who died of a stroke three weeks after Nast's last diminutive cartoon of him appeared in print. Hendricks was commenting on spoilsman David Hill's election as New York Governor.

HW May 2, 1885 288

TOO OFFICE-IOUS.
"Little boy, don't fool with that chair; you have one of your own."

HW November 14, 1885 743

THE PART OF THE ADMINISTRATION THAT FEELS VERY MUCH INDORSED.
Mr. Hendricks. "I regard the result in New York as a straight-out Democratic victory, *with all that that implies.*"

HW October 3, 1885 645

A CIVIL SERVICE REFORM LETTER.

* * * It is a source of congratulation that there are so many friends of civil service reform marshalled on the practical side of the question, and that the number is not greater of those who profess friendliness for the cause, and yet mischievously, and with supercilious self-righteousness, discredit every effort not in exact accord with their attenuated ideas, decry with carping criticism the labor of those actually in the field of reform, and, ignoring the conditions which bound and qualify every struggle for a radical improvement in the affairs of government, demand complete and immediate perfection. * * *

I believe in civil service reform, and its application in the most practicable form attainable, among other reasons, because it opens the door for the rich and the poor alike to a participation in public place-holding. And I hope the time is at hand when all our people will see the advantage of a reliance for such an opportunity upon merit and fitness, instead of a dependence upon the caprice or selfish interest of those who impudently stand between the people and the machinery of their government. In the one case, a reasonable intelligence and the education which is freely furnished or forced upon the youth of our land are the credentials to office; in the other, the way is found in favor secured by a participation in partisan work, often unfitting a person morally, if not mentally and physically, for the responsibilities and duties of public employment. * * *

GROVER CLEVELAND.

HOLDING HIM UP TO RIDICULE.
Columbia. "Do you imagine, you hungry, thirsty office-seeker, that fifty-five million people are going to be ruled by a handful of chaps like you?"

In this trite cartoon, the diminutive office-seeker was labeled "Anti-Civil Service Reform," and Hendricks was labeled "The Vice President of Office-Seeker," while Cleveland was "The President of the People."

A year later, Nast lauded Cleveland for ignoring the patronage requests of Henry Watterson, the Democratic publisher of the *Louisville Courier-Journal.* Again, he emphasized Cleveland's physical dominance over an insignificant adversary. Nast needled Watterson — still his personal friend — for his excessive drinking, by italicizing the word "drop."

HW October 2, 1886 640

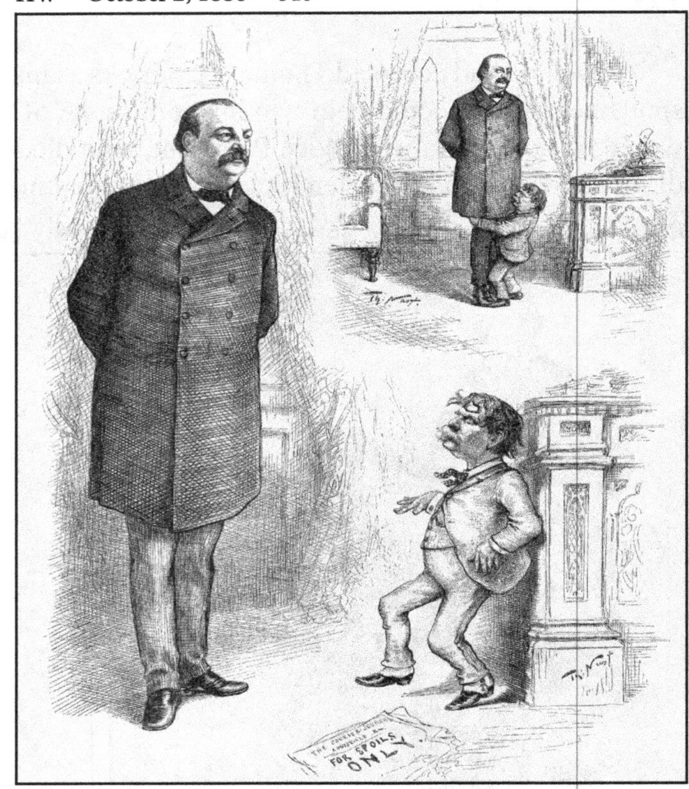

ONLY A *DROP*, AFTER ALL, MY COUNTRYMEN.

After Nast returned from Europe, he featured the starving Democratic Tiger, as the President stood firm against the horde of Democratic office-seekers who besieged him. Two cartoons showed the beast vainly trying to get inside the White House.

HW October 10, 1885 673

THAT EVERLASTING HUNGRY WAIL.

HW November 21, 1885 768

SLAM-BANG!

"It looks as though Mr. Cleveland meant business when he ordered the doors permanently closed against office-seekers."—*Elmira Advertiser*.

Nast related two intervening cartoons directly to his climactic Tammany Tiger mauling Lady Liberty in the Colosseum, while Tweed and his Ring cohorts looked on in 1871.* Now — 14 years later — new Tammany chief Richard Croker and his Irving Hall partner-in-crime were trying to push Columbia off the White House steps onto the arena floor. The Tiger was caged as New York Governor David Hill, up for reelection in two weeks, watched under a Spoils banner.

Lieutenant-Governor Hill had succeeded Cleveland as Governor. The two men never got along because Hill was a machine politician for whom spoils were a way of life. After Hill won the election by a landslide over a weak Republican candidate, Cleveland rebuffed him and Croker. Although Columbia was now on the Colosseum floor, she was being handed a sword to slay the Tiger if he got loose. Meanwhile Hill and Croker were barred from the White House, as Nast quoted Cleveland's policy of "No Change."

HW October 31, 1885 709

"THIS WOULD, INDEED, BE A *BACKWARD STEP*!"

I BELIEVE IN CIVIL SERVICE REFORM.
Of course there should be no surrender of principle nor
BACKWARD STEP,
and all laws for the enforcement of the reform should be rigidly executed.
G. CLEVELAND.

NO CHANGE.
"I can not rid myself of the idea that this civil service reform is something intended to do practical good, and not a mere sentiment invented for the purpose of affording opportunity to ventilate high-sounding notions and fine phrases. My plan of giving it the greatest possible usefulness involves the removal of stumbling-blocks from the way of good, honest men, who are inclined to its support, and demonstrate in every public manner its value as adapted to the every-day affairs of the government."
G. CLEVELAND.
November 5.

HW November 14, 1885 741

DOES THIS MEAN THE INDORSEMENT OF THE PRESIDENT!

"It means, above all, that the fact that Governor Hill was the representative of real Democracy and not of sham Mugwump Democracy secured his election by a majority probably fifteen or twenty times greater than the State gave Mr. Cleveland last year. This is the lesson of the election."— *New York World, November 4.*

Hedden — Sterling

The first and most important challenge to Cleveland's Civil Service policy occurred about six months after he took office. In late June 1885, he appointed Edward Hedden as Collector of the Port of New York to replace William Robertson — President Garfield's controversial 1881 choice — whose term had expired.** Cleveland wanted a non-politician to fill the office which controlled more than 1,300 patronage jobs. Hedden qualified because he had dealt with the Custom-house for 35 years as customs manager for a recently dissolved import company.

Hedden turned out to be a front for Boss Hubert Thompson, the Brooklyn Commissioner of Public Works, who split with John Kelly and Tammany Hall in 1877, founded the County Democracy Party, and firmly supported Cleveland's candidacy. Ineligible for Collector by Cleveland's ethical standard, Hedden became Thompson's puppet.

---

* See p. 278-279
** See p. 512

On September 14, Hedden fired George Bacon, the highly regarded sixteen-year veteran chief weigher for Brooklyn from his $2,500 a year position without cause or notice. He replaced Bacon with George Sterling, a saloon-keeper and political hack, who would now control a number of lesser patronage positions.

After returning from his two-month European vacation, Nast finally had some specific targets to attack — depicting Hedden as a cunning rabbit and Sterling as a whisky bottle.

HW September 25, 1885 635

COLLECTOR HEDDEN'S NEW *"WHISKEY."*

HW October 3, 1885 651

THE CUSTOM-HOUSE HARE.
"It is a wonderfully cunning animal, and is said, by many who have closely studied its habits, to surpass the fox in ready ingenuity."—*Natural History.*

HW October 3, 1885 655

TAKE HIM OFF THE LIST.
"For he never would be missed."

Note: From *The Mikado*

When Cleveland found out, he immediately ordered Treasury Secretary Daniel Manning to suspend Sterling, just a week after his appointment. Although the vacant weigher position wasn't covered by Civil Service regulations, it was decided to have candidates for it take a competitive examination. Sterling refused and went back to his saloon, where Nast had him confronting newly-elected Governor David Hill.

HW October 3, 1885 656

SUCH MONOTONOUS BREAKFASTS, AND STILL HE STAYS.

Treasury Department,
Washington, D.C., Sept. 21, 1885.
Office of the Secretary.
Collector of Customs, New York, N. Y.:
Sir,—In view of all the information received at this department, and pending an examination of the subject, you will suspend from duty George H. Sterling as Weigher No. 50, Class 4, at your port.
Very respectfully,
D. Manning, Secretary.

(Extract from upper left)

HW November 28, 1885 784

VETERAN SOLDIERS ARE NOT AFRAID OF CIVIL-SERVICE EXAMINATIONS.

HW December 5, 1885 808

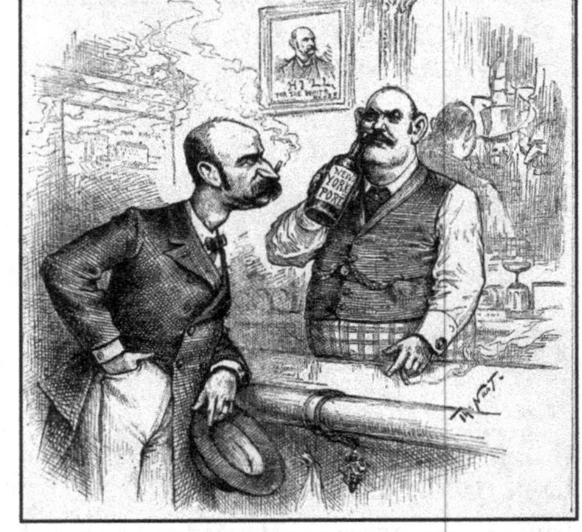

MOST AT HOME WHERE HE IS.
The Sterling Brooklyn Alderman. "Why, Governor, there is no vacancy here; this is full."

This normally-irrelevant incident demonstrated to both political parties that the President was deadly serious about Civil Service reform. Nast's cartoons emphasized that a local issue had national implications.

Cleveland fired Hedden in July 1886, the same month Hubert Thompson unexpectedly died at age 37, although the two events were not related. He was replaced by Daniel Magone, an upstate lawyer with an admirable reputation.[3]

Puck

Eugene (Zim) Zimmerman surpassed Nast in portraying twelve identifiable characters assailing the President for embracing Civil Service, in a cartoon reminiscent of (his boss) Keppler's *Forbidding the Banns*.* They included Hedden, Hubert Thompson, Hill, Hendricks, Eustis, Kelly and publishers Dana, McLean and Pulitzer, whose Democratic *World* had turned against Cleveland after strongly supporting him for election.

PUCK October 21, 1885

NO WELCOME FOR THE LITTLE STRANGER.
Father Cleveland Adopts the Abandoned Infant of the Republican Home, to the Great Discomfort of the Jeffersonian Household.

* See p. 492

As he approached the end of his first year in office, Nast depicted Cleveland as Hercules, with a firm grip on the reptilian spoilsmen of both parties. (He removed 643 individuals during that year.) However, a month later, Curtis criticized him for making too many changes without legitimate cause.[4] The President marched to his own drummer so there was no way he could keep from antagonizing even his friends.

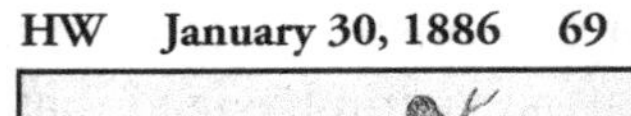

THE PRESIDENTS GRIP; OR, OUR INFANT HERCULES.

Tenure of Office

In the spring of 1884, Curtis and other Mugwumps had backed Republican Senator George Edmunds of Vermont for the Presidential nomination. At that time, he had been president pro tempore of the Senate, and was followed in that role by John Sherman of Ohio. In December 1885, Edmunds — now Chairman of the Judiciary Committee — along with Sherman, launched a massive attack to humble and embarrass Cleveland for his Civil Service Reform policy and successes.

Their weapon was the Tenure of Office Act, which 39-year old Edmunds had helped draft and enact in 1867 with the goal of impeaching President Andrew Johnson.* After President Grant took office in 1869, the Act was weakened — over Edmunds's objections — in two respects: the Senate had no authority whatsoever over dismissals, and it had no right to demand "reasons or evidence" for them.

After the new Congress convened in December 1885, Senate Republicans agreed not to approve Cleveland's sub-cabinet appointments unless he provided complete documentation of dismissed office-holders. Cleveland instructed his Cabinet not to comply; moreover, with regard to new nominations, he told them to submit all formal papers and open endorsements, but not confidential letters or memoranda. His rationale was that not knowing most nominees, he was dependent on truthful references, and couldn't expect those unless his informants were assured of confidentiality.

The test case involved the dismissal of a Republican district attorney in Alabama and his replacement by a Democrat in late December 1885. Attorney General Augustus Garland submitted limited papers on the appointment, but not on the removal. A month later, the Judiciary Committee voted to censure Garland and to withhold all further Presidential nominations. (The test case became moot when it was revealed that the dismissed official's term had expired.)

Cleveland made his point in a March 1 "Special Message" to the Senate, which offended the humorless, aristocratic Edmunds, who was accustomed to winning power struggles. Edmunds made a serious mistake when he compared this jurisdictional dispute to that between tyrannical King Charles I of England and Parliament, which cost the monarch his head in 1649. Neatly turning the metaphor about, the President reminded the Senator about the perversity of parliaments, and of Oliver Cromwell, who dissolved Parliament in 1651 and became "Lord Protector" in 1653.

That provided Nast with the inspiration for two covers and a full-page cartoon over six weeks. He was the Nast of yore, a flair in his final year at the *Weekly* — perhaps influenced by Keppler's and Gillam's artistry at *Puck*.

* See p. 180-181

HW March 13, 1886 161 C

LIKE CROMWELL—*NOT* "LIKE CHARLES THE FIRST,"—MR. EDMUNDS!
Now Open The Doors All Around, And Let The People Judge Where The Responsibility Lies.

His initial cover portrayed the President, representing the public and dressed as Cromwell — not Charles I — pitching his Message into the Star Chamber of the House/Senate of Lords. A crown-capped emblematic mace of Senate power lay on a bench, while Senators (via their feet) appeared to be fleeing in consternation. (The Star Chamber referred to the vindictive and arbitrary King's tribunal held in Westminster Palace in a secret room with stars on its ceiling.) The following week, Nast tweaked Edmunds as a fly outside his Star Chamber.

HW March 20, 1886 192

THE SECRET CHAMBER OF BARGAINS.
Fly—open the doors! or—fly—in the face of the public.

Nast's next small cartoon showed the Star Chamber in action, considering removals and replacements in executive session, closed to the public and the press. The previous week, Curtis had editorialized that the Senate was playing "A Losing Game," sharply criticizing Edmunds whom he had nominated for President two years before.

Nast dressed Edmunds in regal ermine, silk and lace, with his scepter pointing to a scrolled declaration that "the people have no right to any part in the government." At the lower right of the document, the "Seal of Secrecy" was thumbing its nose, one of several clever Nast touches.

Another was New York Senator William Evarts, sitting to Edmunds's left, looking glum and with no apparent mouth. Evarts had strongly opposed the Tenure of Office Act, while representing Johnson during his impeachment, so he couldn't support Edmunds's position now.

Behind Edmunds, Senator John Logan of Illinois, James Blaine's running mate in 1884, was spitting into an upturned crown as though it was a cuspidor. His action implied both his disrespect for Edmunds and his reputed crudeness.

Presiding over the Senate was John Sherman as president pro tempore. Above him, the royal shield was emblazed with "The People Be Duped," a reference to railroad tycoon William Vanderbilt's notorious 1882 remark, "The Public Be Damned." To Sherman's right a banner proclaimed "Royal Spoils at Auction This Day — Bargains."

HW April 3, 1886 221

OUR ROYAL RULERS (BY DIVINE RIGHT) IN SECRET SESSION.

By the end of March, the battle was essentially over as many Republicans broke from Edmunds. Some of them had quietly gone to Cleveland in the past, asking him to remove Republican office-holders whom they disliked. If he made their requests public, they would suffer politically, and he included a quiet hint to that effect in his message. Others resented Edmunds for his irritating manner and malignant sarcasm as the arbiter of Constitutional questions in the Senate.[5]

Nast took a final swipe at Edmunds in a post-dated cover appearing in late April — Oliver Cromwell and Charles I. Cleveland was gesturing to Edmunds that he should place his head on the chopping block, where masked executioners Logan and Blaine were ready to wield their axes. Nast's pun about *The only headway they are making in Washington* was a perfect finish.

HW May 1, 1886 273 C

OLIVER CROMWELL AND CHARLES I.
The Only Headway They Are Making In Washington.

For Edwards, this was a personal tragedy because he never regained his authority and power in the Senate. Salt was rubbed into his open wound when the Senate, later in the year, voted to repeal the Tenure of Office Act, with his being the only no vote on the Judiciary Committee. In 1891, he resigned his Senate set after 25 years, went into private practice, and lived another 28 years.

The Garland Scandal

At the same time the Tenure of Office controversy was brewing, a scandal involving Attorney General Augustus Garland was making headlines and giving Nast material for 22 cartoons. The case was a rare occurrence where both he and Curtis were openly critical of the President, much to the latter's expressed displeasure.

The keynote involved ownership of the basic telephone patent that Alexander Graham Bell had originally filed on February 14, 1876, and the U.S. Patent Office subsequently granted. Other inventors, especially Elisha Gray, who filed later the same day, and their companies claimed prior invention and sued Bell Telephone to invalidate its patents. Over several decades, Bell defended more than 600 lawsuits, all of which the company won.

While Garland was a U.S. Senator from Arkansas (1877-1885), six "impecunious men," as he described them in 1886 testimony to the Senate, organized the Pan-Electric Telephone Company in Tennessee. Its purposes was to form regional phone companies that utilized equipment developed by J. Harris Rogers. Bell sued it for patent infringement.

To strengthen its risky legal premise, Pan-Electric offered stock to members of Congress — some of whom accepted — in hope of gaining political influence when needed. Nast and others would make the obvious references to Credit Mobilier and the Mulligan letters.

Senator Garland was offered and accepted 500,000 shares. The only way those shares would ever have value was if Bell's patent was invalidated. Consequently, less than a year after Garland became Attorney General, Pan-Electric's owners asked him to sue Bell Telephone to make that happen. Garland refused, before returning home to Arkansas for a lengthy stay. He didn't tell his Solicitor General — the decision-maker in his absence — about either the request or his significant stock ownership.

Pan-Electric tried again, this time with the Solicitor General, who approved the lawsuit, not knowing of Garland's personal interest. When that became public in late January, Nast attacked the Attorney General in a cover cartoon using an ornamental pictorial symbol of his name, and an animated telephone effectively.

HW February 13, 1886 97 C

THAT GARLAND HAS SLIPPED.
His *Various Channels Of Usefulness* In *Public Trust*—Are At An End!

HW February 13, 1886 107

THE TELEPHONE SCANDAL.
Hello! Hello!! Hello!!!

President Cleveland was upset and advised Garland to give away his stock, but he couldn't find anybody to take it off his hands. Nast followed up with another cover, suggesting the Attorney General resign, and also portrayed him as a pawnbroker.

HW February 27, 1886 129 C

THE "SOMETHING" (THAT) "SHOULD BE DONE BY ME TO RELIEVE MYSELF AND THE ADMINISTRATION.
Garland. "Nobody will take the stock off my hands."
Columbia. "Can't you get somebody to take you off my hands?

HW February 20, 1886 116

DEFACING THE ADMINISTRATION SIGN.
We Cannot Allow This Mis-*Construction*.

HW April 3, 1886 215

A GARLAND OF HONOR.
Fame. "Mr. Lamar, pick out the real inventor from among the frauds, that he may wear this."

Additionally, Cleveland reprimanded the Solicitor General for not following the usual procedure by referring the matter to Secretary of the Interior Lucius Lamar, who had jurisdiction over patents. That happened, and after the lawsuit ruling was revoked, Lamar reinstated the lawsuits, and Nast's telephone threw up its hands.

As the case headed toward the Supreme Court, Nast enjoyed punning with a Bell and a frying Pan tangling with each other. Once again, he alluded to the Mikado.

HW March 3, 1886 159

THE MASQUERADING TELEPHONE PUZZLE.
Bell and Pan still at their tricks,
Trying to scare me out of my wits,
Ringing and banging me into fits;
But in this court I've got them on the list—
I'm sure they'd not be missed.

HW March 13, 1886 165

THE TELEPHONE RIVALS WERE FIGHTING FOR A *SHADOW*, AND THE SUBSTANCE WAS LOST.

HW March 20, 1886 177 C

ONE THING YOU ARE ACCOUNTABLE TO THE PUBLIC FOR.
An Exacting House-Keeper. "The reason you have this position is on account of your reputation for not leaving any rubbish like this around in dark corners."

After Garland's explanations to the Senate committee, he somehow disposed of his stock, and the Cleveland administration dropped its case against Bell. Nast, with strong support from Curtis, pressed the unwilling President to fire Garland, beginning with a cover depicting his cabinet with a "Garland" and his stock burning in its grate, as Columbia admonished him.

Nast followed with two smaller cartoons depicting Cleveland cooking with a long-handled frying Pan-Electric, with a smelly Garland in it. In spite of his Attorney General's negative press, however, Cleveland believed that he had made an "amazing indiscretion" and error of judgment, but that his integrity was not compromised. Stubbornly, he kept Garland on for the rest of his term.

HW April 24, 1886 272

"UNDER FIRE."
It is not gammon and spinach.

HW May 15, 1886 319

OH! THE GARLAND OF IT!
***We all* "regret it has not panned out better."**

Marriage

After his law partner Oscar Folsom died in 1875, Cleveland saw himself as a virtual guardian of his daughter Frances (Frankie) Folsom, then 13. He corresponded with her at Wells College and sent her flowers on occasion. During her spring vacation in April 1885, Frankie and her mother visited him at the White House, a month or so after his Inauguration. She graduated that spring.[6]

In August, Grover and Frances became engaged after he wrote her proposing marriage. The nuptials took place in the White House on Wednesday June 2, 1886. Nast celebrated the happy union with a reference to Civil Service Reform, and a starving tiger looking on wistfully outside the White House. As Nast noted in a scrapbook, the strange-looking Cupid delivering the marriage certificate was thinking "I understand you, old fellow."[7]

Frances, only 22, was universally admired, and made her husband brighter and more companionable. The happy couple eventually had five children, all raised with minimal publicity.

Nast followed his cover cartoon with a smaller one the next week, needling Garland for not resigning.

HW June 12, 1886 369 C

BLESSED BE THE UNION.
More Civil Service Reform.

HW June 19, 1886 395

PERHAPS THIS IS THE REASON WHY THE ATTORNEY-GENERAL DID NOT WISH TO CHANGE HIS COAT.

Nast's clipping service must have sent him a short article from the Logansport, Indiana paper — dated August 1, 1886 and entitled *Our Statuesque Chief* — which he pasted in his scrapbook.[8]

> *The Critic* (a New York magazine) *has no objection to our President, but rather an admiration, particularly since he showed the good sense to marry a young and lovely girl. But if somebody could put Thomas Nast in the stocks for the next two years, the President would have a better chance of a second term. Kings sometimes unbend, but Cleveland, as depicted by Nast, never. We have grown so very tired, and so, probably, have several thousand readers of Harper's Weekly, of seeing the President, week after week, posing as for a statue, his form rigid and unbending, and upon his face that mingled look of the bull-dog and mule which seems to say, "though the Heavens fall Cleveland will not yield." If Mr. Nast would but permit him to smile occasionally, or let him down from those heights of sternness whereon he has been so long immured, it would place him before the public in a more human light. Even in his wedding picture, though somewhat softened by the unusual elegance of his dress, his face wore the same adamantine look. Looked he thus, one wonders, when he wooed? Looked he thus when he won? If so, Miss Folsom was capable of loving the Sphinx. Were we within elbow reach of Mr. Nast, we would beg him, for the love he bears to mankind, now that Mr. Cleveland is married to soften down his saturnine features and introduce hint of the lovable.*

Chapter 46
President Cleveland: Labor Issues

Chinese Labor

Although the Chinese Exclusion Act had been signed by President Arthur in 1882,* the Union Pacific still used both white and Chinese laborers to mine coal in Wyoming three years later. Western coal was closer to the surface, cheaper and less dangerous to mine, and nearer to the railroad's routes. Management responded to a strike by firing the white strikers and then using white contract workers, as well as non-striking Chinese laborers, to operate the mines.

In Rock Springs, about 600 Chinese and 300 whites worked in the same close spaces, all paid the same piece rate. With separate languages and cultures a divisive factor, the willingness of the Chinese to work for less money in a depressed economy enraged the whites.

On September 2, 1885, a quarrel inside a mine resulted in four Chinese casualties; all miners abruptly fled to their homes. A few hours later, an armed group of more than 100 whites entered Chinatown and ordered everyone to leave immediately. Growing impatient, they killed 28 Chinese, injured 15, and burned their dwellings. Most got away, but were later tricked into returning and, with escape almost impossible, were forced to go back into the mines.

Nast's response to the Rock Springs massacre was in print a week later.

HW September 19, 1885 623

"HERE'S A PRETTY MESS!" (IN WYOMING.)
Chinese Satirical Diplomatist. "There's no doubt of the United States being at the head of enlightened nations!"

---

* See p. 530-531

The white miners belonged to the Knights of Labor which, of course, backed them and claimed the Union Pacific was responsible for the massacre because its contractor employed the Chinese. Governor Francis Warren of the Wyoming Territory tried to support the Chinese by using federal troops to maintain order, but refused to pay indemnities. Six months later, Congress finally appropriated $150,000 to settle the Chinese claims after the State Department refused them. Both editor Curtis and Nast were outspoken on behalf of the Chinese.

HW March 20, 1886 191

IF WE WERE ENOUGH OF A NATION TO DEMAND, — WE OUGHT TO BE ENOUGH OF A NATION NOW TO PAY.

U. Sam. "We, as a Nation, are not responsible; it is the State; and as the murders were all committed by *unnaturalized foreigners*, you should go to their native lands for indemnity."

Anti-Chinese sentiment also boiled over in the Northwest. On February 7, a mob in Seattle, Washington Territory, carefully planned and attacked 400 Chinese in their homes at night, and marched them to a dock with a steamer waiting to take them to San Francisco. The Governor quickly deputized concerned citizens and ordered the mob to disperse. The militia guarded the Chinese and a judge ordered all to return to their homes, except those who bought steamer tickets and wanted to leave. A mob of 2,000 then attacked the militia. In response, President Cleveland sent troops to maintain order.

Not long after an "Anti-Chinese Congress" was held in Portland, and a resolution adopted calling upon the people in every town in the Northwest "peaceably to assemble and politely request the Mongolian race to remove." As the *Weekly* noted, the experience of Seattle may at any time be repeated in other towns.[1] Nast followed up with three cartoons depicting the violence.

HW March 20, 1886 183

MURDERERS STOP AT NOTHING.

Portland, Oregon, March 7—The bodies of M. Coleman and Wilson Patten , well-known citizens of Seattle, W.T., arrived here from Lake Washington yesterday. They were assassinated by some unknown persons. Coleman was foreman of the Grand Jury that indicted a number of men for participating in the recent Seattle riot, and also those who shot and killed several Chinamen at the New Castle coal mines.

HW March 27, 1886 208

JUSTICE FOR THE CHINESE.

"It seems to be high time for all good people to come out and show the disreputable outlaws that the local authorities will be sustained by the people, and that law and order must and will be maintained in Portland."—Mayor Gates of Portland, Oregon.

HW May 15, 1886 319

THE CHINESE PUZZLED.

"Is it because we don't do deeds like that, that *we 'must go' and they stay!*"

Communism and Anarchy: 1878

Labor agitation incited by Communists in the United States was not a new subject for Nast. He first depicted it in 1874, using "Death" to personify radicals.* Three years later, the great railroad strikes began on July 14, and effectively shut down the country's transportation system for ten weeks before federal troops finally restored order. There were major riots in Baltimore, Pittsburgh, Chicago, St. Louis and other cities, thousands of casualties, and extensive property damage to railroad cars, depots and equipment. The turmoil made 1877 a momentous year for the American labor movement.

Harper's provided plenty of commentary, including two covers (August 11 and 18). Unfortunately, it couldn't call on Nast because he was on his own three-month strike against Curtis for the editor's abrupt and unreasonable rejection of his already scheduled cartoon.**

The following year, Nast vigorously attacked Communism as the insidious motivator behind continuing labor unrest, with at least eight cartoons. Usually, he portrayed Communism as an animal, or as a skeleton representing Death. Here, he made an exception by personally depicting Indiana Senator Daniel Voorhees as a Communist agitator who refused to take responsibility for backing the strikers and their horrific outcomes. (Nast disliked the Democrat whom he had ridiculed as a Copperhead Congressman during the Civil War.)

HW March 16, 1878 205 C

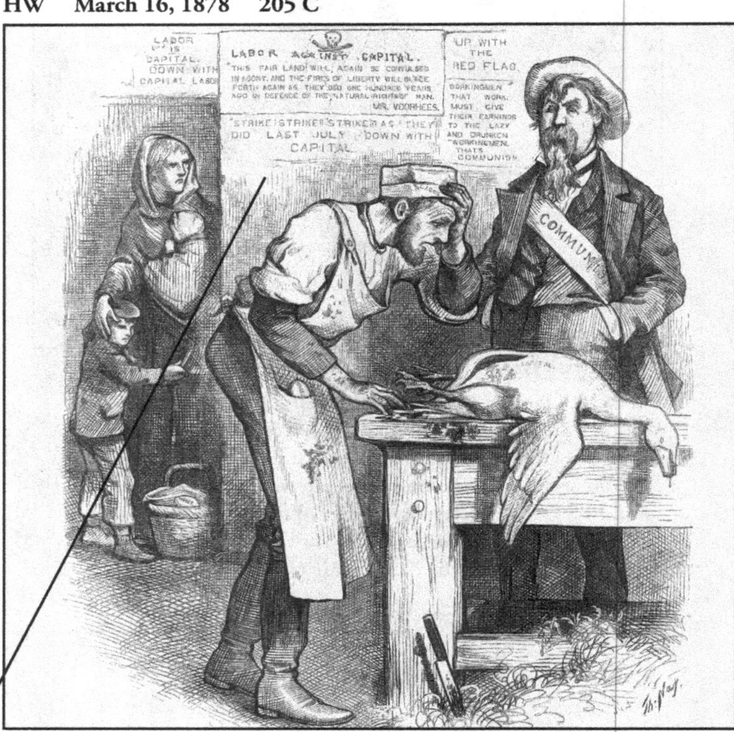

ALWAYS KILLING THE GOOSE THAT LAYS THE GOLDEN EGG.
Communistic Statesman *(without responsibility)*. "Nothing in it, after all; it's too bad; now I thought he was just full of them."

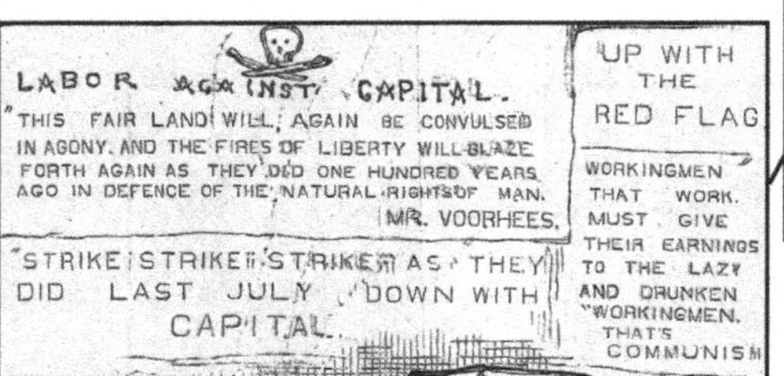

HW May 25, 1878 413

THE QUACK FROG.
Fox. "How can you pretend to prescribe for others, who are unable to heal your own lame gait and wrinkled skin!"

HW June 1, 1878 440

THE REPTILE.
If he don't burst himself, we must do it.

* See p. 390
** See p. 440

HW June 22, 1878 496

"HOME, SWEET HOME! THERE'S NO PLACE LIKE HOME?"

Destroyer of All. "Home ties are nothing. Family ties are nothing. Every thing that is— is nothing."

Anarchy joined Communism and Socialism as a triple threat to Capitalism in mid-1878, when German anarchists unsuccessfully attempted to assassinate 81-year old Kaiser Wilhelm I on two separate occasions. Now Nast added anarchistic sayings and symbolic Death to his labor/Communist full-page cartoons.

With the above as background, fast forward eight years when labor strife exploded and anarchy became a violent and visible threat all over the country.

HW November 23, 1878 936

ONE AND INSEPARABLE.

Capital Makes Labor, And Labor Makes Capital.

HW February 1, 1879 92

VERY SOCIAL.

First D.H. Conspirator. "After we have killed all Kings and Rulers, *we shall be the Sovereigns.*"
Second D.H. Conspirator. "And then we can kill each other. What sport!"

Johann Most

Most was a German-born Socialist and Anarchist. Expelled from the German Parliament (Reichstag) and then from Germany because of extremism, he moved to England and re-started the *Freiheit* (Freedom) newspaper. After publishing an article rejoicing over the assassination of Czar Alexander II in March 1881, he was jailed for 18 months.

After his release, Most moved to New York in 1882, re-established the *Freiheit*, and gave speeches calling for violence against governments and for abolition of private property and free markets. In 1885, he published *The Science of Revolutionary Warfare*, a how-to manual on bomb-making, and became known as *Dynamost*. The year before, he had offered "medicine" — dynamite — to August Spies, also a German-born anarchist, who spearheaded labor strikes and riots in Chicago.

On April 22, 1886, Most advocated murder and violence to a large audience in Germania Hall. After a warrant was issued for his arrest, he was found hiding under his bed. He was indicted, released on bail on May 14, and apparently not imprisoned. However, Nast, who despised Most, ridiculed him in successive issues as much for his cowardice as for his beliefs.

HW May 22, 1886 335

WHEN HIS SKIN IS NOT IN DANGER, AND —

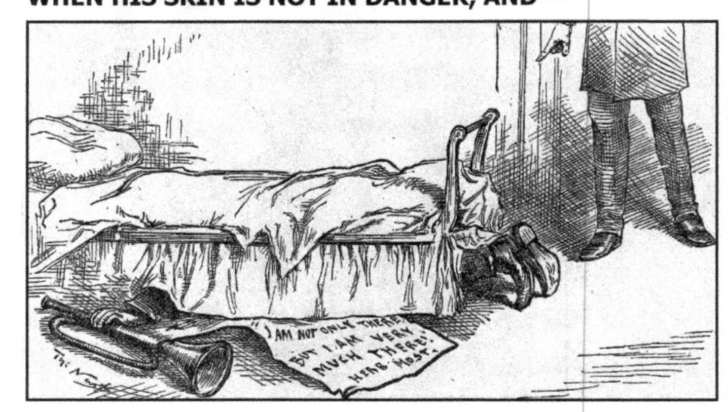

WHEN IT IS.

HW May 29, 1886 351

ANARCHISTS' DRILL, NEW TACTICS.
Generalissimo. "Double quick, under the bed, march!"

Knights of Labor

The Knights formed America's first dominant national union. Founded in 1869, it had 10,000 members when Terence Powderly became its president a decade later. Under his leadership, its membership increased to more than 100,000 by 1886. His primary objective was to secure an eight-hour day.

Harper's respected Powderly as "intelligent and cool-headed," but he wasn't strong enough to control all his local unions. After 1886. Powderly's influence and membership were superseded by the newly-formed American Federation of Labor, which organized workers by craft.

During the 1880s, Jay Gould controlled several railroads, including the Texas & Pacific and the Missouri Pacific. By 1886, the T&P was in bankruptcy and operated by the Federal government. Trouble broke out on March 1 when its workers went on strike until management reinstated a discharged mechanic.

A rebellious hothead, Martin Irons, was the Knights District Chief in St. Louis, responsible for the Missouri Pacific. He told the MoPac Vice President to get the T&P mechanic back on the payroll, or he would call strikes on the MoPac and other Gould railroads. The MoPac VP no longer had any authority over the T&P, so Irons ordered an 18-day strike without notifying Powderly or asking for permission; he knew that Powderly strongly favored arbitration and disapproved of strikes.

Harper's railed against the strikes week after week, calling them boycotts because the Knight's only legitimate grievance was with the T&P. It compared the impacted workers to slaves who didn't know why they couldn't work or support their starving families. Nast led with a cover cartoon depicting Powderly holding a pair of red-hot "Irons" while perched on a powder barrel, and followed "Irons Grip" as "boss of the U.S.," with an analogy to slavery. Nast's targets' names encouraged him to pun, pun, pun.

HW April 10, 1886 225 C

WHAT'S IN A NAME!
There Is A Great Deal In *His Name*, And Great Responsibility In The Way In Which He Guards It.

HW April 17, 1886 253

WILFUL SLAVERY MAKES WOFUL SUFFERING.
Colored Labor To White Labor. "No sooner am I really set free than you enslave yourselves, and at the expense of your families, too."

HW May 8, 1886 293

THE ROOT OF THE MATTER.
Boycotter. "*You* must stop work, because *I* have a grievance against your employer, no matter whether you have any, or whether your family suffers meanwhile. *I must show my power*."

However, there was no humor in the St. Louis blockade of freight trains on the "Gould system," which created critical shortages of food, coal and other necessities as perishables rotted, flour mills closed, factories shut down and violence flared up.[2] *Harper's* ran an illustration of endless freight cars piled up in St. Louis,[3] and Nast commented as well.

On March 26, five Western governors issued proclamations calling for managers to send out trains as usual, with police and troops to protect them. The strikers responded by disabling engines, decoupling cars, and raising violence levels and fatalities. The country was paralyzed by boycotts of all kinds of businesses, along with lockouts. Powderly's direct negotiations with Gould failed. Congress investigated and the House passed a bill to help pay for voluntary arbitration of labor disputes.

By the end of April the strike broke down and the Knights surrendered as its devastated workers could hold out no longer. It was formally terminated on May 4. Gould's Missouri Pacific took back only about one out of five former employees.

One particular boycott of Mrs. Gray's Bakery caught the *Weekly's* attention because her shop was in New York, and the Harpers and their staff probably patronized it. The editorial columns referred to it in four issues, and Nast featured it in three consecutive ones.

HW April 24, 1886 271

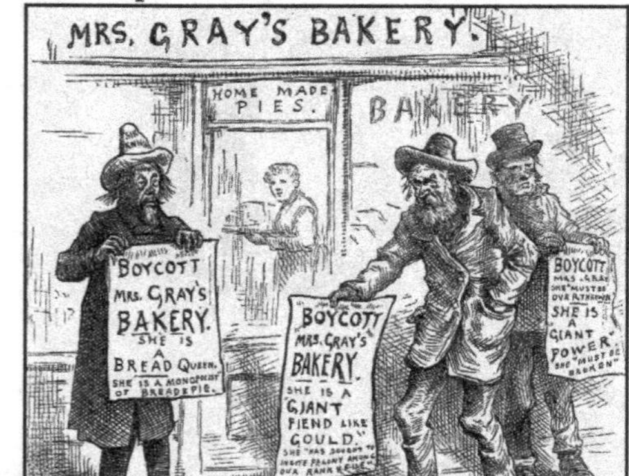

THE CHIVALRY OF MODERN KNIGHTS.

HW May 1, 1886 287

ILL-BRED GERMAN "SANDWICH" KNIGHTS.

HW May 8, 1886 303

HIGHWAY BOYCOTTING.
"We have ruined your business, now you must pay us a ransom for doing it."

Haymarket

On the same date, one of the worst, and certainly the most notorious, labor riots in American history took place in Haymarket Square in Chicago. It was precipitated by a lockout and subsequent violence at Cyrus McCormick's Reaper Works the preceding day, Monday, May 3. The Knights of Labor workers had been planning to strike for an eight-hour day, but were locked out and replaced by strikebreakers, guarded by a large police force. When the shift changed, the strikers heckled their replacements and some threw rocks. The police protectors fired into the mob, killing two and critically wounding several men.

Chicago's labor force in 1886 was mostly immigrants, primarily German and Czech (then called Bohemians.) They earned $1.50 a day for a six-day week. Several thousand were Anarchists, or Communist or Socialist sympathizers.

The Anarchist leader was August Spies, 30, who published the *Arbeiter-Zeitung* (*Workers' Times*), a daily German-language newspaper. He and an associate, Michael Schwab, had addressed the locked-out McCormick workers on the Saturday before the Monday blow-up. On Monday night, Spies and Schwab printed 20,000 handbills — in both German and English — calling for a rally at 7 pm Tuesday, May 4, at Haymarket Square (where Desplaines and Randolph streets intersected). Its key message called "Workingmen to Arms!"

Widely distributed, the fliers, plus word-of-mouth, brought an estimated 2,000 workers and radicals to Haymarket, along with about 150 police. In addition to Spies who led off, the speakers included Alabama-born, ex-Confederate soldier Albert Parsons, and English-born Samuel Fielden, both close associates and conspirators. Rain arrived as the evening wore on, and the crowd dwindled to about 300. As Fielden was winding down about 10:20, with a threat "to lay hands on Law and throttle it," the police captain ordered the crowd to disperse and Fielden agreed.

Suddenly a dynamite bomb was thrown from the area of the speakers' stand (a wagon) into the advancing police, killing seven and wounding sixty of them. Gunfire broke out. Four in the crowd died at the scene, at least 70 were injured, and more than 100 arrested. The mob disappeared in five minutes or so.

An on-the scene correspondent for *Harper's* quickly sent sketches and photographs to New York. Probably by holding its presses for two or three days, the post-dated *Weekly* contained a dramatic double-page illustration by Thure de Thulstrup, along with a descriptive article, in its May 15 issue.

HW May 15, 1886 312-313

THE ANARCHIST RIOT IN CHICAGO — A DYNAMITE BOMB EXPLODING AMONG THE POLICE.

HW May 15, 1886 305 C

Nast had three cartoons in the issue, including the cover. All were submitted before he knew about the Haymarket riot.

HW May 15, 1886 315

HW May 15, 1886 320

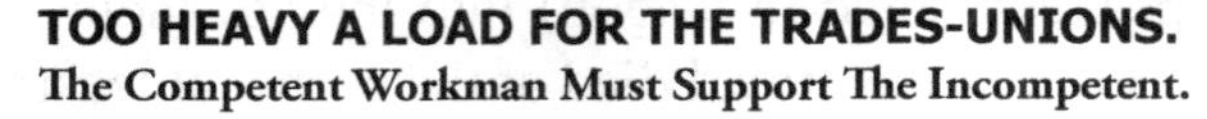

TOO HEAVY A LOAD FOR THE TRADES-UNIONS.
The Competent Workman Must Support The Incompetent.

A WARNING IN TIME.
Uncle Sam. "Ours is a large country, but there is room in it for only *one* flag."

THE EVOLUTION OF THE AMERICANIZED FOREIGNER.
Alderman Pat Boodle. "Go on, Hans Socialist, you'll be an Alderman some day; I used to be a rioter myself."

Police found dynamite bombs in the *Arbeiter* offices and at the home of employee Louis Lingg, who had written a "how-to" manual on bomb making. The day before he was scheduled to be hanged, Lingg committed suicide by biting a dynamite cap in his cell. (The actual bomb-thrower, indiscernible in the dark, probably was German-born Rudolph Schnauble, also an *Arbeiter* employee; he was arrested, released and then disappeared — probably fleeing to Europe.

A grand jury indicted eight men later in May. The trial began in July and finished August 20, with guilty verdicts against all eight. One was sentenced to 8-15 years, and seven ordered to be hanged on November 11. (The day before, Illinois Governor Richard Olglesby commuted the sentences of Fielden and Schwab to life imprisonment. In 1893, they were pardoned by Governor John P. Altgeld, along with Oscar Neebe who was serving the 8-15 year sentence.)[4]

Note: Today, some historians believe that several of the men should not have been charged or convicted. That was not the opinion of *Harper's*, Nast or most of the press at the time.

Nast never commented on the trial directly, but he did mock the anarchists and strikers in a number of small cartoons before its conclusion.

HW May 8, 1886 304

IS THIS THE TRIUMPH OF OUR REPUBLICAN FORM OF GOVERNMENT?
Must the honest laborer, satisfied with his employer, his wages, his hours, go to his daily work like this?

HW May 22, 1886 333

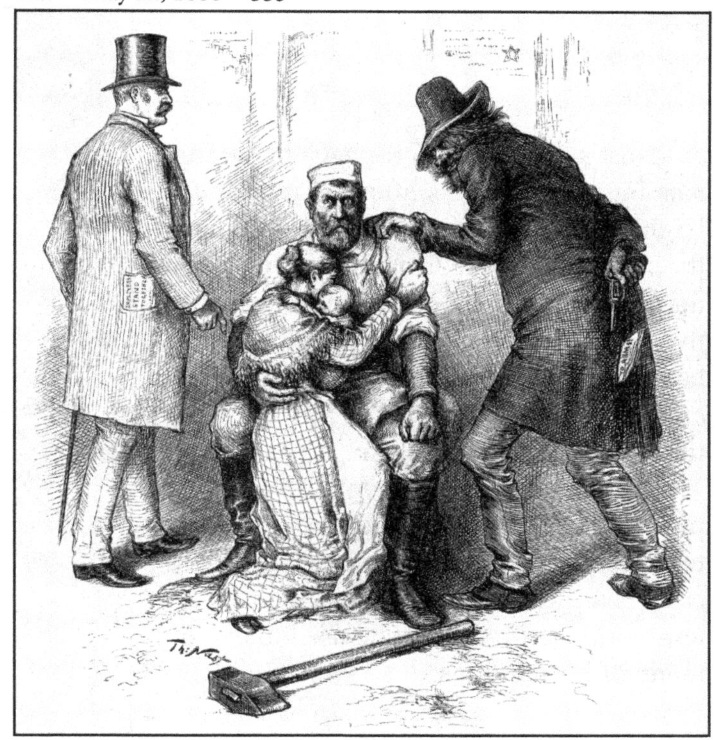

BETWEEN TWO FIRES.
Employer. "If you don't go to work, I must fill your place."
Anarchist. "If you go to work, I'll make it hot for you."

HW June 5, 1886 363

THE HARDEST BLOW YET TO THE ANARCHISTS.
Deprived of a privilege of which they were never known to avail themselves.

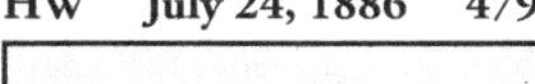

HW July 24, 1886 479

THOSE FOREIGN SAVAGES
Have even fired on our flag while we were celebrating Independence Day.

HW July 31, 1886 495

THE WORST THREAT YET.
First Boycotter. "I will not drink drop of any beer, for all brewers are bloated capitalists."
Second Boycotter. "What! commit suicide by keeping sober!"

Nast's classical full-page illustration was in print five days after the trial ended. Highly uncharacteristic of him, it depicted the seven condemned anarchists writhing in the giant right hand of a symbolic Justice, the hand traditionally used for balancing her scales. However, their faces appeared as recognizable portraits in this combination of allegory and realism.[5]

Liberty is Not Anarchy was a short, punchy title, appropriate for this final masterpiece of Nast's quarter-century at *Harper's*. That, in itself, contrasted with the often-wordy sub-titles that he used to explain many of his cartoons.

HW September 4, 1886 564

LIBERTY IS NOT ANARCHY.

Nast closed out Haymarket as a subject with two small gallows scenes, one in the same issue and one in the next.

HW September 4, 1886 571

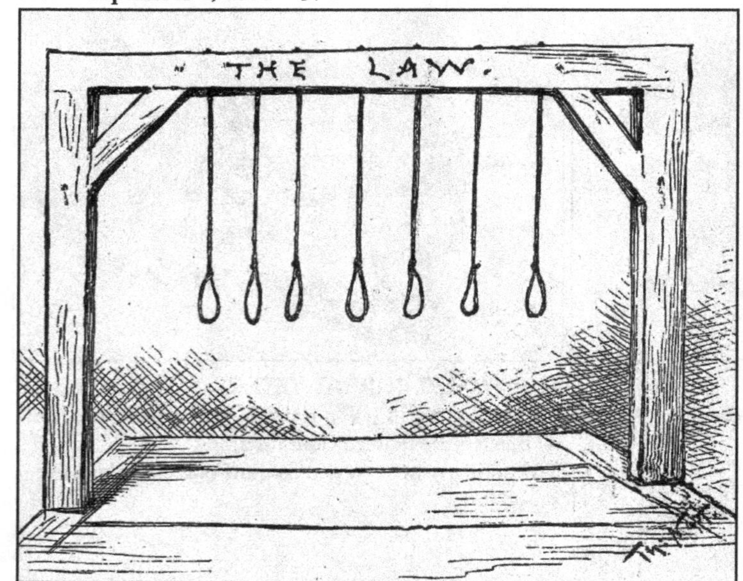

EQUAL TO THE ANARCHISTS.
They Will Have All The Rope They Want, And More Too.

HW September 11, 1886 592

THE SHADOW OF A COMING EVENT.
Justice. "Do any more of you wish to become '*Martyrs?*'"

Chapter 47
President Cleveland: Other Issues

Unity

Immediately after Cleveland's electoral victory, Nast praised him as a unifier of North and South — as well as blacks and whites — in two cover cartoons. He periodically reinforced the theme over the next two years.

HW November 22, 1884 763 C

ONE OF THE FIRST-FRUITS OF THE VICTORY.
President-Elect Cleveland. "Shake heartily, boys!"
The Atlanta (Georgia) *Constitution* (Democratic) says: "The negro will find that his best friend is the Southern Democrat. President Cleveland is his friend. The Southern people are his friends. Every right that they have as freemen and citizens will be jealously protected by the white men of the South, who have been their neighbors for years. In their schools, at the ballot-boxes, everywhere, they have their full rights. That man is the best Southerner and the best Democrat who stands by this doctrine and shows the negro that we are his true friends."

HW December 27, 1884 851 C

"ON EARTH PEACE, GOOD-WILL TOWARD MEN."

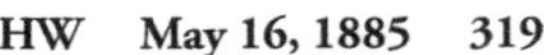
HW May 16, 1885 319

GETTYSBURG, MAY 4th, 1885.
"While the South and the North proclaim in one voice,
The flag of the Union is the flag of our choice."

HW July 25, 1885 484

THE TIME HAS COME.
Uncle Sam. "With this corner-stone, I bury the bloody shirt, or the party. Choose!"

During his first two years in particular, Cleveland had to deal with recalcitrant ex-Confederates, who still mourned the Last Cause even though they finally had a Democratic President. Conversely, a few Northern Republicans like Ohio Senator John Sherman and *Tribune* publisher Whitelaw Reid continued to taunt the former rebels. Nast strongly backed the President without reservation.

HW August 29, 1885 576

A DEAD ISSUE.
South. "I should like to oblige you by killing a few negroes, Mr. Tribune, but I am too busy."

HW September 12, 1885 604

A FAIR CHALLENGE TO A POLITICIAN.
Ex-Confederate Brigadier. "Take this, and if you can find any rebellion within our Union, ***I'll help you put it down.***"

Cleveland made several smart political appointments to discourage the unreconstructed Southerners. First, he appointed Mississippi's Lucius Lamar and Arkansas's Augustus Garland to his Cabinet. Then, influenced by their advice, he gradually distributed patronage in the South to Democrats who were in accord with his own full-reconciliation policy. A new South continued to evolve, with its primary interest in business.[1]

Rebuilding the Navy

When Cleveland took office, the United States Navy was in deplorable condition from top to bottom. There were 35 cruising vessels in the entire navy, none of them first-rate warships, and many in need of, or under, repair. A lot of the problems originated under George Robeson, President Grant's Secretary of the Navy, who was accused of gross misconduct by Congress in 1876 and 1878, and narrowly escaped impeachment.*

William Chandler, a seasoned Republican lawyer and politician, held the post during President Arthur's administration. He favored a defensive Navy which would keep peace by showing the American Flag to protect American lives, property and commerce around the world. However, the Pacific Fleet, which had to cover the coasts of Africa, the Indian Ocean, China and South and Central America, had only six or eight sea-going ships.[2]

Naval administration was an uncoordinated mess, with eight semi-autonomous, jealous, turf-protective bureaus, and no coordinating senior officer in command. Steam Engineering was responsible for engines; Construction and Repair for hulls; and Ordnance for guns. David Dixon Porter, the Civil War hero, was the top Admiral in the Navy; while his rank and prestige gave him significant influence, he had no line authority.[3]

In addition to fundamental administrative reorganization, the Navy needed major transitions from wooden hulls to steel-plated armor, and from sail to steam. The latter wasn't easy because it required coaling stations around the world, as well as acceptance of the international understanding that if the U.S. was a belligerent, it couldn't take on coal at a neutral port. Therefore, it still needed sail power to save coal for actual fighting.[4]

Prior to becoming Secretary in 1882, Chandler's clients included shipbuilder John Roach, for whom he did lobbying as well as legal work. Roach, an immigrant Irish orphan, began as an iron laborer at 16, and became the owner of multiple iron works and a shipyard in Chester, PA. Basically illiterate, he was a skilled businessman, and was one of the "Money Kings" at Belshazzar's Feast (the Blaine dinner fiasco on October 29, 1884).**

Chandler awarded contracts for three new cruisers and a dispatch-ship (for carrying messages) to Roach's shipyard, in addition to multiple contracts for repairs. With work underway, the House under the leadership of Democratic Speaker Samuel Randall, refused to approve money to complete their construction because of a "pretense of economy," as well as impugning Republicans Robeson and Chandler. Nast commented with a cover cartoon — in conjunction with editor Curtis's unusually harsh editorial — shortly before the electoral campaigns began in 1884.

HW April 26, 1884 261 C

THE GREAT DEMOCRATIC "PROTECTIONIST" OF HIS COUNTRY'S INTERESTS.
We May Have A *"Spirited Foreign Policy."*
We May Have A *Spirited Foreign War.*
We May Have A *Spirited Foreign Bombardment.*

* See p. 377
** See p. 585

Curtis pointed out that the armament for the four new ships would cost about $450,000, while re-armament of existing ships would cost about $600,000. A Naval investigation found that it was useless to preserve the wooden ships. Nast duly held Robeson and Chandler responsible. (Many years later, historians gave them some credit for beginning a long overdue process of providing the United States with a Navy almost as up to date and nearly as powerful as that of Turkey or Chile.[5])

HW June 20, 1885 399

PRESERVED LUMBER.
The board of investigation was forced to the following conclusion: "That the art of preserving timber has no practical value whatever."

Well aware of the need for action, Cleveland appointed William Whitney, a successful New York businessman, as Secretary of the Navy. Whitney reorganized the Navy Department into three principal branches: Personnel; Construction and Materials; and Finance, Contracts and Purchasing — all ultimately reporting to him. He scuttled most repairs; assisted new American companies with contracts to make steel for armor-plate, rifled cannons, gun forging, and other metal basics; and spread orders for new ships (which Congress finally approved) to seven diverse shipyards. Nast acknowledged Whitney's progress as it became apparent.

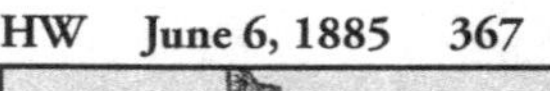
HW June 6, 1885 367

Penitentiary

"REPAIRS."
Turn the Rascals in.

HW June 13, 1885 383

ROUGH ON "REPAIRS."

HW December 19, 1885 847

THE REMEDY FOUND.
Commander Whitney. "Substantially thrown away."

Whitney faced a significant test immediately after he took office. The new dispatch-boat *Dolphin* was ready for its sea trial. John Roach & Son had signed its contract, awarded by Chandler, on July 23, 1883. To be accepted by the Navy, it had to meet strict specifications, including a sustained sea speed of fifteen knots. It failed the first two trials for mechanical reasons, and the third when it couldn't sustain the required speed. (A comparable British boat built at the same time, was more powerful, weighed less, and was two knots faster.)

Roach claimed he built the *Dolphin* to the specifications that the Government's naval architects had provided, and that he was not responsible for its failure. A Navy investigating board basically agreed, and the ship had to be accepted. Chandler, attempting to avoid blame, issued a public statement that "Secretary Whitney's dissatisfaction with the boat has a political and personal meaning."

Nast animated the *Dolphin* and backed Whitney with two cover cartoons that stood out from most of his other work (during Cleveland's Presidency) for their simple, captivating humor. He followed with a wordier cartoon quoting a three-paragraph explanation of the controversy by Curtis underneath.

Roach soon went bankrupt, both from the delay in getting paid for the Dolphin, and from problems with the three cruisers that Chandler ordered when Roach significantly underbid his competitors; the government took over and finished them. Whitney spread new orders over several shipyards.

HW June 6, 1885 353 C

CRUELTY.
Dolphin. "What! go to sea, Secretary Whitney? Why, that might make me seasick!"

HW July 4, 1885 421 C

DOLPHIN. "Put me into a heavy sea, Secretary Whitney! Why, you'll want me to fire off a gun next!"
"The trials of the *Dolphin* are not yet ended. Her trips on the Sound and beyond Sandy Hook are not sufficient. The sea was not heavy enough on Thursday to suit the official critics, and the dispatch-boat must try it again."—*New York Tribune*.

HW July 11, 1885 449

A DOLPHIN AND A MONKEY TIME.

What Mr. Roach, in his testimony before Congress (1882), meant by "sea speed":

"I think that we ought to build no ships of less than fifteen knots speed, and that a portion of your fleet should have a speed of eighteen knots; and when I speak of speed I don't mean speed according to the English standard. Their plan is to take the speed of the vessel in running a measured mile, and count that as the speed. But the speed I mean is the average speed of the ship in ordinary fair weather, and she must be able to keep it up for twenty-four hours if necessary. Twenty-four hours is about as long as you want to chase an enemy or run away from him. If you do not succeed in that time you may as well give the thing up."

(Bottom Left)

Mr. Chandler writes, June 23, 1885:

"This provision of law was complied with, and Mr. Roach bid upon designs of the Navy Department, and justly and properly was compe to guarantee only good workmanship. He guaranteed neither spe horse-power, nor anything else, except that the materials should be 'fi class and of the very best quality,' and well and faithfully put toget according to the plans and specifications of the department, and under inspection and supervision of the Naval Advisory Board. There is 'looseness of the contract' nor 'absence of effective stipulations,' as Whitney asserts, but all the provisions are to be found necessary to c out the fundamental idea upon which the contract was based, nam good work on Mr. Roach's part applied to the department's designs."

(Bottom Right)

Russia

While United States affairs were relatively calm during Cleveland's first year, Europe had enough going on for Nast to take notice. Great Britain, Russia and Germany were scrambling to absorb or colonize as much African and Asian territory as possible without provoking major wars. Here, John Bull, Czar Alexander III and German Chancellor Otto Von Bismarck were grabbing what they could.

A potential major problem began in 1881, when illiberal, autocratic Alexander III succeeded his assassinated father. His expansionist objective was to gradually absorb Central Asian territory — much of today's Turkestan — and he achieved that by 1884. His next goal was to take over independent Afghanistan; the first step was to conquer Herat, its northwestern fortress. On March 30, 1885, his general fought and won a battle inside Afghan territory, in which he lost 11 men while killing 500 Afghan defenders. (Battle of Panjdeh).

Britain understood that India (including today's Pakistan) — its "Crown Jewel" — would be in peril if Russia captured Afghanistan, and was ready to go to war if necessary. Nast deployed his animal kingdom — Lion, Bear and even a Lamb — to portray the potential combatants, while Curtis called the Russians "cheaters" among other harsh names.

HW June 20, 1885 399

THE WORLD'S PLUNDERERS.
"It's English, you know."

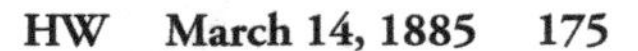
HW March 14, 1885 175

THE ANGLO-RUSSIAN TROUBLE.
Something else to "smash."

HW April 25, 1885 272

A BARE "EXPLANATION."
As a Bear was lapping at the head of a running brook, he spied a stray Lamb paddling at some distance down the stream. Having made up his mind to seize her, he bethought himself how he might justify his violence. "Villain!" said he, running up to her, "how dare you muddle the water that I was drinking?" "Indeed!" said the Lamb humbly. "I do not see how I can disturb the water, since it runs from you to me, not from me to you." "Be that as it may," replied the Bear, "it was but a year ago that you called me ill names." "Oh, sir!" said the Lamb, trembling, "a year ago I was not born." "Well," replied the Bear, "if it was not you, it was your father, and that is all the same; but it is no use trying to argue me out of my supper;" and without another word he fell upon the poor helpless Lamb and tore her to pieces.—Aesop

HW May 9, 1885 304

LET HIM GO!
"We say it is a case for preparation."—*Mr. Gladstone's Speech.*

British honor was at stake, and Prime Minister William Gladstone asked Parliament for a large war appropriation. A last-minute, face-saving agreement kept the peace when the Russians backed off.

HW May 16, 1885 309

THE FIGHT'S OFF—(FOR THE PRESENT).

However, the Russians were allowed to keep the borderline Afghan villages of Panjdeh. In one of his more humorous cartoons, Nast depicted the British Lion with a blindfold on, as the Bear grabbed his territory.

HW June 6, 1885 368

BEAR AN FOR-BEAR.
During the peace negotiations.

Egypt

In order to protect its control of the Suez Canal, England had established a "veiled" de facto protectorate over Egypt in 1882. However, Egypt was not part of the British Empire; it remained an autonomous province of the Ottoman Empire under the rule of a khedive. Nast had attacked England in 25 cartoons that year for its bombardment of Alexandria and conquest of the country.*

* See p. 542

By 1884, Chancellor Bismarck was expanding the German Empire by colonizing several African countries, as well as New Guinea in the Pacific. In early 1885, Nast parodied a cartoon from London's *Punch* as a springboard to depict both countries as greedy hogs grabbing Egypt and New Guinea, respectively.

HW February 7, 1885 96

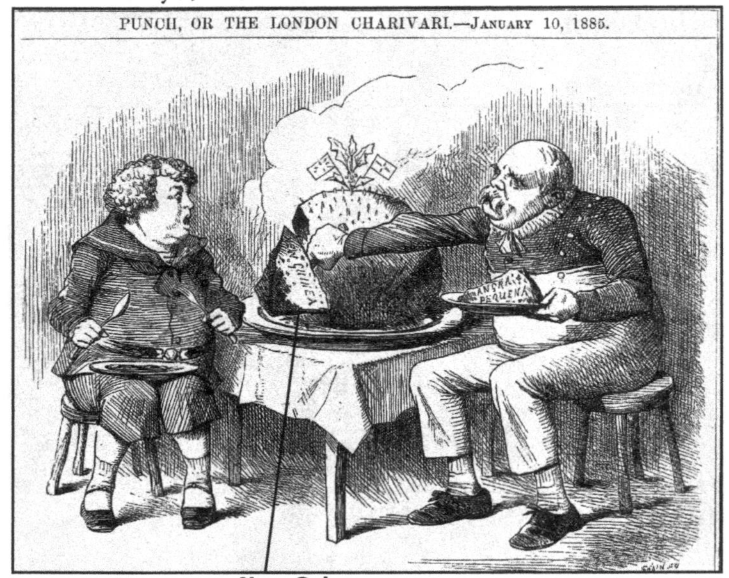

New Guinea

THE GREEDY BOY.

New Guinea

THE GREEDY — WHICH?

Sudan, which was part of Egypt, came under attack from a militant Islamist named Muhammad Ahmad, who proclaimed himself the Mahdi. He conquered various parts in 1883, and laid siege to Khartoum, the strategic capital where the White and Blue Nile Rivers met. General Charles Gordon was sent to Khartoum in February 1884 with orders to evacuate the British garrison. Instead, he began to administer the city, prepared defenses for what turned out to be a ten-month siege, and then requested a relief expedition.

Food supplies ran low, mass starvation became common, and the Mahdi attacked with 50,000 men on the night of January 25-26, 1885. Gordon and all his troops were slaughtered. The delayed relief expedition was in Sudan but didn't get to Khartoum; in fact, its presence probably triggered the Mahdi's attack. England was in an uproar, Gordon was a martyr, and Prime Minister William Gladstone was forced to resign.

Three months after the battle, Nast drew a low-key cartoon depicting the British Lion transiting from Egypt to Afghanistan, while a wary Sphinx and a hungry Nile crocodile watched him depart. The Russian Bear was asleep outside his newly-acquired fortress. Nast's wit was at its subtle best with the Lion wearing a mask to cover his bloody nose.

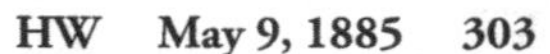
HW May 9, 1885 303

THE BRITISH LION MUST GO! HE SAYS HE IS WANTED ELSEWHERE.

Bulgaria

In 1878, Turkey lost its war against Russia. The resultant Treaty of Paris established Bulgaria as a self-governing principality with a Christian government, nominally under control of the Ottoman Sultan. Russia, Austria-Hungary, England, Germany, France and Italy all had the right to approve Bulgaria's ruler (called the Kynaz). Czar Alexander II installed his German-born nephew, Prince Alexander, as the first Kynaz.

Eight years later, current Czar Alexander III wanted to capture Constantinople (today's Istanbul), but Bulgaria was in the way and its Prince Alexander opposed Russian dominance. The Czar organized a plot against his cousin, the Prince. He bribed the palace guards, who seized Alexander and sailed away with him into exile on August 9, 1886. A counter-coup brought him back on August 17, but he abdicated on August 26 to calm relations with Russia. England and Austria-Hungary were disturbed, but helpless to intervene, as Nast illustrated with a pun.

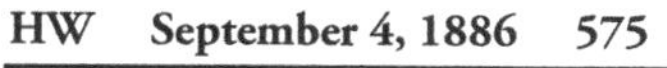
HW September 4, 1886 575

ENGLAND
Grin and—

RUSSIA
Bear it.

Once the throne was empty, Russia was unable to fill it. Nast commented, but he left *Harper's* six months before Emperor Franz Joseph I of Austria-Hungary succeeded in placing his nephew, Ferdinand I, on it.

HW September 18, 1886 612

THE WHOLE THING IS BEARISH.
Sophia, Sept 4—Prince Alexander has publicly announced his intention of abdicating. He says he cannot remain in Bulgaria on account of the objections of the Czar. Before leaving he will establish a regency.

HW November 27, 1886 767

ANYTHING BUT AN EASY CHAIR—TO FILL.

Pensions

Cleveland was the first post-Civil War President who was not a military officer. Drafted in 1863, he hired a substitute to serve in his place in order to support his widowed mother and younger siblings. While legal, it made him unpopular with Union veterans during his Presidency.

By 1886, pensions for veterans consumed one quarter of the Federal budget, second only to interest on the national debt; that was up from one-tenth a decade earlier. Previous presidents had opposed any reduction. In fact, Rutherford Hayes signed the Arrears of Pensions Act in 1879, which retroactively broadened benefits and also applied to future claims.

There were about 325,000 pensioners on the rolls when Cleveland took office. An estimated quarter of the list was fraudulent. When the Pension Bureau denied petitions, veterans and their claims agent, went to their Congressmen for special bills which overwhelmed the President. For example, one day he received 240 bills of which more than 80% had been previously rejected.[6]

On May 8, 1886, Cleveland issued a veto message about the special pension bills, and took action against dozens of them; however, he signed far more than he rejected. Nast took note in a couple of cartoons in the same issue.

HW July 3, 1886 421

AT HIS POST.
President Cleveland. "I am so thoroughly tired of disapproving gifts of public money to individuals who in my view have no right or claim to the same, not withstanding apparent Congressional sanction."

HW July 3, 1886 431

A POLITICAL "TIE-UP."
Practical Politician. "This seems to work *contrari-wise*."

During his first term, he vetoed 414 bills, more than double the number issued by all his predecessors combined. Most of them dealt with pension ineligibility.

Silver

In 1886, free coinage of silver became a major legislative topic once again. The Bland-Allison Act, which Congress passed eight years earlier over President Rutherford Hayes's veto, was still in effect; it required the government to purchase $2-4 million of silver every month. Treasury Secretary John Sherman and his successors stayed with the lower limit.*

* See p. 470-473

Cleveland strongly supported the gold standard and opposed free silver, thereby clashing with members of his own party. One of his comments got into the press: “Whenever I see a Bland dollar, I am reminded of the aphorism about the cloud with the silver lining — it is 80% silver and 20% mist.”[7] In his first message to Congress in December 1885, he called for suspension of the annual silver purchase.

Then the President made a big mistake. Instead of pressing Congressmen for action, he held back and advised them to legislate as they saw fit. What he got back from Representative Richard Bland and others was a bill for free and unlimited coinage of silver. If passed, it would have devastated the Treasury, which had $165 million in silver dollars filling its vaults while only $50 million of coins were in circulation.[8]

Unlike in 1878, Nast only drew one cartoon about silver, depicting Bland confronting John Sherman, now the Senate’s presiding officer, with a basket of silver eggs. Behind his back, Sherman was holding an “Act to Make Eggs Golden.” while a sign pointed toward U.S. Sorcery.

Usually Sallie Nast corrected her husband’s misspellings, but “A bran new silver act” got past her or Tom Jr., 20, who now assisted his father on occasion.

Six months of proposed bills followed, with a final approved act pocket-vetoed by Cleveland in August 1886. Despite what was frequently referred to as a “silver blizzard,” Nast was too busy with other more cartoonable topics to comment again.

HW February 13, 1886 112

WHY NOT PREPARE THE WAY FOR THIS?

Indians

When Cleveland took office, there were about 250,000 Indians in the country, most of them living peacefully on scattered reservations. The public viewed them either as whiskey-drinking nuisances or as much-cheated and neglected fellow residents. (They didn’t receive citizenship until 1924 and voting rights until 1948, or later in some states.

The President strongly wanted Indians not only to be treated fairly, but also to be awarded individual land grants of up to 160 acres so they could farm. He believed that owning inheritable land would help them assimilate into American culture. The land grants required about eleven million acres, only eight percent of the 138 million total acres of reservation land.[9]

Western settlers were clamoring for that excess land to be made available to them, and Cleveland was sympathetic. He also forced the railroads like the Northern Pacific to disgorge 81 million acres which had been granted to them under stipulations they no longer met. The Dawes Act (sponsored by Congressman Henry Dawes) accomplished both of the President’s objectives when it passed in February 1887, two months after Nast left the *Weekly*. He never commented on the events that brought it about.

The Apache War

Major exceptions to the growing tranquility with the Indians were the sporadic Apache uprisings in the New Mexico and Arizona Territories led by the legendary Geronimo. He escaped from the San Carlos Reservation in Arizona four times between 1877 and May 1885, terrorizing settlers, and hiding out in Mexico's remote canyons.

His last escape evidently inspired Nast's only cartoon about Indians during the Cleveland administration. His caption was totally inappropriate, considering the terrible publicized atrocities attributed to Geronimo.

HW July 4, 1885 436

THE USUAL SUMMER ERUPTION.

The Army went all out to capture Geronimo. When General Richard Crook, who had captured him four times, couldn't find him in Mexico, he was forced to retire, then replaced by General Nelson Miles. With 5,000 soldiers and 500 Apache scouts, Miles finally caught up with Geronimo and his band of 24 men in a remote Mexican canyon in September 1886. The major Apache attacks came to an end, although skirmishes broke out over the next several years.

Frederic Remington

In early 1882, a sketch drawn on wrapping paper, and crammed into a small envelope with a Wyoming postmark, arrived at the *Weekly* from Frederic Remington, an unknown 20-year old artist. Entitled *Cow-Boys of Arizona — Roused by a Scout*, the sketch was turned into an illustration by W.A. Rogers, and *Harper's* sent Remington a check and a tearsheet.[10] An accompanying article explained that the Cow-Boys were lawless cattle-rustlers based in Tombstone, and protected by the local sheriff, police and newspapers. (Wyatt Earp was a saloon guard and his brother Virgil was marshal.)

HW February 25, 1882 120

COW-BOYS OF ARIZONA—ROUSED BY A SCOUT.—Drawn by W.A. Rogers from a sketch by Frederic Remington.—**[See page 118.]**

Three years later, Remington submitted another sketch entitled *Ejecting an "Oklahoma Boomer."* This time, Thure de Thulstrup used it to draw a cover illustration. A related article explained how the 1,000 so-called Boomers were settlers who were prohibited from moving into the Indian Territory, which ultimately became the state of Oklahoma.

HW March 28, 1885 193 C

EJECTING AN OKLAHOMA BOOMER."— **Drawn by T. de Thulstrup from a sketch by Frederic Remington.**

After receiving the second sketch, the Harpers realized that Remington could provide them with first-hand coverage of the Apache War and the West. His illustrations and descriptive articles about the military campaign to capture Geronimo would appeal to its diminished readership, and hopefully attract back some of their lost Republican circulation. Accordingly, they hired him to go West and illustrate the soldiers, cowboys, Indians, Mexicans and horses that comprised most of his carefully drawn pictures.

As 1886 dawned, Remington's cover became the first commissioned picture that he ever sold. In total, nine of his illustrations appeared in the *Weekly* in 1886, while the Apache War was discussed in fifteen different issues. All told, the fledgling artist earned more than $1,000 from *Harper's* in his first year.

HW January 9, 1886 17

THE APACHE WAR—INDIAN SCOUTS ON GERONIMO'S TRAIL.—Drawn by Frederic Remington. [See page 23.]

In effect, Remington phased in at the *Weekly* as Nast phased out. He became the "living-history" painter that Nast originally had hoped to become.* With Remington on board as a star attraction, the Harpers could be more cavalier in reducing the size — and related cost — of Nast's cartoons, or rejecting them entirely. Rogers and Thulstrup earned $75 to $100 for a full page, and Remington probably was in the same range, while Nast still earned about $150, although his full pages decreased in number.[11]

Nast still received $5,000 for exclusivity. While Remington had an arrangement with the Harpers not to draw or write for any other publication, he was free to paint and sculpt as he chose. However, it is likely that Nast saw Remington's emergence as a threat to his own future income.

Remington stayed with Harper and Brothers for fifteen years, becoming a mainstay of the *Monthly Magazine*, as well as the *Weekly*. The firm published his sketches, illustrations, articles, stories, and pictures of his paintings and sculptures, as well as five books. He covered all sorts of special happenings first-hand, including the Spanish-American War in Cuba. After the company went bankrupt at the end of 1899, it let him go for economic reasons. He began publishing regularly in *Collier's Weekly* in 1901.

* See p. 185

Jacob Sharp

In the early 1880s, New York City had 32 horse-drawn streetcar companies providing transportation. None of them accepted transfers, making travel difficult. The cars were usually filthy and vermin-infested, and the poorly-paid drivers and conductors worked shifts as long as 16 hours. In 1883, the New York Cable Railroad Company was formed to replace the horse-cars with electric cable-cars.[12]

That precipitated reaction from Jacob Sharp, 70, an entrepreneurial schemer. Back in the early 1850s, he had been awarded a Wall Street ferry franchise over higher-bidding competitors, by bribing the Board of Aldermen (known as the "40 Thieves.") He also obtained a franchise to build a surface railroad along Broadway, but was blocked by property owners from constructing it over the next 32 years.

Now, New York Cable forced the issue. Sharp out-bribed his competitor by paying New York State legislators $400,000 to shift the authority to grant a current franchise from Albany to New York City; his lawyer drafted the bill. Next, in August 1884, he paid $500,000 ($25,000 each) to 20 Aldermen to give him the franchise free (with percentages later); only two Aldermen refused the bribes. Mayor Franklin Edson vetoed the bill twice, but his second veto was overridden in December 1884.

The public was outraged. Newspapers, led by Joseph Pulitzer's *World*, created an unquenchable uproar which forced the State Senate to investigate; it hired Roscoe Conkling as lead counsel. The *Weekly* noted that during Conkling's questioning, "Mr. Sharp held a bottle of milk in his hand from which he frequently sought solace and refreshment." Sharp couldn't remember who received his checks made out to cash for amounts of $200,000 and $300,000.[13] More light was shed by three of the bribed Aldermen, who confessed and provided evidence.

The timing in February 1886 coincided with Nast's attacks on Attorney General Augustus Garland for his role in the Pan-Electric scandal. He also went after Sharp in four humorous cartoons and the Aldermen in two.

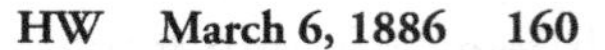
HW March 6, 1886 160

A MUSIC LESSON.
How a *sharp* could be *flat*.

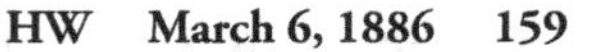
HW March 6, 1886 159

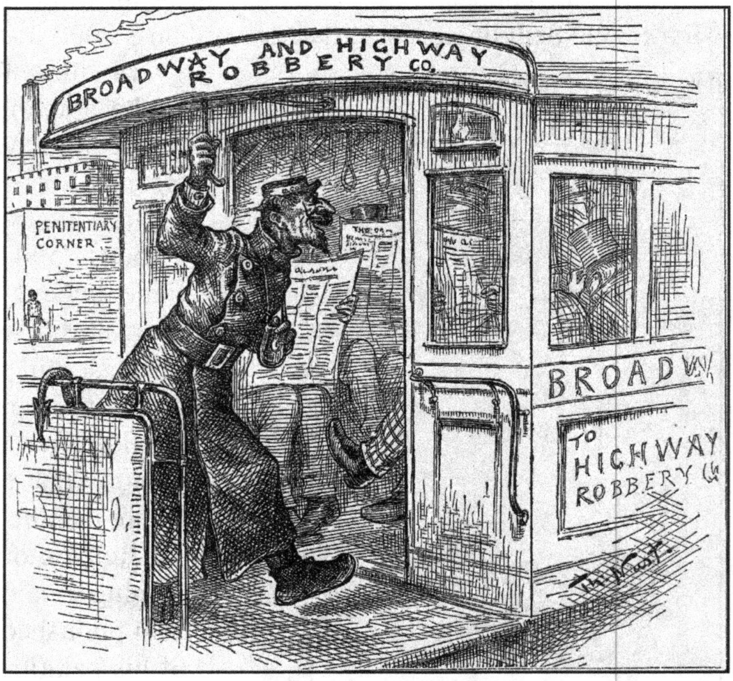

THIS CONDUCTOR TO PAY ON THIS LINE.
"Who '*squealed*' to stop here?"

HW March 13, 1886 176

LET THIS FRANCHISE BE GIVEN TO THE ALDERMEN.
Police Conductor. "More room still!"

Henry Jachne, Vice President of the Board, was the first Alderman convicted. Judge George Barrett sentenced him and 19 others to Sing Sing prison. Nast took note.

HW May 24, 1886 352

AN ALDERMANIC BOODLEFUL SUIT.
Judge Barrett. "Instead of 'a stay,' let me give you a 'short cut.'"

HW March 27, 1886 207

THE ONLY WAY TO HAVE THEM ABOVE SUSPICION.
Let us take our city officials direct from their natural home — and return them when their official duties have been performed.

Sharp was arrested and sent to Ludlow Street jail, where he occupied the same luxurious suite that housed Boss Tweed during the previous decade. His trial was delayed until June 15, 1887. By then, three Aldermen were in Sing Sing; nine were out on bail awaiting action by the District Attorney; two were dead; one was insane; three were fugitives in Canada and one in Germany. Two convicted middlemen-bribers also fled to Canada. Nast got his last licks in at the Aldermen with another pun.

HW August 28, 1886 559

IF ALL ARE OF ONE STRIPE, THE MORE THE "FUNNIER."
They say they will drag others in with them.

When Nast voluntarily left *Harper's* at the end of 1886, he had drawn seven post-dated 1887 cartoons, six of which appeared in December. **His final cartoon** — out of more than 2,200 (including illustrations) that the *Weekly* published — was a humdrum effort that pictured Sharp getting his milk refreshment, and subjected his audience to a couple of poor puns.

Judge Barrett convicted Sharp, but was reversed by a Court of Appeals on a technicality. Sharp died in 1888 before his scheduled retrial could be held.

HW January 22, 1887 56

SHAKE SHARP NEXT!
Justice. "You say it has *turned against you*, and you would like to try it in another county. It is true it has been abused, but you'll find it about the same everywhere. And it will be proved to you that in this case it is *not* better to give than to receive."

Chapter 48
After Harper's Weekly: The Election of 1888

Separation

Nast's hard work in producing an average of one cartoon every two days — 350 overall during two calendar years after Cleveland's election — left him exhausted. Compounding his stress, *Harper's* generally accepted his smaller cartoons at $40 each while rejecting his larger ones at $150 per page; only 15% were large compared to the previous 22-year average of about half. Of course, the *Weekly's* circulation and revenue had dropped sharply after it deserted its Republican base by supporting Cleveland, so it probably was pinching pennies, as well as casting a more critical eye over its former premier artist's relatively weak work.

Once again, Nast faced the same stay-or-leave decision that he made four years earlier* — but with two major differences: his physical and emotional health, and his financial health after his failed investments. His doctor's advice to take a year off from work proved decisive. When he told the Harpers in late 1886, they paid him his $5,000 annual retainer to ensure that he wouldn't work for any other publication.

During his sabbatical, he planned to complete a book of his Christmas pictures, and then begin work on a second book about the Tweed campaign. However, fate intervened with a second financial calamity, so *Christmas Drawings for the Human Race* didn't appear until late 1889 and the Tweed book not at all.

Travel

Nast spent most of the first six weeks of his recuperation as a touring sportsman. A Canadian executive invited him and fellow cartoonists Joseph Keppler, Bernhard Gillam and Eugene Zimmerman among others, to go snowshoeing, tobogganing and caribou-hunting in the wilderness. The evening before they left, Nast gave a dinner for the group at his Morristown home. Gillam, who knew Nast from when he worked at the *Weekly*, attended, but Keppler — his former arch-rival — sent regrets "with bleeding heart." [1] Tom Jr. joined him at Montreal's Winter Carnival in early February.

In mid-March, Tommy and Sallie took what turned out to be their last extended trip together. (Their youngest child Cyril was only seven, so Sallie's travel was limited). They stopped in Washington on their way to and from Jacksonville, Florida, where Nast interviewed President Cleveland on both occasions, and his new wife Frances took them to a memorable White House reception.

In a subsequent interview, Nast made an interesting comment on the hand-shaking style of the three presidents whom he had observed up close:[2]

> "Now, I knew Grant," he said, "and I loved him — I'm not criticizing Grant, but Grant would come in and stand grim and cold as an iceberg, and let any one who wished to shake his hand."
>
> "Mr. Arthur, he was suave and courtly and very kind to folks, but his dignity was predominant; you couldn't forget that you were addressing the August Presence.
>
> "But with Mr. Cleveland it was very different. There was no ostentation or formality. He shook hands briefly with the haughty and spoke most kindly to the timid."

---

* See p. 539-544.

Another Disastrous Investment

As mentioned previously, while Nast's conflicts with the Harpers increased during the eighties, he continued almost obsessively to focus on somehow obtaining his own publication where he would have the same freedom of expression that Keppler had at *Puck*. He needed capital — especially after the Grant and Ward debacle — to make that happen.

Accordingly, in early 1886 (while still working for the *Weekly*), Nast took the approximate $60,000 savings he had left and bought a controlling interest in two silver mines near Silver Cliff, Colorado: the Leavenworth Lode in Ross Basin and the Pearl Lode in Eureka Green. After his multi-year attacks on the use of silver currency at a pegged rate, it was an ironic investment for him as *Harper's* pointed out on its April 17, 1886 editorial page:

> The *Indianapolis Journal*, accepting as true the report now going the rounds of the press that Mr. Thomas Nast has recently bought the controlling interest in a couple of silver mines out West, says, in friendly comment: "Thomas Nast uses his pencil to show that Uncle Sam is lame in one leg because of the silver surplus, but he turns right around and puts his own money into Colorado mines. The caricaturist has just bought a half interest in two lodes." To all of which Mr. Nast simply replies: "*If* I owned a 'half interest' in every silver mine in the United States, I would not change my mind as to the absurdity of Congress having the power to make seventy-nine cents a dollar."

Shortly after this article appeared, Nast had 21 year-old Tom, Jr. learn about assaying, and sent him west to manage the Colorado properties. With permission from the Harpers, he went out to inspect his investment for several weeks during September and October, preparing five cartoons in advance for the nine issues published during his absence. At some point, he took another mortgage on his house and put up an additional $3,000.

Even more ironically, Nast's judgment about investing in silver mining was sound. Four years later, Congress passed the Sherman Silver Purchase Act of 1890, obligating the government to buy 4.5 million ounces every month — almost the entire supply. The Treasury Department bought the silver, using paper money which then could be redeemed for gold. That helped bring on the Panic of 1893 and the repeal of the Act. If his investment had panned out, he probably would have had the money to start his own paper on a sound financial basis — but with the odds of success strongly against him.

Almost 15 years later — about the time he accepted his consular post in Ecuador — Nast drew a cartoon of himself as a pistol-packing Colorado Springs cowboy, astride a spring-driven hobby-horse. As noted previously, the hobby-horse was Nast's symbol for fakes. His mining investment came home to roost one final time — as another bitter memory.

Macculloch Hall Historical Museum

Lecturing

When Nast recovered his health, he desperately needed to generate income. His reputation preceded him in the West, paving the way for an extended lecture tour covering about three dozen cities in eleven states and Western Canada. Tom Jr. accompanied him on part of the seven-month tour ending in the late spring of 1888.

Unlike his three earlier lecture circuits, Nast had good reason to keep politics out of this one. Two hours of sketches, scenic paintings and witty remarks followed the same pattern. Often he sketched and sometimes painted a small befuddled British lion looking warily at a grinning Uncle Sam; the American eagle had the lion's tail in its mouth.

Macculloch Hall Historical Museum

Macculloch Hall Historical Museum

NAST ON TOUR

The Final Break

When Nast finally returned home in July 1888 after ten months away, the Presidential campaign was underway. The Democrats had met in St. Louis on June 5 and nominated Grover Cleveland by acclamation for a second term. Two weeks later, the Republicans chose compromise candidate Benjamin Harrison on the eighth ballot.

Harper's Weekly continued to back Cleveland, as did *Puck*. The Harpers reached out to Nast by telegram "for consideration of a new contract" but he turned them down. Much as he disliked editor Curtis and was unhappy with the Harpers' treatment of him, **it was one of the worst decisions he ever made**. Effectively, he cut off his nose to spite his face when he had nothing to gain by doing so.

His judgment must have been clouded by his battered pride, unaffordable financial losses, long absence from home, and resultant depressed mental state. He voluntarily gave up *Harper's* still considerable circulation and whatever impact it provided, as well as more potential income than he was able to earn elsewhere. Moreover, he did so even though he agreed with *Harper's* political support for Cleveland and its opposition to New York Governor David Hill (who also was on the Democratic ticket for reelection).

The Harpers probably didn't really care because they knew that William A. Rogers, a fine illustrator and competent cartoonist could fill Nast's worn-out shoes capably. Moreover, Nast was no longer reliable; his book of Christmas drawings was overdue, and still more than a year away from completion and publication

Benjamin Harrison

Two months before the nominating conventions, Keppler drew a *Puck* cartoon reminiscent of Nast at his best. Cleveland was dominant over eight Republican pretenders to his throne, including James Blaine, Ohio Senator John Sherman and Chauncey Depew (New York's favorite son). Harrison wasn't among them.

Initially, Blaine was expected to be the Republican nominee in a re-run of the 1884 election. However, as a hypochondriac with health problems, he didn't have the spark or the stomach for another fatiguing campaign, although he still almost totally controlled his Party. Blaine spent the first seven months of 1888 in Europe to avoid domestic politics, sending declination letters in January and again in May, and approving Harrison while blocking Sherman, Depew and other favorite son candidates.

PUCK April 11, 1888

QUALITY COUNTS.

Harrison, an Indiana lawyer, became the last Union general (after Grant, Hayes and Garfield) to win the Presidency; he had served under William Sherman in his Atlanta and March-to-the-Sea campaigns. After a single term in the Senate, he was not reelected by the Legislature in 1886. Known as the "Iceman" for his frigid personality, he didn't have many friends or accomplishments.

Positively during his campaign — and negatively during his Presidency — "Little Ben" Harrison (5 feet, 6 inches tall) was compared to his grandfather, the ninth President. William Henry Harrison became a War of 1812 hero after routing the Indians (who sided with the British) at the hard-fought, pre-war, November 1811 Battle of Tippecanoe, and was elected in 1840 (along with Vice President John Tyler) on a "Tippecanoe and Tyler Too" ticket. Unfortunately, he caught pneumonia at his inauguration and, a month later, became the first President to die in office.

Immediately after his nomination, *Harper's Weekly* praised Harrison's character, but opposed him and the Republican Party because of its high tariff platform. Rogers showed Uncle Sam holding a "Young Tip" jug while toasting him with a dubious look; "Free Whiskey" would become a key element of the tariff debate. The elephant had broken loose from the "Chicago Circus" (the Republican National Convention). To enlist support from Boss Tom (formerly "Me Too") Platt of New York — a crucial Electoral College state along with Indiana — Levi Morton was chosen as Vice President, and shown as a small pennant on the elephant's tail. (Reminiscent of Nast's Gratz Brown tag during the 1872 Greeley campaign.)

HW June 30, 1888 468

"BROKEN LOOSE."

Harrison worked hard, giving 94 speeches from the front porch of his home in Indianapolis. Pennsylvania political boss Matthew Quay managed the campaign well, and wealthy Philadelphia retailer John Wanamaker raised substantial money from his fellow millionaires. Blaine, who returned from Europe in August and was then designated as Secretary of State if Harrison won, kept potential dissenters in line.

Keppler came up with the imaginative idea of featuring "Little Ben" as a midget in his grandfather's hat, which was much too large for him. He used it both before and after the election to depict him as weak and in Blaine's thrall. Here, Blaine (as Edgar Allen Poe's *Raven*) cast a shadow over his Presidency.

PUCK August 13, 1890

THE RAVEN
And the lamplight o'er him streaming
Throws his shadow on the floor—
And my soul from out that shadow
That lies floating on the floor.
Shall be lifted — Nevermore!

Tariffs

The tariff issue had been building since the 1880 campaign when Democratic candidate Winfield Hancock flubbed his answer to a reporter's question: "The tariff is a local question."* Four years later, Blaine tried in vain to win with Tariff Protection as his principal plank. No meaningful changes were made by Congress after Cleveland won in 1884. The Republican platform, championed by Blaine, was "uncompromisingly in favor of the American system of protection."

A fundamental problem with the current 47% (average) tariff structure was that it brought in far more revenue than was needed to run the country. The surplus was a potential grab-bag for Congress; it could fund undeserved pension benefits, personal earmarks (in current terminology), or controversial infrastructure projects. As Cleveland stated in his second annual message to Congress: it "invited schemes of public plunder." Accordingly, the Democratic platform called for "Tariff for Revenue only."

* See p. 507

On December 8, 1886, **Nast's last major political cartoon** of his quarter-century at *Harper's Weekly* appeared on its post-dated cover, featuring a weary Uncle Sam struggling with a $125,000 surplus.

HW December 18, 1886 821 C

"AN UNNECESSARY BURDEN."—PRESIDENT'S MESSAGE.
"Don't *over-tax* yourself, for it only leads *them* into temptation."

Working for the Democrats

Not long after Nast returned from his lecture tour in July 1888 — and it was known that his affiliation with *Harper's Weekly* was over — he was hired by the Democratic National Committee to draw syndicated cartoons backing Cleveland. The anchor paper responsible for paying him was the *Daily Graphic*. Others in the syndicate included the *New York Evening Post*, the *Louisville Courier-Journal*, and the *Memphis Commercial Appeal*.

Cleveland's widely acclaimed annual message to Congress in December 1887 focused on tariff reform and the surplus. Nast was on his Western tour when Cleveland made his speech. Keppler's contemporary cartoon converted Nast's Elephant symbol — long since adopted by his fellow cartoonists — into the "dragon in the room," representing the bloated surplus, with the "Tariff Question" as its tail.

PUCK December 7, 1887

THE OPENING OF THE CONGRESSIONAL SESSION
Tariff Monster—Here I am again! What are you going to do with me?

Cleveland's speech was published as a booklet during the 1888 campaign and featured 19 run-of-the-mill Nast illustrations. The same Uncle Sam image that he used in his final political cartoon for the *Weekly* almost two years before, reappeared on the cover. Nast was probably paid by the Democratic National Committee rather than the publisher.

September 1888

Another reprinted excerpts from the speech, and depicted the President as a fighter against War Taxes, Trusts and Monopolies — but not crusading for Free Trade. Although not especially creative, it was blown up into a widely-distributed campaign poster.

OUR CHAMPION INFANT ON REAL PROTECTION.

The *Daily Graphic* was 15 years old and fading rapidly. (It would expire a year later.) Founded on a proprietary process which enabled fast reproduction of photographs, drawings and cartoons, it peaked at a circulation of about 10,000, but was mortally wounded by 1884 when Joseph Pulitzer's *World* adopted similar reproduction techniques. Financial and other mismanagement compounded its vulnerability, and even a new owner couldn't save it. Consequently, Nast's mediocre cartoons were further diminished by being printed on inferior quality paper.[3]

Nast's first of a dozen or so syndicated cartoons appeared in the *Graphic* on August 4, along with an explanation. **"Mr. Nast comes to the Democratic side on the tariff issue. He is not a Democrat except in matters of this campaign . . . He has enlisted for the entire fight."**

The *Evening Post* was edited by self-righteous Edwin Godkin, who had been the subject of Nast's most scatological cartoon when he edited the *Nation* a dozen years before.* (In 1881, the *Nation* was merged into the *Evening Post* and became its Saturday edition under its own name.) The *Daily Post* had a circulation of about 20,000 and the weekly *Nation* had half of that. In addition to Nast working for Godkin, a man he despised, there were other ironies as Nast's former foes now fed the hand that repeatedly had hammered them. The long-serving Chairman of the Democratic National Committee was former Senator William Barnum of Connecticut, derogatorily referred to as "Seven Mule" Barnum; that came from his attempt to buy electoral votes for Samuel Tilden in the aftermath of the 1876 election. Nast had depicted him carrying a large check to Florida.** Moreover, the *Louisville Courier-Journal* was published by Nast's personal friend and frequent public enemy, Henry Watterson, whom he skewered on a score of occasions as a leading Democratic politician.***

Congressman William "Pig Iron" Kelley of Philadelphia was the embodiment of Protectionism and Trusts — in fact, and in Nast's and other cartoons — as he aggressively defended Pennsylvania's basic iron and steel monopolies. Nast had depicted Kelley as one of the wrongdoers in the 1873 Credit Mobilier scandal, and five subsequent times, always negatively, but with more creativity than now.

MEMPHIS COMMERCIAL APPEAL October 17, 1888

NY EVENING POST October 30, 1888

* See p. 437
** See p. 414
*** See p. 412

In May 1888, James Foster, President of the Republican League of the U.S., a protectionist lobbying group funded by manufacturers, sent out a letter to his members, demanding money for support. He threatened to "fry all the fat out of the manufacturers of Pennsylvania" if they didn't pay up. Nast responded with *The "Fat" Secret,* which his employer's syndicate published and promoted.

The *Evening Post* published at least eight Nast cartoons in its October 30 issue. Editor Godkin believed that they were detrimental to the quality of his paper — perhaps remembering the artist's 1876 "Blue Pills" attack on him — and ended his participation. The *Daily Graphic* followed, and Nast never received all his contractual pay; that probably was due to the paper's financial condition, a dimming outlook for Cleveland in New York state, and the new owner's rabid support for the reelection of Democratic Governor David Hill, whom Nast scorned and had brutally caricatured in *Harper's* in 1885-6. Cleveland lost New York but Hill won easily.

While Nast's cartoons continued to lose impact, Rogers replaced him at *Harper's* with clever ideas and more than adequate execution. For example, about the time Nast began with the *Graphic*, Rogers depicted leading protectionist Congressmen Thomas Reed and Kelley as weeping little boys complaining to a consoling Uncle Sam that their protection hedge was being chopped down to allow in Free Trade. Cleveland was only trimming the surplus while keeping the labeled "Protection Hedge" in place.

THE DIFFERENCE BETWEEN TRIMMING A HEDGE AND CUTTING IT DOWN.
Uncle Sam. "Now don't come around tellin' me that old story about cuttin' down the hedge and bein' eat up by the free-trade b'ars."

The following month, Rogers attacked the Republican plank by displaying nine consumer products with their specific "War Taxes . . . for the sole benefit of Trust, Monopoly & Co." Rates were in the 80% range for necessities like salt, sugar and woolen clothing; the 40% range for hand tools; and the 20% range for Bibles and soap. No luxury items were included.

He also called out Trust, Monopoly & Co. for importing "duty-free" immigrants to undercut American wages. However, there wasn't much difference between the parties on that issue.

HW September 29, 1888 725 C

A QUESTION OF LABOR.
***"This question is from first to last, from the beginning to the end, from skin to core and from core back to skin again, a question of labor."*—James G. Blaine at Madison Square, August 10, 1888.**

"Free" Whiskey

Both parties favored getting rid of internal excise taxes on tobacco, but the idea of eliminating whiskey taxes and thereby encouraging insobriety, was a potential powder keg. The Prohibition Party received 2.2% of the national vote in both 1884 and 1888, enough to threaten either party that actually promoted "Free Whiskey."

The excise tax on spirits averaged about 90 cents a gallon. Eliminating it would make whiskey available at 20 cents a gallon. In 1884, Blaine had taken the moral high ground to retain the tax, reasoning that removing it "would increase consumption enormously," but lost the Prohibitionist Party's decisive vote due to Republican Party campaign blunders.*

Four years later, however, the Republican platform stated: "If there still remains a larger revenue than is requisite for the wants of the government, we favor the entire repeal of internal taxes rather than surrender any part of our protective system at the joint behest of the whiskey trusts and the agents of foreign manufacturers."

Rogers followed up his elephant cartoon from three weeks earlier — showing Uncle Sam drinking Free Whiskey — with a small masterpiece — reminiscent of Nast — by referring to its predecessor. This time the drunken elephant, piloted by a plastered Harrison, had a banner reading "Tippecanoe and Tariff Scare Too." The man with the jug possibly was Robert Ingersoll, a Chicago lawyer and powerful voice in the Republican party, who had dubbed Blaine the "plumed knight" when he nominated him at the 1876 convention. Ingersoll, a prominent trial lawyer, had defended Federal officials in the Whiskey Ring and Star Route scandals. Alternatively, he could also have been a symbol for pro-Harrison *Judge* magazine. (A bound volume of *Judge* was on the man's desk.)

* See p. 575

Two months later, Rogers attacked Harrison on three counts: He was carrying a jug of free whiskey "presented by Bob Ingersoll;" wearing a much larger hat "presented by friends of his grandfather," over his own; and encased in the plumed knight's armor in "defence of trusts" presented by J.G. Blaine. His breastplate depicted an octopus symbolizing the size and power of Standard Oil and other trusts and monopolies.

HW July 21, 1888 539

THE VICTIM OF HIS FRIENDS.

HW September 15, 1888 699

FIRST EFFECTS OF "FREE WHISKEY."
Marvellous conception of a stimulated contemporary evolved from our modest cartoon "Broken Loose."

The Cartoon

While working for the *Daily Graphic* and its Democratic syndicate, Nast also had a few cartoons published in *The Cartoon*, a short-lived weekly available for five cents, during September and October 1888. They were closer to his old style and talent than anything else he drew but had a minute audience compared to *Puck, Judge* and *Harper's*. His almost unrecognizable elephant had the "Free Whiskey" platform plank spelled out on its side — drawn by a lifelong temperance advocate.

SATURDAY CARTOON October 6, 1888

NEVERTHELESS IT IS AN ELEPHANT.
Uncle Sam

SATURDAY CARTOON September 15, 1888

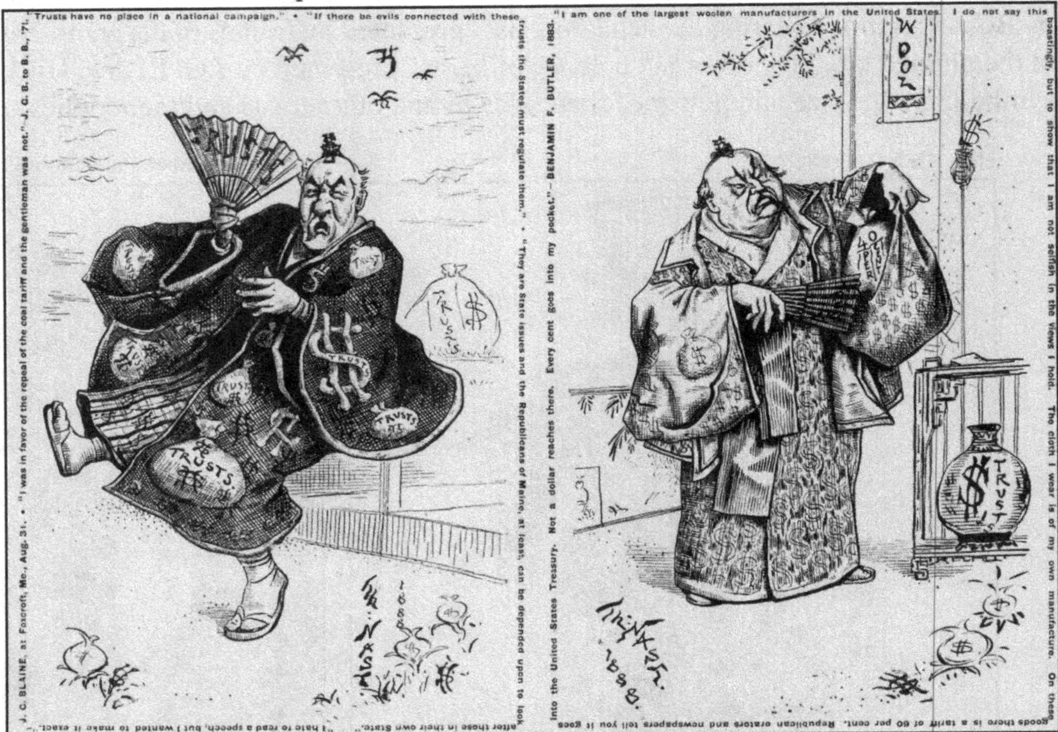

THE TRUSTS IN THE "KO-KO" NUT. THE "POOH-BAH" BUT.

Nast's best cartoon featured Gilbert & Sullivan's Mikado. Blaine was the Emperor of all trusts, demanding state rather than federal control of them. (The Sherman Anti-trust Act of 1890 foreclosed that idea.) The other vignette showed Benjamin Butler — former Senator, Governor and Presidential candidate, with a reputation for dishonesty and guile — as the Pooh-Bah of the Wool Trust, benefiting from a 58% tariff, (Butler came from Lowell, Massachusetts, home to many woolen mills).

SATURDAY CARTOON October 27, 1888

OUR PORTRAIT GALLERY. THOS. NAST.
"What Are You Laughing At?"

After caricaturing Butler more than 60 times over 25 years, and Blaine more than 90 times over 12 years in *Harper's Weekly*, these were probably Nast's last shots at them. Artistically among his best, few of his former fans saw them.

Nast himself was targeted in *The Cartoon*, probably after his last accepted drawing. Thomas Fleming portrayed him sitting on a book of his cartoons, looking disturbed and holding an earlier depiction of "Sir James" Blaine in England with his "brown box." Blaine apparently was declining the nomination, but Nast didn't believe him and was later proved wrong.

At this point, the publishing company probably had ended its relationship with Nast by not paying or under-paying him. However, the look on his face almost certainly reflected his post-*Harper's Weekly* mood.[4]

In retrospect, Nast had virtually no influence on the 1888 campaign. His cartoons lacked impact — especially because he could no longer sequence them — and their circulation was insignificant; Keppler and Rogers shone in comparison. Their audiences dwarfed Nast's and their work appeared on better quality paper.

If Nast was depressed going into the campaign, he had to be more so coming out of it — probably first because of his diminished public stature and difficulty in earning a living, and then because he finally knew that he could no longer play in the big leagues unless he could somehow acquire his own paper and make a financial success out of it. Although his 1888 income from lecturing and the Democrats exceeded his expenses, his future prospects were bleak. Exhausted, he and Tom Jr. took a six-week trip to England returning in time for Christmas.[5]

Chapter 49
After Harper's Weekly: Freelancing in the Early '90s

Although his cartoons were mediocre at best during 1888, Nast's prior reputation was sufficient to attract — as a freelancer — eight publishers over the next eight years. The first was his only daily newspaper client.

San Francisco Examiner

George Hearst acquired the *San Francisco Examiner* in 1880 in payment of a gambling debt. After he was elected Senator in late 1886, he gave the paper to his son William Randolph Hearst. In March 1889, Hearst hired Thomas Nast with an editorial splash full of praiseworthy biographical misinformation. It included a profiled silhouette.

An early cartoon showed the Standard Oil Trust, based in Cleveland, stomping supreme over publisher Murat Halstead's *Cincinnati Commercial*, which had criticized John D. Rockefeller's business, as well as other trusts. Nast may have figured that Ohio was safe territory to lampoon, especially because Halstead was an old friend. Senator Hearst, now in Congress, probably disagreed.

Three weeks later, Nast poked fun at a wealthy, overweight, local friend of the Hearsts, (most likely George Nickel) in connection with an invitation — or not — to a ball celebrating the Centennial of George Washington's first Inauguration.

March 1889

Nast Scrapbook, Morristown Library, p. 28

DAILY EXAMINER April 8, 1889

ABOVE CRITICISM.

DAILY EXAMINER April 30, 1889

"WHO SAYS I AM NOT ONE OF THE 400? IS THERE ANY DOUBT ABOUT IT?"

Nast's cartoons were published from mid-March to mid-May, when he evidently had a disagreement with young Hearst about their content. His scrapbook contained a satirical article about a hypothetical conversation between Nast and Hearst, in which the publisher rejected all of the cartoonist's ideas about attacking "political, corporation and newspaper rascalities" because they might embarrass his father, the Senator.[1]

The farce was written by Joseph Howard and published in his *New York Weekly Star*. Howard had a tarnished reputation, from his 1861 phony story about Lincoln disguising himself at a Baltimore station on his way to Washington,* and his subsequent prison time at Fort Lafayette in 1864 for a financial scheme affecting the price of gold. However, Howard was a good reporter and writer, and his satire probably was close to the truth.

DAILY EXAMINER May 19, 1889

THE GUARDIAN OF THE GOLDEN GATE.

Nast finished on a positive note. In what was probably his last cartoon for the *Examiner*, Nast lauded Adolph Sutro, a generous benefactor to San Francisco. He made his money from the Comstock silver lode in Nevada, expanded it in real estate to where he owned about one-twelfth of the city's land, including Sutro Heights and part of the Golden Gate Recreational Area (which he donated to the city). Five years later, he became Mayor. Nast probably had extra respect for Sutro because of his silver mining success.

After Hearst ended his relationship with Nast, Joseph Pulitzer's *World* commented on June 23: **"It seems to be the consensus of opinion on the Pacific Coast that Mr. Nast's pencil had been worn to a stub."**

America

While he was working for the *San Francisco Examiner*, Nast signed on with *America*, a year-old Chicago anti-immigrant paper. His 16-month run from April 4, 1889 through August 14, 1890, was his longest unbroken engagement with any post-*Harper's* general news publication. He produced 74 prominently placed cartoons: 28 covers, 45 center-spreads, and one full interior page.

America was started by a wealthy young entrepreneur, just two years out of college. He sold it to one of his editors after six months — and several expensive failed ideas like celebrity contributors and free samples. The new owner hired Nast as the paper's first political cartoonist, but downgraded the quality of the paper stock that featured his work. Circulation peaked at about 25,000.[2]

In addition to his renown, the probable reason that Nast was chosen over cheaper but capable local Chicago cartoonists, was the intense Protestant nativism of *America*. It was strongly anti-immigrant in general, anti-Irish in particular, and anti-Catholic Church — all over "what it regards as the curse of alien interference and alien insolence in American politics."[3]

As discussed previously, during the 1860s and 1870s, Nast's harsh treatment of the Irish, Pope Pius IX, and sectarianism over funding and curricula for public schools were based on the events and commonly held Protestant views of the time. However, during Nast's last years at the *Weekly*, Curtis and the next generation of Harpers probably discouraged or bottled up most of his dealing with those subjects. Their prime motivation may have been to protect their important school textbook business, where increased Catholic representation on local boards and book selection committees could have hurt them financially.

* See p. 88-89

Nast's innate but dormant prejudices matched up well with most of *America's*. (Not so much with its anti-German bias.) More than half of his 74 uninhibited cartoons continued his 20-year battles against the ruffian Irish and sectarian Catholic Church, but the violent Irish mafia-like Clan-Na-Gael Society was a new target. Others featured foreign policy and social issues, domestic politics and holidays.

However, modern critics of his bigotry base their denunciations on his *Harper's Weekly* cartoons which seemed justifiable when he drew them, and not on his *America* work which few people are aware of and fewer have seen.

July 18, 1889

THE POPE'S TOE IS OF SOME USE AFTER ALL—"IN REMOVAL."

August 8, 1889

WHICH IS THE TRUE SOURCE (OR SALT) OF AMERICAN GREATNESS?

August 1, 1889

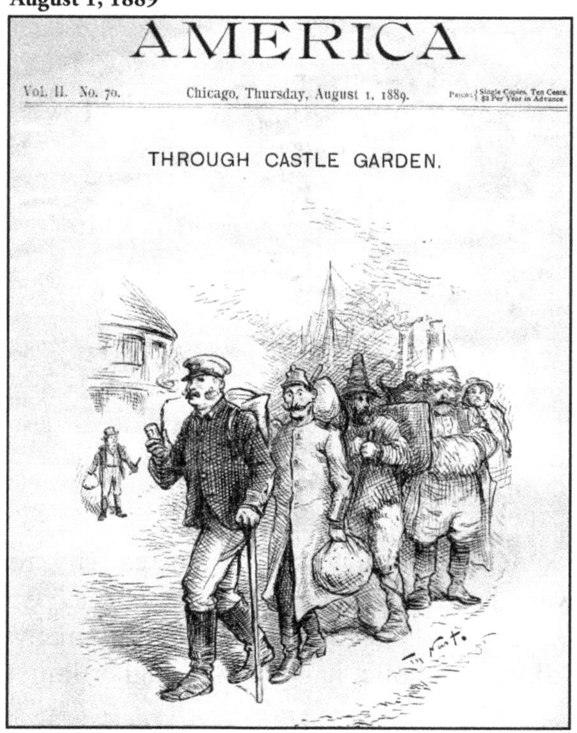

FREE TRADE EVERY DAY TO COMPETE WITH OUR LABOR.

August 1, 1889

WHAT IS OUR COUNTRY WITHOUT OUR FLAG?
Ex-American. "Soon you'll know how it is yourself."

Time

Nast's third freelance connection in 1889 was with *Time*, a weekly humor publication. It had been founded five years earlier as *Tid-Bits*. Under new ownership in June 1888, it changed its name and raised its price from a nickel to a dime to compete with *Puck* and *Judge*. *Time* considered itself as "Liberal Republican," but wasn't a political advocate like *America*.

Nast's employment lasted about seven months, from June 29,1889 through February 1, 1890; three weeks later, *Time* disappeared when it merged into *Munsey's Weekly*, another Republican humor magazine. While at *Time*, Nast redesigned the cover and produced about 63 cartoons — 32 covers and 31 center-spreads. His tenure coincided with the publication of his book, *Christmas Drawings for the Human Race,* in November 1889.[4]

Most of his cartoons dealt with politics — hammering the trusts and Democratic New York Governor David Hill, an alcoholic who had visions of running for the Presidency three years hence. Some were up to his old standard; others were well below it. Few of them had the strong conviction of his work for *America*, much less that of most of his *Harper's* cartoons, as evident in the covers below.

October 19, 1889 C

THE WHITE QUADRUPED ON UNCLE SAM'S HANDS.

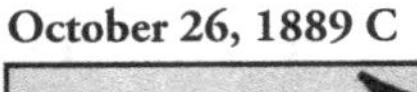
October 26, 1889 C

ALCOHOL VERSUS WATER.

However, the double-page spreads inside those issues were close to his old level of creativity, reminiscent of his Tweed and Greeley campaigns In the first one, Hill was carrying a slate with "White House" written on it while getting electrically charged as he strode on two storage batteries labeled Alco Hall and Tammany Hall. The batteries were based on a loose plank of Hill's platform. Hill, an alcoholic, had opposed higher liquor taxes, as well as Civil Service reform.

The sequential cartoon depicted Hill as a painter in the Sour-Mash Art Saloon, where he was trying to paint approval for his 1892 candidacy into the brain of Tammany Boss Richard Croker. Hill did run against Cleveland but lost on the first ballot.

TIME October 19, 1889 8-9

ONE SORT OF WALK OVER.
"From beginning to end the platform adopted by the Syracuse Convention yesterday is a labored defence of Governor Hill. If he did not write the entire document it is safe to assume that he dictated it. Its language is conclusive proof that *the Governor by demagogism and shallow trickery in his high office, has put the Democratic party of this State into an apologetic position.*"—*N.Y. Herald, Oct. 2nd.*

TIME October 26, 1889 8-9

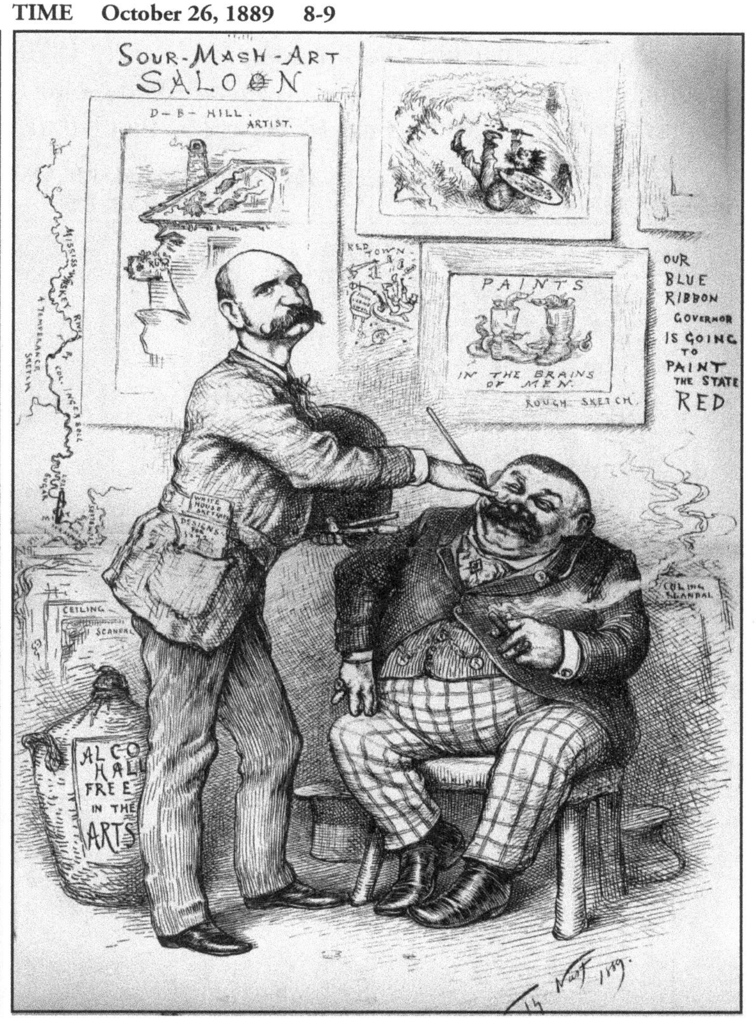

OUR ARTISTIC SOUR MASHER.
***Saloon Statesman*: Oh! how he does tickle me!**

The *Illustrated American*

The same day that *Time* died, February 22, 1890, the *Illustrated American* was born. Its wealthy founder, Lorillard Spencer, who was prominent in Newport society, wanted a first-class magazine featuring illustrated current events; lengthy, often negative profiles; and solid, serialized literature. In many respects, he aped *Harper's Weekly*.

But where his well established competitors *Puck, Judge* and *Harper's* charged 10 cents an issue, the *Illustrated American* cost a quarter. It gained a circulation of 40,000 by 1892, then cut its price to a dime, and lasted until 1900.

Nast drew cartoons and illustrated articles and stories for the *Illustrated American*, beginning in August 1890 and continuing off and on into July 1891, appearing in 14 issues altogether. Lengthy personal profiles gave him an opportunity to demonize current politicians like Chauncey Depew and Matthew Quay.

Tweed

Nast was initially hired by the *Illustrated American* to provide illustrations for the serialization — in eleven issues — of Edgar Fawcett's novel *A New York Family*. Though Nast rarely illustrated novels, in this case, he was the logical choice because the story was set in early 1870s New York and Boss Tweed was a major character in it. Nast included his old question — "What Are You Going to Do About It?" that he haunted Tweed with in 1871 (on the playing card), as well as his 1876 cartoon that led to Tweed's capture in Spain (lower right corner).

THE ILLUSTRATED AMERICAN

August 23, 1890

August 23, 1890

TRAPPED.

September 6, 1890

TWEED ROARED AT THIS, AND SLAPPED HIS FACETIOUS ARTIST RESONANTLY ON THE BACK.

September 6, 1890

THE TRAPPER TRAPPED! AT PORT OF VIGO, SPAIN, SEPTEMBER 6 1876.

Chauncey Depew

Although Depew was a powerful Republican politician in New York State during the 1870s, Nast never portrayed him in *Harper's Weekly*. Depew supported Horace Greeley against Grant in 1872, but since his political role was secondary to his position as general counsel of the New York Central Railroad, Nast omitted him from his Liberal Republican targets. After the death of William Vanderbilt in 1885, Depew became President of the New York Central. The following year, he and Nast interacted at an intimate dinner given by a Philadelphia publisher in honor of a British duke.

Depew's avocation — he called it "my recreation" — was giving public speeches several times a week, primarily at banquets. He claimed that he had a "natural facility" for it, and that he obtained "reciprocal business" for his railroad by doing so. His talks were full of puns, jokes and unseemly humor.

Consequently, Depew was depicted as a costumed fool, clown, or strutting court jester by leading cartoonists and journalists across the board including in *Harper's* and *Puck*. His unsuccessful efforts to secure the Republican Presidential nomination in 1888 and 1892, along with his predilection for European royalty, provided plenty of ammunition.

HW June 16, 1888 440

AN EXPERIENCED PERFORMER.
Ring-Master Platt. "Now, Chauncey, have you ever had any experience with an elephant before, sir?"
Clown. "No, sir, but I had a great deal of 'experience' with a mule once."

HW June 30, 1888 480

A GOOD SAFE TOY TO FALL BACK ON.

In his first cartoon, far left, Rogers referred to Depew's support of Greeley and the Democratic Donkey in 1872. Two weeks later, after his favorite son candidacy fizzled, Depew consoled himself by tinkering with his toy New York Central engine.

PUCK November 2, 1892

THE LAST THREE HOPES OF THE REPUBLICAN PARTY— BUFFOONERY, BOODLE AND BLUFF.

In 1892, Frederick Opper depicted Depew as a buffoon. The verse read: *A little nonsense now and then may help the cause of Brother Ben.* Unfortunately, it didn't when Harrison lost to Cleveland in their re-match.

In his first comprehensive serial assault on a living target since he left *Harper's* four years earlier, Nast went after Depew twice in five months within illustrated articles. The first — *"Royal Chauncey": Adventures and Misadventures of a Court Jester* — needled Depew for his Presidential ambitions; his courtship of European royalty, especially the Prince of Wales (the future Edward VII, still ten-plus years away from the English throne); and his tiresome speeches.

October 11, 1890 C

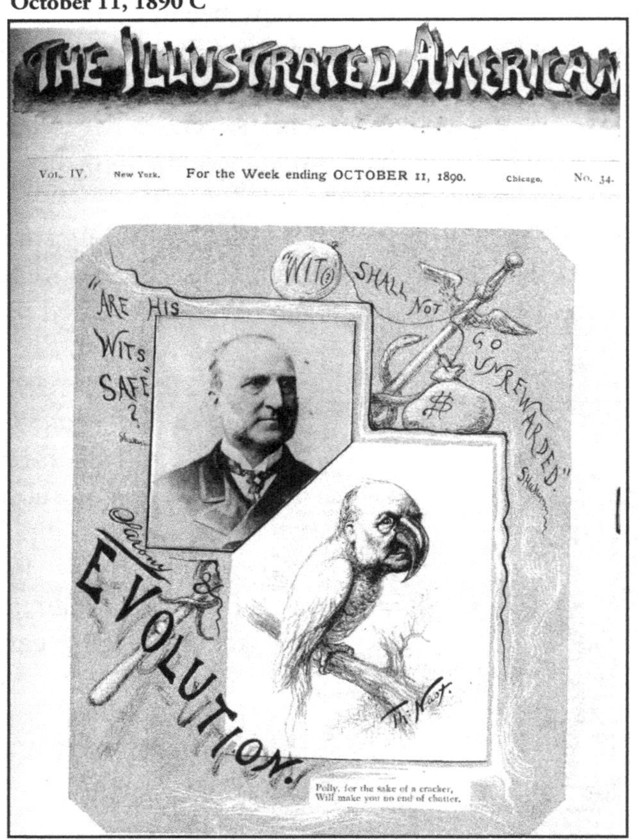

"ROYAL CHAUNCEY."
Mr. Depew Is Not The Jester Of America Alone: He Wears His Motley For The Universe.

October 11, 1890 75

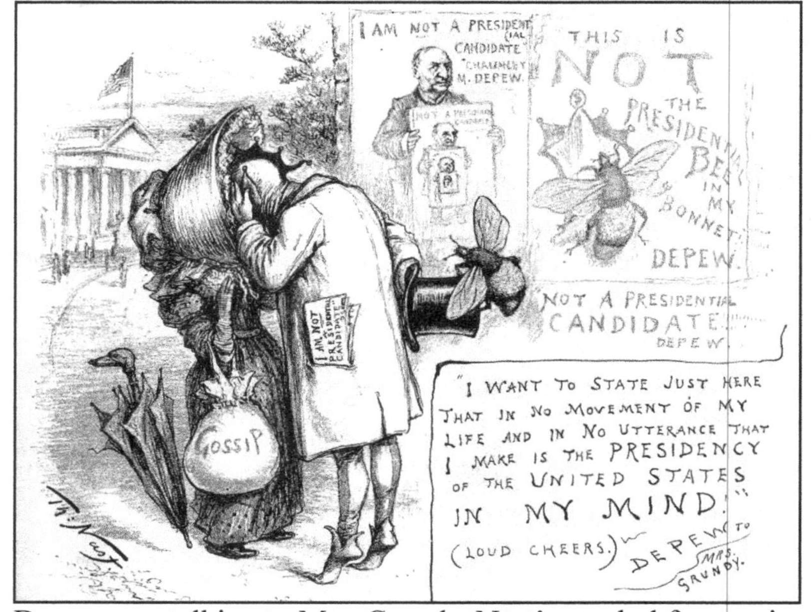

Depew was talking to Mrs. Grundy, Nast's symbol for gossip. (See p. 155-157)

In contrast, the second Depew article on March 28, 1891 — entitled *Has a Corporation a Soul?* — was deadly serious. Five weeks earlier, a railroad maintenance car in the tunnel from Grand Central, was struck from the rear by a four-car train with 60 passengers just after 7 A.M. Six people in the maintenance car died. A coroner's 12-man jury — which included a former mayor and two bank presidents — indicted Depew and the New York Central for second degree manslaughter.

Depew claimed that the engineer of the passenger train was responsible because he missed a signal. The jury said the air in the tunnel was so dense (because the railroad hadn't provided enough vents for adequate light and circulation) that signals weren't visible. Additionally, the maintenance car had an illegal stove which caught fire in the crash and created a fatal inferno.

With a $50,000 salary, top level political influence, unsurpassed public speaking ability — and an ego to match — Depew joked throughout the trial, and was shocked by the indictment. How could the great Chauncey be held personally liable for a lowly engineer's mistake? Chairman Cornelius Vanderbilt II put up his $25,000 bail, and a jury ultimately acquitted him at trial.

Nast, who had blasted various railroads impersonally over the years for their many fatal accidents, augmented the article's text and photographs with searing personal attacks on Depew.

ILLUSTRATED AMERICAN March 28, 1891 286

MR. DEPEW'S IDEA OF IT.
"I haven't a word to say against Coroner Levy. He's all right. It was a great day for Levy, and I shouldn't wonder if it would make him a Police Justice, and perhaps send him to Congress. He wasn't responsible for the finding of the jury, and when the jury made itself ridiculous, I suppose he had to swallow it."—*From an interview with Mr. Depew.*

ILLUSTRATED AMERICAN March 28, 1891 289

MR. DEPEW MUST GIVE BAIL.
What! Arrest a railroad president, drawing fifty thousand dollars a year, and let a humble wretch of an engineer go free? The thought was sacrilegious!

ILLUSTRATED AMERICAN March 28, 1891 290

MR. DEPEW MISUNDERSTOOD.
Manslaughter in the second degree is defined by the Penal Code to be "causing the death of one person by the culpable negligence of another, with a penalty for imprisonment for not less than one year and not more than fifteen years, or by a fine of not more than one thousand dollars, or both."

Of all Nast's major domestic multi-cartoon targets — Jeff Davis, Andrew Johnson, Boss Tweed, Horace Greeley, Samuel Tilden, John Kelly and James Blaine — Depew apparently was the only one who actively sought revenge, and he waited until two months after Nast died. In the first of his two terms in the Senate (1899-1911), Depew put into the Congressional Record a totally fabricated story about his being alone with Greeley shortly before the 1872 election. According to Depew, Greeley glanced at Nast's "vile" cartoons, bemoaned his fate, "snapped his brain and went into an asylum the next day, where he died."

As Albert Paine put it in Nast's biography: "Unluckily for Senator Depew, he did not wait long enough. There was still one man living who could refute his testimony . . . and set the matter right before the world." Whitelaw Reid in an editorial "To keep the Record Straight" in the *Tribune*, somewhat surprisingly did just that. Paine was so incensed by Depew's slander of his deceased hero that he used more than a page of small type for a footnote containing the full text of Depew's calumny and Reid's rebuttal.[5] In Depew's 400-page detailed autobiography written 30 years later — *My Memories of Eighty Years* — Depew never mentioned the accident, trial or Nast, while describing many less significant events in his life.

During his time at *Harper's*, Nast disparaged or vilified Reid 54 times: 33 during the Greeley fiasco, 15 more during the vitriolic 1884 Blaine campaign (when he called Reid a liar), and another half-dozen during Cleveland's first term.

However, in 1892 when Harrison ran unsuccessfully for a second term, and Reid replaced Levi Morton as the Vice Presidential nominee, Nast reversed course and supported the Republican ticket, high tariffs and all, in his own *Nast's Weekly*. He actually complimented Reid: "He improves upon intimate acquaintance." Reid repaid the support and new friendship with his editorial.

Matthew Quay

Two weeks after it first ridiculed Depew as a jester, the *Illustrated American* went after Matt Quay, the political boss of Pennsylvania for the past two decades. Currently Chairman of the Republican National Committee, Quay had been Harrison's campaign manager, although Harrison attributed his victory to "Providence." In response, Quay told Philadelphia reporters: "He ought to know that Providence hadn't a damn thing to do with it, and that his nominee would never know how many Republicans were compelled to approach the gates of the penitentiary to make him President."

Like Depew, Nast had never portrayed Quay in *Harper's Weekly*, even when Quay was involved in a huge financial scandal in 1880. As State Treasurer, he misused State funds for bribes, loans, vote-buying, and deposits in favorite banks which lent interest-free money to him and his associates; he then tried to replace the stolen money with stock market speculations that went bad. A new Treasurer discovered a $260,000 loss.

After considering suicide, Quay threw himself upon the tender mercies of Senator Don Cameron, whose father, Simon, had started a political dynasty in the 1860s that superseded even Quay's control. Cameron put up the last $100,000 repayment after Quay and his associate scraped up what they could; the associate then killed himself. Nast illustrated the crime, using a skull for the stock tape feeder.

ILLUSTRATED AMERICAN October 25, 1890

DON CAMERON SAVING QUAY FROM EXPOSURE AND THE PENITENTIARY.
"I don't do this to save you, Quay," said the senator, "but for the sake of your wife and your children."
The money was paid.

In 1885, Quay was again elected State Treasurer and once more gambled with $400,000 of State money, this time in bonds. It worked and Quay made a fortune. His fellow conspirator, a bank president, soon drank himself to death. The *Times*, *World*, *Evening Post*, and *Harper's Weekly* all played up Quay's conspiracies in August 1890, and Nast's current publication followed suit on October 25.

However, there was another current angle: Quay was trying to elect a governor he could "own," one George Delamater. As the *Illustrated American* concluded its article: "The election of Delamater would be the vindication of Quay. Are you willing to be 'bossed' any longer by a man who has been denounced in the House of Representatives as a branded criminal?" The answer on Election Day was no; Delamater lost.

Nast went back to his Tweed roots in portraying Quay as a vulture sitting on a nest of the people's money with the eggs below representing his confederates who died shortly after their frauds were discovered. The artist's pen still couldn't spell as Birds of a "fetter" proved. (He meant "feather," of course).

Ultimately, Quay won. He had been a Senator in 1887-8, failed to win reelection, but then won again in 1900 and served until his death three years later.

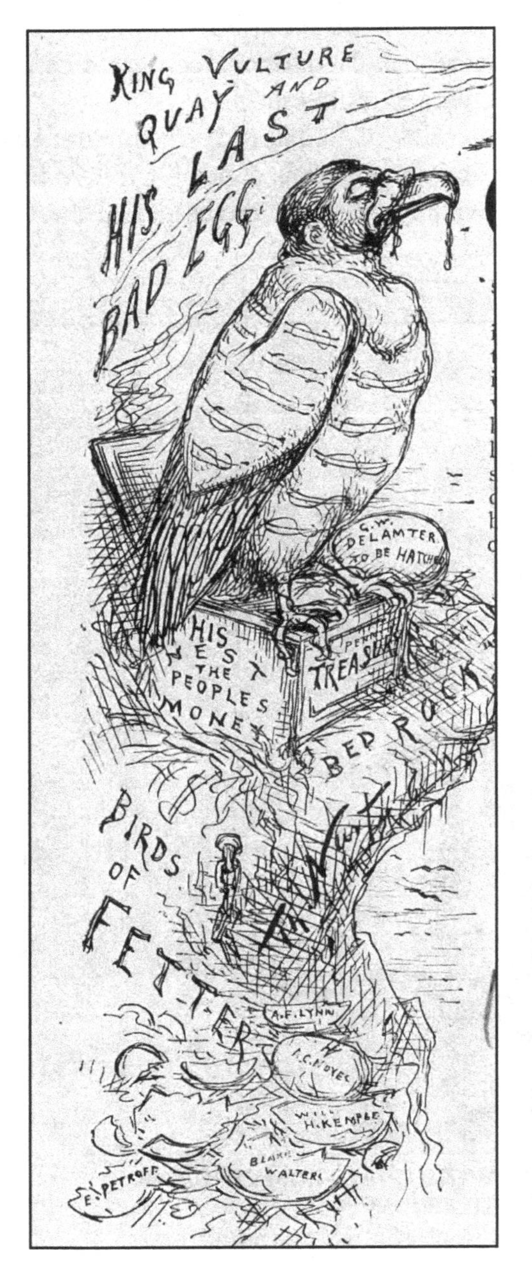

HIS DIGNIFIED AND SILENT GALLERY.
"I Want To Know How It Feels To Own A Governor Just For ONCE."—*Matt Quay*

The Latest Dream of Santa Claus

Four and a half years later, Nast made a final appearance in the *Illustrated American's* post-dated Christmas issue of January 4, 1896. Coincidentally, the man who created the modern Santa Claus, illustrated a 45-stanza poem entitled *The Latest Dream of Santa Claus*. His seven cartoons highlighted clever verse satirizing five of his familiar targets — Cleveland, Harrison, Quay, David Hill and Chauncey Depew.

"First of all I saw him, the sincere, brave and truthful,
The strong man with feet planted firm on a hill—
Stout Grover; and toward him with brow bland and youthful,
Though needing a wig for the dome of his will,

"Came Democracy's David, dressed up like a waiter
(He has waited in sooth for his turn, like the worm),
And he offered to Cleveland a goose on a platter
And whispered, 'O Duck-hunter, take a Third-Term.'

"As this pair from my *camera magica* faded,
Ben Harrison loomed, hat in hand, through the shade;
He looked like a deacon, devoted, though jaded
By passing the plate, foreign missions to aid.

"Close to him was Matt Quay, like the skin of banana,
A slippery customer, toting a bag;
'Take this, Ben,' he said, 'to help fix Indiana,
Which pious John sends lest your courage should flag."

"'Twas Vanderbilt, Duke of New York, and he handed
His bouquet, with a bow—not to George Francis Train—
But to Chauncey Depew, that Demosthenes candied,
Whose heart is as sweet as the fun of his brain.

"'Take a life-term as President, sir, of my railway,'
Thus Vanderbilt murmured, 'O Wit never tame!
For tho' toward the White-House you make but a snail-way,
You deserve, sir, to get there, at last, just the same.'

Once A Week

On April 8, 1890, two-year old *Once A Week* published the first of Nast's 26 cartoons. They were mostly topical — Wall Street, baseball, temperance — rather than political. Two were self-caricatures, one as an inebriate. Evidently, his personal aversion to alcohol gave way to his financial and occupational pressures on occasion, although he apparently was ashamed of his lapses.

OAW November 11, 1891 OAW December 8, 1891

BACCHUS' SLAVES BECOME PLUTO'S SUBJECTS.

OAW October 13, 1891

GOOD AND BAD FORM

OAW October 13, 1891

THE ROBBED – STOCKED PUNISHED TOGETHER

Nast contributed through 1891, focused in the *Gazette* and his own paper in 1892, and returned for eight cartoons after his own paper failed in March 1893. *Once A Week* prospered, reaching a circulation of 25,000 in 1892 when it became more of a news magazine with extensive photo-journalism, and changed its name to *Collier's Weekly* in 1895 when Robert Collier, son of the founder, took charge. (It lasted until 1957, when it could no longer compete for advertising and circulation with booming television.)

The two cartoons above, both in the same issue, also reflected Nast's despondent mood. He pictured himself reaching to grab the proverbial crow, probably to eat it. Side-by-side, were Wall Street pigs at the trough, overlooked by waiting vultures. The lettering at the top read: "He that withholds corn, the people will curse him." The bottom read: "The robbed stocked. Punished together." This may have been the only time Nast personalized his financial debacle with Grant and Ward in a publication.

Chapter 50
After Harper's Weekly: Nast's Weekly

New York Gazette

The *Gazette* was a thinly-capitalized four-page daily newspaper that began publishing in 1889. In March 1892, it reached out to Nast to become its illustrator and cartoonist, promising him free reign. Needing income, he accepted.

Some of Nast's work was pure illustration, like a cover portrait of Republican statesman William Evarts, now 74, and recently retired from public life because of illness. A cartoon in the same issue depicted Senator Henry Cabot Lodge as a porcupine, unsuccessfully trying to get a Free Elections Bill passed. (It would have added Federal protection for black voters in the South, thereby helping to achieve Republican victories.) Nast also drew advertisements for Knox Hats and others.

NEW YORK GAZETTE June 25, 1892

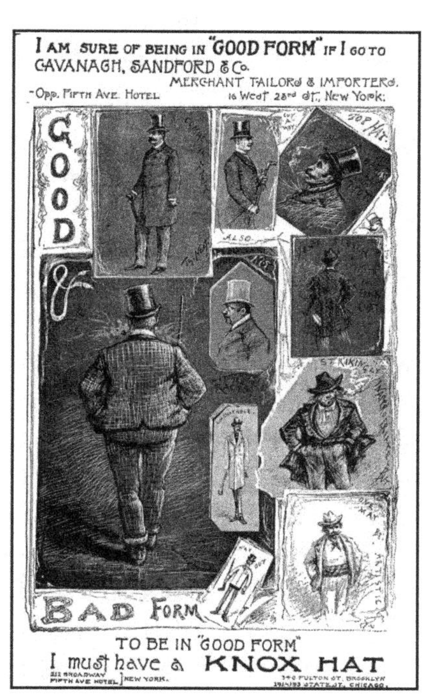

A FEDERAL BAYONETTE AND SABER LODGE PORCUPINE

For its efforts in attacking Tammany Hall and the police, the *Gazette's* owners attracted potential support from two wealthy municipal reform backers, but the death of the key principal washed that prospect away by July. In response, Tammany ordered the city's leading newspaper distributor to discontinue non-mail distribution of the paper. The *Gazette* expired on August 13, 1892, leaving Nast as its largest creditor. If he so desired, he could inherit the shell, and finally achieve his long quest for his own paper.

Into the Fire

Nast quickly swallowed the spoiled bait in his third terrible financial decision, after losing all his savings in the Grant and Ward Ponzi scheme, and his Colorado "non-silver" mines. Unlike the first two, this time he probably thought he was playing in familiar territory. Five weeks later, the first issue of *Th. Nast's Weekly* appeared on September 17, 1892, selling for a nickel — half the price of *Harper's Weekly*, *Puck* and the *Illustrated American.*[1]

His objective was to take advantage of his new editorial freedom to compete with Joseph Keppler at Democratic-leaning *Puck*. He evidently ignored *Puck's* overwhelming advantages: 15 years of history; close to six-figure circulation; color lithography; superb personnel like cartoonist Frederick Opper, editor H.C. Bunner, and business manager Adolph Schwarzmann; and a multitude of satisfied advertisers.

Judge, the Republican-oriented version of *Puck*, was an even greater barrier to Nast's success because its current ex-*Puck* cartoonists, Bernhard Gillam and Eugene Zimmerman, were about as talented as Keppler. With solid financial support and a circulation close to 85,000, *Judge* was a strong Harrison backer.

Against competition like that, Nast had nothing to offer in the way of management, finances, marketing, editorial strength or expertise. He made 27-year old Tom, Jr. the publisher, and hired Morrison Renshaw as editor. None of the three had publishing experience. Desperate for both artistic and financial success, Nast plunged ahead with the hopeless venture.

Moreover, the financial panic of 1893 was about to upset the national economy. Hundreds of banks and commercial companies failed. By 1897, a third of all railroad mileage was in bankruptcy.

Funding

To raise capital, he took out an additional mortgage on his house[2] (either a second or a third) and probably raised $5,000 to $10,000. However, the Presidential election was two months away — eight issues to be exact — and Nast evidently understood the Republican Party agreed to guarantee 100,000 circulation ($5,000 a week) in return for his backing the Benjamin Harrison and Whitelaw Reid ticket.

Doing so required Nast to totally reverse his 1888 support for Cleveland and tariff reform (as a freelancer), and his 1884 backing for Cleveland (as a Mugwump at the *Weekly)*. The editorial notes in his first pro-Harrison issue stated: "Fact. 'His grandfather's hat' really does fit the grandson. If anything, it is a trifle small." He praised Reid — the *Tribune* publisher, whom he had targeted 54 times over 20 years as a snobby nose-in-the-air editor — as "a good running mate with the sure-footed Harrison," and predicted "a bigger victory for Harrison than that which he won in 1888."

In addition to the vital financial funding that the Party's circulation guarantee would provide, Nast could support the Republican ticket proactively for the first time in 20 years (when Grant trounced Greeley), with a clear conscience. Equally important, he was disillusioned with 7\41, and no Democratic offers came his way after his ineffective efforts on behalf of the President's failed reelection bid.

Moreover, James Blaine — Nast's principal Republican arch-enemy during the past four Presidential elections, and Harrison's enabler four years earlier — was no longer associated with the President. As Secretary of State, he had tangled with Harrison over the President's support for reciprocal free trade treaties versus Blaine's all-out protective tariffs, and resigned three days before the Republican Convention met in June 1892. In poor health from gout and Bright's Disease, he made only a single campaign speech for Harrison, and died less than three months after the election. If Blaine's health had allowed him to be a candidate, he would have easily won the nomination, and Nast probably would have avoided his third financial disaster.

As it turned out, the 100,000 circulation guarantee evaporated after three issues. On the last page of the fourth issue (October 8), Nast guaranteed circulation of 50,000 for the next five weeks — through the election — based on "closed contracts." Previous verbal understandings (or misunderstandings) were now in writing.

However, while the Republican Party paid Nast for its guaranteed circulation — first, a questionable $5,000, then $2,500 a week — it probably never came close to reaching those numbers. Nast's on-going attacks on Tammany Hall and its current Boss, Richard Croker, resulted in the continuing loss of local newsboy circulation and possibly more, when a key distributor affiliated with Tammany, refused to handle the paper. Less damaging but still important, Chauncey Depew's New York Central (and probably other railroads) extended its boycott of the *Illustrated American* to *Nast's Weekly* in continued retaliation for his 1890 attacks.*

NAST'S WEEKLY March 4, 1893

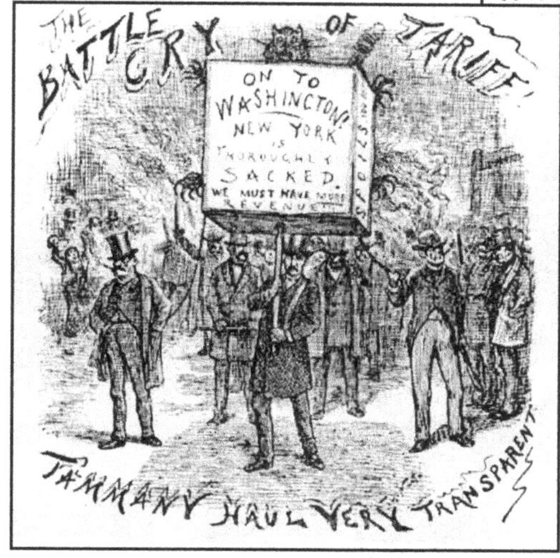

Curtis

One surprise in the first issue was a reprint from the *Herald* of a flowery tribute to George William Curtis, who had died on August 31, about two weeks before Nast's paper went to press. Nast made no comment among the "Editorial Notes," and almost certainly didn't attend Curtis's funeral; however, to his credit, he did recognize the passing of his nemesis in a public, positive, but totally impersonal manner.

GEORGE WILLIAM CURTIS

Yes, the world is less melodious than it was, for a tuneful voice is hushed forever and a magic pen will write no more.

In the death of George William Curtis, the sweetest singer who ever sang in prose, a bright light is quenched, a star of the first magnitude goes out of our earthly firmament to shine in the skies of the glorious hereafter. He was a man we loved, not for the enemies he made, but for the friends. He was an American of Americans, and in his well spent, useful, luminous life it is hard to find a single blemish. He possessed that rarest of good gifts, character, and he never left it at home when he went abroad or lost it when it was needful to him.

—N.Y. Herald.

---

* See p. 653-656

The Owl

Nast's masthead revealed his qualms by portraying himself as a symbolic wise owl, but with doubt and sadness in his eyes. His owl history went back to 1859 when he illustrated a children's book. In 1885, he sketched himself as an owl on a palate, holding a pen with the English *Punch* (magazine) mascot at one end, and a neutral look of passive inquiry in its staring eyes.

The current owl had a jester's cap on its head; Nast probably would have called it a fool's cap to illustrate his current self-image, as well as the comic aspect of his publication. His other facial features were accurate.

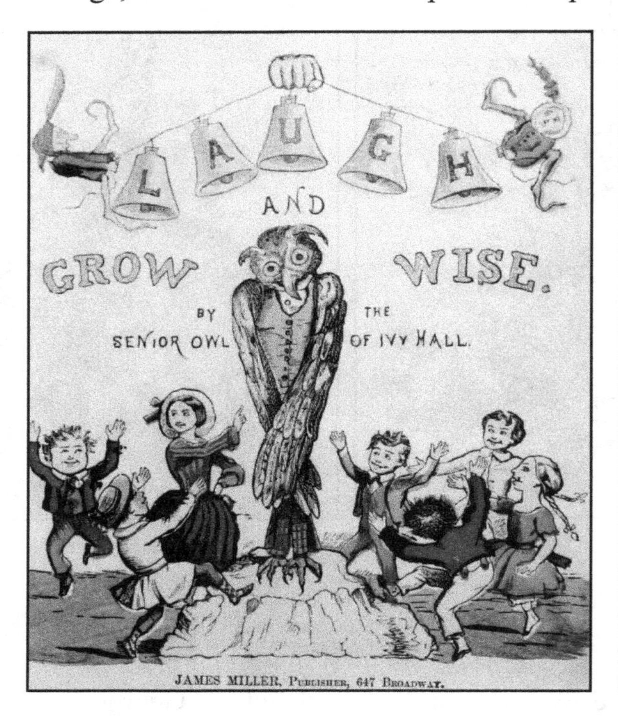

Advertising

Four weeks after it should have appeared in his first issue, Nast finally got around to publishing a mission statement, along with a personal pitch to advertisers and the lowered 50,000 guarantee: "Special attention given to Cartoon and Illustrated Advertisements." That was an area that conceivably could have brought in revenue, but only with a credible, established circulation base. In actuality, Nast drew a total of only seven illustrated ads in his 25 issues. Moreover, his advertising agent demanded, and received commissions on contracts which ultimately proved worthless.[3]

October 15, 1892

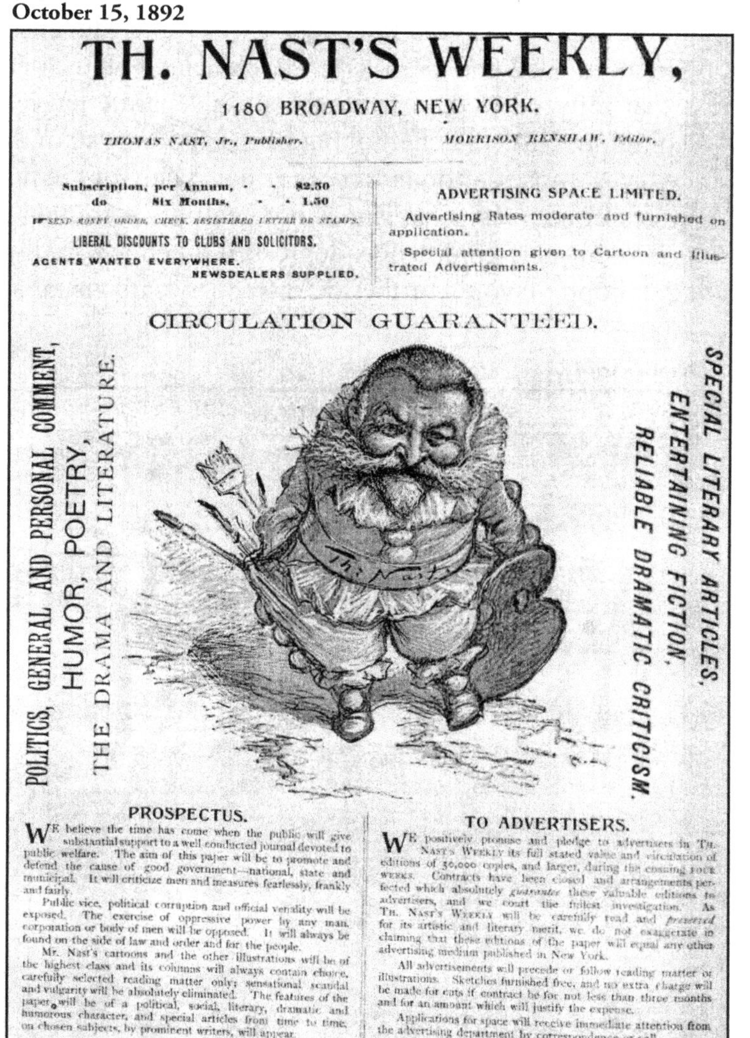

TH. NAST'S WEEKLY,

1180 BROADWAY, NEW YORK.

THOMAS NAST, Jr., Publisher. *MORRISON RENSHAW, Editor.*

Subscription, per Annum, - - $2.50
do Six Months, - - 1.50

SEND MONEY ORDER, CHECK, REGISTERED LETTER OR STAMPS.

LIBERAL DISCOUNTS TO CLUBS AND SOLICITORS.

AGENTS WANTED EVERYWHERE.
NEWSDEALERS SUPPLIED.

ADVERTISING SPACE LIMITED.

Advertising Rates moderate and furnished on application.

Special attention given to Cartoon and Illustrated Advertisements.

CIRCULATION GUARANTEED.

POLITICS, GENERAL AND PERSONAL COMMENT,
HUMOR, POETRY,
THE DRAMA AND LITERATURE.

SPECIAL LITERARY ARTICLES,
ENTERTAINING FICTION,
RELIABLE DRAMATIC CRITICISM.

PROSPECTUS.

WE believe the time has come when the public will give substantial support to a well conducted journal devoted to public welfare. The aim of this paper will be to promote and defend the cause of good government—national, state and municipal. It will criticize men and measures fearlessly, frankly and fairly.

Public vice, political corruption and official venality will be exposed. The exercise of oppressive power by any man, corporation or body of men will be opposed. It will always be found on the side of law and order and for the people.

Mr. Nast's cartoons and the other illustrations will be of the highest class and its columns will always contain choice, carefully selected reading matter only; sensational scandal and vulgarity will be absolutely eliminated. The features of the paper will be of a political, social, literary, dramatic and humorous character, and special articles from time to time, on chosen subjects, by prominent writers, will appear.

TO ADVERTISERS.

WE positively promise and pledge to advertisers in TH. NAST'S WEEKLY its full stated value and circulation of editions of 50,000 copies, and larger, during the coming FOUR WEEKS. Contracts have been closed and arrangements perfected which absolutely *guarantee* these valuable editions to advertisers, and we court the fullest investigation. As TH. NAST'S WEEKLY will be carefully read and *preserved* for its artistic and literary merit, we do not exaggerate in claiming that these editions of the paper will equal any other advertising medium published in New York.

All advertisements will precede or follow reading matter or illustrations. Sketches furnished free, and no extra charge will be made for cuts if contract be for not less than three months and for an amount which will justify the expense.

Applications for space will receive immediate attention from the advertising department by correspondence or call.

The Election

Cleveland won the election handily, with a 122 vote margin in the electoral college and a three-point edge in the popular vote. Populist Party candidate James Weaver drew almost 10%.

Nast's Weekly managed to survive until Cleveland was inaugurated on March 4, 1893. It cut back from sixteen to eight pages after the election, and editor Morrison Renshaw disappeared from the masthead a month later.

As he had done in the five Presidential elections at *Harper's Weekly*, Nast focused his cartoons on the opposition candidate. That wasn't difficult with Horatio Seymour and Horace Greeley against Ulysses Grant (in 1868 and 1872); Samuel Tilden against Rutherford Hayes (whom he never portrayed) in 1876; and James Blaine (in 1884). He went easy on his friend, Winfield Hancock (in 1880) and never depicted James Garfield (in 1880). All except the politically naive and inexperienced Hancock, had plenty of political and personal sins to provide impalement.

Cleveland was different. Nast had supported him once for Governor and twice for President. He had commented to a journalist on his informal and collegial style in shaking constituents' hands, which he personally observed and contrasted with Grant and Chester Arthur.*

---

* See p. 635

All he could come up with now was Cleveland's corpulence, which translated into "His Dignity." Nast obviously wasn't convinced that he was backing the right candidate. His only funny cartoon was his last one on Inauguration Day, when Vice President-Elect Adlai Stevenson (grandfather of Adlai II, Dwight Eisenhower's losing opponent in 1952 and 1956) conked Cleveland on the head with a spoils-system axe. However, the inane editorial text that referred to the cartoon — on a separate page — was sophomoric but typical: "We prefer the story of Washington's little hatchet to that of the spoils-system that Adlai wields."

At least those cartoons were original. Many of the rest were retreads from *Harper's Weekly*, the *Daily Graphic*, or lesser sources. Nast's missing creativity stemmed from a variety of roots: obvious lack of political conviction, missing self-confidence, depressed mental state, financial insecurity, and dominant competitors in *Puck* and *Judge*. Sloppy layouts further detracted from its visual appeal.

October 15, 1892

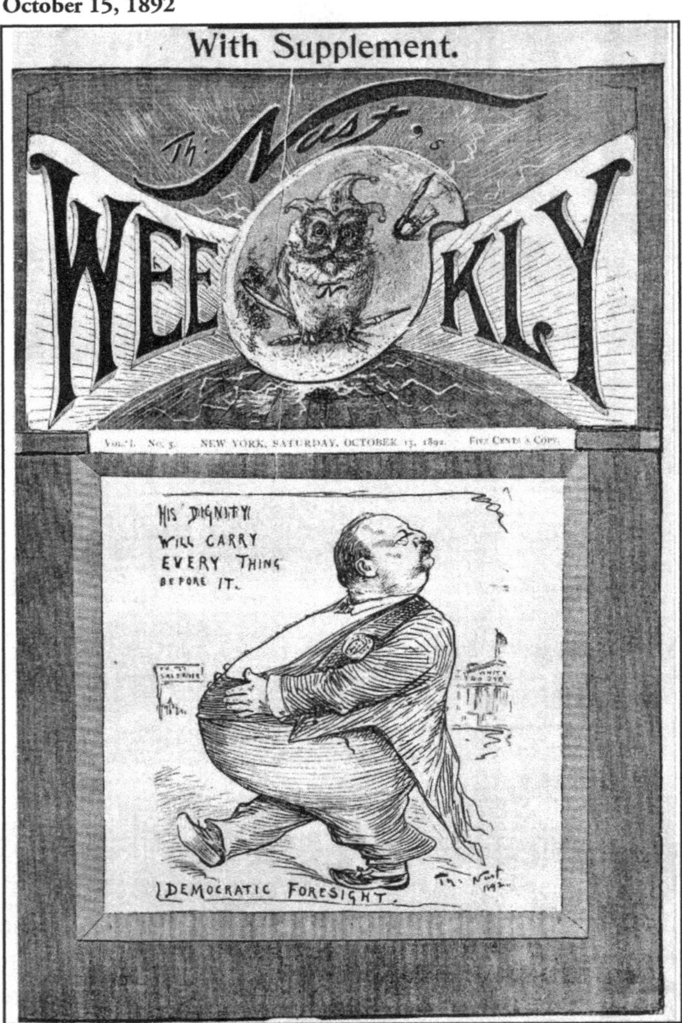

March 4, 1893

Theatre

Theatre had always been Nast's principal avocation, beginning when his father took him to see productions while he played trombone in the orchestra.* He had belonged to the Players Club on Gramercy Square for many years, where he hobnobbed with actors and producers; long before and after his influence and stature declined, the Club was his New York "home away from home." His cartoons were full of theatrical characters, plots and settings — primarily from Shakespeare.

Consequently, the only area in which *Nast's Weekly* had something original and potentially interesting to offer was its theatre page, entitled "The Players," and featuring Shakespeare attended by Comedy and Tragedy figures in its heading. It featured more than a dozen reviews and announcements, some with admirable negative candor.

ROBERT MANTELL celebrated his fiftieth performance of "A Face in the Moonlight" at Proctor's Theatre, Wednesday evening, October 5th, by presenting to the ladies in the audience a souvenir in the shape of a transparent lamp shade, which when placed upon a lighted lamp gives a brilliant picture of Mr. Mantell's various scenes in the play. Mr. Mantell will take his company on the road, and "Ye Earlie Trouble" will be presented on October 10th.

HENRY E. DIXEY closed his prosperous engagement at Palmer's Theatre last Saturday and was succeeded by Mr. John Drew in Bisson & Carres', "The Masked Ball." The play is a delightful one and will probably be popular.

MR. MANSFIELD'S production of the "Scarlet Letter" which, by the way, was more successful in a financial way than was anticipated, has been succeeded at Daly's Theatre by "Little Miss Million."

THE Fifth Avenue Theatre has been visited in large numbers by people anxious to see Miss Hall's new comedy "Puritania." There have been several theatre parties during the week and Miss Hall has no reason to complain of her receptions. The singing of the opera has improved, and in many other respects it goes smoother and better. The absence of vulgar horse play, which is generally a disagreeable feature of similar productions, is entirely lacking.

AT the Standard Theatre large audiences have been the rule. "Jane" does not seem to lose in interest. Lottie Collins continues to do her little act, but it is said that the London priestess of "Ta-ra-boom-de-ay" is not altogether pleased with her reception in New York. It is certain that New York audiences would prefer that music hall specialties should not be thrown into light comedy in quite so promiscuous a way as Mr. Hill has seen fit to do with this rather stale acrobatic dancer.

"A FAIR REBEL" is still presented at the Fourteenth Street Theatre, and the audiences are good. It is a tale of war life something after the style of "Shenandoah" and "Across the Potomac." There are, however, some incompatibilities of stage presentation which might just as well be eliminated. War times are not quite ancient history as yet.

AT the Union Square Theatre, the Liliputians have had a most successful week with "Candy." These midgets certainly present a very interesting entertainment, which grown people may enjoy with quite as much enthusiasm as do the youngsters.

THERE is some truth in the advertised saying of Evans and Hoey, that if you have not seen their "Parlor Match," "you have not seen it." At least, a great many people have crowded the Bijou Theatre to find out whether they had "seen it" or not, and most of them have come away with the impression that other productions have lacked that distinctive forcefulness which Hoyt's plays require and which marks Evans and Hoey's conception of it.

AT the Casino the change from "the home of comic opera" to a mild sort of London music hall has had its trial for two weeks. There is not much to say about it. The change in the theatre has evidently been made with a view of being able to change back again, if necessary, at very little expense. In other words, the alterations have by no means a permanent look. This was probably wise on the part of the promoters of the new scheme. The audiences have been large, but any novelty will attract large audiences in New York for a while, and the concensus of opinion among men about town is, that unless radical changes are made in the character of the programme, the new music hall will not long enjoy public favor. The specialties, with one or two exceptions, are decidedly not up to the mark of critical taste.

"THE Black Crook" still continues its gorgeous presentations at the Academy of Music. There is no diminution in the attendance, and it is extremely likely that this attraction will have a very prolonged run and hold its audiences as strongly as it does now throughout the whole season. There have been some changes and all for the better.

IN "Capt. Lettarblair," E. H. Sothern, beyond a doubt, has secured a play that will prove a bonanza. The Lyceum is filled to overflowing every evening. His interpretation of the character is wonderfully artistic and clever, and the cast is thoroughly acceptable. The jolly Irish captain will certainly live in memory as one of Mr. Sothern's best rôles.

DE WOLF HOPPER certainly has no reason to complain. "Wang" not only still holds the boards at the Broadway Theatre, but is not likely to be changed for some time to come.

KOSTER AND BIAL announce an entirely reorganized company. This information will give some satisfaction. It is a fact that this place of amusement has been trading upon its former reputation for several seasons. The programmes presented for several months past, with few exceptions, have been extremely dreary. For the last three or four weeks the only act worth witnessing was Amanns character sketches, or rather, impersonations. The much advertised "Vanoni," instead of being "The Great Parisian Success," appears to be a variety actress at one time well known in the Bowery. Koster and Bial will learn sometime that the public tire of novelties whose principal attractiveness is their cheapness—to the proprietors of the theatre. Theatre goers are not exacting as a rule, but audiences should be given something for their money.

MODJESKA'S production of "Henry VIII." in which she presents her conception of Katharine of Arragon, will be welcomed by play-goers. This actress has always been a favorite with the public, and her presentation of Shakespeare's great play will undoubtedly meet with success. She is painstaking, conscientious, and her performances are never mediocre. Her companies are likewise always of good material, and she, like Sarah Bernhardt, is never satisfied to leave rehearsals to others, and gives the parts of her company that personal attention which is always necessary to insure thoroughness. She is said to be very ambitious to succeed in this *rôle*. Should she do so she will have reason, and very good reason, to feel very highly complimented, as the rôle was one of Charlotte Cushman's greatest. There is every reason therefore to expect that Madame Modjeska will do her best, and her best means much.

"A TRIP TO CHINATOWN" still fills the Madison Square Theatre. It is really a remarkable success, and critics are somewhat at a loss how to account for it. Many reasons have have been given of all kinds and all descriptions, but when simmered down to cold hard fact there is no doubt that Harry Conor's magnetic personality is the mainspring of this phenomenal run. Talking about the "skit"—for it does not deserve the name of a play—afterwards, it is seldom that anybody remembers anything else except Conor's delightful humor. It is to be hoped that the talent he undoubtedly possesses for a higher order of character will soon have an opportunity to display itself. A chance this for a new author.

At the Standard Theatre large audiences have been the rule. "Jane" does not seem to lose in interest. Lottie Collins continues to do her little act, but it is said that the London priestess of "Ta-ra-boom-de-ay" is not altogether pleased with her reception in New York. It is certain that New York audiences would prefer that music hall specialties should not be thrown into light comedy in quite so promiscuous a way as Mr. Hill has seen fit to do with this rather stale acrobatic dancer.

"A Fair Rebel" is still presented at the Fourteenth Street Theatre, and the audiences are good. It is a tale of war life something after the style of "Shenandoah" and "Across the Potomac." There are, however, some incompatibilities of stage presentation which might just as well be eliminated. War times are not quite ancient history as yet.

Looking back at Nast's career at age 48 — after he lost his mining investment, finished his long Western lecture tour, and turned down *Harper's Weekly* projected offer to work on the 1888 election campaign — was there any venture at which he might have been successful if his ego, physical and mental health, and minimal financing capability had permitted? A weekly or bi-weekly theatrical paper — including reviews, cartoons, profiles and, especially ads — might have worked if production and printing was subcontracted, and politics was limited to within the theatrical community. The right partner — not Tom Jr. — conceivably could have made it happen.

---

* See p. 8-10

Bankruptcy

After Nast closed his lifelong dream at the end of February 1893, he paid off all its debts. None of the paper's creditors lost money, except possibly a few subscribers who had paid in advance. He himself was deeply in debt, and had no current prospect of making enough to sustain his cost of living.[4]

Five months after *Nast's Weekly* died, 21-year old Mabel Nast — Tommy and Sallie's fourth child and youngest daughter (of three) — was married in Morristown to John Crawford. Who paid for the wedding is not known, but the father of the bride drew a sketch on the back of the announcement. It showed him waving a "Bankruptcy Auction Sale" banner, using a similar forlorn image of himself as he doodled after he lost his money with Grant and Ward ten years earlier.*

Mr. & Mrs. Thomas Nast
announce the marriage of their daughter,
Mabel,
to
Mr. John William Roy-Crawford,
on Thursday, July the twenty-seventh,
eighteen hundred and ninety-three.
Morristown, New Jersey.

Morristown and Morris County Library

* See p. 546

Chapter 51
After Harper's Weekly: Nast's Final Decade

Herman Kohlsaat

In early June 1892, Nast attended the Republican National Convention in Minneapolis, which re-nominated Benjamin Harrison for President on the first ballot. While there, Nast met and became friendly with Herman Kohlsaat and Art Young. Kohlsaat was the controlling owner, and 26-year old. Young was the principal cartoonist, for the Chicago-based *Inter Ocean* newspaper

Kohlsaat, a wealthy businessman, grew rich as the proprietor of the city's largest bakery. He wanted to become influential in politics, and backed William McKinley who chaired the Convention. Nast had contributed some trite cartoons to the *Inter Ocean* prior to the Convention. Subsequently, Kohlsaat invited Nast to Chicago to judge a graphic contest.

THE INTER OCEAN

May 8, 1892

WHEREVER UNCLE SAM INTRODUCES THE WORLD'S FAIR

May 28, 1892

JUSTICE "TAKE NOT THE LAW INTO YOUR OWN HANDS, FOR WHERE WILL THAT END"

April 3, 1892

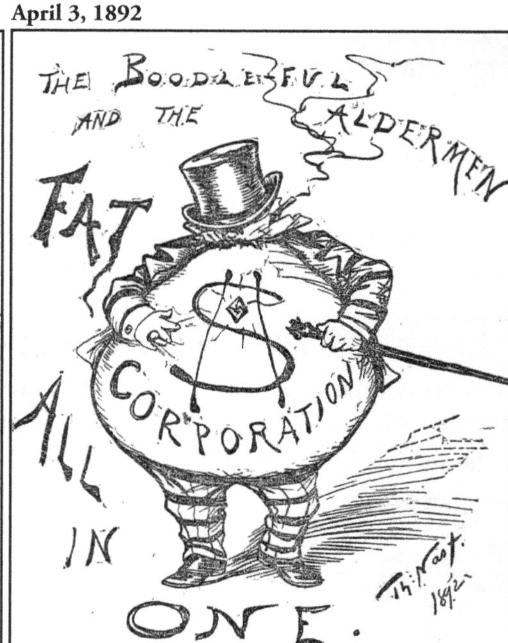

THAT'S WHAT THEY LIVE FOR AND THAT'S WHAT THEY ARE HERE FOR.

While he was in Paris the previous year, Kohlsaat had seen a recently-invented press which was capable of printing high-speed color supplements. He ordered one — the first in America — for the *Inter Ocean*, with the upcoming Chicago World's Fair, celebrating the 400th anniversary of Columbus discovering America, in mind. Nast drew several full color cartoons, the only known time he did so for a publication.

October 16, 1892

October 30, 1892

April 30, 1893

Called the Columbian Exposition, its delayed opening was May 1, 1893. Nast's cartoon was on the cover of the Supplement date (dated April 30).

Nast and Kohlsaat shared an important bond in their mutual reverence of Grant. Kohlsaat had been raised in Grant's hometown of Galena, Illinois, until he turned 12 in 1865, and probably met Sam Grant in 1860 when the future President worked in his family's leather goods store. Their bond would result in a meaningful Grant-related project for both of them a few years later.

Art Young, who drew almost all the cover cartoons for the Inter Ocean, was thrilled to be associated with Nast, his childhood idol. Their friendship remained close until Nast left for Guayaquil 10 years later. One of Young's memories, noted in his autobiography, was accompanying Nast in 1897 or 1898 to see the first movie exhibited in New York. Nast continually commented "Marvellous," as they watched the French Cavalry perform drills.

London

In 1894, Nast traveled to London to search for new revenue. Rudyard Kipling, the famous English author and poet, was a fellow passenger on the steamer. Nast sketched him playing shuffleboard, pushing American coins at a "penny-a-line."

While Nast contributed some work to the *Pall Mall Gazette* in London, evidently nothing else materialized in the way of cartoons. However, he lucked out when two old friends separately commissioned him to paint significant pictures of two of his personal idols — Ulysses Grant and William Shakespeare.

MR. KIPLING ON THE STEAMER, 1894

Paine, p. 545

Peace in Union

First, he met with Kohlsaat, who ordered a large (nine-by-twelve-foot) painting of General Robert E. Lee surrendering to Grant at Appomattox. Kohlsaat wanted to commemorate that culminating national event in all their lives — Grant's, Kohlsaat's and Nast's — on its forthcoming thirtieth anniversary. In addition to Grant, Kohlsaat probably was acquainted with Galenans John Rawlings and Ely Parker, and with Orville Babcock, who had married Galenan Anne Campbell in 1866. Nast completed the painting on the exact date — April 9, 1895 — and Kohlsaat proudly presented it to the "Citizens of Galena" on April 27, what would have been Grant's 73rd birthday.*

Galena & U.S. Grant Museum, Galena, IL.

PEACE IN UNION

Nast earned a $5,000 fee, probably more than he made in any of the last five years. Its relative value to him can be measured against the $3,000 salary that he accepted in desperation seven years later — to knowingly face death from yellow fever as Consul General in Guayaquil, Ecuador. Critically for him, Kohlsaat paid half the fee up front.[1]

The following year, Nast painted another reconciliation picture, showing an angelic Columbia in Washington, holding a large flag at the graves of Grant and Lee. Grant's tombstone was marked "Harmony and Good Feeling Between the Sections;" Lee's inscription stated "Restoration of Peace Should Be the Sole Object of All."[2]

Rutherford B. Hayes Library, Fremont, OH.

* See p. 141 and related footnotes for identifications and more details on the 13 recognizable men in the picture

Sir Henry Irving

Nast's second commission came from his English friend, Henry Irving, the greatest Shakespearean actor and producer of the past quarter-century. Irving, who would be knighted a year later, and Nast knew each other well from their previous trans-Atlantic travels, and shared a deep appreciation of Shakespeare's characters and plays with each other.

So when the two experts dined at Irving's club one evening after theatre, Nast suggested painting a tribute to their idol, and Irving sparked to the idea. The project lay fallow until Nast met his deadline for *Peace in Union*. On July 20, 1895, Irving responded to Nast's preliminary sketch with perhaps the cheeriest encouragement in the artist's last decade: "Love and greetings, old friend. Delighted at the suggestion. Paint it for me."

THE ILLUSTRATED AMERICAN September 14, 1895 327

Nast's dark setting for The *Immortal Light of Genius* was the small room where Shakespeare was born on April 23, 1564. The only light emanated from the smouldering logs in the fireplace behind his bust. Two hard-to-discern spirits — Comedy, dressed as a jester, and Tragedy, in Roman garb — advanced to lay laurel wreaths on the bust's brow.

Two months after Irving's approval, Nast published the sketch in the *Illustrated American*, where he was once again freelancing.

The picture was completed on the bard's birthday in 1896, and presented to the William Winter Memorial on Staten Island, where it was later destroyed by fire.[3]

Nast also painted a replica the following year, borrowing the original from Mr. Winter to do so.[4] It passed through private hands, fell into poor condition, and ultimately was acquired and restored by the Morristown and Morris Township Public Library, where it hangs today.

THE IMMORTAL LIGHT OF GENIUS

ILLUSTRATED AMERICAN November 16, 1895 625

What remuneration Nast received for each of the Shakespeare pictures is unknown. They are much smaller than *Peace in Union*, so three to five thousand dollars for both would seem likely.

While he was working on the preliminary phases of Irving's picture during the last half of 1895, Nast freelanced for both the *Illustrated American* and *Harper's Weekly*. Irving had been knighted prior to a lengthy American tour, so Nast celebrated Sir Henry accepting an international loving cup from Uncle Sam, as Shakespeare looked on, flanked by the British Lion and the American Eagle. Nast gave him the original drawing at a New York Press Club banquet.

Two weeks before that drawing appeared, Nast and Irving must have watched host Princeton beat Harvard in football — maybe the only occasion when either of them saw a game. The cartoonist celebrated the win by portraying his symbolic tiger — and Princeton's mascot — in a *positive* manner, probably for the only time.

THE ILLUSTRATED AMERICAN November 23, 1895 652-653

Harper's Weekly Redux

Beginning in June 1895, *Harper's* published 23 Nast cartoons over the next eight months. Two of them provided his final opportunity to resurrect Boss Tweed (17 years after Tweed's 1878 death) to guilt-by-association current political figures. (25 post-mortem appearances vs. 120 while he lived.) Here, the late Democratic boss was used to impugn disreputable Republican bosses — New York's Tom Platt and Pennsylvania's Matt Quay. Most of the other cartoons attacked Nast's old targets: Tammany Hall, soft money, intemperance and British imperialism.

HW June 15, 1895 574

"WHO IS MR. PLATT, ANYHOW?"— *NEW YORK HERALD.*

HW September 21, 1895 904

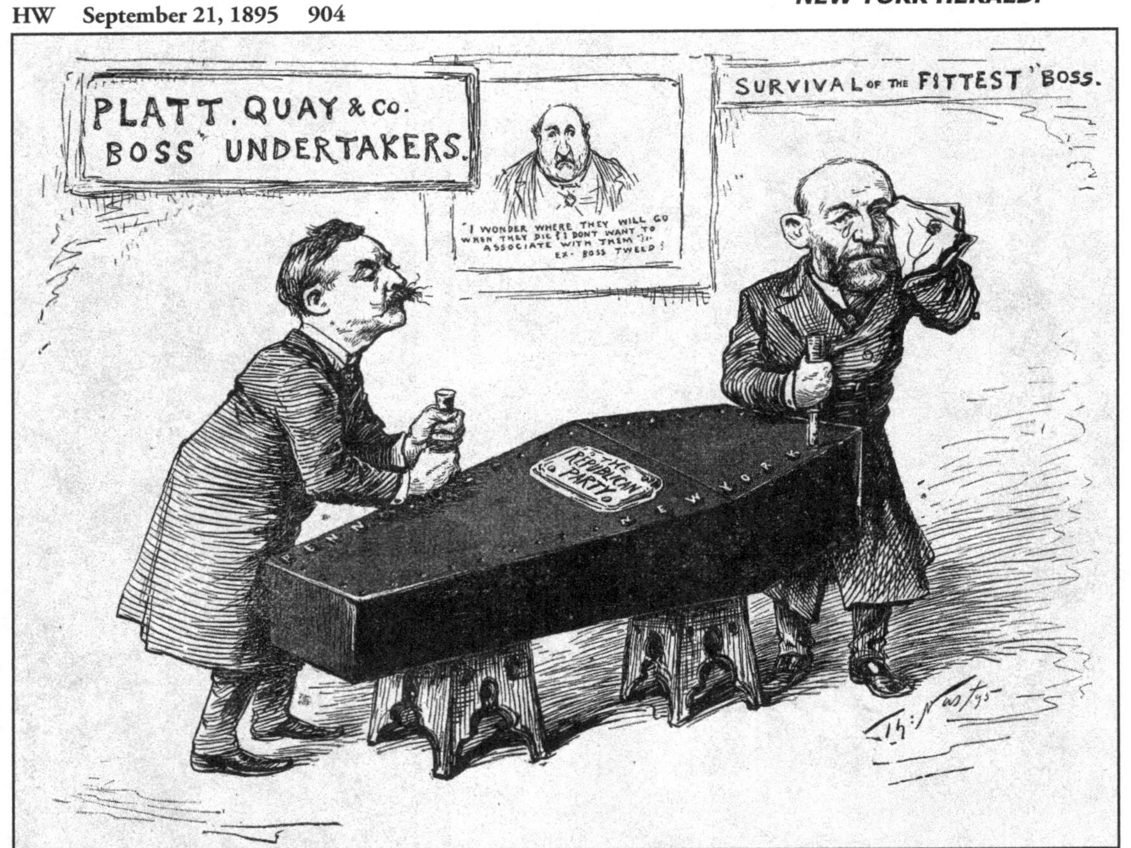

IT'S FUN FOR THEM, BUT DEATH TO THE PARTY THEY ARE SCREWING DOWN.
"It's too bad, but we must live." "That's what we're here for."

A rare positive portrayal featured Theodore Roosevelt, who was appointed President of the New York City Police Board in 1895. His strict enforcement of laws, especially the prohibition of liquor sales on Sunday, gave Nast a comic opening which he used three times. One was his final career shot at the press: His first and only depiction of Joseph Pulitzer (*World*) and his last of James Gordon Bennett, Jr. (*Herald*) — "Chimmy" in Pulitzer's German accent.

HW July 27, 1895 702

HW August 31, 1895 838

ANYTHING TO PUT THE POLICE BOARD "IN A HOLE."

Roundsman Smirk (*giving reporter the wink*). "I must '*carry out the law*' and arrest him. This is Sunday, and he gave a glass of ice-water to his poor, sick mother. *I know my business*!"
Reporter. "Bully for you, cop! *We will have a double-leaded editorial on this*!"

HW September 14, 1895 886

GETTING EVEN WITH "TEDDY."

"Say, Chimmy, ve von't let 'Teddy' Roosevelt '*slide down our cellar door*,' vill ve?"

One morning, Nast called on Roosevelt to exchange mutual compliments. The future President reportedly told him: "Well, Nast, I ought to make a good official. I learned my politics of your cartoons."[5] Unfortunately, the personal relationship didn't help much seven years later when Nast sought a healthier, less remote diplomatic post than Guayaquil, Ecuador.

The *Insurance Observer*

Nast's last regular client for his cartoons was the *Insurance Observer*, a prosperous New York trade journal. About half its pages contained essential (for them) insurance company ads, helping ensure its profitability. Nast's cover and back page cartoons took aim at company presidents, state commissioners, relevant judges, and politicians involved in legislation or scandals. A typical target was John McCall, President of New York Life.

BEFORE
HE HEARD FROM COLORADO.
No one responsible for the management of those sacred trusts should fail to denounce the financial heresies of the Chicago platform, or refuse to join in bringing about the defeat of their advocate.—
(John A. McCall.)

AFTER
HE HEARD FROM COLORADO.
No circular has been sent by any of our officials to the policy holders on the political situation. I would not consider such a document a proper one to make official.—
(John A. McCall.)

THE POLITE LETTER WRITER
Writes 54,000 letters a year, or 176 a day, to policy holders to let them know that they may consider themselves "at liberty to address ME."
N.B.—When is a member a "prospective member?"

Apparently, Nast was confident and comfortable when he drew these cartoons, a quality lacking ever since he left *Harper's* almost a decade earlier. His cordial relationship with the *Observer* lasted from April 1896 until he left for Guayaquil six years later in July 1902.

Industry Changes

The publishers whom Nast had worked for and competed against struggled, especially during the latter part of the decade. *Puck's* key cartoonists were no longer there. Joseph Keppler died in February 1894 at 66, and editor H.C. Bunner in 1896. Bernhard Gillam and Eugene Zimmerman had left for Republican-leaning *Judge* in 1885, but Gillam, only 39, died in January 1896 from typhoid fever.

Harper & Brothers went downhill during the 1890s and collapsed by the end of the decade. As the five second-generation sons died or retired, they drained the firm of accumulated capital as it bought back their partnership shares. Foreseeing a need for more capital, the profitable schoolbook business was opportunistically sold for $550,000 in 1890; it was producing almost half of that in annual gross profit.[6]

Those events, in conjunction with slumping sales of its periodicals, saw the partnership end after 79 years with the formation of a stock company in November 1896. J.P. Morgan, who thought the firm too important to disappear, lent it $850,000 over the next three years. When it couldn't meet the interest payments, it went into receivership on December 4, 1899.[7]

The reorganized company hired 36-year old George Harvey to become its chief. Harvey had a strong background in the publishing business, most recently as Joseph Pulitzer's managing editor at the *World*. He found that revenues, which exceeded $4 million in the 1880s, were now less than $800,000, with a consequent loss larger than that.

To his great credit, Harvey made the firm profitable again and paid off its debt. With the exception of Nast's friend J. Henry Harper, the other nine members of the third generation of Harpers were demoted, fired or retired. Harvey, a strong Democrat, found a place in history by being the first person to promote Woodrow Wilson (then president of Princeton) as a potential candidate for his Party's 1912 Presidential nomination.[8]

Daily Cartoons

As discussed previously, a concomitant change that affected Nast's potential market was that the daily newspapers began printing editorial cartoons as a regular feature, following the pioneering *Daily Graphic* and the *World*. Nast's short-lived 1888 appearance in the *New York Evening Post* and 1889 flirtation with Hearst's *San Francisco Examiner* gave him first-hand experience but he couldn't capitalize on it.

Around Election Day in 1896, he drew a sad, self-pitying cartoon of himself being rejected by the publisher of the *Philadelphia Evening Telegraph*. He wrote "Poor Nast" four times, with the number of exclamation points increasing after each.

Morristown and Morris County Library

Fading Away

Morristown and Morris County Library

Other than the *Insurance Observer*, Nast really had no place to go with his cartoons. From 1896 on, he drew and submitted his work to various publications, but almost all were rejected. Returning to his roots, he did sell a few full-page cartoons to *Leslie's Weekly* from 1898 to 1900. Depressed and without zeal, both his creativity and execution were far below the standards he set for himself when he made his reputation. Even when his work was accepted, it wasn't always easy to get paid.

In retrospect, Republican-oriented *Judge* conceivably could have been a logical outlet for him, especially because Gillam's untimely death left an opening. Although Nast probably would have supported the Republican ticket in 1896 (William McKinley vs. William Jennings Bryan), his anti-Blaine, pro-Cleveland stance in 1884 and 1888 may have been too much for *Judge* to overcome, even if steady work had inspired cartoons that came closer to his former quality standards. Another potential barrier was his lack of experience with lithography.

Poverty

By 1896 (if not before), it became clear to Nast that he couldn't earn enough income to support his family. He had completed his Shakespeare painting, and no other commissions would appear until 1899 when William Keese, a fellow member of the Players Club, paid for a portrait of William Burton to be hung in the Club. (Burton was the actor and theatre owner who had given young Tommy his own seat in the theatre, where he portrayed the comical Toodles and Nast's father played in the orchestra; Keese was a drama historian and Burton's biographer.) Nast, who credited Burton for inspiring his career as a caricaturist, must have appreciated the opportunity for emotional payback, as well as the fee.*

Long before, Nast had cut back his overhead, and eliminated the family servants and other luxuries.[9] He sometimes paid for his doctor, dentist and lawyer by painting their portraits.[10] Cyril, his youngest child, was 17 in August 1896, and the only one still living at home. Although he had paid off all liabilities incurred by *Nast's Weekly* to its creditors, his personal debts continued to haunt and depress him.

Equally distressing, many of his former fans and readers believed he was dead — a thought almost worse than death itself for a supreme egotist. All he could do was sketch denials to send to offenders.

1897

Morristown and Morris County Library

1901

Paine, p. 553

WHEN REFERRED TO AS "THE LATE THOMAS NAST"

* See p. 9

By 1899, Nast was displaying his empty pockets to the world in a pose he had used for Tweed's Mayor Oakey Hall (here with Horace Greeley), and others over the years. However, his distorted facial expression was new. He had maintained his membership in the prestigious Union League Club, which sent out a solicitation for funding the family of a general (and member) recently killed in heroic action in the Philippines. Nast returned the card without a contribution; on the reverse side, he was hanging by a rope, from a pawnbroker's sign, with a caption reading "Th: Nast knows how it is himself."[10]

HW December 9, 1871 1152

HG DIOGENES HAS FOUND THE HONEST MAN.

1899

SOURCE UNKNOWN June 15, 1900

Nast used the same facial image in 1900 to William Smedley, Jr., who probably gave Nast a hard time over a debt and received a similar response: "Th. Nast is Glad "your nose is out of Joint."

Tobacco

As previously discussed, Nast's aversion to alcohol cracked under the pressures that enveloped him in his last decade.* But his abhorrence of tobacco smoke grew even stronger because it affected his chronic catarrh, a throat condition causing inflammation of the respiratory tract. His throat probably bothered him more as he aged. While he didn't attack smoking continuously like he did drinking, Nast showed his distaste in a few cartoons like these in his final year at *Harper's*.

Especially during his last years, he generally stayed away from dinners and smokers. Instead of attending, he usually sent a sketch to whomever had invited him.[11]

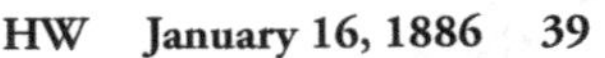

HW January 16, 1886 39

THE NEXT THING TO ABOLISH.
Member. "I say, is life worth living?"

HW January 16, 1886 48

SLAVES TO THE WEED—
Forget that they can't serve two masters.

---

* See p. 660

Theatre

In addition to his family, perhaps the principal positive in Nast's life during his last decade was his continuing interest in the theatre. He did manage to keep up his membership in the Players Club, where he mingled with friends and acquaintances, and eventually met his biographer, Albert Bigelow Paine. Although he could no longer afford to pay for tickets, his actor and producer friends supplied him with "Annie Oakleys" (as free tickets were called because they had holes punched in them).

Producer Daniel Frohman sent him tickets for a play in October 1893, while Nast was still in the after-shock of his paper's failure and daughter Mabel's wedding. Nast wrote that "he had to stay home and mind the house." His note showed "Nast sitting with the house upon his lap . . . pulling his whiskers and otherwise misbehaving."[12]

Paul Loblang

Morristown and Morris County Library

"I was playing Hot Stuff in Hoyt's 'Black Sheep' at the Madison Square Theatre, when Mr. Nast, whom I knew very well, asked me to get him two seats, but insisted upon paying for them. Naturally, I declined to accept anything for them.

"Then I'm a deadhead!' exclaimed the great cartoonist; and the following day I received this cartoon, bearing the skull and crossbones on the back of Mr. Nast's orchestra chair. It is an excellent likeness of him, and one that has never before been published."

Three years later, an actor named Otis Harlan received a similar note, along with an acceptance.

The Last Paintings

In the year before he died, Nast painted two tragic portraits, both relating to the gloom that enveloped him. In the first, he depicted himself contemplating a similarly bleak future to that of Napoleon facing abdication and exile to Elba. It was based on Paul Delaroche's *Napoleon at Fontainbleau*, which he had adapted for several cartoons over a decade.* Here, his handlebar mustache was in full flair, as his furious gaze focused on the pitiless mirror from which he was painting. Tellingly, his back was to a curtained vignette of Wall Street and Trinity Church.

The painting currently is in the Smithsonian Institution's collection. During the Nixon Administration, it hung in Daniel Moynihan's office at the White House where it was humorously referred to as ***Nast Contemplating the Bust of Ward***, a subtle word-play on Rembrandt's 1653 *Aristotle Contemplating the Bust of Homer*.

Nast's last picture wasn't completed before he left for Guayaquil. Here too, he could relate to the subject, and likely the title as well — *The Lost Cause: Lee Waiting For Grant April 9, 1865*. He probably identified with the circumstances that Lee — as a loser — faced at Appomattox, and, accordingly, showed empathy to a Confederate for this first and only time.

American Antiquarian Society

His grandson, Thomas Nast St. Hill, included a photograph of artist and subject in his article. "One wonders," he said, "who looks the sadder."[13]

* See p. 231

Chapter 52
After Harper's Weekly: Nast's Last Year

In February 1902, Thomas Nast took his oldest grandson on their first outing to New York City. Thomas Nast St. Hill — known as Buddy (or Budy, as his grandfather misspelled it) — was Edith's seven year-old son. At age 78, he reminisced about three sketches that his grandfather sent him to commemorate the treasured occasion.[1]

> *The first of these, sent on Valentine's Day, 1902, announced in rhyme that we were to go on a spree the following Wednesday. My mother had arranged to provide the necessary funds for the outing. The next sketch, five days later, is a message that speaks for itself. It shows my grandfather sitting on the edge of his chair, hat on, cane in hand, ready and eager to be off. But the dollar sign and the question mark on his travelling bag tell the story. The check has not arrived! The problem was apparently solved before the big day, however, as the final sketch shows us marching joyfully down the street after attending a matinee at the Broadway Theatre. The description of our first spree as having been "done up Brown" refers to our luncheon at Brown's, a well-known chophouse for men in New York at the time.*

Guayaquil

About three weeks later, Nast received a letter from John Hay, whom he first met in the White House when Hay was President Lincoln's secretary. Now he was Theodore Roosevelt's Secretary of State.

Department of State
Washington, March 10, 1902

My Dear Nast:

The President for some months has been anxious to offer you some place in the consular service, but no vacancy has turned up exactly filling the requirements. There is to be a vacancy in Guayaquil on the Pacific coast of Ecuador. It is worth, I believe, some four thousand dollars. The President would like to put it at your disposition, but if you think it too far away and too little amusing to a man with the soul of an artist, please say so frankly, and he will keep you in mind if anything better should turn up: but it is heartbreaking business waiting for vacancies. Our service is so edifying and preservative that few die and nobody resigns.

Please let me know what you think about Guayaquil, and believe me always,

Sincerely yours,
John Hay.

Nast had become friendly with Roosevelt when he portrayed him as head of the New York City Police Board in 1895.* These two old acquaintances probably were aware of Nast's financial troubles and wanted to help him as best they could. However, in addition to what Hay wrote in his letter to Nast, he was having a hard time getting consular appointments approved in what he referred to as "the vast Senatorial suck."[2]

Guayaquil, Ecuador's largest city and port, then and now, was a hell-hole. Ravaged by fire not long before Nast arrived, it was noisy, filthy and extremely unsanitary. Yellow fever was prevalent, along with malaria and bilious fever.

Nast was familiar with the scourge of yellow fever. After Memphis, New Orleans and other Southern cities had been devastated by it in 1878, Congress appointed a Commission to investigate and recommend what should be done. When it advocated extensive quarantining the following year, Nast used a dramatic double-page to depict "Federal Interference" with the States Rights of the South — two years after President Rutherford Hayes had withdrawn Federal troops.** The headstone of the skeletons representing the South was engraved with defiance in response to Columbia's spear of National Quarantine. (In this instance, Columbia was dubbed Athena, Hygeia, Goddess of Wisdom and Health.)

HW April 19, 1879 308-309

ANOTHER "FEDERAL INTERFERENCE."
The Struggle Between Athena Hygeia And Yellow Jack.

* See p. 675
** See p. 424 & 453-455

Although Nast was desperate for any position which would pay him $4,000 a year, Guayaquil left him in a quandary. He exchanged letters with Hay and visited him in Washington in April, aiming for a consulship in healthier Germany or England, where he knew the language and the climate wouldn't make his bad health worse.

Hay confirmed that only Guayaquil was open, but gave him two months to arrange his affairs. Nast was nominated on May 1, and on May 23 he was sent an oath of office to be executed and returned. He received another blow when the acceptance letter stated that the salary of the office "is fixed by law at $3,000 per annum." Shortly after, he sent Hay a sketch, noting: "Say the word and I am off!"

Macculloch Hall Historical Museum

Before he sailed on July 1, he drew several prophetic sketches for his friends. One given to a *New York Herald* reporter depicted Nast standing on a red hot equator, melting under a burning sun. Local features included an erupting volcano, a hungry crocodile, a hissing snake, and a skeletonized yellow jack-in-the box (yellow fever) that "will D.H. (Dead Head) you."

After arriving in Guayaquil on July 17, he detailed his unhappy life as Consul General to Sallie in about fifty letters, full of misspellings, poor grammar and complaints about the misery he had to endure, along with small doodles and sketches to illustrate them. Four weeks in, he wrote:

> *Mice, rats, bats, mosquitoes, fleas, spiders and dirt thrive here. Water for washing is scarce and hot water is not known here but in coffee. Then it is nearly all water. I tried hanging bread and fruit on a rope from the ceiling but the rats continue to get to it; there isn't enough water to fill my bathtub.*
>
> *The more one sees of these so called Americans, the less I care for them. They are worse than the native — they cheat, lie, get drunk, make spit and don't wash.*[3]

In addition to filth and stink, noise was a major problem for Nast, especially at night. He listed the sources: the army with their drums and bugles out every morning about 4:30 A.M.; the church bells which start earlier; the police whistling all night long; the toy railroad that the custom house runs; the whistles of the steamboats; the construction of tin houses; and the dogs. None of the windows had glass panes, so the noise was not filtered or blocked.[4]

Minimal correspondence from Sallie added to Nast's unhappiness. British steamers from the North often refused to deliver cargo to Guayaquil because of the threat of yellow fever. They went South, and sometimes stopped on the way back to drop off the mail and pick up outgoing shipments. Her Tommy got only a few letters from his Sallie during the four months that he could have received them.[5]

Yellow fever was his dominant concern and topic. Beginning in August, almost every letter mentioned people dying. When a German neighbor down the hall died, Nast spread carbolic acid and chloride of lime around his room and the halls of his boarding house. He continued to tell Sallie he didn't expect to get yellow fever, but he obviously was extremely apprehensive.[6]

Nast was proud of his status as Consul General, but he didn't have much official business to do because the steamers didn't call, and there was little if any trade. One case involved mediating between an obnoxious American ship captain and a mutinous sailor. He did submit periodic reports to the State Department, which apparently was well satisfied with his performance.

Painting wasn't easy because the constant humidity made pictures slow to dry; however, he did complete and send a couple of commissioned portraits. He also spent enjoyable time reading the *Encyclopedia Britannica*.

The last cartoon Thomas Nast ever drew was sent to *Bohemia*, a magazine in Havana, in late November. It celebrated Nueve de Octobre, the Cuban equivalent of America's Fourth of July. (After four years of American military occupation following the Spanish-American War, Cuba gained its independence in 1902.)

On Thanksgiving, before having a turkey dinner with the British Vice-Consul, John Ashton, and his wife, Tommy wrote Sallie his last long letter. He followed with a brief note on Sunday, November 30. The next day he felt nauseous and grew worse as the week progressed. He died on Sunday morning, December 7, from what the doctors described as "the fever in its worst form." Ashton gave the eulogy.[7]

Nast was cremated and his ashes buried in Guayaquil. Four years later, they were re-buried in Woodlawn Cemetery in the Bronx, where his family's remains also are interred. Although they were not close in life, Joseph Keppler's grave lies not too far away.

After Nast's death, his family found a prophetic sketch in his roll-top desk — drawn before his departure. It depicted his drawing materials, with his pen and pencil tied with black ribbon.[8]

Paine, p. 583

December 20, 1902 1961

HARPER'S WEEKLY

Vol. XLVI. *New York, Saturday, December 20, 1902—Illustrated Section* No. 2400

Photograph by Pirie MacDonald, photographer of men

THOMAS NAST

Born in Landau, Bavaria, September 27, 1840. Died of yellow fever in Guayaquil, Ecuador, December 7, 1902

The post-dated December 20, 1902 issue of *Harper's Weekly* — now edited by George Harvey after the firm's reorganization in 1899 — devoted seven of its 44 pages to their illustrious cartoonist. However, Nast had to share top billing with Thomas Reed, the revered former Speaker of the House and 1896 Presidential candidate (losing to William McKinley), who died unexpectedly the same day from appendicitis and Bright's Disease.

Nast's obituary was wrapped around a cartoon drawn many years before by Baron De Grimm. The *Weekly* explained that Nast and De Grimm (who died in 1896 at 51) were in a competition. When the freelancer won, he "drew this picture as a compliment to Mr. Nast, imitating his style, and executing this historic portrait." The issue also reproduced three pages of Nast's cartoons; six dealt with the Tweed Ring and one with the Greeley campaign.

HW December 20, 1902 1972

THOMAS NAST died of yellow fever at noon on December 7, at Guayaquil, Ecuador, where he was consul-general of the United States. His illness lasted three days. He was buried a few hours after his death, in the cemetery at Guayaquil. The British consul read a prayer over his grave.

He has been called, perhaps not with accuracy, but with substantial justice, the Father of American Caricature. He won by far the greatest reputation that has yet been won in this country by a maker of political cartoons, and won it by his work in HARPER'S WEEKLY. It speaks for the substantial quality of that reputation that it has lasted so well, for it is fifteen years now since his contributions to the periodical press have been frequent or important. He belongs so much to the past that the impression has naturally spread that he was an old man, but he was born (in Landau, Bavaria) in 1840, so that he was but sixty-two when he died. He was a famous man thirty years ago, when he was hardly more than thirty years old.

The story of his life is not long to tell. He was brought to this country in 1846. His acquaintance with art is said to have begun when, as a young lad, he got a place as door-keeper of a picture-gallery on Broadway in New York, and was allowed to make copies of the paintings. When he was fourteen, he spent about six months in the drawing classes of Theodore Kaufmann. Not very long after, he found employment as a draughtsman with Frank Leslie, with whom he stayed about four years, going from him to the *Illustrated News*, which sent him forthwith to make pictures of the Heenan-Sayers prize-fight. These pictures of a great international sporting event made some stir in New York, and were the beginning of Nast's reputation as an illustrator. Next he followed Garibaldi in southern Italy and Sicily, and sent back war sketches to papers in New York, London, and Paris. He got back to New York in 1861, and in July, 1862, began making war pictures for HARPER'S WEEKLY. Following his natural bent, he soon broke out into political caricature, for which he showed marked aptitude. His political satires hit hard and gained influence and popularity. He kept them up. After the war, in due time came the great fight in New York against Tweed, in which the WEEKLY and Nast took a conspicuous part. His caricatures of Tweed, Sweeny, Connolly, and Hall are vividly remembered to-day. They were extremely distasteful to their victims, who threatened the Harpers, and Nast himself, with all imaginable penalties, but the caricatures kept on. Nast made the Tammany Ring known to every one who had eyes to see, and the Tammany Ring in turn made Nast a very famous man. When the Ring finally collapsed, it left him at the height of a great and honorable reputation. At this time he lectured and did more or less work outside of his labors for the WEEKLY. While the civil war lasted, and afterwards through the fight with Tammany, politics were plain sailing. As time went on there came to be another side to most political questions, and it was not so easy for the conscientious satirist to satisfy himself which side to take. Nast went on with the WEEKLY for fifteen years after the downfall of Tweed, but finally withdrew from active political work, and turned to lecturing and other employments. He never wholly gave up drawing, and in 1894 he went to London to do some pictures for the *Pall Mall Gazette*, but during the latter years of his life he appeared more often on the lecture platform, where he illustrated his talk with sketches, than in the press. Last May President Roosevelt appointed him Consul-General to Ecuador.

Many of Mr. Nast's inventions are now part of the stock in trade of the contemporary cartoonists. He is credited with originating the Tammany tiger and the Republican elephant. On Tammany he put his mark so deep and black that it will never be effaced. He was an honest, conscientious man, of a courage proof against all temptation and all disaster. At one time he was possessed of a fairly comfortable fortune, a large part of which he had the misfortune to lose. Men who knew him well speak with admiration of the fortitude and good-humor with which he bore the reverses of fortune. He never was soured, nor ever complained unduly, but faced every situation with a good heart. He was honored in 1879 by the officers of the army and navy, who presented to him a silver vase in recognition of his important public labors. It was a fit tribute to a patriot, for a patriot Nast was in an intense degree. He was not born an American, but he lived and worked and died a true lover of his country and a stalwart warrior in her behalf.

Some time ago Mr. Nast and Mr. De Grimm entered into a competition for drawing cartoons. Mr. De Grimm won, and then drew this picture as a compliment to Mr. Nast, imitating his style, and executing this historic portrait

Four years later, *Harper's Weekly* celebrated its Fiftieth Anniversary with a 36-page commemorative issue, eight of which pictured Nast.

- W.A. Rogers drew the whimsical cover, featuring Nast as a knight with his foot on Boss Tweed's throat.
- The De Grimm cartoon reappeared, this time with a glowing tribute to Nast underneath.
- Albert Paine wrote a five-page article, including four Tweed cartoons. Another contributor used a different Tweed cartoon.

HW January 5, 1907 2

THOMAS NAST, THE ILLUSTRIOUS CARTOONIST OF "HARPER'S WEEKLY," WHOSE GENIUS OVERTHREW THE TWEED "RING," AND FOR YEARS WAGED A MEMORABLE FIGHT IN THE COUNTRY'S POLITICAL WARFARE

DRAWN BY C. DE GRIMM

January 5, 1907 1 C

Chapter 53
Nast's Legacy: Santa Claus

Family

As mentioned in the Introduction,* of all the symbols Nast created, popularized or inspired, Santa Claus is the most endearing, and probably will be the most enduring, as an irresistible holiday image — for both hearts and pocketbooks. Santa was extremely personal to him and his family; they appeared in many of the 33 Santa Claus cartoons he drew for *Harper's Weekly* and the 21 he drew for the *Bazar* over 24 years.

Tommy and Sallie Nast had five children whom they doted on, and spaced over 17 years. As they grew older, they showed up regularly in their father's Christmas illustrations — usually, but not always, for the better. For Christmas 1879, when baby Cyril was only four months old, they all appeared together on the cover of the post-dated *Harper's Bazar*.

	Born
Julia	July 1, 1862
Tom, Jr.	April 28, 1865
Edith	July 3, 1868
Mabel	December 5, 1871
Cyril	August 28, 1879

Harper's Bazar January 3, 1880

MERRY CHRISTMAS.

On a personal note, Cyril's son, Thomas Nast III, was born in 1914, twelve years after his grandfather died. I met with Tom several times before he passed away in 2002. We shared a common interest in New Rochelle, New York, where Sallie, Cyril, Mabel and Tom lived after they left Morristown, and where I grew up and went to school. (Tom is buried in Woodlawn Cemetery in the Bronx, near his grandfather).

---

* See p. xix

Tom sent me a few Christmas cards with his grandfather's imagery on them. My favorite was this oil painting from 1895, which contains his features as Santa Claus. Two years later, he painted a self-portrait for the 100th Anniversary of the Morristown Volunteer Fire Department with the same nose and pudgy cheeks. (Both are in the Macculloch Hall Historical Museum in Morristown.)

Self-portrait for the 100th Anniversary of the Morristown Volunteer Fire Department

St. Nicholas

Of course, the modern concept of Santa Claus began to take shape almost 60 years before Nast drew his first Santa cartoon. Santa's American conceptualists were John Pintard, founder of the New-York Historical Society; Washington Irving, considered the father of American literature; and Clement Moore, author of *A Visit From St. Nicholas*, better known as *'Twas the Night Before Christmas*.[1]

The real St. Nicholas was a fourth-century Roman Catholic bishop, born in what is now Turkey; he died on December 6, 342, a day which was — and still is, in some countries — celebrated. Among the legendary good deeds and miracles that led to his sainthood, was a custom of giving presents in secret on a special day. As a saint, however, he was envisioned as one of God's representatives on earth — a powerful and dignified figure who not only rewarded good children, but punished bad ones. (Nast would reiterate that theme when his young son misbehaved).

Ultimately, St. Nicholas became the patron saint of New York, but not because of any Dutch heritage. Rather, he became a counter-figure to England's St. George about the time of the Revolution — somewhat comparable to Ireland's St. Patrick and Scotland's St. Andrew. While retaining some religious overtones, he was more secular and mercantile than the Roman Catholic saints.

The Dutch Sint Nikolass evolved into Sinter Klass, Sancte Claus, Sante Claus and similar variations before he became Americanized as St. Nick or Santa Claus. Santa may also have been derived from the German Sanct Herr, phonetically pronounced.

John Pintard

New-York Historical Society

Pintard first referred to Saint Nicholas in his diary in 1793. Six years after he founded the New-York Historical Society in 1804, he commissioned and gave to the Society a broadside portrait of St. Nicholas, whose life was still celebrated on December 6 (the date he died). The rather stern saint was drawn with a halo, cross and bishop's scepter. Underneath was a parallel poem written in both Dutch and English, which began "Sancte Claus" and St. Nicholas, respectively.[2]

The legendary and judgmental St. Nicholas dropped coins and presents down the chimneys of his flock; the recipients hung stockings by their fireplaces to catch them. Here, a good little girl had a full stocking, while the tearful little boy had only switches in his. (Both appeared as miniature adults in the style of the day.)

Washington Irving

American Antiquarian Society

Washington Irving was the critical link between John Pintard and Clement Moore in the literary evolution of Santa Claus from religious icon to mobile gift-giver. He was only 24 (and eleven years away from publishing his better known *Rip Van Winkle*) when he and his brother Peter began writing their *Knickerbocker History of New York* in early 1808; he deliberately published it on St. Nicholas Day, December 6, 1809. It is generally considered as the first American book based on imagination.

The fanciful account included 25 references to St. Nicholas as seen in a dream. It described him bringing gifts on his horse and wagon, parking on a roof, sliding down a chimney, and "laying a finger beside his nose." The frontispiece featured three Dutch gentlemen smoking long pipes in a tavern; one had his finger beside his nose, a gesture meaning "don't tell." It had future significance for Clement Moore and Santa Claus.[3]

John Pintard and Washington Irving were friends. Irving belonged to the Historical Society and dedicated his book to that organization.

Innovations

In 1821, a small book called *The Children's Friend* included an eight-stanza poem with each verse illustrated. Old Santeclaus was still a bishop — kinder-looking than his predecessor from a decade earlier — but who still left birch rods for parents to discipline their bad children, as well as rewards for good ones.[4]

However, the otherwise inconsequential book had three innovations that Clement Moore incorporated into his keynote poem the following year: a reindeer, a sleigh and Christmas Eve (replacing December 6).

Clement Moore

The publisher of *The Children's Friend* was a neighbor of Clement Clark Moore. Moore's inherited 94-acre estate covered uptown Manhattan from Eighth to Tenth Avenues, 19th to 24th Streets; it was called Chelsea then (and now, with some geographical expansion). Moore, 43, was a generous and genial professor of Hebrew and ancient languages at the Episcopal Theological Seminary which he had established on his property. He enjoyed his nine children.

HW January 3, 1863 C

SANTA CLAUS IN CAMP.

Moore wrote his legendary *A Visit From St. Nicholas* in 1822. Better known as *'Twas the Night Before Christmas*, his authorship remained unknown until 1837. However, another friend sent it to the *Troy* (New York) *Sentinel*, which published it anonymously on December 23, 1823. Today, it is perhaps the best known poem by any American author, and probably the most frequently recited.[5]

Moore undoubtedly was influenced by Washington Irving; in fact he only referred to St. Nicholas, not to Santa Claus. But his St. Nick was jolly, not religious or austerely saintly. He was not a punisher of bad children, but a gift-bringer to all.

Although his poem wasn't illustrated, four of Moore's fourteen stanzas provided visual cues that were subsequently incorporated piecemeal into depictions of Santa Claus by Nast and others. He was small — an elf — so that he could fit in a chimney; chubby and plump with a round little belly. (Not unlike Nast himself.)

He was dressed in fur (a bear or other animal skin). As a young boy who spent his first five Decembers in Germany, Tommy Nast celebrated "Pelz-Nicol" or "Furry Nicholas." At 22, his first Santa Claus for *Harper's* still wore a fur suit as he distributed toys to Union soldiers in 1862.*

Santa's "broad face" was described in detail: twinkling eyes, dimples, nose like a cherry, a droll little mouth and a white beard. At a time when wealthy people in New Amsterdam smoked much longer pipes than working class men, he had the stump of a pipe between his teeth. Importantly, he looked like a peddler with his sack of toys, and no trace of a bishop's garb.

However, some elements from the bishop portrayals remained: stockings; gifts; chimney; miniature sleigh; and tiny reindeer, now expanded from one to eight, and named. The secrecy of the occasion remained, as evidenced by Santa's "laying his finger aside of his nose" as he rose up the chimney; the well-known meaning was more specific than with the Dutch gentlemen: Not only "keep quiet," but also "don't tell that I'm not real."

'Twas the night before Christmas, when all through
the house
Not a creature was stirring, not even a mouse;
The stockings were hung by the chimney with care,
In hopes that St. Nicholas soon would be there;

* * *

He spoke not a word, but went straight to his work,
And fill'd all the stockings; then turned with a jerk,
And laying his finger aside of his nose,
And giving a nod, up the chimney he rose;
He sprang to his sleigh, to his team gave a whistle,
And away they all flew like the down of a thistle.
But I heard him exclaim, ere he drove out of sight,
"Happy Christmas to all, and to all a good night."

Clement C. Moore.

* See p. 116

In 1837, *A Visit From St. Nicholas* was included in an anthology of verses by local poets. Entitled *The New-York Book of Poetry*, Clement Moore's authorship finally surfaced.

His poem attracted the attention of Robert Walter Weir, a 34-year old painter who taught art at West Point. Weir read the poem to his wife and two young sons, and was inspired to paint a portrait of the old saint while illustrating the next to last verse of the poem. This was the first known picture of Moore's Santa Claus.

New-York Historical Society

SANTA CLAUS, OR ST. NICHOLAS
By Robert Walter Weir, West Point, 1837

Beardless St. Nicholas wore a red cape trimmed in white fur and a matching stocking cap. His pack contained both toys and switches. The left stocking, with his older son Walter's initials (W.W.) was full of switches, but had a compensating jumping jack below; Robert's (R.W.) stocking had toys; his wife's stocking (far right) displayed a ball of yarn and knitting needles. However, Santa's mythical New Amsterdam heritage from Washington Irving's *Knickerbocker History* was affirmed by his Dutch boots, the Delft fireplace tiles, and a half-eaten orange. (Symbol of the House of Orange, then ruling Holland.)[6]

The first known drawing of Santa Claus in this country appeared as a full-page woodcut in January 1841 in *Dollar Magazine*, a short-lived New York publication. It depicted *Santa Claus, or, St. Nicholas, in the Act of Descending Brother Jonathan's Chimney on New Year's Eve*. Santa's face and hat resembled Weir's. Two reindeer stood by.

American Antiquarian Society

In December 1844, another ephemeral literary magazine, the *New Mirror,* published a Christmas card sub-titled *The Night Before New Year*. Sitting by a fireplace at the base of a chimney, a familiar-looking younger Santa had a religious cross on his ski hat and what looked like switches, along with gifts, in his small backpack and large pocket.

SANTA CLAUS.
The Night Before New Year.

In 1848, Clement Moore's timeless verse finally was published in book-length form under his name. St. Nick was dressed as a peddler, but didn't look particularly warm or jolly in seven illustrations by Theodore Boyd.

Harper's Weekly Before Nast

The *Weekly* observed four Christmases before Nast arrived in 1862 with his furry *Santa Claus in Camp*. Its first (hyphenated) Santa-Claus in 1857 "was born in Germany" according to a long accompanying poem, but appeared pretty much as Moore described him in 1822.

It's second Santa Claus looked more like Moore's 1848 version, drawn in his sleigh by a turkey and small children. Wine was featured on the sleigh, along with Christ the King, in a religiously-oriented *My Christmas Song* featured on the cover.

HW December 26, 1857 820

HW December 25, 1858 817

SANTA CLAUS PAYING HIS USUAL CHRISTMAS VISIT TO HIS YOUNG FRIENDS IN THE UNITED STATES.

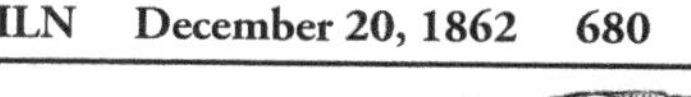
ILN December 20, 1862 680

OLD CHRISTMAS.

Secession and the Civil War preempted Santa Claus until Nast showed him in camp in 1862. That year, the *Illustrated London News* depicted an unnamed Christmas religious figure in a monk's habit, with a crown of mistletoe, and holding a prominent cross.

Santa Claus and His Works

Other than Nast's January 1881 *Merry Old Santa Claus* (which has become Santa's de facto portrait),* Nast's most impressive holiday cartoon was published fifteen Christmases earlier. Its twenty vignettes utilized the essence of *'Twas the Night Before Christmas*, embodied the good vs. bad children theme that preceded the poem, and created Santa's home life from Nast's own imagination.

The centerpiece of the 1866 double-page featured Clement Moore's elfin, fur-suited Santa standing on a chair to reach the stockings hung on the mantle. To his left, he was using hand tools to make toys in his work-shop, while at the lower right, he was hand-sewing dollies' clothes; four other vignettes depicted dollies' kitchen, parlor, tea party and costume assortments. Nast's oldest child Julia was four, so his mind was focused on gifts for her.

In small letters at the top of the central circular enclosure, "Santaclaussville, N.P." encompassed the farmyard, stables and household pets, as well as his sleigh and reindeer on Christmas Eve. At the lower left, Santa was on a ladder, cutting gift toys off "The Christmas Tree."

As discussed previously, John Pintard's religious St. Nicholas was harsh on badly-behaved children, while Clement Moore treated every child as good. Nast resurrected Santa's judgmental role impersonally, in *Santa's Workshop*.

At the upper left, Santa — leaning on an icy parapet — was using his telescope "on the lookout for good children." Below, his bad children's jack-in-the-box Santa symbol, made its initial appearance. For emphasis at the upper right, Santa was studying the "record of behavior" in his account book.

---

* See p. xx

HW December 29, 1866 824-825

"N.P." was another Nast creative landmark: the **North Pole** as Santa's workshop and residence — geographically isolated, politically neutral, and a natural tie-in to reindeer and snow. The pole had been in the news intermittently for two decades — since British Admiral Sir John Franklin's ill-fated 1845 Arctic expedition — so the *Weekly's* audience could readily relate to it.

Beginning after the Workshop cartoon appeared, Nast's images of Santa appeared on thousands of Christmas cards over the next several decades. In this early card of unknown date, Santa was still clad in brown fur.

About four years after this pivotal cartoon appeared, Nast illustrated a children's picture book with the same title for McLaughlin Bros., the first of several editions over a dozen or more years. The author, George P. Webster, wrote a long poem, plagiarizing the exact meter used by Clement Moore.

On the cover of some editions, Santa wore a golden brown bearskin. However, on the inside pages, his furry costume was red — a first, and mostly unchanged since. Whether the idea for red came from Nast, McLaughlin Bros., or an imaginative lithographer is unknown.

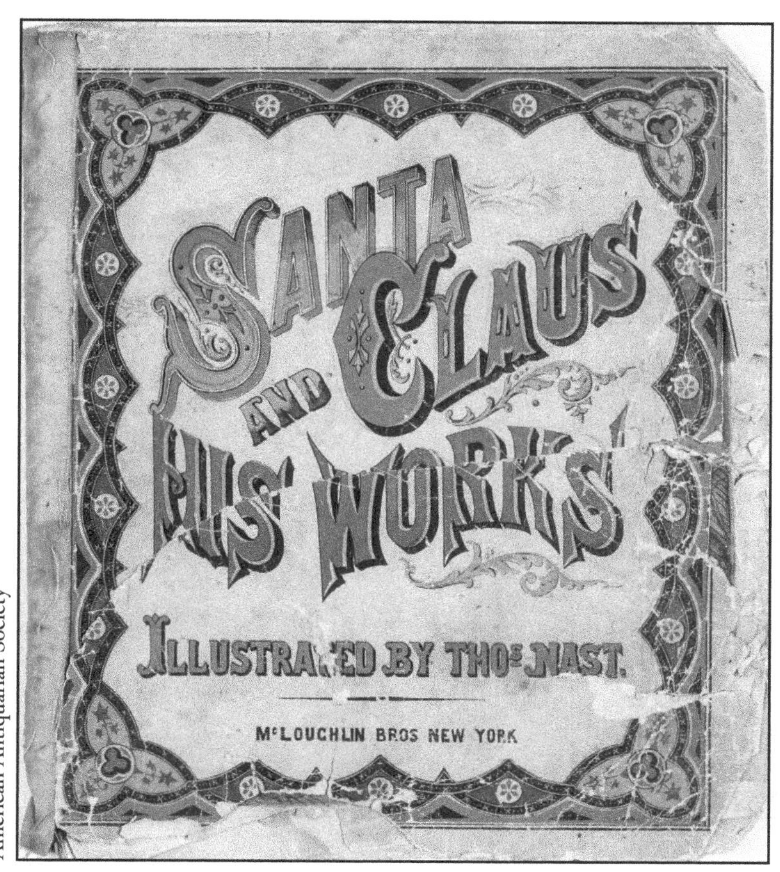

American Antiquarian Society

1869

American Antiquarian Society

1882

Santa as Disciplinarian

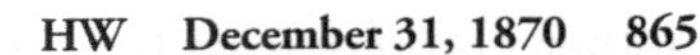
HW December 31, 1870 865

When Tom, Jr. was five, bad Santa chastised him and his sister (probably Julia because Edith was only two).

A year later, young Tommy must have been really "naughty," as Papa and Mamma complained to Santa in *Harper's Bazar*. The similarly-dated *Weekly* showed Santa receiving about six times more letters from "naughty children's parents" while pictures of good and naughty children hung prominently on the wall behind him.

Nast, of course, was still finishing up his attacks on the Tweed Ring members in the lead-up to his 1871 Christmas cartoons. Producing 50 cartoons — many of them complex — over 12 weeks was extremely stressful, so patience with his six-year old son may have been in short supply.

Fletcher Harper took full advantage of his 31-year old artist's celebrity for ousting Tweed by putting Nast on the cover of both his publications.

December 30, 1871

SANTA CLAUS'S MAIL.

December 30, 1871

SANTA CLAUS'S REBUKE.

"I'll never do it again."

Even though the tensions of the Greeley campaign resulted in Nast's physical collapse after Grant's November 1872 victory, his depictions of Santa as a disciplinarian were over. His loving double-page cartoon showed four-year old Edith and seven-year old Tommy blissfully dreaming about more than a dozen of their favorite fairy tales, nursery rhymes and other stories like Gulliver, Robinson Crusoe and Ali Baba. Santa, with his sleigh and reindeer, was about to unload his overflowing pack. All of the fabled miniature characters were readily recognizable. **Its level of detail and complexity mark *The Same Old Christmas Story Over Again* as one of the best non-political cartoons Nast ever drew for *Harper's Weekly*.** However, the title was apt because it reprised some of the same tales and format that he originated in *Mother Goose Melodies* for *Harper's Bazar* two years before.*

HW January 4, 1873 8-9

THE SAME OLD CHRISTMAS STORY OVER AGAIN.

* See p. 208

Protecting the Legend

As his children grew older, Nast struggled to keep the mystery of Santa alive for them. Technological improvements like gas lighting enabled middle-class families to stay awake well past sunset. His post-dated 1873 Christmas cover illustration showed a still-smiling Santa waiting on the roof for the children to get to sleep, but an accompanying poem encapsulated his problem.

What! not yet asleep?—No, their voices I hear:
How little they guess their old friend is so near!
I hope they won't keep me cooped here half the night,
For I've a long journey to make before light.

I never had to wait in the old-fashioned days,
Before people put on these new-fangled ways,
When the children were pillowed by daylight's decline,
And the household was wrapped in sound slumber by nine.

Less seriously, Nast referred to how the introduction of coal heating affected Santa Claus.

And, then, down the wide-throated chimney I'd slip,
With my knapsack in hand, never fearing a trip,
Now dreading to stick in some narrow-mouthed flue,
And break half my presents before I got through;

Two years later, he followed up with:

The sprite that you love is all blackened with soot
Poor Santa Claus' coat is as black as your boot.

HW January 3, 1874 1 C

CHRISTMAS-EVE—SANTA CLAUS WAITING FOR THE CHILDREN TO GET TO SLEEP.

Emphasis on Family

In 1875, Nast drew two post-dated cartoons about his children trying to see Santa. One featured ten-year old Tommy and either seven-year old Edith or four-year old Mabel waiting up in vain, along with the family dog. In the other, a discouraged Santa hid on top of the chimney, while young Tommy and an unseen friend tried to find him.

HW January 1, 1876 8-9

THE WATCH ON CHRISTMAS EVE.

HW January 1, 1876 17

SEEING SANTA CLAUS.

Beginning with Christmas 1876, and continuing for the next four years, Nast focused on family member rather than Santa Claus. That year, Tommy (probably), now 11, extended himself to hang his mother's stocking in hopes of getting a bigger haul. The following year, Edith, 9, and Mabel, just 7, were up at 5 A.M. looking at what Santa had left. In 1878, Edith was mailing a letter to Santa as the Nast family dog watched.

HW December 30, 1876 1056

"'TWAS THE NIGHT BEFORE CHRISTMAS."
A Chance To Test Santa Claus' Generosity.

HW January 5, 1878 4

A CHRISTMAS SKETCH—"FIVE O'CLOCK IN THE MORNING."

HW January 4, 1879 1 C

CHRISTMAS POST.

As noted, Cyril was born on August 28, 1879 — an unexpected "accident," probably conceived the previous Thanksgiving. Nast celebrated with *Another Stocking to Fill*, perhaps the tenderest illustration he ever drew. A ten-stanza poem began with "What Mama Thinks" and closed with "Santa Claus's View of It," including these foreboding lines:

"Sleep away my little man, ***trouble*** comes with years; ***you are bound to get your share in this*** vale of tears."

Nast's depressive mood apparently was similar to his unhappiness four years earlier as the 1876 election loomed. 1880 would be the last year of Rutherford Hayes's single-term Presidency, which Nast had suffered through while clashing with Curtis. Once again, it looked as if his political enemy Blaine would be the probable Republican nominee. That, combined with Curtis's censorship, comprised his current "vale of tears."

HW January 3, 1880 8-9

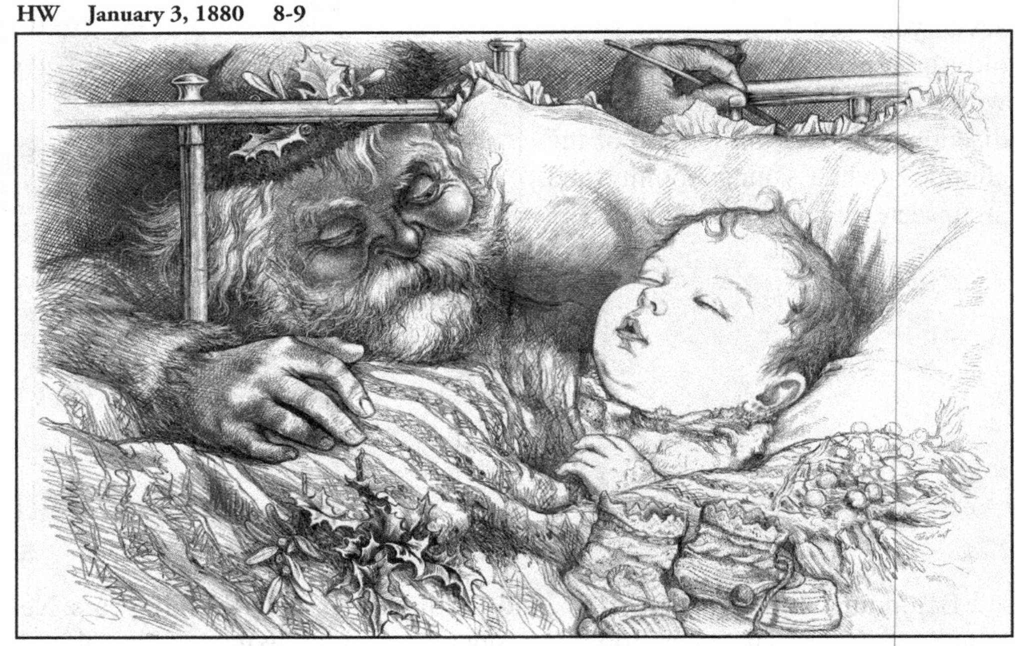

"ANOTHER STOCKING TO FILL."

A year later, Nast pictured his everlasting *Merry Old Santa Claus.* During his remaining six years at the *Weekly*, he drew his children, both as they were currently and at younger ages.

- Julia, 20, standing under the mistletoe in *Christmas Flirtation* in 1882, looking expectantly at a potential kisser.
- Mabel, 14, and Cyril, 6, carefully tracing *Santa Claus's Route* from the North Pole to their house in Morristown in 1885.

HW December 23, 1882 826-827

CHRISTMAS FLIRTATION.

HW December 19, 1885 840-841

SANTA CLAUS'S ROUTE.

• In 1884, Nast pictured Mabel, 13, talking to Santa directly on a new-fangled telephone. (Alexander Graham Bell's patent had been granted in 1876, and the first switchboard was established two years later in New Haven.)

HW December 20, 1884 842-843

"HELLO! SANTA CLAUS!" **"HELLO! LITTLE ONE!"**

Finale

Appropriately, Nast's last Christmas cartoon for *Harper's Weekly* appeared on its cover, post-dated at the start of his final week at the publication. It included a beaming Santa Claus portrait with Nast's features, and another portrait of seven-year old Cyril.

Once more, he played off *'Twas the Night Before Christmas*, but he now featured the sleeping mice in *their* beds and *their* house. The book of "Christmas Sketches" in the cartoon alluded to Nast's illustrated work for McLoughlin Bros., beginning almost two decades earlier. Among Nast's imaginative fantasies were a miniature telephone on the wall behind Papa Mouse's fashionable iron bed, as well as a watch set at midnight and a bottle of croup medicine on the night table beside it. (Nast probably used that medicine frequently for his chronic throat problems.)

HW December 25, 1886 837 C

"'TWAS THE NIGHT BEFORE CHRISTMAS,
and all through the house
Not a creature was stirring, *not even a mouse.*"

Nast's Book

When Cyril was 10 in 1889, Nast finally published *Christmas Drawings for The Human Race*, his compilation of 54 cartoons from *Harper's Weekly* and *Bazar*. They were scattered randomly through the pages, and Santa wasn't seen or mentioned in a dozen of them. However, his tender picture of Cyril as a baby was the first illustration in his book — opposite the title page — and, in retrospect, perhaps the best outward demonstration of how important his family always was to him.

However, his copyright notice wasn't so loving. Nast knew he was in the Harpers' doghouse, both for rejecting its offer to work for the *Weekly* on Cleveland's 1888 campaign, and for delivering his book more than a year late. He depicted an unhappy Santa passing judgment on two of the unnamed Harpers.

Why Christmas was so important

In summary, Christmas was a special time for Nast — a celebration of and with his children. The public sphere and strife that occupied the remainder of the year were irrelevant and excluded. Religious aspects were minimal, with an occasional manger scene or a casual "Peace on Earth and Good Will . . ." The holiday was all about family and peaceful domesticity.

Moreover, Nast self-identified with Santa Claus, well before he blended his own features into Santa's face. He proved repeatedly — sometimes to his financial detriment, as when he rejected a lucrative 1877 lecture tour with Mark Twain — that being with Sallie and his children was the most important value in his life. Working at home solidified that, and Christmas was its annual summit.

Somewhat ironically, while Nast's influence and reputation were predicated primarily on the effectiveness of his negative attacks on Confederates, the Tweed Ring, Horace Greeley and Democratic Presidential candidates, it is his jolly Santa Claus image which has become his principal legacy in today's fast-changing world.

Chapter 54
Nast's Legacy: Political Symbols

As previously discussed, Nast's legacy includes four symbolic images which are in common use today: the Republican Elephant, the Democratic Donkey, Uncle Sam and Santa Claus. The Elephant is the only one he invented from scratch, and it appeared just 27 times in his *Harper's Weekly* cartoons.* The Democratic Donkey, which he popularized, made even fewer appearances.**

Of course, national political symbols were in use for many decades before Nast was born. For example, John Bull represented England early in the eighteenth century. (Nast drew him more than 100 times). On occasion, Britain was also depicted as a Lion, an image that went back centuries to heraldry.

The Flag

America's first self-created symbols were the Flag and the Bald Eagle. The Continental Congress passed the Flag Act on June 1, 1777. The Eagle with its wings spread, and the flag on a shield in front, was incorporated into the Great Seal of the United States five years later. However, the eagle had been employed as an emblem by many countries and provinces since Roman times. Nast used it 25 times, often in conjunction with Uncle Sam and/or Columbia.

The first cartoon featuring the American flag (in the Library of Congress Collection) appeared as the cover for a patriotic song in 1836.

Nast considered himself a super-patriot, so the American Flag was especially important to him. In times of trouble, he flew it upside down, sometimes listing military victories or other accomplishments on its stripes, while detailing negatives on Confederate, Tammany or other "enemy" banners.

---

* See p. 357 and 361

** See p. 224

Columbia

In July 1790, President George Washington established the District of Columbia (a feminized derivation of Columbus for whom the District was named) on land annexed from Maryland and Virginia. It took ten years for enough construction to be completed for the Federal Government to move from Philadelphia. President John Adams first slept in what would be called the White House in December 1800.

Columbia soon became a national symbol of America. She generally was dressed in a classic gown and a close-fitting cap (worn by ancient Phrygians and adopted as a symbol of Liberty during the first French Republic.) In this 1813 cartoon entitled *Columbia TEACHING John Bull his new LESSON*, both the eagle and her stars-and-stripes shield were prominent accompaniments.[1]

Library of Congress

During the opening years of the Civil War, one artist depicted Columbia in Revolutionary War era clothing, while another utilized her as a prop for the Flag (white tunic, red sash, blue gown with stars) in a Union sheet music illustration.

Library of Congress

Nast decided early on that his wife Sallie's classic beauty made her an ideal model for Columbia. Beginning about a year after he joined the *Weekly*, Sallie appeared 158 times as Columbia, but also 53 times as Justice, 14 as Peace, 10 as New York, and even 5 as Britannia.

HW October 24, 1863 680-681

HONOR THE BRAVE

Macculloch Hall Historical Museum

1878 Portrait by Nast

HW December 5, 1863 766-767

THANKSGIVING DAY NOVEMBER 26, 1863

Brother Jonathan

Uncle Sam was preceded as the national symbol of the United States by Brother Jonathan, a derisive caricature created by English cartoonists in the latter part of the eighteenth century to ridicule their former colonists. Along with the tune and verses of *Yankee Doodle*, their aim was to embody all the crudeness, pretension and ignorance of the assertive, cocky young country into the figure of a rustic New Englander.[2]

However, their contemptuous image and verse backfired. Americans adopted Brother Jonathan as a positive national symbol, and *Yankee Doodle* as a patriotic song. (Its tune went back centuries, and the original disparaging English verses pre-dated the Revolutionary War.)

A key battle of the War of 1812 took place on September 10, 1813, when Oliver Perry destroyed the British naval flotilla on Lake Erie and secured control of the Great Lakes. The following month, artist/engraver Amos Doolittle drew *BROTHER JONATHAN Administering a Salutary Cordial to JOHN BULL*. The beverage was labeled "Perry;" its distressed recipient's balloon conversation referred to him as "This D_____d Yankee Perry." Neither figure had developed to its later recognizable caricatured appearance.

Library of Congress

By the time of the Mexican War, Brother Jonathan had evolved into a more standardized figure: tall, thin, beardless, and relatively young. He wore pantaloons (often striped), a vest, a well-worn swallow-tailed coat, and a stovepipe hat — somewhat of a Yankee Doodle Dandy. In 1846, well known artist Edward Clay depicted a jaunty Jonathan as he strode across the Rio Grande to cut Mexico in two with a huge scissors; one blade represented the regular army, and the other was the volunteers.[3]

Greene County Historical Journal

Early in the Civil War, an American naval commander seized two Confederate diplomats, James Mason and John Slidell, from a British steamer which had evaded the Union blockade. The action violated international law, and the resultant controversy almost provoked hostilities with England in December 1861. President Lincoln reportedly said "One war at a time," and had Mason and Slidell released. Frank Bellew (triangle signature) had Brother Jonathan comment on the crisis in *Harper's Weekly*. Jonathan had aged since the Mexican War, wore striped pants, and was deadly serious.

HW January 11, 1862 32

JONATHAN ON THE MASON AND SLIDELL AFFAIR.

Brother Jonathan. "Well, Johnny, if you want 'em very bad, you can take 'em—and tell yer what, if you feel like going into that kinder Business, I can let yer have just as many more as you like from a little Establishment of mine called Sing Sing!"

About the same time, Bufford's (the Boston publisher which first employed Winslow Homer) produced a fanciful company of *Yankee Volunteers Marching into Dixie*. All were dressed in stovepipe hats and striped trousers, while singing and playing *Yankee Doodle*.

Library of Congress

Nast left the *New York Illustrated News* in May 1862 for a short return to *Leslie's* before joining *Harper's* in August.* In June, the *Illustrated News* printed an unsigned cartoon showing Brother Jonathan confronting John Bull over an Armstrong gun — potentially more powerful and safer because it was breech-loaded rather than muzzle-loaded. Nast almost certainly drew the cartoon, which showed Jonathan with long hair as Nast's Uncle Sam images did after the Civil War ended. This probably was the prototype for his future Uncle Sam, although he didn't yet acquire striped trousers or a goatee.

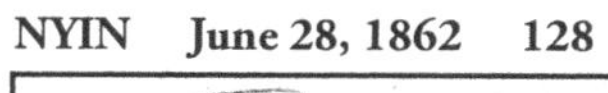
NYIN June 28, 1862 128

UNPLEASANT SUBJECT FOR J. B.
***Jonathan to J. Bull.*—How about that Armstrong gun of yours, that won't work?**
***J. B. to Jonathan.*—Harmstrong gun! vot's a Harmstrong gun? I hain't 'eard nothink of no Harmstrong gun!**

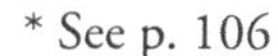

* See p. 106

Harper's Weekly depicted Brother Jonathan in cartoons as late as 1882, primarily interacting with John Bull. However, Nast only used him once in his 25 years there, and then in an unorthodox manner.

In the spring of 1869, recently inaugurated President Grant unsuccessfully attempted to settle the *Alabama* Claims controversy, left over from Civil War marauders unlawfully provided to the Confederacy by English shipbuilders.* Nast reacted to a cartoon in *London Punch* depicting Grant as Jonathan, dressed as a British squire. He counter-attacked sharply a month later, trumping the *Punch* cartoon (which he included) by pointing out that John Bull (Falstaff) had grown too fat from his ill-gotten wealth, obtained by violating neutrality. Not too subtly, the British icon angrily crumpled a speech by Senator Charles Sumner, who had recently demanded that Britain cede Canada to the United States as part of a $2 billion proposed settlement.[4]

HW June 26, 1869 413

SIR JONATHAN FALSTAFF.
Prince of Wales. "Sirrah, Do I Owe You A Thousand Pound?" Sir Jonathan. A Thousand Pound, Al'?—Four Hundred Million! Thy Love Is Worth Four Hundred Million: Thou Owest Me Thy Love.'—Shakespeare *(slightly altered)*

SIR JOHN BULL FALSTAFF.
Prince Jonathan. "Here Comes Lean Jack; Here Comes Barebones! How Now, My Sweet Creature Of Bombast? How Long Is't Ago, Jack, Since Thou Sawst Thine Own Knee?"—Shakespeare *(not altered)*

Uncle Sam before Nast

Although Nast created the image of today's Uncle Sam about 150 years ago, he had nothing to do with the concept whose appellation was first expressed in 1810, 30 years before Nast was born.[5] However, the creation of Uncle Sam's name in historic legend is generally traced to Samuel Wilson, a meat packer in Troy, New York, who supplied meat products to the Army during the War of 1812.

---

* See p. 225-228

His barrels of meat were labeled "EA-US." When Wilson's slaughterhouse was inspected by Governor Daniel Tompkins in October 1812, the official asked the worker who was branding the barrels what the initials stood for; that joker told him that E.A. stood for Elbert Anderson, the Army's contractor, and U.S. for Uncle Sam. "Who is Uncle Sam?" the Governor asked. "Why Uncle Sam Wilson, who feeds the Army" was the humorous response. (As the middle child of 13 siblings, Wilson was known as Uncle Sam to numerous nieces and nephews, so there may have been a less fanciful basis for his quick-witted answer.)

Greene County Historical Journal, 2011

THE ORIGINAL UNCLE SAM.

UNCLE SAM SICK WITH LA GRIPPE.

Library of Congress

Over time, the name took hold, and Uncle Sam became interchangeable with Brother Jonathan, although generally as an older, more mature figure. In 1837, during Martin Van Buren's Presidency, Uncle Sam was in an eighteenth century sickroom, wearing a liberty cap, a stars-and-stripes dressing gown and moccasins. Brother Jonathan was in a separate room. The artist was Edward Clay.

In 1844, President John Tyler ran unsuccessfully for a second term against James Polk and Henry Clay. Uncle Sam was portrayed as an old man, wearing knee breeches and a wide-brimmed straw hat.

Library of Congress

In 1852, Frank Bellew drew Uncle Sam and John Bull observing as their shipping companies competed. A relatively young Sam was beardless, apparently long-haired, and dressed in pin-striped trousers and a vest. The cartoon appeared in the short-lived (1852-3) humor magazine, *The Lantern*.

Greene County Historical Journal

COLLINS AND CUNARD COMPETITION.

By the 1860 Presidential campaign, Uncle Sam had matured. Louis Maurer, a prominent artist for Currier & Ives, drew Columbia spanking Stephen Douglas for "being a bad boy." Uncle Sam — in knee breeches, beardless, bald and with long hair in back — encouraged Columbia to ". . . give him the Stripes until he sees Stars."

In another following cartoon depicting Lincoln, and his three competitors (Douglas, John Bell, and John Breckinridge) and departing President James Buchanan, artist Maurer portrayed Uncle Sam with shorter hair in back. (Maybe he had a haircut in the interim.)

Uncle Sam

STEPHEN FINDING "HIS MOTHER."

Uncle Sam

"UNCLE SAM" MAKING NEW ARRANGEMENTS.

Nast's Re-creation

Nast generally made Uncle Sam an active participant in his cartoons rather than just an on-looker. Thin, tall, with an angular face, tousled long hair, goatee, high hat, striped pantaloons, swallow-tailed coat and gaudy vest, his avuncular figure almost always emanated a proper dignity and morality. The exceptions came when Uncle Sam dealt with a shameful political event (as Nast saw it).

Nast had just turned 29 when he depicted an Uncle Sam, about his own age, presiding at Thanksgiving dinner in 1869. Unusually, he was hatless.*

HW November 20, 1869 745

UNCLE SAM'S THANKSGIVING DINNER
(Extract)

HW December 2, 1871 1124

TO WHOM IT MAY CONCERN.
***New York.* "Now You See What I DID ABOUT IT. Go And Do Likewise."**

Two years later, Uncle Sam was celebrating Boss Tweed's defeat — up on a ladder painting a sign. This time Sallie was New York (rather than Columbia), gesturing to European leaders from Italy, Austria and Germany to do to the Pope what she had done to the Ring. Tweed, Oakey Hall and Peter Sweeny were all crushed and compressed under the weight of the ballot box.

* See p. 221

As Horace Greeley's campaign was gearing up the following year, Nast apparently substituted Uncle Sam for himself. Sam was whittling a stick from the Republican oak; the frontal view showed how his pantaloons were held in place over his boots.

However, the subtle message was that Nast was sharpening his pencil for the forthcoming battle. Another clue was the sign on Greeley's symbolic white coat: "Notice to caricaturists. Hands off. These are SACRED."

The predictive cover cartoon referred to the Liberal Republican candidate's alliance with Tammany Democrats and ex-Confederates, including the Ku Klux Klan. The rotten Democratic tree featured "Corruption, Tammany, Slavery, Rebellion, KKK and Lost Cause." Although the sign in Greeley's coat pocket said "What I Know About Splitting," "Massa Horrors Greedey" couldn't separate his party from those elements.*

HW June 29, 1872 505 C

THE SAGE OF CHAPPAQUA.
Uncle Tom. **"I say, Uncle Sam, Massa Horrors Greedey will find it a Tough Job when he tries his Hand at this Tree."**

Other cartoonists at *Puck*, *Judge*, *Harper's Weekly* and subsequent publications adopted Nast's caricature of Uncle Sam, and, of course, it survives today. In his iconic World War I recruiting poster, James Montgomery Flagg enshrined the image forever.

* See p. 321-328

Chapter 55
Epilogue

Looking over Nast's life and legacy, the key to his success was his ability to persuade without lecturing by using images instead of dialogue. Handicapped by his dyslexia and inability to spell, he couldn't readily employ the "looped speech" as the political cartoonists before him did, and the comic strip and comic book authors of today do. Forced by necessity, he created a symbolic pictorial language which ancestored television sound bites and the Internet's emojis.

Animal symbols, depicted in caves, go back to the Stone Age, 35,000 to 40,000 years ago. Most of them had to do with hunting or supernatural themes.

Aesop, a Greek slave who lived about 2,500 years ago, created 725 *Fables*, almost all of which featured animals to imply or teach moral lessons. Today's examples include *sour grapes* (from a fox) and *a wolf in sheep's clothing*. Nast sourced Aesop at least 19 times.

Two exemplary innovators whose names come to mind when relating Nast's creativity and impact to today, are Leo Burnett and Steve Jobs. Nast is widely recognized as the father of American political cartooning, but his heritage goes beyond that; he can be considered as the foster father of both symbolic print and television advertising, and Internet emojis.

Leo Burnett

Many years ago, an NBC president aptly summarized the power of television advertising: "You could take a low-interest product and make it dramatic and compelling to the average person."[1] Leo Burnett, who founded his eponymous advertising agency in 1935, did just that with a symbolic approach reminiscent of Nast.

Prime examples included the Jolly Green Giant (canned peas and corn)[2], Kellogg's Tony Tiger, Keebler's Elves, Pillsbury's Doughboy, Maytag's Lonely Repairman and the Marlboro Man among others, as television advertising exploded from the 1950s on.

Charlie the Tuna

As discussed early on,* my initial interest in *Harper's Weekly* was sparked by my ground-breaking experience in measuring the relative effectiveness of various television advertising alternatives for more than 100 grocery store brands — what worked and what didn't.[3]

Of more than 300 tests, the most memorable — unintentionally and indelibly — proved the importance of visual symbols at the point of sale. H.J. Heinz Company, which owned StarKist, wanted to find out what would happen if it doubled its television advertising weight. StarKist and Ralston's Chicken of the Sea brand each controlled about one-third of the canned tunafish market; Bumble Bee and private label shared the rest.

The Burnett Agency had created Charlie the Tuna as a symbolic mascot for StarKist in 1961, and its print ads featured Charlie. During the test, StarKist's volume went up 16%, but the whole category went up 17%, so StarKist's market share was unchanged. Why?

The answer was obvious. Charlie was in the ads but not on the can or package label. The additional advertising apparently motivated consumers to buy more tunafish, but they couldn't always distinguish (remember? identify?) StarKist from its competitors on the shelf. Needless to say, Charlie has been on the package labels ever since.

Nike

If Nast had been asked which modern product symbol he liked best, he might well have chosen Nike's Swoosh for several reasons. First, Nike was named after the Greek Winged Goddess of Victory; he had incorporated classical mythology into 69 cartoons, so both her name (also Athena, on occasion) and what it stood for were familiar to him. Second, the Swoosh — created in 1971 as a symbolized fluid wing emphasizing speed, strength and power — would have fit right in with his artistic inventiveness.

Third, the Swoosh blended well with Nike's slogan *Just Do It*, and implies the words in its omnipresence on athletic shoes and clothing, enhanced by endorsements from star athletes from a wide variety of sports. Constant Swoosh visualization — both paid directly and indirectly (on uniforms) — continues to provide Nike with impact on purchase decisions — equivalent to Nast's influence over political actions during his Tweed and Greeley heydays.

Steve Jobs

Nast's runner-up in a symbols contest conceivably would have been Apple, which became the corporate name for Steve Jobs's company, as well as its symbol. Jobs and Nast had a lot in common: the ability to visualize projects and issues in a novel manner; an insistence on getting artistic details just right; and an exceptional talent for persuasion. Accordingly, each significantly changed the use and effectiveness of leading media to promote their ideas/products visually.

* See p. xxiv

Emojis

Originally invented in Japan around 1999, Apple introduced emojis with its iPhone in late 2008, and released them to all users in 2011. Today, there are thousands of general emojis, and tens of thousands of private ones.

Emojis were initially developed to express shades of emotions pictorially; the word means "image (or picture) character" in Japanese. Smiling or frowning faces, and thumbs up or down, were early examples. Used primarily on social media, they simplify messaging by conveying context and intent without words. Going back to Scandinavian runes and Egyptian hieroglyphics, symbolic communication has come full circle for ordinary internet conversation and communication.

In essence, Steve Jobs fostered today's common use of emojis, but their ancestral debt to Nast should be noted.

Neurology: The Connection to Nast

A recent neurological study showed that emojis — with their eyes, eyebrows and mouths portraying human emotions — were processed in the same area of the brain as faces.[4] That finding sheds light on why Nast's caricatures were so effective. He, of course, had cartes de visite or other photographs of almost all the men who populated his cartoons, and exaggerated their faces or other physical features as he saw fit. But he never thought of his work as "linguistic inventiveness" per se, as a scholar of digital communication discussed emojis in her recent book.[5]

While Nast did not create entirely new communications industries — like Johannes Gutenberg did in the mid-15th Century; or Alexander Graham Bell and Thomas Edison did in the late 19th; or Bill Gates and Steve Jobs did in the late 20th; or the founders of Google, Facebook, Twitter and many apps did earlier in this century — he did envision a more technological future for the country. His 1886 cartoon was reasonably accurate in forecasting the cable-crowded poles and wires of today.

HW January 9, 1886 32

WHAT THE TELEGRAPH COMPANIES WILL DO NEXT.

Nast's Public Profile

At a time when the names and faces of most journalists were not well known, Nast became the first celebrity cartoonist in the United States. He accomplished this through promotion by his employers — first, the *New York Illustrated News* when he reported from England and Italy — and then by *Harper's Weekly*. He augmented that with 38 self-caricatures in the *Weekly*; numerous news stories about him, his cartoons, his friendships with public figures, or battles with well known opponents; and his lecture tours. A poet, John Yates, summarized his celebrity.

AN OLD MAN'S WORD FOR NAST

Well, Betsey, here's your Harper's, with its pictures in, by Nast!
His shots for truth are heavy, and he sends them thick and fast.
The Devil, and corruptionists, all, wear a troubled look,
When T. Nast takes his crayons up to make a picture book.

I've been to hear him lecture—been with these old eyes to see
The man who did so much to break the rule of Tammany.
It was a treat to see his hand bring out with lighting speed
The NOSE of Andy Johnson and the CLOTHES of Billy Tweed.

Some men are born with riches, and they keep on hoardin' gains;
Some men come into bein' with nothin' but their brains;
This Nast was born an artist, who needeth not a school,
And the man who butts agin' him was only born a—fool.

Some men preach from the pulpit in defense of righteousness;
Some clothe their thoughts with burnin' words and preach them
thro' the press;
T. Nast's is ***picture-preachin'****, and he cannot well be beat,*
For we've seen the vilest sinners sittin' on his anxious seat.

Hurrah for Harper's Weekly and its witty artist—Nast!
Corruption falls before them like a reed before the blast.
Of the paper and its pictures, you nor I will never tire;
Now, Betsey, read aloud, while I smoke before the fire!

Then there was the other side, which appeared in a literary magazine called *The Arcadian* in 1874.

PROPOSED EPITAPH FOR THOMAS NAST

Here lies Tom Nast
Who's gone at last
Below he now holds revel
'Mid groans and moans
And dead men's bones
He caricatures the devil.

Henry Watterson

Most obituaries about Nast were impersonally factual and positive, including those in *Harper's* and the *Times*. The one he would have enjoyed most appeared in publisher Henry Watterson's *Louisville Courier-Journal* four days after he died.

The two same-age journalists had tweaked and blasted each other over the years, but remained close friends. After the ardent Democrat backed Liberal Republican Horace Greeley in 1872 — and lost — he pulled no punches in negatively giving Nast credit.

It cannot be denied that he was Grant's best pleader before the masses of the people. Always striking, often amusing, sometimes unfeeling, sure to be regardless alike of amenities and consequences, he has won his spurs. There are times when Nast's drawing runs close upon high art — but there is no time when he stirs the better emotions at the expense of the lower . . . Very likely he has put his talent — we were almost going to say his genius — to its best uses. He has certainly employed himself profitably; he is celebrated; he is growing rich. But if he were an old man, he would find little pleasure in looking over a career devoted to unjust partisan assaults and virulent personal defamation; and being a young one, though considerations of this sort are likely to weigh little in a nature so ungentle in itself, and so heedless of consequences.[6]

In the fourteen remaining years before he left the *Weekly*, Nast depicted Watterson 23 times, all but once negatively. (The exception: when Watterson became a father.) Frequently, liquor bottles highlighted the Democrat's heavy drinking as a sideline to his politics. Nevertheless, Watterson's feelings for his friend stood out in his obituary.[7]

To him a spade was a spade and he never hesitated to call it so. He had the simple, childlike faith of the artist, crossed upon the full-confident spirit of the self-made man. To the younger generations the name of Thomas Nast is but a shade. Yet a century hence his work will be sought as an essential sidelight upon the public life in the United States during the two decades succeeding the great sectional war. His satire flashed upon a rogue and discovered a rascal like a policeman's lantern. Always unsparing and direct, sometimes cruel, he was the old Saxon warrior over again. Yet to those who knew him with his armor off and his battle axe hung upon the wall, one of the heartiest and healthiest of men; quick to requite the proven wrong; ready to give and take, to live and let live, an ideal comrade and model of the domestic virtues.

Nast's Own Impression

Nast's view of his legacy was off the mark. Depressed and despondent, shortly before he left for Guayaquil, Nast told an interviewer that "Some day I may become famous, but it will be after I am dead."

'But do you not think that you have reached fame already?' asked the reporter.

'No' was the reply, 'fame is lasting. I have had notoriety, but not fame. A dozen years ago my name was on the tip of the tongue of millions of people. Today, I am forgotten, a back number, out of existence and most people do not believe that I am living.

'What?' they say, 'Thomas Nast alive? Nonsense, he has been dead for years.' And so I have in a sense. No one has heard of me. No one has thought of me for over a decade. I am a part of history.

'What do you expect your fame to rest on?' [asked the reporter].

'On my historical paintings, said Mr. Nast. Few people realize the significance of the work I have done, but in years to come, when time shall have given men a chance to think over the events of the last century, they will come to a realizing sense of the value of history as depicted by pen and brush. Then the name of Nast will go down to posterity as a painter. Other men have told the story of the Civil War in books and stories, but I have told it in pictures . . . But time will tell.

'But what does it matter, . . . My life's work is done . . . I assuredly would not go were it not for the fact that I have got to do something.'[8]

Time did tell. His paintings are obscure but his symbols and many of his cartoons will live on.

GOOD NIGHT *

AU REVOIR **

HARPER'S BAZAR Date Unknown

"MERRY CHRISTMAS TO ALL, AND TO ALL A GOOD-NIGHT."

* See p. 353
** See p. 197

Endnotes

Introduction

1. *Hustler Magazine* Inc. vs. Jerry Falwell. 485 U.S. 46 (1988). S.Ct. 876, 99 L.Ed.2d 41. Argued December 2, 1987. Decided February 24, 1988.
2. *The Times* tribute was published March 30, 1872, almost five months after Tweed lost power in the November 1871 election. The newspaper, and Nast played off each other's work to help bring down the Tweed Ring.
3. The clipping quoted an otherwise unknown Gertrud Garrison and is in a Nast scrapbook in the New York Public Library.
4. The September 29, 1871 note was from Neosho, Missouri *Journal* editor Alfred M. Williams, and was pasted in a Nast scrapbook. The late Draper Hill found it there, but didn't note where the scrapbook was located.
5. Pat Oliphant, perhaps the most influential political cartoonist of his generation, was the most widely syndicated political cartoonist in the world at the time he wrote this tribute for the *Journal of the Thomas Nast Society*, as he and his fellow cartoonists saluted Nast.
6. This sketch is reproduced from *The Bookman* of March 15, 1902; Nast resketched it for a *Bookman* article called *Thomas Nast and His Cartoons*. His original sketch is in the John Hay Library at Brown University.
7. Politically, McClellan also knew that New York and Pennsylvania — which accounted for half the electoral votes he needed to win — would never accept the "war is a failure" plank.
8. The last — and probably the most famous — critical victory was General Phil Sheridan's melodramatic defeat of Confederate General Jubal Early at the Battle of Cedar Creek, in the Shenandoah Valley on October 19. The timing — less than three weeks before Election Day — was perfect for giving Northern morale and electoral effort a final meaningful boost.

   With Sheridan away for a strategy conference, Early made a successful surprise attack at dawn, capturing 1,300 prisoners and 18 guns, and causing may stragglers to flee. Sheridan, having returned ahead of schedule from his conference, was 15 miles away in Winchester. Hearing the unexpected sounds of battle, he covered the distance to the front in a couple of hours, rallied his defeated soldiers, counter-attacked and routed Early's forces.

   Sheridan's Ride, a stirring poem by Thomas B. Read, helped verbalize his heroic battlefield leadership and enshrine it at the forefront of the public's memory. While Nast never portrayed it, he became a good friend of Sheridan's after the war and pictured him a dozen times in future cartoons and paintings. For *Harper's Weekly*, it was the perfect cover story — two issues before the election. With military success no longer as troublesome an issue, Nast and *Harper's Weekly* could focus on attacking McClellan and his Copperhead sponsors.
9. The Nast take-offs were collected by the late Draper Hill for a 2002 *Salute to Thomas Nast*, published by the Thomas Nast Society to commemorate the 100th anniversary of his death. They are reprinted here with the permission of the original cartoonists via Draper Hill.

Sources and Acknowledgments

1. In 2012, Dr. Fiona Deans Halloran published *Thomas Nast: The Father of Political Cartooning* with the University of North Carolina Press which promoted it as "a thoroughgoing and lively biography." I refer to her book because reviewers and readers may compare it with mine.

   Among Ms. Halloran's principle sources were Albert Bigelow Paine's 1904 biography and my proprietary **HarpWeek** database, as well as several of my free websites at **HarpWeek.com**. She wrote: "With the advent of the internet, Nast's vast body of work became far easier to catalog. **HarpWeek.com**, a website that has made *Harper's Weekly* available to the public, has embraced Nast as its primary celebrity. The site features a "Cartoon of the Day" that provides a brief explanation of the cartoon and places it in historical context. Before **HarpWeek**, many of Nast's lesser known drawings were hidden in the back pages of dusty bound volumes.

HarpWeek made Nast's work searchable, so that any subscriber interested in cartoons containing references to Carl Schurz, for example, need only to enter his name, and the pertinent cartoons pop up, listed in chronological order." (See p. xxiv of my biography.)

To her credit, Ms. Halloran is a good writer and a diligent researcher. She visited many of the diverse resources that Draper Hill and I did, and a few that we didn't. Her extensive bibliography is impressive. As an academic book focused on an analysis of Nast in relation to the Gilded Age, politics, and society, reviewers agree that Halloran's work is well-done, but as a biography of Nast, it falls well short.

"... useful, if rather strange biography. . .one comes to the end of this book knowing a good deal more about the work than about the man." (Jonathan Yardley, *The Washington Post,* February 15, 2013.)

"For readers unfamiliar with the life and work of Thomas Nast, Halloran's book does not offer a comprehensive look at Nast. . .her efforts (as a biographer) have failed." (Christine Jochem, *The Journal of the Civil War Era,* December 14, 2014, p. 613. Ms. Jochem was the curator emeritus of the Thomas Nast Collection at the Morristown and Morris Township Library and former president of the Thomas Nast Society.)

"It is a credible account of some of Nast's career, but needs more on Nast himself to be a biography." (J.A. Lent, CHOICE Current Reviews for Academic Libraries, 1825.)

Close examination of Halloran's book reveals at least 50 erroneous factual statements, as well as 20 or more significant omissions. For example, her misinterpretation of the premise behind Nast's most important cartoon: "*Compromise with the South* was a hammer blow for Lincoln and *against* peace." (my italics)

Indeed it was a hammer blow — but against a *Rebel* peace — which would have resulted in the restoration of slavery within an independent Confederacy. Less important but worth noting, Ms. Halloran didn't identify Jeff Davis, a key caricature and the dominant element in the cartoon, and certainly recognizable to most of Nast's readers. (Explained on p. x of my Introduction.)

In summary, Halloran's book was written for an academic audience, is filled with academic jargon, and lacks the solid focus expected in a traditional complete biography. With plenty of editorializing, it reads somewhat like a series of meditations on phases, events, or cartoons in Nast's life. Moreover, it contains only 60 cartoons, all from *Harper's Weekly* squeezed into pages half the size of mine — in contrast to the 800 images from the *Weekly* and 200 from other publications in my biography. Her book is not what it purports to be.

2. Julia Nast, 36, was living by herself in a New York boarding house at 31 East 22nd Street, when she was found dead on April 28, 1899. She was a trained nurse. Initially suicide by an overdose of cocaine was suspected and received some publicity, including in the April 30 *Times*. However, the coroner subsequently affirmed that Julia died of natural causes, probably related to kidney disease. The circumstances must have caused tremendous upset and grief in her family.

3. Letter dated January 27, 1908. The late Draper Hill referred to it without identifying its current location.

4. Letter from Paine to Nast dated May 16, 1902 at the Huntington Library, San Marino, CA. Paine found the letter in Nast's home after his death, and wrote his comments on it in pencil.

5. Paine, p. 90.

6. HW. April 4, 1863, p. 219.

7. Paine, p. 118.

8. Paine, p. 109, 202.

9. Paine, p. 225. The original letter is at The Huntington Library, San Marino, CA.

10. Paine, p. 204-5. The other artists were Englishmen, William Hogarth (1697-1764); George Cruikshank (1792-1878); John Leech (1817-1864); and Frenchman Gustave Doré (1832-1883). Nast knew and admired Leech and Doré.

11. *Harper's Weekly* was sold in 1913 and had little resemblance to its former self; it disappeared entirely in 1916. While I own the last four volumes, it made no sense to include their drastically different content in a cumulative index.

12. In 2008, I published *Doomed by Cartoon: How Cartoonist Thomas Nast and The New-York Times Brought Down Boss Tweed and His Ring of Thieves*. About 60% of the interpretive content, as well as the narrative, came from Draper Hill's commissioned writings, and I credited him on the cover and within the book. (Morgan James Publishing, LLC. Garden City, NY.)

13. Richard Samuel West published *Satire on Stone: The Political Cartoons of Joseph Keppler.* (1988. University of Illinois Press) and co-authored *Puck: What Fools These Mortals Be* (2014. IDW Press, San Diego). The latter has been an invaluable source for the *Puck* cartoons.

14. Paine, p. 24.

15. In 1997, I planned to include these essays on a CD-ROM about Nast, before that technology became outdated. Much of its planned content eventually migrated into this biography.

16. *The Battle for Christmas*. 1996. Alfred A Knopf, Inc., New York.

17. Dr. John Hope Franklin met with me at Duke University in 1995, when I sought his advice in connection with indexing my HarpWeek database. As a former president of both the Organization of American Historians and the American Historical Association, he was revered by his colleagues as *the* authority figure to provide a decisive answer to my query. Several years ago, when my biography was almost complete, the word "Black" was capitalized (as Negro had been all along). However, because both Nast's cartoons and *Harper's Weekly* had used lower case, we retained its authenticity (except in the Introduction)

    Separately, more than 20 years ago, HarpWeek created a free website called *Toward Racial Equality: Harper's Weekly Reports on Black America: 1957-1874*. Concerned about derogatory language in general and the use of the N-word in particular, I consulted with Dr. Randall Kennedy of Harvard Law School, who had written widely on the topic. Dr. Kennedy who is Black, advised me not to censor anything to ensure an accurate picture of the 19th Century portrayals — even though current viewers might be offended.

Chapter 1 Growing Up

1. Englishman Thomas Butler Gunn lived in a series of New York boarding-houses from 1855 to 1863. He generally moved with his current landlady every May 1 (Moving Day when leases expired), which gave him the grist for his book.

    Fortunately for this biography, Gunn kept a daily diary full of unvarnished descriptions of Thomas Nast (whom he didn't like) and Gunn's other social and business companions who interacted with Nast. His "Dutch Uncle" relationship with Sallie Edwards, Tommy's future wife, provides candid, dispassionate observations of key psychological perceptions and actual events in Nast's life as they occurred. Gunn's digitized diaries are at the Missouri Historical Society in St. Louis and are utilized here with the Society's permission and assistance.

2. Paine. P. 15.

3. Other titles among the eight pictures included *Primitive Fear of a Superior Being*; *Monotheism Replacing Polytheism*; *The Death of Socrates, an Original Thinker*; and *Reason Triumphant in a Democratic World.* Calamitously for Kaufmann, all the paintings were consumed in the fire, although a set of etchings completed the previous year did survive and is in the Library of Congress.

4. Kaufmann himself had been trained by two German artists, Peter Cornelius and Wilhelm von Kaulbach, who painted historical subjects in a grandiose style. Cornelius executed large frescoes of Greek mythology and the New Testament, while Kaulbach's murals highlighted monumental pictorial cycles.

5. Deuteronomy: "Thou shalt not deliver unto the master his servant which has escaped from his master unto thee. He shall dwell with thee. Even among you in that place which he shall choose in one of thy gates where it liketh him best. Thou shalt not oppress him."

    Declaration of Independence: "We hold that all men are created equal, that they are endowed by their Creator with certain unalienable rights, that among these are life, liberty and the pursuit of happiness."

6. While his pupil went on to stardom, Kaufmann's career as a painter was not successful. He served in the Union army, and then became an itinerant photographer who also painted portraits on commission, along with a few historical pictures. One of them called *On to Liberty*, painted in 1867, showed a group of former slaves fleeing to Union lines, and is in the Metropolitan Museum of Art today.
7. The Academy of Design was then located on 13th Street just west of Broadway. Founded in 1825, membership was considered to be an academic honor. Its first president was painter Samuel F.B. Morse, who went on to invent the telegraph. Its second and current president was Asher B. Duran; Duran and Academy co-founder Thomas Cole were leaders of the Hudson River school of painting.
8. The cartoons were drawn and submitted to *Yankee Notions* before Nast left for Europe in mid-February 1860 — well in advance of the June publishing date.

Chapter 2 The Emergence of Frank Leslie

1. From an affidavit located in the municipal records of New York City's Court of Common Pleas, as part of Leslie's divorce from Sarah Ann Leslie, 1868-1871.
2. The information about Charles Wells came from *Pictures in the Papers*, an article by Roger Butterfield in the June 1862 issue of *American Heritage*, p. 32, 34.
3. The boxwood logs were sawed off from the end, and then squared and smoothed in an exact manner. The thickness of the rectangular blocks had to be the same as the length of the type — generally one inch — so they were uniform in that respect. The engraving was done by carving into the end grain, which was smooth and hard, and could be cut rapidly with exquisite detail. The wood was whitened before it was used.
   Engravers used sandbags to rest their blocks on. Most of them used a magnifying glass in a frame, which could be set at any angle to focus on their work. The artists' sketches and lettering had to be drawn or traced on the wood **in reverse**, so the printed images would appear correctly. As mentioned previously, that may have been the only circumstance where Thomas Nast's apparent dyslexia proved beneficial to him.
   The engravers faced the light as much as possible. For night work, an ordinary glass globe filled with water focused the light from a lamp on the block. Four basic tools were used, all of which were available in a range of sizes: gravers, tint tools, scrapers and chisels. Mistakes could be corrected by replacing the damaged area with a plug of wood.
4. Gleason sold his *Pictorial* to his editor, Maturin Ballou in 1855. It continued as *Ballou's Pictorial Drawing-Room Companion* until the end of 1859, when it expired of "editorial anemia." Among its artists were Winslow Homer and Alfred Waud. The latter went by Alfred Hill to avoid discovery while living with another man's wife.
5. Much of the only detailed information on Leslie's early life resides in 26 hand-written affidavits, depositions, rulings and similar documents located in the municipal records of New York City's Court of Common Pleas.
6. Paine, p. 14.
7. William T. Coggeshall, *The Newspaper Record*, p. 149-150 Philadelphia, 1856, as footnoted in *The Newspaper Revolution: 1830-1860* by James L. Crouthamel, published by The New York State Historical Association, April 1964.
8. George Jones put up $25,000, as did his partner Edward B. Wesley, and Jones raised the rest of the money from other investors whom he knew from his time as a banker.

Chapter 3 Learning at Leslie's

1. Charles Parsons, 35, later became head of the art department at *Harper's*, Leslie's principal rival; Jacob Dallas unfortunately died at age 32 in September 1857.
2. Gunn Diaries, April 1862.
3. Ibid.

4. Paine, p. 28.
5. "Artists and Counsellors.

To the Editor of Frank Leslie's Illustrated Newspaper:

Mr. Graham said in his defence of the Aldermen, before Judge Welsh, the other day, that the persons most to blame for the caricature of the swill cow stable whitewashers were the artists, who, for the sake of hire, degraded themselves to libel honorable men; adding that he should like to send them to the Penitentiary. Without pausing to inquire how far such men as the signers of a solemn report, given in contradiction of all evidence, deserve that appellation – not even stopping to point out what an admirable Attorney-General Mr. Graham would have made for King George the Third of blessed memory, and would still make for King Bomba* of equal blessed existence – I trust you will allow me space in your paper to consider the distinctive characteristics of the two professions – that of the artist and the lawyer – and since the honest exercise of our talents is the foundation of all personal independence and honor, to see how far the calling of an artist is inferior to that of the lawyer.

That eminent moralist, Dr. Samuel Johnson, defined an advocate to be a man who gained a disreputable living by the indiscriminate defence of right and wrong, and marked his contempt of the vocation by affirming seriously to Boswell, that a counsel was bound to do for his client what his client would do for himself if he had his legal knowledge. I will not make any personal application of this undoubtedly truthful definition to Mr. Graham; but I may ask him, since he is somewhat famous as a criminal lawyer, if he has never defended a man, knowing him to be a notorious villain; whether he has not screened, for hire, murderers, forgers and thieves, or any other of those law breakers who make up so large a portion of a lawyer's business? Has Mr. Graham never protested the innocence of some of his patrons, when he knew all the time they were notorious villains, and that the welfare of society demanded their imprisonment or death? Even Mr. John Graham's legal disregard of truth would hardly embolden him so far as to answer this question in the negative! And indeed it would seem to require a long preparation of such indiscriminate sympathy with crime to nerve any man to undertake the desperate and unpopular task of advocating the cause of corrupt officials – men, if they deserve that name, Mr. Editor, who, for hire, endeavor to fasten upon the people of New York a poison which slays its thousands every year.

If Mr. Graham has on lingering touch of his original nature, which was cherished at his mother's breast, but now, I fear, obliterated by the leprous distillment of swill milk, let him follow the remorseful but noble example of the man who, having sold a righteous cause for thirty pieces of silver, returned the money to the Tuomey and Reed of those days, and then executed justice on himself.

Mr. Graham expressed great indignation against artists for libeling such respectable gentlemen as the Aldermen; although this is probably some of Mr. John Graham's delicate irony, and conceived in the same spirit as manifested by those writers who, when they allude to the devil, facetiously call him "the *gentleman* in black." I shall, however, consider it in its literal sense, and ask Mr. Graham if he has never insulted a witness – even modest and timid ladies – by putting questions implying crimes which Mr. Graham well knew were to be mere impudent inventions, and the putting which is one of those foul tricks belonging only to *his* trade? I will not tell him what my definition of such *artistic* proceedings is, for its truth and severity might disturb those well-combed and exquisitely arranged locks of that fair and possibly frail face, which really seems more fitted to adorn a millinery establishment than to grace a court of law.

Surely Mr. Graham cannot have confused his moral perceptions so far by this adoring contemplation of his manifold charms in a mirror, as not to know such conduct is *almost* as deserving the Penitentiary as to sketch a harmless and innocent illustration, calculated to shame the guardians of the public health into withdrawing their unholy protection from the vendors of a poison, sold under the false pretence of being a nutritious article of food. If anything could stamp the defenders of the swill milk interest, whether they be corrupt aldermen or hireling lawyers, with deep damnation, it is the unblushing fact that these wholesale poisoners can only get parents to force it down their infants' throats under the lying pretence that it is something else.

The druggist who knowingly sells laudanum for tincture of rhubarb is hanged, and every honest man thinks a similar punishment should also fall upon those child-slayers. What is the villainy of passing bogus coin to that of passing off a slow poison as milk? And yet, for hire, Mr. Graham has thrown the shield of his wit, virulence and legal lore over this infamous traffic. If Mr. Graham's personal admiration of himself and undoubted charms has so far confused his notions of right and wrong, I can only drop a tear on the melancholy mental condition of the Narcissus of the New York bar. But the spectacle of a mighty mind overthrown is not a pleasant one, and I conclude by asking him, almost in his own words, that if an artist who carries out Mr. Leslie's idea for the purpose of saving infant life, by bringing the force of ridicule to bear upon men, who, hardened by a long course of official depravity are insensible to all human sympathies, and all that generally touches the heart of man – if an artist, I say, is to blame for employing his talent for the holy purpose of saving life, what condemnation is sufficiently strong for one of Mr. Graham's profession, who, for the sake of a paltry fee, openly defends in a court of justice those who falsify evidence, and recommend the public to drink what they confess they would not knowingly drink themselves, or suffer their families to drink, and which I dare say Mr. Graham would not give even to a favorite dog? If to save life by these means, for hire, be deserving of the Penitentiary, what does not that man deserve who defends the murderer, and does his best to perpetuate the sale of a slow poison vended under the alluring name of 'pure Orange county grass-fed milk?' The public voice has spared Mr. Graham the necessity of a reply. Yours, AN ARTIST"

6. Gunn Diaries, October 1858.

Chapter 4 Freelancing

1. Nast's 1860 diary is in the Rutherford B. Hayes Presidential Library, Fremont, OH.
2. FLIN April 23, 1859.
3. The entire existing police force was replaced with a new consolidated Metropolitan unit from New York — Manhattan, Kings (Brooklyn), Richmond (Staten Island) and Westchester counties. The superseded police became part of the new force, but the Republicans in Albany controlled its board and the Metropolitans effectively were turned into a state-controlled police entity. Complaints about its allegedly poor administration and performance culminated in a scathing report presented to the New York State Senate on March 4, 1859.
4. Nast also drew *Phunny Phellow* cartoons with Greeley in them that appeared in March and May 1860, after he had sailed to England to cover the champion boxing match between John Heenan and Tom Sayers (for the *New York Illustrated News*). Thirteen years later, Nast would skewer Greeley serially for months when Greeley ran for president against Nast's unsurpassed hero, Ulysses Grant.
5. *On My Way: Being the Book of Art Young in Text and Picture*. Horace Liveright. New York. 1928.
6. Haney sold his half-interest in Nick-Nax to his partner, Mary Levinson, in 1860.

Chapter 5 When Tommy Met Sallie

1. Paine, p. 32.
2. Paine, p. 33.
3. June 22, 1860 Courtesy of The Huntington Library, San Marino, CA.
4. Gunn Diaries, June 5, 1859.
5. Fanny Fern's first husband, Charles Eldredge, died from typhoid fever; her second, Samuel Farrington, was divorced after she left him. Fanny died in 1872, and four years later James Parton married her younger daughter Ellen Eldredge (by her first husband) in an unusual twist. Her older daughter, Grace Eldredge, married Mortimer "Doesticks" Thomson in 1859, about six months after his first wife "Chips" died in childbirth. Grace too died in childbirth three years later, and Jim raised her daughter Ethel, first with Fanny and then with Ellen.
6. See footnote 3. By then Nast was in Italy with Garibaldi.
7. Gunn Diaries, April 13, 1861.

Chapter 6 *New York Illustrated News*

1. When Frank Luther Mott published his definitive five-volume *A History of American Magazines* in 1938, he erroneously wrote that John King was the first proprietor; King didn't take over until January 1861 when the *Illustrated News* was fourteen months old. However, King was its advertising agent through 1860, and possibly was related to Lexow by marriage. (After Lexow left Germany, he went to England and married Caroline King of Hull.) King was an Englishman, who emigrated to New York City in 1852 and established an advertising agency. It is reasonable to conclude that King, as advertising agent, was owed large amounts and took over the total publishing business at the end of 1860 in payment of his debts and to protect his future advertising income.
2. Paine, p. 34.
3. Gunn Diaries, August 10, 1860.
4. A copy of this chart in Sallie Nast's hand-writing is in the Rutherford B. Hayes Presidential Library in Fremont, Ohio, along with Nast's 1860 diary. "Tommy studied Sallie's chart too, attaching a great importance to it," according to Gunn.
5. Paine, p. 35.

Chapter 7 Garibaldi

1. Meucci incorporated the New-York Paraffine Candle Company and, in 1859, patented a candle made from the distillation of coal which claimed to give better illumination and last longer than the sperm whale oil candles of that time.
2. This was the achievement that led to Nast's illustrating *Garibaldi, the Hero of Italy* for Street & Smith's *New York Weekly*.
3. NYIN, June 30, 1860.
4. Paine, p. 48.
5. ILN, July 7, 1860.
6. Paine, p. 49.
7. *The Fat Boy* is from *The Pickwick Papers* by Charles Dickens. Dickens later wrote a separate story about *The Fat Boy* which Nast illustrated. The illustration is from Paine, p. 56.
8. The tales Nast told Paine about Naples are on p. 56-61.
9. Nast's letters to Sallie are at The Huntington Library, San Marino, CA.
10. HW, April 22, 1865, p. 243.
11. Paine, p. 66. This is a solid example of the unreliability of Nast's memory in what he told Paine. The diary is in the Rutherford B. Hayes Library in Fremont, OH.

Chapter 8 The Civil War Begins

1. One source was Allan Pinkerton, a detective employed by the railroad. The other was Frederick Seward, son of about-to-be Secretary of State William Seward, who had found out about the plot through separate undercover detectives put on the case by the New York City Police Commissioner at the senior Seward's request.
2. Three years later, Howard was convicted of another forgery and sent to prison.
3. Taney, then 80, wrote the notorious 1857 Dred Scott decision that "Negroes, whether slave or free . . . are not citizens of the United States." He died in 1864.
4. The note and the sketch are in Nast's sketchbook at the John Hay Library at Brown University.

5. The April 19, 1862 issue of the *Illustrated News* quoted the *New York World*: "All correspondents connected with the army divisions are ordered by Secretary Stanton to return, and are prohibited from remaining under penalty of arrest and imprisonment. All news from rebeldom and of the success or defeat of our own forces will be obtained through chance public rumors and other channels until official reports are made."

   The daily papers weren't the only publications that got in trouble with Stanton. The April 26 issue of *Harper's Weekly* — available about ten days earlier but post-dated — contained two full-page illustrations of Yorktown fortifications with details pointed out, which were prepared by an officer of the Topographical Engineers. That may have been the straw that broke Stanton's camel's back, because sales of *Harper's Weekly* were suspended at Fortress Monroe, and his general order was issued. *Harper's Weekly* protested vigorously in print — complaining, explaining and defending its discretion. Fletcher Harper made a hurried trip to Washington to see Stanton, and the suspension was lifted. Not coincidentally, the May 17 issue contained a glowing tribute to Stanton and his military censor, Colonel E. S. Sanford.

6. The Laocoon was an antique marble statue representing the Trojan priest Laocoon and his two sons being crushed to death by snakes for warning the Trojans against the wooden horse of the Greeks. Nast may have seen the Laocoon when he stopped briefly in Rome after completing his tour with Garibaldi sixteen months earlier.

7. The slaves' owner was Confederate Colonel Charles Mallory.

8. Ironically, Fortress Monroe was the historic place where the first twenty African slaves landed in America. A Dutch ship brought them over to the Virginia colonists in 1619. It took 242 years for the first significant crack to appear in that dike, right where it was originally established. When Jefferson Davis was imprisoned there after the Civil War, the symbolism was complete. Nast had a lot to say about that too.

9. King, an Englishman, must have worsened his pre-existing financial problems with additional circulation and advertising revenue losses resulting from his pro-slavery and pro-Southern independence editorials in February and March; he supported slavery because it was Constitutional, and proposed an England-Scotland-type affiliation for the North and the South. However, exactly why King left or what he did next is unknown.

10. Williamsburg was a rear guard delaying action under Confederate General James Longstreet after the evacuation of Yorktown in Union Commander George B. McClellan's ill-fated Peninsular Campaign, and resulted in almost 4,000 casualties among the 73,000 troops who fought there.

11. When the fleeing Union troops reached Centerville, they ran into the 8th New York, a German regiment commanded by the two former employees and minority owners of the *New York Illustrated News* and its German-language affiliate. Colonel Louis Blenker and Lieutenant-Colonel Julius Stahel received public commendations and promotions (to general and colonel, respectively) for their role in slowing down the runaway army in the late afternoon and evening, and in turning back a troop of pursuing Confederate cavalry about an hour before midnight. That stalwart action closed off any Confederate chance of advancing towards Washington.

12. Before they left, *Harper's Weekly* authorized Davis to go, and Russell knew without a doubt that Davis was representing *Harper's*. *Harper's* then announced in print that "we have dispatched an artist to the South in company with William H. Russell, Esq., LL.D., Barrister at Law, Correspondent of the *London Times*."

    When Confederate officials read that, they reacted strongly. Russell lied and said he believed Davis was representing only the *Illustrated London News*. Davis was threatened on several occasions, and *Harper's Weekly* angrily printed a detailed record of all the relevant correspondence in its July 20 issue, available to its 120,000 subscribers the week before Bull Run. A month earlier, *Harper's Weekly* had featured Russell on its cover, including a sketch of him by Davis.

13. August Belmont, a War Democrat, subsequently acquired great wealth, became chairman of the Democratic National Party and, in 1862, purchased the *New York World* and installed Manton Marble as editor. Nast despised Marble and the *World*, a feeling that was mutual.

14. Jeff Davis was at the top, of course, with Robert E. Lee on the far left and Governor Henry Wise of Virginia to the right of Davis. The two generals to the left of Davis, Ben McCulloch and Sterling Price, had led the Confederacy to victory at the Battle of Wilson's Creek on August 10, 1861, and elsewhere in Missouri through November, so they were prominent at the time when the only significant fighting after Bull Run was in the West. Wise had overseen the imprisonment, trial and execution of John Brown two years earlier.

15. Coincidentally, Grant and Buckner had been friends at West Point, and Buckner had loaned Grant money eight years earlier when Grant was in financial trouble. He also served as a pallbearer at Grant's funeral in 1885.

16. That did not stop Beauregard from wiring Jeff Davis that he had won a "glorious victory," which provided great fodder for Northern cartoonists and ridicule from both sides.

17. Poor Henri Lovie's immediate "reward" for his exceptional coverage was an extreme case of battle fatigue. Recuperating in Mississippi afterwards, he described his experience in the same May 17, 1862 issue of Leslie's in which most of his sketches appeared: "Riding from 10 to 15 miles daily, through mud and underbrush, and then working until midnight by the dim light of an attenuated tallow dip," caused him to be "nearly played out." Not long after his resultant rest and recreation break, Lovie invested in a cotton venture and unexpectedly became wealthy enough to return to Cincinnati and give up battlefield sketching for a much easier and safer life.

18. In January 1864, proprietor Thomas B. Leggett gave up and sold the paper to W. Jennings Demorest. *Demorest's New York Illustrated News* added fashions and other women's features, but disappeared by August when it merged with *Demorest's Mirror of Fashion.*

Chapter 9 *Harper's Weekly*

1. Nast didn't sign an exclusivity contract with Harper & Brothers until the fall of 1873. After the Tweed (1871) and Greeley (1872) campaigns established him as the Harpers' principal circulation magnet, the firm needed to protect itself against potential poachers, old and new.

2. In addition, the prominence of the publication attracted sketches from many military men (as did *Leslie's* and, to a lesser extent, the *Illustrated News.*) Alfred Waud traveled with the Army of the Potomac in Virginia and at Antietam and Gettysburg, covering about half of the war's 120-plus named battles. Theodore Davis accompanied the Western armies under Generals Ulysses Grant, William Sherman and others. Each had more than 200 sketches in the *Weekly*, bringing the war home to its readers as fast as special couriers or the mail could get them to New York. Of course, the written accounts arrived one to three weeks earlier, sent by reporters for the daily papers by telegraph.

   Their reportorial illustrations were complemented and buttressed by the incisive editorials and commentary of George William Curtis. Fletcher Harper maintained a close eye over the illustrations, and Charles Parsons who became superintendent of the art department in April 1863, provided overall guidance. Curtis remained editor until his death in 1892, and Parsons retired in 1889, thereby giving *Harper's* a consistency that *Frank Leslie's Illustrated Newspaper* could never come close to matching.

3. Another 14 Homer sketches dealt with the political and home fronts, six of which were published prior to the start of the war. Not all of them were worthy of the Homer who is idolized today; some were hastily drawn and others were poorly engraved.

4. In this instance, Homer's painting was created first but was not exhibited until several months later. The most interesting difference between the two works is that the soldier in the illustration had his canteen hanging from a branch, indicating that he could stay up in the tree all day if necessary; the painting had no canteen. The idea for the *Sharp-Shooter* came from Homer's experience at Yorktown, where he saw Colonel Hiram Berdan's crack riflemen in action, and sent a sketch of them to the *Weekly.*

5. Unlike Nast, Homer never depicted himself in the *Weekly*. However, after the war he made a set of 24 colored lithographed cards for pasting in albums which were printed and distributed by Louis Prang, his Boston friend, for $1.50 a set. One of these *Life in Camp* cards showed Homer himself as "Our Special."
6. *The Mail and Express*, New York. April 12, 1884. "Thomas Nast in His Workshop."
7. Major General Winfield Scott Hancock was a hero of Gettysburg and participated in many other campaigns. Nast had great respect for him and, unable to resist an obvious pun, depicted him as a fighting cock.
   Nast depicted George Armstrong Custer as *The Pet of the Army* because he had been commissioned a Brigadier General of Volunteers at the age of 23 in June 1863, and Major General of Volunteers in April 1865. As a cavalry officer in the Army of the Potomac, he fought in all but one battle from First Bull Run to Appomattox, while eleven horses were killed under him. However, Custer is usually remembered for his disastrous defeat and annihilation at Little Big Horn on June 25, 1876, and not for his Civil War service. He probably was the most flamboyantly dressed officer in the army which, along with his elaborate hair style, Nast captured in his caricature.
8. Unlike regular soldiers, guerillas generally were not paid wages by the Confederate government. Instead, they could dispose of their captured supplies for their own benefit, with the government as primary purchaser.
9. The losing Confederates generals included Sterling Price and Ben Mcculloch who had been figuratively hung on Nast's *Christmas Tree of the Federal Army* about two months earlier (see p. 102). Mcculloch predictively met his fate on the field. Albert Pike grew up in Massachusetts, moved to Arkansas and became a lawyer before the war. He represented the Creeks in a victorious lawsuit, and was "Confederate Commissioner to the Indians" at the time of the battle.
10. A protocol was worked out whereby a lieutenant was worth four privates, a commanding general was worth thirty sergeants, etc.
11. In the Nast scrapbook at the John Hay Library at Brown University.
12. "Letters from every corner of the Union came to the Harper office with messages of thanks for that inspired picture. A colonel wrote to tell how it had reached him on Christmas Eve and had been unfolded by the light of his own camp-fire, and how his tears had fallen upon the page . . . It was only a picture but thousands besides the colonel had shed tears upon those pages and had been enabled and strengthened in their high resolve." Paine, p. 86.
13. Forbes, a battlefield artist, was paid only for the sketches that Leslie actually published.
14. Clem was discharged a year later at age 13, made the army his career as an adult, and retired in 1915 as Major General John Lincoln Clem.

Chapter 10 Emancipation

1. The Border States, as well as slaves in Union-occupied Rebel territory (Coastal Carolina and Virginia, Western Tennessee, and New Orleans), were not included in the decree.
2. On a familial sidenote, Thomas Butler Gunn noted in his October 17, 1862 diary entry — less than a month after the Proclamation — that Tommy's father-in-law, George Edwards, "has become agent for sending 500 negroes, with their families, to Australia to cultivate cotton." Like others of his ad hoc business schemes, George's venture never happened.
3. At the John Hay Library, Brown University.
4. According to historian Joshua Brown of the City University of New York, there were 233 children in the Asylum on that day.
5. Four years later when Grant received the Republican nomination for president (vs. Democrat Horatio Seymour), the same picture graced the cover of *Harper's* June 6, 1868 issue.

Chapter 11 The Election of 1864

1. Grant's identity is not certain, but a sketch in Nast's scrapbook at the John Hay Library, Brown University, tends to confirm it.
2. *The Old Guard* actually began as a 24-page pamphlet in June 1862, but was suppressed after three issues. It reemerged in January 1863.
3. There are preliminary sketches of Angel of Peace in a Nast scrapbook at the Morgan Library in New York, so he put a lot of thought into it.
4. As *Harper's* cover story also detailed, every state in the Union had to pass legislation to allow its absentee soldiers to vote. Copperheads "made Patriotism a crime" by blocking permission in New York when Governor Horatio Seymour vetoed the legislature's bill; a state constitutional amendment overruled him. Another constitutional amendment in Pennsylvania, and a state Supreme Court decision in Vallandigham's Ohio, enabled their soldiers to vote, while Copperheads prevailed in Connecticut, New Jersey, Delaware, Indiana and Illinois.
5. The Emancipation Proclamation did not apply to the four Border states. Under pressure from Lincoln and some Congressmen who wanted to ensure that slavery would ab abolished permanently, the Senate passed the 13th Amendment on April 8, 1864, and the House on January 31, 1865. It was finally ratified on December 6, 1865. Missouri had freed its slaves in January 1865, but Kentucky and Delaware resisted until ratification by 27 of the 36 states — including most of the readmitted Confederate states — forced them to conform.

Chapter 12 Victory and Assassination

1. Technically, Nast had difficulties drawing the tall figure of Lincoln exactly the way he wanted, and was dissatisfied enough with the two (of thirty-six) woodblocks that comprised the essence of Lincoln to replace them in the completed engraving. The two new blocks — of Lincoln's head to his waist, and his waist to his knee — had tonal variations and occasional white lines apparent to a viewer, which distinguished them from the other blocks.
2. Letter dated December 9, 1864 from Curtis "To the President. My dear sir." Photocopy in files at Macculloch Hall Historical museum, as well as private collector Richard Stack who kindly brought it to my attention.
3. Charles Coffin, a reporter for the *Boston Journal*, was near Lincoln as he *walked* through the city. He wrote Nast: "Your conception is very fine and would answer quite well as most pictures for the historical truth." Nast also sketched the scene for Coffin's 1866 book, *Four Years of Fighting* (which undoubtedly is why Coffin corresponded with him). Leslie's "imaginary" illustration showed Lincoln by himself riding in a coach with a black driver on the box. Coffin's letter is at the William C. Clements Library at the University of Michigan.

   The illustration also became the genesis of one of Nast's best actual history paintings when he recreated it two years later and valued it at $250. He traded it to New York's Union League Club in exchange for membership initiation and annual dues.
4. Coincidentally, McLean's previous house and estate were part of the Confederate defenses and battlefield at First Bull Run. Apocryphally, he is rumored to have said: "The war began in my front yard and ended in my parlor."
5. Rawlins, a Galena native nine years younger than Grant, handled legal affairs for the Grant family leather goods store where 38-year old Sam worked as a clerk in 1860, and had been his chief staff officer and closest advisor for four years. After Grant was elected President in 1868, Rawlins served as his Secretary of War before his untimely death from tuberculosis in 1869.
6. Ely Parker, who lived in Galena, also was a friend of store clerk Sam Grant, and ultimately became Grant's military secretary. At Appomattox, Parker transcribed the official copies of the surrender documents. The son of a Seneca chief, he became the first Native American to hold the office of Commissioner of Indian Affairs when President Grant appointed him to that position.

While Parker was at work, Grant introduced Lee to his staff — Colonels Orville Babcock (whose wife was from Galena), Adam Badeau, Horace Porter and Theodore Bowers — all of whom would play a role in his presidential administrations. Lee also spoke with General Seth Williams, the only man in the room he knew, who had served under him at West Point when Lee was Superintendent. The other generals Lee shook hands with were Rufus Ingalls, Grant's supply chief, and Edward Ord.

General George Armstrong Custer was at Appomattox but not in the room. Nast edged him into his picture anyway, about twenty years after Custer's tragic death in the massacre at Little Big Horn.

7. Nast had no cartoons in *Harper's Weekly* from December 31, 1864 (*The Union Christmas Dinner*) to April 29, 1865 (*The Eve of War — The Dawn of Peace*).
8. Francis Bicknell Carpenter is best known for his painting of Lincoln reading the Emancipation Proclamation to his Cabinet in July 1862.
9. The editorial appeared on May 27, 1865. That issue also contained General James Wilson's formal report of the capture of Davis on its cover page.
10. *Harper's Weekly* editor George William Curtis wrote that Greeley bailed Davis for several reasons: to help the country, to help the Republican party, and to help himself by winning personal good will in the Southern states, as well as "a certain love of notoriety."

Chapter 13 President Johnson: First Year

1. Twelve years later, on May 30, 1877 — Decoration Day — Pryor made a passionate *Plea for Reconciliation* at the Brooklyn Academy of Music. In his speech, he made a rarely expressed point that "the Constitution of the Confederacy made express provision for its own dissolution (by) conceding the right of any State to secede at will." He also stressed that a Southerner's allegiance was to his state while a Northerner's was to the *United* States.
2. When Nast wasn't sure about somebody, he usually drew him in shadow in the background. Secretary of State Judah Benjamin (left rear) never applied for a pardon, but fled to England through Florida and the Bahamas, and built a successful legal practice there. Being Jewish could have made his postwar life difficult in America, and he did have English ancestors.
3. Reportedly Johnson was suffering from typhoid fever and dosed himself with too much whiskey. However, there would be future public appearances where he also was drunk.
4. Clement Moore wrote his timeless poem in December 1822. It was first published anonymously a year later in a Troy, New York newspaper. His authorship didn't surface until 1837. The poem didn't appear in book form until 1848.
5. Personal Memoirs of P.H. Sheridan, Volume II, p. 210, Jenkins & McCowan, New York 1888.
6. The Rutherford B. Hayes Presidential Library in Fremont, Ohio, has a collection of a dozen or so cartes de visite of the Nast caricatures, some of which are used here with great appreciation. Other names were printed in the April 13, 1866 *New York Times*, reporting on the auction sales from the night before at the Somerville Art Gallery. Additional information, including the $250 watch, came from the October 1867 *American Phrenological Journal*.
7. *The Youth's Companion*, June 18, 1896. Article by Nast entitled *Caricatures and Caricatured*. Reprinted in *Journal of the Thomas Nast Society*, Vol. 6, No. 1, 1992.

Chapter 14 President Johnson: King Andy

1. All but 500 had their rights restored in 1872.
2. 27 of the 36 states, including 8 of the 11 seceded states approved the Fourteenth Amendment; Mississippi, Texas, and Florida were the laggards. However, it took two more years for final ratification by the 28th of the now 37 states; Nebraska ratified it when admitted on June 15, 1867.

3. Nast had sketched the Coliseum in December 1860 on his way home from Garibaldi, and probably was inspired by a full-page engraving of its exterior which appeared in the *Weekly's* issue of October 6. His sketchbook at the Morgan Library in New York reveals that he finished the picture in October 1866, but withheld it from publication for five months until Johnson's potential impeachment pot was beginning to simmer in the wake of a Congressional report on the riot.
4. HW, September 22, 1866, p. 594.
5. About three weeks earlier, four blacks, convicted of larceny, were sold at auction in Annapolis; one bought himself for $35. In Raleigh, General Daniel Sickles, the military commander, had issued an order forbidding public whipping. The provisional governor went to Washington to appeal personally to the President, who then overruled Sickles. Free blacks were lashed immediately after conviction by a jury of former rebels and sentencing by a judge appointed for his Confederate views.
6. *Harper's Weekly*, April 13, 1867, p. 226; April 27, 1867, p. 258, 263 (*Winglets* column).
7. Redding's Russia Salve, a Boston company, had not advertised in the *Weekly* since 1864. After this cartoon, its ad appeared in four of the next six issues.
8. Nast's May 20, 1867 letter to Locke is in the Locke Collection at the Rutherford B. Hayes Library in Fremont, OH.
9. As the trial dragged on and Johnson's acquittal became probable, Nast gave the unengraved block to his host, Norton Chipman. About forty years later, Chipman presented it to the *Sacramento Bee* newspaper owned by the McClatchy family. Draper Hill found it there and wrote it up in the Winter 1999 *Notebook of the Association of American Editorial Cartoonists.*
10. Edmund Ross was an accidental senator — his predecessor, James Lane, committed suicide — and his post-trial successful patronage requests to Johnson kindled suspicions.
11. Instead Nast saved the engraved block whose origin was dated by two things: the signature of Joseph Spear, the New York engraver whom Nast hired specifically for his Chicago cartoons; and the appearance of Thaddeus Stevens exiting at the far right, who had died in August 1868.

Chapter 15 Historical Painter

1. *Nast's Historical Paintings* by Leigh Leslie. *National Magazine,* September 1906, p. 595. The comments on Nast's knowledge of European art are from the author's commissioned essay by the late Albert Boime, Professor of Art at UCLA.
2. 1903 letter from John Parker Davis to Albert Bigelow Paine in the Nast collection at the Morgan Library, New York.
3. Letter dated September 24, 1869, from Nast to Colonel Norton Chipman, in Chipman papers in the California State Library, Sacramento.
4. March 14, 1869 letter from Nast to Colonel Norton Chipman. Courtesy of Princeton University Special Collections Library.
5. *The Art-Idea: Painting, Sculpture, and Architecture in America.*
6. HW, April 30, 1864, p. 275.
7. HW, May 13, 1865, p. 291. Re-titled *The Halt*, Nast did get his picture into a Chicago exhibition. *Harper's Weekly* continued to publicize its artist by devoting a June 1866 cover to his picture, along with praise from the *Chicago Tribune.* His attempts to get it exhibited at a Boston gallery and in the 1867 Paris Exhibition were unsuccessful. The best he could do was a reproduction in the *Illustrated London News* a year and a half later, courtesy of William Luden Thomas, his friend from the Heenan-Sayers and Garibaldi days of 1860. (October 21, 1866).

8. Ironically, his painting was acquired by fellow member James H. Ingersoll and presented to the Regiment. The following year Ingersoll turned out to be a prominent player in Boss Tweed's gang of thieves, and was memorably skewered by Nast.
9. After Nast severed his ties with *Harper's* after 1886, he again occasionally turned to painting, with a few commissions during the 1890s adding to his meager income. (See Chapter 49.)
10. John Banvard's tour featured thirty-eight scenes depicting sights along the Mississippi River shoreline from St. Louis to the Gulf of Mexico (about 1845), lasted five years, and was viewed by an estimated two million people, some of them in London and Paris. Banvard lectured on the sights while his wife played the piano. Banvard then developed a huge (more than twenty-five feet high) *Panorama of the Holyland* which ran from 1854 to 1859 at his "Georama" theatre on Broadway, as well as in Boston and Philadelphia. Other moving panoramas depicted Niagara Falls, which toured for a dozen years from 1853 to 1865, and the 1835 Arctic explorations of Elisha Kent Kane.
11. March 30, 1867 letter to David Ross Locke. Locke Collection, Rutherford B. Hayes Presidential Library, Fremont, OH.
12. Nast illustrated a third Nasby book in 1871, but with a different publisher, I.N. Richardson of Boston.
13. Nast's March 23, 1867 letter to Locke is also in the Locke Collection at the Hayes Library.
14. Nast's sketchbook is at the Morgan Library in New York.
15. Even though Locke didn't collaborate with Nast on the Caricaturama, the two continued to work together. In 1871, Locke moved to New York and became managing editor of the *New York Evening Mail*, as well as a partner in the advertising agency of Bates and Locke. He and Nast became closer friends, and the artist illustrated *The Struggles of Petroleum V. Nasby with Illustrations by Thomas Nast* which was published the following year by the *Toledo Blade*. Locke soon returned to Toledo where he played an active role in both the civic and economic life of that city.
16. Nast's May 20, 1867 letter to Locke is also in the Locke Collection at the Hayes Library.
17. Mark Twain's November 12, 1877 letter to Nast is in Albert Bigelow Paine's scrapbook (in the Nast Collection) at the Hayes Library; it is contained in an article from the *New York Herald*, April 1, 1906, about the upcoming auction of Nast memorabilia.
18. December 5, 1867.
19. After Nast moved his family to Morristown, New Jersey in 1871, the Caricaturama panels were stored in a shed behind his house until a local sign painter acquired them, primarily for drop cloths. Today, only eight of the thirty-three survive: five in storage at the Smithsonian Institution, two at the Macculloch Hall Historical Museum in Morristown, and *Swinging Round the Circle* on the wall of the Morristown and Morris Township Public Library. The Library, which acquired the panel through a 1948 donation, had it carefully restored in 1990. Macculloch Hall Historical Museum has a complete set of photographs of the panels, which it kindly licensed to the author for use in this book.
20. *Radiant with Color and Art: McLoughlin Brothers and the Business of Picture Books, 1858-1920*. By Lauren B. Hewes and Laura E. Wasowicz. P. 112. American Antiquarian Society, Worcester, MA. Original footnote No. 20 source, p. 143, was "Galaxy Advertiser," *The Galaxy 10*, December 1870.

Chapter 16 *Harper's Bazaar* (No Endnotes)

Chapter 17 The Election of 1868

1. Later that summer, Chipman served as judge advocate in the military trial of Henry Wirz, who was hanged on November 10 for his crimes at Andersonville prison.
2. Nast was inspired by the crouching figure in French artist Ernest Meissonier's 1852 painting of *The Hired Assassins*.

3. *"First with the Most" Forrest* by Robert Selph Henry. The Bobbs-Merrill Company, New York, 1944, p. 442-448.
4. *The Cruise of The Alabama and the Sumter* (from the private journals and other papers of Commander R. Semmes, CS.N.). George W. Carleton, New York, 1864.
5. *The Political Andersonville*, HW October 24, 1868, p. 681.
6. *Reconstruction 1863-1877* by Eric Foner, p. 292, Harper & Row, New York, 1988.
7. *The Worcester Spy* (MA), October 3, 1868.
8. Grant carried Alabama, Arkansas, Florida, North and South Carolina, and Tennessee; Seymour captured Georgia and Louisiana. Mississippi, Texas and Virginia had not yet approved black suffrage, so were ineligible to vote. Seymour won the border states of Kentucky, Maryland and Delaware; Missouri and West Virginia went to Grant. Seymour also carried New York, New Jersey and Oregon.

Chapter 18 President Grant: First Term

1. While not using any direct quotations, much of the insightful material in this chapter came from *Hamilton Fish: The Inner History of the Grant Administration* by Allan Nevins, published by Dodd, Mead & Company, New York, in 1936. Fish, Grant's Secretary of State in both terms, kept a detailed diary, which Professor Nevins referred to or quoted from throughout his book.

   Another useful source was *Grant, A Biography*, by William McFeeley. A third was a commissioned essay by prominent Grant historian Brooks Simpson (Arizona State) entitled: *The Idol as Icon: Thomas Nast and Ulysses S. Grant.*
2. Paine, p. 137.
3. HW, July 10, 1869, p. 437.
4. HW, April 22, 1871, p. 363. Congress did not provide citizenship to Native Americans until 1924. Individual states could then allow them to vote. The last states waited until 1957 to do so.
5. St. Crispin was the patron saint of shoemakers. "Shoo Fly, don't bother me" was the best known song from the famous minstrel act of Dan Bryant (1833-1875).

   Harper's Weekly opposed mass importation of Chinese laborers, but supported "the operation of natural laws, free from all forcing. We doubt if any honest American laborer need fear the result." (July 16, 1870, p. 451).

   In 1870, fewer than 50,000 Chinese lived in California, 14,000 in the rest of the country, and a miniscule number in New York City.
6. *The Treaty of Washington* by Caleb Cushing, p. 15-16, Harper & Brothers, New York, 1873.
7. *Fighting Politician: Major General N.P. Banks*, p. 191-2, by Fred H. Harrington, U. of Pennsylvania Press, 1948.

   HW, July 2, 1870, p. 418.
8. This content is extracted from a privately-commissioned article by the late Albert Boime, Professor of Art History at UCLA.
9. It was written by Reverend Henry Williams and published by Francis B. Felt & Co., New York, 1871.

Chapter 19 The Pope

1. Drawing a fine line to gauge Nast's depth of emotional antagonism toward his other major villains, Nast scorned — but probably did not hate — Andrew Johnson and Horatio Seymour (Confederate sympathizers); Napoleon III (Pope's protector); the Tweed Ring (partners with Irish-American and Catholic supporters of the Pope); and Horace Greeley (bailed Jeff Davis and ran against Grant). His common thread was that all of them were threats to stable, honest government and the fundamental liberties it guaranteed.

2. Letter to Frank Sadler, Esq. dated April 15, 1870. Reprinted in *The House of Harper* by J. Henry Harper. P. 307. Harper & Brothers, New York, 1912.
3. *Miss Columbia's Public School or Will It Blow Over?* Published by Francis B. Felt & Co., New York, 1871, p. 81-2. Someone other than Nast —possibly Eugene Lawrence — may have authored the statement.
4. Ibid p. 9.
5. Nast's letter of November 26, 1871, is in the Norton Chipman file at the California State Library in Sacramento.
6. *Immigrants, Temperance and Tammany Hall*, by W.J. Rorabaugh. *Civil War History,* June 1976, p. 138-54.
7. HW, November 24, 1866, p. 742.
8. HW October 24, 1885.
9. Nast may have borrowed the analogy from English cartoonist John Leech, who had used a single crocodile-bishop in *Punch* 20 years before. Entitled *Remarkable Crocodile Found in Ireland*, it appeared on September 6, 1851.
10. *New York Times*, September 24, 1871.
11. Having illustrated Garibaldi's biography in 1859, Nast may have known that his hero was educated by priests and married his first two wives in Catholic churches, but despised the Papacy and its temporal power. Garibaldi believed in personal immortality and considered himself a good Christian.
12. HW February 25, 1871, p. 114-5.
13. The site of the new St. Patrick's Cathedral was selected by Archbishop John Hughes, but the Cathedral wasn't completed until 1879, 15 years after his death.

Chapter 20 Tweed: The Rise of the Ring

1. *The Election and Naturalization Frauds in New York City 1860-1870* by John Davenport, 1895, p. 274-5.
2. Albert Boime, UCLA art historian and professor, believed that the composition, pose, gesture, informality of bearing, and even the wastebasket of Nast's *Universal Suffrage* influenced Edgar Degas's famous painting of his uncle's *Cotton Office at New Orleans*, begun a year later in that city. Source: Privately commissioned essay for the author by Professor Boime.
3. *Tammany Hall* by M.R. Werner, p. 104-106, Doubleday, Doran & Co., Inc., New York, 1928. The quote is from *North American Review*, Vol. CXIX, p. 363-364.
4. In 1977, revisionist historian Leo Hershkowitz of Queens College, CUNY, published *Tweed's New York: Another Look* (Anchor Press, Doubleday). His book was primarily based on city records that were about to be discarded, and on correspondence between Tweed and his brother Richard that Richard's descendants showed him.

   Professor Hershkowitz's thesis was that the whole Tweed story is a myth. "Tweed was no saint but he was not the Nast creature. He was more a victim than a scoundrel or thief." (p. xviii). "At no time did such a 'Ring' dominate New York City politics. . . The problem with Tweed and the myth is that it is all so much vapor and so little substance." (p. xvi).

   Nast, of course, was "a bigot, a panderer to the coarsest tastes and morals of society, for depicting the Irish as drunken, brawling ape-like creatures, Catholic clergymen as alligators, and Tweed like a thieving vulture" (after p. 244). He also referred to Nast as a "Swiss immigrant."

   To make his story fit his thesis, Hershkowitz ignored vote fraud and John L. Davenport's 1894 book, *The Election and Naturalization Frauds in New York City: 1860-1870*, which documented the actual records. Davenport was United States Commissioner, and Chief Supervisor of Elections for the Southern District of New York. Hershkowitz skipped past the fact that Tweed bribed Orange Winans of Chatauqua County to win a key legislative vote, and claims Tweed didn't control the legislature.

In spite of his dozens of factual and chronological errors and omissions, Hershowitz's inside-cover summary was reasonably accurate although its gruel was thin. "It was during Tweed's time and often under his direction, that the Metropolitan Museum of Art was incorporated, Central Park developed, Broadway made into a boulevard, and a modern system of social services planned. It was Tweed who championed the interests of the city (?) and the immigrant and challenged an entrenched anti-urban establishment. It was Tweed who was the catalyst in New York's transition from a small town to a major metropolis."

5. Hall paid a dollar a line compared to the normal 20 to 40 cents. Over the 18 months ending in September 1870, monthly payments averaged $130,000. In 1875, after the Ring was long gone, the annual total was $100,000.
6. *History of American Magazines, 1865-1885*, p. 440-442, by Frank Luther Matt. 1857. Harvard University Press, Cambridge, MA.
7. *Journal of The Thomas Nast Society*, Volume 6, 1992, p. 18, by Jeffrey Eger. Napoleon Sarony often posed Nast in carious costumes, including this one.

Chapter 21 Tweed: Attacking the Ring

1. HW, November 3, 1866, p. 690-691.
2. *The Greek Slave* represented a Christian woman put up for sale by Turks for sexual purposes. It had a profitable 1847-8 tour in this country and was the centerpiece of the American exhibit at the 1851 World's Fair in London.
3. HW. September 14, 1861, p. 579. Mozart Hall was Mayor Fernando Wood's rival to Tammany Hall.
4. Minutes of the American Bar Association, New York, May 1, 1871.

Chapter 22 Tweed: Breaking the Ring

1. Paine, p. 165.
2. Paine, p. 181.
3. *When Dana Was The Sun*, p. 209. Charles J. Rosebault. Greenwood Press, Westport, CT, 1970. (Reprint of 1931 book published by Robert M. McBride & Company, New York).
4. Paine, p. 179. HW, May 30, 1874, p. 450 (Editorial by Curtis).
5. In millions: James Ingersoll, $5.7; Andrew Garvey, $2.9; Carpenter John Keyser, $1.2. Board Clerk Elbert Woodward, on a salary of $1,500, built a park in which all the houses were located, along with a lavish house and farm for himself.
6. *The Nation*, August 31, 1871.
7. Nast's source was a dog-eared plate in his copy of *Illustrated Natural History*, Vol. II, London, 1862.
8. Young Oliver Twist was forced to accompany two of master criminal Fagin's young thieves on an unsuccessful robbery. When discovered and pursued, his companions joined the mob as it captured Oliver, yelling "stop thief" as they ran.
9. Probably no political cartoon ever published by anyone had the influence that *Compromise with the South* did in helping to reelect Lincoln in the country's most critical election ever. Interestingly, both symbolic themes featured smirking leaders — Jeff Davis and Boss Tweed — breaking their oppositions' swords of power as Columbia was almost destroyed. (See p. v).
10. Carthage was near Tunis, capital of Tunisia. Vanderlyn's painting won a gold medal in Paris, reportedly at the direction of Napoleon I.

Chapter 23 Tweed: Aftermath

1. Nast's reference was to *The Last Rose of Summer* written by Irish poet Thomas Moore in 1805. In actuality, Connolly jumped bail and fled to France four days before the pre-drawn and post-dated cartoon appeared on January 3, 1872.
2. In fact, Nast had the source of his quotation wrong, a rare if not singular occurrence. It actually came from the last two lines of Thomas Gray's 1742 poem, *Ode on a Distant Prospect of Eton College*. Professor Harry Rusche of Emory University noted the discrepancy in a privately commissioned essay: *Oh for a Muse of Fire: Thomas Nast and William Shakespeare*.
3. *The Diary of George Templeton Strong, 1865-1875*, p. 416. Edited by Allan Nevins and Milton H. Thomas. 1952. The MacMillan Company. New York.
4. Paine, p. 353.
5. The cars were labeled for: John A. Dix, its new president; lawyer Samuel Barlow, General Daniel Sickles, General William Sherman, and A.O.P. Archer — the new directors of the Erie. *The Life and Legend of Jay Gould*, p. 121-126. The Johns Hopkins University Press. Baltimore. 1986.
6. HW, November 25, 1871 (in print, November 15). The *Times*, November 16, 1871.
7. *The Nation*, November 23, 1871.

Chapter 24 The Election of 1872: The Liberal Republicans

1. The letter is in the Nast Collection at The Huntington Library, San Marino, CA. Biographer Albert Paine (p. 225) mistranscribed the last sentence as "The power I have *here* frightens *me*," which totally changed the meaning.
2. Deputy editor Charles Dana wrote the actual editorial while Greeley was in Chappaqua nursing an injury. "Forward to Richmond! Forward to Richmond! The Rebel Congress must not be allowed to meet there on the 20th of July. By that date the place must be held by the National Army."
3. HW May 18, 1872, p. 306.
4. The Credit Mobilier/Pacific Railway Scandal, which roiled Congress and the public, and involved both of Grant's vice presidents, bubbled up in September but didn't boil over until after the election.
5. Nast to Sallie, February 6, 1872. The Huntington Library. See Footnote 1.
6. Grant's December 4, 1871 message to Congress: "If bad men have secured places, it has been the fault of the system established by law and custom for making appointments, or the fault of those who recommend for government positions persons not sufficiently well known to them personally, or who give letters endorsing the character of office-seekers without a proper sense of the grave responsibility which such a course devolves upon them. A civil service reform which can correct this abuse is much desired." George Wilkes, next to Greeley, was publisher of *Wilkes' Spirit of the Times*; Nast knew him from the Heenan-Sayers fight which Wilkes promoted. (See p. 62). Nast also met Matt Morgan in 1860.
7. HW May 18, 1872, p. 306.
8. *The House of Harper* by J. Henry Harper, p. 302. Harper & Brothers, New York. 1912.
9. Ibid p. 304.

Chapter 25 The Election of 1872: The Nomination

1. George Washington, who could have exercised great political power after defeating the British, instead returned to cultivating his lands. A group of army officers then formed The Society of the Cincinnati, for which the Liberals' convention city was named.
2. HW May 18, 1872, p. 306.

3. Based on an 1819 poem by Lord Byron, the 1830 play climaxed with a final scene in which a young Polish nobleman was stripped of his clothing by a villainous count and tied to the back of a spirited stallion. An 1861 New York production featured boxer John Heenan's erstwhile mistress, Adah Isacs Menken, as the male hero, wearing a flesh-colored body-stocking that created the illusion she was totally naked. Nast undoubtedly saw the play, read long illustrated articles about Menken in the *New York Illustrated News* (published in March 1860 while he was in England covering the Heenan-Sayers fight), and drew Jeff Davis as *The Modern Mazeppa* for *Phunny Phellow* in June 1862. Greeley attacked Menken for "shocking and revolting decent people by exposing her body in the nude." Now he was playing the role, courtesy of Nast.
4. *Woodhull & Claflin's Weekly,* March 16, 1872, p. 9.
5. Frank Leslie's *Budget of Fun*, January 1872.
6. The *Woodhull & Claflin Weekly* ran out of money in June 1872 and shut down. With funding from an undisclosed source, it regenerated in a single issue dated November 2. Victoria wrote a scathing four-page exposé of the Beecher-Tilton scandal which shocked the city and nation. Copies resold for as much as $10 each when the publication became available on October 28, nine days before the election.

   Victoria and Tennie ended up winners. When Cornelius Vanderbilt died in 1877, he reportedly left $90 million to his son William Henry, and $15 million to be divided among William's many siblings. Threatened by potential lawsuits from them, bolstered by testimony from the sisters, William paid them off generously to move to England. There they married rich men, then abandoned free love, and lived in luxury into the 1920s.

   Tilton ended up a loser. He sued Beecher in 1874, but after a six-month trial the following year, a hung jury's 9-3 verdict favored Beecher. Both men lied under oath.

   Tilton struggled to make a living, moved to Paris in 1893 and died in poverty 14 years later. Beecher returned to his pulpit somewhat bruised in reputation. Nast depicted him preaching in 1886, looking hale and hearty, in the year before his death.

   While other cartoonists reveled in the licentiousness of the testimony, Nast ignored it. Social controversy was for others; he was busy promoting and defending Grant and his administration on strictly political issues.

Chapter 26 The Election of 1872: The Campaign

1. According to the quote, it was from the *Tribune* of November 26, 1860. The *Tribune* declared it a deliberate forgery. Actually, the *Harper's* printer erred on the date; it was from May 1, 1861 — after the war began. The *Weekly* corrected the date two weeks later, and stressed the accuracy of Greeley's statement in response to the *Tribune's* denial — keeping the story and the cartoon in the news.
2. HW, August 17, 1872, p. 634.
3. Frenchman Auguste Biard painted "Le Bateau Pirate" in 1851.
4. The "Go West" advice originated in an 1851 editorial in the Terre Haute, IN *Express* by J.L.B. Soule.
5. The cartoons from Nast's collection are in the New York Public Library, and are included here, courtesy of that institution.

Chapter 27 Credit Mobilier

1. Letter dated January 30, 1873 from Nast to Norton Chipman. Chipman papers in the California State Library, Sacramento.
2. Nast had moved his family to Morristown in the summer of 1871 (see p. 270), but rented until he bought a seven-year old house on Macculloch Avenue for $21,250 in April 1872. It was expensive for that time and he was worried about the large mortgage. However, his principles took precedence over any implied future obligation to the Republican Party, a wise judgment in view of his antipathy toward its next three presidential election candidates.
3. Paine, p. 266.

4. *My Life in Many States and in Foreign Lands* by George Francis Train, p. 284-286. D. Appleton and Company. New York. 1902.
5. *The Era of Good Stealings* by Mark Wahlgren Summers, p. 50-54. Oxford University Press. New York. 1993.
6. *The Tribune Since the Civil War* by Harry W. Baehr, Jr., p. 111. Dodd, Mead & Company. New York. 1936.
7. HW, September 28, 1872, p. 747.
8. HW, June 28, 1873, p. 546; July 17, 1880, p. 450; July 31, 1880, p. 483.
9. Paine, p. 269-270.
10. See Footnote 1.
11. Paine, p. 272.
12. Howard, then a *Times* reporter, had made up the "Lincoln in disguise" story as the President-elect covertly changed his route to avoid assassins on his way to Washington in 1861 (see p. 88). In May 1864, Howard and a co-conspirator bought gold, then issued a false story about Lincoln conscripting 400,000 men; it sent the stock market down and the price of gold up to their profitable advantage. Both were convicted of forgery and served time in Fort Lafayette. After several jobs as a reporter, he bought the *New York Star*, to which Nast added *Forger* for the cartoon.

Chapter 28 President Grant: Caesarism

1. *The Era of Good Stealings* by Mark Wahlgren Summers, p. 255. Oxford University Press. New York. 1993.
2. *Philadelphia Times and Dispatch*, November 27, 1873, in Nast Collection at the New York Public Library.
3. Letter to Sallie in the Nast Collection at The Huntington Library, San Marino, CA.
4. Commissioned essay from Professor Mark W. Summers, University of Kentucky, 1997.
5. Other cartoonists never let Bennett forget the incident; in *Puck*, he usually had a bandage across his nose to cover the scar from his whipping. Nast, surprisingly, didn't do so.
6. Paine, p. 296.
7. My thanks go to Seth Kaller, who brought Grant's elephant to my attention.
8. Six weeks earlier, George Templeton Strong, a prominent New York lawyer, noted in his diary: "I hope and believe that Grant is rather pachydermous. Were he in the least sensitive, he would be stung to death by the envenomed proboscises of this swarm of minute black flies, like the *World* and the *Sun*" (and the *Tribune*).
   The Diary of George Templeton Strong. Edited by Allan Nevins and Milton Thomas. Volume IV, p. 436. The MacMillan Company. New York. 1952.
9. *New Language of Politics: An Anecdotal Dictionary of Catchwords, Slogans and Political Usage*, Revised Edition, Collier Books, New York, 1972.
10. "To see the elephant" dated back to the 1840s when it referred to Barnum's Museum, and then became synonymous with seeing battle during the War with Mexico.
11. Both Belknap and Robeson would be exposed in separate scandals before Grant left office.

Chapter 29 President Grant: Scandals

1. Privately commissioned 1997 essay by Professor Mark W. Summers of the University of Kentucky. His source: Jay Cooke to Henry D. Cooke, February 14, 1872, Henry D. Cooke to Jay Cooke, February 15, 1872, Jay Cooke MSS, Historical Society of Pennsylvania.
2. Same essay. His source: Orville E. Babcock to Thomas Nast, March 11, 1873, Nast to Babcock, March 15, 1873, Orville E. Babcock MSS, Newberry Library, Chicago.

Chapter 30 President Grant: Second Term Issues

1. Instead of using woodblocks, David Croly initially developed a printing innovation, where his artists or cartoonists would draw on a metal plate and etch away all but the lines of the drawing using acid. Photographs could be taken, brought to the *Daily Graphic* office, redrawn on metal, and reproduced faster than if engraved on woodblocks. In March 1880, a further improvement enabled pictures to be reproduced directly from photographic plates without being redrawn, a break-through which made Croly famous. The new process would affect Nast's work in a negative manner when he was forced to convert to it. Source: *The Yellow Press and Gilded Age Journalism* by Sidney Kobre, p. 39-42. Undated but probably written in the 1930s and published by Florida State University.
2. *The Diary of George Templeton Strong*, Volume IV, p. 536. Edited by Allan Nevins and Milton Thomas. The MacMillan Company. New York. 1952.
3. HW, January 23, 1875, p. 70.
4. Paine, p. 306.
5. HW, May 30, 1874, p. 450.
6. Paine, p. 293.
7. HW, February 7, 1874, p. 122.

Chapter 31 The Election of 1876: Tilden

1. Paine, p. 332 contains the text of the complete letter.
2. HW, April 10, 1875, p. 294. One contractor received 16 times his bid. Another charged the state twice: once for excavations never made and a second time for putting the earth back as embankments. (See also August 28, 1875, p. 694).
3. Commemorating the approaching Centennial, Grant's speech to the Army of the Tennessee stressed the importance of public education and the separation of church and state. Nast printed it in its entirety in *The Plank-Hitting the Nail on the Head*, and excerpted from it in *The Pope's Big Toe.*
4. *The Unexpected President: The Life and Times of Chester A. Arthur*, p. 95. By Scott S. Greenberger. Da Capo Press, Hachette Book Group. New York. 2017.

Chapter 32 The Election of 1876: Electoral Scramble

1. *The Diary of George Templeton Strong,* Vol. 4, p. 422. By Allan Nevins and Milton Thomas. The Macmillan Company, 1952. New York.
2. *Fraud of the Century,* p. 11-13 by Roy Morris, Jr. Simon & Schuster, New York, 2003.
3. Ibid p. 14-18.
4. Ibid p. 161. In fact, the 14th Amendment specifically prohibited either the federal government or any state government assuming or paying any debt or obligation incurred in aiding resurrection or rebellion against the U.S.
5. Ibid p. 11. The phrase originated in 1868 when Congressman Ben Butler waved a torn, bloody shirt on the floor of the House which came from a Federal tax collector whipped by the Ku Klux Klan in Mississippi.
6. *The Diary of George Templeton Strong*, Vol. 4, p. 536-8.
7. Paine, p. 344.
8. *The Life of Samuel J. Tilden*, Vol. II, p. 183, 210, by John Bigelow. Harper & Brothers. 1895 (Tilden's testimony to Congress).
9. *Fraud of the Century,* p. 183-4 by Roy Morris, Jr. Simon & Schuster, New York, 2003.

10. *Tilden*, Vol. II, p. 201. The $8,000 was actually advanced by The Third National Bank of New York.
11. *Fraud of the Century*, p. 189. The author commented on the possibility of a Republican bribe which indirectly surfaced a year later, but was never investigated or substantiated.
12. *The Civil War and Reconstruction in Florida*, p. 717. By William Davis. Columbia University Studies in History, Economics and Public Law. New York. 1913.
13. Ibid p. 708.
14. *Lucius Q.C. Lamar* by Wirt A. Cate, p. 277. U. of North Carolina Press, Chapel Hill, N.C. 1935.
15. Nast's classical caption referred to the so-called "Pyrrhic victory" of the King of Epirus over the Romans at Asculum in 279 B.C., in which he suffered overwhelming losses.

Chapter 33 Power Struggle with Curtis: Early Rounds

1. Paine, p. 217. Curtis's letter was received by Nast on January 28 or 29, 1872, when he was being recruited in Washington by Grant's associates.
2. Letter to Sallie dated January 29, 1872. In Nast collection at The Huntington Library, San Marino, CA.
3. HW. July 18, 1874. P. 594. Letter to Curtis, July 9, 1874, in Rutherford B. Hayes Library, Fremont, OH.
4. *George William Curtis* by Edward Cary, p. 160, 165, 189. Houghton, Mifflin & Co., New York, 1894. Cary was a reporter for the *New York Times*.
5. Cary, p. 191. Letter to Charles Eliot Norton dated April 20, 1865, in response to an offer to potentially take over a prospective, unfunded new paper.
6. *Raymond of the Times* by Francis Brown. P. 325. W.W. Norton & Company Inc. New York, 1951. Also *The House of Harper* by J. Henry Harper. p. 258. Harper & Brothers., New York. 1912.
7. Anna Shaw's brother Robert achieved posthumous fame for bravely leading the first regiment of black soldiers (54th Massachusetts) in a disastrous attack on Fort Wagner at the entrance to Charleston Harbor on July 18, 1863. Their heroic efforts convinced Unionists that black soldiers could be important to their eventual victory. Curtis extolled his brother-in-law in the *Weekly*.
8. Cary, p. 147. Letter to John Pinkerton dated July 9, 1861.
9. Cary, p. 198. Undated letter to John Pinkerton.
10. The letter is in the Nast Collection in the Rutherford B. Hayes Library, Fremont, OH.
11. Paine, p. 267.
12. Paine, p. 243.
13. Paine, p. 244.
14. Paine, p. 265.
15. *Journal of the Thomas Nast Society*, Vol. 8, No. 1, 1994. p. 3. Reprint of talk by Alfred Mills, Morristown's Mayor in the 1870's.
16. Paine, p. 254.
17. *The House of Harper* by J. Henry Harper, p. 304. Harper & Brothers, New York. 1912.
18. Paine, p. 265.

Chapter 34 Power Struggle with Curtis: Tipping Point

1. *The House of Harper* by Eugene Exman, p. 86. Harper & Row. New York. 1967.
2. Nast was probably stimulated by a speech Curtis made on December 22, 1876 at Delmonico's Restaurant to the New England Society of New York, in which he discussed the Hayes-Tilden electoral crisis.

3. Paine, p. 349.
4. HW, November 18, 1876, p. 926.
5. HW, February 3, 1877, p. 86. The reference was to the December issue of *The Leisure Hour*, "a widely circulated London magazine."
6. *Twelfth Night*, Act II, Scene 5. Fabian, a servant, urged Sir Toby Belch: "Nay patience, or we break the sinews of our plot." The plot was an elaborative love hoax to be played on the steward Malvolio who had just reprimanded Sir Toby for his drunkenness. Previously, Sir Toby had referred to Malvolio as "the little villain," who was absurd, gullible and self-absorbed. Nast probably had Curtis in mind for Malvolio's role, a subtlety understandable to his erudite oppressor.
7. Paine, p. 355.
8. *George William Curtis* by Edward Cary, p. 254. Houghton, Mifflin & Co., New York. 1894.
9. Paine, p. 363-4.
10. Paine, p. 367.
11. Paine, p. 366. Letter dated September 25, 1877, written from Newburyport, MA.
12. HW, December 13, 1879, p. 996.
13. Paine, p. 369.
14. *Life and Letters of Roscoe Conkling* by Alfred R. Conkling, p. 540 Charles L. Webster & Co. New York. 1889. Extracted from the full text of Conkling's speech.
15. HW, November 10, 1877, p. 891.
16. Paine, p. 367-8. In this instance, Paine had both his chronology and his resultant interpretation wrong. Twain's letter was dated November 21, 1877, a month *after* Nast returned to the *Weekly*. Paine (p. 368) said Nast "did not wish to close an engagement to travel, unless the Harper problem remained too long unsolved." That was a careless and critical misstatement, affecting a more critical time in Nast's life than his subject knew, and his biographer should have realized if he got his time sequence correct.

    Paine also deleted part of the letter. Fortunately, the full text, including the date, was available from a copy of the *New York Herald* for Sunday, April 1, 1906, reporting on the Merwin-Clayton auction sale of Nast's letters and cartoons to be held the next two days.
17. I am indebted to my friend Richard Samuel West for his knowledge of and insights into the life and work of Joseph Keppler. Rich authored *Satire on Stone: The Political Cartoons of Joseph Keppler* (University of Illinois Press, 1988) and co-authored *What Fools These Mortals Be: The Story of Puck* (IDW Publishing, San Diego, 2014). They have been my principal sources for the *Puck* cartoons and character identifications within them.
18. *Satire on Stone,* p. 112-3.
19. *Satire on Stone,* p. 128.
20. *Periodyssey*, Richard West's business periodical. Undated.

Chapter 35 President Hayes: Civic Issues

1. HW, December 15, 1877, p. 978.
2. *The Unexpected President: The Life and Times of Chester A. Arthur*, p. 72. By Scott S. Greenberger. Da Capo Press, Hatchette Book Group. New York. 2017.
3. Paine, p. 409.
4. Quote from Hayes letter to editor Murat Halstead of the *Cincinnati Commercial*, his close friend. *Rutherford B. Hayes* by Ari Hoogenbaum, p. 395. University Press of Kansas. 1995.
5. Hoogenbaum, p. 396-402.

6. HW, March 6, 1880, p. 146.
7. *Lucius G.C. Lamar* by Wirt A. Cate, p. 1-7. U. of North Carolina Press. Chapel Hill, NC 1935.
8. *The Reconstruction Presidents* by Brooks D. Simpson, p. 212. University Press of Kansas. 1998.
9. HW, March 9, 1878, p. 186. Also, Cate p. 310-11.
10. HW, November 29, 1879, p. 934; December 6, 1879, p. 950; March 6, 1880, p. 150.
11. *Reconstruction: America's Unfinished Revolution 1803-1877* by Eric Foner. P. 559. Harper & Row. New York. 1988.
12. Hoogenbaum, p. 387-389.
13. *The Public Career of William M. Evarts* by Brainerd Dyer, p. 221-223. U. of California Press. 1933.

Chapter 36 President Hayes: The Money Question

1. *From Hayes to McKinley* by H. Wayne Morgan, p. 44. Syracuse University Press. 1969.
2. Paine, p. 380.
3. HW, April 2, 1881, p. 211.
4. *American Ulysses* by Ronald C. White, p. 251-2. Random House, New York. 2016.
5. Ibid p. 467-8.

Chapter 37 The Election of 1880: The Candidates

1. The original letter is at The Huntington Library, San Marino, CA.
2. HW. June 5, 1880, p. 354.
3. The letter was printed in the Sunday, *New York Herald*, of April 1, 1906, when Nast's effects were about to be auctioned. It is in the Nast collection at the Rutherford B. Hayes Library in Fremont, OH. Paine reprinted the letter on p. 420, but erroneously called Joshua Chamberlain "George" instead of "General."
4. *The Unexpected President: The Life and Times of Chester A. Arthur*, p. 125, by Scott S. Greenberger. Da Capo Press, Hachette Book Group. 2017.
5. *Hayes to McKinley: National Party Politics 1877-1896.* By H. Wayne Morgan. P. 80. Syracuse University Press. 1969.
6. HW July 31, 1880, p. 482. P. 458, para 2.

Chapter 38 1880: The Campaign

1. The article was printed in the Sunday, *New York Herald*, of April 1, 1906, when Nast's effects were about to be auctioned. It is in the Nast collection at the Rutherford B. Hayes Library in Fremont, OH, and in the Princeton University Special Collections Library.
2. HW, July 17, 1880, p. 450.
3. HW, June 28, 1873, p. 546.
4. HW, September 18, 1880, p. 595.
5. *The Life, Speeches and Public Services of Gen. James A. Garfield of Ohio* by Russell H. Conwell, p. 248-305. B.B. Russell & Co. Philadelphia. 1880.
6. *Satire on Stone* by Richard S. West. P. 198. University of Illinois Press. 1988.
7. Paine, p. 434-5.
8. *The Life, Speeches and Public Services of Gen. James A. Garfield of Ohio* by Russell H. Conwell, p. 305-17. B.B. Russell & Co. Philadelphia. 1880.

9. Ibid. P. 246-248. The $5,000 fee is noted on p. 167 of *The Press Gang* by Mark Summers. University of North Carolina Press. 1994.

10. This is a print from the original painting, copyrighted in 1865 by Johnson Fry & Co., New York. Courtesy of Rutherford B. Hayes Library, Fremont, OH.

11. *Grover Cleveland: A Study in Courage*. Footnote on p. 418 by Allan Nevins. Dodd Mead & Company, New York. 1932. Source: *The Nation,* November 8, 1888. W.W. Dudley, an Indiana politician, "helped disburse $400,000 in the State in buying votes, hiring repeaters, and bribing election officers to stuff ballot-boxes and falsify returns." (Shades of Boss Tweed.)

12. *From Hayes to McKinley* by H. Wayne Morgan. p. 118. Syracuse University Press. 1969.

Chapter 39 President Garfield

1. Paine, p. 449. An upstate editor wrote to Nast, telling him about his daughter's question.
2. Paine p. 487
3. *William Chandler, Republican* by Leon B. Richardson, p. 340. Dodd, Mead & Co., New York. 1940. Taken from the *Nation*, April 23, 1881.
4. HW, Friday, July 8, 1881, p. 479.

Chapter 40 President Arthur

1. There is evidence that Nast could have received an extra day — October 6th instead of the 5th — for his final submission date. That did happen with the January 13, 1883 issue where an in-cartoon message referred to an event of January 4, only nine days before the issue date. (See p. 527).
2. HW, March 7, 1885. P. 146.
3. HW, October 6, 1877. P. 782.
4. *What Fools These Mortals Be!* by Richard S. West and Alexander Kahn. P. 210. IDW Publishing. San Diego. 2014.
5. HW, May 20, 1882. P. 306.
6. *Rum, Romanism and Rebellion* by Mark W. Summers, p. 71. The University of North Carolina Press. 2000.

Chapter 41 Irreparable Losses

1. *The House of Harper* by J. Henry Harper, p. 650. Harper & Brothers. New York. 1912.
2. *The House of Harper* by Eugene Exman, p. 148. Harper & Row. New York. 1967,
3. Paine, p. 417-8.
4. *Zim. The Autobiography of Eugene Zimmerman*. Edited by Walter M. Brasch. Selinsgrove: Susquehanna University Press. P. 78.
5. *Mrs. Frank Leslie's Illustrated Newspaper* by Lynne Vincent Cheney. *American Heritage*, October 1975. P. 48.
6. Paine, p. 465-6.
7. Ibid. p. 467.
8. Ibid. p. 468.
9. Ibid. p. 470.
10. Ibid. p. 472.
11. *A Disposition to Be Rich* by Geoffrey C. Ward, p. 152. Alfred A. Knopf. New York. 2012.

12. Ibid. Ferdinand Ward was well-known author Geoffrey C. Ward's great-grandfather. Utilizing research and correspondence available only to himself, Mr. Ward described in minute detail "How a small-town pastor's son ruined an American President, brought on a Wall Street crash, and made himself the best-hated man in the United States."

    I am grateful to Mr. Ward for his detailed findings and masterful presentation of them. His ancestor's fraud also marked a significant turning point in Thomas Nast's life. Unlike General Grant's family, Nast and his heirs never recovered their financial independence.
13. Ibid. p. 162.
14. Ibid. p. 168.
15. Ibid. p. 185, 194-5.
16. Ibid. p. 178-9, 266.
17. Ibid. p. 222.
18. Ibid. p. 256.
19. Inside back corner of scrapbook at Morristown and Morris Township Library.
20. The sketchbook was privately owned. About 20 years ago, I paid the anonymous owner to copy its 300 or so drawings. Nast probably took the stupefied Grant image from an 1872 cartoon by Matt Morgan in *Frank Leslie's Illustrated Newspaper*, which supported Horace Greeley against Grant. (See p. 306).
21. HW January 24, 1885, p. 51.
22. Paine, p. 518.

Chapter 42 The Election of 1884: Blaine

1. Interview with a reporter for the Jacksonville, Florida *Morning News*, reprinted in the *Mail and Express*, New York, May 30, 1887. *Fickle Thomas Nast. How he changed from Republican to Mugwump.* Source: Nast Scrapbook, p. 26, in the Morristown and Morristownship Library.
2. *The House of Harper* by J. Henry Harper, p. 498. Harper & Brothers. New York. 1912. Paine, p. 495-6.
3. HW, June 14, 1884. P. 374.
4. *James G. Blaine: A Political Idol of Other Days* by David Saville Muzzey, p. 255. Dodd, Mead & Co. New York. 1934. (Letter from Andrew Carnegie to former Prime Minister William Gladstone of England, dated June 29, 1887.)
5. Muzzey, p. 235. The quote is from a letter Blaine wrote to Jay Cooke on November 10, 1869, beseeching him for an investment and indicating that both would benefit. Cooke turned him down. The letter is in the Jay Cooke papers at the Pennsylvania Historical Society in Philadelphia.
6. Ibid, p. 236.
7. Ibid, p. 300-1.
8. Ibid, p. 303-4.
9. HW, May 10, 1884, p. 295.
10. *From Hayes to McKinley*: *National Party Politics 1877-1896* by H. Wayne Morgan, p. 69. Syracuse University Press, 1969. Morgan's Source was *The Politicos* by Matthew Josephson, p. 336. Harcourt, Brace. New York. 1938.
11. *Political Discussions: Legislative, Diplomatic and Popular* by James G. Blaine, p. 154. The Henry Hill Publishing Company, Norwich, CT. 1887. The Democrats' failure to exempt Davis from a bill which would have pardoned 750 remaining ineligible Confederates stopped the bill and should have been a plume on Blaine's hat.

Chapter 43 The Election of 1884: The Other Candidates

1. *Ben Butler and the New York Election of 1884* by Hans L. Trefoussse. P. 192. New York State Historical Association, 1956.
2. *Grover Cleveland: A Study in Courage* by Allan Nevins, p. 148. Dodd, Mead & Company, New York, 1932.
3. *The Yellow Press: Gilded Age Journalism* by Sidney Kubre, p. 46. Florida State University. No date. (Probably 1963-1965).
4. Ibid, p. 46.
5. Ibid, p. 58.
6. *Rum, Romanism & Rebellion: The Making of a President* by Mark W. Summers, p. 295. The University of North Carolina Press, Chapel Hill, 2000.

Chapter 44 The Election of 1884: The Campaign

1. *Grover Cleveland: A Study in Courage* by Allan Nevins, p. 162-9. Dodd, Mead & Company. New York. 1932. Professor Nevins made a careful study of the Maria Halpin affair, even speaking to some of the principals who were still alive almost 50 years later, and carefully assessed the facts through letters, original documents, contemporary Buffalo and New York papers, and relevant books about other men with specific insights.

   In 1895, when Maria had remarried and was living in New Rochelle, NY, she sent Cleveland two letters asking for money and threatening to publish facts in her possession. The President, then in his second term, apparently took no action. Nevins read the letters.

   Since 1932, Professor Nevins' biography has been considered the definitive account of Maria Halpin's story. In 2000, Professor Mark Summers of the University of Kentucky published *Rum, Romanism and Rebellion: The Making of a President* (University of North Carolina Press) in which he described the 1884 campaign in detail. I have made substantial use of his book in writing this chapter, as well as the commissioned essay that he wrote for me 25 years ago, *Thomas Nast and the Paper Tigers*.
2. On pages 281 and 285 of his book, Professor Summers describes two affidavits signed by Maria which appeared in the *Chicago Tribune* on October 30-31, 1884, just before the election. In the second one, she accused Cleveland of rape, and conceiving their child on that occasion. The Chicago paper was owned and edited by Joseph Medill, who had been a founder of the Republican Party in 1854; he was doing everything he could to help Blaine by giving credence to Maria's sensational charges. The Democratic *World's* reporter interviewed Maria, who denied the rape charge, admitted their sex was consensual, and praised Cleveland,

   In 2018, Patricia Miller devoted a chapter in her book *Bringing Down the Colonel*, to accusing Cleveland of rape and describing Maria as a victim. (Farrar, Straus & Giroux. Sarah Crichton Books. New York).

   The author did extensive research, made a solid case, and explained her position well in an interview on C-Span. However her "Wanton Woman" conclusion is almost entirely predicated on the actively pro-Blaine, anti-Cleveland *Chicago Tribune*. Weighed against the evidence in the Nevins and Summers books, I believe Ms. Miller is mistaken.
3. *Rum, Romanism and Rebellion*, p. 146.
4. Ibid, p. 183.
5. Ibid, p. 188.
6. *James G. Blaine: A Political Idol of Other Days* by David Saulle Muzzey, p. 299. Dodd, Mead & Company. New York. 1934.
7. *Rum, Romanism and Rebellion*, p. 296.
8. HW, July 23, 1904, p. 1140-2. All the information about "The Three R's" meeting and its aftermath in this section came from Frank Mack's first-hand account.

9. *Rum, Romanism and Rebellion*, p. 295.
10. Paine. p. 507.
11. HW. October 1, 1881, p. 659.
12. *The House of Harper* by J. Henry Harper, p. 503. Harper Brothers, New York. 1912.

Chapter 45 President Cleveland: Civil Service Reform

1. HW May 16, 1885, p. 306.
2. *Grover Cleveland: A Study in Courage* by Allan Nevins, p. 256. Dodd, Mead & Company, New York, 1932.
3. HW August 21, 1886, p. 530.
4. HW March 6, 1886, p. 192.
5. Nevins, p. 263-5.
6. Ibid, p. 302-4.
7. Nast Scrapbook, p. 7 in the Morristown and Morristownship County Library.
8. Ibid.

Chapter 46 President Cleveland: Labor Issues

1. HW March 6, 1886, p. 155.
2. *Grover Cleveland: A Study in Courage* by Allan Nevins, p. 346-7. Dodd, Mead & Company, New York, 1932.
3. HW April 3, 1886, p. 218.
4. *Famous Trials: An Account of the Haymarket Trial* by Douglas Linder, University of Missouri/Kansas City School of Law. 1995. Professor Linder filled in details that *Harper's Weekly* and Allan Nevins didn't know or include.
5. Where did Nast source the portraits? Probably not from the *Weekly*, which ran a sketch of the trial in the July 31 issue without identifying the individuals. Leslie's did have all seven portraits separately displayed in an earlier issue (date unknown), so Nast probably utilized that page from his first employer.

Chapter 47 President Cleveland: Other Issues

1. *Grover Cleveland: A Study in Courage* by Allan Nevins, p. 322-3. Dodd, Mead & Company, New York, 1932.
2. *American Gunboat Diplomacy and the Old Navy 1877-1889* by Kenneth J. Hagon, p. 186. Greenwood Press, Westport, CT. 1973.
3. Ibid, p. 16.
4. Ibid, p. 19.
5. Commissioned Essay by Professor Mark W. Summers, University of Kentucky. 1997.
6. Nevins, p. 326-7.
7. Ibid, p. 302.
8. Ibid, p. 267-70.
9. Ibid, p. 357-9.
10. *The House of Harper* by Eugene Exman, p. 114-5. Harper & Rowe. New York. 1967.
11. Ibid, p. 117.
12. The first commercial electric cable streetcar line began operating in Cleveland in 1884. Power was transmitted from an overhead line, tapped through a connecting pole from the streetcar.

13. HW, February 20, 1886, p. 123.
11. Paine, p. 526.

Chapter 48 After *Harper's Weekly*: The Election of 1888

1. Paine, p. 529.
2. Interview with the *Jacksonville Morning News*, quoted in the *New York Mail and Express*, May 30, 1887. From p. 17 of Nast scrapbook at the Morristown and Morris Township Library.
3. *The Yellow Press and Gilded Age Journalism* by Sidney Kobre, p. 42. Florida State University. (No date).
4. The only reference to The Cartoon Publishing Company is on p. 25 of the Nast scrapbook in the Morristown and Morris Township Library. The cartoons were in the collection of the Goethe Institute in Boston in 1983. They were published by Northeastern University (made possible by a grant from the Morristown Library) in a catalog of an exhibition of Nast's work by the University's Fine Arts Department. Author's collection.
5. Paine, p. 533.

Chapter 49 After *Harper's Weekly*: Freelancing in the Early 90's

1. All the material and cartoons relating to the *San Francisco Examiner* is in the Morristown and Morris Township Library Scrapbook and relevant print collection.
2. Most of the descriptive information on *America* is in *Thomas Nast and "America": The Journal for Americans* by Richard S. West in the 2000 issue (Vol. 14) of the *Journal of the Thomas Nast Society*. Some of the specific detail is in the Nast scrapbook in Morristown. The cartoons are from the author's collection.
3. *America*, August 8, 1889, p. 585.
4. Some of the information on *Time* is in *Nast on the Cover of "Time"* by Richard S. West in the 1999 issue (Vol. 13) of the *Journal of the Thomas Nast Society*. Some of the specific detail is in the Nast scrapbook in Morristown. The cartoons are from the author's collection.
5. Paine, p. 536-9.

Chapter 50 After *Harper's Weekly*: Nast's Weekly

1. The only complete set of *Nast's Weekly* is at the Wilson Library (part of James Ford Bell Libraries) at the University of Minnesota in Minneapolis.
2. Paine, p. 538.
3. Paine, p. 539.
4. Paine, p. 540.

Chapter 51 After *Harper's Weekly*: Nast's Final Decade

1. *Peace in Union* was originally displayed in the Galena Customhouse, then moved to the public library, and since 1938 has been in the Galena & U.S. Grant Museum. The Museum staff graciously provided me with a copy of the picture and looked up the amount Nast was paid. The fact that half was paid up front is in an article that his son Cyril published in *The American Art Student and Commercial Artist*, probably in the mid-1950s.
2. What happened to the painting is unknown, but an untitled print is at the Rutherford B. Hayes Library in Fremont, Ohio.
3. William Winter was the dean of American drama critics, had written frequently for both *Harper's Weekly* and the *Tribune*, and had featured Henry Irving in a series of articles in both publications after the actor's 1885 New York performances. (Nast was still at *Harper's*.)
4. Letter from Nast to Frank Partington, Mr. Winter's Head Master, dated January 30, 1897, at the Morristown and Morris County Library. The Library graciously provided me with a copy of the picture.

5. Paine, page 553.
6. *The House of Harper* by Eugene Exman. Harper & Row. New York 1967. p. 170-73.
7. Ibid, p. 180-3.
8. *Harper's Weekly* lasted until May 1913 when it was sold to Norman Hapgood, the former editor of *Collier's Weekly*, and completely changed its character and content. Three years later, its mailing list was sold to the *Independent*, and it disappeared. The firm's book business continues today as Harper Collins, while *Harper's Magazine* and *Harper's Bazaar* (now with a double "a" in *Bazaar*) maintain their individual presences. *Harper's Magazine*, launched in 1850 and the second oldest in the country, is published by a private foundation. The *Bazaar* dates to 1867, and is owned by the Hearst Communications.
9. Paine, p. 535.
10. *The Life and Death of Thomas Nast* by Thomas Nast St. Hill. *American Heritage*, October 1971, p. 93.
11. The information comes from an undated article in *The American Art Student and Commercial Artist* by Nast's son Cyril.
12. *Daniel Frohman Presents*. (His autobiography) Kendal & Sharp. New York. 1935, p. 199. Thanks to my good friend Paul Leblang, whose grandfather Joseph Leblang was a theatre ticket broker, and was given an autographed copy by Frohman's wife.
13. See footnote 10, above.

Chapter 52 After *Harper's Weekly*: Nast's Last Year

1. *The Life and Death of Thomas Nast* by Thomas Nast St. Hill. *American Heritage*, October 1971, p. 91.
2. *The Last Days of Thomas Nast* by Richard C. Simon. *The Journal of the Thomas Nast Society*, 1992, p. 57.
3. August 12, 1902 letter to Sallie, in The Huntington Library, San Marino, CA. (I supplied first-person pronouns in the second sentence.)
4. See Endnote 2 above. Page 60.
5. Ibid.
6. Paine, p. 570.
7. Paine, p. 572-3.
8. Paine, p. 583.

Chapter 53 Nast's Legacy: Santa Claus

1. I used three basic sources for my *pre-Nast* introductory material for this chapter. The mother-lode of St. Nicholas, Santa Claus and related material is at the American Antiquarian Society in Worcester, MA. Although I have been an AAS member for 27 years, I utilized AAS illustrations and related text through the following secondary sources for this chapter.
    - *The Battle for Christmas* by Stephen Nissenbaum. Alfred A. Knoph, New York. 1997. Chapter 2. Also, a commissioned essay "Nast and Christmas" that Professor Nissenbaum wrote for me not long after he published his book.
    - *Santa Claus Visits the Hudson* by R.W.G. Vail. The *New-York Historical Society Quarterly*. October 1951, p. 337-343.
    - *Knickerbocker Santa Claus* by Charles W. Jones. The *New-York Historical Society Quarterly*. October 1954. P. 356-383.
2. *Santa Claus Visits the Hudson* by R. G. Vail, *New-York Historical Society Quarterly*, October 1951, p. 342.
3. *The Battle for Christmas*. P. 80.

4. *Thomas Nast's Christmas Drawings* by Thomas Nast St. Hill. Harper & Row. New York. 1971, p. 34. *The Battle for Christmas*. P. 72-74.
5. About 20 years ago, revisionist academics, using digital word-analysis techniques, claimed that Clement Moore was not the author; they credited Henry Livingston, patriarch of an old New York family. Historical document expert Seth Keller, who once owned the only original copy of Moore's manuscript, painstakingly and effectively refuted the revisionists in an article in the Winter 2004 *New York Journal of American History*.
6. See Footnote 2.

Chapter 54 Nast's Legacy: Political Symbols

1. The War of 1812 lasted until 1815. Here, in its second year, Columbia was telling John Bull to stop impressment of American sailors (whom the British considered deserters) and impeding trade with France (with whom England was at war.) She also warned Napoleon to learn respect and avoid retribution.
2. Several of the images in this chapter were taken from the *Greene County Historical Journal* of 2011, a four-part publication of the New York County's Historical Society. Andrew Bittner's article was entitled *The Man Who Evolved into a National Symbol: The Story of Uncle Sam.*
3. *A Century of Political Cartoons* by Allan Nevins and Frank Weitenkampf. P. 64-5. Charles Scribner's Sons. New York. 1944.
4. The *Punch* cartoon was drawn by John Tenniel, its principal cartoonist, whom Nast knew. This was a bit of repartee between them, probably because Tenniel ridiculed Grant.
5. Isaac Mayo, a 16-yeat old seasick sailor wrote in his diary in March 1810 that if he "could have got on shore in the hight (sic) of it (a storm), I swear that Uncle Sam, as they call him, would certainly forever lose the services of at least one sailor." The U.S.S. Constitution Museum in Boston discovered the reference in 2013, and Sam Roberts wrote about it in *The New York Times* of April 20, 2016, p. A21.

Chapter 55 Epilogue

1. Don Durgin, NBC President from 1966-1973, quoted in *Advertising Age* (Special Collection Edition, 50 Years of TV Advertising), Spring 1995, p. 54.
2. The Minnesota Valley Canning Company (later re-named Green Giant) first depicted its Green Giant in 1928 as a scowling caveman wearing a bearskin, to emphasize the large size of its canned peas. A dark Brothers Grimm fairy tale from the early nineteenth century played a role in its origin. Copy writer Leo Burnett traded the scowl and bearskin for a smile and a leafy suit, and added "Jolly" to the Green Giant's name in 1935. Its first TV appearance was in 1954.
3. My AdTel clients included 13 of the top 16 and 27 of the top 50 packaged goods television advertisers. After my focal point switched to Nast 20 years later (1995), I was able to correlate his creative imagery, personalized symbolic caricatures, catchy slogans and sequential repetition with what I had learned from eight years of testing.
4. Researchers from Columbia University published their study in the June 2019 issue of *Behavior and Information Technology*.
5. *Because Internet: Understanding the New Rules of Language* by Gretchen McCulloch, 2019 Riverhead Books. New York. Reviewed in *The New York Times Book Review* by Clay Shirky. September 1, 2019, p. 15.
6. *Louisville Courier-Journal*, November 19, 1872.
7. Paine, p. 575.
8. Privately commissioned article by Draper Hill. I don't know his source.

Index

This manually-created index is predicated on Nast's 1,000 depicted cartoons, illustrations, sketches and paintings. It has 3 sections.

- **Nast's work is bolded.**
- Related content, context, and explanatory references — plus about 100 relevant cartoons by other artists — appear in ordinary type. There are three sections.

Ten major categories and dozens of sub-classifications comprise this section. Where applicable, Nast's characters are also referenced under their relevant categories, as well as in the People/ Characters section.

Nast drew more than 450 different characters. All but five were identified in the research for this biography; many were portrayed only once or twice, and they generally appeared in individual, non-serialized cartoons which were not selected for this biography. About half his characters are included here; all but two political figures (Anna Elizabeth Dickinson and Victoria Woodhull) were men. (Nast drew fewer than ten women, primarily actresses or opera singers.)

Nast Index

Personal Aspects

Family

Friendships

Finances (Personal)

How Nast Portrayed Himself

Portrayals of Nast by Other Artists

Art

Art Education

Nast's Paintings

Artistic and Literary Sources

American Artists

Bible

Classical Mythology

Charles Dickens

Fictional Characters

French Artists

Gilbert & Sullivan

William Shakespeare

During Nast's era, Shakespeare's plays were an inherent part of the school curriculum. In addition to reading and writing, Shakespeare was used to help teach history, civics, elocution and ethics. Even relatively uneducated people were attracted to Shakespearean theatre after their schooling ended.

Nast idolized Shakespeare and referenced 23 of his 37 plays in more than 100 cartoons — sometimes with just a recognizable line or two, but generally with pictorial content. Thirteen of his plays are indexed below.

Theatre

Illustrated Books

Nast illustrated more than 100 books, and alluded to dozens of other literary works in his cartoons. Nine of his books are discussed in these pages.

Other Publications to Which Nast Contributed

Nast's Symbols

Impersonal Political Symbols

Personal Political Symbols: Presidential Election Losers

International

Derivative Symbols (Long after Nast)

Cartoons by Other Artists (By publication)

Frank Leslie's Illustrated Newspaper (FLIN)

New York Illustrated News (NYIN)

Harper's Weekly (HW)

Newspapers/Publishers

Nast delighted in attacking opposing publishers — many of whom were or had been active politicians — whose views differed from his. Only George Jones of the *Times* and William Cullen Bryant of the *Post* generally agreed with Nast and were never targeted.

Major New York City Nast Targets

Herald

Other New York City Dailies

Other Newspapers

Topics/Issues Index

Civil War

Battles (In chronological order)

Union Politicians

Confederate Generals

Confederate Politicians

Reconstruction

Historians generally consider Reconstruction as the period from 1865 through 1877. However, Nast's cartoons clearly depicted the endless conflicts between North and South — which evolved into most Republicans versus most Democrats — as continuing through the 1884 election when Republican James Blaine continued to wave the Bloody Shirt in his campaign in Nast's negative depictions of him. It was a more substantive issue in 1880 when Democratic candidate Winfield Scott Hancock actually was allied with ex-Confederates.

Accordingly, most of Nast's Reconstruction Era cartoons have been separately indexed under Presidents — Andrew Johnson, Ulysses Grant, and Rutherford Hayes; or under Presidential Election Losers — Horatio Seymour, Horace Greeley, Samuel Tilden and Hancock.

Nast strongly supported Blacks, Indians and Chinese emigrants, except when he thought their behavior was wrong — e.g., corruption or massacres. In rare circumstances, he used the N-word to ridicule whites, not to demean Blacks. Although the term was in common use by both races, Fletcher Harper discouraged its employment in his publications but understood why it could be appropriate for emphasis in a few of Nast's satires.

General Issues/Topics

Black-Oriented Issues/Topics

Reconstructed States

Presidents

Ulysses S. Grant (1869-1877)

Presidential Election Losers

Front for the Ring

Other Key Insiders

Fringe Players

Tammany Hall: Post-Tweed

Ethnic/Religious/Radical Politics

Chinese

German-Americans

Indians (Native Americans)

Recurring Political Issues

Foreign Affairs and Countries

People/Characters Index

Bibliography

Adler, John and Draper Hill. *Doomed by Cartoon: How Cartoonist Thomas Nast and The New-York Times Brought Down Boss Tweed and His Ring of Thieves*. Morgan James Publishing, LLC. Garden City, NY. 2008.

America. August 8, 1889.

American Bar Association. Minutes of the American Bar Association. New York. May 1, 1871.

Baehr, Harry W., Jr. *The Tribune Since the Civil War*. Dodd, Mead & Company. New York. 1936.

Behavior and Information Technology. Columbia University. June 2019.

Bigelow, John. *The Life of Samuel J. Tilden*, Vol. II. Harper & Brothers. 1895.

Blaine, James G. *Political Discussions: Legislative, Diplomatic and Popular*. The Henry Hill Publishing Company. Norwich, CT. 1887.

Blaine, James G. *Twenty Years of Congress: 1861-1881*. The Henry Hill Publishing Company. Norwich, CT. 1887.

Boime, Albert. Privately-commissioned article.

Butterfield, Roger. *Pictures in the Papers. American Heritage.* June 1862.

Bookman, March 15, 1902. John Hay Library, Brown University.

Brasch, Walter M. *Zim. The Autobiography of Eugene Zimmerman*. Selinsgrove: Susquehanna University Press.

Bittner, Andrew. *The Man Who Evolved into a National Symbol: The Story of Uncle Sam. Greene County Historical Journal.* 2011.

Brown, Francis. *Raymond of the Times*. W.W. Norton & Company Inc. New York. 1951.

Budget of Fun. January 1872.

Cary, Edward. *George William Curtis*. Houghton, Mifflin & Co. New York. 1894.

Cate, Wirt A. *Lucius Q.C. Lamar*. U. of North Carolina Press. Chapel Hill, N.C. 1935.

Cheney, Lynne Vincent. *Mrs. Frank Leslie's Illustrated Newspaper*. *American Heritage*. October 1975.

The Cruise of The Alabama and the Sumter (from the private journals and other papers of Commander R. Semmes, CS.N.). George W. Carleton. New York. 1864.

Coggeshall, William T. *The Newspaper Record*, Philadelphia, 1856.

Conkling, Alfred R. *Life and Letters of Roscoe Conkling*. Charles L. Webster & Co. New York. 1889.

Conwell, Russell H. *The Life, Speeches and Public Services of Gen. James A. Garfield of Ohio*. B.B. Russell & Co. Philadelphia. 1880.

Curtis, George William. "To the President. My dear sir." Letter. December 9, 1864. Macculloch Hall Historical Museum, and private collection of Richard Stack.

Cushing, Caleb. *The Treaty of Washington*. Harper & Brothers. New York. 1873.

Davenport, John. *The Election and Naturalization Frauds in New York City 1860-1870*. 1895.

Davis, William .*The Civil War and Reconstruction in Florida*. Columbia University Studies in History, Economics and Public Law. New York. 1913.

Durgin, Don. Quoted in *Advertising Age* (Special Collection Edition, 50 Years of TV Advertising). Spring 1995.

Dyer, Brainerd. *The Public Career of William M. Evarts*. U. of California Press. 1933.

Eger, Jeffrey. *Journal of The Thomas Nast Society*. Volume 6, 1992.

Exman, Eugene. *The House of Harper*. Harper & Row. New York. 1967.

Fickle Thomas Nast. How he changed from Republican to Mugwump. Mail and Express. New York. May 30, 1887.

Fischer, Robert. Privately commissioned essay.

Foner, Eric. *Reconstruction 1863-1877.* Harper & Row. New York. 1988.

Frank Leslie's Illustrated News. April 23, 1859.

Garrison, Gertrud. Nast Scrapbook. New York Public Library.

Greenberger, Scott S. *The Unexpected President: The Life and Times of Chester A. Arthur*. Da Capo Press, Hachette Book Group. New York. 2017.

Grodinsky, Julius. *Jay Gould: His Business Career*. University of Pennsylvania Press. 1957.

Gunn, Thomas Butler. Diaries. Missouri Historical Society, St. Louis. October 1858, June 5, 1859, August 10, 1860, April 13, 1861, April 1862, October 17, 1862.

Hagon, Kenneth J. *American Gunboat Diplomacy and the Old Navy 1877-1889*. Greenwood Press, Westport, CT. 1973.

Harper, J. Henry. *The House of Harper*. Harper & Brothers. New York. 1912.

Harrington, Fred H. *Fighting Politician: Major General N.P. Banks*. University of Pennsylvania Press. 1948.

Haynes, Fred E. *Third Party Movements*. The State Historical Society of Iowa. 1916.

Henry, Robert Selph. *"First with the Most" Forrest*. The Bobbs-Merrill Company. New York. 1944.

Hershkowitz, Leo. *Tweed's New York: Another Look.* Anchor Press, Doubleday. 1977.

Hewes , Lauren B. and Laura E. Wasowicz. *Radiant with Color and Art: McLoughlin Brothers and the Business of Picture Books, 1858-1920*. American Antiquarian Society, Worcester, MA. December 1870.

Hill, Draper. Privately commissioned articles.

Hoogenbaum , Ari. *Rutherford B. Hayes*. University Press of Kansas. 1995.

Illustrated London News. July 7, 1860.

Jones. Charles W. *Knickerbocker Santa Claus*. The *New-York Historical Society Quarterly*. October 1954.

Jordan, David M. *Roscoe Conkling of New York: Voice in the Senate*. Cornell University Press. 1971.

Katz, Irving. *August Belmont, A Political Biography*. Columbia University Press. 1968.

Kobre, Sidney. *The Yellow Press and Gilded Age Journalism*. Florida State University. No publication date.

Leonard, Thomas C. *The Power of the Press*. Oxford University Press. 1986.

Leonard, Thomas C. Privately commissioned essay.

Linder, Douglas. *Famous Trials: An Account of the Haymarket Trial.* University of Missouri/Kansas City School of Law. 1995.

Louisville Courier-Journal. November 19, 1872.

The Mail and Express. "Thomas Nast in His Workshop." New York. April 12, 1884.

Matt, Frank Luther. *History of American Magazines, 1865-1885 (Volume II and III)*. Harvard University Press, Cambridge, MA. 1938.

McFeeley, William. *Grant, A Biography*.

McJimsey, George T. Genteel Partisan Manton Marble 1834-1917. Iowa State University Press, Inc. 1971.

Mills, Alfred. *Journal of the Thomas Nast Society*. 1994.

Miss Columbia's Public School or Will It Blow Over? Francis B. Felt & Co. New York. 1871.

Morgan, H. Wayne. *From Hayes to McKinley*. Syracuse University Press. 1969.

Morris, Roy, Jr. *Fraud of the Century*. Simon & Schuster. New York. 2003.

Mushkat, Jerome. *The Reconstruction of New York Democracy 1861-74*. Associated University Presses, Inc. 1981. Chapter 7.

Muzzey, David Saville. *James G. Blaine: A Political Idol of Other Days*. Dodd, Mead & Co. New York. 1934.

Nast, Tomas. Letters to David Ross Locke. Locke Collection, Rutherford B. Hayes Presidential Library, Fremont, OH. March 23 & 30, 1867, May 20, 1867.

Nast, Thomas. Letter to Norton Chipman. The Norton Chipman file, California State Library, Sacramento, CA. November 26, 1871.

Nast, Thomas. Letter to Curtis. Rutherford B. Hayes Library, Fremont, OH. July 9, 1874.

Nast, Thomas. Letters to Sallie. The Huntington Library, San Marino, CA.

Nast, Thomas. Personal scrapbook. John Hay Library, Brown University.

Nast, Thomas. Letter to Frank Partington. Morristown and Morris County Library. January 30, 1897.

Nast's Weekly. Wilson Library (part of James Ford Bell Libraries), University of Minnesota, Minneapolis.

The Nation. August 31, 1871, May 18, 1872.

Nevins, Allan. *Grover Cleveland: A Study in Courage*. Dodd Mead & Company. New York. 1932.

Nevins, Allan. *Hamilton Fish: The Inner History of the Grant Administration*. Dodd, Mead & Company. New York. 1936.

Nevins, Allan and Frank Weitenkampf. *A Century of Political Cartoons*. Charles Scribner's Sons. New York. 1944.

Nevins, Allan and Milton H. Thomas. *The Diary of George Templeton Strong, 1865-1875*. The MacMillan Company. New York. 1952.

New Language of Politics: An Anecdotal Dictionary of Catchwords, Slogans and Political Usage, Revised Edition. Collier Books. New York. 1972.

New York Illustrated News. April 19, 1862, June 30, 1860.

New York Times. September 24, 1871, November 16, 1871.

Nissenbaum, Stephen. *The Battle for Christmas*. Alfred A. Knoph. New York. 1997. Chapter 2.

Nissenbaum, Stephen. Privately commissioned essay.

Oliphant, Pat. *Journal of the Thomas Nast Society. 2002.*

Paine, Albert Bigelow. *Thomas Nast: His Period and His Pictures*. Reprint. Pyne Press. Princeton. 1974.

Philadelphia Times and Dispatch. Nast Collection. New York Public Library. November 27, 1873.

Platt, Thomas C. *The Autobiography of Collier Platt*. BW Dodge & Company. New York. 1910.

Richardson, Leon B. *William Chandler, Republican*. Dodd, Mead & Co. New York. 1940.

Roberts, Sam. *The New York Times.* April 20, 2016.

Rorabaugh, W.J. *Immigrants, Temperance and Tammany Hall. Civil War History.* June 1976.

Rosebault, Charles J. *When Dana Was The Sun*. Greenwood Press. Westport, CT. 1970.

Rusche, Harry (Professor Emory University). *Oh for a Muse of Fire: Thomas Nast and William Shakespeare*, Privately commissioned essay.

St. Hill, Thomas Nast. *The Life and Death of Thomas Nast*. *American Heritage*. October 1971.

Salute to Thomas Nast. The Journal of the Thomas Nast Society. 2002.

San Francisco Examiner. Morristown and Morris Township Library Scrapbook and relevant print collection.

Semmes, Commander R., CS.N. *The Cruise of The Alabama and the Sumter* (from the private journals and other papers). George W. Carleton. New York. 1864.

Simon, Richard C. *The Last Days of Thomas Nast*. *The Journal of the Thomas Nast Society*. 1992.

Simpson, Brooke. *The Idol as Icon: Thomas Nast and Ulysses S. Grant.* Commissioned essay.

Simpson, Brooks D. *The Reconstruction Presidents*. University Press of Kansas. 1998.

Soule, J.L.B. Editorial in the Terre Haute, IN *Express.* 1851.

Summers, Mark W. *The Press Gang*. University of North Carolina Press. 1994.

Summers, Mark W. Commissioned essay. University of Kentucky, 1997.

Summers, Mark W. *Rum, Romanism and Rebellion.* The University of North Carolina Press. 2000.

Summers, Mark W. *The Era of Good Stealings*. Oxford University Press. New York. 1993.

Swanberg, W.A. *Jim Fisk: The Career of an Improbable Rascal*. Charles Scribner's Sons. New York. 1959.

Train, George Francis. *My Life in Many States and in Foreign Lands*. D. Appleton and Company. New York, 1902.

Trefoussse, Hans L. *Ben Butler and the New York Election of 1884*. New York State Historical Association. 1956.

Twain, Mark. Letter to David Ross Locke. Locke Collection, Rutherford B. Hayes Presidential Library, Fremont, OH. November 12, 1877.

Vail, R.W.G. *Santa Claus Visits the Hudson*. The *New-York Historical Society Quarterly*. October 1951.

Ward, Geoffrey C. *A Disposition to Be Rich*. Alfred A. Knopf. New York. 2012.

Werner, M.R. *Tammany Hall*. Doubleday, Doran & Co., Inc. New York. 1928. Quote is from *North American Review*, Vol. CXIX,

West, Richard Samuel and Michael Alexander Kahn. *Puck: What Fools These Mortals Be.* IDW Press. San Diego. 2014.

West, Richard Samuel. *Satire on Stone: The Political Cartoons of Joseph Keppler.* University of Illinois Press. 1988.

West, Richard Samuel. *Nast on the Cover of "Time." Journal of the Thomas Nast Society*. 1999.

West, Richard Samuel. Privately commissioned essay.

West, Richard Samuel. *Thomas Nast and "America": The Journal of the Thomas Nast Society.* 2000.

White, Ronald C. *American Ulysses*. Random House. New York. 2016.

Williams, Alfred M. Nast Scrapbook, location unknown.

Williams, Reverend Henry. *The Fight at Dame Europa's School, Showing How the German Boy Thrashed the French Boy and How the English Boy Looked On.* Francis B. Felt & Co. New York. 1871.

Woodhull & Claflin's Weekly. March 16, 1872.

The Worcester Spy (MA). October 3, 1868.

Young, Art. *On My Way: Being the Book of Art Young in Text and Picture*. Horace Liveright. New York. 1928.

Harper's Weekly:
September 14, 1861, p. 579.
April 4, 1863, p. 219.
April 22, 1865, p. 243.
November 3, 1866, p. 690-691.
November 24, 1866, p. 742.
The Political Andersonville. October 24, 1868, p. 681.
July 10, 1869, p. 437.
July 2, 1870, p. 418.
July 16, 1870, p. 451
February 25, 1871, p. 114-5.
April 22, 1871, p. 363.
November 25, 1871
May 18, 1872, p. 306.
August 17, 1872, p. 634.
September 28, 1872, p. 747.
June 28, 1873, p. 546.
February 7, 1874, p. 122.
July 18, 1874. P. 594.
May 30, 1874, p. 450 (Editorial by Curtis).
January 23, 1875, p. 70.
April 10, 1875, p. 294.
November 18, 1876, p. 926.
February 3, 1877, p. 86.
November 10, 1877, p. 891.
October 6, 1877. P. 782.
December 15, 1877, p. 978.
March 9, 1878, p. 186.
November 29, 1879, p. 934.
December 6, 1879, p. 950.
December 13, 1879, p. 996.
March 6, 1880, p. 146, 150.
June 5, 1880, p. 354.
July 17, 1880, p. 450.
July 31, 1880, p. 458, 483, 482.
September 18, 1880, p. 595.
April 2, 1881, p. 211.
July 8, 1881, p. 479.
October 1, 1881, p. 659.
May 10, 1884, p. 295.
May 20, 1882. P. 306.
June 14, 1884. P. 374.
January 24, 1885, p. 51.
March 7, 1885. P. 146.
October 24, 1885.
February 20, 1886, p. 123.
March 6, 1886, p. 155, 192.
August 21, 1886, p. 530.
July 23, 1904, p. 1140-2.

CPSIA information can be obtained
at www.ICGtesting.com
Printed in the USA
JSHW042008150922
30346JS00004BA/14